Rick Steves'

ITALY

2014

CONTENTS

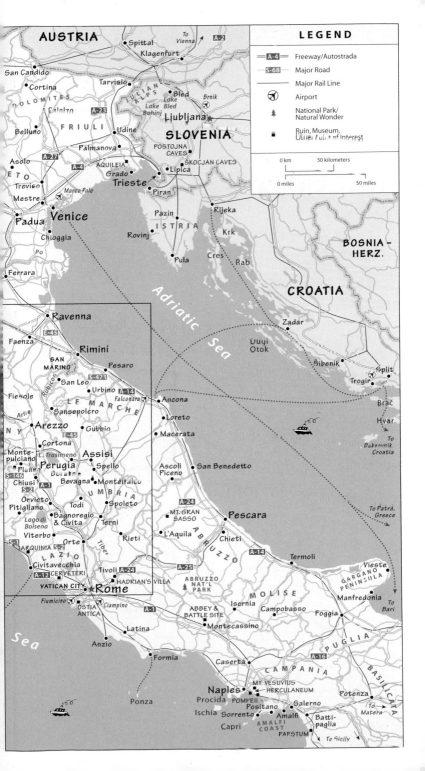

LEGEND

- ===A-4=== Freeway/Autostrada
- [S-68] Major Road
- —— Major Rail Line
- ✈ Airport
- ▲ National Park/ Natural Wonder
- ■ Ruin, Museum, Other Point of Interest

0 km   50 kilometers

0 miles   50 miles

AUSTRIA

Spittal

To Vienna A-2

Klagenfurt

San Candido

Cortina

Tarvisio

JULIAN ALPS

Bled

Lake Bled

Brnik ✈

DOLOMITES

Caldzo

Belluno

FRIULI

Udine

Lake Bohinj

Ljubljana ★

SLOVENIA

Asolo

A-27

PALMANOVA

ETO

Treviso

A-4

AQUILEIA

Grado

POSTOJNA CAVES

SKOCJAN CAVES

Mestre

Marco Polo ✈

Trieste

Lipica

Padua

Venice

Chioggia

Piran

Pazin

Rijeka

Po

Rovinj

ISTRIA

Krk

BOSNIA-HERZ.

Ferrara

Pula

Cres

Rab

CROATIA

Adriatic Sea

Zadar

Dugi Otok

Ravenna

E-45

Faenza

Rimini

SAN MARINO

Pesaro

Šibenik

Split

Rubicon

S-423

San Leo

Trogir ✈

Fiesole

Urbino

A-14

Brač

LE MARCHE

Falconara ✈

Ancona

Hvar

Arlia

Sansepolcro

Loreto

To Dubrovnik Croatia

NY

Arezzo

E-45

Gubbio

Macerata

Montepulciano

Cortona

L. Trasimeno

Assisi

Spello

To Patrà, Greece

Chiusi

S-146

Plum

Perugia

Duruio

Bevagna

Montefalco

Ascoli Piceno

San Benedetto

S-2

A-1

UMBRIA

Orvieto

Pitigliano

Todi

Spoleto

A-24

Lago di Bolsena

Bagnoregio & Civita

Terni

MT. GRAN SASSO

Pescara

Viterbo

Orte

Rieti

L'Aquila

Chieti

A-14

Termoli

Vieste

S-1

LAZIO

Tibet

ABRUZZO

A-24

GARGANO PENINSULA

TAROUINIA

Civitavecchia

A-25

CERVETERI

Tivoli A-24

A-12

HADRIAN'S VILLA

ABRUZZO NAT'L PARK

Manfredonia

VATICAN CITY ★ Rome

MOLISE

To Bari

Fiumicino ✈

OSTIA ANTICA

Ciampino ✈

A-1

ABBEY & BATTLE SITE

Isernia

Campobasso

Foggia

PUGLIA

Sea

Latina

Montecassino

Caserta

A-16

Anzio

CAMPANIA

BASILICATA

Formia

Ponza

Naples

MT. VESUVIUS

HERCULANEUM

Procida

POMPEII

Positano

Salerno

Potenza

To Matera

Ischia

Sorrento

Amalfi

Batti-paglia

Capri

AMALFI COAST

PAESTUM

To Sicily

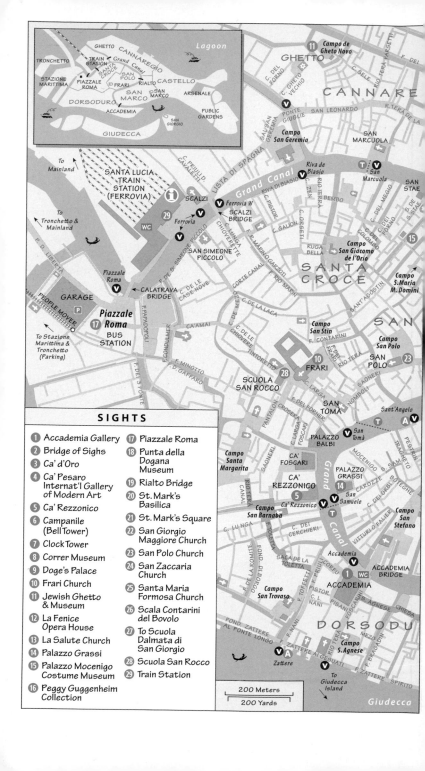

SIGHTS

1. Accademia Gallery
2. Bridge of Sighs
3. Ca' d'Oro
4. Ca' Pesaro Internat'l Gallery of Modern Art
5. Ca' Rezzonico
6. Campanile (Bell Tower)
7. Clock Tower
8. Correr Museum
9. Doge's Palace
10. Frari Church
11. Jewish Ghetto & Museum
12. La Fenice Opera House
13. La Salute Church
14. Palazzo Grassi
15. Palazzo Mocenigo Costume Museum
16. Peggy Guggenheim Collection
17. Piazzale Roma
18. Punta della Dogana Museum
19. Rialto Bridge
20. St. Mark's Basilica
21. St. Mark's Square
22. San Giorgio Maggiore Church
23. San Polo Church
24. San Zaccaria Church
25. Santa Maria Formosa Church
26. Scala Contarini del Bovolo
27. To Scuola Dalmata di San Giorgio
28. Scuola San Rocco
29. Train Station

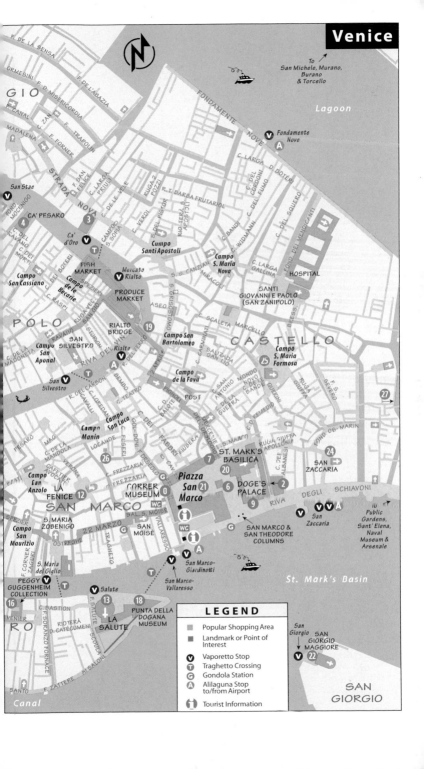

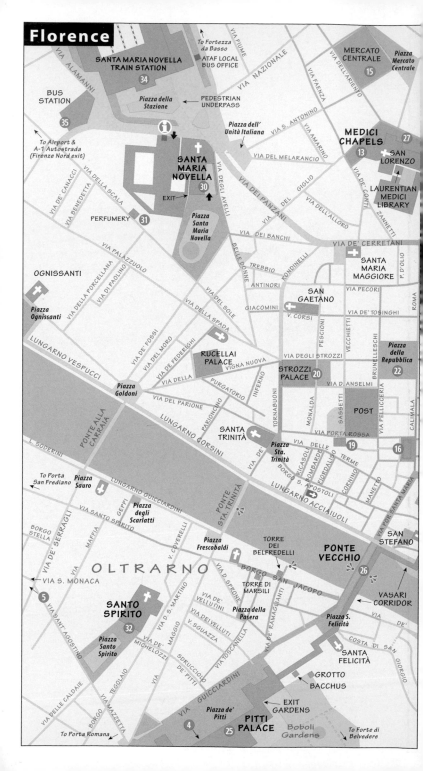

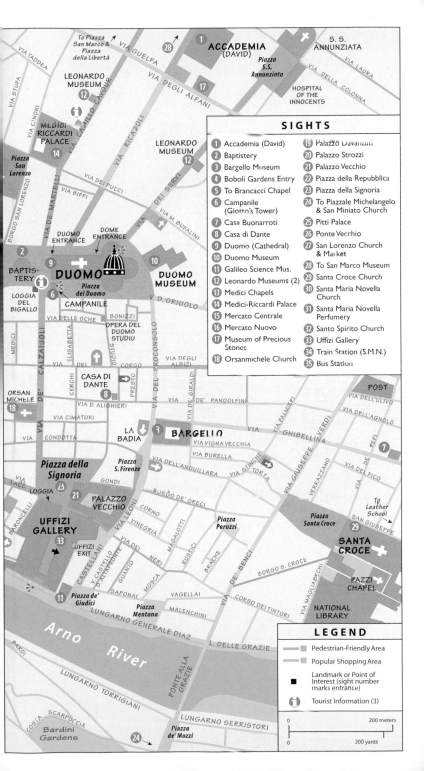

SIGHTS

1 Accademia (David)	**19** Palazzo Davanzati
2 Baptistery	**20** Palazzo Strozzi
3 Bargello Museum	**21** Palazzo Vecchio
4 Boboli Gardens Entry	**22** Piazza della Repubblica
5 To Brancacci Chapel	**23** Piazza della Signoria
6 Campanile (Giotto's Tower)	**24** To Piazzale Michelangelo & San Miniato Church
7 Casa Buonarroti	**25** Pitti Palace
8 Casa di Dante	**26** Ponte Vecchio
9 Duomo (Cathedral)	**27** San Lorenzo Church & Market
10 Duomo Museum	**28** To San Marco Museum
11 Galileo Science Mus.	**29** Santa Croce Church
12 Leonardo Museums (2)	**30** Santa Maria Novella Church
13 Medici Chapels	**31** Santa Maria Novella Perfumery
14 Medici-Riccardi Palace	**32** Santo Spirito Church
15 Mercato Centrale	**33** Uffizi Gallery
16 Mercato Nuovo	**34** Train Station (S.M.N.)
17 Museum of Precious Stones	**35** Bus Station
18 Orsanmichele Church	

LEGEND

- Pedestrian-Friendly Area
- Popular Shopping Area
- ■ Landmark or Point of Interest (sight number marks entrance)
- Tourist Information (3)

0 — 200 meters
0 — 200 yards

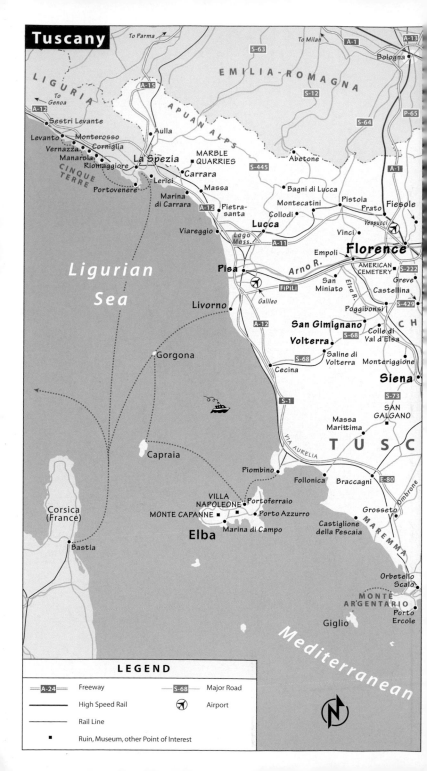

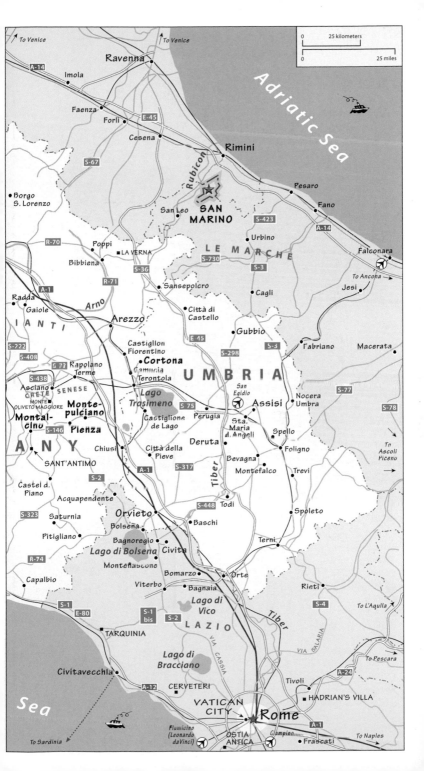

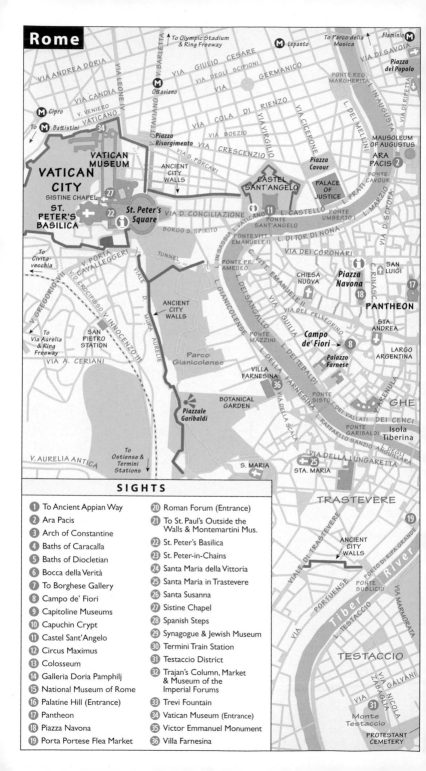

Rome

- To Olympic Stadium & Ring Freeway
- To Parco della Musica
- Flaminio Ⓜ
- Lepanto Ⓜ
- VIA DI SAVOIA
- VIA ANDREA DORIA
- VIA GIULIO CESARE
- VIA DEGLI SCIPIONI
- GERMANICO
- Piazza del Popolo
- Ⓜ Ottaviano
- VIA CANDIA
- V. VENIERO
- VATICANO
- VIA LEONE IV
- VIA COLA DI RIENZO
- VIA BOEZIO
- VIA CRESCENZIO
- VIA CICERONE
- PONTE REG. MARGHERITA
- L. IN AUGUSTA
- VIA DI RIPETTA
- Ⓜ Cipro
- Ⓜ Battistini
- To
- OTTAVIANO
- VIA S. PORCARI
- MAUSOLEUM OF AUGUSTUS
- ARA PACIS ②
- Piazza Risorgimento
- Piazza Cavour
- PALACE OF JUSTICE
- PONTE CAVOUR
- L. DEL MELLINI
- L. MARZIO
- L. DI SCROFA
- VATICAN MUSEUM
- ③④
- ANCIENT CITY WALLS
- CASTEL SANT'ANGELO
- VATICAN CITY
- VIA L. PRATI
- SISTINE CHAPEL
- ②⑦
- ②②
- St. Peter's Square
- VIA D. CONCILIAZIONE
- L. CASTELLO
- L. TOR DI NONA
- PONTE UMBERTO I
- ST. PETER'S BASILICA
- BORGO S. SPIRITO
- PONTE SANT'ANGELO
- VIA DEI CORONARI
- SAN LUIGI
- To Civita-vecchia
- TUNNEL
- IN SASSIA L. VATICANO
- PONTE VITT. EMANUELE II
- C. VITT. EMANUELE II
- CHIESA NUOVA
- Piazza Navona
- ①⑦
- VIA S. GREGORIO VII
- V. PORTA CAVALLEGGERI
- V. D. CROCIFISSO
- V. INNOCENZO III
- PONTE PR. AMEDEO
- VIA GIULIA
- VIA DEL PELLEGRINO
- ①⑧
- PANTHEON
- ANCIENT CITY WALLS
- SAN PIETRO STATION
- VIALE D. MURA AURELIE
- L. GIANICOLENSE
- VIA DEI BANCHI
- VIA DI PANICO
- STA. ANDREA
- To Via Aurelia & Ring Freeway
- VIA A. CERIANI
- Parco Gianicolense
- PONTE MAZZINI
- L. DEI TEBALDI
- Campo de' Fiori ⑧
- LARGO ARGENTINA
- VIA DELLA LUNGARA
- Palazzo Farnese
- Piazzale Garibaldi
- BOTANICAL GARDEN
- VILLA FARNESINA
- ③⑥
- PONTE SISTO
- L. DEI VALLATI
- PONTE GARIBALDI
- GHE
- DEI CENCI
- Isola Tiberina
- L. RAFFAELLO SANZIO
- VIA DELLA SCALA
- VIA DELLA LUNGARETTA
- ②⑤
- S. MARIA
- STA. MARIA
- TRASTEVERE
- ①⑨
- VIALE DI TRASTEVERE
- ANCIENT CITY WALLS
- PORTO DI RIPA GRANDE
- Tiber River
- VIA PORTUENSE
- PONTE SUBLICIO
- TESTACCIO
- L. TESTACCIO
- VIA MARMORATA
- VIA NICOLA ZABAGLIA
- ③①
- Monte Testaccio
- VIA GALVANI
- PROTESTANT CEMETERY
- To Ostiense & Termini Stations

SIGHTS

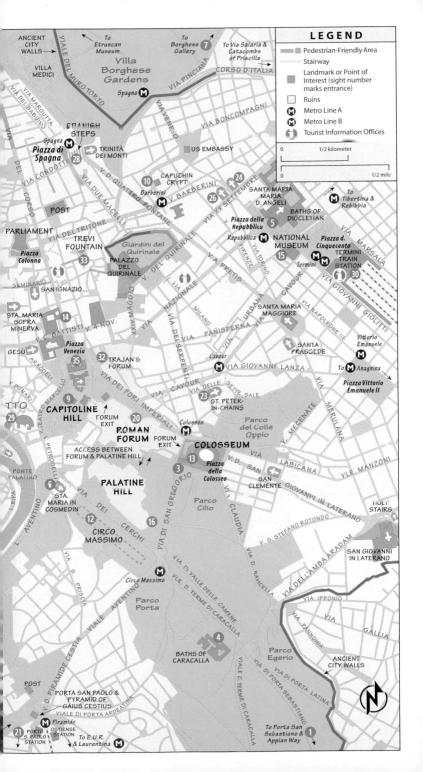

Italy

Italia

Bella Italia! Italy has Europe's richest, craziest culture. If you take Italy on its own terms, you'll experience a cultural keelhauling that actually feels good.

Some people, often with considerable effort, manage to hate this country. Italy bubbles with emotion, corruption, stray hairs, inflation, traffic jams, strikes, rallies, holidays, crowded squalor, and irate ranters shaking their fists at each other one minute and walking arm-in-arm the next. Have a talk with yourself before you cross the border. Promise yourself to relax and accept it all as a package deal.

After all, Italy is the cradle of European civilization— established by the Roman Empire and carried on by the Roman Catholic Church. As you explore Italy, you'll stand face-to-face with some of the world's most iconic images from this 2,000-year history: the Colosseum of Ancient Rome, the medieval Leaning Tower of Pisa, Michelangelo's *David* and Botticelli's *Venus*, the playful Baroque exuberance of the Trevi Fountain...and the Italian city that preserves this legacy in a state of elegant decay: Venice.

Beyond these famous sights, though, Italy offers Europe's richest culture. Traditions still live within a country that is vibrant and fully modern. Go with an eye open to both the Italy of the past and of the present.

Italy is diverse, encompassing German-flavored Alps; Mediterranean beaches; sun-baked Sicily; romantic hill towns; the urban jungle of Naples; the business center of Milan; and the art-drenched cities of Venice, Florence, and Rome. The country is reasonably small and laced with freeways and train lines, so you're never more than a day's journey from any of these places. Each of Italy's 20 regions has its own distinct character, whether it's scenic Tuscany,

busy Lombardy, chaotic Campania, or the place where it all mixes together—Lazio, home of the capital, Rome.

Many travelers discover that there are two Italys: The North is industrial, aggressive, and "time is money" in its outlook. The weather is temperate, and the people are more like Northern Europeans. The South is hot and sunny, crowded, poor, relaxed, farm-oriented, and traditional. Families here are very close-knit and usually live in the same house for many generations. Loyalties are to family, city, region, soccer team, and country—in that order. (For more on the two Italys, see "Rome vs. Milan: A Classic Squabble" on page 326.)

Economically, Italy has had its problems, but somehow things have always worked out. Today, Italy is the world's eleventh-largest industrial power, and the fifth-largest in Europe. Ferraris, Fiats, Maseratis, and Lamborghinis are world-renowned (though they're not really major exports). Tourism is big business—Italy is considered the world's fifth-most-visited tourist destination.

Cronyism, which complicates my work, is an integral part of the economy. Much of Italy's business is hidden in a large "black market" unreported to government officials. Labor unions are strong, strikes are frequent, and the country today is faced with pressure to compete globally.

While most Italians are nominally Catholic, the true dominant religion is life: motor scooters, soccer, fashion, girl-watching, boy-watching, good coffee, good wine, and *il dolce far niente* (the sweetness of doing nothing). The Italian character shows itself on the streets, in the maniacal yet skilled drivers and the classy dressers who star in the ritual evening stroll, or *passeggiata*.

Italians are more social and communal than most other Europeans. In small towns, everyone knows everyone. People get out of their apartments to socialize on the main square. Young women walk hand in hand, and young teenagers shove or punch each other playfully or hang all over each other.

Because they're so outgoing and their language is so fun, Italians are a pleasure to communicate with. Be melodramatic and talk with your hands. Hear the melody; get into the flow. Italians want to connect, and they try harder than any other Europeans. Play with them. Even in non-touristy towns, where English is rare and Italian is the norm, showing a little warmth lets you hop right over the language barrier. If a local starts chattering at you in Italian, don't resist. Go with it. You may find you understand more than you'd expect.

Like most Europeans (and Americans), Italians enjoy watching TV (game shows, sitcoms, etc.), going to movies (American films are almost always dubbed, not subtitled), and listening to their homegrown pop music. Though Italy is the birthplace of opera and much classical music, it's not much more "cultured" today than America is.

Italy Almanac

Official Name: Repubblica Italiana (Italian Republic), or Italia for short.

Population: 61 million, comprised almost entirely of indigenous Italians who speak Italian (German and French are spoken in some Alpine regions) and are nominally Roman Catholic (80 percent).

Latitude and Longitude: 43°N and 12°E (similar to Oregon and Maine).

Area: 116,000 square miles, including the islands of Sicily, Sardinia, and others.

Geography: Italy is shaped like a boot, 850 miles long and 150 miles wide, jutting into the central Mediterranean. (By comparison, Florida is 500 miles long.) The terrain is generally mountainous or hilly, with the Alps in the north and a north-south "spine" of the Apennine Mountains. The highest point is Mont Blanc (15,771 feet), on the border with France. Outside the Alps, the highest point is Monte Cimone (7,100 feet). Italy has 5,000 miles of coastline. Major rivers include the Po (the longest at 400 miles), Arno, Adige, and Tiber. Italy has three active volcanoes: Vesuvius, Etna, and Stromboli.

Regions: Italy is divided into 20 regions (including Tuscany, Umbria, Veneto, and Lazio). Locally, there are some 8,200 "communes," each with a community council and mayor.

Major Cities: Rome (the capital, 2.7 million), Milan (1.3 million), and Naples (1 million).

Economy: The Gross Domestic Product is $1.8 trillion; the GDP per capita is $30,100. About 68 percent of the economy consists of service jobs (especially tourism), 28 percent is industry (textiles, chemicals), and 4 percent is agriculture (fruit, vegetables, olives, wine, plus fishing). There are 12,500 miles of train lines (mostly government-run) and 4,300 miles of expressway (autostrada).

Government: Italy is a republic, with three branches of government. The chief executive is Prime Minister Erico Letta. The bicameral legislature is elected by (mostly) direct voting. Since World War II, the fragmented country has had 62 national governments.

Flag: Three vertical bands of green, white, and red.

Italian Inventions: Opera, cologne, thermometer, barometer, pizza, wireless telegraph, espresso machine, typewriter, batteries, nitroglycerin, yo-yos...and the ice-cream cone.

Museums: 3,800.

Average "Gio": The average Italian is 43 years old, has 1.3 kids, and will live to the ripe old age of 82 (1 in 5 Italians is older than 65). Every day, he or she consumes two servings of pasta, a half-pound of bread, and two glasses of wine. Despite Italian cuisine, Gio isn't fat—only 10 percent of Italians are considered obese.

Italian food, however, is a cut above. If America's specialty is fast food, Italy's is slow food: locally grown ingredients, in

season, bought daily, prepared with love, and enjoyed in social circumstances with friends and family. Even in modern cities, big supermarkets are rare. Instead, people buy their bread from the baker and their meats from the butcher, enjoying a chance to catch up on gossip with the shopkeeper. Italians buy foods in season, celebrating the arrival of fresh artichokes in the spring and porcini mushrooms in the fall.

The three-hour meal is common. For many Italians, dinner is the evening's entertainment. They eat in courses, lingering over each one. A typical meal might start with an antipasto plate of cold cuts and veggies. Next comes the pasta *(primo),* then the meat dish *(secondo),* then a salad. No meal is complete without dessert (Italian gelato is considered the best ice cream in the world), accompanied by coffee or a digestif.

Wine complements each course. Italy is the world's number-one wine producer (just ahead of France). It'd be a shame to visit Italy without sampling the specialties from each region, whether it's the famous Chianti from central Italy, a white Soave from the Veneto, Bardolinos from the North, or a Lacryma Christi from the South.

Italian "bars" are not taverns, but cafés...and social watering holes. In the morning, they serve coffee, orange juice, and croissants to workers on the go. At lunch, it's sandwiches *(panini)* and mini-pizzas for university students. In the afternoon, housewives might drop in for an ice-cream bar. At night, men and women enjoy a glass of wine and watch TV while the kids play a video game in the corner.

Besides food, travelers enjoy sampling Italy's other wares. While no longer a cheap country, Italy is still a hit with shoppers. Find glassware in Venice; gold, silver, leather, and prints in Florence; and high fashion in Rome and Milan.

Italians are obsessed with sports—though not American sports. Italian sports idols are soccer players (Francesco Totti, Antonio Cassano), skiers (Giorgio Rocca), and cyclists (Paolo Savoldelli). Motor racing—Formula 1/Grand Prix—is huge. And since many Italians grow up zipping through narrow streets on small Vespas, it's little wonder that motorcycle racing (*moto,* led by Valentino Rossi) is a major sport here. A favorite participant sport is bocce, played casually at parks throughout Italy. The players take turns tossing small metal balls on a dirt court, aiming at a small wooden ball.

Italy's undisputed number-one sport is soccer (called *il calcio*). Soccer fans *(tifosi)* are passionate. Star players are paid millions and treated like movie stars. Little kids everywhere grow up pretending to score the winning goal just like them. On big game nights, bars are packed with men crowded around TV sets. After a loss, they drown their sorrows. After a victory, fans celebrate by driving through the city streets honking horns and waving team flags. Many Italians place their national, regional, and personal pride on the backs of their athletes. It's a cliché that remains true: In a Europe at peace, the soccer field is the battleground.

But even as Europe evolves, Italy remains a mix of old and new. Appreciate the extreme changes Italian society has gone through in just half a century: the "economic miracle" of the 1950s and 1960s, a wave of domestic terrorism (from the left and the right) in the 1970s and 1980s, stronger integration in the European Union in the 1990s, and the current economic downturn and debt crisis. Italian politics are a reckless pendulum that swings between right- and left-wing extremes. It seems that nobody holds office for very long, but it's always possible to bounce back.

Italy, home of the Vatican, is still mostly Catholic...but not particularly devout. Most people would never think of renouncing their faith, but they don't attend church regularly. They baptize their kids at the local church (there's one every few blocks), but they hold modern opinions on social issues, often in conflict with strict Catholic dogma.

Italy is now the land of legalized abortion, the lowest birth rate in Europe, nudity on TV, socialist politics, and a society whose common language is decidedly secular.

For Italians, it's very important to exhibit a positive public persona—a concept called *la bella figura*. While some Americans don't think twice about going to the supermarket in sweats, Italians dress well any time they leave the house—and they'd rather miss their bus than get all sweaty and mussed-up rushing to catch it. An elderly woman will do her hair and carefully put on makeup for her monthly doctor's appointment, and no matter how hot it gets, Italian men wear long pants—never shorts (except at the beach). At a restaurant, few Italians would ask for tap water or request a "doggy bag" for uneaten food—which, to them, comes off as cheap. This thinking is partly a holdover from the very lean postwar years, when Italians were self-conscious about their poverty and wanted to put their best foot forward.

Some traditions thrive. Italian families and communities are still more close-knit than many others in the modern world. Many Italians, especially in rural regions and small towns, still follow the traditional siesta schedule (called *reposo* in Italy). At about 13:00, shops close and people go home for a three-hour break to have lunch, socialize with friends

and family, and run errands. (While a few old-timers take a short nap in front of the TV, most Italians are quite busy during this time.) And on festival days, locals still dress up in medieval garb to paddle gondolas (Venice), race horses (Siena), battle over a bridge (Pisa), or play rugby or soccer (Florence). But these days, the traditional ways are carried on by choice. Italians are wary of the dangers of a fast-paced global lifestyle. Their history is long, and they're secure in their place in the world.

Accept Italy as Italy. Zero in on the fine points. Don't dwell on the problems. Savor your cappuccino, dangle your feet over a canal (if it smells, breathe through your mouth), and imagine what it was like centuries ago. Ramble through the rabble and rubble of Rome and mentally resurrect those ancient stones. Look into the famous sculpted eyes of Michelangelo's *David* and understand Renaissance Man's assertion of himself. Sit silently on a hilltop rooftop. Get chummy with the winds of the past. Write a poem over a glass of local wine in a sun-splashed, wave-dashed Riviera village. If you fall off your moral horse, call it a cultural experience. Italy is for romantics.

INTRODUCTION

This book will help you make the most of your trip. It breaks Italy into its top destinations—offering a balanced, comfortable mix of exciting cities and cozy towns, from brutal but *bella* Rome to *tranquillo,* traffic-free Riviera villages. It covers the predictable biggies and stirs in a healthy dose of "Back Door" intimacy. Along with marveling at Michelangelo's masterpieces, you'll enjoy a snack of bruschetta (fresh garlic rubbed on toast) prepared by a village boy. I've been selective, including only the most exciting sights and experiences. For example, after visiting many hill towns, I recommend just my favorites.

You'll get all the specifics and opinions necessary to wring the maximum value out of your limited time and money. If you plan a month or less in Italy, and you have a normal appetite for information, this book is all you need. If you're a travel-info fiend like me, you'll find that this book sorts through all the superlatives and provides a handy rack upon which to hang your supplemental information.

Italy is my favorite European country. Experiencing its culture, people, and natural wonders economically and hassle-free has been my goal for three decades of traveling, tour guiding, and writing. With this book, I pass on to you the lessons I've learned, updated for 2014.

The best of Italy is, of course, only my opinion. But after spending half my adult life researching Europe, I've developed a sixth sense for what travelers enjoy.

INTRODUCTION

Map Legend

↳	Viewpoint	✈	Airport	🍦	Gelato
↟	Entrance	ⓣ	Taxi Stand		Pedestrian Zone
ℹ	Tourist Info	🇹	Tram Stop		Railway
WC	Restroom	ⓑ	Bus Stop		Ferry/Boat Route
✿	Synagogue	🅿	Parking		
⛪	Church	)(	Mtn. Pass	⊢—⊣	Tram
V	Vaporetto Dock		Park		Stairs
T	Traghetto Crossing	▪	Statue/Point of Interest	· · · · ·	Walk/Tour Route
G	Gondola Station				
A	Alilaguna Stop	🏰	Castle	- - - - -	Trail

Use this legend to help you navigate the maps in this book.

About This Book

Rick Steves' Italy 2014 is a personal tour guide in your pocket. This book is organized by destinations. Each is a mini-vacation on its own, filled with exciting sights, strollable neighborhoods, affordable places to stay, and memorable places to eat. In the following chapters, you'll find these sections:

Planning Your Time suggests a schedule for how to best use your limited time.

Orientation includes specifics on public transportation, helpful hints, local tour options, easy-to-read maps, and tourist information.

Sights describes the top attractions and includes their cost and hours.

Self-Guided Walks take you through interesting neighborhoods, with a personal tour guide in hand.

Sleeping describes my favorite hotels, from good-value deals to cushy splurges.

Eating serves up a range of options, from inexpensive cafés to fancy restaurants.

Connections outlines your options for traveling to destinations by train, bus, plane, and cruise ship. When describing car-friendly regions, I've included route tips for drivers.

The **Italian History** chapter gives you a helpful overview of Italy's history, art, and architecture.

The **appendix** is a traveler's tool kit, with telephone tips, useful phone numbers and websites, transportation basics (on trains, buses, boats, car rentals, driving, and flights), recommended books and films, a festival list, a climate chart, a handy packing checklist, and Italian survival phrases.

Browse through this book, choose your favorite destinations, and link them up. Then have a *buono* trip! Traveling like a tempo-

Key to This Book

Updates
This book is updated every year—but as soon as you pin down Italy, it wiggles. For the latest, visit www.ricksteves.com/update. For a valuable list of reports and experiences—good and bad—from fellow travelers, check www.ricksteves.com/feedback.

Abbreviations and Times
I use the following symbols and abbreviations in this book:
Sights are rated:

▲▲▲ **Don't miss**
▲▲ **Try hard to see**
▲ **Worthwhile if you can make it**
No rating **Worth knowing about**

Tourist information offices are abbreviated as **TI,** and bathrooms are **WCs.** To categorize accommodations, I use a **Sleep Code** (described on page 23).

Like Europe, this book uses the **24-hour clock.** It's the same through 12:00 noon, then keeps going: 13:00, 14:00, and so on. For anything over 12, subtract 12 and add p.m. (14:00 is 2:00 p.m.).

When giving **opening times,** I include both peak season and off-season hours if they differ. So, if a museum is listed as "May-Oct daily 9:00-16:00," it should be open from 9 a.m. until 4 p.m. from the first day of May until the last day of October (but expect exceptions).

For **transit** or **tour departures,** I first list the frequency, then the duration. So a train connection listed as "2/hour, 1.5 hours" departs twice each hour, and the journey lasts an hour and a half.

rary local, you'll get the absolute most out of every mile, minute, and dollar. As you visit places I know and love, I'm happy that you'll be meeting some of my favorite Italian people.

Planning

This section will help you get started planning your trip—with advice on trip costs, when to go, and what you should know before you take off.

Travel Smart
Many people travel through Italy thinking it's a chaotic mess. They feel that any attempt at efficient travel is futile. This is dead wrong—and expensive. Italy, which seems as orderly as spilled spa-

Top Destinations in Italy

DOLOMITES

THE LAKES

MILAN

TOWNS NEAR VENICE

VENICE

RIVIERA TOWNS NEAR CINQUE TERRE

CINQUE TERRE

PISA & LUCCA

FLORENCE

SIENA

HILL TOWNS OF CENTRAL ITALY

ASSISI

ORVIETO & CIVITA

ROME

NAPLES

POMPEII

SORRENTO & CAPRI

AMALFI COAST & PAESTUM

100 Kilometers

100 Miles

ghetti, actually functions quite well. Only those who understand this and travel smart can enjoy Italy on a budget.

This book can save you lots of time and money. But to have an "A" trip, you need to be an "A" student. Read it all before your trip, noting holidays, specific advice on sights, and days when sights are closed. A smart trip is a puzzle—a fun, doable, and worthwhile challenge.

When you're plotting your itinerary, strive for a mix of intense and relaxed stretches. To maximize rootedness, minimize one-night stands. It's worth taking a long drive after dinner (or a train ride with a dinner picnic) to get settled in a town for two nights. Hotels are more likely to give a better price to someone staying more than one night. Every trip—and every traveler—needs slack time (laundry, picnics, people-watching, and so on). Pace yourself. Assume you will return.

Reread this book as you travel, and visit local tourist information offices (abbreviated as TI in this book). Upon arrival in a new town, lay the groundwork for a smooth departure; get the schedule for the train, bus, or boat that you'll take when you depart. Drivers can study the best route to their next destination.

Get online at Internet cafés or your hotel, and carry a mobile phone (or use a phone card) to make travel plans: You can find tourist information, learn the latest on sights (special events, English tour schedule, etc.), book tickets and tours, make reservations, reconfirm hotels, research transportation connections, and keep in touch with your loved ones.

Enjoy the friendliness of the Italian people. Connect with the culture. Set up your own quest for the best piazza, bell tower, or gelato. Slow down and be open to unexpected experiences. Ask questions—most locals are eager to point you in their idea of the right direction. Keep a notepad in your pocket for noting directions, organizing your thoughts, and confirming prices. Wear your money belt, learn the currency, and figure out how to estimate prices in dollars. Those who expect to travel smart, do.

Trip Costs

Six components make up your trip costs: airfare, surface transportation, room and board, sightseeing and entertainment, shopping and miscellany, and gelato.

Airfare: A basic round trip flight from the US to Milan or Rome can cost, on average, about $800-1,700 total, depending on where you fly from and when (cheaper in winter). Smaller budget airlines provide bargain service from several European capitals to many cities in Italy. If your trip covers a wide area, consider saving time and money in Europe by flying into one city and out of another—for instance, into Milan and out of Rome.

Surface Transportation: For a three-week whirlwind trip of my recommended destinations, allow $550 per person for buses and second-class trains ($750 for first-class trains). For a three-week car rental, allow $750 per person (based on two people sharing), not including tolls, gas, and insurance. Leasing is worth considering for trips of three weeks or more. Car rentals and leases are cheapest if arranged from the US. Train passes normally must be purchased outside of Europe, but aren't necessarily your best option—you may save money by simply buying tickets as you go. Don't hesitate to consider flying, as budget airlines can be cheaper than taking the train (check www.skyscanner.com for intra-European flights). For more on public transportation and car rental, see "Transportation" in the appendix.

Room and Board: You can thrive in Italy in 2014 on $125 a day per person for room and board (more in big cities). This allows

Italy's Best Three-Week Trip
(by Train and Bus)

Day	Plan	Sleep in
1	Arrive in Milan	Milan
2	Milan to Lake Como	Varenna
3	Lake Como	Varenna
4	To Dolomites via Verona	Bolzano/Castelrotto
5	Dolomites	Bolzano/Castelrotto
6	To Venice	Venice
7	Venice	Venice
8	To Cinque Terre	Vernazza
9	Cinque Terre	Vernazza
10	Pisa, then to Florence	Florence
11	Florence	Florence
12	Florence, late to Siena	Siena
13	Siena	Siena
14	To Assisi (by bus)	Assisi
15	To Orvieto and Civita	Orvieto
16	To Sorrento	Sorrento
17	Naples and Pompeii	Sorrento
18	Capri or Amalfi Coast	Sorrento
19	Morning to Rome	Rome
20	Rome	Rome
21	Rome	Rome
22	Fly home	

With limited time: Skip the Dolomites.

To modify for drivers: The big sights of Italy (Rome, Florence, Venice, Sorrento/Naples/Capri/Amalfi, and Cinque Terre)

$5 for breakfast, $15 for lunch, $25 for dinner, and $80 for lodging (based on two people splitting the cost of a $160 double room). Students and tightwads can enjoy Italy for as little as $65 a day ($35 for a bed, $30 for meals and snacks).

Sightseeing and Entertainment: In big cities, figure about $15-22 per major sight (museums, Colosseum), $7-10 for minor ones (climbing church towers), and $30 for splurge experiences (such as walking tours and concerts). An overall average of $35 a day works for most people. Don't skimp here. After all, this category is the driving force behind your trip—you came to sightsee, enjoy, and experience Italy.

Shopping and Miscellany: Figure $3 per postcard (including postage) and $5 per coffee, soft drink, or gelato. Shopping can vary

Italy's Best Three-Week Trip

(LAKES) VARENNA
CASTELROTTO (DOLOMITES)
MILAN
VERONA
VENICE
100 Kilometers
100 Miles
RAVENNA
CINQUE TERRE
PISA
FLORENCE
SIENA
ASSISI
CIVITA
ORVIETO
Adriatic Sea
ROME
Mediterranean Sea
NAPLES
POMPEII
SORRENTO
PAESTUM
AMALFI COAST
● Overnights
• Other Stops

are inconvenient by car and easy by public transportation. Those wanting to drive in Italy will find a car most helpful for the hill towns of Tuscany and Umbria and the Dolomites. I'd start by touring most of the country by train, then use a car to explore a region or two (even if it means backtracking a few extra hours by train or car).

in cost from nearly nothing to a small fortune. Good budget travelers find that this category has little to do with assembling a trip full of lifelong and wonderful memories.

Sightseeing Priorities

Depending on the length of your trip, and taking geographic proximity into account, here are my recommended priorities:

4 days:	Florence, Venice
6 days, add:	Rome
8 days, add:	Cinque Terre
10 days, add:	Civita and Siena
14 days, add:	Sorrento, Naples, Pompeii, Amalfi Coast, Paestum

18 days, add: Milan, Lake Como, Varenna, Assisi
21 days, add: Dolomites, Verona, Padua
    This includes nearly everything on the map on the previous page.

When to Go

Italy's best travel months (also its busiest and most expensive) are May, June, September, and October. These months combine the convenience of peak season with pleasant weather.

The most grueling thing about travel in Italy—particularly in the south—is the summer heat in July and August, when temperatures hit the high 80s and 90s. Most mid-range hotels come with air-conditioning—important in the summer—but it's usually available only from June through September.

Peak season (roughly May-Oct in the north and May-June and Sept-Oct in the south) offers the longest hours and the most exciting slate of activities—but terrible crowds. During peak times, many resort-area hotels maximize business by requiring that guests take half-pension, which means buying a meal per day (usually dinner) in their restaurants. August, the month when many Italians take their summer vacations, isn't as bad as many make it out to be, but big cities tend to be quiet (with discounted hotel prices), and beach and mountain resorts are jammed (with higher hotel prices). Note that Italians generally wear shorts only at beach resort towns. If you want to blend in, wear lightweight long (or Capri) pants in Italy, even in summer, except at the beach.

Between November and April, you can usually expect pleasant weather, and you'll miss most of the sweat and stress of the tourist season. Off-season, expect shorter hours, more lunchtime breaks, and fewer activities. However, spring and fall can be cool, and many hotels—thanks to a national interest in conserving energy—aren't allowed to turn on their heat until winter. In the winter, it often drops to the 40s in Milan and the 50s in Rome (see the climate chart in the appendix).

Know Before You Go

Your trip is more likely to go smoothly if you plan ahead. Check this list of things to arrange while you're still at home.

You need a **passport**—but no visa or shots—to travel in Italy. You may be denied entry into certain European countries if your passport is due to expire within three to six months of your ticketed date of return. Get it renewed if you'll be cutting it close. It can take up to six weeks to get or renew a passport (for more on passports, see www.travel.state.gov). Pack a photocopy of your passport in your luggage in case the original is lost or stolen.

Book rooms well in advance if you'll be traveling during peak season (spring and fall) and any major holidays (see page 1189).

Rick Steves' Audio Europe

If you're bringing a mobile device, be sure to check out **Rick Steves Audio Europe,** where you can download free audio tours and hours of travel interviews (via the Rick Steves Audio Europe smartphone app, www.ricksteves.com/audioeurope, Google Play, or iTunes).

My self-guided **audio tours** are user-friendly, easy-to-follow, fun, and informative, covering the major sights and neighborhoods in Venice, Florence, Assisi, and Rome. Compared to live tours, my audio tours are hard to beat: Nobody will stand you up, the quality is reliable, you can take the tour exactly when you like, and they're free.

Rick Steves Audio Europe also offers a far-reaching library of intriguing **travel interviews** with experts from around the globe. The interviews are organized by destination, including many of the places in this book.

Call your **debit- and credit-card companies** to let them know the countries you'll be visiting, to ask about fees, request your PIN code (it will be mailed to you), and more. See page 16 for details.

Do your homework if you want to buy **travel insurance.** Compare the cost of the insurance to the likelihood of your using it and your potential loss if something goes wrong. Also, check whether your existing insurance (health, homeowners, or renters) covers you and your possessions overseas. For more tips, see www.ricksteves.com/insurance.

If you're taking an **overnight train** and need a couchette *(cuccetta)* or sleeper—and you must leave on a certain day—consider booking it in advance through a US agent (such as www.raileurope.com), even though it may cost more than buying it in Italy. Other Italian trains, including the high-speed Frecce trains, require a seat reservation, but for these it's usually possible to make arrangements in Italy just a few days ahead. (For more on train travel, see the appendix.)

If you're planning on **renting a car** in Italy, bring your driver's license and an International Driving Permit (see page 1178). Driving is prohibited in some city centers; obey the signage or risk getting a huge fine (see page 1181).

While you can stroll right in at plenty of sights, the famous ones come with long lines. These lines are often avoidable if you follow the strategies in this book, often by **buying tickets or making reservations in advance.** Book at least a month in advance for **Florence**'s Uffizi Gallery (Renaissance paintings) and a few days ahead for the Accademia (Michelangelo's *David*)—or buy a Firenze Card when you arrive in Florence (see page 516). For **Milan,** try to book several months ahead for da Vinci's *Last Supper* (see page 349);

Italy at a Glance

These attractions are listed (as in this book) roughly from north to south.

▲▲▲**Venice** Romantic island city, powerful in medieval times; famous for St. Mark's Basilica, the Grand Canal, and singing gondoliers.

▲**Near Venice** Several interesting towns: Padua (with Giotto's gloriously frescoed Scrovegni Chapel), Verona (Roman amphitheater plus Romeo and Juliet sights), and Ravenna (top Byzantine mosaics).

▲**The Dolomites** Italy's rugged rooftop with a Germanic flair, featuring Bolzano (home of Ötzi the Iceman), Castelrotto (charming village), and Alpe di Siusi (alpine meadows laced with lifts and hiking trails).

▲**The Lakes** Two relaxing lakes, each with low-key resort towns and a mountainous backdrop: Lake Como, with quaint Varenna and upscale Bellagio; and Lake Maggiore, with straightforward Stresa, manicured islands, and elegant villas.

▲▲**Milan** Powerhouse city of commerce and fashion, with the prestigious La Scala opera house, Leonardo's *The Last Supper*, and three airports.

▲▲▲**The Cinque Terre** Five idyllic Riviera hamlets along a rugged coastline (and part of a national park), connected by scenic hiking trails and dotted with beaches.

Riviera Towns near the Cinque Terre More Italian Riviera fun, including the beach towns of Levanto, Sestri Levante, the larger Santa Margherita Ligure, and trendier Portofino nearby; and to the south, resorty Portovenere and workaday La Spezia (transportation hub).

▲▲▲**Florence** The cradle of the Renaissance, with the world-class Uffizi Gallery, Brunelleschi's dome-topped Duomo, Michelangelo's *David*, and Italy's best gelato.

for **Padua,** book at least two days in advance for Giotto's Scrovegni Chapel (see page 171); and for **Rome,** a week ahead for the Borghese Gallery (Bernini sculptures; see page 920). Reservations let you skip the line at Rome's Vatican Museum (see page 910), as do advance tickets or the Roma Pass for the Colosseum (see page 882) and Forum (see page 890).

▲**Pisa and Lucca** Two classic towns: Pisa, with its famous Leaning Tower and surrounding Field of Miracles, and Lucca, with a charming walled old center.

▲▲▲**Siena** Florence's smaller and (some say) more appealing rival, with its grand Il Campo square and striking striped cathedral.

▲▲**Hill Towns of Central Italy** Picturesque, wine-soaked villages of Italy's heartland, including San Gimignano, Volterra, Montalcino, Pienza, Montepulciano, and Cortona.

▲▲**Assisi** St. Francis' hometown, perched on a hillside, with a divinely Giotto-decorated basilica.

▲▲**Orvieto and Civita** More hill-town adventures, featuring Orvieto's classic views and ornate cathedral, plus the adorable pocket-sized village of Civita di Bagnoregio.

▲▲▲**Rome** Italy's capital, the Eternal City, studded with Roman remnants (Forum, Colosseum, Pantheon), romantic floodlit-fountain squares, and the Vatican –home to one of Italy's top museums and the Sistine Chapel.

▲▲**Naples** Gritty, in-love-with-life port city featuring vibrant street life and a top archaeological museum.

▲**Pompeii and Nearby** Famous ruins of the ancient towns of Pompeii and Herculaneum, stopped in their tracks by the eruption of Mount Vesuvius.

▲**Sorrento and Capri** The seaside resort port of Sorrento, and a short cruise away, the jet-set island getaway of Capri, with its Blue Grotto.

▲**Amalfi Coast and Paestum** String of seafront villages—including hilly Positano and workaday Amalfi—tied together by a scenic mountainous coastal road, plus nearby Paestum, with its well-preserved ancient Greek temples.

If you plan to hire a **local guide,** reserve ahead by email. Popular guides can get booked up.

If you're bringing a **mobile device,** download any apps you might want to use on the road, such as translators, maps, and transit schedules. Check out **Rick Steves Audio Europe,** featuring audio tours of major sights, hours of travel interviews on Italy, and more (via www.ricksteves.com/audioeurope, iTunes, Google Play, or the Rick Steves Audio Europe smartphone app; for details, see the sidebar on page 9).

Check the **Rick Steves guidebook updates** page for any recent changes to this book (www.ricksteves.com/update).

Because **airline carry-on restrictions** are always changing, visit the Transportation Security Administration's website (www. tsa.gov) for an up-to-date list of what you can bring on the plane with you...and what you must check.

If you're planning some Riviera **beach** time (such as in the Cinque Terre), be aware that many Italian beaches are pebbly or rocky rather than sandy. In addition to your swimsuit, you may want to pack (or buy in Europe) a pair of water shoes for wading.

Practicalities

Emergency and Medical Help: In Italy, dial 113 for English-speaking police help. To summon an ambulance, call 118. If you get sick, do as the Italians do and go to a pharmacist for advice. Or ask at your hotel for help—they'll know of the nearest medical and emergency services.

Theft or Loss: To replace a passport, you'll need to go in person to your embassy (see page 1164). If your credit and debit cards disappear, cancel and replace them (see "Damage Control for Lost Cards" on page 17). File a police report, either on the spot or within a day or two; you'll need it to submit an insurance claim for lost or stolen railpasses or travel gear, and it can help with replacing your passport or credit and debit cards. For more information, see www. ricksteves.com/help. Precautionary measures can minimize the effects of loss—back up your digital photos and other files frequently.

More Help: A service of the Italian government, **EasyItalia,** offers English-language tourist information, emergency assistance, and help with everything from flight cancellations to car-rental trouble (call toll-free 800-000-039 from a land line or pay phone, otherwise call 039-039-039, phone answered daily 9:00-22:00; or use their online form at www.easy-italia.com for a response within 48 hours).

Avoiding Theft and Scams: Although violent crime is rare in Italy, petty theft is rampant in Italy's large cities. With sweet-talking con artists meeting you at the station, well-dressed pickpockets on buses, and thieving gangs of children roving ancient sites, tourists face a gauntlet of rip-offs. Although it's not as bad as it was a few years ago, and pickpockets don't want to hurt you—they usually just want your money—green or sloppy tourists will be scammed.

Thieves strike when you're distracted. Don't trust kind strangers. Keep nothing important in your pockets. Be most on guard while boarding and leaving buses and subways. Thieves crowd the door, then stop and turn while others crowd and push from behind. You'll find less crowding and commotion—and less risk—waiting for the end cars of a subway rather than the middle cars. The sneakiest thieves pretend to be well-dressed businessmen (generally with something in their hands) or tourists wearing fanny packs and toting cameras and even Rick Steves guidebooks.

Scams abound: Always be clear about what paper money you're giving someone, demand clear and itemized bills, and count your change. Don't give your wallet to self-proclaimed "police" who stop you on the street, warn you about counterfeit (or drug) money, and ask to see your cash. If a bank machine eats your ATM card, see if there's a thin plastic insert with a tongue hanging out that thieves use to extract it.

If you know what to look out for, fast-fingered moms with babies and gangs of children picking the pockets and handbags of naive tourists are not a threat, but an interesting, albeit sad, spectacle. Pickpockets troll through the tourist crowds around major sights and and train and Metro stations. Watch them target tourists who are overloaded with bags or distracted with a video camera. The kids look like beggars and hold up newspapers or cardboard signs to confuse their victims. They scram like stray cats if you're on to them.

This all sounds intimidating, and perhaps I'm overstating the dangers. Don't be scared—just be aware and be smart, and you'll be fine.

Time Zones: Italy, like most of continental Europe, is generally six/nine hours ahead of the East/West Coasts of the US. The exceptions are the beginning and end of Daylight Saving Time: Europe "springs forward" the last Sunday in March (two weeks after most of North America), and "falls back" the last Sunday in October (one week before North America). For a handy online time converter, see www.timeanddate.com/worldclock.

Business Hours: Traditionally, Italy used the siesta plan. People worked from 9:00 to 13:00 and from 15:30 to 19:00, Monday through Saturday. But many businesses have now adopted the government's recommended 8:00 to 14:00 workday (although in tourist areas, shops are open longer). Still, expect small towns and villages to be more or less shut tight during the midafternoon. Stores are also usually closed on Sunday, and often on Monday, as well as for a couple of weeks around August 15. Banking hours are generally Monday through Friday from 8:30 to 13:30 and 15:30 to 16:30, but can vary wildly.

Saturdays are virtually weekdays, with earlier closing hours. Sundays have the same pros and cons as they do for travelers in the US: Sightseeing attractions are generally open, while shops and banks are closed, public transportation options are fewer (for example, no bus service to or from the smaller hill towns), and there's no rush hour. Rowdy evenings are rare on Sundays.

Watt's Up? Europe's electrical system is 220 volts, instead of North America's 110 volts. Most newer electronics (such as laptops, battery chargers, and hair dryers) convert automatically, so you won't need a converter, but you will need an adapter plug with two round prongs, sold inexpensively at travel stores in the US. Avoid bringing older appliances that don't automatically convert voltage; instead, buy a cheap replacement in Europe.

Discounts: Discounts are not listed in this book. However, many sights offer discounts for youths (up to age 18), students (with proper identification cards, www.isic.org), families, seniors (loosely defined as retirees or those willing to call themselves a senior), and groups of 10 or more. Always ask. Italy's national museums generally offer free admission to children under 18, but some discounts are available only for citizens of the European Union (EU).

Tobacco Shops: Tobacco shops (known as *tabacchi*, often indicated with a big *T* sign) are ubiquitous across Italy as handy places to pay for street parking, and to buy postage or tickets for city buses and subways.

Online Translation Tip: You can use Google's Chrome browser (available free at www.google.com/chrome) to instantly translate websites. With one click, the page appears in (very rough) English translation. You can also paste the URL of the site into the translation window at www.google.com/translate.

Money

This section offers advice on how to pay for purchases on your trip (including getting cash from ATMs and paying with plastic), dealing with lost or stolen cards, VAT (sales tax) refunds, and tipping.

What to Bring

Bring both a credit card and a debit card. You'll use the debit card at cash machines (ATMs) to withdraw local cash for most purchases, and the credit card to pay for larger items. Some travelers carry a third card as a backup, in case one gets demagnetized or eaten by a temperamental machine.

For an emergency stash, bring several hundred dollars in hard cash in $20 bills. If you have to exchange the bills, go to a bank; avoid using currency exchange booths because of their lousy rates and/or outrageous fees.

Cash

Cash is just as desirable in Europe as it is at home. Small businesses (hotels, restaurants, shops, etc.) prefer that you pay your bills with

> ## Exchange Rate
>
> ### 1 euro (€) = about $1.30
>
> To convert prices in euros to dollars, add about 30 percent: €20 = about $26, €50 = about $65. (Check www.oanda.com for the latest exchange rates.) Just like the dollar, one euro is broken down into 100 cents. Coins range from €0.01 to €2, and bills from €5 to €500.

cash. Some vendors will charge you extra for using a credit card, and many restaurants and some sights won't take credit cards at all. Cash is the best—and sometimes only—way to pay for bus fare, taxis, and local guides.

Throughout Europe, ATMs are the standard way for travelers to get cash. But stay away from "independent" ATMs such as Travelex, Euronet, and Forex, which charge huge commissions and have terrible exchange rates.

To withdraw money from an ATM (known as a *bancomat*), you'll need a debit card (ideally with a Visa or MasterCard logo for maximum usability), plus a PIN code. Know your PIN code in numbers; there are only numbers—no letters—on European keypads. Although you can use a credit card for an ATM transaction, it only makes sense in an emergency, because it's considered a cash advance (borrowed at a high interest rate) rather than a withdrawal. Try to withdraw large sums of money to reduce the number of per-transaction bank fees you'll pay.

For increased security, shield the keypad when entering your PIN code, and don't use an ATM if anything on the front of the machine looks loose or damaged (a sign that someone may have attached a "skimming" device to capture account information). It's a good idea to monitor your account while traveling to detect any unauthorized transactions.

Pickpockets target tourists. To safeguard your cash, wear a money belt—a pouch with a strap that you buckle around your waist like a belt and tuck under your clothes. Keep your cash, credit cards, and passport secure in your money belt, and carry only a day's spending money in your front pocket.

Credit and Debit Cards

For purchases, Visa and MasterCard are more commonly accepted than American Express. Just like at home, credit or debit cards work easily at larger hotels, restaurants, and shops. I typically use my debit card to withdraw cash to pay for most purchases. I use my credit card only in a few specific situations: to book hotel reservations by phone, to cover major expenses (such as car rentals, plane tickets, and long hotel stays), and to pay for things near the end of my trip (to avoid another visit to the ATM). While you could use a debit card to make most large purchases, using a credit card offers a greater degree of fraud protection (because debit cards draw funds directly from your account).

Ask Your Credit- or Debit-Card Company: Before your trip, contact the company that issued your debit or credit cards.

• Confirm your **card will work overseas,** and alert them that you'll be using it in Europe; otherwise, they may deny transactions if they perceive unusual spending patterns.

• Ask for the specifics on transaction **fees.** When you use your credit or debit card—either for purchases or ATM withdrawals— you'll typically be charged additional "international transaction" fees of up to 3 percent (1 percent is normal) plus $5 per transaction. If your card's fees seem high, consider getting a different card just for your trip: Capital One (www.capitalone.com) and most credit unions have low-to-no international fees.

• If you plan to withdraw cash from ATMs, confirm your daily **withdrawal limit,** and, if necessary, ask your bank to adjust it. Some travelers prefer a high limit that allows them to take out more cash at each ATM stop (saving on bank fees), while others prefer to set a lower limit in case their card is stolen. Note that foreign banks also set maximum withdrawal amounts for their ATMs.

• Get your bank's emergency **phone number** in the US (but not its 800 number, which isn't accessible from overseas) to call collect if you have a problem.

• Ask for your credit card's **PIN** in case you need to make an emergency cash withdrawal or encounter Europe's "chip-and-PIN" system (described next); the bank won't tell you your PIN over the phone, so allow time for it to be mailed to you.

Chip and PIN: While much of Europe is shifting to a "chip-and-PIN" security system for credit and debit cards, Italy still uses the old magnetic-swipe technology. (European chip-and-PIN cards are embedded with an electronic security chip, and require the purchaser to punch in a PIN rather than sign a receipt.) If you happen to encounter chip and PIN, it will probably be at auto-mated payment machines, such as those at toll roads or self-serve gas pumps. On the outside chance that a machine won't take your card, find a cashier who can make your card work (they can print a receipt for you to sign), or find a machine that takes cash. But don't panic. Most travelers who are carrying only magnetic-stripe cards never encounter any problems. You can always use an ATM with your magnetic-stripe card, even in countries where people predom-inantly use chip-and-PIN cards.

Dynamic Currency Conversion: If merchants offer to con-

vert your purchase price into dollars (called dynamic currency conversion, or DCC), refuse this "service." You'll pay even more in fees
for the expensive convenience of seeing your charge in dollars.

Damage Control for Lost Cards

If you lose your credit, debit, or ATM card, you can stop people
from using your card by reporting the loss immediately to the respective global customer-assistance centers. Call these 24-hour
US numbers collect: Visa (tel. 303/967-1096), MasterCard (tel.
636/722-7111), and American Express (tel. 336/393-1111). European toll-free numbers (listed by country) can also be found at the
websites for Visa and MasterCard.

Providing the following information will allow for a quicker
cancellation of your missing card: full card number, whether you
are the primary or secondary cardholder, the cardholder's name
exactly as printed on the card, billing address, home phone number, circumstances of the loss or theft, and identification verifica-
tion (your birth date, your mother's maiden name, or your Social
Security number—memorize this, don't carry a copy). If you are
the secondary cardholder, you'll also need to provide the primary
cardholder's identification-verification details. You can generally
receive a temporary card within two or three business days in Europe (see www.ricksteves.com/help for more).

If you report your loss within two days, you typically won't
be responsible for any unauthorized transactions on your account,
although many banks charge a liability fee of $50.

Tipping

Tipping in Italy isn't as automatic and generous as it is in the US,
but for special service, tips are appreciated, if not expected. As in
the US, the proper amount depends on your resources, tipping philosophy, and the circumstances, but some general guidelines apply.

Restaurants: In Italy, a service charge *(servizio)* is usually
built into your bill, so the total you pay already includes a basic tip.
It's up to you whether to tip beyond this. For details on restaurant
tipping, see page 33.

Taxis: To tip the cabbie, round up. For a typical ride, round up
your fare a bit (to pay a €4.50 fare, give €5). If the cabbie hauls your
bags and zips you to the airport to help you catch your flight, you
might want to toss in a little more. But if you feel like you're being
driven in circles or otherwise ripped off, skip the tip.

Services: In general, if someone in the service industry does
a super job for you, a small tip (the equivalent of a euro or two) is
appropriate...but not required. If you're not sure whether (or how
much) to tip for a service, ask your hotelier or the TI.

Getting a VAT Refund

Wrapped into the purchase price of your Italian souvenirs is a Value-Added Tax (VAT) of about 22 percent. You're entitled to get most of that tax back if you purchase more than €155 (about $200) worth of goods at a store that participates in the VAT-refund scheme. Typically, you must ring up the minimum at a single retailer—you can't add up your purchases from various shops to reach the required amount.

Getting your refund is usually straightforward and, if you buy a substantial amount of souvenirs, well worth the hassle. If you're lucky, the merchant will subtract the tax when you make your purchase. (This is more likely to occur if the store ships the goods to your home.) Otherwise, you'll need to:

Get the paperwork. Have the merchant completely fill out the necessary refund document. You'll have to present your passport. Get the paperwork done before you leave the store to ensure you'll have everything you need (including your original sales receipt).

Get your stamp at the border or airport. Process your VAT document at your last stop in the European Union (such as at the airport) with the customs agent who deals with VAT refunds. Arrive an additional hour early before you need to check in for your flight, to give you time to find the local customs office—and to stand in line. Keep your purchases readily available for viewing by the customs agent (ideally in your carry-on bag—don't make the mistake of checking the bag with your purchases before you've seen the agent). You're not supposed to use your purchased goods before you leave. If you show up at customs wearing your new Italian leather shoes, officials might look the other way—or deny you a refund.

Collect your refund. You'll need to return your stamped document to the retailer or its representative. Many merchants work with services, such as Global Blue or Premier Tax Free, that have offices at major airports, ports, or border crossings (either before or after security, often strategically located near a duty-free shop). These services, which extract a 4 percent fee, can refund your money immediately in cash or credit your card (within two billing cycles). If the retailer handles VAT refunds directly, it's up to you to contact the merchant for your refund. You can mail the documents from home or, more quickly, from your point of departure (using an envelope you've prepared in advance or one that's been provided by the merchant). You'll then have to wait—it can take months.

Customs for American Shoppers

You are allowed to take home $800 worth of items per person duty-free, once every 30 days. You can also bring in duty-free a liter of alcohol. As for food, you can take home many processed and packaged foods: vacuum-packed cheeses, dried herbs, jams, baked goods, candy, chocolate, oil, vinegar, mustard, and honey. Fresh fruits and vegetables and most meats are not allowed. Any liquid-containing foods must be packed in checked luggage, a potential recipe for disaster. To check customs rules and duty rates, visit http://help.cbp.gov.

Sightseeing

Sightseeing can be hard work. Use these tips to make your visits to Italy's finest museums meaningful, fun, efficient, and painless.

Plan Ahead

Set up an itinerary that allows you to fit in all your must-see sights. For a one-stop look at opening hours, see the "At a Glance" side-bars for each major city (Venice, Milan, Florence, Siena, and Rome). Most sights keep stable hours, but you can easily confirm the latest by checking with the TI or visiting museum websites. Or call sights in the morning and ask: "Are you open today?" (*"Aperto oggi?"*; ah-PER-toh OH-jee) and "What time do you close?" (*"A che ora chiuso?"*; ah kay OH-rah kee-OO-zoh). I've included telephone numbers for this purpose.

Use the suggestions in this book to avoid waiting in line to buy tickets or enter sights. Sometimes you can make reservations for an entry time (for example, at Florence's Uffizi Gallery or Rome's Vatican Museum). Some cities offer museum passes for admission to several museums (e.g., Roma Pass and Firenze Card) that let you skip ticket-buying lines. At some popular places (such as Rome's Colosseum or Venice's Doge's Palace), you can get in more quickly by buying your ticket or pass at a less-crowded sight (Rome's Palatine Hill or Venice's Correr Museum). Booking a guided tour can help you avoid lines at many popular sights.

Don't put off visiting a must-see sight—you never know when a place will close unexpectedly for a holiday, strike, or restoration. Many museums are closed or have reduced hours at least a few days a year, especially on holidays such as Christmas, New Year's, and Labor Day (May 1). A list of holidays is on page 1189; check museum websites for possible closures during your trip. In summer, some sights may stay open late. Off-season, many museums have shorter hours.

Going at the right time helps avoid crowds. This book offers tips on the best times to see specific sights. Try visiting popular sights very early or very late. Evening visits are usually peaceful, with fewer crowds.

Study up. To get the most out of the sight descriptions in this book, read them before you visit.

At Sights

Here's what you can typically expect:

Entering: You may have to pay cash for the admission fee; some sights don't take credit cards. Be warned that you may not be allowed to enter if you arrive within 30 to 60 minutes of closing time. And guards start ushering people out well before the actual closing time, so don't save the best for last.

Important sights often have a security check, where you must open your bag or send it through a metal detector. Some sights require you to check daypacks and coats. (If you'd rather not check your daypack, try carrying it tucked under your arm like a purse as you enter.)

Photography: If the museum's photo policy isn't clearly posted, ask a guard. Generally, taking photos without a flash or tripod is allowed. Some sights—especially churches—ban photos altogether.

Temporary Exhibits: Some sights have found a clever way to squeeze more money out of visitors by hosting special exhibits in addition to their permanent collection. Most of these come at an extra cost (which you'll likely have to pay even if you don't want to see the special exhibit). The prices I've listed in this book generally include these obligatory temporary exhibits. Come expecting this higher price...and consider yourself lucky if you happen to visit between exhibitions, when you can get in for less.

Expect Changes: Artwork can be on tour, on loan, out sick, or shifted at the whim of the curator. To adapt, pick up a floor plan as you enter, and ask museum staff if you can't find a particular item. Say the title or artist's name, or point to the photograph in this book and ask, *"Dov'è?"* (doh-VEH; meaning "Where is?").

Audioguides: Many sights rent audioguides, which generally offer dry-but-useful recorded descriptions in English (about $5). If you bring your own earbuds, you can enjoy better sound and avoid holding the device to your ear. To save money, bring a Y-jack and share one audioguide with your travel partner. Increasingly, sights are offering apps (often free) that you can download to your mobile device. I've produced free downloadable audio tours of some of Italy's major sights; see page 9.

It helps to know the terms. Art historians and Italians refer to the great Florentine centuries by dropping a thousand years. The Trecento (300s), Quattrocento (400s), and Cinquecento (500s) were the 1300s, 1400s, and 1500s. The Novecento (900s) means modern art (the 1900s). Also, in Italian museums, art is dated with *sec* (for *secolo*, or century, often indicated with Roman numerals), A.C. (for *avanti Cristo*, or B.C.), and D.C. (for *dopo Cristo*, or A.D.). O.K.?

Services: Important sights may have an on-site café or cafeteria (usually a handy place to rejuvenate during a long visit). The WCs at sights are free and generally clean.

Before Leaving: At the gift shop, scan the postcard rack or thumb through a guidebook to be sure that you haven't overlooked something that you'd like to see.

Every sight or museum offers more than what is covered in this book. Use the information in this book as an introduction, not the final word.

Find Religion

Churches offer some amazing art (usually free), a cool respite from heat, and a welcome seat.

A modest dress code (no bare shoulders or shorts for anyone, even kids) is enforced at larger churches, such as Venice's St. Mark's and the Vatican's St. Peter's, but is often overlooked elsewhere. If you are caught by surprise, you can improvise, using maps to cover your shoulders and a jacket for your knees. (I wear a super-lightweight pair of long pants rather than shorts for my hot and muggy big-city Italian sightseeing.)

Some churches have coin-operated audioboxes that describe the art and history; just set the dial on English, put in your coins, and listen. Other coin boxes illuminate the art (and present a better photo opportunity). I pop in a coin whenever I can. It improves my experience, is a favor to other visitors trying to appreciate a great piece of art in the dark, and is a little contribution to that church and its work. Whenever possible, let there be light.

Sleeping

I favor hotels and restaurants that are handy to your sightseeing activities. Rather than list hotels scattered throughout a city, I describe two or three favorite neighborhoods and recommend the best accommodations values in each, from fancy hotels with all of the comforts to budget hostels.

Sleeping in Italy is expensive, and cheap big-city hotels can be depressing. Tourist information services cannot give opinions on quality of hotels. A major feature of this book is its extensive and opinionated listing of good-value rooms. I like places that are clean, central, relatively quiet at night, reasonably priced, friendly, small enough to have a hands-on owner and stable staff, run with a respect for Italian traditions, and not listed in other guidebooks. (In Italy, for me, six out of these eight criteria means it's a keeper.) Some places listed are old and rickety, and I've described them as such. I'm more impressed by a convenient location and a fun-loving philosophy than flat-screen TVs and a pricey laundry service.

Book your accommodations well in advance if you'll be traveling during busy times. See page 1189 for a list of major holidays and festivals in Italy; for tips on making reservations, see page 26.

Sleep Code

(€1 = about $1.30, country code: 39)

Price Rankings

To help you easily sort through my listings, I've divided the accommodations into three categories based on the price for a double room with bath during high season:

$$$	**Higher Priced**
$$	**Moderately Priced**
$	**Lower Priced**

I always rate hostels as $, whether or not they have double rooms, because they have the cheapest beds in town. Prices can change without notice; verify the hotel's current rates online or by email. For the best prices, always book direct.

Abbreviations

To pack maximum information into minimum space, I use the following code to describe accommodations in this book. Prices listed are per room, not per person. When a price range is given for a type of room (such as double rooms listing for €100-150), it means the price fluctuates with the season, size of room, or length of stay; expect to pay the upper end for peak-season stays.

S = Single room (or price for one person in a double).

D = Double or twin room. "Double beds" can be two twins sheeted together and are usually big enough for nonromantic couples.

T = Triple (generally a double bed with a single).

Q = Quad (usually two double beds; adding an extra child's bed to a T is usually cheaper).

b = Private bathroom with toilet and shower or tub.

s = Private shower or tub only (the toilet is down the hall).

According to this code, a couple staying at a "Db-€140" hotel would pay a total of €140 (about $180) for a double room with a private bathroom. Unless otherwise noted, breakfast is included, hotel staff speak basic English, and credit cards are accepted. Some cities charge a hotel tax of €1-4 per person, per night. If the city adds a room tax, it generally isn't included in the rates I list.

There's almost always Wi-Fi and/or a guest computer available, either free or for a fee.

INTRODUCTION

Rates and Deals

I've described my recommended accommodations using a Sleep Code (see sidebar). Prices listed are for one-night stays in peak season, and assume you're booking direct (rather than using an online hotel-booking engine or going through a TI). Booking services extract a commission from the hotel, which logically closes the door on special deals. Book direct. For most of the hotels I list, I provide a website (which often has a built-in booking form) and an email address; you can expect an English response within a day (and often sooner).

Some cities—such as Venice, Florence, Padua, and Rome—levy a tax on hotel rooms to generate income for municipal projects. This tax is generally not included in the prices in this book and must be paid in cash at checkout. It varies from €1 to €4 per person, per night, depending on the city and how many stars the hotel has.

Given the economic downturn, hoteliers are often willing and eager to make a deal. I'd suggest emailing several hotels to ask for their best price. Comparison-shop and make your choice.

Some hotels use "dynamic pricing," which means room rates change from day to day depending on demand. This makes it difficult to predict what you will pay. When possible, I've tried to list just one price, which is what you'll most likely pay for a standard room during the busy season (but ignoring the dramatically inflated rates hotels charge for special events a few days each year). This rate is intended as a rough guideline, and may vary significantly based on demand—check the hotel's website, or email them, to find out specifics for the date of your visit. For other hotels, I list a range of prices; if the rate you're offered is at or near the bottom of this range, it's likely a good deal.

As you look over the listings, you'll notice that some accommodations promise special prices to Rick Steves readers who book directly with the hotel. To get these rates, you must book direct (that is, *not* through a booking site like TripAdvisor or Booking.com), mention this book when you reserve, and then show the book upon arrival. Rick Steves discounts apply to readers with ebooks as well as printed books. Because we trust hotels to honor this, please let me know if you don't receive a listed discount. Note, though, that discounts understandably may not be applied to promotional rates.

In general, prices can soften if you do any of the following: offer to pay cash, stay at least three nights, or mention this book. You can also try asking for a cheaper room or a discount, or offer to skip breakfast.

Types of Accommodations
Hotels

Double rooms listed in this book range from about €50 (very simple, toilet and shower down the hall) to €450 (maximum plumbing and more), with most clustered around €140 (with private bathrooms). Prices are higher in big cities and heavily touristed cities, and lower off the beaten path.

Solo travelers find that the cost of a *camera singola* is often only 25 percent less than a *camera doppia*. Three or four people can economize by requesting larger rooms. (If a double room is €110, a quad may be about €150.) Most listed hotels have a variety of rooms that can accommodate from one to five people. If there's space for an extra cot, they'll cram it in for you (charging you around €25).

The Italian word for "hotel" is *hotel*, and in smaller, non-touristy towns, *albergo*. A few places have kept the old titles *locanda* or *pensione*, indicating that they offer budget beds. English works in all but the cheapest places.

Nearly all places offer at least some rooms with private bathrooms. You'll save €30/night if you request a room with the shower down the hall. Generally rooms with a bath or shower also have a toilet and a bidet (which Italians use for quick sponge baths). The cord that dangles over the tub or shower is not a clothesline. You pull it when you've fallen and can't get up.

Double beds are called *matrimoniale*, even though hotels aren't interested in your marital status. Twins are *due letti singoli*. Convents offer cheap accommodation, but only *letti singoli*.

When you check in, the receptionist will normally ask for your passport and keep it for anywhere from a couple of minutes to a couple of hours. Hotels are legally required to register each guest with the police. Relax. Americans are notorious for making this chore more difficult than it needs to be.

Hotels and B&Bs are sometimes located on the higher floors of a multipurpose building with a secured door. In that case, look for your hotel's name on the buttons by the main entrance. When you ring the bell, you'll be buzzed in. Hotel elevators, while becoming more common, are often very small—pack light, or you may need to send your bags up separately.

Assume that a basic breakfast is included in the prices I've listed, unless otherwise noted. If the breakfast costs money, you may want to skip it. While convenient, it's usually expensive—€5-8 per person for a simple continental buffet with (at its most generous) bread, ham, cheese, yogurt, juice, and unlimited caffè latte. A picnic in your room followed by a coffee at the corner café can be a lot cheaper. (For more on Italian breakfasts, see page 31.)

More pillows and blankets are usually in the closet or available on request. Towels and linen aren't always replaced every day. Hang your towel up to dry. Some hotels use lightweight "waffle" or very thin tablecloth-type towels; although less absorbent, these take less water and electricity to launder and are preferred by many Italians.

Most hotel rooms have a TV, phone, and Wi-Fi (although

Chill Out

In general, all but the cheapest hotels have air-conditioning. Because Europeans are generally careful with energy use, you'll find government-enforced limits on air-conditioning and heating. There's a one-month period each spring and fall when neither is allowed. Air-conditioning sometimes costs an extra per-day charge, is worth seeking out in summer (though it may be on only at certain times of the day), and is rarely available from fall through spring. Fancier hotel rooms usually include air-conditioning in the price. Conveniently, many business-class hotels drop their prices in July and August, just when the air-conditioned comfort they offer is most important.

Most hotel rooms with air conditioners come with a remote control that generally has the same symbols and features: fan icon (click to toggle through wind power, from light to gale); louver icon (choose steady airflow or waves); snowflake and sunshine icons (cold air or heat, depending on season); clock ("O" setting: run x hours before turning off; "I" setting: wait x hours to start); and the temperature control (21 degrees Celsius is comfortable).

in old buildings with thick walls, the Wi-Fi signal doesn't always make it to the rooms; sometimes it's only available in the lobby). Sometimes there's a guest computer with Internet access in the lobby. Simpler places rarely have a room phone, but often do have Wi-Fi. Pricier hotels are more likely to have elevators and small stocked mini-fridges in the rooms called *frigo bars* (FREE-goh; pay for what you use).

Hotels in resort areas will often charge you for half-pension, called *mezza pensione*, during peak season (which can run from May through mid-October for resorts). Half-pension means that you pay for one meal per day per person (lunch or dinner, though usually dinner), whether you want to or not. Wine is rarely included. If half-pension is required, you can't opt out and pay less. Some places offer half-pension as an option, and it can be worth considering. If they charge you less per meal than you've been paying for an average restaurant meal on your trip, half-pension is a fine value—if the chef is good. Ask other guests about the quality or check out their restaurant yourself.

If you're arriving early in the morning, your room probably won't be ready. You can drop your bag safely at the hotel's front desk and dive right into sightseeing.

Hoteliers can be a great help and source of advice. Most know their city well, and can assist you with everything from public transit and airport connections to finding a good restaurant, the nearest launderette, or an Internet café.

Making Hotel Reservations

Reserve your rooms several weeks in advance—or as soon as you've pinned down your travel dates—particularly if you'll be traveling during peak times. Note that some national holidays jam things up and merit your making reservations far in advance (see "Holidays and Festivals" on page 1189).

Requesting a Reservation: It's usually easiest to book your room through the hotel's website. Many have a reservation-request form built right in. (For the best rates, be sure to use the hotel's official site and not a booking agency's site.) Simpler websites will generate an email to the hotelier with your request. If there's no reservation form, or for complicated requests, send an email (for an example, see the sample request on the next page). Most recommended hotels are accustomed to guests who speak only English.

The hotelier wants to know:
- the number and type of rooms you need
- the number of nights you'll stay
- your date of arrival
- your date of departure
- any special needs (such as bathroom in the room or down the hall, cheapest room, twin beds vs. double bed, crib, air-conditioning, quiet, view, ground floor or no stairs, and so on)

If you request a room by email, use the European style for writing dates: day/month/year. For example, for a two-night stay in July of 2014, ask for "1 double room for 2 nights, arrive 16/07/14, depart 18/07/14." Make sure you mention any discounts—for Rick Steves readers or otherwise—when you make the reservation.

Confirming a Reservation: When the hotel replies with its room availability and rates, just email back to confirm your reservation. Most places will request a credit-card number to hold your room. While you can email it (I do), it's safer to share that confidential info via a phone call, two emails (splitting your number between them), or the hotel's secure online reservation form. On the small chance that a hotel loses track of your reservation, bring along a hard copy of their confirmation.

Canceling a Reservation: If you must cancel your reservation, it's courteous—and smart—to do so with as much notice as possible, especially for smaller family-run places. Simply make a quick phone call or send an email. Request confirmation of your

Even at the best places, mechanical breakdowns occur: Air-conditioning malfunctions, sinks leak, hot water turns cold, and toilets gurgle and smell. Report your concerns clearly and calmly at the front desk. For more complicated problems, don't expect instant results.

If you suspect night noise will be a problem (if, for instance, your room is over a café or faces a busy street), ask for a quieter room

From: rick@ricksteves.com
Sent: Today
To: info@hotelcentral.com
Subject: Reservation request for 19-22 July

Dear Hotel Central,

I would like to reserve a double room for 2 people for 3 nights, arriving 19 July and departing 22 July. If possible, I would like a quiet room with a bathroom inside the room.

Please let me know if you have a room available and the price.

Thank you!
Rick Steves

cancellation in case you are accidentally billed.

Be aware that cancellation policies can be strict; read the fine print or ask about these before you book. For example, if you cancel on short notice, you could lose your deposit or be billed for one night or even your entire stay. Internet deals may require prepayment, with no refunds for cancellations.

Reconfirming a Reservation: Call to reconfirm your room reservation a few days in advance. Smaller hotels and B&Bs appreciate knowing your estimated time of arrival. If you'll be arriving late (after 17:00), let them know.

Reserving Rooms as You Travel: You can make reservations as you travel, calling hotels a few days to a week before your arrival. If you'd rather travel without any reservations at all, you'll have greater success snaring rooms if you arrive at your destination early in the day. When you anticipate crowds (weekends are worst), call hotels at about 9:00 or 10:00 on the day you plan to arrive, when the receptionist knows who'll be checking out and which rooms will be available. If you encounter a language barrier, ask the fluent receptionist at your current hotel to call for you.

Phoning: For tips on how to call hotels overseas, see page 1156.

in the back or on an upper floor. To guard against theft in your room, keep valuables out of sight. Some rooms come with a safe, and other hotels have safes at the front desk. I've never bothered using one.

Checkout can pose problems if surprise charges pop up on your bill. If you settle your bill the afternoon before you leave, you'll have time to discuss and address any points of contention (before 19:00, when the night shift usually arrives).

INTRODUCTION

Above all, keep a positive attitude. Remember, you're on vacation. If your hotel is a disappointment, spend more time out enjoying the city you came to see.

Hostels

You'll pay about €25-30 per bed to stay at a hostel. Travelers of any age are welcome if they don't mind dorm-style accommodations and meeting other travelers. Most hostels offer kitchen facilities, guest computers, Wi-Fi, and a self-service laundry. Nowadays, concerned about bedbugs, hostels are likely to provide all bedding, including sheets. Family and private rooms may be available on request.

Independent hostels tend to be easygoing, colorful, and informal (no membership required); www.hostelworld.com is the standard way backpackers search and book hostels these days, but also try www.hostelz.com, www.hostels.com, and www.hostelbookers.com.

Official hostels are part of Hostelling International (HI) and share an online booking site (www.hihostels.com). HI hostels typically require that you either have a membership card or pay extra per night.

Private Rooms and Apartments

In small towns, there are often few hotels to choose from, but an abundance of *affitta camere,* or rental rooms. This can be anything from a set of keys and a basic bed to a cozy B&B with your own Tuscan grandmother. Local TIs can give you a list of possibilities (or try the free Ciao Italia Bed & Breakfast, which books B&Bs and hostels in Rome, Florence, and Venice; www.ciaoitalia-bb.com). These rooms are usually a good budget option, but since they vary in quality, shop around to find the best value. It's always OK to ask to see the room before you commit.

Whether you're in a city or the countryside, renting an apartment, house, or villa can be a fun and cost-effective way to delve into Europe. Apartment rentals, a great value for families or multiple couples traveling together, are also listed at TIs and are common in small towns. Websites such as HomeAway.com and its sister site vrbo.com let you correspond directly with European property owners or managers. Also browse through www.wantedinrome.com. Rentals are generally by the week, with prices starting around €100 per day. A bigger place for a group of four to five rents for around €200. Apartments generally offer a couple of bedrooms, a sitting area, and a teensy *cucinetta* (kitchenette), usually stocked with dishes and flatware. After you check in, you're basically on your own. While you won't have a doorman to carry your bags or a maid to clean your room each day, you will get an inside peek at an Italian home, and you can save lots of money—especially if you take advantage of the cooking facilities—with no loss of comfort.

Cross-Pollinate, an online booking agency, represents B&Bs and apartments in a handful of European cities, including Rome, Venice, and Florence. Search their website for a listing you like, then submit your reservation online. If the place is available, you'll be charged a small deposit and emailed the location and check-in details. Policies vary from owner to owner, but in most cases you'll pay the balance on arrival in cash (US tel. 800-270-1190, www.cross-pollinate.com, info@cross-pollinate.com). Frederick of **Tournights** runs a similar apartment-finding service in Rome and Florence (www.tournights.com).

Agritourism

Agriturismo (agricultural tourism), or rural B&Bs, began in the 1980s as a way to encourage small farmers in the countryside to survive in a modern economy where, like in the US, so many have been run out of business by giant agricultural corporations. By renting rooms to travelers, farmers can remain on their land and continue to produce food. A peaceful home base for exploring the region, these rural Italian B&Bs are ideal for those traveling by car—especially families.

It's wise to book several months in advance for high season (May-Sept). Weeklong stays are preferred in July and August, but shorter stays are possible off-season. To sleep cheaper, avoid the peak season for *agriturismi*. A farmhouse that rents for as much as $2,000 a week at peak times can go for as little as $700 in late September or October. In the winter, you might be charged extra for heat, so confirm the price ahead of time. Payment policies vary, but generally a 25 percent deposit is required (lost if you cancel), and the balance is due one month before arrival.

As the name implies, *agriturismi* are in the countryside, although some are located within a mile of town. Most are family-run. *Agriturismi* vary wildly in quality—some properties are rustic, while others are downright luxurious, offering amenities such as swimming pools and riding stables. The rooms are usually clean and comfortable. Breakfast is often included, and *mezza pensione* (half-pension, which in this case means a home-cooked dinner) might be built into the price whether you want it or not. Most places serve tasty homegrown food; some are vegetarian or organic,

INTRODUCTION

others are gourmet. Kitchenettes are often available to cook up your own feast.

To qualify officially as an *agriturismo,* the farm must still generate more money from its farm activities, thereby ensuring that the land is worked and preserved. Some farmhouse B&Bs aren't actual farms, though they are fine places to stay. But if you want the real thing, make sure the owners call their place an *agriturismo.*

In this book, I've listed a broad range of options under the towns that they're nearest to, but there are many, many more. Local TIs can give you a list of farms in their area, and many *agriturismi* have their own websites. For a sampling, visit www.agriturismoitaly.it or search online for *agriturismo.* One booking agency among many is Farm Holidays in Tuscany (closed Sat-Sun, tel. 0564-417-418, www.byfarmholidays.com, info@byfarmholidays.com).

Other Options

Airbnb.com makes it reasonably easy to find a place to sleep in someone's home. Beds range from air-mattress-in-living-room basic to plush-B&B-suite posh. If you want a free place to sleep, Couchsurfing.com is a vagabond's alternative to Airbnb. It lists millions of outgoing members, who host fellow "surfers" in their homes.

Eating

The Italians are masters of the art of fine living. That means eating long and well. Lengthy, multicourse meals and endless hours sitting in outdoor cafés are the norm. Americans eat on their way to an evening event and complain if the check is slow in coming. For Italians, the meal is an end in itself, and only rude

waiters rush you. When you want the bill, mime-scribble on your raised palm or request it: *"Il conto, per favore."* You may have to ask for it more than once. If you're in a hurry, request the check when you receive the last item you've ordered.

A highlight of your Italian adventure will be this country's cafés, cuisine, and wines. Trust me: This is sightseeing for your palate. Even if you liked dorm food and are sleeping in cheap hotels, your taste buds will relish an occasional first-class splurge. You can eat well without going broke. But be careful: You're just as likely to blow a small fortune on a disappointing meal as you are to dine wonderfully for €25.

Eating with the Seasons

Italian cooks love to serve you fresh produce and seafood at its tastiest. If you insist on having porcini mushrooms outside of fall, they'll be frozen. Each region in Italy has its specialties, which you'll see displayed in open-air markets. To get a plate of the freshest veggies at a fine restaurant, request "*Un piatto di verdure della stagioni, per favore*" ("A plate of veggies in season, please").

Here are a few examples of what's fresh when:

April-May:	Calamari, squid, fava beans, romanesco (similar to cauliflower), asparagus, artichokes, and zucchini flowers
April-May and Sept-Oct:	Black truffles
May-June:	Mussels, asparagus, zucchini, cantaloupe, and strawberries
May-Aug:	Eggplant
Oct-Nov:	Mushrooms, white truffles, and chestnuts
Nov-Feb:	Radicchio
Fresh year-round:	Clams, meats, and cheese

Italians take fresh, seasonal ingredients so seriously that a restaurant cooking with frozen ingredients must note it on the menu—look for *congelato*.

In general, Italians eat meals a bit later than we do. At 7:00 or 8:00 in the morning, they have a light breakfast (coffee and a roll, often standing up at a café). Lunch, which is usually the main meal of the day, begins around 13:00 and can last for a couple of hours. Then they eat a late, light dinner (around 20:00-21:30, or maybe earlier in winter). To bridge the gap, people drop into a bar in the late afternoon for a *spuntino* (snack) and aperitif.

Most restaurant kitchens close between their lunch and dinner service. Good restaurants don't reopen for dinner before 19:00.

Breakfast

Italian breakfasts, like Italian bath towels, are small: The basic, traditional version is coffee and a roll with butter and marmalade. These days, many places also have juice, yogurt, maybe cereal, possibly cold cuts and sliced cheese, and sometimes eggs (typically hard-boiled; scrambled or fried eggs are rare). Small budget hotels may leave a basic breakfast in a fridge in your room (stale croissant, roll, jam, yogurt, coffee). In general, the pricier the hotel, the bigger the breakfast.

The strong coffee at breakfast is often mixed about half-and-half with heated milk. At your hotel, refills are usually free. The delicious blood orange juice *(spremuta di arance rosse)* is made from Sicilian blood oranges.

If you want to skip your hotel breakfast, consider browsing for a morning picnic at a local open-air market. Or do as the Italians do: Stop into a bar or café to drink a cappuccino and munch a *cornetto* (croissant) while standing at the bar. While the *cornetto* is the most common pastry, you'll find a range of *pasticcini* (pastries, sometimes called *dolci*—"sweets"). Look for *otto* ("8"-shaped pastry, often filled with custard, jam, or chocolate), *sfoglia* (can be fruit-filled, like a turnover), or *ciambella* (doughnut filled with custard or chocolate)—or ask about local specialties.

Restaurants

While the word *ristorante* is self-explanatory, you'll also see other types of Italian eateries: A *trattoria* or an *osteria* (which can be more casual) is generally a family-owned place serving home-cooked meals, often at moderate prices. A *locanda* is an inn, a *cantina* is a wine cellar, and a *birreria* is a brewpub. *Pizzerie*, *rosticcerie* (delis), *tavola calda* ("hot table") bars, *enoteche* (wine bars), and other alternatives are explained later.

When restaurant hunting, choose a spot filled with locals, not the place with the big neon signs boasting, "We speak English and accept credit cards." Restaurants parked on famous squares generally serve bad food at high prices to tourists. Locals eat better at lower-rent locales. Family-run places operate without hired help and can offer cheaper meals. Venturing even a block or two off the main drag leads to higher-quality food for less than half the price of the tourist-oriented places.

Cover and Tipping

Before you sit down, look at a menu to see what extra charges a restaurant tacks on. Two different items are routinely factored into your bill: the *coperto* and the *servizio*.

The **coperto** (cover charge), sometimes called *pane e coperto* (bread and cover), offsets the restaurant's overhead expenses—from the basket of bread on your table to the electricity for running the dishwasher. It's not negotiable, even if you don't eat the bread. Think of it as covering the cost of using the table for as long as you like. (Italians like to linger.) Most restaurants add the *coperto* onto your bill as a flat fee (€1-3.50 per person; the amount should be clearly noted on the menu).

The *servizio* (service charge) of about 10 percent pays for the waitstaff. At most legitimate eateries, the words *servizio incluso* are written on the menu and/or the receipt—indicating that the listed prices already include the fee. You can add on a tip, if you choose, by including a euro or two for each person in your party. While Italians don't think about tips in terms of percentages—and many don't tip at all—this extra amount usually comes out to about 5 percent (10 percent is excessive for all but the very best service).

If you see the words *servizio non incluso* on the menu or bill, you are expected to add a tip of about 10 percent. A few trendy restaurants don't include the service in the menu prices, but will automatically tack on a 10 percent *servizio* charge to your bill.

Most good-value eateries have a cover charge, and the service is already included in the menu prices (i.e., *servizio incluso*). Places with *both* a cover and a tacked-on service charge are best avoided— that's a clue that a restaurant is counting on a nonlocal clientele who can't gauge value. The same goes for the opposite: Places that advertise "no cover, no service charge" to attract tourists are likely raising their prices to compensate.

Courses: Antipasto, *Primo,* and *Secondo*

A full Italian meal consists of several courses:

Antipasto (usually €5-10): An appetizer such as bruschetta; grilled veggies; deep-fried tasties; thin-sliced meat (for example, prosciutto or *carpaccio*); or a plate of olives, cold cuts, and cheeses. A plate of *antipasti misti* ("mixed"—an assortment) could make a light meal in itself.

Primo piatto (usually €7-15): A "first dish" generally consist- ing of pasta, rice, or soup. If you think of pasta when you think of Italy, you can dine well here without ever going beyond the *primo*.

Secondo piatto (usually €10-25): A "second dish," equivalent to our main course, of meat or fish/seafood. Italians freely admit the *secondo* is the least interesting part of their cuisine.

A vegetable side dish *(contorno)* may come with the *secondo*, but more often must be ordered separately (€5-6).

The euros can add up in a hurry, and for most travelers, a com- plete meal with all three courses (plus *contorni*, dessert, and wine) is simply too much food. To avoid overeating (and to stretch your budget), share dishes. A good rule of thumb is for each person to order any two courses. For example, a couple can order and share one *antipasto*, one *primo*, one *secondo*, and one dessert; or two *anti- pasti* and two *primi*; or whatever combination appeals.

Pasta, Pasta!

Italy is famous for its cuisine, but above all, it's known for pasta. Each of the more than 600 varieties of Italian pasta has a reason for being—usually as the perfect platform for highlighting the sauce, meat, or regional ingredients of a particular dish. While we think of pasta as a main dish, in Italy it's considered a *primo piatto*—first course. Italian pasta falls into two broad categories: long and short.

Long pasta (*pasta lunga*) is long enough to twist around a fork. Aside from the universally familiar spaghetti, you'll find *capellini* (thin "little hairs"); *vermicelli* (slightly thicker "little worms"); and long, hollow *bucatini*. Flattened versions of *pasta lunga* include *linguine* (narrow "little tongues"), *fettuccine* (wider "small ribbons"), *tagliatelle* (even wider), and *pappardelle* (very wide, best with meat sauces).

Short pastas (*pasta corta*) can be speared or scooped with a fork. The most common *pasta corta* are short tubes, such as *penne*, *rigatoni*, *ziti*, *manicotti*, and *cannelloni*; while similar, these differ in how long they are, how thick they are, whether they're square-cut or angle-cut, and whether they're *lisce* (smooth) or *rigate* (grooved—better to catch and cling to sauce). Many short pastas are named for their unique shapes: *conchiglie* (shells), *farfalle* (butterflies), *cavatappi* (corkscrews), *ditali* (thimbles), *gomiti* ("elbow" macaroni), *lumache* (snails), *marziani* (spirals resembling "Martian" antennae), and even *strozzapreti* (priest stranglers)...to name just a few.

Some short pastas are designed to be filled *(ripieni)*. Aside from the familiar ravioli and tortellini, this category includes *gnocchi* (shell-shaped, hand-rolled potato dumplings), *tortelli* (C-shaped, stuffed ravioli), and *angolotti* or *mezzelune* (stuffed pasta shaped like "priest's hats" or "half-moons").

Most types of pasta can come in slight variations: If it's a bit thicker, *-one* is added to the end; if it's a bit thinner, *-ine*, *-ette*, or *-elle* is added. For example, *tortellini* are smaller *tortelli,* while *tortelloni* are bigger.

Regional variations are enticing. Tuscany (Siena in particu-

Another good option is sharing an array of *antipasti*—either by ordering several specific dishes or, at restaurants that offer self-serve buffets, by choosing a variety of cold and cooked appetizers from an *antipasti* buffet spread out like a salad bar. At buffets, you pay per plate; a typical serving costs about €8 (generally Italians don't treat buffets as all-you-can-eat, but take a one-time moderate serving; watch others and imitate).

To maximize the experience and flavors, small groups can mix *antipasti* and *primi* family-style (skipping *secondi*). If you do this

lar) specializes in *pici,* thick, hand-formed noodles. Umbria feasts on *umbricelli,* a thick, chewy, rolled pasta. And the Riviera digs into *trenette,* a long, flat, thin noodle similar to linguine.

As for what to put on that pasta, the options are almost as endless as the shapes. The following terms are usually preceded by *alla* (in the style of) or *in* (in):

aglio e olio: garlic and olive oil

alfredo: butter, cream, and parmesan

amatriciana: pork cheek, pecorino cheese, and tomato

arrabbiata: "angry," spicy tomato sauce with chili peppers

bolognese: meat and tomato sauce

boscaiola: mushrooms and sausage

burro e salvia: butter and sage

carbonara: bacon, egg, cheese, and pepper

carrettiera: spicy and garlicky, with olive oil and little tomatoes

diavola: "devil-style," spicy hot

funghi: mushrooms

frutti di mare: seafood

genovese: pesto (basil ground with parmigiano cheese, garlic, pine nuts, and olive oil)

gricia: cured pork and pecorino romano cheese

marinara: usually tomato, often with garlic and onions, but can be a seafood sauce ("sailor's style")

norma: tomato, eggplant, and ricotta cheese

pajata (or *pagliata*): calf intestines

pescatora: seafood ("fisherman style")

pomodoro: tomato only

puttanesca: "harlot-style" tomato sauce with anchovies, olives, and capers

ragù: meaty tomato sauce

scoglio: mussels, clams, and tomatoes

sorrentina: "Sorrento style," with tomatoes, basil, and mozzarella (usually over gnocchi)

sugo di lepre: rich sauce made of wild hare

tartufi (or *tartufate*): truffles

umbria: sauce of anchovies, garlic, tomatoes, and truffles

vongole: clams and spices

right, you can eat well in better places for less than the cost of a tourist *menù* in a cheap place.

Ordering

Seafood and steak may be sold by weight (priced by the kilo—1,000 grams, or just over two pounds; or by the *etto*—100 grams). The abbreviation *s.q. (secondo quantità)* means an item is priced "according to quantity." Unless the menu indicates a fillet *(filetto),* fish is usually served whole with the head and tail. However, you can always ask your waiter to select a small fish for you. Sometimes, especially for steak, restaurants require a minimum order of four or five *etti* (which diners can share). Make sure you're really clear on the price before ordering.

Some special dishes come in larger quantities meant to be shared by two people. The shorthand way of showing this on a menu is "X2" (for two), but the price listed generally indicates the cost per person.

If you order a pasta dish and a side salad—but no main course—the waiter may ask when you want the salad served (Italians prefer it after the pasta, believing that it enhances digestion). If you want the salad with your pasta, specify *insieme* (een-see-YEH-meh, "together").

Because pasta and bread are both starches, Italians consider them redundant. If you order only a pasta dish, bread may not come with it; you can request it, but you may be charged extra. On the other hand, if you order a vegetable antipasto or a meat *secondo*, bread is provided to balance the ingredients.

At places with counter service—such as at a bar or a freeway rest-stop diner—you'll first order and pay at the *cassa* (cashier). Then take your receipt over to the counter to claim your food.

Fixed-Price Meals

You can save by getting a fixed-priced meal, which is frequently exempt from cover and service charges. Avoid the cheapest ones (often called a *menù turistico*), which tend to be bland and heavy, pairing a very basic pasta with reheated schnitzel and roast meats. Look instead for a genuine *menù del giorno* (menu of the day), which offers diners a choice of appetizer, main course, and dessert. It's worth paying a little more for an inventive fixed-price meal that shows off the chef's creativity.

MENU € 19,00
TURISTICO

ANTIPASTO di MARE

PRIMI PIATTI
RISOTTO alla PESCATORA
SPAGHETTI alla MARINARA
SPAGHETTI allo SCOGLIO
TRENETTE al PESTO

SECONDI PIATTI
PESCE ai FERRI
FRITTO MISTO
GRIGLIATA di CARNE

CONTORNI
PATATE FRITTE o INSALATA

While fixed-price meals can be easy and convenient, galloping gourmets order à la carte with the help of a menu translator. (The *Rick Steves' Italian Phrase Book & Dictionary* has a menu decoder with enough phrases for intermediate eaters.) When going to an especially good restaurant with an approachable staff, I like to find out what they're eager to serve, or I'll simply say, *"Mi faccia felice"* (Make me happy) and set a price limit.

Budget Eating

Italy offers many budget options for hungry travelers, but beware of cheap eateries that sport big color photos of pizza and piles of different pastas. They have no kitchens and simply microwave disgusting prepackaged food.

Self-service cafeterias offer the basics without add-on charges. Travelers on a hard-core budget equip their room with a pantry stocked at the market (fruits and veggies are remarkably cheap) or pick up a kebab (or the equivalent), then dine in at picnic prices. Bars and cafés, described in detail later, are another good place to grab a meal on the go.

Pizzerias

Pizza is cheap and readily available. Stop by a pizza shop for stand-up or take-out pizza (*pizza al taglio* means "by the slice"). While some

shops sell individual slices of round, Naples-style pizza, you'll more likely see *pizza rustica*—thick pizza baked in a large rectangular pan and sold by weight. If you simply ask for a piece, you may be handed a gigantic slab and charged top euro. Instead, clearly indicate how much you want: 100 grams, or *un etto*, is a hot and cheap snack; 200 grams, or *due etti*, makes a light meal. Or show the size with your hands—*tanto così* (TAHN-toh koh-ZEE; this much).

Key pizza vocabulary: *capricciosa* ("chef's choice," generally prosciutto, mushrooms, olives, and artichokes), *funghi* (mushrooms), *marinara* (tomato sauce, oregano, garlic, no cheese), *napoletana* (mozzarella, anchovies, and tomato sauce), *vegetariana* or *ortolana* ("greengrocer-style," with vegetables), *quattro formaggi* (four different cheeses), and *quattro stagioni* (different toppings on each of the four quarters, for those who can't choose just one menu item). If you ask for pepperoni on your pizza, you'll get *peperoni* (green or red peppers, not sausage); request *diavola* or *salsiccia piccante* instead (the closest thing in Italy to American pepperoni). Kids like the bland *margherita* (tomato sauce, mozzarella, and basil—the red, white, and green of the Italian flag). *Pizza bianca* (or *pizza ciaccina*) is "white" pizza, with no tomatoes.

Bars/Cafés

Italian "bars" are not taverns, but inexpensive cafés. These neighborhood hangouts serve coffee, mini-pizzas, premade sandwiches, and drinks from the cooler. Many dish up plates of fried cheese and vegetables from under the glass counter, ready to reheat. This budget choice is the Italian equivalent of English pub grub.

Food: For quick meals, bars usually have trays of cheap, premade sandwiches (*panini,* made with a baguette; *piadini,* on flatbread; or *tramezzini,* on crustless white bread)—some are delightful grilled. (Others have too much mayo.) To save time for sightseeing and room for dinner, stop by a bar for a light lunch, such as a ham-and-cheese sandwich (called *toast*); have it grilled twice if you want it really hot. To get food "to go," say, "*da portar via*" (for the road). Many bars are small—if you can't find a table, you'll need to stand up or find a ledge to sit on outside. Most charge extra for table service (see next). All bars have a WC *(toilette, bagno)* in the back, and customers—and the discreet public—can use it.

Prices and Paying: You'll notice a two- or three-tiered pricing system. Drinking a cup of coffee while standing at the bar is cheaper than drinking it at an indoor table (you'll pay still more at an outdoor table). Many places have a *lista dei prezzi* (price list) with two columns—*al bar* and *al tavolo* (table)—posted somewhere by the bar or cash register. If you're on a budget, don't sit down without first checking out the financial consequences. Ask, "Same price if I sit or stand?" by saying, "*Costa uguale al tavolo o al banco?*" (KOH-stah oo-GWAH-lay ahl TAH-voh-loh oh ahl BAHN-koh). Throughout Italy, you can get cheap coffee at the bar of any establishment, no matter how fancy, and pay the same low, government-regulated price (generally only a euro if you stand).

If the bar isn't busy, you can probably just order and pay when you leave. Otherwise: 1) Decide what you want; 2) find out the price by checking the price list on the wall, the prices posted near the food, or by asking the barista; 3) pay the cashier; and 4) give the receipt to the barista (whose clean fingers handle no dirty euros) and tell him or her what you want.

For more on drinking, see "Beverages," later.

Kebab Shops

In big cities like Venice and Florence, perhaps the best value for a cheap, hot meal is a *döner kebab*. (While these came to Europe from Turkey—by way of immigrants in Germany—they've been enthusiastically embraced by Italians as a "local" fast food.) Look for little hole-in-the-wall kebab shops, where you can get a hearty take-out dinner wrapped in pita bread for €3.50. Pay an extra euro to super-size it, and it'll feed two. Ask a local for the favorite place in your neighborhood, as the quality can vary substantially.

Ordering Food at *Tavola Calda* Bars and *Rosticcerie*

plate of mixed veggies	*piatto misto di verdure*	pee-AH-toh MEE-stoh dee vehr-DOO-ray
Heated, please.	*Scaldare, per favore.*	skahl-DAH-ray, pehr fah-VOH-ray
A taste, please.	*Un assaggio, per favore.*	oon ah-SAH-joh, pehr fah-VOH-ray
artichoke	*carciofi*	kar-CHOH-fee
asparagus	*asparagi*	ah-spah-RAH-jee
beans	*fagioli*	fah-JOH-lee
breadsticks	*grissini*	gree-SEE-nee
broccoli	*broccoli*	BROH-koh-lee
cantaloupe	*melone*	may-LOH-nay
carrots	*carote*	kah-ROT-ay
green beans	*fagiolini*	fah-joh-LEE-nee
ham	*prosciutto*	proh-SHOO-toh
mushrooms	*funghi*	FOON-ghee
potatoes	*patate*	pah-TAH-tay
rice	*riso*	REE-zoh
spinach	*spinaci*	spee-NAH-chee
tomatoes	*pomodori*	poh-moh-DOH-ree
zucchini	*zucchine*	zoo-KEE-nay

(Excerpted from *Rick Steves' Italian Phrase Book & Dictionary*)

Tavola Calda Bars and *Rosticcerie*

For a fast and cheap lunch, find an Italian variation on the corner deli: a *rosticceria* (specializing in roasted meats and accompanying *antipasti*) or a *tavola calda* bar ("hot table" point-and-shoot cafeteria with a buffet spread of meat and vegetables; sometimes called *tavola fredda,* or "cold table," in the north). For a healthy light meal, ask for a mixed plate of vegetables with a hunk of mozzarella *(piatto misto di verdure con mozzarella).* Don't be limited by what's displayed. If you'd like a salad with a slice of cantaloupe and a hunk of cheese, they'll whip that up for you in a snap. Belly up to the bar and, with a pointing finger and key words in the chart in this chapter, you can get a fine plate of mixed vegetables. If something's a mystery, ask for *un assaggio* (oon ah-SAH-joh) to get a little taste.

Wine Bars

Wine bars *(enoteche)* are a popular, fast option for lunch. Surrounded by the office crowd, you can get a fancy salad, a plate of cold cuts and cheeses, and a glass of fine wine (see blackboards for the day's selection and price per glass). A good *enoteca* aims to impress visitors with its wine, and will generally choose excellent-quality ingredients for the simple dishes it offers with the wine (though prices can add up quickly—be careful with your ordering to keep this a budget choice).

Groceries and Delis

Another budget option is to drop by an *alimentari* (neighborhood grocery) or *salumeria* (delicatessen) to pick up some cold cuts, cheeses, and other supplies for a picnic. Some *salumerie,* and any *paninoteca* or *foccaceria* (sandwich shop), can make you a sandwich to order. Just point to what you want, and they'll stuff it into a *panino;* if you want it heated, say, *"Scaldare, per favore"* (skahl-DAH-ray pehr fah-VOH-ray). To get a sampler plate of cold cuts and cheeses in a restaurant, ask for *affettato misto* (mixed cold cuts), *antipasto misto* (cold cuts, cheeses, and marinated vegetables), or—in Tuscany—*tagliere* (a sampler "board").

Salumi ("salted" meats), also called *affettati* ("cut" meats), are an Italian staple. Whereas most American cold cuts are cooked, in Italy they're far more commonly cured by air-drying, salting, and smoking. (Don't worry; these so-called "raw" meats are safe to eat, and you can really taste the difference.)

The two most familiar types of *salumi* are *salame* and prosciutto. **Salame** is an air-dried, sometimes spicy sausage that comes in many varieties, including *finocchiona* (with fennel seeds), *salame piccante* (spicy hot, similar to pepperoni), and *salame di Sant'Olcese* (what we'd call "Genoa salami"). When Italians say *"prosciutto,"* they usually mean *prosciutto crudo*—the "raw" ham that air-cures on the hock and is then thinly sliced. Produced mainly in the north of Italy, prosciutto can be either *dolce* (sweet) or *salato* (salty). Purists say the best is *prosciutto di Parma.*

Other *salumi* may be less familiar. Air-cured pork variations include *culatello* (prosciutto made with only the finest cuts of meat), *capocollo* (or *coppa*, peppery pork shoulder), *speck* (smoked pork shoulder), *guanciale* (tender pork cheek), and *lonzino* (cured pork loin). *Pancetta*—which can be eaten raw or added to cooked dishes—is salt-cured, peppery pork belly meat (similar to bacon). *Mortadella,* a finely ground pork loaf, is similar to our baloney, and *bresaola* is air-cured beef. But look out for *testa in cassetta* (head-cheese—organs in aspic) and *lampredotto*—cow stomach that re-sembles a lamprey (eel)—a traditional budget food in Tuscany.

As for **formaggio** (cheese), you're probably already familiar with several Italian favorites: *asiago* (hard cow cheese that comes either *mezzano*—young, firm, and creamy; or *stravecchio*—aged, pungent, and granular); *fontina* (semi-hard, nutty, Gruyère-style mountain cheese); *gorgonzola* (pungent, blue-veined cheese, either *dolce*—creamy, or *stagionato*—aged and hard); *mascarpone* (sweet, buttery, spreadable dessert cheese); *parmigiano-reggiano* (hard, crumbly, sharp, aged cow cheese with more nuanced flavor than American "parmesan"; *grana padano* is a less expensive variation); *pecorino* (either *fresco*—fresh, soft, and mild; or *stagionato*—aged and sharp, sometimes called *pecorino romano*); *provolone* (rich, firm, aged cow cheese); *ricotta* (soft, airy cheese made by "recooking" leftover whey); and, of course, mozzarella. The best mozzarella is *mozzarella di bufala,* made from the milk of water buffaloes; other variations include *burrata* (a creamy mozzarella) and *scamorza* (similar to mozzarella, but often smoked).

Picnic Tips

Picnicking saves lots of euros and is a great way to sample regional specialties. A typical picnic for two might be fresh rolls, 100 grams (*un etto,* EH-toh, plural *etti,* EH-tee—about a quarter-pound) of cheese, and 100 grams of meat (sometimes ordered by the slice—*fetta,* or piece—*pezzi;* for two people, I might get *cinque pezzi*—five pieces—of prosciutto). Add two tomatoes, three carrots, two apples, yogurt, and a liter box of juice. Total cost: about €10.

In the process of assembling your meal, you get to deal with the Italians in the market scene. For a colorful experience, gather your ingredients in the morning at a produce market; you'll prob-ably need to hit several stalls to put together a complete meal (note that many close in the early afternoon).

While it's fun to visit the small specialty shops, an *alimen-tari* is your one-stop corner grocery store (most will slice and stuff your sandwich for you if you buy the ingredients there). The rare *supermercato* (look for the Conad, Despar, and Co-op chains) gives you more efficiency with less color for less cost. At busier supermar-kets, you'll need to take a number for deli service.

Juice lovers can get a liter of O.J. for the price of a Coke or coffee. Look for "100% *succo*" (juice) or "*senza zucchero*" (without sugar) on the label—or be surprised by something diluted and sugary sweet. Hang on to the half-liter mineral-water bottles (sold everywhere for about €1). Buy juice in cheap liter boxes, then drink some and store the extra in your water bottle. (I refill my water bottle with tap water—*acqua del rubinetto*.)

Picnics can be an adventure in high cuisine. Be daring. Try the fresh mozzarella, *presto* pesto, shriveled olives, and any UFOs the locals are excited about. If ordering *antipasti* (such as grilled or marinated veggies) at a deli counter, you can ask for *una porzione* in a plastic take-away container *(contenitore)*. Use gestures to show exactly how much you want. The word *basta* (BAH-stah)—"enough"—works as a question or as a statement.

Shopkeepers are happy to sell small quantities of produce, but it's customary to let the merchant choose for you. Say *"per oggi"* (pehr OH-jee; for today) and he or she will grab you something ready to eat. To avoid being overcharged, know the cost per kilo and study the weighing procedure as if you're doing the arithmetic.

Gelato

Gelato is an edible art form—and it's one souvenir that can't break and won't clutter your luggage. While American ice cream is made with cream and has a high butterfat content, Italian gelato is made with milk. It's also churned more slowly, making it denser. Connoisseurs believe that because gelato has less air and less fat (which coats the mouth and blocks the taste buds), it's more flavorful than American-style ice cream.

Stop by a *gelateria* and survey your options. A key to gelato appreciation is sampling liberally and choosing flavors that go well together. Ask, as Italians do, for *"Un assaggio, per favore?"* (A taste, please?; oon ah-SAH-joh pehr fah-VOH-ray) and *"Quali gusti stanno bene insieme?"* (What flavors go well together?; KWAH-lee GOO-stee STAH-noh BEH-nay een-see-EH-may).

Most *gelaterie* clearly display prices and sizes. But in the textbook *gelateria* scam, the tourist orders two or three flavors—and the clerk selects a fancy, expensive chocolate-coated waffle cone, piles it high with huge scoops, and cheerfully charges the tourist €10. To avoid rip-offs, point to the price or say what you want—for example, *"Una coppetta da tre euro"* (OO-nah koh-PEH-tah dah tray eh-oo-roh; a €3 cup).

Not all *gelaterie* are created equal. The best ones display signs reading *artiginale, nostra produzione,* or *produzione propia,* indicating that the gelato is made on the premises. Seasonal flavors are also a good sign. Gelato stored in covered metal tins (rather than white plastic) is more likely to be homemade. Gelato aficionados avoid colors that don't appear in nature; for fewer chemicals and real flavor, go for mellow hues.

As far as flavors, the sky's the limit. Most *gelaterie* label each tub with the flavor (in Italian and, often, in English) and, sometimes, a little picture to help identify it. Aside from the typical *crema* (vanilla), *cioccolato* (chocolate), and *fragola* (strawberry), here are a few flavors worth trying: After Eight (chocolate and mint), *bacio* (chocolate hazelnut, named for Italy's popular "kiss" candies), *croccantino* ("crunchy," with toasted peanut bits), *cassata* (with dried fruits), *fior di latte* (sweet milk), *macedonia* (mixed fruits), *riso* (with actual bits of rice mixed in), *malaga* (similar to rum raisin), *tartufo* (super chocolate), *zuppa inglese* (sponge cake, custard, chocolate, and cream), and the popular *stracciatella* (vanilla with chocolate chips). Flavors named Snickers, Lion, and Bounty resemble their namesake candy bars.

Gelato variations or alternatives include *sorbetto* (sorbet—made with fruit, but no milk or eggs); *granita* or *grattachecca* (a cup of slushy ice with flavored syrup); and *cremolata* (a gelato-*granita* float).

Beverages

Italian bars serve great drinks—hot, cold, sweet, caffeinated, or alcoholic. Chilled bottled water, still *(naturale)* or carbonated *(frizzante)*, is sold cheap in stores. Coffee and wine—two Italian specialties—are covered in greater depth later.

Juice: *Spremuta* means freshly squeezed, as far as *succo* (fruit juice) is concerned (order *una spremuta*—don't confuse it with *spumante*, sparkling wine). It's usually orange juice *(arancia)*, and February through April it's almost always made from blood oranges *(arance rosse)*.

Beer: Beer on tap is *alla spina*. Get it *piccola* (33 cl, 11 oz), *media* (50 cl, about a pint), or *grande* (a liter). Italians drink mainly lager beers. You'll find local brews (Peroni and Moretti) and imports such as Heineken as well. A *lattina* (lah-TEE-nah) is a can and a *bottiglia* (boh-TEEL-yah) is a bottle.

Cocktails and Spirits: Italians appreciate both *aperitivi* (palate-stimulating cocktails) and *digestivi* (after-dinner drinks designed to aid digestion). Popular *aperitivo* options include Campari (dark-colored bitters with herbs and orange peel), Americano (vermouth with bitters, brandy, and lemon peel), Cynar (bitters flavored with artichoke), and Punt e Mes (sweet red vermouth and red wine). Widely used vermouth brands include Cinzano and Martini. *Digestivo* choices are usually either a strong herbal bitters or something sweet. Many restaurants have their own secret recipe for a bittersweet herbal brew called *amaro;* popular commercial brands are Fernet Branca and Montenegro. If your tastes run sweeter, try *amaretto* (almond-flavored liqueur), Frangelico (hazelnut liqueur), *limoncello* or *limoncino* (lemon liqueur), *nocino* (dark, sweet walnut liqueur), and *sambuca* (syrupy, anise-flavored liqueur; *con moscha* adds "flies"—three coffee beans). *Grappa* is a brandy distilled from grape skins and stems; *stravecchio* is an aged, mellower variation.

Coffee and Other Hot Drinks

The espresso-based style of coffee so popular in the US was born in Italy. If you ask for *"un caffè,"* you'll get a shot of espresso in a little cup; the closest thing to American-style drip coffee is a c*affè americano.* Most Italian drinks begin with espresso, to which is added varying amounts of hot water and/or steamed or foamed milk. Milky drinks, like cappuccino or *caffè latte,* are served to locals before noon and to tourists any time of day (to an Italian, cappuccino is a breakfast drink). If they add any milk after lunch, it's just a splash, in a *macchiato* (mah-kee-AH-toh). Italians like their coffee only warm—to get it very hot, request *"Molto caldo, per favore"* (MOHL-toh KAHL-doh pehr fah-VOH-ray). Any coffee drink is available decaffeinated—ask for it *decaffeinato* (deh-kah-feh-ee-NAH-toh).

Experiment with a few of the options:

- **Cappuccino:** Espresso with foamed milk on top
- *Caffè latte:* Espresso mixed with hot milk, no foam, in a tall glass (ordering just a "latte" gets you only milk)
- *Caffè macchiato:* Espresso "marked" with just a splash of milk, in a small cup
- *Latte macchiato:* Layers of hot milk and foam, "marked" by an espresso shot, in a tall glass
- *Caffè corto/lungo:* Concentrated espresso diluted with a tiny bit of hot water, in a small cup (*lungo* is more diluted than *corto*)
- *Caffè americano:* Espresso diluted with even more hot water, in a larger cup
- *Caffè corretto:* Espresso "corrected" with a shot of liqueur (normally grappa, amaro, or Sambuca)
- *Marocchino:* "Moroccan" coffee with espresso, foamed milk, and cocoa powder; the similar *mocaccino* has chocolate instead of cocoa
- *Caffè freddo:* Sweet and iced espresso
- *Cappuccino freddo:* Iced cappuccino
- *Caffè hag:* Instant decaf

Notice that there's a big difference between *caffè macchiato* and *latte macchiato.* If you order simply a *"macchiato,"* you'll probably get the coffee version...and have to get your milk fix elsewhere.

More Hot Drinks: *Cioccolato* is hot chocolate. *Tè* is hot tea. *Tè freddo* (iced tea) is usually from a can—sweetened and flavored with lemon or peach.

Wine

The ancient Greeks who colonized Italy more than 2,000 years ago called it Oenotria—land of the grape. Centuries later, Galileo wrote, "Wine is light held together by water." Wine *(vino)* is certainly a part of the Italian culinary trinity—grape, olive, and wheat. (I'd add gelato.) Ideal conditions for grapes (warm climate, well-draining soil, and an abundance of hillsides) make the Italian peninsula a paradise for grape growers, winemakers, and wine drinkers. Italy makes and consumes more wine per capita than any other country.

To order a glass *(bicchiere;* bee-kee-EH-ree) of red *(rosso)* or white *(bianco)* wine, say, *"Un bicchiere di vino rosso/bianco." Corposo* means full-bodied. House wine *(vino della casa)* comes in a carafe; choose from a quarter-liter pitcher (8.5 oz, *un quarto),* half-liter pitcher (17 oz, *un mezzo),* or one-liter pitcher (34 oz, *un litro).*

Wine Labels and Lingo

Even if you're clueless about wine, the information on an Italian wine label can help you choose something decent. Terms you may

see include *classico* (from a defined, select area), *annata* (year of harvest), *vendemmia* (harvest), and *imbottigliato dal produttore all'origine* (bottled by producers). To figure out what you like—and what suits your pocketbook—visit an *enoteca* (wine bar)

and sample wines side-by-side.

In general, Italy designates its wines by one of four official categories:

Vino da Tavola (VDT) is table wine, the lowest grade, made from grapes grown anywhere in Italy. It's inexpensive, but Italy's wines are so good that, for many people, a basic *vino da tavola* is just fine with a meal. Many restaurants, even modest ones, take pride in their house wine *(vino della casa),* bottling their own or working with wineries.

Denominazione di Origine Controllata (DOC) meets national standards for high-quality wine. Made from grapes grown in a defined area, it's usually quite affordable, and can be surprisingly good. Hundreds of wines have earned the DOC designation. In Tuscany, for example, many such wines come from the Chianti region, located between Florence and Siena.

Denominazione di Origine Controllata e Guarantita (DOCG), the highest grade, meets national standards for the highest-quality

Describing Wine in Italian

As you can see from many of the words listed below, adding a vowel to the English word often gets you close to the Italian one. Have some fun, gesture like a local, and you'll have no problems speaking the language of the *enoteca*. *Salute!*

dry	*secco*	SEH-koh
sweet	*dolce*	DOHL-chay
earthy	*terroso*	teh-ROH-zoh
tannic	*tannico*	TAH-nee-koh
young	*giovane*	JOH-vah-nay
mature	*maturo*	mah-TOO-roh
sparkling	*spumante, frizzante*	spoo-mahn-tay, freed-ZAHN-tay
fruity	*fruttato*	froo-TAH-toh
full-bodied	*corposo, pieno*	kor-POH-zoh, pee-EH-noh
elegant	*elegante*	eh-leh-GAHN-tay

wine (made with grapes from a defined area whose quality is "guaranteed"). These wines can be identified by the pink or green label on the neck...and the scary price tag on the shelf. Only a limited number of wines in Italy can be called DOCG. They're generally a good bet if you want a quality wine, but you don't know anything else about the winemaker. (*Riserva* indicates a DOC or DOCG wine matured for a longer, more specific time.)

Indicazione Geographica Tipica (IGT) is a broad group of wines that range from basic to some of Italy's best. These wines don't follow the strict "recipe" required for DOC or DOCG status, but they give local vintners creative license. This category includes the Super Tuscans, wines made from a mix of international grapes (such as cabernet sauvignon) grown in Tuscany and aged in small oak barrels for only two years. The result is a lively full-bodied wine that dances all over your head...and is worth the steep price for aficionados.

Regional Wines

In almost every part of Italy, you'll find wine varieties designed to go with the regional cuisine.

Tuscany (Florence, Siena, and Nearby): Many Tuscan wines are made with sangiovese ("blood of Jupiter") grapes, including the well-known Chiantis, which range from cheap, acidic basket-bottles of table wine (called *fiaschi*) to the hearty Chianti Classico. Vino Nobile di Montepulciano is a high-quality dry ruby red that pairs well with meat, especially chicken. One of Italy's top reds is Brunello di Montalcino (smooth, dry, aged at least four years in wood); a cheaper, younger "baby Brunello" is Rosso di Montalcino. Pricey Super Tuscans blend traditional grapes with locally grown non-Italian grapes (such as cabernet or merlot). A decent white choice is Vernaccia di San Gimignano (medium-dry, pairs well with pasta and salad). Trebbiano and vermentino are two other local white grapes. Vin Santo is a sweet, syrupy, "holy" dessert wine, often served with a cookie for dipping.

Veneto (near Venice): Valpolicella grapes are used to make a light, fruity, dry, red table wine as well as Amarone (full-bodied red made from partially dried—*passito*—grapes, then aged for at least four years in oak) and Recioto (sweet dessert wine made with high-sugar grapes that are also dried and aged). Bardolino is a light, fruity, Beaujolais-like picnic wine. Whites include Soave (crisp, dry white that goes well with seafood; the best is Soave Classico), Pinot Grigio, and Bianco di Custoza. If you like bubbles, try Fragolino (sweet, slightly fizzy dessert wine made from a strawberry-flavored grape) or Prosecco (connoisseurs say the best hails from Valdobbiadene).

Umbria (Assisi, Orvieto, and Nearby): Trebbiano is this region's main white grape. Look for Orvieto Classico (a golden, dry white). For reds, consider Sagrantino de Montefalco (dark, tannic) or Torgiano Rosso Riserva (elegant, smooth). Wines from the quality producer Lungarotti are worth trying.

Liguria (Italian Riviera, including Cinque Terre). This coastal region produces light, delicate whites (using mostly bosco grapes) that go well with seafood. Dolceacqua is a medium-bodied red. After dinner, try Sciacchetrà (shok-ee-trah, a silky sweet, potent, amber-colored wine made with raisins).

Lazio (Rome and Nearby): Wines to try here include Frascati (inexpensive dry white); Castelli Romani, Marino, Colli Albani, and Velletri (all light and fairly dry); and Torre Ercolana (balanced, medium-bodied, best-quality red).

Dolomites: While beer is king here, look for reds like St. Magdalaner (light, dry, made from schiava grapes); Lagrein Scuro (full-bodied, dry and fruity, similar to a cabernet sauvignon or merlot); or whites like Pinot Grigio, Gewürztraminer, and Pinot Blanc. Nosiola is an aromatic local grape used for dessert and sparkling wine.

Piedmont (near Milan and the Lakes): This region specializes in bold, dry reds that go with the rich, local cuisine. Nebbiolo

How Was Your Trip?

Were your travels fun, smooth, and meaningful? If you'd like to share your tips, concerns, and discoveries, please fill out the survey at www.ricksteves.com/feedback. I value your feedback. Thanks in advance—it helps a lot.

is the main red grape. Wine lovers drool over Barolo (big, tannic, aged three years or more) or its "little brother," Barbaresco (elegant, aged two years). For lighter, less tannic reds, try Barbera or Dolcetto (soft, fruity). Whites include Gavi (light, fruity) and Arneis (flowery, medium-bodied). For bubbly wines, try Brachetto (crimson, sweet, berry notes, excellent aperitif), Moscato d'Asti (semisweet, slightly fizzy), and Asti Spumante (dry).

Campania (Naples, Sorrento, and Nearby): Plentiful sun and Mt. Vesuvius' volcanic soils provide great wine-growing conditions. Taurasi is an excellent ruby-colored, tannic, aged, full-bodied red from the aglianico grape. Lacryma Christi ("tears of Christ") comes in both red (medium body) and white (dry and fruity, great with seafood). Other whites are Greco di Tufo (dry, pale yellow) and Fiano di Avellino (soft, flavorful, dry).

Sicily: The main red is Nero d'Avola (jammy, full-bodied, tannic). Corvo, Regaleali, and Planeta are some established producers. White wines use indigenous grapes like grillo, inzolio, and catarrato. Try Bianca d'Alcamo (dry, fresh, fruity) and Etna Bianco (dry, lemon flavors, pairs well with shellfish). Marsala is a (usually) sweet fortified dessert wine.

Traveling as a Temporary Local

We travel all the way to Italy to enjoy differences—to become temporary locals. You'll experience frustrations. Certain truths that we find "God-given" or "self-evident," such as cold beer, ice in drinks, bottomless cups of coffee, and bigger being better, are suddenly not so true. One of the benefits of travel is the eye-opening realization that there are logical, civil, and even better alternatives. A willingness to go local ensures that you'll enjoy a full dose of Italian hospitality.

Europeans generally like Americans. But if there is a negative aspect to Italians' image of Americans, it's that we are loud, wasteful, ethnocentric, too informal (which can seem disrespectful), and a bit naïve. Think about the rationale behind "crazy" Italian decisions. For instance, many hoteliers turn off the heat in spring and don't turn on the air-conditioning until summer. The point is to conserve energy, and it's mandated by the Italian government. You could complain about being cold or hot...or bring a sweater in winter, and in summer, be prepared to sweat a little like everyone else.

While Italians, flabbergasted by our Yankee excesses, say in disbelief, *"Mi sono cadute le braccia!"* ("I throw my arms down!"), they nearly always afford us individual travelers all the warmth we deserve.

Judging from all the happy feedback I receive from travelers who have used this book, it's safe to assume you'll enjoy a great, affordable vacation—with the finesse of an independent, experienced traveler.

Thanks, and *buon viaggio!*

Back Door Travel Philosophy

From *Rick Steves' Europe Through the Back Door*

Travel is intensified living—maximum thrills per minute and one of the last great sources of legal adventure. Travel is freedom. It's recess, and we need it.

Experiencing the real Europe requires catching it by surprise, going casual..."through the Back Door."

Affording travel is a matter of priorities. (Make do with the old car.) You can eat and sleep—simply, safely, and enjoyably—anywhere in Europe for $120 a day plus transportation costs. In many ways, spending more money only builds a thicker wall between you and what you traveled so far to see. Europe is a cultural carnival, and time after time, you'll find that its best acts are free and the best seats are the cheap ones.

A tight budget forces you to travel close to the ground, meeting and communicating with the people. Never sacrifice sleep, nutrition, safety, or cleanliness to save money. Simply enjoy the local-style alternatives to expensive hotels and restaurants.

Connecting with people carbonates your experience. Extroverts have more fun. If your trip is low on magic moments, kick yourself and make things happen. If you don't enjoy a place, maybe you don't know enough about it. Seek the truth. Recognize tourist traps. Give a culture the benefit of your open mind. See things as different, but not better or worse. Any culture has plenty to share.

Of course, travel, like the world, is a series of hills and valleys. Be fanatically positive and militantly optimistic. If something's not to your liking, change your liking.

Travel can make you a happier American, as well as a citizen of the world. Our Earth is home to seven billion equally precious people. It's humbling to travel and find that other people don't have the "American Dream"—they have their own dreams. Europeans like us, but with all due respect, they wouldn't trade passports.

Thoughtful travel engages us with the world. In tough economic times, it reminds us what is truly important. By broadening perspectives, travel teaches new ways to measure quality of life.

Globetrotting destroys ethnocentricity, helping us understand and appreciate other cultures. Rather than fear the diversity on this planet, celebrate it. Among your most prized souvenirs will be the strands of different cultures you choose to knit into your own character. The world is a cultural yarn shop, and Back Door travelers are weaving the ultimate tapestry. Join in!

VENICE

Venezia

Soak all day in this puddle of elegant decay. Venice is Europe's best-preserved big city. This car-free urban wonderland of a hundred islands—laced together by 400 bridges and 2,000 alleys—survives on the artificial respirator of tourism.

Born in a lagoon 1,500 years ago as a refuge from barbarians, Venice is overloaded with tourists and is slowly sinking (not because of the tourists). In the Middle Ages, the Venetians became Europe's clever middlemen for East-West trade and created a great trading empire. By smuggling in the bones of St Mark (San Marco) in A.D. 828, Venice gained religious importance as well. With the discovery of America and new trading routes to the Orient, Venetian power ebbed. But as Venice fell, her appetite for decadence grew. Through the 17th and 18th centuries, Venice partied on the wealth accumulated through earlier centuries as a trading power.

Today, Venice is home to 58,000 people in its old city, down from about twice that number just three decades ago. While there are about 270,000 people in greater Venice (counting the mainland, not counting tourists), the old town has a small-town feel. Locals seem to know everyone. To see small-town Venice away from the touristic flak, escape the Rialto-San Marco tourist zone and savor the town early and late, without the hordes of vacationers day-tripping in from cruise ships and nearby beach resorts. A 10-minute walk from the madness puts you in an idyllic Venice that few tourists see.

VENICE

Venice Overview

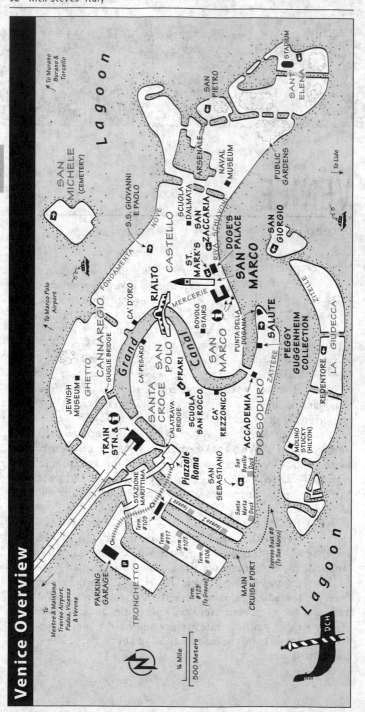

Planning Your Time

Venice is worth at least a day on even the speediest tour. Hyper-efficient train travelers take the night train in and/or out. Sleep in the old center to experience Venice at its best: early and late. For a one-day visit, cruise the Grand Canal, do the major sights on St. Mark's Square (the square itself, Doge's Palace, Correr Museum, and St. Mark's Basilica), see the Frari Church for art, and wander the back streets on a pub crawl. Enjoy an evening gondola ride. Venice's greatest sight is the city itself. While doable in a day, Venice is worth two. It's a medieval cookie jar, and nobody's looking. Make time to simply wander.

Orientation to Venice

The island city of Venice is shaped like a fish. Its major thorough-fares are canals. The Grand Canal winds through the middle of the

fish, starting at the mouth where all the people and food enter, passing under the Rialto Bridge, and ending at St. Mark's Square (Piazza San Marco). Park your 21st-century perspective at the mouth and let Venice swallow you whole.

Venice is a carless kaleidoscope of people, bridges, and odorless canals. It's made up of more than a hundred small islands—but for simplicity, I refer to the whole shebang as "the island."

There are six districts (*sestieri,* shown on map on page 52): **San Marco** (from St. Mark's Square to the Accademia Bridge), **Castello** (the area east of St. Mark's Square), **Dorsoduro** (the "belly" of the fish, on the far side the Accademia Bridge), **Cannaregio** (between the train station and the Rialto Bridge), **San Polo** (west of the Rialto Bridge), and **Santa Croce** (the "eye" of the fish, across the canal from the train station).

The easiest way to navigate is by landmarks. Many street corners have a sign pointing you to *(per)* the nearest major landmark, such as San Marco, Accademia, Rialto, and Ferrovia (train station). Obedient visitors stick to the main thoroughfares as directed by these signs...and miss the charm of back-street Venice.

Beyond the city's core lie several other islands, including San Giorgio (with great views of Venice), Giudecca (more views), San Michele (old cemetery), Murano (famous for glass), Burano (lace-making), Torcello (old church), and the skinny Lido (with Venice's beach).

Tourist Information

With this book, a free city map from your hotel, and the events schedule on the TI's website, there's little need to make an in-person visit to a TI in Venice. That's fortunate, because the city's TIs can be crowded and don't have many free printed materials to hand out. If you need to check or confirm something, try phoning the TI at 041-529-8711 or visit www.turismovenezia.it (click on "Venezia," then the English icon). This website can be more helpful than the actual TI office.

VENICE

If you must visit a TI, you'll find two convenient branches near **St. Mark's Square** (one in the far-left corner with your back to the basilica, the other next to the Giardinetti Reali park near the San Marco vaporetto stop; both of these are open daily 9:00-19:00). There's also a TI desk at the **airport** (daily 9:00-20:00).

At the **train station,** you'll find TI staffers in a big, white kiosk out front near the vaporetto #2 stop most of the year (from Carnevale—falling sometime in Feb—through Oct daily 9:00-14:30, closed off-season; as this kiosk is shared with the private Alilaguna boat company, be sure to seek out a TI representative). The TI inside the station is open on summer afternoons (daily 13:00-19:00) and all day long in winter (daily 9:00-19:00; likely near track 1, though this may change with station renovation).

Maps: Of all places, you need a good map in Venice. Hotels give away freebies (no better than the small color one at the front of this book). The TI sells a decent €2.50 map and miniguide—but you can find a wider range at bookshops, newsstands, and postcard stands. The cheap maps are pretty bad, but if you spend €5, you'll get a map that shows you everything. Investing in a good map can be the best €5 you'll spend in Venice. Map lovers should look for the book *Calli, Campielli e Canali,* sold at bookstores for €22.50, with 1:2,000 maps of the whole city.

Also consider a mapping **app** for your smartphone, which uses GPS to pinpoint your location—extremely useful if you get lost in twisty back streets. To avoid data-roaming charges, look for an offline map that can be downloaded in its entirety before your trip. **City Maps 2Go** has a huge number of searchable offline maps, including a fairly good Venice version ($2 pays for any/all of their maps).

Helpful History Timelines: For historical orientation, local guide Michael Broderick (listed later, under "Tours in Venice") has produced three poster-size timelines that cleverly map the city's history and art (sold at local bookstores; see www.venicescapes.org).

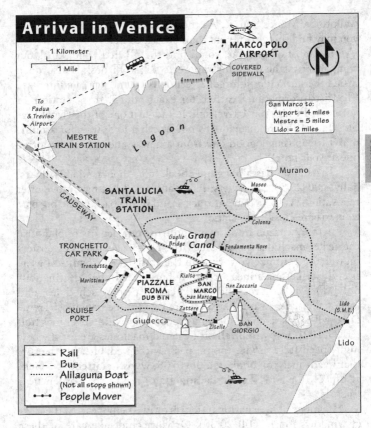

Arrival in Venice

A two-mile-long causeway (with highway and train lines) connects Venice to the mainland. Mestre, the sprawling mainland section of Venice, has fewer crowds, cheaper hotels, and plenty of inexpensive parking lots, but zero charm. Don't stop in Mestre unless you're parking your car, changing trains, or sleeping there.

By Train

All trains to "Venice" stop at Venezia Mestre (on the mainland). Most continue on to Santa Lucia Station (a.k.a. Venezia S.L. or Ferrovia) on the island of Venice itself. If your train only stops at Mestre, worry not. Your train ticket to Venice will get you to Santa Lucia. Just hop any train coming by and finish your journey (6/hour, 10 minutes). If, for some reason, you need a ticket from Mestre to Santa Lucia, you can buy one at a machine for €1.20.

Santa Lucia train station plops you right into the old town on the Grand Canal, an easy vaporetto ride or fascinating 45-minute walk to St. Mark's Square. As the station has just been renovated, you may find things different than described here.

For most of the year, you'll find the **TI** in a white kiosk out front, next to the dock for vaporetto #2; a TI desk is also open inside the station on summer afternoons and all day in winter (see "Tourist Information," earlier, for exact hours). If the station TI is crowded when you arrive, skip it and visit one of the two TIs at St. Mark's Square instead. It's not worth a long wait for a minimal TI map (buy a good one from a newsstand or pick up a free one at your hotel).

The station has a **baggage check** (€5/5 hours, €11/24 hours, daily 6:00-23:50, no lockers; likely at track 1 but may move after renovation). **WCs** (€1) are at track 1 and in the back of the big bar/cafeteria area inside the station.

Before heading into town, confirm your departure plan (use the ticket machines or just study the *partenze*/departures posters on walls). Minimize your time in the station—the banks of user-friendly ticket machines are handy but cover Italian destinations only. They take euros and credit cards, display schedules, and issue tickets. Be aware that there are two train companies: Trenitalia, with most connections, has green-and-white machines (toll tel. 892-021, www.trenitalia.it); the red machines are for the new high-speed Italo service (no railpasses accepted, cheaper the further in advance you book, tel. 06-0708, www.italotreno.it). Ticket offices (for both Trenitalia and Italo) are in the corner, near track 14.

If you need international tickets or live help, head to the ticket windows (open 6:00-20:30). Or you could take care of these tasks online or at a downtown travel agency (€4 fee per ticket, see page 62).

Getting from the Train Station to Downtown: Walk straight out of the station to the canal. You'll see vaporetto docks and ticket booths on both sides. For vaporetto #2 (fast boat down Grand Canal), go left. For vaporetto #1 (slow boat down Grand Canal), go right. See page 66 for details on vaporetto tickets and passes. A water taxi from the train station to a hotel in central Venice costs about €60-70 (the taxi dock is straight ahead).

By Bus

Venice's "bus station" is actually an open-air parking lot called Piazzale Roma. The square itself is a jumble of different operators, platforms, and crosswalks over busy lanes of traffic. But bus stops are well-signed. The ticket windows for ACTV (local public buses, including #5 to Marco Polo Airport) are by the vaporetto stop. The ATVO ticket office (for express buses to Marco Polo and Treviso airports and to Padua) is in the big, white building, on the right side of the square as you face away from the canal (office open daily 6:40-19:35).

Piazzale Roma also has three big parking garages and the People Mover monorail (€1, links to the cruise port and then the parking-lot island of Tronchetto). A baggage-storage office is next to the monorail at #497m (€7/24 hours, daily 6:00-21:00).

If you arrive here, find the vaporetto docks (just left of the modern bridge) and take #1 or the faster #2 down the Grand Canal to reach the Rialto, Accademia, or San Marco (St. Mark's Square) stops. Electronic boards direct you to the letter of the dock you want. Before buying a single-ride vaporetto ticket, consider getting a transit pass (see page 66). If your hotel is near the train station, you can simply walk there by crossing the modern Calatrava Bridge.

By Car

The freeway dead-ends after crossing the causeway to Venice. At the end of the road you have two parking choices: garages at Tronchetto or Piazzale Roma. As you drive into the city, signboards with green and red lights indicate which lots are full. (You can also park in Mestre, on the mainland, but this is less convenient.)

Parking at Tronchetto: This garage is much bigger, a bit farther out, a bit cheaper, and well-connected by vaporetto (€3-4/hour, €21/24 hours, discounts for longer stays, tel. 041-520-7555, www.veniceparking.it).

After parking in the big Tronchetto garage, cross the street. While you can head left for a long walk to the People Mover monorail (described below), it's easiest to go right to the vaporetto dock (not well-signed, look for ACTV). At the dock, catch vaporetto #2 in one of two directions: via the Grand Canal (more scenic, stops at Rialto, 40 minutes to San Marco), or via Giudecca (around the city, faster, no Rialto stop, 30 minutes to San Marco).

Don't be waylaid by aggressive water-taxi boatmen. They'll charge €100 to take you where the vaporetto will take you for €7. Also avoid the travel agencies masquerading as TIs; deal only with the ticket booth at the vaporetto dock or the HelloVenezia public transport office. If you're going to buy a local transport pass, do it now.

If you're staying near the train station and don't mind a walk, you can take the €1 **People Mover** instead of paying €7 for the two-stop vaporetto ride. The monorail brings you from Tronchetto to the bus station at Piazzale Roma, from which it's a five-minute walk across the Calatrava Bridge to the train station (buy monorail tickets with coins from machine, 3-minute trip, runs Mon-Sat 7:00-23:00, Sun 8:30-21:00).

Parking at Piazzale Roma: The two garages here are closer in and more convenient—but a bit more expensive and likelier to be full. Both garages face the busy square (Piazzale Roma) where the road ends. The big white building on your right is a 2,200-space public parking garage, the Autorimessa Communale (€26/24 hours, TI office in payment lobby, tel. 041-272-7211, www.asmvenezia.it). In a back corner of the square is the private Garage San Marco (€30/24 hours, tel. 041-523-2213, www.garagesanmarco.it). At either of these, you'll have to give up your keys. Near the Garage San Marco, avoid the Parcheggio Sant'Andrea, which charges obscene rates (€72/24 hours).

Parking in Mestre: Parking in the Parcheggio Stazione garage across from the train station in Mestre (on the mainland) only makes sense if you have light bags and are staying within walking distance of Santa Lucia Station (€10/day Mon-Fri, €14-16/day Sat-Sun; www.sabait.it).

By Plane or Cruise Ship

For information on Venice's airport and cruise terminal, see the end of this chapter.

Helpful Hints

Theft Alert: The dark, late-night streets of Venice are generally safe. Even so, pickpockets (often elegantly dressed) work the crowded main streets, docks, and *vaporetti*. Your biggest risk of pickpockets is inside St. Mark's Basilica, near the Accademia or Rialto bridges (especially if you're preoccupied with snapping photos), or on a tightly packed vaporetto.

A handy *polizia* station is on the right side of St. Mark's Square as you face the basilica (at #63, near Caffè Florian). To call the police, dial 113. The Venice TI handles complaints—which must be submitted in writing—about local crooks, including gondoliers, restaurants, and hotel rip-offs (fax 041-523-0399, complaint.apt@turismovenezia.it).

It's illegal for street vendors to sell knockoff handbags, and it's also illegal for you to buy them; both you and the vendor can get big fines.

Medical Help: Venice's Santi Giovanni e Paolo hospital (tel. 118) is a 10-minute walk from both the Rialto and San Marco neighborhoods, located behind the big church of the same name on Fondamenta dei Mendicanti (toward Fondamente Nove). You can take vaporetto #4.1 from San Zaccaria, or #5.2 from the train station or Piazzale Roma, to the Ospedale stop.

VENICE

Daily Reminder

Sunday: While anyone is welcome to worship, most churches are closed to sightseers on Sunday morning. They reopen in the afternoon: St. Mark's Basilica (14:00-17:00, until 16:00 Nov-March), Frari Church (13:00-18:00), and the Church of San Zaccaria (16:00-18:00). The Church of San Polo and Naval Museum are closed all day, and the Rialto open-air market consists mainly of souvenir stalls (fish and produce sections closed). It's a bad day for a pub crawl, as most pubs are closed.

Monday: All sights are open except the Rialto fish market, Ca' Pesaro, Palazzo Mocenigo Costume Museum, Lace Museum (on the island of Burano), and Torcello Museum (on the island of Torcello). The Accademia and Ca' d'Oro close at 14:00. Don't side-trip to Verona today, as most sights there are closed in the morning, if not all day.

Tuesday: All sights are open except the Peggy Guggenheim Collection, Ca' Rezzonico (Museum of 18th-Century Venice), and Punta della Dogana.

Wednesday/Thursday/Friday: All sights are open.

Saturday: All sights are open except the Jewish Museum.

Notes: The Accademia is open earlier (daily at 8:15) and closes later (19:15 Tue-Sun) than most sights in Venice. Some sights close earlier off-season (such as the Correr Museum, Campanile bell tower, St. Mark's Basilica, and the Church of San Giorgio Maggiore). Modest dress is recommended at churches and required at St. Mark's Basilica—no bare shoulders, shorts, or short skirts.

Crowd Control: The city is inundated with cruise-ship passengers and tours from mainland hotels daily from 10:00 to about 17:00. While major sights are busiest in the late morning, it's a delightful time to explore the back lanes. The sights that have crowd problems get even more packed when it rains.

To avoid the worst of the crowds at **St. Mark's Basilica,** go early or late. You can bypass the line if you have a bag to check (see page 90).

At the **Doge's Palace,** purchase your ticket at the never-crowded Correr Museum across St. Mark's Square. You can also visit later in the day.

For the **Campanile,** ascend first thing in the morning or go late (it's open until 21:00 July-Sept), or skip it entirely if you're going to the similar San Giorgio Maggiore bell tower.

For the **Accademia,** you'll enjoy fewer crowds by going early or late.

Be Prepared to Splurge: Venice is expensive for residents as well as tourists, as everything must be shipped in and hand-trucked to its destination. But it's a unique place that's worth paying a premium to fully experience. I find that the best way to enjoy Venice is just to succumb to its charms and blow through a little money.

Take Breaks: Venice's endless pavement, crowds, and tight spaces are hard on tourists, especially in hot weather. Schedule breaks in your sightseeing. Grab a cool place to sit down, relax, and recoup—meditate on a pew in an uncrowded church, or stop in a café.

Etiquette: As ever-growing waves of tourists wash over Venice every year, its residents are struggling to ward off the trash (and trashiness) left in their wake. Picnicking is illegal anywhere on St. Mark's Square, and offenders can be fined. (The only place nearby for a legal picnic is in Giardinetti Reali, the small park along the waterfront west of the Piazzetta near St. Mark's Square. Elsewhere in Venice, picnicking is no problem.) On St. Mark's Square, police admonish snackers and sunbathers. You may see friendly guidelines posted around town discouraging litter, pigeon-feeding, and beachwear (or rather, "encouraging" good behavior, as city officials are hoping that sweet talk will prove more effective).

Dress Modestly: When visiting St. Mark's Basilica or other major churches, men, women, and even children must cover their shoulders and knees (or risk being turned away). Remove hats when entering a church.

Public Toilets: Handy public WCs (€1.50) are near major landmarks, including St. Mark's Square (behind the Correr Museum and at the waterfront park, Giardinetti Reali), Rialto, and the Accademia Bridge. Use free toilets whenever you can—any museum you're visiting, or any café you're eating in. You could also get a drink at a bar (cheaper) and use their WC for free.

Best Views: A slow vaporetto ride down the Grand Canal on a sunny day—or a misty early morning—is a shutterbug's delight (try to sit in the front seats, available on some older boats; for narration, see my self-guided Grand Canal cruise, later). On St. Mark's Square, enjoy views from the soaring Campanile or the balcony of St. Mark's Basilica (both require admission). The Rialto and Accademia bridges provide free, expansive views of the Grand Canal, along with a cooling breeze. Or get off the main island for a view of the Venetian skyline: Ascend San Giorgio Maggiore's bell tower, or venture to Giudecca Island to visit the swanky bar of the Molino Stucky

Hilton Hotel (free shuttle boat leaves from near the San Zac-caria-M.V.E. vaporetto dock).

Pigeon Poop: If your head is bombed by a pigeon, resist the initial response to wipe it off immediately—it'll just smear into your hair. Wait until it dries, and it should flake off cleanly. But if the poop splatters on your clothes, wipe it off immediately to avoid a stain.

Water: I carry a water bottle to refill at public fountains. Venetians pride themselves on having pure, safe, and tasty tap water piped in from the foothills of the Alps. You can actually see the mountains from Venice's bell towers on crisp, clear winter days.

Updates to This Book: For news about changes to this book's coverage since it was published, see www.ricksteves.com/update.

Services

Internet Access: Almost all hotels have Wi-Fi, many have a computer that guests can use, and most provide these services for free. Otherwise, handy if pricey little Internet places are scattered around town (usually on back streets, marked with an @ sign, and charging €5/hour).

Post Office: Use post offices only as a last resort, as simple transactions can take 45 minutes if you get in the wrong line. You can buy stamps from tobacco shops and mail postcards at any of the red postboxes in town.

The main post office is just north of the Rialto Bridge—on the San Marco side, near the Teatro Malibran on Calle de le Acque (Mon-Fri 8:30-19:10, Sat 8:30-12:30, closed Sun, Castello 5016). You'll find branch offices with shorter hours (generally mornings only) around town, including a handy one right behind St. Mark's Square (near the TI).

Bookstores: In keeping with its literary heritage, Venice has classy and inviting bookstores. The small **Libreria Studium**, a block behind St. Mark's Basilica, has a carefully chosen selection of new English books, including my guidebooks (Mon-Sat 9:00-19:30, Sun 9:30-13:30 & 14:00-18:00, on Calle de la Canonica at #337—see map on page 89, tel. 041-522-2382). Used-bookstore lovers shouldn't miss the funky **Acqua Alta** ("high water") bookstore, whose quirky owner, Luigi, has  prepared for the next flood by displaying his wares in a selection of vessels, including bathtubs and a gondola. Look for the "book stairs" in his back garden (daily 9:00-21:00, large and classically disorganized selection includes prints of Venice, just beyond Campo Santa Maria Formosa on Calle Lunga Santa Maria Formosa at #5176—see map on page 125, tel. 041-296-0841). For a solid selection of used books in English, visit **Marco Polo,** on Calle del Teatro o de l'Opera, close to the St. Mark's side of the Rialto Bridge, just past the Coin department store and behind the church (Mon-Sat 9:30-13:00 & 15:30-19:30, closed Sun, Cannaregio 5886a—see map on page 125, tel. 041-522-6343).

Laundry: You'll find coin-operated launderettes near the train station and off Campo Santa Maria Formosa. I've listed details for a self-service *lavanderia* and a competitively priced full-service laundry near St. Mark's Square (see page 119), and for a self-serve laundry near the train station (page 132). Or ask your hotelier for the nearest launderette.

Travel Agencies: If you need to get train tickets, make seat reservations, or arrange a *cuccetta* (koo-CHET-tah—a berth on a night train), save a time-consuming trip to Venice's crowded train station by using a downtown travel agency. Most trains between Venice, Florence, and Rome require reservations, even for railpass holders. A travel agency can also give advice on cheap flights (book at least a week in advance for the best fares). Both of the following agencies charge a €4 per-ticket fee.

Along the embankment near St. Mark's Square (facing the San Zaccaria vaporetto stop), look for **Oltrex Change and Travel** (daily 9:00-13:00 & 14:00-18:00, closed Sun Nov-April; on Riva degli Schiavoni, one bridge past the Bridge of Sighs at San Marco 5097b—see map on page 89; tel. 041-524-2828, Luca and Beatrice).

Near Rialto, try **Kele & Teo Travel** (Mon-Fri 9:00-18:00, Sat 9:00-12:00, closed Sun; leaving the Rialto Bridge heading for St. Mark's, it's half a block away, tucked down a side street on the right—see map on page 125; tel. 041-520-8722).

English Church Services: San Zulian Church offers a Mass in English (generally May-Sept Mon-Fri at 9:30 and Sun at 11:30, Sun only Oct-April, 2 blocks toward Rialto off St. Mark's Square, tel. 041-523-5383). **St. George's Anglican Church** welcomes all to its English-language Eucharist (Sun at 10:30, located on Campo San Zio in Dorsoduro, midway between Accademia and Peggy Guggenheim Collection, www.stgeorgesvenice.com).

Getting Around Venice
On Foot

The city's "streets" are narrow pedestrian walkways connecting its docks, squares, bridges, and courtyards. To navigate, look for yellow signs on street corners pointing you to *(per)* the nearest major landmark. The first landmarks you'll get to know are San Marco (St. Mark's Square), Rialto (the bridge), Accademia (another bridge), Ferrovia (the train station), and Piazzale Roma (the bus station). Determine whether your destination is in the direction of a major signposted landmark, then follow the signs through the maze.

Dare to turn off the posted routes and make your own discoveries. While 80 percent of Venice is, in fact, not touristy, 80 percent of the tourists never notice. Escape the crowds and explore on foot. Walk and walk to the far reaches of the town. Don't worry about getting lost—in fact, get as lost as possible. Keep reminding yourself, "I'm on an island, and I can't get off." When it comes time to find your way, just follow the arrows on building corners or simply ask a local, *"Dov'è San Marco?"* ("Where is St. Mark's?") People in the tourist business (that's most Venetians) speak some English. If they don't, listen politely, watch where their hands point, say *"Grazie,"* and head off in that direction. If you're lost, refer to your map, or pop into a hotel and ask for their business card—it probably comes with a map and a prominent "You are here."

Every building in Venice has a house number. The numbers relate to the district (each with about 6,000 address numbers), not the street. Therefore, if you need to find a specific address, it helps to know its district, street, house number, and nearby landmarks.

Some helpful street terminology: *Campo* means square, a *campiello* is a small square, *calle* (pronounced "KAH-lay" with an "L" sound) means "street," and a *ponte* is a bridge. A *fondamenta* is the embankment along a canal or the lagoon. A *rio* is a small canal, while a *rio terà* is a street that was once a canal and has been filled in (and a *piscina* is a filled-in former pond). A *sotoportego* is a covered passageway. *Salizzada* means "laid with cobblestones" (indicating it's among the first Venetian streets ever paved). Don't get hung up on the exact spelling of street and square names, which may sometimes appear in the Venetian dialect and other times in standard Italian.

By Vaporetto

Venice's public transit system, run by a company called ACTV, is a fleet of motorized bus-boats called *vaporetti*. They work like city buses except that they never get a flat, the stops are docks, and if you get off between stops, you might drown.

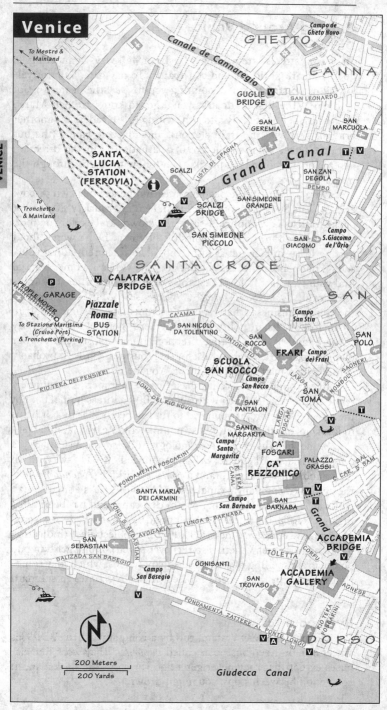

Venice

To Mestre &
Mainland

Canale de Cannaregio

GHETTO

CANNA

SANTA
LUCIA
STATION
(FERROVIA)

SCALZI

To
Tronchetto
Mainland

SCALZI
BRIDGE

SAN SIMEONE
GRANDE

SAN SIMEONE
PICCOLO

LISTA DI SPAGNA

Grand Canal

GUGLIE
BRIDGE

SAN LEONARDO

SAN
GEREMIA

SAN
MARCUOLA

SAN ZAN
DEGOLÀ
BEMBO

SAN
GIACOMO

Campo
S.Giacomo
de l'Orio

SANTA   CROCE

SAN

PEOPLE MOVER

GARAGE

CALATRAVA
BRIDGE

Piazzale
Roma
BUS
STATION

To Stazione Marittima
(Cruise Port)
& Tronchetto (Parking)

CA'AMAI

SAN NICOLÒ
DA TOLENTINO

TINTORETTO

Campo
San Stin

SAN
POLO

SAN
ROCCO

FRARI

Campo
dei Frari

NOMBOLI

SAONERI

LARGA

RIO TERÀ DEI PENSIERI

FOND. DEL RIO NOVO

SCUOLA
SAN ROCCO

Campo
San Rocco

SAN
PANTALON

SANTA
MARGARITA

Campo
Santa
Margarita

SAN
TOMÀ

C. LARGA
FOSCARI

CA'
FOSCARI

CA'
REZZONICO

R. TERÀ
CANAL

PALAZZO
GRASSI

C. CAR.   SAL.
S. SAM.

FONDAMENTA FOSCARINI

FOND. S. SEBASTIAN

SANTA MARIA
DEI CARMINI

Campo
San Barnaba

SAN
BARNABA

Grand Canal

C. LUNGA S. BARNABA

SALIZADA SAN BASEGIO

SAN
SEBASTIAN

C. AVOGARIA

OGNISANTI

Campo
San Basegio

TOLETTA

CORFU

ACCADEMIA
BRIDGE

ACCADEMIA
GALLERY

SAN
TROVASO

AGNESE

FONDAMENTA ZATTERE AL PONTE LONGO

RIO TERÀ
FOSCARINI

DORSO

Giudecca Canal

200 Meters

200 Yards

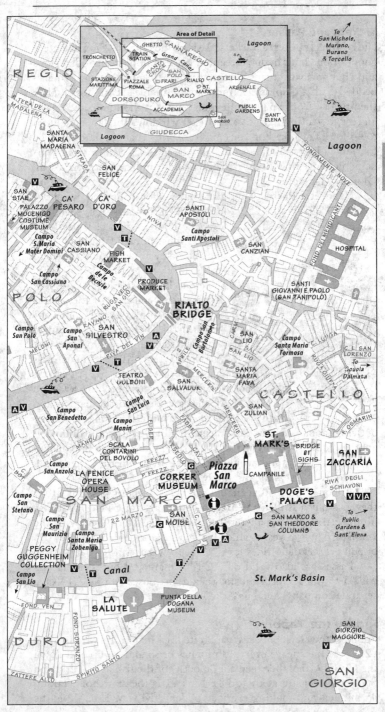

VENICE

Tickets and Passes

Individual Vaporetto Tickets: A single ticket costs €7. Tickets are good for one hour in one direction; you can hop on and off at stops and change boats during that time. Your ticket (a plastic card embedded with a chip) is electronic and refillable—don't toss it after the first use. You can put more money on it at the automated kiosks and avoid waiting in line at the ticket window. The fare is reduced to €4 for a few one-stop runs *(corsa semplice)* that are hard to do by foot, including the route from San Marco to La Salute, from Fondamente Nove to Murano-Colonna, and from San Zaccaria to San Giorgio Maggiore.

Vaporetto Passes: You can buy a pass for unlimited use of *vaporetti:* €18/12 hours, €20/24 hours, €25/36 hours, €30/48 hours,

€35/72 hours, €50/7-day pass. All passes must be validated each time you board by touching it to the small white machine on the dock. Because single tickets cost a hefty €7 a pop, these passes can pay for themselves in a hurry. Think through your Venice itinerary before you step up to the ticket booth to pay for your first vaporetto trip. The 48-hour pass pays for itself with five rides (for example: to your hotel, on a Grand Canal joyride, into the lagoon and back, and to the train station). Keep in mind that smaller and/or outlying stops, such as Sant'Elena and Biennale, are unstaffed—another good reason to buy a pass. It's fun to be able to hop on and off spontaneously, and avoid long ticket lines. On the other hand, many tourists just walk and rarely use a boat.

Anyone under 30 years old can get a 72-hour pass for €18 if they also buy a **Rolling Venice** discount card for €4 (see page 88). Those settling in for a longer stay can ride like a local by buying the **Imob** card (€40/5 years, which lets you either ride for €1.30 per trip or buy a *carnet* of 10 rides for €11). See www.actv.it for details.

Passes are also valid on ACTV's mainland buses, including bus #5 to the airport (but not the airport buses run by ATVO, a separate company) and bus #2 to Mestre.

Riding the *Vaporetti*

For most travelers, only two vaporetto lines matter: line #1 and line #2. These lines leave every 10 minutes or so and go up and down the Grand Canal, between the "mouth" of the fish at one end and St. Mark's Square at the other. Line #1 is the slow boat, taking 45 minutes and making every stop along the way. Line #2 is the fast boat that zips down the Grand Canal in 25 minutes, stopping only at Tronchetto (parking lot), Piazzale Roma (bus station), Ferrovia (train station), Rialto Bridge, San Tomà (Frari Church), San Samuele (opposite Ca' Rezzonico—an easy *traghetto* ride across), Accademia Bridge, and San Marco (west end of St. Mark's Square, end of the line).

Catching a vaporetto is very much like catching a city bus. You can buy either single-ride tickets (valid for 1 hour) or passes (valid for a variety of durations, from 12 hours to 7 days) from any ticket window or HelloVenezia office. HelloVenezia, run by ACTV, is a string of shops selling tickets and passes at the same prices as ticket windows (www.hellovenezia.com).

Before you board, validate your ticket by holding it up to the small white machine on the dock until you hear a pinging sound. The machine readout shows how long your ticket is valid—and inspectors do come by now and then to check tickets. If you board without a ticket (because ticket windows may be closed at odd hours or small stops), seek out the conductor immediately to buy a single ticket on board (or risk a €50 fine). If you purchase a vaporetto pass, you need to touch the pass to the machine each time you board the boat.

Most stops have at least two docks. Signs on each dock show the vaporetto lines that stop there and the direction they are headed. For example, along the Grand Canal, a #1 or #2 boat might be headed toward St. Mark's Square (signposted *Lido* or *San Marco*), or back toward the mainland (signposted *Ferrovia, Piazzale Roma*, or *Tronchetto*). Helpful electronic boards at most stops display which boats are coming next, and when. Make a point to take advantage of these. Most boats also have electronic boards displaying this information.

Large stops—such as San Marco, San Zaccaria, Rialto, Ferrovia (train station), and Piazzale Roma—have multiple docks. At these, each berth is assigned a letter (clearly marked above the door to the dock, along with the numbers of the vaporetto lines that use that dock). Electronic boards will direct you to the letter of the dock you want.

Sorting out the different directions of travel can be confusing. Some boats have circular routes traveling in one direction only (true for lines #5.1 and #5.2, plus the non-Murano sections of lines #4.1 and #4.2). Be careful of the otherwise-handy express line #2, which runs in both directions and is almost, but not quite, a full loop. The #2 boat leaving from the San Marco stop goes in one direction (up the Grand Canal), whereas from the San Zaccaria stop—just a five-minute walk away—it goes in the opposite direction (around the tail of the "fish"). Make sure you use the correct stop to avoid taking the long way around to your destination.

Handy *Vaporetti* from San Zaccaria, near St. Mark's Square

Several *vaporetti* leave from the San Zaccaria docks, located 150 yards east of St. Mark's Square. There are four separate San Zaccaria docks spaced about 70 yards apart, with a total of six different berths, lettered A to E: Danieli (E and F), Jolanda (C and D), M.V.E. (B), and Pietà (A). While this may sound confusing, in practice it's simple: Check the big electronic board (next to the Jolanda C/D dock), which indicates the departure time, line number, destination, and berth letter of upcoming *vaporetti*. Once you've figured out which boat you want, go to that letter berth and hop on. They're all within about a five-minute stroll of each other.

- **Line #1** goes up the Grand Canal, making all the stops, including San Marco, Rialto, Ferrovia (train station), and Piazzale Roma (but it does not go as far as Tronchetto). In the other direction, it goes from San Zaccaria to Arsenale and Giardini before ending on the Lido.
- **Line #2** zips over to San Giorgio Maggiore, the island church across from St. Mark's Square (5 minutes, €4 ride). From there, it continues on to stops on the island of Giudecca, the parking lot at Tronchetto, and then down the Grand Canal. Note: You cannot ride the #2 up the Grand Canal (for example, to Rialto or the train station) directly from this stop—you'll need to walk five minutes along the waterfront, past St. Mark's Square, to the San Marco-Giardinetti dock, and hop the #2 from there.
- **Line #4.1** goes to San Michele and Murano in 45 minutes.
- **Line #7** is the summertime express boat to Murano (25 minutes).
- The **Molino Stucky shuttle boat** takes even nonguests to the Hilton Hotel, with its popular view bar (free, 20-minute ride, leaves at 0:20 past the hour from near the San Zaccaria-

You may notice some *vaporetti* sporting a *corsa bis* sign, indicating that it's running a shortened or altered route, and that riders may have to hop off partway and wait for the next boat. If you see a *corsa bis* sign, before boarding ask the conductor whether it's going to your desired destination.

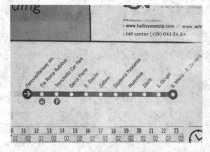

To clear up any confusion, ask a ticket-seller or conductor for help (sometimes they're stationed on the dock to help confused

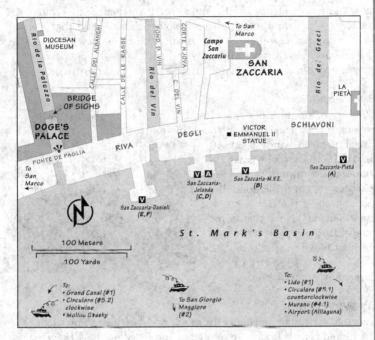

M.V.E. dock).
- **Lines #5.1** and **#5.2** are the *circulare* (cheer-koo-LAH-ray), making a loop around the perimeter of the island, with a stop at the Lido—perfect if you just like riding boats. Line #5.1 goes counterclockwise, and #5.2 goes clockwise.
- The **Alilaguna** shuttle to and from the airport stops here as well.

tourists), or look at the most current ACTV timetable (in English and Italian, free at ticket booths but often unavailable—can be downloaded from the ACTV website, www.actv.it).

More Vaporetto Tips
For fun, follow my self-guided cruise on the Grand Canal. But be warned: Grand Canal *vaporetti* in particular can be absolutely jam-packed, especially during the tourist rush hour (during mornings heading in from Piazzale Roma, and in evenings heading out to Piazzale Roma). Riding at night, with nearly empty boats and chandelier-lit palace interiors viewable from the Grand Canal, is an entirely different experience.

Vaporetto dell'Arte: Twice hourly, these specially designated *vaporetti* (marked *VA*) go up and down the Grand Canal. For an extra €10 per pass, you get audioguide commentary, video screens, more comfortable seats, Wi-Fi, and so on. If you believe that tourists should be sorted into higher and lower classes—and that it's worth paying extra for elite status—be my guest (see www.vaporettoarte.com)...but I'll save my euros and stick with the public *vaporetti*, which reach all the same places and run far more often.

By *Traghetto*

Only four bridges cross the Grand Canal, but *traghetti* (shuttle gondolas) ferry locals and in-the-know tourists across the Grand Canal at seven handy locations (marked on the color map of Venice at the front of this book). Just step in, hand the gondolier €2, and enjoy the ride—standing or sitting. Note that some *traghetti* are seasonal, some stop running as early as 12:30, and all stop by 18:00. *Traghetti* are not covered by any transit pass.

By Water Taxi

Venetian taxis, like speedboat limos, hang out at busy points along the Grand Canal. Prices are regulated and listed on the TI's website: €15 for pickup, then €2 per minute; €5 per person for more than four passengers; and €10 between 22:00 and 6:00. Extra bags cost €3 apiece. (For information on taking the water taxi to/from the airport, see page 156.) Despite regulation, prices can be soft; negotiate and settle on the price or rate before stepping in. For travelers with lots of luggage or small groups who can split the cost, taxi boat rides can be a worthwhile and time-saving convenience—and skipping across the lagoon in a classic wooden motorboat is a cool indulgence. For a little more than €100 an hour, you can have a private, unguided taxi-boat tour. You may find more competitive rates if you prebook through the Consorzio Motoscafi water taxi association (tel. 041-522-2303, www.motoscafivenezia.it).

By Gondola

If you're interested in hiring a gondolier for your own private cruise, see page 112.

Tours in Venice

Avventure Bellissime Venice Tours

This company offers several English-only two-hour walks, including a basic St. Mark's Square introduction called the "Original  Venice Walking Tour" (€22, includes church entry, most days at 11:00, Sun at 14:00; 45 minutes on the square, 15 minutes in the church, 1 hour along back streets), a 70-minute private boat tour of the Grand Canal (€43, daily at 16:30, 8 people maximum), a "Hidden Venice" tour (€22, in summer 3/week at 11:30, less off-season), and excursions on the mainland (10 percent discount for Rick Steves readers, see descriptions at www. tours-italy.com, tel. 041-970-499, info@tours-italy.com, Monica or Jonathan).

VENICE

Classic Venice Bars Tour

Debonair guide Alessandro Schezzini is a connoisseur of Venetian *bacari*—classic old bars serving wine and traditional *cicchetti* snacks. He organizes two-hour Venetian pub tours (€30, any night on request at 18:00, depart from top of Rialto Bridge, better to book by email—alessandro@schezzini.it—than by phone, mobile 335-530-9024, www.schezzini.it). Alessandro's tours include sampling *cicchetti* with wines at three different *bacari*. (If you think of this tour as a light dinner with a local friend, it's a particularly good value.)

Artviva Tours

This company offers a comprehensive program of tours, including Venice in a day, five themed tours (Grand Canal, Venice Walk, Doge's Palace, Gondola Tour, Food and Wine Tour with a sommelier), and a "Learn to Be a Gondolier" tour (for details, see www. italy.artviva.com).

Venicescapes

Michael Broderick's private theme tours of Venice are intellectually demanding and beyond the attention span of most mortal tourists. But travelers with a keen interest and a desire to learn find him passionate and engaging. Your time with Michael is like a rolling, graduate-level lecture (see his website for various 4-6-hour itineraries, 2 people-$250-290 or the euro equivalent, $60/person after that, admissions and transport not included, book in advance, tel. 041-850-5742, mobile 349-479-7406, www.venicescapes.org, info@venicescapes.org).

VENICE

Is Venice Sinking?

Venice has battled rising water levels since the fifth century. But today, the water seems to be winning. Several factors, both natural and man-made, cause Venice to flood about 100 times a year—usually from October until late winter—a phenomenon called the *acqua alta*.

On my last trip I asked a Venetian how much the city is sinking. He said, "Less than the sea is rising." Venice sits atop sediments deposited at the ancient mouth of the Po River, which are still compacting and settling. Early industrial projects, such as offshore piers and the railroad bridge to the mainland, affected the sea floor and tidal cycles in ways that made the city more vulnerable to flooding. Twentieth-century industry worsened things by pumping out massive amounts of groundwater from the aquifer beneath the lagoon for nearly 50 years before the government stopped the practice in the 1970s. In the last century, Venice has sunk by about nine inches.

Meanwhile, the waters around Venice are rising, a phenomenon that's especially apparent in winter. The highest so far was in November 1966, when a huge storm (the same one that famously flooded Florence) raised Venice's water level to more than six feet above the norm. The notorious *acqua alta* happens when an unusually high tide combines with strong sirocco winds and a storm. Although tides are miniscule in the Mediterranean, the narrow, shallow Adriatic Sea has about a three-foot tidal range. When a storm—an area of low pressure—travels over a body of water, it pulls the surface of the water up into a dome. As strong sirocco winds from Africa blow storms north up the Adriatic, they push this high water ahead of the front, causing a surging storm tide. Add to that the worldwide sea-level rise that's resulted from recent climate change (melting ice caps, thermal expansion of the water, more frequent and more powerful storms), and it makes a high sea that much higher.

Local Guides

Plenty of licensed, trained guides are available. If you organize a small group from your hotel at breakfast to split the cost (figure on €70/hour with a 2-hour minimum), the fee becomes more reasonable. The following guides work with individuals, families, and small groups:

Walks Inside Venice is a dynamic duo of women—and their tour-guide colleagues—enthusiastic about teaching (€225/3 hours per group of up to 6 with this book, 3-hour minimum; Roberta: mobile 347-253-0560; Sara: mobile 335-522-9714; www.walksin-

If the *acqua alta* appears during your visit, you'll see the first puddles in the center of paved squares, pooling around the limestone grates at the square's lowest point. These grates cover cisterns that long held Venice's only source of drinking water. That's right: Surrounded by the lagoon and beset by constant flooding, this city had no natural source of fresh water. For centuries, resi-

dents carried water from the mainland with much effort and risk. In the ninth century, they devised a way to collect rainwater by using paved, cleverly sloped squares as catchment systems, with limestone filters covering underground clay tubs. Venice's population grew markedly once citizens were able to access fresh water by simply dropping buckets down into these "wells." Several thousand cisterns provided the city with drinking water up until 1886, when an aqueduct was built (paralleling the railroad bridge) to bring in water from nearby mountains. Now the wells are capped, the clay tubs are rotted out, and rain drains from squares into the lagoon—or up from it, as the case may be.

So what is Venice doing about the flooding? Since the 1966 flood, officials knew something had to be done, but it took about four decades to come up with a solution. In 2003, a consortium of engineering firms began construction on the MOSE Project. Named for the acronym of its Italian name, *Modulo Sperimentale Elettromeccanico,* it's also a nod to Moses and his (albeit temporary) mastery over the sea.

Underwater "mobile" gates are being installed on the floor of the sea at the three inlets where the open sea enters Venice's lagoon. When the seawater rises above a certain level, air will be pumped into the gates, causing them to rise and shut out the Adriatic. The first gates are already installed, and the project is scheduled to finish by 2016. Will it work? There are many doubters.

sidevenice.com, info@walksinsidevenice.com). Roberta has been a big help in the making of this book. They also do side-trips to outlying destinations and offer regularly scheduled small-group, English-only walking tours (€62.50, departs daily at 14:30, 2.5 hours).

Alessandro Schezzini, mentioned earlier for his Classic Venice Bars Tour, isn't a licensed guide, so he can't take you into sights. But his relaxed, 1.5-hour back-streets tour gets you beyond the clichés and into off-beat Venice (€15/person, departs daily at 16:30, mobile 335-530-9024, www.schezzini.it, alessandro@schezzini.it). He also does lagoon tours in the morning.

Tour Leader Venice, a.k.a. **Treviso Car Service,** offers small-group tours beyond Venice to 16th-century villas, wine-and-cheese tastings, and the Dolomites. Within Venice, their guided excursions include visits to "Venice off the beaten path," the Rialto produce market, the lagoon, and artisan shops (also provides airport transfers—see page 156, mobile 348-900-0700 or 333-411-2840; in Venice: www.tourleadervenice.com, info@tourleadervenice.com; beyond Venice: www.trevisocarservice.com, tvcarservice@gmail.com; Igor, Andrea, and Marta).

Another good option is **Venice with a Guide,** a co-op of 10 good guides (www.venicewithaguide.com), including **Corine Govi** (mobile 347-966-8346, corine_g@libero.it) and **Elisabetta Morelli** (€70/hour, 2-hour minimum, tel. 041-526-7816, mobile 328-753-5220, bettamorelli@inwind.it).

Weekend Tour Packages for Students

Andy Steves (my son) runs Weekend Student Adventures, offering active and experiential three-day weekend tours from €199, designed for American students studying abroad (www.wsaeurope.com for details on tours of Venice and other great cities).

Self-Guided Cruise

▲▲▲Welcome to Venice's Grand Canal Cruise

Take a joyride and introduce yourself to Venice by boat. Cruise the Canal Grande all the way to San Marco, starting at the train station (Ferrovia) or the bus station (Piazzale Roma).

If it's your first trip down the Grand Canal, you might want to stow this book and just take it all in—Venice is a barrage on the senses that hardly needs narration. But these notes give the cruise a little meaning and help orient you to this great city.

This tour is designed to be done on the slow boat #1 (which takes about 45 minutes). The express boat #2 travels the same route, but it skips many stops and takes only 25 minutes, making it hard to sightsee.

You can break up the tour by hopping on and off at various sights described in greater depth elsewhere in this chapter (but remember, a single-fare vaporetto ticket is good for just one hour; passes let you hop on and off all day).

To help you enjoy the visual parade of canal wonders, I've organized this tour by boat stop. I'll point out both what you can see from the current stop, and what to look forward to as you cruise to the next stop. You can download this self-guided cruise as a free Rick Steves audio tour (see page 9).

Where to Sit: You're more likely to find an empty seat if you catch the vaporetto at Piazzale Roma—the stop *before* Ferrovia.

Some *vaporetti* have seats in the bow (in front of the captain's bridge), which is the perfect vantage point for spotting sights left, right, and forward. However, many boats lack these seats, so you have to settle for another option: Sit inside (and view the passing sights through windows), stand in the open middle deck (you can try to move back and forth—almost impossible if the boat is crowded), or sit outside in the back (where you'll miss the wonderful forward views). If you have to commit to one side, consider this: The left side has a slight edge, with more sights and the best light late in the day.

Overview

The Grand Canal is Venice's "Main Street." At more than two miles long, nearly 150 feet wide, and nearly 15 feet deep, it's the city's largest canal, lined with its most impressive palaces. It's the remnant of a river that once spilled from the mainland into the Adriatic. The sediment it carried formed barrier islands that cut Venice off from the sea, forming a lagoon.

Venice was built on the marshy islands of the former delta, sitting on wood pilings driven nearly 15 feet into the clay (alder was the preferred wood). About 25 miles of canals drain the city, dumping like streams into the Grand Canal. Technically, Venice has only three canals: Grand, Giudecca, and Cannaregio. The 45 small waterways that dump into the Grand Canal are referred to as rivers (e.g., Rio Novo).

Venice is a city of palaces, dating from the days when the city was the world's richest. The most lavish palaces formed a grand architectural cancan along the Grand Canal. Once frescoed in

reds and blues, with black-and-white borders and gold-leaf trim, they made Venice a city of dazzling color. This cruise is the only way to truly appreciate the palaces, approaching them at water level, where their main entrances were located. Today, strict laws prohibit any changes in these buildings, so while landowners gnash their teeth, we can enjoy Europe's best-preserved medieval city—which also is slowly rotting. Many of the grand buildings are now vacant. Others harbor chandeliered elegance above mossy, empty (often flooded) ground floors.

The Grand Canal Cruise Begins

This tour starts at the Ferrovia vaporetto stop (at Santa Lucia train station). It also works—and the boat can be less crowded—if you board upstream from Ferrovia at Piazzale Roma, a short walk from Ferrovia over the Calatrava Bridge. At Piazzale Roma, check the electronic boards to see which dock the next #1 or #2 is leaving from, hop on board to get your pick of seats, and start reading the tour when your vaporetto reaches Ferrovia.

Ferrovia: The **Santa Lucia train station,** one of the few modern buildings in town, was built in 1954. It's been the gate-

way into Venice since 1860, when the first station was built. "F.S." stands for "Ferrovie dello Stato," the Italian state railway system.

More than 20,000 people a day commute in from the mainland, making this the busiest part of Venice during rush hour. The **Calatrava Bridge,** spanning the Grand Canal between the train station and Piazzale Roma upstream, was built in 2008 to alleviate some of the congestion and make the commute easier (see page 107).

Opposite the train station, atop the green dome of **San Simeon Piccolo** church, St. Simeon waves *ciao* to whoever enters or leaves the "old" city. The pink church with the white Carrara-marble facade, just beyond the train station, is the **Church of the Scalzi** (Church of the Barefoot, named after the shoeless Carmelite monks), where the last doge (Venetian ruler) rests. It looks relatively new because it was partially rebuilt after being bombed in 1915 by Austrians aiming (poorly) at the train station.

Riva de Biasio: Venice's main thoroughfare is busy with all kinds of **boats:** taxis, police boats, garbage boats, ambulances, construction cranes, and even brown-and-white UPS boats. Somehow they all manage to share the canal in relative peace.

About 25 yards past the Riva de Biasio stop, look left down the broad **Cannaregio Canal** to see what was the **Jewish Ghetto** (described on page 105). The twin, pale-pink, six-story "skyscrapers"—the tallest buildings you'll see at this end of the canal—are reminders of how densely populated the world's original ghetto was. Set aside as the local Jewish quarter in 1516, this area became extremely crowded. This urban island developed into one of the most closely knit business and cultural quarters of all the Jewish communities in Italy and gave us our word "ghetto" (from *geto,* the copper foundry located here).

San Marcuola: At this stop, facing a tiny square just ahead, stands the unfinished Church of San Marcuola, one of only five churches fronting the Grand Canal. Centuries ago, this canal was a commercial drag of expensive real estate in high demand by wealthy merchants. About 20 yards ahead on the right (across the

Grand Canal) stands the stately gray **Turkish "Fondaco" Exchange,** one of the oldest houses in Venice. Its horseshoe arches and roofline of triangles and dingleballs are reminders of its Byzantine heritage. Turkish traders in turbans docked here, unloaded their goods into

the warehouse on the bottom story, then went upstairs for a home-style meal and a place to sleep. Venice in the 1500s was very cosmopolitan, welcoming every religion and ethnicity, so long as they carried cash. (Today the building contains the city's Museum of Natural History—and Venice's only dinosaur skeleton.)

Just 100 yards ahead on the left, Venice's **Casinò** is housed in the palace where German composer Richard *(The Ring)* Wagner died in 1883. See his distinct, strong-jawed profile in the white plaque on the brick wall. In the 1700s, Venice was Europe's Vegas, with casinos and prostitutes everywhere. *Casinòs* ("little houses" in Venetian dialect) have long provided Italians with a handy escape from daily life. Today they're run by the state to keep Mafia influence at bay. Notice the fancy front porch, rolling out the red carpet for high rollers arriving by taxi or hotel boat.

San Stae: The San Stae Church sports a delightful Baroque facade. Opposite the San Stae stop is a little canal opening—on the second building to the right of that opening, look for the peeling plaster that once made up **frescoes** (you can barely distinguish the scant remains of little angels on the lower floors). Imagine the facades of the Grand Canal at their finest. Most of them would have been covered in frescoes by the best artists of the day. As colorful as the city is today, it's still only a faded, sepia-toned remnant of a long-gone era, a time of lavishly decorated, brilliantly colored palaces.

Just ahead, jutting out a bit on the right, is the ornate white facade of **Ca' Pesaro** (which houses the International Gallery of

Modern Art—see page 102). *"Ca'"* is short for *casa* (house). Because only the house of the doge (Venetian ruler) could be called a palace *(palazzo),* all other Venetian palaces are technically *"Ca'."*

In this city of masks, notice how the rich marble facades along the Grand Canal mask what are generally just simple, no-nonsense brick buildings. Most merchants enjoyed showing off. However, being

Grand Canal

GUGLIE BRIDGE

Canale de Cannaregio

To Jewish Ghetto

STRADA

PALAZZO CORRER CONTARINI

SAN MARCUOLA

SAN GEREMIA

LISTA DI SPAGNA

Canal

PALAZZO GRITTI

CASINÒ

PALAZZO VENDRAMIN CALERGI

SANTA LUCIA TRAIN STATION (FERROVIA)

SCALZI

PALAZZO CALBO-CROTTA

PALAZZO FLANGINI

Grand

PALAZZO MARCELLO

PALAZZO GIOVANELLI

TURKISH "FONDACO" EXCHANGE

PAL. GRITTI

SCALZI BRIDGE

SAN ZAN DEGOLÀ

PALAZZO DONA BALBI

PALAZZO CA' TRON

SAN SIMEONE PICCOLO

SANTA CROCE

CALATRAVA BRIDGE

SAN

PIAZZALE ROMA
& PEOPLE MOVER
TO STAZIONE MARITTIMA
& TRONCHETTO

FRARI

PALAZZO CAPPELLO-LAYARD

Vaporetto Stops

① Ferrovia
② Riva de Biasio
③ San Marcuola
④ San Stae
⑤ Ca' d'Oro
⑥ Mercato Rialto
⑦ Rialto
⑧ San Silvestro
⑨ Sant'Angelo
⑩ San Tomà
⑪ Ca' Rezzonico
⑫ Accademia
⑬ Santa Maria del Giglio
⑭ Salute
⑮ San Marco
⑯ San Zaccaria

SAN TOMÀ

PALAZZO GIUSTINIANI

PALAZZO BARBARIGO

PALAZZO BALBI

FIRE STATION

CA' FOSCARI

PALAZZO GIUSTINIAN

CA' REZZONICO

PALAZZO MOCENIGO

PALAZZO VECCHIA

PALAZZO MORO LIN

PALAZZO GRASSI

PALAZZO MALIPIERO-CAPPELLO

PALAZZO LOREDAN

PALAZZO FALIER

PALAZZO CONTARINI DEGLI SCRIGNI

PALAZZO QUERINI

PALAZZO GIUSTINIAN LOLIN

ACCADEMIA BRIDGE & GALLERY

PALAZZO BARBARO

PALAZZO BARBARIGO

FONDAMENTA ZATTERE AL PONTE LONGO

Giudecca Canal

DORSODURO

To Zattere

VENICE

VENICE

smart businessmen, they only decorated the side of the buildings that would be seen and appreciated. But look back as you pass Ca' Pesaro. It's the only building you'll see with a fine side facade. Ahead, on the left, with its glorious triple-decker medieval arcade (just before the next stop) is Ca' d'Oro.

Ca' d'Oro: The lacy **Ca' d'Oro** (House of Gold) is the best example of Venetian Gothic architecture on the canal. Its three

stories offer different variations on balcony design, topped with a spiny white roofline. Venetian Gothic mixes traditional Gothic (pointed arches and round medallions stamped with a four-leaf clover) with Byzantine styles (tall, narrow arches atop thin columns), filled in with Islamic frills. Like all the palaces, this was originally painted and gilded to make it even more glorious than it is now. Today the Ca' d'Oro is an art gallery (described on page 107).

Look at the Venetian chorus line of palaces in front of the boat. On the right is the arcade of the covered **fish market,** with the open-air **produce market** just beyond. It bustles in the morning but is quiet the rest of the day. This is a great scene to wander through—even though European Union hygiene standards have made it cleaner, but less colorful, than it once was.

Find the *traghetto* gondola ferrying shoppers—standing like Washington crossing the Dela-

ware—back and forth. There are seven *traghetto* crossings along the Grand Canal, each one marked by a classy low-key green-and-black sign. Driving a *traghetto* isn't these gondoliers' normal day jobs. As a public service, all gondoliers are obliged to row the *traghetto* a few days a month. Make a point to use them. At €2 a ride, *traghetti* offer the cheapest gondola ride in Venice (but, at this price, don't expect them to sing to you).

Mercato Rialto: This stop was opened in 2007 to serve the busy market (boats only stop here between 8:00 and 20:00). The long and officious-looking building at this stop is the Venice courthouse. Straight ahead in the distance, rising above the huge post office, is the tip of the Campanile (bell tower), crowned by its golden angel at St. Mark's Square, where this tour will end. The **German**

Exchange (100 yards directly ahead, on left side) was the trading center for German metal merchants in the early 1500s (once a post office, it will soon be a shopping center).

You'll cruise by some trendy and beautifully situated wine bars on the right, but look ahead as you round the corner and see the impressive Rialto Bridge come into view.

A major landmark of Venice, the **Rialto Bridge** is lined with shops and tourists. Constructed in 1588, it's the third bridge built on this spot. Until the 1850s, this was the only bridge crossing the Grand Canal. With a span of 160 feet and foundations stretching 650 feet on either side, the Rialto was an impressive engineering feat in its day. Earlier Rialto Bridges could open to let big ships in, but not this one. When this new bridge was completed, much of the Grand Canal was closed to shipping and became a canal of palaces.

When gondoliers pass under the fat arch of the Rialto Bridge, they take full advantage of its acoustics: *"Volare, oh, oh..."*

Rialto: Rialto, a separate town in the early days of Venice, has always been the commercial district, while San Marco was the religious and governmental center. Today, a winding street called the Mercerie connects the two, providing travelers with human traffic jams and a mesmerizing gauntlet of shopping temptations. This is the only stretch of the historic Grand Canal with landings upon which you can walk. They unloaded the city's basic necessities here: oil, wine, charcoal, iron. Today, the quay is lined with tourist-trap restaurants.

Venice's sleek, black, graceful **gondolas** are a symbol of the city (for more on gondolas, see page 112). With about 500 gondoliers joyriding amid the churning *vaporetti*, there's a lot of congestion on the Grand Canal. Pay attention—this is where most of the gondola and vaporetto accidents take place. While the Rialto is the highlight of many gondola rides, gondoliers understandably prefer the quieter small canals. Watch your vaporetto driver curse the better-paid gondoliers.

Ahead, 100 yards on the left, two gray-colored **palaces** stand side by side (the City Hall and the mayor's office). Their horseshoe-shaped, arched windows are similar and their stories are the same height, lining up to create the effect of one long balcony.

San Silvestro: We now enter a long stretch of important **merchants' palaces,** each with proud and different facades. Because ships couldn't navigate beyond the Rialto Bridge, the biggest palaces—with the major shipping needs—line this last stretch of the navigable Grand Canal.

Palaces like these were multifunctional: ground floor for the warehouse, offices and showrooms upstairs, and the living quarters above the offices on the "noble floors" (with big windows designed to allow in maximum light). Servants lived and worked on the top floors (with the smallest windows). For fire-safety reasons, the kitchens were also located on the top floors. Peek into the noble floors to catch a glimpse of their still-glorious chandeliers of Murano glass.

Sant'Angelo: Notice how many buildings have a foundation of waterproof white stone *(pietra d'Istria)* upon which the bricks sit high and dry. Many canal-level floors are abandoned as the rising water level takes its toll.

The **posts**—historically painted gaily with the equivalent of family coats of arms—don't rot underwater. But the wood at the waterline, where it's exposed to oxygen, does. On the smallest canals, little blue gondola signs indicate that these docks are for gondolas only (no taxis or motor boats).

San Tomà: Fifty yards ahead, on the right side (with twin obelisks on the rooftop), stands **Palazzo Balbi,** the palace of an early-17th-century captain general of the sea. These Venetian equivalents of five-star admirals were honored with twin obelisks decorating their palaces. This palace, like so many in the city, flies three flags: Italy (green-white-red), the European Union (blue with ring of stars), and Venice (a lion on a field of red and gold). Today it houses the administrative headquarters of the regional government.

Just past the admiral's palace, look immediately to the right, down a side canal. On the right side of that canal, before the bridge, see the traffic light and the **fire station** (the 1930s Mussolini-era building with four arches hiding fireboats parked and ready to go).

The impressive **Ca' Foscari,** with a classic Venetian facade (on the corner, across from the fire station), dominates the bend in the

canal. This is the main building of the University of Venice, which has about 25,000 students. Notice the elegant lamp on the corner—needed in the old days to light this intersection.

The grand, heavy, white **Ca' Rezzonico,** just before the stop of the same name, houses the Museum of 18th-Century Venice (described on page 102). Across the canal is the cleaner and leaner **Palazzo Grassi,** the last major palace built on the canal, erected in the late 1700s. It was purchased by a French tycoon and now displays part of Punta della Dogana's contemporary art collection.

Ca' Rezzonico: Up ahead, the Accademia Bridge leads over the Grand Canal to the **Accademia Gallery** (right side), filled with the best Venetian paintings (described on page 99). The bridge was put up in 1934 as a temporary structure. Locals liked it, so it stayed. It was rebuilt in 1984 in the original style.

Accademia: From here, look through the graceful bridge and way ahead to enjoy a classic view of **La Salute Church,** topped by

a crown-shaped dome supported by scrolls (described on page 101). This Church of St. Mary of Good Health was built to thank God for delivering Venetians from the devastating plague of 1630 (which had killed about a third of the city's population).

The low, white building among greenery (100 yards ahead, on the right, between the Accademia Bridge and the church) is the **Peggy Guggenheim Collection.** The American heiress "retired" here, sprucing up a palace that had been abandoned in midconstruction. Peggy willed the city her fine collection of modern art (described on page 101).

As you approach the next stop, notice on the right how the fine line of higgledy-piggledy palaces evokes old-time Venice. Two

doors past the Guggenheim, Palazzo Dario has a great set of characteristic **funnel-shaped chimneys.** These forced embers through a loop-the-loop channel until they were dead—required in the days when stone palaces were surrounded by humble, wooden buildings, and a live spark could make a merchant's workforce homeless. Notice this early Renaissance building's flat-feeling façade with "pasted-on" Renaissance motifs. Three doors later is the **Salviati building,** which once served as a glassworks. Its fine mosaic, done by Art Nouveau in the early 20th century, features Venice as a queen being appreciated by the big shots of society.

Santa Maria del Giglio: Back on the left stands the fancy Gritti Palace hotel. Hemingway and Woody Allen both stayed here (but not together).

Take a deep whiff of Venice. What's all this nonsense about stinky canals? All I smell is my shirt. By the way, how's your captain? Smooth dockings? To get to know him, stand up in the bow and block his view.

Salute: The huge La Salute Church towers overhead as if squirted from a can of Catholic Reddi-wip. Like Venice itself, the church rests upon pilings. To build the foundation for the city, more than a million trees were piled together, reaching beneath the mud to the solid clay. Much of the surrounding countryside was deforested by Venice. Trees were imported and consumed locally—to fuel the furnaces of Venice's booming glass industry, to build Europe's biggest merchant marine, to form light and flexible beams for nearly all of the buildings in town, and to prop up this city in the mud.

As the Grand Canal opens up into the lagoon, the last building on the right, with the golden ball, is the 17th-century **Customs House,** which now houses the Punta della Dogana contemporary art museum (listed on page 102). Its two bronze Atlases hold a statue of Fortune riding the ball. Arriving ships stopped here to pay their tolls.

San Marco: Up ahead on the left, the green pointed tip of the Campanile marks **St. Mark's Square,** the political and religious

center of Venice...and the final destination of this tour. You could get off at the San Marco stop and go straight to St. Mark's Square. But I'm staying on the boat for one more stop, just past St. Mark's Square (it's a quick walk back).

Survey the lagoon. Opposite St. Mark's Square, across the water, the ghostly white church with the pointy bell tower is **San Giorgio Maggiore,** with great views of Venice (described on page 99). Next to it is the residential island Giudecca, stretching from close to San Giorgio Maggiore past the Venice youth hostel (with a nice view, directly across) to the Hilton Hotel (good nighttime view, far right end of island).

Still on board? If you are, as we leave the San Marco stop, prepare for a drive-by view of St. Mark's Square. First comes the bold white facade of the old mint (marked by a tiny cupola, where Venice's golden ducat, the "dollar" of the Venetian Republic, was made) and the library facade. Then come the twin columns topped by St. Theodore and St. Mark, who've welcomed visitors since the 15th century. Between the columns, catch a glimpse of two giant figures atop the **Clock Tower**—they've been whacking their clappers every hour since 1499. The domes of **St. Mark's Basilica** are soon eclipsed by the lacy facade of the **Doge's Palace.** Next you'll see the **Bridge of Sighs** (leading from the palace to the prison—check out the maximum security bars), many gondolas with their green breakwater buoys, and then the grand harborside promenade—the **Riva.**

Follow the Riva with your eye, past elegant hotels to the green area in the distance. This is the largest of Venice's few **parks,** which hosts the annual Biennale festival (see page 114). Much farther in the distance is the **Lido,** the island with Venice's beach. Its sand and casinos are tempting, but its car traffic disrupts the medieval charm of Venice.

San Zaccaria: OK, you're at your last stop. Quick—muscle your way off this boat! (If you don't, you'll eventually end up at the Lido.)

At San Zaccaria, you're right in the thick of the action. A number of other *vaporetti* depart from here (see page 68). Otherwise, it's a short walk back along the Riva to St. Mark's Square. Ahoy!

Sights in Venice

Venice's city museums offer youth and senior discounts to Americans and other non-EU citizens.

Also, be sure to check www.ricksteves.com/update for any significant changes that may have occurred since this book was printed.

Sightseeing Passes for Venice

Venice offers a dizzying array of combo-tickets and sightseeing passes. Determine roughly what you plan to see, do the math, and pick the pass that best suits your plans. For most people, the best choice is the Museum Pass, which covers entry into the Doge's Palace, Correr Museum, and more. Note that some major sights are not covered on any pass, including the Accademia, Peggy Guggenheim Collection, Scuola San Rocco, and Campanile, along with the three sights within St. Mark's Basilica that charge admission.

All of the passes described below are sold at the TI (except for the combo-ticket), and most are also available at participating sights.

Venice at a Glance

▲▲▲**St. Mark's Square** Venice's grand main square. **Hours:** Always open. See page 88.

▲▲▲**St. Mark's Basilica** Cathedral with mosaics, saint's bones, treasury, museum, and viewpoint of square. **Hours:** Mon-Sat 9:45-17:00, Sun 14:00-17:00 (until 16:00 Nov-March). See page 90.

▲▲▲**Doge's Palace** Art-splashed palace of former rulers, with prison accessible through Bridge of Sighs. **Hours:** Daily April-Oct 8:30-18:30, Nov-March 8:00-17:30. See page 94.

▲▲▲**Rialto Bridge** Distinctive bridge spanning the Grand Canal, with a market nearby. **Hours:** Bridge—always open; market—souvenir stalls open daily, produce market closed Sun, fish market closed Sun-Mon. See page 103.

▲▲**Correr Museum** Venetian history and art. **Hours:** Daily April-Oct 10:00-19:00, Nov-March 10:00-17:00. See page 96.

▲▲**Accademia** Venice's top art museum. **Hours:** Mon 8:15-14:00, Tue-Sun 8:15-19:15. See page 99.

▲▲**Peggy Guggenheim Collection** Popular display of 20th-century art. **Hours:** Wed-Mon 10:00-18:00, closed Tue. See page 101.

▲▲**Frari Church** Franciscan church featuring Renaissance masters. **Hours:** Mon-Sat 9:00-18:00, Sun 13:00-18:00. See page 103.

▲▲**Scuola San Rocco** "Tintoretto's Sistine Chapel." **Hours:** Daily 9:30-17:30. See page 105.

▲**Campanile** Dramatic bell tower on St. Mark's Square with elevator to the top. **Hours:** Daily Easter-June and Oct 9:00-19:00, July-Sept 9:00-21:00; Nov-Easter 9:30-16:45. See page 97.

▲**Bridge of Sighs** Famous enclosed bridge, part of Doge's Palace, near St. Mark's Square. **Hours:** Always viewable. See page 98.

▲**La Salute Church** Striking church dedicated to the Virgin Mary. **Hours:** Daily 9:00-12:00 & 15:00-17:30. See page 101.

▲**Ca' Rezzonico** Posh Grand Canal palazzo with 18th-century Venetian art. **Hours:** April-Oct Wed-Mon 10:00-18:00, Nov-March Wed-Mon 10:00-17:00, closed Tue year-round. See page 102.

▲**Punta della Dogana** Museum of contemporary art. **Hours:** Wed-Mon 10:00-19:00, closed Tue. See page 102.

▲**Ca' Pesaro International Gallery of Modern Art** in a canalside palazzo. **Hours:** April-Oct Tue-Sun 10:00-18:00, Nov-March Tue-Sun 10:00-17:00, closed Mon year-round. See page 102.

▲**Scuola Dalmata di San Giorgio** Exquisite Renaissance meeting house. **Hours:** Mon 14:45-18:00, Tue-Sat 9:15-13:00 & 14:45-18:00, Sun 9:15-13:00. See page 108.

Church of San Zaccaria Final resting place of St. Zechariah, plus a Bellini altarpiece and an eerie crypt. **Hours:** Mon-Sat 10:00-12:00 & 16:00-18:00, Sun 16:00-18:00. See page 98.

Church of San Polo Ninth-century church with works by Tintoretto, Veronese, and Tiepolo. **Hours:** Mon-Sat 10:00-17:00, closed Sun. See page 105.

Nearby Islands

▲**San Giorgio Magglore** Island facing St. Mark's Square, featuring church with Palladio architecture, Tintoretto paintings, and fine views back on Venice. **Hours:** April-Oct Mon-Sat 9:00-19:00, Sun 9:00-11:00 & 12:00-19:00; Nov-March daily 9:00-17:30. See page 99.

San Michele Cemetery island on the lagoon. **Hours:** Daily April-Sept 7:30-18:00, Oct-March 7:30-16:30. See page 109.

▲**Murano** Island famous for glass factories and glassmaking museum. **Hours:** Glass Museum open daily April-Oct 10:00-18:00, Nov-March 10:00-17:00 (may be under renovation when you visit). See page 109.

▲▲**Burano** Sleepy island known for lacemaking and a lace museum. **Hours:** Lace Museum open April-Oct Tue-Sun 10:00-18:00, Nov-March Tue-Sun 10:00-17:00, closed Mon year-round. See page 109.

▲**Torcello** Near-deserted island with old church, bell tower, and museum. **Hours:** Church open daily March-Oct 10:30-18:00, Nov-Feb 10:00-17:00, museum closed Mon. See page 112.

Combo-Ticket: A €16 combo-ticket covers both the Doge's Palace and the Correr Museum; to bypass the long line at the Doge's Palace, buy your combo-ticket at the never-crowded Correr Museum. The two sights are also covered by the Museum Pass and Venice Card.

Museum Pass: Busy sightseers may prefer this more expensive pass, which covers these museums: the Doge's Palace; Correr Museum; Ca' Rezzonico (Museum of 18th-Century Venice); Palazzo Mocenigo Costume Museum; Casa Goldoni (home of the Italian playwright); Ca' Pesaro (modern art); Museum of Natural History in the Santa Croce district; the Glass Museum on the island of Murano; and the Lace Museum on the island of Burano. At €24, this pass is the best value if you plan to see the Doge's Palace/Correr Museum and even just one of the other covered museums. (Families get a price break on multiple passes—ask.) You can buy it at any of the participating museums.

Chorus Pass: This pass gives church lovers admission to 16 of Venice's churches and their art (generally €3 each)—including the Frari Church—for €10, although the typical tourist is unlikely to see more than two of them.

Venice Card: This pass combines the 11 city-run museums and the 16 churches covered by the Chorus Pass, plus a few minor discounts, for €40. A cheaper variation, the Venice Card San Marco, is more selective: It covers the Correr Museum, Doge's Palace, and your choice of any three churches for €25. But it's hard to make either of these passes pay off.

Rolling Venice: This youth pass offers discounts at dozens of sights and shops, but its best deal is for transit. If you're under 30 and want to buy a three-day transit pass, it'll cost you just €18—rather than €35—with the Rolling Venice pass (€4 for ages 14-29, sold at TIs and HelloVenezia shops).

Transportation Passes: Venice sells transit-only passes that cover *vaporetti* and mainland buses. For a rundown on these, see "Getting Around Venice" on page 63.

San Marco District
▲▲▲St. Mark's Square (Piazza San Marco)
This grand square is surrounded by splashy, historic buildings and sights: St. Mark's Basilica, the Doge's Palace, the Campanile bell tower, and the Correr Museum. The square is filled with music, lovers, pigeons, and tourists by day, and is your private rendezvous with the Venetian past late at night, when Europe's most magnificent dance floor is *the* romantic place to be.

With your back to the church, survey one of Europe's great urban spaces, and the only square in Venice to merit the title "Pi-

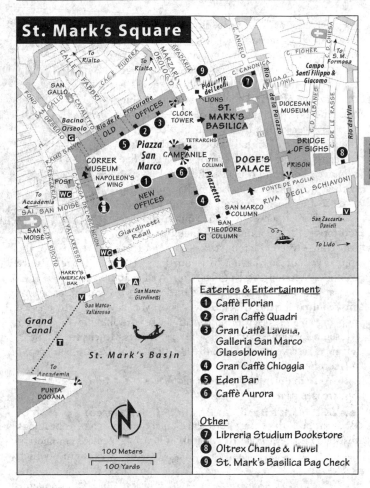

St. Mark's Square

Eateries & Entertainment
1. Caffè Florian
2. Gran Caffè Quadri
3. Gran Caffè Lavena, Galleria San Marco Glassblowing
4. Gran Caffè Chioggia
5. Eden Bar
6. Caffè Aurora

Other
7. Libreria Studium Bookstore
8. Oltrex Change & Travel
9. St. Mark's Basilica Bag Check

VENICE

azza." Nearly two football fields long, it's surrounded by the offices of the republic. On the right are the "old offices" (16th-century Renaissance). At left are the "new offices" (17th-century High Renaissance). Napoleon called the piazza "the most beautiful drawing room in Europe," and added to the intimacy by building the final wing, opposite the basilica, that encloses the square.

For a slow and pricey evening thrill, invest €12-22 (including the cover charge for the music) for a drink at one of the elegant cafés with the dueling orchestras (see "Cafés on St. Mark's Square" on page 94). For an unmatched experience that offers the best people-watching, it's worth the small splurge.

The **Clock Tower** (Torre dell'Orologio), built during the Renaissance in 1496, marks the entry to the main shopping drag, called

VENICE

the Mercerie (or "Marzarie," in Venetian dialect), which connects St. Mark's Square with the Rialto Bridge. From the piazza, you can see the bronze men (Moors) swing their huge clappers at the top of each hour. In the 17th century, one of them knocked an unsuspecting worker off the top and to his death—probably the first-ever killing by a robot. Notice one of the world's first "digital" clocks on the tower facing the square (with dramatic flips every five minutes). You can go inside the Clock Tower with a prebooked guided tour that takes you close to the clock's innards and out to a terrace with good views over the square and city rooftops (€12.50 combo-ticket includes Correr  Museum—where the tour starts—but not Doge's Palace; €7 for the tour if you already have a Museum Pass or Correr/Doge's Palace combo-ticket; tours in English Mon-Wed at 10:00 and 11:00, Thu-Sun at 14:00 and 15:00; no kids under age 6). While reservations are required for the Clock Tower tour, you have a decent chance of being able to "reserve" on the spot—try dropping by the Correr Museum for same-day (or day-before) tickets. To ensure a spot in advance, reserve by calling 848-082-000, or book online at http://torreorologio.visitmuve.it.

You can download a free Rick Steves audio tour of St. Mark's Square (see page 9).

▲▲▲St. Mark's Basilica (Basilica di San Marco)
Built in the 11th century to replace an earlier church, this basilica's distinctly Eastern-style architecture underlines Venice's connection

with Byzantium (which protected it from the ambition of Charlemagne and his Holy Roman Empire). It's decorated with booty from returning sea captains—a kind of architectural Venetian trophy chest. The interior glows mysteriously with gold mosaics and colored marble. Since about A.D. 830, the saint's bones have been housed on this site.

Cost and Hours: Basilica entry is free, three interior sights charge admission (see below), open Mon-Sat 9:45-17:00, Sun 14:00-17:00 (Sun until 16:00 Nov-March), interior brilliantly lit daily 11:30-12:30, St. Mark's Square, vaporetto: San Marco or San

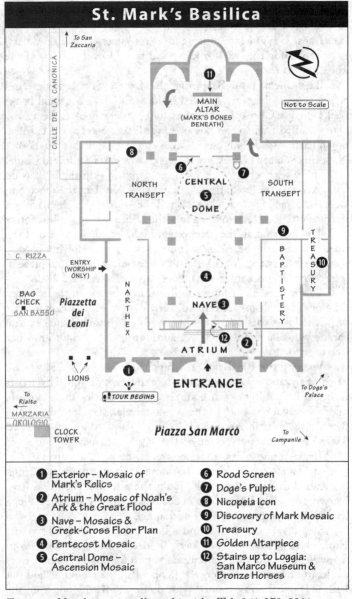

St. Mark's Basilica

To San Zaccaria

CALLE DE LA CANONICA

Not to Scale

VENICE

11 MAIN ALTAR (MARK'S BONES BENEATH)

8

6

7

NORTH TRANSEPT

CENTRAL DOME **5**

SOUTH TRANSEPT

9 TREASURY **10**

C. RIZZA

ENTRY (WORSHIP ONLY)

NARTHEX

4

BAPTISTERY

BAG CHECK SAN BASSO

Piazzetta dei Leoni

NAVE **3**

12 **2**

ATRIUM

LIONS

To Rialto

1

ENTRANCE

To Doge's Palace

MARZARIA OROLOGIO

TOUR BEGINS

CLOCK TOWER

Piazza San Marco

To Campanile

---

1 Exterior – Mosaic of Mark's Relics
2 Atrium – Mosaic of Noah's Ark & the Great Flood
3 Nave – Mosaics & Greek-Cross Floor Plan
4 Pentecost Mosaic
5 Central Dome – Ascension Mosaic

6 Rood Screen
7 Doge's Pulpit
8 Nicopeia Icon
9 Discovery of Mark Mosaic
10 Treasury
11 Golden Altarpiece
12 Stairs up to Loggia: San Marco Museum & Bronze Horses

Zaccaria. No photos are allowed inside. Tel. 041-270-8311, www. basilicasanmarco.it.

Three separate exhibits within the church charge admission: the **Treasury** (€3, includes free audioguide), **Golden Altarpiece** (€2), and **San Marco Museum** (€5). The San Marco Museum has the original bronze horses (copies of these overlook the square), a balcony offering a remarkable view over St. Mark's Square, and various works related to the church.

Dress Code: Modest dress (no bare knees or bare shoulders) is strictly enforced, even for kids. Shorts are OK if they cover the knees.

Bag Check (and Skipping the Line): Small purses and shoulder-slung bags are allowed inside, but larger bags and backpacks are not. Check them for free for up to one hour at the nearby church called Ateneo San Basso, 30 yards to the left of the basilica, down narrow Calle San Basso (see map page 91; daily 9:30-17:00). Note that you can't check small bags that would be allowed inside.

Those with a bag to check actually get to skip the line, as do their companions (up to three or so). Leave your bag at Ateneo San Basso and pick up your claim tag. Take your tag to the basilica's tourist entrance. Keep to the left of the railing where the line forms and show your tag to the gatekeeper. He'll let you in, ahead of the line. After touring St. Mark's, come back and pick up your bag.

Theft Alert: St. Mark's Basilica is the most dangerous place in Venice for pickpocketing—inside, it's always a crowded jostle.

Tours: Free, hour-long English **tours** (heavy on the mosaics' religious symbolism) are offered many days at 11:00 (meet in atrium, schedule varies, see schedule board just inside entrance). You can download a free Rick Steves **audio tour** of St. Mark's Basilica (see page 9).

Visiting the Basilica: St. Mark's Basilica has 4,750 square yards of Byzantine mosaics, though many were designed by artists from the Italian Renaissance and later. Start outside in the square, far enough back to take in the whole facade. Then zero in on the details. The mosaic over the far left door shows the theft of ❶ **St. Mark's relics** that put Venice on the pilgrimage map.

The best and oldest mosaics are in the atrium (turn right as you enter and stop under the last dome). Facing the piazza, look domeward for the story of ❷ **Noah, the ark, and the flood** (two by two, the wicked being drowned, Noah sending out the dove, a happy rainbow, and a sacrifice of thanks).

Step inside the church and follow the one-way tourist route. Notice how the marble floor is richly decorated in mosaics. As in many Venetian buildings, because the best foundation pilings were made around the perimeter, the floor rolls. The church is laid out with four equal arms, topped with domes, radiating out from the center to form a ❸ **Greek cross** (+). Those familiar with Eastern Orthodox churches will find common elements in St. Mark's: a central floor plan, domes, mosaics, and iconic images of Mary and Christ as Pantocrator—ruler of all things.

Find the chandelier near the entrance doorway, and run your eyes up to the ❹ **Pentecost** mosaic in the dome above. In a golden heaven, the dove of the Holy Spirit shoots out a pinwheel of spiritual lasers, igniting tongues of fire on the heads of the 12 apostles below.

Shuffle under the central dome, and look up for the ❺ **Ascension** mosaic. Christ—having lived his miraculous life and having been crucified for man's sins—ascends into the starry sky on a rainbow.

Look around at the church's furniture: the ❻ **rood screen**, topped with 14 saints, separates the congregation from the high altar. The ❼ **pulpit** on the right was reserved for the doge, who led prayers and made important announcements.

In the north transept, today's Venetians pray to a painted wooden icon of Mary and baby Jesus known as ❽ **Nicopeia,** or "Our Lady of Victory." This Madonna has helped Venice persevere through plagues, wars, and crucial soccer games.

In the south transept (to right of main altar), find the dim ❾ **Discovery of Mark** mosaic high up on the west wall. This mosaic re-creates the happy scene in 1094 when Mark's misplaced relics were found within a hollow column.

Additional Sights: The ❿ **Treasury** (Tesoro; ask for the included and informative audioguide when you buy your ticket) and ⓫ **Golden Altarpiece** (Pala d'Oro) give you the easiest way outside of Istanbul or Ravenna to see the glories of the Byzantine Empire. Venetian crusaders looted the Christian city of Constantinople and brought home piles of lavish loot (perhaps the lowest point in Christian history until the advent of TV evangelism). Much of this plunder is stored in the Treasury of San Marco. As you view these treasures, remember that most were made in about A.D. 500, while Western Europe was stuck in the Dark Ages. Beneath the high altar lies the body of St. Mark ("Marco") and the Golden Altarpiece, made of 250 blue-backed enamels with religious scenes, all set in a gold frame and studded with 15 hefty rubies, 300 emeralds, 1,500 pearls, and assorted sapphires, amethysts, and topaz (c. 1100).

In the ⓬ **San Marco Museum** (Museo di San Marco) upstairs you can see an up-close mosaic exhibition, a fine view of the church interior, a view of the square from the balcony with bronze horses, and (inside) the original horses. Art historians don't know how old the horses are—they could be from ancient Greece (fourth century B.C.) or from ancient Rome, during its Fall (fourth century A.D.). Legend says these well-traveled horses were taken to Rome by Nero. We know they were taken to Constantinople/Istanbul by Constantine, to Venice by crusaders, to Paris by Napoleon, back "home" to Venice when Napoleon fell, and finally indoors and out of the acidic air. The staircase up to the museum is in the atrium, near the basilica's main entrance, marked by a sign that says *Loggia dei Cavalli, Museo.*

VENICE

VENICE

Cafés on St. Mark's Square

In the Venetian culture, coffee was huge. It was said that the freedoms a gentleman could experience in Venice went far beyond what any one person could actually indulge in. But one extravagance all could enjoy was the ritual of coffee's public consumption: showing off with an affordable luxury, participating in something new and trendy, sharing the ideas of the Enlightenment.

Exotic coffee was made to order for the fancy café scene. Traders introduced coffee, called the "wine of Islam," from the East. The first coffeehouses opened in the 17th century, and by 1750 there were dozens of cafés lining Piazza San Marco and 200 operating in Venice.

Today, several fine old cafés survive and still line the square. Those with live music feature similar food, prices, and a three-to five-piece combo playing a selection of classical and pop hits, from Brahms to "Bésame Mucho." If you sit outside and get just a drink, expect to pay €12-22, including a €6 cover charge when the orchestra is playing (no cover charge otherwise). A coffee—your cheapest option—costs about €6 if you sit at an outside table, plus the €6 cover charge when the music plays, bringing it to €12 total (the venerable Caffè Florian charges a little more). It's per-

▲▲▲Doge's Palace (Palazzo Ducale)

The seat of the Venetian government and home of its ruling duke, or doge, this was the most powerful half-acre in Europe for 400 years. The Doge's Palace was built to show off the power and wealth of the Republic. The doge lived with his family on the first floor up, near the halls of power. From his once-lavish (now sparse) quarters, you'll follow the one-way tour through the public rooms of the top floor, finishing with the Bridge of Sighs and the prison. The place is wallpapered with masterpieces by Veronese and Tintoretto. Don't worry too much about the great art. Enjoy the building.

Cost and Hours: €16 combo-ticket includes Correr Museum, also covered by Museum Pass—see page 85, daily April-Oct 8:30-18:30, Nov-March 8:00-17:30, last entry one hour before clos-

fectly acceptable to nurse a cappuccino for an hour—you're paying for the music with the cover charge. Do remember that a law limits what a café can charge for coffee at the bar—no matter how fancy the place or how high the demand. So, you can sip your coffee at the bar at a nearly normal price—even with the orchestra playing. For locations of the following cafés, see the map on page 89.

Caffè Florian (on the right as you face the church) is the most famous Venetian café and one of the first places in Europe to serve coffee (daily 10:00-24:00, shorter hours in winter). It's been a popular spot for a discreet rendezvous in Venice since 1720. The orchestra here plays a more classical repertoire than at the other cafés. The outside tables are the main action, but do walk inside through the richly decorated, old-time rooms where Casanova, Lord Byron, Charles Dickens, and Woody Allen have all paid too much for a drink.

Gran Caffè Quadri, opposite the Florian, has an equally illustrious roster of famous clientele, including the writers Stendhal and Dumas, and composer Richard Wagner.

Gran Caffè Lavena, near the Clock Tower, is newer and less storied. Drop in to check out its dazzling but politically incorrect chandelier.

Gran Caffè Chioggia, on the Piazzetta facing the Doge's Palace, charges slightly less, with one or two musicians, usually a pianist, playing cocktail jazz.

Eden Bar and **Caffè Aurora** are less expensive and don't have live music.

ing, café, no photos inside, next to St. Mark's Basilica, just off St. Mark's Square, vaporetto stops: San Marco or San Zaccaria, tel. 041-271-5911, http://palazzoducale.visitmuve.it.

Avoiding Lines: If the line is long at the Doge's Palace, buy your combo-ticket at the Correr Museum across the square; then you can go straight to the Doge's Palace turnstile, skirting along to the right of the long ticket-buying line and entering at the "prepaid tickets" entrance. It's also possible to buy your ticket online—at least 48 hours in advance—on the museum website (€0.50 fee).

Tours: The **audioguide** tour is dry but informative (€5, 1.5 hours, need ID or credit card for deposit). For a 1.25-hour live guided tour, consider the Secret Itineraries Tour, which takes you into palace rooms otherwise not open to the public (€20, includes Doge's Palace admission but not Correr Museum admission; €14 with combo-ticket; three English-language tours each morning). Though the tour skips the palace's main hall, you're welcome to visit the hall afterward on your own. Reserve ahead for this tour in peak season—it can fill up as much as a month in advance. Book online (http://palazzoducale.visitmuve.it, €0.50 fee), or reserve by phone (tel. 848-082-000, from the US dial 011-39-041-4273-0892), or you can try just showing up at the info desk.

Visiting the Doge's Palace: You'll see the restored facades from the **courtyard.** Notice a grand staircase (with nearly naked Moses and Paul Newman at the top). Even the most powerful visitors climbed this to meet the doge. This was the beginning of an architectural power trip.

In the **Senate Hall,** the 120 senators met, debated, and passed laws. Tintoretto's large *Triumph of Venice* on the ceiling (central painting, best viewed from the top) shows the city in all its glory. Lady Venice is up in heaven with the Greek gods, while barbaric lesser nations swirl up to give her gifts and tribute.

The **Armory**—a dazzling display originally assembled to intimidate potential adversaries—shows remnants of the military might that the empire employed to keep the East-West trade lines open (and the local economy booming).

The giant **Hall of the Grand Council** (175 feet by 80 feet, capacity 2,600) is where the entire nobility met to elect the senate and doge. It took a room this size to contain the grandeur of the Most Serene Republic. Ringing the top of the room are portraits of the first 76 doges (in chronological order). The one at the far end that's blacked out (in the left corner) is the notorious Doge Marin Falier, who opposed the will of the Grand Council in 1355. He was tried for treason, beheaded, and airbrushed from history.

On the wall over the doge's throne is Tintoretto's monster-piece, *Paradise,* the largest oil painting in the world. Christ and Mary are surrounded by a heavenly host of 500 saints. The painting leaves you feeling that you get to heaven not by being a good Christian, but by being a good Venetian.

Cross the covered **Bridge of Sighs** over the canal to the **prisons.** Circle the cells. Notice the carvings made by prisoners—from olden days up until 1930—on some of the stone windowsills of the cells, especially in the far corner of the building.

Cross back over the Bridge of Sighs, pausing to look through the marble-trellised windows at all of the tourists.

▲▲Correr Museum (Museo Correr)

This uncrowded museum gives you a good, easy-to-manage overview of Venetian history and art. The doge memorabilia, armor, banners, statues (by Canova), and paintings (by the Bellini family and others) re-create the festive days of the Venetian Republic. And it's all accompanied—throughout the museum—by English descriptions and breathtaking views of St. Mark's Square. But the Correr Museum has one more thing to offer, and that's a quiet refuge—a place to rise above St. Mark's Square when the piazza is too hot, too rainy, or too overrun with tourists.

Cost and Hours: €16 combo-ticket also includes the Doge's Palace and the two lesser museums inside the Correr (National Archaeological Museum and the Monumental Rooms of the Marciana National Library); daily April-Oct 10:00-19:00, Nov-March 10:00-17:00, last entry one hour before closing; bag check free and mandatory for bags bigger than a large purse, no photos, elegant café, enter at far end of square directly opposite basilica, tel. 041-240-5211, http://correr.visitmuve.it.

Avoid long lines at the crowded Doge's Palace by buying your combo-ticket at the Correr Museum. For €12.50 you can see the Correr Museum and tour the Clock Tower on St. Mark's Square, but this ticket doesn't include the Doge's Palace (and the €16 combo-ticket mentioned above doesn't include the Clock Tower). For more on reserving a Clock Tower tour, see page 89.

see page 89.

VENICE

▲Campanile (Campanile di San Marco)

This dramatic bell tower replaced a shorter tower, part of the original fortress that guarded the entry of the Grand Canal. That

tower crumbled into a pile of bricks in 1902, a thousand years after it was built. Today you'll see construction work being done to strengthen the base of the rebuilt tower. Ride the elevator 325 feet to the top of the bell tower for the best view in Venice (especially at sunset). For an ear-shattering experience, be on top when the bells ring. The golden archangel Gabriel at the top always faces into the wind. Beat the crowds and enjoy the crisp morning air at 9:00 or the cool evening breeze at 18:00.

Cost and Hours: €8, daily Easter-June and Oct 9:00-19:00, July-Sept 9:00-21:00, Nov-Easter 9:30-16:45, tel. 041-522-4064, www.basilicasanmarco.it.

La Fenice Opera House (Gran Teatro alla Fenice)

During Venice's glorious decline in the 18th century, this was one of seven opera houses in the city, and one of the most famous in Europe. For 200 years, great operas and famous divas debuted here, applauded by ladies and gentlemen in their finery. Then, in 1996, an arson fire completely gutted the theater. But La Fenice ("The Phoenix") has risen from the ashes, thanks to an eight-year effort to rebuild the historic landmark according to photographic archives of the inte-

rior. To see the results at their most glorious, attend an evening **performance** (theater box office open daily 10:00-17:00, tel. 041-2424, www.teatrolafenice.it).

During the day, you can take an **audioguide tour** of the opera house. All you really see is the theater itself; there's no "backstage" tour of dressing rooms or an opera museum, and the dry 45-minute guide mainly recounts two centuries of construction. But the auditorium, ringed with box seats, is impressive: pastel blue with sparkling gold filigree, muses depicted on the ceiling, and a starburst chandelier. It's also a bit saccharine and brings sadness to Venetians who remember the place before the fire. Other than a minor exhibit of opera scores and Maria Callas memorabilia, there's little to see from the world of opera.

Cost and Hours: €8.50 audioguide tours, generally open daily 9:30-18:00, but can vary wildly, depending on the performance schedule—to confirm, call box office number (listed above) or check www.festfenice.com. La Fenice is on Campo San Fantin, between St. Mark's Square and the Accademia Bridge.

Palazzo Grassi

This former palace, gleaming proudly on the San Marco side of the Grand Canal, holds a branch of the Punta della Dogana contemporary art museum (for details, see "Punta della Dogana," later).

Behind St. Mark's Basilica

▲Bridge of Sighs

This much-photographed bridge connects the Doge's Palace with the prison. Travelers popularized this bridge in the Romantic 19th century. Supposedly, a condemned man would be led over this bridge on his way to the prison, take one last look at the glory of Venice, and sigh. Though overhyped, the Bridge of Sighs is undeniably tingle-worthy—especially after dark, when the crowds have dispersed and it's just you and floodlit Venice.

Getting There: The Bridge of Sighs is around the corner from the Doge's Palace. Walk toward the waterfront, turn left along the water, and look up the first canal on your left. You can walk across the bridge (from the inside) by visiting the Doge's Palace.

Church of San Zaccaria

This historic church is home to a sometimes-waterlogged crypt, a Bellini altarpiece, a Tintoretto painting, and the final resting place of St. Zechariah, the father of John the Baptist.

Cost and Hours: Free, €1 to enter crypt, €0.50 coin to light

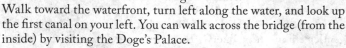

up Bellini's altarpiece, Mon-Sat 10:00-12:00 & 16:00-18:00, Sun 16:00-18:00 only, 2 canals behind St. Mark's Basilica.

Across the Lagoon from St. Mark's Square

▲San Giorgio Maggiore

This is the dreamy church-topped island you can see from the waterfront by St. Mark's Square. The striking church, designed by Palladio, features art by Tintoretto, a bell tower, and good views of Venice.

Cost and Hours: Free entry to church; April-Oct Mon-Sat 9:00-19:00, Sun 9:00-11:00 & 12:00-19:00; Nov-March daily

9:00-17:30. The bell tower costs €6 and is accessible by elevator (runs until 30 minutes before the church closes).

Getting There: To reach the island from St. Mark's Square, take the five-minute ride on vaporetto #2 (€4, 6/ hour, ticket valid for one hour;

leaves from San Zaccaria stop—check the readerboard to see which dock/berth it leaves from, direction: Tronchetto).

Dorsoduro District

▲▲Accademia (Galleria dell'Accademia)

Venice's top art museum, packed with highlights of the Venetian Renaissance, features paintings by the Bellini family, Titian, Tintoretto, Veronese, Tiepolo, Giorgione, Canaletto, and Testosterone. It's just over the wooden Accademia Bridge from the San Marco action.

Cost and Hours: €9, dull audioguide-€6, Mon 8:15-14:00, Tue-Sun 8:15-19:15, last entry 45 minutes before closing, no photos allowed. At Accademia Bridge, vaporetto: Accademia, tel. 041-522-2247, www.gallerieaccademia.org.

Avoiding Lines: Just 360 people are allowed into the gallery at one time, so you may have to wait. It's most crowded on Monday mornings and whenever it rains; it's least crowded Tue-Sun mornings (before about 10:00) and late afternoons (after about 17:00). While it's possible to book tickets in advance (€1.50/ticket surcharge; either book online at www.gallerieaccademia.org or call 041-520-0345), it's generally not necessary if you avoid the busiest times.

Renovation: This museum seems to be in a constant state of disarray. A major expansion and renovation has been dragging on for years. Paintings come and go, but the museum always contains sumptuous art—the best in Venice. If you can't find one of the

VENICE

VENICE

Accademia

To Zattere

HIGH RENAISSANCE

ROOM 11   ROOM 10

To Eateries & Zattere

Camp. Calbo

ROOM 9

RIO TERÀ ANTONIO FOSCARINI

ROOM 12

Courtyard

(Not to Scale)

ROOM 6   ROOM 8

ROOM 7

ROOM 13

ROOM 5

ROOM 2

ROOM 14

ELEGANT DECAY

ROOM 4   EARLY REN.

ROOM 3

RIO TERÀ DE LA CARITÀ

ROOM 16

ROOM 20

Courtyard

ROOM 15

ROOM 19   ROOM 21

MEDIEVAL ROOM 1

To Cafés, Peggy Guggenheim Collection & La Salute

ROOM 17   WC

ROOM 18   ROOM 22   ROOM 24

ROOM 23 "DISPLACED HIGHLIGHTS"

STAIRS

ENTRANCE (BELOW)   CAFE

To Frari & Ca' Rezzonico

PIZZA   WC   Campo de la Carità

To San Marco & Rialto   ACCADEMIA BRIDGE   V Accademia   Grand Canal

items noted below, check in Room 23 at the end, where they tend to shuffle pieces that have been displaced by the renovation.

Visiting the Accademia: The Accademia is the greatest museum anywhere for Venetian Renaissance art and a good overview of painters whose works you'll see all over town. Venetian art is underrated and, I think, misunderstood. It's nowhere near as famous today as the work of the florescent Florentines, but—with historical slices of Venice, ravishing nudes, and very human Madonnas—it's livelier, more colorful, and simply more fun. The Venetian love of luxury shines through in this collection, which starts in the Middle Ages and runs to the 1700s. Look for grand canvases of colorful, spacious settings, peopled with happy locals in extravagant clothes having a great time.

Medieval highlights include elaborate altarpieces and golden-haloed Madonnas, all painted at a time when realism, depth of field, and emotion were considered beside the point. Medieval Venetians, with their close ties to the East, borrowed techniques such as gold-leafing, frontal poses, and "iconic" faces from the religious icons of Byzantium (modern-day Istanbul).

Among early masterpieces of the Renaissance are Mantegna's studly *St. George* and Giorgione's mysterious *Tempest*. As the Renaissance reaches its heights, so do the paintings, such as Titian's magnificent *Presentation of the Virgin*. It's a religious scene, yes, but it's really just an excuse to display secular splendor (Titian was the most famous painter of his day—perhaps even more famous than Michelangelo). Veronese's sumptuous *Feast in the House of Levi* also has an ostensibly religious theme (in the middle, find Jesus eating his final meal)—but it's outdone by the luxury and optimism of Renaissance Venice. Life was a good thing and beauty was to be enjoyed. (Veronese was hauled before the Inquisition for painting such a bawdy Last Supper...so he fine-tuned the title.) End your tour with Guardi's and Canaletto's painted "postcards" of the city—landscapes for visitors who lost their hearts to the romance of Venice.

▲▲Peggy Guggenheim Collection

The popular museum of far-out art, housed in the American heiress' former retirement palazzo, offers one of Europe's best reviews of the art of the first half of the 20th century. Stroll through styles represented by artists whom Peggy knew personally—Cubism (Picasso, Braque), Surrealism (Dalí, Ernst), Futurism (Boccioni), American Abstract Expressionism (Pollock), and a sprinkling of Klee, Calder, and Chagall.

Cost and Hours: €14, usually includes temporary exhibits, audioguide-€7, Wed-Mon 10:00-18:00, closed Tue, pricey café, 5-minute walk from the Accademia Bridge, vaporetto: Accademia or Salute, tel. 041-240-5411, www.guggenheim-venice.it.

▲La Salute Church (Santa Maria della Salute)

This impressive church with a crown-shaped dome was built and dedicated to the Virgin Mary by grateful survivors of the 1630 plague.

Cost and Hours: Free entry to church, €3 to enter the Sacristy; daily 9:00-12:00 & 15:00-17:30. It's a 10-minute walk from the Accademia Bridge; the Salute vaporetto stop is at its doorstep, tel. 041-241-1018, www.seminariovenezia.it.

VENICE

▲Ca' Rezzonico (Museum of 18th-Century Venice)

This grand Grand Canal palazzo offers the most insightful look at the life of Venice's rich and famous in the 1700s. Wander under ceilings by Tiepolo, among furnishings from that most decadent century, enjoying views of the canal and paintings by Guardi, Canaletto, and Longhi.

Cost and Hours: €8, audioguide-€4; April-Oct Wed-Mon 10:00-18:00, Nov-March Wed-Mon 10:00-17:00, closed Tue year-round; ticket office closes one hour before museum does, no photos, café, at Ca' Rezzonico vaporetto stop, tel. 041-241-0100, http://carezzonico.visitmuve.it.

▲Punta della Dogana

This museum of contemporary art, opened in 2009, makes the Dorsoduro a major destination for art lovers. Housed in the former Customs House at the end of the Grand Canal, it features cutting-edge 21st-century art in spacious rooms. This isn't Picasso and Matisse, or even Pollock and Warhol—those guys are ancient history. But if you're into the likes of Jeff Koons, Cy Twombly, Ra-chel Whiteread, and a host of newer artists, the museum is world-class. The displays change completely about once a year, drawn from the museum's large collection—so large it also fills Palazzo Grassi, farther up the Grand Canal.

Cost and Hours: €15 for one locale, €20 for both; Wed-Mon 10:00-19:00, closed Tue, last entry one hour before closing; audioguide-€5 or €8 for both museums, small café, tel. 199-139-139, www.palazzograssi.it.

Getting There: Punta della Dogana is near La Salute Church (Dogana *traghetto* or vaporetto: Salute). Palazzo Grassi is a bit upstream, on the east side of the Grand Canal (vaporetto #2: San Samuele, or vaporetto #1 to Ca' Rezzonico then *traghetto* across the canal).

Santa Croce District

▲Ca' Pesaro International Gallery of Modern Art

This museum features 19th- and early 20th-century art in a 17th-century canalside palazzo. The collection is strongest on Italian (especially Venetian) artists, but also presents a broad array of other well-known artists. While the Peggy Guggenheim Collection is Venice's undisputedly best modern collection, Ca' Pesaro comes in a clear second—and features a handful of recognizable masterpieces (most notably Klimt's *Judith II*, Kandinsky's *White Zig Zags*, and Chagall's *Rabbi of Vitebsk*).

Cost and Hours: €8; April-Oct Tue-Sun 10:00-18:00, Nov-March Tue-Sun 10:00-17:00, closed Mon year-round, last entry 1 hour before closing, 2-minute walk from San Stae vaporetto stop, tel. 041-524-0695, http://capesaro.visitmuve.it.

Palazzo Mocenigo Costume Museum
The Museo di Palazzo Mocenigo offers a walk through six rooms of a fine 17th-century mansion with period furnishings, family por-traits, ceilings painted (c. 1790) with family triumphs (the Moceni-gos produced seven doges), Murano glass chandeliers in situ, and a paltry collection of costumes with sparse descriptions.

Cost and Hours: €5; April-Oct Tue-Sun 10:00-17:00, Nov-March Tue-Sun 10:00-16:00, closed Mon year-round, last entry one hour before closing, a block in from San Stae vaporetto stop, tel. 041-721-798, http://mocenigo.visitmuve.it.

San Polo District

▲▲▲Rialto Bridge

One of the world's most
famous bridges, this dis-
tinctive and dramatic
stone structure crosses the
Grand Canal with a single
confident span. The ar-
cades along the top of the
bridge help reinforce the
structure...and offer some

enjoyable shopping diversions, as does the **market** surrounding the bridge (produce market closed Sun, fish market closed Sun-Mon).

▲▲Frari Church
(Basilica di Santa Maria Gloriosa dei Frari)

My favorite art experience in Venice is seeing art in the setting for which it was designed—as it is at the Frari Church. The Fran-ciscan "Church of the Brothers" and the
art that decorates it are warmed by the
spirit of St. Francis. It features the work
of three great Renaissance masters: Donatello, Giovanni Bellini, and Titian—
each showing worshippers the glory of
God in human terms.

Cost and Hours: €3, Mon-Sat
9:00-18:00, Sun 13:00-18:00, last entry
30 minutes before closing, modest dress
recommended, no photos, on Campo dei
Frari, near San Tomà vaporetto and *tra-ghetto* stops, tel. 041-272-8618, www.basilicadeifrari.it.

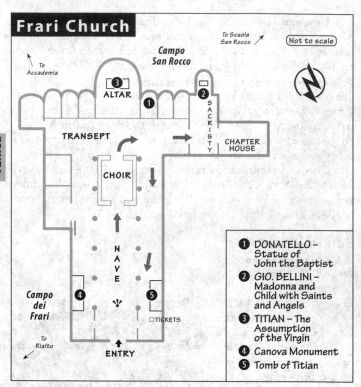

Frari Church

To Scuola
San Rocco

Not to scale

To
Accademia

Campo
San Rocco

3
ALTAR

1

2

S
A
C
R
I
S
T
Y

TRANSEPT

CHAPTER
HOUSE

CHOIR

N
A
V
E

Campo
dei
Frari

4

5

☐ TICKETS

To
Rialto

ENTRY

1 DONATELLO –
Statue of
John the Baptist

2 GIO. BELLINI –
Madonna and
Child with Saints
and Angels

3 TITIAN – The
Assumption
of the Virgin

4 Canova Monument

5 Tomb of Titian

Audioguides: You can rent an audioguide for €2, or you can download a free Rick Steves audio tour of the Frari (see page 9).

Concerts: The church occasionally hosts evening concerts and small theatrical performances (usually around €15, buy tickets at church, for details see the church's website, earlier).

Visiting the Frari Church: In **Donatello's wood statue of St. John the Baptist** (just to the right of the high altar), the prophet of the desert—dressed in animal skins and nearly starving from his diet of bugs 'n' honey—announces the coming of the Messiah. Donatello was a Florentine working at the dawn of the Renaissance.

Bellini's *Madonna and Child with Saints and Angels* painting (in the sacristy farther to the right) came later, done by a Venetian in a more Venetian style—soft focus without Donatello's harsh realism. While Renaissance humanism demanded Madonnas and saints that were accessible and human, Bellini places them in a physical setting so beautiful that it creates its own mood of serene holiness. The genius of Bellini, perhaps the greatest Venetian painter, is obvious in the pristine clarity, rich colors (notice Mary's clothing), believable depth, and reassuring calm of this three-paneled altarpiece.

Finally, glowing red and gold like a stained-glass window over the high altar, **Titian's** *Assumption of the Virgin* sets the tone of exuberant beauty found in the otherwise sparse church. Titian the Venetian—a student of Bellini—painted steadily for 60 years... you'll see a lot of his art. As stunned apostles look up past the swirl of arms and legs, the complex composition of this painting draws you right to the radiant face of the once-dying, now triumphant Mary as she joins God in heaven.

Feel comfortable to discreetly freeload off passing tours. For many, these three pieces of art make a visit to the Accademia Gallery unnecessary (or they may whet your appetite for more). Before leaving, flanking the nave just inside the main entrance, check out the Neoclassical pyramid-shaped Canova monument and (opposite that) the grandiose tomb of Titian. Compare the carved marble *Assumption* behind Titian's tombstone portrait with the painted original above the high altar.

▲▲Scuola San Rocco

Sometimes called "Tintoretto's Sistine Chapel," this lavish meeting hall (next to the Frari Church) has some 50 large, colorful Tintoretto paintings plastered to the walls and ceilings. The best paintings are upstairs, especially the *Crucifixion* in the smaller room. View the neck-breaking splendor with the mirrors available in the Grand Hall.

Cost and Hours: €10, includes audioguide, daily 9:30-17:30, last entry 30 minutes before closing, no photos, tel. 041-523-4864, www.scuolagrandesanrocco.it.

Church of San Polo

This nearby church, which pales in comparison to the two sights just listed, is only worth a visit for art lovers. One of Venice's oldest churches (from the ninth century), San Polo features works by Tintoretto, Veronese, and Tiepolo and son.

Cost and Hours: €3, Mon-Sat 10:00-17:00, closed Sun.

Cannaregio District

Jewish Ghetto

Tucked away in the Cannaregio District is the ghetto where Venice's Jewish population once lived, segregated from their non-Jewish neighbors. While today's Jewish population is dwindling, the neighborhood still has centuries of history, not to mention Jewish-themed sights and eateries.

In medieval times, Jews were grudgingly allowed to do business in Venice, but they weren't permitted to live here until 1385 (subject to strict laws and special taxes). Anti-Semitic forces tried to oust them from the city, but in 1516, the doge compromised by restricting Jews to a special (undesirable) neighborhood. It was located on an easy-to-isolate island near the former foundry *(geto)*. In

VENICE

A Dying City?

Venice's population (58,000 in the historic city) is half what it was just 30 years ago, and people are leaving at a rate of a thousand a year. Of those who stay, 25 percent are 65 or older.

Sad, yes, but imagine raising a family here: Apartments are small, high up, and expensive. Humidity and occasional flooding make basic maintenance a pain. Home-improvement projects require navigating miles of red tape, and you must follow regulations intended to preserve the historical ambience. Everything is expensive because it has to be shipped in from the mainland. You can easily get glass and tourist trinkets, but it's hard to find groceries or get your shoes fixed. Running basic errands involves lots of walking and stairs—imagine crossing over arched bridges while pushing a child in a stroller and carrying a day's worth of groceries.

With millions of visitors a year (150,000 a day at peak times), on any given day Venetians are likely outnumbered by tourists. Despite government efforts to subsidize rents and build cheap housing, the city is losing its residents. The economy itself is thriving, thanks to tourist dollars and rich foreigners buying second homes. But the culture is dying. Even the most hopeful city planners worry that in a few decades Venice will not be a city at all, but a museum, a cultural theme park, a decaying Disneyland for adults.

time, the word "ghetto" caught on across Europe as a term for any segregated neighborhood.

The population swelled with immigrants from elsewhere in Europe, reaching 5,000 in the 1600s, the Golden Age of Venice's Jews. Restricted within their tiny neighborhood (the Gheto Novo—"New Ghetto"), they expanded upward, building six-story "skyscrapers" that still stand today. The community's five synagogues were built atop the high-rise tenements. (As space was very tight and you couldn't live above a house of worship, this was the most practical use of precious land.) Only two synagogues are still active; you can spot them (with their five windows) from the square.

The **Jewish Museum** (Museo Ebraico), at #2902b, is small, but modern and well-presented—a worthwhile stop. Exhibits include silver menorahs, cloth covers for Torah scrolls, and a concise bilingual exhibit on the Venetian Jewish community (€4, June-Sept

Sun-Fri 10:00-19:00, Oct-May Sun-Fri 10:00-17:30, closed Jewish holidays and Sat year-round, bookstore, small café, Campo de Gheto Novo, tel 041-715-359, www.museoebraico.it). You can see three of the ghetto's five synagogues with the 45-minute English tour (€10, includes museum admission, tours run hourly on the half-hour June-Sept Sun-Fri 10:30-17:30, Oct-May Sun-Fri 10:30-16:30, no tours Sat and Jewish holidays). Group sizes are limited (the 11:30 and 12:30 tours are the most popular), so show up 20 minutes early to be sure you get in.

Getting There: From either the San Marcuola vaporetto stop or the train station, walk five minutes to the Ponte de Guglie bridge that crosses the Cannaregio Canal. Cross the bridge and turn left. About 50 yards north of the bridge, a small covered alleyway (Calle del Gheto Vechio) leads between the *farmacia* and the Gam-Gam Kosher Restaurant, through a newer Jewish section, across a bridge, and into the historic core of the ghetto at Campo de Gheto Novo.

Calatrava Bridge (a.k.a. Ponte della Costituzione)

This controversial bridge, designed by Spanish architect Santiago Calatrava, is just upstream from the train station. Only the fourth

bridge to cross the Grand Canal, it carries foot traffic between the train station and bus terminal at Piazzale Roma.

Twhe bridge draws snorts from Venetians. Its modern design is a sore point for a city with such rich medieval and Renaissance architecture. With an original price tag of €4 million, the cost rose to around €11 million by the time it finally opened, after lengthy delays, in 2008. Then someone noticed that people in wheelchairs couldn't cross, so the bridge was retrofitted with a special carriage on a track. And, to add practical insult to aesthetic injury, critics say the heavy bridge is crushing the centuries-old foundations at either end, threatening nearby buildings.

Ca' d'Oro

This "House of Gold" palace, fronting the Grand Canal, is quintessential Venetian Gothic (Gothic seasoned with Byzantine and Islamic accents—see "Ca' d'Oro" on page 80). Inside, the permanent collection includes a few big names in Renaissance painting (Ghirlandaio, Signorelli, and Mantegna), a glimpse at a lush courtyard, and a grand view of the Grand Canal.

Cost and Hours: €6, dry audioguide-€4, Mon 8:15-14:00, Tue-Sat 8:15-19:15, Sun 10:00-18:00, free peek through hole in door of courtyard, Cannaregio 3932, vaporetto: Ca' d'Oro, www.cadoro.org.

Castello District

▲Scuola Dalmata di San Giorgio

This little-visited *scuola* (which can mean either "school" or, as in this case, "meeting place") features an exquisite wood-paneled chapel decorated with the world's best collection of paintings by Vittorio Carpaccio (1465-1526).

The Scuola, a reminder that cosmopolitan Venice was once Europe's trade hub, was one of a hundred such community centers for various ethnic, religious, and economic groups, supported by the government partly to keep an eye on foreigners. It was here that the Dalmatians (from a region of Croatia) worshipped in their own way, held neighborhood meetings, and preserved their culture.

Cost and Hours: €5, Mon 14:45-18:00, Tue-Sat 9:15-13:00 & 14:45-18:00, Sun 9:15-13:00, midway between St. Mark's Square and the Arsenale on Calle dei Furlani at #3259a, tel. 041-522-8828.

Naval Museum and Arsenale

The mighty Republic of Venice was home to the first great military industrial complex: a state-of-the-art shipyard that could build a powerful warship of standardized parts in an assembly line (and did so to intimidate visiting heads of state). While the Arsenale is still a military base and is therefore closed to the public, its massive and evocative gate, the Porta Magna, is worth a look (to see the gate, turn left at the Naval Museum and follow the canal). At the waterfront end of the canal, in front of the Arsenale, stands the Naval Museum (Museo Storico Navale). It's very old-school and military-run, but anyone into maritime history or sailing will find its several floors of exhibits interesting. You'll see the evolution of warships, displays on old fishing boats, and gondolas (all described in English).

Cost and Hours: Museum-€1.55, Mon-Sat 8:45-13:30, closed Sun, Castello 2148, tel. 041-244-1399.

Getting There: From the Doge's Palace, hike six bridges east along the waterfront to the Naval Museum. To see the gate, turn left at the museum and follow the canal.

Sant'Elena

For a pleasant peek into a completely nontouristy, residential side of Venice, walk or catch vaporetto #1 from St. Mark's Square to the neighborhood of Sant'Elena (at the fish's tail). This 100-year-old suburb lives as if there were no tourism. You'll find a kid-friendly park, a few lazy restaurants, and beautiful sunsets over San Marco.

La Biennale

From roughly June through November, Venice hosts an annual world's fair—contemporary art in odd years, modern architecture in even years—in buildings and pavilions scattered throughout Giardini park and the Arsenale. The festival is an excuse for temporary art exhibitions, concerts, and other cultural events around the city (for more information, see page 114 and www.labiennale. org).

Venice's Lagoon

The island of Venice sits in a lagoon—a calm section of the Adriatic protected from wind and waves by the natural breakwater of the Lido. Beyond the church-topped island of San Giorgio Maggiore (directly in front of St. Mark's Square—see page 99), four interesting islands hide out in the lagoon: San Michele, Murano, Burano, and Torcello.

San Michele (a.k.a. Cimitero) is the cemetery island—the final resting place of Venetians and a few foreign VIPs, from poet Ezra Pound to composer Igor Stravinsky. The stopover is easy, because boats come every 10 minutes. If you even half-enjoy wandering through old cemeteries, you'll dig this one—it's full of flowers, trees, scurrying lizards, and birdsong, and has an intriguing chapel (cemetery open daily April-Sept 7:30-18:00, Oct-March 7:30-16:30; reception to the left as you enter, free WC to the right, no picnicking).

Murano is famous for its glassmaking. From the Colonna vaporetto stop, skip the glass shops in front of you, walk to the

right, and wander up the street along the canal, **Fondamenta dei Vetrai** (Glassmakers' Embankment). The Faro district of Murano, on the other side of the canal, is packed with factories *(fabriche)* and their furnaces *(fornaci)*. You'll pass dozens of **glass shops** along the canal. Early along this promenade, at #47, is the venerable **Venini** shop, with glass that's a cut above much of what else is on offer here, and with an interior showing off the ultimate in modern Venetian glass design (Mon-Sat 9:30-18:00, closed Sun).

Murano's **Glass Museum** (Museo Vetrario) traces the history of this delicate art (details may change during or after renovation—but likely €8, daily April-Oct 10:00-18:00, Nov-March 10:00-17:00, last entry 30 minutes before closing, tel. 041-739-586, http://museovetro.visitmuve.it).

Burano, known for its lacemaking and countless lace shops, offers a delightful, vibrantly colorful village alternative to big, bustling Venice. The tight **main drag** is packed with tourists and lined with shops, some of which sell Burano's locally produced white wine. Wander to the far side of the island, and the mood shifts. Explore to the right of the leaning tower for a peaceful yet intensely

VENICE

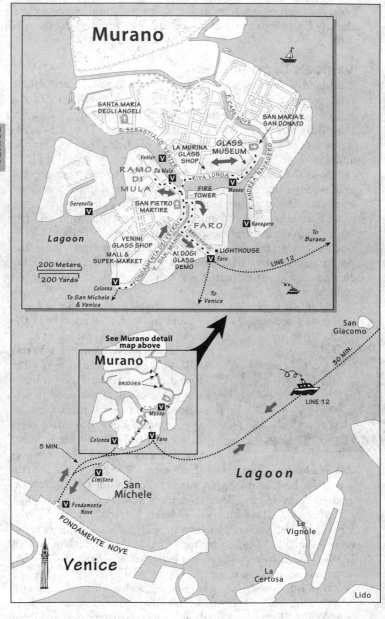

Murano

SANTA MARIA
DEGLI ANGELI

F. SEBASTIANO

F. CASE NOVE

SAN MARIA E
SAN DONATO

LA MURINA
GLASS
SHOP

GLASS
MUSEUM

Venier

Da Mula

RAMO
DI
MULA

RIVA LONGA

Museo

F. ANDREA NAVAGERO

FIRE
TOWER

Serenella

SAN PIETRO
MARTIRE

FARO

Navagero

Lagoon

VENINI
GLASS SHOP

MALL &
SUPER-MARKET

AI DOGI
GLASS
DEMO

LIGHTHOUSE

Faro

LINE 12

To
Burano

FONDAMENTA DE VETRAI

F. DAN. MANIN

BRESSAGIO

200 Meters

200 Yards

Colonna

To San Michele
& Venice

To
Venice

See Murano detail
map above

Murano

BRIDGES

Museo

Colonna

Faro

San
Giacomo

30 MIN

LINE 12

5 MIN.

Cimitero

San
Michele

Lagoon

Fondamente
Nove

FONDAMENTE NOVE

Venice

Le
Vignole

La
Certosa

Lido

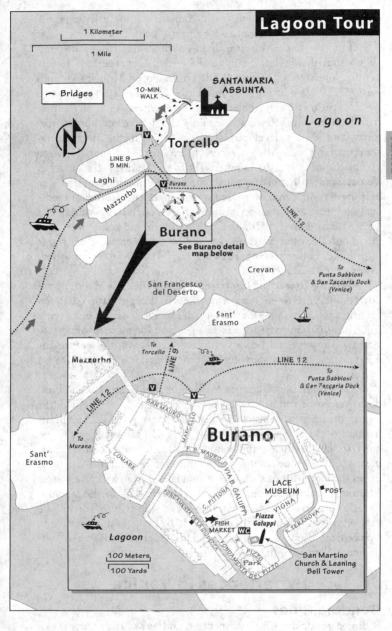

VENICE

colorful, small-town lagoon world. Benches lining a little promenade at the water's edge make for a pretty picnic spot.

Burano's **Lace Museum** (Museo del Merletto di Burano)
shows the island's lace heritage (€5, April-Oct Tue-Sun 10:00-
18:00, Nov-March Tue-Sun 10:00-17:00, closed Mon year-round,
tel. 041-730-034, http://museomerletto.visitmuve.it).

Torcello is the birthplace of Venice, where some of the first
mainland refugees settled, escaping the barbarian hordes. Yet
today it's the least-developed island (pop. 20) in the most natural
state, marshy and shrub-covered. There's little for tourists to see
except the church (a 10-minute walk from the dock; the oldest in
Venice, and still sporting some impressive mosaics), a climbable
bell tower, and a modest museum of Roman sculpture and medieval sculpture and manuscripts (€5; church open daily March-Oct
10:30-18:00, Nov-Feb 10:00-17:00, museum and campanile close
30 minutes earlier, museum closed Mon; last entry to all sights
30 minutes before closing; museum tel. 041-730-761, church/bell
tower tel. 041-730-119).

Getting There: You can travel to any of the four islands by vaporetto. Because single vaporetto tickets (€7) expire after one hour,
getting a vaporetto pass for this lagoon excursion makes more sense
(such as a 12-hour pass for €18; see page 66 for more on vaporetto
tickets). *Vaporetti* can be very crowded; if you want a seat for the
longer rides, consider showing up at the boat dock a bit early to get
in line.

For a route that takes you to all four islands, start at the **Fondamente Nove** vaporetto stop on the north shore of Venice (the
"back" of the fish). Lines #4.1 and #4.2 converge here before heading out to Murano. Catch either one (every 10 minutes); you'll first
cross to San Michele (whose stop is called Cimitero) in six minutes, then continue another three minutes to Murano-Colonna.
Stroll through Murano, then leave that island from a different stop:
Murano-Faro, where you can board vaporetto #12 for the 30-min-
ute trip to Burano. From Burano, you can side-trip to Torcello on
vaporetto #9 (5-minute trip each way). To make a quick return to
Venice from Burano, hop vaporetto #12, which returns you to Fondamente Nove (45 minutes).

Experiences in Venice

Gondola Rides

Riding a gondola is simple, expensive, and one of the great experiences in Europe. Gondoliers hanging out all over town are eager
to have you hop in for a ride. While this is rip-off for some, it's a
traditional must for romantics.

The price for a gondola starts at €80 for a 40-minute ride dur-

ing the day. You can divide the cost—and the romance—among up to six people per boat, but only two get the love seat. Prices jump about 30 percent after 19:00—when it's most romantic and relaxing. Adding a singer and an accordionist will cost an additional €120. If you value budget over romance, you can save money by recruiting fellow travelers to split a gondola. Prices are standard and listed on the gondoliers' association website (go to www. gondolavenezia.it, click on "Using the Gondola," and look under *"charterage"*).

Dozens of gondola stations *(servizio gondole)* are set up along canals all over town. Because your gondolier might offer narration or conversation during your ride, talk with several and choose one you like. You're welcome to review the map and discuss the route. Doing so is also a good way to see if you enjoy the gondolier's personality and language skills. Establish the price, route, and duration of the trip before boarding, enjoy your ride, and pay only when you're finished. While prices are pretty firm, you might find them softer during the day. Most gondoliers honor the official prices, but a few might try to scam you out of some extra euros, particularly by insisting on a tip. (While not required or even expected, if your gondolier does the full 40 minutes and entertains you en route, a 5-10 percent tip is appreciated; if he's surly or rushes through the trip, skip it.)

If you've hired musicians and want to hear a Venetian song *(un canto Veneziano)*, try requesting *"Venezia La Luna e Tu."* Asking to hear *"O Sole Mio"* (which comes from Naples) is like asking a lounge singer in Cleveland to sing "The Eyes of Texas."

Glide through nighttime Venice with your head on someone's shoulder. Follow the moon as it sails past otherwise unseen buildings. Silhouettes gaze down from bridges while window glitter spills onto the black water. You're anonymous in the city of masks, as the rhythmic thrust of your striped-shirted gondolier turns old crows into songbirds. This is extremely relaxing (and, I think, worth the extra cost to experience at night). Suggestion: Put the camera down and make a point for you and your partner to enjoy a threesome with Venice. Warning: Women, beware...while gondoliers can be extremely charming, local women say that anyone who falls for one of these Venetian Romeos "has slices of ham over her eyes."

For cheap gondola thrills during the day, stick to the €2 one-minute ferry ride on a Grand Canal *traghetto*. At night, *vaporetti* are nearly empty, and it's a great time to cruise the Grand Canal on the slow boat #1. Or hang out on a bridge along the gondola route and wave at romantics.

Festivals

Venice's most famous festival is **Carnevale,** the celebration Americans call Mardi Gras (Feb 22-March 4 in 2014, www.carnevale. venezia.it). Carnevale, which means "farewell to meat," originated centuries ago as a wild two-month-long party leading up to the austerity of Lent. In Carnevale's heyday—the 1600s and 1700s—you could do pretty much anything with anybody from any social class if you were wearing a mask. These days it's a tamer 18-day celebration, culminating in a huge dance lit with fireworks on St. Mark's Square. Sporting masks and costumes, Venetians from kids to businessmen join in the fun. Drawing the biggest crowds of the year, Carnevale has nearly been a victim of its own success, driving away many Venetians (who skip out on the craziness to go skiing in the Dolomites).

Every year, the city hosts the **Venice Biennale International Art Exhibition,** a world-class contemporary fair, alternating between art in odd years and architecture in even years. The exhibition spreads over the Arsenale and Giardini park. When the Biennale focuses on visual art, representatives from 70 nations offer the latest in contemporary art forms: video, computer art, performance art, and digital photography, along with painting and sculpture (take vaporetto #1 or #2 to Giardini-Biennale; for details and an events calendar, see www.labiennale.org). The actual exhibition usually runs from June through November, but other events loosely connected with the Biennale—film, dance, theater—are held throughout the year (starting as early as Feb) in various venues on the island.

Other typically Venetian festival days filling the city's hotels with visitors and its canals with decked-out boats are **Feast of the Ascension Day** (May 29 in 2014), **Feast and Regatta of the Redeemer** (Festa del Redentore) on the third weekend in July (with spectacular fireworks show Sat night), and the **Historical Regatta** (old-time boats and pageantry, first Sat and Sun in Sept). **Vogalonga** is a colorful regatta that attracts more than 1,500 human-powered watercraft; teams of often-costumed participants follow a 20-mile course through the canals and lagoon (late May-early June, www.vogalonga.it). Smaller regattas include the **Murano Regatta** (early July) and the **Burano Regatta** (mid-Sept).

Venice's patron saint, **St. Mark,** is commemorated every April 25. Venetian men celebrate the day by presenting roses to the women in their lives (mothers, wives, and lovers).

Every November 21 is the **Feast of Our Lady of Good Health.** On this local "Thanksgiving," a bridge is built over the Grand Canal so that the city can pile into La Salute Church and remember how Venice survived the gruesome plague of 1630. On this day, Venetians eat smoked lamb from Dalmatia (which was the cargo of the first ship admitted when the plague lifted).

Shopping in Venice

Shoppers like Murano glass (described earlier), Burano lace (fun lace umbrellas for little girls), Carnevale masks (fine shops and artisans all over town), art reproductions (posters, postcards, and books), prints of Venetian scenes, traditional stationery (pens and marbled paper products of all kinds), calendars with Venetian scenes, silk ties, scarves, and plenty of goofy knickknacks (Titian mousepads, gondolier T-shirts, and little plastic gondola condom holders).

In touristy areas, shops are typically open from 9:00 to 19:30 (sometimes with a break from about 13:00 until 15:00 or 16:00), and more stores are open on Sunday here than in the rest of the country. If you're buying a substantial amount from nearly any shop, bargain—it's accepted and almost expected. Offer less and offer to pay cash; merchants are very conscious of the bite taken by credit-card companies.

Popular **Venetian glass** is available in many forms: vases, tea sets, decanters, glasses, jewelry, lamps, mod sculptures (such as solid-glass aquariums), and on and on. Shops will ship it home for you, but you're likely to pay as much or more for the shipping as you are for the item(s), and you may have to pay duty on larger purchases. Make sure the shop insures their merchandise *(assicurazione),* or you're out of luck if it breaks. If your item arrives broken and it has been insured, take a photo of the pieces, send it to the shop, and they'll replace it for free.

Some visitors feel that because they're in Venice, they ought to grab the opportunity to buy glass. Remember that you can buy fine glass back home, too (Venice stopped forbidding its glassblowers from leaving the republic a few centuries ago)—and under less time pressure.

Also be aware that much of the cheap glass you'll see in Venice is imported (a sore point for local vendors dealing in the more expensive, authentic stuff). Venetian glass producers, up in arms about the influx of Chinese glass, claim that a big percentage of the glass tourists buy is actually not Venetian. Genuine Venetian glass comes with the Murano seal.

If you'd like to watch a quick glassblowing demonstration, try **Galleria San Marco,** a tour-group staple on St. Mark's Square at #139, which offers great demos every few minutes. They let individual travelers flashing this book sneak in with tour groups to see the show (and sales pitch). If you buy anything, show this book and they'll take 20 percent off the listed price. The gallery faces the square behind the orchestra nearest to the church; come to the door at #139, go through the shop, and climb the stairs (daily 9:00-18:00, tel. 041-271-8671, info@galleriasanmarco.it, manager Marino Busetto).

If you're serious about glass, visit the island of **Murano,** its glass museum, and many shops (see page 109). You'll find greater variety on Murano, but prices are usually the same as in Venice.

Nightlife in Venice

You must experience Venice after dark. The city is quiet at night, as tour groups stay in the cheaper hotels of Mestre on the mainland, and the masses of day-trippers return to their beach resorts and cruise ships. Gondolas cost more, but are worth the extra expense (see page 112). At night, *vaporetti* are nearly empty, and it's a great time to cruise the Grand Canal on the slow boat #1. Venice has a busy schedule of events, church concerts, festivals, and entertainment. Check at the TI or the TI's website (www.turismovenezia. it) for listings. The free monthly *Un Ospite di Venezia* lists all the latest happenings in English (free at fancy hotels, or check www. unospitedivenezia.it).

Baroque Concerts

Venice is a city of the powdered-wig Baroque era. For about €25, you can take your pick of traditional Vivaldi concerts in churches throughout town. Homegrown Vivaldi is as ubiquitous here as Strauss is in Vienna and Mozart is in Salzburg. In fact, you'll find frilly young Vivaldis hawking concert tickets on many corners. Most shows start at 20:30 and generally last 1.5 hours. You'll see posters in hotels all over town (hotels sell tickets at face value). Tickets for Baroque concerts in Venice can usually be bought the same day as the concert, so don't bother with websites that sell tickets with a surcharge. The general rule of thumb: Musicians in wigs and tights offer better spectacle; musicians in black-and-white suits are better performers.

The **Interpreti Veneziani orchestra,** considered the best group in town, generally performs 1.5-hour concerts nightly at 21:00 inside the sumptuous San Vidal Church (€26, church ticket booth open daily 9:30-21:00, north end of Accademia Bridge, tel. 041-277-0561, www.interpretiveneziani.com).

Other Performances

Venice's most famous theaters are **La Fenice** (grand old opera house, box office tel. 041-2424, see page 97), **Teatro Goldoni** (mostly Italian live theater), and **Teatro della Fondamenta Nuove** (theater, music, and dance).

Musica a Palazzo is a unique evening of opera at a Venetian palace on the Grand Canal. You'll spend about 45 delightful minutes in each of three sumptuous rooms (about 2.25 hours total) as eight musicians (generally four instruments and four singers) perform. They generally present three different operas on successive nights—enthusiasts can experience more than one. With these kinds of surroundings, under Tiepolo frescoes, you'll be glad you dressed up. As there are only 70 seats, you must book by phone or online in advance (€60, nightly at 20:30, Palazzo Barbarigo Minotto, Fondamenta Duodo Barbarigo, vaporetto: Santa Maria del Giglio, San Marco 2504, mobile 340-971 7272, www.musicapalazzo.com).

Venezia is advertised as "the show that tells the great story of Venice" and "simply the best show in town." I found the performance to be slow-moving and a bit cheesy, and the venue disappointing (€39, nightly May-Oct at 20:00, Nov-April at 19:00; 80 minutes, just off St. Mark's Square on Campo San Gallo, San Marco 1097, tel. 041-241-2002, www.teatrosangallo.net).

St. Mark's Square

For tourists, St. Mark's Square is the highlight, with lantern light and live music echoing from the cafés. Just being here after dark is a thrill, as **dueling café orchestras** entertain (see sidebar on page 94). Every night, enthusiastic musicians play the same songs, creating the same irresistible magic. Hang out for free behind the tables (allowing you to move easily on to the next orchestra when the musicians take a break), or spring for a seat and enjoy a fun and gorgeously set concert. If you sit awhile, it can be €12-22 well spent (for a drink and the cover charge for music). Dancing on the square is free—and encouraged.

Several venerable cafés and bars on the square serve expensive drinks outside but cheap drinks inside at the bar. The scene in a bar like **Gran Caffè Lavena** (in spite of its politically incorrect chandelier) can be great. The touristy **Bar Americano** is lively until late (under the Clock Tower). You'll hear people talking about the famous **Harry's American Bar,** which sells overpriced food and American cocktails to dressy tourists near the San Marco-Vallaresso vaporetto stop. But it's a rip-off...and the last place Hemingway would drink today. It's far cheaper to get a drink at any of the bars just off St. Mark's Square; you can get a bottle of beer or even prosecco-to-go in a plastic cup.

Wherever you end up, streetlamp halos, live music, floodlit history, and a ceiling of stars make St. Mark's magic at midnight. You're not a tourist, you're a living part of a soft Venetian night...an alley cat with money. In the misty light, the moon has a golden hue. Shine with the old lanterns on the gondola piers, where the sloppy lagoon splashes at the Doge's Palace...reminiscing.

Sleeping in Venice

For hassle-free efficiency and the sheer magic of being close to the action, I favor hotels that are handy to your sightseeing activities. I've listed rooms in four neighborhoods: St. Mark's bustle, the Rialto action, the quiet Dorsoduro area behind the Accademia art museum, and near the train station.

Book your accommodations well in advance if you'll be traveling during busy times. Note that hotel websites are particularly valuable for Venice, because they often include detailed directions that can help you get to your rooms with a minimum of wrong turns in this navigationally challenging city.

The prices I've listed are for one-night stays in peak season (April, May, June, Sept, and Oct) and assume you're booking directly (not through a TI or online hotel-booking engine). Prices can spike during festivals. Almost all places drop prices from November through March (except during Christmas and Carnevale—Feb 22-March 4 in 2014) and in July and August. A €180 double can cost €80-90 in winter. Off-season, don't pay the rates I list.

Over the past decade, Venice has seen the opening of several big new hotels, countless little boutique hotels, and the conversion of many private homes to short-term rental apartments, nearly doubling Venice's hotel capacity. Now the city is overbuilt for hotels. Demand is soft and, therefore, so are the prices.

To save money during a relatively slow time, consider arriving without a reservation and dropping in at the last minute. Big, fancy hotels put empty rooms on an aggressive push list, offering great prices. Many hotels in Venice list rooms on www.venere.com, especially for last-minute vacancies (two to three weeks before the date). Before you bite, check to see if rates are lower than the prices in this book.

For tips on making reservations, see page 26.

Sleep Code

(€1 = about $1.30, country code: 39)
S = Single, **D** = Double/Twin, **T** = Triple, **Q** = Quad, **b** = bathroom, **s** = shower only. Unless otherwise noted, breakfast is included, hotel staff speak basic English, and credit cards are accepted. There's almost always Wi-Fi and/or a guest computer available, either free or for a fee. Venice charges a hotel tax of €1-4 per person, per night. This tax is typically not included in the prices I've listed here.

To help you easily sort through these listings, I've divided the accommodations into three categories based on the price for a double room with bath during high season:

$$$ **Higher Priced**—Most rooms €180 or more.
$$ **Moderately Priced**—Most rooms between €130-180.
$ **Lower Priced**—Most rooms €130 or less.

Prices can change without notice; verify the hotel's current rates online or by email. For the best prices, always book direct.

Near St. Mark's Square

To get here from the train station or Piazzale Roma bus station, ride the vaporetto to San Zaccaria—either the slow #1 or the fast #2 (from the Tronchetto parking lot, it's #2 only). Consider using your ride to follow my tour of the Grand Canal (see page 74); to make sure you arrive via the Grand Canal, confirm that your boat goes "*via Rialto.*"

Nearby Laundries: Lavanderia Gabriella offers full service a few streets north of St. Mark's Square (€15/load includes wash, dry, and fold; drop off Mon-Fri 8:00-12:30, closed Sat-Sun; pick up 2 hours later or next working day, on Rio Terà de le Colonne, look for #985, tel. 041-522-1758, Elisabetta).

Effe Erre, a modern self-service *lavanderia*, is near the recommended Hotel al Piave on Ruga Giuffa at #4826 (€12/load, daily 6:30-24:00, mobile 349-058-3881, Massimo).

East of St. Mark's Square

Located near the Bridge of Sighs, just off the Riva degli Schiavoni waterfront promenade, these places rub drainpipes with Venice's most palatial five-star hotels. To locate the following hotels, see the map on page 120.

$$$ Hotel Campiello, lacy and bright, was once part of a 19th-century convent. Ideally located 50 yards off the waterfront on a tiny square, its 16 rooms offer a tranquil, friendly refuge for

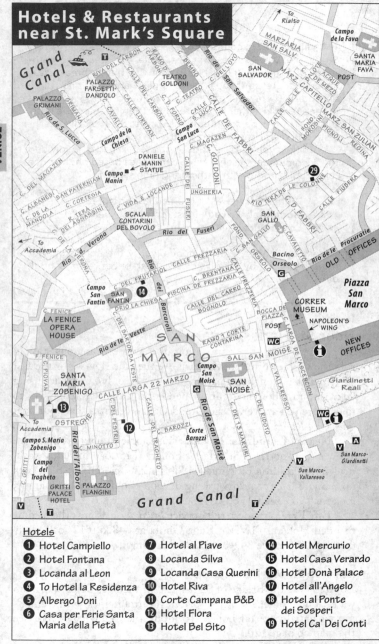

Hotels & Restaurants near St. Mark's Square

Hotels

1. Hotel Campiello
2. Hotel Fontana
3. Locanda al Leon
4. To Hotel la Residenza
5. Albergo Doni
6. Casa per Ferie Santa Maria della Pietà
7. Hotel al Piave
8. Locanda Silva
9. Locanda Casa Querini
10. Hotel Riva
11. Corte Campana B&B
12. Hotel Flora
13. Hotel Bel Sito
14. Hotel Mercurio
15. Hotel Casa Verardo
16. Hotel Donà Palace
17. Hotel all'Angelo
18. Hotel al Ponte dei Sosperi
19. Hotel Ca' Dei Conti

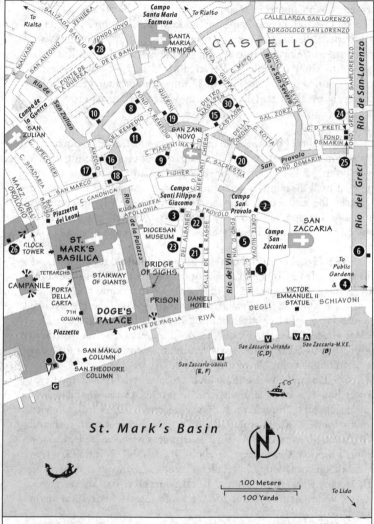

VENICE

Eateries & Other

- ⑳ Ristorante Antica Sacrestia
- ㉑ Birreria Forst Café
- ㉒ Bar Verde
- ㉓ Ristorante alla Basilica
- ㉔ Ristorante alla Conchiglia
- ㉕ Trattoria da Giorgio ai Greci
- ㉖ Gran Caffè Lavena (Gelato)
- ㉗ Todaro Gelateria
- ㉘ Co-op Supermarket
- ㉙ Lavanderia Gabriella
- ㉚ Lavanderia Effe Erre

travelers who appreciate comfort and professional service (Sb-
€130, Db-€180, bigger "superior" rooms €20-30 more, 10 percent
discount with this book if you reserve direct and pay cash on arrival, air-con, elevator, free Wi-Fi; just steps from the San Zaccaria
vaporetto stop, Castello 4647; tel. 041-520-5764, www.hcampi-
ello.it, campiello@hcampiello.it; family-run for four generations,
currently by Thomas, Nicoletta, and Marco). They also rent three
modern family apartments, under rustic timbers just steps away (up
to €380/night).

$$$ Hotel Fontana, two bridges behind St. Mark's Square, is
a pleasant family-run place with 15 sparse but classic-feeling rooms
overlooking a lively square (Sb-€120, Db-€180, family rooms, 10
percent cash discount, quieter rooms on garden side, 2 rooms have
terraces for €20 extra, air-con, elevator, free Wi-Fi in common
areas, on Campo San Provolo at Castello 4701, tel. 041-522-0579,
www.hotelfontana.it, info@hotelfontana.it, cousins Diego and Ga-
briele).

$$$ Hotel la Residenza is a grand old palace facing a peace-
ful square. It has 16 small rooms on three levels (with no elevator)
and a huge, luxurious lounge that comes with a piano and a stingy
breakfast. This is a good value for romantics—you'll feel like you're
in the Doge's Palace after hours (Sb-€105, Db-€205, view Db-
€215, air-con, free Wi-Fi, on Campo Bandiera e Moro at Castello
3608, tel. 041-528-5315, www.venicelaresidenza.com, info@ven-
icelaresidenza.com, Giovanni).

$$ Locanda al Leon, which feels a little like a medieval
tower house, is conscientiously run and rents 13 reasonably priced
rooms just off Campo Santi Filippo e Giacomo (Db-€160, Db with
square view-€180, Tb-€200, Qb-€240, these prices with cash and
this book, air-con, free Wi-Fi, 2 apartments with kitchens, Campo
Santi Filippo e Giacomo, Castello 4270, tel. 041-277-0393, www.
hotelalleon.com, leon@hotelalleon.com, Giuliano and Marcella).
Their down-the-street annex, **B&B Marcella,** has three newer,
classy, and spacious rooms for the same rates (check in at main
hotel).

$ Albergo Doni, situated along a quiet canal, is dark and
quiet. This time-warp—with 13 well-worn, once-classy rooms up a
creaky stairway—is run by friendly Tessa and her brother, an Ital-
ian stallion named Nikos (S-€70, D-€105, Db-€130, T-€135, Tb-
€170, €5 discount in 2014 with this book, ceiling fans, three Db
rooms have air-con, free Wi-Fi in common areas, 3 nice overflow
apartments are same price but no breakfast, on Fondamenta del
Vin at Castello 4656, tel. 041-522-4267, www.albergodoni.it, al-
bergodoni@hotmail.it).

$ Casa per Ferie Santa Maria della Pietà is a wonderful
church-run facility renting 53 beds in 15 rooms just a block off the

Riva, with a fabulous lagoon-view roof terrace that could rival the most luxurious hotels in town. Institutional with generous public spaces and dorm-style comfort, there are no sinks, toilets, or showers in any of its rooms, but there's plenty of plumbing down the hall (€40 beds in 4-8-bed dorms, S-€55, D-€100, straight price all year, only twin beds, reserve with credit card but pay cash, aircon, free Wi-Fi, profits go to church care for poor, 100 yards from San Zaccaria-Pietà vaporetto dock, down Calle de la Pietà from La Pietà Church at Castello 3701, take elevator to third floor, tel. 041-883-0111, www.bedandvenice.it, info@bedandvenice.it).

North of St. Mark's Square

To locate the following hotels, see the map on page 120.

$$ Hotel al Piave, with 28 fine, air-conditioned rooms above a bright and classy lobby, is fresh, modern, and comfortable. You'll enjoy the neighborhood and always get a cheery welcome (Db-€155, larger "superior" Db-€200, Tb-€200, Qb-€260; family suites-€280 for 4, €300 for 5, or €310 for 6; €10 Rick Steves discount when you book direct and pay in cash, free Wi-Fi, on Ruga Giuffa at Castello 4838, tel. 041-528-5174, www.hotelalpiave.com, info@hotelalpiave.com; Mirella, Paolo, Ilaria, and Federico speak English).

$$ Locanda Silva is a big, basic, beautifully located hotel with a functional 1960s feel, renting 23 decent old-school rooms that are particularly worth considering if you're willing to share a bathroom to save some money (S-€70, Sb-€85, D-€85, D with toilet but shared shower-€90, Db-€140, Tb-€160, Qb-€180, book direct and request 10 percent Rick Steves discount, another 10 percent off if you stay at least 2 nights, discounts valid only with cash, closed Dec-Jan, air-con, lots of stairs, pay Wi-Fi, on Fondamenta del Remedio at Castello 4423, tel. 041-522-7643, www.locandasilva.it, info@locandasilva.it; Sandra, Katia, and Massimo).

$$ Locanda Casa Querini rents six bright, high-ceilinged rooms on a quiet square tucked away behind St. Mark's. You can enjoy your breakfast or a sunny happy-hour picnic sitting at their tables right on the sleepy little square (Db-€155, Tb-€180, one cheaper small double, these prices promised in 2014 for Rick Steves readers who book direct and pay cash, €5 additional discount if you book on their website, air-con, free Wi-Fi, halfway between San Zaccaria vaporetto stop and Campo Santa Maria Formosa at Castello 4388 on Campo San Zaninovo/Giovanni Novo, tel. 041-241-1294, www.locandaquerini.com, info@locandaquerini.com; Silvia, Patrizia, and Caterina).

$ Hotel Riva, with gleaming marble hallways, big exposed beams, fine antique furnishings, and lots of stairs, is romantically situated on a canal along the gondola serenade route. This has long

VENICE

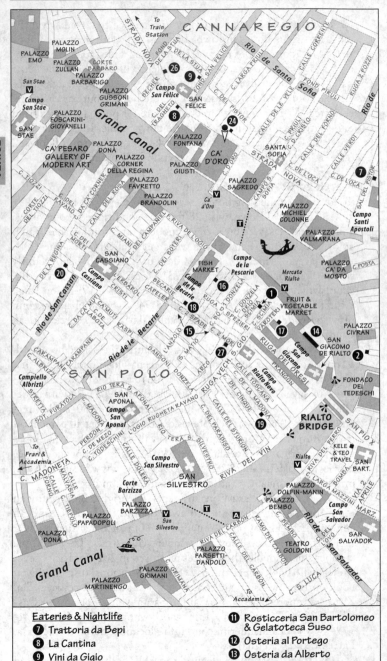

Hotels & Restaurants near the Rialto Bridge

Hotels

1. Pensione Guerrato
2. Hotel al Ponte Antico
3. Locanda la Corte
4. To Alloggi Barbaria
5. Hotel Giorgione
6. Foresteria della Chiesa Valdese

---

16. Pronto Pesce
17. Al Mercà
18. Ristorante Vini da Pinto
19. Trattoria alla Madonna
20. Trattoria Pizzeria al Nono Risorto
21. Osteria alle Testiere

22. Osteria al Mascaron
23. Peter Pan Kebabs
24. Grom Gelateria
25. Co-op Supermarket
26. Billa Supermarket
27. Small Deli

been a standby in this book, but how it'll stack up when it reopens after a major renovation remains to be seen (see website for latest prices, on Ponte de l'Anzolo at Castello 5310, tel. 041-522-7034, www.hotelriva.it, info@hotelriva.it, Daniella).

$ Corte Campana B&B, run by enthusiastic and helpful Ric-cardo, rents three quiet and characteristic rooms up a few flights of stairs just behind St. Mark's Square. One room has a private bath down the hall (Db-€125, Tb-€165, Qb-€190, prices are soft, cash only, 2-night minimum, at least €10/night less for stays of 4 nights, air-con, pay Wi-Fi but free guest computer, on Calle del Remedio at Castello 4410, tel. 041-523-3603, mobile 389-272-6500, www.cortecampana.com, info@cortecampana.com).

Near Campo Santa Maria Formosa
A bit farther north of the options listed above, these are in a pleas-ant, somewhat less touristy neighborhood near the inviting Campo Santa Maria Formosa. For locations, see the map on page 125.

$$ Locanda la Corte is perfumed with elegance without being snooty. Its 17 attractive, high-ceilinged, wood-beamed rooms—Venetian-style, done in earthy pastels—circle a small, quiet courtyard (standard Db-€150, deluxe Db-€170, 10 percent discount with cash and this book, suites and family rooms avail-able, air-con, free Wi-Fi, on Calle Bressana at Castello 6317, tel. 041-241-1300, www.locandalacorte.it, info@locandalacorte.it, Marco and Tommy the cat).

$ Alloggi Barbaria rents eight backpacker-type rooms on one floor around a bright but institutional-feeling common area. Beyond Campo San Zanipolo/Santi Giovanni e Paolo, it's a long walk from the action, in a residential neighborhood, and only a step above a youth hostel (Db-€90-100, third or fourth person-€25 each, pay cash for best price, family deals, limited breakfast, air-con, free Wi-Fi, on Calle de le Capucine at Castello 6573, tel. 041-522-2750, www.alloggibarbaria.it, info@alloggibarbaria.it, Gior-gio and Fausto).

West of St. Mark's Square
To locate the following hotels, see the map on page 120.

$$$ Hotel Flora sits buried in a sea of fancy designer bou-tiques and elegant hotels almost on the Grand Canal. It's formal, with uniformed staff and grand public spaces, yet the 40 rooms have a homey warmth, and the garden oasis is a sanctuary for well-heeled, foot-weary guests (generally Db-€260, check website for special discounts or email Sr. Romanelli for 10 percent Rick Steves discount off standard prices, air-con, elevator, free Wi-Fi, fitness room, family apartment, on Calle Bergamaschi at San Marco 2283a, tel. 041-520-5844, www.hotelflora.it, info@hotelflora.it).

$$$ **Hotel Mercurio,** a lesser value a block in front of La Fenice Opera House, offers 29 peaceful, comfortable rooms (Sb-€180, Db-€240, Tb-€290, Qb-€320, about €30 extra for a canal view, €10 discount on any room when booked direct and paid in cash, air-con, lots of stairs, free Wi-Fi, on Calle del Fruttariol at San Marco 1848, tel. 041-522-0947, www.hotelmercurio.com, info@hotelmercurio.com; Monica, Vittorio, Natale, and Giacomo).

$$$ **Hotel Bel Sito** offers pleasing yet well-worn Old World character, 34 rooms, generous public spaces, a peaceful courtyard, and a picturesque location—facing a church on a small square between St. Mark's Square and the Accademia (Sb-€110, Db-€185, €20 extra for "superior" room with view of canal or square, air-con, elevator, free Wi-Fi; near Santa Maria del Giglio vaporetto stop—line #1, on Campo Santa Maria Zobenigo/del Giglio at San Marco 2517, tel. 041-522-3365, www.hotelbelsitovenezia.it, info@hotelbelsito.info, manager Rossella).

Near the Rialto Bridge

These two places are on opposite sides of the Grand Canal, each within a short walk of the Rialto Bridge. Vaporetto #2 brings you to the Rialto quickly from the train station, the Piazzale Roma bus station, and the parking-lot island of Tronchetto. You can also take the slower vaporetto #1 (but not from Tronchetto). To locate the following hotels, see the map on page 125.

East of the Rialto Bridge: $$$ **Hotel al Ponte Antico** is exquisite, professional, and small. With nine plush rooms, a velvety royal living/breakfast room, and its own dock for water taxi arrivals, it's perfect for a romantic anniversary. Because its wonderful terrace overlooks the Grand Canal, Rialto Bridge, and market action, its non-canal-view rooms may be a better value (Db-€320, "superior" Db-€400, deluxe canal-front Db-€490, air-con, free Wi-Fi, 100 yards from Rialto Bridge at Cannaregio 5768, tel. 041-241-1944, www.alponteantico.com, info@alponteantico.com, Matteo makes you feel like royalty).

West of the Rialto Bridge: $$ **Pensione Guerrato,** above the colorful Rialto produce market and just two minutes from the Rialto Bridge, is run by friendly, creative, and hardworking Roberto and Piero. Their 800-year-old building—with 24 spacious, charming rooms—is simple, airy, and wonderfully characteristic (D-€95, Db-€135, Tb-€155, Qb-€175, Quint/b-€185, these prices with this book and cash, check website for special discounts, Rick Steves readers can ask for €5/night discount below online specials, air-con, free Wi-Fi in lobby, on Calle drio la Scimia at San Polo 240a, tel. 041-528-5927, www.pensioneguerrato.it, info@pensioneguerrato.it, Monica and Rosanna). My tour groups book this place for 60 nights each year. Sorry. The Guerrato also rents family apartments in the old center (great for groups of 4-8) for around €60 per person.

Near the Accademia Bridge

As you step over the Accademia Bridge, the commotion of touristy Venice is replaced by a sleepy village laced with canals. This quiet area, next to the best painting gallery in town, is a 15-minute walk from the Rialto or St. Mark's Square.

The fast vaporetto #2 connects the Accademia Bridge with the train station (15 minutes), Piazzale Roma bus station (20 minutes), Tronchetto parking lot (25 minutes), and St. Mark's Square (5 minutes). For hotels south of the Accademia Bridge, a good option is vaporetto #5.1 to Zattere (or the Alilaguna speedboat from the airport to Zattere).

To locate the following hotels, see the map on page 131.

South of the Accademia Bridge, in Dorsoduro

$$$ **Pensione Accademia** fills the 17th-century Villa Maravege like a Bellini painting. Its 27 comfortable, elegant rooms gild the lily. You'll feel aristocratic gliding through its grand public spaces and lounging in its wistful, breezy gardens (Sb-€80-160, standard Db-€145-295, bigger "superior" Db-€210-390, Tb-€340, Qb-€370, 5 percent Rick Steves discount on balance when booked direct and paying in cash—mention when reserving and show this book, air-con, cheap Wi-Fi in rooms, free Wi-Fi in lobby, on Fondamenta Bollani at Dorsoduro 1058, tel. 041-521-0188, www.pensioneaccademia.it, info@pensioneaccademia.it).

$$$ **Pensione la Calcina,** the home of English writer John Ruskin in 1876, maintains a 19th-century formality. It comes with three-star comforts in a professional yet intimate package. Its 27 nautical-feeling rooms are squeaky clean, with nice wood furniture, hardwood floors, and a peaceful canalside setting facing Giudecca Island (Sb-€140, Sb with view-€170, Db-€150-250, Db with view-€290-330, price depends on size, air-con, free Wi-Fi, rooftop terrace, buffet breakfast outdoors on platform over lagoon, near Zattere vaporetto stop at south end of Rio de San Vio at Dorsoduro 780, tel. 041-520-6466, www.lacalcina.com, info@lacalcina.com).

$$$ **Hotel Belle Arti,** with a stiff, serious staff, lacks personality but has a grand entry, an inviting garden terrace, and 64 heavily decorated rooms (Sb-€150, Db-€240, Tb-€270, air-con, elevator, pay Wi-Fi in common areas, 100 yards behind Accademia art museum on Rio Terà A. Foscarini at Dorsoduro 912a, tel. 041-522-6230, www.hotelbellearti.com, info@hotelbellearti.com).

$$ **Casa Rezzonico,** a tranquil getaway far from the crowds, rents seven inviting, nicely appointed rooms with a grassy private

garden terrace. All of the rooms overlook either the canal or the garden (Sb-€130, Db-€170, Tb-€200, Qb-€230, ask for Rick Steves discount when you book, air-con, free Wi-Fi, near Ca' Rezzonico vaporetto stop—line #1, a few blocks past Campo San Barnaba on Fondamenta Gherardini at Dorsoduro 2813, tel. 041-277-0653, www.casarezzonico.it, info@casarezzonico.it, brothers Matteo and Mattia).

$$ Hotel Galleria has nine tight, old-fashioned, velvety rooms, most with views of the Grand Canal. Some rooms are quite narrow. It's run with a family feel by Luciano and Stefano (S-€85, D-€130, Grand Canal view D-€150, skinny Grand Canal view Db-€160, palatial Grand Canal view Db-€185, breakfast in room, ceiling fans, free mini-bar, free Wi-Fi, 30 yards from Accademia art museum, next to recommended Foscarini pizzeria at Dorsoduro 878a, tel. 041-523-2489, www.hotelgalleria.it, info@hotelgalleria. it).

$$ Don Orione Religious Guest House is a big cultural center dedicated to the work of a local man who became a saint in modern times. With 80 rooms filling an old monastery, it feels cookie-cutter-institutional (like a modern retreat center), but is also classy, clean, peaceful, and strictly run. It's beautifully located, comfortable, and a good value supporting a fine cause: Profits go to mission work in the developing world (Sb-€96, Db-€160, Tb-€207, Qb-€248, groups welcome, air-con, elevator, free Wi-Fi, on Rio Terà A. Foscarini, Dorsoduro 909a, tel. 041-522-4077, www.donorione-venezia.it, info@donorione-venezia.it). From the Zattere vaporetto stop, turn right, then turn left. It's just after the church at #909a.

$ Ca' San Trovaso rents seven simple rooms split between the main building and a nearby annex. The location is peaceful, on a small, desolate-feeling canal (Sb-€90, Db-€115, Db with bigger canal view and air-con-€130, Tb-€145, breakfast in your room, air-con in most rooms, free Wi-Fi, no common space except small roof terrace, near Zattere vaporetto stop, off Fondamenta de le Romite at Dorsoduro 1350/51, tel. 041-277-1146, mobile 339-445-8821, www.casantrovaso.com, info@casantrovaso.com, Mark and Cristina).

$ Casa di Sara, a colorfully decorated B&B, is hidden in a leafy courtyard in a humble back-street area overlooking a canal. Their four quiet rooms and tiny roof terrace offer the maximum in privacy (Sb-€85, Db-€110, Tb-€130, air-con, free Wi-Fi, along Fondamenta de le Romite at Dorsoduro 1330, mobile 342-596-3563, www.casadisara.com, info@casadisara.com, Aniello).

VENICE

VENICE

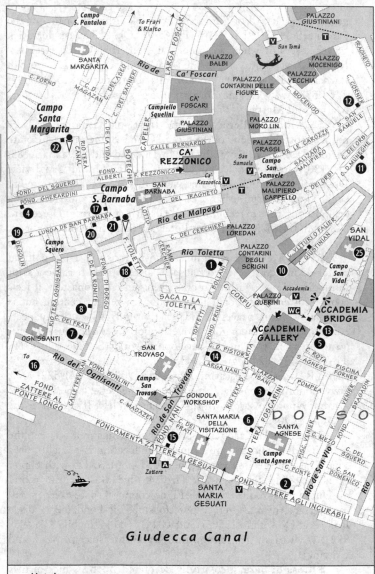

Hotels

1. Pensione Accademia
2. Pensione la Calcina
3. Hotel Belle Arti
4. Casa Rezzonico
5. Hotel Galleria
6. Don Orione Religious Guest House
7. Ca' San Trovaso
8. Casa di Sara
9. Novecento Hotel
10. Foresteria Levi
11. Istituto Ciliota
12. Albergo San Samuele

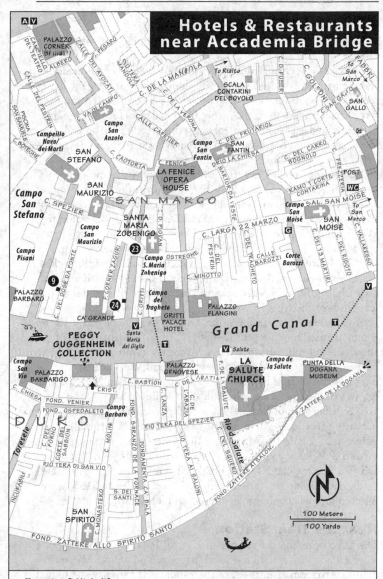

Hotels & Restaurants near Accademia Bridge

VENICE

Eateries & Nightlife

13 Bar Foscarini
14 Enoteca Cantine del Vino Già Schiavi
15 Terrazza del Casin dei Nobili
16 To Ae Oche Pizzeria & Billa Supermarket
17 Ristoteca Oniga
18 Osteria Enoteca Ai Artisti
19 Pizzeria al Profeta
20 Enoteca e Trattoria la Bitta
21 Grom Gelateria
22 Il Doge Gelateria
23 Small Deli
24 Musica a Palazzo
25 Interpreti Veneziani Orchestra

North of the Accademia Bridge

These places are between the Accademia Bridge and St. Mark's Square.

$$$ Novecento Hotel rents nine plush rooms on three floors, complemented by a big, welcoming lounge and an elegant living room. This boutique hotel has a tasteful sense of style, mingling Art Deco with North African and Turkish decor (Db-€270, bigger "superior" Db-€290, air-con, lots of stairs, free Wi-Fi, on Calle del Dose, off Campo San Maurizio at San Marco 2683, tel. 041-241-3765, www.novecento.biz, info@novecento.biz).

$$$ Foresteria Levi, run by a foundation that promotes research on Venetian music, offers 20 quiet, institutional yet comfortable and spacious rooms (some are lofts). Prices vary wildly—ask for the Rick Steves deal (generally around Db-€190, fans, elevator, free Wi-Fi, family loft rooms, on Calle Giustinian at San Marco 2893, tel. 041-786-711, www.fondazionelevi.it, info@foresterialevi.it).

$$ Istituto Ciliota is a big, efficient, and sparkling-clean place—well-run, well-located, and church-owned—with an Ikea-style charm, 30 dorm-like rooms, and a peaceful garden. If you want industrial-strength comfort at a good price with no stress and little character, this is a fine value. During the school year, half the rooms are used by students (Sb-€90, Db-€130, cheaper with longer stays, air-con, mini-fridges in each room, elevator, free Wi-Fi in some areas, on Calle de le Muneghe just off Campo San Stefano near the Accademia Bridge and vaporetto stop, San Marco 2976, tel. 041-520-4888, www.ciliota.it, info@ciliota.it).

$ Albergo San Samuele is a backpacker place that's dumpy but in a great locale. It rents 10 basic rooms in a crumbling old palace near Campo San Stefano. Sleep here only if their price is far less than what you can get at my other listings (S-€70, D-€90, Db-€115, extra bed-€15, no breakfast, fans, free Wi-Fi, on Salizada San Samuele at San Marco 3358, tel. 041-520-5165, www.hotelsansamuele.com, info@hotelsansamuele.com).

Near the Train Station

I don't recommend the train station area. It's crawling with noisy, disoriented tourists with too much baggage and people whose life's calling is to scam visitors out of their money. It's so easy just to hop a vaporetto upon arrival and sleep in the Venice of your dreams. Still, some like to park their bags near the station, and if so, these places stand out. The farther you get from the station, the more pleasant the surroundings (for locations, see the map on page 134).

Nearby Laundry: The nearest self-service **launderette** is across the Grand Canal from the station (€14/load, daily 7:30-22:30, on Ramo de le Chioverete, Santa Croce 665b).

Close to the Station

$$$ Hotel Abbazia, in the dreary hotel zone near the train station, fills a former abbey with both history and class. The refectory makes a grand living room for guests, a garden fills the old courtyard, and the halls leading to 50 rooms are monkishly wide (Db-€200, larger "superior" Db-€230—choose Venetian or modern style, ask for 10 percent Rick Steves discount when you book direct, air-con, no elevator but plenty of stairs, free Wi-Fi, fun-loving staff, 2 blocks from the station on the very quiet Calle Priuli dei Cavaletti, Cannaregio 68, tel. 041-717-333, www.abbaziahotel. com, info@abbaziahotel.com).

$ Albergo Marin has a humdrum lobby, but its 19 rooms are a good value. It's across the Grand Canal from the train station — close enough to be convenient, but far enough to be quiet, sane, and residential (Sb-€120, D-€110, Db-€130, big "superior" Db with fancy showers-€160, Tb-€160, 5 percent discount if you pay cash, air-con, free Wi-Fi, on Ramo de le Chioverete at Santa Croce 670b, tel. 041-718-022, www.albergomarin.it, info@albergomarin. it, brothers Giacomo and Filippo).

$ Hotel S. Lucia, 150 yards from the train station, is oddly modern and sterile, with bright and spacious rooms and tight showers. Its 13 rooms are simple and clean. Guests enjoy their sunny garden area out front (S-€60, D-€90, Db-€110, Tb-€130, 5 percent discount if you pay cash, breakfast-€5, air-con, free Wi-Fi, closed Nov-Feb, on Calle de la Misericordia at Cannaregio 358, tel. 041-715-180, www.hotelslucia.com, info@hotelslucia.com, Gianni and Alessandra).

$ Hotel Rossi, sitting quietly at the end of a dead-end street, rents 14 tired, well-worn rooms that are cheap in every sense (S-€59, D-€83, Db-€98, Tb-€118, air-con, free Wi-Fi in common areas, a short walk from the station and a block off the main street at Lista di Spagna, Cannaregio 262, tel. 041-715-164, www.hotelrossi.ve.it, into@hotelrossi.ve.it).

Farther from the Station, Toward the Jewish Ghetto and Rialto

While still walkable from the station, these listings are just outside the chaotic station neighborhood, in a far more pleasant residential zone close to the former Jewish Ghetto. The nearest Grand Canal vaporetto stop is San Marcuola.

$$ Locanda Ca' San Marcuola is a peaceful, characteristic, good-value oldie-but-goodie renting 14 fine rooms a few steps from the Grand Canal (Db-€140, €10 more for slightly bigger room overlooking small canal, air-con, elevator, pay Wi-Fi, next to San Marcuola vaporetto stop on Campo San Marcuola, Can-

VENICE

Hotels & Restaurants near the Train Station

1 Hotel Abbazia
2 Albergo Marin & Launderette
3 Hotel S. Lucia
4 Hotel Rossi
5 Locanda Ca' San Marcuola
6 Locanda Herion
7 Hotel Henry
8 To Osteria L'Orto dei Mori

9 To Osteria Ai 40 Ladroni
10 Timon Enoteca Osteria
11 To Osteria al Bacco
12 Pizzeria Vesuvio
13 Enoteca Cicchetteria Do Colonne
14 Antica Birraria la Corte
15 Brek Cafeteria
16 Grom Gelateria

Road to Mestre & Mainland

To Road to Mestre & Mainland

To Tronchetto

SANTA LUCIA TRAIN STATION (FERROVIA)

FOND. DE

CALLE DE LA 2 CORTI

C. DE LA 2 CORTI

CALLE DE LA MISERICORDIA

3

RAMO DEI SCALZI

1

C. PRIULI DEI CAVALETI

PHARMACY

15

SCALZI

RIO

Ferrovia W

V

Ferrovia Scalzi

V

SCALZI BRIDGE

Ferrovia

V

WC

SAN SIMEONE PICCOLO

CAMP DE LE CHIOVERETE

CALLE NOVA DE S

FOND. DE SAN SIMEONE PICCOLO

C. DEI BERGAMASCHI

2

To Stazione Marittima & Tronchetto

RAMPA SAN BASILIO

PONTE DELLA LIBERTA

Canale de Santa Chiara

Canale de la Liberta

PEOPLE MOVER

CO-OP SUPER-MARKET

Piazzale Roma

V

CALATRAVA BRIDGE

FOND. DE LA CROCE

F. DEI TOLENTINI

CASE NOVE

CAMPO D. L.

PARKING GARAGE

P

RIO TERA SAN ANDREA

Piazzale Roma

BUS STATION

Campiello de Lana

Rio Novo

F. PAPADOPOLI

F. CONDULMER

Giardino Papadopoli

C. DE CA'AMAI

SAN NICOLO DA TOLENTINO

PHARMACY

SANTA   CROCE

Canale de Santa Maria Maggiore

F. DEL MAGAZEN

FONDAMENTA DEI 3 PONTE

F. MINOTTO

F.D. GAFFARO

C. D. S. BIACCA

C. BABEGO

GALLO

F. DEL RIO NUOVO

100 Meters
100 Yards

Rio de la Cazziola

VENICE

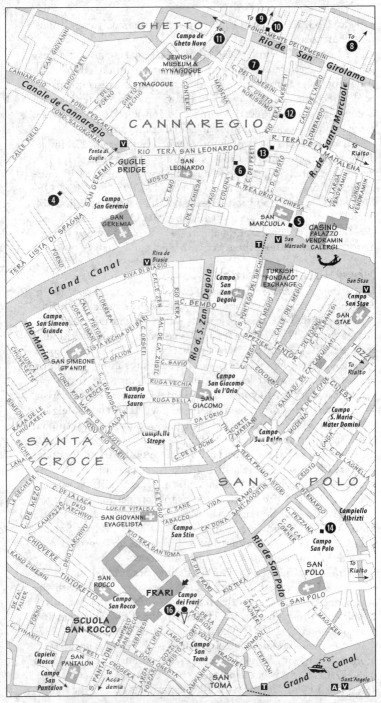

GHETTO

To ⑨ ⑩
Campo de
Gheto Novo ⑪
To

FONDAMENTE DEI ORMESINI

Rio de San

To
⑧

Girolamo

JEWISH
MUSEUM &
SYNAGOGUE

C. DEI CUMESINI

⑦

SYNAGOGUE

GHETO
VECHIO

C. GHETO
NOVISSIMO

RIO TERA FARSETTI

CALLE DE L'OCA

R. de Santa Marcuole

CALLE DE L'OCA

LOMBARDO

CANNAREGIO

⑫

Canale de Cannaregio

FOND. PESCARIA

C. DEL
FORNO

Ponte di
Guglie

CALLE RIELO

FOND. SAVORGNAN

GUGLIE
BRIDGE

SAN GEREMIA

RIO TERA SAN LEONARDO

SAN
LEONARDO

C. DEI PRETI

C. DE CRISTO

⑬

R. TERA DE LA MADALENA

To
Rialto

MOSTO

C. EMO

R. TERA DRIO LA CHIESA

C. LARGA
VENDRAMIN

C. LONGA
VENDRAMIN

⑥

④

Campo
San Geremia

SAN
GEREMIA

C. DE LA CHIESA

PIAGIA

C. COLONA

SAN
MARCUOLA ⑤

CASINÒ
PALAZZO
VENDRAMIN
CALERGI

T

San
Marcuola

Grand Canal

Riva de
Biasio

RIVA DI BIASIO

TURKISH
"FONDACO"
EXCHANGE

San Stae

V

Campo
San Stae

C. DE LA CROCE

CALLE ZEN

RIO TERA

C. BEMBO

Campo
San Zan
Degolà

S. PONTEGO DEI TURCHI

C. DEL MEGIO

SAN
STAE

Campo
San Simeon
Grande

CORREGA

CORTE
PISTOR

CALLE PISANI

LISTA VECHIA DEI BARI

SAL. DE CA. ZUSTO

C. ORSEOLI

RIO a. S. ZANDO
Degola

SPEZIER

C. DEL FORNO

SALIZADA DE CA CARMINATI

C. DEI ALBANESI

TIOZZA

To
Rialto

Rio Marin

C. LUNGA

C. CHIOVERETE

SAN SIMEONE
GRANDE

C. GALION

RUGA VECHIA

C. SAVIO

Campo
Nazario
Sauro

RUGA BELLA

Campo
San Giacomo
de l'Oria

SAN
GIACOMO

DA L'ORIO

COLOKOB

TENTOR

LARGA

C. DEL FORNO

MODENA

F. DE LE G. DE CHIESA

Campo
S. Maria
Mater Domini

C. DE L'AGNELA

SANTA

CROCE

SIMEON DELE CHIOVERETE

FOND. RIO MARIN

C. DE LA GRADISCA

FOND. RIO MARIN O. G. PALDAN

Campiello
Strope

INT. CORTE
MARIANI

C. DE LE OCHE

Campo
San Boldo

CRISTO

R. TERA PRIMO ASTORI

C. LARGA

SAN   POLO

RAJA DE LE
CHIOVERETE

SEGHERA

LANA

CAMPAZZO

C. DE MEZO

C. DE LA LACA

DRIO

C. L'ARCHIVO

CURTE VITALBA

C. ZANE

TABACCO

VIDA

RAMO
SANT'AGOSTIN

CA DONA

C. DE CA
CORNER

C. PEZZANA

C. BERNARDO

Campiello
Albrizti

⑭

CHIOVERE

RAMO CIMESIN

TINTORETTO

SAN GIOVANNI
EVAGELISTA

RIO TERA SAN TOMA

Campo
San Stin

Campo
San Polo

SAN
POLO

To
Rialto

DE CA
FALIER

C. FORNO

SAN
ROCCO

FRARI

Campo
dei Frari ⑯

F. DEI FRARI

RIO TERA

S. SAN POLO

C. DE LA
PASSION

S. SAN POLO

C. MAGAZEN

C. VINANTI

SCUOLA
SAN ROCCO

Campo
San Rocco

C. DEI ALBANESI

LARGA

C. TIPOLI

CORT' VOLTO

Campo
San Tomà

NOMBOLI

C. CENTANI

Capielo
Mosca

C. PRETI

SAN
PANTALON

C. PANTALON

CROSERA

C. DONA ONESTA

Campo
San
Pantalon

To
Accademia

LARGA FOSCARI

CAMPANIEL

SAN
TOMÀ

TRAGHETO

T

Grand Canal

Sant'Angelo

A V

naregio 1763, tel. 041-716-048, www.casanmarcuola.com, info@ casanmarcuola).

$ **Locanda Herion,** tucked down a sleepy lane just off a busy shopping street, rents 15 beige-tiled, homey rooms (Db-€130, larger rooms available at higher rates, 10 percent discount if you book direct, air-con, pay Wi-Fi in lobby, a few shared terraces, on Campiello Augusto Picutti, Cannaregio 1697a, tel. 041-275-9426, www.locandaherion.com, info@locandaherion.com).

$ **Hotel Henry,** a tiny family-owned hotel, rents 15 simple, flowery, nicely maintained rooms with few public spaces. It's in a sleepy residential neighborhood near the Jewish Ghetto, a 10-minute walk from the train station (D-€80, Db-€95, Tb-€130, Qb-€160, these prices good with cash and this book through 2014, breakfast-€10, air-con, free Wi-Fi, on Calle Ormesini at Campiello Briani, Cannaregio 1506e, tel. 041-523-6675, www.alloggi-henry.com, info@alloggihenry.com, Manola and Henry).

More Hotels in Venice

Big, Fancy Hotels that Discount Shamelessly: Several big, plush, $$$ places with greedy, sky-high rack rates (around Db-€300-350) frequently have steep discounts (often around Db-€220-250, and as low as Db-€120 or less off-season) if you book through their websites. All of the ones I've listed here are on the map on page 120, except Hotel Giorgione. If you want sliding-glass-door, uniformed-receptionist kind of comfort and formality in the old center, these are worth considering: **Hotel Giorgione** (big, garish, shiny, near Rialto Bridge—see map on page 125; www.hotelgior-gione.com); **Hotel Casa Verardo** (elegant and quietly parked on a canal behind St. Mark's, more stately, 22 rooms, www.casaverardo. it); **Hotel Donà Palace, Hotel all'Angelo,** and **Hotel al Ponte dei Sosperi** (three sister hotels sitting like Las Vegas in the touristy zone a few blocks behind St. Mark's Basilica, with stiff service and renting a total of 100 overpriced rooms that are getting a bit long in the tooth, all on Calle Larga San Marco, www.donapalace.it); and **Hotel Ca' Dei Conti** (5 minutes northeast of St. Mark's Square, palatial and perfectly located but €500 rooms are worth it only when deeply discounted, www.cadeiconti.com).

Other Options: If all my other listings are full, try one of the following $$ hotels. Rates for these places vary widely with the season and demand (generally around Db-€160-190 for a standard double room in high season): **Hotel Violino d'Oro** is a beautiful boutique hotel (Via XXII Marzo, San Marco 2091, tel. 041-277-0841, www.violinodoro.com). Its sister hotel, **Hotel Anastasia,** is more modest, with limited reception staff (San Marco 2141, tel. 041-277-0776, www.hotelanastasia.com). **Hotel American Dine-sen** offers 30 plush rooms with all the comforts (near Peggy Guggenheim Collection at Fondamenta Bragadin, Dorsoduro 628, tel. 041-520-4733, www.hotelamerican.com). **Hotel La Fenice et des Artistes** has 68 classy but unpretentious rooms on a sleepy square (near opera house at Campiello della Fenice, San Marco 1936, tel. 041-523-2333, www.fenicehotels.it). **Hotel dei Dragomanni** is modern, stylish, and pricey (facing Grand Canal at San Marco 2711, tel. 041-277-1300, www.hoteldragomanni.com).

Cheap Dormitory Accommodations

$ Foresteria della Chiesa Valdese is ramshackle, chilly, and run-down yet charming. It rents 70 beds—mostly in tight (6-10-bed) dorms, but with nine fine doubles and some larger private rooms sleeping up to six. It comes with generous public spaces and classic paintings on the walls and ceilings. Its profits support the charity work of the Methodist Church. They take reservations for the rooms, but only accept walk-ins for the dorms (dorm bed-€35, Db-€105-140, Tb-€120-140, Qb-€155-170, Quint/b-€185-220, €5/person less for multi-night stays; includes breakfast, sheets, towels, and lockers; must check in and out when office is open—8:30-19:30, no air-con, elevator, near Campo Santa Maria Formosa on Fondamenta Cavagnis at Castello 5170, see map on page 125, tel. 041-528-6797, www.foresteriavenezia.it, info@foresteriavenezia.it).

$ Venice's youth hostel, on Giudecca Island with 260 beds and grand views across the Bay of San Marco, is a godsend for backpackers shell-shocked by Venetian prices. Though the facility was recently renovated, at heart it's a classic hostel—big rooms stacked with bunk beds (€27 beds with sheets and breakfast in 8-20-bed dorms, €2 extra the first night for nonmembers, free Wi-Fi, lockers, towels-€5, room lock-out 10:00-13:30, office open 24 hours, Fondamenta Zitelle 86, tel. 041-523-8211, www.ostellovenezia.it, info@ostellovenezia.it). Take vaporetto #4.1 from the bus or train stations (from the Tronchetto parking lot, take vaporetto #2) to the Zitelle stop, then walk right along the embankment to #86.

Eating in Venice

While touristy restaurants are the scourge of Venice, the following places are popular with actual Venetians and respect the tourists who happen in. First trick: Walk away from triple-language menus. Second trick: For freshness, eat fish. Most seafood dishes are the catch-of-the-day. (But remember that

seafood can be sold by weight—per 100 grams or *etto*—rather than a set price.) Third trick: Eat later. A place may feel really touristy at 19:00, but if you come back at 21:00, it can be filled with locals. Tourists eat barbarically early, which is fine with the restaurants because they fill tables that would otherwise be used only once in an evening.

Near the Rialto Bridge

For locations, see the map on page 125.

North of the Bridge

These restaurants are located beyond Campo Santi Apostoli, on or near the Strada Nova, the main drag going from Rialto toward the train station.

Trattoria da Bepi, bright and alpine-paneled, feels like a classic, where Loris carries on his mother's passion for good, traditional Venetian cuisine. Ask for the seasonal specialties: The seafood appetizer plate and crab dishes are excellent. There's good seating inside and out. If you trust Loris, you'll walk away with a wonderful dining memory (€7-12 pastas, €14-20 *secondi,* Fri-Wed 12:00-14:30 & 19:00-22:00, closed Thu, half a block off Campo Santi Apostoli on Salizada Pistor at #4550, tel. 041-528-5031).

La Cantina is an elegant *enoteca,* both rustic and sophisticated—you won't find a menu here. Rather than cook (there's no kitchen), Francesco and Andrea prepare wonderful gourmet cold plates of meat, cheese, and fish. Though it's not cheap (meat-and-cheese plates-€15/person, seafood plates-€30/person), you'll enjoy the very best ingredients paired with fine wines. You can sit inside and watch the preparation scene, or enjoy the parade of passersby from great seats right on the Strada Nova. For a budget alternative, have a *cicchetto* at the bar with a glass of fine wine (€1.50 for ham-and-cheese *cicchetti,* €2.50 for seafood, Mon-Sat 10:00-22:00, closed Sun, facing Campo San Felice on Strada Nova near Ca' d'Oro, Cannaregio 3688, tel. 041-522-8258).

Vini da Gigio has an enthusiasm for good food and a traditional Venetian menu, with a classy but un-snooty setting that's a pleasant mix of traditional and contemporary (€13-18 pastas, €19-24 *secondi,* Wed-Sun 12:00-14:30 & 19:00-22:30, closed Mon-Tue, 4 blocks from Ca' d'Oro vaporetto stop on Fondamenta San Felice at #3628a—behind the church on Campo San Felice, tel. 041-528-5140).

East of the Rialto Bridge

The next few places hide away in the twisty lanes between the Rialto Bridge and Campo Santa Maria Formosa. Osteria da Alberto is a tad farther north of the others, in Cannaregio.

Osteria di Santa Marina, serving pricey, near-gourmet cuisine in a dressy dining room, is highly regarded by Venetians. The presentation is impressive, but you feel there's more pretense than love of food. Cheap-eating tricks are frowned upon in this elegant, borderline stuffy restaurant (€16 pastas, €27-30 *secondi*, €75-80 fixed-price meals, Mon-Sat 12:30-14:30 & 19:30-22:00, closed Sun, reserve for dinner, eat indoors or outdoors on the pleasant square, between Rialto Bridge and Campo Santa Maria Formosa at Campo Marina 5911, tel. 041-528-5239, www.osteriadisantamarina.com).

Rosticceria San Bartolomeo is a cheap—if confusing—self-service diner. This throwback budget eatery has a surly staff: Don't take it personally. Notice that the different counters serve up different types of food—pastas, *secondi*, fried goodies, and so on. You can get it to go, grab one of the few tiny tables, or munch at the bar—but I'd skip their upper-floor restaurant option (€7-8 pastas, great fried *mozzarella al prosciutto* for €1.60, fruit salad, €2 glasses of wine, prices listed on wall behind counter, no cover and no service charge, daily 9:00-21:30, San Marco 5424, tel. 041-522-3569). To find it, imagine the statue on Campo San Bartolomeo walking backward 20 yards, turning left, and going under a passageway—now, follow him.

Osteria al Portego is a friendly neighborhood eatery. Carlo serves good meals and excellent €1-3 *cicchetti*—best enjoyed early, around 18:00 (from 19:00 to 21:00, their six tables are reserved for those ordering from the menu; the *cicchetti* are picked over by 21:00). The *cicchetti* here can make a great meal, but consider sitting down for a dinner from their fine menu. Reserve ahead if you want a table (€13 pastas, €1 glasses of house wine, daily 10:30-15:00 & 18:00-22:00, near Campo Santa Marina at #6015 on Calle de la Malvasia, tel. 041-522-9038). From Rosticceria San Bartolomeo (listed above), continue over a bridge to Campo San Lio, turn left, and follow Calle Carminati straight 50 yards over another bridge.

Osteria da Alberto, up near Campo Santa Maria Novo, is one of my standbys. They offer up excellent daily specials, €11-18 seafood dishes, €9-12 pastas, and a good house wine in a woody and characteristic interior (although it's set along a canal, you can't see it from the dining area). It's smart to reserve at night—I'd request a table in front (Mon-Sat 12:00-14:30 & 18:30-22:30, closed Sun; on Calle Larga Giacinto Gallina, midway between Campo Santi Apostoli and Campo San Zanipolo/Santi Giovanni e Paolo, and next to Ponte de la Panada bridge at #5401; tel. 041-523-8153, www.osteriadaalberto.it, run by Graziano and Giovanni).

Rialto Market Area

As with market neighborhoods anywhere, you'll find lots of hard-

Venetian Cuisine

Even more so than the rest of Italy, Venetian cuisine relies heavily on fish, shellfish, risotto, and polenta. Along with the usual pizza-and-pasta fare, here are some typical foods you'll encounter.

Popular **antipasti** include *antipasto di mare* (a marinated mix of fish and shellfish served chilled), *asiago* cheese (a cow's-milk cheese that's either *mezzano*—young, firm, and creamy—or *stravecchio*—aged, pungent, and granular), and *sarde in saor* (sardines marinated with onions). *Cicchetti* are Venetian tapas, the finger-food appetizers served in some pubs (see sidebar on page 144).

On the **first-course** *(primi)* front, Venice's favorite dish is risotto, a short-grain rice simmered in broth and often flavored with fish and seafood (*risotto seppia al nero* is risotto made with cuttlefish ink; *risotto ai porcini* contains porcini mushrooms). Other first courses are *risi e bisi* (rice and peas), *pasta e fagioli* (bean and pasta soup), and *bigoli in salsa* (a long, fat, whole-wheat noodle with anchovy sauce). Pasta is commonly served *alla buzzara* (with a rich seafood-tomato sauce). You'll also see plenty of polenta—cornmeal boiled into a mush and served soft or cut into firm slabs and grilled. Polenta is a standard accompaniment with cod (*baccalà*—see next) or calf liver and onions (*fegato alla veneziana*).

For **second courses** *(secondi)*, it's mostly *frutti di mare* (seafood). The most common fish on Venetian plates—such as *branzino* (sea bass, grilled and served whole), *orata* (sea bream), *salmone* (salmon), and *rombo* (turbot, a flounder-like flatfish)—are farmed, not wild. The weirder the animal (eel, octopus, frogfish), the more

working hole-in-the walls with a line on the freshest of ingredients and catering to local shoppers needing a quick, affordable, and tasty bite. This area is very crowded by day, nearly empty early in the evening, and packed with young Venetian clubbers later.

Most of these places are informal, serving *cicchetti* and/or light meals. At each place, look for the list of snacks and wine by the glass at the bar or on the wall. When you're ready for dessert, try dipping a Burano biscuit in a glass of strawberry-flavored *fragolino* or another sweet dessert wine. Most bars are closed 15:00-18:00 and offer glasses of house wine for under €1, better wine for around €2.50, and *cicchetti* for €1-2.

My listings below include a strip of trendy places fronting the Grand Canal, a stretch of dark and rustic pubs serving regional tapas, a few little places on the market, a venerable old Venetian diner, and a couple of solid places for pasta and pizza. Most of these eateries are within 200 yards of the market and each other.

local it is. *Baccalà* is a dried Atlantic salt cod that's rehydrated and served with polenta (or, as *baccalà mantecato*, chopped up and mixed with mayonnaise as an antipasto topping). Other sea life on Venetian menus include calamari, *cozze* (mussels, often steamed in an herb broth with tomato), *gamberi* (shrimp), *moleche col pien* (fried soft-shell crabs), *pesce spada* (swordfish), *rospo* (frogfish, a small marine fish), *seppia* (cuttlefish, a squid-like creature; can be served in its own ink, often over spaghetti); *sogliola* (sole, served poached or oven-roasted), *vitello di mare* ("sea veal," like sword-fish—firm, pink, mild, and grilled), and *vongole* (small clams, often steamed with fresh herbs and wine). *Pesce fritto misto* is assorted deep-fried seafood (often calamari and prawns). *Zuppa di pesce* is seafood stew.

For *dolci* (desserts), dive into the familiar *tiramisù* (literally "pick-me-up")—spongy ladyfingers soaked in coffee and sweet Marsala wine, layered with mascarpone cheese and bitter choco-late. Venetians also love cookies, which come in many varieties.

Another popular Venetian tradition takes place before the meal, when people enjoy sipping *aperitivi* (before-dinner cock-tails). The dominant option is *spritz*, which mixes white wine, soda, and ice with either Campari (bitter) or Aperol (sweeter), garnished with an olive or skewer of fruit. Other options include the *bellini* (cocktail of Prosecco and white-peach puree) and *tiziano* (grape juice and Prosecco). A popular *digestivo* (after-dinner drink) is *sgroppino*: squeezed lemon juice, lemon gelato, and vodka.

The Bancogiro Stretch:
Five Places Overlooking the Grand Canal
Just past the Rialto Bridge, between Campo San Giacomo and the Grand Canal, this strip of five popular places has some of the best canalside seating in Venice. I call this the "Bancogiro Stretch" (Bancogiro is the strip of old banking buildings they front).

Each place has a unique character and formula. Unless other-wise noted, all of these are open daily; while you can get a drink anytime, dinner is typically served only after 19:00 or 19:30. Dur-ing meals, they charge more and limit table seating to those order-ing full lunches or dinners; but between meal times you can enjoy a drink or a snack at fine prices. After dinner hours, the Banco-giro Stretch—and especially in the surrounding alleys that house low-rent bars—becomes a youthful and trendy nightspot. Before or after dinner, this strip is one of the best places in town for a *spritz*.

Here's the rundown (in the order you'll reach them from the Rialto Bridge): **Bar Naranzaria** serves Italian dishes with a few

Japanese options (€12-14 pastas, €17-23 *secondi*). **Caffè Vergnano,** your cheapest option—especially during meal times—is just a café with no cover (€10-12 salads, pizzas, and pastas—and a busy microwave oven). **Osteria al Pescador** is a more serious restaurant (€13-18 pastas, €23-27 *secondi*). **Bar Ristorante Bancogiro** is really good, with romantic dining upstairs (no canal views), a passion for the best cheese, and good *cicchetti* options at the bar (€15-18 pastas, €22-26 *secondi*, nice €15 cheese plate, closed Mon, tel. 041-523-2061). The more modern **Bar Ancòra** seems to be most popular with the local bar crowd, with a live piano player crooning lounge music during busy times (€13 pastas, €17 *secondi*, *cicchetti* at the bar).

The *Cicchetti* Strip: Four Venetian Tapas Bars

The 100-yard-long stretch starting two blocks inland from the Rialto Market (along Sotoportego dei Do Mori and Calle de le Do Spade) is beloved among Venetian *cicchetti* enthusiasts for its delightful bar munchies, good wine by the glass, and fun stand-up conviviality. These four places serve food all day, but the spread is best at around noon (generally open daily 12:00-15:00 & 18:00-20:00 or 21:00; two of the places I list are closed Sun). While each place offers a fine bar-and-stools scene, you might instead choose to treat one like a restaurant, order from their rustic menu, and grab a table. Scout these four places in advance (listed in the order you'll reach them, if coming from the Rialto Bridge) to help decide which ambience is right for the experience you have in mind. Then pick one, dig in, and drink up.

Bar all'Arco, a bustling one-room joint, is particularly enjoyable for its tiny open-face sandwiches (closed Sun, San Polo 436; Francisco, Anne, Matteo).

Cantina Do Mori has been famous with locals (since 1462) and savvy travelers (since 1982) as a convivial place for fine wine. They serve a forest of little edibles on toothpicks and *francobolli* (a spicy selection of 20 tiny, mayo-soaked sandwiches nicknamed "stamps"). Go here to be abused in a fine atmosphere—the frowns are part of the shtick (closed Sun, San Polo 430).

Osteria ai Storti, with a cool photo of the market in 1909, is run by Alessandro, who speaks English and enjoys helping educate travelers, and his sister Baby—pronounced "Bobby" (€8 pastas, €12-13 *secondi*, daily except closed Sun off-season, around the corner from Cantina Do Mori on Calle San Matio—follow signs, San Polo 819).

Cantina Do Spade is expertly run by Francesco, who clearly lists the *cicchetti* and wines of the day (also good for sit-down meals, 30 yards down Calle de le Do Spade from Osteria ai Storti at San Polo 860, tel. 041-521-0583).

VENICE

Other Good Eateries near the Rialto Market

Pronto Pesce is the perfect place to sample fish while watching the market action. Umberto and his staff speak English and like to explain what's good. They serve a €10 mixed-fish plate with bread (daily from 13:00 until it's sold out) that locals plan their day around. Consider their "express plates" of pasta (€12-15, served daily 12:45-14:15), fish risotto specials, artful fish hors d'oeuvres, and many other fresh fish tidbits. This fancy hole-in-the-wall is fun for a quick bite—eat standing up or take it to go (Mon 11:30-15:00, Tue-Sat 10:00-15:00, closed Sun, generally open in the evenings only for groups, facing the fish market on Calle de le Becarie o Panataria, San Polo 319, tel. 041-822-0298).

Al Mercà ("At the Market"), a few steps away and off the canal, is a lively little nook with a happy crowd, where law-office workers have lunch and young locals gather in the evening for drinks and little snacks. The price list is clear, and I've found the crowd to be welcoming to tourists interested in connecting (stand at the bar or in the square—there are no tables and no interior, Mon-Sat 9:30-14:30 & 18:00-21:00, closed Sun, on Campo Cesare Battisti, San Polo 213).

Ristorante Vini da Pinto is a cheap, tourist-friendly eatery with a basic menu and forgettable food at decent prices. It has good service and relaxing outdoor seating (€8-12 pastas, €9-19 *secondi*, €13 fixed-price meal, open long hours daily, facing the fish market, San Polo 367a, tel. 041-522-4599).

Trattoria alla Madonna is a big, bustling, classic Italian eatery with old-school formal waiters, a huge menu, and about a hundred tables. Tour groups find it efficient, and local families have come here for lunch after church for generations. There's no romance—just solid, reliable, traditional food from a menu that hasn't changed since World War II (€11-13 pastas, €13-16 *secondi*, closed Wed, tucked away on Calle de la Madona, 2 minutes west of Rialto Bridge, San Polo 592, tel. 041-522-3824).

Farther West, Toward Ca' Pesaro: **Trattoria Pizzeria al Nono Risorto** is unpretentious, inexpensive, youthful, and famous for serving good pizza in a nice setting. You'll sit in a gravelly garden under a leafy canopy, surrounded by Italians enjoying huge €8-10 salads, €9-12 pastas and pizzas, and €12-18 grilled meat or fish dishes (Thu 19:00-22:30, Fri-Tue 12:00-14:30 & 19:00-22:30, closed Wed, reservations smart on weekends; from Rialto fish market, get out your map and walk 3 minutes away from the Rialto to Campo San Cassiano—it's just over the bridge on Sotoportego de Siora Bettina at #2338; tel. 041-524-1169).

Between the Rialto Bridge and Frari Church: **Antica Birraria la Corte** is an everyday eatery on the delightful Campo San Polo. Popular for its €8-11 pizza, calzones, and wonderful selection of

The Stand-Up Progressive Venetian Pub-Crawl Dinner

My favorite Venetian dinner is a pub crawl *(giro d'ombra)*—a tradition unique to Venice, where no cars means easy crawling. *(Giro* means stroll, and *ombra*—slang for a glass of wine—means shade, from the old days when a portable wine bar scooted with the shadow of the Campanile bell tower across St. Mark's Square.)

Venice's residential back streets hide plenty of characteristic bars *(bacari)* with countless trays of interesting toothpick munchies *(cicchetti)* and blackboards listing the wines that are uncorked and served by the glass. This is a great way to mingle and have fun with the Venetians. Bars don't stay open very late, and the *cicchetti* selection is best early, so start your evening by 18:00. Most bars are closed on Sunday. For a stress-free pub crawl, consider taking a tour with the charming Alessandro Schezzini (see page 71).

Cicchetti **bars** have a social stand-up zone and a cozy gaggle of tables where you can generally sit down with your *cicchetti* or order from a simple menu. In some of the more popular places, the crowds happily spill out onto the street. Food generally costs the same price whether you stand or sit.

I've listed plenty of pubs in walking order for a quick or ex-

hearty €10-13 salads, it fills the far side of this cozy, family-filled square. The interior is a sprawling beer hall, making it a joy to eat on the square, where metal tables teeter on the cobbles, the wind plays with the paper mats, and children run free (€11-13 pastas, €12-20 *secondi*, daily 12:00-14:30 & 18:00-22:30, Campo San Polo 2168—see map on page 134, tel. 041-275-0570).

Near St. Mark's Square

While my first listing is a serious restaurant, the other places listed here are cheap-and-cheery options convenient to your sightseeing. For locations, see the map on page 120.

Ristorante Antica Sacrestia is a classic restaurant where the owner, Pino, takes a hands-on approach to greeting guests. His staff serve creative €33-50 fixed-price meals and a humdrum €20 *menù del giorno*. (Be warned: These meals seem designed to overwhelm you with too much food. You will not leave hungry.) You can also order à la carte; try the delightful €21 antipasto spread,

tended crawl. If you've crawled enough, most of these bars make a fine one-stop, sit-down dinner.

While you can order a plate, Venetians prefer going one-by-one...sipping their wine and trying this...then give me one of those...and so on. Try deep-fried mozzarella cheese, gorgonzola, calamari, artichoke hearts, and anything ugly on a toothpick. *Crostini* (small toasted bread with a topping) are popular, as are marinated seafood, olives, and prosciutto with melon. Meat and fish (*pesce*; PESH-ay) munchies can be expensive; veggies (*verdure*) are cheap, at about €3 for a meal-sized plate. In many places, there's a set price per food item (e.g., €1.50). To get a plate of assorted appetizers for €8 (or more, depending on how hungry you are), ask for "*Un piatto classico di cicchetti misti da €8*" (oon pee-AH-toh KLAH-see-koh dee cheh-KET-tee MEE-stee dah OH-toh ay-OO-roh). Bread sticks (*grissini*) are free for the asking.

Bar-hopping Venetians enjoy an *aperitivo*, a before-dinner drink. Boldly order a Bellini, a *spritz con Aperol*, or a Prosecco, and draw approving looks from the natives.

Drink the house wines. A small glass of house red or white wine (*ombra rosso* or *ombra bianco*) or a small beer (*birrino*) costs about €1. The house keg wine is cheap—€1 per glass, about €4 per liter. *Vin bon*, Venetian for "fine wine," may run you from €2 to €6 per little glass. There are usually several fine wines uncorked and available by the glass. A good last drink is *fragolino*, the local sweet wine—*bianco* or *rosso*. It often comes with a little cookie (*biscotti*) for dipping.

which looks like a lagoon aquarium spread out on a plate. The entrance courtyard is a great place to sip a drink if you have to wait for a table. While the food isn't high cuisine, the service is animated, and the experience is memorable. My readers are welcome to a free *sgroppino* (lemon vodka after-dinner drink) upon request (€13-18 pastas and pizzas, €20-30 *secondi,* Tue-Sun 11:30-15:00 & 18:00-23:00, closed Mon, behind San Zaninovo/Giovanni Novo Church on Calle Corona at Castello 4463, tel. 041-523-0749).

"Sandwich Row": On Calle de le Rasse, just steps away from the tourist intensity at St. Mark's Square, is a handy strip I call "Sandwich Row." Lined with sandwich bars, it's the closest place to St. Mark's to get a decent sandwich at an affordable price with a place to sit down (most places open daily 7:00-24:00, €1 extra to sit; from the Bridge of Sighs, head down the Riva and take the second lane on the left). I particularly like **Birreria Forst,** a pleasantly unpretentious café that serves a selection of meaty €3 sandwiches with tasty sauce on wheat bread, or made-to-order sandwiches for

€4 (daily 9:30-22:00, air-con, rustic wood tables, Castello 4540, tel. 041-523-0557), and **Bar Verde,** a more modern sandwich bar with fun people-watching views from its corner tables (big €4-5 sandwiches, splittable €9 salads, fresh pastries, at the end of Calle de le Rasse at #4526, facing Campo Santi Filippo e Giacomo).

Ristorante alla Basilica, just one street behind St. Mark's Basilica, is a church-run, indoor, institutional-feeling place that serves a solid €14 fixed-price lunch (including water). It's not self-serve—you'll be seated and can choose a pasta, a *secondi,* and a vegetable side dish off the menu (Tue-Sun 11:45-15:00, closed Mon, air-con, Calle dei Albanesi 4255, tel. 041-522-0524).

Picnicking: Though you can't picnic on St. Mark's Square, you can legally take your snacks to the nearby Giardinetti Reali, the small park along the waterfront west of the Piazzetta.

North of St. Mark's Square, near Campo Santa Maria Formosa

For a (marginally) less touristy scene, walk a few blocks north to the inviting Campo Santa Maria Formosa. For locations, see the map on page 125.

Osteria alle Testiere is my top dining splurge in Venice. Hugely respected, Luca and his staff are dedicated to quality, serving up creative, artfully presented market-fresh seafood (there's no meat on the menu), homemade pastas, and fine wine in what the chef calls a "Venetian Nouvelle" style. With only 22 seats, it's tight and homey, with the focus on food and service. They have daily specials, 10 wines by the glass, and one agenda: a great dining experience. This is a good spot to let loose and trust your host. They're open for lunch (12:30-14:30), and reservations are a must for their two dinner seatings: 19:00 and 21:30 (€20 pastas, €26 *secondi,* plan on spending €50 for dinner, closed Sun-Mon, on Calle del Mondo Novo, just off Campo Santa Maria Formosa at Castello 5801, tel. 041-522-7220; you can also reserve online at www.osterialletestiere.it).

Osteria al Mascaron is where I've gone for years to watch Gigi, Momi, and their food-loving band of ruffians dish up rustic-yet-sumptuous pastas with steamy seafood to salivating foodies. The seafood pastas seem pricey at €26-36, but they're meant for two (it's OK to ask for single portions). The €16 *antipasto misto* plate—have fun pointing—and two glasses of wine make a terrific light meal (€16-20 main dishes, Mon-Sat 12:00-15:00 & 19:00-23:00, closed Sun, reservations smart Fri-Sat; on Calle Lunga Santa Maria Formosa, a block past Campo Santa Maria Formosa, at #5225; tel. 041-522-5995, www.osteriamascaron.it).

Fast and Cheap Eats: The veggie stand on Campo Santa Maria Formosa is a fixture. For *döner kebabs* (€3.50) and pizza to go (€2/

slice), head down Calle Lunga Santa Maria Formosa to **Peter Pan,**
at #6249 (daily 11:00-24:00).

In Dorsoduro

All of these recommendations are within a 10-minute walk of the
Accademia Bridge (for locations, see the map on page 131). Dorsoduro is great for restaurants and well worth the walk from the more
touristy Rialto and San Marco areas. The first two listings are near
the Accademia (and best for lunch). The next two are in Zattere,
overlooking the Giudecca Canal. And the last four (best for dinner)
are near Campo San Barnaba.

Near the Accademia Bridge

Bar Foscarini, next to the Accademia Bridge and Galleria, offers decent €8-15 pizzas and €8-10 *panini* in a memorable Grand
Canal-view setting. The food is decent but forgettable, and pricey
drinks pad your tab, but you're paying a premium for this premium
location. On each visit to Venice, I grab a pizza lunch here while
I ponder the Grand Canal bustle. They also serve a €10 break
fast (Wed-Mon 7:00-22:30, until 21:00 Nov-April, closed Tue
year-round, on Rio Terà A. Foscarini at #878c, tel. 041-522-7281,
Paolo).

Enoteca Cantine del Vino Già Schiavi, with a wonderfully
characteristic *cicchetti*-bar ambience, is much-loved for its €1 *cic-*

chetti, €3.50 sandwiches (order from
list on board), and €1-2 glasses of
wine. You're welcome to enjoy your
wine and finger food at the bar or
out on the sidewalk. This is primarily a wine shop with great prices for
bottles to go—and plastic glasses
for picnickers (Mon-Sat 8:00-20:30,
closed Sun, 100 yards from Acca-
demia art museum on San Trovaso canal; facing Accademia, take
a right and then a forced left at the canal to the second bridge—it's
at #992, tel. 041-523-0034).

In Zattere

Terrazza del Casin dei Nobili takes full advantage of the warm,
romantic evening sun. They serve finely crafted, regional specialties
with creativity at tolerable prices. The canalside seating is breezy and
beautiful, but comes with the rumble of *vaporetti* from the nearby
stop. The interior is bright and hip (good €8-10 pizzas, €13-15 pastas, €14-18 *secondi,* daily 12:00-23:00 except closed Thu off-season;
from Zattere vaporetto stop, turn left to #924; tel. 041-520-6895,

Romantic Canalside Settings

Of course, if you want a meal with a canal view, it generally comes with lower quality and/or a higher price. But if you're determined to take home a canalside memory, these places can be great.

Near the Rialto Bridge: The five places I call the "Banco-giro Stretch" offer wonderful canalside dining and a great place to enjoy a drink and/or a snack be-tween meals or after dinner (see page 141).

Rialto Bridge Tourist Traps: Venetians are embarrassed by the lousy food and aggressive "service" at the string of joints dominating the best romantic, Grand Canal-fringing real estate in town. Still, if you want to linger over dinner with a view of the most famous bridge and the songs of gondoliers oaring by (and don't mind eating with other tourists), this can be enjoyable. Don't trust the waiter's recommendations for special meals. The budget ideal would be to get a simple pizza or pasta and a drink for €15, and savor the ambience without getting ripped off. But few restaurants will allow you to get off that easy. To avoid a dispute over the bill, ask if there's a minimum charge before you sit down (most places have one).

Near the Accademia: Bar Foscarini, next to the Accademia Bridge, offers decent pizzas overlooking the canal with no cover or service charge (see page 147).

Ruggiero and Eleonora). On Wednesday and Sunday evenings in summer, there's live music nearby on the Zattere promenade.

Ae Oche Pizzeria is playful, with casual tables on the canal and a sprawling pizza-parlor interior. It's a hit with young Venetians for its fun atmosphere and good prices (daily 12:00-15:00 & 19:00-23:00, a couple of hundred yards from the Zattere vaporetto stop, Dorsoduro 1414, tel. 041-520-6601).

On or near Campo San Barnaba

This small square is a delight—especially in the evening. As these places are within a few steps of each other—and the energy and atmosphere can vary—I like to survey the options before choos-ing (although reservations may be necessary to dine later in the evening).

Ristoteca Oniga is all about fresh fish, with a chic-and-ship-shape interior, great tables on the square, and the enthusiastic direc-tion of Raffaele. The menu is accessible and always includes a good

East of St. Mark's Square: Ristorante alla Conchiglia and **Trattoria da Giorgio ai Greci,** several blocks behind St. Mark's, both have a few tables next to one of the smaller canals frequented by gondoliers. While tourist traps, they are lit up like Venetian Christmas trees after dark, and you can't argue with their set-

ting (€17-20 fixed-price meals, €6-17 pastas and pizzas, €10-25 *secondi,* cover and service charge extra; on Fondamenta San Lorenzo near the Ponte dei Greci bridge).

Overlooking the Giudecca Canal: **Terrazza del Casin dei Nobili** is located in Zattere—on the Venice side of the wide Giudecca Canal—and is particularly nice just before sunset (vaporetto: Zattere, see page 147). For a cheaper perch on the same canal, consider **Ae Oche Pizzeria,** described on page 148. **I Figli delle Stelle Ristorante,** on the island of Giudecca, is a classy restaurant offering romantic canalside seating and a wonderful experience (vaporetto: Zitelle, see page 151).

On Fondamente Nove with a View of the Open Lagoon: **Ristorante Algiubagiò** offers a good opportunity to eat well while overlooking the north lagoon (see page 151).

On Burano: **Trattoria al Gatto Nero** sits on a tranquil canal under a tilting bell tower in the pastel townscape of Burano. If you're touring the lagoon and want to enjoy Burano without the crowds, go late and consider a dinner here (see page 109).

vegetarian dish (€12-14 pastas, €18-22 *secondi,* Wed-Mon 12:00-14:30 & 19:00-22:30, closed Tue, reservations smart, Campo San Barnaba, Dorsoduro 2852, tel. 041-522-4410, www.oniga.it).

Osteria Enoteca Ai Artisti serves well-presented quality dishes either in its tight little wine-snob interior or at a few petite, romantic canalside tables. They serve good wines by the glass from their prize-winning list (€13-15 pastas, €20-25 *secondi,* closed Sun, Fondamenta de la Toletta, Dorsoduro 1169a, tel. 041-523-8944).

Pizzeria al Profeta is a casual place popular for great pizza and steak. Its large interior seems to stoke conviviality, as does its leafy garden out back (€8-10 pizzas, Wed-Mon 12:00-14:30 & 19:00-23:00, closed Tue; from Campo San Barnaba, walk to the end of Calle Lunga San Barnaba; Dorsoduro 2671, tel. 041-523-7466).

Enoteca e Trattoria la Bitta is dark and woody, with a soft-jazz bistro feel, tight seating, and a small, forgettable back patio. They serve beautifully presented, traditional Venetian food with—

proudly—no fish. Their helpful waitstaff and small, handwritten daily menu are clearly focused on quality, with local ingredients and a "slow food" ethic. As it has an avid following, they do two dinner seatings (19:00 and 21:00), reservations are required, and service can be intense (€10-11 pastas, €16-27 *secondi*, dinner only, Mon-Sat 18:30-23:00, closed Sun, cash only, just off Campo San Barnaba on Calle Lunga San Barnaba, Dorsoduro 2753a, tel. 041-523-0531, Debora and Marcellino).

In Cannaregio

Cannaregio, along the fish's "back," offers the classic chance in Venice to get off the beaten path. I've listed restaurants both near the Jewish Ghetto and near a main thoroughfare (see map on page 134; these zones are about a 10-minute walk apart). Also listed here are a few convenient, last-resort options next to the train station.

Behind the Jewish Ghetto

This sleepy neighborhood—more residential than touristic—features a grid layout with straight and spacious canalside walks (part of an expansion from the 1400s). Although it lacks the higgledy-piggledy feel of the older part of town, it's worth the long walk for a look. Rather than come here just for a meal, I'd make time to explore and then grab a bite while in the neighborhood. Cannaregio is most peaceful at sunset.

Osteria L'Orto dei Mori is a chic place serving nicely presented, creative Venetian cuisine. You can eat in the elegant, modern interior or on a great neighborhood square with 10 tables surrounded by a classic scene of wellhead, bridges, and canal (€14 pastas, €19-23 *secondi*, smart to reserve for dinner, Wed-Mon 12:30-15:30 & 19:00-24:00, closed Tue; on Campo dei Mori, facing a bridge on Fondamenta dei Mori, Dorsoduro 3386; tel. 041-524-3677, www.osteriaortodeimori.com).

Osteria Ai 40 Ladroni ("The 40 Thieves") is a characteristic, unpretentious old standby with a few tables on the canal, a rustic interior, and a convivial garden out back. The action is near the bar (€9-12 pastas, €10-15 *secondi*, they're proud of their mixed seafood *antipasti*, Tue-Sun 12:00-14:30 & 19:00-22:00, closed Mon, on Fondamenta de la Sensa near the start of Calle del Capitello at Dorsoduro 3253, tel. 041-715-736).

Timon Enoteca Osteria, while nothing earthshaking, has a relaxing canalside setting with nice wines and *cicchetti* (a block past the Jewish Ghetto on Fondamenta Ormesini near the corner with Calle de la Malvasia at Dorsoduro 2754, tel. 041-524-6066).

Osteria al Bacco is simple and rustic, with a typical Venetian menu and a couple of canalside tables (€10 pastas, €16 *secondi*, closed Mon, on Fondamenta Capuzine near the corner with Calle Girolamo at Dorsoduro 3054, tel. 041-721-415).

Along the Main Drag
Just a few blocks closer to the Grand Canal from the options listed above, the following places are a few steps from the main drag connecting the train station to the Rialto/San Marco area, near the San Marcuola vaporetto stop.

Pizzeria Vesuvio serves some of the best and most popular pizza in town. A neighborhood favorite, it has classy indoor seating and pleasant tables outside (€6-9 pizzas, daily 9:30-23:30 except closed Tue off-season, on Rio Terà Farsetti, Cannaregio 1837, tel. 041-795-688).

Enoteca Cicchetteria Do Colonne is a local dive with a loyal following and a good spread of *cicchetti* and sandwiches. It's handy for a drink and a snack. While the food is mediocre, the scene— both at the bar and at the tables outside—feels real and is fun (daily 10:00-22:00, on Rio Terà del Cristo, Cannaregio 1814, tel. 041-524-0453).

Near the Train Station
There are piles of cateries near the station. The buffet in the station itself is quite good, with peaceful garden seating out back in summer, big €3-4 sandwiches, and slices of pizza for €3. A block away is a small branch of the efficient and economic **Brek,** a popular self-service cafeteria chain (€6 pastas, €7-12 *secondi*, daily 11:30-22:00, head left as you leave the station and walk about 50 yards past the bridge along Rio Terà Lista di Spagna to #124).

Splurging on a Water View
On Giudecca Island, with a View of St. Mark's Square: **I Figli delle Stelle Ristorante** offers a delightful dining experience with an excuse to ride the boat from St. Mark's Square across to the island of Giudecca. Simone and his staff artfully serve Venetian classics with a dash of Rome and Puglia and a passion for fish and lamb. While they have inside seating, the reason to venture here is to sit canalside with fine views of Venice across the broad Giudecca Canal and all the water traffic. Reserve ahead to specify "first line" seating along the water, "second line" seating a few steps away, or a table inside (€15 pastas, €22 *secondi*, daily 12:30-14:30 & 19:00-22:30, 50 yards from Zitelle vaporetto dock—from San Marco ride line #4.2 or #2, Giudecca 70/71, tel. 041-523-0004, www.ifiglidellestelle.it).

On Fondamente Nove, with a Lagoon View: **Ristorante Algiubagió,** though not cheap, is a good place to eat well overlooking the northern lagoon. The name is a combination of the owners' four names—Alberto, Giulio, Barbara, and Giovanna—who strive to impress visitors with quality, creative Venetian cuisine made using the best ingredients. Reserve a table on the lagoon facing the island of San Michele or in their classy cantina dining room (€16-19 pastas, €20-28 *secondi*, €35-54 fixed-price meals, daily 12:00-15:00 & 19:00-22:30, between the two sets of vaporetto docks on Fondamente Nove, Cannaregio 5039—see map on page 111, tel. 041-523-6084, www.algiubagio.net). This is a convenient place to eat if you're taking the vaporetto out to the islands in the lagoon.

Picnics

You're legally forbidden from picnicking anywhere on or near St. Mark's Square except for Giardinetti Reali, the waterfront park near the San Marco vaporetto docks. Though it's legal to eat outdoors elsewhere around town, you may be besieged by pigeons.

Venice has one main produce market and several convenient supermarkets:

Outdoor Market near the Rialto: The **fruit and vegetable market** that sprawls for a few blocks just past the Rialto Bridge is a fun place to assemble a picnic (best Mon-Sat 8:00-13:00, liveliest in the morning, closed Sun). The adjacent **fish market** is wonderfully slimy (closed Sun-Mon). Side lanes in this area are speckled with fine little hole-in-the-wall munchie bars, bakeries, and cheese shops.

Neighborhood Deli near the Rialto: One tiny *alimentari* just around the corner from the Rialto market sells a flavorful concoction of cheese, Kalamata olives, sun-dried tomatoes, olive oil, and hot peppers that they call *intruglio*. It goes great with a fresh roll (€2.70). It's at the end of my favorite strip of *cicchetti* bars, near the fruit-and-vegetable market at the San Polo end of the Rialto Bridge (Mon-Sat 9:00-20:00, Sun 11:00-19:00, San Polo 414, see map on page 125).

Neighborhood Deli near the Accademia Bridge: A small deli hides along the main route between the Accademia and St. Mark's Square (at #2512, on the zigzag bridge near the Church of Santa Maria Zobenigo/del Giglio—see map on page 131).

Produce Stands: Many squares have a dedicated produce stand. To find the one nearest St. Mark's Square, face St. Mark's Basilica, then walk along its left side, heading east down Calle de la Canonica. Cross the bridge and turn left at Campo Santi Filippo e Giacomo. There are also stands on Campo Santa Maria Formosa and Campo Santa Margherita.

Supermarket near St. Mark's Square: A handy (but often mobbed) **Co-op** supermarket is between St. Mark's and Campo Santa Maria Formosa, on the corner of Salizada San Lio and Calle del Mondo Novo at #5817. It has a great selection of picnic supplies, including packaged salads for €3 (daily 8:30-20:30).

Other Supermarkets: The largest supermarket in town is the **Co-op** at Piazzale Roma, next to the vaporetto stop at #504-507 (daily 8:30-20:00). It's an easy walk from the train station, as is the **Billa** supermarket on Campo San Felice (daily 8:00-23:00, along the Strada Nova between the train station and Rialto area, Cannaregio 3660). Another **Billa** supermarket is convenient for those staying in Dorsoduro: It's at #1492, as far west as possible on the Zattere embankment, by the San Basilio vaporetto stop and the cruise-ship docks (Mon-Sat 8:30-23:00, Sun 8:30-21:00).

Good Gelato Spots

You'll find good *gelaterie* in every Venetian neighborhood, offering one-scoop cones for about €1.50. Look for the words *artigianale* or *produzione propria*, which indicates that a shop makes its own gelato. All of these are open long hours daily.

The popular, inventive, upscale **Grom** ice-cream chain has three branches in Venice: on Campo San Barnaba at #2761 (beyond the Accademia Bridge); on the Strada Nova at #3844, not far from the Rialto; and on Campo dei Frari at #3006, facing the Frari Church (all open long hours daily). A competing gourmet gelato shop, **Gelatoteca Suso,** serves up delectable flavors such as fig and nut (next to recommended Rosticceria San Bartolomeo on Calle de la Bissa, San Marco 5453). **Il Doge,** on the big and bustling Campo Santa Margarita, has a wide range of homemade flavors, as well as Sicilian-style *granita* (slushy ice flavored with fresh fruit; Dorsoduro 3058a, tel. 041-523-4607).

On St. Mark's Square, two venerable cafés have gelato counters: **Gran Caffè Lavena** (April-Oct daily until 24:00, no gelato Nov-March, at #134) and **Todaro** (on the corner of the Piazzetta at #5, near the water and just under the column topped by St. Theodore slaying a crocodile).

Venice Connections

By Train

From Venice by Train to: Padua (2/hour, 30-50 minutes), **Vicenza** (2/hour, 45-75 minutes), **Verona** (2/hour, 1.25-1.75 hours), **Ravenna** (roughly hourly, 3-3.5 hours, transfer in Ferrara or Bologna), **Florence** (hourly, 2 hours, often crowded so make reservations), **Bolzano/Dolomites** (to Bolzano about hourly, 3-3.5 hours, transfer in Verona; catch bus from Bolzano into mountains), **Milan** (hourly, 2.5-3.5 hours), **Cinque Terre/Monterosso** (5/day, 6 hours, change in Milan), **Rome** (roughly hourly, 3.5 hours, also 1 night train, 9 hours with change in Verona), **Naples** (almost hourly, 5.5-7 hours with changes in Bologna or Rome), **Brindisi** (5/day, 9 hours, change in Rome or Bologna).

Note that these departures are operated by Trenitalia; a competing private rail company called Italo offers additional high-speed connections to major Italian cities (including **Padua, Bologna, Florence,** and **Rome**). While Italo is often cheaper (particularly if you book long in advance), it doesn't accept railpasses (for details on Italo, see page 1168 or visit www.italotreno.it).

International Destinations: Interlaken (5/day, 6-8.5 hours, 2-5 changes, no pleasant overnight option), **Luzern** (7/day, 6.5-7 hours, change in Milan and Arth-Goldau), **Bern** (3/day, 6 hours, change in Milan or Brig), **Munich** (4-6/day, 7 hours, change in Verona; 1 direct night train, 9 hours; most trains reservable only via www.bahn.de), **Salzburg** (5/day, 6-7 hours, 1-2 changes, 1 direct night train, 7 hours), **Paris** (2/day, 10-12 hours with change in Milan; 1 direct night train, 13.5 hours, reserve up to 4 months in advance, no railpasses accepted, www.thello.com), **Ljubljana** (2/day, 6.75 hours—buy ticket at train station, take bus from Piazzale Roma to Villach in Austria, then transfer to train; faster by direct DRD bus from Mestre—1/day, 3.75 hours, www.drd.si; also possible by private shuttle—see www.goopti.com), **Vienna** (4/day, 8-9 hours—same bus-to-train connection system as Ljubljana; 1 direct night train, 11 hours).

By Plane

Marco Polo is Venice's main airport. Some budget flights, including Ryanair, use the smaller airport in the nearby city of Treviso. (For more on budget carriers, see page 1183.)

Marco Polo Airport

Venice's small, modern airport is on the mainland shore of the lagoon, six miles north of the city (airport code: VCE). There's one sleek terminal, with a TI (daily 9:00-20:00), car-rental agencies, ATMs, a bank, and a few shops and eateries. For flight information, call 041-260-9260, visit www.veniceairport.com, or ask your hotel.

Getting Between the Airport and Venice

You can get between the airport and downtown Venice one of four ways:

• Alilaguna boats—Slowest trip, medium cost
• Water taxis—Fastest trip, most expensive
• Airport shuttle buses to Piazzale Roma (Venice's bus station)—Faster than Alilaguna, slower than water taxi, least expensive, requires change to vaporetto to reach most hotels
• Land taxi or private minivan to Piazzale Roma—Medium speed, medium cost, requires change to vaporetto to reach most hotels

Each of these options is explained in detail here. An advantage of the Alilaguna boats is that you can reach most of this book's recommended hotels very simply, with no changes—except hotels near the train station, which are better served by the bus to Piazzale Roma.

Both Alilaguna boats and water taxis leave from the airport's boat dock, an eight-minute walk from the terminal. Exit the arrivals hall and turn left, following signs along a paved, level, covered sidewalk (easy for wheeled bags).

When flying out of Venice, allow yourself plenty of time to get to the airport. Water transport can be slow. Plan to arrive at the airport two hours before your flight, and remember that getting there can easily take up to two hours. Alilaguna boats are small and can fill up. In an emergency, you can always hop in a water taxi and get to the airport in 30 minutes.

Alilaguna Airport Boats

These boats make the scenic (if slooooow) journey across the lagoon, each shuttling passengers between the airport and a number of different stops on the island of Venice (€15, €27 round-trip, €1 surcharge if bought on boat, roughly 2/hour, 1-1.5-hour trip depending on destination). Alilaguna boats are not part of the ACTV vaporetto system, so they aren't covered by city transit passes. But they do use the same docks and ticket windows as the regular *vaporetti*.

There are two Alilaguna lines—blue and orange—which take about the same amount of time to reach St. Mark's Square. From the airport, the **blue line** *(linea blu)* heads first to Fondamente Nove (on the "back" of Venice's fish, 40 minutes), then loops around the "tail" of the fish to San Zaccaria and San Marco (about 1.5 hours) before continuing on to Zattere and the cruise terminal (almost 2 hours). The **orange line** *(linea arancio)* runs down the Grand Canal, reaching Guglie (handy for Cannaregio hotels, 45 minutes), Rialto (1 hour), and San Marco (1.25 hours). For a full schedule, visit the TI, see the website (www.alilaguna.it), call 041-240-1701, ask your hotelier, or scan the schedules posted at the docks.

From the Airport to Venice: You can buy Alilaguna tickets at the airport's TI, the ticket desk in the terminal, and at the ticket booth at the dock. Any ticket seller can tell you which line to catch to get to your destination. Boats from the airport run roughly twice an hour (blue line from 6:10, orange line from 8:00, both run until about midnight).

From Venice to the Airport: Ask your hotelier what dock and what line is best. Blue-line boats start leaving Venice as early as 3:40 in the morning for passengers with early flights. Scope out the dock and buy your ticket in advance to avoid last-minute stress.

Water Taxis

Luxury taxi speedboats zip directly between the airport and the closest dock to your hotel, getting you to within steps of your final destination in about 30 minutes. The official price is €115 for up to four people; add €10 for every extra person (10-passenger limit). You may get a higher quote—politely talk it down. A taxi can be a smart investment for small groups and those with an early departure.

From the airport, arrange your ride at the water-taxi desk or with the boat captains lounging at the dock. From Venice, book your taxi trip the day before you leave. Your hotel will help (since they get a commission), or you can book direct with the Consorzio Motoscafi water taxi association (tel. 041-522-2303, www.motoscafivenezia.it).

Airport Shuttle Buses

Buses between the airport and Venice are fast, frequent, and cheap. They take you across the bridge from the mainland to the island, dropping you at Venice's bus station, at the "mouth" of the fish on a square called Piazzale Roma. From there, you can catch a vaporetto down the Grand Canal—convenient for hotels near the Rialto Bridge and St. Mark's Square. If you're staying near the train station, you can walk from Piazzale Roma to your hotel.

Two bus companies run between Piazzale Roma and the airport: ATVO and ACTV. ATVO buses take 20 minutes and go nonstop. ACTV buses make a few stops en route and take slightly longer (30 minutes). They are equally good; just jump on whichever one's leaving next (either bus: €6, runs about 5:00-24:00, 2/hour, drops to 1/hour early and late, check schedules at www.atvo.it or www.actv.it).

From the Airport to Venice: Both buses leave from just outside the arrivals terminal. Buy tickets from the TI, the ticket desk in the terminal, ticket machines, or the driver. ATVO tickets are not valid on ACTV buses and vice versa. Double-check the destination; you want Piazzale Roma. If taking ACTV, you want bus #5.

From Venice to the Airport: At Piazzale Roma, buy your ticket from the ACTV windows or ATVO office before heading out to the platforms. The newsstand in the center of the lot also sells tickets. ACTV buses leave from platform A1; ATVO buses leave from platforms near the center of the lot and are well-signed.

Land Taxi or Private Minivan

It takes about 20 minutes to drive from the airport to Piazzale Roma. A **land taxi** can get you from the airport to Piazzale Roma for about €40. **Treviso Car Service** offers a private minivan service between the airport and Piazzale Roma or the cruise port (minivan-€55, seats up to 8; car-€50, seats up to 3; mobile 348-900-0700 or 333-411-2840, www.tourleadervenice.com, info@tourleader-venice.com). They also offer transfers to Treviso airport (see below), as well as guided tours (see page 74).

Treviso Airport

Several budget airlines, such as Ryanair, Wizz Air, and German-wings, use Treviso Airport, 12 miles northwest of Venice (airport code: TSF, tel. 042-231-5111, www.trevisoairport.it). The fastest option into Venice (Tronchetto parking lot) is on the **Barzi express bus,** which does the trip in just 40 minutes (€7, buy tickets on board, 1-2/hour, www.barziservice.com). From Tronchetto, hop on the People Mover monorail to Piazzale Roma for €1. **ATVO buses** are a bit more frequent and drop you right at Piazzale Roma (saving you the People Mover ride), but take nearly twice as long because they make more stops (€7, about 2/hour, 1.25 hours, www.atvo.it; buy tickets at the ATVO desk in the airport and stamp them on the bus). **Treviso Car Service** offers minivan service to Piazzale Roma (minivan-€75, seats up to 8; car-€65, seats up to 3; for contact info, see listing above).

By Cruise Ship

More than 1.5 million passengers visit Venice by cruise ship every year. For more detailed port arrival instructions and sightseeing tips tailored to arriving cruise passengers, consider my guidebook, *Rick Steves' Mediterranean Cruise Ports.*

Most cruise ships visiting Venice dock at **Stazione Marittima** (also called Terminal Crociere, Venezia Terminal Passeggeri, or VTP), which is roughly between the Tronchetto parking garage and Santa Lucia train station. The terminal forms "the fish's mouth" of Venice. Some smaller ships also tie up at the Santa Marta and San Basilio docks, to the south of the main port. The Venice port website has a map of the different docks (www.port.venice.it/en/terminals.html).

The main cruise port consists of one long, wide, rectangular pier and a narrower, adjacent pier; together these form a harbor. There are six terminal buildings: #117 (along the north side of the main pier), #107 and #108 (along the south/harbor side of the main pier), #103 (at the top of the harbor), and Isonzo 1 and Isonzo 2 (along the narrower pier, used mostly by the MSC cruise line).

Wherever you arrive, the best strategy is to make your way to terminal #103 (the long, low-slung, modern, red building with the tall gray tower in the middle) at the top of the harbor. The water-front strip in front of this terminal includes the dock for both *vaporetti* and taxi boats; the People Mover monorail is a five-minute walk beyond this building.

VENICE

Getting into Town

The handy Alilaguna express boat (blue line) conveniently connects the cruise port directly to St. Mark's Square (San Marco-Giardinetti dock) in just 30 minutes (€8 one-way, €15 round-trip, €3/big bag, 2/hour in each direction; before boarding at the cruise terminal, buy ticket at kiosk in front of building #103; www.alilaguna. it). Because this service is understandably popular, the boats can fill up; if you're arriving on a cruise ship, get to this dock as quickly as possible.

To reach the Grand Canal (and the start of my self-guided Grand Canal Cruise) from Stazione Marittima, take your cruise line's free shuttle bus, if offered, or hop on the People Mover (€1) to Piazzale Roma. The People Mover station is a five-minute walk inland from the port (you'll see its elevated platform).

If money is no object, you can spring for a water taxi to anywhere in town (€70-80).

If all of these options are jammed up (as can happen when multiple cruise ships arrive all at once), you can walk to the Grand Canal in about 15 minutes, or all the way to St. Mark's Square in about 45 minutes.

If your ship arrives at the Santa Marta or San Basilio docks, take vaporetto #2 from San Basilio to get downtown.

Getting to Marco Polo Airport

Buses between Piazzale Roma and the airport are quick and inexpensive (described earlier). From the cruise port, take the People Mover to Piazzale Roma to catch the airport bus. To go from Stazione Marittima to the airport, you can also take a land taxi (€40) or the Alilaguna blue line (€15, 1.25 hours). From the Santa Marta or San Basilio docks, you can take a land taxi to the airport (€40).

NEAR VENICE

Padua • Verona • Ravenna

Venice is just one of many towns in the Italian region of Veneto (VEN-eh-toh), but few visitors venture off the lagoon. That's a shame, as there's much to see within a very short hop of Venice. The trip from Venice westward to Milan is a route strewn with temptations: the Dolomite peaks, Italy's famous lakes, and—closest to Venice—the important and worthwhile towns of **Padua, Verona,** and **Ravenna.** This trio of towns gives visitors a low-key slice of Italy that complements the intensity and earth-shaking (yet exhausting) sightseeing thrills of Venice, Florence, and Rome. If you can't make it to all three, pick the one that most interests you. Art lovers will want to head to Padua to see Giotto's celebrated Scrovegni Chapel, or to Ravenna for its sumptuous Byzantine mosaics. History buffs should see Verona's impressive Roman ruins. Verona is also the pick for star-crossed lovers retracing Romeo and Juliet's steps. Architecture fans could consider a quick trip to Palladio-designed Vicenza, located about halfway between Padua and Verona.

Spending a day as a side-trip from Venice or town-hopping between Venice and Milan is exciting and efficient. Padua and Verona are on the same train line and only 40-60 minutes apart. Connected by at least two trains per hour, they're easy to visit. Of the towns included in this chapter, only Ravenna (2.5 hours from Padua and 3-3.5 hours from Venice) is not on the main Venice-Milan train line.

If you're Padua-bound, remember that you need to reserve ahead to see the Scrovegni Chapel. Don't bother visiting Vicenza on a Monday, when many of the top sights are closed; in Verona, several sights don't open until 13:30 on Mondays.

Padua

Living under Venetian rule for four centuries seemed only to sharpen Padua's independent spirit. Nicknamed "The brain of Veneto,"

Padua (Padova in Italian) is home to the prestigious university (founded in 1222) that hosted Galileo, Copernicus, Dante, and Petrarch. Pilgrims know Padua as the home of the Basilica of St. Anthony, where the reverent line assembles to touch his tomb and ogle his remarkably intact lower jaw and tongue. And lovers of early-Renaissance art come here to make a pilgrimage of their own: to gaze at the remarkable frescoes of Giotto in the Scrovegni Chapel. But despite the fact that Padua's museums and churches hold their own in Italy's artistic big league, its hotels are reasonably priced, and the city doesn't feel touristy. Padua's old town center is elegantly arcaded, filled with students, and sprinkled with surprises, including some of Italy's most inviting squares for lingering over an *aperitivo* as the sun slowly dips low in the sky.

Planning Your Time: Padua in Six Hours

Day-trippers can do a quick but enjoyable blitz of Padua—including a visit to the Scrovegni Chapel—in six hours. Trains from Venice are cheap, take 30-50 minutes, and run frequently. Once in Padua, everything is a 10-minute walk or a quick tram ride apart.

Your Scrovegni Chapel reservation will dictate the order of your sightseeing (see "Reservations" on page 171). When planning your day, also consider these factors: The station has a reliable baggage check desk; the open-air markets are vibrant in the morning, dead in the evening; student life is best at the university late in the day; and the Basilica of St. Anthony is open all day, but the reliquary chapel closes midday, from 12:45 to 14:45.

Ideally, I'd do it this way: 9:00—market action and sightseeing in town center, 11:00—Basilica of St. Anthony, 13:00—lunch, 15:00—Scrovegni Chapel tour.

Orientation to Padua

Padua's main tourist sights lie on a north-south axis through the heart of the city, from the train station to Scrovegni Chapel to the market squares (the center of town) to the Basilica of St. Anthony. It's roughly a 10-minute walk between each of these sights, or about 30 minutes from end to end. Padua's wonderful, single tram line makes lacing things together quick and easy (see "Getting Around Padua," later).

Tourist Information

Padua has two TIs: in the **center** (in the alley behind Caffè Pedrocchi at Vicolo Cappellatto Pedrocchi 9, Mon-Sat 9:00-13:30 & 15:00-19:00, closed Sun, tel. 049-876-7927), and at the **train station** (Mon-Sat 9:15-19:00, Sun 9:00-12:30, tel. 049-875-2077). Be aware that one or both of these TIs may close in 2014 due to Italy's budget problems.

At any TI, pick up a map and the seasonal *Padova Today* entertainment listing (with a list of sights in the back). The TI's free I-PADova audio tour is creative and works well; you can download it to your smartphone or tablet for free from their website and follow any of the five routes in town (www.turismopadova.it; smart to print out audio tour map ahead of time). You can also borrow a device preloaded with the tour (leave ID as deposit).

The **Padova Card** includes entry to all the recommended sights—except the university's Anatomy Theater and the Oratory of St. George—and unlimited tram rides (€16/48 hours, €21/72 hours). The card covers the Scrovegni Chapel and Civic Museums, but you still need to make a reservation in advance to enter (€1 extra reservation fee). This pass only makes sense if you're visiting a covered sight in addition to the Scrovegni Chapel (for example, the Palazzo della Ragione)—and even then, it may only save you a euro or two. You can buy the card at TIs, at participating sights, and at the Scrovegni Chapel website (www.cappelladegliscrovegni.it; consider buying card when reserving chapel entry, then picking it up when checking in at chapel's ticket office).

Arrival in Padua

By Train: The efficient station is a user-friendly shopping mall with whatever you may need (Despar supermarket open daily 7:00-21:00). Along track 1 are WCs and baggage deposit (€3.87—yes,

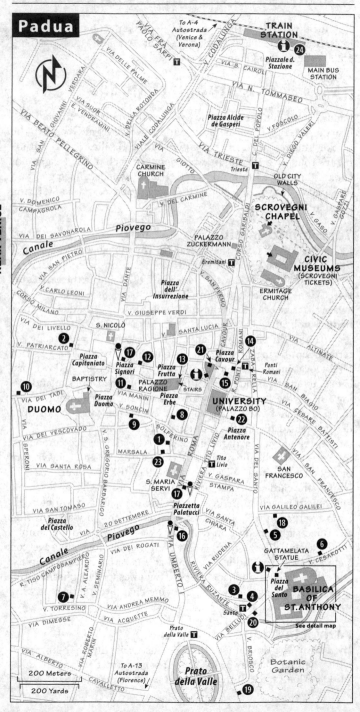

Padua

To A-4
Autostrada
(Venice &
Verona)

TRAIN STATION

24

Piazzale d.
Stazione

MAIN BUS
STATION

VIA FRA PAOLO SARPI

VIA DELLE PALME

V. CODALUNGA

VIA N. TOMMASEO

VIA B. CAIROLI

Piazza Alcide
de Gasperi

V. DIEGO VALERI

V. DEL TODOLO

VIA DELLA ROTONDA

VIALE CODALUNGA

VIA GIOTTO

VIA TRIESTE

Trieste

VIA SUOR E. VENDRAMINI

VIA SAN GIOVANNI VERDARA

VIA BEATO PELLEGRINO

CARMINE
CHURCH

VIA DEL CARMINE

OLD CITY
WALLS

SCROVEGNI
CHAPEL

V. GASPARE GOZZI

V. GASO

V. DOMENICO CAMPAGNOLA

VIA DEI SAVONAROLA

Piovego

Canale

VIA SAN PIETRO

PALAZZO
ZUCKERMANN

CORSO GARIBALDI

CIVIC
MUSEUMS
(SCROVEGNI
TICKETS)

Eremitani

CORSO MILANO

V. CARLO LEONI

VIA DANTE

Piazza
dell'
Insurrezione

V. SAN FERMO

ERMITAGE
CHURCH

VIA DEI LIVELLO

V. GIUSEPPE VERDI

S. NICOLÒ

V. SANTA LUCIA

2

V. PATRIARCATO

Piazza
Capitaniato

17   12

Piazza
Signori

BAPTISTRY

11

Piazza
Frutta

13

21

Piazza
Cavour

14

ZABARELLA

Ponti
Romani

VIA CAVOUR

FONTI ROMANI

VIA ALTINATE

VIA SAN BIAGIO

10

VIA DEI TADI

PALAZZO
RAGIONE

STAIRS

15

VIA CESARE BATTISTI

DUOMO

Piazza
Duomo

V. MANIN

V. SONCIN

Piazza
Erbe

8

UNIVERSITY
(PALAZZO BO)

V. S. GREGORIO BARBARIGO

VIA DEL VESCOVADO

9

SOLFERINO

22

Piazza
Antenore

VIA SANTA ROSA

MARSALA

1

ROMA

RIVIERA TITO LIVIO

Tito
Livio

SAN
FRANCESCO

VIA SAN FRANCESCO

VIA GALILEO GALILEI

B.SPERONI

23

S. MARIA
SERVI

17

V. GASPARA
STAMPA

VIA DEL SANTO

VIA SAN TOMASO

Piazza
del Castello

20 SETTEMBRE

Piazzetta
Palatucci

16

VIA SANTA
CHIARA

18

5

6

V. CESAROTTI

Piovego

Canale

VIA DEI ROGATI

VIA UMBERTO

RIVIERA RUZANTE

VIA RUDENA

GATTAMELATA
STATUE

R. TISO CAMPOSAMPIERO

V. A. ALEARDO

VIA SEMINARIO

3

4

Piazza
del Santo

BASILICA
OF ST.
ANTHONY

See detail map

7

V. TORRESINO

VIA ANDREA MEMMO

Santo

20

VIA DIMESSE

VIA ACQUETTE

Prato
della Valle

BRIOSCO

Botanic
Garden

200 Meters

VIA ALBERTO

VIA ROBERTO MARIN

CAVALLETTO

To A-13
Autostrada
(Florence)

Prato
della Valle

19

200 Yards

Padua Key

1. Hotel Majestic Toscanelli
2. Albergo Verdi
3. Hotel Al Fagiano
4. Hotel Belludi 37
5. Hotel Al Santo & Antica Trattoria dei Paccagnella
6. Hotel/Rist. Casa del Pellegrino
7. Ostello Città di Padova
8. Osteria dei Fabbri
9. Osteria L'Anfora
10. Enoteca dei Tadi
11. Rist. Dante alle Piazze
12. La Lanterna Ristorante
13. Bar dei Osei
14. Brek Cafeteria
15. PAM Supermarket & Brek
16. Gelato Pretto
17. Gelateria Grom (2)
18. Pizzeria Pago Pago
19. Zairo Rist./Pizzeria
20. Pollodoro la Gastronomica
21. Caffè Pedrocchi
22. Feltrinelli's Int'l Bookstore
23. Launderette
24. Buses to Venice & Marco Polo Airport

NEAR VENICE

that's right, they're stubbornly sticking with the exact lire-to-euro conversion from 2002; daily 6:30-18:00, bring photo ID).

For a travel agency, go to **Leonardi Viaggi-Turismo,** which is only a block from the station and offers ticketing services for trains, planes, and boats for a small fee (Mon-Fri 9:00-13:00 & 14:30-19:00, Sat 9:00-13:00, closed Sun, up the main drag, Corso del Popolo 14, tel. 049-650-455).

To get downtown, simply hop on Padua's handy **tram** (see "Getting Around Padua" on page 164). Purchase your ticket (€1.20) at one of the shops inside the station. Leaving the station, the tram stop is 100 yards to the right at the foot of the bridge. A **taxi** into town (a good option after dark) costs about €8-10.

By Bus: The bus station is 100 yards east of the train station. Buses arrive here from Venice's Piazzale Roma and Marco Polo Airport.

Helpful Hints

Pronunciation: You say Padua (PAD-joo-wah), they say Padova (PAH-doh-vah). The city's top sight, Scrovegni Chapel, is pronounced skroh-VEHN-yee.

Internet Access: All of the hotels I list offer free Wi-Fi. Padua has few Internet cafés (ask your hotel for the nearest). The central TI has an Internet point where you can get online for 15 minutes (free, fill out a form and show your passport).

Bookstore: Feltrinelli's International Bookstore, with books in English, is one block from the main university building (Mon-Sat 9:00-19:30, Sun 10:00-13:00 & 15:30-20:00, Via San Francesco 7, tel. 049-875-4630).

Launderette: Lavami is modern and entirely automated (€5/wash,

€4/dry, daily 7:00-22:00, Via Marsala 22 near intersection with Via dell'Arco, tel. 049-876-4532).

Local Guide: Charming and helpful **Cristina Pernechele** is a great teacher (€110/half-day, mobile 338-495-5453, cristina@pernechele.eu).

Getting Around Padua

Ignore the city buses; pretend there is only the **tram** and rely on it. There's just one line, which efficiently and without stress connects everything you care about (€1.20 ticket good for 1.25 hours; buy tickets from machines at stops, tobacco shops, or newsstands; departs every 8 minutes during the day Mon-Sat, every 20 minutes evenings and Sun). The rubber-wheeled trams run on a single rail.

Before boarding, note the tram direction on posted schedules and above the front window (Pontevigodarzere is northbound, Capolinia Sud is southbound). Stops that matter to tourists include: Stazione FS (train and bus stations), Eremitani (Scrovegni Chapel), Ponti Romani (old town center, market squares, university), Tito Livio (ghetto, old town center, Hotel Majestic Toscanelli), Santo (Basilica of St. Anthony and neighborhood hotels), and Prato della Valle (hostel).

Padua's **hop-on, hop-off tour buses** are not worth the time or money.

Sights in Padua

Sights in the Center

Padua's two main sights (Basilica of St. Anthony and Scrovegni Chapel) are, respectively, at the southern and northern reaches of downtown. But its atmospheric, cobbled core—with bustling markets, vibrant student life, and inviting sun-and-café-speckled piazzas—is its own ▲▲▲ attraction. You could simply stroll the area aimlessly, or seek out some of the following spots.

▲▲Market Squares: Piazza delle Erbe, Piazza della Frutta, and Piazza dei Signori

The stately Palazzo della Ragione (described later) provides a dramatic backdrop for Padua's almost exotic-feeling produce market that fills the surrounding squares—**Piazza delle Erbe** and **Piazza della Frutta**—each morning and all day Saturday (Mon-Fri roughly 8:00-13:00, Sat 8:00-19:00 but a bit quieter in the afternoon, closed Sun). Second only to the produce market in Italy's gastronomic capital of Bologna, this market has been renowned for centuries as having the freshest and greatest selection of herbs, fruits, and vegetables. The presentation is an art in itself. As you wander, appreciate the local passion for good food: Residents can tell the month by the seasonal selections, and merchants share recipe tips with shoppers. You'll notice quite a few Sri Lankans working here (Italy took in many refugees from Sri Lanka's civil war).

Don't miss the **indoor market** zone on the ground floor of the Palazzo della Ragione. Wandering through this H-shaped arcade—where you'll find various butchers, *salumerie* (delicatessens), cheese shops, bakeries, and fishmongers at work—is a sensuous experience. For centuries, this was a market for luxury items (furs, fine fabrics, silver, and gold—notice the imposing iron gates used to lock it up each evening). Then, the devastating loss to the French in 1797 marked the end of good times, and with no market for luxury items, the arcade was used to sell perishables—meat and cheese—out of the sun.

Students gather in the squares after the markets have closed, spilling out of colorful bars and cafés, drinks in hand. Pizza by the slice is dirt cheap. For pointers on a recommended local sandwich stand, **Bar dei Osei,** and a neighboring seafood-snack stand, see page 188. Just a few steps away from these is a classic old pharmacy that dates to 1841: The licorice-perfumed **Ai Due Cantini d'Oro,** which stocks retail items like it did before World War II, sells odd foods and specialty items for every dietary need (Piazza della Frutta 46, tel. 049-875-0623).

Piazza dei Signori, just a block away, is a busy clothing market in the morning and the most popular gathering place in the

evening for students out for a drink (see next listing). The circa-1400 clock decorates the former palace of the ruling family. The aggressive lion with unfurled wings on the column was a reminder of the Venetian determination to assert its control. Today that lion can be seen as representing the Veneto region's independence from Rome: Italy's North (Veneto and Lombardy) is tired of subsidizing the South. Grumbling about this issue continues to stir talk of splitting the country.

Drinking a *Spritz* with the Student Crowd
Each early evening, before dinner, students enliven Padua by enjoying a convivial drink in their favorite places. Piazza dei Signori is trendier, with people of all ages, while the scene on Piazza della Erbe is more bohemian and alternative. Or you could sit in front

NEAR VENICE

of the university, nurse your drink, and watch the graduates get roasted with their crazy gangs of friends (see "Graduation Antics in Padua" sidebar, later).

The drink of choice is a *spritz*, an aperitif generally made with Campari (a red liqueur infused with bitter herbs), white wine, and sparkling water, and garnished with a blood-orange wedge. Traditionally, men opt for the heavier and bitterer Campari *spritz*, while women prefer a sweeter and lighter *spritz* made with Aperol (an orange-flavored liqueur with less alcohol content).

Grab a table and be part of the scene. This is a classic opportunity to enjoy a real discussion with smart, English-speaking students who see tourists not as pests, but as interesting people from far away. For an instant conversation starter, ask about the current political situation in Italy, the right-wing party's policy on immigrants, or the cultural differences between Italy's North and South.

Palazzo della Ragione

Looming over Padua's two big central market squares (Piazza delle

Erbe and Piazza della Frutta), this grand 13th-century palazzo—commonly called *il Salone* (the great hall)—once held the medieval law courts. Its first floor consists of a huge hall— 265 feet by 90 feet—that was at one time adorned with frescoes by Giotto. A fire in 1412 destroyed those paintings, and the palazzo was redecorated with the 15th-century art you see today: a series of 333 frescoes depicting the signs of the zodiac, labors of the month, symbols representing characteristics of people born under each sign, and, finally, figures of saints to legitimize the power of the courts in the eyes of the Church.

The hall is topped with a hull-shaped roof, which helps to support the structure without the use of columns—quite an architectural feat in its day, considering the building's dimensions. The biggest thing in the hall is the giant, very anatomically correct horse. Its prominent placement represents the pride locals feel for the Veneto's own highly respected breed of horse. (After the bronze ones in St. Mark's Basilica, these are the favorite horses in the region.) The curious black stone in the corner opposite the big wooden horse is the "Stone of Shame," which was the seat of debtors being punished during the Middle Ages. It was introduced as a compassionate alternative to prison by St. Anthony in 1230. Instead of being executed or doing prison time, debtors sat upon this stone, surrendered their possessions, and denounced themselves publicly before being exiled from the city. The computer kiosks provide excellent information with entertaining videos.

Cost and Hours: €4, more during special exhibitions; Feb-Oct Tue-Sun 9:00-19:00, Nov-Jan Tue-Sun 9:00-18:00, closed Mon year-round; enter through the east end of Piazza delle Erbe and go up the long staircase, Ponti Romani tram stop, tel. 049-820-5006. The WCs are through the glass doors at the opposite end of the hall from the wooden horse.

Caffè Pedrocchi

The white-columned, Neoclassical Pedrocchi building is much more than just a café on the ground floor. A complex of meeting rooms and entertainment venues, it stirs the Italian soul (or the patriotic Italian soul, at least). Built in 1831 during the period of Austrian rule, Caffè Pedrocchi was inaugurated for the fourth Italian Congress of Scientists, which convened during the mid-19th century to stir up nationalistic fervor as Italy struggled to become a united nation. As a symbol of patriotic hope, it was the target (no surprise) of a student uprising plot in 1848.

Each of the café's three dining rooms is decorated and furnished in a different color (denoted by the hue of velvet on the chairs): red, white, or green—representing the colors of the Italian flag. In the outer, unheated Sala Verde (Green Room), people are welcome to sit and relax without ordering anything or having to pay. This is where Italian gentlemen read their newspapers and gather with friends to chat about the old days. In the Sala Rossa (Red Room), the clock over the bar is flanked by marble reliefs of morning and night, signaling that it was once open 24 hours a day (in the 19th century). In the rooms on either side, the maps of the hemispheres with south up top reflect the anticonventional spirit of the place. The menu offers teahouse fare, including €13 salads, €7.50 sandwiches, and the writer Stendhal's beloved *zabaglione*, a creamy custard made with *marsala* wine. Remember that in Italy, you can order a basic coffee standing up at the bar of any place, no matter how fancy, and pay the same low, government-regulated price. In the Sala Bianca (White Room), you can still see a bullet hole (framed in tarnished silver) in the wall, where one of the insurgents in that ill-fated 1848 uprising was killed.

Cost and Hours: Café interior free, Sun-Tue 9:00-21:00, Wed-Sat 9:00-23:00, two entrances across from Via VIII Febbraio 14 and 20 near Ponti Romani tram stop, tel. 049-878-1231.

Piano Nobile: To see the café's even more elaborate upstairs, you can pay to enter this "noble floor" of the Pedrocchi building (€4, Tue-Sun 9:30-12:30 & 15:30-18:00, closed Mon; to find entrance, head outside to Piazza Cavour, face café, and go through the door on the right; tel. 049-878-1231). Each room is a different style, such as Greek, Etruscan, or Egyptian, with good English descriptions throughout. These rooms were intended to evoke memories of the glory of past epochs, which a united Italy had hopes of reliving.

The Piano Nobile also hosts the small **Museum of the Risorgimento,** which traces Padua's role in Italian history, from the downfall of the Venetian Republic (1797) to the founding of the Republic of Italy (1948). Exhibits, a few with English descriptions, include uniforms, medals, weaponry, old artillery, Fascist propaganda posters, and a 30-minute propagandistic video (in Italian, but mostly fascinating footage without narration). The video, played on demand, is a "Luce" production (meaning a Mussolini production) and features great scenes of the town in the 1930s, including clips of Il Duce's visit and later WWII bombardments. The war and propaganda posters in the last room are haunting. An old woman pleads to those who question the Fascist-driven war effort: "Don't betray my son." Another declares, "The Germans are truly our friends." And another asks, "And you...what are *you* doing?"

University of Padua

The main building of this prestigious university, known as Palazzo Bò, is adjacent to Caffè Pedrocchi. Founded in 1222, it's one of the first, greatest, and most progressive universities in Europe. Back when the Church controlled university curricula, a group of professors and students broke free from the University of Bologna to create this liberal school, which would be independent of Catholic constraints and accessible to people of alternative faiths.

A haven for free thought, the university attracted intellectuals from all over Europe, including the great astronomer Copernicus, who realized here that the universe didn't revolve around him. And Galileo—notorious for disagreeing with the Church's views on science—called his 18 years on the faculty here the best of his life.

Cost and Hours: While it's free to visit the university (weekdays and Sat mornings only), you must sign up for a 30-minute tour (€5) to see the Anatomy Theater. Only 30 people may enter at a time. Tours run three times a day (March-Oct Mon, Wed, and Fri at 15:15, 16:15, and 17:15; Tue, Thu, and Sat at 9:15, 10:15, and 11:15; no tours on Sun, reduced schedule Nov-Feb—call number below, Ponti Romani tram stop, www.unipd.it). School groups often book the entire visit, and many of the guides do not speak English.

Confirm tour times and availability by calling 049-827-3047 or stopping by the ticket window (opens 15 minutes before each tour, located just inside the palace, in the hall reached from the

Graduation Antics in Padua

With 60,000 students, Padua's university always seems to be hosting graduation ceremonies. There's a constant trickle of happy grads and their friends and families celebrating the big event.

During the school year, every 20 minutes or so, a student steps into a formal room (upstairs, above the university courtyard) to officially meet with the leading professors of his or her faculty. When they're finished, the students are given a green laurel wreath. They pose for ceremonial group photos and family snapshots. It's a sweet scene. Then, craziness takes over.

The new graduates replace their somber clothing with raunchy outfits, as gangs of friends gather around them on Via VIII Febbraio, the street in front of the university. The roast begins. The gang rolls out a giant butcher-paper poster with a generally obscene caricature of the student and a litany of *This Is Your Life* photos and stories. The new grad, subject to various embarrassing pranks, reads the funny statements out loud. The poster is then taped to the university wall for all to see. (Find the plastic panels to the right of the main entry, facing Via VIII Febbraio. Graduation posters are allowed to stay there for 24 hours. The panels are emptied each morning, but by nighttime a new set of posters is affixed to the plastic shields.)

During the roast, the friends sing the catchy but obscene local university anthem, reminding their newly esteemed friend not to get too huffy: *Dottore, dottore, dottore del buso del cul. Vaffancul, vaffancul* (loosely translated, "Doctor, doctor. You're just a doctor of the a-hole...go f-off, go f-off"). After you've heard this song (with its fanfare and oom-pah-pah catchiness) and have seen all the good-natured fun, you can't stop singing it.

The crazy show is usually staged late in the afternoon. Outdoor café tables afford great seats to enjoy the spectacle.

Fascist-era courtyard described next). The bar there is fun for a cheap drink and to see photos of university life.

Visiting the University: The gawking public is not really welcomed in the university, but on weekdays and Saturday mornings, you can poke into two **courtyards** (when closed, just peer through the gate). Find the entrance at Via VIII Febbraio 7, under the "Gymnasium" inscription (30 yards from Caffè Pedrocchi, facing City Hall). You'll pop into a 16th-century courtyard, the school's historic core. It's littered with the coats of arms of important faculty and leaders of the university over the ages. Classrooms, which open onto the square, are still used. Today, students gather here, surrounded by memories of illustrious alumni, including the first woman in the world to receive a university degree (in 1678).

A passageway leads from here to an adjacent second courtyard from the Fascist era (c. 1938). The relief celebrates heroic students in World War I. Off of this courtyard, notice the richly decorated stairway, frescoed Fascist-style in the 1930s with themes celebrating art, science, and the pursuit of knowledge.

The big attraction among tourists is Europe's first great **Anatomy Theater** (from 1594), which you can visit

only on a guided tour. Try to get a ticket, but keep in mind that it's not worth any heroics to see. The first two rooms of the tour are underwhelming: One features the supposed "pulpit of Galileo" (c. 1550) and portraits of 40 famous alums. The second is the Aula Magna, a ceremonial room for festivities. The historic Anatomy Theater itself is more impressive. Despite the Church's strict ban on autopsies, more than 300 students would pack this theater to watch professors dissect human cadavers (the bodies of criminals from another town). This had to be done in a "don't ask, don't tell" kind of way, because the Roman Catholic Church only started allowing the teaching of anatomy through dissection in the late 1800s.

▲Baptistery

This richly frescoed little building was originally the private chapel of Padua's ruling family. Then, in 1405, Venice took over, killing the family, and making the building a baptistery. Located next to Padua's skippable Duomo, the Baptistery was frescoed (c. 1370) by Giusto de' Menabuoi.

Although the Baptistery was created 70 years after Giotto, it feels older. Because de' Menabuoi was working for a private family, he needed to be politically correct and not threaten or offend the family's allies—especially the Church. While still mind-blowing, the Baptistery's art seems relatively conservative compared to Giotto's Scrovegni Chapel. Giotto, supported by the powerful Scrovegni family and the Franciscans, could get away with being more progressive and bold.

The Baptistery's complex design must have made perfect and cohesive sense to the faithful in centuries past. Almighty Christ is in majesty on top, while approachable Mary and the multitude of saints provide the devout with access to God. Find the world as it was known in the 14th century (the disk below Mary's feet). It kicks off a cycle of scenes illustrating creation (clockwise from the creation of Adam). The four evangelists (Matthew, Mark, Luke, and John) with their books and symbols fill the corners. A vivid crucifixion scene faces a gorgeous annunciation. And the altar niche features a dim, blue-toned, literal Apocalypse from the book of Revelation.

Cost and Hours: €2.80, daily 10:00-18:00, on Piazza Duomo.

▲▲▲Scrovegni Chapel (Cappella degli Scrovegni) and Civic Museums

Wallpapered with Giotto's beautifully preserved cycle of nearly 40 frescoes, the glorious, renovated Scrovegni Chapel holds scenes de-

picting the lives of Jesus and Mary. You must make reservations in advance to see the chapel. Scrovegni Chapel tickets also cover the Civic Museums, featuring the worthwhile Pinacoteca and Multimedia Room, as well as the skippable Archaeological Museum and the little-visited Palazzo Zuckermann.

Cost and Hours: The €13 ticket covers the Scrovegni Chapel and Civic Museums. Chapel tickets drop to €8 when most of the museums are closed (after 19:00 and on Monday). It's €10 for just the museums. The **chapel** is open March-Oct Mon 9:00-19:00, Tue-Sun 9:00-22:00; Nov-Feb daily 9:00-19:00; tel. 049-201-0020, www.cappelladegliscrovegni.it. The **Pinacoteca** and **Archaeological Museum** are open Tue-Sun 9:00-19:00, closed Mon; the **Multimedia Room** is open daily 9:00-19:00; **Palazzo Zuckermann** is open Tue-Sun 10:00-19:00, closed Mon; museums tel. 049-820-4551, palazzo tel. 049-820-5664.

Chapel Entry Times: To protect the paintings from excess humidity, only 25 people are allowed in the chapel at a time. Every 15 minutes (on the quarter-hour), a new group is admitted for a 15-minute video presentation in an anteroom, followed by 15 minutes in the chapel itself. After 19:00, visitors can enter every 20 minutes and get 20 minutes inside (last entry at 21:40).

Reservations: Prepaid reservations are required. It's wise to reserve at least two days in advance. It's easiest to reserve online at www.cappelladegliscrovegni.it (website also sells Padova Cards—described on page 161, tel. 049-201-0020).

NEAR VENICE

Without a reservation, it's sometimes possible to buy a ticket for the same day at the ticket office (especially for single visitors), but don't count on it. If you neglected to make a reservation and really want to see the chapel, drop by and see if anything is available (a Post-it note stuck to the desk indicates the next available entry time). Tickets for daytime visits are generally released at 9:00, and for evening visits at 17:00 (or at 16:00 on Sun); showing up at one of these times will increase your chances of getting a slot (likely for later in the day). You can't book next-day reservations in person—only online or by phone. Local tour guides, who have to book blocks of tickets, are generally happy to unload unneeded tickets to those who ask.

Helpful Hint: If you packed binoculars, bring them along for a better—and more comfortable—view of the uppermost frescoes. No photos are allowed.

Getting There: From the train station, it's a 10- to 15-minute walk, or a quick, two-stop tram ride to the Eremitani stop.

Getting In: To reach the chapel, enter through the Eremitani building, where you'll find the museums, ticket office, and a free but mandatory bag check. Though you're instructed to pick up your tickets at the ticket office at least one hour before your visit, in practice, I've found that you can arrive later. Still, give yourself a minimum of 30 minutes to weather any commotion at the desk. Present your confirmation number at the ticket desk, verify your time, pick up your ticket, and check any bags or purses.

While waiting for your reserved time, blitz the Pinacoteca and Multimedia Room (described later). Read the chapel description before you enter, since you'll only have a short time in the chapel itself.

The chapel is well-signed: From the ticket office, go outside and walk 100 yards down the path, passing some ruins of Roman Padua (described later). Be at the chapel doors at least five minutes before your scheduled visit. The doors are automatic, and if you're even a minute late, you'll forfeit your visit and have to rebook and repay to enter.

At your appointed time, you first enter an anteroom to watch a very instructive 15-minute video (with English subtitles) and to establish humidity levels before continuing into the chapel. Although you have only a short visit inside the chapel, it is divine. You're inside a Giotto time capsule, looking back at an artist ahead of his time.

Scrovegni Chapel

Painted by Giotto and his assistants from 1303 to 1305 and considered by many to be the first piece of modern art, this work makes it

Scrovegni Chapel

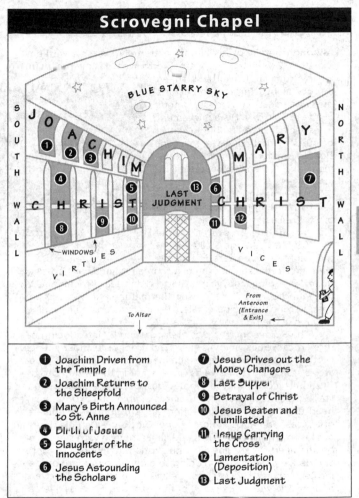

BLUE STARRY SKY

SOUTH WALL

NORTH WALL

J O A C H I M

M A R Y

C H R I S T

C H R I S T

LAST JUDGMENT

VIRTUES

VICES

WINDOWS

To Altar

From Anteroom (Entrance & Exit)

① Joachim Driven from the Temple

② Joachim Returns to the Sheepfold

③ Mary's Birth Announced to St. Anne

④ Birth of Jesus

⑤ Slaughter of the Innocents

⑥ Jesus Astounding the Scholars

⑦ Jesus Drives out the Money Changers

⑧ Last Supper

⑨ Betrayal of Christ

⑩ Jesus Beaten and Humiliated

⑪ Jesus Carrying the Cross

⑫ Lamentation (Deposition)

⑬ Last Judgment

clear: Europe was breaking out of the Middle Ages. A sign of the Renaissance to come, Giotto placed real people in real scenes, expressing real human emotions. These frescoes were radical for their 3-D nature, lively colors, light sources, emotion, and humanism.

The chapel was built out of guilt for white-collar crimes. Reginaldo degli Scrovegni (skroh-VEHN-yee) charged sky-high interest rates at a time when the Church forbade the practice. He even caught the attention of Dante, who placed him in one of the levels of hell in his *Inferno*. When Reginaldo died, the Church denied him a Christian burial. His son Enrico tried to buy forgiveness for his father's sins by building this superb chapel. After seeing

Giotto di Bondone (c. 1267-1337)

Although details of his life are extremely sketchy, we know that the 12-year-old shepherd Giotto was discovered painting pictures of his father's sheep on rock slabs. He grew to become the wealthiest and most famous painter of his day. His achievement is especially remarkable because painters at that time weren't considered anything more than craftsmen—and weren't expected to be innovators.

After making a name for himself by painting frescoes of the life of St. Francis in Assisi, the Florentine tackled the Scrovegni Chapel (c. 1303-1305). At age 35, he was at the height of his powers. His scenes were more realistic and human than anything that had been done for a thousand years. Giotto didn't learn technique by dissecting corpses or studying the mathematics of 3-D perspective; he had innate talent. And his personality shines through in the humanity of his art.

The Scrovegni frescoes break ground by introducing nature—rocks, trees, animals—as a backdrop for religious scenes. Giotto's people, with their voluminous, deeply creased robes, are as sturdy and massive as Greek statues, throwbacks to the Byzantine icon art of the Middle Ages. But these figures exude stage presence. Their gestures are simple but expressive: A head tilted down says dejection, an arm flung out indicates grief, clasped hands indicate hope. Giotto created his figures not just by drawing outlines and filling them in with single colors; he filled the outlines in with subtle patchworks of lighter and darker shades, and in doing so pioneered modern modeling techniques. Giotto's storytelling style is straightforward, and anyone with knowledge of the episodes of Jesus' life can read the chapel like a comic book.

The Scrovegni represents a turning point in European art and culture—away from scenes of heaven and toward a more down-to-earth, human-centered view.

Giotto's frescoes for the Franciscan monks of St. Anthony, Enrico knew he'd found the right artist to decorate the interior (and, he hoped, to save his father's soul). The Scrovegni residence once stood next to the chapel, but was torn down in 1824.

Giotto's Frescoes in the Scrovegni Chapel

Giotto painted the entire chapel in 200 working days over two years, but you'll get only 15 minutes to see it.

As you enter the long, narrow chapel, look straight to the far end—the rear wall is covered with Giotto's big *Last Judgment*. Christ in a bubble is flanked by crowds of saints and by scenes of heaven and hell. This is the final, climactic scene of the story told in the chapel's 38 panels—the three-generation history of Jesus, his mother Mary, and Mary's parents.

The story begins with Jesus' grandparents, on the long south wall (with the windows) in the upper-left corner. ❶ In the first frame, a priest scolds the man who will be Mary's father (Joachim, with the halo) and kicks him out of the temple for the sin of being childless. ❷ In the next panel to the right, Joachim returns dejectedly to his sheep farm. ❸ Meanwhile (next panel), his wife is in the bedroom, hearing the miraculous news that their prayers have been answered—she'll give birth to Mary, the mother of Jesus.

From this humble start, the story of Mary and Jesus spirals clockwise around the chapel, from top to bottom. The top row (both south and north walls) covers Mary's birth and life.

Jesus enters the picture in the middle row of the south (windowed) wall. ❹ The first frame shows his birth in a shed-like manger. In the next frame, the Magi arrive and kneel to kiss his little toes. Then the child is presented in the tiny temple. Fearing danger, the family gets on a horse and flees to Egypt. ❺ Meanwhile, back home, all the baby boys are slaughtered in an attempt to prevent the coming of the Messiah (*Slaughter of the Innocents*).

Spinning clockwise to the opposite (north) wall, you see (in a badly damaged fresco) ❻ the child Jesus astounding scholars with his wisdom. Next, Jesus is baptized by John the Baptist. His first miracle, at a wedding, is turning jars of water into wine. Next, he raises a mummy-like Lazarus from the dead. Riding a donkey, he enters Jerusalem triumphantly. ❼ In the temple, he drives out the wicked money changers.

Turning again to the south wall (bottom row), we see scenes from Jesus' final days. ❽ In the first frame, he and his followers gather at a table for a Last Supper. Next, Jesus kneels humbly to wash their feet. ❾ He is betrayed with a kiss and arrested. Jesus is tried. ❿ Then he is beaten and humiliated.

⓫ Finally (north wall, bottom row), he is forced to carry his own cross, is crucified, and prepared for burial, while his followers mourn (⓬ *Lamentation*). Then he is resurrected and ascends to heaven, leaving his disciples to carry on.

⓭ The whole story concludes on the rear wall, where Jesus reigns at the Last Judgment. The long south wall (ground level) features the Virtues that lead to heaven, while the north wall has the (always more interesting) Vices. And all this unfolds beneath the blue, starry sky overhead on the ceiling.

Some panels deserve a closer look:

Joachim Returns to the Sheepfold (south wall, upper left, second panel): Though difficult to appreciate from ground level, this oft-reproduced scene is groundbreaking. Giotto—a former shepherd himself—uses nature as a stage, setting the scene in front of a backdrop of real-life mountains, and adding down-home details like Joachim's jumping dog, frozen in midair.

Betrayal of Christ, a.k.a. *Il Bacio*, "The Kiss" (south wall, bottom row, center panel): Amid the crowded chaos of Jesus' arrest, Giotto skillfully creates a focus upon the central action, where Judas ensnares Jesus in his yellow robe (the color symbolizing envy), establishes meaningful eye contact, and kisses him.

Lamentation, a.k.a. *Deposition* (north wall, bottom row, middle): Jesus has been crucified, and his followers weep and wail over the lifeless body. John the Evangelist spreads his arms wide and shrieks, his cries echoed by anguished angels above. Each face is a study in grief. Giotto emphasizes these saints' human vulnerability.

Last Judgment (big west wall): Christ in the center is a glorious vision, but the real action is in hell (lower right). Satan is a Minotaur-headed ogre munching on sinners. Around him, demons give sinners their just desserts in a scene right out of Dante...who was Giotto's friend and fellow Florentine. Front and center is Enrico Scrovegni, in a violet robe (the color symbolizing penitence), donating the chapel to the Church in exchange for forgiveness of his father's sins.

Before the guard scoots you out, take a look at the actual altar. Though Enrico's father's tomb is lost, Enrico Scrovegni himself is in the tomb at the altar. The three statues are by Giovanni Pisano— Mary (in the center) supports baby Jesus on her hip with a perfectly natural, maternal, S-shape. She's flanked by anonymous deacons.

Nearby: Between the museum and the chapel are the scant remains of **Roman Padua**. The remnants are from the wall of an arena and nicely fitting pipes that once channeled water so that the arena could be flooded for special spectacles.

Civic Museums (Musei Civici Agli Eremitani)

The Eremitani, the building next to the Scrovegni Chapel, was once an Augustinian hermit's monastery and now houses several museums. While you can skip the ground-floor Archaeological Museum (with Roman and Etruscan artifacts and no English descriptions), the Pinacoteca and the Multimedia Room are worth visiting. Another part of the museum, Palazzo Zuckermann, is across the street.

Pinacoteca

The museum's highlight is upstairs, in the Pinacoteca (picture gallery). The collection has 13th- to 18th-century paintings by Titian, Tintoretto, Giorgione, Tiepolo, Veronese, Bellini, Canova, Guariento, and other Veneto artists. But I'd make a beeline for the room with the Giotto crucifix (upstairs and to the right, through the upper gallery). Ask for *"La Croce di Giotto?"* (lah KROH-cheh dee JOH-toh?).

Originally hung in the Scrovegni Chapel between the Scrovegni family's private zone and the public's worshipping zone, this crucifix is painted on wood by Giotto. If you actually sit on the floor and look up, the body really pops. The adjacent "God as Jesus" piece *(L'Eterno)* was the only painting in the otherwise frescoed chapel. (This is hung here because of preservation concerns. Its copy is the only non-original art in the chapel.) Studying these two masterpieces affirms Giotto's greatness.

Behind the crucifix room is a collection of 14th- and 15th-century art. While the works here are exquisite—and came well after Giotto—they're clearly not as modern.

Multimedia Room

Dedicated to taking a closer look at the Scrovegni Chapel, this small but interesting exhibit is downstairs. To head straight from the museum entrance to the Multimedia Room, use the entrance to the right of the main entry, step into the courtyard, make a sharp right, go through the glass doors at the end of the corridor, and head down the stairs.

Rows of computer screens offer a virtual Scrovegni Chapel visit and provide cultural insights into daily life in the Middle Ages. You'll find explanations of the individual panels, Giotto's fresco technique, close-ups of the art, and a description of the restoration. You'll also see a life-size re-creation of the house of Mary's mother, St. Anne, as depicted in Giotto's fresco. They show a 12-minute video (English headphones available) about the history of the chapel that is similar—but not identical—to the one that precedes your chapel visit. For me, it's worth just taking some time to enjoy a second video that features a mesmerizing, slow montage of close-ups of the Giotto frescoes.

Palazzo Zuckermann

This overlooked wing of the Civic Museum is just across a busy street. Its first two floors offer a commotion of applied and decorative arts—such as clothes, furniture, and ceramics—from the Venetian Republic (1600s-1700s). On the top floor, the Bottacin collection takes you to the 19th century, with coins and delightful (but no-name) pre-Impressionist paintings.

▲▲▲Basilica of St. Anthony

Friar Anthony of Padua, "Christ's perfect follower and a tireless preacher of the Gospel," is buried here. Construction of this

impressive Romanesque/Gothic church (with its Byzantine-style domes) started immediately after St. Anthony's death in 1231. As a mark of his universal appeal and importance in the medieval Church, he was sainted within a year of his death. Speedy. And for nearly 800 years, his remains and this glorious church have attracted pilgrims to Padua.

Cost and Hours: The **basilica** is free and open April-Oct daily 6:20-19:45; Nov-March Mon-Fri 6:20-19:00, Sat-Sun 6:20-19:45. The various sights within the basilica have slightly different hours: The important **Chapel of the Reliquaries** (free) is open when the basilica is, except that it closes for lunch (12:45-14:45). Other, less important sights include a **museum** (€2.50, Tue-Fri 9:00-13:00, Sat-Sun 9:00-13:00 & 14:00-18:00, closed Mon), a **multimedia exhibit** (free, daily 9:00-12:30 & 14:00-17:30), and the **Oratory of St. George and Scuola del Santo** (€3 apiece or €5 together, same hours as basilica but closed 12:30-14:30). The nearest tram stop is Santo.

Dress Code: A modest dress code is enforced.

Information: Information desks are at both entrances to the cloisters. Each desk has a free pamphlet in English on the saint's life and the basilica; make a donation in the Chapel of the Reliquaries to get a more detailed booklet. Tel. 049-822-5652, www.basilicadelsanto.org.

Church Services: The church hosts six separate Masses each morning (all before 10:00), as well as ones at 11:00, 17:00, and 18:00; on Sundays, additional services are at 12:15, 16:00, and 19:00.

Services: WCs and a picnic area are inside the cloisters.

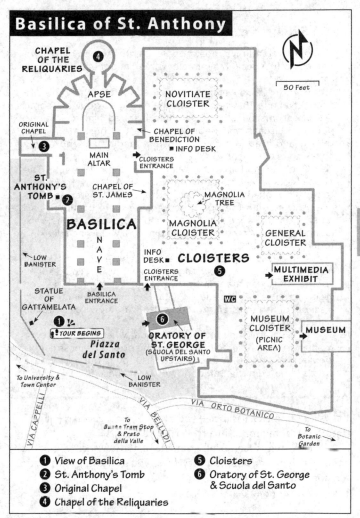

Basilica of St. Anthony

CHAPEL OF THE RELIQUARIES ❹

APSE

NOVITIATE CLOISTER

50 Feet

ORIGINAL CHAPEL

❸

CHAPEL OF BENEDICTION
■ INFO DESK

MAIN ALTAR

CLOISTERS ENTRANCE

ST. ANTHONY'S TOMB ■ ❼

CHAPEL OF ST. JAMES

MAGNOLIA TREE

BASILICA

N A V E

MAGNOLIA CLOISTER

GENERAL CLOISTER

INFO DESK ■
CLOISTERS
❺

LOW BANISTER

CLOISTERS ENTRANCE

MULTIMEDIA EXHIBIT

STATUE OF GATTAMELATA

BASILICA ENTRANCE

WC

MUSEUM CLOISTER (PICNIC AREA)

MUSEUM

❶ ⚑
🚶 TOUR BEGINS

Piazza del Santo

❻

ORATORY OF ST. GEORGE (SCUOLA DEL SANTO UPSTAIRS)

To University & Town Center

LOW BANISTER

VIA CAPELLI

VIA BELLUDI

To Guizza Tram Stop & Prato della Valle

VIA ORTO BOTANICO

To Botanic Garden

NEAR VENICE

❶ View of Basilica
❷ St. Anthony's Tomb
❸ Original Chapel
❹ Chapel of the Reliquaries
❺ Cloisters
❻ Oratory of St. George & Scuola del Santo

Basilica Exterior

St. Anthony looks down from the red-brick facade and blesses all. He holds a book, a symbol of all the knowledge he had accumulated as a quiet monk before starting his preaching career.

A golden angel—the weathervane atop the spire—points her trumpet into the wind. (While you can never really be sure with angels, locals say they know it's a woman because she always tells the truth.)

Guarding the church is Donatello's life-size equestrian statue of the Venetian mercenary general, Gattamelata. Though it looks like a thousand other man-on-a-horse statues, it was a landmark in

St. Anthony of Padua (1195-1231)

One of Christendom's most popular saints, Anthony is known as a powerful speaker, a miracle worker, and the finder of lost articles.

Born in Lisbon to a rich, well-educated family, his life changed at age 25, when he saw the mutilated bodies of some Franciscan martyrs. Their sacrifice inspired him to join the poor Franciscans and dedicate his life to Christ. He moved to Italy and lived in a cave, studying, meditating, and barely speaking to anyone.

One day, he joined his fellow monks for a service. The appointed speaker failed to show up, so Anthony was asked to say a few off-the-cuff words to the crowd. He started slowly, but, filled with the Spirit, he became more confident and amazed the audience with his eloquence. Up in Assisi, St. Francis heard about Anthony and sent him on a whirlwind speaking tour.

Anthony had a strong voice, he knew several languages, had an encyclopedic knowledge of theology, and could speak spontaneously as the Spirit moved him. It's said that he even stood on the shores of the Adriatic Sea in Rimini and enticed a school of fish to listen. Anthony also was known as a prolific miracle worker.

In 1230, Anthony retired to Padua, where he founded a monastery and initiated reforms for the poor. An illness cut his life short at age 36. Anthony said, "Happy is the man whose words issue from the Spirit and not from himself!"

Italy's budding Renaissance—the first life-size, secular, equestrian statue cast from bronze in a thousand years.

The church is technically outside of Italy. When you pass the banisters that mark its property line, you're passing into Vatican territory.

• *Enter the basilica.*

Interior

Grab a pew in the center of the nave and let your eyes adjust. Sit and appreciate the space. Gaze past the crowds and through the incense haze to Donatello's glorious crucifix rising from the altar, and realize that this is one of the most important pilgrimage sites in Christendom.

Along with the crucifix, Donatello's bronze statues—Mary with Padua's six favorite saints—grace the high altar. Late in his career, the great Florentine sculptor spent more than a decade in Padua (1444-1455), creating the altar and Gattamelata.

• *Head to the left side of the nave to find the gleaming marble masterpiece that is the focus of the visiting pilgrims—the tomb of St. Anthony.*

St. Anthony's Tomb

Pilgrims file slowly through this side chapel around the tomb, so focused on the saint that they hardly notice the nine fine marble reliefs. (While the long queue looks intimidating, these folks are just waiting their turn to touch the tomb; you can easily skirt around the side of this group for a closer look at each panel.) These Renaissance masterpieces were carved during the 16th century, and show scenes and miracles from the life of the saint. As you enjoy each scene, notice the Renaissance mastery of realism and 3-D perspective and the intricate frames, which celebrate life with a burst of exuberance. Note also the vivid faces with their powerful emotions.

First Relief: This depicts St. Anthony receiving the Franciscan tunic. The architectural setting (such as the perspective of the arches on the left and the open door) illustrates the new ability to show depth by using mathematics. The cityscape above is Padua in about 1500.

Second Relief: A jealous husband has angrily stabbed his wife. Notice the musculature, the emotion, and the determination in the faces of loved ones. Above, Anthony intercedes with God to bring the woman back to life.

Third Relief: This panel shows Anthony bringing a young man back to life. Above is the Palazzo della Ragione looking as it still does today.

Fourth Relief: This scene, by the famous Florentine sculptor Jacopo Sansovino, shows three generations: a dead girl, her distraught mom, and a grandmother who's seen it all. A boy on the right realistically leans on his stick. Of course, Anthony will eventually change the mood, but right now it's pretty dire. Above is a relief of this basilica.

Fifth Relief: A fisherman holds a net, sadly having retrieved a drowned boy. The mother looks at Anthony, who blesses and revives the boy. Across from here is the saint's actual tomb. Under thoughtful lighting, it reads *Corpus S. Antonii*. Prayer letters are dropped behind the iron grill.

Sixth Relief: This shows "the miracle of the miser's heart." Anthony's helper dips his hand into a moneylender's side to demonstrate the absence of his heart. At his foot, the square tray with coins and a heart illustrates the scriptural verse "for where your treasure is, there your heart will be also."

Seventh Relief: Anthony holds the foot of a young man who confessed to kicking his mother. Taking a lesson from the saint about respecting your mother a little too literally, the man had cut off his own foot. The hysterical mother implores Anthony's help, and the saint's prayers to God enabled him to reattach the foot.

Stand in the corner for a moment, observing the passionate devotion that pilgrims and Paduans alike have for Anthony. Touching his tomb or kneeling in prayer, the faithful believe Anthony is their protector—a confidant and intercessor for the poor. And they believe he works miracles. Believers leave offerings, votives, and written prayers to ask for help or to give thanks for miracles they believe Anthony has performed. By putting their hands on his tomb while saying silent prayers, pilgrims show devotion to Anthony and feel the saint's presence.

Popular Anthony is the patron saint of dozens of things: travelers, amputees, donkeys, pregnant women, infertile women, and flight attendants. Most pilgrims ask for his help in his role as the "finder of things"—from lost car keys to a life companion. You'll see dozens of photos posted on his tomb in prayer or as thanks, including many of fervently wished-for newborns.

Eighth Relief: This scene makes the point that—unlike St. Francis, who was a rowdy youth—Anthony was holy even as a toddler. He tosses the glass (representing his faith), which, rather than shattering, breaks the marble floor.

Ninth Relief: A jealous husband (the bearded man behind Anthony) accuses his wife of cheating. The wife asks Anthony to identify her baby's father. Anthony asks the child, who speaks and says that the husband is his real dad and his mother was not messing around. Everyone is relieved—whew!

Before leaving, stand in the corner and take a moment to appreciate how the entire chapel is an integrated artistic wonder.

• *Leave the chapel (between scenes eight and nine) and step into the oldest part of the church. This is the...*

Original Chapel

This is where Anthony was first buried in 1231. To the left of the altar, note the fine (and impressively realistic for the 14th century) view of medieval Padua, with this church outside the wall (finished by 1300 and looking like it does today). Below the cityscape, in a circa-1380 fresco, Anthony on his cloud promises he'll watch over Padua.

As you exit this chapel, you'll notice many tombs nearby. People wanted to be buried near a saint. If you could afford it, this was about the best piece of real estate a dead person could want. (The practice was ended with Napoleonic reforms in 1806.)

• *Continue your circuit of the church by going behind the altar into the apse, to the Chapel of the Reliquaries. (At busy times, you may have to line up and trudge slowly up the stairs past the reliquaries.)*

Chapel of the Reliquaries

The most prized relic is in the glass case at center stage—Anthony's tongue. When Anthony's remains were exhumed 32 years after his death (in 1263), his body had decayed to dust, but his tongue was found miraculously unspoiled and red in color. How appropriate for the great preacher who, full of the Spirit, couldn't stop talking about God.

Entering the chapel, join the parade of pilgrims working their way clockwise around the chapel and up the stairs. First, on the left, look for the red, triangular vestment in which Anthony's body was wrapped. Next is his rough-hewn wood coffin. Then, up the stairs, is his pillow—a comfy rock (chest level in first glass case). The center display case contains (top to bottom) the saint's lower jaw with all his teeth impressively intact *(il mento,* located about 8 feet high), his uncorrupted tongue *(lingua,* at about eye level), and, finally, his vocal chords *(apparato vocale,* at about waist level) discovered intact when his remains were examined in 1981. In the last display case, a fragment of the True Cross *(la croce)* is held in a precious cross-shaped reliquary. Finally, descend the stairs and pass St. Anthony's holy, and holey, tunic *(tonaca)*.

Above the relics, decorating the cornice, is the *Glorification of St. Anthony.* In this Baroque fantasy—made in 1691 of carved marble and stucco—a cloud of angels and giddy *putti* tumble to the left and right in jubilation as they play their Baroque-era musical instruments to celebrate Anthony's arrival in heaven.

• *Leaving this relic chapel, continue circling the apse. You'll come to the* **Chapel of Benediction.** *Here, under a powerful modern fresco of the Crucifixion (by Pietro Annigoni, who died in 1982), a priest is waiting to bless anyone who cares to be blessed.*

Next, past the sacristy (where you can peek in at priests preparing for Mass), is a door leading to the cloisters. But before heading out, walk just beyond this passage to the...

Chapel of St. James

Exactly opposite the tomb of St. Anthony, this chapel features an exquisite 14th-century fresco by Altichiero da Zevio. Study the vivid commotion around the Crucifixion, clearly inspired by Giotto (this was created 70 years after the Scrovegni Chapel). The faces are real—right off the streets of 14th-century Padua.

• *Next, head out into the cloisters. From the right side of the nave as you face the altar, follow signs to* chiostro; *from outside, find signs on the right side of the church.*

Cloisters

The main cloister is dominated by an exceptionally bushy magnolia tree, planted in 1810 (the magnolia tree was exotic for Europe when it was imported from America in 1760). Also in the cloister are the graves of the most illustrious Paduans, such as Gabriel Fallopius, the scientist who gave his name to his discovery, the Fallopian tube. When Napoleon decreed that graves should be moved out of cities, this once grave-covered courtyard was cleared of tombstones. But the bodies were left in the ground, perhaps contributing to the magnolia tree's fecundity. Today the tree remains an explosion of life.

Wander around the series of three cloisters. Picnic tables invite pilgrims and tourists to enjoy meals within the solitude of one of the cloisters (it's covered and suitable even when rainy, also has WCs).

The **multimedia exhibit** on the life of St. Anthony is kitschy, as pilgrimage multimedia exhibits tend to be (30 minutes, free, you move three times as you use headphones to listen to the story of each tableau).

At the far end, a fascinating little **museum** is filled with votives and folk art recounting miracles attributed to Anthony. The abbreviation *PGR* that you'll see on many votives stands for *per grazia ricevuta*—for answered prayers.

Oratory of St. George and Scuola del Santo

The small but sumptuous **Oratory of St. George** faces the little square in front of the basilica. The oratory ("ora" means prayer) is not actually a church, though it's certainly a fine place to pray—it's filled with vivid, circa-1370 frescoes showing scenes not of Anthony, but from the life of St. Catherine. Because many lovers credit St. Anthony with finding them their partners—and this is the closest place to St. Anthony where you can be married—it's popular for weddings. While you can see it all from the door, paying the entry fee lets you sit and enjoy this peaceful spot.

Next door and upstairs (buy ticket and get info sheet in the oratory) is the skippable **Scuola del Santo** (a.k.a. La Scoletta), the former meeting hall of the Confraternity of Anthony, with frescoes and paintings by various artists—including some by Titian.

Near the Basilica

Prato della Valle

The square is 150 yards southwest of the basilica (down Via Luca Belludi). Once a Roman theater and later Anthony's preaching grounds, this square claims to be the largest in Italy. It's a pleasant, 400-yard-long, oval-shaped piazza with fountains, walkways, dozens of statues of Padua's eminent citizens, and grass. It's also a lively

market scene: fruit and vegetables (Mon-Fri 8:00-13:00); clothing, shoes, and household goods (Sat 8:00-19:00); and antiques (third Sun 8:00 19:00) This place is often busy with special events and festivals. Ask at the TI or your hotel if anything's going on at Prato della Valle.

Botanic Garden (Orto Botanico)

Green thumbs appreciate this nearly five-acre botanical garden, which contains the university's vast collection of rare plants. Founded in 1545 to cultivate medicinal plants, it's the world's oldest academic botanical garden still in its original location. A visitors center—in a little cottage to the right of the garden's entrance—houses models of the garden's layout and computer terminals that describe the history and composition of the garden in English.

Cost and Hours: Garden—€5; April-Oct Mon-Sat 9:00-19:00, Sun 10:00-19:00; Nov-Feb Mon-Sat 9:00-15:00, closed Sun; March Mon-Sat 9:00-15:00, Sun 10:00-16:00; entrance 150 yards south of Basilica of St. Anthony—with your back to the facade, take a hard left; Santo tram stop, tel. 049-827-2119, www.ortobotanico.unipd.it.

Sleeping in Padua

Rooms in Padua's hotels are more spacious and a better value than those in Venice. Keep in mind that when large conventions take over the town—several times a year—all hotels raise prices. Generally, prices are very flexible and are often lower than what I've written here; check hotel websites for *offerti* (specials). I've listed two hotels in the center and a group of accommodations near the basilica. All are reachable from the station by the tram; only Albergo Verdi is more than a five-minute walk from the nearest tram stop.

In the Center

$$$ Hotel Majestic Toscanelli, an old-fashioned, borderline-gaudy, family-run, 34-room hotel, owns a perfectly convenient location right in the town center—buried in the characteristic ghetto with wonderful cobbled ambience. At night, this area is popular with noisy students; request a quiet room on the back side (Sb-€95-110 depending on size, Db-€149, ask for 10 percent Rick Steves discount, book direct for the best rates, check their website for routine special discounts, spacious attic "loft" rooms with kitchenettes and low beams, air-con, elevator, free Wi-Fi, parking-€12/day for Rick Steves readers, Via dell'Arco 2, Tito Livio tram stop, tel. 049-663-244, www.toscanelli.com, majestic@toscanelli.com, Mario Morosi and family). From the tram stop, follow the passageway next to #26, then jog left down Via Marsala and turn right on Via dell'Arco.

Sleep Code

(€1 = about $1.30, country code: 39)
S = Single, **D** = Double/Twin, **T** = Triple, **Q** = Quad, **b** = bathroom, **s** = shower only. Unless otherwise noted, credit cards are accepted, breakfast is included, and English is spoken. Many cities in Italy levy a hotel tax of about €2 per person, per night, which must be paid in cash (not included in the rates I've quoted).

To help you easily sort through these listings, I've divided the accommodations into three categories based on the price for a standard double room with bath:

$$$ **Higher Priced**—Most rooms €125 or more.
  $$ **Moderately Priced**—Most rooms between €90-125.
   $ **Lower Priced**—Most rooms €90 or less.

Prices can change without notice; verify the hotel's current rates online or by email. For the best prices, always book direct.

$$ Albergo Verdi, an Ikea-mod little place, is crammed into an old building on a small back street beyond Piazza dei Signori. While public spaces are tight, the 14 rooms are comfortable (Sb-€80, Db-€110, extra person-€30, air-con, tiny elevator, free guest computer, free Wi-Fi, Via Dondi dall'Orologio 7, Ponti Romani tram stop, tel. 049-836-4163, www.albergoverdipadova.it, info@albergoverdipadova.it). From Piazza dei Signori, walk through the arch under the clock tower and go to the far end of Piazza del Capitaniato; the hotel is on the side street to your right.

Near Basilica of St. Anthony
Santo is the nearest tram stop for the following hotels. Use the Prato della Valle tram stop for the hostel.

$$ Hotel Al Fagiano feels like an art gallery with crazy, sexy, modern art everywhere. The hotel is all about the union of a man and a woman (quite romantic). They rent 40 bright and cheery air-conditioned rooms, each uniquely decorated with Rossella Fagiano's canvases (Sb-€64, Db-€100, Tb-€115, 10 percent Rick Steves discount if you book direct, €7/person less without breakfast, air-con, elevator, free Wi-Fi, parking-€10/day, 50 yards from the Santo tram stop at Via Locatelli 45, tel. 049-875-3396, www.alfagiano.com, info@alfagiano.com; Anita, artist Rossella, and husband Amato).

$$ Hotel Belludi 37 is a slick, stylish, borderline pretentious place renting 15 modern rooms shoehorned into an old building.

The decor is dark, woody, and fresh (S-€57, Sb-€80, Db-€125, bigger Db-€145, ask for 10 percent Rick Steves discount, €7/person less without breakfast, air-con, lots of stairs with no elevator, free Wi-Fi, a block from the Santo tram stop at Via Beato Luca Belludi 37, tel. 049-665-633, www.belludi37.it, info@belludi37.it).

$ Hotel Al Santo, run with charm by Valentina and Antonio, offers 15 spacious rooms with all the comforts on two floors above their restaurant, a few steps from the basilica. Given the warm welcome and pleasant location, it's a fine value (Sb-€60, Db-€85, Tb-€110, Qb-€130, double-paned windows, quieter rooms off street, some rooms have views of basilica, air-con, elevator, free Wi-Fi, parking-€14/day, Via del Santo 147, tel. 049-875-2131, www.alsanto.it, alsanto@alsanto.it).

$ Hotel Casa del Pellegrino, with 147 spotless, cheap, institutional rooms and straight pricing, is owned by the friars of St. Anthony. It's home to the pilgrims who come to pay homage to the saint in the basilica next door. Any visitor to Padua is welcome, making it popular with professors and students. "Superior" rooms cost €5 extra; some of these are regular rooms with basilica views (but these also come with more noise—both from the street, and, starting at 6:00 in the morning, the church bells), while others are in *dipendenza,* the hotel's modern wing (S-€44, Sb-€59, D-€58, Db-€71, Tb-€85, Qb-€100, Quint/b-€110, ask for a room off the street, breakfast-€5, air-con, elevator, free Wi-Fi, parking-€5/day, Via Cesarotti 21, tel. 049-823-9711, www.casadelpellegrino.com, info@casadelpellegrino.com).

Hostel: **$ Ostello Città di Padova,** near Prato della Valle, is well-run and has 90 beds in 6-bed rooms (beds with sheets and breakfast-€19, family rooms-€88, free Wi-Fi, laundry-€5.50/load, lockers, reception open 7:00-9:30 & 15:30-23:00, rooms locked during afternoon but reception staffed if you need to leave bags, 23:00 curfew, Via Aleardi 30, Prato de Valle tram stop, tel. 049-875-2219, www.ostellopadova.it, ostellopadova@ctgveneto.it). From the tram stop, exit the square ahead of you to the right and make an immediate left down Via Memmo; after the church, continue straight one block on Via Torresini and turn right on Via Aleardi.

Eating in Padua

The university population means cheap, good food abounds. My recommended restaurants are all centrally located in the historic core. You'd think there would be fine dining on the charming market squares, but on the piazzas it's a take-out-pizza-and-casual-bar scene (dominated by students after dark). La Lanterna, at the neighboring Piazza dei Signori, is the best on-square option—but they only offer functional Italian classics. The dreamily atmospheric ghetto neighborhood (just two blocks off the market squares) thrives after dark with trendy bars and a lively student *spritz* scene.

Dining near the Center

Osteria dei Fabbri, with shared rustic tables, offers a good mix of class and accessibility, quality, and price. The dining room is spacious, and the dishes are traditional Venetian and Paduan. Ask to peek into their back courtyard, where you can see the door of an old synagogue (€9 pastas, €15-17 *secondi*, Mon-Sat 12:30-14:30 & 19:30-22:30, closed Sun except sometimes open for lunch in the springtime, Via dei Fabbri 13, on a side street on south side of Piazza Erbe, tel. 049-650-336).

Osteria L'Anfora is a classic place serving classic dishes in an informal, fun-loving space. Don't be put off by the woody, ruffian decor and the fact that it's a popular hangout for a pre-meal drink. They take food seriously and serve it at good prices, and the energy and commotion add to a great dining experience (€8-10 pastas, €14-16 *secondi*, meals served Mon-Sat 12:30-15:00 & 19:30-22:30, closed Sun, reservations smart for dinner, Via dei Soncin 13, tel. 049-656-629).

Enoteca dei Tadi is a small place with seven tables filling a cozy back room behind a convivial little bar (avoid their basement). Roberta and Anna serve traditional Paduan dishes and have earned a local following for their small but tasty menu. The selection is driven by what's fresh and in season, and they offer good wines by the glass (€7-10 dishes, Tue-Sun 18:00-24:00, closed Mon, Via dei Tadi 16, mobile 338-408-3434).

Ristorante Dante alle Piazze is a respected fixture in town for its dressy white-tablecloth dining. They are passionate about their meat and fish dishes. Reservations are smart at night (€9-11 pastas, €16-18 *secondi*, Tue-Sat 12:00-15:00 & 18:30-24:00, Sun 12:00-15:00, closed Mon, Via Daniele Manin 8, tel. 049-836-0973, www.dadanteallepiazze.com).

Cheap Eats near the Center

Affordable Meals in Padua's Living Room, Piazza dei Signori: **La Lanterna** has a forgettable interior and a predictable menu of pizzas, pastas, and *secondi*. But its prime location on Piazza dei Signori provides a rare-in-Padua chance to sit in a grand square under the stars, surrounded by great architecture. Its pizzas are a local favorite—takeaway available—and reservations are recommended (€6-9 pizzas, €8-11 pastas, €15-20 *secondi*, Fri-Wed 12:00-14:30 & 18:00-24:00, closed Thu, Piazza dei Signori 39, tel. 049-660-770, www.lalanternapadova.it).

Light Local Meals on Piazza della Frutta: **Bar dei Osei,** on Piazza della Frutta, is a very simple sandwich bar with some of

the best outdoor seats in town. While Paduans love their delicate *tremazzini*—white bread sandwiches with crusts cut off
(€1.50/€1.80 with table service)—I'd choose their *porchetta*—savory roasted pork sandwiches (€3.50/€3.80). You'll find a two-foot-
long mother lode waiting on the counter for you; tell friendly Marco
how big a slice you'd like. Wines are listed on the board (Mon-Sat
7:00-21:00, closed Sun, Piazza della Frutta 1, tel. 049-875-9606).
In the evenings, just a few feet away, a typical **snack stand** selling
all kinds of fresh, hot, and ready-to-eat seafood appetizers sets up
between 17:00 and 20:30 (daily except Sun). Belly up to the bar
with your drink and try whatever Massimiliano's serving.

Fast Food: **Brek,** with one entrance next to the Ponti Romani
tram stop and another tucked into a corner of Piazza Cavour at
#20, is an easy self-service chain *ristorante* with healthy and afford-
able choices. It's big, bright, practical, and family-friendly (€4-7
pastas, €5-9 *secondi*, daily 11:30-15:00 & 18:30-22:00, tel. 049-
875-3788). **Brek Foccacceria** (part of the same chain), across from
Caffè Pedrocchi and next door to the PAM supermarket, is a café
selling big €3-5 sandwiches and slices of pizza that you can eat at
outdoor tables. During happy hour (18:30-20:30), you can buy a
drink and pay €1 more to fill a plate at their *antipasti* buffet, which
can easily turn into a light dinner (open daily 8:00-22:00, Piazzetta
della Garzeria 6, tel. 049-876-1651).

Groceries: Stock up on picnic items at the outdoor markets, or
visit the **PAM supermarket,** in the tiny *piazzetta* east of Caffè Pedrocchi (Mon-Sat 8:00-21:00, Sun 9:00-19:00, Piazzetta Garzeria 3).

Gelato: If eating dinner out, consider skipping dessert and
instead licking a gelato while strolling the wonderful streets and
piazzas of Padua. My favorite *gelateria* is **Gelato Pretto,** the creation of Michelin three-star chefs who wanted to bring gourmet
to gelato. Their exclusive taste creations cost a bit more than the
already expensive standard flavors. Ask for several tastes before
choosing your favorite (daily 12:00-23:00, Via Umberto 1, tel. 049-
875-0776). **Grom** is also popular for its unusual flavors and exotic
ingredients. While it's tasty, organic, and green, it's also part of a
big chain—the Starbucks of Italian gelato joints (two locations: Via
Roma 101, tel. 049-876-4262; and Piazza dei Signori 33, tel. 049-
875-4373).

Near the Basilica of St. Anthony

Antica Trattoria dei Paccagnella, the most serious restaurant near
the basilica, serves up nicely presented, seasonal local dishes with
modern flair and an impressive attention to ingredients. The place
has friendly service, modern art on the walls, and no pretense. It's
thoughtfully run by two brothers, Raffaele and Cesare, who happily explain why they are so excited about local hen (€8-10 pastas,

€13-18 *secondi*, daily 12:00-14:30 & 19:00-22:00, Via del Santo 113, tel. 049-875-0549).

Pizzeria Pago Pago dishes up wood-fired Neapolitan pizzas (a local favorite) and daily specials depending on what's in season. Get there early for dinner or wait (€5-8 pizzas, €9 salads, Wed-Mon 12:00-14:00 & 19:00-24:00, closed Tue; 2 blocks from Basilica of St. Anthony, up Via del Santo and right onto Via Galileo Galilei to #59; tel. 049-665-558, Gaetano and Modesto).

Casa del Pellegrino Ristorante caters to St. Anthony pilgrims with simple, basic, and hearty meals, served in a cheery dining room just north of the basilica (€5-8 pastas, €9-10 *secondi*, €15 fixed-price meal, €2 cover, daily 12:00-14:00 & 19:30-21:30, Via Cesarotti 21, tel. 049-876-0715).

Zairo is a huge indoor/outdoor *ristorante*/pizzeria with reasonable prices, delicious homemade pastas, Veneto specialties, snappy service, and a local clientele. As it's next to the vast and inviting Prato della Valle square/park, consider combining dinner here with a relaxing stroll through the park (€5-10 pizzas, €7-8 pastas, €9-16 *secondi*, Tue-Sun 11:30-15:00 & 19:00-24:00, closed Mon, east side of Prato della Valle at #51, tel. 049-663-803).

Pollodoro la Gastronomica, my pick of the take-out delis near the basilica, sells roast chicken, pastas, pizza, and veggies. They'll also make sandwiches (Wed-Sat and Mon 8:30-20:00, Sun 8:30-14:00 only, closed Tue, 100 yards from basilica at Via Belludi 34, tel. 049-663-718). You can picnic at the nearby cloisters of the basilica.

Padua Connections

From Padua by Train to: Venice (at least 2/hour, 30-50 minutes), **Vicenza** (at least 2/hour, fewer on weekends, 15-25 minutes), **Milan** (1-2/hour, 2-3 hours), **Verona** (at least 2/hour, 40-60 minutes), **Ravenna** (roughly hourly, change in Bologna or Ferrara, 2.5-3.5 hours).

Note that the departures listed above are operated by Trenitalia; a competing private rail company called Italo offers additional high-speed connections to major cities (including **Venice, Bologna, Florence,** and **Rome**). While Italo is often cheaper (particularly if you book long in advance), it doesn't accept railpasses (for details on Italo, see page 1168 or visit www.italotreno.it).

By Bus to: Venice (45 minutes, hourly at :25 past the hour from 5:25 to 20:25), and Venice's **Marco Polo Airport** (65 minutes, €8, €10 if bought on board, buses depart at :25 past each hour from platform 11 at Padua's bus station, next to the train station; recheck times at www.fsbusitalia.it). If flying into the airport, take this bus to get directly to Padua (buy tickets at windows in arrivals hall or at airport TI).

By Minibus to Airports: A minibus service runs from Padua to **Marco Polo Airport** (€32/person) or **Treviso Airport** (€41/person, reservations required, tel. 049-870-4425, www.airservicepadova.it).

Near Padua: Vicenza

To many architects, Vicenza (vih-CHEHN-zah) is a pilgrimage site. Entire streets look like the back of a nickel. This is the city of Andrea Palladio (1508-1580), the 16th-century Renaissance architect who defined the Palladian style that is now so influential in countless British country homes. But as grandiose as Vicenza's Palladian facades may feel, there is little marble here because the city lacked the wealth to build with much more than painted wood and plaster.

If you're an architecture buff, Vicenza merits a quick day trip on any day but Monday, when major sights are closed. If you're packing light, it's an easy stop, located on the same train line as Padua, Verona, and Venice. However, because you can't store bags at the train station, it's not worth stopping here if you have lots of luggage.

Tourist Information: The TI is next to the Olympic Theater at Piazza Matteotti 12 (daily 9:00-13:30 & 14:00-17:30, tel. 0444-320-854, www.visitvicenza.org). Ask for the free brochure on Palladio's buildings. Architecture fans appreciate the €2.50 *Vicenza and the Villas of Andrea Palladio*.

Arrival in Vicenza: From the **train station,** I'd head straight for the most distant sight, the Olympic Theater (with a TI next door), and then see other sights on the way back. Go straight out the train station's front door, and use the crosswalk on the right side of the roundabout. From here, it's a five-minute walk straight up wide Viale Roma to the PAM supermarket at the bottom of Corso Palladio; turn right through the gate, and then it's a good 10 minutes more down the Corso to the Olympic Theater (a taxi costs €8). **Drivers** can park in one of the cheap parking lots (Parcheggio Bassano and Parcheggio Cricoli) and catch a free shuttle bus to the center.

Helpful Hints: All of the sights mentioned (except the villas outside of town) are covered by the **Museum Card** combo-ticket (€10, €14 family pass, good for 3 days, sold at Olympic Theater and Palazzo Leoni Montanari). In a pinch, the TI may be willing to store bags for you while you walk around town.

Vicenza

NEAR VENICE

Sights in Vicenza

Helpful bilingual signs in front of Palladio's buildings explain their history. Arrows around town point you to his major works, and you can also pick up a map from the TI.

▲▲Olympic Theater (Teatro Olimpico)

Palladio's last work, one of his greatest, shouldn't be missed. This indoor theater is a wood-and-stucco festival of classical columns, statues, and an oh-wow stage bursting with perspective tricks. When you step back outside, take another look at the town's main drag—named after Palladio. It's the same main street you saw on the stage of his theater.

Cost and Hours: Entry only with €10 Museum Card, which also covers other Vicenza sights; Tue-Sun 9:00-17:00, closed Mon, last entry 30 minutes before closing, very occasionally closed when theater is in use, audioguide available, entrance to left of TI at Piazza Matteotti 11, tel. 0444-222-800, www.olimpico-vicenza.it.

▲Church of Santa Corona and Diocesan Museum

A block away from the Olympic Theater, this "Church of the Holy Crown" was built in the 13th century to house a thorn from the Crown of Thorns, given to the Bishop of Vicenza by the French King Louis IX. The church has two artistic highlights: the art embellishing its high altar and Giovanni Bellini's fine painting, *Baptism of Christ*.

Cost and Hours: €5, Tue-Sun 9:00-12:00 & 15:00-18:00, closed Mon, Piazza Duomo 12, tel. 0444-226-400, www.museo-diocesanovicenza.it.

Archaeological and Natural History Museum

Located next door to the Church of Santa Corona, this museum's ground floor features Roman antiquities (mosaics, statues, and artifacts excavated from Rome's Baths of Caracalla, plus swords) and a barbarian warrior skeleton complete with sword and helmet. Prehistoric scraps are upstairs. Look for English description sheets near exhibit entryways throughout.

Cost and Hours: Covered by Museum Card, Tue-Sun 9:00-17:00, closed Mon, Contrà Santa Corona 4, tel. 0444-222-815, www.museicivicivicenza.it.

Palazzo Leoni Montanari

Across the street from the Church of Santa Corona, this small museum is a palatial riot of Baroque, with cherub-cluttered ceilings jumbled like a preschool in heaven. A quick stroll shows off Venetian paintings and a floor of Russian icons.

Cost and Hours: €5, Tue-Sun 10:00-18:00, closed Mon, last entry 30 minutes before closing, Contrà Santa Corona 25, tel. 800-578-875, www.palazzomontanari.com.

Piazza dei Signori

Vicenza's main square has been the center of town ever since it was the site of the ancient Roman forum. The commanding **Basilica Palladiana,** with its 270-foot-tall, 13th-century tower, dominates the square. This was once the meeting place for local big shots. It was young Palladio's proposal—to redo Vicenza's dilapidated Gothic palace of justice in the Neo-Greek style—that established him as the city's favorite architect. The rest of Palladio's career was a one-man construction boom. The basilica hosts special exhibitions that sometimes involve a fee, but you can often pop in for a free look.

Villas on the Outskirts of Vicenza

Vicenza is surrounded by dreamy Venetian villas. Venice's commercial empire receded in the 1500s, when trade began to pick up along the Atlantic seaboard and dwindle in the Mediterranean. Venice redirected its economic agenda to agribusiness, which led to the construction of lavish country villas, such as **Villa la Rotonda,** the inspiration for Thomas Jefferson's Monticello (www. villalarotonda.it) and **Villa Valmarana ai Nani** (www.villavalmarana.com). Located southeast of the town center, both houses are furnished with period pieces and come with good English descriptions (closed Mon). Pick up the free English brochure on Palladio's villas from the TI if you plan to visit.

Vicenza Connections

From Vicenza by Train to: Venice (at least 2/hour, 45-75 minutes), **Padua** (at least 2/hour, fewer on weekends, 15-25 minutes), **Verona** (at least 2/hour, 25-60 minutes), **Milan** (1-2/hour, 1.75-2 hours). Unless you crave speed or need to burn a railpass day, you'll save a lot of money by taking the slow R trains to Vicenza instead of the fast Frecce trains.

Verona

Romeo and Juliet made Verona a household word. Alas, a visit here has nothing to do with those two star-crossed lovers. You can pay  to visit the house that falsely claims to be Juliet's (with an almost believable balcony and a courtyard swarming with tour groups), join in the tradition of rubbing the breast of Juliet's statue to help find a lover (or to pick up the sweat of someone who can't), and even make a pilgrimage to what isn't "La Tomba di Giulietta."

Fiction aside, Verona has been an important crossroads for 2,000 years and is, therefore, packed with genuine history. R&J fans will take some solace in the fact that two real feuding families, the Montecchi and the Cappellos, were the models for Shakespeare's Montagues and Capulets. And, if R&J had existed and were alive today, they would still recognize much of their "hometown."

Verona's main attractions are its wealth of Roman ruins; the remnants of its 13th- and 14th-century political and cultural boom brought about by its leading family, the Scaligeri; its 21st-century, pedestrian-only ambience; and its world-class opera festival, held each summer. After Venice's festival of tourism, the Veneto region's second city is a cool and welcome sip of pure Italy, where dumpsters are painted by schoolchildren as class projects and public spaces are primarily the domain of locals, not tourists. If you like Italy but don't need blockbuster sights, this town is a joy.

Orientation to Verona

Verona's old town fills an easy-to-defend bend in the River Adige. The vibrant and enjoyable core of Verona lies along Via Mazzini between Piazza Brà (pronounced "bra") and Piazza Erbe, Verona's market square since Roman times. Each evening the two main streets from Piazza Brà to Piazza Erbe, Via Mazzini and Corso Porta Borsari, are enlivened by a wonderful *passeggiata*...bustling with a slow and elegant parade of strollers. For a good day trip to Verona, take my self-guided walk, beginning with a visit to the Roman Arena.

Tourist Information

Verona's helpful TI is just off **Piazza Brà**—from the square, head to the big yellow building with columns and cross the street to Via degli Alpini 9 (Feb-Nov Mon-Sat 9:00-19:00, Dec-Jan Mon-Sat 9:00-18:00; Sun 10:00-16:00 year-round; tel. 045-806-8680, www.tourism.verona.it). Pick up the free city map and confirm the walking-tour schedule.

Verona Card: This tourist card covers entrance to all the recommended Verona sights (€15/2 days, €20/5 days, sold at the TI and at participating sights). If you visit the Roman Arena (€6), climb Torre dei Lamberti (€6), explore Castelvecchio (€6), and tour two churches (€5), you'll pay €23. At €15, the card saves day-trippers intent on blitzing the city almost a third off their sightseeing costs. (However, the card does not cover city transportation, nor does it include the expensive ArenaMuseOpera museum.)

The €6 **Church Card,** sold at four churches that require admission (San Zeno, Duomo, Sant'Anastasia, and San Fermo, normally €2.50 each), pays off if you visit three (www.chieseverona.it). There's no need to get both tourist cards.

If you're staying the night, ask the TI about concerts, or stop by a newsstand to pick up the €2 monthly entertainment guide, *Carnet Verona*.

Arrival in Verona

By Train: Verona's main train station is called Verona Porta Nuova. In the main hall, you'll find WCs (€0.80) and a baggage check office (€5/5 hours, €12.50/24 hours, daily 8:00-20:00). Buses and taxis are immediately outside.

Avoid the boring 15-minute walk from the station to Piazza Brà. Buses are cheap, easy, and leave every few minutes. Buy a ticket from the tobacco shop inside the station (€1.30/90 minutes, €4 day pass valid until midnight), or buy one from the driver for €0.20 more. Leaving the station, angle right across the street to the bus stalls, find platform A, and hop on a bus: #11, #12, and #13 run Monday-Saturday before 20:00; #90, #92, and #98 run after 20:00 and all day Sunday; and #510 runs daily, even after 20:00. If in doubt, confirm that your bus is headed to the city center by asking, *"Per il centro?"* (pehr eel CHEN-troh). Validate your ticket by stamping it in the machine on the bus.

Drivers don't announce stops, but you'll know Piazza Brà because of the mass exodus and the can't-miss-it Roman Arena (bus stops in front of big, yellow, Neoclassical building). The TI is just a few steps beyond the bus stop, against the medieval wall. You can catch return buses to the station (same numbers) from the stop on the piazza side of the street, or from another bus stop just outside the city wall on Corso Porta Nuova (on the right, in front of McDonald's).

Taxis pick up only at taxi stands (at Piazza Brà, Piazza Erbe, and the train station) and cost about €8 for the quick ride between the train station and the center of town (€3 more on Sundays and after 22:00, €1/big bag).

If you're in downtown Verona and need train tickets or reservations, drop by World Travel (see "Helpful Hints," later).

By Car: The old town center (where nearly all my recommended hotels are located) is closed to traffic. Your hotel can get you permission to drive in—ask when you book. Otherwise your license plate will be photographed, and a €100 ticket might be waiting in the mail when you get home.

Drivers will find reasonably priced parking in well-marked lots and garages just outside the center. The underground **Cittadella garage,** at Piazza Cittadella (a block off Piazza Brà, behind the TI), is huge, convenient, and easy to find (€2/hour, €15/24 hours). The lot in front of the **train station** costs less (€8.50/24 hours), but you'll spend your savings on the bus to the center. The **Città di Nimes** parking lot (a 5-minute walk from the train station, near the wall) costs €5/day. **Street parking** is limited to two hours and costs €1/hour (spaces marked with blue lines, buy ticket at a tobacco shop or ticket machine, place ticket on dashboard; some hotels can give you a free street-parking permit—ask).

By Plane: Efficient buses connect Verona's airport (known as Catullo or Verona-Villafranca, 12 miles southwest of the city, airport code: VRN, tel. 045-809-5666, www.aeroportoverona.it) with

NEAR VENICE

its train station (€6, buy tickets on board or at tobacco shop, daily about 5:15-23:00, 3/hour, 15 minutes, bus stop is by front door of train station).

Helpful Hints

Sightseeing Schedules: Most sights (except churches) are closed on Monday mornings, and typically open at 13:30.

Opera: From mid-June through early September, Verona's opera festival brings the city to life, with 15,000 music fans filling the Roman Arena for almost nightly performances (cheap upper-level seats-€25, day-of-show tickets often available). The city is packed and festive—restaurants have prescheduled seatings for dinner, and hotels jack up their prices. You can book tickets at the TI (no extra charge) or through the official box office (buy online at www.arena.it or call 045-800-5151; box office open Mon-Fri 9:00-12:00 & 15:15-17:45, Sat-Sun 9:00-12:00; during opera season, open daily 10:00-17:45, or until 21:00 on performance days; Via Dietro Anfiteatro 6B). If you're not here for the festival, you can still explore the arena (at the start of my self-guided walk) and/or visit Verona's opera-focused ArenaMuseOpera museum (described later).

Internet Access: Just outside the wall from Piazza Brà is **Play Internet Point** (20 Internet terminals inside a casino, €2/hour, daily 10:00-24:00, to the left of the TI at 49 Via Adigetto, follow signs for *Piazza Cittadella*).

Travel Agency: If you need train tickets or reservations, stop by **World Travel** (small fee added to tickets but saves a trip to the station, Mon-Fri 9:00-19:00, Sat 9:30-12:30 & 15:00-18:00, closed Sun, Corso Porta Nuova 11, tel. 049 806-0111)

Tours in Verona

Walking Tours

The TI organizes 1.5-hour tours in English (March-Oct Sat-Sun 11:30, no tours off-season, €10/person). Tours meet inside the Piazza Brà TI and stroll all the way through the old town (call to confirm schedule, no reservation necessary, tel. 045-806-8680).

Private Guides

Three excellent and enthusiastic Verona guides enjoy giving private tours of the town and region to readers of this book (€115/2 hours, €230/5 hours, prices are per group, tours tailored to your interests—villas, wine tasting, and so on). They are **Marina Menegoi** (mobile 328-958-1108, www.marinamenegoi.com, mmenegoi@gmail.com), **Valeria Biasi** (mobile 348-903-4238, www.aguidein verona.com or www.veronatours.com for small groups, valeria@aguideinverona.com, also offers interactive city Safari game for

NEAR VENICE

families—€130/2.5 hours), and **Franklin Baumgarten** (franklin_baumgarten@web.de, mobile 347-566-6765).

Self-Guided Walk

Welcome to Verona

This walk covers the essential sights in the town core, starting at Piazza Brà and ending at the cathedral. Allow two hours (including the tower climb and dawdling).

❶ Piazza Brà

If you're wondering about the name, it comes from the local dialect and means "big open space." A generation ago this piazza was noisy with cars. Now it's open and people friendly—it's become the community family room and natural festival grounds.

Grab a bench near the central **fountain** called "The Alps." This was a gift from Verona's sister city Munich, which is just over the mountains to the north. You'll see in the middle of the fountain the symbols of the two cities separated by the Alps, carved out of pink marble from this region. In general, Verona has a bit of an alpine feel; historically it was the place where people rested and prepared before crossing the mountains, and to this day it's the place where the main west-east, Milan-Venice train line meets the north-south line up to Bolzano, the Dolomites, and Austria.

The ancient **arena** looming over the piazza is a reminder that the city's history goes back to Roman times. On this walk we'll meander across what was the ancient city, from the arena on this side to the theater across the river.

With the fall of Rome in the fifth century, Verona became a favored capital of barbarian kings. In the Middle Ages, noble families had to choose sides in the civil struggles between emperors (Ghibellines) and popes (Guelphs). During this time (1200s), the town bristled with several hundred San Gimignano-type towers, built by different families to symbolize their power. When the Scaligeri family rose to power here in the 14th century, they established stability on their terms and made the other noble families lop off their proud towers—only the Scaligeri were allowed to keep theirs. To add insult to injury, the Scaligeri paved the city's roads with bricks from the other families' toppled towers. But inter-family feuds made it impossible for the Scaligeri to maintain a stable government, and in 1405 the town essentially gave itself to Venice,

NEAR VENICE

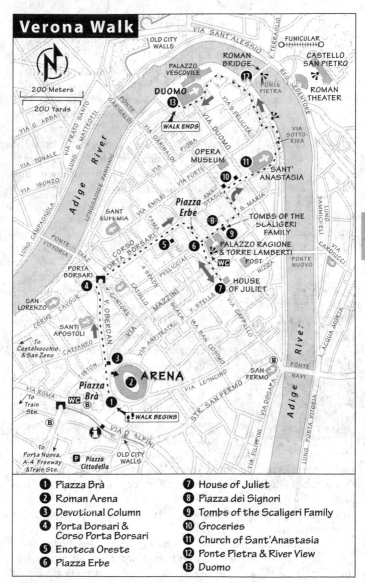

Verona Walk

200 Meters
200 Yards

OLD CITY WALLS

VIA SANT'ALESSIO

FUNICULAR

CASTELLO SAN PIETRO

PALAZZO VESCOVILE

ROMAN BRIDGE

ROMAN THEATER

DUOMO ⓭

WALK ENDS

OPERA MUSEUM

SANT' ANASTASIA

Piazza Erbe

TOMBS OF THE SCALIGERI FAMILY

SANT EUFEMIA

PALAZZO RAGIONE & TORRE LAMBERTI

WC POST

HOUSE OF JULIET ⑦

PORTA BORSARI

SAN LORENZO

SANTI APOSTOLI

To Castelvecchio & San Zeno

⓭ ⓬ ⓫ ⓾ ⑨ ⑧

ARENA

Piazza Brà

WC

To Train Stn.

SAN FERMO

WALK BEGINS

To Porta Nuova, A-4 Freeway & Train Stn.

OLD CITY WALLS

Piazza Cittadella

NEAR VENICE

① Piazza Brà
② Roman Arena
③ Devotional Column
④ Porta Borsari & Corso Porta Borsari
⑤ Enoteca Oreste
⑥ Piazza Erbe
⑦ House of Juliet
⑧ Piazza dei Signori
⑨ Tombs of the Scaligeri Family
⑩ Groceries
⑪ Church of Sant'Anastasia
⑫ Ponte Pietra & River View
⑬ Duomo

which ruled Verona until Napoleon stopped by in 1796. During the 19th century, a tug-of-war between France and Austria actually divided the city for a time, with the river marking the border of each country's domain. Eventually Verona, like Venice, fell into Austrian hands. Reminders of Austrian rule remain: The huge yellow Neoclassical **city hall** facing Piazza Brà (look for the flags) was built by the Austrians to serve as their 19th-century military headquarters. Their former arsenal stands just across the river, and an Austrian fortress caps the hill looking over the city. But the big **equestrian statue** is of Italy's first king, Victor Emmanuel II, celebrating Italian independence and unity, won in the 1860s. The **statue of a modern soldier** striking a *David* pose, with a machine gun instead of a sling over his shoulder, honors Verona's war dead.

Apart from all its history, Piazza Brà is about strolling—the evening *passeggiata* is a national sport in Italy. The broad, shiny sidewalk (named "Liston" after a Venetian promenade; note the fine Venetian-style marble pavement slabs) was built by 17th-century Venetians, who made it big and wide so that promenading socialites could see and be seen in all their finery.

❷ Roman Arena

The Romans built this stadium outside their town walls, just as modern stadiums are usually located outside downtown districts.

With 72 aisles, this elliptical 466-by-400-foot amphitheater is the third largest in Italy (and it was originally 50 percent taller). Most of the stone you see is original. Dating from the first century A.D., it looks great in its pink marble. Over the centuries, crowds of up to 25,000 spectators have cheered Roman gladiator battles, medieval executions, rock concerts, and modern plays, all taking advantage of the arena's famous acoustics. This is also where the popular opera festival is held every summer. Started in 1913, the festival has run continuously ever since, except for brief breaks during both World Wars, when the arena was used as a bomb shelter. While there's little to see inside except the impressive stonework, it's memorable to visit a Roman arena that is still a thriving concert venue. If you climb to the top, you'll enjoy great city views.

The gladiators posing with tourists out front are mostly from Albania, and part of a local gang; they're notorious for overcharging for photos. While they're a nuisance, the police say it's better that they're scamming a living here than finding even more disreputable ways to get by.

Cost and Hours: €6, don't bother with the combo-ticket that includes the unimpressive Maffei Museum, Tue-Sun 8:30-19:30, Mon 13:30-19:30, closes earlier—likely around 16:00—during mid-June-early Sept opera season, last entry one hour before closing, WC near entry, tel. 045-800-3204.

• *As you exit the arena, look to your right. Where the street splits you'll see a column.*

❸ Devotional Column

In the Middle Ages, this column blessed a marketplace held here. Ten yards in front of it, a bronze plaque in the sidewalk shows the Roman city plan—a town of 20,000 placed strategically in the bend of the river, which provided protection on three sides. A wall enclosed the peninsula. The center of the grid was the forum, today's Piazza Erbe. (Look down Via Mazzini, the busy main pedestrian drag—the bell tower in the distance marks Piazza Erbe.)

• *After viewing the bronze plaque, turn around so your back is to the arena. Head straight down Via Oberdan (bearing left at the fork) and continue a couple of blocks (passing a derelict Fascist-era theater, the Astra, set back from the street on the left, at #13) until you see an ancient gate to your right, the Porta Borsari. Walk up to it.*

❹ Porta Borsari and Corso Porta Borsari

You're standing before the main entrance to Roman Verona; back then, this gate functioned as a tollbooth (*borsari* means "purse," referring to the collection of tolls

here). Below the spiral, fluted columns (which parents nickname *"tortiglioni"*—a pasta kids can relate to), carved into the rock, is a tribute to the emperor who restored this gate. Outside the adjacent Caffè Rialto, the stone on the curb is from a tomb: In Roman times, the roads outside the walls were lined with tomb-stones, because burials were not allowed within the town itself. Turn around, look down Corso Cavour, and imagine it in Roman times, leading away from the city gate and lined with tombs. Step into the café. A glass panel in the floor shows the original Roman foundations and pavement stones.

Back outside, cross under the Roman gate and head into the ancient city. Walk down Corso Porta Borsari, the Roman main drag, toward what was the forum. Make it a scavenger hunt. As you walk, discover bits of the town's illustrious past—chips of Roman columns, medieval reliefs, fine old facades, fossils in marble—as well as its elegant present of fancy shops, in a setting that prioritizes pedestrians over cars. On the right, you'll pass the recommended Osteria del Bugiardo, at #17, a popular wine bar and a good place to take a break and hang out with Verona's young and trendy.

• *Between Corso Porta Borsari 13 and 15, detour right down Vicolo San*

NEAR VENICE

Marco in Foro, following the Pozzo dell'Amore *sign. Twenty yards ahead on your right, you'll find...*

❺ Enoteca Oreste

This funky wine-and-grappa bar is still run by Oreste (with his Chicagoan wife, Beverly) like a 1970s, old-style *enoteca*. Browse and sample and clown around with Oreste. This historic *enoteca* was once the private chapel of the arch-bishop of Verona. Traces of the past hide between the bottles—ask Beverly to tell you the story (light food, Tue-Sun 9:00-22:00, closed Mon, Vicolo San Marco in Foro 7, tel. 045-803-4369).

• *Return to Corso Porta Borsari and continue one block until you hit a big square.*

❻ Piazza Erbe

This bustling market square is a photographer's delight. Its pastel buildings corral the fountains, pigeons, and peo-

ple who have congregated here since Roman times, when this was a forum. Notice the Venetian lion hovering above the square atop a column, reminding locals of the conquest of 1405. Wander into the market, to the fountain in the middle. A fountain has bubbled here for 2,000 years. The original Roman statue lost its head and arms. After a sculptor added a new head and arms, the statue became Verona's Madonna. She holds a small banner that reads, roughly, "The city of Verona deserves respect and justice." During medieval times, the stone canopy in the center of the square (past the fountain) held the scales where merchants measured the weight of goods they bought and sold, such as silk and wool.

If you were standing here in the Middle Ages, you would have been surrounded by proud noble family towers. Medieval nobles showed off with towers. Renaissance nobles showed off with finely painted facades on their palaces. Find remnants of the 16th-century days when Verona was nicknamed "the painted city."

Locals like to start their evening with an *aperitivo* here. Each bar caters to a different market segment. Survey the scene and, if or when the time is right, choose the terrace that suits you and join in the ritual. It's simple: Grab a spot, adjust your seat for the best view, and order a *spritz* to drink (€4 with a plate of olives and chips).

• *At the far end of Piazza Erbe is a market column featuring St. Zeno, the patron of Verona, who looks at the crazy crowds flushing into the city's silly claim to touristic fame: the House of Juliet (100 yards down Via Cappello to #23, on the left—just follow the crowds). Side-trip there now (but watch your wallet—it's a pickpocket's haven).*

❼ House of Juliet

The tiny, admittedly romantic courtyard is a spectacle: Tourists from all over the world pose on the balcony, while those hoping for love wait their turn to polish Juliet's

bronze breast. Residents marvel that each year, about 1,600 Japanese tour groups break their Venice-Milan ride for an hour-long stop in Verona just to see this courtyard (free, gates open roughly 9:00-19:30 or longer). It's fun to stand in the corner and observe the scene, knowing that all of this commotion was started by a clever tour guide in the early 1970s as a way to attract visitors to Verona.

The courtyard walls have long been filled with amorous graffiti. The latest trend is to affix a paper note to the gates or walls with chewing gum. The wall of padlocks is another gimmick, enabling lovers to blow money in an attempt to prove that their hearts are thoroughly locked up. (The shop that sells the locks also sells pens to write on them.) The red mailbox is for love letters to Juliet. There's actually a Juliet Club that reviews these—and all the letters mailed from around the world to "Juliet, Verona, Italy." Each year, the club awards the author of the sweetest letter a free vacation to Verona.

Even those who milk their living out of this sight freely admit that "While no documentation has been discovered to prove the truth of the legend, no documentation has disproved it either." The "museum," which displays art inspired by the love story, plus costumes and the bed from Franco Zeffirelli's film *Romeo and Juliet*, is certainly not worth the €6 entry fee.

Was there ever a real Juliet Capulet? You just walked down Via Cappello, the street of the cap makers. Above the courtyard entry (looking out) is a coat of arms featuring a hat—representing a family that made hats and which would be named, logically, Capulet.

The public's interest in a fictional Romeo and Juliet—or at least Juliet—is a sign that there's a hunger for a Juliet in our world. Observing the mobs clamoring to polish her breast or blow kisses from her bogus balcony, I try to appreciate what she means to people, and to psychoanalyze what she provides to those who come to Verona specifically for this: the message that love will prevail. In love, you can lose and still be a winner. Juliet is brave, tragic, honest, outspoken, timeless, and passionate. She's a mover and a shaker, a dreamer, and a fighter. In a way, this is a pagan temple where the spirit of Juliet gives people something to believe in...or maybe it's just a bunch of baloney appreciated by a simple-minded crowd.

• *Return to Piazza Erbe. From the middle of the piazza, head right on Via della Costa. Walk down Via della Costa, into the big square.*

❽ Piazza dei Signori

Literally the "Lords' Square," this is Verona's sitting room, quieter and more harmonious than Piazza Erbe. The buildings—which span five centuries—define the square and are all linked by arches. From one arch dangles a whale's rib. It was likely a souvenir brought home by a traveling merchant from a trip to the Orient, reminding the townspeople that there was a big world out there. The long portico on the left is inspired by a building in Florence: Brunelleschi's Hospital of the Innocents, considered the first Renaissance building.

Locals call the square Piazza Dante for the statue of the Italian poet **Dante Alighieri** that dominates it. Dante—always pensive, never smiling—seems to wonder why the tourists choose Juliet over him. Dante was expelled from Florence when that city sided with the pope (who didn't appreciate Dante's writing) and banished its greatest poet. Verona and its ruling Scaligeri family, however, were at odds with the pope (siding instead with the Holy Roman Emperor), and granted Dante asylum.

With the whale's rib behind you, you're facing the brick, crenellated, 14th-century Scaligeri residence. Behind Dante is the yellowish, 15th-century Venetian Renaissance-style Portico of the Counsel. At Dante's two o'clock is the 12th-century Romanesque **Palazzo della Ragione** (closed to the public, except for its tower).

Looking back the way you came, follow the white *toilette* signs into the courtyard of the Palazzo della Ragione. The impressive stairway is the only surviving Renaissance staircase in Verona. For a grand city view, you can climb to the top of the palazzo's 13th-century **Torre dei Lamberti** (€6 for stairs or elevator, daily June-Sept 8:30-20:30, Oct-May 8:30-19:30, ticket office next to staircase). The elevator saves you 243 steps—but you'll still need to

climb 46 more to get to the first viewing platform. It's not worth continuing up 79 more spiral stairs to the second viewing platform.
• *Exit the courtyard the way you entered and turn right, continuing downhill. Within a block, you'll find the...*

❾ Tombs of the Scaligeri Family

These exotic and very Gothic 14th-century tombs, with their fine, original, wrought-iron protective cages, evoke the age when one

family ruled Verona. The Scaligeri were to Verona what the Medici family was to Florence. These were powerful people. They changed the law so that they could be buried within the town. They forbade the presence of any noble family's towers but their own. And, by building tombs atop pillars, they arranged to be looked up to, even in death.

• *Continue 15 yards to the next corner and take a left on Vicolo Cavalletto. At the first corner, turn right along Corso Sant'Anastasia toward the big, unfinished brick facade of Verona's largest church. For a fragrant and potentially tasty diversion, pop*

into ❿ *two classic grocery stores: Gastronomia (on the opposite corner at the start of the street, at #33, closed Sun afternoon) and Albertini, located on your left in the next block. Gastronomia can rustle up tasty sandwiches (about €3-4).*

⓫ Church of Sant'Anastasia

This church was built from the late 13th century through the 15th century. Although the facade was never finished (the builders ran

out of steam), the interior was—and still is—brilliant. Step inside to see the delightful way this region's medieval churches were painted. Note the grimacing hunchbacks holding basins of holy water on their backs (near main entrance at base of columns). And don't miss Pisanello's fresco of *St. George and the Princess of Trebizond* (1438; at the tip of the arch, high above chapel to right of altar). Once colorful, it has oxidized over time to its current monochrome state. For a closer look at its wonderful detail, check out the images on the computer terminal below the fresco. Ask for the English brochure, which describes the story of the church.

Cost and Hours: €2.50; March-Oct Mon-Sat 9:00-18:00,

NEAR VENICE

Sun 13:00-18:00; Nov-Feb Mon-Sat 9:00-13:00 & 13:30-17:00, Sun 13:00-17:00; www.chieseverona.it.

• *Leaving the church, make two lefts, and walk along the right side of the church to Via Sottoriva. To the right, the Sottoriva arcade was once busy with colorful wine bars and* osterie, *some of which still exist (see "Eating in Verona," later). But for now, head to the left on Via Sottoriva. In a block, you'll reach a small riverfront area with stone benches that usually have a few modern-day Romeos and Juliets gazing at each other rather than at the view. Belly up to the river view.*

⑫ Ponte Pietra and River View

The white stones of the Ponte Pietra footbridge are from the original Roman bridge that stood here. After the bridge was bombed in World War II, the Veronese fished the marble chunks out of the river to rebuild it. From here you can see across the river to the Roman Theater, built into the hillside behind the green hedge (see page 209). Way above the theater (behind the cypress trees) is the fortress, Castello San Pietro.

The wide spot in the river here was called the "Millers' Widening," where boats stopped and unloaded grain to be milled. Water wheels once lined the river and powered medieval Verona, employing technology imported from the Holy Land by 10th-century Crusaders.

Continue up the river toward the bridge. You'll pass the recommended **Gelateria Ponte Pietra,** where Mirko, Mariam, and Stefano dish out fine gelato. Walk to the high point on the bridge and enjoy the view.

• *From the bridge, look back 200 yards at the tall white spire...that's where you're heading. Walk back off of the bridge, then turn right, keeping an eye on the left for the steeple of the...*

⑬ Duomo

Started in the 12th century, this church was built over a period of several hundred years. Before entering, note the fine Romanesque carvings on its facade.

Step inside, pick up the leaflet that

explains the church's highlights, and head to the back-left corner of the church. In the last chapel on the left is Titian's 16th-century *Assumption of the Virgin*. Mary calmly rides a cloud—direction up—to the shock and bewilderment of the crowd below. Notice a handful of tombs embedded in the walls about 15 feet above floor level—an unusual feature. (Generally, tombs are found in the floor of the church or in crypts below.)

Now head up the aisle to the last door on the left (left of high altar), where you'll find the **ruins** of an older church. These are the 10th-century foundations of the Church of St. Elena, turned intriguingly into a modern-day chapel featuring exposed fourth-century mosaic floors from the Roman church that originally stood here.

From there, pass through the little open-air courtyard into the adjacent **baptistery,** with its clean Romanesque lines, hanging 14th-century crucifix, and fine marble font. Try to identify the eight biblical scenes carved on its panels before referring to my answers. (Answers, starting with the panel just to the right of center and working counterclockwise: Annunciation; first Christmas, with animals licking baby Jesus and giving him a barnyard welcome; announcement to shepherds of Jesus' birth, with their flock stacked on one side; Epiphany, with the Three Kings giving their gifts to Baby Jesus; Herod commanding that all male infants be killed; Slaughter of the Innocents; flight to Egypt; and, finally, facing the entry door, John the Baptist baptizing Christ.)

Finally, after leaving the church, circle around its left side (as you face the main facade) to find the peaceful Romanesque **cloister** *(chiostro),* with mosaics from a fifth-century Christian church exposed below the walk.

Cost and Hours: €2.50; March-Oct Mon-Sat 10:00-17:30, Sun 13:30-17:30; Nov-Feb Mon-Fri 10:00-13:00 & 13:30-17:00, Sat 10:00-16:00, Sun 13:30-17:00.

Sights in Verona

In the Town Center

▲▲Evening *Passeggiata*

For me, the highlight of Verona is the *passeggiata* (stroll)—especially in the evening. Make a big circle from Piazza Brà through the old town on Via Mazzini (one of Europe's many "first" pedestrian-only streets) to the colorful Piazza Erbe, and then back down Corso Porta Borsari to Piazza Brà. This is a small town, where people know each other, and they're all out on parade. Like peacocks, the young and nubile spread their wings. The classy shop windows are integral to the *passeggiata* as, for the ladies, shopping is a sport. Their never-finished wardrobes are considered a work in progress,

NEAR VENICE

and this is when they gather ideas. If you're going to complement your stroll with a stop in a café or bar, the best plan is to enjoy a *spritz* drink—not on Piazza Brà, but on Piazza Erbe (the oldest and most elegant bars are on the end farthest from Juliet's balcony).

ArenaMuseOpera (AMO)

This slick museum, which opened in 2013 to celebrate the 100th anniversary of the city's renowned opera festival, fills the old Palazzo Forti in the sleepy streets at the northern edge of downtown. The underwhelming permanent exhibit, swaddled in red velvet, uses a few scant artifacts, sparse descriptions, and a handful of interactive touchscreens to trace the creation of an opera from words *(libretto)* to score *(partitura)* to staging *(rappresentazione,* including designers' sketches, along with actual sets and costumes from some of the performances that have graced the arena's stage). Although the museum is vastly overpriced, opera lovers may enjoy it—particularly if the temporary exhibits, which can be excellent, are of interest.

Cost and Hours: €10-15 depending on special exhibits, daily 9:00-19:30, Via Massalongo 7, tel. 045-803-0461, www.arena-museopera.com.

West of Piazza Brà and the Arena

▲Castelvecchio

Verona's powerful Scaligeri family built this castle (1343-1356) as both a residence and a fortress. The castle has two parts: the family

palace and the quarters for their private army (separated, for the nervous family's security, by a fortified wall and an internal moat). Today, it houses the city's art gallery, with an extensive, enjoyable collection of sculpture and paintings. (Religious statues were Verona's medieval forte, while paintings were the city's Renaissance forte.) Meanwhile, kids (and kids at heart) enjoy the chance to scramble across the delightfully crenellated parapets, with fine views over Verona.

From the entrance, you'll head right toward the **statues,** once brightly painted. Cross to the next wing and head upstairs to walk through two floors that trace the evolution of **painting** from the 13th through the 17th centuries, including minor works by many major masters (such as Bellini, Mantegna, and Veronese). You'll also pass by a small armory collection; en route, watch for the chance to roam the **ramparts** with fine views of the city, river, and

Ponte Scaligero (described next). Verona was an independent city-state from 1176 to 1387. Then came a long period of subjugation under other powers that, in more modern times, included the Austrians. From the ramparts you can see remnants of Austrian rule: the arsenal across the river and the castle atop the distant hill.

Cost and Hours: €6, Tue-Sun 8:30-19:30, Mon 13:30-19:30, last entry 45 minutes before closing, Corso Castelvecchio 2, tel. 045-806-2611, see map on page 211 for location. Info sheets with good English descriptions are available throughout, but the €4 audioguide (€6/2 people) is still worthwhile.

Nearby: Next to Castelvecchio, the picturesque red-brick bridge called **Ponte Scaligero**—fortified and crenellated, as if a continuation of the castle—is free, open to the public, and fun to stroll across. Destroyed by the Germans in World War II, it was rebuilt in the 1950s using many of its original bricks, which were dredged out of the river. Today it's understandably a favorite for wedding-day photos.

▲Basilica of San Zeno Maggiore

This church, outside the old center, is dedicated to the patron saint of Verona, whose remains are buried in the crypt under the main altar. In addition to being a fine example of Italian Romanesque, the basilica features Mantegna's *San Zeno Triptych* (1456-1459) with its marvelous perspective, peaceful double-columned cloisters, and a set of 48 paneled 11th-century bronze doors nicknamed "the poor man's Bible." Pretend you're an illiterate medieval peasant and do some reading. Facing the altar, on the walls of the right-side aisle, you can see frescoes painted on top of other frescoes and graffiti dating from the 1300s. These were done by people who fled into the church in times of war or flooding and scratched prayers into the walls. Druidic-looking runes are actually decorated letters typical of the Gothic period, like those in illuminated manuscripts.

Cost and Hours: €2.50, March-Oct Mon-Sat 8:30-18:00, Sun 12:30-18:00; Nov-Feb Mon-Sat 10:00-13:00 & 13:30-17:00, Sun 13:00-17:00; located on Piazza San Zeno, a 15-minute walk upriver beyond Castelvecchio, www.chieseverona.it.

Across the Roman Bridge, North of the Center

Roman Theater (Teatro Romano)

Dating from about the time of Christ, this ancient theater was discovered in the 19th century and restored. Admission includes the Roman Museum, located high in the building above the theater (reach it via elevator—start at the stage and walk up the middle set of stairs, then continue straight on the path through the bushes).

The museum displays a model of the theater, a small chapel, and Roman artifacts, including mosaic floors, busts and other statuary, clay and bronze votive figures, and architectural fragments. There's not much to see. Unless you've never seen a Roman ruin, I'd skip it.

Cost and Hours: €4.50, Tue-Sun 8:30-19:30, Mon 13:30-19:30, last entry one hour before closing, theater located across the river near Ponte Pietra footbridge, tel. 045-800-0360. From mid-June through August, the theater stages Shakespeare plays—only a little more difficult to understand in Italian than in Elizabethan English.

Giusti Garden (Giardino Giusti)

You'll see this picturesque Renaissance garden capping the steep hilltop just across the Roman Bridge at the northern edge of the city. It's a little oasis with manicured box hedges, towering cypress trees, and a city view from the top of its hill. For most people, however, it's not worth the hike, time, or money.

Cost and Hours: €6, daily April-Sept 9:00-20:00, Oct-March 9:00-17:00, across the river, beyond Ponte Nuovo.

Sleeping in Verona

I've listed rates you'll pay in the regular season—most of April through May, and September through October. Prices soar (at least €20-30 more per night) from mid-June through early September (opera season), in early April (during the Vinitaly wine festival—see "The Wines of Verona" sidebar, later), and during big trade fairs or major holidays. Unless your goal is opera, consider coming before mid-June or after early September. Prices are lower from November to March. Hotel websites clearly explain their rates.

Near Piazza Erbe

$$$ Hotel Aurora, at the corner of Piazza Erbe and Via Pelliciai, has friendly family management, attention to detail, a welcoming terrace with wonderful piazza views, and 18 fresh, modern rooms (Sb-€140, Db-€170, Tb-€200, Qb-€300, Db rates can peak at €240 during opera season, elevator, air-con, free Wi-Fi, Piazzetta XIV Novembre 2, tel. 045-594-717, www.hotelaurora.biz, info@

Verona Hotels & Restaurants

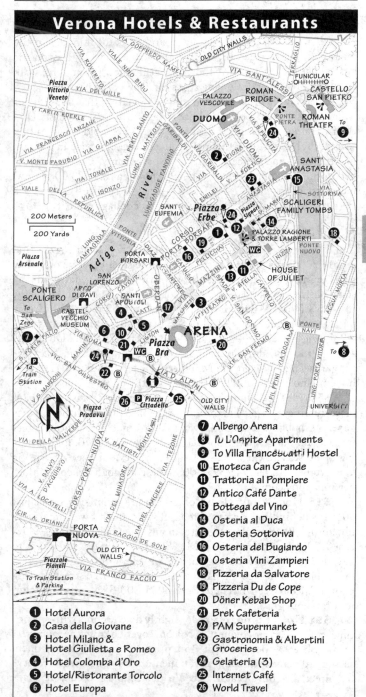

1 Hotel Aurora
2 Casa della Giovane
3 Hotel Milano & Hotel Giulietta e Romeo
4 Hotel Colomba d'Oro
5 Hotel/Ristorante Torcolo
6 Hotel Europa

7 Albergo Arena
8 To L'Ospite Apartments
9 To Villa Francescatti Hostel
10 Enoteca Can Grande
11 Trattoria al Pompiere
12 Antico Café Dante
13 Bottega del Vino
14 Osteria al Duca
15 Osteria Sottoriva
16 Osteria del Bugiardo
17 Osteria Vini Zampieri
18 Pizzeria da Salvatore
19 Pizzeria Du de Cope
20 Döner Kebab Shop
21 Brek Cafeteria
22 PAM Supermarket
23 Gastronomia & Albertini Groceries
24 Gelateria (3)
25 Internet Café
26 World Travel

NEAR VENICE

hotelaurora.biz, Rita). Coming from the train station, you can hop off at Piazza Brà, cross the square, and walk 10 minutes up the main pedestrian street; or, for a slightly shorter walk, stay on the bus two stops longer until the San Fermo stop (from here, walk away from the river, following signs for *Piazza Erbe*).

$ Casa della Giovane, run by an association that houses poor women, also rents rooms and dorm beds to female tourists (and their children up to age 10). Buried deep in the old town and up several flights of stairs, this place offers 20 cheap beds in a clean, institutional, and peaceful setting (women only, €22/bed in 11-bed dorm, Sb-€35, Db-€60, Tb-€90, no breakfast, 23:00 curfew, reception open 9:00-21:00, free Wi-Fi, self-service laundry, Via Pigna 7, tel. 045-596-880, www.protezionedellagiovane.it).

Near Piazza Brà

You'll find several options in the quiet streets just off Piazza Brà, within 200 yards of the bus stop. From the square, white or yellow signs point you to the hotels. Most of these are big, fairly impersonal business-class places; the Torcolo is more homey and friendly.

$$$ Hotel Milano is an arty hotel with 52 rooms. The lobby and fancier rooms are tricked out in black and chrome (rates vary wildly—see website—generally about Sb-€75-100, Db-€120-150, up to €280 during opera season, air-con, elevator, free Wi-Fi, garage-€20, Vicolo Tre Marchetti 11, tel. 045-596-011, www.hotelmilano-vr.it, info@hotelmilano-vr.it).

$$$ Hotel Colomba d'Oro is a sprawling, stately, elegant place renting 51 spacious rooms with Baroque flourishes. It has generous public spaces and overlooks a quiet and central street (prices vary but generally Sb-€110-130, Db-€150-170, higher during opera season, extra bed-€30, air-con, elevator, pay Wi-Fi, Via C. Cattaneo 10, tel. 045-595-300, www.colombahotel.com, info@colombahotel.com).

$$$ Hotel Giulietta e Romeo is on a quiet side street just 50 yards behind the Roman Arena. It's stylish and well-managed; nine of its 40 sexy, ultra-modern rooms have balconies (Sb-€110, Db-€130, bigger "superior" Db-€30 more, prices shoot up to €200/€260 during opera season, air-con, elevator, free Wi-Fi, free loaner bikes, fitness room, garage-€20 or ask for free street parking permit, Vicolo Tre Marchetti 3, tel. 045-800-3554, www.hotelgr.it, info@hotelgr.it).

$$$ Hotel Europa offers 46 slightly dated rooms with springtime colors. Try to request a balcony overlooking the *piazzetta* below (Sb-€90-100, Db-€130-150, prices up to €206 during opera season, 10 percent discount if you mention this book when reserving direct, air-con, elevator, free Wi-Fi, a couple of blocks off Piazza Brà at Via Roma 8, tel. 045-594-744, www.veronahoteleuropa. com, info@veronahoteleuropa.com).

$$ Hotel Torcolo offers 19 comfortable, lovingly maintained rooms with Grandma's furnishings (Sb-€75, Db-€100 most of the year but up to €150 during opera season, breakfast-€14, air-con, fridge in room, elevator, Wi-Fi, garage-€16; from Piazza Brà promenade, head down the alley to the right of #16 and walk to Vicolo Listone 3; tel. 045-800-7512, www.hoteltorcolo.it, hoteltorcolo@virgilio.it, well-run by Silvia, Diana, and helpful Caterina).

Near Castelvecchio
$ Albergo Arena, while dreary, is a good value for those on a budget. Located in a peaceful courtyard off a busy street a few blocks from Piazza Brà, it offers 15 very basic, quiet rooms (S-€45, Sb-€60, Db-€85, air-con, elevator, free Wi-Fi, just west of Castelvecchio at Stradone Porta Palio 2, tel. 045-803-2440, www.albergoarena.it, info@albergoarena.it, Francesco and Elena).

Across the River
$$ L'Ospite, a 10-minute walk across the river from Piazza Erbe, has six cozy, immaculate, fully equipped apartments and lots of stairs. The rooms, warmly managed by English-speaking Federica De Rossi, sleep from two to four, with air-conditioning and free Wi-Fi (Db-€95, Tb/Qb-about €40-55/person, discounts for cash and longer stays, no reception or daily cleaning; Via XX Settembre 3; tel. 045-803-6994, mobile 329-426-2524, www.lospite.com, info@lospite.com). Coming from the station by bus (ride same buses as those headed downtown—see "Arrival in Verona," earlier), get off three stops past Piazza Brà, just after crossing the bridge, at the XX Settembre stop (across the street from the apartments).

$ Villa Francescatti is a good, church-affiliated hostel in a pretty hillside setting (€18/bed in 6- or 8-bed sex-segregated rooms with hall bath, €20/bed in family rooms with private bathrooms, cash only, includes breakfast and sheets, €8 dinners, laundry €5/load, free Wi-Fi in common areas, rooms closed from 9:00 to 17:00 but reception open all day, 24:00 curfew; Salita Fontana del Ferro 15, bus #73 or #91 from station to Piazza Isolo plus short steep walk, tel. 045-590-360, www.ostelloverona.it, info@villafrancescatti.it).

Eating in Verona

Every restaurant listed here is within a 10-minute walk of the others. They're mostly small and intimate, and found along side streets. It's tempting to grab a table next to the *passeggiata* action along Piazza Brà, but you'll be sacrificing service, value, and quality for your view of the floodlit Roman Arena and Verona on parade (perhaps a fair trade-off). Except for Brek Cafeteria, restaurants on the piazza tend to charge a cover and service fee, making even pizza a pricey choice.

Fine Dining

Enoteca Can Grande is enthusiastically run by Giuliano and Corrina, who enjoy turning people on to great, well-matched food and wine. You can sit on a quiet street or in a plush little dining area inside. Their star offering is a €40 set menu, a festival of *antipasti* treats, an imaginative pasta, your choice of a meat or fish course, and dessert. They also offer a junior version at lunch for €20: a pasta and your choice of salad or dessert (Wed-Mon 12:00-15:30 & 18:00-22:30, closed Tue, closed Mon instead of Tue during opera season; a block off Piazza Brà at Via Dietro Liston 19D—if the equestrian statue jogged slightly right, he'd head straight here; tel. 045-595-022).

Trattoria al Pompiere, which has a commitment to regional traditions, is bigger, with formal waiters weaving among its tight tables and walls plastered with photos of big shots from the area. This bustling place is a favorite of local foodies. Marco and his gang serve gourmet meats and cheeses as *antipasti* from their larger-than-life back counter, ideal for a mixed plate to complement the huge selection of fine wines. Reservations are wise (€10-14 pastas, €16-19 *secondi*, Mon-Sat 12:40-14:00 & 19:40-22:30, closed Sun, chivalry lives—ladies' menus come without prices; halfway between Piazza Erbe and Juliet's courtyard—head down narrow side street next to Via Cappello 8 to Vicolo Regina d'Ungheria 5; tel. 045-803-0537, www.alpompiere.tv).

Antico Café Dante is a high-end place with a 19th-century pedigree and elegant service on the coziest and classiest square in town. You can enjoy a memorable meal of classic Veneto cuisine either at romantic tables on the square, or inside. While it's not cheap, if you want to dress up and enjoy a slow, romantic, memorable meal, this can be a good value (€15-16 pastas, €22-25 *secondi*, daily 12:30-14:30 & 19:30-23:00, Piazza dei Signori 2, tel. 045-800-0083, www.caffedante.it). For something a little more affordable, duck into their shaded alley next door to order from a more casual menu (from lunchtime through 18:00).

Bottega del Vino is pricey, venerable, and a bit pretentious. Under a high ceiling and walls of wine bottles, brisk black-vested waiters match traditional dishes (polenta, duck, game) with glasses of fine wine. Choose from 20 open bottles. The waitstaff, ambience, and food have deep roots in local culture. I like their front room best. Reservations are smart for dinner (€16 pastas, €20-24

The Wines of Verona

Wine connoisseurs love the high-quality wines of the Verona area. The hills to the east are covered with grapes to make Soave; to the north is Valpolicella country; and Bardolino comes from vineyards to the west.

Valpolicella grapes, which are used to make the fruity, red Valpolicella table wine (found everywhere), are also the basis for full-bodied red Amarone and the sweet dessert wine Recioto. To produce Amarone, grapes are partially dried (*passito*) before fermentation, then aged for a minimum of four years in oak casks, resulting in a rich, velvety, full-bodied red. Recioto, which in local dialect means "ears," uses only the grapes from the top of the cluster (so they sort of look like the "ears" of the cluster's "head"). Because these grapes get the most sun, they mature the fastest and have the highest concentration of sugar. Before pressing, the grapes are dried for months until all moisture has gone out; the wine is then aged for one to three years.

Bardolino, from the vineyards near Lake Garda, is a light, fruity wine, like a French Beaujolais. It's a perfect picnic wine.

Soave, which might be Italy's best-known white wine, goes well with seafood and risotto dishes. While Soave can vary widely in quality, the best are called "Soave Classico" and come from the heart of the region, near the Soave Castle. Soave is sometimes aged in oak casks, giving it a mellow, rounded flavor.

Sample these and many others at the numerous *enoteche* (wine-tasting bars) or at any restaurant around town. In early April, Verona hosts Vinitaly, the most important international convention of domestic and international wines. Vintners vie for prestigious awards for the past year's vintage. Tourists are welcome to attend at the end of the week, and are shuttled to the convention hall from Piazza Brà. Hotels book up months in advance. Check with the TI and www.vinitaly.com for details.

If you're visiting the area in the fall, consider a day trip to nearby Monteforte d'Alpone, east of Verona. The town hosts a fun, raucous wine festival in September—ask at the TI for more information on this and other regional wine festivals.

secondi, good daily specials, daily 12:00-23:00, off Via Mazzini at Via Scudo di Francia 3, tel. 045-800-4535, www.bottegavini.it).

Budget Restaurants

Osteria al Duca is a fun, family-run place with a lively atmosphe and good traditional dishes. Locals line up for its affordable, tv course, €17 fixed-price meal with lots of choices. I much pr their ground floor (*piano terra*—worth requesting). Reserva are advised (Mon-Sat 12:00-15:00 & 18:30-22:30, closed Sun, half-block east of Scaligeri family tombs at Via Arche Scaligere 2, tel. 045-594-474, Alessandro or Daniela).

Ristorante Torcolo is a family restaurant, with mom (Paola) running the kitchen, and father and son (Roberto and Luca) serving the meals. While it feels a bit dressy, it lacks pretense. They serve all the classic dishes, with an accessible menu and an extensive wine list. Eat in their dining hall or on the tiny courtyard outside (€9-12 pastas, €15-18 *secondi*, €35 fixed-price meal featuring traditional Verona dishes, Tue-Sun 12:00-15:00 & 19:00-22:30, closed Mon, just behind the Piazza Brà scene on a quiet street, Via Carlo Cattaneo 11, tel. 045-803-3730).

Eating in *Osterie* (Old Bars)

Wandering around the old town, you'll see plenty of Verona's thriving little watering holes. While these characteristic old bars focus more on wine than on food, most serve memorable, characteristic, and affordable plates. Menus are simple and rustic—sometimes just bar munchies and the daily pasta. Service is relaxed and the clientele is young and local. For drinks it's mostly wine or water—fine wines are served by the glass, with bottles open and prices listed on blackboards. (I saw one sign suggesting that patrons "don't drive too much to drink.")

I've listed three places below: a classic antique *osteria* with more of a menu; a trendy, more modern place in the old center; and a small one-man show just off Piazza Brà, where you're most likely to make a new friend.

Osteria Sottoriva survives from an era when Verona's river served as the town thoroughfare, and business deals could be made over a glass of wine at rustic riverside eateries. Located in a fine old covered arcade (the portico of Via Sottoriva), Sottoriva offers simple soups and pastas, with both cozy indoor and outdoor seating (€7-13 dishes, Thu-Tue 11:00-15:00 & 18:30-22:30—but open all day long in summer, closed Wed, behind the Church of Sant'Anastasia at Via Sottoriva 9, tel. 045-801-4323).

Osteria del Bugiardo is jammed with a hip, young crowd that spills out onto the pedestrian-filled Corso Porta Borsari. They have a buffet of little sandwiches, can whip up a plate of top-quality cheeses, and serve a good pasta-of-the-day. They showcase their own Buglioni wines and are proud to tell you more about them (€7 pastas, €11 *secondi*, daily 10:00-23:00, Corso Porta Borsari 17, tel. 045-591-869).

Osteria Vini Zampieri, with a tiny bar and five tables, keeps tradition of stoking conviviality with good wine since 1937. Its young and energetic manager, Leo, is passionate about organic wines, slow food, and his own home-brewed beer. As the drinks

A Mobile Feast Through Verona

Verona is a great town to sample the *aperitivo* ritual. All over town, locals enjoy a refreshing *spritz*, ideally on Piazza Erbe, between 18:00 and 20:00. Choose a nice perch, and then, for about €4, you'll get the drink of your choice, a few nibbles (olives and/or potato chips), and a chance to feel very local as you enjoy the *passeggiata* scene.

Consider this for a fun sampling of many dimensions of the Verona eating and socializing scene: Start with an *aperitivo* on **Piazza Erbe** (the most refined bars are the farthest from Juliet's balcony), then walk across Ponte Nuovo to **Pizzeria da Salvatore** and enjoy the town's best pizza. If you have to wait for a table, have another *spritz* at the neighboring bar. Then stroll along the river to **Osteria Sottoriva** and enjoy a little sampling of bar food with a glass of Amarone (wine to meditate with) under the old arcade. Finish by meandering through the old center back to Piazza Brà for a gelato at **Gelateria Savoia**. *Buon appetito!*

NEAR VENICE

are their priority, they don't serve much food—just some bar munchies and a nice *antipasti* plate—but at lunchtime, Leo can whip up a simple pasta to complement your wine (daily 11:00-late, a few steps off Piazza Brà and next to Via Mazzini at Via Alberto Maria 23, tel. 045-597-053). You're welcome to play foosball downstairs on what Italians call the *calcio balilla* ("the little boy soldiers of Mussolini").

Pizza

Pizzeria da Salvatore, Verona's first pizzeria, opened in 1961, when pizza was considered a foreign food...from Naples. They serve the best pizza in town, and a visit here gives a nice excuse to stroll across the river into a part of town with no tourists. It's family-friendly, not fancy or romantic, and you'll squeeze into a tight row of tiny tables, rubbing elbows with your neighbors. While it's not quite Naples, it's justifiably popular—come early, or plan to leave your name on the list and wait awhile (no reservations, €6-10 pizzas, Mon-Sat 12:30-14:30 & 19:00-23:00, Sun 19:00-23:00 on across Ponte Nuovo to Piazza San Tomaso 6, tel. 045-803-036

Pizzeria Du de Cope is a colorful, high-energy, info place (with paper placemats) that buzzes with smartly attired waiters and locals who keep coming back for the pizza (€10- zas, big €10-16 salads, daily 12:00-14:30 & 19:00-23:00, f ant desserts, families welcome, no reservations, at Galleri 10, tel. 045-595-562).

Cheap Eats

Döner kebab shops all over town serve hearty, cheap kebabs to munch on from a stool or to take out (most open daily roughly noon-midnight). *Piadine* (pita-bread) kebabs are worth the €4, and the super-sized kebabs can fill a couple on a very tight budget for a total of €6. The best kebabs, according to local assessments, are behind the Roman Arena at Via Leoncino 44. There's another good place on the other side of Piazza Brà, near Hotel Europa, at Via Teatro Filarmonico 6. The benches in the center of Piazza Brà are handy for a scenic place to munch your cheap meal.

Brek Cafeteria, a well-run and modern chain right on Piazza Brà, offers a cheap and easy self-serve option inside (€5 pastas, €7 *secondi,* cheap salad plates). Or, if you want to sit out on the square, you can order off the pricier menu (€9 pastas, €13 *secondi*) and enjoy a view that's worth paying a little extra for (daily 11:30-15:00 & 18:30-22:00, longer hours for outdoor seating during summer, facing equestrian statue at Piazza Brà 20).

Groceries: **PAM supermarket** is just outside the historic gate on Piazza Brà (Mon-Sat 8:00-21:00, Sun 9:00-20:00, exit Piazza Brà through the gate and take the first right to Via dei Mutilati 3). Near the Church of Sant'Anastasia are two classic grocery stores, **Gastronomia** and **Albertini** (described on page 205).

Gelato: The venerable **Gelateria Savoia** has been a local favorite since 1939. It's in an arcade just off Piazza Brà, marked by a happy crowd licking their distinctive *semi-freddo*—a specialty of bitter-almond amaretto, cream, and cookie (open long hours daily, just off Piazza Brà at Via Roma 1). On the other side of town, near Ponte Pietra and the Duomo, is **Gelateria Ponte Pietra** (Tue-Sun 14:30-19:30, until 23:00 in summer, closed Mon, at #23; see the end of my self-guided walk, earlier). **Gelato Pretto,** the pricey gourmet *gelateria* from Padua, also has a prime location here in Verona—right on Piazza Erbe (at #40; see description on page 189).

Verona Connections

You have three options for getting train tickets in the Verona station: the standard station ticket office (with slow-moving lines, ...ly 6:00-21:00), a bank of modern machines (good English de-...tions, cash and credit cards accepted), and the Deutsche Bahn ... office (20 yards from baggage check office in the tunnel, of-...tickets at the same cost as the station office but with German ...y and no lines, Mon-Sat 8:00-18:00, closed Sun).

...y hour, at least two trains connect Verona with Venice, ...d Vicenza: One's a slow, cheap, regional train; the other ... Venice faster but costs twice as much and requires reservations—meaning you need to choose a particular departure when you buy your ticket.

From Verona by Train to: Venice (at least 2/hour, 1.25-1.75 hours), **Padua** (at least 2/hour, 40-60 minutes), **Vicenza** (at least 2/hour, 25-60 minutes), **Florence** (*Firenze*, about hourly, 1.5 hours direct or 2.5 hours with transfer in Bologna), **Bologna** (hourly, 1.25-1.5 hours), **Milan** (about 2/hour, 1.5-2 hours), **Rome** (at least hourly, 4-5 hours, often with transfer in Bologna, also 1 direct night train, 6.5 hours), **Bolzano** (hourly, 1.75-2.25 hours, avoid "fast" trains that take the same amount of time but cost much more). For more information, visit www.trenitalia.com.

Ravenna

Ravenna is on the tourist map for one reason: its 1,500-year-old churches, decorated with best-in-the-West Byzantine mosaics.

The city's churches and mosaics date from the time (c. A.D. 400-600) when it was the center of Western civilization—a civilization in transition, from Roman to barbarian to Byzantine to medieval. You'll see all these layers in Ravenna.

In 402, barbarian tribes were zeroing in on the city of Rome. The Roman emperor moved his capital to Ravenna, a city well-known as a home port for the imperial navy (today's Classe). Because of its location, Ravenna kept close ties with the other Roman capital at Constantinople (called Byzantium).

Ravenna was conquered by the Goths (via Hungary) in 476, and the 1,000 years of the Roman Empire came to an end. But Ravenna continued on as the Goths' capital. They kept much of the Roman infrastructure and legitimized their rule by buildin sophisticated palaces and churches in the Roman style.

In 540, the Byzantine emperor Justinian conquered the Go This reunited Italy with the still-thriving Empire to the east tinian turned Ravenna into a pinnacle of civilization. It rema flickering light in Europe's Dark Ages for another 200 yea the Lombard tribes of Germany booted out the Byzar 751). Ravenna melted into the backwaters of medieval I ing out of historical sight for a thousand years.

In your sightseeing, you'll see art from each o ods: Roman (Mausoleum of Galla Placidia, Neonia Gothic (Arian Baptistery, Basilica di Sant'Apollin

Byzantine (Basilica di San Vitale, House of Stone Carpets, Church of Sant'Apollinare in Classe), and medieval (Tomb of Dante, Basilica di San Francesco).

Today, Ravenna's economy booms with a big chemical industry, the discovery of offshore gas deposits, and the construction of a new ship canal. From a traveler's perspective, Ravenna has a delightful workaday quality, providing relief from the touristic intensity of Venice and Florence. The bustling town center is Italy's best for bicyclists. Residents go about their business, while busloads of tourists (mostly cruise-ship passengers and Italian school groups) slip quietly in and out of town for the best look at the glories of Byzantium this side of Istanbul—specifically, the richest collection anywhere of mosaics from the fifth and sixth centuries. Many are pleasantly surprised by the peaceful charm of this low-key town. If it seems less prettied-up than some of the more famous Italian towns, well...that's sort of the point.

Planning Your Time

Ravenna is a worthwhile four-hour stop, or even an overnight, particularly for mosaic lovers. Its inexpensive lodgings offer good value for your money, and its restaurants are good and affordable. You could stop here on your way between Venice (or Padua) and Florence. The town is also a doable, though long, day trip from Florence, Venice, or Padua. Ravenna is busiest between March and mid-June—prime field-trip season.

Orientation to Ravenna

Particularly because its sights are concentrated right downtown, Ravenna feels surprisingly small for a city of 160,000. Central Ravenna is quiet, with a pedestrian-friendly core and more bikes than cars. Subtle white-brick paving down the center of "pedestrian" streets indicates the bike lane: Keep to the sides and listen for the outta-my-way bells (while watching local pedestrians flagrantly stroll right down the middle). To join the two-wheeled crowd, you an rent a bike right next to the station, or borrow one from your tel or the TI.

On a quick visit to Ravenna, follow my self-guided walk and the Basilica di San Vitale, its adjacent Mausoleum of Galla ia, and the Basilica di Sant'Apollinare Nuovo (all covered by bo-ticket).

Information

15-minute walk (or a 5-minute pedal) from the train Sat 8:30-19:00, until 18:00 Oct-March, Sun 10:00-

NEAR VENICE

16:00 year-round, Via Salara 8, tel. 0544-35404, www.turismo. ra.it).

Combo-Ticket: Five of Ravenna's best mosaic sights are covered by a single combo-ticket; just pay €11.50 at the first sight you visit (€9.50 July-Feb). Included are the Basilica di San Vitale, Mausoleum of Galla Placidia, Basilica di Sant'Apollinare Nuovo, Archiepiscopal Museum (with its Chapel of Sant'Andrea), and Neonian Baptistery. All five sights are church-run and have virtually the same hours (daily April-Sept 9:00-19:00, Oct-March 9:00 or 9:30-17:00).

Arrival in Ravenna

By Train: The compact, manageable train station has all of the basic services (ticket windows open 6:00-20:55, ATMs, fast food, newsstand). The only ticket machines are just for regional trips. While there's no baggage storage inside the station, if you exit to the left and walk two minutes, you can **check your bag** at the Co-op San Vitale bike-rental shop, listed below (€3-5/24 hours).

The station is just a few minutes' walk east of the main pedestrian street: Exit out the front of the station and keep going straight ahead until you hit the main square, Piazza del Popolo (my self-guided walk begins with this same stroll from the station). If you prefer to bike, you can rent wheels at the Co-op San Vitale.

By Car: Don't drive into the center, as you'll be fined. Two inexpensive lots are near the historic core: one accessible from the west side of Via Roma, at Piazzale Torre Umbriatica (€1.80/day), and another at Largo Giustiniano just north of the Basilica di San Vitale (€3/day). Or find a free lot south of the station, on Circonvallazione Piazza d'Armi; another is north of the Piazzale Torre Umbriatica lot, on Via Monsignore F. Lanzoni. Many lots are free overnight (20:00-8:00) and most are free on Sunday.

Helpful Hints

Laundry: The self-service **Fastclan Lavanderia** is a five-minute walk from the train station (€3.50 wash, €3.50 dry, daily 7:00-22:00, go left as you exit the station, then take your first left over the rail crossing to Via Candiano 16, mobile 331-130-2072).

Bike Rental: Co-op San Vitale, in front of the train station, re bikes (€1.50/hour, €12/day, Mon-Fri 7:00-19:00, closed Sun, photo ID required, tel. 054-437-031). Many hotels loaner bikes. The **TI** loans 20 yellow one-speed bikes f on a first-come, first-served basis (bring your passport, under 18, must return bike 30 minutes before closing

NEAR VENICE

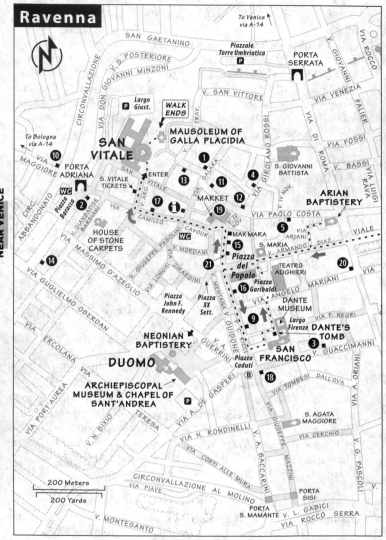

Ravenna

To Venice
via A-14

Piazzale
Torre Umbriatica

PORTA
SERRATA

SAN GAETANINO

V. S. POSTERIORE

V.S. POSTERIORE

VIA DON GIOVANNI MINZONI

CIRCONVALLAZIONE

V. SAN VITTORE

TRAV.

Largo
Giust.

WALK
ENDS

MAUSOLEUM OF
GALLA PLACIDIA

SAN
VITALE

To Bologna
via A-14

VIA
MAGGIORE

PORTA
ADRIANA

S. VITALE
TICKETS

ENTER

V. SAN

V. ARG.

VIA

CAMILLO

WC

Piazza
Baracca

V. GIANBATTISTE
BARBIANI

HOUSE
OF STONE
CARPETS

V. MASSIMO D'AZEGLIO

VIA GUGLIELMO OBERDAN

VIA ERCOLANA

VIA PORT AUREA

V.N. BIXIO

CIRC.

ABBANDONATO

S. GIOVANNI
BATTISTA

VIA GIROLAMO ROSSI

VIA SALARA

V. DI IV NOV.

ARIAN
BAPTISTERY

VIA PAOLO COSTA

VIA
ARIANI

V. MARIA
V. ARMANDO DIAZ

MAX MARA

S. MARIA

VIA GIUSEPPE PASCOLI

V. GIUSEPPE PASCOLI

V. MORDANI

WC

VIA LONGHI ZIRARDINI

MENTANA V. GUIDONE

V. ANGELO MARIANI

Piazza
del
Popolo

Piazza
Garibaldi

TEATRO
ALIGHIERI

VIA

Piazza
John F.
Kennedy

Piazza
XX
Sett.

DANTE
MUSEUM

Largo
Firenze

DANTE'S
TOMB

NEONIAN
BAPTISTERY

V. A.
GUERRINI

V. C. RICCI

SAN
FRANCISCO

V. GUACCIMANNI

VIA A. ORIANI

DUOMO

Piazza
Caduti

ARCHIEPISCOPAL
MUSEUM & CHAPEL OF
SANT'ANDREA

VIA A. DE GASPERI

TERESA

VIA TOMBESI DALL'OVA

S. AGATA
MAGGIORE

VIA N. RONDINELLI

VIA A. BACCARINI

VIA GIUSEPPE MAZZINI

VIA CERCHIO

200 Meters

200 Yards

VIA CORTI ALLE MURA

CIRCONVALLAZIONE AL MOLINO

VIA PIAVE

V. MONTESANTO

PORTA
S. MAMANTE V. L. GABICI

PORTA
SISI

VIA ROCCO SERRA

V.

VIA G. G. PASCOLI

Local Guide: Private guide Claudia Frassineti is excellent (€100/
half-day, mobile 335-613-2996, claudia.frassineti@gmail.com).

Self-Guided Walk

come to Ravenna (A Four-Hour Tour)

` to Ravenna can be as short as a four-hour loop from the
`tion. This 45-minute walk brings you from the train station
`na's top draw (Basilica di San Vitale), quickly taking in a

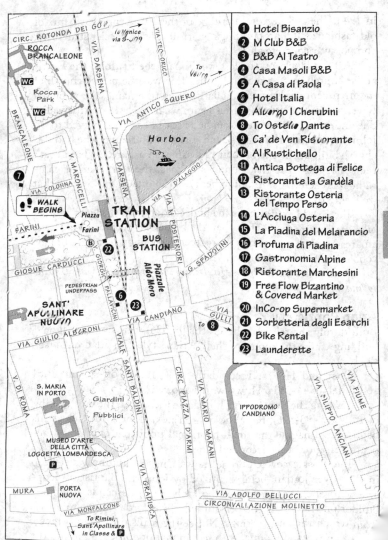

NEAR VENICE

1. Hotel Bisanzio
2. M Club B&B
3. B&B Al Teatro
4. Casa Masoli B&B
5. A Casa di Paola
6. Hotel Italia
7. Albergo I Cherubini
8. To Ostello Dante
9. Ca' de Ven Ristorante
10. Al Rustichello
11. Antica Bottega di Felice
12. Ristorante la Gardèla
13. Ristorante Osteria del Tempo Perso
14. L'Acciuga Osteria
15. La Piadina del Melarancio
16. Profuma di Piadina
17. Gastronomia Alpine
18. Ristorante Marchesini
19. Free Flow Bizantino & Covered Market
20. InCo-op Supermarket
21. Sorbetteria degli Esarchi
22. Bike Rental
23. Launderette

few other sights on the way. When done, you'll be well-ori
and can use any remaining time to visit more of Ravenna's
Start at the train station, and walk (or pedal) directly into
the main drag...

Viale Farini

The station and surrounding neighborhood were bor
War II, when Ravenna was right on the so-called "C
the Nazis' last line of defense against an encroach

in 1944. The architectural heritage of the 20th century is a mix of old-fashioned Italian buildings, stern interwar Fascist structures, and postwar concrete gloom.

After a block, on the left, you'll pass the **St. John the Evangelist** church, with a rebuilt facade. This was the palace church of the fifth-century Empress Galla Placidia (the namesake of one of Ravenna's major sights, a mausoleum we'll see later on this walk). She and her children were caught at sea in a storm, prayed to St. John (the protector of sailors), and survived. In thanks, she had this church built at the site of their first safe step ashore. At least that's the story. It is true that in ancient times, the town harbor came right up to here. Historic churches are so abundant in Ravenna that we'll skip this one.

The next big building is the high school, with students' motorbikes parked in front. After that, the boulevard becomes **Via Diaz,** an arcaded pedestrian shopping street. Remember that the lighter cobbles are for the bikes.

• *At the intersection with Via degli Ariani, side-trip to the right 50 yards to find the...*

Arian Baptistery
Built during the reign of the Goths (c. 526), this small octagonal building marks the center of their Arian-style Christian faith (see sidebar).

Cost and Hours: Free, daily 8:30-19:30, off-season until 16:00, tel. 0544-543-711, www.turismo.ra.it.

Visiting the Baptistery: Theodoric the Great, the Gothic king of Italy (r. 493-526), built the church next door, with this as his baptistery. Imagine the small baptismal pool that once stood beneath this gloriously decorated dome.

The mosaic-covered dome shows Christ standing waist-deep in the River Jordan, being baptized by John the Baptist (in leopard-skin robe), as the dove of the Holy Spirit descends. The body builder on the left is the personified River Jordan, next to a vase from which the river springs. Notice the realism in John's stance. The 12 apostles, dynamic, with feet in motion, proceed around the dome. The empty throne between Paul (with scroll) and Peter (with key) is a reminder that Judgment Day will come.

The mosaic is Arian, stressing Jesus' human rather than divine. Jesus is naked, with his genitals only partly obscured by the water. This emphasizes his mortal body, not his divine spirit. He's a youth, suggesting his recent creation by God. The descending dove pours water to purify Jesus, marking the exact moment when Arians believed Jesus' divine nature emerged. Besides heretical theological touches, there's also the pagan river god, shown in (pagan) human form as a bearded old man with a vase and river plant.

To modern eyes, these subtle details mean little. But to Byzantine Emperor Justinian and the Nicenes, these were red flags announcing heresy. While most Arian art was destroyed when Justinian took control, this ceiling is one of the rare survivors.

The adjacent church is closed to the public. It was the cathedral of the Goths, with a simple main structure surviving from the sixth century and a Renaissance portico.

• *Now, return to the pedestrian boulevard, turn right, and continue to...*

Piazza del Popolo

Marking the town center, this square was created by Ravenna's Venetian rulers in the 15th century. Today's shipping canal was once a river that flowed to about where the two columns stand. But it got mucky and full of mosquitoes. (Dante died here...of malaria.) One column was topped by a Venetian lion until 1509 when, with the support of Rome, Ravenna won its independence from Venice. Ravenna's citizens pulled down that symbol of Venetian rule and did the local equivalent of tarring and feathering it. The lion was replaced by St. Vitale (a first-century Christian martyr). The column on the left is topped by Ravenna's first bishop, St. Apollinare. This square is a fine place to join the old guys on benches, watching the community parade by.

• *At the end of Piazza del Popolo, turn left down Via Cairoli and walk two blocks—crossing a busy street and passing some heavy-handed Fascist architecture—to find the...*

Basilica di San Francesco

Pop into this basilica to see its flooded mosaic-covered crypt below the main altar. Today's water table is about three feet above the

Roman crypt's floor level—so there's a pond with goldfish over the fifth-century mosaics (insert a €1 coin to turn on the light). The interior is simple and Franciscan; the altar features a fourth-century Christian sarcophagus with Jesus in the center and the 12 apostles.

Cost and Hours: Free, daily 7:00-12:0(& 15:00-19:00, Piazza San Francesco, t 054-433-256.

• *With your back to the church, cut right thr the small wooded park. On your right, next double archway, is the...*

Tomb of Dante

After he was exiled from Florence for his political beli lived out the rest of his life in Ravenna. The Florenti Dante posthumously and wanted to bring their famous

NEAR VENICE

The Arian Heresy

Ravenna's art reflects a centuries-long battle of ideas among Europe's Christians that came to a violent head right here. As you wonder at the beauty of Ravenna's mosaics, you're also witnessing an epic clash between two different interpretations of Christianity.

Around A.D. 320 in Alexandria, a devout Christian priest named Arius (c. 256-336) began preaching a seemingly simple idea: Jesus, being the Son of God, was therefore created by God the Father. This idea touched off a firestorm of debate and division unmatched in Christianity until the Protestant Reformation. Arius had raised questions about the very nature of the Christian God: Is God a single entity (as the head of a monotheistic religion should be), three different persons (God the Father, Jesus Christ, and the Holy Spirit), or something in between?

To keep the peace, Roman Emperor Constantine convened a Council at Nicea (in A.D. 325, near modern Istanbul). Arius was accused of doubting the divinity of Christ, by making him separate from and inferior to God the Father. The Council branded Arius a heretic and burned his books. After splitting many theological hairs, they issued the Nicene Creed, which defined God as a Trinity: There was one God, existing in three persons "of the same substance." (Don't make me try to explain it further, or this book may end up getting burned by some sect somewhere.) The three-in-one Trinity became the standard throughout the Empire, and Arian sects were brutally suppressed. (Don't confuse the Arian sect with Nazi Germany's idea of an Aryan race.)

But that didn't settle the matter. Constantine's own son, a fervent Arian, sent missionaries north across the Danube to convert the barbarian Goths to Arian-style Christianity. A century later, as Rome was falling, those same Goths came knocking on Italy's doorstep. They overran Ravenna (476) and made Arian Christianity the official religion of state, though they tolerated the Nicene Christianity of their Italian subjects.

The churches the Goths built—including the Arian Baptistery and Basilica di Sant'Apollinare Nuovo—reflected their Arian faith. Arian mosaics of Jesus emphasized his humanness rather than his divinity.

In 540, the Byzantine Emperor Justinian drove out the Goths. To unite his empire, he demanded both political and theological conformity. Anything with the slightest whiff of Arianism was wiped out. Mosaics were stripped from the walls, statues defaced, and churches were renamed for saints famous for fighting heretics. In their place came art that reflected Byzantine tastes and Trinitarian theology. You'll see evidence of this shift at many of Ravenna's top sights.

Ravenna was Arianism's Waterloo. Sects were snuffed, Trinitarians triumphed, and the Nicene Creed (in some forms) is still said in many Christian churches today.

home to rest. To protect Dante's relics from theft by the Florentines, in 1519 Ravenna hid his bones inside the wall of the Monastery of San Francesco. There the bones lay forgotten for three centuries, until they were rediscovered and eventually placed here in 1865. (Florence's Santa Croce Church has a Dante memorial that's often mistaken for a tomb—but it's empty.)

The mausoleum is loaded with symbolism. High above the door, for example, the bronze snake eating its own tail—a symbol of eternity—suggests that Dante's soul (or, at least, his works) will have everlasting life. Capping the structure is an allegorical pinecone: A tasty pine nut hides inside the cone's desiccated, lifeless exterior—a reminder of how our spirits can transcend the death of our earthly form.

Just to the right of the tomb, peer through the clever hanging fence (give it a jiggle) to the garden with the mound *(tumulo)* where Dante's bones were briefly hidden during World War II.

Cost and Hours: Free, daily April-Sept 9:30-18:30, Oct-March 9:00-12:00 & 14:00-17:00, Via D. Alighieri 9, tel. 0544-33662.

Nearby: The door to the left of the tomb leads into the peaceful twin cloisters of a former Franciscan monastery (attached to the Basilica di San Francesco, which we saw earlier). Today this complex houses a fascinating-to-Italians **Dante Museum**, which is worth a visit if you're a fan (otherwise, save your sightseeing stamina for what's coming up; museum described on page 235).

• *Turn your back to Dante's tomb and walk straight ahead until you pop out into...*

Piazza Garibaldi

With a statue of the namesake Italian patriot in the center and the stately, vivid-yellow Alighieri Theater (named for Dante) on the right, this is the humbler of Ravenna's two main squares. On the wall on your left, look for the plaques honoring patriots from Ravenna *(patrioti ravennati)* who died in **World War II.** You'll both *morti sul patibolo nelle carceri in esilio* (died in prisons in e and *caduti sui campo di battaglia* (killed on the field of battle the summer and fall of 1944, the Nazis—steadily losing the on Italy—dug in near Ravenna and fought determinedly on. The countryside surrounding Ravenna is dotted with WWII cemeteries, as well as a few remaining "bailey temporary bridges erected quickly by Allies on the ma

Next to the plaque listing the war dead is one listing the names of the Nazis' Jewish victims *(ebrei)* and their age at death. Notice just how young many of them were.

Continue under the arcade back into Piazza del Popolo, and look at the *Il Comune di Ravenna* plaque on the towered building to your right, dedicated *ai suoi caduti per la liberta* (to those "fallen for freedom"). Those killed included *partigiani caduti in combattimento* (patriots lost in battle) and *per rappresaglia*—killed by the Nazis in retribution for Allied successes. Ravenna was ultimately liberated by mostly Canadian forces.

• *With your back to the tower, turn and cross to the far-right corner of the piazza. Turn right and head one block up Via IV Novembre. On your right, at #37, peek into the Max Mara shop. At the back of this space, notice the brick apse of what was once a church. Backing up into the square and looking up, you can see the still-standing bell tower, marking what had been a sixth-century basilica.*

Turning left puts you face-to-face with Ravenna's colorful...

Covered Market

The Mercato Coperto, built in 1921, is good for picnic fixings (Mon-Sat 7:00-14:00, closed Sun) and has a busy self-serve cafeteria (closed Sat-Sun, more seating and WC upstairs). While for decades this has been the home of many local producers and vendors, it was recently purchased by the Co-op supermarket chain, which plans to convert at least part of the structure into a modern shopping center—prompting many long-term shopkeepers to preemptively move out.

• *With your back to the market's front door, jog to the right around the building onto Via Cavour, Ravenna's favored street for evening strolling and shopping. One block along is Via Salara—turn right here if you'd like to visit the TI (for information or free loaner bikes).*

Otherwise, continue down Via Cavour. Halfway down the long block, on the right, at #43, peek into the courtyard that holds Gastronomia Alpine, a deli selling top-quality local meats and cheeses—you could pull together a classy picnic here (see shop listing on page 241).

As you approach the end of the block, the yellow Porta Adriana city gate comes into view (straight ahead). A few steps later, turn right onto Via Argentario. Halfway down this block on the left, at #22, is the ticket office for Ravenna's big sights; the first of these is through the gateway at the end of this block. Buy your ticket here, then continue down the street to Ravenna's crown jewel, the...

Basilica di San Vitale

It's A.D. 540. The city of Rome has been looted, the land crawling with barbarians, and the infrastructure of Rome's

thousand-year empire is crumbling fast. Into this chaotic world comes the emperor of the East (Justinian), bringing order and stability, briefly reassembling the empire, and making Ravenna a beacon of civilization. Of Ravenna's many impressive and important buildings from this time, we'll begin with two of the finest: First the basilica itself, with its dazzling mosaics, and then, across the yard, the small but poignant Mausoleum of Galla Placidia.

Cost and Hours: The Basilica di San Vitale is covered by a combo-ticket that includes (and is also sold at) four other worthwhile sights: the Mausoleum of Galla Placidia, Basilica di Sant'Apollinare Nuovo, Archiepiscopal Museum, and Neonian Baptistery. The ticket costs €11.50 during peak school-group season (March-mid-June), and €9.50 the rest of the year.

Hours: The church is open daily April-Sept 9:00-19:00, March and Oct 9:00-17:30, Nov-Feb 9:30-17:00 (as is Galla Placidia; the other sights open 30 minutes later, but all close at the same time). Last entry to San Vitale is 15 minutes before closing time (likewise for the other included sights except the Archiepiscopal Museum, which stops selling tickets 30 minutes before closing).

Information: Tel. 0544-541-688, www.ravennamosaici.it.

➲ **Self-Guided Tour:** Going through the ornamental gateway, show your ticket, and step down into the church. Circle around to the middle of the nave and take it all in.

The basilica—standing as a sanctuary of order in the midst of the madness after the fall of Rome—is covered with lavish mosaics: gold and glass chips the size of your fingernail. It's impressive enough to see a 1,400-year-old church, but it's rare to see one decorated in such brilliant mosaics, which still manage to convey their intended message: "This sense of peace and stability was brought to you by your emperor and God." The art is an intricate ensemble of images that, with the help of a medieval priest, would teach volumes.

First, let's get the big picture: The centerpiece, high above the altar, is God in heaven, portrayed as Christ sitting on a celestial orb. He oversees his glorious creation, symbolized by the four rivers.

Get closer to the altar so you can see the side walls flanking it. Running the show on earth is Justinian

NEAR VENICE

(left side), sporting both a halo and a crown to indicate that he's both leader of the Church and the state. Here Justinian brings together the military leaders and the church leaders, all united by the straight line of eyes. The bald bishop of Ravenna—the only local guy in this group—is portrayed most realistically (with a name tag above reading *Maximanus*).

On the opposite wall, facing the emperor, is his wife, Theodora, flanked by her entourage. Decked out in jewels and pearls, the former dancer who became Justinian's mistress (and then empress) carries a chalice with which to consecrate the new church.

The border inside the apse's arch, high above, is decorated with horns of plenty (cornucopia), promising prosperity in return for the people's obedience to the Church and State (Justinian and Theodora).

Back up a bit to let this space work its magic. Sit in a wooden pew, front and center. Get in a medieval frame of mind and study the scene: On the floor between the pews, a 16th-century inlaid marble labyrinth leads to the center of the building—evocative of the belief that the pilgrimage of life on earth leads to salvation through Christ. The scallop-shell designs ringing the center of the floor mosaic symbolize St. James, the patron saint of pilgrims.

While the decor behind you is Baroque and of no particular artistic importance, the walls and ceilings above and in front sparkle with colorful biblical scenes told with a sixth-century exuberance. (Viennese artist Gustav Klimt sat right here around 1900 and was inspired by the glint of the light on the gold leaf.)

OK. Now take a longitudinal, ground-up tour from your seat: The inlaid floor leads to the sixth-century marble altar (busy with iconography). High on the wall above that is Christ on the globe. Appreciate the symmetry. At the top of the arch, the circle with the monogram of Christ (*I* for Jesus and *X* for Christ) symbolizes perfection and eternity. Floating above the arch, two angels hold rays of sun (Christ is the origin of light). The scene is bookended by two cities: Bethlehem and Jerusalem (where Jesus was born and died). Above each city are potted grape vines producing wine, symbols of the blood of Christ.

The ceiling above is a festive celebration of God's creation, with different birds from the sixth century—most still flying near Ravenna today. (Bird-watchers—who visit with binoculars, no doubt—can easily identify these by their exquisitely detailed and accurate feathers.) All creation swirls around Christ as the sacrificial lamb, supported by four angels.

Framing the entire apse, arcing high above, is a triumphal arch. Its 15 medallions depict 12 apostles, 2 sons of St. Vitale, and a medieval bearded Christ.

The mid-sixth century was a time of transition, and many consider Ravenna's mosaics to be both the last ancient Roman and the first medieval European works of art. Standing here, we can witness a culture suddenly lurching forward out of antiquity and into the Middle Ages. Notice, for example, that the Christ who hovers above the altar is beardless (per standard ancient-Roman depiction), whereas it's the usual medieval bearded Jesus who's encircled atop the arch—and yet these mosaics were created within the same generation.

The church's octagonal design—clearly Eastern in origin—inspired at least two influential churches, including Hagia Sofia, the church-turned-mosque-turned-museum built 10 years later in Constantinople (today's Istanbul). Hagia Sofia, in turn, became the classic architectural model for mosques around the world. In A.D. 787, Emperor Charlemagne traveled to Ravenna, and was so impressed with San Vitale that he returned to Aix-la-Chapelle (now Aachen, Germany) and built a new palace—the power base for his vast empire—with a San Vitale-esque chapel at its core. It still stands as part of Aachen Cathedral, making it the oldest great stone building in northern Europe.

The pilasters surrounding you are brick, covered by sliced marble veneers. Similar marble sheets once covered all the walls. Many were scavenged by Charlemagne to provide flooring for his grand church.

• *When you're ready, exit through the door on the left (as you face the altar) and head across the grounds to the much smaller Mausoleum of Galla Placidia. Look to the right to see a bit of contemporary mosaic art—a glassy round of hay (described on the adjacent plaque). Left over from a recent international festival of mosaics, it reminds visitors that the art form survives today.*

▲▲Mausoleum of Galla Placidia

Just across the courtyard from the Basilica di San Vitale is a humble-looking mausoleum, with the oldest—and, to many most precious—mosaics in Ravenna. Ninety-five percent mosaics here are originals, dating from the late Roman when Ravenna was capital of a declining West.

NEAR VENICE

Cost and Hours: Covered by Basilica di San Vitale combo-ticket, same hours and contact info as listed earlier for the basilica.

Visiting the Mausoleum: The Mausoleum of Galla Placidia (plah-CHEE-dee-ah) was likely designed to be the burial place of this daughter, sister, and mother of emperors, who died around A.D. 450. But Galla Placidia died in Rome, and wasn't buried here. The three sarcophagi, built for the imperial family but likely only used by later Christian leaders, stand empty today. The original floor was about four feet lower, explaining the stunted feel of the interior. The art's realistic portrayal of tunics and sandals gives us a peek at the fashions of fifth-century Romans.

The little light that sneaks through the thin alabaster panels brings a glow and a twinkle to the early Christian symbolism that fills the small room. Opposite the door is St. Lawrence being martyred on a fiery grill. He's legendary for mocking his executors, reportedly saying something like, "I'm done on this side. You can turn me over now." He was famous as an example of the strength of the feisty early Christians. Note the four Gospels clearly labeled on the bookshelf, another inspiration for these first believers as they were persecuted by the Romans.

The dome is filled with stars. Along with Mark's lion, Luke's ox, Matthew's Archangel, and John's eagle, the golden cross rises from the east, bringing life to all. Doves drink from fountains, symbolic of souls finding nourishment in the Word of God. In both transepts are deer, reminding worshippers of Psalms 42: "Like the thirsty deer longs for spring water, so my soul longs for you, my God."

Look toward the back of the mausoleum. Cover the light from the door with this book (or close the curtain) to see the stan-

dard Roman portrayal of Christ—beardless and as the Good Shepherd. Jesus, dressed in gold and purple like a Roman emperor, is the King of Paradise—receiving the faithful (represented by lambs). The Eastern influence (perhaps inspired by the designs on fine Persian carpets or silks) is apparent the vault's decorative patterns.

ur walk is done. Got a train to catch? Head straight back to the n. If you have more time, visit the other sights included on your a ticket on your way: the Neonian Baptistery, the Archiepiscopal n, and the Basilica di Sant'Apollinare Nuovo.

More Sights in Ravenna

East of Piazza del Popolo

The only noteworthy sight in this part of town, the Basilica di Sant'Apollinare Nuovo, is on Via di Roma, just a short detour off the main road back to the train station.

▲▲Basilica di Sant'Apollinare Nuovo

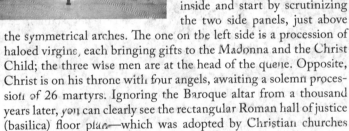

This austere sixth-century church has a typical early-Christian-basilica floor plan and two huge and wonderfully preserved side panels.

Cost and Hours: Covered by Basilica di San Vitale combo-ticket—for cost, hours, and contact information, see page 228.

Visiting the Basilica: Head inside and start by scrutinizing the two side panels, just above the symmetrical arches. The one on the left side is a procession of haloed virgins, each bringing gifts to the Madonna and the Christ Child; the three wise men are at the head of the queue. Opposite, Christ is on his throne with four angels, awaiting a solemn procession of 26 martyrs. Ignoring the Baroque altar from a thousand years later, you can clearly see the rectangular Roman hall of justice (basilica) floor plan—which was adopted by Christian churches and used throughout the Middle Ages.

This basilica started (c. 500) as an Arian church—the palace church of King Theodoric of the Goths. Theodoric decorated it with scenes of himself and his royal palace amid Christ and the saints. Look for original, surviving Arian art in the front (on the left, Mary and Baby Jesus; on the right, Jesus and four angels) and in the rear (two cityscapes: *Civi Classis*—Classe; and *Palatium*, for the palace in Ravenna).

When Justinian arrived, he transformed the church in the Byzantine (and Nicene) style. If you study the arcades in the Ravenna cityscape, you can see where Arian figures were erased, leaving only bits of hands and fingers on the columns, and blotted-out haloes behind the curtains. The brilliant white-robed figures parading on both sides were remade in the mid-500s with a Byzantine rather than an Arian message. But the uppermost panels (hard to see without binoculars) are original Theodoric Arian: prophets (between windows), miracles of Christ (top row on the left), scenes from the last week of Jesus' life and his Resurrection (top row on the right).

Nearby: You can have a quick lunch at the air-cond

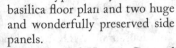

NEAR VENICE

NEAR VENICE

efficient Sant'Apollinare self-serve cafeteria on the church grounds (€5-6 pastas and *secondi*, Mon-Fri 12:00-14:30, closed Sat-Sun).

South of Piazza del Popolo

The first three sights described below cluster near Ravenna's modest Duomo, about a 10-minute walk from Piazza del Popolo. The last sight, the Dante Museum, is a few minutes' walk east of here, right next to the Basilica di San Francesco and Dante's tomb (both described earlier, on my self-guided walk).

▲Archiepiscopal Museum

This museum, in Ravenna's Duomo, contains the sixth-century Chapel of Sant'Andrea. Built as the private prayer chapel for the

Catholic bishop during Theodoric's time (c. 500), today it anchors a fine collection of Roman, Byzantine-Christian, and pagan statues, reliefs, and mosaics.

Cost and Hours: Covered by Basilica di San Vitale combo-ticket—for cost, hours, and contact information, see page 228.

Visiting the Museum: From the museum entrance on Piazza Arcivescovado, follow signs to the *Cappella di Sant'Andrea*, in Room IE. Enter the room, turn around, and look above the door to see a sixth-century mosaic showing Christ as a religious warrior, stepping triumphantly on a lion and snake (ancient symbols of evil) and carrying the cross as if it were a weapon. The book he holds reads in Latin, "I am the way, the truth, and the life." This is a strong pro-Trinity statement (Jesus, God, and the Holy Spirit are one) against the Arian heresy. The main chamber of the charming chapel is covered in rich mosaics, with lots of sixth-century symbolism and realistic portrait medallions. Topping the arch just over the door is another clean-shaven Jesus.

Exiting the chapel, turn left into Room IF to see the museum's other highlight, an exquisite sixth-century Byzantine ivory throne, decorated with scenes from the life of Christ. It was carved for Bishop Maximian, Justinian's Trinitarian appointee, the man who ...rsaw construction of the Basilica di San Vitale, and whose bald ...d appears in its mosaics. Nearby, in Room IG, is an interesting ...lar calendar designed to keep track of the dates for Easter be- ...n the years 532 and 626.

...ng the museum, turn left to find the...

▲Neonian Baptistery

Also known as the Baptistery of the Orthodox, this octagonal space dates from about the year 400. Imagine pagan adults immersed

in the pool under glorious ceiling mosaics as they convert to Christianity. The mosaic portrays the common baptistery theme: John the Baptist baptizing Christ, with the personification of the River Jordan looking on. The scene is ringed by empty chairs waiting to welcome you into the eternal heavenly banquet. Twelve apostles with dancing feet—their tunics and cloaks alternating between gold and white—give the room a joyful visual sense of rhythm. The acanthus flowers dividing the apostles were the botanic inspiration for the Corinthian capital, the Roman capital of choice. Decoration on the lower walls features dark purple disks made of precious porphyry stone and a gold leafy arcade creating almond frames for the prophets.

Cost and Hours: Covered by Basilica di San Vitale comboticket—for cost, hours, and contact information, see page 228.

• *While you're here, consider at least popping into Ravenna's Duomo for a quick peek. From the Baptistery, walk away from the Archiepiscopal Museum and hook left to reach the front door of the...*

Duomo

Ravenna's main church is a typically big, Baroque house of worship. Like everything else in this town, it's built on much older rubble. In the 18th century, to make way for the current structure, its builders razed the gigantic five-nave Basilica Ursiana—but pragmatically repurposed big chunks of the old church to build the new one. Pay close attention to the inlaid floors, made with cross-sections of columns, capitals, and other decorations from the previous church, all neatly sliced and joined together. Just before the right transept, notice the fine sixth-century marble-carved pulpit, covered with two-dimensional images of animals (typical of the Byzantine style). The Latin inscription, referring to the bishop who reconsecrated the Arian churches, reads, "Agnellu made this pulpit."

Cost and Hours: Free, daily 7:00-12:00 & 14:30-18:30.

Nearby: Exiting the Duomo, turn right and walk up Via C sponi to return to Piazza del Popolo. After one block, turn on Via Guerrini to find the entrance to a free-to-enter **bo garden** (Giardino Rasponi) with a great view of the cathe delightful spot to rest after so much sightseeing.

Dante Museum (Museo Dantesco)

This new museum celebrates Dante Alighieri, "the Ita speare," who spent the last three years of his life in F now rests next door in the former Monastery of San Francesco. It was here that a 19th-century bricklayer stumbled upon the author's long-lost remains, tucked in a wooden box—now displayed in the museum—simply marked *Dantis ossa* ("Dante's bones"). While most of the museum's information is available in English, it takes a strong background on Dante and his *Divine Comedy* to make a visit here worthwhile. If you do go in, request an English showing of the seven-minute film. Then be prepared to visit hell, purgatory, and paradise (or at least halls representing each of these). Outside, enjoy the two restful, grassy courtyards, one of them with modern statues of St. Francis and St. Claire.

Cost and Hours: €3, March-Oct Tue-Sun 10:00-18:00, Nov-Feb Tue-Sun 10:00-16:00, closed Mon year-round, Via—what else?—Dante Alighieri 4, tel. 0544-215-676, www.classense.ra.it.

North of Piazza del Popolo

House of Stone Carpets (Domus dei Tappeti di Pietra)

Discovered in 1993, the stone mosaic floors of this sixth-century Byzantine house show both pictorial images and abstract designs. Excavations revealed many layers, dating back to the second century B.C. All were peeled away and preserved elsewhere. Only the sixth-century floor (12 rooms on one level) was put back and exhibited here, very close to its original location. Because this was a private home, its art could break from the conservative norms for public art of the age. The highlight is the wonderfully realistic *Dance of the Four Seasons* (displayed on the wall on your right as you descend the stairs). Don't miss the fourth-century *Christ as a Shepherd*, which some consider the earliest portrayal of Jesus (it's on the wall facing the *Four Seasons;* part of the face was lost to modern excavations). A visit here is almost meaningless without the €1 audioguide.

Cost and Hours: €4; March-Oct daily 10:00-18:30, July-Aug Tue and Fri until 22:30; Nov-Feb Tue-Fri 10:00-17:30, Sat-Sun 10:00-18:00, closed Mon; ask for the 10-minute English-language video—the computer-generated images help visitors envision the place in action; entrance through Church of Sant'Eufemia, on Via Barbiani just off Via Cavour near Piazza Baracca, tel. 0544-32512, vw.domusdeitappetidipietra.it.

More Mosaics: The same association that runs the House of e Carpets also runs two other mosaic sights: **TAMO** has little way of historical artifacts, but tells the story of mosaic-mak- daily 10:00-18:30, shorter hours off-season, Via Rondinelli oni Crypt displays a floor of mosaics pieced together from sites, crazy-quilt style (€2, Tue-Sun 10:00-18:30, closed er hours off-season, Piazza San Francesco).

Near Ravenna

▲▲Church of Sant'Apollinare in Classe

The final major sight for Byzantine mosaic fans is a sixth-century church standing a few miles outside of Ravenna in the suburb of Classe. It's impressive, but comes in fourth place after the Basilica di San Vitale, Mausoleum of Galla Placidia, and Basilica di Sant'Apollinare Nuovo. On a quick day trip, it's certainly skippable.

Cost and Hours: €3, Mon-Sat 8:30-19:30, Sun 13:00-19:30, last entry at 19:00, Via Romea Sud, tel. 0544-473-569, www.turismo.ra.it.

Getting There: The church is three miles out of town—an easy bike ride. To go by bus, buy two local bus tickets (€1.20 each) at any tobacco shop, then catch bus #4 across the street from the train station (on the corner by the park; 3/hour Mon-Sat, 1/hour on Sun, 15 minutes; save second ticket for return trip). The bus also leaves from Piazza Caduti (stop is on the corner). To return to Ravenna from the church, walk back toward town along the main road about 100 yards to find the bus shelter on the right. You could also pay for a taxi (figure around €12 one-way, or €25 round-trip if your visit is quick).

Visiting the Church: The statue of Emperor Augustus, standing in front of the church, is a reminder that Classe was a strategic navy base in Roman times. In early Christian days, Classe was a big pilgrimage destination and home to a large Christian community. Today little remains other than its church, and even that was nearly bombed-out in World War II when the Germans used its medieval tower as a lookout.

The artistic treasure here is the mosaic work in the apse, 90 percent of which is original from the sixth century. The scene is an abstract portrayal of the Transfiguration of Jesus. The cross with a tiny portrait of Christ in its center beams light. God's hand above affirms that "This is the Truth." The three lambs represent James, John, and Peter. The landscape is of pine trees, which once forested the region. And St. Apollinare, the first local bishop, is celebrated because it was he who brought Christianity to the area.

The rest of the church—its mosaics lost to time—is pretty plain. While many churches this old have settled and the bases of their columns are no longer visible, here the floor level remains unchanged and you can admire the columns' original bases. Near the entrance, a bilingual display panel gives detailed information on the church.

Famous-but-Skippable Nearby Towns

Nearly all train travelers to Ravenna change in the regional of **Bologna.** While it might be tempting to check your bag gna's station and spend a few hours in town, I'd resist—

much more pleasant. Though well-preserved, Bologna is also huge (three times the size of Ravenna), congested, and relatively charmless. If you decide to stop off here anyway, head straight to Piazza Maggiore (a 20-minute walk from the station), home to the Town Hall, the TI, and a famous statue of Neptune. The big Gothic building across the square is the unfinished 14th-century Basilica di San Petronio—destined to be one of the biggest churches in Christendom until the Vatican put the brakes on the project. A few blocks west are Bologna's twin symbols, a pair of leaning brick towers.

The nearby beach town of **Rimini** is an overrated, crowded mess.

Sleeping in Ravenna

In the Pedestrian Zone, near Piazza del Popolo

$$ Hotel Bisanzio is a business-class hotel with dated public spaces and 38 rooms in the city center (Sb-€86, small Db-€108, mid-size Db-€124, large Db-€136, prices soft, air-con, elevator, free Wi-Fi, usually free on-street parking with hotel permits; Via Salara 30, tel. 054-421-7111, www.bisanziohotel.com, info@bisanziohotel.com).

$$ M Club B&B is a creative, comfortable, and stylish five-room place with an elegant breakfast room, spacious bedrooms, and thoughtful touches. Its website describes each unique room in detail (straight pricing: Db-€80-130 depending on size, big Qb suite-€150, free Wi-Fi, loaner bikes, Piazza Baracca 26, mobile 333-955-6466, www.m-club.it, info@m-club.it, Michael). The M Club faces the Porta Adriana gate at the far end of the old town from the train station (a 15-minute walk).

$ B&B Al Teatro fills an elegant townhouse with three rooms, one two-level apartment, and shared lounges that invite you to linger (Sb-€60-75, Db-€75-90, price depends on size, extra bed-€20, air-con, elevator, free Wi-Fi, Via Guaccimanni 38, tel. 0544-188-1011, mobile 348-708-3867, www.bbalteatroravenna.com, info@bbalteatroravenna.com).

$ Casa Masoli B&B's six elegantly outfitted rooms include ̱ant bathrooms in a wood-paneled Art Deco style (Sb-€40-50, ̱-€70-80, higher prices are for weekends, Tb-€90, 4th and 5th ̱on-€20 each, peaceful garden, air-con, free Wi-Fi, library, Via ̱ossi 22, tel. 0544-217-682, www.casamasoli.it, info@casa-̱i.it).

̱A Casa di Paola is a converted private home (Paola's mother ̱partment on the ground floor) with eight nicely decorated ̱mfy common spaces, and a treehouse floor plan (Sb-€50,

Db-€70, Tb-€90, Qb-€120, Quint/b-€140, air-con, free Wi-Fi, free drinks, loaner bikes, Via P. Costa 31, tel. 0544-39425, mobile 347-730-6386, www.acasadipaola.it, info@acasadipaola.it). They also rent three rooms in their art-cluttered home a half-block away, at #26 (same prices and contact information; one room has private bathroom down the hall).

Near the Train Station

These places are convenient, but have less atmosphere.

$$ Hotel Italia, just 100 yards from the train station, feels like a chain hotel but is actually family-owned. Its 45 rooms lack character but provide comfort and lots of space (Sb-€60, Db-€90, Tb-€115, Qb-€135, air-con, elevator, free Wi-Fi, loaner bikes, free parking on first-come, first-served basis, turn left out of station, Viale Pallavicini 4/6, tel. 0544-212-363, www.hotelitaliaravenna. com, info@hotelitaliaravenna.com, Mauro).

$ Albergo I Cherubini, near the train station, is a last-resort budget option with 18 basic, no-frills rooms and dark hallways. Ask for a room off the street (S-€30, D-€50, Db-€65, Tb-€75, Qb-€90, fans, free Wi-fi, Via R. Brancaleone 42, tel. 0544-39403, www. albergoristoranteicherubini.it, info@albergoristoranteicherubini.it, Donatella).

Hostel: **$ Ostello Dante,** a 15-minute walk from the station, has 110 beds, free Wi-Fi, loaner bikes, and a game room (€18/bed in 4-bed rooms, Db-€48, family rooms with bath-€22/person, €2/night extra for non-hostel members, includes breakfast and sheets, towels-€1, laundry-€5/load, 11:00-14:30 lockout, 23:30 curfew or pay €1 for magnetic entrance key, closed Nov-Feb, Via Nicolodi 12, bus #1 or #70 from train station, tel. & fax 0544-421-164, www. hostelravenna.com, hostelravenna@hotmail.com).

Eating in Ravenna

Located in the cuisine-crazy Emilia-Romagna region—famous for its cheeses and *salumi*—Ravenna has more than its share of great restaurants. Emilia-Romagna, nestled between farm fields and the sea, boasts seafood that's as good as its landfood. A local staple—served at carryout stands as well as fine restaurants—is *piadir* (pee-ah-DEE-nah), unleavened flatbread served plain or with wide variety of fillings. At the top of every pasta menu is *cappell* little doughy pockets of cheese in a variety of sauces. Chefs also make ample use of *squacquerone*, a soft cream cheese. (Fo on *salumi* and other Italian treats, see page 40.)

Ca' de Ven ("House of Wine"), the most famous rest town, is surprisingly affordable. It fills a 16th-century with communal seating and residents enjoying quality

NEAR VENICE

traditional regional cuisine. Up front is a bar with tables under ornately decorated Baroque domes, with 15-foot-tall wine cabinets towering above; in back is a huge hall under rough barrel vaults. For a light meal, order one of their €4-6 *piadine*. Their dessert specialty, *torta di marzapane*—a decadent almond-and-cocoa brownie—is good with sweet red wine. Reserve ahead for dinner (€8-10 pastas, €12-14 *secondi*, €38 fixed-price meal, no cover, Tue-Sun 11:00-14:15 & 18:30-22:00, closed Mon, 2-minute walk from Piazza del Popolo on Via Cairoli, which turns into Via C. Ricci, Via C. Ricci 24, tel. 0544-30163, www.cadeven.it).

Al Rustichello, a classic trattoria just outside the Porta Adriana city gate, has cozy ambience under heavy timbers. While you can ask for a printed menu, the owner ignores it—he just comes to your table and rattles off the options. Few diners can resist their *cappelletti*, served in the pan it was cooked in. Their €7 *antipasti* plate is a fun, splittable starter, with enticing samples of four local dishes (closed Sat lunch and all day Sun, €9-10 pastas, €10-14 *secondi*, Via Maggiore 21, tel. 0544-36043).

Antica Bottega di Felice, behind the covered market, has a cheese-and-meat shop in the front, and in back, an unpretentious sit-down eatery serving up delicious local cuisine made with many of those same ingredients. While the space is more functional than atmospheric, the cuisine more than compensates (€8-10 pastas, €11-18 *secondi*, Mon-Sat 12:00-22:00, closed Sun, Via Ponte Marino 23/25, tel. 0544-240-170).

Ristorante la Gardèla is a local fixture—if Ravenna had a town dining room, this would be it. The fun-loving waitstaff has been here for years, and the restaurant has all the nice touches without the pretense. While there are a few tables outside and upstairs, I like the jolly main floor. Their *cappelletti* is served *in brodo* (soup) or *al ragù* (with meat sauce; €6-8 pastas, €9-16 *secondi*, €15 and €25 fixed-price meals, Fri-Wed 12:00-24:00, closed Thu, tucked behind the covered market at Via Ponte Marino 3, tel. 0544-217-147).

Fish and Seafood

Ristorante Osteria del Tempo Perso is a red-velvet-romantic choice for seafood, with service as warm as its color scheme, mellow jazz on the soundtrack, and a grown-up vibe. I'd ignore the forgettable outdoor seating (€10-12 pastas, €16-24 *secondi*, Mon 19:30-23:00, Sat-Sun 12:30-15:00 & 19:30-23:00, Via Gamba 12, tel. 0544-215-393).

Acciuga Osteria ("Anchovy"), hiding at the back of a courtyard on a residential street just outside the old town, is well-respected for its intentionally short menu of fresh seafood. Because everything is fresh and priced by the weight, this can get expensive, but it's worth a splurge for seafood lovers. The restaurant is done up like the lower holds of a submarine, but—thanks to the tasteful, dressy decor—seems stylish rather than tacky (€10-12 pastas, €15-30 *secondi*, €30 fixed-price meal, Tue-Sat 12:00-16:00 & 19:00-22:00, Sun 12:00-16:00 only, closed Mon, Viale Baracca 74, tel. 0544-212-713).

Quick Snack Spots

Piadina Stands: For the best cheap, traditional lunch in Ravenna, skip the pizza and instead grab a *piadina*. These tasty flatbread sandwiches are stuffed with a variety of local meats, vegetables, and cheeses (including *squacquerone*), then folded over and grilled. You'll see several take-out windows in the downtown pedestrian zone selling them for €3.50-5; consider **La Piadina del Melarancio** (between Piazza del Popolo and the covered market at Via IV Novembre 31) and the popular-with-students **Profuma di Piadina** (on the way from Piazza del Popolo to the Basilica di San Francesco, at Via Cairoli 24).

Local Products: **Gastronomia Alpine,** a "gastronomic boutique" selling regional cheeses, *salumi,* and other products, treats in-the-know picnic shoppers to the bounty of Emilia-Romagna. It's conveniently located right along the main pedestrian street (Fri-Wed 8:00-13:00 & 16:00-19:30, Thu 8:00-13:00 only, Via Cavour 43, tel. 0544-32594). **Antica Bottega di Felice,** recommended earlier as a restaurant, also has a fine cheese and *salumi* shop up front.

Supermarkets: For lunch, assemble a picnic at the **covered market** (Mon-Sat 7:00-14:00, closed Sun) and enjoy your feast in the shady gardens of the Rocca Brancaleone fortress (daily until 18:00; 5-minute walk from station, follow Via Maroncelli until you see the walls). If the covered market is closed, visit **InCo-op,** on Via di Roma at the corner of Via A. Moriani (Mon-Sat 8:00-20:30, Sun 9:00-13:30 & 16:30-20:30).

Self-Service Cafeterias: **Ristorante Marchesini,** near the Basilica di San Francesco, is an upscale self-serve restaurant (over a delicatessen) offering delicious salads and homemade pastas (€ pastas, €10 *secondi*, €1.50 cover, Mon-Sat 12:00-14:30, closed Su 5-minute walk from Piazza del Popolo, on corner of Piazza Ca at Via Mazzini 6—ride elevator to first floor, tel. 0544-212- **Free Flow Bizantino,** inside the covered market, is a self-cafeteria serving lunch only (€3-5 pastas, €5-6 *secondi*, €8.50 course lunch, Mon-Fri 11:45-14:45, closed Sat-Sun, te 32073).

Gelato: **Sorbetteria degli Esarchi,** right on the m

trian street between Piazza del Popolo and the covered market, is both convenient and tasty (Via IV Novembre 11).

Ravenna Connections

From Ravenna by Train to: Venice (roughly hourly, 3-3.5 hours), **Padua** (roughly hourly, 2.5 hours), **Florence** (about hourly, 2.5 hours by fast train, no slow train option). All of these trips require a change in either Ferrara or Bologna.

THE DOLOMITES

Dolomiti

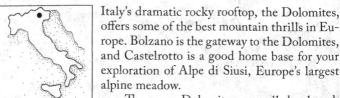

Italy's dramatic rocky rooftop, the Dolomites, offers some of the best mountain thrills in Europe. Bolzano is the gateway to the Dolomites, and Castelrotto is a good home base for your exploration of Alpe di Siusi, Europe's largest alpine meadow.

The sunny Dolomites are well-developed, and the region's famous valleys and towns suffer from après-ski fever. The cost for the comfort of reliably good weather is a drained-reservoir feeling. Lovers of other parts of the Alps may miss the lushness that comes with the unpredictable weather farther north. But the bold, light-gray cliffs and spires flecked with snow, above green meadows and beneath a blue sky, offer a powerful, unique, and memorable mountain experience. Dolomite, a sedimentary rock similar to limestone, gives these mountains their distinctive shape and color.

A hard-fought history has left the region bicultural, with an emphasis on the German. Most locals speak German first, and some wish they were still part of Austria. In the Middle Ages, as part of the Holy Roman Empire, the region faced north. Later, it was firmly in the Austrian Habsburg realm. By losing World War I, Austria's South Tirol became Italy's Alto Adige. Mussolini d what he could to Italianize the region, including giving each to an Italian name. But even as recently as the 1990s, secessi groups agitated violently for more autonomy—with some s (see sidebar).

The government has wooed locals with economic which have made this one of Italy's richest areas (as lo attest), and today all signs and literature in the provin Adige/Südtirol are in both languages. Many include ;

DOLOMITES

guage, Ladin—an ancient Romance language still spoken in a few traditional areas. (I have listed both the Italian and German, so the confusion caused by this guidebook will match that experienced in your travels.)

In spite of all the glamorous ski resorts and busy construction cranes, the regional color survives in a warm, blue-aproned, ruddy-faced, felt-hat-with-feathers way. There's yogurt and yodeling for breakfast. Culturally, as much as geographically, the area is reminiscent of Austria. In fact, the Austrian region of Tirol is named for a village that is now part of Italy.

Planning Your Time

Train travelers can side-trip into the mountains from Bolzano (1.5 hours north of Verona). To get a feel for the alpine culture, spend at least one night in Castelrotto. But with two nights there, you can really get out and hike. Tenderfeet ride the bus, catch a cable car, and stroll. For serious mountain thrills, do a six-hour hike. And for a thrill that won't soon fade away, spend a night in a mountain

Ich bin ein Italiener

With the exception of Bolzano, where Italian has become the primary language, you'll hear mostly German in Dolomite vil-

lages. Overall, seven in ten Italians living in the South Tirol speak German as their mother tongue. Many are fair-skinned and blue-eyed, prefer dumplings and strudel to pasta and gelato, and feel a closer bond with their ancestors in Austria than with their swarthy countrymen to the south. Most have a working knowledge of Italian, but they watch German-language TV, read newspapers *auf Deutsch,* and live in Tirolean-looking villages.

At the end of World War I, the region was ceded by Austria (loser) to Italy (winner). Mussolini suppressed the Germanic cultural elements as part of his propaganda campaign to praise all things Italian. Many German-speakers hoped that Hitler would "liberate" them from Italy, but Hitler's close alliance with Mussolini prevented that from happening. Instead, in June of 1939, residents were given six months to make a hard choice—move north to the Fatherland and become German citizens, or stay in their homeland *(Heimat)* under Italian rule. The vast majority (212,000, or 85 percent) made the decision to leave, but because of the outbreak of World War II, only 75,000 actually moved.

At the war's end, German speakers were again disappointed when the Allied powers refused to grant them autonomy or the chance to become Austrian citizens. Instead, the victors decided to stick with the prewar arrangement.

The region rebuilt and the two linguistic groups patched things up, but for the remainder of the 20th century, there was always an underlying problem: German speakers were continually outvoted by the Italian-speaking majority in the regional government (comprising two provinces, Italian-speaking Trentino and German-speaking Alto Adige/Südtirol). German speakers lobbied the national government for more control on the provincial (not regional) level, even turning to demonstrations and violence. Over the years, Rome has slowly and grudgingly granted increased local control.

Today, Alto Adige/Südtirol has a large measure of autonomy written into the country's 2001 constitution, though it's still officially tied to Trentino. Roads, water, electricity, communications, and schools are all under local control, including the Free University of Bozen-Bolzano, founded in 1998.

hut. Always remember to check the latest transportation timetables before you embark on an outing.

If you have a car, you can drive the three-hour loop from Bolzano or Castelrotto (Val Gardena-Sella Pass-Val di Fassa) and ride one of the lifts to the top for a ridge walk. Connecting Bolzano and Venice by the Great Dolomite Road takes two hours longer than by the autostrada, but is far more scenic (see "More Sights in the Dolomites" at the end of this chapter).

Hiking season is mid-June through mid-October. The region is particularly crowded, booming, and blooming from mid-July through mid-September (but once you're out on the trails, you'll leave the crowds behind). It's packed with Italian vacationers in August. Spring is usually dead, with lifts shut down, huts closed, and the most exciting trails still under snow. Many hotels and restaurants close in April and November. Ski season (Dec-Easter) is busiest of all. For more information, visit www.visitdolomites.com.

Bolzano

Willkommen to the Italian Tirol! If Bolzano ("Bozen" in German) weren't so sunny, you could be in Innsbruck. This enjoyable old town of 100,000 is the most convenient gateway to the Dolomites, especially if you're relying on public transportation. It's just the place to take a Tirolean stroll.

Orientation to Bolzano

Tourist Information

Bolzano's TI is helpful (Mon-Fri 9:00-19:00, Sat 9:30-18:00, closed Sun, Piazza Walther/Waltherplatz 8, tel. 0471-307-000, www.bolzano-bozen.it). Pick up the city map and the *Historic and Cultural Route* brochure (also downloadable from website).

Consider buying the **Museummobil Card,** which covers most museums in the South Tirol (including the archaeology museum, with its famous Iceman), plus trains, buses, the Funivia del Renon/ Rittner Seilbahn cable car, and more (€28/3 days, available at local TIs and some hotels, www.mobilcard.info). This card saves you several euros if you visit the Iceman, ride the cable car, take the round-trip from Bolzano to Klobenstein, and take the bus round-trip from Bolzano to Castelrotto. The **Mobilcard** is a transit pass that covers trains, buses, and lifts (€15/1 day, €23/3 sold at TIs and transit offices, www.mobilcard.info).

serious hikers visit the **Alpine Information Center** (Alpine run by the Alpenverein Südtirol, a local hiking club. It offers a map library (also available at http://trekking.suedtirol.info) and advice on trails and mountain huts. It's deep in the old town in an arcade that you enter at Via Dr. Streiter/Dr. Streiter-Gasse 16; ring the bell and go upstairs (Mon-Thu 9:00-12:00 & 13:00-17:00, Fri 9:00-12:00, closed Sat-Sun, tel. 0471-999-955, www.alpine-auskunft.it).

Arrival in Bolzano

There are two train stations for Bolzano—you want just *Bolzano*, not *Bolzano Süd*. To get to the TI and downtown from the train station, veer left up the tree-lined Viale della Stazione/Bahnhof-sallee, and walk past the bus station (on your left) two blocks to **Piazza Walther/Waltherplatz.** You'll see the TI on the right side of the square. The medieval heart of town is on the far side of the square: The arcaded Via dei Portici/Laubengasse is Bolzano's old main street. It leads to Piazza Erbe/Obstplatz, which has an open-air produce market (see "Markets," below); the Iceman is a couple of blocks farther beyond.

Helpful Hints

Sleepy Sundays: The city is really dead on Sunday (young locals add, "and during the rest of the week, too").

Markets: Piazza Erbe/Obstplatz hosts an ancient and still-thriving open-air produce market (Mon-Fri all day, Sat morning only, closed Sun). Wash your produce in the handy drinking fountain in the middle of the market. Another market (offering more variety, not just food) is held Saturday mornings on Piazza della Vittoria.

Internet Access: Multi Kulti Internet Point is a short walk from Piazza Walther/Waltherplatz at Via Dr. Streiter/Dr.-Streiter-Gasse 9 (€3/hour, Mon-Sat 9:00-22:00, closed Sun, tel. 0471-056-056).

Baggage Storage: While there's no baggage-storage service at the train station, there is a tiny *deposito bagagli* at the bus station just a block away (€3/24 hours, €10 refundable deposit, out back from where the buses leave, at the entrance to the bathrooms, daily 7:00-13:00 & 14:00-19:30).

Laundry: Lava e Asciuga launderette is at Via Rosmini/Rosmin Strasse 81, about two blocks west of the South Tirol Museum of Archaeology (€3 wash, €3 dry, English instructions, d 7:30-22:30, last wash 21:00, mobile 340-220-2323).

Bike Rental: The city has a well-developed bike-trail system. al bikes are curiously cheap here. Plenty of bikes are av for rent just off Piazza Walther/Waltherplatz on Via Stazione/Bahnhofsallee, on the right side (€1/6 hou 24 hours, €5/24 hours, €10 refundable deposit, ID

DOLOMITES

April-Sept Mon-Sat 7:30-19:50, Oct until 18:50, closed Sun and Nov-March, tel. 0471-997-578). The TI also has 10 bikes to rent for €5 per day (€10 refundable deposit, ID required, ask for a map).

Local Bus: A tourist shuttle called **BoBus,** leaving Piazza Walther/Walterplatz about every 1.5 hours, does a loop through town, stopping at major sightseeing points (€1.50, buy ticket on bus, daily 9:00-17:00).

Self-Guided Walk

Welcome to Bolzano

Everything mentioned in Bolzano is a 10-minute walk from the train station and the main square, Piazza Walther/Waltherplatz.

• *Start in...*

Piazza Walther/Waltherplatz: The statue in the center honors the square's namesake, Walther von der Vogelweide, a 12th-century politically incorrect German poet who courageously stood up to the pope in favor of the Holy Roman (German) Emperor. Walther's spunk against a far bigger power represents the Germanic pride of this region. The statue is made of marble quarried in the village of Laas, north of Bolzano. The US chose this same marble for the 86,000 crosses and Stars of

David needed to mark the WWII dead buried at Normandy and other battlefields across Europe.

When not hosting Bolzano's Christmas market, flower market (May Day), or Speck Fest (a spring ham festival), Piazza Walther/Waltherplatz is simply the town's living room. And locals care about it. It was the site of Italy's first McDonald's, which, in the early 1990s, became the first McDonald's to be shut down by locals protesting American fast food. Today the square is home to trendy cafés such as Café Walther, where (outside of meal times) you're welcome to nurse a "Venetian" *spritz* or a pricier cocktail as long as you like.

• *Cross the street to the big church.*

The Cathedral: The cathedral's glazed-tile roof is typical of the ~~G~~ermanic world, a reminder that from the sixth century until 1919, ~~Ger~~man was the region's official language. Then, suddenly: *Buon ~~gior~~no!* Walk around to the right, to the Romanesque Lion's Gate. ~~This c~~hurch was flattened in World War II (a distinct downside of ~~being l~~ocated near a train station in 20th-century Europe). As you ~~wander insi~~de, the place feels Teutonic, not Italian. The mostly Gothic ~~lines are~~ broken by an impressive Baroque tabernacle. Most of the art here is by Bavarian artists. There's a stiff, pre-Michelangelo, 15th-century *pietà* to the left of the altar. The sandstone pulpit (c. 1500), with its reliefs of the four Church fathers (whose presence gave credibility to sermons preached here), is reminiscent of Vienna's St. Stephen's Cathedral.

• *Leaving the church, walk diagonally across Piazza Walther/Waltherplatz and find the street to the right of the big Sparkasse bank building. Go down it for one block, to...*

Piazza del Grano/Kornplatz: Nine hundred years ago, this was Bolzano's main square. The building to your right was the bishop's castle. The traditional food stand selling *Vollkornbrot* (dense, whole-grain bread) and pretzels is another reminder of German heritage. Find the flower beds at the top of the square; a bronze relief on a large stone shows Bolzano's street plan in the 12th century—a one-street arcaded town huddled within a fortified wall.

• *Continue uphill into the original medieval town, passing the "Wurstel Boutique" on your left (yet another reminder of this region's Germanic orientation).*

Via dei Portici/Laubengasse: This was the only street in 12th-century Bolzano. Step into the center (dodging bikes). Looking

east and west, you see the width of the original town. Thirty yards to the left is the old City Hall—the street's only Gothic building (with frescoed pointed arches). The other buildings are all basically the same: Each had a storm cellar, cows out back, a ground-level shop, and living quarters upstairs. Bay windows were designed for maximum light—just right for clerks keeping track of accounts and for women doing their weaving. The arcades *(Lauben)*, typical of Tirol, sheltered merchants and their goods from both snow and sun. Narrow side passages lead to neighboring streets. The only balcony marks the one Baroque building—once the mercantile center (with a fine worth-a-look courtyard), now a skippable museum.

• *Turn left on Via dei Portici/Laubengasse and continue to the end, where you'll find a bustling market.*

Piazza Erbe/Obstplatz: This square hosts an open-air produce market, liveliest in the morning (Mon-Fri all day, Sat mornings, closed Sun). The historic market fountain gives Bolzano only hint of the sea—a 17th-century statue of Neptune. S around and see what's in season. All of the breads, strudel hams *schmecken sehr gut.*

• *From the market, Via Museo/Museumstrasse (called Butche until the 19th century, when a museum opened) leads straight t Fritz.*

Bolzano

NEW BOLZANO

To 14

CORSO DELLA LIBERTÀ

VIA BATTISTI

Piazza della Vittoria

VICTORY MONUMENT

PONTE TALVERA

Petrarcha Park

To Maretsch & Runkelstein Castles

SOUTH TIROL MUSEUM OF ARCHAEOLOGY (ÖTZI THE ICEMAN)

VIA MUSEO

MUSEO CIVICO

EUROPA GALLERY

VIA LEONARDO

Piazza Sernesi

FREE UNIVERSITY OF BOLZANO

VIA OSPEDALE

VIALE SAN QUIRINO

VIALE VENEZIA

VIA FLUME

VIA ZARA

Talvera River

VIA ROSMINI

VIA CASSA DI RISPARMIO

VIA CARDUCCI

VIA DANTE

VIA CARDUCCI

VIA MARCONI

VIALE DRUSO

VIALE TRISTE

VIA VERONA

Bike

Isarco/

- ① Hotel Figl
- ② Hotel Greif
- ③ Stadt Hotel Città
- ④ Parkhotel Laurin
- ⑤ Hotel Feichter
- ⑥ Kolpinghaus Bozen
- ⑦ Youth Hostel Bolzano
- ⑧ Weisses Rössl Restaurant
- ⑨ Ca' de Bezzi/Gasthaus Batzenhäusl
- ⑩ Hopfen & Co. Restaurant
- ⑪ Paulaner Stuben
- ⑫ Enoteca Il Baccaro
- ⑬ Gasthaus Fink
- ⑭ To Avalon Gelato
- ⑮ DeSpar Supermarkets (3)
- ⑯ Internet Café
- ⑰ Alpine Info Center
- ⑱ Launderette
- ⑲ Bike Rental

DOLOMITES

Sights in Bolzano

▲▲South Tirol Museum of Archaeology (Museo Archeologico dell'Alto Adige/Südtiroler Archäologiemuseum)

This excellent museum, which illuminates the prehistory of the region, boasts a unique attraction: the actual corpse of Ötzi the Iceman, who spent more than five millennia stuck in a glacier.

Cost and Hours: €9, €37.50 guided tour for up to 15 people (must reserve ahead), Tue-Sun 10:00-18:00, closed Mon except July-Aug and Dec, last entry 30 minutes before closing, no photos, no café, near the river at Via Museo/Museumstrasse 43, tel. 0471-20-100, www.iceman.it.

Visiting the Museum: Ötzi's frozen body was discovered high he mountains on the Italian/Austrian border by a German couple 91. Police initially believed the corpse was a lost hiker, and Ötzi hopped roughly out of the glacier, damaging his left side. But discovering his pre-Bronze Age hatchet, officials realized what d found: a 5,300-year-old, nearly perfectly preserved man

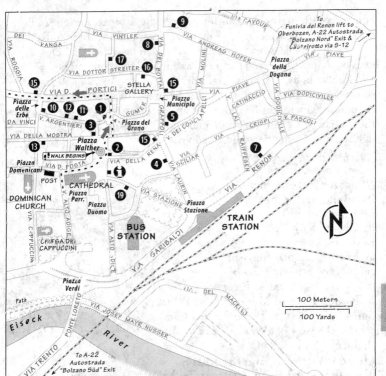

with clothing and gear in excellent condition for his age. Later, researchers pinned down the cause of death—an arrowhead buried in Ötzi's left shoulder.

You'll see Ötzi himself—still frozen—as well as an artist's reconstruction of what he looked like when he was alive. In his mid-40s at the time of his death, Ötzi was 5 feet, 3 inches tall with brown hair and brown eyes. He weighed about 110 poun and likely had trouble with his knees.

Glass cases display his incredibly well-preserved and fasc ing clothing and gear, including a finely stitched two-colo his goathide loincloth, a fancy hat, shoes, a well-crafted hate arrows, a bow, and fire-making gadgets.

With Ötzi as the centerpiece, the museum takes intriguing journey through time, recounting the ev humanity—from the Paleolithic era to the Roman period and finally to the Middle Ages—in vivid detail. The exhibit offers informative displays and models, video demonstrations of Ötzi's extraction and his personal effects, and interactive computers.

As the body was found right on the border, Austria and Italy squabbled briefly over who would get him. Tooth enamel studies have now shown that he did grow up on the Italian side. An Austrian journalist dubbed him Ötzi, after the Ötztal valley, where he was discovered.

Dominican Church (Chiesa dei Domenicani/ Dominikanerkirche)

Drop by this 13th-century church to see its Chapel of St. John (San Giovanni/St. Johannes; chapel is through the archway and on the right), frescoed in the 14th century by the Giotto School.

Cost and Hours: Free, €0.50 coin lights dim interior, Mon-Sat 9:00-17:00, Sun 12:00-18:00, on Piazza Domenicani, two blocks west of Piazza Walther/Waltherplatz.

Lift to Oberbozen and the Ritten

The **Funivia del Renon/Rittner Seilbahn** cable car whisks you over the hills from Bolzano to the touristy resort village of Oberbozen, where Sigmund Freud and his wife once celebrated their wedding anniversary. The reasonably priced, 12-minute ride itself is the main attraction, offering views of the town, surrounding mountains, made-for-yodeling farmsteads, and 18-wheelers downshifting along the expressway from Austria. While the cable car is fun, it is no replacement for a trip to Castelrotto and Alpe di Siusi.

Cost and Hours: €10 round-trip, departures year-round Mon-Sat 6:30-22:38, Sun 7:10-22:38; leaves every 4 minutes, or every 12 minutes after 21:00; closes for maintenance for a week in March and Nov; for info call regional transport hotline at tel. 840-000-471 or visit www.sii.bz.it.

Getting There: The cable car's valley station is a five-block walk east from the Bolzano train station along Via Renon/Rittner strasse or from Piazza Municipio/Rathausplatz in the old center.

At the Top: Oberbozen (elevation 4,000 feet) is mostly a collection of resort hotels. From Oberbozen, a narrow-gauge train makes the 16-minute trip to **Klobenstein,** a larger and slightly less touristy village at 3,800 feet (€3.50 one-way, €6 round-trip, €12 round-trip for both cable car and train, leaves daily at least hourly). The local TI has branches in both villages (www.ritten. com). In Oberbozen, the TI is in the train station building, just steps from the lift station (Mon-Fri 9:00-12:30 & 15:00-18:00, Sat 9:00-12:30, closed Sun in summer, tel. 0471-345-245). The Klobenstein TI is a five-minute walk from the train station (Mon-Fri 8:30-18:00, Sat 8:30-12:00, closed Sun, tel. 0471-356-100).

The lift station and TIs have brochures suggesting short walks. More interesting than Oberbozen itself (though not a must-see) are the nearby **"earth pyramids,"** which are a 30-minute walk downhill from the cable-car station and can be glimpsed from the cable car itself. The pyramids, created by eroding glacial debris dumped at the end of the last ice age, are Bryce Canyon-like pinnacles that rise out of the ridge. Klobenstein has its own earth pyramids a 45-minute walk from town. Another walk is the Freud-

promenade, a fairly level, 1.5-hour stroll between Oberbozen and Klobenstein (you can take the train back).

New Bolzano (Nuova Bolzano)

Just across the river from the Museum of Archaeology, the fascist-style **Victory Monument** (Monumento alla Vittoria) glistens in white Zandobbio marble. It marks the beginning of the "new" city built by the fascist government in the 1920s, in an effort to Italianize the otherwise Germanic-looking city. Indeed, you won't hear German spoken here as often as in the old town, and the shops and bars along the colonnaded Corso della Libertà feel a world away from the old town.

The grand plans for this part of the city were never completed. Even so, there are several blocks of buildings constructed in a repetitive Modernist design, following the idea of imperial monumentalism that was meant to impress and announce the dawn of a new era in Italy. Most of the structures were intended to house state institutions and highly desirable apartments for state employees. A few blocks down on Piazza Tribunale, you can still find the somewhat faded image of Mussolini waving from one of the building

Runkelstein Castle (Castel Roncolo/Schloss Runkelstei

This 13th-century "illustrated manor" perches above the river north of downtown. Inside is an impressively large collecti secular medieval frescoes, with scenes from the everyday l knights and ladies. To get here, either hop on the BoBus shuttle (see "Helpful Hints," earlier) or walk the promenade along the Talvera River (see "Bolzano Walks," next).

Cost and Hours: €8, Tue-Sun 10:00-18:00, closed Mon, last entry 30 minutes before closing, 2 miles north of Ponte Talvera on Kaiser-Franz-Josef Weg, tel. 0471-329-808, www.runkelstein.com.

Bolzano Walks

Pick up a map at the TI for scenic, accessible strolls that provide a different perspective on the region. One popular option is to stroll the easy, shaded **Talvera promenade** just west of the Museum of Archaeology, following the river embankment north. This route has great people-watching in the summer, with views of vineyards and Maretsch Castle (Castello Mareccio/Burg Maretsch) to the right. In about 20 minutes, you'll reach the Bridge of St. Antonio, where you can cross and follow the river for another 20 minutes to the impressive Runkelstein Castle (described previously).

If you want to extend your hike, walk away from the river (staying on the same side) and head up the hill about 45 minutes for the **St. Oswald** walk. This route takes you to the church of Santa Magdalena (with its 14th-century frescoes), offering great views back to the city.

More ambitious hikers can continue about 20 minutes farther downhill to the **Isarco/Eisack River.** Cross the river to see the Colle cable car, the first in the world to carry passengers, in 1908. At Virgil Hill, take the Passeggiata Virgolo path about 1.5 miles to see the 12th-century Haselburg Castle (Castel Flavon), now home to one of Bolzano's most scenic restaurants.

Sleeping in Bolzano

All of the listed hotels are in the city center, within walking distance of the train and bus stations.

$$$ Hotel Figl, warmly run by Anton and Helga Mayr, has 23 comfy, bright, modern rooms and an attached café on a pedestrian square located a block from Piazza Walther/Waltherplatz. With rooms better than its humble public spaces and exterior, it's a fine value (Sb-€90-95, Db-€125-135, junior suite-€135-145, discount with this book for longer stays—ask when you reserve, breakfast-€4-14, air-con, elevator, non-smoking, free guest computer and Wi-Fi, parking-€15/day, Piazza del Grano/Kornplatz 9, l. 0471-978-412, www.figl.net, info@figl.net, include a backup one number if you email).

$$$ Hotel Greif, a luxury boutique hotel, is right on Piazza her/Waltherplatz. Each of the 33 individually designed rooms s you feel like you're in a modern-art installation (its fine web- es a room-by-room tour). It's not cozy, but it is striking, and

---

Sleep Code

(€1 = about $1.30, country code: 39)

S = Single, **D** = Double/Twin, **T** = Triple, **Q** = Quad, **b** = bathroom, **s** = shower only. Unless otherwise noted, credit cards are accepted, English is spoken, and breakfast is included. Many cities in Italy levy a hotel tax of €2 per person, per night, which must be paid in cash (not included in the rates I've quoted).

To help you sort easily through these listings, I've divided the accommodations into three categories based on the price for a standard double room with bath:

$$$ Higher Priced—Most rooms €100 or more.

$$ Moderately Priced—Most rooms between €60-100.

$ Lower Priced—Most rooms €60 or less.

Prices can change without notice; verify the hotel's current rates online or by email. For the best prices, always book direct.

---

a stay here comes with one of the best breakfasts in Italy (comfort Sb-€123, Db-€185, comfort Db-€215, superior Db-€261, includes buffet breakfast, most rooms non-smoking, air-con, guest computer and Wi-Fi, Piazza Walther/Waltherplatz, entrance on Via della Rena/Raingasse, tel. 0471-318-000, www.greif.it, info@greif.it). Drivers follow signs to P3-*Parking Walther* (€19/day) and enter the hotel from level 1 of the garage.

$$$ Stadt Hotel Città, a venerable old hotel with 99 modern if basic rooms, is ideally situated on Piazza Walther/Waltherplatz. The hotel's café spills out onto the piazza, offering a prime spot for people-watching (Sb-€104-124, Db-€150-230, bigger Db with view-€194, Tb-€194, air-con, elevator, free guest computer and Wi-Fi, parking-€16/day, Piazza Walther/Waltherplatz 21, tel. 0471-975-221, www.hotelcitta.info, info@hotelcitta.info, Francesco and Alessandra). This place is an especially good value if you plan to spend an afternoon in their free-for-guests Wellness Center (mid-Sept-May Mon-Sat 16:30-22:00, likely closed Sun; closed May-mid-Sept; Turkish bath, whirlpool, Finnish sauna, biosauna, massage by appointment)—a fine way to unwind after a day of hiking in the Dolomites.

$$$ Parkhotel Laurin is an Old World luxury hotel located very close to the train station, with 100 tastefully decorated rooms, marble bathrooms, a chic dining room and terrace, a swimming pool, an extensive garden, attentive staff, and frescoes throughout the grand lobby depicting the legend of King Laurin (see

€113, standard Sb-€128, standard Db-€164, comfort Db-€203, discounted Sat-Sun by request, guest computer and Wi-Fi, parking-€16/day, Via Laurin/Laurinstrasse 4, tel. 0471-311-000, www.laurin.it, info@laurin.it).

$$ Hotel Feichter is an inexpensive, well-kept, family-run place with simple but sufficient amenities in a great location. Some of the 30 rooms share a communal terrace overlooking the rooftops of Bolzano. Papà Walter, Mamma Hedwig, Hannes, Irene, and Wolfi Feichter have run this homey hotel since 1969 (Sb-€60, Db-€95, Tb-€115, parking-€5/day, Wi-Fi, ground-floor café serves lunches Mon-Fri; from station, walk up Via Laurin/Laurinstrasse, which becomes Via Grappoli/Weintraubengasse—hotel is on the right at #15; tel. 0471-978-768, www.hotelfeichter.it, info@hotelfeichter.it).

$$ Kolpinghaus Bozen, modern, clean, and church-run, has 34 rooms with two twin beds (placed head to toe) and 71 air-conditioned single rooms with all the comforts. Though institutional, it's a great deal...and makes me feel thankful (Sb-€65, Db-€99, Tb-€140, elevator, free guest computer or Wi-Fi—varies by floor, laundry-€6/big load, parking-€13, 4 blocks from Piazza Walther/Waltherplatz near Piazza Domenicani at Largo A. Kolping/Adolph-Kolping-Strasse 3, tel. 0471-308-400, www.kolping-bozen.it, info@kolpingbozen.it). The line of people in front of the building at lunchtime consists mainly of office workers waiting for the cafeteria to open (€10.50 three-course lunch, Mon-Fri 11:45-14:00, Sat 12:00-13:30, closed Sun).

$ Youth Hostel Bolzano is the most comfortable and inviting hostel that I've seen in Italy. It has 18 four-bed rooms (each with two bunk beds and a full bathroom) and 10 delightful singles with bath. The bright, clean, modern rooms make it feel like a dorm in a fancy university. With no age limit, easy reservations online, great lockers, and cheap guest computer, it is the utopian hostel (bed in quad-€21, Sb-€28, €2 extra for 1-night stays, includes linens and buffet breakfast, towels-€2, laundry-€4/load, Wi-Fi, kitchen, free luggage storage, 9:00 checkout; 100 yards to the right as you leave the train station at Via Renon/Rittner Strasse 23; tel. 0471-300-865, www.ostello.bz, bolzano@ostello.bz).

Eating in Bolzano

of these recommendations are in the center of the old town. es are consistent (you can generally get a good plate of meat eggies for €10). While nearly every local-style place serves a Germanic/Tirolean and Italian fare, I favor eating Tirolean Bozen.

sses **Rössl** ("White Horse") offers affordable, mostly Tirolean food with meat, fish, and fine vegetarian options. Located in a traditional woody setting, it's good for dining indoors among savvy locals (€11-14 main courses, €7-12 lunch specials, Mon-Fri 11:00-15:00 & 17:30-23:30—light meals only available between 15:00-17:30, Sat 11:00-15:00 only, closed Sun, 2 blocks north of Piazza Municipio at Via Bottai/Bindergasse 6, tel. 0471-973-267).

Ca' de Bezzi/Gasthaus Batzenhäusl is historic. It's Bolzano's oldest inn, with two Teutonic-feeling upper floors; by contrast, the patio and back room are refreshingly modern and untouristy. They make their own breads and pastas and serve traditional Tirolean fare (€12-14 main courses, daily 11:00-24:00, limited menu outside mealtimes, one of the rare places open on Sun, Via Andreas Hofer/Andreas-Hofer-Strasse 30, tel. 0471-050-950).

Hopfen and Company fills an 800-year-old house with happy eaters, drinkers, and the beer lover's favorite aroma: hops *(Hopfen)*. A tavern since the 1600s, it's a stylish, fresh microbrewery today. This high-energy, boisterous place is packed with locals who come for its homemade beer, delicious Tirolean food, and reasonable prices. You'll enjoy the friendly, English-speaking waitstaff (€10-15 main courses, €7-11 heavy traditional beer dumplings with salad, great €8 salads, Mon-Sat 9:30-24:00, Sun 9:30-12:00, limited menu outside of mealtimes, Piazza Erbe/Obstplatz 17, tel. 0471-300-788).

Paulaner Stuben is a restaurant-pizzeria-*Bierstube* serving good food and a favorite Bavarian beer. It has good outside seating and a take-me-to-Germany *Stube* (€6-7 pizzas and pastas, €7-8 salads, €10-14 main courses, Mon-Sat 11:30-24:00, limited menu from 15:00-18:00, closed Sun, Via Argentieri/Silbergasse 16—or use back entrance at Via dei Portici/Laubengasse 51, tel. 0471-980-407).

Enoteca Il Baccaro, a nondescript hole-in-the-wall wine bar, is an intriguing spot for a glass of wine (€1-4) and bar snacks amid locals. Wines available by the glass are listed on the blackboard (Mon-Fri 8:30-14:00 & 16:30-20:30, Sat 9:00-14:30, closed Sun, located a half-block east of Hopfen and Company on a hidden alley off Via Argentieri/Silbergasse 17, look for *vino* or *wein* sign next to fountain on south side of street and enter courtyard, tel. 0471-971-421).

Gasthaus Fink, a busy diner, serves typical Tirolean and Italian dishes. It has both indoor and outdoor seating on a quiet pedestrian street a few doors off Piazza Walther/Waltherplatz (€ pastas, €10 antipasto plates, €14 *secondi*, Fri-Tue 9:00-22:00, W 9:00-15:00 only, closed Thu, Via della Mostra/Mustergasse 9, 0471-975-047).

Gelato: **Officina del Gelo Avalon,** tucked away in an u suming corner of the colonnaded street, is one of Bolzano's

Tirolean Cuisine

During your visit to the Dolomites, take a break from Italian-style pizzas and pastas to sample some of the region's traditional cuisine...with a distinctly Austrian flavor. For simplicity, I've generally listed Italian names here, though local menus are in both Italian and German (and usually also English).

Wurst and sauerkraut are the Tirolean clichés. More adventurous eaters seek out *speck*, a raw (prosciutto-style) ham smoked for five months then thinly sliced and served as an antipasto or in sandwiches. *Canederli*—large dumplings with bits of *speck,* liver, spinach, or cheese—are often served in broth, or with butter and cheese. (Never cut a dumpling with a knife—it'll destroy the chef.)

The stars of Tirolean cuisine are the hearty meat dishes—which, unlike traditional Italian main courses, are nearly always served with side dishes of doughy dumplings or vegetables and potatoes. Try *stinco di maiale* (roasted pork shank, usually garnished with potatoes) and *crauti rossi* (a sweetish sauerkraut made from red cabbage). *Carrè affumicato* is pork shank that is first smoked, then boiled. *Selvaggine*, or wild game, comes in the form of *capriolo* (fawn), *cervo* (venison), or *camoscio* (chamois/antelope). Game is eaten smoked and thinly sliced in *antipasti;* in meat sauce *(ragù)* with fresh pasta or as ravioli stuffing; or in entrées, as tender chunks grilled or roasted in a rich sauce *(spezzatino)*.

For dessert, strudel is everywhere, filled with the harvest from this region's renowned apple orchards. Cakes and pies are loaded with other locally grown fruits, raisins, and nuts. *Kaiserschmarrn* is an interesting alternative: a tall, eggy crêpe prepared with raisins and topped with powdered sugar and red currant jam.

Bier (birra) is king in the Alto Adige (the best-known brand, Forst, is brewed in nearby Merano), but the wines of the area are well-matched to the local fare. *Magdalaner* is a light, dry red made from Schiava grapes. *Lagrein scuro* is a full-bodied red, dry and fruity, similar to a cabernet sauvignon or merlot. *Gewürztraminer* is a dry white wine with a spicy fruit flavor. For something stronger, try grappa made from Williams pears (and served with a wedge of fresh pear), or *grappa nocino*—a darker, sweeter brew similar to Jägermeister. *Guten Appetit und Prost!*

kept secrets, setting new standards in the art of gelato making. The passionate, proud owner, Paolo, happily expounds on its natural ingredients sourced from carefully chosen organic producers from around the world. Lighted signs indicate which of the gelataria's always-fresh flavors are available. Try one of half a dozen kinds of chocolate, or embark on a near-religious experience by tasting the pistachio (€1.50/scoop, daily 13:00-22:30, Corso della Libertà 44, tel. 0471-260-434).

Picnics: Assemble the ingredients at the **Piazza Erbe/Obstplatz** market and dine in the park along the Talvera River (the green area with benches past the museum). Or visit one of the three **Despar supermarkets:** The largest, with longest hours, is at the end of the Galleria Greif arcade (enter arcade from Piazza Walther/Waltherplatz by Hotel Greif and walk to far end—the supermarket is downstairs; Mon-Fri 8:30-19:30, Sat 8:30-19:00, closed Sun). Smaller branches are on Piazza Erbe/Obstplatz and at Via Bottai/Bindergasse 29 (both open Mon-Fri 8:30-19:15, Sat 8:30-18:00, closed Sun).

Bolzano Connections

From Bolzano by Train to: Milan (about hourly, 3.5-4 hours, change in Verona), **Verona** (about hourly, 1.75-2.25 hours, take the "R" trains—avoid fast trains that take same time for double the cost), **Venice** (about hourly, 3-3.5 hours, change in Verona), **Florence** (every 1-2 hours, 3.5-5 hours, change in Verona and/or Bologna), **Innsbruck** (1-2/hour, 2-2.5 hours, some change in Brennero), **Munich** (called "Monaco" in Italy, 5/day direct, 3.75 hours).

By Bus to: Castelrotto (2/hour Mon-Fri, 1-2/hour Sat, hourly Sun, 50 minutes, last departure Mon-Fri at 20:10, Sat-Sun at 19:10, pick up free schedule at bus station, €3.80 each way, buy tickets from driver, toll-free tel. 800-846-047 or toll tel. 840-000-471, www.sii.bz.it). The bus leaves from Bolzano's bus station (one block west of train station), stops at the train station, and then winds high into the mountains, dropping you in the center of Castelrotto.

If you're heading directly to **Alpe di Siusi,** take the same bus, get off just past the Seiseralm Bergbahn cable-car station, and ascend on the cable car. For more on Alpe di Siusi, see page 269.

Castelrotto

The ideal home base for exploring Alpe di Siusi, Castelrotto (Kastelruth in German; town population: 2,000; district population: 6,000; altitude: 3,475 feet) has more village character than any other town I know in the region. With a traffic-free center, a thousand years of history, an oversized and hyperactive bell tower, and traditionally clad locals, it seems lost in another world. Against a backdrop of mountains, Castelrotto conveys the powerful message that simple pleasures are enough. Stay two nights.

Orientation to Castelrotto

Tourist Information

The helpful TI is on the main square at Piazza Kraus 2 (Mon-Sat 8:30-12:00 & 14:30-18:00, closed Sun except June-Aug 10:00-12:00, shorter hours off-season, tel. 0471-706-333, www.seiseralm. it). If you plan to do any hiking, pick up the TI's list of suggested hikes, which includes estimated walking times and trail numbers.

For a longer stay, consider the **Combi-Card** (€38/any 3 days out of a 7-day validity period, €48/unlimited usage for 7 days, expires 1 week after time stamp). This card covers the Alpe di Siusi Express bus, Seiseralm Bergbahn cable car, Compatsch-Saltria shuttle bus (Almbus #11), other shuttle buses, regional orange SAD buses—such as the one to Bolzano from Castelrotto—and all trains in the Südtirol/Alto Adige region.

Helpful Hints

Annual Events: The Oswald-von-Wolkenstein Riding Tournament, held on the first weekend of June, features equestrian medieval-style tournament games, followed by a feast. The town also holds religious processions with locals dressed in traditional costumes, usually on Corpus Christi (June 19 in 2014); the feast day of the village protectors, Sts. Peter and Paul (June 29); and on the local Thanksgiving (first weekend in Oct). Mid-October is packed for Kastleruther Spatzenfest, a concert weekend for local musical heartthrobs, Kastleruther Spatzen.

ares: The periods between ski season and hiking season (April d Nov) are quiet, with lifts closed for maintenance and most

Castelrotto

CALVARIO STROLL

100 Meters
100 Yards

To San Michele, Val Gardena, Sella Pass & ❻

CHURCH
Main Square
BUS STATION
BELL TOWER
WC

MARINZEN CHAIR LIFT

To Pool, Alpe di Siusi, Siusi Village (Cable Car to Alpe di Siusi), Bolzano via S-12

POST

DOLOMITES

❶ Alla Torre (Gasthof zum Turm) Hotel, Rest. & Internet Café
❷ Hotel Cavallino d'Oro (Goldenes Rössl) & Rest.
❸ Hotel Wolf (Hotel al Lupo)
❹ Residence Garni Trocker & Internet Café
❺ Haus Trocker
❻ To Tirler Hof B&B
❼ To Villa Pircher, Residence Burghof, Sasso's Wine Bar & Santners

❽ Saalstuben Restaurant
❾ Zur Alten Schmiede Pizzeria
❿ Storm Café
⓫ Rubin's Wine Bar
⓬ Supermarkets (3)
⓭ Library (Internet)
⓮ RC Sports & Rent
⓯ ATM, WC & Phones
⓰ Mendel Haus
⓱ Kastelruther Spatzen-Laden Shop

hotels and restaurants shut down so locals can take their own vacations.

Internet Access: You'll find a free Wi-Fi hotspot in the main square. If you need an Internet terminal, stop by the recommended **Alla Torre** hotel, which has an Internet café (Thu-T 8:00-23:00, closed Wed, closed April-May and Nov, beh TI at Kofelgasse 8, tel. 0471-706-349), or the recommer **Residence Garni Trocker** (daily 8:00-20:00, on Fostlw

Or visit the public **library** (Mon 14:00-18:00, Tue 9:00-12:00, Thu 15:00-19:00, Fri 9:00-12:00, tel. 0471-708-023).

Recreation: A heated outdoor swimming pool with alpine views and nearby tennis courts is near town (€6.50 mid-May-mid-Sept 9:00-21:00, tel. 0471-705-090, ask at your hotel for details). You can rent a horse at **Unter-Lanzinerhof Telfen** (tel. 339-868-6868, Karin speaks some English).

For more excitement, tandem paragliding flights—you and the pilot—depart from Alpe di Siusi and land either where you started or in Castelrotto (tel. 335-603-6400, www. tandem-paragliding.com, Ruben and Kurt). You can rent skis and snowboards at **RC Sports and Rent** (Via Panider/Panid-erstrasse 10, tel. 0471-711-079, Robert—mobile 339-293-9725, Christian—mobile 328-303-8045).

Arrival in Castelrotto

The **bus station** *(Bushof)* is a few steps below the town's main square. The bus parking lot has a shelter with timetables. An ATM, WC, and phones are located in a building to the right. Take the stairs or elevator to get to the main square and TI.

Drivers can park in one of the two underground parking lots: One is near the bus station, and the other is on Wolkensteinstrasse just past the recommended Saalstuben Restaurant (first hour free). Each of the recommended hotels also has free parking (ask for details when you book).

Self-Guided Walk

Welcome to Castelrotto

Castelrotto has little to distract you other than the surrounding mountains and hikes. This quick walk will trace the town's history, from the ruling Krauses to yodelers who rule. Note that shops in Castelrotto close for siesta from 12:00 to 15:00—a good time for a long lunch, a hike in the hills...or a siesta of your own.

• *Start in the...*

Main Square: Piazza Kraus is named for the family who ruled the town from 1550 to 1800. Their palace, now the City Hall and TI, overlooks the square and sports the Kraus family coat of arms.

Castelrotto uses its square well. The farmers' market takes place here on Friday mornings in the summer (June-Oct), and a clothing market fills the square most Thursday mornings. Before and after Sunday Mass, the square is crowded with villagers and farmers (who fill the church) dressed in traditional clothing. The main Mass (Sat at 20:00—or at 19:30 in winter—and Sun at 10:00) is in German. Another Mass takes place in Italian throughout the tourist season (at 11:00) for visitors.

• *A landmark in the square is the...*

Bell Tower: At 250 feet, the freestanding bell tower dominates the town. It was once attached to a church, which burned in

1753. While the bell tower was quickly rebuilt,
the present-day church was constructed a century later next to the gutted church (which was
then torn down to make space for the square).
The wire between the church and tower connects the noisy bells. The sacristan can easily
ring them using an electric switch.

When you feel the pride that the locals
have in their tower—which symbolizes their
town—you'll better understand why Italy is
called "the land of a thousand bell towers." The
bells of Castelrotto, which are a big part of the
town experience, ring on the hour from 6:00 until 22:00. While
sleepy tourists wonder why they clang so very early in the morning, locals who grew up with the chimes find them comforting.
The bells mark the hours, summon people to work and to Mass,
announce festivals, and warn when storms threaten. In the days
when people used to believe that thunder was the devil approaching, the bells called everyone to pray. (Townspeople thought the
bells' sound cleared the clouds.) Bells ring big at 7:00, noon, and
19:00. The biggest of the eight bells (7,500 pounds) peals only on
special days. On Fridays, the bells ring at 15:00, commemorating
Christ's sacrifice at the supposed hour of his death. The colorful
poles in front of the church (yellow-and-white for the Vatican, red-
and-white for Tirol) fly flags on festival days.

• *Also on the square is the...*

Church: Before entering, notice the plaque on the exterior.
This commemorative inscription honors the tiny community's
WWI dead—*Dorf* means from the village itself, and *Fraktion* is
from an outlying district. Stepping into the church, you're surrounded by harmonious art from about 1850. The church is dedicated to Sts. Peter and Paul, and the paintings that flank the high
altar show how each was martyred (crucifixion and beheading).
The pews (and smart matching confessionals) are carved of walnut
wood.

• *Back outside, belly up to the...*

Fountain: Opposite the bell tower, Castelrotto's fountain
dates from 1884. St. Florian, the protector against fires, keeps a
eye on it today as he did when villagers (and their horses) first car
here for a drink of water.

• *With your back to the bell tower, look a half-block down the lane t
the finely frescoed...*

Mendel Haus: This house has a traditional facade and a

DOLOMITES

The Dramatic Dolomites

Located in northeastern Italy, the Dolomites have been called the most beautiful mountains on earth, and certainly they are

among the most dramatic. They differ from the rest of the Alps because of their dominant rock type, dolomite, which forms sheer vertical walls of white, gray, and pink that rise abruptly from green valleys and meadows. There is one national park (Dolomiti Bellunesi National Park) in this region, and many regional parks, such as Alpe di Siusi. Rail lines, roads, and a huge system of lifts make this group of mountains very accessible.

Once dubbed the "Pale Mountains" or the "Venetian Alps," this mountain range was named after French mineralogist Dolomieu, who in the late 1700s first described the rock type responsible for the region's light-colored bluffs and peaks. These sedimentary rocks (similar to limestone) were formed in warm tropical seas during the Triassic Period (about 250 million years ago). The marine sediments, along with the fossilized remains of coral reefs and other animals, were buried, hardened, and later scooped upward along with the rest of the Alps by the tectonic-plate action of Africa slowly smashing into Europe. Today, marine fossils are found atop the region's highest peaks, including the skyscraping, nearly 11,000-feet-high Marmolada (east of Bolzano).

During World War I, the front line between the Italian and Austro-Hungarian forces ran through these mountains, and many paths were cut into the range for military use. Today mountaineers can follow a network of metal rungs, cables, and ladders called a *via ferrata*. One famous wartime trail is the "Road of Tunnels," which passes through 52 tunnels. Along with being a paradise for hikers and climbers, the Dolomites are a popular skiing destination. The 1956 Olympics in Cortina di Ampezzo put the region on the map. A popular winter activity for intrepid skiers is the "Sella Ronda"—circling the Sella massif using a system of lifts and 28 miles of ski runs.

Whether you experience the Dolomites with your hand on a walking stick, a ski pole, or an *aperitivo* while mountain-gazing from a café, it's easy to enjoy this spectacular region.

carvers' shop. Its frescoes (from 1886) include many symbolic figures, as well as an emblem of a carpenter above the door—a relic om the days when images, rather than address numbers, identified house. Notice St. Florian again; this time, he's pouring water small painting of this very house engulfed in flames. Inside del Haus are fine carvings, a reminder that this region—espe-

cially nearby Val Gardena—
is famous for its woodwork.
You'll also see many witches,
folk figures that date back
to when this area was the
Salem of this corner of Europe. Women who didn't fit
society's mold—including

midwives, healers, redheads, and so on—were sometimes burned
as witches.

• *Walk downhill to the left of Mendel Haus, then turn right and climb
the stairs. At the top of the stairs, turn left on Dolomitenstrasse. In 20
yards, on the left at the end of the street, is a shop dedicated to Castelrotto's hometown heroes...*

Kastelruther Spatzen-Laden: The ABBA of the Alps, the
folk-singing group Kastelruther Spatzen is a gang of local boys
who put Castelrotto on the map. They have a huge following here
and throughout the German-speaking world. The lead singer, Nor-
bert, is a Germanic heartthrob on par with Tom Jones. At the big
Castelrotto festival on the second weekend in October, they put on
hometown concerts, filling this place with fans from as far away as
the Alsace, Switzerland, and the Netherlands. They also have an
open-air concert in June and a Christmas concert.

Inside this shop—where you'll undoubtedly hear their inimi-
table music—is a folk musician's Carnaby Street. Downstairs is a
folksy little museum slathered with gifts, awards, and gold records.
The group has won 13 Echo Awards..."more than Robbie Williams." Watch the continuously playing video (€2 museum downstairs, refunded if you spend €5 in the shop, Mon-Fri 9:00-12:00
& 14:00-18:00, Sat 9:00-12:00, closed Sun, Via Dolomitenstrasse
21, tel. 0471-707-439, www.spatzenladen.it).

Sights in Castelrotto

Calvario Stroll

For a scenic stroll, take a short walk around the town's hill, originally the site of the ancient Roman fortress and later the fortified
home of the medieval lord. One lane circles the hill while another
spirals to the top past seven little chapels, each depicting a scene
from Christ's Passion and culminating in the Crucifixion. Facing
the TI, take the road under the arch to the right, and then follow signs to *Kofel* (to go around the hill) or *Kalvarienberg* (to ge
directly to the top). This 15-minute stroll is great after dark—ro
mantically lit and under the stars. (The lead singer of Kastelruth
Spatzen enjoyed his first kiss right here.) On a warm day, take
Friedensweg (Peace Trail) from the top of the hill to go bac

the town square or below the village. This 30-minute forest walk is decorated with peace-themed artwork by local elementary students.

Marinzen Lift

The little Marinzen chairlift zips you up the mountain to the Marinzenhütte café, which has an animal park for kids (open when the cable car runs). You can come back on the lift, or it's a one-hour hike down.

Cost and Hours: €7 one-way, €9 round-trip, runs daily late May-mid-Oct 9:00-17:00, July-Aug Wed until 22:00, closed off-season and rainy mornings, tel. 0471-707-160, www.seiseralm.it.

Getting There: From the town square, head downhill toward Wolkensteinstrasse, turn left and go another 50 yards down the road toward San Michele, and find the chairlift a few steps off the road on the right, behind the Co-op supermarket.

Nightlife in and near Castelrotto

If you're here on the weekend, the "Nightliner" shuttle bus connects you with local hot spots (Fri-Sat hourly 20:40-4:00 in the morning, schedules at TI and hotels; €2.50/ride, €4/all-night pass). **Rubin's,** next door to the Hotel Schgaguler in Castelrotto (tel. 0471-712-100), and **Sasso's,** on Schlernstrasse in the nearby town of Siusi/Seis (tel. 0471-708-068), are trendy wine bars. A popular hangout for the younger crowd in Siusi/Seis is **Santners,** at the Seiseralm Bergbahn cable-car station (tel. 0471-727-913).

Sleeping in Castelrotto

$$$ Alla Torre (in German, **Gasthof zum Turm**) is comfortable, clean, and alpine-traditional, with great beds and modern bathrooms (small Db-€80-120, big Db-€100-140, Tb-€150-210, one-night stay-€4 extra, price depends on season—highest in Aug, elevator, free Wi-Fi, free parking, closed April and Nov, behind TI at Kofelgasse 8, tel. 0471-706-349, www.zumturm.com, info@zumturm.com, Gabi and Günther).

$$$ Hotel Cavallino d'Oro (in German, **Goldenes Rössl**), on the main square, has plenty of Tirolean character and plush, welcoming public rooms. Run by friendly and helpful Stefan and Susanne, the entire place is dappled with artistic, woodsy touches and historic photos. If you love antiques by candlelight, this 700-year-old hotel is the best in town (Sb-€55-77, Db-€94-154,

Db suite-€130-190 depending on season, 2 percent discount with cash, discount for 4-night stay, elevator, free guest computer and Wi-Fi, laundry, free parking, Piazza Kraus 1, tel. 0471-700 337, www.cavallino.it, cavallino@cavallino.it). Stefan converted his wine cellar into a Roman steam bath and Finnish sauna (free for guests, great after a hike, can book an hour for exclusive use)—complete with heated tile seats, massage rooms, a solarium for tanning, and tropical plants.

$$$ Hotel Wolf (in Italian, **al Lupo**) is pure Tirolean, with all the comforts in 23 neat-as-a-pin rooms, most with balconies (Sb-€57-72, Db-€95-120, prices vary with season and view, elevator, pay Wi-Fi, coin-op laundry, free parking, closed April-mid-May and Nov-mid-Dec, a block below main square at Wolkensteinstrasse 5, tel. 0471-706-332, www.hotelwolf.it, info@hotelwolf.it, Arno).

$$ Residence Garni Trocker is run by the Moser family, who rent 11 great rooms in a place that's bomb-shelter solid yet warm-wood cozy. Their compound is beautifully laid out with a café-bar, garden, and top-notch plumbing (Sb-€40-55, Db-€60-90 depending on season, apartments available, pay Wi-Fi, Fostlweg 3, tel. 0471-705-200, www.residencetrocker.com, garni@residence-trocker.com, Stefan). Sunday afternoon is the family's time of rest; if you're coming on a Sunday, be sure to let them know in advance what time you'll arrive.

$ Haus Trocker, on the edge of town, is a modern home where the delightful Frau Trocker rents two lovely rooms that share one WC. Frau Trocker doesn't speak English, but after you meet her you won't care. Her son Roland can translate for you if he's around (D-€50; from the bus station, walk away from the church spire, past Hotel Kastel Seiseralm to Fostlweg 6, then look for yellow *Zimmer* sign at top of steps; mobile 348-921-0335).

$ Tirler Hof, the storybook Jaider family farm, has 40 cows, four Old World-comfy guest rooms, and a great mountain view. The ground-floor double has a private bath. The top-floor rooms share a bathroom and a great balcony. Take a stroll before breakfast (D/Db-€60, discount for stays longer than one night, cash only, open year-round, free kitchen use on request, definitely most practical for drivers; it's the first farm outside of town on the right on road to San Michele, Via Panider/Paniderstrasse 44; tel. 0471-706-017, info@tirlerhof.it).

Near Castelrotto, in Siusi/Seis

These two accommodations are in the hamlet of Siusi/Seis, just five minutes from Castelrotto by bus (see "By Bus from Castelrotto" on page 272). Siusi/Seis has shops, restaurants, a TI, and other services—and the cable car to Alpe di Siusi. Both places listed below will pick you up from the Siusi/Seis bus station.

$$ At **Villa Pircher,** the friendly Pircher family rents out two view apartments just a short walk or bus ride from the cable-car station. Numerous trails begin nearby (Db-€49-75, price varies by season and number of people, no minimum stay, laundry service, parking, one stop past the Siusi/Seis bus station at Laranzweg 13, tel. 0471-707-440, mobile 339-191-3063, www.villapircher.com, info@villapircher.com, Thomas speaks some English).

$$ Residence Burghof offers eight fully equipped apartments in a rural setting with beautiful views only 10 minutes from the village. When he's not teaching skiing, English-speaking Patrick Fill and his family run this Tirolean retreat (Sb-€48-64, Db-€51-91, Tb-€70-131, price depends on season, discounts for 3-night stay, family rates, sauna, pay Wi-Fi, free parking, rental bikes available, Burgfriedenstrasse 20, tel. 0471-706-243, www.residence-burghof.com, info@residence-burghof.com).

Eating in Castelrotto

Note that the first two options are also listed earlier under "Sleeping in Castelrotto."

Cavallino d'Oro Restaurant offers a variety of beautifully presented, homemade Tirolean cuisine—including wild game, *canederli* dumplings, and strudel—in a dressy but relaxed and woodsy ambience. The waiters, Marco and Monica, are very helpful; quiz them before you order. Reservations are smart (€30 meals, daily 18:00-21:00, tel. 0471-706-337).

Alla Torre Restaurant, homier and with the best terrace in town, is another fine option for traditional and international dishes (Thu-Tue 12:00-14:00 & 18:00-20:45, closed Wed, closed April-May and Nov, tel. 0471-706-349).

Saalstuben Restaurant dishes up a selection of reasonably priced Austrian-Italian dishes indoors or on their terrace. If you believe in dessert first, try the *Kaiserschmarrn* (€9.30), a favorite of Austrian Emperor Franz Josef. You won't need anything else (summer daily 11:30-14:00 & 17:30-21:00, closed Thu in winter, Wolkensteinstrasse 12, tel. 0471-707-394).

Zur Alten Schmiede Pizzeria is a great place to enjoy an evening drinking Forst, the local beer, and playing darts (€6-9 pizzas and pastas, Tue-Sun 12:00-14:00 & 17:30-24:00 but kitchen closes at 23:00, closed Mon, outdoor seating, near bus station entrance at Paniderstrasse 7, tel. 0471-707-390).

Dessert: For strudel, locals like the no-nonsense **Stern** café, with its terrace seating (Tue-Sun 7:30-19:00, closed Mon; on Plattenstrasse—facing TI, go left through arch; tel. 0471-706-382).

Picnics: You can put together a picnic at **Euro Spar** (Mon-at 8:00-19:00, closed Sun, on Wolkensteinstrasse, tel. 0471-706-

222), **M-Preis** (Mon-Sat 8:00-19:00, closed Sun, Paniderstrasse 21, tel. 0471-710-014), or **Co-op/Konsum-Market** (sells locally produced food, Mon-Sat 7:30-12:30 & 15:00-19:00, closed Sun and off-season Sat afternoons, Paniderstrasse 24, tel. 0471-706-330).

Castelrotto Connections

From Castelrotto by Bus to: Bolzano (2/hour Mon-Fri, 1-2/hour Sat, hourly Sun, 50 minutes, runs Mon-Sat 6:15-19:00, Sun 7:00-19:00; in Bolzano, the bus stops at the more central Bahnhofplatz, or train station—get off here to avoid the 200-yard walk from the bus station, where the bus terminates), **Canazei** (late June-mid-Sept only, 3-4/day, 2-2.25 hours), and **Ortisei/St. Ulrich** and **St. Cristina** (8/day, 30 minutes to Ortisei, then another 10 minutes to St. Cristina). Get bus schedules at the TI, call toll-free tel. 800-846-047, toll tel. 840-000-471, or check www.sii.bz.it or www.silbernagl.it. For **Alpe di Siusi** connections, see "Orientation to Alpe di Siusi," later.

    To Munich: On Saturdays only from June to late September and mid-December to late March, a bus departs Alpe di Siusi (Compatsch) at 6:00 and Castelrotto at 6:25, and heads for Munich's main bus station (arrives 11:00, €42) and airport (arrives 12:00, €50). You can be picked up at your hotel for an extra €5. For information and booking, contact the Castelrotto TI.

Alpe di Siusi

Europe's largest high-alpine meadow, Alpe di Siusi (Seiser Alm in German), separates two of the most famous Dolomite ski-resort

valleys. Eight miles wide, 20 miles long, and soaring up to 6,500 feet high, Alpe di Siusi is dotted by farm huts and wildflowers (mid-June-July), surrounded by dramatic—if distant—Dolomite peaks and cliffs, and much appreciated by hordes of walkers.

    Compatsch, the modern little tourist town at the entrance of the meadow, has a TI, food, two small shopping streets, and services (described later). Don't confuse the village of S

Alpe di Siusi

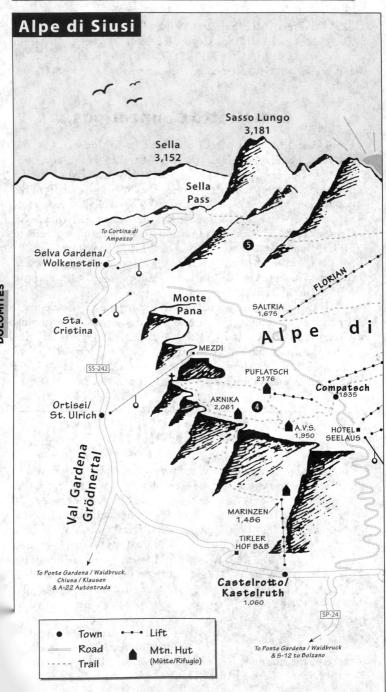

Sasso Lungo
3,181

Sella
3,152

Sella
Pass

To Cortina di
Ampezzo

Selva Gardena/
Wolkenstein

FLORIAN

SALTRIA
1,675

Monte
Pana

Alpe di

Sta.
Cristina

MEZDI

PUFLATSCH
2176

SS-242

Compatsch
1835

ARNIKA
2,061

4

Ortisei/
St. Ulrich

A.V.S.
1,950

HOTEL
SEELAUS

MARINZEN
1,486

TIRLER
HOF B&B

To Ponte Gardena / Waidbruck,
Chiusa / Klausen
& A-22 Autostrada

Castelrotto/
Kastelruth
1,060

SP-24

DOLOMITES

Val Gardena
Grödnertal

● Town	•••• Lift	
—— Road	▲ Mtn. Hut	
- - - Trail	(Mütte/Rifugio)	

To Ponte Gardena / Waidbruck
& S-12 to Bolzano

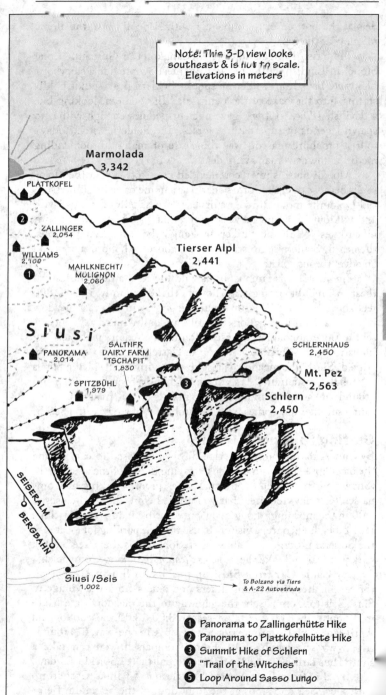

Note: This 3-D view looks southeast & is not to scale. Elevations in meters

Marmolada
3,342

PLATTKOFEL

2

ZALLINGER
2,054

WILLIAMS
2,100

1

MAHLKNECHT/
MULIGNON
2,060

Tierser Alpl
2,441

S i u s i

PANORAMA
2,014

SALTNER
DAIRY FARM
"TSCHAPIT"
1,830

SPITZBÜHL
1,979

3

SCHLERNHAUS
2,450

Mt. Pez
2,563

Schlern
2,450

SEISERALM
BERGBAHN

Siusi /Seis
1,002

To Bolzano via Tiers
& A-22 Autostrada

DOLOMITES

1 Panorama to Zallingerhütte Hike
2 Panorama to Plattkofelhütte Hike
3 Summit Hike of Schlern
4 "Trail of the Witches"
5 Loop Around Sasso Lungo

Seis at the bottom of the cable car with Alpe di Siusi, the alpine meadow at the top.

The Sasso Lungo Mountains (Langkofel in German, "Long Stone" in English) at the head of the meadow provide a storybook Dolomite backdrop, while the spooky Schlern peak stands boldly staring into the haze of the peninsula. The Schlern, looking like a devilish *Winged Victory,* gave ancient peoples enough willies to spawn legends of supernatural forces. The Schlern witch, today's tourist-brochure mascot, was the cause of many a broom-riding medieval townswoman's fiery death.

Alpe di Siusi is my recommended one-stop look at the Dolomites because of Castelrotto's charm as a home base; its quintessential Dolomite mountain views; its easy accessibility for those with and without cars; and its variety of walks, hikes, and mountain-bike routes. While most hikers will enjoy the easy meadow strolls, the nearby Schlern tempts and rewards those with more energy and an adventurous spirit.

The meadow is famous for its wildflowers—a fragrant festival (best in June) blooming with flowers that grow only 5,900-7,800 feet above sea level. The cows munching away in this vast meadow produce 2.5 million gallons of milk annually, much of which is sent to Bolzano to make cheese. After tourism, dairy is the leading industry here. While cows winter in Castelrotto, they summer in Alpe di Siusi. The meadow is also dotted with small, idyllic hotels and chalet restaurants. It's extremely family-friendly, with playgrounds at each stop and plenty of animals to pet. Being here on a sunny summer day comes with the ambience of a day at the beach.

Getting to Alpe di Siusi

By Car: A nature preserve, Alpe di Siusi is closed to cars during the day (9:00-17:00), unless you're staying in one of the area hotels. (Show your reservation confirmation as proof.) Parking at Compatsch (€14/day) requires that you arrive before the road closes at 9:00 in the morning, though you can drive back down at any time. Park officials encourage visitors to use the free parking lot located at the Seiseralm Bergbahn cable-car station in Siusi/Seis (see below); park your car and take the cable car *(cabinovia)* up to Compatsch.

By Cable Car from Siusi up to Alpe di Siusi: A cable car (Seiseralm Bergbahn) runs hikers and skiers from the village of Siusi/Seis to Compatsch, the gateway to the meadow (late May-mid-Sept daily 8:00-19:00, off-season 8:00-18:00, closed Nov and April-late May, 15-minute ride to the top, €10 one-way, €14 round-trip, www.seiseralmbahn.it). From Compatsch, you can take a shuttle bus farther into Alpe di Siusi to Saltria (€1.50/ride, €3/day).

By Bus from Castelrotto: Shuttle bus #3 links Castelrotto with Siusi/Seis and stops at the front door of the Seiseralm Bergbalm cable-car station (4/hour mid-June-mid-Oct during morning and afternoon peak times, otherwise 2/hour, 5 minutes). Less-frequent bus #4 connects the cable-car station with Siusi/Seis, Castelrotto, and Ortisei/St. Ulrich (2/hour, June-Oct only). Buses cost €1-4 per ride (buy tickets at the vending machines, not from the driver).

Regional buses (such as the orange SAD bus to and from Bolzano) stop at Siusi/Seis and just below the cable-car station (frequent in summer, 4/day in each direction off-season, €2 one-way).

The Alpe di Siusi Express is a shuttle bus that runs from Castelrotto all the way to Compatsch—denying you the fun experience of approaching the high meadow by cable car (6/day, 20 minutes, €10 one-way, €14 round-trip, see www.silbernagl.it for schedules).

Getting Around Alpe di Siusi

Shuttle Buses: Because the meadow is essentially car-free, the park's buses shuttle visitors to and from key points along the tiny road all the way from Compatsch—at the entry to the meadow—to the end of the line at Saltria, at the foot of the postcard-dramatic Sasso peaks (every 20 minutes 9:00-18:30, 15 minutes from Compatsch to Saltria, €1.50, buy at vending machines at the station or directly from the driver). At the end of the day, buses can be jam-packed.

Cable Cars and Chair Lifts: The entire meadow is served by various lifts (marked on maps). These are worth the roughly €5-8 per ride to get you into the higher and more scenic hiking areas (or back to the shuttle buses quickly). Keep in mind that lifts stop running fairly early (typically at about 17:00), which can be a major disappointment if you're running out of steam and time and are still high up after a long day's hike. Check schedules and plan your day accordingly.

Orientation to Compatsch Town

This tourist village (6,048 feet) at the entrance to the meadow is served by the Seiseralm Bergbahn cable car from the town of Siusi/Seis. You can drive to Compatsch only if you are staying at a hotel in Alpe di Siusi (or if you arrive very early or leave very late, outside of park opening hours). Parking costs €14 per day.

Compatsch has a **TI** (Mon-Fri 8:15-12:30, Sat 8:15-12:00, closed Sun, tel. 0471-727-904, www.seiseralm.it/en). The cable-car station has WCs, sporting-goods stores, and restaurants. In the center of Compatsch, you'll also find a tiny grocery store (open early-June-mid-Oct), ATMs, hotels, restaurants, and shops.

DOLOMITES

Helpful Hints

Bike Rental: You can rent mountain bikes at **Sporthaus Fill** (€8/1 hour, €25/day, mid-May-mid-Oct, at the bottom of the stairs of the cable-car station, tel. 0471-729-063, www.sporthausfill. com). There's a world of tiny paved and gravel lanes to pedal on. Pick up their suggested routes and consider the ones I describe later. Rentable baby buggies are popular for those hiking with toddlers.

Horse Rides: Trocker rents horses and provides guides (about €28/1 hour, €38/2 hours, €54/3 hours, mid-June-Sept, near cable-car station, follow gravel road between Pensione Animone and station to end, tel. 0471-727-807, no English spoken).

    Horse-drawn carriage rides are available to the left of the TI (May-Oct 9:00-16:00). Prices vary widely; check the sign near the road for details.

Local Guide: American transplant **Kat Reno** loves sharing her knowledge of South Tirol history and folklore. She offers private walks, hikes, and other alpine adventures (half-day walking tour-€140, mobile 346-663-8340, dolomitefun@live. com).

Hiking in Alpe di Siusi

Easy meadow walks abound in Alpe di Siusi, giving novice hikers classic Dolomite views from baby-stroller trails. Experienced hikers should consider the tougher, more exciting treks. Before attempting a hike, call or stop by the TI to confirm your understanding of the time and skills required. As always, when hiking in the mountains, assume weather can change quickly, and pack accordingly. Many lifts operate only mid-June through mid-October, so check with the TI for specifics on open lifts. Meadow walks, for flower lovers and strollers, are pretty—for advanced hikers, they're pretty boring. Chairlifts are springboards for more dramatic and demanding hikes. Trails are very well-marked, and the brightly painted numbers are keyed into local maps. Signs also display the next mountain hut along the trail, which serve as helpful navigational landmarks. (When asked for directions, most locals will know the trail by the huts it connects rather than its number.) For simple hikes, you can basically string together three or four hut names. For anything more serious, invest in a good map, about €6 at the TI. The Kompass Bolzano map #54 covers everything in this chapter (scale 1:50,000). The Wanderkarte map of Alpe di Siusi (produced by Tabacco) offers more detail and focuses on just Alpe di Siusi (scale 1:25,000).

Walks and Hikes from Compatsch

Panorama to Zallingerhütte: The "Easy" Route

This is a basic four-hour walk that is moderately strenuous. It promises fine vistas from both ends of the meadow, fun stops along the way, and lifts up and down on each end. Start by riding the €5 lift to Panorama (6,600 feet), then hike 1.25 hours to Mahlknecht-thütte/Molignonhütte (6,725 feet)—from the chairlift, follow trail #2 across the meadow to the paved road and then join trail #7. Continue hiking two hours to Zallingerhütte (6,725 feet). From here it's a 10-minute walk to Williamshütte (6,888 feet), where you catch the €8 Florian lift back to Saltria and the shuttle-bus stop (for Compatsch). Both Mahlknechthütte and Zallingerhütte have great restaurants for a drink or meal. For shorter or cheaper versions, you can ride the lift up and stroll back down.

Panorama to Plattkofelhütte: The High Route

For a more thrilling two-hour extension of the previous hike, climb from Mahlknechthütte (6,725 feet) up to Plattkofelhütte (7,544 feet), follow the high trail #4 along the ridge for an hour, with commanding views both left and right, and then take a steep hike back down to Williamshütte (6,888 feet).

Summit Hike of Schlern (Sciliar)

For a challenging 12-mile (six-hour) hike—with a possible overnight in a traditional mountain refuge (generally open mid-June–Sept)—consider hiking to the summit of Schlern and spending a night in Rifugio Bolzano/Schlernhaus. This route is popular with serious hikers as the best hike in the region.

Start at the Spitzbühl chairlift (€5 one-way, €7 round-trip, 5,659 feet, free parking lot, first bus stop in park, www.seiseralm.it), which drops you at Spitzbühl (6,348 feet). Trail #5 takes you through a high meadow, down to the Saltner dairy farm (6,004 feet—you want the Saltner dairy farm at Tschapit, not the one near Zallingerhütte), across a stream, and steeply up the Schlern mountain. About three hours into your hike, you'll meet trail #1 and walk across the rocky tabletop plateau of Schlern to the mountain hotel **Rifugio Bolzano/Schlernhaus** (7,544 feet, €24-30 bunks, some double rooms available, breakfast-€8, open early June-Oct, no hot water, summer-only tel. 0471-612-024, off-season tel. 0471-724-094, can reserve by email before hut opens in June, www.schlernhaus.it, info@schlernhaus.it). From this dramatic setting, you can enjoy a meal and get a great view of the Rosengarten range

Hike 20 more minutes up the nearby peak (Monte Pez, 8,400 feet), where you'll find a lofty meadow, cows in the summer, and the region's ultimate 360-degree alpine panorama. From Rifugio Bolzano/Schlernhaus, you can hike back the way you came or walk farther along the Schlern (7 miles, 2 hours; past **Rifugio Alpe di Tires/Tierser Alpl,** 8,006 feet, €23-34 bunks, half-board available for €42-53, open June-mid-Oct, showers-€3, tel. 0471-727-958 or 0471-707-460, mobile 333-654-6865, www.tierseralpl.com, info@tierseralpl.com) and descend back into Alpe di Siusi, to the road where the bus or cable car will return you to your starting point or hotel.

The "Trail of the Witches"

Take the cable car from Compatsch to Puflatsch (€5 one-way, €7 round-trip) for the two-hour loop north to Arnikahütte (with a café) and back (elevation gain about 660 feet). An engraved map at the Engelrast (Angel's Rest) observation point near the top of the lift gives the names of the surrounding mountains. Walking among the legendary stone seats of witches, you'll enjoy fine views of the valley all the way down to Castelrotto. With an hour more to spare, you can continue past Arnikahütte to Puflatschhütte and downhill all the way back to Comapatsch, giving you even more amazing views to the valley below.

Loop Around Sasso Lungo

Another dramatic but medium-difficulty hike is the eight-hour walk around the Sasso Lungo (Langkofel) mountains, called the Federico Augusto/Friederich August trail. The trail has sections of loose rocks; good shoes are essential. Ride the bus to Saltria (end of the line), take the chairlift to Williamshütte, walk past the **Zallingerhütte** (overnight possible, €48/person in dorm room, Db-€62, includes breakfast and dinner, open late-May-mid-Oct, tel. 0471-727-947, www.zallinger.com), and circle the Sasso Lungo group (get details and advice from the TI). On the opposite side, at Sella Pass, you ride a lift up Sasso Lungo to the Leo Demetz hut (8,790 feet), cross the saddle between Sasso Lungo and Sasso Piatto, and zigzag back into Alpe di Siusi with breathtaking views of rock climbers.

Trail Running

The Running Park Seiser Alm includes 46 miles of signed running trails in the meadow. Year after year, the clean air and high mountain altitude attract many international runners, including the Kenyan marathon team (during a one-day event usually held in July, they invite the public to run with them...or at least try). Contact the Compatsch TI for trail info and maps.

Biking in Alpe di Siusi

Mountain bikes are easy to rent, welcome on many lifts, and permitted on Alpe di Siusi lanes. The Compatsch TI has a good information flier that lists the best routes (I've listed three here). Get local advice to confirm difficulty levels and your plan before starting any ride.

Mountain-Bike Rides from Compatsch

Easy High Alp Ride (2.5 Hours, Moderate)

This ride stays in Alpe di Siusi and gives you the best basic look at this high meadow, with little altitude gain and easy lanes throughout.

Start from Compatsch (6,048 feet), bike or ride the lift to Panorama (6,600 feet), and take road #7, which runs generally uphill to Punta d'Oro/Goldknopf, and then follows a series of hills and dips to Mahlknechthütte/Molignonhütte (6,725 feet). Then take road #8 downhill to Saltria (5,575 feet) and back to Compatsch (6,048 feet).

Alpe di Siusi Meadow and Val Gardena
(4 Hours, Moderate to Difficult)

This route covers the great views of the Alpe di Siusi meadow, gets you into Val Gardena (a classic Südtirol valley) to see two resort towns, and then a lift gets you easily back to your starting point.

Start at Compatsch (6,048 feet), and take the road to Saltria (5,575 feet); from the bus stop, ride the unpaved road down to Monte Pana (5,366 feet). From here, an asphalt road zigzags steeply to St. Cristina (4,592 feet on valley floor far below), then heads down the valley to Ortisei/St. Ulrich (4,264 feet), where you take the cable car to Mezdi (6,560 feet, runs late May-Oct, €10.50 one-way, €15.20 round-trip). Complete your loop by rolling back down on a good road to Compatsch (6,048 feet).

Dramatic High Ridge Ride (4 Hours, Difficult)

This ride takes you into the dramatic rocks so characteristic of the Dolomites, with grand views and only the sound of your hardworking body and the rocks under your tires. If you get an early start, you can leave the bike at the Alpe di Tires/ Tierser Alpl hut (8,006 feet) while you hike to Rifugio Bolzano/Schlernhausern near the summit of the mighty Schlern—Monte Pez (2 hours, 8,400 feet).

Start at Compatsch (6,048 feet), ride the paved road downhill for 3.5 miles to Saltria (5,575 feet), then take road #8 for a huge uphill slog to the Tierser Alpl hut (8,006 feet; or you can ride the lift to Williamshütte to avoid half the altitude gain). From the Tierser Alpl hut, return the way you came until just below Hotel Floralpina/Seiser Alm Haus, where you'll take the left fork and follow road #7 to Mahlknechthütte/Molignonhütte (6,725 feet) and on

DOLOMITES

through Punta d'Oro/Goldknopt (6,560 feet), and back down to Compatsch (6,048 feet).

Sleeping in Alpe di Siusi

There are many chalets and huts with rooms for rent in Alpe di Siusi, which generally cost as much as a normal hotel. A few high-altitude options are mentioned under "Hiking in Alpe di Siusi," earlier; for additional choices, ask at the TI. For a bigger hotel near the park entrance, consider this option:

$$$ Hotel Seelaus, a 10-minute walk downhill from Compatsch, is a cozy, friendly, family-run place with an Austrian feel and down comforters (Sb-€65-130, Db-€120-240, Tb-€165-330, suite-€140-265; prices vary with season and type of room; family rates and week-stay discounts; includes buffet breakfast and hearty dinner, free and easy parking, and use of Wellness Center with sauna, hydro-massage, and mini-pool; free Wi-Fi, Via Compatsch 8, tel. 0471-727-954, www.hotelseelaus.it, info@hotelseelaus.it, Roberto). If you arrive in Siusi/Seis by bus, Roberto can pick you up—arrange in advance.

More Sights in the Dolomites

▲▲Great Dolomite Road (Grande Strada delle Dolomiti)
This is the definitive Dolomite drive: Belluno-Cortina-Pordoi Pass-Val di Fassa-Bolzano (about 125 miles). Connecting Venice with Bolzano this way (the Venice-Belluno autostrada is slick) takes two hours longer than the direct Venice-Verona-Bolzano autostrada. No public transit does this trip. In spring and early summer, passes labeled "closed" are often bare, dry, and, as far as local drivers are concerned, wide open. Call 0471-200-198 for road conditions (in Italian or German only).

▲▲Abbreviated Dolomite Loop Drive
See the biggies in half the miles (allow four hours, Bolzano-Castel-rotto-Val Gardena-Sella Pass-Val di Fassa-Bolzano). Val Gardena (Grodner Tal) is famous for its skiing and hiking resorts, traditional Ladin culture, and wood-carvers (the wood-carving company ANRI is from the Val Gardena town of St. Cristina). It's a bit over-rated, but even if its culture has been suffocated by the big bucks of hedonistic European fun-seekers, it remains a good jumping-off point for trips into the mountains. Within an hour, you'll reach Sella Pass (7,349 feet). After a series of tight hairpin turns a half-mile or so over the pass, you'll see some benches and cars. Pull over and watch the rock climbers.

The town of Canazei, at the head of the valley and the end of the bus line, has the most ambience and altitude (4,642 feet). From there, a lift (€5 one-way, €8.50 round-trip) and a gondola (€6.50 one-way, €11 round-trip; or both lifts for €10 one-way, €17 round-trip; late April-late Oct daily 8:30-12:30 & 14:00-17:30, both closed late Oct-late April) take you to Col dei Rossi Belvedere, where you can hike the Bindelweg trail past Rifugio Belvedere along an easy but breathtaking ridge to Rifugio Viel del Pan (Canazei TI for lift info: Tel. 0462-609-600, www.fassa.com). This three-hour round-trip hike has views of the highest mountain in the Dolomites—the Marmolada—and the Dolo-mighty Sella range.

▲▲Reifenstein Castle

For one of Europe's most intimate looks at medieval castle life, let the friendly lady of Reifenstein (Frau Steiner) show you around her wonderfully preserved castle. She leads a one-hour tour in German and Italian, squeezing in whatever English she can.

Cost and Hours: €7, open April-Oct; tours Sun-Fri at 10:30, 14:00, and 15:00; mid-July-mid-Sept also at 16:00, closed most Sat, best to call ahead to reserve tour, minimum of 4 people needed for tour to run, picnic spot at drawbridge, tel. 339-264-3752, or TI tel. 0472-765-325, www.sterzing.com.

Getting There: To drive to the castle, follow the A-22 autostrada toward Brenner Pass, exit at Vipiteno (Sterzing), and follow signs toward *Bolzano*, taking three rights. The castle is just west of the freeway; park at the base of the castle's rock. Of the two castles here, Reifenstein is the one to the west. While this is easy by car, it's probably not worth the trouble by train (6/day from Bolzano, one-hour train ride followed by a one-hour hike).

▲Glurns

Drivers connecting the Dolomites and Lake Como by the high road via Meran and Bormio can spend the night in the amazing little town of Glurns (45 minutes west of touristy Meran, between Schluderns and Taufers). Glurns still lives within its square wall on the Adige River, with a church bell tower that has a thing about ringing, and real farms rather than boutiques. The town's short archways seem to cause the locals, whose families go back eons, to take on a Quasimodo-like posture. There are several small hotels in the town, but I'd stay in a private home (such as **Family Hofer,** 4 rooms, €29/person with breakfast, less for 3 nights or longer, cash only, 100 yards from town square, near church, just outside wall on river, Via Adige 1, tel. 0473-831-597, www.hofer.bz.it, privatzimmer.hofer@rolmail.net).

THE LAKES

Commune with nature where Italy is joined to the Alps, in the lovely Italian lakes district. In this land of lakes, the million-euro question is: Which one? For the best mix of accessibility, scenery, and offbeatness, the village of Varenna on Lake Como is my top choice, followed by Stresa on Lake Maggiore. In either place, you'll get a complete dose of Italian-lakes wonder and aristocratic-old-days romance. Bustling Milan, just an hour away from either lake, doesn't even exist. Now it's your turn to be *chiuso per restauro* (closed for restoration). If relaxation's not on your agenda, the lakes shouldn't be either. If you must choose between Lake Como and Lake Maggiore, the former is a better place to linger, while the latter makes a good day trip from Milan.

Lake Como

Lake Como (Lago di Como)—lined with elegant 19th-century villas, crowned by snowcapped mountains, and busy with ferries, hydrofoils, and slow, passenger-only boats—is a good place to take a break from the intensity and obligatory-turnstile culture of central Italy. It seems like half the travelers you'll meet have tossed their itineraries into the lake and are actually relaxing.

Lake Como is Milan's quick getaway, and the sleepy mid-lake village of Varenna is the gateway to the lake and the handiest base of operations. With good connections to Milan, Malpensa Airport, and mid-lake destinations, Varenna is my favorite home base for the lakes. Today, the hazy, lazy lake's only serious industry is tour-

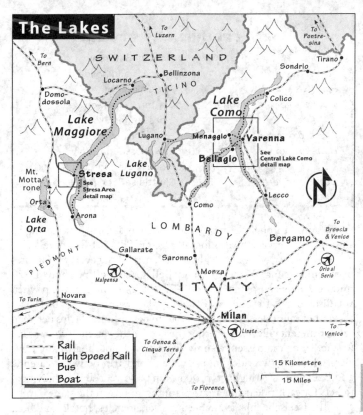

The Lakes

To Luzern • To Pontresina

SWITZERLAND

To Bern
To Bellinzona
Locarno
Tirano
Sondrio
TICINO
Domo-dossola
Colico
Lake Maggiore
Lake Como
Lugano
Menaggio
Varenna
Lake Lugano
Bellagio
See Central Lake Como detail map
Mt. Mottarone
Stresa
See Stresa Area detail map
Orta
Lecco
Lake Orta
Como
Arona
To Brescia & Venice
LOMBARDY
Bergamo
PIEDMONT
Gallarate
Saronno
Orio al Serio
Malpensa
Monza
ITALY
To Turin
Novara
Milan
Linate
To Venice
To Genoa & Cinque Terre
To Florence

- - - · Rail
—— High Speed Rail
- - - Bus
········ Boat

15 Kilometers
15 Miles

ism. Thousands of lakeside residents travel daily to nearby Lugano, in Switzerland, to find work. The lake's isolation and flat economy have left it pretty much the way the 19th-century Romantic poets described it: heaven on earth.

Planning Your Time

Even though there are no essential activities, plan for at least two nights so you'll have an uninterrupted day to see how slow you can get your pulse.

Getting Around Lake Como

By Boat: Lake Como is well-served by boats and hydrofoils. The lake service is divided into three parts: south-north from Como to Colico; mid-lake between Varenna, Bellagio, Menaggio, and Cadenabbia (Villa Carlotta); and the southwestern arm to Lenno (Villa del Balbianello). Unless

Boat Schedule Literacy Tips

Feriali	Monday-Saturday
Festivi	Sundays and holidays
Partenze da...	Departing from
Traghetto or *autotraghetto*	Car ferry (walk-on passengers, too)
Aliscafo or *servizio rapido*	Hydrofoil
Battello ship	Slow passenger-only boat going to Como
Battello navetta	Shuttle serving mid-lake only

you're going through Como, you'll probably limit your cruising to the mid-lake service (boat info: toll-free tel. 800-551-801 or tel. 031-579-211, www.navigazionelaghi.it). Boats go about every 30 minutes between Varenna, Menaggio, and Bellagio (€4.60 per hop, 15-20 minutes, daily approximately 7:00-22:30, confirm return trip when you disembark). The one-day €15 mid-lake pass saves you a little over the cost of four rides. It can be used to make unlimited trips between seven different villages bordering the lake, either on the *autotraghetto* (car ferry) or the passenger-only *battello* (but note that many travelers take only two rides in a day—a round-trip between Varenna and Bellagio). Overnight stopovers aren't allowed, so buy individual tickets for each ride if you aren't planning to return the same day.

The free schedule (available at travel agencies, hotels, and boat docks) lists boat times. Rates are displayed on posters at ticket windows. Confusingly, the schedule requires you to scan four different timetables to know all the departures:

- car and passenger ferry (mid-lake ferryboat, or *autotraghetto*)
- hydrofoil (*servizio rapido*, costs a third more, enclosed, stuffy, speedy, less scenic)
- all-lake slow boat *(battello ship)*
- mid-lake shuttle ferry *(battello navetta)*

If you find the schedule impossible to decipher, simply ask at each dock when the next boat is leaving and which slip it's leaving from (Bellagio has several docks). When checking schedules, be sure to pay attention to whether you're traveling on a weekday (*feriali*, Mon-Sat) or a Sunday or holiday *(festivi)*. Review your possible connections (ask your hotelier for help) before you set out so you can pace your day smartly. It'd be a shame to miss a boat and lose out on a hike or an eagerly anticipated meal because of confusing timetables.

By Car: With scarce parking, traffic jams, and expensive car ferries, this is no place to drive if you don't have to. While you can drive around the lake, the road is narrow, congested, and lined with privacy-seeking walls, hedges, and tall fences. Parking in Bellagio is more difficult than in Varenna. If you have a car in Varenna, leave it there and use the boat.

While you can rent cars in Bellagio, for most travelers, it's best to take the train to Milan and pick up a car there, either at the central train station or at one of Milan's three airports.

Varenna

This community of 800 people offers the best of all lake worlds. Easily accessible by train, on the less-driven side of the lake, Va-

renna has a romantic promenade, a tiny harbor, narrow lanes, and its own villa. It's just the right place to savor a lakeside cappuccino or *aperitivo*. There's wonderfully little to do here, and it's very quiet at night... unless you're here during one of the hundred or so annual American wedding parties. The *passerella* (lakeside promenade, lit at foot level and safe after dark) is adorned with caryatid lovers pressing silently against each other in the shadows. Varenna is a popular destination with my readers and European vacationers—book well in advance for visits in summer (May-Oct). Between November and mid-March, Varenna practically shuts down; hotels close for the winter, and restaurants and shops reduce their hours.

Orientation to Varenna

Tourist Information
The TI (called Proloco Varenna Information Point), on the **main square**, is generally open only during high season (May-Sept Tue-Sat 10:00-12:00 & 15:00-18:00, Sun 9:00-12:00, closed Mon and Oct-April, just past the bank, tel. 0341-830-367, www.discovervarenna.com). The travel agency, a block from the train station, is a good backup if the TI is closed. Your hotel may have the latest edition of the *Varenna Tourist Info* booklet, with updated info on sights around Varenna and a list of restaurants, services, and day trips.

Arrival in Varenna
By Train: From any destination covered in this book, you'll get to Lake Como via Milan. The quickest, easiest, and cheapest Milan connection to any point mid-lake (Varenna, Bellagio, or Menag-

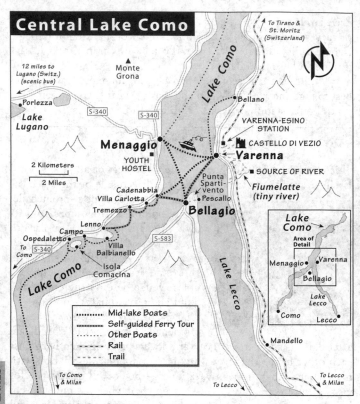

Central Lake Como

To Tirano &
St. Moritz
(Switzerland)

12 miles to
Lugano (Switz.)
(scenic bus)

Monte
Grona

Lake Como

Porlezza

Lake
Lugano

S-340

S-340

Bellano

VARENNA-ESINO
STATION

Menaggio

YOUTH
HOSTEL

CASTELLO DI VEZIO

Varenna

SOURCE OF RIVER

2 Kilometers

2 Miles

Cadenabbia

Villa Carlotta

Tremezzo

Lenno

Campo

Ospedaletto

To
Como

S-340

Villa
Balbianello

Isola
Comacina

Lake Como

Punta
Sparti-
vento

Pescallo

Bellagio

S-583

Fiumelatte
(tiny river)

Lake Lecco

Lake
Como

Area of
Detail

Menaggio

Varenna

Bellagio

Lake
Lecco

Como

Lecco

Mandello

·········· Mid-lake Boats
━━━━━━ Self-guided Ferry Tour
·········· Other Boats
─·─·─ Rail
─ ─ ─ Trail

To Como
& Milan

To Lecco

To Lecco
& Milan

gio) is via the train to Varenna. Once here, limit your activities to the scenic mid-lake area (Varenna and Bellagio).

Here are the specifics: Leaving from Milan's central train station, catch a train heading for Sondrio or Tirano—sometimes the departure board also says "Lecco/Tirano." (Tirano is often confused with Torino...wrong city. And, if you're heading for Varenna, be sure you don't accidentally catch a train to Verona.) All Sondrio-bound trains stop in Varenna, as noted in the fine print on the *partenze* (departures) schedule posted at Milan's train station. Trains leave Milan about every one to two hours (€6.40, 1 hour, likely schedule—but confirm these times: 6:20, 7:20, 8:20, 9:20, 10:20, 12:20, 14:20, 16:20, 17:20, 19:20, 20:20, and 21:20; railpasses accepted). Get a second-class ticket, since first-class wagons are rare on the Sondrio-Tirano route. If you plan to head back to Milan on the train, also buy a return ticket—Varenna's station has no ticket office or ticket machine (though it does have a travel agency that sells train tickets). Stamp the ticket in the yellow box at the front of the tracks or risk a €50 fine. If you run into a problem or need to validate your railpass at Milan's train station, find the helpful Trenitalia Customer Care office in front of track 21 (daily 6:00-24:00).

Leaving Milan, sit on the left for maximum lake-view beauty. Get off at Varenna-Esino. Even though train schedules list only Varenna, Varenna-Esino is what you'll see at the platform—same place.

Long trains serve Varenna's tiny station and stop only briefly. Know what time you're supposed to arrive in Varenna, so you can be ready to disembark with luggage in hand. Because trains can be longer than the station, your car may actually stop before or after the platform. Look out the window. If even part of the train is at the station, you'll need to get out and walk. Tips: Board midtrain to land next to a platform. Leave from the door through which you entered, since you know it's working. You may have to open the train door yourself: If necessary, pull hard on the red handle to open the door.

From Varenna's train station, follow the signs for the ferry boat. Once you reach the ferry dock, walk up to the main road to avoid carting your luggage across the cobblestones that line the lakeside promenade. A taxi from the station costs about €9.

By Train from Milan's Airports: It's a two-step process: First, take the Malpensa Express train from Malpensa Airport or the Starfly bus from Linate Airport to Milan's central train station (see pages 372-373), then transfer to a Varenna-bound train (described earlier).

By Boat via Como: For a less convenient, much slower, but more scenic trip, you can also get to Varenna from Milan via the town of Como (or vice versa). Trains take you from Milan to Como (hourly, 30-90 minutes). It's a 10-minute walk to the dock, where you catch either the speedy hydrofoil or the leisurely *battello* (slow boat—great for enjoying the scenery) for the ride up the lake to Varenna (slow boat: 3/day, €11.60, 2 hours, last departure about 15:00; hydrofoil: 5/day Mon-Sat, 2/day Sun, €16.20, 1 hour, last departure about 19:00).

By Taxi: A taxi costs roughly €130-165 between Varenna and downtown Milan or Milan's airports. For a reputable taxi service, see "By Taxi" page 286.

By Car: In Varenna, the easiest (though most expensive) option for parking is the new multilevel lot at the end of town, across from Villa Monastero (€2/hour, €20/24 hours). Save yourself the time and headache of looking for public parking (described next), and just park in the garage.

In town, you can look for the color-coded lines to decipher the parking options: White is free anytime; yellow is for residents only; and blue means you pay (look for signs, €2/hour, payment times vary during holidays and high season—often Mon-Fri 8:00-20:00,

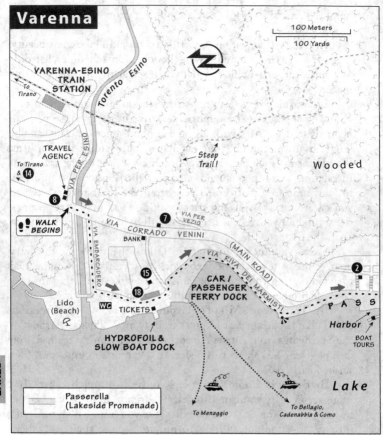

daily in Aug, otherwise free). Buy tickets from meters or at Albergo Beretta. Leave the ticket on your dashboard; overnight until 8:00 is OK. Parking on the main square is for residents only.

At the train station, parking is free Monday-Friday, but you'll have to pay on Saturdays and Sundays during high season and every day in August (8:00-19:00, feed coins into meter in center of lot and put printed ticket on dashboard).

If you park elsewhere in town and aren't sure if your spot is legal, check with your hotelier.

Getting Around Varenna

Varenna is small, and everything is within a 15-minute walk (except for the Eremo Gaudio hotel). If you'd prefer a taxi, you'll find them waiting at the train station and dock. From either arrival point, a taxi should charge about €9 for a ride to your hotel.

By Taxi: Reliable **Marco Barili** (or his wife Nelly) will meet

1 Hotel du Lac
2 Albergo Milano & Ristorante la Vista
3 Villa Cipressi & Ristorante la Contrada
4 To Eremo Gaudio
5 Albergo/Ristorante del Sole
6 Villa Elena
7 Hotel/Rist. Montecodeno
8 Albergo Beretta
9 Ristorante il Cavatappi
10 Varennamonamour
11 Osteria Quatro Pass
12 Nilus Bar & Bar il Molo
13 Gelateria Riva
14 To Ristorante il Caminetto & Cooking Course
15 Pub l'Orso
16 Ristorante Isola Nuova
17 Vecchia Varenna
18 Hotel/Ristorante Olivedo
19 Grocery Stores (2)
20 Ornithology & Natural Science Museum; Proloco Info Point
21 Laundry
22 Barilott (Train Tickets)
23 Villa Monastero Entrance

you at the train station if you know your exact arrival time in Varenna. Look for a flashing sign with your name on it. He can also get you to Milan and its airports and, unlike other drivers, he doesn't add surcharges for baggage or early/late departures (€135 to central Milan or Linate Airport, €150 to Malpensa Airport for up to 4 people—or €210 for 5-8 passengers in a minibus, €130 to Bergamo's Orio al Serio Airport, tel. 0341-815-061, taxi.varenna@tiscali.it).

Helpful Hints

Train Tickets: I Viaggi del Tivano travel agency, Barilott, and Albergo Beretta are the only places in town that sell train tickets to Milan; no tickets are sold at the small train station.

Money: One bank is near Varenna's main square; another is located inland from the boat dock. Both have ATMs (see town map).

Internet Access: Try **Barilott,** which also sells some train and local bus tickets, fresh *panini,* and wines by the glass (Internet access-€4/hour, free for customers, Mon-Sat 7:00-20:00, closed Sun, Via IV Novembre 6, tel. 0341-815-045, Claudia and Fabrizio).

Post Office: It's just off the main square (Tue, Thu, and Sat 8:00-13:00).

Laundry: Lavanderia Pensa Barbara can wash and dry your laundry within 24 hours (€3.50/kilo—about 2 pounds, no self-service, Mon-Fri 9:00-12:00 & 15:00-19:30, Sat 9:00-12:30, closed Sun, Via Venini 31, tel. 0341-830-478, mobile 340-466-2977).

Travel Agency: For bus and boat tours, consider Varenna's travel agency, **I Viaggi del Tivano,** next to Albergo Beretta, a block below the train station. They book planes, trains, and automobiles, and can offer half-day and daylong tours of the region and into Switzerland from April through September (book tours by noon the day before; open Mon-Fri 9:00-18:30, Sat 9:00-16:00, closed Sun, shorter hours off-season, can book rental cars here but pick up in Lecco, no service charge for regional train tickets, €5 service charge for long-distance train tickets, Via Esino 3, tel. 0341-814-009, www.tivanotours.com, info@tivanotours.com, helpful Cristina and Eleonora).

Self-Guided Walk

Welcome to Varenna

Since you came here to relax, this short walk gives you just the town basics.

Bridge Just Below Train Station: This main bridge spans the tiny Esino River, which divides two communities: Perledo (which sprawls up the hill—notice the church spire high above) and the old fishing town of Varenna (huddled around its harbor). The train station, called Varenna-Esino, is named for a third community that sits eight miles higher in the hills.

Cross the bridge and follow the river down to the small square, which hosts a market on Wednesdays. The town's public beach (or *lido*) is just over the cute pedestrian bridge (€2 entry). The inn facing the ferry dock, Hotel Olivedo, has greeted ferry travelers since the 19th century and is named for the olive groves you can see growing halfway up the hill. Natives claim this is the farthest north that olives grow in Europe.

• *Across from Hotel Olivedo is Varenna's...*

Ferry Landing: Since the coming of the train in 1892, Varenna has been *the* convenient access point from "mid-lake" (the communities of Bellagio, Menaggio, and Varenna) to Milan. From this viewpoint, you can almost see how Lake Como is shaped like a man. The head is the north end (to the right, up by the Swiss Alps). Varenna is the man's left hip (to the east). Menaggio, across the lake, is the right hip (to the west). And Bellagio (hiding behind the smaller wooded hill to your left) is the crotch—or, more poetically, Punta Spartivento ("Point that Divides the Wind"). In a more colorful description, a traditional poem says, "Lake Como is a man, with Colico the head, Lecco and Como the feet, and Bellagio the testicles." (In the regional dialect, this rhymes—ask a native to say it for you.)

The farthest ridges high above the right hip mark the border of Switzerland. This region's longtime poverty shaped the local character (much like the Great Depression shaped the outlook of a generation of Americans). Many still remember that this side of the lake was the poorest, because those on the Menaggio side controlled the lucrative cigarette-smuggling business over the Swiss border. Today, the entire region is thriving—thanks to tourism.

• *Walk past the ferry dock toward a small playground, to Varenna's elevated shoreline walk, called the...*

Passerella: A generation ago, Varenna built this elegant lakeside promenade, which connects the ferry dock with the old town

center. Strolling this lane, you'll come to the tiny, two-dinghy, concrete breakwater of a villa. Lake Como is lined with swanky 19th-century villas; their front doors face the lake to welcome visitors arriving by boat. At this point, the modern *passerella* cuts between this villa's water gate and its private harbor. From here, enjoy a good Varenna town view. These buildings are stringently protected by preservation laws; you can't even change the color of your villa's paint.

Just over the hump (which allows boats into a covered moorage), look up at another typical old villa— with a private *passerella*, a lovely veil of wisteria, and a prime lakeview terrace. Many of these villas are owned by the region's "impoverished nobility." They were bred and raised not to work and, therefore, are now unable to pay for the upkeep of their sprawling houses. Lately, these villas are being bought by the region's nouveau riche.

• *At the community harbor, walk to the end of the pier for a town overview, then continue under the old-time arcades toward the multihued homes facing the harbor.*

Varenna Harborfront: There are no streets in the old town— just the characteristic stepped lanes called *contrade*. Varenna was originally a fishing community. Even today, old-timers enjoy Lake Como's counterpart to Norwegian lutefisk: *missoltino*, air-dried

and salted lake "sardines." They're served with the region's polenta (different from Venice's, because buckwheat is mixed in with the corn).

Imagine the harbor 200 years ago—busy with coopers expertly fitting chestnut and oak staves into barrels, stoneworkers carving the black marble that was quarried just above town, and fishing boats dragged onto the sloping beach. The little stone harbor dates from about 1600. Today, the fishing boats are just for recreation, and residents gather here with their kids to relax by the lake.

At the south end of the harbor (across from the recommended Bar il Molo *gelateria*), belly up to the banister of the terrace for a colorful town view. Another traditional ditty goes, "If you love Lake Como, you know Bellagio is the pearl...but Varenna is the diamond."

• *Continue straight, leaving the harbor. A lane curves around Hotel du Lac (its fine lakeside terrace welcomes even non-guests for a drink), finishing with an unexpected hill. Finally you'll reach the tiny pebbly town beach below. From here, climb the stairs and go through the yellow arch to the square, called...*

Piazza San Giorgio: Several churches face Varenna's town square. The main church (Chiesa di San Giorgio) dates from the 13th century. Romantic Varenna is an understandably popular spot for weddings—rice often litters the church's front yard. Stepping inside, you'll find a few humble but centuries-old bits of carving and frescoes. The black floor and chapels are made from the local marble.

Across from the square, to the right of the municipal building, is the Proloco Varenna Information Point (TI) and the Ornithology and Natural Science Museum, with its small collection of stuffed birds and other wildlife (open April-Sept, Sat-Sun only).

The Hotel Royal Victoria, also on the main square, recalls the 1839 visit of Queen Victoria, who registered herself as the Countess of Clare in an attempt to remain anonymous.

The trees in the square are planted to make a V for Varenna. The street plan survives from Roman times, when gutters flowed down to the lake. The little church on the lake side of the square is the baptistery. Dating from the ninth century, it's one of the oldest churches on the lake, but is rarely open for visits.

Your walk is over. Facing the church, you can head right to

visit the gardens or hike up to the castle (both described later, under "Sights in Varenna"); left to go to the train station or ferry dock; or back downhill to enjoy the beach (take either of the lanes flanking the Hotel Royal Victoria down to the water).

Sights in Varenna

Castle
A steep and stony trail leads to Varenna's ruined hilltop castle, Castello di Vezio, located in a peaceful, traffic-free, one-chapel town. Take the small road, Via per Vezio (about 100 feet south of—and to the right of—Hotel Montecodeno), and figure on a 20-minute walk one-way. The castle is barren, but enlivened by occasional art exhibits and a falconry-training center.

Cost and Hours: €6, April-Sept Mon-Fri 10:00-18:00, Sat-Sun 10:00-19:00, March and Oct closes one hour earlier, closed Nov-Feb and in bad weather, low-key falconry shows usually around 15:30, but check website or call in morning for times, bar and restaurant at entrance, dinner by reservation only, mobile 333-448-5975, www.castellodivezio.it, info@castellodivezio.it, Nicola.

Gardens
Two separate manicured lakeside gardens—the terraces of Villa

Cipressi and the adjacent, more open grounds of Villa Monastero—are open to the public. Formerly a noble residence, Villa Monastero, filled with overly ornate furnishings from the late 1800s, is also open to the public as a museum.

Cost and Hours: Villa Cipressi—€4, May-Nov daily 8:00-18:00, closed Dec-April; Villa Monastero—gardens-€5, gardens and museum-€8; gardens open March-Oct daily 9:00-18:00, until 19:00 May-Sept, closed Nov-Feb; museum open March-April and Oct daily 9:00-18:00, May-Sept Mon-Thu & Sat-Sun 9:00-19:00, Fri 9:00-14:00, closed Nov-Feb; bar in garden serves snacks, tel. 0341-295-450, www.villamonastero.eu.

Swimming
There are three spots to swim in Varenna: the free little beach behind the Hotel Royal Victoria off Piazza San Giorgio, the central lakefront area by Nilus Bar, and the *lido*. The *lido* is by far the best-equipped for swimmers. Just north of the boat dock, it's essentially a wide concrete slab with sand and a swimming area off an old boat ramp. It has showers, bathrooms, a restaurant, a bar, and lounge chairs for rent (entry-€2, umbrellas-€4, lounge chairs-€6, tel.

0341-815-3700). Swimming by the boat dock is strictly forbidden for safety reasons.

Boat Tours
Taxi Boat Varenna organizes hour-long central lake tours (€30/ person), 30-minute "Varenna seen from the water" tours (€10/ person), and 50-minute romantic private tours (€150/couple). Ask Luca about his special "Tour George"; book direct on their website (April-Oct, mobile 349-229-0953, www.taxiboatlecco.com, info@ taxiboatlecco.com). A similar company works out of Bellagio.

Near Varenna

▲▲Self-Guided Ferry Tour: Lake Como
The best simple day out is to take the *battello navetta* (mid-lake

ferry) on its entire 50-minute Varenna-Bellagio-Cadenab-bia-Villa Carlotta-Tremezzo-Lenno route. On the return trip, stop at any sights that interest you (Lenno to see Villa del Balbianello, Tremezzo for Villa Carlotta, and/or Bellagio). This commentary describes what you'll see along the way.

Leaving Varenna: Looking back at Varenna from the lake, you'll see the castle rising above the town, with new Varenna on the left (bigger buildings and mod-ern ferry dock), and old Varenna on the right (tighter, more color-ful buildings). The big develop-ment high on the hillside is an ugly example of cronyism (with-out the mayor involved, this would never have happened). Under the castle is a grove of ol-ives (reputedly the northernmost

ones grown in Italy). Because the lake is protected from the north wind, exotic flowers grow well in the lake's many fine gardens. To the right of Varenna's castle are the town cemetery, a lift up to the Eremo Gaudio hotel (a former hermitage), and a spurt of water gushing out of the mountain just above lake level. This is the tiny Fiumelatte, Italy's shortest river.

Mid-Lake: The Swiss Alps rise to the north. Across the lake is Menaggio, and just over the ridge from that are Lugano and the "Swiss Riviera." The winds alternate between north and south. In pre-industrial times, traders harnessed the wind to sail up and down the lake. Notice the V-shaped, fjord-like terrain. Lake Como is glacier-cut. And, at more than 1,200 feet deep, it's Europe's deepest lake. You'll cruise past the Punta Spartivento, the point that literally "splits the wind," and where the two "legs" of the lake join (Lake Lecco is on the left/east, and Lake Como on the right).

Approaching Bellagio: Survey the park to the left of Punta Spartivento—it's a pleasant walk from town. Bellagio has three

times the number of hotel rooms as Varenna, as you can see upon approach. The town, with its strip of swanky hotels, is bookended by Villa Serbelloni (five stars) on the left, dominating the lakefront, and the sprawling Grand Hotel Bretagne (four stars) on the right. In the 19th century, aristocratic Russians hung out in the Serbelloni, and well-heeled English chose the Bretagne. These days, the Serbelloni is the second-most-luxurious hotel on the lake after Villa d'Este, while Bretagne is mired in a long renovation project.

Approaching Cadenabbia: From Bellagio, you cross the lake to Cadenabbia. Above Cadenabbia, the Church of St. Martin seems stranded halfway up the mountain. This side of the lake has nearly all the area's traffic, thanks to a big road that ended up separating many fine lakefront gardens from their villas. Farther north is the village of Dongo, where Mussolini and his girlfriend were captured in the last months of World War II as they tried to escape into Switzerland. They were shot here on the lake, and their bodies were hung ingloriously in Milan for public viewing.

Villa Carlotta: Because of lake taxes and high maintenance costs, owners of once-elite villas have been forced to turn them into hotels or to open their doors to the paying public. This is an example of the latter. One of the finest properties on the lake, Villa Carlotta is most visited for its Canova statue and lush garden (see listing on page 308).

Tremezzo: Notice the Grand Hotel Tremezzo, with its striking Liberty-style (Art Nouveau) facade and swimming pool floating on the lake. Above the town is a villa built in the 19th-century Romantic Age to resemble a medieval castle. After the Tremezzo stop (just before the Tremezzo church), you'll see a fine public park with a fountain. When the road separated this land from its villa, its owners gave it to the community. Here the lake is dotted by a string of fine old villas with elegant landings and gated boathouses. Built in the days before motors, they are now too small for most modern lake boats. Tullio Abbate is famous in this area for building speedy, high-end lake boats.

Lenno: This is your last stop. About 400 yards farther along the shore is a tiny dock for shuttle boats headed for Villa del Balbianello (of *Star Wars: Episode II* and *Casino Royale* fame— see page 308).

Sailing Home: Get off the boat at Lenno; from here you can return to Bellagio or Varenna, stopping along the way as you like.

Hiking

The town of Fiumelatte, about a half-mile south of Varenna, was named for its "milky river." It's the shortest river in Italy (at 800 feet) and runs—like most of the area tourist industry—only from April through September (though even then it may be dry, depending on the weather). The *La Sorgente del Fiumelatte* brochure, available at Varenna's travel agency, lays out a walk from Varenna to the Fiumelatte, then to the castle, and back. It's a 30-minute hike to the source *(sorgente)* of the river (at Varenna's monastery, take the high road, drop into the tranquil and evocative cemetery, and climb steps to the wooded trail leading to the peaceful and refreshing cave from which the river spouts).

For a longer hike in the opposite direction with lake views, ask the travel agency about the Wayfarers' Path (hike one-way up the lake, about 1.5 hours, not quite as steep as Fiumelatte hike). You can return by train from Bellano (€1.30, Bellano not included on mid-lake pass, check schedule before you go), or take the ferry to Menaggio and catch a connecting boat back to Varenna.

▲Cooking Course

Chef Moreno of the recommended Ristorante il Caminetto picks you up in Varenna, zips you up the mountain to his restaurant (experience Italian driving!), and then teaches you some basics of Italian cooking. Learn how to handcraft fresh pasta or prep regional specialties. Classes last about three hours, plus time to *mangiare*. People love the experience and find Moreno a charming teacher and host (€50 includes trip, lesson, recipes, and lunch complete with wine, cookies, and coffee; Mon, Tue, Thu, and Fri; 10:00 pickup from Varenna landing, return by 16:00, reservations mandatory, tel. 0341-815-225, www.ilcaminettoonline.com, info@ilcaminettoonline.com).

Sleep Code

(€1 = about $1.30, country code 39)
S = Single, **D** = Double/Twin, **T** = Triple, **Q** = Quad, **b** = bathroom, **s** = shower only. Unless otherwise noted, credit cards are accepted, English is spoken, and breakfast is included. Varenna, like many cities in Italy, charges a tourist tax (€1 per person per night, must be paid in cash at check-out).

To help you sort easily through these listings, I've divided the accommodations into three categories based on the price for a standard double room with bath:

$$$ **Higher Priced**—Most rooms €150 or more.
$$ **Moderately Priced**—Most rooms between €100-150.
$ **Lower Priced**—Most rooms €100 or less.

Prices can change without notice; verify the hotel's current rates online or by email. For the best prices, always book direct.

Sleeping in Varenna

Reservations are tight in August, snug May through October, and wide open most of the rest of the year. Many places close in winter. High-season prices are listed here; prices get soft off-season (Nov-April).

$$$ Hotel du Lac, filling a refined and modernized 19th-century villa, is the finest hotel in town. From its exclusive private perch on the point, it offers a quiet lakefront breakfast terrace; generous public spaces; a friendly, professional staff; and 16 delightful rooms—all but 3 with lake views (standard Db-€195, bigger Db-€250, these high-season prices are for May-mid-Oct, €20 less in shoulder season, closed Nov-March, air-con, free Wi-Fi, parking-€16, Via del Prestino 11, tel. 0341-830-238, www.albergodulac.com, info@albergodulac.com).

$$$ Albergo Milano, located right in the old town, is graciously run by Egidio and his Swiss wife, Bettina. Fusing the best of Italy with the best of Switzerland, this well-run, romantic hotel has eight comfortable rooms with extravagant views, balconies, or big terraces (Sb-€125, Db-€150-170, €10 extra for view terrace, €5/day cash discount, closed mid-Nov-Feb, no elevator, free Wi-Fi; from the station, take main road to town and turn right at steep alley where sidewalk and guardrail break; Via XX Settembre 35, tel. 0341-830-298, www.varenna.net, hotelmilano@varenna.net). This place whispers *luna di miele*––honeymoon (see website for 3-night honeymoon deal). Nearby is **$$ Casa Rossa,** an annex with six comfortable rooms and two apartments that work well for families (Db-€135-165, proportionately more for third or fourth person, breakfast served at main hotel). Their recommended Ristorante la Vista is worth considering for dinner.

$$ Villa Cipressi is a sprawling, centuries-old lakeside mansion with 33 warmly outfitted, modern rooms. Its public spaces are often busy with wedding parties. Rooms without views face the street and can be noisy. The villa sits in a huge, quiet terraced garden that non-guests pay to see (Sb-€140, non-view Db-€170, view Db-€195, extra cot-€40, extra bed-€60, ask for Rick Steves discount, elevator, guest computer, free Wi-Fi, garden access, Via IV Novembre 22, tel. 0341-830-113, www.hotelvillacipressi.it, info@ hotelvillacipressi.it, Davide).

$$ Eremo Gaudio stands out with a commanding lake view high above Varenna. Once an orphanage, it became a hermitage run by the Catholic Church, and then—since 2000—a modern hotel accessed by a private funicular. Perfect for monks with champagne tastes, it's peaceful, with awe-inspiring view balconies and a breakfast terrace. Thirteen bright, plain-but-comfy rooms climb up the main building, and 15 less dramatic but equally comfortable rooms huddle below at the foot of the funicular. Suppers are served on the terrace (upper rooms: Sb-€110, Db-€130, Db with balcony-€148; lower rooms: Db-€120-148; closed Nov-Feb, all rooms have lake views, air-con May-Oct, requires walking up steep hills and steps—taking a taxi from station is recommended, quarter-mile south of Varenna's main square at Via Roma 25, tel. 0341-815-301, www.eremogaudio.it, eremogaudio@yahoo.it).

$$ Albergo del Sole is a no-frills hotel over a restaurant right on the town square. Run by fun-loving Enzo, the hotel has eight comfy rooms and no hint of a lake view (Sb-€90; Db-€130, €105 off-season; fans, hardwood floors, shiny bathrooms, elevator, free Wi-Fi, Piazza San Giorgio 17, tel. 0341-815-218, www.albergodelsolevarenna.it, albergo.sole@virgilio.it).

$ Villa Elena, a grandmotherly, low-energy place on the main square, offers a tranquil rest and the best budget beds in town. English-speaking Signora Seta ("Silk") Vitali, who lives downstairs, rents three characteristic, antique-filled rooms that all share one bathroom and an updated kitchen/dining room with a view terrace. With only twin beds, it's not for romantics, but it is a great value (D-€70, cash only, no breakfast, it's the house with the vine-covered pergola at Piazza San Giorgio 7 near Via San Giovanni, tel. 0341-830-575, www.villaelenavarenna.it, info@villaelenavarenna.it).

$ Albergo Beretta, on the main road a block below the station, has 10 pleasant rooms, several with balconies (and street noise). Second-floor rooms are quietest. This place, above a coffee shop that doubles as the reception, feels homey but lacks any lake-side glamour (D-€60, Db-€70, larger room-€80, extra bed-€12, breakfast-€6 but free with 2-night stay and this book, no elevator, Via per Esino 1, tel. 0341-830-132, hotelberetta@iol.it).

$ Hotel Montecodeno, with 11 decent rooms and no views, is a functional concrete box just off the main road between the train station and lake (Sb-€80, Db-€105, extra bed-€10, air-con, guest computer and free Wi-Fi, attached restaurant serves fresh fish and a €23 "Rick Steves" fixed-price meal if you show this book before-hand; if you stay 3 nights and pay cash, you get 1 meal included per guest or a 15 percent cash discount—take your pick; Via della Croce 2, tel. 0341-830-123, www.hotelmontecodeno.com, info@hotelmontecodeno.com, kind Marina Castelli and Lucia).

Eating in Varenna

Dining with a Lake View

Ristorante la Vista, at Albergo Milano, feels like a private hotel restaurant but also welcomes non-guests. On a balmy evening, their terrace overlooking the town and the lake is hard to beat. Egidio (or Egi—pronounced "edgy") and his staff give traditional cuisine a creative twist, and his selection is great for foodies with discerning tastes. I'd go with his €38 three-course fixed-price din-ner (Mon and Wed-Sat 19.00-22:00, closed Sun and Tue, reserva-tions required, Via XX Settembre 35, tel. 0341-830-298).

Ristorante la Contrada, with its terrace-side location, is run by the Villa Cipressi and takes advantage of the villa's elegant gar-den, trickling fountain, and lake view. Indoor seating glows with a warm and romantic air, and the garden is a delight on warm summer evenings. Fresh daily specialties and professional service make this a worthwhile splurge. However, weddings and confer-ence groups can crowd the place and distract from the service (€40 meals plus wine, daily 12:30-14:00 & 19:15-21:30, may close for weddings, Via IV Novembre 22, tel. 0341-830-113).

Dining Without a Lake View

Ristorante il Cavatappi, a tiny place on a quiet lane just off the town square, serves old-time specialties, such as spaghetti with *missoltino*, the air-dried lake fish that natives like more than tour-ists do. Helpful owner-chef Mario is happy to be considered a lunatic gourmet. With just five tables, he can connect personally with diners. Talk with him, make a plan, then let him loose. Plan on spending €28-38 plus wine (daily 12:30-14:30 & 19:30-21:45, reservations recommended for dinner, Via XX Settembre 10, tel. 0341-815-349).

LAKES

Varennamonamour, an upscale eatery hiding just up from the water, is popular with fashionable Italians. Its seasonal menu has a nouvelle cuisine flair, with a few popular mainstays fresh from the lake. The cream-and-brown modern decor harmonizes well with the original exposed stone walls to create a classy, welcoming space (€13-15 pastas, €13-18 *secondi*, hours/days can vary—generally daily in high season, Contrada Scoscesa 7, tel. 033-181-4016).

Osteria Quatro Pass is a welcoming bistro known for its homemade pasta and fish. It offers 14 candlelit tables under picturesque vaults, plus sidewalk seating (€12-20 pastas, €10-20 *secondi*, daily 12:00-14:00 & 19:00-22:00, closed Wed outside of peak season, Via XX Settembre 20, tel. 0341-815-091, Lollo).

Eating Simply on the Harbor
The harborfront is lined with several simple eateries, all with great lakefront seating.

Nilus Bar, with a young waitstaff, serves crêpes, pizzas, big mixed salads, hot sandwiches, soup of the day, and cocktails with a smile (Wed-Mon 12:00-22:30, hours can vary and bar open longer, closed Tue and Dec-Feb, cash only, tel. 0341-815-228, Fulvia and Giovanni).

Bar il Molo, next door, is good for a casual meal on the harbor or a gelato with a view (€9-10 pizzas, €7-9 pastas, €5-8 salads, €6 toasted sandwiches, daily 11:00-24:00, closed Nov-March, tel. 0341-830-070). They also have a room full of gifty edibles for sale.

At **Gelateria Riva,** you can get a cup or cone to go, then grab a pillowy seat on the bulkhead. Duillo is the only guy in town who prepares his gelato fresh every day. Try his *nocciola* (hazelnut) before making your choice. Ask the day before if you want to watch the gelato being made (daily 12:00-19:00, open later June-Sept, closed off-season).

Eating Simply Without a Lake View
Ristorante del Sole, facing the town square, serves respectable, well-priced meals and Neapolitan-style pizzas. Making few concessions to the tourist crowds, this family-friendly restaurant caters to residents, providing a fun atmosphere, a cozy, walled-in garden in back, and tables on the square (€7-9 pizzas, €6-10 pastas, €10-19 *secondi*, daily 12:00-14:30 & 18:30-22:30, Piazza San Giorgio 21, tel. 0341-815-218).

Ristorante il Caminetto is a homey, backwoods mountain trattoria in Gittana, a tiny town high above Varenna. Getting there entails a curvy 10-minute drive—they'll pick you up for free in Piazza San Giorgio at 19:30, deliver you to the restaurant, and then dish up classic fare at small-town prices. Husband-and-wife team Moreno and Rossella take pride in their specialties, including grilled meats and risotto with porcini mushrooms and berries. This is a good place to set a price and trust your host to bring whatever's best (€16-25 *dégustation* menu, wine extra, Thu-Tue 12:30-14:30 & 19:30-21:30, closed Wed, reservations mandatory to confirm pick-up from Varenna at 19:30, Viale Progresso 6, tel. 0341-815-225 or 0341-815-127, mobile 347-331-2238).

Other Eateries

Pub l'Orso is the hotspot in town for wine or beer and a light meal. Oozing character, it's behind Hotel Olivedo in a renovated shed that used to be a marble-polishing shop (closed Mon). At **Ristorante Montecodeno,** a cozy little place on the big road, chef Ferruccio serves a plate of eight different tasty lake fish specialties (including *missoltino*). **Ristorante Isola Nuova** is a newish restaurant with a fresh atmosphere, buried in the old town with no sea view (closed Tue). The venerable **Vecchia Varenna** is the only classy restaurant actually on the harbor (old place with new management). And at **Hotel Olivedo,** a grand old hotel facing the ferry dock, you can eat in a classic dining hall.

   Picnics: Varenna's two little grocery stores have all you need for a tasty balcony or breakwater picnic-dinner. The *salumeria* on the square is best for meats, cheese, and bread; try their homemade salami (Tue-Sat 8:00-12:30 & 16:00-19:30, Sun-Mon 8:00-12:30 only). The store just north of the main square by the pharmacy stocks fresh fruits, veggies, and a few essentials (daily 7:30-12:30, Tue-Sat also 16:00-19:30).

Varenna Connections

Remember, if leaving Varenna by train, you can't purchase tickets at the station. Instead, you can buy them from the travel agency (I Viaggi del Tivano), Albergo Beretta next door, or Barilott just off the main square (see "Helpful Hints," earlier). Stamp your ticket in the yellow machine at the station before boarding. If those places are closed, win the sympathy of the conductor and buy your ticket as soon as you get on board for an additional fee. (Find him before he finds you—or you'll likely be charged an even stiffer penalty.)

   Varenna to Milan by Train: Trains leave Varenna for Milano Centrale (1 hour, €6.40, likely schedule for daily and direct trains: 5:36, 6:23, 6:35, 7:37, 8:37, 10:37, 12:37, 14:37, 16:37, 17:37, 18:37, 20:37, 21:37, and 22:21; if you board a train at a time not listed here, it's likely a local milk-run train that will take twice as long).

   Varenna to Stresa by Train: Trains run about every two hours (2.75-4 hours, transfer in Milan).

   Varenna to St. Moritz in Switzerland by Train: From Varenna, you have easy access to the Bernina Express scenic train to St. Moritz. Note that this is only realistic from April through October. First, take the train to Tirano, and then transfer to the Bernina Express train to St. Moritz (4/day, allow 4-5 hours with transfer; for details see www.rhb.ch). For information and a time-table for this route, stop by the I Viaggi del Tivano travel agency (see "Helpful Hints," earlier), or ask your hotelier for the handy tourist information book produced by local travel agencies. Don't forget your passport for trips into Switzerland.

Bellagio

The self-proclaimed "Pearl of the Lake" is a classy combination of tidiness and Old World elegance. If you don't mind that "tramp

in a palace" feeling, it's a fine place to shop for ties and umbrellas while surrounding yourself with the more adventurous posh travelers. Heavy curtains between the harborfront arcades create welcome shade and keep visitors and their poodles from sweating. Thriving yet still cute, Bellagio is a much more substantial town than Varenna (which has one-third the number of hotel beds and almost no shops).

Orientation to Bellagio

Tourist Information
The TI is right downtown, at the slow boat and hydrofoil dock (April-Oct Mon-Sat 9:00-12:30 & 13:00-18:00, Sun 10:00-14:00; Nov-March shorter hours and closed Tue and Sun; tel. 031-950-204, www.bellagiolakecomo.com).

Arrival in Bellagio
Bellagio is best reached via ferry from Varenna (€4.60); or by ferry, hydrofoil, or slow boat from Como. (For ferries, see page 281; for hydrofoils and slow boats, see page 285.)

By Boat: Bellagio has two docks a few minutes' walk apart. The northern docks are for the passenger-only slow boat (*battello* or *battello navetta*) and the hydrofoil (*servizio rapido*). The southern dock is for all "ferry boats" (*traghetti*): both the car ferry (cars and foot passengers) and the passenger-only ferry. Ask around to make sure you're waiting at the correct dock. Remember that if you want to know all your departure options beyond Varenna, Cadenabbia, and Menaggio, you need to study four different timetables (see

"Getting Around Lake Como," page 281). Confirm your intentions at the kiosk near either dock.

By Car: Parking is difficult, but you can try for a spot near the lake or in the parking lot at the ferry dock (white lines are always free, yellow lines are for residents only, blue lines cost €1.50/hour—pay with coins in gray or blue machines and stick ticket in car window).

Helpful Hints

Internet Access: Bellagio Point has a slick Internet café, complete with great sandwiches, wine-tasting options, and free Wi-Fi if you buy a drink (€2/30 minutes, daily 10:00-22:00, Salita Plinio 8, tel. 031-950-437, www.bellagiopoint.com). Julio also rents apartments (see "Sleeping in Bellagio," later).

Laundry: La Lavandera is bright and new. Don't be discouraged if it looks closed; the lights come on automatically when you enter (€8.50 wash/dry, open daily 24 hours, Salita Carlo Grandi 21—this street is also marked as Via Specula, tel. 339-410-6852).

Sights in Bellagio

Villa Serbelloni Park

If you need a destination, you can take a guided tour of this park, which overlooks the town. The villa itself, owned by the Rockefeller Foundation, is not open to the public.

Cost and Hours: €9, April-Oct, tours Tue-Sun at 11:00 and 15:30, no tours Mon or when rainy, 1.5 hours, first two-thirds of walk is uphill, show up at the little tour office in the medieval tower on Piazza della Chiesa 15 minutes before tour time to buy tickets, confirm time at office, tel. 031-951-555.

Strolling

Explore the steep-stepped lanes rising from the harborfront. While Johnnie Walker and jewelry sell best at lake level, the natives shop up the hill. Piazza della Chiesa, near the top of town, has a worth-a-look church (with its art described in an English-language handout).

The administrative capital of the mid-lake region, Bellagio is located where the two southern legs of the lake split off. For an easy break in a park with a great view, wander right out to the crotch. Meander past the rich and famous Hotel Villa Serbelloni, and walk five minutes to Punta Spartivento ("Poi

LAKES

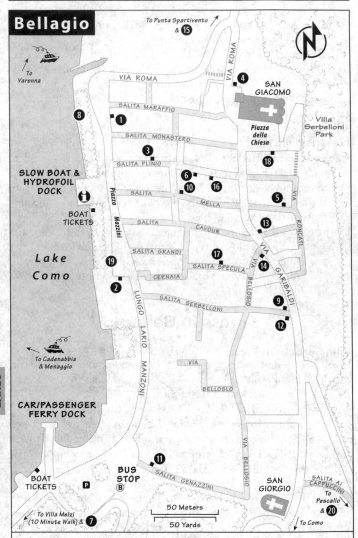

Bellagio

1 Hotel Florence
2 Hotel/Rist./Snack Bar Metropole
3 Hotel Centrale
4 Albergo Europa
5 Bellagio B&B Apartments
6 Il Borgo Apartments
7 To Giardini di Villa Melzi Apartments
8 The Florence Ristorante
9 Trattoria San Giacomo
10 Rist. Terrazza Barchetta
11 Enoteca Cava Turacciolo
12 Aperitivo Et Al
13 Gelateria del Borgo
14 Caligari Alimentari
15 To La Punta Ristorante
16 Internet Café
17 Launderette
18 Villa Serbelloni Park Tickets
19 Bellagio Water-Taxi Lake Tours
20 To Bellagio Water Sports (Kayak Tours)

that Divides the Wind"). You'll find a Renoir atmosphere complete with an inviting bar-restaurant (see "Eating in Bellagio," later), a tiny harbor, and a chance to sit on a park bench and gaze north past Menaggio, Varenna, and the end of the lake to the Swiss Alps.

For another stroll, head south from the car-ferry dock down the tree-shaded promenade. Ten minutes later, you'll pass the town's concrete swimming area. The grassy, pebbly, public San Giovanni beach (no showers) is another 20 minutes farther south from there.

Villa Melzi Gardens

A 10-minute walk south from the ferry dock, this picture-perfect lakeside expanse of exotic plants, flowers, trees, and Neoclassical sculpture was assembled by the vice president of Napoleon's Italian Republic in the early 19th century.

Cost and Hours: €6.50, April-Oct daily 9:30-18:30, last entry at 18:00, closed Nov-March, mobile 339-457-3838, www.giardin-idivillamelzi.it.

Hikes and Walks

The TI has free brochures for three well-crafted walking tours, varying from one to three hours, all of which explore the city and environs. Sites include villas, gardens, churches, an old-fashioned dairy shop, medieval towers, and a nautical instruments museum. The TI also sells a hiking map for €3 that shows four different hikes ranging in difficulty and duration.

Bellagio Water-Taxi Lake Tours

With a small stand at the boat docks, Jennine and Luca offer tours and private service in their luxurious and powerful boat. Their basic 2.5-hour tour, guided by Luca, includes a fun hour at mid-lake, with a float-by of Richard Branson's villa, as well as a stop at Villa del Balbianello (see listing on page 308), where you'll take an English tour.

Cost and Hours: €50, 10 percent discount if you reserve direct and bring this book, price includes entry and tour of villa—worth €13, generally runs at 13:30 but check blackboard for day's offerings or call, mobile 338-524-4914, www.bellagiowatertaxis.com, bellagiowatertaxis@gmail.com.

Bellagio Water Sports

Friendly Michele offers kayaking tours within a 10-minute walk of the town center. His popular 1.5- and 2-hour tours cover the Bellagio coast, while his 3-hour tour includes a stop at Villa Melzi. He also rents kayaks for those willing to go solo.

Cost and Hours: €25/1.5-hour tour, €30/2-hour tour, €35/3-hour tour; kayak rentals €15/1.5 hours, €17.50/2 hours, €22.50/3 hours; no tours on Sun, located on Pescallo Bay at via Sfondrati 1 near Hotel La Pergola, mobile 340-394-9375, www.bellagiowater-sports.com, info@bellagiowatersports.com.

Sleeping in Bellagio

This is a "boom or bust" lake resort, with high-season prices (those listed here) straight through from May to September, plus a brief shoulder season (with discounted prices) in April and from October to November. Off-season (Dec-March), nearly everything is closed down.

$$$ Hotel Florence has a prime lakefront setting in the center of town. The 150-year-old, family-run place features 30 rooms, hardwood floors, bold earth tones, and a rich touch of Old World elegance (Sb-€125, Db-€145-210, Db suite-€150-270, prices depend on view and balcony, closed Nov-March, fans available on request, handheld showers, elevator, free Wi-Fi, Piazza Mazzini 46, tel. 031-950-342, www.hotelflorencebellagio.it, info@hotel-florencebellagio.it, run by the Austrian Ketzlar family).

$$$ Hotel Metropole, dominating Bellagio's waterfront between the ferry docks, is a grand old place with plush public spaces. Its modern rooms have all the comforts, but with a bit of an institutional feel. Many of its 42 rooms have lake views (Sb-€120, €140 with balcony, Db-€160, €190 with balcony, €220 with terrace, aircon, elevator, free Wi-Fi, stunning roof terrace, Piazza Mazzini 1, tel. 031-950-409, www.albergometropole.it, info@albergometro-pole.it).

$$ Hotel Centrale, managed with pride and care by Giacomo Borelli, warmly welcomes its guests into a true-blue family operation: Signore Borelli's two sons help out, his mama painted the art, and grandpa crafted much of the Art Deco-era furniture. This place has generous public spaces and many thoughtful touches—and its 17 comfortable rooms are a great value, even without lake views (Sb-€110, Db-€130, €5/night discount with this book, aircon, elevator, guest computer, free Wi-Fi, Salita Plinio 7, tel. 031-951-940, www.hc-bellagio.com, info@hc-bellagio.com).

$ Albergo Europa, run with low energy, is in a concrete annex behind a restaurant, away from the waterfront. Its 10 rooms have no charm but are comfortable (Sb-€60, Db-€80, no elevator, free parking, Via Roma 21, tel. 031-950-471, www.hoteleuropabella-gio.it, info@hoteleuropabellagio.it, Marchesi family).

$ Bellagio B&B Apartments, with three units for rent, are located behind the *gelateria* at the top of town. Julio also runs the Bellagio Point Internet café, which serves as the reception (Db-€60, more for additional people, 2-night minimum, no breakfast, free Wi-Fi, reception at Salita Plinio 8, apartments at Salita Cavour 37, tel. 031-951-680, www.bellagiobedandbreakfast.com, info@bellagiobe-dandbreakfast.com). Julio also has five large apartments a 15-minute walk from Bellagio (toward Como, Db-€80-100 for 4 people).

$ Il Borgo Apartments rents seven modern *Better Homes and Gardens*-quality apartments with kitchenettes in the old center at great prices. Easygoing Flavio is available for check-in daily 9:00-12:00, or by appointment (Db-€100, 2 bigger apartments for up to 6 people-€120, cash discount, no breakfast, 3-night minimum required, air-con, Wi-Fi, Salita Plinio 4, tel. 031-952-497, mobile 338-193-5559, www.borgoresidence.it, info@borgoresidence.it).

$ Giardini di Villa Melzi Apartments provides modern lodgings in three double bedrooms and three studios with kitchenettes in the little harbor of Loppia, about a 15-minute walk south of Bellagio. A free pass allows guests to take a shortcut to Bellagio through the Villa Melzi Gardens (€50/person, usually 3-night minimum—ask, guest computer, free parking, Via Melzi d'Eril 23, tel. 339-221-4394, www.bellagiowelcome.com, info@bellagiowelcome.com, Ornella).

Eating in Bellagio

On the Lakefront

These places (also listed under "Sleeping in Bellagio," earlier) offer wonderful lakeside tables and, considering the setting, reasonable prices.

Hotel Metropole Ristorante, while a mediocre food value, has a full menu and is a relaxing delight with good service (€12-16 pastas, €14-22 *secondi*, April-Oct daily 12:00-14:30 & 19:00-21:30, closed Nov-March, Piazza Mazzini 1, tel. 031-950-409). **Hotel Metropole Snack Bar,** next to the restaurant, is quite good, with simple €9 pastas and sandwiches and fine €7-12 salads (April-Oct daily 12:00-21:30, bar open later, closed Nov-March, good service, great locale).

The Florence is nicely situated under a trellis of flowers across from the Florence Hotel, away from the ferry fumes. This is a lovely perch for a drink or meal (€16 pastas, €22 *secondi*, simpler lunch menu of salads and lighter fare, April-Sept daily 12:00-14:30 & 19:00-22:00, bar open all day).

In the Old Town, Without Lake Views

Trattoria San Giacomo is a high-energy place that's respected for its traditional cuisine, such as *riso e filetto di pesce* (rice and perch fillet in butter and sage). It has daily seasonal specials and an inviting €25 fixed-price meal based on regional specialties. Choose between fun seating on a steep, cobbled lane or tight seating inside (Mon and Wed-Thu 12:00-14:30 & 19:00-21:30, Fri-Sun open later midday and evenings, closed Tue and Dec-Feb, Salita Serbelloni 45, tel. 031-950-329, Aurelio).

LAKES

Ristorante Terrazza Barchetta, set on a terrace with no lake view and bedecked with summery colors, puts a creative twist on regional favorites such as lake fish. Don't confuse it with the street-level bar-trattoria—head up the stairs to the second floor. Reservations are recommended (€15 pastas, €20 *secondi*, Wed-Mon 12:00-14:30 & 19:00-22:30, closed Tue, Salita Mella 13, tel. 031-951-389).

Other Options

Wine-Tasting: Step into the vaulted stone cellar of the funky **Enoteca Cava Turacciolo** to taste three regional wines with a sampling of cheeses, meats, and breads (€19/person with this book, Thu-Tue April-Oct 10:30-1:00, Nov-Dec and March 18:00-24:00, closed Wed and Jan-Feb, Salita Genazzini 3, tel. 031-950-975, Norberto and Rosy). **Aperitivo Et Al,** slick and jazzy, is a trendier wine bar, offering mixed *salumi* and *formaggi* plates (€8-12), big fresh salads (€9-12), and light lunches, along with a great selection of wines by the glass (€14-18/three-glass tasting—totaling a half-bottle of wine per person, add antipasto plate for €24, also Super Tuscan wine-tastings, daily 11:30-24:00, closed Dec-Feb and Tue off-season, free Wi-Fi, Salita Serbelloni 34, tel. 031-951-523).

Gelato: Residents agree that you won't find the best *gelateria* in town among the sundaes served on the waterfront. Instead, climb to the top of town to **Gelateria del Borgo** (daily 10:00-22:30, shorter hours off-season, closed Nov-March, Via Garibaldi 46, tel. 031-950-755, Stefania and Gianfranco).

Picnics: You'll find benches at the park, along the waterfront in town, and lining the promenade south of town. Pick up your picnic supplies at **Caligari Alimentari.** They have roast chicken, ribs, and focaccia, and are happy to make fresh sandwiches to order (Tue-Sat 7:30-13:00 & 16:00-19:30, Sun 7:30-13:00, closed Mon, shorter hours off-season, on corner of Via Garibaldi and Via Carlo Bellosio, tel. 031-951-815).

Punta Spartivento: This dramatic natural park, a 10-minute walk north of town (see "Strolling," page 301), is a great place for either a picnic or a meal at **La Punta Ristorante** (€9 pastas, €13 fish, €22 meat courses, March-Oct daily 12:00-14:30 & 19:00-22:00, bar open 14:30-19:00 for snacks only, closed Nov-Feb, tel. 031-951-888).

Menaggio

Menaggio has more urban bulk than its neighbors, but visitors are charmed by its lovely lakefront park. Since many find Lake

Como too dirty for swimming, consider spending time in Menaggio's fine public pool (look for the *lido*). This is the starting point for a few hikes. (Just a few decades ago, cigarette smugglers used these trails at night to sneak back into Italy from Switzerland with their tax-free booty.) The TI has information about mountain biking and catching the bus to trailheads on nearby Mount Grona. Ask for the free *Walking in the Province of Como* booklet, with information on 18 different walks detailing historical, artistic, and natural features (TI in Piazza Garibaldi open Mon-Sat 9:00-12:30 & 14:30-18:00, closed Wed Nov-March, closed Sun year-round, tel. 0344-32 924, www.menaggio.com).

Sleeping in Menaggio

$ La Marianna B&B has eight rooms and a fine restaurant in Cadenabbia, about a mile south of Menaggio on a busy road (Db with view-€98, lakeside terrace at restaurant—guests receive a 25 percent restaurant discount, air-con, tel. 0344-43095, www.la-marianna.com, info@la-marianna.com, Ty and Paola). The hourly Como-Menaggio bus #C10 stops here, and the ferry dock for mid lake towns via Bellagio is 300 yards away.

$ La Primula Youth Hostel has a great location on the lake, a two-minute walk from the ferry dock (€20/person in dorm room, Db-€54, family room with bathroom and 4 beds-€80, €2 extra for nonmembers, pizzas from €6, guest computer, Wi-Fi, sailing school, kayak and mountain bike rentals, cooking classes, tel. 0344-32356, www.lakecomohostel.com, info@lakecomohostel.com). The hourly Como-Menaggio bus #C10 stops right by the hostel.

Menaggio Connections

From Menaggio to Milan: It's a 20-minute ferry to Varenna (boats hourly), where trains connect to Milan (every 1-2 hours, 1 hour, see "Varenna Connections," page 299). More fast trains depart from Como than Varenna. From Menaggio, take hourly local bus #C10

(€3.50, 1-2/hour, 1 hour) to Como, where you can catch the train (hourly, 30-90 minutes). If you need to reach Malpensa Airport, you could take bus #C10 to Como, then take a train to Saronno, which is on the Malpensa Express train line (see page 373).

From Menaggio to Switzerland: Public bus #C12 departs about every hour or two from Piazza Roma for Lugano (€10 round-trip, 1 hour, buy tickets at bus stop on Via Calvi). In summer, the yellow Palm Express bus runs once daily to **Lugano** (1 hour) and **St. Moritz** (3 hours). Off-season (mid-Oct-mid-June), the bus runs only on weekends. Advance reservations are required (www.post-bus.ch)—and remember to bring your passport.

More Sights on Lake Como

Villa Carlotta

If you plan to tour one of Lake Como's famed villas, this is the best for gardens and flowers (its forte). I see the lakes as a break from Italy's art, but if you're in need of a place that charges admission, Villa Carlotta offers an elegant Neoclassical interior, Antonio Canova's famous *Maddalena Penitente* statue, and a garden (at its best in spring).

Cost and Hours: €9, daily April-mid-Oct 9:00-18:00, last 2 weeks of March and mid-Oct-mid-Nov 10:00-17:00, closed mid-Nov-mid-March, no photos inside the villa, tel. 034-440-405, www.villacarlotta.it.

Nearby: Tremezzo and **Cadenabbia** are pleasant lakeside resorts, each one an easy walk away. Boats serve both places (5-minute walk from either dock to the villa) and are reached by *traghetto* (ferry, dock in Cadenabbia) or the *battello* (slow boat, dock in Tremezzo).

To visit **Villa del Balbianello** (described next) after you see Villa Carlotta, catch the blue bus #C10 (turn right when exiting the villa and walk to the trash cans; bus departs at 10:50, 11:10, 11:58, 13:05, 13:57, 14:36, 15:06, and 15:36; €1.50, pay on bus). Get off at the second stop in Lenno, walk 30 yards, turn left, and follow the lakeside south to the lido of Lenno.

Villa del Balbianello

The dreamiest villa on the lake perches on a romantic promontory overlooking Lake Como and facing Bellagio. Built for a cardinal at the end of the 18th century on the remains of an old Franciscan church, the villa was the cardinal's palace of delights, where he could study and brainstorm with his friends. Today it reflects the exotic vision of its last owner, explorer Guido Monzino, who died in 1988—leaving his villa, his rich art collection, and mementos of his expeditions to the state. The upper floor serves as a museum of his expeditions, with memorabilia from his North Pole and Mount Everest adventures. The real masterpiece here is the terraced garden and elegant loggia, where the land fits the architecture and landscaping in a lovely way. This is a favorite choice for movie directors when they need a far-out villa to feature; scenes from *Casino Royale* and *Star Wars: Episode II* were filmed here.

Cost and Hours: Garden only-€7, garden with villa tour-€13, tours depart hourly Thu-Sun and Tue 10:00-18:00, closed Mon and Wed and mid-Nov-mid-March, tel. 034-456-110, www.fondoambiente.it.

Getting There: You can reach it on **foot** (on Tue and Sat-Sun only) by walking a half-mile from Lenno through the park. Otherwise, catch the more glamorous **speedboat shuttle** from Lido di Lenno (€5 one-way, €6 round-trip, Igor can also be hired for private tours, mobile 333-410-3854).

Isola Comacina

This remote little island, just south of Bellagio, offers peace, ancient church foundations, a small archaeological museum, swans, ducks, nice swimming, and a lovely view of Lake Como. It takes 30-45 minutes to walk around the island, but longer to savor it. Bring a picnic or try the snack bar at the dock.

Cost and Hours: €6, daily July-Aug 10:00-18:30, mid-March-June and Sept-Oct 10:00-17:00, closed Nov-mid-March, information at TI in mainland town of Ossuccio, tel. 034-456-369, www.isola-comacina.it, info@isola-comacina.it.

Getting There: The *isola* can be reached by ferry from Varenna (1 hour), Menaggio (50 minutes), or Bellagio (35 minutes). Look for trips to Isola Comacina (€5) on the Colico-Como *battello* schedule (listed in Lago di Como boat timetable, free at ticket booths at ferry docks, see page 281). Check return times carefully (Como-Colico direction) and don't miss your boat. Usually only one trip a day each way works out for a visit. Allow about six hours, including travel time.

Como

On the southwest tip of the lake, Como has a good, traffic-free old town, an interesting Gothic/Renaissance cathedral, and a pleasant lakefront with a promenade (TI open Mon-Sat 9:00-13:00 & 14:00-17:00, closed Sun, tel. 031-269-712, www.lakecomo.it). It's an easy 10-minute walk from the boat dock to the train station (trains to Milan depart hourly, 30-90 minutes). Boats leave Como about hourly for mid-lake (ferries-€10, 2 hours, departures 7:35-16:45; hydrofoils-€15, 1 hour, departures 8:45-19:20, fewer on Sun; tel. 031-579-211, www.navigazionelaghi.it).

Sleeping in Como: For a cheap overnight, try the **$ Villa Olmo**

LAKES

Hostel (€18 bunks, family room-€20.50/person, includes breakfast and sheets, €2/night extra for nonmembers, dinners-€5.50-12, pay guest computer, free Wi-Fi, laundry service available, baggage storage, free parking, bike rental, reception open 7:00-10:00 & 16:00-24:00, lockout 10:00-16:00, 24:00 curfew, closed mid-Nov-Feb, 20-minute walk from train station or dock, Via Bellinzona 2, tel. 031-573-800, www.ostellocomo.it, ostellocomo@tin.it).

All-Day Lugano Side-Trip

From Varenna or Bellagio, you can make a loop that lets you nip into Switzerland to see the elegant lake resort of Lugano, pass through the town of Como, and cruise a good part of Lake Como. Here's a good day plan: 9:00—ferry to Menaggio; 10:00—bus to Lugano (45 minutes, bring your passport); 11:30—explore Lugano, then train to Como (2/hour); 16:00—fast boat from Como to Varenna (departures also at about 17:00, 18:00, and 19:00). For information on Lugano, see www.ricksteves.com/lugano.

Lake Maggiore

Lake Maggiore is ringed by mountains, snowcapped in spring and fall, and lined with resort towns such as Stresa. While crassly touristic, Stresa is a handy base from which to explore the exotic garden islands of Lake Maggiore. And many consider it a pleasant last stop before flying home from nearby Malpensa Airport.

A visit to this region is worth the trouble for two islands, both with exotic gardens and lovely villas built by the Borromeo family. The Borromeos—through many generations since 1630—lovingly turned their islands into magical retreats, with elaborate villas and fragrant gardens. Isola Bella has a palace and terraced garden; Isola Madre has a villa and sprawling English-style (more casual) garden. A third island, Isola Superiore (a.k.a. Isola Pescatori), is simply small, serene, and residential. The Borromeos, who made their money from trade and banking, enjoyed the arts—from paintings (hung in lavish abundance throughout the palace and villa) to plays (performed in an open-air theater on Isola Bella) and marionette shows (you'll see the puppets that once performed here).

Tourists flock to the lakes in May and June, when flowers are in bloom, and in September. Concerts held in scenic settings draw music lovers, particularly during the summer Stresa Festival (get details from Stresa TI). For fewer crowds, visit in April, July, August (when Italians prefer the Mediterranean beaches), or October. In winter, the snow-covered mountains (with resorts a 1.5-hour drive away) attract skiers.

Planning Your Time

This region is best visited on a sunny day, when the mountains are clear, the lake is calm, and the heat of the sun brings out the scent of the blossoms. The two top islands for sightseeing are Isola Bella and Isola Madre. Isola Superiore has no sights, but is a peaceful place for lunch. You can stay the night in Stresa (accommodations listed later), but a day trip is sufficient for most.

Day Trip from Milan: Catch the one-hour, early train from Milan to Stresa (usually at 8:25, may require reservations; the next departure isn't until 11:25). Upon arrival in Stresa, walk 10 minutes downhill to the boat dock, and catch a boat to Isola Madre. Then work your way back to Isola Superiore for a lazy lunch, and on to Isola Bella for the afternoon, before returning to the town of Stresa and back to Milan.

Getting Around Lake Maggiore

Boats link the islands and Stresa, running about twice hourly. Allow roughly 10 minutes between stops. Since short round-trip hops add up fast (€7.80 each for Isola Bella and Isola Superiore, €10 for Isola Madre), it's best to simply buy the **all-day pass:** €10.10 for two islands (Bella and Superiore), or €16.90 for all the islands plus Pallanza (a town on the opposite shore) and Villa Taranto. An €18 **combo-ticket** combining the villas on Isola Bella and Isola Madre can be purchased at the boat dock (credit cards accepted).

Boats run daily April through September. The map on page 316 shows the route: Stresa, Carciano/Lido, Isola Bella, Isola Superiore, Baveno (lakeside town), Isola Madre, Pallanza, and Villa Taranto. This route is part of a longer one. To follow the boat schedule (free, available at boat docks, TI, and maybe your hotel), look at the Arona-Locarno timetable for trips from Stresa to the islands, and the Locarno-Arona timetable for the return trip to Stresa. Off-season, the boats cover a shorter route; check the timetable (public boat info: toll-free tel. 800-551-801, tel. 0322-233-200, www.navigazionelaghi.it, infomaggiore@navigazionelaghi.it).

Buy boat tickets directly from the dock ticket booth under the gallery to the left of the TI. Don't be fooled by the private taxi-boat drivers, most dressed in navy-blue uniforms and white hats (they look like Italian traffic cops); with their little sales booth on the sidewalk in front of the public boat launch, they'll try to talk you into paying way too much for private tours on their smaller boats.

Stresa

Stresa—which means "thin stretch"—was named for the original strip of fishermen's huts that lined the shore. Today, grand old hotels run along that same shore. The old town—basically a traffic-free touristy shopping mall—is just a few blocks deep, stretching inland from the main boat dock. A fine waterfront promenade leads past the venerable old hotels to the Lido (with the Carciano boat dock and a mountain cable car). Stresa's stately 19th-century lakeside hotels date back to the days when this town was on the "Grand Tour" circuit. In any Romantic-age resort like Stresa, hotels had names designed to appeal to Victorian aristocrats...like Palace (rather than Palazzo), Astoria, Bristol, and Victoria.

Nineteen-year-old Ernest Hemingway first came to Stresa in 1918. Wounded in Slovenia as an ambulance driver for the Italian Red Cross, he was taken to the Grand Hotel des Iles Borromees. This was the first hotel on the shore (from 1862), and it served—like its regal neighbors—as an infirmary during World War I. Hemingway returned to the same hotel in 1948, stayed in the same room (#205, now called the "Hemingway suite"—you can stay there for a couple of thousand dollars a night), and signed the guest book as "an old client." Another "old client" was Winston Churchill, who honeymooned here.

Orientation to Stresa

Tourist Information

The helpful TI, located to the right of the ticket window at the boat dock, has free maps and boat schedules (March-Oct daily 10:00-12:30 & 15:00-18:30; Nov-Feb Mon-Fri 10:00-12:30 & 15:00-18:30, Sat 10:00-12:30, closed Sun; Piazza Marconi 16, tel. 0323-30150, www.stresaturismo.it).

Helpful Hints

Internet Access: The **Newdata Internet Point** is a block off Piazza Cadorna in the old center (Mon-Sat 9:00-12:00 & 15:00-19:00, closed Sun, Via de Vit 15A, tel. 0323-30323, www.newdata.too.it).

Arrival in Stresa

At the train station, ask for a free city map at the newsstand (to the far right of the tracks as you exit the train). To get downtown, exit right from the station and take your first left (on Viale Duchessa di Genova). This takes you straight down to the lake (the boat dock is about four blocks to your right; ask for boat schedule at ticket window). The TI is next door on the same dock. Taxis charge a fixed rate of €8 for even the shortest ride in town.

Sights in Stresa

Islands and Gardens

▲▲Isola Bella

This island, nearest Stresa, has a formal garden and a fancy Baroque palace. Looking like a stepped pyramid from the water,

the island was named by Charles Borromeo (sponsor of Milan's Duomo) for his wife, Isabella. The island itself is touristy, with a gauntlet of souvenir stands and a corral of restaurants. A few back streets provide evidence that people actually live here. While the Borromeo family now lives in Milan, they spend a few weeks on Isola Bella each summer (when their blue-and-red family flag flies from the top of the garden).

Cost and Hours: Palace and garden-€13, picture gallery-€3 extra, €18 combo-ticket includes the villa at Isola Madre (but not Isola Bella's picture gallery), daily late-March-late-Oct 9:00-18:00, closed late-Oct-late-March, last entry 30 minutes before closing, no photos in villa, tel. 0323-30556, www.borromeoturismo.it.

Audioguide: A fine €3 audioguide describes the palace, which also has posted English descriptions.

Services: A WC is at the garden entrance. Note that there are two docks on this island (one for each direction). Departure times are indicated by clocks at each dock. Picnicking is not allowed in the garden, but you can picnic at the point of the island (free and open to the public); take the black-and-white mosaic sidewalk to the left of the palace entrance.

Visiting the Island: Your visit is a one-way tour, starting with the palace and finishing with the garden. (There's no way to see the garden without the palace.) From the dock, head left to the huge palace, passing the public WCs.

In the lavishly decorated Baroque **palace,** stairs lead to stucco crests of Italy's top families (balls signify the Medici, bees mean the Barberini, and a unicorn symbolizes the Borromeos' motto: Humility). Here, you can choose to pay for a supplementary ticket to walk through the picture gallery (containing 130 beautifully restored 16th-century paintings from the Borromeo family's private collection, followed by an ornate throne room). Otherwise, continue right into the next room, where you'll see a portrait of the first Borromeo, and into a richly stuccoed grand hall, with an

80-foot-high dome and featuring an 18th-century model of the villa, including a grand entry that never materialized. The next room was the site of the 1935 Stresa Conference, in which Mussolini met with British and French diplomats in a united attempt to scare Germany out of starting World War II. Look for a copy of the treaty with Mussolini's signature on the wall next to the exit. Unfortunately, the "Stresa Front" soon fizzled when Mussolini attacked Ethiopia and joined forces with Hitler.

Next, Napoleon's bedroom comes with an engraving that depicts his 1797 visit (Napoleon is on a bench with his wife and sister enjoying festivities in his honor). The last rooms display souvenirs and gifts that the Borromeo family picked up over the generations.

Downstairs, many of the famous Borromeo marionettes are on display. (A larger collection is on Isola Madre.) The 18th-century grotto, decorated from ceiling to floor with shell motifs and black-and-white stones, still serves its original function of providing a cool refuge from Italy's heat. The dreamy marble statues are by Gaetano Monti, a student of Canova. Climbing out of the basement, look up at the unique cantilevered stairs; they're from a 16th-century fortress that predates this building.

Pass through the mirrored corridor and follow the path until you come to the ornate hall of 16th-century Flemish tapestries. This leads to the finale of this island visit: the beautiful **garden,** complete with Chinese white peacocks, which give it an exotic splash. Baroque—which is exactly what you see here—is all about controlling nature. Climb the stairs to see the terraced gardens, which are crowned by the Borromeo family unicorn. Back downstairs, follow the signs (hidden in the bushes) to the café/bookshop to get a 360-degree glimpse of the gardens. Then follow the signs to the exit. Gardeners continue on to the second exit to pass through Elisa's Greenhouse, named for Napoleon's sister and home to tropical plants.

▲Isola Superiore (Pescatori)

This sleepy island—home to 35 families—is the smallest and most residential of the three. It has a couple of good seafood restaurants, picnic benches, views, and, blissfully, nothing much to do—all under arbors of wisteria. A delight for photographers and painters, the island is never really crowded, except at lunchtime.

▲▲Isola Madre

Don't come here unless you intend to tour the sight, because that's all there is: an interesting furnished villa and a lovely garden filled with exotic birds and plants.

Cost and Hours: Villa and garden—€11, €18 combo-ticket includes Isola Bella, late-March-late-Oct daily 9:00-18:00, closed late-Oct-late-March, last entry 30 minutes before closing, no photos in villa, tel. 0323-31261, www.borromeoturismo.it.

Audioguide: A fine €3 audioguide is devoted almost entirely to the garden—a good investment to properly appreciate the plantings.

Services: A WC is next to the chapel. You'll also find a cafe/bookshop just outside the villa.

Visiting the Island: Visiting is a one-way affair. The sightseeing route is clearly signed, with a long stroll through the garden, villa, and chapel.

Eight gardeners (with the help of water continually pumped from the lake) keep this English-style **garden** paradise lush. It's a

joy, even for those bored by flowers and foliage. You'll see trees from around the world, and an exotic bird menagerie with golden and silver pheasants and Chinese peacocks. In front of the villa, a once-magnificent Himalayan cypress tree paints your world a streaky green. The 150-year-old tree, knocked down by a tornado in 2006 but successfully saved, is an attraction in its own right, with steel guy-wires now anchoring it firmly in place.

The 16th-century **villa** is the first of the Borromeo palaces. A century older than the

Isola Bella villa, it's dark, somber, and dates from the Renaissance. The clever angled hinges keep the doors from flapping in the lake breeze. The family's huge collection of dolls, marionettes, and exquisite 17th-century marionette theater sets—painted by a famous La Scala opera set designer—fills several rooms. A corner room is painted to take you into an 18th-century Venetian Rococo sitting room under a floral greenhouse. Some of the garden's best flowers are in view immediately after leaving the villa.

Eating: While eating is best on Isola Superiore, Isola Madre has one eatery, **La Piratera Ristorante Bar** (€25 fixed-price tourist meal, daily 8:00-18:00, sit-down meals 12:00-15:30, simple sandwiches and slices of pizza to go anytime, picnic at rocky beach a minute's walk from restaurant, just to your right as you exit the gardens, tel. 0323-31171).

▲Villa Taranto Botanical Gardens

Garden lovers will enjoy this large landscaped park, located on the mainland a 10-minute boat ride beyond Isola Madre (across the lake from Stresa). The gardens are a Scotsman's labor of love. Starting in the 1930s, Neil McEacharn created this garden of delights—bringing in thousands of plants from all over the world—

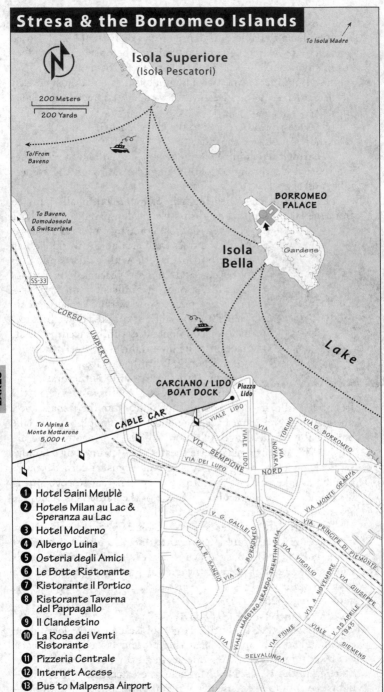

Stresa & the Borromeo Islands

Isola Superiore
(Isola Pescatori)

To Isola Madre

200 Meters
200 Yards

To/From Baveno

To Baveno, Domodossola & Switzerland

BORROMEO PALACE

Isola Bella

Gardens

SS-33

CORSO UMBERTO I

Lake

CARCIANO / LIDO BOAT DOCK

Piazza Lido

CABLE CAR

To Alpina & Monte Mottarone 5,000 f.

VIALE LIDO

VIA SEMPIONE

VIA DEL LUPO

VIALE LIDO

VIA NOVARA

VIA TORINO

NORD

VIA G. BORROMEO

VIA MONTE GRAPPA

VIA PRINCIPE DI PIEMONTE

V. G. GALILEI

VIA R. SANZIO

VIA F. BORROMEO

VIALE MAESTRO ERARDO TRENTHAGLIA

VIA VIRGILIO

VIA 4. NOVEMBRE

VIA GIUSEPPE

VIA FIUME

VIALE V. 28 APRILE

VIA 1945

SIEMENS

SELVALUNGA

LAKES

① Hotel Saini Meublè
② Hotels Milan au Lac & Speranza au Lac
③ Hotel Moderno
④ Albergo Luina
⑤ Osteria degli Amici
⑥ Le Botte Ristorante
⑦ Ristorante il Portico
⑧ Ristorante Taverna del Pappagallo
⑨ Il Clandestino
⑩ La Rosa dei Venti Ristorante
⑪ Pizzeria Centrale
⑫ Internet Access
⑬ Bus to Malpensa Airport

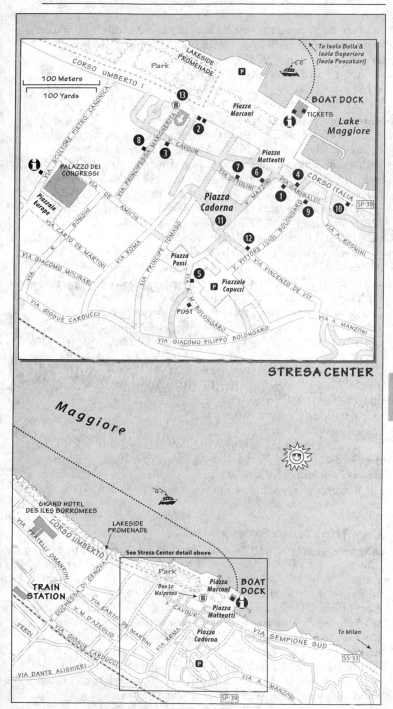

and here he stays, in the small mausoleum. The park's highlight is a terraced garden with a series of cascading pools. Villa Taranto is directly across the street from the boat dock.

Cost and Hours: €10, boat from Stresa-€12.40, daily mid-March-Oct 8:30-18:30, closed Nov-mid-March, tel. 0323-404-555, www.villataranto.it.

Mountain Cable Car

From Stresa's Lido, a cable car takes you up—in 2 stages and a 20-minute ride—to the top of Mount Mottarone (about 5,000 feet). From here, you get great views of neighboring peaks and, by taking a short hike, a bird's-eye view of the small, neighboring Lake Orta.

Cost and Hours: €18 round-trip, €11 one-way, daily 9:30-17:40 in summer, 8:10-17:20 in winter, 2-3/hour, bar midway up, tel. 0323-30295, www.stresa-mottarone.it.

Activities: To visit the **Alpine Gardens,** get off at the midway Alpina stop, where a 10-minute walk leads to the gardens (turn left as you leave; €3, April-Oct daily 9:30-18:00, closed Nov-March). The gardens come with great lake views and picnic spots, but can't compare to what you'll see on the islands.

If you plan to **hike** down, pick up the *Trekking Map* from the TI and allow four hours from the top of Mount Mottarone, or two hours from the Alpine Gardens.

You can rent a **bike** at the base of the cable-car lift (ask TI for details) and bring it on the cable car with you. It's a treacherous ride, enjoyable only for serious bikers. While the ride is nice on top, you'll fight traffic on congested, rough, and windy roads for the rest of the descent.

Day Trips from Stresa

▲Scenic Boat and Rail Trip to Locarno and Centovalli

This enjoyable all-day excursion from Stresa involves three segments. Before you embark on the trip, confirm all times, particularly the departure of the last boat from Locarno. Take the train from Stresa to Domodossola, then catch the "Centovalli" train for a 1.5-hour ride that links together remote mountain villages on your way to Locarno, in the Italian-speaking Swiss canton of Ticino (bring your passport). Spend an hour or so exploring this town, on the far end of Lake Maggiore. Then take the boat past loads of small lakeside hamlets back to Italy. As a relaxing finale, you'll cruise into your home port of Stresa. The trip can also be done in reverse (with the boat trip first). A special €32 "Lago Maggiore Express" ticket covers both the train and boat (purchase at the ferry dock in advance or email ahead of time if you want to eat on board; toll-free tel. 800-551-801, tel. 0322-233-200, www.lagomaggiore-express.com, infomaggiore@navigazionelaghi.it).

▲Lake Orta

Just on the other side of Mount Mottarone is the small lake of Orta. The lake's main town, Orta San Giulio, has a beautiful lakeside

piazza ringed by picturesque buildings. The piazza faces the lake with a view of Isola San Giulio. Taxi boats (€4 round-trip) make the five-minute trip throughout the day. The island is worth a look for the Church of San Giulio and the circular "path of silence," which takes about 10 minutes. In peak season, Orta is anything but

silent, but off-season or early or late in the day, this place is full of peace and magic (TI open Sat-Sun 9:30-17:30, closed Mon-Fri, on Via Panoramica next to the parking lot downhill from the train station, tel. 0322-905-163).

Getting There: The train ride from Stresa to Orta-Miasino (a short walk from the lakeside piazza) takes 1.5-2 hours and requires a change or two (9/day). Public buses from Stresa's Piazza Marconi to Orta depart from near the TI (around €9 round-trip, 3/day mid-June-mid-Sept, confirm schedule at TI or at www.safduemila.com).

Sleeping in Stresa

Because Stresa's town is just a resort, I'd day-trip from Milan. But here are some good options if you'd like to stay.

$$ Hotel Saini Meublè is a cozy, 14-room place with rustic stonework and hardwood floors, located in a pedestrian zone a couple of blocks from the boat dock in the old center (Sb-€82, Db-€105, lower prices off-season, these rates promised to Rick Steves readers through 2014, elevator, guest computer and free Wi-Fi; Via Garibaldi 10, from Piazza Matteotti head up Via Mazzini and turn left on Via Garibaldi, tel. 0323-934-519, www.hotelsaini.it, info@hotelsaini.it). Gianni (Johnny) greets you at reception.

$$ Hotel Milan au Lac and its sister hotel next door, the yellow-brick **Speranza au Lac,** are impersonal four-star corporate-style hotels that cater mostly to tour groups, with 167 predictably comfortable rooms across from the boat dock (to the right as you leave the boat). Reception for both hotels is in Hotel Milan au Lac (Db-€125-160 depending on season and view, air-con, elevator, pay guest computer and Wi-Fi, laundry service, generally closed Nov-

March, Piazza Marconi 6/9, tel. 0323-31178, www.milansperanza.
it, info@milansperanza.it).

$$ Hotel Moderno offers 54 peaceful and well-maintained
pastel rooms on a pedestrian street a block from the main square
(Sb-€98, Db-€150, discount for Rick Steves readers depending
on availability, air-con, elevator, guest computer and free Wi-Fi,
closed Nov-mid-March, Via Cavour 33; from the main square,
with your back to the lake, find the church—hotel is behind the
church on pedestrian street parallel to main road; tel. 0323-933-
773, www.hms.it, moderno@hms.it).

$ Albergo Luina offers seven basic rooms above a restaurant
(Sb-€62, Db-€95, breakfast-€4; 2 blocks off Piazza Matteotti—
with back to lake, go left up small street; Via Garibaldi 21, tel.
0323-30285, luinastresa@yahoo.it, Cattia).

Eating in Stresa

Osteria degli Amici serves up tasty €10 risottos and pastas, with
fast and friendly service under a canopy of grape and kiwi leaves (€7
wood-fired pizzas, daily 12:00-14:15 & 18:30-22:30, closed Wed
Sept-June, deep in the old town past Piazza Cadorna at Via Bolon-
garo 33, tel. 0323-30453).

Le Botte offers a variety of Piedmont's regional specialties
in a pub-grub casual atmosphere (€7-9 pastas, €9-15 *secondi*, daily
12:00-15:00 & 19:00-22:30 in summer, closed Thu Oct-March and
all of Jan-Feb, Via Mazzini 6/8, tel. 0323-30462).

Ristorante il Portico is a cheerful, energetic place featur-
ing several €16-26 multicourse tasting samplers and daily market
specials on sidewalk tables or in their airy, fresh dining room. It's
smart to reserve (piping-hot €6-10 pizzas, €7-10 pastas, €12-16
secondi, daily 12:00-16:00 & 19:00-24:00, closed off-season, Via
Ottolini 9, tel. 0323-934-510).

Ristorante Taverna del Pappagallo is a bustling place with
hardworking servers and happy locals. A glass case of desserts
tempts you on the way in, but first try one of their shareable dishes,
such as risotto with fish fresh from the lake, or their "moneybags"
ravioli with pears and cheese (€6-10 pizzas, €7-10 pastas, €8-16
secondi, Thu-Tue 12:00-14:30 & 18:30-22:30, closed Wed, Via
Principessa Marghertia 46, tel. 0323-30411).

Il Clandestino is a classy splurge. Lively Franco serves up
creative fish and pasta dishes made with only the freshest ingredi-
ents (€15-18 pastas, €20 *secondi*, more expensive fixed-price menu
available, Wed-Mon 19:15-23:00, Fri-Sun also 12:30-14:30, closed
Tue, Via Rosmini 5, tel. 0323-30399).

La Rosa dei Venti, on the touristy main drag, has €5-8 pizzas
and lakefront dining. They offer homemade pastas and creative ri-

sottos for €8-11 (big €8-10 salads, €14-19 *secondi*, daily 12:00-14:30 & 19:00-22:30, closed Tue off-season, 2 blocks south of the boat dock at Corso Italia 50, tel. 0323-31431).

The main square, **Piazza Cadorna,** is a carnival of residents selling things to tourists. Still, at night it has a certain charm. It seems anyone who claims to be a musician can get a gig singing for diners. **Pizzeria Centrale** (on a platform in the center) is a good place to enjoy the ambience. Their pizzas are decent, but don't order any serious food here.

Stresa Connections

From Stresa by Train to: Milan (about hourly, 1-hour fast train—but there can be gaps in service so check timetable carefully, 1.5-hour slow train), **Varenna** (roughly every two hours, 2.75-4 hours, transfer in Milan), **Venice** (7/day, 4-4.5 hours, transfer in Milan), **Domodossola** (near the Swiss border, almost hourly, 30 minutes).

To Malpensa Airport: For a **train-bus combination,** take the train toward Milan (departs hourly) and get off at Gallarate (after about 40 minutes), where cheap shuttle buses run to Malpensa's Terminal 1 (€2, pay driver, about 1-2/hour, 25 minutes). From Gallarate, the bus departs from the train station and runs 5:55-19:20; from Malpensa's Terminal 1, the bus runs 5:34-19:00 (tel. 0331-258-411, www.sea-aeroportimilano.it/en). For an early-morning flight, the first Stresa-Milan train departs at 5:45, connecting with Gallarate's second or third bus departure for Malpensa (confirm schedules locally).

Alibus Airport buses run between Stresa and Malpensa (€12, mid-April-Sept, 50 minutes, leaves Stresa from in front of the church next to Hotel Milan au Lac—near the ferry dock and TI—at 6:30, 9:30, 11:30, 13:30, 16:30, and 19:30, leaves airport from bus stop 22 outside Terminal 1 at 8:30, 11:30, 13:30, 15:30, 18:30, and 21:00; confirm schedule, must reserve by 11:00 the previous day or by 11:00 Sat if booking for Sun or Mon bus—call 0323-552-172, book online at www.safduemila.com, or email alibus@safduemila.com).

Taxis to the airport cost €100 (1-5 people, €110 if traveling at night, 22:00-7:00) and take about an hour; your hotel can arrange the taxi for you, but will charge extra for booking it. It's easy to arrange a taxi on your own at the train station's taxi stand. Salvo Taxi is reliable (mobile 335-707-8894).

MILAN

Milano

For every church in Rome, there's a bank in Milan. Italy's second city and the capital of Lombardy, Milan is a hardworking, fashion-conscious, time-is-money city of 1.3 million. It's a melting pot of people and history. Milan's industriousness may come from the Teutonic blood of its original inhabitants, the Lombards, or from the region's Austrian heritage. Milan is Italy's fashion, industrial, banking, TV, publishing, and convention capital. The economic success of postwar Italy can be attributed, in part, to this city of publicists and pasta power lunches.

As if to make up for its rough, noisy big-city-ness, the Milanesi people are works of art. Milan is an international fashion capital with a refined taste. Window displays are gorgeous, cigarettes are chic, and even the cheese comes gift-wrapped. Yet thankfully, Milan is no more expensive for tourists than other Italian cities.

Three hundred years before Christ, the Romans called this place Mediolanum, or "the central place." By the fourth century A.D., it was the capital of the western half of the Roman Empire. Emperor Constantine issued the Edict of Milan from here, legalizing Christianity. After some barbarian darkness, medieval Milan became a successful mercantile city, eventually rising to regional prominence under the Visconti and Sforza families. By the time of the Renaissance, it was nicknamed "the New Athens," and was enough of a cultural center for Leonardo da Vinci to call it home. Then came 400 years of foreign domination (Spain, Austria, France, more Austria). Milan was a center of the 1848 revolution against Austria, and helped lead Italy to unification in 1870.

Mussolini left a heavy fascist touch on the architecture here (such as the central train station). His excesses also led to the

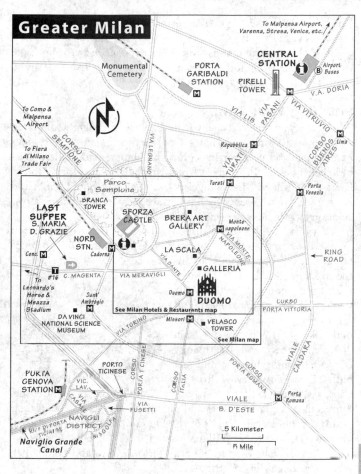

WWII bombing of Milan. But the city rose again. The 1959 Pirelli Tower (the skinny skyscraper in front of the station) was a trendsetter in its day. Today, Milan is people-friendly, with a great transit system and inviting pedestrian zones. And the city is busy with construction projects in an effort to beef up both its infrastructure and cultural offerings as it prepares to host the 2015 World's Fair in the Rho-Pero district. The area is revamping its layout with new parks, museums, and American-style skyscrapers to welcome the expected 20 million visitors. An estimated 130 to 150 countries will display exhibits about their contributions to sustainable development (for more information, see http://en.expo2015.org).

Many tourists come to Italy for the past. But Milan is today's Italy, and no trip to this country is complete without visiting it. While it's not big on the tourist circuit, the city has plenty to see.

And fortunately, seeing Milan—so manageable and well-organized—is not difficult.

For pleasant excursions from the city, consider visiting Lake Como or Lake Maggiore—both are about an hour from Milan by train (see The Lakes chapter).

Planning Your Time

OK, it's a big, intense city, so you probably won't linger. Compared to Rome and Florence, Milan's art is mediocre, but the city does have unique and noteworthy sights: the Duomo and Galleria Vittorio Emanuele II, Pinacoteca Ambrosiana, La Scala Opera House, Brera Art Gallery, Michelangelo's last *Pietà* in Sforza Castle, and Leonardo's *Last Supper* (which is hard to see without making a reservation long in advance—see page 349).

With two nights and a full day, you can gain an appreciation for the town and see the major sights. On a short visit, I'd focus on the center. Tour the Duomo, hit the art you like, browse through the elegant shopping area and the Galleria Vittorio Emanuele II, and try to see an opera. Technology buffs like the Leonardo da Vinci National Science and Technology Museum, while history and art buffs dig the city's early Christian churches, Brera Gallery, Pinacoteca Ambrosiana, and Museo del Novecento. People-watchers and pigeon-feeders could spend their entire visit never losing sight of the Duomo. And if you dig burial grounds, rattle through Milan's evocative Monumental Cemetery. To maximize your time in Milan, use the Metro and note which places stay open through the siesta.

Since Milan is a cold Italian plunge, and most flights to the US leave Milan early in the morning, you could save it for the end of your trip and start your journey softly by going directly by train from Milan to Lake Como (one-hour ride to Varenna) or the Cinque Terre (3-4 hours to Monterosso). Then spend the last night or two of your trip in Milan before flying home.

Monday is a terrible sightseeing day, since many museums are closed (including the church that houses Leonardo's *Last Supper*). August is oppressively hot and muggy, and locals who can vacate at this time do, leaving the city pretty quiet. Those visiting in August find that the nightlife is sleepy and many shops and restaurants are closed. Some hotels are closed; other hotel rooms are on the discounted push list.

A Three-Hour Tour: If you're just changing trains in Milan's Centrale Station (as, sooner or later, you probably will), consider catching a later train and taking this blitz tour: Check your bag at the station, pick up a city map at the station TI, ride the subway to the Duomo, peruse the square, explore the cathedral's rooftop and interior, have a scenic coffee in the Galleria Vittorio Emanuele II, spin on the floor mosaic of the bull for good luck, see a museum or two (most are within a 10-minute walk of the main square), and return by subway to the station. Art fans could make time for *The Last Supper* (if they've made reservations), the Michelangelo *Pietà* in Sforza Castle (no reservations necessary), the Brera Art Gallery, or the Pinacoteca Ambrosiana (with its Leonardo exhibit).

Orientation to Milan

My coverage focuses on the old center. Most sights and hotels are within a 10-minute walk of the cathedral (Duomo), which is a straight eight-minute Metro ride from the central train station.

Tourist Information

Milan has two TIs: The main TI is at Piazza Castello 1 (near Sforza Castle), and the other is at the Milano Centrale train station, in front of track 13 (both share the same hours: Mon-Fri 9:00-17:00, Sat-Sun 9:00-12:30, main TI tel. 02-7740-4343, train-station TI tel. 02-7740-4318, www.visitamilano.it). You can book Autostradale and Zani Viaggi city tours (see "Tours in Milan," later) at the companies' offices on Piazza Castello, near the main TI.

I've listed enough sights to keep you very busy for two days, but there's much more to see in Milan. Its many thousand-year-old churches make it clear that Milan was an important beacon in the Dark Ages. The TI and local guidebooks can point you in the right direction if you have more time.

Arrival in Milan

By Train at Milano Centrale: The huge, sternly decorated, fascist-built (in 1931) central train station is a sight in itself. Recently cleaned, the halls feel more monumental than ever. Notice how the art makes you feel small—it emphasizes that a powerful state is a good thing. In the front lobby, heroic people celebrate "modern" transportation (circa-1930 ships, trains, and cars) opposite reliefs depicting old-fashioned sailboats and horse carts.

The station has three levels of **shops and services.** The WCs are by track 22 (€1, daily 6:00-24:00). Stepping out of the platform area and into the shopping corridor, you'll find the big neon-green cross of the 24-hour pharmacy to your left. If you ride the moving walkways down two more levels, you'll reach the **Trenitalia ticket office** (daily 5:50-22:20) and user-friendly ticket sales machines (gray-and-blue for local train services only, red-white-and-green

Rome vs. Milan: A Classic Squabble

In Italy, the North and South bicker about each other, hurling barbs, quips, and generalizations. All the classic North/South traits can be applied to Milan (the business capital) and Rome (the government and religious capital). People like to say that people come to Milan to sin and go to Rome to ask for forgiveness. Although the differences have become less pronounced lately, the sniping continues.

The Milanesi say the Romans are lazy. Roman government jobs come with short hours—cut even shorter by too many coffee breaks, three-hour lunches, chats with colleagues, and phone calls to friends and relatives. Milanesi contend that "Roma *ladrona*" (Rome, the big thief) is a parasite that lives off the taxes of people up North. There's still a strong Milan-based movement seriously promoting secession from the South.

Romans, meanwhile, dismiss the Milanesi as uptight workaholics with nothing else to live for—gray like their foggy city. Romans do admit that in Milan, job opportunities are better and based on merit. And the Milanesi grudgingly concede the Romans have a gift for enjoying life.

While Rome is more of a family city, Milan is the place for

for all Italian trains, credit cards and cash accepted, you can't buy international tickets from machines). Also on this level, you'll find taxis, travel agencies, shuttle buses to the airports, and a baggage check (marked *deposito bagagli*, €5/5 hours, €13/24 hours, 5-day maximum, daily 6:00-23:00, passport required, 45-pound bag limit). Just outside the front entrance of the station are car-rental offices and the Metro (clearly marked). An ATM is on the lower Metro level.

The **365 Travel Agency**—which sells train tickets, supplements, and night-train berth reservations—has three offices at the station. One is across from the baggage-check *deposito* desk (has longest hours, daily 7:00-21:00, agency tel. 02-6738-2603, www.agenzie365.it); another is outside facing the airport shuttle buses on Piazza Luigi di Savoia; and a third is on the opposite side of the station near the Sisley fashion store (with your back to the tracks, exit right). Their 7 percent commission can be a reasonable price to pay to skip the Trenitalia ticket lines.

Taking the Metro from Milano Centrale to the Duomo and Back: For a quick visit, it's a straight shot on the underground from Centrale Station to the Duomo: Buy a €1.50 ticket at a kiosk or

high-powered singles on the career fast track. Milanese yuppies mix with each other...not the city's longtime residents. Milan is seen as wary of foreigners and inward-looking, and Rome as fun-loving, tolerant, and friendly. In Milan, bureaucracy (like social services) works logically and efficiently, while in Rome, accom-

plishing even small chores can be exasperating. Everything in Rome—from finding a baby-sitter to buying a car—is done through friends. Meanwhile, people in Milan are more private.

Milanesi find Romans vulgar. The Roman dialect is considered one of the coarsest in the country. Much as they try,

Milanesi just can't say "Damn your dead relatives" quite as effectively as the Romans. Still, Milanesi enjoy Roman comedians and love to imitate the accent.

The Milanesi feel that Rome is dirty and Roman traffic nerve-wracking. But despite the craziness, Rome maintains a genuine village feel. People share family news with their neighborhood grocer. Milan lacks people-friendly piazzas, and entertainment comes at a high price. But in Rome, *la dolce vita* is as close as the nearest square, and a full moon is enjoyed by all.

from the machines, follow signs for yellow line 3 (direction: San Donato), and after an eight-minute ride (four stops), you'll be facing the cathedral. To return, ride the same yellow line 3 back the other way (direction: Comasina).

By Train at Milano Cadorna: You're most likely to use this humble little commuter railway station for its airport shuttle train. Malpensa Express generally uses track 1. The station has WCs, taxis, and handy eateries; the Cadorna Metro station is directly in front.

By Train at Milano Porta Garibaldi: Italo trains—Italy's new, privately run high-speed service to Florence, Rome, and Naples (see page 1166)—use Porta Garibaldi Station, north of the city center and not far from Milano Centrale (see map on page 323). High-speed TGV trains from Paris also use this station. As Milan's busiest commuter station, Porta Garibaldi is also served by many bus lines and Metro line 2 (green).

By Car: Leonardo never drove in Milan. Smart guy. Driving is bad enough in Milan to make the €20/day fee for a downtown garage a blessing. If you're driving, do Milan (and Lake Como) before or after you rent your car, not while you've got it. If you have a car, use the well-marked suburban *parcheggi* (parking lots), which offer affordable (€6/day) and safe parking at city-edge subway stations, with easy access to the center by Metro.

By Plane: Frequent shuttle trains and buses connect the airports and Milano Centrale train station both conveniently and economically. See "Milan Connections" at the end of this chapter.

Helpful Hints

Theft Alert: Be on guard. Milan's thieves target tourists, especially at the central train station, getting in and out of the subway, and around the Duomo. They can be dressed as tourists, businessmen, or beggars, or they can be gangs of too-young-to-arrest children. Watch out for ragged people carrying newspaper and cardboard—they'll thrust this item at you as a distraction while they pick your pocket. If you're ripped off and plan to file an insurance claim, fill out a report with the police (Police Station, "Questura," Via Fatebenefratelli 11, Metro: Turati, open daily 24 hours, tel. 02-62261). For police emergencies, call 113. For lost or stolen credit cards, see page 17.

US Consulate: It's at Via Principe Amedeo 2/10 (Metro: Turati, tel. 02-290-351 for recorded info and phone tree, http://milan.usconsulate.gov).

Medical Help: Dial 118 for medical emergencies. There are two medical clinics with emergency care facilities: the **International Health Center** in Galleria Strasburgo (Mon-Thu 9:00-19:00, Fri 9:00-18:00, closed Sat-Sun, between Via Durini and Corso Europa, at #3, third floor, Metro: San Babila, tel. 02-7634-0720), and the **American International Medical Center** at Via Mercalli 11 (Mon-Fri 9:00-17:30, closed Sat-Sun, Metro: Missori or Crocetta, call for appointment, tel. 02-5831-9808, mobile 335-570-1055). A 24-hour pharmacy is in the central train station; look for the neon-green cross.

Street Markets: Milan has two very popular flea markets. **Fiera di Sinigallia** spills into a lot at Porta Genova every Saturday (8:30-17:00, Metro: Porta Genova). If you continue along Viale d'Annunzio to Viale Papiniano, you'll run into the **Papiniano** market (Tue 7:00-13:00 and Sat 7:30-17:00). Small street markets are held every morning except Sunday in various neighborhoods; *Hello Milano* has a complete listing (www.hellomilano.it).

Internet Access: Underground, in the Duomo Metro station, the **Secure Money Center** offers Internet access (€2/30 minutes).

Bookstores: The handiest major bookstore, with fiction and guidebooks in English, is **La Feltrinelli,** under the Galleria Vittorio Emanuele II (daily 10:00-23:00, enter through Autogrill restaurant on Piazza del Duomo, tel. 02-8699-6903).

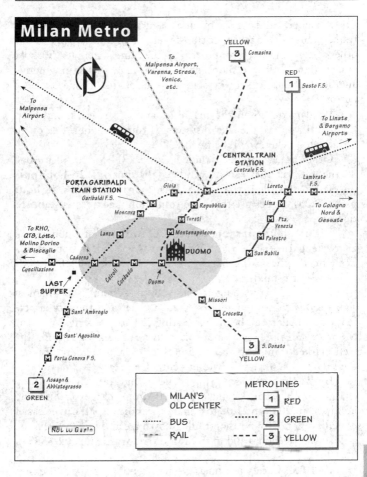

Milan Metro

YELLOW 3 Comasina

RED 1 Sesto F.S.

To Malpensa Airport, Varenna, Stresa, Venice, etc.

To Malpensa Airport

To Linate & Bergamo Airports

CENTRAL TRAIN STATION
Centrale F.S.

PORTA GARIBALDI TRAIN STATION
Garibaldi F.S.

Gioia

Lambrate F.S.

Loreto

Repubblica

Lima

To Cologno Nord & Gessate

Moscova

Turati

Pta. Venezia

To RHO, QT8, Lotto, Molino Dorino & Bisceglie

Lanza

Montenapoleone

Palestro

Cadorna

DUOMO

San Babila

Conciliazione

Cairoli Cordusio

Duomo

LAST SUPPER

Missori

Sant'Ambrogio

Crocetta

Sant'Agostino

Porta Genova F.S.

3 S. Donato
YELLOW

2 Assago & Abbiategrasso
GREEN

Not to Scale

MILAN'S OLD CENTER

BUS

RAIL

METRO LINES

1 RED

2 GREEN

3 YELLOW

The **American Bookstore** is at Via Camperio 16, near Sforza Castle (Mon-Sat 10:30-19:00, closed Sun, tel. 02-878-920).

Travel Agencies: You can buy train tickets and reserve an overnight berth *(cuccetta)* at the **365 Travel Agency**'s train station locations (listed earlier, under "Arrival in Milan") or at any number of downtown travel agencies.

Getting Around Milan

By Public Transit: Use Milan's great subway system. The clean, spacious, fast, and easy three-line Metro zips you nearly anywhere you may want to go, and trams and city buses fill in the gaps. The handiest Metro line for a quick visit is the yellow line 3, which connects the central train station to the Duomo. The other lines are red (1) and green (2). "ATM" is the acronym for the Milan public transit system. Public transit usually runs until about midnight.

A **ticket,** valid for 75 minutes, can be used for one subway, tram, or bus ride, including a transfer either within the same or another system, but not a round-trip on the same system (€1.50; sold at newsstands, tobacco shops, shops with *ATM* sticker in window, and at machines in subway stations—select the "Urban Tickets" button).

Validate tickets in the machines at the turnstiles, and keep them until you exit the Metro system. If you're caught riding on an unvalidated ticket, you'll be fined €33.

Other ticket options include a *carnet* (€14 for 10 rides—one magnetic ticket that can be validated 10 times); a **24-hour pass** (€4.50, worthwhile if you take at least four rides); and a **48-hour pass** (€8.25). Passes use the same validation machines as standard tickets.

For transit information, visit the **ATM Point** (at Duomo stop, near Arengario exit, to right of Duomo as you face it, opposite La Scala ticket office, Mon-Sat 7:45-19:15, closed Sun, tel. 800-808-181, www.atm-mi.it).

I've keyed sightseeing to the subway system. Though most sights are within a few blocks of each other and the city is perfectly flat, Milan can be an exhausting city for walking. With the Metro, you'll rarely wait more than five minutes for a train. The well-marked trams can also be useful, especially to get to *The Last Supper* (tram #16) and the Monumental Cemetery (#12 or #14).

By Taxi: Small groups go cheap and fast by taxi (drop charge-€3.20, €1.10/kilometer; €5.20 drop charge on Sun and holidays, €6.20 from 21:00 to 6:00 in the morning). It can be easier to walk to a taxi stand than to flag down a cab. Handy stands are at Piazza del Duomo and in front of Sforza Castle (tel. 02-8585 or 02-6969).

By Bike: Locals use bikes to get around quickly and easily. Like many big cities in Europe, Milan has a public bike system, **BikeMi**. You can set up a temporary subscription (€6/week or €2.50/day) online or at an "ATM Point" public transit info office (a handy one is in the Duomo Metro station—see earlier). You'll receive a user code and password, allowing you to pick up a bike at any BikeMi station, generally located near Metro stations. Enter your code and password on the keypad, grab the assigned bike, and you're on your way. The system is designed for short uses (first 30 minutes free, then €0.50/each 30 minutes up to 2 hours, then €2/hour, www.bikemi.com, toll-free tel. 800-808-181).

Tours in Milan

Bus Tours

The three-hour **Autostradale** bus-and-walking tour is a good value, has a live guide describing the city's monuments in English, and guarantees you'll see Leonardo's *Last Supper*—useful if you haven't booked ahead for this important sight. The jam-packed itinerary also includes visits to the Duomo, Galleria Vittorio Emanuele II, Sforza Castle, and La Scala Opera House (€60, departs Tue-Sun at 9:30 and Fri-Sat at 13:00, no Mon tours). They also offer an express version of the same tour, which skips the walking portion and lasts 1.5 hours (€35, Tue-Sun at 11:00). Tours leave from Piazza del Duomo, next to the taxi stand at the far end of the square from the church. There are four ways to reserve this tour: Book online at least two days in advance at www.autostradale.it; ask your hotelier to book it for you; call the main TI at 02-7740-4343; or drop into the Autostradale office next to the TI at Piazza Castello 1 (Mon-Fri 8:30-18:00, Sat-Sun 9:00-16:00). Tickets may be available for the same-morning departure. To confirm details, call 02-7200-1304 or 02-3391-0794.

Zani Viaggi does a similar tour that includes *The Last Supper*. Guides lead two-language tours (always English, plus one other), departing Tuesday through Sunday at 9:30 and 14:30 from their office at Foro Bonaparte 76, near Sforza Castle (€65, 3.5 hours, no Mon tours; ticket office open Mon-Fri 9:00-19:00, Sat-Sun 9:00-15:00; online reservations must be made at least two days in advance, tel. 02-867-131, www.zaniviaggi.it, excursions @zaniviaggi.it)

CitySightseeing Milano has hop-on, hop-off buses that do a circuit of the major sights accompanied by a recorded commentary. With one ticket, you can get off at a stop, tour the sight, and hop back on the bus to resume your tour. While you can hop on at any of their stops, it's handiest at the Duomo (next to the taxi stand) and La Scala (€20/day—valid until 18:00, €25/48 hours, buy on board; April-Oct daily 9:30-19:25, 2/hour; Nov-March daily 9:30-17:30, hourly; tel. 02-867-131. www.city-sightseeing.it).

Local Guide

Lorenza Scorti is a hardworking young guide who knows her city's history and how to teach it (€135/3-hour tour, €270/day, same price for individuals or groups, evenings OK, mobile 347-735-1346, lorenza.scorti@libero.it). **Sara Cerri** is another good licensed local guide who enjoys teaching (€175/3 hours, then €50/hour, mobile 380-433-3019, www.walkingtourmilan.it, walkingtourmilan@gmail.com).

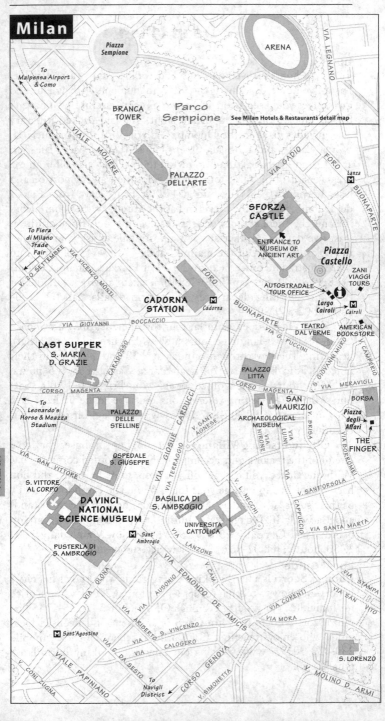

Milan

Piazza Sempione

ARENA

VIA LEGNANO

To Malpansa Airport & Como

Parco Sempione

BRANCA TOWER

VIALE MOLIERE

PALAZZO DELL'ARTE

See Milan Hotels & Restaurants detail map

VIA GADIO

FORO

Lanza M

VIA BUONAPARTE

SFORZA CASTLE

ENTRANCE TO MUSEUM OF ANCIENT ART

Piazza Castello

To Fiera di Milano Trade Fair

V. 20 SETTEMBRE

VIA VICENZO MONTI

FORO

ZANI VIAGGI TOURS

AUTOSTRADALE TOUR OFFICE

Largo Cairoli

M Cairoli

CADORNA STATION

M Cadorna

BUONAPARTE

VIA GIOVANNI BOCCACCIO

TEATRO DAL VERME

VIA G. PUCCINI

AMERICAN BOOKSTORE

V. CAMPERIO

LAST SUPPER

S. MARIA D. GRAZIE

V. CARADOSSO

VIA GIOSUE CARDUCCI

PALAZZO LITTA

S. GIOVANNI MURO

VIA MERAVIGLI

CORSO MAGENTA

CORSO MAGENTA

SAN MAURIZIO

BORSA

Piazza degli Affari

To Leonardo's Horse & Meazza Stadium

PALAZZO DELLE STELLINE

V. SANT' AGNESE

ARCHAEOLOGICAL MUSEUM

V. NIRONE

VIA LUINI

V. BRISA

VIA BORROMEI

THE FINGER

VIA SAN VITTORE

OSPEDALE S. GIUSEPPE

VIA TERRAGGIO

S. VITTORE AL CORPO

DA VINCI NATIONAL SCIENCE MUSEUM

BASILICA DI S. AMBROGIO

V. L NEGRI

V. SANT'ORSOLA

VIA CAPPUCCIO

VIA SANTA MARTA

UNIVERSITA CATTOLICA

PUSTERLA DI S. AMBROGIO

M Sant' Ambrogio

VIA LANZONE

VIA OLONA

V. CAM...

VIA EDMONDO DE AMICIS

VIA CORENTI

VIA STAMPA

VIA SAN VITO

VIA MORA

M Sant'Agostino

VIA ARIBERTO

S. VINCENZO

VIA G. DA SESTO

VIA CALOGERO

CORSO GENOVA

VIA SIMONETTA

S. LORENZO

VIALE PAPINIANO

V. CONI ZUGNA

To Navigli District

V. MOLINO D. ARMI

MILAN

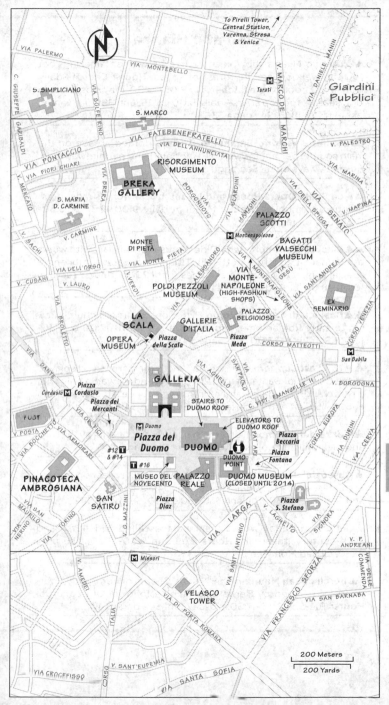

Milan at a Glance

▲▲**Duomo** Milan's showpiece cathedral, with an amazing roof you can walk on, amid a forest of spires. **Hours:** Church—daily 7:00-19:30, rooftop elevator—daily 9:00-18:00, may close later in high season; rooftop stairs—daily 9:00-20:15, until 19:30 in winter, last entry at 18:15. See page 336.

▲▲**Galleria Vittorio Emanuele II** Glass-domed arcade on the main square, perfect for window-shopping and people-watching. **Hours:** Always open. See page 341.

▲▲**La Scala Opera House and Museum** The world's most prestigious opera house. **Hours:** Museum daily 9:00-12:30 & 13:30-17:30. See page 343.

▲▲**Pinacoteca Ambrosiana** Oldest museum in Milan, with works by Raphael, Leonardo, Botticelli, Titian, and Caravaggio, and a special exhibit of Leonardo sketches (until 2015). **Hours:** Tue-Sun 10:00-18:00, closed Mon. See page 345.

▲▲**Basilica di Sant'Ambrogio** Historic, art-packed church dating to early Roman times. **Hours:** Mon-Sat 10:00-12:00 & 14:30-18:00, Sun 15:00-17:00. See page 348.

▲▲*The Last Supper* Leonardo da Vinci's masterpiece, displayed in the Church of Santa Maria delle Grazie, and viewable only with a reservation—book several months in advance. **Hours:** Tue-Sun 8:15-18:45 (last entry), closed Mon. See page 349.

▲**Piazza del Duomo** Milan's main square, full of energy, history, and pickpockets. **Hours:** Always open. See page 340.

▲**Museo del Novecento** Milan's 20th-century art collection, housed in the fascist-era City Hall. **Hours:** Mon 14:30-19:30, Tue-Wed, Fri, and Sun 9:30-19:30, Thu and Sat 9:30-22:30. See page 342.

▲**Gallerie d'Italia** Two adjacent palaces filled with 19th- and 20th-century Italian art. **Hours:** Tue-Sun 9:30-19:30, Thu until 21:30, closed Mon. See page 344.

▲**Church of San Maurizio** The "Sistine Chapel of Lombardy," gorgeously frescoed by Bernardino Luini, a follower of Leonardo. **Hours:** Tue-Sun 9:30-17:30, closed Mon. See page 347.

MILAN

▲**Leonardo da Vinci National Science and Technology Museum**
Leonardo's designs illustrated in wooden models, plus a vast collection of historical, scientific, and technological bric-a-brac and
machines. **Hours:** Tue-Fri 9:30-17:00, Sat-Sun 9:30-18:30, closed
Mon. See page 349.

▲**Brera Art Gallery** World-class collection of Italian paintings
(13th-20th century), including Raphael, Caravaggio, Gentile da
Fabriano, Piero della Francesca, Mantegna, and the Bellini brothers. **Hours:** Tue-Sun 8:30-19:00, closed Mon. See page 352.

▲**Risorgimento Museum** History of Italian unification. **Hours:**
Tue-Sun 9:00-13:00 & 14:00-17:30, closed Mon. See page 353.

▲**Sforza Castle** Milan's castle containing a museum whose highlight is an unfinished Michelangelo *Pietà*. **Hours:** Tue-Sun 9:00-
17:30, closed Mon. See page 354.

▲**Via Dante** Human traffic frolics to lilting accordions on one
of Europe's longest pedestrian-only boulevards. **Hours:** Always
open. See page 356.

▲**Naviglio Grande** Milan's old canal port—once a working-class
zone, now a trendy, atmospheric nightspot for dinner or drinks.
Hours: Always open. See page 357.

▲**Monumental Cemetery** Evocative outdoor art gallery with
tombs showcasing expressive art styles from 1870 to 1930. **Hours:**
Tue-Sun 8:00-18:00, closed Mon. See page 358.

Poldi Pezzoli Museum Italian paintings (15th-18th century), weaponry, and decorative arts. **Hours:** Wed-Mon 10:00-18:00, closed
Tue. See page 353.

Bagatti Valsecchi Museum 19th-century Italian Renaissance furnishings. **Hours:** Tue-Sun 13:00-17:45, closed Mon. See page 353.

Leonardo's Horse Gargantuan equestrian monument built according to Leonardo's designs. **Hours:** Tue-Sun 9:00-17:30,
closed Mon. See page 357.

MILAN

Sights in Milan

▲▲Duomo (Cathedral)

The city's centerpiece is the fourth-largest church in Europe (after the Vatican's, London's, and Seville's). At 525 by 300 feet, the place

is immense, with more than two thousand statues inside (and another thousand outside) and 52 one-hundred-foot-tall, sequoia-size pillars representing the weeks of the year and the liturgical calendar. If you do two laps, you've done your daily walk. It was built to hold 40,000 worshippers, the entire population of Milan when construction began. Ride the elevator or hike to the rooftop for a stroll through its forest of jagged spires.

Cost and Hours: Free entry; separate charges for treasury (€2), baptistery (€4), and roof climb (by **elevator**-€12, daily 9:00-18:00, may close later in high season, enter outside at north or south transept; or take **stairs**-€7, daily 9:00-20:15, until 19:30 in winter, last stair entry at 18:15, enter outside on north side, across from La Rinascente department store). Church open daily 7:00-19:30, Metro: Duomo, tel. 02-7202-2656, www.duomomilano.it.

Crowd-Beating Tips: The Duomo Point info center, behind the cathedral on the right-hand side, sells tickets for the Duomo's elevator and stairs. To avoid long ticket lines at the church, buy your ticket here, then go directly through the turnstile (daily 9:00-18:00, tel. 02-7202-3375, staff are helpful and speak English). The outdoor kiosk in front of, but not affiliated with, the info center also sells tickets for the same price during the same hours.

Dress Code: Modest dress is required. Don't wear shorts or anything sleeveless. Even kids with bare shoulders or knees are likely to be turned away at the door.

Audioguide: €5, Mon-Sat 8:30-17:00, no rentals Sun, 1.5 hours, available from kiosk immediately inside church.

Photography: The Duomo charges €2 for a special wristband (sold at audioguide kiosk) that allows you to take pictures.

Background

Back when Europe was fragmented into countless tiny kingdoms and dukedoms, the dukes of Milan wanted to impress their counterparts in Germany and France. Their goal was to earn Milan recognition and respect from both the Vatican and the kings and

princes of northern Europe by building a massive, richly orna-
mented cathedral. Even after Renaissance-style domes were in
vogue elsewhere in Italy, conservative Milan's cathedral stayed on
Gothic target. The dukes—thinking northerners would relate better to Gothic—loaded it with pointed arches and spires. For good
measure, the cathedral was built not from ordinary stone, but from
marble, top to bottom. Pink Candoglia marble was rafted in from
a quarry about 60 miles away, across Lake Maggiore and down a
canal to a port at the cathedral.

Built from 1386 to 1810, with the final touches added in 1965,
this construction project originated the Italian phrase for "never-
ending": "like building a cathedral." It started out Gothic (best
seen in the apse behind the altar) and was finished in the early
1800s under Napoleon (particularly the noteworthy west façade,
which is wonderful late in the day, with the sun low in the sky).
While the church is a good example of the Flamboyant, or "flame-
like," overripe final stage of Gothic, architectural harmony is not
its forte.

Self-Guided Tour of the Duomo

Begin by looping around the Duomo's exterior, then head inside to
enjoy its remarkable bulk, fine stained-glass windows, and Baroque
altar.

Exterior

Walk around the entire church exterior and notice the statues,
made between the 14th and 20th centuries by sculptors from all
over Europe. There are hundreds of these statues—each different and quite creative. Look at the statues on the tips of the many
spires...they seem so relaxed, like they're just hanging out, waiting
for their big day. Functioning as drain spouts, the 96 fanciful gar-
goyle monsters are especially imaginative.

As you stand outside at the back of the church, behind the
altar, imagine the glory of this first wall. These were the earliest
stones, laid in 1390. The sun-in-rose window was the proud symbol
of the city's leading Visconti family; it's flanked by the angel telling
Mary she's going to bear the Messiah. And behind you is a shrine
to the leading religion of the 21st century: soccer. The Football
Team store is filled with colorful vestments and relics of local soccer saints (go upstairs, daily 10:00-19:00).

Continue circling the cathedral. Back at the front, enjoy the
statues enlivening the facade. The lower ones—full of energy and
movement—are early Baroque, from about 1600. Of the five doors,
the center one is biggest. Made in 1907 in the Liberty Style, it features the Joy and Sorrow of the Virgin Mary. Sad scenes are on the
left, joyful ones on the right, and on top is the coronation of M

in heaven by Jesus, with all the saints and angels looking on. Step up close and study the fine reliefs.

Interior

Enter the church. Stand at the back of the fourth-longest nave in Christendom. The apse at the far end was started in 1386. The wall behind you wasn't finished until 1520. Even though the Renaissance had begun, builders stuck with the Gothic style. The two single stone-marble pillars behind you are the most precious ones in the church.

Notice two tiny lights: The little red one on the cross above the altar marks where a nail from the cross of Jesus is kept. This relic was brought to Milan by St. Helen (Emperor Constantine's mother) in the fourth century, when Milan was the capital of the Western Roman Empire. It's on display for three days a year (in mid-Sept). Now look high to the right, in the rear corner of the church, and find a tiny pinhole of white light. This is designed to shine a 10-inch sunbeam at noon onto the bronze line that runs across the floor, indicating where we are on the zodiac (but local guides claim they've never seen it work).

Stained-Glass Windows: Wander deeper into the church, up the right aisle. Check out the windows: 15th-century mosaics of brilliant and expensive colored glass (stained, not painted). Bought by wealthy families seeking the Church's favor, they face the south and get the most light. The altars below generally honor the patron who made each window possible. Pick out familiar scenes in the windows. The purpose was to teach the illiterate masses the way to salvation through stories of the Old Testament and the life of Jesus. On the opposite wall (left side), many of the windows are more modern—from the 16th to the 20th century—and are either made of dimmer, cheaper painted glass or are replacements for ones destroyed by the concussion of WWII bombs that missed the church but fell nearby.

There are a couple of stops of interest along the right aisle. Under the third window, you can trace the uninterrupted rule of 144 local archbishops back to A.D. 51.

The fifth window dates from 1470, just 90 years after the first stone of the cathedral was laid. The window shows the story of Jesus, from Annunciation to Crucifixion. In the bottom window, as the angel Gabriel tells Mary the news, the Holy Spirit (in the form of a dove) enters Mary's window and world. Compare the exquisite beauty of this window to the cruder 19th-century window on the right.

While construction up to this point was very fast, the church wasn't finished for centuries. Below this fifth window, check out the 1888 proposed plan for the west facade. (This plan wasn't used; the west front of the church was finally finished around 1900.)

The seventh window is modern, from the 1980s. Bright and bold, it celebrates two local cardinals (whose tombs and bodies are behind glass). This memorial to Cardinal Ferrari and Cardinal Schuster, who heroically helped the Milanese out of their post-WWII blues, is a reminder that this great church is more than a tourist attraction—it's a living part of Milan.

Altar: Belly up to the bar facing the high altar. While the church is Gothic, the area around the altar is Baroque—a dramatic stage-like setting, in the style of the Vatican in the 1570s (a Roman Catholic statement to counter the Protestant churches of the north, which were mostly Gothic). Napoleon crowned himself King of Italy under this dome in 1805. Now look to the rear up at the ceiling and see the fancy "carving" (between the ribs)—nope, that's painted. It looks expensive, but paint is more affordable than carved stone.

St. Bartolomeo Statue: Find the bald statue lit by the open door, by the wall in the south transept. This is a grotesque 16th-century statue of St. Bartolomeo, an apostle and first-century martyr skinned alive by the Romans. Walk behind the poor guy wearing his own skin like a robe to see his face, hands, and feet. Carved by a student of Leonardo da Vinci, this is a study in human anatomy learned by dissection, forbidden by the Church at the time.

Floor: Walk toward the altar and around the corner 30 steps, to a gate blocking entry to the apse. Look down at the fine 16th-century inlaid-marble floor. The pieces around the altar are original. You can tell that the black marble (quarried from Lake Como) is harder because it looks and feels less worn than the other colors (the white is from Lake Maggiore, the pink from Verona).

Windows: The apse is lit by three huge windows, all 19th-century painted copies. The originals, destroyed in Napoleonic times, were made of precious stained glass.

Other Sights in the Duomo

Crypt of St. Charles Borromeo and Treasury: Steps lead under the altar to the treasury and to the tombs of St. Charles Borromeo (1538-1584, the economic power behind the church) and his family. Charles was bishop of Milan, and the second most important hometown saint after St. Ambrose. Tarnished silver reliefs around the ceiling show scenes from Charles' life. The treasury, or *tesoro*, features empty reliquaries and carved ivories.

Paleo-Christian Baptistery: In the rear of the church (buy ticket at bookshop kiosk, same hours as the Duomo), you can climb down into the church that stood here long before the present one. Milan was an important center of early Christianity. In Roman times, Mediolanum's street level was 10 feet below today's level. You'll see the scant remains of an eight-sided baptistery (where saints Augustine and Ambrose were baptized) and a little church. Back then, since you couldn't enter the church until you were baptized (which didn't happen until age 18), churches had a little "holy zone" just outside for the unbaptized. This included a baptistery like this one.

Cathedral Rooftop: This is the most memorable part of a Duomo visit. You'll wander through a fancy forest of spires with great views of the city, the square, and—on clear days—the crisp and jagged Alps to the north. And, 330 feet above everything, La Madonnina overlooks it all. This 15-foot-tall gilded Virgin Mary is a symbol of the city.

You can climb the stairs or take the elevator; the entrances to both are outside the church (for specifics, see "Cost and Hours," earlier).

Near the Duomo, on or near Piazza del Duomo

▲▲Duomo Museum (Museo del Duomo)
This fine museum, currently closed for extensive renovation, offers an excellent opportunity to understand Milan's cathedral and see its original art close up. It may reopen as early as 2014; inquire locally for details.

▲Piazza del Duomo
Milan's main square is a classic European scene and a popular local gathering point. Professionals scurry, fashion-conscious kids loiter, and young thieves peruse.

Standing in the square (midway between the statue and the Galleria), you're surrounded by history. The **statue** is Victor Emmanuel II, first king of Italy. He's looking at the grand Galleria named for him. The words above the triumphal arch entrance read: "To Victor Emmanuel II, from the people of Milan."

Opposite the Galleria are the twin fascist buildings of the Arengario Palace, which houses the new **Museo del Novecento** (described later). Mussolini made grandiose speeches from their balconies. Study the buildings' relief panels, which tell—with fascist melodrama—the history of Milan. Between these buildings and the cathedral (set back a bit) is the historic ducal palace, **Palazzo Reale.** This building, now a venue for temporary art exhibits, was redone in the Neoclassical style by Empress Maria Theresa in the late 1700s, when Milan was ruled by the Austrian Habsburgs. For a fine view of the Duomo and the piazza, enter the fascist-style building closest to the cathedral through the museum, and go to the bar on the first floor (no ticket necessary, fine *aperitivo* happy hour). Behind the Duomo is a vibrant pedestrian shopping zone along Corso Vittorio Emanuele.

Behind the Victor Emmanuel II statue (opposite the cathedral, about a block beyond the square), hiding in a small courtyard, is **Piazza dei Mercanti,** the center of medieval Milan (described later).

▲▲Galleria Vittorio Emanuele II

A symbol of Milan is its great four-story glass-domed arcade on the cathedral square. This great iron-and-glass structure (part of

the age of Eiffel) was symbolic of a new modern era. Built during the heady days of Italian unification (c. 1870), it was the first building in town to have electric lighting, and from its inception, it provided an elegant and popular meeting place. (Sadly, its designer, Giuseppe Mengoni, died the day before the gallery opened.) Here you can turn an expensive cup of coffee into a good value by enjoying some of Europe's best people-watching.

The venerable **Bar Camparino** (at the entry), with a friendly staff and a Liberty-style interior typical of the age, is the former haunt of famous opera composer Giuseppe Verdi and conductor Arturo Toscanini, who used to stop by after their performances at La Scala. It's a fine place to enjoy a drink and people-watch (€3.50 for an espresso is a great deal if you relax and enjoy the view, or €1 at the bar just to enjoy the sumptuous interior). Once called the Campari café (after the wealthy family who originally owned it), this is considered the birthplace of the famous Campari bitter (€4.50 standing or €10 seated, Tue-Sun 7:30-20:00, closed Mon and Aug, tel. 02-8646-4435).

Wander around the gallery. Its art celebrates the establishment of Italy as an independent country. Around the central dome, patriotic mosaics symbolize the four major continents (sorry, Australia). The mosaic floor is also patriotic. The white cross in the center represents the king. The she-wolf with Romulus and Remus (on the south side—facing Rome) honors the city that, since 1870, has been the national capital. On the west side (facing Torino, the provisional capital of Italy from 1861-1865), you'll find that city's symbol: a *torino* (little bull). For good luck, locals step on his irresistible little testicles. Two local girls explained to me that it works better if you spin—two times, and it must be clockwise. Find the poor little bull and observe for a few minutes...it's a cute scene. With so much spinning, the mosaic is replaced every few years.

The gallery has held luxury shops from the beginning. Along with Gucci, Louis Vuitton, and Prada, you'll find Borsalino (at the end near Piazza della Scala), which has been selling hats here since the gallery opened in 1877.

If you cut through the Galleria to the other side, you'll pop out at Piazza della Scala, with its famous opera house and the Gallerie d'Italia (all described later).

▲Museo del Novecento

Milan's 20th-century art fills the twin buildings of Arengario Palace, Mussolini's fascist-era City Hall, facing Piazza del Duomo. In the beautifully laid-out museum, you'll work your way up the escalators and through the last century, one decade at a time. The first painting, at the top of spiral staircase, is *The Fourth Estate* by Pellizza da Volpedo, painted in 1901. It celebrates the socialism and humanitarian spirit that came with the arrival of the new century, preparing you for the spirit of the collection. The first rooms feature the work of Umberto Boccioni, a seminal Futurist working in Milan when the city was at the artistic forefront. His abstract scenes convey the speed and intensity of the new modern age. Along with paintings, there are sculptures from the 1930s by Arturo Martini and Fausto Melotti. Each section is well-described in English, and the capper is a fine panoramic view over Piazza del Duomo through grand fascist-era arches.

Cost and Hours: €5, audioguide-€5, Mon 14:30-19:30, Tue-Wed, Fri, and Sun 9:30-19:30, Thu and Sat 9:30-22:30, last admission one hour before closing, Pallazzo dell'Arengario at Via Marconi 1, tel. 02-8844-4061, www.museodelnovecento.org.

Piazza dei Mercanti

This small square, the center of political power in 13th-century Milan, hides one block off Piazza del Duomo (directly opposite the cathedral). A strangely peaceful place today, it offers a fine smattering of historic architecture that escaped the bombs of World War II.

The arcaded, red-brick building that dominates the square was the City Hall (Palazzo dei Regione). The market was held under the arcades below, with six gates representing the six main guilds. Facing the square (opposite the wellhead), the balcony with the coats of arms is where new laws were announced. Eventually two big families—Visconti and Sforza—took power, Medici-style, in Milan; the snake is their symbol. Running the show in Renaissance times, these dynasties shaped much of the city we see today, including the Duomo and the fortress. In 1454, the Sforza family made peace with Venice while enjoying a friendship with the Medici in Florence (who counseled them on becoming dominant as bankers), and ushered in a time of stability and peace, as the region's major city-states were run by banking families. This freed up money for that Renaissance generation to make art, not war.

This square also held the Palace of Justice (the 16th-century courthouse with the clock tower), the market (not food, but crafts: leather, gold, and iron goods), the bank, the city's first university, and its prison. All the elements of a great city were right here on the "Square of the Merchants."

On Piazza della Scala

To reach these sights, simply cut through the Galleria Vittorio Emanuele II from Piazza del Duomo.

Piazza della Scala

This smart little traffic-free square, out the back between the Galleria and the opera house, is dominated by a statue of Leonardo da Vinci. The statue (from 1870) is a reminder that Leonardo spent his best 20 years in Milan, with well-paid, steady work. He was the brainy darling of the Sforza family (who dominated Milan as the Medici family dominated Florence). Under the great Renaissance genius stand four of his greatest "Leonardeschi." (He apprenticed a sizable group of followers.) The reliefs show his various contributions as painter, architect, and engineer. Leonardo, wearing his hydro-engineer hat, re-engineered Milan's canal system, complete with locks. (Until the 1920s, Milan was one of Italy's major ports, with canals connecting the city to the Po River and Lake Maggiore. For more on this footnote of Milan's history, read about the Naviglio Grande on page 357.)

The statue of Leonardo is looking at a plain but famous Neoclassical building, arguably the world's most prestigious opera house (described next).

▲▲La Scala Opera House and Museum

Milan's famous Teatrale alla Scala opened in 1778 with an opera by Antonio Salieri (of *Amadeus* fame). Today, opera buffs can get

MILAN

a glimpse of the theater and tour the adjacent museum's extensive collection.

Cost and Hours: Museum—€6, daily 9:00-12:30 & 13:30-17:30, last entry 30 minutes before closing, Piazza della Scala, tel. 02-8879-7473, www.teatroallascala.org.

Museum: Well-described in English, the collection features things that mean absolutely nothing to the hip-hop crowd: Verdi's top hat, Rossini's eyeglasses, Toscanini's baton, Fettuccini's pesto, original scores, diorama stage sets, costumes, busts, portraits, and death masks of great composers and musicians. The museum allows you to peek into the actual theater. The stage is as big as the seating area on the ground floor. (You can see the towering stage box from Piazza della Scala across the street.) A recent five-year renovation corrected acoustical problems caused by WWII bombing and subsequent reconstruction. The royal box is just below your vantage point, in the center rear. Notice the massive chandelier made of Bohemian crystal.

Events in the Opera House: The show goes on at the world-famous La Scala Opera House. Schedules vary, but the opera season is nearly year-round (show time 20:00), and ballet and classical concerts are held from October through June. No performances are held in August (for information, call Scala Infotel Service, daily 9:00-18:00, tel. 02-7200-3744; for automated booking, call 02-860-775 and press 2 for English; or book online at www.teatroallascala.org). On the opening night of an opera, a dress code is enforced for men (suit and tie).

Tickets generally go on sale one month before a performance. Seats sell out quickly. On performance days, 140 sky-high gallery tickets are sold at a discount only at the box office (located down the left side of the theater toward the back on Via Filodrammatici, and marked with *Biglietteria Serale* sign). If you want a same-day discounted (but still not cheap) ticket, show up at 13:00 to get your name on the list. Return at 17:00 for the roll call. You must be present when your name is called in order to receive a voucher, which you'll then show at the ticket window to purchase a discounted ticket. One hour before show time, the box office sells any remaining tickets at a 25 percent discount. You can also buy tickets—but not the discounted ones—at a handy ticket office in the Duomo Metro station (daily 12:00-18:00, entrance is to right of the Duomo as you face it, underground, follow signs to *ATM Point*), as well as on the Internet (Web sales end one hour before show time).

▲Gallerie d'Italia

This museum fills two adjacent palaces on Piazza della Scala with the amazing art collections of two banks that once occupied these buildings. One palace dates from the 19th century and boasts the nicest Neoclassical interior I've seen in Milan; the other is 20th-century, Tiffany-like Historicism, with a hint of the coming Liberty Style. Impressive buildings in their own right, they are filled with the exquisite work of 19th- and 20th-century Italian painters. One has Romantic landscapes; Hyperrealistic, time-travel scenes of folk life; and Impressionism. And in the adjacent palace, marble reliefs by Antonio Canova are displayed in appropriately Neoclassical rooms, while upstairs you'll find dramatic scenes from the Risorgimento—showing the thrilling story of the unification of Italy. You can even go downstairs and peer into the original bank vault, which now stores racks and racks of paintings not on display.

Cost and Hours: Free entrance, free audioguides (for as long as the bank is feeling generous), Tue-Sun 9:30-19:30, Thu until 21:30, closed Mon, across from La Scala Opera House at Piazza della Scala 6, toll-free tel. 800-167-619, www.gallerieditalia.com.

West of the Duomo

These are listed roughly in the order you'll reach them, as you travel west from Piazza del Duomo. The first one is just a few short blocks from the cathedral, while the last is just over a mile away.

▲▲Pinacoteca Ambrosiana (with Leonardo exhibit)

This oldest museum in Milan was inaugurated in 1618 to house Cardinal Federico Borromeo's painting collection. And until 2015, the museum is both more expensive and more important, thanks to a long-running special exhibit displaying 22 pages from Leonardo's notebook. Think of your visit in two parts: the permanent collection of paintings (including the Leonardo Hall), and the last room, which has the notebook pages. While it's exciting to see the pages, the permanent material is still the highlight. Pick up the English-language map locating major works, and rent the €1 audioguide (80 minutes), which explains highlights of both the permanent and special exhibits.

Cost and Hours: €15, Tue-Sun 10:00-18:00, closed Mon, last entry at 17:00, near Piazza del Duomo at Piazza Pio XI 2, tel. 02-8069-2221, www.ambrosiana.eu.

Visiting the Museum: Pinacoteca Ambrosiana began as a teaching academy, which explains its many replicas of famous works of art. Highlights include original paintings by Botticelli, Caravaggio, and Titian.

As Cardinal Borromeo was a friend of **Jan Brueghel,** you'll find an entire room (#7) filled with delightful works by Brueghel and other Flemish masters. Study the wonderful detail in Brueghel's *Allegory of Fire* and *Allegory of Water*. The Flemish paintings are extremely detailed—many painted on copper to heighten the effect—and offer an insight into the psyche of the age. If the cardinal were asked why he enjoyed paintings that celebrated the secular life, he'd likely say, "Secular themes are God's book of nature."

Filling an entire wall, **Raphael's cartoon** served as an outline for the famous *School of Athens* fresco at the Vatican Museum. (A cartoon—*cartone* in Italian—is a large charcoal-on-canvas sketch that functions as a model for the making of a fresco.) While the Vatican's much-adored fresco is attributed entirely to Raphael, it was painted mostly by his students. But this *cartone* was wholly sketched by the hand of Raphael. To make the fresco, his assistants riddled this cartoon with pinpricks along the outlines of the characters, stuck it to the wall of the pope's study, and then applied a colored powder. When they removed the *cartone*, the characters' shapes were marked on the wall, and completing the fresco was a lot like filling in a coloring book. If you've seen the original fresco at the Vatican, you'll notice that the figure of Michelangelo (as a brooding stonecutter lounging on the steps in the foreground) is missing from the cartoon. Raphael added him to the fresco as a tribute after seeing Michelangelo's awe-inspiring work on the ceiling of the Sistine Chapel.

As Leonardo da Vinci spent many of his most productive years working in Milan, the city has an affinity for the Renaissance genius. The **Leonardo Hall,** with more of the gallery's permanent collection, features Leonardo's *Portrait of a Musician,* a copy of *The Last Supper,* and several fine Leonardo-type paintings by Bernardino Luini and other disciples. During his Milan years, Leonardo created *The Last Supper* and painted several other famous canvases. Of these other paintings, only the *Portrait of a Musician*—as delicate, mysterious, and thought-provoking as the *Mona Lisa*—remains in Milan. The large fresco filling the far wall—with Christ receiving the crown of thorns—is by Luini. I find the painting of *The Last Supper* most interesting. When the cardinal realized that Leonardo's marvelous frescoed original was fading, he commissioned a careful copy to be created here for posterity. Today, this copy gives a rare chance to appreciate the original colorful richness of the now-faded masterpiece.

The Leonardo Hall leads into the somber library called Federiciana Hall, where you'll find the special **Leonardo exhibit.** The gallery, which owns Leonardo's *Codex Atlanticus,* is showing 22 of its 1,119 pages in themed exhibits changing quarterly until 2015. Soft period music accompanies your time with the 22 glass cases, each displaying a well-lit page from the notebook (the audioguide, which explains each page of the current exhibit, is essential to fully enjoy your visit). Don't enter the special exhibit until you are done with the permanent collection, as it's a one-way system and re-entry isn't allowed.

Piazza degli Affari and a Towering Middle Finger

This square and monument mark the center of Milan's financial district. The bold fascist buildings in the neighborhood were built

MILAN

in the 1930s under Mussolini. Italy's major stock exchange, the Borsa, faces the square. Stand in the center, appreciate the modern take on ancient aesthetics (you're standing atop the city's ancient Roman theater), and find the stern statues representing various labors and occupations, and celebrating the nobility of workers—typical whistle-while-you-work fascist themes. Then notice the equally bold modern statue in the center. After a 2009 contest to find the most appropriate sculpture to grace the financial district, this was the winner. Of course, Italy has its financial problems, and a similar sentiment that powers the Occupy Movement in the US rumbles in this society as well. Here we see how "the 99 percent" feel when they stand before the symbol of corporate power in Italy. (Notice how the finger is oriented—it's the 1 percent, and not the 99 percent, that's flipping the bird.) The 36-foot-tall, Carrara marble digit was made by Maurizio Cattelan, the most famous—or, at least, most controversial—Italian sculptor of our age. *L.O.V.E.*, as the statue is titled, was temporary at first. But locals liked it, and, by popular demand, it's now permanent.

▲Church of San Maurizio

This church, part of a ninth-century convent built into a surviving bit of Milan's ancient Roman wall, dates from around 1500. Despite its simple facade, it's a hit with art lovers for its amazing cycle of Bernardino Luini frescos. Stepping into this church is like stepping into the Sistine Chapel of Lombardy.

Cost and Hours: Free, Tue-Sun 9:30-17:30, closed Mon, Corso Magenta 15 at the Monastero Maggiore, tel. 02-8645-0011.

Visiting the Church: Bernardino Luini (1480-1532), a follower of Leonardo, was also inspired by his contemporaries Michelangelo and Raphael. Sit in a pew and take in the art, which has the movement and force of Michelangelo and the grace and calm beauty of Leonardo.

Maurizio, the patron saint of this church, was a third-century Roman soldier who persecuted Christians, then converted, and eventually worked to stop those same persecutions. He's the guy standing on the pedestal in the upper-right, wearing a bright yellow cape. The nobleman who paid for the art is to the left of the altar. His daughter, who joined the convent here and was treated as a queen (as nuns with noble connections were), is to the right. And all around are martyrs—identified by their palm fronds.

The adjacent **Hall of Nuns,** where sisters were cloistered, is also full of fine paintings. Stepping into this fine room, behind the altar you'll find more amazing art, including fine Luini frescos above and around the wooden crucifix. The Annunciation scene on the arch features a cute Baby Jesus zooming down from heaven. The organ dates from 1554, and the venue, with its fine acoustics, is popular for concerts with period instruments. Explore the pictorial

Bible behind the wooden chairs. Luini's landscapes, which line the walls, were groundbreaking in the 16th century. Leonardo incorporated landscapes into his paintings, but Luini was among the first to make landscape the main subject of the painting.

In the adjacent archaeological museum, you can see part of the ancient city wall and a third-century Roman tower.

▲▲Basilica di Sant'Ambrogio

One of Milan's top religious, artistic, and historic sights, this church was first built on top of an early Christian martyr's cemetery by St. Ambrose around A.D. 380, when Milan had become the capital of the fading (and Christian) Western Roman Empire.

Cost and Hours: Free, Mon-Sat 10:00-12:00 & 14:30-18:00, Sun 15:00-17:00, Piazza Sant'Ambrogio 15, tel. 02-8645-0895, www.basilicasantambrogio.it.

❍ **Self-Guided Tour:** Ambrose was a local bishop and one of the great fathers of the early Church. He helped establish the Church by convincing Augustine, a pagan, to become Christian. (Augustine himself later became another great Church father.) The original fourth-century church was later (in the 12th century) rebuilt in the Romanesque style you see today.

The entry is an arcaded **atrium**—standard in many churches back when you couldn't actually enter the church until you were baptized. The non-baptized waited here during Mass. The courtyard is textbook Romanesque, with playful capitals and fanciful animals. Inset into the wall (right side, above the pagan sarcophagi) are stone markers of Christian tombs—a reminder that this church, like St. Peter's at the Vatican, is built upon an ancient Roman cemetery.

From the atrium, marvel at the elegant 12th-century **facade,** or west portal. It's typical Lombard medieval style. The local bishop would bless crowds from its upper loggia. As two different monastic communities shared the church and were divided in their theology, there were also two different bell towers.

Step into the **nave** and grab a pew. The mosaic in the apse features Jesus Pantocrator (creator of all) in the company of Milanese saints. Around you are pillars with Romanesque capitals and surviving fragments of 12th-century frescos that once covered the church.

The 12th-century **pulpit** sits atop a Christian sarcophagus dating from the year 400. Study its late-Roman and early-Christian iconography—Apollo on his chariot morphs into Jesus on a chariot. You can see the moment when Jesus gave the Old Testament (the first five books, anyway) to his apostles.

The precious, ninth-century golden **altar** has four ancient porphyry columns under an elegant Romanesque 12th-century canopy. The entire ensemble was taken to the Vatican during World

War II to avoid destruction. That was smart—the apse took a direct hit in 1943. The 13th-century mosaic was destroyed; today we see a reconstruction.

Step into the **crypt,** under the altar, to see the skeletal bodies of three people: Ambrose (in the middle, highest) and two earlier Christian martyrs whose tombs he visited before building the church.

Nearby: For a little bonus after visiting the church, consider this: The **Benedictine monastery** next to the church is now Cattolica University. With its stately colonnaded courtyards designed by Renaissance architect Donato Bramante, it's a fine student environment. It's fun to poke around and imagine being a student here.

▲Leonardo da Vinci National Science and Technology Museum (Museo Nazionale della Scienza e Tecnica "Leonardo da Vinci")

The spirit of Leonardo lives here. Most tourists visit for the hall of Leonardo—the core of the museum—with designs illustrated in wooden models. But Leonardo's mind is just as easy to appreciate by paging through a coffee-table edition of his notebooks in any bookstore. The rest of this immense collection of industrial cleverness is fascinating, with planes, trains, automobiles, ships, radios, old musical instruments, computers, batteries, telephones, chunks of the first transatlantic cable, interactive science workshops, and a 1960s "pocket-sized" submarine. Many exhibits include English descriptions. Some of the best exhibits (such as the Marconi radios) branch off the Leonardo hall. Ask for an English museum map from the ticket desk—you'll need it. Allow at least 1.5 hours here. On weekends, this museum is very popular with families, so come early or be prepared to wait in line.

Cost and Hours: €10, guided tour of submarine-€8; Tue-Fri 9:30-17:00, Sat-Sun 9:30-18:30, closed Mon; Via San Vittore 21, bus #50 or #58 from Sforza Castle, or tram #16—catch it just off Piazza del Duomo in direction: San Siro, or Metro: Sant'Ambrogio; tel. 02-485-551, www.museoscienza.org.

▲▲Leonardo da Vinci's *The Last Supper (Cenacolo)*

Housed in the Church of Santa Maria delle Grazie, this is one of the ultimate masterpieces of the Renaissance. Milan's leading family, the Sforzas, hired da Vinci to decorate the dining hall of the Dominican monastery that adjoins the church. This gift was essentially a bribe to the monks so that the Sforzas could locate their family tomb in the church. Ultimately, the French drove the Sforzas out of Milan, they were never buried here, and the Dominicans got a great fresco for nothing. Note that this is a small but very popular sight, and entry must be booked several months in advance (see "Reservations," later).

MILAN

Cost and Hours: €8, includes €1.50 reservation fee (9:30 and 15:30 visits require €3.25 extra for provided guided English tour). Open Tue-Sun 8:15-18:45 (last entry), closed Mon. Show up 20 minutes before your scheduled entry time. When an attendant calls your time, get up and move into the next room.

Reservations: Reservations are mandatory. Even though the hype surrounding *The Da Vinci Code* novel and movie has died down, spots are still booked several months in advance—so plan ahead. To minimize the humidity problem—even though the damage has already been done—only 900 visitors a day are allowed in. That's 25 tourists popping in every 15 minutes for exactly 15 minutes. Prior to your appointment time, you wait in several rooms to dehumidify, while doors close behind you and open up slowly in front of you. The posted information about Leonardo is mainly in Italian.

If you book by **phone,** you'll have a greater selection of days and time slots to choose from, since the website doesn't reflect cancellations, but you won't be able to reserve same-day tickets (tel. 02-9280-0360, or from the US dial 011-39-02-9280-0360, office open Mon-Sat 8:00-18:30, closed Sun; the number is often busy—once you get through, dial 2 for an English-speaking operator; the process takes about two minutes and you'll hang up with an appointed entry time and a number; pay with credit card upon booking).

If you book **online** using the official website, www.cenacolovinciano.net, choose "Cenacolo Vinciano." You'll see a calendar that shows available time slots for the current month. If the days are blank, it means that all the slots for those days have been filled. Be careful when you select the date—on European calendars, the first day of the week is Monday. If you can't find a spot when you need it, try calling instead, because cancellations show up on the website as booked slots.

Last-Minute Tickets: While "reservations are required," if spots are available (more likely on weekdays and first thing in the morning), you can sometimes book one at the desk (even if the *Sold Out* sign is posted). If fewer than 25 people show up for a particular time slot, you may get lucky. But those who show up without a reservation generally kill lots of time waiting around. Note that the Autostradale and Zani Viaggi bus tours (see "Tours in Milan," earlier) include entry to *The Last Supper*.

Audioguide: Consider the fine €3 audioguide. Its spiel fills every second of the time you're in the room—so try to start listening to it just before you enter (ideally in the waiting room while studying the reproduction of *The Last Supper*).

Photography: No photos are allowed.

Getting There: Take the Metro to Cadorna or Conciliazione (plus a 5-minute walk), or hop on tram #16 (catch it just off Piazza del Duomo on corner of Via Mazzini and Via Dogana), which drops you off in front of the Church of Santa Maria delle Grazie. The Science and Technology Museum (previous listing) is two blocks away.

Visiting *The Last Supper*: Because of Leonardo's experimental fresco technique, deterioration began within six years of *The Last Supper's* completion. The church was bombed in World War II, but—miraculously, it seems—the wall holding *The Last Supper* remained standing. A 21-year restoration project (completed in 1999) peeled away 500 years of touch-ups, leaving Leonardo's masterpiece faint but vibrant.

In a big, vacant whitewashed room, you'll see faded pastels and not a crisp edge. The feet under the table look like negatives. But the composition is dreamy—Leonardo captures the psychological drama as the Lord says, "One of you will betray me," and the apostles huddle in stressed-out groups of three, wondering, "Lord, is it I?" Some are scandalized. Others want more information. Simon (on the far right) gestures as if to ask a question that has no answer. In this agitated atmosphere, only Judas (fourth from left and the only one with his face in shadow)—clutching his 30 pieces of silver and looking pretty guilty—is not shocked.

The circle meant life and harmony to Leonardo. Deep into a study of how life emanates in circles—like ripples on a pool hit by a pebble—Leonardo positioned the 13 characters in a semicircle. Jesus is in the center, from whence the spiritual force of God emanates, or ripples out.

The room depicted in the painting seems like an architectural extension of the church. The disciples form an apse, with Jesus as the altar—in keeping with the Eucharist. Jesus anticipates his sacrifice, his face sad, all-knowing, and accepting. His feet even foreshadowed his death by crucifixion. Had the door, which was cut out in 1652, not been added, you'd see how Leonardo placed Jesus' feet atop each other, ready for the nail.

MILAN

The room was a refectory or dining room for the Dominican friars. Traditionally, they'd gather here to eat, with a Last Supper scene on one wall facing a Crucifixion scene on the opposite wall.

The perspective is mathematically correct. In fact, restorers found a tiny nail hole in Jesus' left eye, which anchored the strings Leonardo used to establish these lines. The table is cheated out to show the meal. Notice the exquisite lighting. The walls are lined with tapestries (as they would have been), and the one on the right is brighter in order to fit the actual lighting in the refectory (which has windows on the left). With the extremely natural effect of the light and the drama of the faces, Leonardo created a masterpiece.

North of the Duomo, in the Brera Neighborhood

▲Brera Art Gallery

Milan's top collection of Italian paintings (13th-20th century) is world-class, but it can't top Rome's or Florence's. Established in 1809 to house Napoleon's looted art, it fills the first floor above a prestigious art college.

Cost and Hours: €6, more during special exhibits, Tue-Sun 8:30-19:00, closed Mon, last entry 45 minutes before closing, free lockers just before the ticket counter, no photos, Via Brera 28, Metro: Lanza or Montenapoleone, tel. 02-722-631, www.brera. beniculturali.it. Since there are no English descriptions, consider renting the audioguide (€5, ID required).

Visiting the Museum: Enter the grand courtyard of a former monastery, where you'll be greeted by the nude *Napoleon with Tinkerbell* (by Antonio Canova). Climb the stairway (following signs to *Pinacoteca,* past all the art students), buy your ticket, and pick up an English map of the museum's masterpieces.

The gallery's highlights include works by late-Gothic master Gentile da Fabriano, hinting at the realism of the coming Renaissance (check out the lifelike flowers and realistic, bright gold paint—he used real gold powder, Room IV). Andrea Mantegna's *The Dead Christ* is a textbook example of feet-first foreshortening (Room VI). Room XVIII hosts a permanent glass-enclosed restoration lab, allowing you to see various restoration works in progress.

In Room XXI, notice how Crivelli employs Renaissance technique (he was a contemporary of Leonardo), yet clings to the mystique of the Gothic Age (that's why I like him so much). Find eight Crivellis. Also, don't miss Raphael's *Wedding of the Madonna,* Piero della Francesca's *Madonna and Child with Four Angels* (Room XXIV), and the gritty-yet-intimate realism of Caravaggio's *Supper at Emmaus* (Room XXIX). Room XXXV features several of Canaletto's picture-postcards of Venetian cityscapes. This is ahead-of-its-time Impressionism—there's not a single line in these works, just strategically placed daubs of paint that render palazzos and canals bathed in Venetian light with photographic precision. To spice things up, look for Francesco Hayez's hot and heavy *The Kiss (Il Bacio)* in Room XXXVII. You'll also find paintings by the great Venetian masters Tintoretto and Veronese.

Java junkies will seek out the great, cheap cappuccino machine: Go through Napoleon's courtyard and straight through the art school to the end of the long hall; the machine's on your left. It's fun to explore the art school on the ground floor, mill about among the many young students, and wonder if there's a 21st-century Leonardo in your midst.

▲Risorgimento Museum

With a quick 30-minute swing through this quiet one-floor museum, you'll get an idea of the interesting story of Italy's rocky road to unity: from Napoleon (1796) to the victory in Rome (1870). However, there isn't much information in English. It's just around the block from the Brera Art Gallery at Via Borgonuovo 23.

Cost and Hours: €2, Tue-Sun 9:00-13:00 & 14:00-17:30, closed Mon, Metro: Montenapoleone, tel. 02-8846-4176, www.museodelrisorgimento.mi.it.

Northeast of the Duomo, near Montenapoleone

Poldi Pezzoli Museum

This classy house of art features top Italian paintings of the 15th through 18th century, old weaponry, and lots of interesting decorative arts, such as a roomful of old sundials and compasses.

Cost and Hours: €9, Wed-Mon 10:00-18:00, closed Tue, last entry one hour before closing, free English audioguides, Via Manzoni 12, Metro: Montenapoleone, tel. 02-794-889, www.museopoldipezzoli.it.

Bagatti Valsecchi Museum

This unique 19th-century collection of Italian Renaissance furnishings was assembled by two aristocratic brothers who spent a wad turning their home into a Renaissance mansion. The beautiful but outrageously expensive café in its Renaissance courtyard might be worth the €5 cover charge just to be seen sipping tea with Milan's stylish elite.

Cost and Hours: €8, half-price on Wed, open Tue-Sun 13:00-17:45, closed Mon, free English audioguides and good English descriptions throughout, Via Gesù 5, Metro: Montenapoleone, tel. 02-7600-6132, www.museobagattivalsecchi.org.

Sforza Castle and Nearby
▲Sforza Castle (Castello Sforzesco)

The castle of Milan tells the story of the city in brick. Built in the late 1300s as a military fortress, it guarded the gate to the city wall and defended Milan from enemies "within and without." It was beefed up by the Sforza duke in 1450 in anticipation of a Venetian attack. Later, the Sforza family made it their residence and built their Renaissance palace into the fortress. It was even home to their in-house genius, Leonardo. (When he applied for a position with the Sforza family, he did so as a military engineer and contributed to the design of the ramparts.) During the time of foreign rule (16th-19th century), it was a barracks for occupying Spanish, French, and Austrian soldiers. And today it houses an array of museums. While your ticket covers all the museums (including Egyptian, music, and furniture), the Museum of Ancient Art is the one to visit.

Cost and Hours: €3, free entry 16:30-17:00 and Fri 14:00-17:00; open Tue-Sun 9:00-17:30, closed Mon, WCs and free lockers at the ticket counter, English info fliers throughout and at information office beside the Porta Umberto entrance, Metro: Cairoli, tel. 02-8846-3700, www.milanocastello.it.

○ Self-Guided Tour: This tour begins outside the fortress, then focuses on the Museum of Ancient Art.

The **gate** facing the city center stands above a ditch that was once filled with water. A relief celebrates Umberto I, the second king of Italy. Above that, a statue of St. Ambrose, the patron of Milan (and a local bishop in the fourth century), oversees the action. Notice the chart, just outside the gate, showing how the city was encircled first by a crude medieval wall, and then by a state-of-the-art 16th-century wall—of which this castle was a key element. It's apparent from the enormity of these walls that Milan was a strategic prize. Today, the walls are gone, giving the city two circular boulevards.

This immense brick fortress—exhausting at first sight—can only be described as heavy. While originally functioning as military parade grounds, today its three huge courtyards host concerts and welcome the public. (The holes in the walls were for scaffolding.)

Just past the ticket counter, the **Museum of Ancient Art** fills the old Sforza family palace with interesting medieval armor, furniture, early Lombard art, and—for your finale—Michelangelo's unfinished *Pietà Rondanini*. While the museum is huge, here are room-by-room highlights leading you to Michelangelo's *Pietà*.

In the first room, among ancient sarcophagi (with early Christian themes), stands a fine 14th-century **equestrian statue**—a memorial to Bernabò Visconti. Of the four virtues, he selected only two (strength and justice) to stand beside his anatomically correct horse, opting out of love and patience.

Next, the room of **tapestries** is dominated by a big embroidery of St. Ambrose defeating the heretical Arians. While that was a fourth-century struggle, 12 centuries later, he was summoned back in spirit to deal with Protestants, in the form of Archbishop Borromeo. As a Counter-Reformation leader, with St. Peter's Basilica behind him, Ambrose stands tall and strong in defense of the Roman Church. The room is lined by 16th-century Flemish tapestries, which were easy to pack up quickly as the nobility traveled. These were typical of those used to warm chilly stone palaces.

Next, you'll come to the **Sala delle Asse,** named for the mulberry garden that was used to feed silkworms. The Visconti family grew rich making silk in the Lake Como area. While plastered over for centuries, this room was restored around 1900. Not much sparkle survives, but you can appreciate the intricate canopy woven with branches and rope in complicated knots—the work of Leonardo himself, in 1498. The tiny Leonardo-esque painting of Madonna and Child is by Francesco Napoletano, a pupil of Leonardo. The painting's structure, anatomy, and subtle modeling of the color with no harsh lines *(sfumato)* are all characteristic of Leonardo. In the upper right, notice the castle, as it looked in 1495.

After browsing a room filled with weapons and armor from the 16th and 17th centuries, you reach the highlight of the mu-

seum—**Michelangelo's** *Pietà Rondanini.* This is a rare opportunity to enjoy a Michelangelo statue with no crowds. Michelangelo died while still working on this piece, his fourth *pietà.* A *pietà,* by definition, is a representation of a dead Christ with a sorrowful Virgin Mary. While unfinished and seemingly a mishmash of corrections and reworks, it's a thought-provoking work by a genius at nearly 90 years old, who knows he's fast approaching the end of his life. The symbolism is of life and of death: Jesus returning to his mother, as two bodies seem to become one.

Michelangelo's more famous *pietà* at the Vatican (carved when he was in his 20s) features a beautiful, young, and astonished Mary. Here, Mary is older and wiser. Perhaps Mary is now better able to accept death as part of life...as is Michelangelo. The *pietà* at the Vatican is simple and clear, showing two different people: the mother holding her dead son. Contemplating the *Pietà Rondanini,* you wonder who's supporting whom. It's confused and complex, each figure seeming to both need and support the other.

This unfinished statue is unique in that it shows the genius of Michelangelo midway through a major rework—Christ's head is cut out of Mary's right shoulder, and an earlier arm is still just hanging there. Above Mary's right ear, you can see the remains of a previous face (eye, brow, and hairline).

And there's a certain power to this rawness. Walk around the back to see the strain in Mary's back (and Michelangelo's rough chisel work) as she struggles to support her son. The sculpture's elongated form hints at the Mannerist style that would follow.

Notice the ancient Roman altar underneath the *Pietà*. Notice, also, the funeral portrait of Michelangelo, showing the artist as he looked when he died in 1564, working on this statue—still vibrant and seeking.

For a quick exit, continue past the *Pietà* exit, out the back side and into Sempione Park (described next).

Parco Sempione

This is Milan's equivalent of Central Park. With its circa 1900 English-style gardens, free Liberty-style aquarium, views of the triumphal arch, and sprawling family-friendly grounds, this park is particularly popular on weekends.

A five-minute walk through the park, on the left, is the erector-set **Branca Tower** (Torre Branca). You'll ride an elevator that takes you as high as the Mary that crowns the cathedral, for a commanding city view (€4, hours are erratic—call or confirm at TI before heading out, closed Mon and in bad weather, tel. 02-331-4120).

At the far end of the park is the monumental **Arco della Pace**. Originally an arch of triumph, it comes with Nike, goddess of victory, commanding a six-horse chariot. It was built facing Paris to welcome Napoleon's rule and to celebrate the ideals of the French Revolution, destined to lift Italy into the modern age. When they learned Napoleon was just another megalomaniac, they turned the horses around, their tails facing France. With Italian unification in the 1860s, its name was changed to "Arch of Peace."

▲Via Dante

This grand pedestrian boulevard and popular shopping street leads from Sforza Castle toward the town center and the Duomo. Via Dante was carved out of a medieval tangle of streets to celebrate Italian unification (c. 1870) and make Milan—the home of the king—a worthy capital city. Consequently, all the facades lining it are relatively new. Over the vigorous complaints of merchants, the street became traffic-free in 1995. Today, they'd have it no other way, and the street is popular with local shoppers and office workers on lunch breaks. Enjoy strolling this beautiful people zone, where you'll hear the whir of bikes and the lilting melodies of accordion players instead of traffic noise. Photo exhibits are frequently displayed up and down the street. In front of Sforza Castle, a commanding statue of Giuseppe Garibaldi, one of the heroes of the unification movement, looks down one of Europe's longest pedestrian zones. From here you can walk to the Duomo and beyond (about 1.5 miles), down streets that are all nearly traffic-free. Stroll and appreciate Italian design both in people and in windows (ignore the Foot Locker).

Away from the Center

▲Naviglio Grande (Canal District)

Milan, although far from any major lake or river, has a sizable port. It's called "The Big Canal." Since 1170, a canal has connected Milan with the Mediterranean via the Ticino River (which flows into the Po River on its way to the Adriatic Sea). Five hundred years ago, Leonardo helped further develop the city's canals and designed a modern lock system. Then, during the booming Industrial Age in the 19th century—and especially with the flurry of construction after Italian unification—the canals were busy shipping in the marble and stone needed to make Milan the great city it is today. In fact, a canal (filled in in the 1930s) once circled the walls of the city, allowing barges to dock with their stone right at the building site of the great cathedral. By the 1950s, landlocked Milan was actually the seventh-biggest port in Italy, as its canals were instrumental in the rebuilding of the bombed-out city. Today, disused train tracks parallel the canal, old warehouse buildings recall the area's working-class heritage, and former workers' tenements—once squalid and undesirable—are much in demand and being renovated smartly. While recently rough and characteristic, today the area is trendy, traffic-free, pricey, and thriving with inviting bars and eateries. The canal district, with its lively restaurants and bars lining the old industrial canal that once so busily served the city, is an understandably popular destination for dinner or evening fun (for recommendations, see "Eating in Milan," later).

Getting There: Ride the Metro to Porta Genova, exit following signs to Via Casale, and walk the length of Via Casale one block

directly to the canal. To the left, on both sides of the canal, are plenty of great places to eat and drink.

Leonardo's Horse

The largest equestrian monument in the world is a modern reconstruction of a model created in 1482 by Leonardo da Vinci for the Sforza family. The clay prototype was destroyed in 1499 by invading French forces, who used it for target practice. In 1982,

American Renaissance-art collector Charles Dent decided to build the 15-ton, 24-foot-long statue from Leonardo's design, planning to present it to the Italians in appreciation for their role in the Renaissance and in homage to Leonardo's genius. Unfortunately, Dent died before the project could be completed. In 1997, American sculptor Nina Akamu created a new clay model that became the template for the final statue; it was unveiled in 1999. The exhibit, described in English, includes statue casts and photos of the construction.

Cost and Hours: Free, Tue-Sun 9:00-17:30, closed Mon, located on outskirts between San Siro racetrack and Meazza soccer stadium; from the corner of Via Mazzini and Via Dogana, take tram #16, direction: San Siro, to Stratico Palatino stop—ask conductor when to get off, then head right on Via Palatino, and left on Piazzale dello Sport to #9; or you can walk a half-mile from Metro: Lotto.

Soccer

The Milanesi claim that their soccer (football, or *calcio*, in Italian) teams are the best in Europe. For a dose of Europe's soccer mania (which many believe provides a necessary testosterone vent to keep Europe out of a third big war), catch a match while you're here. A.C. Milan and Inter Milan are the ferociously competitive home teams (tickets-€10-350).

A.C. Milan tickets are sold at Intesa Sanpaolo banks (one's at Via Verdi 8, Mon-Fri 8:45-13:45 & 14:45-15:45, closed Sat-Sun), online at www.acmilan.com, or at the Milan Point Shop (Tue-Sat 10:00-19:00, closed Sun-Mon, Piazza XXVI Maggio next to Via San Gottardo). Inter Milan tickets are sold at Banca Popolare di Milano banks (one's at Piazza Meda 4, Metro: San Babila; Mon-Fri 8:45-13:45 & 14:45-15:45, closed Sat-Sun) or online at www.inter.it.

Games are held in the 85,000-seat Meazza stadium most Sunday afternoons from September to June (Metro: Lotto, or tram #16—catch it just off Piazza del Duomo, on corner of Via Mazzini and Via Dogana, direction: San Siro; take it to last stop, where you'll find the stadium). You'll need to have your passport when you buy your ticket and bring it with you to the stadium for security reasons. For more on the Italian passion for soccer, see page xxi.

▲Monumental Cemetery (Il Cimitero Monumentale)

Europe's most artistic and dreamy cemetery experience, this grand place was built just after unification to provide a suitable final resting spot for the city's "famous and well-deserving men." Any cemetery can be evocative, but this one—with its super-emotional portrayals of the deceased and their heavenly escorts (in art styles c. 1870-1930)—is in a class by itself. It's a vast garden art gallery of proud busts and grim reapers, heartbroken angels and weeping widows, too-young soldiers and countless old smiles, frozen on yellowed black-and-white photos.

Cost and Hours: Free, Tue-Sun 8:00-18:00, closed Mon, last entry at 17:30, pick up map at the entrance gate, a long walk from Metro: Garibaldi FS, or catch tram #12 or #14 (stop: Bramante) from the corner of Via Orefici and Via Cantu' near the Duomo, tel. 02-8846-5600, www.monumentale.net.

Shopping in Milan

High Fashion in the Quadrilateral

For world-class window-shopping, visit the "Quadrilateral," an elegant high-fashion shopping area around Via Montenapoleone, northeast of La Scala. This was the original Beverly Hills of Milan. In the 1920s, the top fashion shops moved in, and today it remains *the* place for designer labels. Most shops close Sunday and for much of August. On Mondays, stores open only after 16:00. In this land where fur is still prized, the people-watching is as entertaining as the window-shopping. Notice also the exclusive penthouse apartments with roof gardens high above the scene. Via Montenapoleone and the pedestrianized Via della Spiga are the best streets.

Whether you're gawking or shopping, here's the best route: From La Scala, walk up Via Manzoni to the Metro stop at Montenapoleone, browse down Via Montenapoleone, and cut left on Via Santo Spirito (lined with grand aristocratic palazzos—peek into the courtyard at #7). Then, opposite #17, step into the elegant courtyard at #10 to check out the café-sitters and their poodles. Turn right to window-shop down Via della Spiga, turn right on Via Sant'Andrea and then left, back onto Montenapoleone, which leads you through a final gauntlet of temptations to Corso Giacomo Matteotti, near the Piazza San Babila. Then (for less-expensive shopping thrills), walk back to the Duomo down the pedestrian-only Corso Vittorio Emanuele. From the Duomo, go down Via Dante to Sforza Castle.

Near the Duomo

For a (slightly) more reasonably priced shopping excursion, next to the Duomo, step into **La Rinascente**—a Nordstrom-type department store with something for everyone and an especially good toy selection. Each floor has a fine collection of designer names sold out of independent shops, all functioning within the walls of this vast and venerable store. Simply riding the escalator up and up gives a fun overview of Italian design and marketing. The seventh floor is a top-end food circus, with terrace views of the Duomo and a public WC. Its name, meaning "the place reborn," fits its history. In an earlier life, it was a fine Liberty-style building until it burned down in 1918. It was rebuilt, only to be bombed in World War II and rebuilt once again (Mon-Thu 9:30-21:00, Fri-Sat 9:30-22:00, Sun 10:00-21:00, has a VAT refund office and recommended restaurants, faces north side of the Duomo on Piazza del Duomo).

Heading away from the Duomo, stroll between the arcades on the Corso Vittorio Emanuele II and feel yourself surrounded by tempting material pleasures. Clothing stores that range from classy and pricey to trendy and inexpensive are sheltered under the arcades.

At Via Passarella, detour to the right to check out **Excelsior,** a bold high-end concept store. A conveyor belt takes you from level to colorful level with pulsing music and electronic art installations. If you're looking for the perfect €1,000 shirt, you've come to the right place. Otherwise, hit **Eat's Food Market** in the basement and pick up a tasty high-design salad—a bargain at €6 (daily 10:00-20:30, Galleria del Corso 4, two long blocks behind the Duomo, tel. 027-630-7301).

Double back to the Corso Vittorio Emanuele II to continue shopping all the way to the San Babila Metro station, or return to the Duomo.

Nightlife in Milan

For evening action, check out the artsy Brera area in the old center, with several swanky sidewalk cafés to choose from and lots of bars that stay open late. Home to Brera's Art University, this district has a sophisticated, lively people-watching scene. Another great neighborhood for nightlife, especially for a younger scene, is Naviglio Grande (canal district), Milan's formerly bohemian, now gentrified "Little Venice" (described earlier; Metro: Porta Genova).

There are always concerts and live music playing in the city at various clubs and concert halls. Specifics change quickly, so it's best to rely on the entertainment information in periodicals from the TI.

Sleeping in Milan

All recommended hotels are within a few minutes' walk of Milan's subway system. With Milan's fine Metro, you can get anywhere in town in a flash.

Any time in March, April, September, and October, the city can be completely jammed by conventions, and hotel prices jump way up. I've listed high-season prices, but not convention-gouging prices. (For the convention schedule, see www.fieramilano.it.) Summer is usually wide-open, and prices are discounted, though many hotels close in August for vacation. Hotels cater more to business travelers than to tourists, so Fridays and Saturdays are generally cheaper and available.

Lately I've noticed a trend in which small family-style hotels in the center are being neglected, and the big, modern business-class hotels around the train station are proliferating. I've tried to collect central places, where travelers feel appreciated and the staff feels like part of the family. If the following places are booked up, go online—there are lots of hotels near the train station.

Near the Duomo

The Duomo area is thick with people-watching, reasonably priced eateries, and the major sightseeing attractions. From Milano Centrale train station to the Duomo, it's just four stops on a direct Metro line (yellow line 3, direction: San Donato) to Metro: Duomo.

$$$ Hotel Grand Duca di York is stuck oddly in the middle of banks and big-city starkness three blocks southwest of Piazza del Duomo. It's got lavish public spaces and 33 modern, bright rooms that are thoughtfully designed and decorated (Sb-€98-128, Db-€170-190, 5 percent Rick Steves discount through 2014 if you book direct, air-con, elevator, free Wi-Fi, free minibar, near Metro stops: Cordusio or Duomo, Via Moneta 1, tel. 02-874-863, www.ducadiyork.com, info@ducadiyork.com).

$$$ Hotel Spadari boasts a modern, Art Deco-inspired interior designed by the Milanese artist Giò Pomodoro ("Joe Tomato" in English). The 40 rooms have billowing drapes, big paintings, and designer doors. It's next door to the recommended Peck Deli, and two blocks from the Duomo (standard Db-€230-260, deluxe Db-€290-360, no need for the pricier suites, 5 percent Rick Steves discount through 2014 when you book direct, air-con, elevator, free Wi-Fi, free minibar, Via Spadari 11, tel. 02-7200-2371, www.spadarihotel.com, reservation@spadarihotel.com).

$ Hotel Vecchia Milano is a humble, clean place buried deep in the old town on a narrow lane. Although the management is indifferent, it rents 27 comfortable rooms at a great price for the location (Sb-€65-80, Db-€90-100, air-con, free Wi-Fi, next to recommended Hostaria Borromei at Via Borromei 4, tel. 02-875-042, www.hotelvecchiamilan.com, hotelvecchiamilano@tiscalinet.it).

Between La Scala and Sforza Castle

$$$ Hotel Star, comfortable and modern, rents 30 sparkling, fresh, and spacious rooms with unexpected artistic touches (Sb-€165, Db-€225, prices drop about €40 outside convention times,

Sleep Code

(€1 = about $1.30, country code: 39)
S = Single, **D** = Double/Twin, **T** = Triple, **Q** = Quad, **b** = bathroom, **s** = shower only. Unless otherwise noted, credit cards are accepted, English is spoken, and breakfast is included. Many cities in Italy levy a hotel tax of about €2 per person, per night, which must be paid in cash (not included in the rates I've quoted).

To help you sort easily through these listings, I've divided the accommodations into three categories based on the price for a standard double room with bath:

$$$ Higher Priced—Most rooms €150 or more.
$$ Moderately Priced—Most rooms between €110-150.
$ Lower Priced—Most rooms €110 or less.

Prices can change without notice; verify the hotel's current rates online or by email. For the best prices, always book direct.

check website for deals, interior rooms are quieter, air-con, free Wi-Fi, usually closed Aug, Via dei Bossi 5, tel. 02-801-501, www.hotelstar.it, info@hotelstar.it, cheeky Vittoria).

$$$ Antica Locanda dei Mercanti offers 15 white, minimalist rooms in an 18th-century palazzo. While the rooms are all different—some with kitchens, others with spacious terraces—all have a clean, fresh-flower vibe, uncommonly romantic for Milan. (Db-€195-265, €30 more for terrace rooms, air-con, free guest computer and Wi-Fi, Via San Tomaso 6, Metro: Cairoli or Cordusio; tel. 02-805-4080, www.locanda.it, locanda@locanda.it, Alex and Eri).

$$ London Hotel, a simple 30-room hotel with a comfy living-room-like lobby and basic rooms, is tucked away on a quiet side street just off vibrant Via Dante. It's warmly run by the friendly Gambino family: mom and pop Elda and Franco don't speak English, but daughters Tanya and Licia do (S-€80-90, Sb-€90-100, D-€110-140, Db-€130-160, Tb-€170-200, prices much higher during conventions, skip their €8 breakfast and grab something on Via Dante, cheaper in July and Aug, book direct for these rates and get an additional 10 percent off with cash, air-con, elevator, pay Wi-Fi, near Metro: Cairoli at Via Rovello 3, tel. 02-7202-0166, www.hotellondonmilano.com, info@hotellondonmilano.com).

Near Centrale Train Station

The train station neighborhood is more practical than characteristic. Its hotels are utilitarian business-class hotels with prices that bounce all over depending upon the convention schedule. You'll find more shady characters than shady trees in the parks, and lots of massage parlors. But you can't beat the convenience (near station, Metro to the center, shuttles to airports), and if you hit it outside of convention times, the prices are hard to beat. Here are two decent options:

$$ Hotel Florida is a comfortable, well-maintained business-class hotel with 55 rooms on a quiet street one block from the station. Prices plummet if you book direct and are not visiting during a convention (rack rate Db-€290 but often more like Sb-€70-100 and Db-€90-130, free Wi-Fi, Via Lepetit 33, tel. 02-670-5921, www.hotelfloridamilan.com, info@hotelfloridamilan.com). With the tracks to your back, leave the station's upper hall to the left, cross the taxi stand, and then cross the road. The hotel is on Via Lepetit, around the corner from Ristorante Giglio Rosso.

$$ Hotel Garda has 55 tidy, spotless rooms two and a half blocks from the station (Sb-€40-140, Db-€60-170; email first to get a promo code for a 10 percent discount when booking on their website; air-con, elevator, Via N. Torriani 21, tel. 02-6698-2626, www.hotelgardamilan.com, info@hotelgardamilan.com). Exit the train station and head straight across the square, veering left onto Via N. Torriani. It's ahead on your right.

Hostels

For beds costing about €21-30, consider Milan's hostels. Most are away from the center, but the first one I've listed is closer to town.

$ Ostello Burigozzo, a good choice, has 83 beds in both private rooms and in shared dorm rooms (€22-27 for beds in 6-, 8-, 16-, and 24-bed dorms; hotel-type rooms on the third floor—Sb-€50-70, Db €70-100, Tb-€90-123; reserve ahead, 14:30-24:00 check-in but can leave bags earlier, curfew at 1:30 in the morning, elevator, free guest computer and Wi-Fi, self-serve laundry, Via Burigozzo 11, Metro: Missori—on yellow line 3, tel. 02-5831-4675, www.ostelloburigozzo11.com, info@ostelloburigozzo11.com).

$ AIG Piero Rotta is larger and offers cheap, basic accommodations with a simple breakfast and self-service laundry (€21-30 beds in 2-6-bed dorms, €23-28 for 2-, 3-, and 4-bed rooms with private bath, €2 extra for nonmembers, near Metro: QT8—on red line 1, at Via Martino Bassi 2, tel. 02-3926-7095, www.hostelmilan.org, milano@aighostels.it).

Eating in Milan

Milan's bars, delis, *rosticcerie*, and self-service cafeterias cater to people with plenty of taste and more money than time. You'll find delightful eateries all over town (note that they take Aug off).

I find the price difference between basic and classy restaurants

MILAN

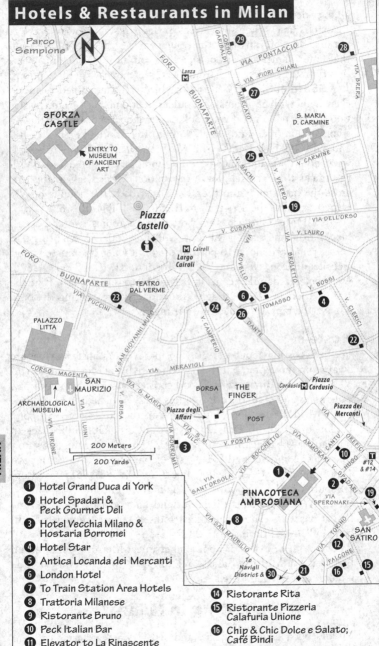

Hotels & Restaurants in Milan

Parco Sempione

SFORZA CASTLE

ENTRY TO MUSEUM OF ANCIENT ART

Piazza Castello

FORO BUONAPARTE

Lanza M

CORSO GARIBALDI

VIA PONTACCIO

VIA FIORI CHIARI

VIA MERCATO

VIA BRERA

S. MARIA D. CARMINE

V. SACHI

V. CARMINE

V. VETERO

VIA DELL'ORSO

V. CUSANI

V. LAURO

V. BOSSI

BROLETTO

ROVELLO

Largo Cairoli

Cairoli M

TEATRO DAL VERME

VIA PUCCINI

PALAZZO LITTA

CORSO MAGENTA

SAN MAURIZIO

ARCHAEOLOGICAL MUSEUM

VIA NIRONE

LUINI

V. BRISA

V. S. MARIA

V. SAN GIOVANNI MURO

VIA MERAVIGLI

VIA DANTE

V. CAMPERIO

V. TOMASSO

V. CLERICI

FORO BUONAPARTE

BORSA

THE FINGER

Piazza degli Affari

POST

Cordusio M Piazza Cordusio

Piazza dei Mercanti

VIA OREFICI

CANTU

V. ARMORARI

V. SPADARI

V. HUGO

VIA POSTA

VIA BOCCHETTO

VIA BORROMEI

V. FUIC.

VIA SANT'ORSOLA

PINACOTECA AMBROSIANA

VIA SPERONARI

SAN SATIRO

VIA SAN MAURIZIO

VIA TORINO

V. FALCONE

To Navigli District &

200 Meters

200 Yards

T #12 & #14

① Hotel Grand Duca di York
② Hotel Spadari & Peck Gourmet Deli
③ Hotel Vecchia Milano & Hostaria Borromei
④ Hotel Star
⑤ Antica Locanda dei Mercanti
⑥ London Hotel
⑦ To Train Station Area Hotels
⑧ Trattoria Milanese
⑨ Ristorante Bruno
⑩ Peck Italian Bar
⑪ Elevator to La Rinascente Dep't Store Eateries
⑫ Latteria Cucina Vegetariana
⑬ Ciao Cafeteria
⑭ Ristorante Rita
⑮ Ristorante Pizzeria Calafuria Unione
⑯ Chip & Chic Dolce e Salato; Café Bindi
⑰ Odeon Gelateria
⑱ Gelateria Grom
⑲ Princi Bakeries (2)

MILAN

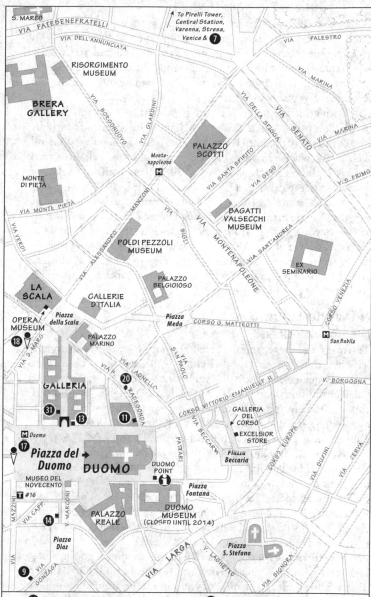

20 Luini Panzerotti & Cioccolati Italiani
21 Supermarket
22 Victoria Ristorante
23 Da Rita e Antonio
24 Antica Osteria Milanese
25 Convivium Ristorante and Pizza
26 Via Dante Eateries
27 Obikà Mozzarella Bar
28 Bar Brera
29 Bottega Caffè Cacao
30 To Naviglio Grande Eateries
31 Bar Camparino

to be negligible, so it's worth springing for the places that offer the best experience. To eat mediocre food on a famous street with great people-watching, choose an eatery on the pedestrian-only Via Dante. To eat with students in trendy little trattorias, explore the Brera neighborhood. To eat well near the Duomo, consider the recommended places listed later.

Locals like to precede a lunch or dinner with an *aperitivo* (while Campari made its debut in Milan, a simple glass of *vino bianco* or prosecco, the Italian champagne, is just as popular). Bars fill their counters with inviting baskets of munchies, which are served free with these drinks, at about 17:00. If you're either likable or discreet, a cheap drink can become a light meal.

Milan's signature dishes (often served together as a *piatto unico*, or "single dish") are *risotto alla milanese* and *ossobuco*. The risotto is flavored with saffron, which gives it its intense yellow color. The subtle flavor of the saffron pairs nicely with the *ossobuco* (meaning "marrow," or, literally "hole in the bone," of the veal shank). The prized marrow is extracted with special little forks and is considered the best part of the meal.

Near the Duomo
Dining with Class

Trattoria Milanese, sophisticated and family-run, is a splurge. It has an enthusiastic and local clientele—the restaurant didn't even bother to get a phone until 1988. Expect a Milanese ambience and quality traditional cuisine (Mon-Fri 12:00-14:45 & 19:00-22:45, closed Sat-Sun and mid-July-Aug, evening reservations recommended, air-con, Via Santa Marta 11, 5-minute walk from the Duomo, near Pinacoteca Ambrosiana, tel. 02-8645-1991).

Ristorante Bruno serves Tuscan cuisine with a passion for fresh fish. This place impresses with its dressy waiters, hearty food, inexpensive desserts, and a fine self-serve antipasto buffet (a plate full of Tuscan specialties for €10). You can eat inside or on the sidewalk under fascist columns (Sun-Fri 12:00-15:00 & 19:00-23:00, closed Sat and Aug, moderate prices, air-con, Via M. Gonzaga 6, reservations wise, tel. 02-804-364, Graziella).

Hostaria Borromei is where Milanese yuppies go for power lunches to impress clients with market-fresh traditional Italian dishes. Dine under an awning of vines in an elegant mellow-yellow interior courtyard or in their cantina-chic dining rooms. Reservations are recommended (€12 pastas, €20 *secondi*, Mon-Fri 12:30-14:45 & 19:30-22:45, Sat-Sun 19:30-22:45, Via Borromei 4, tel. 02-8645-3760).

Peck Italian Bar is a hit with the sophisticated office crowd, which mobs the place at lunch for its fast, excellent meals with im-peck-able service. It's owned by the same people who run the recommended high-end Peck Gourmet Deli (listed later), so be prepared to spend—this place's classiness alone makes it worth the money. Any time you find yourself among such a quality-conscious group of Milanesi, you know you're getting good food (€14 pastas, €18 *secondi*, Mon-Fri 7:30-23:00, Sat 9:00-23:00, closed Sun, Via Cantù 3, tel. 02-869-3017).

Dining at the Top of a Top-End Department Store with a Duomo View

The seventh floor of the La Rinascente department store, alongside the Duomo, has a Milanese-style food court. Of its many eateries, three enjoy a sunny outdoor terrace. You'll dine accompanied by views of the cathedral's rooftop (though anyone can pop up for a look at the cathedral). All three of the terrace-seating establishments recommended below are open 9:00-24:00, and can be accessed after store hours from elevators on Via S. Radegonda: **Obikà** is a swanky mozzarella bar offering this heavenly cheese in all its various forms—cow's milk, buffalo, and smoked—in salads or on splittable €12-20 antipasto sampler plates, accompanied by *salumi*, tapenades, and vegetables. Study their English menu to choose cheeses and accompaniments. (Another Obikà is north of the Duomo—see "In the Brera Neighborhood," later.) **Ristorante Maio** has pricey full-meal service (€13 pastas and pizzas, €25 *secondi*). And **Il Bar,** living room cozy with cushy divans and low coffee tables, serves light meals (salads, pasta), coffee, desserts, and cocktails.

Eating Simply

Latteria Cucina Vegetariana, with a 50-year history, is a bright hole-in-the-wall that serves a good vegetarian Italian lunch. This busy joint—with tight seating in front and behind the kitchen—is overrun with tables where neighborhood workers enjoy soup, salads, pastas, and imaginative veggie entrées at affordable prices. Try the €13 *piatto misto al forno* for a delicious assortment of soufflés, quiches, and roasted and sautéed veggies (€6-12 *panini* and salads, €13-15 meals, Mon-Sat 12:00-16:00, closed Sun, just off Via Torino at Via dell'Unione 6, 2 blocks southwest of the Duomo, tel. 02-874-401).

Ciao, a self-service cafeteria, offers a low-stress, affordable meal above a fast-food arcade on Piazza del Duomo (daily 11:30-23:00, sometimes closes at 22:30, inexpensive pasta and good salad bar, easy public WC). It's to the right of the Galleria entrance—enter through the ground floor Autogrill and go up to the second floor.

Ristorante Rita is a smart budget option (€5 pastas and *secondi*) without the Italian fast-food feel. While the downstairs has a take-out place, there's a sleek, modern restaurant upstairs with good food and cafeteria prices. Their happy hour is a bargain, with a buffet of savory snacks (Mon-Sat 12:00-15:00 & 17:00-20:00, closed Sun, on Via Marconi between Piazza del Duomo and Piazza Diaz, tel. 02-8699-7387).

Ristorante Pizzeria Calafuria Unione is a thriving Milanese-style eatery popular with locals and tourists alike for its pizza and local dishes (€9 pizzas and pastas, €16-20 *secondi*, closed Sun, Metro: Missori, a few blocks south of Piazza del Duomo at Via dell'Unione 8, tel. 02-866-103).

Chip & Chic Dolce e Salato's name says it all: cheap and chic with sweets and salads. This fun little place is a hit with local office workers for its €6 salads in edible bowls, pastas, and fresh pastries (Mon-Sat 12:00-15:00, closed Sun, a couple of blocks south of Piazza del Duomo at Galleria Unione 7, Metro: Missori, mobile 347-035-4761). The **Café Bindi**, across the gallery, has a similar style and charm.

Gelato: Floodlit Mary gazes down on the **Odeon Gelateria** from the top of the Duomo for good reason (next to McDonald's, on far side of square opposite Duomo facade, open nightly until 24:00, closes earlier off-season). While Odeon is convenient, **Gelateria Grom,** two blocks toward La Scala, is the connoisseurs' choice (daily 11:30-23:30, Via Santa Margherita 16).

Picnics Milan-Style, Near the Duomo

Princi bakery is mobbed with locals vying for focaccia, olive breadsticks, and luscious pastries. Notice the stacked-wood-oven action in the back. For most pastry items (like the brioche), pay the cashier first; for items sold by weight (such as pizza and cake), get it weighed before you pay. Consider a pasta lunch (12:00-15:00 only) for €6 per plate (open Mon-Sat 7:00-20:00, Sun 10:00-19:30, on Via Speronari, off Via Torino, a block southwest of Piazza del Duomo; a larger Princi bakery, more like a café, is near Sforza Castle and is listed later).

Peck Gourmet Deli is an aristocratic deli with a fancy café/lunchroom/pastry and gelato shop upstairs, a gourmet grocery and *rosticceria* on the main level, and an expensive *enoteca* wine cellar in the basement. Even if all you can afford is the aroma, peek in. Check out the classic circa-1930 salami slicers and the gourmet assembly line in the kitchen in the back. The *rosticceria* serves fancy food to go for a superb picnic dinner in your hotel. It's delectable, beautiful, sold by weight (order by the *etto*—100-gram unit, 250 grams equals about a half-pound), and pricey (Mon 15:30-19:30, Tue-Sat 9:15-19:30, closed Sun, Via Spadari 9, tel. 02-802-3161).

Luini Panzerotti serves up piping-hot mini-calzones *(panzerotti)* stuffed with mozzarella, tomatoes, ham, or whatever you like for €3-5 (Mon 10:00-15:00, Tue-Sat 10:00-20:00, closed Sun and Aug, Via S. Radegonda 16, tel. 02-8646-1917). From the back of the Duomo, head north and look for the lines of hungry locals out front. Order from the small menus posted behind the cash registers. Traditionally, Milanesi munch their hot little meals on nearby Piazza San Fedele. Don't overlook the *dolce* half of their menu— Panzerotti is popular for its sweets all day long. Across the street is another local hit, **Cioccolati Italiani,** for chocoholics in search of a sweet treat.

Billa Superfresco Supermarket is within a few blocks of the Duomo (Mon-Sat 8:00-23:00, Sun 9:00-21:00, small deli on ground level, big supermarket in basement, on Via Torino at intersection with San Maurilio).

Near La Scala Opera House

Victoria Ristorante is casually elegant, with a modern yet nostalgic atmosphere. It offers creative reinterpretations of traditional Italian dishes for loyal locals and visitors in the know. Its thoughtfully presented dishes, while pricey, are a good value (Mon-Fri 12:30-14:30 & 19:30-24:00, Sat 19:30-24:00, closed Sun, Metro: Cordusio or Duomo, Via Clerici 1, tel. 02-869-0834).

Near Sforza Castle

Da Rita e Antonio is a favorite neighborhood restaurant, serving up well-prepared, reasonably priced Milanese specialties such as *costoletta* (breaded veal chop) and *ossobuco* (veal shank and risotto), as well as delicious €9 Neapolitan-style pizzas. It's a high-energy, brightly lit, dressy place, complete with waiters in bow ties and vests (€10 pastas, €20 *secondi*, great tiramisu, Tue-Sun 12:00-14:30 & 19:00-23:30, closed Mon, Via G. Puccini 2a, tel. 02-875-579). Facing Sforza Castle from the end of Via Dante, it's about 100 yards to your left, built into the far side of the pink-and-white theater.

Antica Osteria Milanese is a hardworking family place with a smart local following and spacious, stylish seating. They serve good-quality typical Milanese favorites (€9 pastas, €14 *secondi*, Mon-Sat 12:15-14:30 & 19:30-22:15, closed Sun, Via Camperio 12, tel. 02-861-367, Alessandro).

Convivium Ristorante and Pizza is popular for its extensive wine list, clever dishes, and conviviality. Classy yet understated, this is a good place for a foodie splurge (€10 pizza and pastas, €22 *secondi*, daily 12:00-14:30 & 19:00-24:00, facing Santa Maria del Carmine church at Via Ponte Vetero 21, tel. 02-8646-3708, Claudio and Nicola).

Princi bakery, near the castle, works the same as the one on Via Speronari (listed earlier), only it's more of a restaurant, with seating both inside and on the street. While the bakery and café are open all day, they serve hot cafeteria-style lunches only 12:00-15:30 (Mon-Sat 7:00-20:00, Sun 9:00-19:30, Via Ponte Vetero 10, tel. 02-7201-6067).

Fancy Via Dante Bars and Cafés: Thriving and central, Via Dante is lined with hardworking eateries where you can join locals for a lively lunch. Or, for about the price of your forgettable hotel breakfast, you can start your day watching the parade of Milanesi heading to work.

In the Brera Neighborhood

The Brera neighborhood, surrounding the Church of St. Carmine, is laced with narrow, inviting pedestrian streets. Make an evening of your visit by having an *aperitivo* (pre-dinner drink) with snacks at recommended Bar Brera or any other bar—most serve munchies with pre-dinner drinks 17:00-21:00. Afterward, stroll along restaurant row on Via Fiori Chiari and Via Brera, or duck into the semicircular lane of Via Madonnina to survey the sidewalk cafés as you pass fortune-tellers, artists, and knock-off handbag vendors. To locate these eateries, see the map on page 364.

Obikà is a trendy mozzarella eatery with a sleek, minimalist, jazzy ambience. For details, see the listing on page 367 (daily 12:00-15:30 & 18:30-24:00, on corner of Via Mercato and Via Fiori Chiari, Via Mercato 28, tel. 02-8645-0568).

Bar Brera, kitty-corner from the Brera Art Gallery, serves salads, sandwiches, and pastas to throngs of art students. Come during the first hour of happy hour (daily 18:00-21:00), have a seat, order an €8 drink, and then help yourself to the buffet (17:00-19:00), which has a generous variety of *antipasti,* from marinated veggies to prosciutto (buffet is free if you buy drinks; €6 salads, €8-10 plates, great streetside seating, Via Brera 23, tel. 02-877-091).

Bottega Caffè Cacao is a quick and handy place for a light meal. In a casually artisan, modern-rustic setting, savor delightful sandwiches (mini and standard size), colorful salads on crispy flatbread, and an array of coffees. Lines can stretch out the door, but the service is quick. Order at the register, then eat at the counter, upstairs, or on the terrace (€1.50 mini-sandwiches, €3 brioche sandwiches, €5 *panini,* €7 salads, daily 7:30-19:30, Corso Garibaldi 16, one block north of Via Tivoli, tel. 02-8050-6589).

In Naviglio Grande (Canal District)

Consider ending your day at the port of Milan. The Naviglio Grande has a bustling collection of bars and restaurants where you have your choice of memorable and affordable options that come with a great people scene.

Getting There: Ride the Metro to Porta Genova and walk down Via Casale, which dead-ends a block away at the canal. Walk halfway across the metal bridge and survey the scene. The street you just walked has plenty of cheap options, including La Vineria, described next. Most of the action—and all of my other recommendations—are to the left, on or near the canal. Consider doing a reconnaissance stroll before settling in somewhere: Walk down the canal on one side to the bridge with cars, then go back on the other side.

La Vineria is a fun place with streetside seating, serving cheap and fun plates of cheese and meats and wine from giant vats to a cool crowd (daily, June-Sept dinner only from 15:30, Oct-May lunch and dinner except no lunch on Mon, Via Casale 4, tel. 02-8324-2440).

Pizzeria Tradizionale is a local favorite for pizza (daily, at the far end of canal walk, Ripa di Porta Ticinese 7).

Ristorante Brellin is the top romantic splurge, with a dressy crowd and fine food. The menu is international while clinging to a bit of tradition (€14 pastas, €24 *secondi*, daily 12:30-15:30 & 19:00-24:00, behind the old laundry tubs at Vicolo dei Lavandai, tel. 02-5810-1351, www.brellin.it).

Osteria Cucina Fusetti is a charming little place serving good Sardinian cuisine. What's that? Giuseppe speaks English, and he enjoys explaining (€8 pastas, €15 *secondi*, closed Sun; near the curved bridge with the zigzag design at the Japanese restaurant, go away from canal to Via Fusetti 1; mobile 340-861-2676).

Pizzeria Spaghetteria La Magolfa is a local fixture offering good, cheap €5 salads, pastas, and pizzas. You can sit inside, on a veranda, or at a table on the street. For €15, two people could split a hearty pizza and a good bottle of wine and get full and a bit drunk (no cover, a long block off canal at end of Via M. Fusetti at Via Magolfa 15, tel. 02-832-1696).

Milan Connections

By Train

From Milano Centrale by Train to: Venice (at least hourly, most departures at :05 or :35 past the hour, most are direct on high-speed ES trains, 2.5-3.5 hours), **Florence** (hourly, 1.75 hours), **Genoa** (about hourly, 1.5-2 hours, also look for trains to La Spezia or Livorno that stop at Genoa), **Rome** (hourly, 3-8 hours, overnight possible), **Brindisi** (4 direct/day, 2 are night trains, 9-15 hours, more with changes), **Cinque Terre/La Spezia** (about hourly, 3 hours direct or with change in Genoa; trains from La Spezia to the villages go nearly hourly), **Cinque Terre/Monterosso al Mare** (8/day direct, otherwise hourly, 3-4 hours, more with change in

MILAN

Genoa), **Varenna** on Lake Como (1 hour; €6.40; small line direct to Lecco/Sondrio/Tirano leaves at 6:20, 7:20, 8:20, 9:20, 10:20, 12:20, 14:20, 16:20, 17:20, 19:20, 20:20, and 21:20; confirm these times—if you take a train at a time not listed here, it will require a change in Lecco and an extra 30 minutes), **Stresa** on Lake Maggiore (about hourly—there can be gaps in service; 1-hour fast train may require reservations; also 1.5-hour slow train; also look for trains to Domodossola and some international destinations that stop at Stresa), **Como** (at least hourly, 30-90 minutes, boats go from Como to Varenna until about 19:00), **Naples** (direct trains hourly, 5 hours, more with change in Rome, overnight possible); see www.trenitalia.com for details.

From Milano Porta Garibaldi by High-Speed Train: While the Centrale Station departures listed above are operated by Trenitalia, a competing private rail company called Italo offers additional high-speed connections to **Florence** (8/day, 2 hours), **Rome** (8/day, 3.5 hours), and **Naples** (5/day, 4.75 hours). While Italo is often cheaper (particularly if you book long in advance), it uses the less convenient Porta Garibaldi Station in Milan, and it doesn't accept railpasses (for details on Italo, see page 1166 or visit www.italotreno.it).

International Destinations: Amsterdam (hourly with several changes, fastest via Basel or Zurich, 15 hours), **Barcelona** (14-20 hours, several with 1-5 changes), **Bern** (change required in Brig, at least 3.5 hours), **Frankfurt** (change in Basel or Zurich, at least 9-10 hours), **London** (3/day, 12-18 hours with changes), **Munich** (7/day, 8-12 hours with changes), **Nice** (5/day with change in Ventimiglia, night train possible, 5-6.5 hours), **Paris** (2-3/day direct from Milano Porta Garibaldi, 7 hours; night train possible from Milano Centrale), **Lyon** (8/day, 6-8.5 hours with changes), **Vienna** (1/day direct, more with 1-3 changes, 11-14 hours). With dozens of budget airlines serving Europe's hub cities, flying to your international destination is often the most efficient and economical option (see "Cheap Flights" on page 1183).

By Plane

To get flight information for Malpensa or Linate airports or the current phone number of your airline, call 02-74851 or 02-232-323 and wait for English options, or check www.sea-aeroportimilano.it.

Malpensa Airport

Most international flights land at the manageable Malpensa Airport (airport code: MXP), 28 miles northwest of Milan. Customs guards fan you through, and even the security dog seems friendly. You'll most likely land at Terminal 1 (international flights), rather

Train Connections from Milan

SWITZERLAND

AUSTRIA

To Basel

To Zürich

To Innsbruck

Chur

Merano

Alpe di Siusi

St. Moritz

Bolzano

Cortina

Lake Maggiore

Lugano

Tirano

Dolomites

Calalzo

Domo.

Trento

Stresa

Lake Como

Varenna

ITALY

Como

Lecco

Bergamo

Orio Al Serio

Lake Garda

Verona

Vicenza

Marco Polo

Gallarate

Malpensa

Linate

Desenzano

Padua

Venice

Milan

Cremona

To Turin

Mantova

Ferrara

Adriatic Sea

30 Kilometers

30 Miles

To Nice

Genoa

S. Margherita

Bologna

Ravenna

Med. Sea

Vernazza

To Florence

Rail

High Speed Rail

Bus

---

than Terminal 2 (low-cost EU flights); buses connect the two. Both have ATMs (at Terminal 1, between exit 4 and 5 at Banca Nazionale del Lavoro), banks, and exchange offices. Terminal 1 has a pharmacy, eateries, and a hotel reservation service disguised as a TI (daily 7.00–20:00; when you exit the baggage-carousel area, go right to reach services and exit; tel. 02-5858-0080).

You have three easy ways to get to downtown Milan: by train, shuttle bus, or taxi.

By Train: The Malpensa Express has two different lines serving downtown Milan. One line serves Milan's central train station, Milano Centrale, with rail links across Italy and beyond (€10, 1-2/hour, 40-50 minutes, usually runs until 22:30). The other line zips between the airport and Milan's Cadorna station, which is both a Metro stop and a small train station; it's relatively close to the Duomo and Sforza Castle (€11, credit cards accepted, not covered by railpasses, 2/hour, 30 minutes; usually departs airport at :26 and :56 past the hour, generally departs Cadorna at :28 and :58 past the hour, very long hours, tel. 800-500-005, www.malpensaexpress.it).

At the airport, as you pop out through customs, you'll see a *Treno per Malpensa* kiosk selling tickets and a big electric board on the wall indicating how many minutes until the next departure. Follow signs (*Treni* and *Malpensa Express*) down the stairs to the tracks. Check to make sure your train is going to the right destination—*Milano Centrale* or *Milano Cadorna*. When you get off the train, turn to "Arrival in Milan," earlier.

If you're leaving Milan to go *to* the airport, either go to Milan's Centrale Station (check the big departure board for the track number) or take the Metro to the Cadorna stop, surface, and buy a ticket (€11) at the Malpensa Express office in the station. Purchase your ticket before you board. Trains depart Cadorna from track 1; note that there are a few late-night departures to and from Cadorna by bus after midnight—ask when you buy your ticket.

Malpensa Airport also has direct, high-speed rail links to **Florence** (2/day, 2.75 hours), **Rome** (1/day, 4.5 hours), and **Naples** (1/day, 6 hours). Check www.trenitalia.com for details.

By Shuttle Bus: Two bus companies offer virtually identical, competing services between Malpensa Airport and Milan's central train station. They each charge about €10 for the one-hour trip (buy ticket from driver) and depart from the same places: in front of the airport (outside exit 4) and from Piazza Luigi di Savoia (on the east side of Milan's central train station—with your back to the tracks, exit to the left). Buses leave about every 20 minutes, every day, from very early until just after midnight (Malpensa Shuttle tel. 02-5858-3185, www.malpensashuttle.it; Autostradale tel. 02-3391-0794, www.autostradale.it). They're almost comically competitive, with one offering three rides for the price of two. Play around a bit and you may save some money.

By Taxi: Taxis into Milan cost a fixed rate of €90; avoid hustlers in airport halls (catch taxis outside exit 6). Considering how far the city is from the airport and how good the train and bus services are, Milan is the last place I'd take an airport taxi.

Getting Between Malpensa and Linate: The Malpensa Shuttle company runs a bus between the airports about hourly (€13, from Malpensa to Linate runs 7:50-24:25, 1.25 hours, catch bus outside Malpensa's exit 3, stop 20, buy tickets from Airport 2000 offices; from Linate to Malpensa buses depart 4:30-21:30, bus stops at Malpensa's Terminal 1—you must request stop if you need Terminal 2; tel. 02-5858-3185, www.malpensashuttle.it).

Linate Airport

Most European flights land at Linate (airport code: LIN), five miles east of Milan. The airport has a bank with an ATM (just past customs) and a hotel-finding service disguised as a TI (daily 7:30-23:30, tel. 02-7020-0443). You can get to downtown Milan by bus or taxi (or to Malpensa Airport by bus; see above).

By Bus: Two different buses—Starfly and ATM—take you from Linate Airport to downtown. The Starfly bus zips you to the central train station (€4, buy ticket from driver, 3/hour, 30 minutes, bus runs from airport 6:00-22:00, from station 6:00-21:30, leaves from east side of train station at Piazza Luigi di Savoia, tel. 02-587-237, www.autostradale.it). The cheaper ATM city bus gets you to the San Babila Metro stop (specifically to Corso Europa, just around the corner from Piazza San Babila and its Metro station; from here it's one stop to the Duomo on red line 1, direction: Molino Dorino or Bisceglie, or a 7-minute walk). The bus costs €1, departs every 10 minutes, and takes 20 minutes (departures leave city center 5:35-24:35, from airport 6:00-01:05, www.atm-mi.it). Either bus company works fine: Wait for the one that's handier to your hotel, or hop on the first one that shows up. From where it drops you off, take the Metro or a taxi to your hotel. Both buses leave the airport from outside the arrivals hall.

By Taxi: Taxis from Linate to the Duomo cost about €25.

Bergamo (Orio Al Serio) Airport

Some budget airlines, such as Ryanair and Wizzair, use Bergamo Airport—about 30 miles from Milan—as their Milan hub (airport code: BGY, tel. 035-326-323, www.sacbo.it).

An express bus, Orioshuttle, connects the airport to Milan's central train station (€10, daily 4:00-23:15, 2/hour, 1 hour, buy tickets from driver or online at http://ticketonline.orioshuttle.com, tel. 035-330-706). A different company, Oriobus Express, covers the same route (€10, €15 round-trip, daily 4:30-1:00 in the morning, 2/hour, 1 hour, tel. 02-3391-0794, www.autostradale.it).

THE CINQUE TERRE

The Cinque Terre (CHINK-weh TAY-reh), a remote chunk of the Italian Riviera, is the traffic-free, lowbrow, underappreciated alternative to the French Riviera. There's not a museum in sight—just sun, sea, sand (well, pebbles), wine, and pure, unadulterated Italy. Enjoy the villages, swimming, hiking, and evening romance of one of God's great gifts to tourism. For a home base, choose among five *(cinque)* villages, each of which fills a ravine with a lazy hive of human activity—calloused locals, sunburned travelers, and no Vespas. While the Cinque Terre is now discovered (and can be unpleasantly crowded midday, when tourist boats and cruise-ship excursions drop by), I've never seen happier, more relaxed tourists.

This chunk of coast was first described in medieval times as "the five lands." In the feudal era, this land was watched over by castles. Tiny communities grew up in their protective shadows, ready to run inside at the first hint of a Turkish Saracen pirate raid. Marauding pirates from North Africa were a persistent problem until about 1400. Many locals were kidnapped and ransomed or sold into slavery, and those who remained built fires on flat-roofed watchtowers to relay warnings—alerting the entire coast to imminent attacks. The last major raid was in 1545.

As the threat of pirates faded, the villages prospered, catching fish and cultivating grapes. Churches were enlarged with a growing population. But until the advent of tourism in this generation, the towns remained isolated. Even today, traditions survive, and each of the five villages comes with a distinct dialect and its own proud heritage.

Sadly, a few ugly, noisy Americans give tourism a bad name here. Even hip, young residents are put off by loud, drunken tour-

The Cinque Terre

To A-12 Autostrada (Carrodano Exit)
SP-566
To Sestri Levante, Santa Margherita & Genoa
Levanto
SP-370
To New Town (Fegina)
To Monterosso's Old Town
SP-38
Monterosso al Mare
SANDY BEACH
Vernazza
Corniglia
CORNIGLIA STATION
Volastra
Manarola
VIA DELL'AMORE ♥
VIA LITORANEA
Riomaggiore

To A-12 Autostrada (Brugnato Exit)
SP-1
To Genoa
A-12
To La Spezia & Pisa
Beverino
SP-1
Pignone
Pian di Barca
SP-1
To La Spezia & A-12
SP-63
These roads likely closed. Inquire locally.
SP-51
To La Spezia & A-12
SP-370
To Portovenere

2 Kilometers
2 Miles

Ligurian Sea

1 Riomaggiore
2 Manarola
3 Corniglia
4 Vernazza
5 Monterosso al Mare

ists. They say—and I agree—that the Cinque Terre is an exceptional place. It deserves a special dignity. Party in Viareggio or Portofino, but be mellow in the Cinque Terre. Talk softly. Help keep it clean. In spite of the tourist crowds, it's still a real community, and we are its guests.

In this chapter, I cover the five towns in order from south to north—from Riomaggiore to Monterosso. Since I still get the names of the towns mixed up, I think of them by number: #1 Riomaggiore (a workaday town), #2 Manarola (picturesque), #3 Corniglia (on a hilltop), #4 Vernazza (the region's cover girl, the most touristy and dramatic), and #5 Monterosso al Mare (the closest thing to a beach resort of the five towns).

Arrival in the Cinque Terre

By Train: Most big, fast trains from elsewhere in Italy speed right

past the Cinque Terre. (There are some exceptions: A few IC trains go directly from Milan to Monterosso and from Pisa to La Spezia and Monterosso). Unless you're coming from a nearby town, you'll most likely have to change trains at least once to reach Manarola, Corniglia, or Vernazza.

Generally, if you're coming from the north, you'll change trains in Sestri Levante or Genoa (specifically, Genoa's Piazza Principe station). If you're coming from the south or east, you'll probably have to switch trains in La Spezia (change at La Spezia Centrale station—don't make the mistake of getting off at La Spezia Migliarina). No matter where you're coming from, it's best to check in the station before you leave to see your full schedule and route options (use the computerized kiosks or ask at a ticket window). Don't forget to validate your ticket by stamping it in the green-and-white machines located on train platforms and elsewhere in the station. Conductors here are notorious for levying stiff fines on forgetful tourists. For more information on riding the train between Cinque Terre towns, see "Getting Around the Cinque Terre," later.

By Car: If you're driving in the Cinque Terre (but, given the narrow roads and lack of parking, I wouldn't), see "Cinque Terre Connections" at the end of this chapter for directions. For parking, see the "By Car" sections in each village.

Planning Your Time

The ideal stay is two or three full days; my recommended minimum stay is two nights and a completely uninterrupted day. The Cinque Terre is served by local trains from Genoa and La Spezia. Speed demons arrive in the morning, check their bags in La Spezia, ride a train to their starting point, take the five-hour hike through all five towns, laze away the afternoon on the beach or rock of their choice, and zoom away on a high-speed evening or overnight train to somewhere back in the real world. But be warned: The Cinque Terre has a strange way of messing up your momentum. (The evidence is the number of Americans who have fallen in love with the region and/or one of its residents...and are still here.) Frankly, staying fewer than two nights is a mistake that you'll likely regret.

The towns are just a few minutes apart by hourly train or boat. There's no checklist of sights or experiences—just a hike, the towns themselves, and your fondest vacation desires. Study this chapter in advance and piece together your best day, mixing hiking, swimming, trains, and a boat ride. For the best light, coolest temperatures, and fewest crowds, start your hike early.

Market days perk up the towns from 8:00 to 13:00 on Tuesday in Vernazza, Wednesday in Levanto, Thursday in Monterosso and Sestri Levante, and Friday in La Spezia. (Levanto, Sestri Levante, and La Spezia are covered in the next chapter.)

The winter is really dead—most hotels and some restaurants close from about January to March. The long Easter weekend (April 18-21 in 2014), May, June, and September are the peak of peak periods—the toughest times to find rooms. July (when the heat keeps away many potential hikers) and August (vacation time hasn't started yet) can be surprisingly light. In spring, the towns can feel inundated with Italian school groups day-tripping on spring excursions (they can't afford to sleep in this expensive region).

For more information on the region, see www.cinqueterre.it.

Cinque Terre Park Cards

Visitors hiking between the towns on coastal trails need to pay a park entrance fee. You have three options: the Cinque Terre Park Card, the Cinque Terre Treno Park Card, and the Cinque Terre Park Card Blu. All are valid until midnight on the expiration date. Write your name on your card or risk a big fine. The configuration and pricing of these cards seem to always be in flux—be aware that the following details may change before your visit. Those under 18 or over 70 get a discount, as do families of four or more (see www. parconazionale5terre.it).

The **Cinque Terre Park Card** costs €6 for one day of hiking or €9.70 for two days (covers trails and shuttle buses but not trains, buy at trailheads and at most train stations, no validation required).

The **Cinque Terre Treno Park Card** covers what the Cinque Terre Park Card does, plus the use of the local trains (from Levanto to La Spezia, including all Cinque Terre towns). It's sold at TIs inside train stations, but not at trailheads (€12/1 day, €23/2 days, validate card at train station by punching it in the machine). With this card, you have to hike and take three train trips every day to break even.

The **Cinque Terre Park Card Blu,** tentatively planned for 2014, would cover trails, trains, and also boats connecting the towns (at least €25/1 day). This pass won't pay for itself unless you take lots of boats (that is, hiking from one end of the Cinque Terre to the other, and then riding a boat all the way back).

Getting Around the Cinque Terre

Within the Cinque Terre, you can connect towns in three ways: by train, boat, or foot. Trains are cheaper, boats are more scenic, and hiking lets you enjoy more pasta. From a practical point of view, you should consider supplementing the often frustrating trains with the sometimes more convenient boats. The Via dell'Amore trail between Riomaggiore and Manarola is a delight and takes just a few minutes (if it's open—see page 386), making the train not worth waiting for.

By Train

By train, the five towns are just a few minutes apart. Along the coast here, trains go in only two directions: *"per* [to] *Genova"* (the

Events in the Cinque Terre in 2014

For more festival information and to confirm dates, check www.cinqueterre.it and www.turismoinliguria.it. The food festivals in particular are subject to change.

April 20-21	All towns: Easter Sunday and Monday
April 25	All towns: Italian Liberation Day (stay away from the Cinque Terre this day, as locals literally shut down the trails)
May 1	All towns: Labor Day (another local holiday that packs the place mostly with day-trippers)
Mid-May	Monterosso: Lemon Festival (usually the third Sunday)
May 29	All towns: Ascension Day
May 30	Monterosso and Vernazza: Feast of Corpus Domini (procession on carpet of flowers at 18:00)
Mid-June	Monterosso: Anchovy Festival
June 24	Riomaggiore and Monterosso: Feast day of St. John the Baptist (procession and fireworks; big fire on Monterosso's old town beach the day before)
June 29	Corniglia: Feast day of Sts. Peter and Paul
July 20	Vernazza: Feast day of patron saint, St. Margaret, with fireworks
Early Aug (first Sun)	Vernazza: Feast of Nostra Signora di Reggio (hike up to Reggio Sanctuary for food and church procession)
Aug 10	Manarola: Feast day of patron saint, St. Lawrence
Aug 14	Monterosso: Fireworks on eve of feast of the Assumption
Aug 15	All towns: Feast of the Assumption (Ferragosto)
Mid-Sept	Monterosso: Anchovies and Olive Oil Festival (usually the second weekend)

Italian spelling of Genoa), northbound; or *"per La Spezia,"* southbound.

Tickets: Most rides within the region cost €2.10. These tickets are good for 75 minutes in one direction, so you could conceivably use one for a brief stopover. (A short hop between very nearby towns—such as Monterosso-Vernazza or Riomaggiore-Manarola—costs €1.80.) A 40-kilometer ticket is good for six hours in

The Cinque Terre National Park: Peaks and Valleys

Founded in 1999, the Cinque Terre National Marine Park was designed to get everyone thinking creatively about how to improve the area for the good of nature, the local communities, and its many visitors. The park designation has brought with it plenty of good things: money (in the form of trail fees), new regulations to protect wildlife, park-sponsored information centers at each train station, shuttle buses to help hikers reach distant trailheads, and improved walkways, trails, beaches, breakwaters, and docks.

But, perhaps predictably, the system has been corrupted by power and money. A charismatic and visionary past park president, nicknamed "The Pharaoh," made great inroads before poisoning the process with cronyism, forcing him to leave office in disgrace. Frequent landslides have cut off trails—the main reason many people come here—and the trails are repaired and reopened with excruciating slowness. Local grassroots movements (including Save Vernazza—see page 419—and a ragtag crew of Manarolans who donated their time to clear a scenic trail) have arguably done more to promote and preserve the Cinque Terre than has the park, even with its substantial budget. The latest park president, a retired sea admiral, is determined to make the park work. But given this region's old-fashioned ways and recent history of bureaucratic failure, success is far from assured.

Keep in mind that the Cinque Terre is a moving target. Don't be surprised if park details (including entrance fees, shuttle buses, information desks, and so on) have changed by the time you visit.

one direction (€4). Buy tickets at the ticket desk or from the ticket machines on the platform. Before you board, stamp your ticket at the green-and-white machine (a Cinque Terre Treno Park Card must be validated only the first time you use it). Riding without a validated ticket can be expensive (usually €50). You can buy several tickets at once and use them as you like, validating as you go. If you have a Eurail Pass, don't spend one of your valuable travel days on the cheap Cinque Terre.

Schedule: Trains run about hourly in each direction, connecting all five towns. Frequency is a bit lower on Sundays, and more trains may be added during the busiest season (June-Sept).

Since the train is the Cinque Terre's lifeline, shops, hotels, and restaurants often post the current schedule, and many also hand out copies of it (one also comes with the Cinque Terre Park Card). I find the printed schedules a bit confusing since certain departures listed are for only weekdays, only Sundays, and so on (check the key carefully). Monitors in the train stations (described next) are your best source of actual, current departure information. Sometimes it's easiest to do as the locals do: Stop by the station and check the screens to see the next departure time; if it's a ways off, enjoy an ice-cream cone, a bit more shopping, or some beach time.

Important: Any train stopping at Vernazza, Corniglia, or Manarola is going to all the towns. Trains from Monterosso, Riomaggiore, or La Spezia sometimes skip lesser stations, so confirm that the train will stop at the town you need.

At the Platform: Convenient TV monitors posted at several places in each station clearly show what times the next trains in each direction are leaving (and, if they're late—*in ritardo*—how many minutes late they are expected to be). On the monitors, northbound trains are marked for *Genova, Levanto,* or *Sestri Levante;* southbound trains are marked for *La Spezia* or *Sarzana.* (Most northbound trains that stop at all Cinque Terre towns will list Sestri Levante as the *destinazione.*) To be sure you get on the right train, it helps to know your train's number and final destination.

Assuming you're on vacation, accept the unpredictability of Cinque Terre trains—they're often late, unless you are, too, in which case they're on time. Relax while you wait—buy a cup of coffee at a station bar. Scout the platform you need in advance, and then, when the train comes, casually walk over and hop on. This is especially easy in Monterosso, with its fine café-with-a-view on track #1 (direction: Milano/Genova), and in Vernazza, where you can hang out at the Blue Marlin Bar with a prepaid drink and dash when the train pulls in.

Getting Off: Know your stop. As the train leaves the town just before your destination, go to the door and get ready to slip out before the mobs flood in (making it impossible to get off). A word to the wise for novice tourists, who often miss their stop: The stations are small and the trains are long, so (especially in Vernazza) you might have to get off deep in a tunnel. Also, the doors don't open automatically—you may have to open the handle of the door yourself (twist the black handle, or lift up the red one). If a door isn't working, go quickly to the next car to leave.

Alternative: Remember that boats connect the towns about as frequently as the trains, though at different times (see next); if you're in a rush, take whichever form of transport is leaving first.

By Boat

From Easter through October, a daily boat service connects Monterosso, Vernazza, Manarola, Riomaggiore, and Portovenere.

Though they can be very crowded, these boats provide a scenic way to get from town to town and survey where you just hiked. And boats offer the only efficient way to visit the nearby resort of Portovenere (see next chapter); the alternative is a tedious train-bus connection via La Spezia. In peaceful weather, the boats can be more reliable than the trains, but if seas are rough, they don't run at all. Because the boats nose in and tourists have to gingerly disembark onto little more than a plank, even a small chop can cancel some or all of the stops.

I see the tour boats as a syringe, injecting each town with a boost of euros. The towns are addicted, and they shoot up hourly through the summer. (Between 10:00 and 15:00—especially on weekends—masses of gawkers unload from boats, tour buses, and cruise ships, inundating the villages and changing the feel of the region.)

Boats depart Monterosso about hourly (10:30-17:00), stopping at the Cinque Terre towns (except at Corniglia) and ending up an hour later in Portovenere. (Portovenere-Monterosso boats run 8:50-17:00.) The ticket price depends on the length of the boat ride (ranging from €2 for a very short ride between towns, to €3.50 between towns farther apart, up to €11 for a five-town, one-way ticket with stops; a five-town all day pass costs €15). Round-trip tickets are slightly cheaper than two one-way trips. You can buy tickets at little stands at each town's harbor (tel. 0187-732-987 and 0187-818-440). Another all-day boat pass for €25 extends to Portovenere and includes a 40-minute scenic ride around three small islands (2/day). Boats are not covered by the standard Cinque Terre Park Card, but the planned Blu card may include them (ask). Boat schedules are posted at docks, harbor bars, Cinque Terre park offices, and hotels (www.navigazionegolfodeipoeti.it).

By Shuttle Bus

Green shuttle buses (which locals call *pulmino*) connect each Cinque Terre town with its distant parking lot and various points in the hills (for example, a shuttle runs from Corniglia's train station to its hilltop town center). Note that these shuttle buses do not connect the towns with each other. Most rides cost €1.50 one-way (buy tickets from driver; buses are also covered by the Cinque Terre Park Card). You can ask about bus schedules at TIs and park info offices, or note the times posted at bus stops, but be aware that shuttle service is quite unreliable. Confirm the details carefully before planning your day around the bus. As you board, it's always smart to tell the driver where you want to go. Departures often coordinate with train arrival times. Some (but not all) departures from Vernazza, Manarola, and Riomaggiore go beyond the parking lots and high into the hills. To soak in the scenery, you can pay €2.50 for a round-trip ride and just cruise both ways (30-45 minutes round-trip).

Hiking the Cinque Terre

All five towns are connected by good trails, marked with red-and-white paint, white arrows, and some signs. *Sentiero* means trail.

The region has several numbered *sentieri*, but most visitors stick to the main coastal trail that connects the villages—that's trail #2 (described in the next section). For extra credit, get local advice for detours to dramatic hilltop sanctuaries. I've outlined my favorite non-#2 hike, from Manarola over Volastra to Corniglia, later.

Trail Closures: Trails can be closed in bad weather or because of landslides. (In fact, in summer of 2013, all four segments of the popular coastal trail were closed for one reason or another.) Before planning your hiking day, carefully confirm whether any of trail segments are closed. Official closures are noted on the national park website (www.parconazionale5terre.it), and the national park information desks in each town's train station post a list. However, sometimes a trail is "officially" closed—meaning that its ticket desk is closed—but still able to be hiked (at your own risk). It's worth asking locals or fellow hikers for the latest on which trails are passable and which aren't.

Hiking Conditions: Other than the wide, easy Riomaggiore-Manarola segment, the coastal trail is generally narrow, steep, rocky, and comes with lots of challenging steps. I get many emails from readers who say the trail was tougher than they'd expected. The rocks and metal grates can be slippery in the rain (I'd avoid the very steep Monterosso-Vernazza stretch if it's wet). And if you venture up on those rocky cliffs without sun protection or water, you deserve the sunburn and dehydration that will result. While the trail is challenging, it's perfectly doable for any fit hiker...and worth the sweat.

When to Go: The coastal trail can be very crowded (and very hot) at midday. The best times to hike are early in the day (before the crowds and heat hit) and late in the day. Before setting out for an evening hike, find out what time the sun sets, and leave yourself plenty of time to arrive at your destination before then; after dark, there's no lighting on the trails.

Navigation: Maps aren't necessary for the basic coastal hikes described here. But for the expanded version of this hike (12 hours, from Portovenere to Levanto) and more serious hikes in the high country, pick up a good hiking map (about €5, sold everywhere). The *Cinque Terre Walking Guide* (by a German publisher, but sold locally in an English-language edition for about €15) is worth seeking out for anyone planning a serious hike. The national park's free, official Cinque Terre ViTour Hiking Guide smartphone app provides trail information (including updates on which trails are open or closed); it is currently available only in Italian, but they hope to launch an English version soon.

Give a Hoot: To leave the park cleaner than you found it, bring a plastic bag *(sacchetto di plastica)* and pick up a little trail trash along the way. It would be great if American visitors—who get so much joy out of this region—were known for this good deed.

Weather: As in many communities whose livelihoods are tied to the sea, locals have names for the different types of winds: *Scirocco* is a cloudy, warm, southeasterly wind from North Africa; it carries sand from the Sahara, which makes a mess as it scatters over the land. The *scirocco* causes a condition called *macaia*—sticky, heavy, wet, still, and overcast weather believed to put everyone in a rotten mood. Conversely, the *tramontana* is a cool, clear, refreshing, northerly breeze that comes "across the mountains," bringing sunny weather and calm seas. The *libeccio* wind, from the southwest (and named for Libya), means "sun but big waves." The *maestrale* is a stiff westerly that generally comes with sunny weather (and isn't as intense as France's notorious mistral). And *grecale* is a strong, cold, northeasterly wind from Russia that produces chilly drizzle and sometimes snow in the mountains.

The Coastal Trail

You'll experience the area's best by hiking from one end of the coastal trail to the other—that means Riomaggiore to Monterosso, or vice versa. (Be aware that segments of this trail can close without warning—see "Trail Closures," earlier.) The entire seven-mile coastal hike (on trail #2) can be done in about four hours, but allow five for dawdling. Germans (with their task-oriented *Alpenstock* walking sticks) are notorious for marching too fast through the region. Take it slow...smell the cactus flowers and herbs, notice the scurrying lizards, listen to birds singing in the olive groves, and enjoy vistas on all sides.

If you're hiking the full five-town route, consider these factors: The trail between Riomaggiore (#1) and Manarola (#2) is easiest.

The hike between Manarola and Corniglia (#3) has minor hills (for a much steeper, more scenic alternative, consider detouring higher up, via Volastra—described later). The trail from Corniglia to Vernazza (#4) is demanding, and the path from Vernazza to Monterosso (#5) is the most challenging. The hike I describe goes from town #1 (Riomaggiore) to #5 (Monterosso), but some hikers prefer the opposite direction. Starting in Monterosso allows you to tackle the toughest section (with lots and lots of steep, narrow stairs) while you're fresh—and to enjoy some of the region's most dramatic scenery as you approach Vernazza. You can also mix-and-match, splitting up the hike over several days, depending on your home base and itinerary, the weather, and the time of day. Remember that hikers need to pay a fee to enter the trails (see "Cinque Terre Park Cards," earlier).

Riomaggiore-Manarola (20 minutes): The popular, easy **Via dell'Amore** (as it's called) was washed out by a landslide in 2013;

they hope to reopen it in early 2014—inquire locally. If it's open, facing the front of the train station in Riomaggiore (#1), go up the stairs to the right, following signs for *Via dell'Amore*. The photo-worthy promenade—wide enough for baby strollers—winds along the coast to Manarola (#2). While there's no beach along the trail, stairs lead down to sunbathing rocks. A long tunnel and mega-nets protect hikers from mean-spirited falling rocks. A recommended wine bar—Bar & Vini A Piè de Mà—is located at the Riomaggiore trailhead and offers light meals, awesome town views, and clever boat storage under the train tracks. There's a picnic zone with a water fountain, shade, and a seagull that must have been human in a previous life hanging out just above the Manarola station (WC at Manarola station). If the trail is closed, you can connect these towns by train...or, far more scenically, with a €2 boat trip.

Manarola-Corniglia (45 minutes): The walk from Manarola (#2) to Corniglia (#3) is a little longer, more rugged, and steeper than the Via dell'Amore. It's also less romantic. To avoid the last stretch (switchback stairs leading up to the hill-capping town of Corniglia), end your hike at Corniglia's train station and catch the shuttle bus to the town center (2/hour, €1.50, free with Cinque Terre Park Card, usually timed to meet the trains).

Corniglia-Vernazza (1.5 hours): The hike from Corniglia (#3) to Vernazza (#4)—the wildest and greenest section of the coast—is very rewarding but very hilly (going the other direction, from Vernazza to Corniglia, is steeper). From the Corniglia station

Via dell'Amore

The Cinque Terre towns were extremely isolated until the last century. Villagers rarely married anyone from outside their town.

After the blasting of a second train line in the 1920s, a trail was made between the first two towns, Riomaggiore and Manarola. The gunpowder warehouses built on each end, safely away from the townspeople, house cute little bars today.

Happy with the trail, the villagers asked that it be improved as a permanent connection between neighbors. But persistent landslides kept the trail closed more often than it was open. After World War II, the trail was reopened and became established as a lovers' meeting point for boys and girls from the two towns. (After one extended closure in 1949, the trail was reopened for a Christmas marriage.) A journalist who noticed all the amorous graffiti along the path coined the trail's now-established name, Via dell'Amore: "Pathway of Love."

This new lane changed the social dynamics between the two villages, and made life much more fun and interesting for courting couples. Today, many tourists are put off by the cluttered graffiti that lines the trail. But it's all part of the history of the Cinque Terre's little lovers' lane.

You'll see padlocks locked to wires, cables, and fences. Closing a padlock with your lover at a lovey-dovey spot—often a bridge—is a common ritual in Italy (it was re-popularized by a teen novel a few years ago). In case you're so inclined, the hardware store next to Bar Centrale in Riomaggiore sells these locks. (You'll notice many of the locks come with the park logo.)

Major construction work—including the addition in 1994 of tunnels—has made the trail safer. Notice how the brick-lined arcades match the train tunnel below. Rock climbers from the north ("Dolomite spiders") were imported to help with the treacherous construction work. As you hike, look up and notice the massive steel netting bolted to the cliffside. Look down at the boulders that fell before the nets were added, and up at the boulders that have been caught...and be thankful for those Dolomite spiders.

Continuing the romance theme, benches along the way are named for lovers from Greek mythology. The many agave plants sport carved love notes—etched by amorous couples who likely don't know that the plant, which flowers once and then dies, is named for a tragic Greek story.

and beach, zigzag up to the town (via the steep stairs, the longer road, or the shuttle bus). Keep going through vineyards toward Vernazza, and after about ten minutes, you'll see Guvano beach far beneath you (once the region's nude beach). The scenic trail leads through a virtually deserted village, past picnic tables, through lots of fragrant and flowery vegetation, into Vernazza. If you need a break before reaching Vernazza, stop by Franco's Ristorante and Bar la Torre; it has a small menu but big views.

Vernazza-Monterosso (1.5 hours): The trail from Vernazza (#4) to Monterosso (#5) is a scenic up-and-down-a-lot trek and the most challenging of the bunch. Trails are narrow, steep, and crumbly, with a lot of steps (some readers report "very dangerous"), but easy to follow. Locals frown on camping at the picnic tables located midway. The views just out of Vernazza, looking back at the town, are spectacular. From there you'll gradually ascend, passing some scenic waterfalls populated by croaking frogs. As you approach Monterosso, you'll descend steeply—on very tall, knee-testing stairs—through vineyards, eventually following a rivulet to the sea. The last stretch into Monterosso is along a pleasant, paved pathway clinging to the cliff. You'll pop out right at Monterosso's refreshing old town beach.

Longer Hikes

While the national park charges admission for the coastal trails, they also maintain a free, far more extensive network of trails higher in the hills. Shuttle buses make the going easier, connecting coastal villages and distant trailheads. For pointers, ask at a TI or park office—or anyone who's helpful (the Manarola-based Cinque Terre Trekking is a good resource; see page 405).

Manarola-Volastra-Corniglia via the High Road (2.5 hours): One option—particularly if the Manarola-Corniglia trail is closed (and, if you're into serious hikes, even if it isn't)—is the hike from Manarola up to the village of Volastra, then north through high-altitude vineyard terraces, and steeply down through a forest to Corniglia (about six miles total). You can shave the two steepest miles off this route by taking the shuttle bus from Manarola up to Volastra (€1.50 or free with Cinque Terre Park Card, schedule at park office, about hourly, 15 minutes). If you prefer to hike, you have two options for getting from Manarola to Volastra. The national park's official route (trail #6) cuts up through the valley, with less scenery. Locals have cleared a more scenic alternate route that begins with the vineyard hike on my self-guided walk for Manarola (page 406). Partway along this walk, when you reach the wooden religious scenes scampering up the hillside, take a sharp right and walk uphill, following the signs for *Volastra panoramica (Corniglia)*. While steeper than the official route, this trail follows the ridge at the top of the vineyard, providing wonderful sea views.

By shuttle bus or by one of the trails, you'll reach Volastra. This tiny village, perched between Manarola and Corniglia, hosts lots of Germans and Italians in the summer. (Just below its town center, in the hamlet of Groppo, is the Cinque Terre Cooperative Winery.) When you're ready to head for Corniglia, make your way to the village church (where the shuttle bus drops off) and look for *Corniglia* signs. You'll circle around to the front door of the church; directly across the piazza, find the trailhead (marked by an iron cross) for trail #6d to Case Pianca. Here begins one of the finest hikes in the region, tight-roping along narrow trails tucked between vineyard terraces, with spectacular bird's eye views over the entire Cinque Terre. You'll cut up and down the terraces a bit—just keep following the red-and-white markings and arrows. After passing a little village (and following the signs through someone's seaview backyard), the trail enters a forest and begins its sharp, rocky descent into Corniglia. (To skip the descent, you could turn around and hike back through the vineyards to Volastra and return by shuttle bus to Manarola.) High above Corniglia, you'll reach a fork, where you turn left to proceed downhill on trail #7a to Corniglia.

Other Longer Hikes: If parts of the main coastal trail are closed and you're here for some serious hiking, get tips from locals on alternative trails. Popular options include **Vernazza to Reggio** (straight up the ridge, along Stations of the Cross, to the Sanctuary of Madonna; about an hour one-way, but easier if you take the shuttle bus from Vernazza); **Monterosso to Levanto** (about 3.5 hours one-way, moderately strenuous); and **Riomaggiore to Portovenere** (about 5 hours one-way, a challenging trek best for serious hikers). Be sure to get specific pointers before you set out.

Swimming, Kayaking, and Biking

Every town in the Cinque Terre has a beach or a rocky place to swim. Monterosso has the biggest and sandiest beach, with umbrellas and beach-use fees (but it's free where there are no umbrellas). Vernazza's main beach is tiny—better for sunning than swimming; the new, flood-created beach there is bigger. Manarola and Riomaggiore have the worst beaches (no sand), but Manarola offers the best deep-water swimming.

Wear your walking shoes and pack your swim gear. Several of the beaches have showers (no shampoo, please). Underwater sightseeing is full of fish—goggles are sold in local shops. Sea urchins can be a problem if you walk on the rocks, and sometimes jellyfish wash up on the pebbles, so water shoes (or at least flip-flops) are essential.

You can rent kayaks or boats in Riomaggiore and Monterosso.

(For details, see individual town listings in this chapter.) Some readers say kayaking can be dangerous—the kayaks tip easily, training is not provided, and lifejackets are not required.

Sleeping in the Cinque Terre

If you think too many people have my book, avoid Vernazza. You get fewer crowds and better value for your money in other towns. Monterosso is a good choice for sun-worshipping softies, those who prefer the ease of a real hotel, and the younger crowd (more nightlife). Hermits, anarchists, wine lovers, and mountain goats like Corniglia. Sophisticated Italians and Germans choose charming but not overrun Manarola, which has a good range of (relatively) professional-feeling small accommodations, but limited dining options. Riomaggiore—bigger than Vernazza and less resorty than Monterosso—has the cheapest beds, but hoteliers there tend to be a bit flakier.

While the Cinque Terre is too rugged for the mobs that ravage the Spanish and French coasts, it's popular with Italians, Germans, and in-the-know Americans. Hotels charge more and are packed on holidays (including Easter); in May, June, and September; and on Fridays and Saturdays all summer. (With global warming, sweltering August is no longer considered peak season on this stretch of the Riviera.) While you can find doubles for €65 or €70 most of the season, you'll pay extra (around €80) in May and June. The prices I've listed are the maximum for April through October. For a terrace or view, you might pay an extra €20 or more. Apartments for four can be economical for families—figure around €120.

It's smart to reserve your room in advance in May, June, July, and September, and on weekends and holidays. At other times,

you can land a double room on any day just by arriving in town (ideally by noon) and asking around at bars and restaurants, or simply by approaching locals on the street. Many travelers enjoy the opportunity to shop around a bit and get the best price by bargaining. Private rooms—called *affitta camere*—are no longer an intimate stay with a family. They are generally comfortable apartments (often with small kitchens), where you get the key and come and go as you like, rarely seeing your landlord. Many landowners rent the buildings by the year to local managers, who then attempt to make a profit by filling them night after night with tourists. While air-conditioning is essential in the summer elsewhere in Italy, in the breezy Cinque Terre you can generally manage fine without it.

For the best value, visit several private rooms and snare the best. Going direct cuts out the middleman and softens prices. Staying more than one night gives you bargaining leverage. Plan on paying cash. Private rooms are generally bigger and more comfortable than those offered by pensions and have the same privacy as a hotel room.

If you want the security of a reservation, make it at a hotel long in advance (smaller places generally don't take reservations very far ahead). If you do reserve, do it by email, and be sure to honor your reservation (or, if you must cancel, do it as early as possible). Since people renting rooms usually don't take deposits, they lose money if you don't show up. The more formal places tend to have strict cancellation policies.

Most of the private rooms don't include breakfast, so I've suggested alternatives in each town. The basic, very Italian choice is simply to drop by a neighborhood bar to buy a coffee and *cornetto* or a croissant. Some pricier places "include breakfast," but this usually consists of a few paltry items (yogurt, instant coffee, stale croissant) in a mini-fridge in your room.

Eating in the Cinque Terre

Hanging out at a seaview restaurant while sampling local specialties could become one of your favorite memories.

The key staple here is anchovies (*acciughe*; ah CHOO-gay)—ideally served the day they're caught. There's nothing cool about being an anchovy virgin. If you've always hated anchovies (the harsh, cured-in-salt American kind), try them fresh here. They can be prepared a variety of ways: marinated, salted, butterflied and deep-fried (sometimes with a delicious garlic/vinegar sauce called *giada*), and so on. *Tegame alla vernazzana* is the most typical main course in Vernazza: a layered, casserole-like dish of whole anchovies, potatoes, tomatoes, white wine, oil, and herbs.

While antipasto means cheese and salami in Tuscany, here you'll get *antipasti frutti di mare* (sometimes called simply *antipasti misti*), a plate of mixed "fruits of the sea" and a fine way to start a meal. Many restaurants are particularly proud of their *antipasti frutti di mare*—it's how they show off. For two diners, splitting one of these and a pasta dish can be plenty.

This region is the birthplace of pesto. Basil, which loves the temperate Ligurian climate, is ground with cheese (half parmigiano cow cheese and half pecorino sheep cheese), garlic, olive oil, and pine nuts, and then poured over pasta. Try it on spaghetti or, better yet, on *trenette* (the long, flat Ligurian noodle ruffled on one side) or *trofie* (short, dense twists made of flour with a bit of potato), both designed specifically for pesto to cling to. Many also like pesto lasagna, always made with white sauce, never red. If you become addicted, small jars of pesto are sold in the local grocery stores and gift shops. If it's refrigerated, it's fresh; this is what you want if you're eating it today. For taking home, get the jar-on-a-shelf pesto.

Pansotti are ravioli with ricotta and a mixture of greens, often served with a walnut sauce...delightful and filling.

Focaccia, the tasty pillowy bread, also originates here in Liguria. Locals say the best focaccia is made between the Cinque Terre and Genoa. It's simply flatbread with olive oil and salt. The baker roughs up the dough with finger holes, then bakes it. Focaccia comes plain or with onions, sage, or olive bits, and is a local favorite for a snack on the beach. Bakeries sell it in rounds or slices by weight (a portion is about 100 grams, or *un etto*).

Farinata, a humble fried-bread snack, is made from chickpea meal, water, oil, and pepper and baked on a copper tray in a wood-burning stove. *Farinata* is sold at pizza and focaccia places.

The *vino delle Cinque Terre,* while not one of Italy's top wines, flows cheap and easily throughout the region. It's white—great with seafood. For a sweet dessert wine, the *Sciacchetrà* wine is worth the splurge (€4 per small glass, often served with a cookie). You could order the fun dessert *torta della nonna* ("grandmother's cake") and dunk chunks of it into your glass. Aged *Sciacchetrà* is dry and costly (up to €12/glass). While 10 kilos of grapes yield 7 liters of local wine, *Sciacchetrà* is made from near-raisins, and 10 kilos of grapes make only 1.5 liters of *Sciacchetrà.* The word means "push and pull"—push in lots of grapes, pull out the best wine. If your room is up a lot of steps, be warned: *Sciacchetrà* is 18 percent alcohol, while regular wine is only 11 percent.

In the cool, calm evening, sit on Vernazza's breakwater with a glass of wine and watch the phosphorescence in the waves.

Nightlife in the Cinque Terre

While the Cinque Terre is certainly not noted for bumping beach-town nightlife like nearby Viareggio, you'll find some sort of travel-tale-telling hub in Monterosso, Vernazza, and Riomaggiore (Manarola and Corniglia are sleepy). Monterosso (where bars can stay open until 2:00 in the morning) has a lively scene, especially in the summertime—but no *discoteca*...yet. In Vernazza, the nightlife centers in the bars on the waterfront piazza, which is the small-town-style place to "see and be seen." A town law requires all bars to shut by midnight. In Riomaggiore, Bar Centrale is the, well, central place for cocktails and meeting fellow travelers. (For details, see the "Nightlife" sections for these three villages.) Wherever your night adventures take you, have fun, but please remember that residents live upstairs.

Helpful Hints for the Cinque Terre

Tourist and Park Information: Each town has a well-staffed park information office, which generally serves as an all-purpose town TI as well (listed throughout this chapter).

Money: Banks and ATMs are plentiful throughout the region.

Baggage Storage: You can store bags at La Spezia's train station (€3/12 hours, 8:00-22:00, see page 491) and at the Wash and Dry Lavarapido in Monterosso (€5/day, see page 443).

Services: Every train station has a handy, free public WC. Otherwise, pop into a bar or restaurant.

Taxi: Cinqueterre Taxi covers all five towns (mobile 334-776-1946 or 347-652-0837, www.cinqueterretaxi.com).

Local Guides: Andrea Bordigoni is both knowledgeable and a delight (€110/half-day, €175/day, mobile 393-133-9409, bordigo@inwind.it). Other local guides are **Marco Brizzi** (mobile 328-694-2847, www.hi-kc.com, marco_brizzi@yahoo.it) and **Paola Tommarchi** (paolatomma@alice.it).

Booking Agency: Miriana at **Cinque Terre Riviera** books rooms in the Cinque Terre towns, Portovenere, and La Spezia for a 10 percent markup over the list price (can also arrange transportation, cooking classes, and weddings; Via Roma 24 in Vernazza or Via Picedi 18 in La Spezia; tel. 0187-520-702, mobile 340-794-7358, www.cinqueterreriviera.com, info@cinqueterreriviera.com, English spoken).

Tours and Activities: ArbaSPàa, which has an office in Manarola, can arrange Cinque Terre experiences that might be tricky to do on your own, such as wine-tasting at a vineyard, cooking classes (6-person minimum), or a fishing trip with local sailors (see website for options and book in advance, tel. 0187-920-785, www.arbaspaa.com; their Explora shop in Manarola, at Via Discovolo 204, is closed Tue).

Riomaggiore (Town #1)

The most substantial non-resort town of the group, Riomaggiore is a disappointment from the train station. But just walk through the tunnel next to the train tracks, and you'll discover a more real, laid-back, and workaday town than its touristy neighbors. The main drag through town, while traffic-free, feels more urban than "village," and surrounding the harbor is a fascinating tangle of pastel homes leaning on each other like drunken sailors.

Orientation to Riomaggiore

Tourist Information

The TI is in the train station at the ticket desk (daily 8:00-18:00, tel. 0187-920-633). If the TI in the station is crowded, buy your hiking pass at the Cinque Terre park shop/information office next door, facing the mural (daily 7:00-19:00, shorter hours off-season, tel. 0187-760-515). For informal information sources, try Ivo and Alberto, who run Bar Centrale (see "Nightlife in Riomaggiore," later) or Amy and Francesco, who run Riomaggiore Reservations (see "Sleeping in Riomaggiore," later).

Arrival in Riomaggiore

By Train: Riomaggiore's train station is separated from the town center by a steep hill (which you can summit for fine views by following my self-guided walk). The easiest way to get into town is to take the pedestrian tunnel that begins by the big mural (and parallels the rail tunnel). You'll exit at the bottom of Via Colombo; most recommended hotels are a short hike up this steep artery. If you're staying near the top of town and want to skip the walk, you can catch the shuttle bus (described next) at the bottom of Via Colombo and ride it partway up.

By Car: Day-trippers are not allowed to drive into Riomaggiore; you'll have to park at the lot above town (€1.50/hour), then walk or ride the shuttle bus downtown (€1.50 one-way, €2.50 round-trip, free with Cinque Terre Park Card, 1-2/hour but almost comically erratic, main stop at the fork of Via Colombo and Via Malborghetto, or flag it down as it passes). If you're staying overnight, seek the advice of your hotelier, who may have a line on their own parking or can fill you in on all the logistics of public parking (which tend to change frequently). Riomaggiore allows overnighters to drive into the town center long enough to drop off your bags, but only during designated times (likely Mon-Fri 6:00-10:00 & 14:00-16:00, Sat 6:00-10:00 only, not on Sun—but confirm with your hotelier).

Helpful Hints

Internet Access: The **park shop/information office** has four Internet terminals upstairs, plus Wi-Fi (€1.50/20 minutes, hours listed earlier, under "Tourist Information"). **La Zorza Café** and **Bar Centrale** both offer free Wi-Fi with the purchase of a drink (see "Nightlife in Riomaggiore," later).

Laundry: A self-service launderette is on the main street (€3.50/wash, €3.50/dry, €1/soap, daily in summer 8:30-20:00, shorter hours off-season, run by Edi's Rooms next door, Via Colombo 111).

Self-Guided Walk

Welcome to Riomaggiore

Here's a partly uphill but fairly easy loop trip that takes the long way around from the station into town. You'll enjoy some fine views before strolling down the main street to the harbor. (If you're arriving for an overnight stay and packing heavy bags, drop them off at your hotel before starting this walk.)

• *Start at the train station. (If you arrive by boat, cross beneath the tracks and take a left, then hike through the tunnel along the tracks to reach the station.) You'll come to some...*

Colorful Murals: These murals, with subjects modeled after real-life Riomaggiorians, glorify the nameless workers who con-

structed the nearly 300 million cubic feet of dry-stone walls (made without mortar) that run throughout the Cinque Terre. These walls give the region its characteristic *muri a secco* terracing for vineyards and olive groves. The murals, created by Argentinean artist Silvio Benedetto, are explained well in English.

Looking left, notice the stairs climbing up just past the station building. These lead to the trail to Manarola, also known as the **Via dell'Amore** (described on page 386).

• *The fastest way into town is to take the pedestrian tunnel (which parallels the tracks from near the murals) straight to the bottom of Via Colombo, just above the marina. But I'd rather take the scenic route, up and over the hill. Before starting, you can check to see if the elevator near the entrance to the tunnel is running (but I doubt it). More likely, you'll have to hoof it: Facing the mural, turn left, then go right up the wide street just before the station café. Watch for the stairs leading through the garden on your right to the upper switchback, then, once on high ground, hook back toward the sea. Soon you'll pass the concrete tower marking the top of the elevator we saw earlier, and a bit farther, a fine viewpoint.*

Top o' the Town: Here you're treated to spectacular sea views. Hook left around the bluff; once you round the bend, ignore the steps marked *Marina Seacoast* (which lead to the harbor) and continue another five minutes along level ground to the church. You'll pass under the city hall, with murals celebrating the heroic grape-pickers and fishermen of the region (also by Silvio Benedetto).

• *Before reaching the church, pause to enjoy the...*

Town View: The major river of this region once ran through this valley, as implied by the name Riomaggiore (local dialect for "river" and "major"). As in the other Cinque Terre towns, the river ravine is now paved over, and the romantic arched bridges that once connected the two sides have been replaced by a practical modern road.

Notice the lack of ugly aerial antennae. In the 1980s, every residence got cable. Now, the TV tower on the hilltop behind the church steeple brings the modern world into each home. The church was rebuilt in 1870, but was first established in 1340. It's dedicated to St. John the Baptist, the patron saint of Genoa, the maritime republic that once dominated the region.

• *Continue straight past the church and along the narrow lane, watching on the right for wide stairs leading down to Riomaggiore's main street...*

Via Colombo: As in the other Cinque Terre towns, the main street of Riomaggiore covers its *rio maggiore*, which carved the canyon now filled by the town's pastel high-rises. Across from where you came down the stairs, notice the handy public WCs. Then start downhill. First you'll pass (on the right, at #62) a good pizzeria/*focacceria*, facing the Co-op grocery store across the street (at #55). Farther down on the left is the town butcher (*marcelleria*, #103). The big covered terrace on the right belongs to Bar Centrale, the town's most popular hangout for international visitors (at #144; see "Nightlife in Riomaggiore," later). Just after the terrace sits a forlorn row of recycling containers, with careful instructions that are ignored by locals and tourists alike.

As you round the bend to the left, notice the old-timey pharmacy just above (on the right). On your left, at #199, peek into the Il Pescato Cucinato shop, where Laura fries up her husband Eduardo's fresh catch; grab a paper cone of deep-fried seafood as a snack. Where the road bends sharply right, notice the bench on your left (just before La Zorza Café)—the hangout for the town's old-timers, who keep a running commentary on the steady flow of people. Straight ahead, you can already see where this street will dead-end. The last shop on the left, Alimentari Franca (at #251), is a well-stocked grocery where you can gather the makings for a perfect picnic out on the harbor or along the Via dell'Amore.

Where Via Colombo dead-ends, look right to see the tunnel leading back to the station (and the Via dell'Amore to Manarola, and eventually to the other Cinque Terre towns). Look left to see two sets of stairs. The "up" stairs take you to a park-like square built over the train tracks, which provides the children of the town a bit of level land on which to kick their soccer balls. The murals above celebrate the great-grandparents of these very children—the salt-of-the-earth locals who earned a humble living before the age of tourism.

• *The "down" stairs take you to the...*

Marina: This most picturesque corner of Riomaggiore features a tight cluster of buildings huddling nervously around a postage-stamp square and vest-pocket harbor. Because Riomaggiore lacks the naturally protected harbor of Vernazza, when bad weather is expected, local fishermen pull their boats up to the safety of the little square. This is quite an operation, so it's a team effort—the signal goes out, and anyone with a boat of their own helps move the whole fleet. Sometimes the fishermen are busy beaching their boats even on a bright, sunny day—an indication that they know something you don't know.

A couple of recommended restaurants—with high prices and memorable seating—look down over the action. Head past them and up the walkway along the left side of the harbor, and enjoy the views of the town's colorful pastel buildings, with the craggy coastline of the Cinque Terre just beyond. Below you, the break-water curves out to sea, providing a bit of protection for the harbor. These rocks are popular with sunbathers by day and romantics and photographers at sunset.

For a peek at Riomaggiore's beach, continue around the bluff on this trail toward the Punta di Montenero, the cape that defines the southern end of the Cinque Terre. As you walk you'll pass the rugged boat landing and eventually run into Riomaggiore's un-comfortably rocky but still inviting beach *(spiaggia)*. Ponder how Europeans manage to look relaxed when lounging on football-sized "pebbles."

Sights in Riomaggiore

Beach

Riomaggiore's rugged and tiny "beach" is rocky, but it's clean and peaceful (to find it, see the end of my self-guided walk, above).

To Manarola

Via dell'Amore
Cliffs

PARK OFFICE
KIOSK
TRAIN
STATION

WALK
BEGINS

MURALS

Ligurian Sea

CINQUE
TERRE INFO

PEDESTRIAN
TUNNEL

VIA PECUNIA
VIA SIGNORINI
VIA SANT'ANTONIO
VIA PUNTA

Cliffs

BOAT DOCK

Harbor

BREAKWATER

VIA SAN GIACOMO

BOAT
TICKETS

1. Riomaggiore Reservations (Office), Il Pescato Cucinato, Giammi Caffè & Co-op Grocery
2. Edi's Rooms & Launderette
3. L'Ancora Rooms
4. Alla Marina Rooms; Enoteca & Ristorante Dau Cila
5. La Dolce Vita Rooms
6. Il BoMa Rooms
7. Locanda del Sole
8. Locanda dalla Compagnia
9. Camere Patrizia
10. La Lanterna Ristorante
11. Trattoria la Grotta & Il Grottino Ristorante
12. Bar Centrale & Gelateria
13. Pizzeria/Focacceria
14. Te La Do Io La Merenda Snack Bar
15. Alimentari Franca
16. Bar & Vini A Piè de Mà
17. La Zorza Café
18. Co-op Grocery

There's a shower here in the summer, and another closer to town by the boat landing—where many enjoy sunning on and jumping from the rocks.

Kayaks and Water Sports

The town has a diving center (scuba, snorkeling, kayaks; office down the stairs and under the tracks on Via San Giacomo, daily May-Sept 9:00-18:00, open in good weather only—likely weekends only in shoulder season, tel. 0187-920-011, www.5terrediving.it).

Hikes

It's possible to hike from here all the way to Portovenere (about 5 strenuous hours). Some easier alternatives are also available. A trail rises scenically from Riomaggiore to the 14th-century Madonna di Montenero sanctuary, high above the town (45 minutes, take the main road inland until you see signs, or ride the green shuttle

CINQUE TERRE

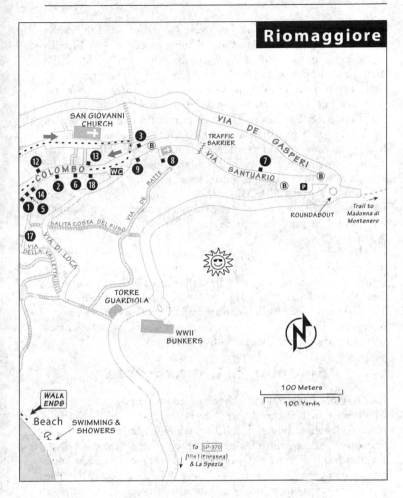

bus 12 minutes from the town center to the sanctuary trail, then walk uphill another 10 minutes; great picnic spot up top). The cliff-hanging Torre Guardiola trail, a steep 20-minute climb from the beach up to old WWII bunkers and a hilltop botanical pathway, has been closed indefinitely because of a rock slide.

Nightlife in Riomaggiore

Bar Centrale, run by sociable Ivo, Alberto, and the gang, offers "nightlife" any time of day—making it a good stop for Italian breakfast and music. Ivo, who lived in San Francisco, fills his bar with San Franciscan rock and a fun-loving vibe. During the day, this is a shaded place to relax with other travelers; it feels a little like the village's living room. At night, it offers the younger set the liveliest action (and best mojitos) in town (daily 7:30-1:00 in the morning, closed Mon in winter, 30 minutes of free Wi-Fi with drink, in the town center at Via Colombo 144, tel. 0187-920-208). They plan to open a restaurant nearby, serving Italian classics as well as comfort food for homesick Americans. The good *gelateria* next door has the same name but different owners.

Enoteca & Ristorante Dau Cila, a cool little hideaway with a mellow jazz-and-Brazilian-lounge ambience down at the miniscule harbor, is a counterpoint to wild Bar Centrale. It's cool for cocktails and open nightly until 24:00 (snacks and meals, fine wine by the glass; see "Eating in Riomaggiore," later).

Bar & Vini A Piè de Mà, at the beginning of Via dell'Amore, has piles of charm, €6 cocktails, frequent music, and stays open until midnight June through September (see "Eating in Riomaggiore," later).

La Zorza Café is a hip, youthful alternative to the other bars in town. The music is thumping, and the cocktails come with a spread of little snacks (€6 cocktails, daily until 1:00 in the morning, free Wi-Fi with drink, tel. 0187-920-036, fun-loving Elenia).

The marvelous **Via dell'Amore** trail (described earlier), lit only with subtle ground lighting so that you can see the stars, welcomes romantics after dark. The trail is free after 19:30.

Sleeping in Riomaggiore

Riomaggiore has arranged its private-room rental system somewhat better than its neighbors. Several agencies—with relatively predictable office hours, English-speaking staff, and email addresses—line up within a few yards of each other on the main drag. Each manages a corral of local rooms for rent—but be aware that quality and specific amenities can vary wildly, so get a complete picture of the room before you commit. These offices sometimes close unexpectedly, so it's smart to settle up the day before you leave in case they're closed when you need to depart. Expect lots of stairs.

Room-Booking Services

Given the relatively lousy value of Riomaggiore's hotels (see next section), I'd contact one of these services first. Keep in mind that very few of these rooms include breakfast; for ideas, see "Breakfast" on page 404.

$$ Riomaggiore Reservations, run with care and smooth communication by American expat Amy and her Italian husband Francesco, offers 12 rooms and 15 apartments (Db-€60-90 depending on view, Db suite with top view-€120, discount if you pay cash, reception open daily 9:00-13:00 & 14:00-17:00 in season, some rooms have air-con, free Wi-Fi at office; parking-€10/

Sleep Code

(€1 = about $1.30, country code: 39)
S = Single, **D** = Double/Twin, **T** = Triple, **Q** = Quad, **b** = bathroom, **s** = shower only. Unless otherwise noted, credit cards are accepted, English is spoken, and breakfast is included (except in Vernazza). Many towns in Italy levy a hotel tax of €2 per person, per night, which must be paid in cash (not included in the rates I've quoted).

To help you sort easily through these listings, I've divided the accommodations into three categories based on the price for a standard double room with bath:

$$$ Higher Priced—Most rooms €100 or more.
$$ Moderately Priced—Most rooms between €50-100.
$ Lower Priced—Most rooms €50 or less.

Prices can change without notice; verify the hotel's current rates online or by email. For the best prices, always book direct.

---

day at the top of town—reserve in advance; Via Colombo 181, tel. 0187-760-575, www.riomaggiorereservations.com, info@riomaggiorereservations.com).

$$ Edi's Rooms manages 20 rooms and apartments. You pay extra for views (Db-€70-100 depending on size/view/location, apartment Qb-€140-180, reserve with credit card, office open daily in summer 8:30-20:00, in winter 10:30-12:30 & 14:30-18:00, some rooms involve climbing a lot of steps—ask, some rooms have air-con and/or free Wi-Fi, reception at Via Colombo 111, tel. 0187-760-842, tel. 0187-920-325, www.appartamenticinqueterre.net, edi-vesigna@iol.it). They also rent three hotelesque but pricey rooms of their own, called **L'Ancora** (Db-€120, air-con, free Wi-Fi, www.lancoracinqueterre.com).

Private Rooms

Another option is to book direct with someone who rents just a few rooms of their own, cutting out the middleman. Here are some options.

$$$ Alla Marina is Riomaggiore's most worthwhile splurge, with three rooms and an apartment (all but one with sea views) at the top of one of the very tall, steep, skinny buildings that rise up from the harbor. The furnishings are a stylish combination of modern and nautical, and friendly Sandro takes pride in running a tight ship (non-view Db-€100, view Db-€120, view Tb-€135, view Qb-€180, includes breakfast in room, air-con, free minibar, free Wi-Fi, parking-€10/day; Via San Giacomo 61—ask Sandro about the easier back-door entrance; mobile 328-013-4077, www. allamarina.com, info@allamarina.com).

$$ La Dolce Vita offers five nice, good-value rooms on the main drag, plus two apartments elsewhere in town (Db-€65-80, open daily 9:30-19:30—if they're closed, they're full; Via Colombo 167, tel. 0187-762-283, mobile 329-099-2741, agonatal@libero.it, helpful Giacomo and Simone).

$$ Il BoMa—named for the owners, American Maddy and her Italian husband Bombetta—has three pricey but well-appointed rooms right along the main drag (Db-€90, includes breakfast in room, one has private bathroom down the hall and fans, the others have air-con, free Wi-Fi, up three flights at Via Colombo 99, tel. 0187-920-395, mobile 320-0748826, www.ilboma.com, info@ilboma.it).

Hotels

Perhaps sensing that they have little "hotel" competition, these options generally offer less value than the room-booking services and private rooms. Breakfast is included in their rates.

$$$ Locanda del Sole has seven modern, basic, and overpriced rooms with a shared and peaceful terrace. Located at the utilitarian top end of town, it's a five-minute walk downhill to the center. Easy (and free with this book) parking makes it especially appealing to drivers (Db-€130, air-con, free Wi-Fi in common areas, Via Santuario 114, tel. 0187-920-773, mobile 340-983-0090, www.locandadelsole.net, info@locandadelsole.net, Enrico).

$$ Locanda dalla Compagnia, loosely run by Allessandro, rents five rooms at the top of town, just 300 yards below the parking lot and the little church. All rooms—decent but rather dim—are on the same tranquil ground floor and share a lounge (Db-€80, air-con, mini-fridge, no views, free Wi-Fi, reception closes at 19:00, Via del Santuario 232, tel. 0187-760-050, www.dallacompa.com, lacomp@libero.it). Allessandro also manages nine apartments scattered around town, which cost the same as his hotel rooms (but don't include breakfast).

Backpacker Dorms

$ Riomaggiore Reservations (also listed earlier) runs a mini-hostel in a fine communal apartment with eight beds in two rooms, a cool living room, a terrace, and a kitchen in a good, quiet location. They also have a four-bed unit with no terrace. Take care of this little treasure so it survives (€25/bed, reception open 9:00-13:00 & 14:00-17:00 in season, free Wi-Fi, Via Colombo 181, tel. 0187-760-575, www.riomaggiorereservations.com, info@riomaggiore reservations.com).

$ **Camere Patrizia,** a suitable last resort, rents cheap doubles (Db-€60, €70 on weekends) and dorm bunk beds (€25/person) from its reception at Via Colombo 25, but books only through www.hostelworld.com or to drop-ins (reception open daily 10:30-20:00, free Wi-Fi in office, mobile 328-309-3727).

Eating in Riomaggiore

On the Harbor

Harborfront dining comes with slightly higher prices but glorious views.

Enoteca & Ristorante Dau Cila (pronounced "dow CHEE-lah") is decked out like a black-and-white movie set in a centuries-old boat shed with extra tables outside on a rustic deck over dinghies. Try their antipasto specialty of several seafood appetizers and listen to the waves lapping at the harbor below (€13-15 pastas, €15-18 *secondi;* for lunch, they also have a simpler menu—€9-12 salads and *bruschette;* daily 12:00-24:00, closed Feb, Via San Giacomo 65, tel. 0187-760-032, Luca).

La Lanterna, with a gray-and-white interior and a few appealing harborview tables outside, is wedged into a niche in the Marina, overlooking the harbor under the tracks. Chef Massimo serves traditional plates, loves anchovies, and bakes fresh bread daily (€10-11 pastas, €12-18 *secondi,* no cover, daily 12:00-22:00, Via San Giacomo 10, tel. 0187-920-589).

On the Main Street, Via Colombo

Trattoria la Grotta, right in the town center (with no view), serves reliably good food with a passion for anchovies and mussels. You'll enjoy friendly service surrounded by historical photos and wonderful stonework in a dramatic, dressy, cave-like setting. Venessa is warm and helpful, while her mother, Isa, is busy cooking (€11-14 pastas, €11-15 *secondi,* 5 percent discount if you pay cash, daily 12:00-14:30 & 17:30-22:30, closed Wed in winter, Via Colombo 247, tel. 0187-920-187). Next door and run by the same family, **Il Grottino Ristorante** is slightly more upscale, with a similar approach and decor and a somewhat different menu (same hours, tel. 0187-920-938). I'd survey both to see which specials look good.

Bar Centrale, the popular bar and expat hangout, plans to begin serving American comfort food; for a break from pizza and pasta, drop by to scope out their menu (see "Nightlife in Riomaggiore," earlier).

Light Meals: Various handy carry-out eateries along the main drag offer good lunches or snacks on the go. At the top of town, the nameless **pizzeria/*focacceria*** at #62 is a reliable standby (€3 slices). For deep-fried seafood in a paper cone, two places face each other across the main street near the bottom of town; of these, I prefer **Il Pescato Cucinato,** where Eduardo fishes and his wife Laura fries (€5-7, chalkboard out front explains what's fresh, daily 11:20-20:30, Via Colombo 199, mobile 339-262-4815). **Te La Do Io La Merenda** has a counter piled with an assortment of munchies, including pizza and focaccia sandwiches (€3 light meals, daily 10:00-20:00, Via Colombo 161, mobile 340-400-3256).

Picnics: Groceries and delis lining Via Colombo sell food to go for a picnic at the harbor or beach. Look for the two *Co-Op* grocery store signs for the best prices. The handy **Alimentari Franca,** at the very bottom of the main street (conveniently located right by the train-station tunnel and stairs down to the marina/beach) has a more appealing selection and good service (Thu-Tue 8:00-12:45 & 15:30-19:30, closed Wed, Via Colombo 251).

Breakfast: While hotels include breakfast, many private rooms don't, and those that do often simply leave some basic continental breakfast fixings in your room's mini-fridge. For a good croissant-and-espresso fix, drop by **Bar Centrale** (which may expand its menu in the future). If you need eggs, consider **Giammi Caffè,** with outdoor tables on the main drag (€5 egg dishes, €13 big breakfast, daily 7:00-24:00, Via Colombo 189, mobile 331-608-3512).

Near the Train Station and Via dell'Amore

Bar & Vini A Piè de Mà, at the trailhead on the Manarola end of town, is good for a scenic light bite or quiet drink at night. The downstairs bar, with all of the great outdoor seating, is self-service: Head into the bar to place your order, then bring it out to your preferred perch (€8-12 dishes, €4 *panini*, daily 10:00-20:00, June-Sept until 24:00, free Wi-Fi—look for password on chalkboard, tel. 0187-921-037). Enjoying a meal at a table on its dramatically situated terrace provides an indelible Cinque Terre memory. In the summer they open a restaurant with table service upstairs—but I prefer the cheaper, simpler terrace.

Manarola (Town #2)

Mellow Manarola fills a ravine, bookended by its wild little harbor to the west and a diminutive hilltop church square inland to the east. Manarola is exceptional for being unexceptional: While Vernazza is prettier, Monterosso glitzier, Riomaggiore bigger, and Corniglia more rustic, each of those towns is also sorely lacking in other regards. Manarola hits a fine balance, giving it the "just right" combination of Cinque Terre qualities. Perhaps that's why it's a favorite among savvy Europeans seeking a relatively untrampled home base. The touristy zone squeezed between the cement-encased train tracks and the harbor can be stressfully congested, but head just a few steps uphill and you can breathe again. The higher you go, the less crowded it gets, culminating in the essentially tourist-free residential zone that clings to the ridge.

Manarola, whose hillsides are blanketed with vineyards, also provides the easiest access to the Cinque Terre's remarkable dry-stone terraces. The trail ringing the town's cemetery peninsula, adjacent to the main harbor, provides some of the most easily accessible and most strikingly beautiful town views anywhere in the region (best light late in the day). For a look at all the facets of  this delightful town, follow my gentle self-guided stroll from the church, through the vineyards, and down to the harborside park.

Orientation to Manarola

Tourist Information: As in other Cinque Terre towns, Manarola's train station has a TI/national park information office (likely daily 7:00-19:00, shorter hours off-season).

Getting Around: The national park's green **shuttle bus** runs from near the post office (halfway up Manarola's main street), stopping first at the parking lots above town, and then going all the way up to Volastra (€1.50 one-way, €2.50 round-trip, buy ticket on board, free with Cinque Terre Park Card, about hourly, just flag it down). Volastra is a great jumping-off point for a scenic hike through vineyards and forests to Corniglia (more challenging—and rewarding—than the official coastal trail; for details, see page 388).

To get to the **dock** and the boats that connect Manarola with the other Cinque Terre towns, find the steps to the left of the harbor view—they lead down to the ticket kiosk. Continue around the left side of the cliff (as you're facing the water) to catch the boats.

Wi-Fi, Laundry, and Hiking Gear and Tips: Cinque Terre Trekking, near the top of the main street (halfway up to the church), fills its cramped little shop with hiking gear; they also sell hiking maps (with free advice), offer pay Wi-Fi, and have a few self-service laundry machines (€10/load wash and dry, daily 9:00-13:00 & 14:00-20:00, shorter hours off-season, Via Discovolo 136, tel. 0187-920-715).

Arrival in Manarola

On Foot: Walking in from Riomaggiore on the Via dell'Amore, you'll pop out at Manarola's train station (see next).

By Train: Like Riomaggiore, Manarola is attached to its station by a 200-yard-long tunnel (lined with interesting photos). During WWII air raids, these tunnels provided refuge and a safe place for rattled villagers to sleep. Walking through the tunnel, you'll reach Manarola's elevated square (created by covering the tracks). To reach the busy harbor (with touristy restaurants, the boat dock, and the start of my self-guided walk), cross the piazza, then go down the other side. To reach the town, hilltop church, and vineyard strolls, turn right.

By Car: Unless you're sleeping here, you're not allowed to drive into Manarola. Park your car in one of the two lots just before town (€1.50/hour), then walk down the road to the church; from there, the street twists down to the main piazza, train-station tunnel (to reach the trailhead for the Via dell'Amore to Riomaggiore), and harbor (the start of my self-guided walk). It's an easy down-hill walk into town, or you can wait for the national park's shuttle bus (described earlier). If you're sleeping here, ask your hotelier for parking advice: You'll likely be allowed to drive into town to drop off your bags—but only during certain hours (likely Mon-Fri 6:00-10:00 & 14:00-16:00, Sat 6:00-10:00 only, not on Sun—confirm locally)—before heading back to the lot to park.

Self-Guided Walk

Welcome to Manarola

From the harbor, this 30-minute circular walk shows you the town and surrounding vineyards and ends at a fantastic viewpoint, perfect for a picnic.

• *Start down at the waterfront. Belly up to the wooden banister overlooking the rocky harbor, between the two restaurants.*

The Harbor: Manarola is tiny and picturesque, a tumble of buildings bunny-hopping down its ravine to the fun-loving waterfront. The breakwater—which attempts to make this jagged harbor a bit less dangerous—was built just over a decade ago. Notice how the I-beam crane launches the boats (which must be pulled ashore when bad weather is expected to avoid being smashed or swept away).

Facing the water, look to the right, at the hillside Punta Bonfiglio cemetery and park. The trail running around the base of the point—where this walk ends—offers magnificent views back on this part of town.

The town's swimming hole is just below you. Manarola has no sand, but offers the best deep-water swimming in the area. The first "beach" has a shower, ladder, and wonderful rocks. The second has tougher access and no shower, but feels more remote and pristine (follow the paved path toward Corniglia, just around the point). For many, the tricky access makes this "beach" dangerous.

• *Hiking inland up the town's main drag—comparison-shopping at the touristy restaurants—you'll climb a steep ramp to reach Manarola's "new" square, which covers the train tracks.*

Piazza Capellini: Built in 2004, this square is an all-around great idea, giving the town a safe, fun zone for kids. Locals living near the tracks also enjoy a little less train noise. Check out the mosaic in the middle of the square, which depicts the varieties of local fish in colorful enamel. The recommended Ristorante di Aristide has an inviting terrace right out on the square.

• *Go down the stairs at the upper end of the square. On your right, notice the tunnel that leads to Manarola's train station (and the trailhead for the Via dell'Amore to Riomaggiore). But for now, head up...*

Via Discovolo: Manarola's sleepy main street twists up through town, lined by modest shops and filled with pooped hikers. Just before the road bends sharply right, watch (on the right) for a waterwheel. This recalls the origin of the town's name—local dialect for "big wheel" (one of many possible derivations). Mills like this once powered the local olive oil industry. As you continue up (all the way to the church), you'll still hear the rushing waters of Manarola's stream. Like the streams in Riomaggiore, Monterosso, and Vernazza, Manarola's rivulet was covered over by a modern sewage system after World War II. Before that time, romantic bridges arched over its ravine. You can peek below the concrete street in several places to see the stream surging below your feet.

Across the street from the waterwheel and a bit farther up, notice the **Cinque Terre Trekking** shop (on your left), which outfits hikers with both information and gear (boots, clothes, walking sticks, and more).

• *Keep switchbacking up until you come to the square at the...*

Top of Manarola: The square is faced by a church, an oratory—now a religious and community meeting place—and a bell tower, which served as a watchtower when pirates raided the town (the cupola was added once the attacks ceased). Behind the church is Manarola's well-run youth hostel, originally the church's schoolhouse. To the right of the oratory, a stepped lane leads to Manarola's sizable tourist-free residential zone.

Check out the **church.** According to the white marble plaque in its facade, the Parish Church of St. Lawrence (San Lorenzo)

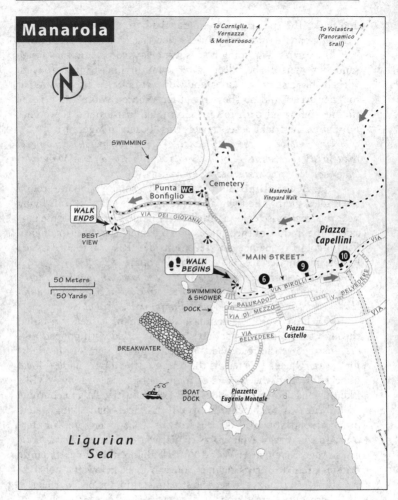

Manarola

To Corniglia,
Vernazza
& Monterosso

To Volastra
(Panoramico
trail)

N

SWIMMING

Punta
Bonfiglio **WC**

Cemetery

Manarola
Vineyard Walk

**WALK
ENDS**

VIA DEI GIOVANNI

*Piazza
Capellini*

BEST
VIEW

VIA

"MAIN STREET"

**WALK
BEGINS**

⑩

50 Meters

⑥

⑨

50 Yards

SWIMMING
& SHOWER

VIA BIROLLI

V. BELVEDERE

DOCK

BALURADO

VIA DI MEZZO

VIA

*Piazza
Castello*

VIA
BELVEDERE

BREAKWATER

BOAT
DOCK

*Piazzetta
Eugenio Montale*

*Ligurian
Sea*

dates from "MCCCXXXVIII" (1338). Step inside to see two altar-piece paintings from the unnamed Master of the Cinque Terre, the only painter of any note from this region (left wall and above main altar). While the style is Gothic, the work dates from the late 15th century, long after Florence had entered the Renaissance. Note the humble painted stone ceiling, which replaced the wooden original in the 1800s. It features Lawrence, patron saint of the Cinque Terre, with his grill, the symbol of his martyrdom (he was roasted on it).

• *With the bell tower on your left, head about 20 yards down the main street below the church and find a wooden railing. It marks the start of a delightful stroll around the high side of town, and back to the seafront. This is the beginning of the...*

1. La Torretta Rooms
2. Aria di Mare Rooms
3. B&B Da Baranin
4. Ostello 5-Terre
5. Albergo Ca' d'Andrean
6. Marina Piccola Rooms & Restaurant
7. Affitta Camere da Paulin
8. To Hotel Il Saraceno
9. Trattoria Il Porticciolo
10. Ristorante di Aristide
11. Via Discovolo Eateries
12. Trattoria dal Billy
13. Cinque Terre Trekking
14. Shuttle Bus to Parking Lot & Volastra

CINQUE TERRE

Manarola Vineyard Walk: Don't miss this experience. Simply follow the wooden railing, enjoying lemon groves and wild red valerian (used for insomnia since the days of the Romans). Along the path, which is primarily flat, you'll get a close-up look at the region's famous dry-stone walls and finely crafted vineyards (with dried-heather thatches to protect the grapes from the southwest winds). Smell the rosemary. Study the structure of the town, and pick out the scant remains of an old fort. Notice the S-shape of the main road—once a riverbed—that flows through town. The town's roofs are traditionally made of locally quarried slate, rather than tile, and are held down by rocks during windstorms.

Halfway along the lip of the ravine, a path marked *Volastra panoramico (Corniglia)* leads steeply up into the vineyards on the right. This path passes a variety of simple wooden religious scenes, the work of local resident Mario Andreoli. Before his father died, Mario promised him he'd replace the old cross on the family's vineyard. Mario has been adding figures ever since. After recovering from a rare illness, he redoubled his efforts. On religious holidays, everything's lit up: the Nativity, the Last Supper, the Crucifixion, the Resurrection, and more. Some of the scenes are left up year-round. High above, a recent fire burned off the tree cover, revealing ancient terraces that line the terrain like a topographic map. This path also marks the start of the scenic route to Volastra (on the hilltop above), and eventually to Corniglia (this challenging alternative to the standard coastal route is described on page 388).

• *Continue on the level trail around the base of the hill. Soon the harbor comes into view. Keep looping around the hill for even better views of town. Once you're facing the sea (with the cemetery peninsula below you), the trail takes a sharp left and heads down toward the water. When you hit the clifftop fence, the T-intersection gives you a choice: right, to the coastal trail to Corniglia, or left, back to town. Turn left for now. Before descending, watch for the turnoff on the right, detouring into...*

The Cemetery: Ever since Napoleon—who was king of Italy in the early 1800s—decreed that cemeteries were health risks, Cinque Terre's burial spots have been located outside the towns. The result: The dearly departed generally get first-class sea views. Each cemetery—with evocative yellowed photos and finely carved Carrara marble memorial reliefs—is worth a visit. (The basic structure for all of them is the same, but Manarola's is the most easily accessible.)

In cemeteries like these, there's a hierarchy of four places to park your mortal remains: a graveyard, a spacious death condo *(loculo)*, a mini bone-niche *(ossario)*, or the communal ossuary. Because of the tight space, a time limit is assigned to the first three options (although many older tombs are grandfathered in). Bones go into the ossuary in the middle of the chapel floor after about a generation. Traditionally, locals make weekly visits to loved ones here, often bringing flowers. The rolling stepladder makes access to top-floor *loculi* easy.

• *The Manarola cemetery is on...*

Punta Bonfiglio: This point offers some of the most commanding views of the entire region. To find the best vantage point, take the stairs just below the cemetery (through the green gate), then walk farther out toward the water through a park (playground, drinking water, WC, and picnic benches). Your Manarola finale is the bench at the tip of the point. Pause and take in the view. The easiest way back to town is to take the stairs at the end of the point, which join the main walking path—offering more spectacular town views on its way back to the harbor, where we started.

Sleeping in Manarola

Manarola's accommodations seem a bit more professional than the other towns (except, perhaps, Monterosso). Like the others, it has plenty of private rooms; ask in bars and restaurants.

In the Residential Zone Above the Church

This area is about a 10-minute uphill hike from the train station—just huff up the main drag to the church. All of these are within a five-minute walk from there.

$$$ La Torretta is a trendy, upscale 13-room place that caters to a demanding clientele. Probably the most elegant retreat in the region, it's a peaceful refuge with all the comforts for those happy to pay, including a communal hot tub with a view. Enjoy a complimentary snack and glass of prosecco on arrival, free wine-tastings during your stay, breakfast in your room, and a free minibar. Each chic room is distinct and described on their website (smaller Db-€145, regular Db-€190, Db suite-€250-400, 10 percent discount when you pay cash, book several months in advance as it's justifiably popular, closed mid-Nov-mid-March, pay Wi-Fi, on Piazza della Chiesa beside the bell tower at Vico Volto 20, tel. 0187-920-327, www.torrettas.com, torretta@cdh.it).

$$$ B&B Da Baranin, with six good rooms and four apartments, is overpriced but nicely located just above the church (Db-€110, bigger "superior" Db-€130, includes breakfast; apartments: Db-€120, Tb-€140, Qb-€160, no breakfast; air-con, free Wi-Fi, Via Aldo Rollandi 29, tel. 0187-920-595, www.baranin.com, info@baranin.com).

$$ Aria di Mare Rooms rents four sunny rooms and an apartment 20 yards beyond Trattoria dal Billy at the very top of town. If you don't mind staying in a mostly residential zone high above the tourists, this is a great value. Three rooms have spacious terraces with knockout views and lounge chairs. Maurizio speaks a little English, while Mamma Franca communicates with lots of Italian and toothy smiles (Db-€85, Db apartment-€90, these prices promised through 2014, includes basic breakfast in room, air-con, free Wi-Fi, upstairs on the left at Via Aldo Rollandi 137, tel. 0187-920-367, mobile 349-058-4155, www.ariadimare.info, info@ariadimare.info, ask at Billy's if no one's home).

$ Ostello 5-Terre, Manarola's modern and pleasant hostel, occupies the former parochial school above the church square and offers 48 beds in four- to six-bed rooms. Nicola runs a calm and peaceful place—it's not a party hostel—and quiet is greatly appreciated. They rent dorm rooms as doubles. Reserve well in advance (dorm beds-€24, Db-€65, Qb-€100; 20 percent less mid-Oct-Easter, not co-ed except for couples and families, no membership necessary, open to all ages, optional €2-5 breakfast and bargain dinners, office closed 13:00-16:00—except maybe in summer, rooms closed 10:00-13:00, check-in until 22:00, elevator, free Wi-Fi, lockers, book exchange, Via B. Riccobaldi 21, tel. 0187-920-039, www.hostel5terre.com, info@hostel5terre.com).

On the Main Street

These options line up along the main street, between the harbor and the church. While in a less atmospheric area than the ones near the church, they're closer to the station—and therefore a bit handier for those packing heavy.

$$$ **Albergo Ca' d'Andrean,** run by Simone, is quiet, comfortable, and modern. It has 10 big, sunny, air-conditioned rooms and a cool garden oasis complete with lemon trees. If you don't mind stairs, try requesting one of their top-floor rooms, with great views from their terraces (Sb-€75, Db-€105, breakfast-€6, free Wi-Fi, up the hill at Via Discovolo 101, tel. 0187-920-040, www.cadandrean.it, info@cadandrean.it).

$$$ **Marina Piccola** offers 13 bright, slick rooms on the water (some with sea views), but the rooms are an afterthought to their busy tourist-trap restaurant. They're planning to renovate their rooms, so prices may increase (Db-€120, air-con, free Wi-Fi, Via Birolli 120, tel. 0187-762-065, www.hotelmarinapiccola.com, info@hotelmarinapiccola.com).

$$ At **Affitta Camere da Paulin,** charming Donatella and Eraldo (the town's retired policeman) rent three very nice, well-equipped rooms with a large and inviting common living room, plus three apartments. It's in a modern setting a few minutes' walk uphill from the train tracks (Db-€100, view apartment Db-€140, Qb-€180, usually requires a 3-night minimum stay, air-con, free Wi-Fi, Via Discovolo 126, tel. 0187-920-706, mobile 334-389-4764, www.dapaulin.it, prenotazioni@dapaulin.it).

High Above Manarola, in Volastra

$$ **Hotel il Saraceno,** with seven spacious, modern, functional rooms, is a deal for drivers. Located above Manarola in the tiny town of Volastra (chock-full of vacationing Germans and Italians in summer), it's serene, clean, and right by the shuttle bus to Manarola (Db-€100, buffet breakfast, free Wi-Fi, free parking, località AVA, tel. 0187-760-081, www.thesaraceno.com, hotel@thesaraceno.com, friendly Antonella).

Eating in Manarola

Restaurant options are limited in Manarola. I've listed these in order, from lowest to highest, in terms of quality and elevation.

The vast majority of the town's restaurants (all of them decidedly touristy) are concentrated in the tight zone between Piazza Capellini and the harbor. While these are mostly interchangeable, the Scorza family works hard at **Trattoria il Porticciolo** (€7-10 pastas, €9-18 *secondi,* Thu-Tue 7:30-23:30, closed Wed, Via Birolli 92, tel. 0187-920-083). At the harborfront itself, **Marina Piccola** is famous for great views, lousy service, and price-gouging naive tourists.

Ristorante di Aristide, right on Piazza Capellini, offers trendy atmosphere and a pleasant, less claustrophobic outdoor setting, with a view of budding soccer stars rather than harborfront glitz (€8-12 pastas, €10-19 *secondi*). Down the stairs, at the bottom of the main street, their simpler **café** has indoor and streetside seating and a simpler menu (€5-7 pizzas, sandwiches, and salads; both open Tue-Sun 8:00-22:30, closed Mon, Via Discovolo 290, tel. 0187-920-000).

Via Discovolo, the main street climbing up through town from Piazza Capellini to the church, is lined with simpler places, including a popular *gelateria* and some small grocery stores where you can browse for a picnic.

Up at the very top of town, in the residential zone above the church, dining options are sparse, but the one place that's here is a good one: **Trattoria dal Billy** offers both good food and impressive views over the valley. With Edoardo and Enrico's black pasta with seafood and squid ink, green pasta with artichokes, mixed seafood starters, and homemade desserts, many find it worth the climb. Dinner reservations are a must (€8-12 pastas, €13-20 *secondi,* generally daily 8:00-15:00 & 19:00-23:30, closed Thu, Via Aldo Rollandi 122, tel. 0187-920-628).

Corniglia (Town #3)

This tiny, sleepy town—the only one of the five not on the water—owns a mellow main square. According to a (likely fanciful) local legend, the town was originally settled by a Roman farmer who named it for his mother, Cornelia (how Corniglia is pronounced). The town and its ancient residents produced a wine so famous that—some say—vases found at Pompeii touted its virtues. Regardless of the veracity of the legends, wine remains Corniglia's lifeblood today. Follow the pungent smell of ripe grapes into an alley cellar and get a local to let you dip a straw into a keg.

Remote and less visited than the other Cinque Terre towns, Corniglia has fewer tourists, cooler temperatures, a few restaurants, a windy overlook on its promontory, and plenty of private rooms for rent (ask at any bar or shop, no cheaper than other towns). Because of the long, steep hike between the town and its train station (give yourself at least 15 minutes to rush down and catch your train, or use the shuttle bus) and Corniglia's lack of a boat dock, it's a less convenient home base for town-hopping. If you think of the Cinque Terre as the Beatles, Corniglia is Ringo.

Orientation to Corniglia

Tourist Information
As in all Cinque Terre towns, a TI/park information office is at the train station (likely daily 7:00-19:00, shorter hours off-season).

Arrival in Corniglia
By Train: From the station, filling a gloomy ravine far below town, a footpath zigzags up 385 steps (and nearly that many switchbacks) to the town. If you'd rather not walk, take the green shuttle bus—generally timed to meet arriving trains—which connects the station with Corniglia's main square, the start of my self-guided walk (€1.50 one-way, €2.50 round-trip, buy ticket as you board, free with Cinque Terre Park Card, 1-2/hour).

By Car: Only residents can park on the main road between the recommended Villa Cecio and the point where the steep switchback staircase meets the road. Beyond that area, parking is €1.50/hour. Fortunately, all parking areas are within an easy and fairly level walk of the town center.

Self-Guided Walk

Welcome to Corniglia
We'll explore this tiny town—population 240—and end at a scenic viewpoint. This walk might take up to 30 minutes...but only if you let yourself browse and lick a gelato cone.

• *Begin near the bus stop, located at a...*

Town Square: The gateway to this community is "Ciappà" square, with an ATM, phone booth, old wine press, and bus stop (shuttle buses timed to coordinate with train schedules). The Cinque Terre's designation as a national park sparked a revitaliza-

CINQUE TERRE

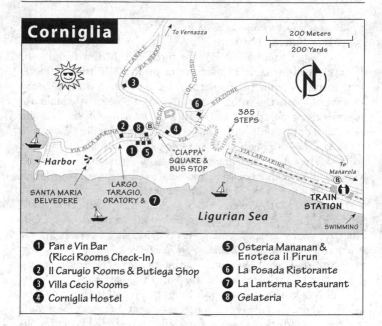

Corniglia

To Vernazza

200 Meters
200 Yards

LOC. CANALE
VIA SERRA

3

LOC. CHIUSO

6

STAZIONE

385 STEPS

2 8 B

4

VIA FIESCHI

VIA

Harbor

1 5

"CIAPPÀ" SQUARE & BUS STOP

VIA ALLA MARINA

VIA LARDARINA

To Manarola
B

SANTA MARIA BELVEDERE

LARGO TARAGIO, ORATORY &

7

TRAIN STATION

Ligurian Sea

SWIMMING

❶ Pan e Vin Bar
 (Ricci Rooms Check-In)

❷ Il Carugio Rooms & Butiega Shop

❸ Villa Cecio Rooms

❹ Corniglia Hostel

❺ Osteria Mananan & Enoteca il Pirun

❻ La Posada Ristorante

❼ La Lanterna Restaurant

❽ Gelateria

tion of the town. Corniglia's young generation is more likely now to stay put, rather than migrate into big cities the way locals did in the past.

• *Look for the arrow pointing to the* centro. *Stroll the spine of Corniglia, Via Fieschi. In the fall, the smell of grapes (on their way to becoming wine) wafts from busy cellars. Along this main street, you'll see...*

Corniglia's Enticing Shops: On the right as you enter Via Fieschi, a pair of neighboring, fiercely competitive *gelaterias* jockey for your business. Both display my book, but my favorite is the second place, **Alberto's Gelateria** (at #74). Before ordering, get a free taste of Alberto's *miele di Corniglia,* made from local honey. His lemon slush *(granita)* takes pucker to new heights.

Farther along, on the left, **Enoteca il Pirùn**—named for a type of oddly shaped old-fashioned wine pitcher designed to aerate the wine and give the alcohol more kick as you squirt it into your mouth—is located in a cool cantina at Via Fieschi 115. Sample some local wines (generally free for small tastes, €3 per glass). If you order wine to drink out of the *pirùn,* Mario will give you a bib. While this is a practical matter (rookies are known to dribble), it also makes a nice souvenir.

In the **Butiega** shop at Via Fieschi 142, Vincenzo sells organic local specialties (daily 8:00-19:30). For picnickers, they offer €4 made-to-order ham-and-cheese sandwiches and a fun *antipasti misti* (priced by the weight). There are good places to picnic farther along on this walk.

• *Following Via Fieschi, you'll end up at the...*

Main Square: On Largo Taragio, tables from two bars and a trattoria spill around a WWI memorial and the town's old well. It once piped in natural spring water from the hillside to locals living without plumbing. What looks like a church is the Oratory of Santa Caterina. (An oratory is a kind of a spiritual clubhouse for a service group doing social work in the name of the Catholic Church. For more information, see "Oratory of the Dead" on page 448.) Up the stairs behind the oratory, you'll find a clearing that local children have made into a soccer field. The stone benches and viewpoint make this a peaceful place for a picnic (less crowded than the end-of-town viewpoint, described next).

• *Opposite the oratory, notice how steps lead steeply down on Via alla Marina to Corniglia's non-beach. It's a five-minute paved climb to sunning rocks, a shower, and a small deck (with a treacherous entry into the water). From the square, continue up Via Fieschi to the...*

End-of-Town Viewpoint: The Santa Maria Belvedere, named for a church that once stood here, marks the scenic end of Corniglia. This is a super picnic spot. From here, look high to the west (right), where the village and sanctuary of San Bernardino straddle a ridge (a good starting point for a hike; accessible by shuttle bus from Monterosso or a long uphill hike from Vernazza). Below is the tortuous harbor, where locals hoist their boats onto the cruel rocks.

Sights in Corniglia

Beaches

This hilltop town has rocky sea access below its train station (toward Manarola). Once a beach, it's all been washed away and offers no services. Look for signs that say *al mare* or *Marina*. A trail leads from the town center steeply down to sunning rocks on the closest thing Corniglia has to a beach (with a shower).

The infamous **Guvano beach** (a bit along the coast toward Vernazza) is now essentially closed down. Guvano was created by an 1893 landslide that cost the village a third of its farmland. Notorious throughout Italy as a nude beach, Guvano was accessed via an unused train tunnel and attracted visitors with an appetite for drug use. Now the tunnel is closed, and the national park wants people to keep their clothes on and forget about Guvano.

Sleeping in Corniglia

(€1 = about $1.30, country code: 39)

Perched high above the sea on a hilltop, Corniglia has plenty of private rooms. To get to the town from the station, catch the shuttle bus or make the 15-minute uphill hike. The town is riddled with humble places that charge too much (generally Db-€65) and have meager business skills and a limited ability to converse with tourists—so it's almost never full.

$$ Cristiana Ricci is an exception to the rule. She communicates well and is reliable, renting four small, clean, and peaceful rooms—two with kitchens and one with a terrace and sweeping view—just inland from the bus stop (Db-€60-70, Tb-€80, Qb-€90, €10/day less when you stay 2 or more nights, free Wi-Fi, check in at the Pan e Vin bar at Via Fieschi 123, mobile 338-937-6547, cri_affittacamere@virgilio.it). Her mom rents two big, modern apartments (€90 for 2-4 people).

$$ Il Carugio has nine modern, sunny rooms right in the center of the village, most with sea views. The communal rooftop terrace offers a commanding view of the coast (Db-€70, Db with seaview balcony-€80, Db apartment-€90 plus €10/extra person, no breakfast, free parking, tel. 0187-812-293, mobile 335-175-7946, www.ilcarugiodicorniglia.com, info@ilcarugiodicorniglia.com, Lidia).

$$ Villa Cecio (pronounced "chay-choe") feels like an abandoned hotel. They offer eight well-worn rooms on the outskirts of town, with saggy beds and little character or warmth. Some rooms have great views, and three have terraces—worth requesting when you check in. All of the rooms share a big rooftop terrace with a grand view (Db-€65 promised in 2014, breakfast-€5, four rooms have air-con, free Wi-Fi, on main road 200 yards toward Vernazza at Via Serra 58, tel. 0187-812-043, mobile 334-350-6637, www.cecio5terre.com, info@cecio5terre.com, Giacinto). They also rent eight similar rooms (Db-€60) in an annex on the square where the bus stops.

$ Corniglia Hostel was formerly the town's schoolhouse. It rents 24 beds in a pastel-yellow building up some steps from the square where the bus stops. The playground in front is often busy with happy kids. Despite its strict and institutional atmosphere, the hostel's prices, central location, and bright and clean rooms ensure its popularity. Its hotelesque double rooms are open to anyone (€24/bed in two 8-bed dorms, four Db-€55—€60 in July-Aug, breakfast-€5, office open 7:00-13:00 & 15:00-1:30 in the morning, dorms closed 10:30-15:00, private rooms closed 13:00-15:00, 1:30 curfew, air-con, lockers, free guest computer and Wi-Fi, self-serve laundry, Via alla Stazione 3, tel. 0187-812-559, www.ostellocorniglia.com, ostellocorniglia@gmail.com).

Eating in Corniglia

Corniglia has few restaurants. The typical array of pizzerias, *focaccerias,* and *alimentari* (grocery stores) line the narrow main drag. For a real meal, consider one of these options.

Osteria Mananan—between the Ciappà bus stop and the main square at Via Fieschi 117—serves what many consider the best food in town in its small, stony, elegant interior (€10 pastas, €10-16 *secondi,* Wed-Mon 12:30-14:30 & 19:30-22:00, closed Tue, no outdoor seating, tel. 0187-821-166).

Enoteca il Pirùn, next door on Via Fieschi, has a small restaurant above the wine bar, where Mario serves typical local dishes (€7-10 pastas, €10-16 *secondi,* €28 fixed-price meal includes homemade wine, daily 12:00-16:00 & 19:30-23:30, tel. 0187-821-075).

La Posada Ristorante offers dinner in a garden under trees, overlooking the Ligurian Sea. To get here, stroll out of town to the top of the stairs that lead down to the station (€8-10 pastas, €10-13 *secondi,* €18 tourist *menù,* daily 12:00-16:00 & 19:00-22:00, tel. 0187-821-174).

The trattoria **La Lanterna,** on the main square, is the most atmospheric, but without particularly charming service (€9-14 pastas, €15-19 *secondi,* daily 12:00-15:00 & 19:30-21:30).

Vernazza (Town #4)

With the closest thing to a natural harbor—overseen by a ruined castle and a stout stone church—Vernazza is the jewel of the

Cinque Terre. Only the occasional noisy slurping up of the train by the mountain reminds you of the modern world.

The action is at the harbor, where you'll find outdoor restaurants, a bar hanging on the edge of the castle, and a breakwater with a promenade, corralled by a natural amphitheater of terraced hills. In the summer, the beach becomes a soccer field, with teams fielded by local bars and restaurants providing late-night entertainment. In the dark, locals fish off the promontory, using glowing bobbers that shine in the waves.

Proud of their Vernazzan heritage, the town's 500 residents like to brag: "Vernazza is locally owned. Portofino has sold out." Fearing the change it would bring, keep-Vernazza-small proponents stopped the construction of a major road into the town and region. Families are tight and go back centuries; several generations live together. In the winter, the population shrinks, as many people return to their more comfortable big-city apartments to spend the money they reaped during the tourist season.

Although Vernazza was hit harder than any other Cinque Terre town by the flood on October 25, 2011 (see sidebar), things are now back to normal. Leisure time is devoted to taking part in the *passeggiata*—strolling lazily together up and down the main street. Sit on a bench and study the passersby doing their *vasche* (laps). Explore the characteristic alleys, called *carugi*. Learn—and live—the phrase *"la vita pigra di Vernazza"* (the lazy life of Vernazza).

Orientation to Vernazza

Tourist Information

There are two information points at the train station, facing each other across the platform between the tracks: One is the gift shop, which can answer basic questions (daily 10:00-13:00 & 14:00-17:00), and the other is the train ticket desk/park office (likely daily 7:00-21:00, shorter hours off-season, tel. 0187-812-533). Public WCs are nearby in the station.

Save Vernazza: Led by a group of American women who married into the community, Save Vernazza brought relief to the town in the immediate aftermath of the 2011 flood and has since morphed into an organization to help preserve and foster healthy tourism. For the latest on their activities, visit www.savevernazza. com

Arrival in Vernazza

By Train: Vernazza's train station is only about three train cars long, but the trains are much longer—so most of the cars come to a stop in a long, dark tunnel. Get out anyway, and walk through the tunnel to the station. From there the main drag flows through town right to the harbor; my self-guided walk begins just above the station.

By Car: Of the five towns, Vernazza is the most difficult to drive to and park in. The best advice: Park your car in La Spezia and take the train. As of mid-2013, two of the three roads into town were officially closed (the one from Monterosso and the one from the main SP-63 highway above town); the third road, from Corniglia, was open but in rough shape and challenging to drive. Anyone driving from Monterosso to Vernazza should drive up and around the SP-38/SP-1 highway to La Spezia, then follow the road above the other Cinque Terre towns.

CINQUE TERRE

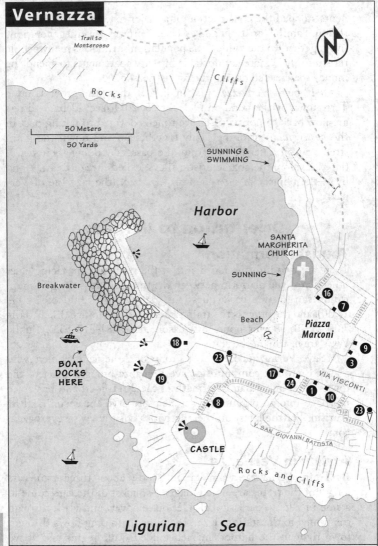

Vernazza

Trail to Monterosso

Cliffs

Rocks

50 Meters
50 Yards

SUNNING & SWIMMING

Harbor

SANTA MARGHERITA CHURCH

SUNNING

Breakwater

Beach

Piazza Marconi

BOAT DOCKS HERE

VIA VISCONTI

V. SAN GIOVANNI BATTISTA

CASTLE

Rocks and Cliffs

Ligurian Sea

1 Trattoria Gianni Reception/Ristorante
2 Pensione Sorriso
3 Albergo Barbara Rooms & Francamaria Reception
4 La Perla delle 5 Terre Rooms, Tonino Basso Rooms & Il Pirata della Cinque Terre Café & Launderette
5 Camere Fontana Vecchia

6 Giuliano Basso Rooms
7 Martina Callo Rooms, Capitano Rooms Reception & Trattoria del Capitano
8 Monica Lercari Rooms
9 Nicolina Rooms Reception & Ristorante Pizzeria Vulnetia
10 Rosa Vitali Rooms
11 Vernazza Rooms Reception & Blue Marlin Bar

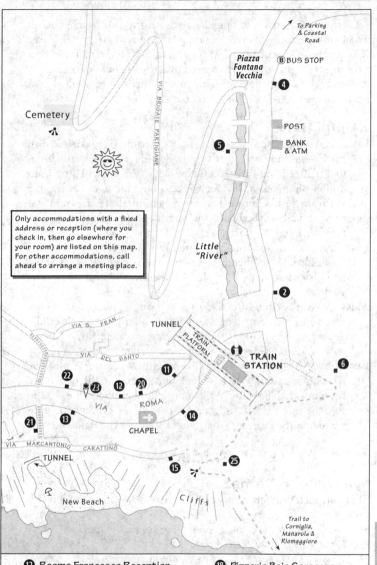

Cemetery

VIA BRIGATE PARTIGIANE

Piazza
Fontana
Vecchia

Ⓑ BUS STOP

To Parking
& Coastal
Road

4

POST

BANK
& ATM

5

Only accommodations with a fixed address or reception (where you check in, then go elsewhere for your room) are listed on this map. For other accommodations, call ahead to arrange a meeting place.

Little
"River"

2

VIA S. FRAN.

TUNNEL

VIA DEL SANTO

TRAIN PLATFORM

TRAIN STATION

6

22

11

23 **12** **20**

VIA ROMA

CHAPEL

14

21

13

VIA MARCANTONIO CARATTINO

TUNNEL

New Beach

15

25

Cliffs

Trail to
Corniglia,
Manarola &
Riomaggiore

CINQUE TERRE

12 Rooms Francesca Reception (Enoteca Sciacchetrà) & Ivo's Camere Reception (Pizzeria Fratelli Basso)

13 Affitta Camere Alberto Basso Reception & Internet Point

14 Eva's Rooms & Trattoria da Sandro

15 Rooms Elisabetta (call first)

16 Ananasso Bar

17 Gambero Rosso Ristorante

18 Pizzeria Baia Saracena

19 Ristorante Belforte

20 Antica Osteria il Baretto

21 Ristorante Incadasè da Piva

22 Forno Bakery

23 Gelaterias (3)

24 Burgus Wine Bar

25 Franco's Ristorante & Bar la Torre

If you must drive, get precise advice from your hotelier about which roads are open, how to drive in, and where to park (see "Cinque Terre Connections" at the end of this chapter). The visitor parking lot high above town, served by a shuttle bus, washed away in the 2011 flood; a replacement may eventually be built, but it could take years. Yellow lines mark parking spots for residents only.

Helpful Hints

Internet Access: The slick, expensive, six-terminal **Internet Point,** run by Alberto and Isabella, is in the village center (daily June-Oct 9:30-23:00, until 20:00 Nov-May, Wi-Fi, will burn your digital photos to a disc for €5, also sells memory cards). The **Il Pirata delle Cinque Terre** bar (behind/above the train station) and **Blue Marlin Bar** (along the main street) both offer free Wi-Fi with a purchase.

Laundry: The town launderette, at the top of town next to the post office, is completely self-serve (coin-op, €5/wash, €5/dry, includes soap, daily 8:00-22:00, operated by Domenico and Barbara at the fish shop).

Massage: Kate Allen offers a super-relaxing fusion of aromatic/ Swedish/holistic massage for €50 per hour in her little studio adjacent to the clinic at the top of Vernazza (tel. 0187-812-537, mobile 333-568-4653, www.vernazzamassage5terre.com).

Best Views: A steep 10-minute hike in either direction from Vernazza gives you a classic village photo op. For the best light, head toward Corniglia in the morning—best views are just before the ticket booth for the national park—and toward Monterosso in the evening—best views are after the ticket booth.

Self-Guided Walk

Welcome to Vernazza

This tour includes Vernazza's characteristic town squares and ends on its scenic breakwater.

• *From the train station, walk uphill along the stream until you hit the small square in front of the Il Pirata delle Cinque Terre bar/café, near the post office. This part of town was particularly damaged during the 2011 flood, but is now being repaired. The stream in this ravine once powered Vernazza's water mill. Shuttle buses run from here to hamlets and sanctuaries in the hills above.*

Walk to the tidy, modern square called...

Fontana Vecchia: Named after a long-gone fountain, this is where older locals remember the river filled with townswomen doing their washing. A lane leads from here up to the cemetery. Imagine the entire village sadly trudging up here during funerals.

(The cemetery is peaceful and evocative at sunset, when the fading light touches each crypt.)

You may see some construction work going on here. Following the 2011 flood, Vernazza attracted worldwide sympathy—including that of prominent architect Richard Rogers (who designed London's Millennium Dome and Lloyd's Building, Wales' National Assembly, and, with frequent collaborator Renzo Piano, Paris' Pompidou Centre). Having enjoyed many relaxing summer vacations in Vernazza, Rogers wanted to give something back. He helped redesign the spine of the town, from here down the main street to the harborfront square (basically the route of this walk). Over the next several years, his plans will help reshape Vernazza. Though Rogers is best known for his dramatically modern designs, his plans for the town are very much in keeping with its traditional soul.

• *Begin your saunter downhill to the harbor. Just before the* Pensione Sorriso *sign, on your right (at #7, with big brown garage doors and a* croce verde Vernazza *sign), you'll see the...*

Ambulance Barn: A group of volunteers is always on call for a dash to the hospital, 40 minutes away in La Spezia. Opposite the barn is a big empty lot. Like many landowners, the owner of Pensione Sorriso had plans to expand, but since the 1980s, the government has said "No." While some landowners are frustrated, the old character of these towns survives. A few steps farther down is the town clinic. The *guarda medica* (emergency doctor—see buzzer) sleeps upstairs.

• *At the corner across from the playground, on a marble plaque in the wall on the left, you'll see a...*

World Wars Monument: This is dedicated to those killed in World Wars I and II. Not a family in Vernazza was spared. Listed on the left are soldiers *morti in combattimento*, who died in World War I; on the right is the WWII section. Some were deported to *Germania;* others—labeled *Part* (for *partigiani*, or partisans, generally communists)—were killed while fighting against Mussolini. Cynics considered partisans less than heroes. After 1943, Hitler called up Italian boys over 15. Rather than die on the front for Hitler, they escaped to the hills and became "resistance fighters" in order to remain free.

The path to Corniglia leaves from here (behind and above the plaque). Behind you is a small square, decorated with a big millstone, once used to grind local olives into oil. There's a good chance you'll see an expat mom here at the village playground with her kids. I've met many American women who fell in love with a local guy, stayed, and are now happily raising families here. (But I've rarely met an American guy who moved in with a local girl.)

From here, Vernazza's tiny river goes underground. Until the

The Cinque Terre Flood and Recovery

On October 25, 2011, after a very dry summer, a freak rainstorm hit the Cinque Terre. Within four hours, 22 inches of rain fell—a third of an average year's total. Flash floods rushed down the hillsides. Topography allowed the water to quickly drain in Riomaggiore, Manarola, and Corniglia, which were mostly undamaged. But Monterosso and Vernazza were devastated, with much of the two towns buried under 10 feet of mud and left without water, electricity, or phone connections.

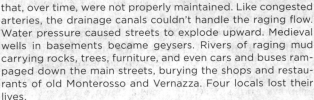

The destruction occurred mostly along former ravines, where, historically, streams ran through the towns. In the last century, the ravines were covered with roads, and the streams channeled into underground canals that, over time, were not properly maintained. Like congested arteries, the drainage canals couldn't handle the raging flow. Water pressure caused streets to explode upward. Medieval wells in basements became geysers. Rivers of raging mud carrying rocks, trees, furniture, and even cars and buses rampaged down the main streets, burying the shops and restaurants of old Monterosso and Vernazza. Four locals lost their lives.

The people of the Cinque Terre were taught a tough lesson. It's their beautiful land that brings the tourists. But with the affluence brought by tourism, locals have abandoned their land—leaving vineyards unplanted and centuries-old dry-stone terracing to crumble—for less physically demanding, more profitable work in town. (Grapevines have far-reaching root systems that help combat erosion, and traditional vintners keep their stone terraces in good order.) After a generation of neglect, the unprotected land was washed down into the towns by the violent weather.

Today, you'll find everything in the Cinque Terre back to normal. You may not even realize that in the affected areas of Vernazza and Monterosso, everything is brand-new: stoves, tables, chairs, plates, walls lined with bottles of wine, and so on, all had to be replaced from scratch. Strolling through these towns today, keep in mind everything these people have been through—and appreciate the resilience of the human spirit.

1950s, the river ran openly through the center of town. Old-timers recall the days before the breakwater, when the river cascaded down and the surf sent waves rolling up Vernazza's main drag. Back then, this place was nicknamed "Little Venice" for the series of romantic bridges that arched over the stream, connecting the two sides of the town before the main road was built.

Corralling this stream under the modern street, and forcing it to take a hard right turn here, contributed to the damage caused by the 2011 flood. After the flood, alpine engineers were imported from Switzerland to redesign this drainage system, so any future floods will be less destructive. They also installed nets above the town to protect it from landslides.

The walls under the tracks serve as a sort of community information center. Look for the bulletin board, with a list of local volunteers and when they are on call to drive the ambulance, and info on current events. Across the way, you'll likely see a giant poster with photos of the 2011 flood *(alluvione)* and the shops that it devastated. "The 25th of October" is a day that will live forever in this town's lore. Vernazza is built around one street—basically a lid over the stream in its ravine. On that fateful day, the surrounding hills acted like a funnel, directing flash-flood waters right through the middle of town. As you stroll from here to the harbor, imagine this street buried under 13 feet of mud. Every shop, restaurant, and hotel on the main drag had to be rewired, replumbed, and re-equipped.

The second set of train tracks (nearer the harbor) was recently renovated to lessen the disruptive noise, but locals say it made no difference.

• *Follow the road downhill to...*

Vernazza's "Business Center": Here, you'll pass many locals doing their *vasche* (laps). Next, you'll pass souvenir shops, wine shops, the Blue Marlin Bar (Vernazza's top nightspot), and the tiny Chapel of Santa Marta (the small stone chapel with iron grillwork over the window, on the left), where Mass is celebrated only on special Sundays. Farther down, you'll walk by a *gelateria*, bakery, pharmacy, a grocery, and another *gelateria*. There are plenty of fun and cheap food-to-go options here.

• *On the left, in front of the second* gelateria, *a stone arch was blasted away by the 2011 flood. Scamper through the hole in the rock to reach Vernazza's...*

"New Beach": This is where the town's stream used to hit the sea back in the 1970s. Older locals remember frolicking on a beach here when they were growing up, but the constant, churning surf eventually eroded it all the way back to the cliff. When the 2011 flood hit, it blew out the passageway and deposited landslide material here from the hills above. In the flood's aftermath, Vernazza's main drag and harbor were filled with mud and silt. Workers barged the first batch away, but then— realizing that was an expensive way to remove so much material—decided instead to use the debris to fill in even more of this beach that Mother Nature had violently created. Now Vernazza has a popular beach that feels a world away from the bustle of the main drag. Like other Cinque Terre beaches, this one has no sand, but instead has small pebbles for wading and big rocks for sunning. You'll also find bits of rubble mixed into the pebbles (fragments of roof tiles, perhaps a bit of rusted metal here and there—this is not a barefoot beach). Locals keep unearthing surprising items here. In what could be interpreted as a miracle, a statue of the Madonna—which had been swept off her pedestal by the flood—was recently unearthed here.

Don't get used to this beach. Locals expect that it, like its predecessor, will eventually be washed away.

• *Back on the main drag, continue downhill to the...*

Harbor Square (Piazza Marconi) and Breakwater: Vernazza, with the only natural harbor of the Cinque Terre, was established as the sole place boats could pick up the fine local wine. The two-foot-high square stone at the foot of the stairs by the Burgus Wine Bar (on the left) is marked *Sasso del Sego* (stone of tallow). Workers crushed animal flesh and fat in its basin to make tallow, which drained out of the tiny hole below. The tallow was then used to waterproof boats or wine barrels. Stonework is the soul of the region. Take some time to appreciate the impressive stonework of the restaurant interiors facing the harbor.

On the far side (behind Ristorante Pizzeria Vulnetia), peek into the tiny street with its commotion of arches. Vernazza's most characteristic side streets, called *carugi,* lead up from here. The narrow stairs mark the beginning of the trail that leads up, up, up to the quintessential view of Vernazza—and, eventually, to Monterosso.

Located in front of the harborside church, the tiny piazza—decorated with a river-rock mosaic—is a popular hangout spot. It's where Vernazza's old ladies soak up the last bit of sun, and kids enjoy a patch of level ball field.

Vernazza's harborfront **church** is unusual for its strange entryway, which faces east (altar side), rather than the more typical western orientation. With relative peace and prosperity in the 16th century, the townspeople doubled the church in size, causing it to overtake a little piazza that once faced the west facade. From the square, use the "new" entry and climb the steps, keeping an eye out for the level necessary to keep the church high and dry. Inside, the lighter pillars in the back mark the 16th-century extension. Three historic portable crosses hanging on the walls are carried through town during religious holiday processions. They are replicas of crosses that (locals like to believe) Vernazza ships once carried on crusades to the Holy Land. In 1998, Vernazza's priest was gruesomely and mysteriously murdered. While circumstantial evidence points to fascinating conspiracy theories, no one knows whodunit (or, at least, no one's telling). Today's priest, Don Giovanni, is popular—he stopped the church bells from ringing through the night (light sleepers rejoiced). In the wake of the 2011 flood, he opened up the church as a staging ground for recovery services.

• *Finish your town tour seated out on the breakwater (perhaps with a glass of local white wine or something more interesting from a nearby bar—borrow the glass, they don't mind). Face the town, and see...*

The Harbor: In a moderate storm, you'd be soaked, as waves routinely crash over the *molo* (breakwater, built in 1972). Waves can rearrange the huge rocks—depositing them from the breakwater

onto the piazza and its benches. Freak waves have even washed away tourists squinting excitedly into their cameras. (I've seen it happen.) In 2007, an American woman was swept away and killed by a rogue wave. Enjoy the waterfront piazza—carefully.

The train line (to your left) was constructed in 1874 to tie together a newly united Italy, and linked Turin and Genoa with Rome. A second line (hidden in a tunnel at this point) was built in the 1920s. The yellow building alongside the tracks was Vernazza's first train station. Along the wall behind the tracks, you can see the four bricked-up alcoves where people once waited for trains. Notice the wonderful concrete sunbathing strip (and place for late-night privacy) laid below the tracks along the rocks.

Vernazza's fishing fleet is down to just a few boats (with the net spools). Vernazzans are still more likely to own a boat than a car, and it's said that you stand a better chance of surviving if you mess with a local man's wife than with his boat.

Boats are on buoys, except in winter or when the red storm flag (see the pole at the start of the breakwater) indicates bad seas. At these times, the boats are pulled up onto the square—which is usually reserved for restaurant tables. In the 1970s, tiny Vernazza had one of Italy's top water polo teams, and the harbor was their "pool." Later, when the league required a real pool, Vernazza dropped out.

The Castle (Castello Doria): On the far right, the castle, which is now a grassy park with great views (and nothing but

stones), still guards the town (€1.50 donation, daily 10:00-18:30; from harbor, take stairs by Trattoria Gianni and follow *Ristorante al Castello* signs, tower is a few steps beyond). This was the town's watchtower back in pirate days, and a Nazi lookout in World War II. The castle tower looks new because it was rebuilt after the

British bombed it, chasing out the Germans. The squat tower on the water is great for a glass of wine or a meal. From the breakwater, you could follow the rope to Ristorante Belforte and pop inside, past the actual submarine door. A photo of a major storm showing the entire tower under a wave (not uncommon in the winter) hangs near the bar.

The Town: Before the 12th century, pirates made the coast uninhabitable, so the first Vernazzans lived in the hills above (near the Reggio Sanctuary). The town itself—and its towers, fortified walls, and hillside terracing—are mostly from the 12th through the 15th century, when Vernazza was allied with the Republic of Genoa.

Vernazza has two halves. *Sciuiu* (Vernazzan dialect for "flowery") is the sunny side on the left, and *luvegu* (dank) is the shady side on the right. Houses below the castle were connected by an interior arcade—ideal for fleeing attacks. The "Ligurian pastel" colors are regulated by a commissioner of good taste in the regional government. The square before you is locally famous for some of the area's finest restaurants. The big red central house—on the site where Genoan warships were built in the 12th century—used to be a guardhouse.

In the Middle Ages, there was no beach or square. The water went right up to the buildings, where boats would tie up, Venetian-style. Imagine what Vernazza looked like in those days, when it was the biggest and richest of the Cinque Terre towns. Buildings had a water gate (facing today's square) and a front door on the higher inland side. There was no pastel plaster—just fine stonework (traces of which survive above the Trattoria del Capitano). Apart from the added plaster, the general shape and size of the town has changed little in five centuries. Survey the windows and notice inhabitants quietly gazing back.

While the town has 1,500 residents in summer, only 500 stay here through the winter. Vernazza has accommodations for about 500 tourists.

Above the Town: The small, round tower above the red guardhouse—another part of the city fortifications—reminds us of the town's importance in the Middle Ages. Back then, its key ally Genoa's enemies (i.e., the other maritime republics, especially Pisa) were Vernazza's enemies. Franco's Ristorante and Bar la Torre, just behind the tower, welcomes hikers who are finishing, starting, or simply contemplating the Corniglia-Vernazza hike, with great town views. That tower recalls a time when the entire town was fortified by a stone wall.

Vineyards fill the mountainside beyond the town. Notice the many terraces. Someone—probably after too much of that local wine—calculated that the roughly 3,000 miles of dry-stone walls built to terrace the region's vineyards have the same amount of stonework as the Great Wall of China.

For six centuries, the economy was based on wine and olive oil. Then came the 1980s—and the tourists. Locals turned to tourism to make a living, and stopped tending the land. Many vineyards were abandoned, and the terraces fell into disrepair. But it's the stonework of the terracing in the surrounding hills that helps prevent flooding—a lesson learned in the worst possible way on October 25, 2011.

Although many locals still maintain their tiny plots and proudly serve their family wines, the patchwork of local vineyards is atomized and complex because of inheritance traditions. Historically, families divided their land between their children. Parents wanted each child to get some good land. Because some lots were "kissed by the sun" while others were shady, the lots were split into increasingly tiny and eventually unviable pieces—another reason why many have been abandoned.

A single steel train line winds up the gully behind the tower. It is for the vintner's *trenino*, the tiny service train. Play "Where's *trenino?*" and see if you can find two trains. The vineyards once stretched as high as you can see, but since fewer people sweat in the fields these days, the most distant terraces have gone wild again.

The Church, School, and City Hall: Vernazza's Ligurian Gothic church, built with black stones quarried from Punta Mesco (the distant point behind you), dates from 1318. Note the gray stone that marks the church's 16th-century expansion. The gray-and-red house above the spire is the local elementary school (about 25 children attend; education through age 14 is obligatory). High-schoolers go to the "big city," La Spezia. The red building to the right of the schoolhouse, a former monastery, is the city hall. Vernazza and Corniglia function as one community. Through most of the 1990s, the local government was Communist. In 1999, residents elected a coalition of many parties working to rise above ideologies and simply make Vernazza a better place. That practical notion of government continues here today.

Finally, on the top of the hill, with the best view of all, is the town cemetery. It's only fair that hardworking Vernazzans—who spend their lives climbing up and down and up and down and up and down the hillsides that hem in their little town—are rewarded with a world-class view for eternity.

Activities in Vernazza

Tuesday-Morning Market
Vernazza's skimpy business community is augmented Tuesday mornings (8:00-13:00), when a meager gang of cars and trucks pulls into town for a tailgate market.

Beaches
The harbor's sandy cove has sunning rocks and showers by the breakwater. There's also a ladder on the breakwater for deep-water access. The sunbathing lane directly under the church also has a shower. And don't miss Vernazza's "new beach," accessed through a hole halfway along its main drag (and described on my self-guided walk, earlier). Note that this beach may be closed periodically for safety reasons. It's safer to hang out closer to the water instead of directly under the cliffs, which experience occasional, minor landslides.

Boat Trips
Vincenzo of **Nord Est** takes people out for mini-cruises (€150/hour, mobile 338-700-0436, info@manuela-vernazza.com). One popular stop is the tiny *acqua pendente* (waterfall) cove between Vernazza and Monterosso; locals call it their *laguna blu*.

Shuttle Bus Joyride
For a cheap and scenic joyride, with a chance to chat about the region with friendly, English-speaking Beppe, Simone, or Pietro, ride the shuttle bus from the top of town (in front of the post office) to the sanctuaries and hamlets San Bernadino and Reggio—the ancient birthplace of Vernazza—and back again (entire route for the cost of a round-trip ticket, generally about 5/day, but times are very unpredictable—try asking at the TI or park office in the train station, or if you see a bus, flag it down and ask for the timetable; €2.50 round-trip, free with Cinque Terre Park Card, churches at sanctuaries are usually closed).

Sustainable Tourism Activities
Save Vernazza, which began as a post-flood relief organization, has now evolved into an all-purpose Vernazza advocacy group, with an emphasis on fostering sustainable tourism. They coordinate "voluntourism" activities regularly through the summer (generally May-July and Sept-Oct, 2/week—usually Wed/Thu and Sat/Sun, 8:30-13:30). If you enjoy the Cinque Terre and would like to give something back, contact them to see if you can join a group working on a project designed to protect and promote traditional Vernazzan lifestyles (www.savevernazza.com, workwithus@savevernazza.com, mobile 349-357-3572).

Nightlife in Vernazza

Vernazza's younger generation of restaurant workers lets loose after-hours. They work hard through the tourist season, travel in the winter, speak English, and enjoy connecting with international visitors. After the restaurants close down, the town is quiet except for a couple of nightspots. For more information on the Blue Marlin, Ananasso, Il Pirata, and Ristorante Incadasè, see their listings under "Eating in Vernazza," later. All Vernazza bars must close by 24:00.

Blue Marlin Bar dominates the late-night scene with a mix of locals and tourists, home-cooked food until 23:00, good drinks, and piano jam sessions. If you're young and hip, this is *the* place to hang out. If you play piano, you're welcome to contribute to the scene. They also host a free book-swap shelf.

Ananasso Bar offers early-evening happy-hour fun and cocktails *(aperitivi)* that both locals and visitors enjoy. Its harborfront tables get the last sunshine of the day.

Burgus Wine Bar, chic and cool with a jazzy ambience, is a popular early-evening and after-dinner harborside hangout, where you can sip local wine or a cocktail (Wed-Mon 7:30-24:00, closed Tue, Piazza Marconi 4).

Il Pirata delle Cinque Terre, behind and above the train station, features the entertaining Cannoli brothers and their devoted tourist clientele. Many come for dinner and end up staying because of these two wild and crazy guys and the camaraderie they create among their diners (erratic hours driven by demand, free Wi-Fi).

Ristorante Incadasè da Piva (tucked up the lane behind the pharmacy) is the haunt of Piva, Vernazza's troubadour. Piva often gets out his guitar and sings traditional local songs as well as his own compositions. If you're looking for a local Hemingway, check here.

Really Late: There's a little cave on the beach just under the church that lends itself to fun in the wee hours, when everything else is closed.

Sleeping in Vernazza

Vernazza, the spindly and salty essence of the Cinque Terre, is my top choice for a home base. Off-season (Oct-March), you can generally arrive without a reservation and find a place, but at other times, it's smart to book ahead (especially June-July and weekends).

People recommended here are listed for their communication skills (they speak English, have email, and are reliable with bookings) and because they rent several rooms. Consequently, my recommendations cost more than comparable rooms you'll find if you shop around. Comparison-shopping will likely save you €10-20 per double per night—and often get you a better place and view to boot. The real Vernazza gems are stray single rooms with owners who have no interest in booking in advance or messing with email. Arrive by early afternoon and drop by any shop or bar and ask; most locals know someone who rents rooms.

Anywhere you stay here requires some climbing, but keep in mind that more climbing means better views. Most do not include breakfast (for suggestions, see "Eating in Vernazza," later). Cash is preferred or required almost everywhere. Night noise can be a problem if you're near the station. Rooms on the harbor come with church bells (but only between 7:00 and 22:00).

Pensions

$$$ Trattoria Gianni rents 27 small rooms and three apartments just under the castle. The rooms are in three buildings—one funky, two modern—up a hundred tight, winding spiral stairs. The funky ones, which may or may not have private baths, are artfully decorated à la shipwreck, with tiny balconies and grand sea views *(con vista sul mare)*. The comfy new *(nuovo)* rooms lack views. Both have modern bathrooms and access to a super-scenic cliff-hanging guests' garden. Steely Marisa requires check-in before 16:00 or a phone call to explain when you're coming. Emanuele (Gianni's son, who now runs the restaurant), Simona, Catarina, and the staff speak a little English  (S-€55, D-€100, Db-€120, Tb-€150, includes breakfast on their gorgeous seaview terrace mid-April-mid-Oct, prices are lower at other times, 10 percent discount when you pay cash and mention this book—request when you reserve, cancellations less than a week in advance are charged one night's deposit, closed Jan-Feb, Piazza Marconi 1, tel. 0187-812-228, tel. 0187-821-003, on Wed call mobile 393-9008-155 instead, www.giannifranzi.it, info@giannifranzi.it). Pick up your keys at Trattoria Gianni's restaurant on the harbor square (on Wed, when the restaurant is closed, call ahead to make other arrangements).

$$$ Pensione Sorriso, the oldest pension in town (where I stayed on my first visit in 1975), rents 19 overpriced rooms above the train station. While the main building has the charm, it comes with train noise and saggy beds; the annex, up the street, is in a quieter apartment that feels forgotten (Sb-€65, D-€70, Db-€110, Db with air-con-€120, T-€90, Tb-€140, breakfast-€15, free Wi-Fi, closed Nov-March, Via Gavino 4, tel. 0187-812-224, www.

pensionesorriso.com, info@pensionesorriso.com, Francesca and Aldo).

$$ Albergo Barbara rents nine basic rooms overlooking the harbor square—most with small windows and small views. It's run by English-speaking Giuseppe and his no-nonsense Swiss wife, Patricia (D-€55, D with private bath down the hall-€65, Db-€70, big Db with nice harbor view-€110, extra bed-€10, 2-night stay preferred, closed Dec-Feb, reserve online with credit card but pay cash, free Wi-Fi, Piazza Marconi 30, tel. 0187-812-398, mobile 338-793-3261, www.albergobarbara.it, info@albergobarbara.it).

Private Rooms (Affitta Camere)
Vernazza is honeycombed with private rooms, offering the best values in town. Owners may be reluctant to reserve rooms far in advance. Doubles cost €55-100, depending on the view, season, and plumbing—you get what you pay for. Apartments (with kitchens) go for a bit more. Most places accept only cash. Some have killer views, come with lots of stairs, and cost the same as a small, dark place on a back lane over the train tracks. Most of these people speak just enough English (or know someone who does).

While a few places have all their beds in one building, most have rooms scattered over town. Better-organized outfits have an informal "reception desk" (sometimes at a restaurant or other business) where you can check in. A few places have no reception at all. (On the Vernazza map, I've marked only places that have a fixed address or reception office; if I say "reception," you'll check in there, then continue on to your actual room.) Because this can be confusing, I strongly recommend clearly communicating your arrival time (by phone or email) and getting clear instructions on where to meet the owner and pick up the keys. In many cases, they'll meet you at the train station—but only if they know when you're coming.

Well-Run Rooms in the Inland Part of Town
Some of my favorite places in town are located in the ravine a five-minute, gently uphill stroll behind the train station. While this sleepy zone is less atmospheric and feels less central than Vernazza's main street, harborfront, and twisty upper lanes, it also has less train and church-bell noise and fewer steep stairs. While none of these places have views, the constant soundtrack of Vernazza's gurgling river is soothing. Il Pirata delle Cinque Terre is the neighborhood hub (offering breakfast and Wi-Fi; see page 437), and Vernazza's self-service launderette is right next door.

$$$ Alessandra runs two different sets of rooms in a single elevator-equipped, modern building: **La Perla delle 5 Terre** (6 clean, sleek rooms with modern style but no air-con, Db-€100, Tb-€120) and **Tonino Basso** (4 rooms decorated with big colorful cutouts,

Db-€120, Tb-€140, air-con, loaner laptop in each room). This is the top choice in town for modern comfort—at a steep price. Both come with free Wi-Fi; La Perla is a better value if you don't need air-conditioning (contact for both: Via Gavino 34, mobile 339-761-1651, www.toninobasso.com, sassarinialessandra@libero.it).

$$ Camere Fontana Vecchia, run by Annamaria, has eight bright, spacious, quiet rooms overlooking the ravine and its rushing river, across the street from the post office (D-€70, Db-€80, Db with terrace-€100, Via Gavino 15, tel. 0187-821-130, mobile 333-454-9371, www.cinqueterrecamere.com, m.annamaria@libero.it).

$$ Giuliano Basso's four carefully crafted rooms are just above town, straddling a ravine among orange trees. It's proudly built out of stone by Giuliano himself—the town's last stone-layer (Db-€80-100, Tb-€120, two rooms have air-con, more train noise than others, above train station, take the ramp just before Pensione Sorriso, mobile 333-341-4792, www.cdh.it/giuliano, giuliano@cdh.it).

Other Reliable Places Scattered Through Town and the Harborside

La Malà, La Marina Rooms, and Memo Rooms are not located on the map in this chapter; arrange a meeting time and/or ask for directions when you reserve.

$$$ La Malà is Vernazza's jetsetter pad. Four pristine white rooms boast fancy-hotel-type extras and a common terrace looking out over the rocky shore. It's a climb—way, way up to the top of town—but they'll gladly carry your bags to and from the station (Db-€160, Db suite-€220, includes breakfast at a bar, air-con, free Wi-Fi, mobile 334-287-5718, www.lamala.it, info@lamala.it, charming Giamba and his mama, Armanda). They also rent the simpler "Armanda's Room" nearby—a great value, since you get Giamba's attention to detail and amenities without paying for a big view (Db-€80, includes simple breakfast in room, air-con, book through La Malà or ring bell at Piazza Marconi 15).

$$$ La Marina Rooms is run by hardworking Christian, who speaks English and happily meets his guests at the station to carry their bags. There are five beautiful, top-end, pricey units, most high above the main street: Three doubles share a fine oceanview terrace (townview Db-€90, seaview Db-€140), and two apartments are more spacious, with fine terraces and views (townview Db-€120, seaview Db with big terrace-€260; mobile 338-476-7472, www.lamarinarooms.com, mapcri@yahoo.it).

$$$ Martina Callo's four simply furnished rooms overlook the square; they're up plenty of steps near the silent-at-night church tower. While the rooms are nothing special, guests appreciate the views (room #1: Tb-€110 or Qb-€120 with harbor view; room #2:

big Qb family room with no view-€110; room #3: Db with grand view terrace-€100; room #4: roomy Db with no view-€60; air-con, free Wi-Fi, ring bell at Piazza Marconi 26, tel. 0187-812-365, mobile 329-435-5344, www.roomartina.com, roomartina@roomartina.com).

$$ Memo Rooms has three clean and spacious rooms that offer good value. They overlook the main street, in what feels like a miniature hotel. Enrica will meet you if you call upon arrival (Db-€70, Via Roma 15, tel. 0187-812-360 but try mobile first, mobile 338-285-2385, www.memorooms.com, info@memorooms.com).

$$ Monica Lercari rents several classy rooms with modern comforts, perched at the top of town. Guests are welcome to borrow the family rowboat or mountain bike (small Db-€80, seaview D-€100, grand seaview terrace D-€120; the previous two rooms can be booked as one big "honeymoon suite" for €180; includes breakfast, air-con, free Wi-Fi, tel. 0187-812-296, mobile 320-025-4515, alcastellovernazza@yahoo.it). For years Monica and her husband, Massimo, had one of Vernazza's most scenic, memorable, and inviting restaurants, Ristorante al Castello, in the old castle tower overlooking town; damaged in the flood, it may reopen in the future—ask around, or try calling tel. 0187-812-296.

$$ Nicolina Rooms consists of seven units in three different buildings. Two rooms are in the center over the pharmacy, up a few steep steps—one has only sleeper sofas (Db-€80-90); another room is on a twisty lane above the harbor (Db-€80); and four more are in a building beyond the church, with great views (D-€100, Db-€140, two-bedroom suite with harborview terrace-€180 plus €30/extra person, free Wi-Fi and loud church bells in these rooms only). Inquire at Pizzeria Vulnetia on the harbor square (all include breakfast, Piazza Marconi 29, tel. 0187-821-193, mobile 333-842-6879, www.camerenicolina.it, camerenicolina.info@cdh.it).

$$ Rosa Vitali rents two four-person apartments across from the pharmacy overlooking the main street (and beyond the train noise). One has a terrace and fridge (top floor); the other has windows and a full kitchen (Db-€85, Tb-€110, Qb-€120, reception just before the tobacco shop near Piazza Marconi at Via Visconti 10, tel. 0187-821-181, mobile 340-267-5009, www.rosacamere.it, rosa.vitali@libero.it).

$$ Francamaria and her kind husband Andrea rent eight sharp, comfortable, and creatively renovated but expensive rooms— all described in detail on her website. While their reception desk is on the harbor square (on the ground floor facing the harbor at Piazza Marconi 30—don't confuse it with Albergo Barbara at same address), the rooms they manage are all over town (Db-€80-120 depending on size and view, Qb-€130-160, extra person-€20,

CINQUE TERRE

tel. 0187-812-002, mobile 328-711-9728, www.francamaria.com, info@francamaria.com).

More Private Rooms in Vernazza

Rooms from Emanuela Colombo, Maria Capellini, and Manuela Moggia are not located on the map in this chapter; arrange a meeting time and/or ask for directions when you reserve.

$$ Vernazza Rooms, run by Daria Bianchi, Chiara, and Davide, rents 13 decent rooms: Five are above the Blue Marlin Bar looking down on the main street, and eight are a steep climb higher up, just under the city hall (Db-€60-95, Qb-€100-120; price depends on view, location, and size; ring bell at Via Roma 41—next to Blue Marlin Bar, some with air-con and others with fans, free Wi-Fi in some rooms, mobile 338-581-4688 or 338-413-8696, www.vernazzarooms.com, info@vernazzarooms.com).

$$ Emanuela Colombo has two rooms—one spacious and basic on the harbor square (Db-€85), the other a *molto* chic split-level apartment located on a quiet side street (Db-€100, Tb-€120; tel. 339-834-2486, www.vacanzemanuela.it, manucap64@libero. it).

$$ Rooms Francesca's three rooms hide out in the steep streets just below the city hall (non-view Db-€70, seaview Db-€80, non-view Tb-€90, 2-room apartment: Db-€90/Qb-€120; check in at Enoteca Sciacchetrà at Via Roma 19, tel. 0187-821-112, www.5terre-vernazza.it, moggia.franco@libero.it, Francesca and Franco).

$$ Ivo's Camere rents two simple no-terrace rooms high above the main street, as well as a studio apartment (Db-€75, air-con, free Wi-Fi, Via Roma 6, reception at Pizzeria Fratelli Basso—Via Roma 1, mobile 333-477-5521, www.ivocamere.com, post@ivocamere.com).

$$ Maria Capellini rents a couple of simple, clean rooms, including one on the ground floor right on the harbor (Db with kitchen-€90, Tb-€110, cash only, fans, mobile 338-436-3411, www.mariacapellini.com, mariacapellini@hotmail.it, Maria and Giacomo).

More Options: **$$ Affitta Camere Alberto Basso** (a clean, modern room with a noisy harbor/piazza view, Db-€80, check in at Internet Point, albertobasso@hotmail.com); **$$ Capitano Rooms** (3 recently remodeled rooms up several flights of stairs above the main drag, Db-€90, includes breakfast, fans, free Wi-Fi at restaurant; ask for Julia, Paolo, or Barbara at the Trattoria del Capitano restaurant on the main square at Piazza Marconi 21; tel. 0187-812-201, www.tavernavernazza.com, info@tavernavernazza.com); **$$ Eva's Rooms** (3 rooms overlooking main street, Sb-€60, D with private bath outside the room-€70, Db-€80, air-con, train noise, ring at Via Roma 56, tel. 0187-821-134, www.evasrooms. it, evasrooms@yahoo.it); **$$ Manuela Moggia** (4 rooms, Db-€80, Db with kitchen or view-€100, Tb-€95, Tb with kitchen or view-€110, Qb with kitchen-€125, some behind the train station at Via Gavino 22, tel. 0187-812-397, mobile 333-413-6374, www.man-uela-vernazza.com, info@manuela-vernazza.com); and **$$ Rooms Elisabetta** (3 tight, tired, simple, casually run rooms at the tip-top of town with Vernazza's ultimate 360-degree roof terrace—come here only for the views, Db-€70, Tb-€95, Qb-€110, these prices if you book direct and pay cash, fans, free Wi-Fi, partway up the Corniglia path at Via Carattino 62, mobile 347-451-1834, www. elisabettacarro.it, carroelisabetta@hotmail.com, Elisabetta and dad Pino).

Eating in Vernazza

Breakfast

Locals take breakfast about as seriously as flossing. A cappuccino and a pastry or a piece of focaccia from a bar or bakery does it. Most of my recommended accommodations don't come with breakfast (when they do, I've noted so in my listings). Assuming you're on your own, you have four basic options: Blue Marlin Bar for its extensive menu, including bacon and eggs; Il Pirata delle Cinque Terre for sugary stuff and a lively welcome; Ananasso Bar for coffee and a sweet roll on the harborfront; or any bakery for picnic goodies.

Blue Marlin Bar (mid-town, just below the train station) serves a good array of clearly priced à la carte items including eggs and bacon (only after 8:15), adding up to the priciest breakfast in town (likely to total €10). It's run by Massimo and Carmen with the capable assistance of Jeff, an American who now lives in Vernazza. If you're awaiting a train any time of day, the Blue Marlin's outdoor seating beats the platform (Thu-Tue 7:00-24:00, closed Wed).

Il Pirata delle Cinque Terre, an endearing tourist trap, is located in the workaday zone behind and above the train station. The dynamic Sicilian duo Gianluca and Massimo (hardworking twins, a.k.a. the Cannoli brothers) enthusiastically offer a wide assortment of Sicilian pastries. Their fun, playful service makes up for the lack of a view. Massimo is a likeable loudmouth, while Gianluca is a pastry artist, hand-painting fanciful sculptured marzipan. Their sweet pastry breakfasts include an array of treats like *panzerotto* (made of ricotta, cinnamon, and vanilla, €2.50) and hot cheese and pesto bruschetta (€3). They proudly serve no bacon and eggs (since "this is Italy"). While the atmosphere of the place seems like suburban Milan, it has a curious charisma among its customers—bringing Vernazza a welcome bit of Sicily (daily 6:30-24:00, Via Gavino 36, tel. 0187-812-047).

Ananasso Bar feels Old World, with youthful energy and a great location with little tables right on the harbor. They offer toasted *panini*, pastries, and designer cappuccino. You can eat a bit cheaper at the bar (you're welcome to picnic on the nearby bench or seawall rocks with a Mediterranean view) or enjoy the best-situated tables in town (Fri-Wed 8:00-late, closed Thu).

Picnic Breakfast: Drop by one of Vernazza's several little bakeries, focaccia shops, or grocery stores to assemble a breakfast to eat on the breakwater. Top it off with a coffee in a nearby bar.

Lunch and Dinner

If you enjoy Italian cuisine and seafood, Vernazza's restaurants are worth the splurge. All take pride in their cooking. Wander around at about 20:00 and compare the ambience, but don't wait too late to eat—many kitchens close at 22:00. (Immigrants, who are doing more and more of the hard work of cooking and cleaning, need to wrap things up in time to catch the last train back to La Spezia, where many of them live.) To get an outdoor table on summer weekends, reserve ahead. Expect to spend around €10-12 for pastas, €12-16 for *secondi*, and €2-3 for a cover charge. Harborside restaurants and bars are easygoing. You're welcome to grab a cup of coffee or glass of wine and disappear somewhere on the breakwater, returning your glass when you're done. If you dine in Vernazza but are staying in another town, be sure to check train schedules before sitting down to eat, as trains run less frequently in the evening. Anchovies (prepared in a dizzying variety of ways) are the specialty. Any restaurant loves to show off with dazzling *antipasti misti* plates of seafood and anchovies. For more details, see "Eating in the Cinque Terre," on page 391.

Harborside

Gambero Rosso ("Red Prawn," the same name as Italy's top restaurant guide) is considered Vernazza's best-regarded restaurant... and charges accordingly. It feels dressier than the others. Try Chef Claudio's namesake risotto, *riso alla Cla* (€10-16 pastas, €16-25 *secondi*, Fri-Wed 12:00-15:30 & 19:00-22:00, closed Thu and Dec-Feb, Piazza Marconi 7, tel. 0187-812-265).

Trattoria Gianni is an old standby for locals and tourists who appreciate the best prices on the harbor, without sacrificing quality cuisine. You'll enjoy well-prepared seafood and receive steady, reliable, and friendly service from Emanuele and Alessandro. Ask about their off-menu specials. While the outdoor seating is basic, the indoor setting is classy (€10-15 pastas, €9-15 *secondi* plus a few €22-24 splurges, check their *menù cucina tipica Vernazza*, Thu-Tue

12:00-15:00 & 19:00-22:00, closed Wed except July-Aug, tel. 0187-812-228).

Trattoria del Capitano, a slightly more affordable option on the square, serves a short menu of straightforward local dishes, including €12 *spaghetti con frutti di mare*—pasta entangled with various types of seafood and €20 *grigliata mista*—a mix of seasonal Mediterranean fish (€8-12 pastas, €15-18 *secondi*, Wed-Mon 12:00-15:00 & 19:00-22:00, closed Tue except in Aug, closed Nov-Dec, tel. 0187-812-201, Paolo speaks English, grandpa Giacomo doesn't need to).

Ristorante Pizzeria Vulnetia is simpler, serving regional specialties such as prizewinning *tegame alla Vernazzana*—anchovies, tomatoes, and potatoes baked in the oven. They also offer pizzas—unlike the three places listed above— making this a good choice for a group with differing tastes (€7-10 pizzas, €8-13 pastas, €12-18 *secondi,* Tue-Sun 12:00-15:30 & 18:30-22:00, closed Mon, Piazza Marconi 29, tel. 0187-821-193, Giuliano).

Pizzeria Baia Saracena ("Saracen Bay") is the only budget option on the harbor, serving pizza and pastas out on the breakwater. Eat here not for high cuisine, but for memorable atmosphere at reasonable prices (€5-9 salads, €9 pizzas and pastas, Sat-Thu 10:30-22:00, closed Fri, tel. 0187-812-113, Luca).

Above the Harbor, by the Castle

Ristorante Belforte's experimental, beautifully presented, creative cuisine includes a hearty *zuppa Michela* (€25 for a boatload of seafood), fishy *spaghetti alla Bruno* (€13), and *trofie al pesto* (hand-rolled noodles with pesto, €15). Their classic *antipasti misto di pesce* (€18 for five plates) can be shared by two people. From the breakwater, follow either the stairs or the rope that leads up and around to the restaurant. You'll find a web of tables embedded in four levels of the lower part of the old castle. For the ultimate seaside perch, call and reserve one of four tables on the *terrazza con vista* (view terrace). Most of Belforte's seating is outdoors—if the weather's bad, the interior can get crowded (€13-16 pastas, €22-28 *secondi,* Wed-Mon 12:00-15:00 & 19:00-22:00, closed Tue and Nov-March, tel. 0187-812-222, Michela).

Inland, on or near the Main Street

Several of Vernazza's inland eateries manage to compete without the harbor ambience, but with slightly cheaper prices.

Trattoria da Sandro, on the main drag, mixes Genovese and Ligurian cuisine with friendly service. It can be a peaceful alternative to the harborside scene. They take pride in their food, and dish up award-winning stuffed mussels (€8-13 pastas, €13-18 *secondi,*

CINQUE TERRE

Wed-Mon 12:00-15:00 & 18:30-22:00, closed Tue, Via Roma 62, tel. 0187-812-223, Gabriella and Alessandro).

Antica Osteria il Baretto is another solid bet for homey, reasonably priced traditional cuisine, run by Simone and Jenny. As it's off the harbor and a little less glitzy than the others, it's favored by locals who prefer less noisy English while they eat great homemade fish ravioli. Sitting deep in their interior can be a peaceful escape (€9-14 pasta, €10-18 *secondi,* Tue-Sat 12:00-22:00, closed Mon, indoor and outdoor seating, Via Roma 31, tel. 0187-812-381).

Ristorante Incadasè da Piva is a rare bit of old Vernazza. For 25 years, charismatic Piva has been known for his *tegame Vernazza,* his *riso Piva* (seafood risotto), and his love of music. The town troubadour, he often serenades his guests when the cooking's done. Piva is now joined by his son, Raphael, who speaks English. *Incadasè* is local dialect for (roughly) "a weary sailor returning home from a long voyage" (€8-13 pastas, €14-18 *secondi,* Fri-Wed 12:00-15:00 & 19:00-22:00, closed Thu, tucked away 20 yards off the main drag, up a lane behind the pharmacy, tel. 0187-812-194).

Other Eating Options

Blue Marlin Bar (on the main street and described under "Breakfast," earlier) busts out of the Vernazzan-cuisine rut with a short, creative menu of more casual dishes. It's a good choice if you just want to grab some reliable food rather than dine. Locals enjoy a meal here when they don't feel like cooking at home (€6-8 pizzas, €9-10 pastas, €10-12 *secondi,* closed Wed).

Il Pirata delle Cinque Terre, popular for breakfast, also attracts many travelers for lunch and dinner (€8-10 pastas, €7-9 salads). Don't come here for the cuisine or for the ambience (it's a simple café/pastry shop), but for a memorable evening with the Cannoli twins, who entertain while they serve, as diners enjoy their meals while laughing out loud. The menu, aimed squarely at American tourists' taste buds, offers a break from more authentic Ligurian fare (at the top of town; for complete description, see listing under "Breakfast," earlier).

Pizzerias, Sandwiches, and Groceries: Vernazza's main-street eateries offer a fine range of quick meals. Two **pizzerias** stay busy, and while they mostly do takeout, each will let you sit and eat for the same cheap price. One has tables on the street, and the other, called Ercole, hides a tiny terrace and a few tables out back. **Forno Bakery** has good focaccia and veggie tarts (at #3), and several bars sell sandwiches and pizza by the slice. **Pino's grocery store** also makes inexpensive sandwiches to order (generally Mon-Sat 8:00-13:00 & 17:00-19:30, closed Sun). Tiny jars of pesto spread give elegance to picnics.

Gelato: The town has three *gelaterias:* **Gelateria Vernazza,** near the top of the main street, takes its gelato seriously, occasion-ally flirting with creative ingredients (soy) and flavors (*riso*—rice, and ricotta and fig). What looks like **Gelateria Amore Mio** (mid-town) is actually Gelateria Stalin—founded in 1968 by a pastry chef with that unfortunate name (now it's run by his niece Sonia and nephew Francesco, with great people-watching tables but the least exciting gelato in town). And out on the harbor, the aptly named **Gelateria Il Porticciolo** ("Marina") is arguably the best; they use fresh ingredients to create intense flavors (try their *cannella*—cinnamon, or their *nocciola*—hazelnut).

Monterosso al Mare (Town #5)

This is a resort with a few cars and lots of hotels, rentable beach umbrellas, crowds, and a little more late-night action than the neighboring towns. Monterosso al Mare—the only Cinque Terre town built on flat land—has two parts: A new town (called Fegina) with a parking lot, train station, and TI; and an old town (Centro Storico), which cradles Old World charm in its

small, crooked lanes. In the old town, you'll find hole-in-the-wall shops, pastel townscapes, and a new generation of creative small-businesspeople eager to keep their visitors happy.

A pedestrian tunnel connects the old with the new, but take a small detour around the point for a nicer walk. It offers a close-up view of two sights: a 16th-century lookout tower, built after the last serious pirate raid in 1545; and a Nazi "pillbox," a small, low concrete bunker where gunners hid. (During World War II, nearby La Spezia was an important Axis naval base, and Monterosso was bombed while the Germans were here.)

Strolling the waterfront promenade, you can pick out each of the Cinque Terre towns decorating the coast. After dark, they sparkle. Monterosso is the most enjoyable of the five for young travelers wanting to connect with others looking for a little evening action. Even so, Monterosso is not a full-blown Portofino-style re-sort—and locals appreciate quiet, sensitive guests.

Monterosso sustained serious damage in the 2011 flood, but within just a few months, it was back up and running at nearly 100 percent. Walking through the town today, you'll have to know where to look to find evidence of the devastation. Big grates on the six roads cover the historic canals (which drain runoff from the surrounding hills into the sea), and the sound of rushing water reassures townsfolk that the streams are flowing unimpeded below.

Orientation to Monterosso

Tourist Information

The TI Proloco is next to the train station (April-Oct daily 9:00-19:00, closed Nov-March, exit station and go left a few doors, tel. 0187-817-506, www.prolocomonterosso.it). For national park tickets and information, head upstairs within the station to the ticket office near platform 1 (likely daily 7:00-19:00, shorter hours off-season). If you arrive late on a summer day, the old town's Internet café is helpful with tourist information (see later).

Rebuild Monterosso: Led by a group of American women who married into the community, Rebuild Monterosso brought relief to the town in the immediate aftermath of the flood and has since evolved into an organization focused on fostering healthy tourism and keeping visitors up to date on the latest in town (www.rebuildmonterosso.com).

Arrival in Monterosso

By Train: Train travelers arrive in the new town, from which it's a scenic, flat 10-minute stroll to all the old town action (leave station to the left; to reach hotels in the new town, turn right out of station). The bar at track 1, which overlooks both the tracks and the beach, is a handy place to hang out while waiting for your train to pull in (salads, sandwiches, drinks). As many trains run late, this can turn a frustration into a blessing.

Shuttle buses run roughly hourly along the waterfront between the old town (Piazza Garibaldi, just beyond the tunnel), the train station, and the parking lot at the end of Via Fegina (*Campo Sportivo* stop). While the buses can be convenient—saving you a 10-minute schlep with your bags—they only go once an hour, and are likely not worth the trouble (€1.50, free with Cinque Terre Park Card).

The other alternative is to take a **taxi** (certain vehicles have permission to drive in the old city center). They usually wait outside the train station, but you may have to call (€7 from station to the old town, mobile 335-616-5842 or 335-628-0933).

By Car: Monterosso is 30 minutes off the freeway (exit: Carrodano-Levanto). Note that about three miles above Monterosso, a fork directs you to either *Centro Storico* (old part of town—Via Roma parking lot with a few spots, and possibly the new Loreto garage) or *Fegina* (the new town and beachfront parking, most likely where you want to go). At this point you must choose which area, because you can't drive directly from the new town to the old center (which is closed to cars without special permits).

Parking is easy (except July-Aug and summer weekends) in the huge beachfront guarded lot in the new town (€18/24 hours). If you're heading to the old town, you'll find the Loreto parking garage on Via Roma, a 10-minute downhill walk to the main square (€1.70/hour, €18/24 hours). For the cheapest Monterosso rates, park along the blue lines (a few minutes farther uphill from the Loreto garage) for €8 per day. See "Cinque Terre Connections" at the end of this chapter for directions from Milan and tips on driving in the Cinque Terre.

Helpful Hints

Thursday Morning Market: Every Thursday morning, trucks pull into the old town and fill the public area by the beach with temporary stalls where locals get the items not otherwise available in this small town.

Medical Help: The town's bike-riding, leather bag-toting, English-speaking physician is **Dr. Vitone,** who charges €50-80 for a simple visit (less for poor students, mobile 338-853-0949).

Internet Access: The Net, a few steps off the old town's main drag (Via Roma), has six high-speed computers (€1/10 minutes) and Wi-Fi (a bit cheaper). Enzo happily provides information on the Cinque Terre, rents rooms (see "Sleeping in Monterosso," later), and can burn your photos onto a DVD for €6 (daily 9:30-23:00, off-season closes at 19:00, Via Vittorio Emanuele 55, tel. 0187-817-288, www.monterossonet.com, info@monterossonet.com).

Baggage Storage: Wash and Dry Lavarapido, two blocks from the station, provides a wonderful bag-check service. Just drop off your bag for €5 (details in next listing).

Laundry: For full-service laundry in the new town, **Wash and Dry Lavarapido** will return your laundry to your hotel (€12/13 pounds, daily 8:00-19:00, Via Molinelli 17, mobile 339-484-0940, Lucia and Ivano).

Boat Trips: Stefano or **Nico** can take you on a cruise around the Cinque Terre (€100/hour, one hour is enough for a quick spin, two hours includes time for swimming stops; longer trips to Portovenere and offshore islands also possible). Stefano's slower boat, *Matilde,* holds up to 6 people, while Nico's fast boat, *Il Delfino,* takes up to 10 and also does taxi boat transfers (€50 one-way to Monterosso, €80 one-way to Riomaggiore, €300 to Portovenere; Stefano's mobile 333-821-2007, Nico's mobile 345-424-9015, www.matildenavigazione.com, info@matildenavigazione.com).

CINQUE TERRE

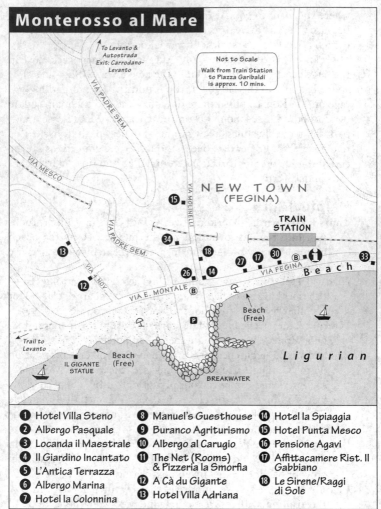

Monterosso al Mare

To Levanto &
Autostrada
Exit: Carrodano-
Levanto

Not to Scale
Walk from Train Station
to Piazza Garibaldi
is approx. 10 mins.

VIA PADRE SEM.

VIA MESCO

VIA PADRE SEM.

VIA 4 NOV.

VIA E. MONTALE

VIA MOLINELLI

NEW TOWN
(FEGINA)

TRAIN
STATION

VIA FEGINA

Beach

Beach
(Free)

Trail to
Levanto

Beach
(Free)

IL GIGANTE
STATUE

BREAKWATER

Ligurian

① Hotel Villa Steno
② Albergo Pasquale
③ Locanda il Maestrale
④ Il Giardino Incantato
⑤ L'Antica Terrazza
⑥ Albergo Marina
⑦ Hotel la Colonnina

⑧ Manuel's Guesthouse
⑨ Buranco Agriturismo
⑩ Albergo al Carugio
⑪ The Net (Rooms)
& Pizzeria la Smorfia
⑫ A Cà du Gigante
⑬ Hotel Villa Adriana

⑭ Hotel la Spiaggia
⑮ Hotel Punta Mesco
⑯ Pensione Agavi
⑰ Affittacamere Rist. Il
Gabbiano
⑱ Le Sirene/Raggi
di Sole

CINQUE TERRE

Massage: Giorgio Moggia, the local physiotherapist, gives good massages at your hotel or in his studio (€60/hour, tel. 339-314-6127, giomogg@tin.it).

Self-Guided Walk

Welcome to Monterosso

This walk will introduce you to Monterosso, beginning with an easy and lazy sweep of the head from the breakwater. Part 1, focusing on the mostly level town center, takes about 30 minutes; for Part 2, summiting the adjacent hill, allow another hour or so.

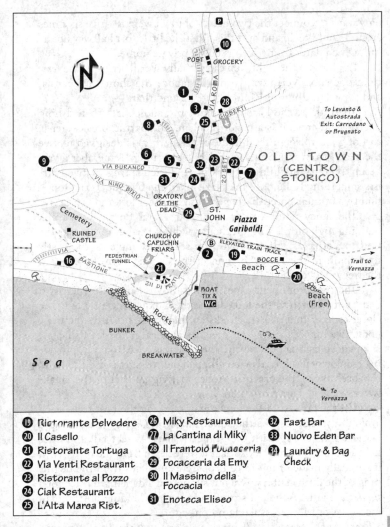

⑲ Ristorante Belvedere	㉖ Miky Restaurant	㉜ Fast Bar
⑳ Il Casello	㉗ La Cantina di Miky	㉝ Nuovo Eden Bar
㉑ Ristorante Tortuga	㉘ Il Frantoio Focacceria	㉞ Laundry & Bag Check
㉒ Via Venti Restaurant	㉙ Focacceria da Emy	
㉓ Ristorante al Pozzo	㉚ Il Massimo della Foccacia	
㉔ Ciak Restaurant		
㉕ L'Alta Marea Rist.	㉛ Enoteca Eliseo	

Part 1: Monterosso Harbor and Town Center

• *Hike out from the dock in the old town and climb five rough steps to the very top of the concrete...*

Breakwater: If you're visiting by boat, you'll start here anyway. From this point you can survey Monterosso's old town (straight ahead) and new town (stretching to the left, with train station and parking lot). Notice the bluff that separates old and new, and imagine how much harder your commute would be if the narrow road tethering these two towns were somehow cut off. It happened in the spring of 2013, when the wall below the Capuchin church (at the top of the hill) gave way, creating a landslide. For a time, the only ways to connect the two halves of town were to drive six miles around…or hike up and over this hill. (The little fort halfway up the hill, which dates from 1550, is now a private home.)

Looking to the right, you can actually see all *cinque* of the *terre* from one spot: Vernazza, Corniglia (above the shore), Manarola, and a few buildings of Riomaggiore beyond that.

These days, the harbor hosts more paddleboats than fishing boats. Sand erosion is a major problem. The partial breakwater (a row of giant rocks in the middle of the harbor) is designed to save the beach from washing away. While old-timers remember a vast beach, their grandchildren truck in sand each spring to give tourists something to lie on. (The Nazis liked the Cinque Terre, too— find two of their bomb-hardened bunkers, near left and far right.)

The fancy €300-a-night, four-star Hotel Porto Roca (pink building high on the hill, on the far right of the harbor) marks the trail to Vernazza. High above, you see an example of the costly roads built in the 1980s to connect the Cinque Terre towns with the freeway over the hills.

The two prominent capes (Punta di Montenero to the right, and Punta Mesco to the left) define the Cinque Terre region. The closer cape, Punta Mesco, marks an important sea-life sanctuary, home to a rare sea grass that provides an ideal home for fish eggs. Buoys keep fishing boats away. The cape was once a quarry, providing employment to locals who chipped out the stones used to build the local towns (the greenish stones making up part of the breakwater below you are from there).

On the far end of the new town, marking the best free beach around, you can just see the statue named *Il Gigante* (hard to spot because it blends in with the gray rock). It's 45 feet tall and once held a trident. While it looks as if it were hewn from the rocky cliff, it's actually made of reinforced concrete and dates from the beginning of the 20th century, when it supported a dancing terrace for a *fin de siècle* villa. A violent storm left the giant holding nothing but memories of Monterosso's glamorous age.

• *From the breakwater, walk into the old town. At the top of the beach, notice the openings of two big drains, ready to let flash floods rip through town without destroying things. Walking under the train tracks, venture right into the square and find the statue of a dandy holding what looks like a box cutter.*

Piazza Garibaldi: The statue honors Giuseppe Garibaldi, the dashing firebrand revolutionary who, in the 1860s, helped unite the people of Italy into a modern nation. Facing Garibaldi, with your back to the sea, you'll see (from right to left) the orange city hall (with the now-required European Union flag beside the Italian one) and a big home and recreation center for poor and homeless elderly. You'll also see A Ca' du Scienza restaurant (with historic town photos inside and upstairs; you're welcome to pop in for a look).

After the 2011 flood, it was on this square that the National Guard set up an emergency tent, used for staging emergency deliveries, community meals, Christmas Eve Mass, and the New Year's Eve disco. In the aftermath of the flood, many moving stories emerged. Old ladies who couldn't help dig, helped cook. People worried that Laura, whose bakery—loved for her secret recipes—was destroyed, wouldn't be able to reopen. But she rebuilt, and that beautiful aroma of her sweet cakes again helps locals greet each new day. The motorbike of Diego's dreams, which he had bought just 10 days before the flood, was buried by the mud. He excavated it, cleaned it up, and—to the cheers of his friends—it started. The local civil protection unit is now named for 40-year-old volunteer Sandro Usai, Monterosso's one death from the flood. Sandro was last seen heroically trying to open up a grate to increase canal drainage. His body washed ashore a week later, and his funeral was the first time the community stopped working and was silent together. Sandro posthumously received the highest civilian award the Italian government gives.

Just under the bell tower (with your back to the sea, it's on your left), a set of covered arcades facing the sea is where the old-timers hang out (they see all and know all). The crenellated bell tower marks the church.

• Go to church (the entrance is on the inland side).

Church of St. John the Baptist (Chiesa di San Giovanni Battista): Before entering, check out the facade. This black-and-white church, with white marble from Carrara and green marble from Punte Mesco, is typical of this region's Romanesque style. Note the lacy, stone rose window above the entrance. It's as delicate as crochet work, with 18 slender mullions (the petals of the rose). The marble stripes get narrower the higher they go, creating the illusion of a church that's taller than it really is.

Step inside for more Ligurian Gothic: original marble columns and capitals with pointed arches to match. The octagonal baptismal font (in the back of the church) was carved from Carrara marble in 1359. Imagine the job getting that from the quarries to here. In the chapel to the right of the high altar, look for the wooden statue of St. Anthony, carved about 1400, which once graced a church that stood atop Punta Mesco. The church itself dates from 1307—see the proud inscription on the left-middle column: "MilleCCCVII." Outside the church, on the side facing the main street, find the high-water mark from an October 1966 flood (the same month as the flood that devastated Florence). Nearly half a century later, the crippling October 2011 flood hit Monterosso. But the church's statues survived, thanks to townspeople who came to their rescue, carrying them through raging waters to safety. Later, when there was enough help in the streets, excess volunteers came into the church and lovingly polished the candlesticks, just to keep caring for their town.

• *Leaving the church, immediately turn left and go to church again.*

Oratory of the Dead (Oratorio dei Neri): During the Counter-Reformation, the Catholic Church offset the rising influence of the Lutherans by creating brotherhoods of good works. These religious Rotary clubs were called "confraternities." Monterosso had two, nicknamed White and Black. This building is the oratory of the Black group, whose mission—as the macabre decor filling the interior indicates—was to arrange for funerals and take care of widows, orphans, the shipwrecked, and the souls of those who ignore the request for a €1 donation. It dates from the 16th century, and membership has passed from father to son for generations. Notice the fine carved choir stalls (c. 1700) just inside the door, and the haunted-house chandeliers. Look up at the ceiling to find the symbol of the confraternity: a skull-and-crossbones and an hourglass...death awaits us all.

• *On that cheery note, if you're in a lazy mood, you can discreetly split off from our walking tour now to enjoy strolling, shopping, gelato-licking, a day at the beach...or all of the above. But if you're up for a hike, continue with me on Part 2. As you face out to sea, look to the right and imagine the views from the top of that hill. Now...go see them.*

Part 2: Capuchin Church and Hilltop Cemetery

• *Return to the beach and find the brick steps that lead up to the hill-capping convent (starting between the train tracks and the pedestrian tunnel, and passing in front of Albergo Pasquale). Approaching the bend in the path, watch for the stairs leading steeply and sharply to the right. This lane (Salita dei Cappuccini) is nicknamed Zii di Frati, or...*

Switchbacks of the Friars: Follow the yellow brick road (OK, it's orange...but I couldn't help singing as I skipped skyward). Pause at the terrace above the castle at a statue of St. Francis and a wolf taking in a grand view. Enjoy another opportunity to see all five of the Cinque Terre towns. From here, backtrack 20 yards and continue uphill.

• *When you reach a gate marked* Convento e Chiesa Cappuccini, *you have arrived at the...*

Church of the Capuchin Friars: The former convent is now manned by a single caretaker friar. Before stepping inside, notice the church's striped Romanesque facade. It's all fake. Tap it—no marble, just cheap 18th-century stucco. Go inside and sit in the rear pew. The high altarpiece painting of St. Francis can be rolled up on special days to reveal a statue of Mary standing behind it. Look at the statue of St. Anthony to the right and smile (you're on convent camera). Wave at the security camera—they're nervous about the precious painting to your left.

This fine painting of the *Crucifixion* is attributed to Anthony van Dyck, the 17th-century Flemish master who lived and worked for years in nearby Genoa (though art historians suspect that, at best, it was painted by someone in the artist's workshop). When Jesus died, the earth went dark. Notice the eclipsed sun in the painting, just to the right of the cross. Do the electric candles work? Pick one up, pray for peace, and plug it in. (Leave €0.50, or unplug it and put it back.)

• *Leave and turn left to hike 100 yards uphill to the cemetery that fills the remains of the castle, capping the hill. Look back from the gate and enjoy the view over the town.*

Cemetery in the Ruined Castle: In the Dark Ages, the village huddled within this castle. Slowly it expanded. Notice the town view from here—no sea. You're looking at the oldest part of Monterosso, tucked behind the hill, out of view of 13th-century pirates. Explore the cemetery, but remember that cemeteries are sacred and treasured places (as is clear by the abundance of fresh flowers). Ponder the black-and-white photos of grandparents past. *Q.R.P.* is *Qui Riposa in Pace* (a.k.a. R.I.P.). Rich families had their own little tomb buildings. Climb to the very summit—the castle's keep, or place of last refuge. Priests are buried in a line of graves closest to the sea, but facing inland, toward the town's holy sanctuary high on the hillside (above the road, with its triangular steeple peeking above the trees). Each Cinque Terre town has a lofty sanctuary, dedicated to Mary and dear to the village hearts.

• *From here, your tour is over—any trail leads you back into town.*

Sights in Monterosso

Beaches

Monterosso's beaches, immediately in front of the train station, are easily the Cinque Terre's best and most crowded. This town is a sandy resort with rentable beach extras: Figure €20 to rent two chairs and an umbrella for the day. Light lunches are served by beach cafés to sunbathers at their lounge chairs. It's often worth the euros to enjoy a private beach. If you see umbrellas on a beach, it means you'll have to pay a rental fee; otherwise the sand is free (all the beaches are marked on this book's Monterosso al Mare map). Prices get very soft in the afternoon. Don't use your white hotel towels; most hotels will give you beach towels—sometimes for a fee. The local hidden beach, which is free, gravelly, and generally less crowded, is tucked away under Il Casello restaurant at the east end of town, near the trailhead to Vernazza. There's another free beach at the far-west end, near the Gigante statue. The bocce ball court (next to Il Casello) is busy with the old boys enjoying their favorite pastime.

Kayaks

Samba rents kayaks on the beach (€7/hour for 1-person kayak, €12/hour for 2-person kayak, cheaper for longer rentals, to the right of train station as you exit, mobile 339-681-2265, Domenico). The paddle to Vernazza is a favorite. The adjacent **La Pineta** beach also rents stand-up paddleboards (€12/hour, Diego).

Shuttle Buses for High-Country Hikes

Monterosso's bus service (described earlier, under "Arrival in Monterosso") continues beyond the town limits, but check the schedules—only one or two departures a day head into the high country (and only in summer). Some buses go to the Sanctuary of Our Lady of Soviore, from where you can hike back down to Monterosso (1.5 hours, moderately steep). Rides cost €2.50 (free with Cinque Terre Park Card, pick up schedule from park office). Or you can hike to Levanto (no Cinque Terre Park card necessary, not as stunning as the rest of the coastal trail, 2.5 hours, straight uphill and then easy decline, follow signs at west end of the new town). For hiking details, ask at the train station TI.

Wine-Tasting

Buranco Agriturismo offers visits to their vineyard and cantina (reserve 2 days ahead). You'll taste two of their wines plus a grappa and a *limoncino*, along with home-cooked food (up to €25/person with snacks, English may be limited, follow Via Buranco uphill to path, 10 minutes above town, tel. 0187-817-677, www.burancocinqueterre.it). They also rent apartments; see "Sleeping in Monterosso," later.

Boat Rides

From the old town harbor, boats run nearly hourly (10:30-17:00) to Vernazza, Manarola, Riomaggiore, and Portovenere. Schedules are posted in Cinque Terre park offices (for details, see "Getting Around the Cinque Terre—By Boat" on page 383).

Nightlife in Monterosso

Enoteca Eliseo, the first (and I'd say best) wine bar in town, comes with operatic ambience. Eliseo and his wife, Mary, love music and wine. You can select a fine bottle from their shop shelf, and for €7 extra, enjoy it and the village action from their cozy tables. If you've ever wanted an education in grappa, talk to Eliseo—he stocks more than a hundred varieties. Wines sold by the glass *(bicchiere)* are posted (Wed-Mon 14:00-24:00, closed Tue, Piazza Matteotti 3, a block inland behind church, tel. 0187-817-308).

Fast Bar, the best bar in town for young travelers and night owls, is located on Via Roma in the old town. Customers mix travel tales with big, cold beers, and the crowd (and the rock 'n' roll) gets noisier as the night rolls on. Come here to watch Italian or American sporting events on TV any time of day (€5 *panini* and €7-9 salads usually served until midnight, open Fri-Wed 9:30-2:00 in the morning, closed Thu except in peak season; Alex, Francisco, and Stefano).

La Cantina di Miky, in the new town just beyond the train station, is a trendy bar-restaurant with an extensive cocktail and grappa menu. The seating is in three zones: overlooking the beach, in the garden, or in the cellar. Run by Manuel, son of well-known local restaurateur Miky, it sometimes hosts live music. Manuel offers a fun "five villages" wine-tasting with local meats and cheeses (€15/person for just wine, €20/person with food). Microbrews are becoming popular in Italy, and this is the best place in town for top-end Italian beers (daily until well after 24:00, Via Fegina 90, tel. 0187-802-525).

Nuovo Eden Bar, overlooking the beach by the big rock just east of the train station, is a fine place to enjoy a cocktail or fancy ice cream with a sea view. During happy hour (16:30-21:00), €6 cocktails come with a snack. Locals consider their ice cream (either to-go from the streetside stand, or fancy and sit-down) the best in town. Consider this place for a pre-dinner drink or dessert with a view (Tue-Sun 7:30-24:00, closed Mon).

Sleeping in Monterosso

Monterosso, the most beach-resorty of the five Cinque Terre towns, offers maximum comfort and ease. The TI Proloco just outside the train station can give you a list of €70-80 double rooms. Rooms in Monterosso are a better value for your money than similar rooms in crowded Vernazza, and the proprietors seem more genuine and welcoming. To locate the hotels, see the Monterosso al Mare map.

In the Old Town
$$$ Hotel Villa Steno is lovingly managed and features great view balconies, panoramic gardens and a roof terrace with sun beds, air-conditioning, and the friendly help of English-speaking Matteo and his wife, Carla. Of their 16 rooms, 12 have view balconies (Sb-€115, Db-€180, Tb-€210, Qb-€260, includes hearty buffet breakfast, €10/night discount in 2014 when you pay cash and show this book, free guest computer and Wi-Fi, laundry, parking-€10—reserve in advance, hike up to the panoramic terrace, Via Roma 109, tel. 0187-817-028 or 0187-818-336, www.villasteno.com, steno@pasini.com). It's a 15-minute hike (or €8 taxi ride) from the train station to the top of the old town. Readers get a free Cinque Terre

info packet and a glass of the local sweet wine, *Sciacchetrà*, when they check in—ask for it.

$$$ Albergo Pasquale is a modern, comfortable place with 15 rooms, run by the same family as the Hotel Villa Steno (above). It's conveniently located just a few steps from the beach, boat dock, tunnel entrance to the new town, and train tracks. While there is some train noise, the soundtrack is mostly a lullaby of waves. Located right on the harbor, it has an elevator and offers easier access than most (same prices and welcome drink as Villa Steno; all rooms with sea view, air-con, elevator, limited free Wi-Fi, Via Fegina 8, tel. 0187-817-550 or 0187-817-477, www.hotelpasquale. com, pasquale@pasini.com, Felicita and Marco).

$$$ Locanda il Maestrale rents six small, stylish rooms in a sophisticated and peaceful little inn. Although renovated with all the modern comforts, it retains centuries-old character under frescoed ceilings. Its peaceful sun terrace overlooking the old town and Via Roma action is a delight (small Db-€115, Db-€145, suite-€170, prices lower off-season, 10 percent Rick Steves discount if you book direct and pay cash, air-con, free Wi-Fi, Via Roma 37, tel. 0187-817-013, mobile 338-4530-531, www.locandamaestrale. net, maestrale@monterossonet.com, Stefania).

$$$ Il Giardino Incantato ("The Enchanted Garden") is a charming and comfortable four-room B&B with impressive attention to detail in a tastefully renovated 16th-century Ligurian home in the heart of the old town. Breakfast is served under lemon trees in a delightful hidden garden, which is illuminated with candles in the evening (Db-€150-170, Db suite-€200, ask for Rick Steves discount, air-con, free Wi-Fi, free minibar and tea and coffee service, laundry service-€15/load, Via Mazzini 18, tel. 0187-818-315, mobile 333-264-9252, www.ilgiardinoincantato.net, giardino_incantato@libero.it, kind and eager-to-please Fausto and Mariapia).

$$$ L'Antica Terrazza rents four classy rooms right in town. With a pretty terrace overlooking the pedestrian street and minimal stairs, Raffaella and John offer a good deal (D with private bath down the hall-€85, Db-€115, these special prices for Rick Steves readers, 5 percent additional discount when you pay cash, air-con, free Wi-Fi, Vicolo San Martino 1, tel. 380-138-0082, mobile 347-132-6213, www.anticaterrazza.com, post@anticaterrazza.com).

$$$ Albergo Marina, creatively run by enthusiastic husband-and-wife team Marina and Eraldo, has 23 decent rooms and a garden with lemon trees. With a free and filling buffet featuring local specialties from 14:00 to 17:00 daily, they offer a fine value (Db-€135, Tb-€160, Qb-€180, 10 percent discount in 2014 when you pay cash and show this book, elevator, air-con, pay Wi-Fi, free use of kayak and snorkel equipment, Via Buranco 40, tel. 0187-817-613, www.hotelmarina5terre.com, marina@hotelmarina5terre.com).

$$$ Hotel la Colonnina has 21 big and pretty rooms (some older, some newer), generous if dated public spaces, and several leafy, peaceful sun terraces. It's buried in the town's fragrant and sleepy back streets (Db-€143-153, Tb-€188, Qb-€233, €5 more for non-view mini-terrace, €15 more for townview terrace, cash only, air-con, free Wi-Fi, fridges, elevator, inviting rooftop terrace with sun beds, garden, in the old town a block inland from the main square at Via Zuecca 6, tel. 0187-817-439, www.lacolonninacinqueterre.it, info@lacolonninacinqueterre.it, Christina).

$$$ Manuel's Guesthouse, perched high above the town among terraces, is a garden getaway run by Lorenzo and his father, Giovanni (and named for their uncle/brother, a disheveled artist who prefers to set up his easels down below these days). They have six big, bright rooms and a grand view. After climbing the killer stairs from the town center, their killer terrace is hard to leave—especially after a few drinks (Db-€110, big Db with grand-view balcony-€130, cash only, air-con, free Wi-Fi, up about 100 steps behind church—you can ask Lorenzo to carry your bags up the hill, Via San Martino 39, mobile 333-439-0809, www.manuels-guesthouse.com, manuelsguesthouse@libero.it).

$$$ Buranco Agriturismo, a 10-minute hike above the old town, has wonderful gardens and views over the vine-covered valley. Its primary business is wine and olive-oil production, but they offer three apartments at a good price. It's a rare opportunity to stay in a farmhouse but still be able to get to town on foot (2-6 people-€60/person including breakfast, €30/child under 12, air-con, €7 taxi from station, tel. 0187-817-677, mobile 349-434-8046, www.burancocinqueterre.it, info@buranco.it, informally run by Loredana, Mary, and Giulietta).

$$ Albergo al Carugio is a simple, practical nine-room place in a big apartment-style building at the top of the old town. It's quiet, comfy, and functional (Db-€80, this price for Rick Steves readers when you book direct and pay cash, no breakfast, air-con, free Wi-Fi, Via Roma 100, tel. 0187-817-453, www.alcarugio.it, info@alcarugio.it, Andrea and Simona).

$ The Net Room Service is run by Enzo, who owns the Internet point in town (and speaks perfect English). He manages several apartments, offering Monterosso's least expensive accommodations. Enzo's office functions as your reception (Db-€60-70 any time of year, 2- or 3-night minimum stay, Via Vittorio Emanuele 55, tel. 0187-817-288, mobile 335-778-5085, www.monterossonet.com, info@monterossonet.com).

In the New Town

$$$ A Cà du Gigante, despite its name, is a tiny yet stylish refuge with nine rooms. About 100 yards from the beach (and surrounded by blocky apartments on a modern street), the interior is tastefully done with modern comfort in mind (Db-€160, Db seaview suite-€180, 10 percent discount with 3-night stay and this book in 2014, occasional last-minute deals, air-con, free Wi-Fi, free parking, Via IV Novembre 11, tel. 0187-817-401, www.ilgigantecinqueterre.it, gigante@ilgigantecinqueterre.it, Claudia).

$$$ Hotel Villa Adriana is a big, modern, bright hotel on a church-owned estate set in a peaceful garden with a pool, free parking, and a no-stress style. They rent 54 rooms—some with terraces and/or sea views—at the same price as much simpler places on the water (Sb-€90, Db-€170, all with showers, air-con, elevator, free Wi-Fi, free loaner bikes, Via IV Novembre 23, tel. 0187-818-109, www.villaadriana.info, info@villaadriana.info).

$$$ Hotel la Spiaggia is a venerable old 19-room place facing the beach and run with attitude by Andrea Poggi and his gentle daughter Maria. Half of the rooms come with air-con and half with sea views, but all are the same price—request what you like when you reserve (Db-€170, extra bed-€30, free parking, cash only, elevator, free Wi-Fi with this book, Via Lungomare 98, tel. 0187-817-567, www.laspiaggiahotel.com, hotellaspiaggia@libero.it).

$$$ Hotel Punta Mesco is a tidy, well-run little haven renting 17 quiet, modern rooms. While none have views, 10 rooms have small terraces. For the price, it may offer the best comfort in town (Db-€143, Tb-€185, 5 percent discount when you pay cash, air-con, free Wi-Fi, free parking, Via Molinelli 35, tel. 0187-817-495, www.hotelpuntamesco.it, info@hotelpuntamesco.it, Diego, Karina, and Manuel).

$$$ Pensione Agavi has 10 spartan, bright, overpriced rooms, about half overlooking the beach near the big rock. This is not a place to party—it feels like an old hospital with narrow hallways (D-€80, Db-€110, Tb-€145, rooms without view can be a bit cheaper, 10 percent discount for 2 nights or more, breakfast-€5, cash only, refrigerators, turn left out of station to Fegina 30, tel. 0187-817-171, mobile 333-697-4071, hotel.agavi@libero.it, Hillary).

$$ Affittacamere Ristorante il Gabbiano is an old-school, family-run restaurant right on the beach, renting five quiet, air-conditioned rooms upstairs. Three rooms face the sea, with small balconies (Db-€100, the largest can be Tb-€130, Qb-€160), while two are at the back, facing a little garden (Db-€90). The Gabbiano family restaurant serves as your reception (cash only, air-con, Via Fegina 84, tel. 0187-817-578, lella-v71@hotmail.it).

$ Le Sirene/Raggi di Sole, with nine simple rooms in two humble buildings, is about the cheapest place in town. It's run from a hole-in-the-wall reception desk a block from the station, just off the water. I'd request the Le Sirene building, which doesn't have train noise and is a bit more spacious and airy than Raggi di Sole (Db-€90, third person-€45, fans, free Wi-Fi in Raggi di Sole only, Via Molinelli 10, mobile 393-935-7683, www.sirenerooms.com, sirenerooms@gmail.com, Ermanna).

Eating in Monterosso

With a Sea View

Of these seaview restaurants, the first two offer reasonable prices right on the old town beach, while the last is a romantic splurge higher up.

Ristorante Belvedere, big and sprawling, is *the* place for a good-value meal indoors or outdoors on the harborfront. Their *amfora belvedere*—mixed seafood stew—is huge, and can easily be split among up to four diners (€48). Share with your group and add pasta for a fine meal. Mussel fans will enjoy the *tagliolini della casa* (€9). Their *misto mare* plate (2-person minimum, €15/person), a fishy treat, can nearly make an entire meal. It's energetically run by Federico and Roberto (€8-10 pastas, €10-16 *secondi*, Wed-Mon 12:00-14:30 & 18:00-22:00, usually closed Tue, on the harbor in the old town, tel. 0187-817-033).

Il Casello is the only place for a fun meal on a terrace overlooking the old town beach. With outdoor tables on a rocky outcrop, it's a pleasant spot for a salad, pasta, or *secondi* (€9-13 pastas, €13-18 *secondi*, daily April-Oct—food and drinks served all day long, closed Nov-March, mobile 333-492-7629, Bacco).

Ristorante Tortuga is the top option in Monterosso for seaview elegance, with gorgeous outdoor seating high on a bluff and an elegant white-tablecloth-and-candles interior. If you're looking for a place to propose, this offers the prettiest and most romantic dining in town. When you're out and about, drop by to consider which table you'd like to reserve for later. House specialties include *cannelloni tortuga* (stuffed not with turtle, but with sea bass) and *filetto Sciacchetrà*—steak with a glaze made of the local sweet wine (€15-19 pastas, €16-21 *secondi*, Tue-Sun 12:00-14:30 & 18:00-22:00, closed Mon, just outside the tunnel that connects the old and new town—or climb up the ramp in front of Albergo Pasquale, tel. 0187-800-065, mobile 333-240-7956, Silvia and Giamba).

In the Old Town

Via Venti is a quiet little trattoria, hidden in an alley deep in the heart of the old town, where Papa Ettore creates imaginative seafood dishes using the day's catch and freshly made pasta. Ilaria and her partner Michele serve up delicate and savory gnocchi (tiny potato dumplings) with crab sauce, tender ravioli stuffed with fresh fish, and pear-and-cheese pasta. There's nothing pretentious here... just good cooking, service, and prices (€11-13 pastas, €14-20 *secondi*, Fri-Wed 12:00-14:30 & 18:30-22:30, closed Thu, Via Venti 32, tel. 0187-818-347).

Ristorante al Pozzo is a favorite among locals. It's family-run, with good old-fashioned quality, as Gino (with his long white beard) cooks, and his engaging English-speaking son, Manuel, serves. They have one of the best wine lists in town, serve only homemade pasta, and are known for their raw fish and wonderful seafood *antipasti misti* (€10-17 pastas, €15-25 *secondi*, Fri-Wed 12:00-15:00 & 18:30-22:30, closed Thu, Via Roma 24, tel. 0187-817-575).

Ciak, high-energy and tightly packed, is a local institution with reliably good food and higher prices. It's known for its huge, sizzling terra-cotta crock for two crammed with the day's catch and accompanied by risotto or spaghetti, or served swimming in a soup *(zuppa).* Other popular choices are fish ravioli with shrimp sauce and the seafood *antipasto Lampara* (€20). Stroll a couple of paces past the outdoor tables up Via Roma to see what Signore Ciak (who wears his Popeye cap in the kitchen) has on the stove (€13-14 pastas, €18-25 *secondi*, Thu-Tue 12:00-15:00 & 19:00-22:30, closed Wed, Via Roma 4, tel. 0187-817-014).

L'Alta Marea offers special fish ravioli, the catch of the day, and huge crocks of fresh, steamed mussels. Young chef Marco cooks with charisma, while his wife, Anna, takes good care of the guests. This place is quieter, buried in the old town two blocks off the beach, and has covered tables out front for people-watching (€9-13 pastas and pizza, €14-20 *secondi*, 10 percent discount with cash and this book, Thu-Tue 12:00-15:00 & 18:00-22:00, closed Wed, Via Roma 54, tel. 0187-817-170).

In the New Town

Even if you're not sleeping in the new town, consider venturing over for dinner at one of these options; as a bonus, the walk is mostly along a scenic and lively beachfront promenade.

Miky is packed with well-dressed locals who know their seafood and want to eat it in a classy environment. For elegantly presented, top-quality food, with subtle flavors that celebrate local ingredients and traditions, this is my Cinque Terre favorite. It's clearly a proud family operation: Miky (dad), Simonetta (mom), charming Sara (daughter, who greets guests), and the attentive but easygoing waitstaff all work hard. All their pasta is "pizza pasta"— cooked normally but finished in a bowl that's encased in a thin pizza crust. They cook the concoction in a wood-fired oven to keep in the aroma, then flambé it at your table. Miky's has a fine wine list with many available by the glass if you ask. If I were ever to require a dessert, it would be their mixed sampler plate, *dolce mista*—€10 and plenty for two (€15-18 pastas, €18-30 *secondi*, €8 sweets, Wed-Mon 12:00-15:00 & 19:00-23:00, closed Tue, reservations wise in summer, diners tend to dress up a bit—but it's not required, in the new town 100 yards north of train station at Via Fegina 104, tel. 0187-817-608).

La Cantina di Miky, a few doors down (toward the station), serves Ligurian specialties that follow in Miky's family tradition of quality. Run by son Manuel—and Christine from New Jersey—it's more trendy, youthful, and informal than Miky's. You can sit downstairs, in the garden, or overlooking the sea (€16 anchovy tasting plate, €10-13 pastas, €12-20 *secondi,* creative desserts, large selection of Italian microbrews, daily 12:00-24:00 or later, Via Fegina 90, tel. 0187-802-525). This place doubles as a cocktail bar in the evenings—see "Nightlife in Monterosso," earlier.

Light Meals, Take-Out Food, and Breakfast

In the Old Town: Lots of shops and bakeries sell pizza and focaccia for an easy picnic at the beach or on the trail. **Pizzeria la Smorfia**—the local favorite for pizza—cooks up good pizza to eat in or take out. Pizzas come in two sizes; the large can feed three (small pizzas-€6-9, large pizzas-€14-19, Fri-Wed 11:30-24:00, closed Thu, Via Vittorio Emanuele 73, tel. 0187-818-395). At **Il Frantoio,** Simone makes tasty pizza and focaccia to go or to munch perched on a stool (Fri-Wed 9:00-13:45 & 16:30-19:30, closed Thu, just off Via Roma at Via Gioberti 1). **Focacceria da Emy** (not to be confused with Pizzeria Ely, up the street) makes airy focaccia and thick-crust pizzas for casual seating or takeout (€5-7 pizza, €3 focaccia, daily 10:30-20:00, until 24:00 in summer, along the skinny street next to the church, Emigliano).

In the New Town, near the Station: For a quick bite right at the train station (or on the beach), consider **Il Massimo della Focaccia.** Massimo and Daniella serve local quiche-like tortes, sandwiches, focaccia pizzas, and desserts. With benches just in front, this is a good bet for a €4 light meal with a sea view (Thu-Tue 9:00-19:00, closed Wed, Via Fegina 50 at the entry to the station).

Breakfast: Most hotels include breakfast in the room rate. But if you're out looking for breakfast, in the new town, consider **Bar Gio,** near the train station on the waterfront (continental breakfasts); in the old town, look for **Bar Davi,** under the arch on Via Roma in the old town (with an American-style option, daily from 7:00).

Cinque Terre Connections

By Train

The five towns of the Cinque Terre are on a pokey milk-run train line (described in "Getting Around the Cinque Terre—By Train" on page 379). Erratically timed but roughly hourly trains connect each town with the others, plus La Spezia, Genoa, and Riviera towns to the north. While a few of these local trains go to more distant points (Milan or Pisa), it's much faster to change in La Spezia, Monterosso, or Sestri Levante to a bigger train (local train info tel. 0187-817-458, www.trenitalia.com).

From La Spezia Centrale by Train to: Rome (7/day, 3-4.5 hours, more with changes, €45; an evening train—departing around 20:00—gives you a complete day in the region while still getting you to Rome that night), **Pisa** (about hourly, 1-1.5 hours, €5), **Florence** (5/day direct, otherwise nearly hourly, 2.5 hours, €11.30), **Milan** (about hourly, 3 hours direct or with change in Genoa, €22), **Venice** (about hourly, 5-6 hours, 1-3 changes, €50).

From Monterosso by Train to: Venice (about hourly, 6-7 hours, 1-3 changes, €52), **Milan** (8/day direct, otherwise hourly with change in Genoa, 3-4 hours, €22), **Genoa** (hourly, 1.2-2 hours, €8), **Turin** (8/day, 3-4 hours, €20), **Pisa** (hourly, 1-2 hours, €6-10), **Sestri Levante** (hourly, 20-40 minutes, most trains to Genoa stop here, €3), **La Spezia** (2-3/hour, 15-30 minutes), **Levanto** (2-3/hour, 4 minutes), **Santa Margherita Ligure** (at least hourly, 45 minutes, €4.50), **Rome** (hourly, 4.5 hours, change in La Spezia, €50). For destinations in **France,** change trains in Genoa.

By Car

Because these towns are close together and have frequent transportation connections, bringing a car to the Cinque Terre is not the best idea. If your plans require it, however, here are some basic tips: Stay in a hotel that includes parking, use public transportation or hike between towns, and for day-trip parking, go to Monterosso (€14-18/day), Riomaggiore (€22/day), or Manarola (€15/day). Don't drive to Vernazza, as the flood blew out its main parking lot. Even if it's rebuilt, finding a spot will likely be tough. Parking anywhere on the Cinque Terre is truly a mess in July and August.

Milan to the Cinque Terre (130 miles): Drivers speed south on autostrada A-7 from Milan, skirt Genoa, and drive a little bit of Italy's curviest and narrowest freeways, passing the Cinque Terre toward the port of La Spezia (A-12). Another option is to take the slightly straighter A-1 via the city of Parma, followed by A-15 to La Spezia. This route takes the same amount of time (about 2.5 hours), even though it covers more miles.

The route from autostrada A-12 depends partly on the status

of repairs to the 2011 flood damage. As of this writing (mid-2013), this is the best approach, but confirm details locally:

To reach **Monterosso** (about 30 minutes from the autostrada), exit A-12 at *uscita Carrodano-Levanto,* northwest of La Spezia. Remember that the highway divides as you approach Monterosso—you must choose between the road to *Centro Storico* (the old town) or the one to *Fegina* (the new town and beachfront parking). Keep in mind that because of road closures (as of mid-2013), you can't reach Monterosso from La Spezia via the other Cinque Terre towns; you'll have to loop up to the SP-1/SP-38 highway.

For **Vernazza, Riomaggiore, Corniglia,** or **Manarola,** leave the freeway at La Spezia and follow the road that parallels the coast (with access to each of these four towns). The drive down to Vernazza is scenic, narrow, and scary; it's much better to park in La Spezia and ride the train in. While there is a secondary road connecting Vernazza and Monterosso, it's likely closed and—even if open—it's not recommended (the main road, SP-63, was washed out by the flood and will likely remain closed indefinitely—ask locally). For more details on the challenges of driving to Vernazza, see page 419. For a map of the region, see page 377.

Within the Cinque Terre: On busy weekends, holidays, and in June, July, and August, both Vernazza and Monterosso fill up, and police at the top of town will deny entry to anyone without a hotel reservation. It's smart to have a confirmation in hand. If you don't, insist (politely) that they allow you to enter—but only if you actually have a room reserved (the police might call your hotel to check your story).

Parking Tips: Riomaggiore, Manarola, and Monterosso each have a parking lot and an hourly shuttle bus to get you into town, though all parking areas are no more than a 10-minute walk uphill from the center.

Blue signs post valid hours for pay parking, which usually don't charge from 24:00 to 8:00 (but read the signs or ask locals to be sure). Anyone can park where there are white lines. Parking is cash only in all towns (except Riomaggiore, where some readers have been overcharged on their credit cards—best to pay in cash).

If you plan to find parking in any of the Cinque Terre towns, try to arrive between 9:00 and 11:00, when overnight visitors are usually departing. Or you can park your car in Levanto or La Spezia (both covered in next chapter), then take the train into the town of your choice. In these bigger towns, confirm that your parking spot is OK, and leave nothing inside to steal.

A few hotels offer parking for free or a daily charge. In **Mon-**

terosso, consider Hotel Villa Steno, A Cà du Gigante, Hotel la Spiaggia, or Hotel Punta Mesco. For **Riomaggiore,** try Locanda del Sole, Locanda Ca' dei Duxi, or Villa Argentina. In Volastra (a shuttle ride above **Manarola**), try Hotel il Saraceno. In **Corniglia,** try Il Carugio. Rooms listed in this book for Vernazza do not offer parking.

RIVIERA TOWNS NEAR THE CINQUE TERRE

Levanto • Sestri Levante • Santa Margherita Ligure •
Portofino • La Spezia • Carrara • Portovenere

The Cinque Terre is tops, but several towns to the north have a breezy beauty and more beaches. Towns to the south offer a mix of marble, trains, and yachts.

Levanto, the northern gateway to the Cinque Terre, has a long beach and a scenic, strenuous trail to Monterosso al Mare. Sestri Levante, on a narrow peninsula flanked by two beaches, is for sun-seekers. Santa Margherita Ligure is more of a real town, with actual sights, beaches, and easy connections with Portofino by trail, bus, or boat. All three towns are a straight shot to the Cinque Terre by train.

South of the Cinque Terre, you'll likely pass through the workaday town of La Spezia (don't stay here unless you're desperate), the southern gateway to the Cinque Terre. Carrara is a quickie for marble lovers who are driving between Pisa and La Spezia. The picturesque village of Portovenere, near La Spezia, has scenic boat connections with Cinque Terre towns.

Public transportation is the best way to get around this region. All the places in this chapter are well connected by train and/or boat.

North of the Cinque Terre

Levanto

Graced with a long, sandy beach, Levanto is packed in summer and popular with surfers. The rest of the year, it's just a small, sleepy town, with less charm and fewer tourists than the Cinque Terre. But with quick connections to Monterosso (4 minutes by train) and better dining options, Levanto makes a decent home base if you can't snare a room in the Cinque Terre.

Levanto has a new section (with a regular grid street plan) and a twisty old town (bisected by a modern street), plus a few pedestrian streets and a castle (not tourable). From Levanto, you can take a no-wimps-allowed hike to Monterosso (2.5 hours) or hop a boat to the Cinque Terre towns and beyond.

Orientation to Levanto

Tourist Information
The helpful TI is on Piazza Mazzini (daily 9:00-13:00 & 15:00-19:00 except Sun until 18:00, tel. 0187-808-125, www.comune.levanto.sp.it). The TI leads a weekly walking tour of Levanto's medieval architecture (free but tips expected, 2 hours, departs Tue at 18:00 from Piazza Cavour, register at TI).

Arrival in Levanto
By Train: It's a 10-minute walk from the Levanto train station to the TI in town (head down stairs in front of station, turn right, cross bridge, then follow Corso Roma to Piazza Mazzini).

By Car: Drivers can use the cheap **short-term parking** in the lots in front of and on either side of the train station (€7.20/8 hours, €10.80/24 hours—pay at machines each day. Another option is the lot across the river from the hospital on the way into town (first left after the hospital, cross bridge and immediately turn left), or north of the church on Via del Mercato (free during high season, except Wed before 14:00). For **long-term parking,** try the lots at Piazza Mazzini or behind the TI (€18/day).

Helpful Hints
Markets: Levanto's modern covered *mercato,* which sells produce and fish, is on Via del Mercato, between the TI and train station (Mon-Sat 8:00-13:00, closed Sun). On Wednesday

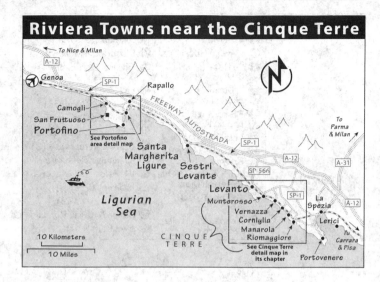

Riviera Towns near the Cinque Terre

morning, an **open-air market** with clothes, shoes, and house-wares fills the street in front of the *mercato*.

Internet Access: Try **Viaggi Beraldi** at Via Garibaldi 102 (€2/30 minutes, Mon-Sat 9:00-12:30 & 15:30-19:30, closed Sun, tel. 0187-800-818).

Baggage Storage: None is available. Try La Spezia (page 491), Monterosso (page 443), or Santa Margherita Ligure (page 476).

Laundry: A **self-service launderette** stuffed with snack and drink vending machines is at Piazza Staglieno 38 (wash-€5 including soap, dry-€5, open 24 hours daily, mobile 338-701-6341). Another self-service place, **Speedy Wash,** is at Via Garibaldi 32 (wash-€4, dry-€2, daily 8:00-21:00, mobile 350-156-5026).

Bike Rental: Cicli Raso North Shore rents bikes (€10-20/day depending on type of bike, daily 9:30-12:30 & 15:30-19:30, closed Sun Nov-April, Via Garibaldi 63, tel. 0187-802-511, www.cicliraso.com). The **Sensafreni Bike Shop** is convenient to the beach boardwalk (€2/hour, €15/24 hours, Mon-Sat 9:30-12:30 & 16:00-19:30, closed Sun, Piazza del Popolo 1, tel. 0187-807-128).

Sports Rentals: Rosa dei Venti rents kayaks, canoes, surfboards, and windsurfing equipment right on the beach (Marco mobile 329-451-1981, www.levantorosadeiventi.it).

Sights in Levanto

Beach

You can access Levanto's beach boardwalk and the sea right behind the TI. As you face the harbor, the boat dock is to your far left, and

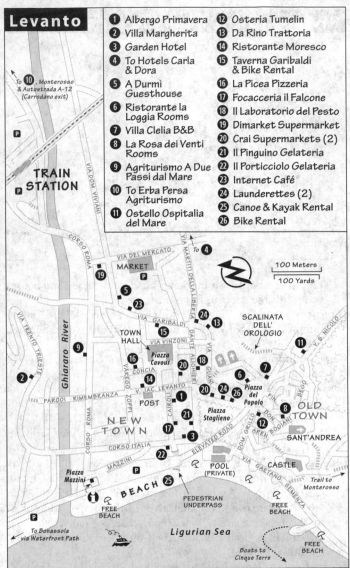

Levanto

1. Albergo Primavera
2. Villa Margherita
3. Garden Hotel
4. To Hotels Carla & Dora
5. A Durmì Guesthouse
6. Ristorante la Loggia Rooms
7. Villa Clelia B&B
8. La Rosa dei Venti Rooms
9. Agriturismo A Due Passi dal Mare
10. To Erba Persa Agriturismo
11. Ostello Ospitalia del Mare
12. Osteria Tumelin
13. Da Rino Trattoria
14. Ristorante Moresco
15. Taverna Garibaldi & Bike Rental
16. La Picea Pizzeria
17. Focacceria il Falcone
18. Il Laboratorio del Pesto
19. Dimarket Supermarket
20. Crai Supermarkets (2)
21. Il Pinguino Gelateria
22. Il Porticciolo Gelateria
23. Internet Café
24. Launderettes (2)
25. Canoe & Kayak Rental
26. Bike Rental

the diving center is to your far right (rental boats available at either place in summer). You can also rent a kayak or canoe on the beach, just below the east end of the Piazza Mazzini parking lot.

During the summer, three parts of the beach are free: both sides of the boat dock, and behind the TI. The rest of the beach is broken up into private sections that charge admission. You can always stroll along the beach, even through the private sections—

just don't sit down. Off-season, roughly October through May, the entire beach is free, and you can lay your towel anywhere you like.

Old Town and Trailhead

The old town, several blocks from the TI and beach, clusters around Piazza del Popolo. Until a few decades ago, the town's open-air market was held at the 13th-century loggia (covered set of archways) in the square. Explore the back streets.

To reach the trailhead to Monterosso: From Piazza del Popolo, head uphill to the striped church, Chiesa di Sant'Andrea (with your back to the loggia, go straight ahead—across the square and up Via Don Emanuele Toso to the church). From the church courtyard, follow the sign to the *castello* (a private residence), go under the stone arch, and continue uphill. Or, if you're coming from the seaside promenade (Via Gaetano Semenza), head under the arches and up the stairs, and follow the signs to the *castello*. Either route leads you to a sign that points you toward Punta Mesco, the rugged tip of the peninsula. From here, you can hike up to Monterosso (2.5 hours). This lovely, rugged-and-wild hike is no joke—bring lots of water and wear good shoes. Most of the trail is a gradual up-and-down, but the last stretch into Monterosso is almost entirely big steps, so those with knee problems might consider starting in Monterosso instead. The elevation gain overall is more than double that of the toughest Cinque Terre hikes. The Cinque Terre hiking pass is not necessary here.

Hike or Bike to Bonassola and Beyond

Cross the river bridge located by the TI to wander along this easy waterfront path, good for walking or cycling. You'll encounter shaded tunnels and two sunny beaches on the way to the small but modern town of Bonassola with its sandy beach (25 minutes by foot, 10 minutes by bike, public beaches located a minute's walk down from trail). From Bonassola, the path continues on to the town of Framura, a 3.5-mile walk/ride from Levanto.

Sleeping in Levanto

In this popular beach town, many hotels want you to take half-pension (lunch or dinner) in summer, especially in July and August. Prices listed here are the maximum for high season (July-Aug); smaller rooms or those without views may be less. Expect to pay €10-30 less per night for April-June and September-October, and even less for the rest of the year. The longer your stay, the greater your bargaining power. The high number of four-person rooms in Levanto makes it particularly welcoming to families who want to explore the Cinque Terre. Many hotels rent out large apartments with kitchenettes (without a half-pension requirement), and parking is free or very reasonable.

Sleep Code

(€1 = about $1.30, country code: 39)
S = Single, **D** = Double/Twin, **T** = Triple, **Q** = Quad, **b** = bathroom, **s** = shower only. Unless otherwise noted, credit cards are accepted, English is spoken, and breakfast is included. Many cities in Italy levy a hotel tax of €2 per person, per night, which must be paid in cash (not included in the rates I've quoted).

To help you sort easily through these listings, I've divided the accommodations into three categories based on the price for a standard double room with bath:

$$$ Higher Priced—Most rooms €110 or more.
$$ Moderately Priced—Most rooms between €50-110.
$ Lower Priced—Most rooms €50 or less.

Prices can change without notice; verify the hotel's current rates online or by email. For the best prices, always book direct.

$$$ Albergo Primavera is family-run, with 17 redecorated, tasteful rooms—10 with balconies but no views—just a half-block from the beach (Db-€140 if you book directly with the hotel, request a quiet room off the street, includes hearty breakfast buffet with local hams and cheeses, air-con, guest computer, Wi-Fi, free loaner bikes, Via Cairoli 5, tel. 0187-808-023, www.primaverahotel.com, info@primaverahotel.com, friendly Carlo, cheerful Daniela, and daughters Giuditta and Gloria). Carlo can arrange airport transfers on request.

$$$ Villa Margherita is 300 yards out of town, but the shady gardens, 11 characteristic colorfully tiled rooms (some with little view terraces), and tranquility are worth the walk (Db-€170, Tb-€185, 5 percent discount with cash and this book, elevator one flight up from street level, guest computer, free Wi-Fi, free parking, 10-minute walk to town with stairs, 5-minute walk to train station, free shuttle service from station if you tell them when you'll arrive, Via Trento e Trieste 31, tel. 0187-807-212, mobile 328-842-6934, www.villamargherita.net, info@villamargherita.net). They also rent apartments around town and a fancy villa (for up to 14 people) set on a peninsula by the sea (www.levanto.net).

$$$ Garden Hotel offers 17 simple, bright, modern rooms, all with balconies (but most lack views due to the elevated street), a block from the beach on busy Corso Italia (Db-€120, newer fifth-floor room with sea views and terrace-Db-€148, 5 percent discount with cash and this book, closed mid-Nov-mid-March, air-con, elevator for fifth floor only, free Wi-Fi, free parking but not on-site—can unload bags and then park near the station, loaner bikes, Corso Italia 6, tel. 0187-808-173, www.nuovogarden.com, info@ nuovogarden.com, Davide and Damiano).

$$$ Hotel Carla's 30 brand-new rooms are decorated in soothing, modish colors. It's located just five minutes from the station and 10 minutes from the beach (Db-€85-140, Via Martiri della Libertà 28, tel. 0187-808-275, www.carlahotel.com, info@ carlahotel.com).

$$ A Durmì is a happy little *affitta camere* (guesthouse) owned by lovely Graziella, Gianni, and their two daughters, Elisa and Chiara. Their sunny patios, green leafy gardens, six immaculate modern new rooms, and five sunlit apartments make a welcoming place to stay (Db-€60-110, extra bed-€20; 3-4 person apartment-€90-160—no minimum stay required; ask about cash discount when you book, rooms cleaned daily, breakfast-€7, air-con, power showers, guest computer, Wi-Fi in lobby, bar, parking-€5/ day, Via D. Viviani 12, tel. 0187-800-823, mobile 349-105-6016, www.adurmi.it, info@adurmi.it).

$$ Ristorante la Loggia has four pleasant, cozy, summery rooms perched above the old loggia on Piazza del Popolo (Db-€70, cash only, request balcony, quieter rooms in back, two basic side-by-side apartments great for families of 4-8, lots of stairs, air-con, free parking, Piazza del Popolo 7, tel. & fax 0187-808-107, mobile 335-641-7701, www.loggialevanto.com, Nerina does not speak English).

$$ Villa Clelia B&B offers six peaceful, dark, air-conditioned rooms (named for the winds—*scirocco, maestrale,* and so on) with mini-fridges and terraces in a garden courtyard just 50 yards from the sea (Db-€75-95, minimal in-room breakfast, Wi-Fi, free parking; with loggia on your left, it's straight ahead at Piazza da Passano 1; tel. 0187-808-195, mobile 329-379-4859, www.villaclelia. it, info@villaclelia.it). They also have seven central apartments that economically sleep up to five (€800/week, 3-night minimum stay). B&B rooms are cleaned daily; you're on your own at the apartments.

$$ La Rosa dei Venti is an *affitta camere* just a couple of blocks from the beach. Enthusiastic Rosanna and her son Marco rent five super-clean rooms with dark hardwood floors, comfy rugs, and a hodgepodge of glittery seashore decor (Db-€110, Tb-€135, includes homemade breakfast, air-con, free Wi-Fi, free parking, behind Enoteca Tumelin across from Piazza del Popolo, Via della Compera, tel. 0187-808-165, Marco's mobile 328-742-8268, www. larosadeiventilevanto.com, info@larosadeiventilevanto.com).

$$ Agriturismo A Due Passi dal Mare is an in-town oasis, just a five-minute walk from the beach or the train station. Friendly Francesca and husband Maurizio rent four crisp, quiet rooms with

468 Rick Steves' Italy

sizeable bathrooms; their back garden is open to guests (Sb-€50, Db-€80, Tb-€100, cheaper in spring and fall, free Wi-Fi and on-site parking, closed Jan-Feb, right on the main drag at Corso Roma 37, tel. 0187-809-177, mobile 338-960-1537, www.a2passidalmare. com, info@a2passidalmare.com).

$$ Hotel Dora has perfectly comfortable (if dated) rooms in a quiet residential neighborhood a 10-minute walk from the beach (Db-€100-120, Via Martiri della Libertà 27, tel. 0187-808-168, www.dorahotel.it, info@dorahotel.it).

$$ Erba Persa Agriturismo, a rustic farmhouse run by sunny Grazia Lizza and her gardener husband Claudio, hosts cats, dogs, pet rabbits, and donkeys among their plots of organic fruits and vegetables. The three rooms are old-fashioned but roomy. It's a 10-minute walk from the train station and about a 20-minute walk from town (D-€50, Db with balcony and countryside view-€70, extra bed-€10, free Wi-Fi, free parking, free mosquitoes, Via N. S. della Guardia 21, mobile 339-400-8587 or 348-344-7695, www. erbapersa.it, erbapersa@alice.it).

Hostel: **$ Ostello Ospitalia del Mare,** a budget gem, is run by the city tourist association. It has 70 basic beds, airy rooms, an elevator, and a terrace in a well-renovated medieval palazzo a few steps from the old town (beds-€19-27 in 4-, 6-, and 8-bed rooms with private bath, Db-€65; includes breakfast, thin towels, and sheets; guest computer, free Wi-Fi, self-service laundry-€7.50, microwave, fridge, nonmembers welcome, co-ed unless you strenuously object, no curfew, no lockout; office open daily April-Oct 8:00-13:00 & 16:00-20:00, until 23:00 weekend nights, slightly shorter hours off-season; may close Nov-March, Via San Nicolò 1, tel. 0187-802-562, www.ospitaliadelmare.it, info@ospitaliadelmare.it).

Eating in Levanto

Osteria Tumelin, a local favorite, is more expensive than other options, but has a dressy, sophisticated ambience and a wide selection of fresh seafood. Reservations are smart on weekends or if you want to dine outside (€12-14 *primi*, €17-23 *secondi*, daily 12:00-14:30 & 19:00-22:30, closed Thu Oct-May, aquarium containing giant lobster and moray eels in first dining room on the right, Via D. Grillo 32, across street from loggia, tel. 0187-808-379).

Da Rino, a small trattoria on a quiet pedestrian lane, dishes up reasonably priced fresh seafood and homemade Ligurian specialties prepared with care. Consider the grilled *totani* (squid), *pansotti con salsa di noci* (ravioli with walnut sauce), and *trofie al pesto* (local pasta with pesto sauce). Dine indoors or at one of the outdoor tables. On busy nights, they open up a second dining room across the street. Sommelier Anna will help you choose a good wine (€8-11 pastas, €13-15 *secondi,* daily 19:00-22:00, closed Tue, Via Garibaldi 10, tel. 0187-813-475).

Ristorante la Loggia, next to the old loggia, makes fine food, including gnocchi with scampi and saffron sauce and a delectable seafood lasagna. Their daily fish specials are served in a homey, wood-paneled dining room or on a little terrace overlooking the square (€10-12 pastas, €15-17 *secondi,* Thu-Tue 12:30-14:00 & 19:00-22:00, closed Wed, closed Nov-Feb, Piazza del Popolo 7, tel. 0187-808-107).

Ristorante Moresco serves large portions of pasta and sea-food at reasonable prices in a vaulted, candlelit room decorated with Moorish-style frescoes. The best value is their €25 four-course tasting *menu* (doesn't include drinks, 2-person minimum). Skip the house white wine and order something more drinkable from their wine list (daily 12:00-14:00 & 19:00-20:00—or until the last diner leaves, may close Sun evenings in winter, reservations appreciated, Via Jacopo 24, tel. 0187-807-253, busy Roberto and Francesca).

Taverna Garibaldi is a good-value, cozy place on the most characteristic street in Levanto, serving focaccia with various top-pings, made-to-order *farinata* (savory chickpea crêpe), 34 types of pizza, and salads (€8-10 light meals, daily in summer 19:00-22:00, likely closed Tue Sept-June, Via Garibaldi 57, tel. 0187-808-098).

La Picea serves up wood-fired pizzas to go, or dine at one of their few small tables (Tue-Sun 16:30-21:45, closed Mon, just off the corner near Via Varego at Via della Concia 18, tel. 0187-802-063).

A Picnic or Bite on the Go: Focaccerie, rosticcerie, and delis with take-out pasta abound on Via Dante Alighieri. **Focacceria il Falcone** has a great selection of focaccia with different toppings (daily 9:30-22:00, Oct-May closes at 20:00 and on Mon, Via Cairoli 19, tel. 0187-807-370). For more picnic options, try the *mercato* (morn-ings except Sun; see "Helpful Hints," page 491). It's fun to grab a crusty loaf of bread, then pair it with a pot of freshly made Geno-vese pesto from **Il Laboratorio del Pesto** (sometimes closed Wed afternoons, Via Dante 14, tel. 0187-807-441). The **Dimarket su-permarket** just below the train station has a good deli counter and opens at 7:00—handy for those taking an early train. There are two **Crai supermarkets.** One is just off Via Jacopo da Levanto at Via del Municipio 5 (Mon-Sat 8:00-13:00 & 17:00-20:00, Sun 8:00-13:00 & 16:30-19:30); the other is nearby on Piazza Staglieno (for a shaded setting, lay out your spread on a bench in the grassy park at this piazza). Another excellent picnic spot is Piazza Cristoforo Colombo, located east of the swimming pool, with benches and sea views.

And for Dessert: Compare **Il Pinguino Gelateria** at Piazza

Staglieno 2 (daily until late) with **Il Porticciolo Gelateria,** at the end of Via Cairoli at Piazzetta Marina (daily in summer, closed Mon Sept-June, mobile 393-228-1570).

Levanto Connections

From Levanto: To get to the Cinque Terre, you can take the **train** (2-3/hour, 4 minutes to Monterosso). A slower, more scenic option is the **boat,** which stops at every Cinque Terre town—except Corniglia—before heading to Portovenere (2/day Easter-Oct, none Nov-Easter; €7 one-way to Monterosso, 10:00 departure includes Cinque Terre, Portovenere, and Lerici Island tour for €28; 14:30 departure includes Cinque Terre and 1-hour stop in Portovenere for €18; 1 return boat each day from Portovenere departs at about 17:00; pick up boat schedule and price sheet from TI or boat dock, tel. 0187-732-987 or on weekends 0187-777-727, www.navigazionegolfodeipoeti.it).

Sestri Levante

This peninsular town is squeezed as skinny as a hot dog between its two beaches. The pedestrian-friendly Corso Colombo, which runs down the middle of the peninsula, is lined with shops that sell take-away pizza, pastries, and beach paraphernalia. Don't be discouraged by the ugly modern town in front of the train station; the peninsula, about a seven-minute walk away, has charm to spare.

Hans Christian Andersen enjoyed his visit here in the mid-1800s, writing, "What a fabulous evening I spent in Sestri Levante!" One of the bays—Baia delle Favole—is named in his honor (*favole* means "fairy tale"). The small mermaid curled on the edge of the fountain behind the TI is another nod to the beloved Danish storyteller.

During the last week of May, the town awards its Hans Christian Andersen Prize, created to celebrate children's literature. Open to professional writers worldwide as well as school children throughout Italy, the competition culminates in a street festival and an awards ceremony for the best fairy tale in four age groups. The "Oscars" are little mermaids.

Orientation to Sestri Levante

Tourist Information: From the train station, it's a five-minute walk to the TI, where you can pick up a map (Tue-Sat 9:30-13:00 & 14:00-17:30, closed Sun-Mon; go straight out of station on Via

Roma, turn left at fountain in park, TI in next square at Piazza Sant'Antonio 10; tel. 0185-457-011). They can also direct you to the trail (south of town) for a one-hour hike to the scenic Punta Manara promontory.

Market Day: It's on Saturday at Piazza Aldo Moro (8:00-13:00). Local producers of olive oil, cheese, jam, and honey also set up on occasional Sundays on Via Asilo Maria Teresa (where Via XXV Aprile and Corso Columbo meet).

Baggage Storage: None is available at the station.

Laundry: There's a self-service launderette not far from the train station (wash-€5, daily 8:30-20:30, Via Costantino Raffo 8, mobile 329-012-8885).

Sights in Sestri Levante

Stroll the Town

From the TI, take Corso Colombo (to the left of Bermuda Bar, eventually turns into Via XXV Aprile, then Via alla Penisola), which runs up the peninsula. Follow this street—lively with shops, eateries, and delightful pastel facades—for about five minutes. Just before you get to Piazza Matteotti with the large white church at the end, turn off for either beach (free Silenzio beach is on your left). Or continue on the street to the left of the church and head uphill. You'll pass the evocative arches of a ruined chapel (bombed during World War II and left as a memorial). A few minutes farther on, past a stony Romanesque church, the road winds to the right to the Grand Hotel dei Castelli. Consider a drink at their view café (so-so view, reasonably priced drinks, daily 10:00-24:00, café entrance is at end of parking lot). The rocky, forested bluff at the end of the town's peninsula is actually the huge private backyard of this fancy hotel.

Beaches

These are named after the bays *(baie)* that they border. The bigger beach, Baia delle Favole, is divided up much of the year (May-Sept) into sections that you must pay to enter. The fees, which can soar up to €30 per day in August (no hourly rate), generally include chairs, umbrellas, and fewer crowds. There are several small free sections: at the ends and in the middle (look for *libere* signs, and ask *"Gratis?"* to make sure that it's free). For less expensive sections of beach (where you can rent a chair for about €8-10), ask for *spiaggia libera attrezzata* (spee-AH-jah LEE-behr-ah ah-treh-ZAHT-tah). The usual beach-town activities are clustered along this *baia*: boat rentals, sailing lessons, and bocce courts—ask if you can get in on a game.

The town's other beach, Baia del Silenzio, is narrow, virtually all free, and packed, providing a good chance to see Italian

Sestri Levante

To Rapallo & Santa Margherita Ligure
To Santa Margherita Ligure
TRAIN STATION
To Santa Margherita Ligure & Portofino
LUNGO G. DESCALZO
VIA OLIVE
VIALE MAZZINI
V. ROMA
VIA EKALDO
Piazza Caduti
To Cinque Terre
To Cinque Terre
L i g u r i a n   S e a
Piazza Italia
VIA NAZIONALE
Giardini Ventre
VIA G. XX SETT
Piazza Sant' Antonio
To A-12 Freeway
Baia delle Favole
VIA RIMEMBRANZA
VIALE TERESA
V. VENETO
V. C. COLOMBO
VIA XXIV APRILE
Piazza Republica
FASCE
Beaches
Piazza Aldo Moro
V. DANTE
BOAT DOCK
PROMENADE & BIKE PATH
VIA PILADE QUEIROLO
V. PENISOLA
VIA XXV
VIA DELLA CHIUSA
VICO CORO
Piazza Matteotti
VIA POZZETTO
GRAND HOTEL DEI CASTELLI
VIA PORT
FREE BEACH
VIA CAPPUCCINI
ROMANESQUE CHURCH
RUINED CHAPEL
Baia del Silenzio
N

200 Meters
200 Yards

1 Hotel Due Mari
2 Hotel Helvetia
3 Hotel Celeste
4 Hotel Mira
5 Hotel Genova
6 Albergo Marina
7 Villa Jolanda
8 L'Osteria Mattana
9 Polpo Mario, Ristorante Mainolla & Minimarket Fabrizio
10 Bacciolo Gelato
11 Ice Cream's Angels
12 Supermarkets (2)
13 Rosticceria Bertolone

families at play. There isn't much more to do here than unroll a beach towel and join in. At the far end of Baia del Silenzio (under Hotel Helvetia) is Citto Beach bar, which offers front-row seats with bay views (drinks daily June-Aug 10:00-24:00, May and Sept-Oct until 20:00, sandwiches and salads at lunchtime only, closed Nov-April, Gilberto).

Sleeping in Sestri Levante

Prices listed here are the maximum for the high season (July-Aug). Prices are €10-20 less per night April-June and September-October, and soft the rest of the year. Some hotels are closed off-season.

$$$ Hotel Due Mari, located in an old Genoese palazzo with sprawling public spaces, has three stars, 65 fine rooms, and a rooftop terrace with a super view of both beaches. Ideally, reserve well in advance. The extra services and grand communal spaces are the draw (small Db-€110, bigger Db-€140-220 depending on view and type of room, €35/person half-pension in aristocratic restaurant required July-Aug, closed mid-Oct-Dec, air-con, guest computer, Wi-Fi, elevator, garden, outdoor and heated indoor seawater swimming pools, wet sauna, small gym, parking-€15/day; take Corso Colombo to the end, hotel is behind church in Piazza Matteotti—take the left-hand alleyway flanking church, Vico del Coro 18; tel. 0185-42695, www.duemarihotel.it, info@duemarihotel.it).

$$$ Hotel Helvetia, overlooking Baia del Silenzio, feels posh and romantic, with 21 bright rooms, a large sun terrace with a heated, cliff-hanging swimming pool, and a peaceful garden atmosphere (viewless Db-€210-230, Db with sea view/balcony-€250-280, closed Nov-March, air-con, elevator, free Wi-Fi, swimming pool, off-site parking-€15/day with free shuttle; from Corso Colombo, turn left on Via Palestro and angle left at the small square to Via Cappuccini 43, tel. 0185-41175, www.hotel-helvetia.it, helvetia@hotelhelvetia.it, Alex).

$$$ Hotel Celeste, a dream for beach lovers, rests along the waterfront. Its 41 rooms are modern and plainly outfitted—you pay for the sea breeze (Db-€165 with view and balcony, €25 optional half-pension, air-con, elevator, guest computer, free Wi-Fi, deals on beach chairs, attached beachside bar, Lungomare Descalzo 14, tel. 0185-485-005, www.hotelceleste.com, info@hotelceleste.com, Franco).

$$$ Hotel Mira is an old-school hotel on the beachfront promenade, just around the corner from the town's charming historical core and handy to the beaches. Rooms are simply furnished, yet have all amenities (Db-€150-160, Tb-€180-190, includes breakfast, Viale Rimembranza 15, tel. 0185-459-404, www.hotelmira.com, info@hotelmira.com).

$$$ Hotel Genova, run by the Bertoni family, is a ship-shape hotel with 27 shiny-clean, modern, and cheery rooms, sunny lounge, rooftop sundeck, free loaner bikes, and a good location just two blocks from Baia delle Favole (Sb-€75, Db-€130, superior Db-€150, Tb-€189, ask for quieter room in back, air-con, elevator, Wi-Fi, parking-€5/day; from the train station, walk straight ahead, turn right at the T-intersection, and find the cream building ahead on the right, Viale Mazzini 126; tel. 0185-41057, www.hotelgenovasestrilevante.com, info@hotelgenovasestrilevante.com, Stefano).

$$ Albergo Marina's friendly Magda and her brother Santo rent 23 bright, peaceful, and clean rooms done in sea-foam green. Though the hotel is located on a busy boulevard, all rooms are at the back, facing a quiet courtyard and parking lots, and priced right (Db-€65-85, half-pension optional, air-con, elevator, Wi-Fi in lobby, self-service laundry, pool table; exit the train station and angle left down Via Eraldo, at Piazza Repubblica, take an easy left onto Via Fasce and find the hotel ahead on the right, Via Fasce 100; tel. 0185-487-332, www.marinahotel.it, marinahotel@marinahotel.it).

$$ Villa Jolanda is a homey, kid-friendly, basic *pensione* with 17 simple rooms, five with little balconies but no views, new bathrooms, and a garden courtyard/sun terrace—perfect for families on a budget...and the owner's cats (Sb-€30-45, Db-€75-95, Qb-€100-120, 3-night minimum stay required with advance reservation, €6.50 breakfast isn't worth it but owner Mario's €23 home-cooked dinners are—available June-Aug only, free parking; located near Baia del Silenzio—take alley just to the right of the church on Piazza Matteotti, Via Pozzetto 15, tel. 0185-41354, www.villajolanda.it, info@villajolanda.it).

Eating in Sestri Levante

Everything I've listed is on classic Via XXV Aprile, which also abounds with *focaccerie*, take-out pizza by the slice, and little grocery shops. Assemble a picnic or try one of the places below.

At **L'Osteria Mattana,** where everyone shares long tables in two dining rooms (the second one is in the back, past the wood oven and brazier), you can mix with locals while enjoying traditional cuisine, listed on chalkboard menus. Handy translations are posted next to the boards (Mon-Fri 19:30-22:00, Sat-Sun 12:30-14:30 & 19:30-22:30, no dinner served Mon Nov-April, cash only; follow Corso Colombo from TI as it turns into Via XXV Aprile, restaurant on right at #36; tel. 0185-457-633, Marco).

Polpo Mario is classier but affordable, with a fun people-watching location on the main drag (€14-16 pastas, €18-22 *secondi*, €40 fixed-price tasting *menu,* Tue-Sun 12:15-15:00 & 19:00-23:00, closed Mon, Via XXV Aprile 163, tel. 0185-480-203).

Ristorante Mainolla offers €4-8 pizzas, big salads, focaccia sandwiches, and reasonably priced pastas near Baia del Silenzio (daily in summer 12:00-16:00 & 19:00-22:00, closed Tue off-season, Via XXV Aprile 187, mobile 338-157-0877).

Gelato: Locals flock to **Ice Cream's Angels** at the intersection of Via XXV Aprile and Via della Chiusa. Riccardo and Elena artfully load up your cone with intermingling flavors, and top it with a dollop of Nutella chocolate-hazelnut cream (open daily until late in summer, closed Tue off-season, mobile 348-402-1604). **Bacciolo** enjoys a similar popularity among residents (closed Thu, Via XXV Aprile 51, on the right just before the church).

Supermarket: You can stock up on picnic supplies at two locations of **Carrefour Express** on Piazza della Repubblica, at #1

(Mon-Sat 8:00-13:00 & 15:30-20:00, closed Sun) and #28 (daily 8:30-20:00). Or pop into the conveniently located **Minimarket Fabrizio** for fresh fruit, *salumi*, and bread (Thu-Tue 8:00-12:30 & 16:00-19:30, closed Wed and sometimes Sun, Via XXV Aprile 177).

Deli: For a take-out meal, head to **Rosticceria Bertolone** for roasted anything—beef, pork, chicken, or vegetables. Assemble an entire meal from their deli and ask them to heat it for you (Mon-Sat 7:30-13:00 & 16:00-19:30, closed Sun, Via Fasce 12, tel. 0185-487-098).

Sestri Levante Connections

By **train,** Sestri Levante is just 20-40 minutes away from Monterosso (hourly connections with Monterosso, nearly hourly with other Cinque Terre towns) and 30 minutes from Santa Margherita Ligure (2/hour).

Boats depart to the Cinque Terre, Santa Margherita Ligure, Portofino, and San Fruttuoso from the dock *(molo)* on the peninsula (boats run Easter-Oct, see "Santa Margherita Ligure Connections," page 485, for details; to get to the dock: facing the church in Piazza Matteotti, take the road on the right with the sea on your right, about halfway down Via Pilade Queirolo; tel. 0185-284-670, mobile 336-253-336, www.traghettiportofino.it).

Santa Margherita Ligure

If you need the Riviera of movie stars, park your yacht at Portofino. Or you can settle down with more elbow room in nearby and personable Santa Margherita Ligure (15 minutes by bus from

Portofino and one hour by train from the Cinque Terre). While Portofino's velour allure is tarnished by a nonstop traffic jam in peak season, Santa Margherita tumbles easily downhill from its train station. The town has a fun Old World resort character and a breezy harborfront.

On a quick day trip from Milan or the Cinque Terre, walk the beach promenade and see the small old town of Santa Margherita Ligure before catching the bus (or boat) to Portofino to see what all the fuss is about. With more time, Santa Margherita makes a fine overnight stop or home base for hiking the Portofino peninsula.

Orientation to
Santa Margherita Ligure

Tourist Information

Pick up a map at the harborside TI on Piazza Veneto (daily April-Sept 9:30-12:30 & 14:30-19:30, Oct-March closes at 17:30 and all day Sun, tel. 0185-287-485, www.turismoinliguria.it).

Arrival by Train

To get from the station to the city center, take the stairs marked *Mare* (sea) down to the harbor; for an easier descent (especially if you're wheeling a suitcase), head down the gentler grade of Via Roma (follow *TI* signs). The harborfront promenade is wider than the skimpy beach. (The real beaches, which are pebbly, are a 10-minute walk farther on, past the port.)

The TI is right on the waterfront at Piazza Veneto (with the roundabout, flags, and park). The pedestrian-friendly old town is a block away: From the piazza, head inland on Largo Antonio Giusti and take a near-immediate left onto Via Torino, which opens onto Piazza Caprera, a square with a church and morning fruit vendors in the midst of traffic-free streets.

Helpful Hints

Internet Access: Papiluc Bar has two terminals (€3/30 minutes, daily 6:30 until late, Via del Arco 20, tel. 0185-282-580).

Post Office: It's just down the road from the train station on Via Roma (Mon-Fri 8:20-19:05, Sat 8:20-12:35, closed Sun, Via Roma 36).

Baggage Storage: There's no official left-luggage office, but day-trippers arriving by train can stash their bags at the station's café-bar (next to the station).

Pharmacy: There's one at Via Roma, near the post office, and another at the corner of Piazza Caprera and Via Pescino, not far from the TI.

Bike Rental: GM Rent is at Via XXV Aprile 11 (€10/5 hours, €20/24 hours, also rents scooters and Smart Cars, daily 10:00-13:00 & 16:30-20:00, mobile 329-406-6274, www.gmrent.it, Francesco).

Taxi: Taxis wait outside the train station and charge €15 for a ride from the station to anywhere in town, €25 to Paraggi beach, and €35 to Portofino (tel. 0185-286-508).

Driver: Helpful taxi driver **Alessandro** is also available for airport transfers and local excursions (mobile 338-860-2349, www.alessandrotaxi.com, alessandrotaxi@yahoo.it).

Parking: The recommended **Hotel Mediterraneo** and **Villa Anita** offer free parking to their guests, and a few hotels have

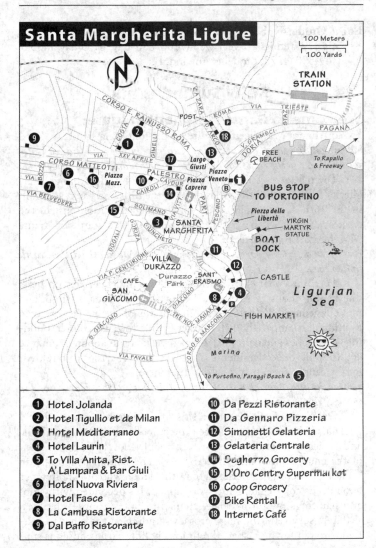

Santa Margherita Ligure

100 Meters
100 Yards

1. Hotel Jolanda
2. Hotel Tigullio et de Milan
3. Hotel Mediterraneo
4. Hotel Laurin
5. To Villa Anita, Rist. A' Lampara & Bar Giuli
6. Hotel Nuova Riviera
7. Hotel Fasce
8. La Cambusa Ristorante
9. Dal Baffo Ristorante
10. Da Pezzi Ristorante
11. Da Gennaro Pizzeria
12. Simonetti Gelateria
13. Gelateria Centrale
14. Seghezzo Grocery
15. D'Oro Centry Supermarket
16. Coop Grocery
17. Bike Rental
18. Internet Café

limited spots for a fee. When you reserve your room, mention that you'll have a car. Otherwise, try a private lot (about €10-15/half-day, €15-20/24 hours) such as **Autopark,** next to the post office (Via Roma 38, tel. 0185-287-818). An hourly parking lot is by the harbor, in front of the fish market (pay at blue machine with big *Ticket* sign overhead, Mon-Sat 8:00-20:00, Sun 8:00-23:00, first hour–€2, successive hours–€2.50). Parking is generally free where there are white lines; blue lines mean you pay.

Local Guide: Roberta De Beni knows the Ligurian Coast, its history, and its art very well (€100/half-day, €165/day, mobile 349-530-4778, diodebe@inwind.it).

Self-Guided Walk

Welcome to Santa Margherita Ligure

Explore Santa Margherita Ligure on the following stroll.

• *Begin on the water at Piazza della Libertà (just beyond Piazza Veneto). Walk out to the tip of the boat dock and turn around to survey the...*

Town View: From here, you can take in all of Santa Margherita Ligure, from the villas dotting the hills and the castle built in the 16th century (closed except for special exhibitions) to the exclusive hotels. Sharing the dock with you is a statue of "Santa Margherita Virgin Martyr."

• *Wander along the harborfront (down Corso Marconi) past the castle and to the...*

Marina: What's left of the town's fishing fleet ties up here. The fishing industry survives, drag-netting octopus, shrimp, and miscellaneous "blue fish"—plus mountains of anchovies attracted to midnight lamps. The fish market (inside the rust-colored building with arches and columns) wiggles weekdays at about, oh, maybe 16:00-20:00 or so. Residents complain that it's easier to buy their locally caught fresh fish in Milan than here.

• *Head up the flight of narrow brick stairs just to the right of the fish market. At the top stands the...*

Oratory of Sant'Erasmo: This small church is named for St. Erasmus (a.k.a. "St. Elmo"), the protector of sailors. Notice the fine and typically local black-and-white pebble mosaic *(riseu)* in front of the church (with maritime themes). The church is actually an "oratory," where a brotherhood of faithful men who did anonymous good deeds congregated and worshipped. It's decorated with ships and paintings of storms that—thanks to St. Erasmus—the local seafarers survived. The huge crosses standing in the nave are carried through town on special religious holidays (the church is supposedly open only during Mass, but often open at other times, too).

• *With your back to the church, find the loooong stairway (Via Tre Novembre) ahead on the right. Climb it to reach the...*

Church of San Giacomo: Even though this is a secondary church in a secondary town, it's impressively lavish (daily 7:30-19:00, may close earlier in winter, avoid visiting during Mass—usually 7:45-9:00). The region's aristocrats amassed wealth from trade in the 11th to the 15th centuries. When Constantinople fell to the Turks, free trade in the Mediterranean stopped, and Genovese traders became bankers—making even more money. A popular saying of the day was, "Silver is born in America, lives in Spain,

Rise of a Resort: The History of Santa Margherita Ligure

This town, like the entire region (from the border of France to La Spezia), was once ruled by the Republic of Genoa. In the

16th century, when Arab pirates from North Africa plagued the entire coastal area, Genoa built castles in the towns and lookout towers in the neighboring hills.

At the time, Santa Margherita was actually two bickering towns—each with its own bay. In 1800, Napoleon came along, took over the Republic of Genoa, and turned the rival towns into one city—naming it Porto Napoleone. When Napoleon fell in 1815, the town stayed united and took the name of the patron saint of its leading church, Santa Margherita.

In 1850, residents set to work creating a Riviera resort. They imported palm trees from North Africa and paved a fine beach promenade. Santa Margherita (and the surrounding area) was studded with fancy villas built by the aristocracy of Genoa (which was controlled by just 35 families). English, Russian, and German aristocrats also discovered the town in the 19th century. Mass tourism only hit in the last generation. Even with the increased crowds, the town decided to stay chic and kept huge developments out. Its neighbor, Rapallo, chose the extreme opposite—giving the Italian language a new word for uncontrolled growth ruining a once-cute town: *rapallizzazione*.

and dies in Genoa." Bankers here served Spain's 17th-century royalty and aristocracy, and the accrued wealth paid for a Golden Age of art. Wander the church and its chapels, noticing the inlaid-marble floors and sparkling glass chandeliers.

• *Step out of the church and enjoy the sea view. Then turn left and step into...*

Durazzo Park (Parco di Villa Durazzo): This park was an abandoned shambles until 1973, when the city took it over (free, daily 9:00-19:00, off-season until 17:00). Today it's a delight, with a breezy café enjoyed mostly by locals (generally daily from 10:30 except closed Tue May-Aug) and free Wi-Fi (ask at the café for the password). The garden has two distinct parts: the carefully coiffed Italian garden (designed to complement the villa's architecture), and the calculatedly wild "English garden" below. The Italian garden is famous for its varied collection of palm trees and an extensive

RIVIERA TOWNS

collection of camellias. It's OK to feed the large turtles in the central pond (they like bits of fish or meat).

• *In the building next to the café, you'll see...*

Villa Durazzo: This was the home of a local journalist and writer, Vittorio G. Rossi (1898-1978), whose office has been preserved as he left it. Typical of the region, this palazzo has some period furniture, several grand pianos, chandeliers, and paintings strewn with cupids on the walls and ceilings. Look for King Umberto's letter offering condolences on Rossi's death. For most people, it's probably not worth the entry fee (€5.50, more for special exhibits; daily 9:00-13:00 & 14:30-18:30, Oct-March until 17:00, last entry 30 minutes before closing, WC opposite entry on left, tel. 0185-293-135, www.villadurazzo.it, villa.durazzo@comunesml.it). Classical music concerts are held here in July and August (ask at TI or villa ticket desk, or call for the schedule).

• *Your self-guided walk is over. Enjoy the park.*

Sights in Santa Margherita Ligure

Basilica of Santa Margherita
(Basilica di Nostra Signora della Rosa)
The town's main church is textbook Italian Baroque. Its 18th-century facade hides a 17th-century interior. The chapels to the right of the high altar contain religious "floats" used in local festival parades. The wooden groups in the niches higher up used to be part of the processions, too. The altar is typical of 17th-century Ligurian altars—shaped like a boat, with lots of shelf space for candles, flowers, and relics. Remember, Baroque is like theater. After the Vatican II decrees of the 1960s, priests began to face their flocks instead of the old altars. For this reason, all over the Catholic world, modern tables serving as post-Vatican II altars stand in front of earlier altars that are no longer the center of attention during the Mass.

Cost and Hours: Free, daily 7:30-12:00 & 15:00-18:30, tel. 0185-286-555.

Via Palestro
This promenade (a.k.a. *caruggio*—"the big street" in local dialect) is *the* strolling street for window-shopping, people-watching, and studying the characteristic Art Nouveau house painting from about 1900. Before 1900, people distinguished their buildings with pastel paint and distinctive door and window frames. Then they decided to get fancy and paint entire exteriors with false balconies, weapons, saints, beautiful women, and 3-D Gothic concentrate.

As you wander from the Basilica of Santa Margherita inland, pop into the fanciest grocer-deli in town—the recommended **Seghezzo** (immediately to the right of the church on Via Cavour).

Locals know that this venerable institution has whatever odd ingredient the most obscure recipe calls for.

Farther up Via Palestro, you might drop into the traditional old **Panificio-Torinese** bakery for a slice of fresh focaccia. Saying *"Vorrei un etto di focaccia"* will get you a Ligurian olive-oily, 100-gram, €1.50 hunk of every kid's favorite beach munchie. Locals claim the best focaccia in Italy is made along this coast.

Markets

On weekday afternoons, fishing boats unload their catch, which is then sold to waiting customers at **Mercato del Pesce** (roughly Mon-Fri 17:00-20:00, opens an hour earlier for wholesalers). Find it in the rust-colored building with arches and columns on Corso Marconi, on the harbor, just past the castle. The open-air market, a commotion of clothes and produce, is held every Friday morning along Corso Matteotti, inland from Piazza Mazzini (8:00-13:00). Piazza Caprera (facing the main church) daily hosts a few farmers selling their produce from stalls.

Beaches

The handiest free Santa Margherita beaches are just below the train station toward the boat dock. But the best beaches are on the south side of town. Among these, I like "Gio and Rino beach" (just before Covo di Nord Est)—not too expensive, with fun, creative management and a young crowd. Also nice is the beach on the south side of Hotel Miramare, which offers a more relaxing sun-worshipping experience. Both beaches have free entry and rentable chairs and umbrellas. They're a 20-minute walk from downtown, or take the bus from either the train station or Piazza Veneto (€1.50 each way if bought in advance from newsstands, tobacco shops, or the green bus ticket kiosk next to the TI; €3 if bought on board).

Paraggi beach, which is halfway to Portofino (with an easy bus connection—see "Portofino," later in this chapter, and the map on page 487), is better than any Santa Margherita beach, but it's *very* expensive. One Paraggi beach operator, Bosetti, offers a reasonable rate (€25/day, no hourly rates, includes umbrella, lounge chair, and towel), while rates at other beaches may soar up to €50 per day in July and August. In high season, the Paraggi beach may be all booked up by big shots from Portofino, which has no beach—only rocks. Off-season, the entire Paraggi beach is all yours and free of charge. A skinny patch of sand smack-dab in the middle of Paraggi beach is free year-round.

Sleeping in Santa Margherita Ligure

All of these accommodations are in the center of town; for specific locations, see the map on page 477. La Locanda di Colombo, Hotel Jolanda, and Hotel Tigullio et de Milan are closest to the station. Prices listed here are the maximum price for the high season of July-August. Expect April-June and September-October to be €10-15 cheaper, and the rest of the year to be cheaper still.

$$$ Hotel Jolanda is a solid, professionally run hotel with 50 rooms, a revolving door, a good breakfast buffet, and a friendly staff. With lavish public spaces and regal colors, this place makes you feel like nobility (Db-€150, superior Db-€170, 10 percent discount if you book directly with the hotel and mention this book when you reserve, air-con, elevator, guest computer, Wi-Fi, free use of small weight room, wet and dry saunas, Jacuzzi, 10 free loaner bikes on request, Via Luisito Costa 6, tel. 0185-287-512, www.hoteljolanda.it, info@hoteljolanda.it).

$$$ Hotel Tigullio et de Milan, run by Giuseppe of Hotel Jolanda, has equally fine rooms with creamy hues and lower prices. You don't get all the luxurious extras, but the breezy sun terrace on top—with a bar in summertime—makes for a relaxing retreat (Db-€140, bigger Db with terrace-€150, 10 percent discount if you book direct with the hotel and mention this book when you reserve, air-con, elevator but lots of stairs down to reception, a few free parking spots, Via Rainusso 3, tel. 0185-287-455, www.hoteltigullio.eu, info@hoteltigullio.eu).

$$$ Hotel Mediterraneo, run by the Melegatti family, offers 30 spacious rooms (a few with balconies or sun terraces) in a family-friendly, creaky, and comfy 18th-century palazzo a five-minute walk from Piazza Veneto. They have a park-like sun garden with lounge chairs and lots of semi-private space. Kindly Pia Pauli presides over the dining room and makes great homemade Ligurian specialties for dinner (Sb-€100, Db-€150, Tb-€180, extensive breakfast, five-course dinner-€30/person, free laundry service with 2-day stay or longer, half the rooms have air-con, Wi-Fi, free parking, free loaner bikes, closed Jan-March, take street immediately to the right of Basilica of Santa Margherita and find hotel straight ahead at Via della Vittoria 18A, tel. 0185-286-881, www.sml-mediterraneo.it, info@sml-mediterraneo.it).

$$$ Hotel Laurin offers slick, modern, air-conditioned, American-style lodgings fixated on harborfront views. All of its 43 rooms face the sea, most have terraces, and there's a small pool on the sundeck, as well as a gym and wet sauna. As it's a Best Western, it feels corporate (Sb-€173, Db-€245, 10 percent discount if you book direct with the hotel and mention this book when you reserve—must show book on arrival, double-paned windows, elevator, 15-yard walk past the castle or €15 taxi ride from station, Corso Marconi 3, tel. 0185-289-971, www.laurinhotel.it, info@ laurinhotel.it).

$$$ Villa Anita is an elegant-yet-homey family hotel run by hospitable Daniela and her friendly son, Sandro. They rent 12 tidy rooms—nearly all with terraces and several with new, high-tech bathrooms—overlooking a peaceful residential neighborhood just a five-minute walk from the seaside boulevard. Daniela makes great cakes, and the in-house chef offers a varying menu of Ligurian specialties (Db-€160, superior Db-€190, dinner-€25/person, family rooms, small heated pool and playground, air-con, free Wi-Fi, free parking, €15 cab ride from station, Viale Minerva 25, tel. 0185-286-543, www.hotelvillaanita.com, info@hotelvillaanita. com).

$$$ Hotel Nuova Riviera is an old villa surrounded by a garden, with nine institutional-feeling rooms, warmly run by the Sabini family (Db-€140, Tb-€160, Qb-€180, 2-night minimum, these prices good in 2014 if you book direct with the hotel and mention this book when you reserve, additional 10 percent discount when you pay cash, fans, some balconies, no elevator, 15-minute walk from station or easy cab ride; if you're driving, follow signs to hospital, then watch for hotel signs on Piazza Mazzini; if you're walking, enter Piazza Mazzini and see signs from there; Via Belvedere 10, tel. 0185-287-403, www.sabinirentals.com, info@sabinirentals.com, chatty Cristina). They also run a nearby annex with six renovated rooms and one apartment with a tiny corner kitchen (Db-€88, Tb-€105, Qb-€125, 2-night minimum, no discounts, cash only, breakfast at Hotel Nuova Riviera is optional and extra, tel. 0185-290-083).

$$$ Hotel Fasce, a 16-room hotel surrounded by flowers and greenery, is run enthusiastically by Florinda and Enrico, whose three kids make this a family-friendly place (Sb-€80, Db-€120, Tb-€150, Qb-€180, two rooms have private bathroom located across the hall, dinner-€20/person, will prepare gluten-free breakfasts, no elevator, free Wi-Fi, free loaner bikes, rooftop garden, laundry service-€15, parking-€20, 10-minute walk or €15 cab ride from station at Via Bozzo 3, tel. 0185-286-435, www.hotelfasce.it, hotelfasce@hotelfasce.it).

Eating in Santa Margherita Ligure

For information on some of the regional specialties, see page 391.

Ristorante "A' Lampara" is the locals' favorite for *casalinga* (home-style) Genovese cuisine, prepared by the endearing Barbieri family: Mamma Maria Luisa oversees the dining room, son Mario cooks, and daughter Natalina serves. Try their specialties, such as *ravioli di pesce*—homemade fish ravioli with red mullet sauce—or *pansotti con salsa di noci*—spinach-stuffed ravioli with walnut sauce (€8-10 pastas, €16-25 *secondi*, Fri-Wed 12:30-14:00 & 19:15-22:00, closed Thu, veggie options, reservations smart for dinner in summer; follow Corso Marconi 4 blocks past the fish market, turn right onto Via Maragliano, and find #33 a block and a half ahead on left; tel. 0185-288-926).

La Cambusa is perched above the culinary heart of Santa Margherita Ligure—the fish market. Popular with tourists and resident romantics, its terrace has an unbeatable view over the harbor. In cooler weather, the terrace is covered and heated. Pick your favorite yacht while tucking into their seafood dishes with a Ligurian twist (€10-13 pasta, €18-22 main dishes, July-Sept daily 9:00-15:00 & 19:00-24:00 except closed Thu morning, Oct-June closed all day Thu, Via T. Bottaro, tel. 0185-287-410; Luciano, wife Antonella, and serious but efficient Vittorio).

Dal Baffo is a bustling mom-and-pop eatery popular for its traditional Ligurian specialties, including homemade pasta, wood-fired pizzas (folks queue up to watch the *pizzaioli* make their €7 pies to go), fresh fish, and grilled steaks at reasonable prices (Wed-Mon 12:00-15:00 & 19:00-23:30, closed Tue; from Piazza Caprera, head inland—both pedestrian streets eventually turn into busy Corso Matteotti; Corso Matteotti 56, tel. 0185-288-987).

Da Pezzi, with a cheap cafeteria-style atmosphere, is packed with locals at midday and at night. They're munching *farinata* (crêpes made from chickpeas, available Oct-May) standing at the bar, or enjoying pesto and fresh fish in the dining room. Consider the deli counter with its Genovese picnic ingredients (Sun-Fri 10:00-14:00 & 17:00-21:00, closed Sat, Via Cavour 21, tel. 0185-285-303, Giancarlo and Giobatta).

Waterfront Dining: All along the harborside of Via Tomaso Bottaro, south of the marina, you'll find restaurants, pizzerias, and bars serving food with a nautical view. **Da Gennaro Pizzeria,** at Piazza della Libertà 30 by the boat dock, makes popular Neapolitan-style pizzas. **Bar Giuli,** the only place actually on the harbor, serves forgettable salads and sandwiches for a reasonable price (about 150 yards south of the fish market, where Via Maragliano meets Via Garibaldi).

Gelato: The best *gelateria* I found in town—with chocolate-truffle *tartufato*—is **Simonetti** (daily 8:30 until late, closed Mon off-season, under the castle, closest to the water at Piazza della Libertà 48). **Gelateria Centrale,** just off Piazza Veneto near the cinema, serves up their specialty—*pinguino* (penguin), a cone with your choice of gelato dipped in chocolate (daily 8:30-late, closed Wed Sept-May).

Groceries: **Seghezzo** is classiest and great for a meal to go—ask them to *riscaldare* (heat up) their white *lasagne al pesto* or dish up their special *carpaccio di polpo*—thinly sliced octopus (daily June-Aug 7:30-13:00 & 15:30-20:00, closed Wed Sept-May, right of the church on Via Cavour, tel. 0185-287-172). The **D'Oro Centry** supermarket, just off Piazza Mazzini at #35, has better prices (Mon-Sat 8:00-13:30 & 15:30-19:30, Sun 8:00-13:00, tel. 0185-286-470), as does the **Co-op** grocery, also off Piazza Mazzini at Corso Giacomo Matteotti 9 (Mon-Sat 8:15-13:00 & 15:30-19:30, Sun 8:30-13:00). Any of these stores is a good place to stock up on well-priced Ligurian olive oil, pasta, and pesto.

Santa Margherita Ligure Connections

From Santa Margherita Ligure by Train to: Sestri Levante (2/hour, 30 minutes), **Monterosso** (at least hourly, 45 minutes), **La Spezia** (hourly, 1-1.5 hours), **Pisa** (1-2/hour, 2-2.5 hours, most connections with transfer, less frequent InterCity/IC goes direct), **Milan** (7/day, 2-2.5 hours, more with transfer in Genoa), **Ventimiglia**/French border (4/day, 4 hours; or hourly with change in Genoa), **Venice** (8/day, 6-7 hours with 1-3 changes). For **Florence,** transfer in Pisa (8/day, 3.5-4 hours). See "Getting Around the Cinque Terre—By Train" on page 379 for details.

By Boat to the Cinque Terre: For the latest, pick up a schedule of departures and excursion options from the TI, visit the ticket shack on the dock, call 0185-284-670 or 335-709-0870, or check online at www.traghettiportofino.it. The routes mentioned below run at least once weekly from May through September or October, increasing in frequency in July and August.

"Tour 3" is an all-day trip that includes two stopovers: one hour in Vernazza and three hours in Portovenere, plus a scenic trip around an island (mid-April-Sept departs Sun at 8:45, plus Thu July-Sept, €22 one-way, €33 round-trip).

The half-day "Tour 4" boat sails to the Cinque Terre with a one-hour stopover in Vernazza (July-Sept departs Tue and Fri at 13:30, €17.50 one-way, €25.50 round-trip).

The "Tour 5 Super Cinque Terre" boat offers day-trip cruises from Santa Margherita Ligure to the Cinque Terre, departing at

8:45 and stopping in three Cinque Terre towns: three hours in Monterosso, and an hour each in Vernazza and Riomaggiore (Wed May-Sept, plus Sat July-Sept, €22 one-way, €33 round-trip).

Portofino

Santa Margherita Ligure, with its aristocratic architecture, hints at old money, whereas nearby Portofino, with its sleek shops, has the sheen of new money. Fortu-

nately, a few pizzerias, *focacce-rie,* bars, and grocery shops are mixed in with Portofino's jewelry shops, art galleries, and haute couture boutiques, making the town affordable. The *piccolo* harbor, classic Italian architecture, and wooded peninsula can turn glitzy Portofino into an appealing package. It makes a fun day trip from Santa Margherita Ligure.

Ever since the Romans founded Portofino for its safe harbor, it has had a strategic value (appreciated by everyone from Napoleon to the Nazis). In the 1950s, *National Geographic* did a beautiful exposé on the idyllic port, and locals claim that's when the Hollywood elite took note. Liz Taylor and Richard Burton came here annually (as did Liz Taylor and Eddie Fisher). During one famous party, Rex Harrison dropped his Oscar into the bay (it was recovered). Ava Gardner came down from her villa each evening for a drink—sporting her famous fur coat. Greta Garbo loved to swim naked in the harbor, not knowing that half the town was watching. Truman Capote also called Portofino home. But VIPs were also here a century earlier. In one of his books, Friedrich Nietzsche wrote about philosophizing with the mythical prophet Zarathustra on the path between Portofino and Santa Margherita.

My favorite Portofino plan: Visit for the evening. Leave Santa Margherita on the bus at about 16:30 and hike the last 20 minutes from Paraggi beach. Explore Portofino. Splurge for a drink on the harborfront, or get a take-out fruity sundae (*paciugo*; pah-CHOO-goh) and sit by the water. Then return by bus to Santa Margherita for dinner (confirm late departures). Portofino offers all kinds of harborside dining, but the quality often doesn't match the high prices. If you do decide to eat in Portofino, **Ristorante lo Stella,** just a few steps from the boat dock, has well-prepared dishes, friendly servers, and portholes in the bathrooms. Opposite the boat dock, little **Solo Gelato** dishes up cones and cups (€3 and up).

Portofino Area

To Cinque Terre & Pisa →

To Genoa

Camogli STATION

Rapallo

See Santa Margherita detail map

PORT

TRAIN STATION

TUNNEL

BUS STOP **B**

CHURCH

Santa Margherita Ligure

To Rapallo

Gulf of Paradise

Portofino Peninsula

BOAT DOCK

Monte Portofino

TRAIL

GIO & RINO BEACHES

San Fruttuoso

Paraggi

Gulf of Tigullio

CHRIST OF THE ABYSS

Portofino

Ligurian Sea

CASTELLO BROWN

LIGHTHOUSE

— · — Rail
- - - Bus
········ Trail

1 Kilometer

1 Mile

Getting to Portofino

Portofino makes an easy day trip from Santa Margherita by bus, boat, hike, or foot.

By Bus: Catch bus #82 from Santa Margherita's train station or at bus stops along the harbor (main stop in front of TI, €1.50, 2-3/hour, 15 minutes, goes to Paraggi or Portofino). Buy tickets at the bar next to the train station, at Piazza Veneto's green bus kiosk (next to the TI; daily 7:00-19:30), from the green machine on the side of the kiosk, or at any newsstand, tobacco shop, or shop that displays a *Biglietti Bus* sign. You can usually buy tickets on the bus—for double the cost. If you're at the Piazza Veneto kiosk, grab a bus schedule, which will come in handy if you travel in the evening (last bus around 23:00, #82).

In Portofino, get tickets at the newsstand or tobacco store on Piazza della Libertà, or from the machine next to the bus stop (go uphill from the harbor and you'll come to the piazza—newsstand and tobacco store on the left side; ticket machine and bus stop on the right, directions in English).

By Boat: The boat makes the 15-minute trip with more class and without the traffic jams (€6 one-way, €9 round-trip, €0.50 more on Sun and holidays; nearly hourly departures daily May-Sept 10:15-16:15, Oct-April at 10:15 and 14:15 only; dock is a

2-minute walk from Piazza Veneto off Piazza Martiri della Libertà, call to confirm or pick up schedule from TI or your hotel, tel. 0185-284-670, mobile 336-253-336, check at www.traghetti-portofino.it). This company also runs boats from Santa Margherita to the Cinque Terre (see page 485). The boat from Portofino back to Santa Margherita departs nearly hourly in summer (May-Sept daily 12:00-18:00; Oct-April at 12:00 and 16:00 only).

By Bike: The 25-minute bike ride from Santa Margherita to Portofino is doable for cautious cyclists. While there are no steep hills to struggle up, the road is narrow, with many blind corners. Many of my recommended hotels provide free loaner bikes (though they may not be in the best condition); you can also rent your own wheels (see page 476).

On Foot: To hike the entire distance from Santa Margherita Ligure to Portofino, you have two options: You can follow the sidewalk along (and sometimes hanging over) the sea (1 hour, 2.5 miles)—although traffic can be noisy, and in places, the footpath disappears. Or, if you're hardy and ambitious, you can take a quieter two-hour hike by leaving Santa Margherita at Via Maragliano, then follow the Ligurian-symbol trail markers (look for red-and-white stripes—they're not always obvious, sometimes numbered according to the path you're on, usually painted on rocks or walls, especially at junctions). This hike takes you high into the hills. Keep left after Cappelletta delle Gave. Several blocks past a castle, you'll drop down into the Paraggi beach, where you'll take the Portofino trail the rest of the way.

Bus and Hike Option: For a shorter hike (20 minutes) into Portofino, ride bus #82 from Santa Margherita only as far as the small but ritzy Paraggi beach. (Ask on board where to get off—watch for an inland bay with green water and a sandy beach.) At the far end of the beach, cross the street, climb the steps, and follow the hilly, paved trail marked *Pedonali per Portofino* high above the road. Twenty minutes later, you'll enter Portofino at a yellow-and-gray-striped church labeled *Divo Martino*—which I figure means "the divine Martin" and has something to do with Dean Martin giving us all "Volare" (which I couldn't get out of my head for the rest of the day).

Orientation to Portofino

Tourist Information: Portofino's TI is uphill from the boat dock and downhill from the bus stop (look for it under a portico—it's on your left coming from the dock, or on your right coming from the bus). Pick up a free town map and a rudimentary hiking map (June-Sept Tue-Sun 10:00-13:00 & 14:00-18:00, closed Mon; Oct-May Tue-Sat 9:30-13:30 & 14:00-17:00, closed Sun-Mon; Via Roma 35, tel. 0185-269-024).

Sights in Portofino

Museo del Parco

For an artsy break, walk around the harbor to the right, where you can stroll around a park littered with 148 contemporary sculptures by mostly Italian artists, including a few top names (€5, June-Oct Wed-Mon 10:00-13:00 & 15:00-19:00, closed Tue, closed Nov-May and in bad weather, mobile 337-333-737, www.museodiportofino.it).

Hikes

One option is the paved stone path that winds up and down to the **lighthouse** *(faro)* at a scenic point with a bar (take the stairs on the right just after Museo del Parco, bar open May-Sept, hedges block views until the end, 25-minute walk). Consider popping into **Castello Brown,** a medieval castle, on the way up or down. It features lush gardens, sweeping viewpoints, and special exhibits about Portofino and its history. Minimal original decorations and exhibits are explained in English (€5, cash only, March-Oct daily 10:00-19:00, Nov-Feb Sat-Sun until 17:00 in winter, tel. 0185-267-101, www.castellobrown.com).

Or you could stroll the hilly pedestrian promenade through the trees from Portofino to **Paraggi beach,** and, if you're lucky, see a wild boar en route (20 minutes, path starts to the right of yellow-and-gray-striped Divo Martino church—look for clock tower, parallels main road, ends at ritzy Paraggi beach, where it's easy to catch bus back to Santa Margherita Ligure).

Another option is to hike out to **San Fruttuoso Abbey** and the nearby underwater Christ statue (described next; the hike there is steep at beginning and end, takes about 2.5 hours from Portofino—pick up the trailhead at the inland-most point of town, past Piazza della Libertà and the *carabinieri* station, you can also hike all the way there from Santa Margherita in about 4.5 hours via Portofino).

The **Parco di Portofino** can provide more information on the many hiking trails that crisscross Portofino's regional parklands (tel. 0185 289-479, www.parcoportofino.it).

Near Portofino

San Fruttuoso Abbey
(Abbazia di San Fruttuoso)

This 11th-century abbey is accessible only by foot (a 2.5-hour hike from Portofino, 4.5 hours from Santa Margherita) or boat (from either Portofino, Santa Margherita, or Camogli; abbey entry-€5, more for special exhibits; June-Sept daily 10:00-17:45; Oct-May daily 10:00-15:45 except closed Mon in winter;

last entry 45 minutes before closing, tel. 0185-772-703, www.
fondoambiente.it). But the abbey itself isn't the main attraction.
The more intriguing draw is 60 feet underwater, offshore from the
abbey, in a specially protected marine area: the statue *Christ of the
Abyss (Cristo degli Abissi)*. A boat will take you out to a spot above
the statue, where you can look down to just barely see the arms of
Jesus—outstretched, reaching upward. Some people bring goggles
and dive in for a better view. The statue was placed there in 1954
for the divine protection of the region's divers (€6, trips depart
from San Fruttuoso at Sat July-Aug at 15:30, some Mon and Wed
sailings—check schedule at www.sopraesottoilmare.net or ask at
Portofino TI).

Getting There: The same boats that link Santa Margherita
Ligure and Portofino continue on to the San Fruttuoso Abbey
(schedule at www.traghettiportofino.it). From Easter through
September, a different company's boats continue north from the
abbey to Camogli (train station), Recco, and Punta Chiappa (€5-8
one-way, can return to Santa Margherita by train from Camogli or
buy round-trip boat tickets, tel. 0185-772-091, schedule at www.
golfoparadiso.it). For details inquire at the TI in Portofino or Santa
Margherita.

South of the Cinque Terre

La Spezia

While just a quick train ride away from the fanciful Cinque Terre
(20-30 minutes), the working town of La Spezia feels like "reality
Italy." Primarily a jumping-off point for travelers, the town is slim
on sights, and has no beaches.

The pedestrian zone on Via del Prione to the gardens along the
harbor makes a pleasant stroll. The nearly deserted **Museo Amedeo
Lia** displays Italian paintings from the 13th to 18th centuries, including minor works by Venetian masters Titian, Tintoretto, and
Canaletto (€7, Tue-Sun 10:00-18:00, closed Mon, last entry 30
minutes before closing, English descriptions on laminated sheets
in most rooms, audioguide-€3, WCs down the hall from ticket
desk, 10-minute walk from station at Via del Prione 234, tel. 0187-
731-100, http://museolia.spezianet.it).

Stay in the Cinque Terre if you can. But if you're in a bind,
I've listed several La Spezia accommodations. I've also listed (under

"Eating in La Spezia") some places to grab a meal while you wait for a train.

Orientation to La Spezia

Tourist Information

The Cinque Terre National Park office is on the platform at track 1 (daily 7:00-21:00, until 19:00 off-season, guest computer-€1.50/20 minutes, tel. 0187-762-600, www.parconazionale5terre.it).

Arrival in La Spezia

By Train: Get off at the La Spezia Centrale stop. You can check your bags at the train station (see "Helpful Hints," next). Exit the station down the road to the left, where several recommended hotels and eateries are located. Another exit takes you out onto Via Fiume by way of the parking garage.

By Car: A handy parking option is under the train station, at the **Park Centro Stazione** (enter from Via Fiume; €1/hour, €6/half-day, about €17/day, or a few euros cheaper with complicated online pre-registration, www.mobpark.it, tel. 0187-187-5303; when returning, punch the code from your ticket into the keypad to open the door). You can park for free at **Piazza d'Armi** (a 20-minute walk to station, or take €1 shuttle bus to Piazza Brin, a 5-minute walk to station; at least 3/hour).

Helpful Hints

Market Days: A colorful covered market sets up in Piazza Cavour (Mon-Sat 7.00-13:00). On Fridays, a huge all-day open-air market sprawls along Viale Garibaldi, about six blocks from the station.

Baggage Storage: A left-luggage service is at the train station along track 1 (facing the tracks on platform 1, go left; it's next to the WC). It's secure, though it isn't always staffed—ring the bell to the left of the doorway to call the attendant. Since you may have to wait, allow plenty of time to pick up your baggage before departing (€3/12 hours, €2 extra per additional 12 hours, daily 8:00-22:00, they'll photocopy your passport).

Laundry: A handy self-service launderette is just below the train station. Head down toward town, and immediately at the first piazza take a sharp right on Via Fiume—it's on your left at #95 (one-hour wash and dry-€8, Mon-Sat 8:30-22:00, Sun 9:00-22:00, mobile 348-543-7924, Edoardo).

Booking Agency: Cinque Terre Riviera books rooms and apartments in La Spezia, the Cinque Terre, and Portovenere for a 10 percent markup (see page 393 for contact info).

Getting to the Cinque Terre: Trains leave at least twice hourly for

the Cinque Terre, though not all trains stop at all towns. The Cinque Terre Treno Park Card (covers train ride to Cinque Terre as well as hiking fee—see page 379) is sold at the train-station ticket window and at the national park office in the station (see "Tourist Information," at the beginning of this section). For more details, see "Getting Around the Cinque Terre" on page 379. It's also possible to take boat excursions to the Cinque Terre, Portovenere, and outer islands from the La Spezia dock; for current schedules, check at the TI, dock, or www.navigazionegolfodeipoeti.it.

Sleeping in La Spezia

Remember, sleep in La Spezia only as a last resort. These hotels and rooms are within a five-minute walk of La Spezia's station—except the last two listings, which are for drivers only. Prices listed are the high-season rates.

1. Hotel Firenze e Continentale
2. Hotel Astoria
3. Mary Hotel
4. Albergo Parma
5. Casa da Nè/Tre Frè Rooms
6. L'Arca di Noè B&B
7. Ristorante Roma da Marcellin
8. Il Pomodoro Pizzeria
9. Covered Market
10. Launderette
11. Piazza d'Armi (Free Parking)
12. Piazza d'Armi Shuttle Drop-Off
13. Portovenere Bus Stop

Hotels

$$$ Hotel Firenze e Continentale is grand and Old World, but newly restored with a mountain-view breakfast room to boot. Just to the left of the station, its 68 rooms have all the usual comforts (prices vary, but generally Sb-€100, Db-€160, email for best rate, 10 percent discount on best available rate if you book direct with the hotel and mention this book when you reserve, cheaper during slow times, double-paned windows, air-con, elevator, free Wi-Fi, parking in garage-€22/day, Via Paleocapa 7, tel. 0187-713 200, www.hotelfirenzecontinentale.it, info@hotelfirenzecontinentale.it).

$$ Hotel Astoria, with 47 decent rooms, has a combination lobby and breakfast room as large as a school cafeteria. It's a fine backup if the hotels nearer the train station are full (older Db without air-con-€80; Db-€95 for the 10 summery, modern superior rooms with air-con; elevator, free Wi-Fi, free parking in garage—reserve ahead; take Via Milano left of Albergo Parma, go 3 blocks, and turn left to reach Via Roma 139; tel. 0187-714-655, www.albergoastoria.com, info@albergoastoria.com).

$$ Mary Hotel, directly across from the train station, has 48 decent rooms above a big lounge/game room (Sb-€65, Db-€100, air-con, elevator, free Wi-Fi, Via Fiume 177, tel. 0187-743-254, www.hotelmary.it, info@hotelmary.it, friendly Luca).

$$ Albergo Parma, a dumpy last resort with 36 rooms, is a dingy slumbermill, but the price is right (D-€50, Db-€60, breakfast-€4, no fans, free Wi-Fi, some street noise, just below train station and down the stairs at Via Fiume 143, tel. 0187-743-010, www.albergoparma.com, albergoparma@libero.it, Aurelio speaks a bit of English, Silvana doesn't).

Private Rooms

Affitta camera—guesthouses or rented rooms with no official reception—abound near the station. Expect good deals, modest English skills, and no breakfast (buy yourself a coffee and pastry at a nearby bar).

$$ Casa da Nè/Tre Frè has 14 chic rooms with comfy linens and orange trees outside the door. It's located so close to the station that some rooms look out at the tracks; luckily, the windows are double-paned (Db-€80, Tb-€100, Qb-€120, includes breakfast at a café, air-con, free Wi-Fi, Via Paleocapa 4, mobile 347-351-3239, www.trefre.it, info@trefre.it, Paolo).

$$ L'Arca di Noè B&B is homey, with three bright and artsy rooms that offer one of the best deals on the Cinque Terre (one has a bathroom inside the room, while the others have private bathrooms down the hall). A group could take the entire massive apartment (D-€55, Tb-€85, includes breakfast, air-con, communal kitchen, 5-minute walk from station at Via Fiume 39, mobile 320-485-2434, montialessandra@email.it, Alessandra).

Near La Spezia

$$ Il Gelsomino, for drivers only, is a another homey B&B in the hills above La Spezia overlooking the Gulf of Poets. It has three tranquil rooms: one with a bay-view terrace, one with hillside views, and a third that lacks views or a terrace (Db-€70, Tb-€90, Qb-€110, reconfirm several days in advance with your arrival time, large breakfast, Via dei Viseggi 9, tel. 0187-704-201, www.ilgelsomino.biz, ilgelsomino@inwind.it, gracious Carla and Walter Massi). Don't confuse this B&B with the one named Il Gelsomino d'Oro.

$ Santa Maria del Mare Monastery, a last resort for drivers, rents 15 comfortable rooms to spiritual travelers high above La Spezia in a scenic but institutional setting (donation only, recommended offerings: dorm bed-€35, Db-€60, includes breakfast, additional €15/person for a meal, Via Montalbano 135B, tel.

0187-711-382, , mobile 347-848-3993, www.santamariadelmare.it, madre@santamariadelmare.191.it).

Eating in La Spezia

Ristorante Roma da Marcellin, a one-minute walk from the station, has a cool, leafy terrace that's ideal for relaxing while you await your train. Grandpa Ottorino cooks up the freshest catch, as well as homemade ravioli and spaghetti *frutti di mare* (€8-12 pastas, €9-15 *secondi*, daily 12:15-15:00 & 19:30-23:00; as you exit the station, turn left—it's across from Hotel Firenze e Continentale at Via Paleocapa 18; tel. 0187-715-921).

Il Pomodoro Pizzeria, just a few doors farther down on the corner of Via Zampino, offers more reasonable prices and an extensive selection of €6-8 pizzas. Practice your Italian with the chalkboard display of pastas of the day (Mon-Fri 12:00-14:00 & 19:00-23:00, Sat 19:00-23:00, closed Sun, Piazza S. Bon 5, tel. 0187-739-911).

La Spezia Connections

From La Spezia by Train to: Monterosso (2-3/hour, 15-30 minutes, €2.60), **Carrara** (2/hour, 25 minutes, €2.40), **Viareggio** (2/hour, 30-60 minutes, €4), **Pisa** (hourly, 1-1.5 hours, €5-9), **Florence** (4/day direct, otherwise nearly hourly, 2.5 hours, change in Pisa, €9), **Rome** (every 2 hours, 3.5-5 hours, €35-45), **Milan** (about hourly, 3 hours direct or with change in Genoa, €22-29), **Venice** (nearly hourly, 5 hours, 1-3 changes, €50-55).

By Bus to Portovenere: City buses generally depart from Viale Garibaldi (bus #P, 2/hour, 30 minutes, €2.50 each way; bus #11 also makes this trip, but only mid-June-mid-Sept and off-season Sat; buy tickets at tobacco shops or newsstands). From the La Spezia train station, exit left and head downhill, following the street to the first square (Piazza S. Bon). Continue down the pedestrian stretch of Via Fiume to Piazza Garibaldi, then turn right at the fountain in the square onto Viale Garibaldi; the bus stop for Portovenere-bound buses is after the first stoplight on the right side of the street. A timetable is posted by the bus stop.

Carrara

What are perhaps the world's most famous marble quarries are just east of La Spezia in Carrara. Michelangelo himself traveled to these valleys to pick out the marble that he would work into his masterpieces. The towns of the region are dominated by marble. The quarries higher up are vast digs that dwarf the hardworking trucks and machinery coming and going. The **Marble Museum** (Museo Civico del Marmo) traces the story of marble-cutting here from pre-Roman times until today (€4.50, May-Sept Mon-Sat 9:30-13:00 & 15:30-18:00, Oct-April Mon-Sat 9:00-12:30 & 14:30-17:00, closed Sun year-round, Viale XX Settembre 85, tel. 0585-845-746, www.museodelmarmo.com).

For a guided visit, **Sara Paolini** is excellent (€80/half-day tour, mobile 373-711-6695, sarapaolini@hotmail.com). She is accustomed to meeting drivers at the Carrara freeway exit, or she can pick you up at the train station.

Portovenere

While the gritty port of La Spezia offers little in the way of redeeming touristic value, the nearby resort of Portovenere is en-

chanting. This Cinque Terre-esque village clings to a rocky promontory that juts into the sea and protects the harbor from the crashing waves. On the harbor, next to colorful bobbing boats, a row of restaurants—perfect for al fresco dining—feature local specialties such as *trenette* pasta with pesto and *spaghetti con frutti di mare.*

Local boats take you on a 40-minute excursion around three nearby islands or over to Lerici, the town across the bay. Lord Byron swam to Lerici (not recommended). Hardy hikers enjoy the five-hour (or more) hike to Riomaggiore, the nearest Cinque Terre town.

Getting There: Portovenere—not to be confused with Portofino—is an easy day trip from the Cinque Terre by **boat** (mid-

June-Oct, 4-6/day, 1 hour, €13 one-way, €25 day pass includes hopping on and off and either Lerici or a jaunt around three small islands near Portovenere, www.navigazionegolfodeipoeti.it). You can also cruise between Portovenere and Santa Margherita Ligure, with stops in Vernazza and Sestri Levante, using another boat line (www.traghettiportofino.it)—see "Santa Margherita Ligure Connections" on page 485. Pick up a schedule of departures and excursion options from the TI, or ask at your hotel. Or you can take the **bus** from La Spezia (bus #P, 2/hour, 30 minutes, €2.50 each way; bus #11 also makes this trip, but only mid-June-mid-Sept and off-season Sat; in La Spezia buy tickets at tobacco shops or newsstands; in Portovenere get tickets at TI; for directions to the bus stop in La Spezia, see page 495). **Parking** is a nightmare here from May through September, but Albergo Il Genio offers free parking. In peak season, buses shuttle drivers from the parking lot just outside Portovenere to the harborside square. Otherwise, test your luck with the spots on the seaside (€2/hour).

Tourist Information: The TI is easy to find in the main square (daily June-Sept 10:00-12:00 & 15:00-19:45; Oct-May Thu-Tue 10:00-12:00 & 15:00-18:00, closed Wed; Piazza Bastreri 7, tel. 0187-790-691, www.prolocoportovenere.it).

Sleeping in Portovenere: If you've forgotten your yacht, try **$$$ Albergo Il Genio,** in the building where the main street hits the piazza (Db-€100, Qb-€130, some rooms with views, no elevator, guest computer, free parking but request when you reserve, Piazza Bastreri 8, tel. 0187-790-611, www.hotelgenioportovenere.com, info@hotelgenioportovenere.com).

FLORENCE

Firenze

Florence, the home of the Renaissance and birthplace of our modern world, has the best Renaissance art in Europe. In a single day, you could look Michelangelo's *David* in the eyes, fall under the seductive sway of Botticelli's *Birth of Venus,* and climb the modern world's first dome, which still dominates the skyline.

Get your bearings with a Renaissance walk. Florentine art goes beyond paintings and statues—enjoy the food, fashion, and street markets. You can lick Italy's best gelato while enjoying some of Europe's best people-watching.

Planning Your Time

If you're in Italy, Florence deserves at least one well-organized day: see the Accademia *(David),* tour the Uffizi Gallery (Renaissance art), visit the underrated Bargello (best statues), and do the Renaissance Walk (explained on page 523; to avoid heat and crowds, do this walk in the morning or late afternoon). Art lovers will want to chisel out another day of their itinerary for the many other Florentine cultural treasures. Shoppers and ice-cream lovers may need to do the same.

Plan your sightseeing carefully; follow the tips and tricks in this chapter to save time and avoid lines. This is particularly important if you'll be in town for only a day or two during the crowded summer months.

The Uffizi Gallery and Accademia nearly always have long ticket-buying lines, especially in peak season (April-Oct) and on holiday weekends. Crowds thin out on weekdays in the off-season. You can easily avoid the wait by making reservations (see page 518) or buying a Firenze Card (see page 516). Note that both of these major sights are closed on Monday.

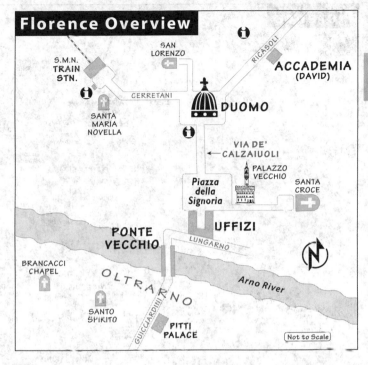

Some sights close early; see the early-closing warning in the "Daily Reminder" on page 506. In general, Sundays and Mondays are not ideal for sightseeing, as many places are either closed or have shorter hours.

Connoisseurs of smaller towns should consider taking the bus to Siena for a day or evening trip (1.25 hours one-way, confirm when last bus returns). Siena is magic after dark. For more information, see the Siena chapter.

Orientation to Florence

The best of Florence lies on the north bank of the Arno River. The main historical sights cluster around the red-brick dome of the cathedral (Duomo). Everything is within a 20-minute walk of the train station, cathedral, or Ponte Vecchio (Old Bridge). The less famous but more characteristic Oltrarno area (south bank) is just over the bridge.

Though small, Florence is intense. Prepare for scorching summer heat, slick pickpockets, few WCs, steep prices, and long lines. Easy tourist money has corrupted some locals, making them greedy and dishonest (check your bill carefully). Visitors to Florence will enjoy the city's newfound passion for traffic-free zones. Once brutal for pedestrians, the city is now a delight on foot.

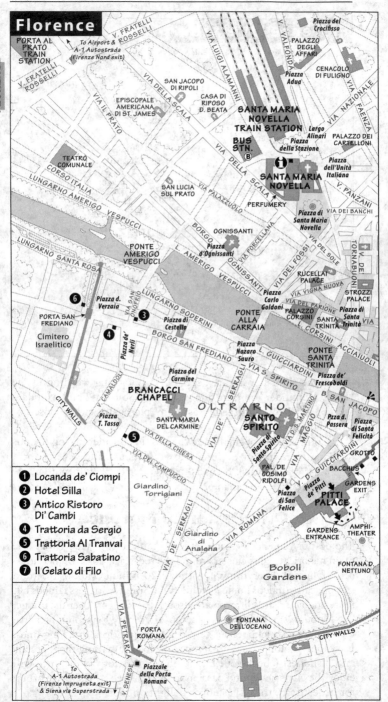

Florence

1 Locanda de' Ciompi
2 Hotel Silla
3 Antico Ristoro Di' Cambi
4 Trattoria da Sergio
5 Trattoria Al Tranvai
6 Trattoria Sabatino
7 Il Gelato di Filo

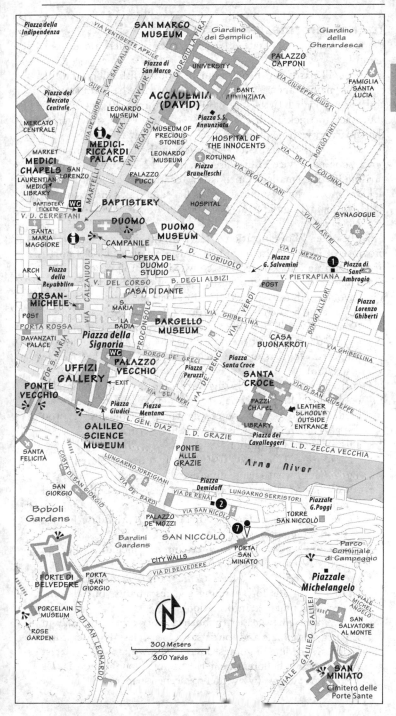

Piazza della Indipendenza

SAN MARCO MUSEUM

Giardino dei Semplici

Giardino della Gherardesca

VIA VENTISETTE APRILE

GIORGIO LA PIRA

PALAZZO CAPPONI

FAMIGLIA SANTA LUCIA

Piazza di San Marco

UNIVERSITY

VIA GIUSEPPE GIUSTI

Piazza del Mercato Centrale

ACCADEMIA (DAVID)

SANT. MINIINZIATA

LEONARDO MUSEUM

VIA DEGLI ARAZZIERI

MERCATO CENTRALE

VIA CAVOUR

VIA RICASOLI

Piazza S.S. Annunziata

MUSEUM OF PRECIOUS STONES

HOSPITAL OF THE INNOCENTS

VIA DELLA COLONNA

MARKET

MEDICI-RICCARDI PALACE

LEONARDO MUSEUM

ROTUNDA

Piazza Brunelleschi

VIA DEGLI ALFANI

BORGO PINTI

MEDICI CHAPELS

SAN LORENZO

PALAZZO PUCCI

VIA PILASTRI

LAURENTIAN MEDICI LIBRARY

MARTELLI

BAPTISTERY TICKETS

WC

BAPTISTERY

HOSPITAL

SYNAGOGUE

V. D. CERRETANI

DUOMO

DUOMO MUSEUM

SANTA MARIA MAGGIORE

CAMPANILE

V. D. L'ORIUOLO

VIA DI MEZZO

OPERA DEL DUOMO STUDIO

Piazza G. Salvemini

POST

Piazza di Sant' Ambrogio

V. PIETRAPIANA

ARCH

Piazza della Repubblica

V. DEL CORSO

B. DEGLI ALBIZI

Piazza Lorenzo Ghiberti

ORSAN-MICHELE

CASA DI DANTE

VIA GHIBELLINA

VIA VERDI

BORGO ALLEGRI

POST

PORTA ROSSA

S. MARIA

LA BADIA

BARGELLO MUSEUM

CASA BUONARROTI

DAVANZATI PALACE

Piazza della Signoria

PROCONSOLO

VIA GHIBELLINA

WC

BORGO DE' GRECI

VIA DE' BENCI

Piazza Santa Croce

VIA DI SAN GIUSEPPE

UFFIZI GALLERY

PALAZZO VECCHIO

Piazza Peruzzi

SANTA CROCE

TOR S. MARIA

EXIT

VIA DEI NERI

PONTE VECCHIO

Piazza Giudici

Piazza Mentana

PAZZI CHAPEL

LEATHER SCHOOL'S OUTSIDE ENTRANCE

L. GEN. DIAZ

LIBRARY

SANTA FELICITÀ

GALILEO SCIENCE MUSEUM

LUNGARNO TORRIGIANI

L. D. GRAZIE

Piazza del Cavalleggeri

L. D. ZECCA VECCHIA

PONTE ALLE GRAZIE

Arno River

COSTA DI SAN GIORGIO

VIA DE' BARDI

Piazza Demidoff

VIA DE' RENAI

Lungarno Serristori

Piazzale G. Poggi

SAN GIORGIO

Boboli Gardens

PALAZZO DE' MOZZI

VIA SAN NICOLÒ

TORRE SAN NICCOLÒ

Parco Comunale di Campeggio

Bardini Gardens

SAN NICCOLÒ

PORTA SAN MINIATO

CITY WALLS

PORTA SAN GIORGIO

VIA DI BELVEDERE

FORTE DI BELVEDERE

PIAZZALE MICHELANGELO

VIALE MICHEL-ANGELO

PORCELAIN MUSEUM

VIA DI SAN LEONARDO

SAN SALVATORE AL MONTE

ROSE GARDEN

N

300 Meters

300 Yards

VIALE GALILEO GALILEI

SAN MINIATO

Cimitero delle Porte Sante

Tourist Information

Florence has two separate TI organizations, which are equally helpful.

One TI has two different branches, both with a focus on the city. The main branch is across the square from the **train station** and very crowded (Mon-Sat 8:30-19:00, Sun 8:30-14:00; with your back to tracks, exit the station—it's 100 yards away, across the square in wall near corner of church at Piazza Stazione 4; if you see a "tourist information" desk inside the train station, it's a hotel-booking service in disguise; tel. 055-212-245, www.firenze-turismo.it). The smaller branch is very centrally located at **Piazza del Duomo,** at the west corner of Via Calzaiuoli (it's inside the Bigallo Museum/Loggia; Mon-Sat 9:00-19:00, Sun 9:00-14:00, tel. 055-288-496).

The other TI organization covers both the city and the greater province of Florence. Its main branch is a couple of blocks **north of the Duomo** and is often less crowded than the others (Mon-Sat 8:30-18:30, closed Sun, just past Medici-Riccardi Palace at Via Cavour 1 red, tel. 055-290-832, international bookstore across street); a second branch is at the **airport** (daily 8:30-20:30).

At any TI, you'll find these free, handy resources in English:

- city map (also ask for the transit map, which has bus routes of interest to tourists on the back; your hotel likely has freebie maps, too)
- current museum-hours listing (very important, since no guidebook—including this one—has ever been able to accurately predict the hours of Florence's sights for the coming year; you can also download this list at www.firenzeturismo.it)
- a list of current exhibitions
- a list of pay (€1) public WCs (generally scarce in Florence)
- a printout of what's happening that day, including concerts
- the compact *Firenze Info* booklet, loaded with useful practical details
- *Firenze: The Places of Interest,* a fold-out with brief descriptions of sightseeing options
- information on events and entertainment, including the TI's monthly *Florence & Tuscany News*
- the glossy monthly *Florence Concierge Information* magazine (stuffed with ads for shopping and restaurants, but also includes some practical information)
- *The Florentine* newspaper (published every other Thursday in English, for expats and tourists, great articles giving cultural insights, schedule of goings-on around town, download latest issue at www.theflorentine.net). A similar publication is *The Florence Newspaper* (www.theflorencenewspaper.com).

The Florence magazine and newspapers just mentioned are often available at hotels throughout town.

The TIs across from the train station and on Via Cavour sell the **Firenze Card,** an expensive but handy sightseeing pass that allows you to skip the lines at top museums (see page 516).

Arrival in Florence
By Train
Florence's main train station is called **Santa Maria Novella** (*Firenze S.M.N.* on schedules and signs). Built in Mussolini's "Rationalism" style back between the wars, in some ways the station seems to have changed little—notice the 1930s-era lettering and architecture.

Florence also has two suburban train stations: **Firenze Rifredi** and **Firenze Campo di Marte.** Note that some trains don't stop at the main station—before boarding, confirm that you're heading for S.M.N., or you may overshoot the city. (If this happens, don't panic; the other stations are a short taxi ride from the center.)

Take advantage of the user-friendly "Fast Ticket" *(Biglietto Veloce)* machines that display schedules, issue tickets, and even make reservations for railpass holders. Some take only credit cards; others take cards and cash. Using them is easy—it actually can be fun; just tap "English." There are two train companies: Trenitalia, with most connections, has green-and-white machines (toll tel. 892-021, www.trenitalia.it); the red machines are for the new high-speed Italo service, run by a private operator (no railpasses accepted, cheaper the further in advance you book, tel. 06-0708, www.italotreno.it).

To get international tickets, you'll need to either go to a ticket window (in the main hall) or a travel agency. To orient yourself to Santa Maria Novella Station and nearby services, stand with your back to the tracks. Look left to see the green cross of a 24-hour pharmacy *(farmacia)* and a small food court. Baggage storage *(deposito bagagli)* is also to the left, halfway down track 16 (€5/5 hours, then €0.70/hour for 6-12 hours and €0.30/hour for over 12 hours, daily 6:00-23:00, passport required, maximum 40 pounds, no explosives—sorry).

Directly ahead of you is the main hall *(salone biglietti,* with ticket windows). WCs (€1) and the Trenitalia information office are to the right, near track 5. The high-speed Italo information office and small waiting room are opposite track 5, near the exit. Avoid the station's fake "Tourist Information" office, funded by hotels, if it's still around. To reach the real TI, walk away from the tracks and exit the station; it's straight across the square, 100 yards away, by the stone church. For cheap eats, the food court near track 16 includes places to get pizza, *paninis,* and simple salads, plus a McDonald's. Alternatively, the handy Margherita/Conad supermarket—with sandwiches and salads to go—is just around the corner (with your back to the tracks, leave the station to the right, go down the steps, and it's immediately on your right on Via Luigi Alamanni; Mon-Sat 7:30-20:30, closed Sun).

Getting to the Duomo and City Center: The Duomo and town center are to your left (with your back to the tracks). Out the doorway to the left, you'll find city buses and the taxi stand. Taxis cost about €8 to the Duomo, and the line moves fast, except on holidays. To walk into town (10-15 minutes), exit the station through the main hall, and head straight across the square outside (toward the Church of Santa Maria Novella). On the far side of the square, keep left and head down the main Via dei Panzani, which leads directly to the Duomo.

By Bus

The bus station is next to the train station, with the TI across the square. Exit the station through the main door, and turn left along the busy street toward the brick dome. The train station is on your left, while downtown Florence is straight ahead and a bit to the right.

By Car

The autostrada has several exits for Florence. Get off at the *Nord, Sud,* or *Certosa* exits and follow signs toward—but not into—the *Centro.*

Don't even attempt driving into the city center. Florence has a traffic-reduction system that's complicated and confusing even to locals. Every car passing into the *Zona Traffico Limitato (ZTL)* is photographed; those who haven't jumped through bureaucratic hoops to get a permit can expect to receive a €100 ticket in the mail (and an "administrative" fee from the rental company). If you get lost and cross the line several times...you get several fines. The no-go zone (defined basically by the old medieval wall, now a boulevard circling the historic center of town—watch for *Zona Traffico Limitato* signs) is roughly the area between the river, main train station, Piazza della Libertà, Piazza Donatello, and Piazza Beccaria. If you think you've crossed the line, and end up parking at a garage, it's worth asking the attendant if there's anything he can do to belatedly register your car (and cancel your ticket).

Parking: The city center is ringed with big, efficient parking lots (signposted with the standard big *P*), each with taxi and bus service into the center. Check www.firenzeparcheggi.it for details on parking lots, availability, and prices. From the freeway, follow

FLORENCE

the signs to *Centro*, then *Stadio*, then *P*. I usually head for "Parcheggio del Parterre," just beyond Piazza della Libertà (€2/hour, €20/day, €65/week, open 24 hours daily, tel. 055-500-1994, 600 spots, automated, pay with cash or credit card, never fills up completely). To get into town, find the taxi stand at the elevator exit, or ride one of the minibuses that connect all of the major parking lots with the city center (see www.ataf.net for routes).

You can park for free along any suburban curb near a bus stop that feels safe and take the bus into the city center from there. Check for signs that indicate parking restrictions—for example, a circle with a slash through it and "*dispari giovedi*, 0,00-06,00" means "don't park on Thursdays between midnight and six in the morning."

Free parking is easy up at Piazzale Michelangelo (see page 546), but don't park where the buses drop off passengers; park on the side of the piazza farthest from the view. To get from Piazzale Michelangelo to the center of town, take bus #12 or #13.

Car Rental: If you're picking up a rental car upon departure, don't struggle with driving into the center. Taxi with your luggage to the car-rental office, and head out from there.

By Plane

Amerigo Vespucci Airport, also called Peretola Airport, is about five miles northwest of the city (open 5:00-23:00, no overnighting allowed, TI, cash machines, car-rental agencies, airport code: FLR, airport info tel. 055-315-874, flight info tel. 055-306-1700—domestic only, www.aeroporto.firenze.it). Shuttle buses (to the far right as you exit the arrivals hall) connect the airport with Florence's BusItalia/SITA bus station, 100 yards west of the train station on Via Santa Caterina da Siena (2/hour, 30 minutes, €6, buy ticket on board and validate immediately, daily 6:00-23:30). If you're changing to a different intercity bus in Florence (for instance, one bound for Siena), stay on the bus through the first stop (at the train station); it will continue on to the bus station nearby. Allow about €25 and 30 minutes for a taxi.

By Cruise Ship

For detailed instructions for arriving at Florence's port, Livorno, see page 582.

Helpful Hints

Theft Alert: Florence has particularly hardworking thief gangs who hang out where you do: near the train station, the station's underpass (especially where the tunnel surfaces), and at major sights. American tourists—especially older ones—are consid-

Daily Reminder

Sunday: The Duomo's dome, Museum of Precious Stones, and Mercato Centrale are closed.

These sights close early: Duomo Museum (at 13:45) and the Baptistery's interior (at 14:00).

A few sights are open only in the afternoon: Duomo (13:30-16:45), Santa Croce Church (14:00-17:30), Church of San Lorenzo (13:30-17:30 except closed Nov-Feb), Brancacci Chapel (13:00-17:00), Church of Santa Maria Novella (12:00-17:00, from 13:00 Oct-June), and Santo Spirito Church (16:00-17:30).

The Museum of San Marco and the Bargello are closed on the first, third, and fifth Sundays of the month. Palazzo Davanzati and the Medici Chapels close on the second and fourth Sundays.

Monday: The biggies are closed, including the Accademia *(David)* and the Uffizi Gallery, as well as the Pitti Palace's Palatine Gallery, Royal Apartments, and Gallery of Modern Art.

The Museum of San Marco and the Bargello close on the second and fourth Mondays. At the Pitti Palace, the Boboli and Bardini Gardens, Argenti/Silverworks Museum, Costume Gallery, and Porcelain Museum close on the first and last Mondays. Palazzo Davanzati and the Medici Chapels are closed on the first, third, and fifth Mondays. The San Lorenzo Market is closed Mondays in winter.

Target these sights on Mondays: the Duomo and its dome, Duomo Museum, Campanile, Baptistery, Medici-Riccardi Palace, Brancacci Chapel, Mercato Nuovo, Mercato Centrale, Casa Buonarroti, Galileo Science Museum, Palazzo Vecchio, and churches (including Santa Croce and Santa Maria Novella). Or take a walking tour.

Tuesday: Casa Buonarroti and the Brancacci Chapel are closed. The Galileo Science Museum closes early (13:00).

Wednesday: All sights are open, except for the Medici-Riccardi

ered easy targets. Some thieves even dress like tourists to fool you. Be on guard at two squares frequented by drug pushers (Santa Maria Novella and Santo Spirito). Bus #7 (to the nearby town of Fiesole, with great Florence views) is a favorite with tourists and, therefore, with thieves.

Medical Help: There's no shortage of English-speaking medical help in Florence. To reach a doctor who speaks English, call **Medical Service Firenze** at 055-475-411; the phone is answered 24/7. Rates are reasonable. For a doctor to come to your hotel within an hour of your call, you'd pay €100-200 (higher rates apply on Sun, holidays, or for late visits). You pay only €50 if you go to the clinic when the doctor's in (Mon-

Palace and Santo Spirito Church.

Thursday: All sights are open, though the following close early: the Palazzo Vecchio (14:00) and, off-season, the Duomo (16:00 May and Oct, 16:30 Nov-April).

Friday: All sights are open.

Saturday: All sights are open, but the Duomo's dome closes earlier than usual, at 17:40.

Early-Closing Warning: Some of Florence's sights close surprisingly early most days. Palazzo Davanzati closes at 13:50, and the Museum of San Marco closes at 13:50 on weekdays (open later on Sat and when open on Sun). Off-season, the Medici Chapels and Bargello close at 13:50. The Museum of Precious Stones closes at 14:00, as does the Mercato Centrale (except in winter, when it stays open until 17:00 on Sat).

Late-Hours Relief: The Accademia and the Pitti Palace's Palatine Gallery, Royal Apartments, and Gallery of Modern Art are open until 18:50 (and the Uffizi until 18:35) daily except Monday.

Several sights are open until 19:00 on certain days: San Lorenzo Market (daily, but closed Mon in winter), the Duomo's dome (Mon-Fri), and the Baptistery (Mon-Sat, except first Sat of month until 14:00).

These sights are open until 19:30: Campanile (daily), Duomo Museum (Mon-Sat), and, in summer, the Pitti Palace's Boboli and Bardini Gardens, Costume Gallery, Argenti/Silverworks Museum, and Porcelain Museum (daily except some Mon, June-Aug only). The Mercato Nuovo is open daily until 20:00, as is the San Miniato Church (but closes at 19:00 in winter).

In summer (April-Sept), the best late-hours sightseeing is at the Palazzo Vecchio, which stays open until 24:00 (except on Thu, when it closes at 14:00); off-season, it's still open relatively late (Fri-Wed until 19:00).

Fri 11:00-12:00, 13:00-15:00 & 17:00-18:00, Sat 11:00-12:00 & 13:00-15:00, closed Sun, no appointment necessary, Via Roma 4, between the Duomo and Piazza della Repubblica).

Dr. Stephen Kerr is an English doctor specializing in helping sick tourists (drop-in clinic open Mon-Fri 15:00-17:00, other times by appointment, €50/visit, Piazza Mercato Nuovo 1, between Piazza della Repubblica and Ponte Vecchio, tel. 055-288-055, mobile 335-836-1682, www.dr-kerr.com). The TI has a list of other English-speaking doctors.

There are 24-hour **pharmacies** at the train station and on Borgo San Lorenzo (near the Baptistery).

Museum Strategies: If you want to see a lot of museums, the pricey

Firenze Card—which saves you from having to wait in line or make reservations for the Uffizi and Accademia—can be a good value (see page 516).

Visiting Churches: Some churches operate like museums, charging an admission fee to see their art treasures. Modest dress for men, women, and even children is required in some churches (including the Duomo, Santa Maria Novella, Santa Croce, Santa Maria del Carmine—with the Brancacci Chapel, and the Medici Chapels). I recommended no bare shoulders, short shorts, or short skirts at any church. Many churches let you borrow or buy a cheap, disposable poncho for instant respectability. Be respectful of worshippers and the paintings; don't use a flash. Churches usually close from 12:00 or 12:30 to 15:00 or 16:00.

Addresses: For reasons beyond human understanding, Florence has a ridiculously confusing system for street addresses, with separate numbering for businesses (red) and residences (black). In print, this designation is sometimes indicated by a letter following the number: "r" = red, for *rosso*; no indication or "n" = black, for *nero*. While usually black, B&Bs can be either. The red and black numbers each appear in roughly consecutive order on streets but bear no apparent connection with one another. While the numbers are sometimes color-coded on street signs, in many cases they appear in neither red nor black, but in blue! I'm lazy and don't concern myself with the distinction (if one number's wrong, I look nearby for the other) and can easily find my way around.

Chill Out: Schedule several breaks into your sightseeing when you can sit, pause, cool off, and refresh yourself with a sandwich, gelato, or coffee. Carry a water bottle to refill at Florence's twist-the-handle public fountains (near the Duomo dome entrance, around the corner from the "Piglet" at the Mercato Nuovo, or in front of the Pitti Palace). Try the *fontanello* (dispenser of free cold water, *frizzante* or *naturale*) on Piazza della Signoria, behind the statue of Neptune (on the left side of the Palazzo Vecchio).

Internet Access: Bustling, tourist-filled Florence has many small Internet cafés. **VIP Internet** has cheap rates, numerous terminals, and long hours (€1.50/hour, daily 9:00-24:00, near recommended hotel Katti House at Via Faenza 49 red, tel. 055-264-5552).

Most hotels have Wi-Fi, as do an increasing number of cafés and restaurants. If you have a smartphone with an Italian mobile number, you can access free Wi-Fi for two hours a day at various hotspots around town, including at most major squares and along the river (the TI can give you a list of hotspots and instructions).

Bookstores: For a good selection of brand-name guidebooks (including mine), try one of these shops. The first two are locally owned and carry only English books. **Paperback Exchange** has the widest selection and also deals in used books (Mon-Fri 9:00-19:30, Sat 10:30-19:30, closed Sun, just south of the Duomo on Via delle Oche 4 red, tel. 055-293-460). **B & M Books & Fine Art** is a bit smaller but also has a great Italian interest section (Tue-Sat 11:00-19:00, closed Sun-Mon, near Ponte alla Carraia at Borgo Ognissanti 4 red, tel. 055-294-575). The local branch of **Feltrinelli International** has a relatively small English section (Mon-Sat 9:00-19:30, closed Sun, a few blocks north of the Duomo, across the street from TI and Medici-Riccardi Palace at Via Cavour 12 red, tel. 055-219-524).

WCs: Public restrooms are scarce. Use them when you can, in any café or museum you patronize. A convenient pay WC (€1) is located near the Duomo, at the Baptistery ticket office.

Laundry: The **Wash & Dry Lavarapido** chain offers long hours and efficient, self-service launderettes at several locations (about €8 for wash and dry, change machine but bring plenty of coins just in case, daily 8:00-22:00, tel 055-580-480). These are close to recommended hotels: Via dei Servi 105 red (near *David*), Via del Sole 29 red and Via della Scala 52 red (between train station and river), Via Ghibellina 143 red (Palazzo Vecchio), and Via dei Serragli 87 red (across the river in Oltrarno neighborhood). For more options, ask the TI for a complete list of launderettes.

Bike Rental: The **city of Florence** rents bikes cheaply at the train station and Piazza Santa Croce (€2/1 hour, €5/5 hours, €10/day, tel. 055-650-5295; information at any TI). **Florence by Bike** rents two-wheelers of all sizes (€3.50/hour, €9/5 hours, includes bike lock and helmet, child seat-€3 extra; Mon-Fri 9:00-13:00 & 15:30-19:30, Sat 9:00-19:00, Sun 9:00-17:00, closed Sun Nov-March; a 15-minute walk north of the Duomo at Via San Zanobi 120 red, tel. 055-488-992, www.florencebybike.it, info@florencebybike.it).

Travel Agency: While it's easy to buy train tickets to destinations within Italy at handy machines at the station, travel agencies can be more convenient and helpful for getting international tickets, reservations, and supplements. The cost may be the same, or there may be a minimal charge. Ask your hotelier for the nearest travel agency.

Updates to this Book: For updates to this book, check www.ricksteves.com/update.

FLORENCE

Getting Around Florence

I organize my sightseeing geographically and do it all on foot. I think of Florence as a Renaissance treadmill—it requires a lot of walking. You likely won't need public transit, except maybe to head up to Piazzale Michelangelo and San Miniato Church for the view, or to Fiesole.

Buses: The city's full-size buses don't cover the old center well (the whole area around the Duomo is off-limits to motorized traffic). The TI hands out a map of transit routes (information also available on their website—www.firenzeturismo.it). Of the many bus lines, I find these to be of most value for seeing outlying sights:

Buses **#12** and **#13** go from the train station to Porta Romana, up to San Miniato Church and Piazzale Michelangelo, and on to Santa Croce.

Bus **#7** goes from Piazza San Marco (near the Accademia and Museum of San Marco) to Fiesole, a small town with big views of Florence.

The train station and Piazza San Marco are two major hubs near the city center; to get between these two, either walk (about 15 minutes) or take bus #1, #6, #14, or #23.

Fun little **minibuses** (many of them electric, *elettrico*) wind through the tangled old center of town and up and down the river—just €1.20 gets you a 1.5-hour joyride. These buses, which run every 10 minutes from 7:00 to 21:00 (less frequent on Sun), are popular with sore-footed sightseers and eccentric local seniors.

Bus **#C1** stops behind the Palazzo Vecchio and Piazza Santa Croce, then heads north, passing near San Marco and the Accademia before ending up at Piazza Libertà.

Bus **#C2** twists through the congested old center from the train station, passing near Piazza della Repubblica and Piazza della Signoria to Piazza Beccaria.

Bus **#C3** goes up and down the Arno River, with stops near Ponte Vecchio, the Carraia bridge to the Oltrarno (including the Pitti Palace), and beyond.

Bus **#D** goes from the train station to Ponte Vecchio, cruises through the Oltrarno (passing the Pitti Palace), and finishes at Ponte San Niccolò.

The minibuses connect many major parking lots with the historical center (tickets sold at machines at lots).

Buy bus tickets at tobacco shops *(tabacchi)*, newsstands, or the ATAF bus office on the west side of the train station (under the "digital" clock) on Piazza della Stazione (€1.20/90 minutes, €4.70/4 tickets, €5/24 hours, €12/3 days, €18/week, day passes aren't always available in tobacco shops, validate in machine on the bus, tel. 800-424-500, www.ataf.net). You can sometimes buy tickets on board, but you'll pay more (€2) and you'll need exact change. City buses are free with the Firenze Card (see page 516). Follow general bus etiquette: Board at front or rear doors, exit out the center.

Taxi: The minimum cost for a taxi ride is €5, or €6 after 22:00 and on Sundays (rides in the center of town should be charged as tariff #1). A taxi ride from the train station to the Duomo costs about €8. Taxi fares and supplements (e.g., €2 extra if you call a cab rather than hail one) are clearly explained on signs in each taxi. Before getting in a cab at a stand or on the street, ask for an approximate cost ("Più o meno, quanto costa?" pew oh MEH-noh, KWAHN-toh KOH-stah). If you can't get a straight answer or the price is outrageous, wait for the next one. It can be hard to find a cab on the street; to call one, dial 055-4390 or 055-4242 (or ask your waiter or hotelier to call for you).

Tours in Florence

Tour companies big and small offer plenty of excursions that go out to smaller towns in the Tuscan countryside (the most popular day trips: Siena, San Gimignano, Pisa, and into Chianti country for wine tasting). Florence city tours are readily available, but for most people, the city really is best on foot (and the book you're holding provides as much information as you'll get with a generic bus tour). To sightsee on your own, download my series of free audio tours that illuminate some of Florence's top sights and neighborhoods: my Renaissance Walk, the Accademia, and the Uffizi Gallery (see sidebar on page 9 for details).

For insight with a personal touch, consider the tour companies and individual Florentine guides listed here. Hardworking and creative, they offer a worthwhile array of organized sightseeing activities. Study their websites for details. If you're taking a city tour, remember that individuals save money with a scheduled public tour (such as those offered daily by Florencetown or ArtViva). If you're traveling as a family or small group, however, you're likely to save money by booking a private guide (since rates are based on roughly €55/hour for any size of group).

Walking (and Biking) Tours
ArtViva Walking Tours
This company offers a variety of tours (up to 12/day year-round) featuring downtown Florence and museum highlights. Their guides are native English speakers. The three-hour "Original Florence" walk hits the main sights while weaving a picture of Florentine life in medieval and Renaissance times. Tours go rain or shine with as few as four participants (€29, daily at 9:15 in high season). Museum tours include the Uffizi Gallery (€49, includes admission,

FLORENCE

Florence at a Glance

▲▲▲**Accademia** Michelangelo's *David* and powerful (unfinished) *Prisoners*. Reserve ahead or get a Firenze Card. **Hours:** Tue-Sun 8:15-18:50, closed Mon. See page 519.

▲▲▲**Duomo Museum** Underrated cathedral museum with sculptures (under renovation until fall of 2015). **Hours:** Mon-Sat 9:00-19:30, Sun 9:00-13:45. See page 531.

▲▲▲**Bargello** Underappreciated sculpture museum (Michelangelo, Donatello, Medici treasures). **Hours:** Tue-Sat 8:15-13:50, until 16:50 during special exhibits (typically April-Oct); also open first, third, and fifth Mon and second and fourth Sun of each month. See page 531.

▲▲▲**Uffizi Gallery** Greatest collection of Italian paintings anywhere. Reserve well in advance or get a Firenze Card. **Hours:** Tue-Sun 8:15-18:35, closed Mon. See page 535.

▲▲**Museum of San Marco** Best collection anywhere of artwork by the early Renaissance master Fra Angelico. **Hours:** Tue-Fri 8:15-13:50, Sat 8:15-16:50; also open 8:15-13:50 on first, third, and fifth Mon and 8:15-16:50 on second and fourth Sun of each month. See page 521.

▲▲**Medici Chapels** Tombs of Florence's great ruling family, designed and carved by Michelangelo. **Hours:** April-Oct Tue-Sat 8:15-16:50, Nov-March Tue-Sat 8:15-13:50; also open second and fourth Mon and first, third, and fifth Sun of each month. See page 524.

▲▲**Duomo** Gothic cathedral with colorful facade and the first dome built since ancient Roman times. **Hours:** Mon-Fri 10:00-17:00, Thu until 16:00 May and Oct, until 16:30 Nov-April; Sat 10:00-16:45, Sun 13:30-16:45. See page 527.

▲▲**Palazzo Vecchio** Fortified palace, once the home of the Medici family, wallpapered with history. **Hours:** Fri-Wed 9:00-19:00, until 24:00 April-Sept, Thu 9:00-14:00 year-round. See page 538.

▲▲**Galileo Science Museum** Fascinating old clocks, telescopes, maps, and three of Galileo's fingers. **Hours:** Wed-Mon 9:30-18:00, Tue 9:30-13:00. See page 540.

▲▲**Santa Croce Church** Precious art, tombs of famous Florentines, and Brunelleschi's Pazzi Chapel in 14th-century church. **Hours:** Mon-Sat 9:30-17:30, Sun 14:00-17:30. See page 540.

▲▲**Church of Santa Maria Novella** Thirteenth-century Dominican church with Masaccio's famous 3-D painting. **Hours:** Mon-Thu 9:00-

17:30, Fri 11:00-17:30, Sat 9:00-17:00, Sun 12:00-17:00 July-Sept (from 13:00 Oct-June). See page 542.

▲▲**Pitti Palace** Several museums in lavish palace plus sprawling Boboli and Bardini Gardens. **Hours:** Palatine Gallery, Royal Apartments, and Gallery of Modern Art open Tue-Sun 8:15-18:50, closed Mon; Boboli and Bardini Gardens, Costume Gallery, Argenti/Silverworks Museum, and Porcelain Museum open daily June-Aug 8:15-19:30, April-May and Sept 8:15-18:30, March and Oct 8:15-17:30, Nov-Feb 8:15-16:30, closed first and last Mon of each month. See page 543.

▲▲**Brancacci Chapel** Works of Masaccio, early Renaissance master who reinvented perspective. **Hours:** Mon and Wed-Sat 10:00-17:00, Sun 13:00-17:00, closed Tue. Reservations required, though often available on the spot. See page 545.

▲▲**San Miniato Church** Sumptuous Renaissance chapel and sacristy showing scenes of St. Benedict. **Hours:** Daily Easter-mid-Oct 8:00-20:00, in winter 8:30-13:00 & 15:30-19:00, closed sporadically for special occasions. See page 547.

▲**Medici-Riccardi Palace** Lorenzo the Magnificent's home, with fine art, frescoed ceilings, and Gozzoli's lovely Chapel of the Magi. **Hours:** Thu-Tue 9:00-18:00, closed Wed. See page 525.

▲**Climbing the Duomo's Dome** Grand view into the cathedral, close-up of dome architecture, and, after 463 steps, a glorious city vista. **Hours:** Mon-Fri 8:30-19:00, Sat 8:30-17:40, closed Sun. See page 527.

▲**Campanile** Bell tower with views similar to Duomo's, 50 fewer steps, and shorter lines. **Hours:** Daily 8:30-19:30. See page 530.

▲**Baptistery** Bronze doors fit to be the gates of paradise. **Hours:** Doors always viewable; interior open Mon-Sat 11:15-19:00 except first Sat of each month 8:30-14:00, Sun 8:30-14:00. See page 530.

▲**Ponte Vecchio** Famous bridge lined with gold and silver shops. **Hours:** Bridge always open (shops closed at night). See page 539.

▲**Casa Buonarroti** Small collection of lesser-known works by Michelangelo. **Hours:** Wed-Mon 10:00-17:00, closed Tue. See page 541.

▲**Piazzale Michelangelo** Hilltop square with stunning view of Duomo and Florence, with San Miniato Church just uphill. **Hours:** Always open. See page 547.

2 hours), Accademia (called "Original *David*" tour, €36, includes admission, 1 hour), and "Original Florence in One Day" (€99, includes admission to Uffizi and Accademia plus 3-hour town walk, 6 hours). Their brochure and website list more activities, including an "Inferno" tour, biking and hiking tours, food and wine tours, and cooking classes. They also offer minibus tours throughout Tuscany (including a villa swim tour) and Cinque Terre day trips (Mon-Sat 8:00-18:00, Sun 8:30-13:30, near Piazza della Repubblica at Via de' Sassetti 1, second floor, above Odeon Cinema, tel. 055-264-5033 during day or mobile 329-613-2730 from 18:00-20:00, www.artviva.com).

Florencetown Tours on Foot or by Bike

This well-organized company runs a variety of English-language tours. The boss, Luca Perfetto, offers student rates (10 percent discount) to anyone with this book, with an additional 10 percent off for second tours (if booking on their website, enter the code "RICKSTEVES2014" when prompted). Three tours—their basic town walk, bike tour, and cooking class—are worth considering: The "Walk and Talk Florence" tour, which takes 2.5 hours, hits all the basic spots, including the Oltrarno neighborhood (€19, daily at 10:00). The "I Bike Florence" tour gives you 2.5 hours on a vintage one-speed bike following a fast-talking guide on a blitz of the town's top sights (€25, daily at 10:00 and 15:00, helmets optional, 15 stops on both sides of the river; in bad weather, the bike tours go as a walking tour). The cooking class includes a market tour (see listing later). Their office is two blocks from the Palazzo Vecchio at Via de Lamberti 1 (find steps off Via de' Calzaiuoli on the river side of Orsanmichele Church); they also have a "Tourist Point" kiosk on Piazza della Repubblica, under the arches at the corner with Via Pellicceria (tel. 055-012-3994, www.florencetown.com).

Walks Inside Florence

Three art historians—Paola Barubiani and her partners Emma Molignoni and Marzia Valbonesi—provide quality guiding. Their company offers a daily 2.5-hour introductory tour (€50/person, 6 people maximum; outside except for a visit to see *David*, Accademia entry fee not included) and three-hour private tours (€180, €60/hour for more time, price is for groups of up to 4 people). They also offer an artisans-and-shopping tour, a guided evening walk, cooking classes with a market visit, private cruise excursions from the port of Livorno, and more—see their website for details (ask about Rick Steves rate for any tour, Paola's mobile 335-526-6496, www.walksinsideflorence.com, paola@walksinsideflorence.it).

Florentia

Top-notch private walking tours—geared for thoughtful, well-heeled travelers with longer-than-average attention spans—are led by Florentine scholars. The tours range from introductory city walks and museum visits to in-depth thematic walks, such as the Oltrarno neighborhood, Jewish Florence, and family-oriented tours (tours start at €250, includes personal assistance by email as you plan your trip, reserve in advance, www.florentia.org, info@florentia.org).

Context Florence

This scholarly group of graduate students and professors leads "walking seminars," such as a 3.5-hour study of Michelangelo's work and influence (€80/person, plus museum admission) and a two-hour evening orientation stroll (€65/person). I enjoyed the fascinating three-hour fresco workshop (€75/person plus materials, you take home a fresco you make yourself). See their website for other innovative offerings: Medici walk, lecture series, food walks, kids' tours, and other programs throughout Europe (tel. 06-9672-7371, US tel. 800-691-6036, www.contexttravel.com, info@contexttravel.com).

Cooking Classes and Market Tours

For something special, consider this five-hour experience offered by **Florencetown.** You'll start with a trip to the Mercato Centrale for shopping and tasting, then settle into their kitchen for a cooking lesson that finishes with a big feast eating everything you cooked. You'll meet butchers and bakers, and make bruschetta, pasta, a main course, and dessert (likely tiramisù). Groups are intimate and small (1-25 people, €85/person, for 10 percent discount use the code "RICKSTEVES2014," Mon-Sat 10:00-15:00, runs rain or shine, chef Giovanni, Via de Lamberti 1, tel. 055-012-3994, www.florencetown.com). They also offer a three-hour pizza- and gelato-making class (€45, daily at 18:00).

Note that most of the tour companies recommended earlier offer similar classes.

Local Guides for Private Tours

Alessandra Marchetti, a Florentine who has lived in the US, gives private walking tours of Florence and driving tours of Tuscany (€60-75/hour, mobile 347-386-9839, aleoberm@tin.it).

Paola Migliorini and her partners offer museum tours, city walking tours, private cooking classes, wine tours, and Tuscan excursions by van—you can tailor tours as you like (€60/hour without car, €70/hour in an 8-seat van, tel. 055-472-448, mobile 347-657-2611, www.florencetour.com, info@florencetour.com); they also do private tours from the cruise-ship port of Livorno.

Roberto Bechi, a great guide based in Siena, can come pick you up in Florence for off-the-beaten-path tours of the Tuscan countryside (see contact information on page 636).

Hop-on, Hop-off Bus Tours

Around town, you'll see big double-decker sightseeing buses double-parking near major sights. Tourists on the top deck can listen to brief recorded descriptions of the sights, snap photos, and enjoy a drive-by look at major landmarks (€20/1 calendar day, €25/48 hours, pay as you board, www.firenze.city-sightseeing.it). As the name implies, you can hop off when you want and catch the next bus (usually every 30 minutes, less frequently off-season). But since the most important sights are buried in the old center where big buses can't go, Florence doesn't really lend itself to this kind of tour bus. Look at the route map before committing.

Driving Tours

500 Touring Club offers a unique look at Florence: from behind the wheel of one of the most iconic Italian cars, a vintage, restored Fiat 500. After a lesson in *la doppietta* (double-clutching), you'll head off in a guided convoy, following a lead car with live radio commentary and photo stops at the best viewpoints. Tours depart from a 15th-century villa on the edge of town; the tiny Fiats are restored models from the 1960s and 1970s. Itineraries vary from basic sightseeing to countryside excursions with wine-making and lunch; see their website for options (classic 2.5 hour tour-€70/person, US tel. 347/535-0030, Italian mobile 346-826-2324, Via Gherardo Silvani 149a, www.500touringclub.com, info@500touringclub.com, Andrea).

Weekend Tour Packages for Students

Andy Steves (my son) runs **Weekend Student Adventures,** offering active and experiential three-day weekend tours from €199, designed for American students abroad (see www.wsaeurope.com for details on tours of Florence and other great cities).

Sights in Florence

Sightseeing Strategies

Florence offers several options to help you bypass the lengthy ticket-buying lines that can plague its most popular sights in peak season. You can spend less time in line and more time seeing the sights if you make use of Florence's official sightseeing pass (the Firenze Card) or make advance reservations.

Firenze Card

The Firenze Card (€72) is pricey but convenient. This three-day sightseeing pass gives you admission to many of Florence's sights, including the Uffizi Gallery and Accademia. Just as important, it lets you skip the ticket-buying lines without making reservations.

FLORENCE

For busy sightseers, the card can save some money. And for anyone, it can certainly save time.

With the card, you simply go to the entrance at a covered sight (if there's a "with reservations" door, use it), show the card, and they let you in (though there still may be  delays at popular sights with bottleneck entryways or capacity limits). At some sights, you must first present your card at the ticket booth or information desk to get a physical ticket before proceeding to the entrance. For people seeing five or six major sights in a short time, the card is well worth it. (But if you only want to see the Uffizi and Accademia, you'll save by making individual reservations instead; see "Advance Reservations," later.)

The Firenze Card is valid for 72 hours from when you validate it at your first museum (e.g., Tue at 15:00 until Fri at 15:00). It covers the regular admission price as well as any special-exhibit surcharges (which are commonly tacked on at major sights such as the Uffizi). The card is good for one visit per sight. It also gives you free use of Florence city buses. The card is not shareable, and there are no family or senior discounts for Americans or Canadians.

Getting the card makes the most sense in peak season, from April through October, when crowds are worst. Off-season travelers could do without it. To figure out if the card is a good deal for you, tally up the entry fees for what you want to see. Here's a sampling of popular sights and their ticket prices:

- Uffizi Gallery (€6.50, €11 with special exhibits, plus €4 fee if reserved ahead)
- Accademia (same as Uffizi, above)
- Palazzo Vecchio (€6.50, €10 with the tower)
- Bargello (€4, €7 with exhibits)
- Medici Chapels (€6, €9 with exhibits)
- Museum of San Marco (€4)
- Medici-Riccardi Palace (€7)
- Duomo sights: Baptistery, Campanile, dome climb, Duomo Museum (€10)
- Pitti Palace sights: Palatine Gallery and Royal Apartments (€8.50), Boboli and Bardini Gardens (€7)

Other covered sights featured in this book include the Brancacci Chapel, Church of Santa Maria Novella (including its museum), Santa Croce Church, Casa Buonarroti, Casa di Dante, Museum of Precious Stones, Palazzo Davanzati, Galileo Science Museum, and the Fiesole Archaeological Area. The card is great for popping into lesser sights you otherwise wouldn't pay for. For a complete list of included sights, see www.firenzecard.it.

Many outlets around town sell the card, including the TIs at the train station and at Via Cavour 1 red (a couple of blocks north of the Duomo) and at some sights: the Uffizi Gallery's door #2 (enter to the left of the ticket-buying line), back entrance of Santa Maria Novella (near the train station), Bargello, Palazzo Vecchio, and Brancacci Chapel. Lines are shortest at the Via Cavour TI and the Church of Santa Maria Novella (around back at Piazza della Stazione 4); if you're doing the Uffizi first, door #2 is relatively quick. You can also pay for the card online (www.firenzecard.it), obtain a voucher, and pick up the card at any of the above locations.

Validate your card only when you're ready to tackle the covered sights on three consecutive days. Make sure the sights you want to visit will be open (many sights are closed Sun or Mon). For details, see the "Daily Reminder" on page 506.

Advance Reservations

If you don't get a Firenze Card, it's smart to make reservations at the often-crowded Accademia and Uffizi Gallery. Some other Florence sights—including the Bargello, Medici Chapels, and Pitti Palace—have reservation systems, but it's not essential to book ahead for these.

The Brancacci Chapel officially "requires" a reservation, but it's usually possible to walk right in and get an entry time on weekdays or any day off-season, especially before 15:30 (for details, see page 546).

Accademia and Uffizi Reservations

Get reservations for these two top sights as soon as you know when you'll be in town. You can generally get an entry time for the Accademia a few days before your visit, but reserve for the Uffizi well in advance. Without a reservation at the Accademia and Uffizi, you can usually enter without significant lines from November through March after 16:00. But from April through October and on weekends, it can be crowded even late in the day. Any time of year, I'd consider reserving a spot.

There are several ways to make a reservation:

• **By Phone:** For either sight, reserve by phone before you leave the States (from the US, dial 011-39-055-294-883, or within Italy call 055-294-883; €4/ticket reservation fee; booking office open Mon-Fri 8:30-18:30, Sat 8:30-12:30, closed Sun). The reservation line is often busy. Be persistent. When you get through, an English-speaking operator walks you through the process—a few minutes later you say *grazie*, having secured an entry time and a confirmation number. You'll present your confirmation number at the museum and pay cash for your ticket. Note that you pay nothing up front when you reserve by phone.

• **Online:** Using a credit card, you can reserve your Accademia or Uffizi visit online through the city's official site (€4/ticket reservation fee, www.firenzemusei.it). To start, click on the gray "B-ticket" strip, and make sure you "Add" your ticket to the cart before you "Buy" it. You'll receive an immediate confirmation email, which is followed within three days by a voucher. Bring your voucher to the ticket desk to swap for an actual ticket.

Pricey middleman sites—such as www.uffizi.com and www.tickitaly.com—are reliable and more user-friendly than the official site, but their booking fees run about €10 per ticket. (Tip: When ordering from these broker sites, don't confuse Florence's Accademia with Venice's gallery of the same name.)

• **Through Your Hotel:** When you make your hotel reservation, ask if they can book your museum reservations for you (some hoteliers will do this for free; others charge a €3-5 fee in addition to the reservation fee; they'll probably give you a confirmation number that you'll take to the museum, where you'll pay cash for your ticket).

• **Private Tour:** Take a tour that includes your museum admission. For example, ArtViva Walking Tours offers tours of the Uffizi (€39/person, 2 hours), Accademia (€35/person, 1 hour), and both museums (€94/person, 6 hours including 3-hour town walk; see listing on page 511).

• **Last-Minute Strategies:** If you arrive without a reservation, call the reservation number (see "By Phone" earlier); ask your hotelier for help; or head to a booking window, either at Orsanmichele Church (€4 reservation fee, daily 10:00-17:00, along Via de' Calzaiuoli—see location on map on page 522) or at the My Accademia Libreria bookstore across from the Accademia's exit (€4 reservation fee, Tue-Sun 8:15-17:30, closed Mon, Via Ricasoli 105 red—see map on page 528). It's also possible to go to the Uffizi's official ticket office (use door #2 and skirt to the left of the long ticket-buying line), ask if they have any short-notice reservations available, and pay cash (€4 fee, Tue-Sun 8:15-18:35).

Sights North of the Arno River
North of the Duomo
▲▲▲Accademia (Galleria dell'Accademia)

This museum houses Michelangelo's *David*, the consummate Renaissance statue of the buff, biblical shepherd boy ready to take on the giant. When you look into the eyes of this magnificent sculpture, you're looking into the eyes of Renaissance Man.

In 1501, Michelangelo Buonarroti, a 26-year-old Florentine, was commissioned to carve a large-scale work. The figure comes from a Bible story. The Israelites are surrounded by barbarian warriors, who are led by a brutish giant named Goliath. When the

FLORENCE

giant challenges the Israelites to send out someone to fight him, a young shepherd boy steps forward. Armed only with a sling, David defeats the giant. This 17-foot-tall symbol of divine victory over evil represents a new century and a whole new Renaissance outlook.

Originally, *David* was meant to stand on the roofline of the Duomo, but it was placed more prominently at the entrance of Palazzo Vecchio (where a copy stands today). In the 19th century, *David* was moved indoors for his own protection, and stands under a wonderful Renaissance-style dome designed just for him.

Nearby are some of the master's other works, including his powerful (unfinished) *Prisoners, St. Matthew,* and a *Pietà* (possibly by one of his disciples). Florentine Michelangelo Buonarroti, who would work tirelessly through the night, believed that the sculptor was a tool of God, responsible only for chipping away at the stone until the intended sculpture emerged. Beyond the magic marble are some mildly interesting pre-Renaissance and Renaissance paintings, including a couple of lighter-than-air Botticellis, the plaster model of Giambologna's *Rape of the Sabine Women,* and a musical instrument collection with an early piano.

Cost and Hours: €6.50, €11 with mandatory special exhibits, additional €4 for recommended reservation, covered by Firenze Card; Tue-Sun 8:15-18:50, closed Mon, last entry 30 minutes before closing; audioguide-€6, Rick Steves audio tour available—see page 9, Via Ricasoli 60, reservation tel. 055-294-883, www.polo-museale.firenze.it. To avoid long lines in peak season, get the Firenze Card or make reservations (see page 518).

Nearby: Piazza S.S. Annunziata, behind the Accademia, displays lovely Renaissance harmony. Facing the square are two fine

buildings: the 15th-century Santissima Annunziata church (worth a peek) and Filippo Brunelleschi's Hospital of the Innocents (Spedale degli Innocenti, not worth going inside), with terra-cotta medallions by Luca della Robbia. Built in the 1420s, the hospital is considered the first Renaissance building. I love sleeping on this square (at the recommended Hotel Loggiato dei Serviti) and picnicking here during the day (with the riffraff, who remind me of the persistent gap— today as in Medici times—between those who appreciate fine art and those just looking for some cheap wine).

▲▲Museum of San Marco (Museo di San Marco)

Located one block north of the Accademia, this 15th-century monastery houses the greatest collection anywhere of frescoes and paintings by the early Renaissance master Fra Angelico. The ground floor features the monk's paintings, along with some works

by Fra Bartolomeo. Upstairs are 43 cells decorated by Fra Angelico and his assistants. While the monk/painter was trained in the medieval religious style, he also learned and adopted Renaissance techniques and sensibilities, producing works that blended Christian symbols and Renaissance realism. Don't miss the cell of Savonarola, the charismatic monk who rode in from the Christian right, threw out the Medici, turned Florence into a theocracy, sponsored "bonfires of the vanities" (burning books, paintings, and so on), and was finally burned himself when Florence decided to change channels.

Cost and Hours: €4, covered by Firenze Card, Tue-Fri 8:15-13:50, Sat 8.15-16:50; also open 8:15-13:50 on first, third, and fifth Mon and 8:15-16:50 on second and fourth Sun of each month; last entry 30 minutes before closing, reservations possible but unnecessary, on Piazza San Marco, tel. 055-238-8608, www.polomuseale.firenze.it.

Museum of Precious Stones (Museo dell'Opificio delle Pietre Dure)

This unusual gem of a museum features room after room of exquisite mosaics of inlaid marble and other stones. The Medici loved colorful stone tabletops and floors; you'll even find landscapes and portraits (find Cosimo I in Room I). Upstairs, you'll see wooden work benches from the Medici workshop (1588), complete with foot-powered power tools. Rockhounds can browse 500 different stones (lapis lazuli, quartz, agate, marble, and so on) and the tools used to cut and inlay them. Borrow the English descriptions in each room.

Cost and Hours: €4, covered by Firenze Card, Mon-Sat 8:15-14:00, closed Sun, last entry 30 minutes before closing, around corner from Accademia at Via degli Alfani 78, tel. 055-265-1357, www.opificiodellepietredure.it.

Church of San Lorenzo

This red-brick dome—which looks like the Duomo's little sister—was the parish church of the Medici and is the burial place of the family's founder, Giovanni di Bicci de' Medici (1360-1429).

FLORENCE

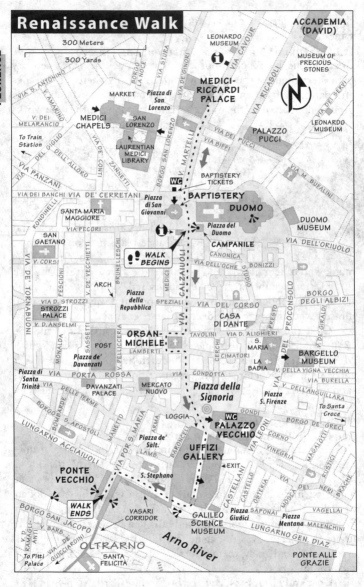

Renaissance Walk

300 Meters
300 Yards

ACCADEMIA (DAVID)

LEONARDO MUSEUM

MUSEUM OF PRECIOUS STONES

VIA STURA

VIA DE'GINORI

VIA CAVOUR

VIA RICASOLI

VIA DEI SERVI

MEDICI-RICCARDI PALACE

VIA S. ANTONINO

V. AMARINO

BORGO LA NOCE

Piazza di San Lorenzo

MARKET

MEDICI CHAPELS

V. DEI MELARANCIO

SAN LORENZO

VIA DE' PUCCI

PALAZZO PUCCI

LEONARDO MUSEUM

VIA M. BUFALINI

To Train Station

DEL GIGLIO

DELL'ALLORO

VIA DE' CONTI

VIA DE' ZANETTI

LAURENTIAN MEDICI LIBRARY

BORGO SAN LORENZO

VIA MARTELLI

VIA BIFFI

VIA PANZANI

WC

BAPTISTERY TICKETS

VIA DEI BANCHI VIA DE' CERRETANI

RONDINELLI

SANTA MARIA MAGGIORE

VIA PECORI

Piazza di San Giovanni

WC

BAPTISTERY

DUOMO

DUOMO MUSEUM

SAN GAETANO

VIA DE' CORSI

VIA DE' VECCHIETTI

BRUNELLESCHI

Piazza del Duomo

CAMPANILE

VIA DELL'ORIUOLO

VIA DE' TORNABUONI

ARCH

VIA D. STROZZI

STROZZI PALACE

V. D. ANSELMI

SASSETTI

FESCIONI

Piazza della Repubblica

MEDICI

SPEZIALI

CANONICA

VIA DELL'OCHE

STUDIO

BONIZZI

WALK BEGINS

VIA CALZAIUOLI

VIA DEL CORSO

CASA DI DANTE

BORGO DEGLI ALBIZI

VIA DEL PROCONSOLO

VIA DE' GIRALDI

POST

MONALDA

ORSAN-MICHELE

LAMBERTI

Piazza de' Davanzati

K. FELLICCERIA

TAVOLINI

VIA D. ALIGHIERI

VERCHI

S. MARIA LA BADIA

CIMATORI

BARGELLO MUSEUM

VIA DELLA VIGNA VECCHIA

VIA BURELLA

Piazza di Santa Trinita

VIA PORTA ROSSA

DAVANZATI PALACE

DELLE TERME

MERCATO NUOVO

CONDOTTA

Piazza della Signoria

Piazza S. Firenze

V. DELL'ANGUILLARA

To Santa Croce

BORGO DE' GRECI

LUNGARNO ACCIAIUOLI

BORGO S. APOSTOLI

MANETTO

VIA POR S. MARIA

PARMA

BARONCELLI

LOGGIA

WC

PALAZZO VECCHIO

GONDI

LEONI

CORNO

VINEGRIA

PONTE VECCHIO

WALK ENDS

VASARI CORRIDOR

Piazza de' Salt.

LAMB.

S. Stephano

UFFIZI GALLERY

EXIT

CASTELLANI

OSTERIA

VIA DEI NERI

BRACHE

MOSCA

BORGO SAN JACOPO

V. D. RAMAGLI ANTI

VIA DE' BARDI

VIA DE' GUICCIARDINI

GALILEO SCIENCE MUSEUM

Piazza Giudici

SAPONAI

Piazza Mentana

MALENCHINI

VAGELLAI

To Pitti Palace

SANTA FELICITA

OLTRARNO

Arno River

LUNGARNO GEN. DIAZ

PONTE ALLE GRAZIE

N

Brunelleschi designed the building, and Donatello worked on the
bronze pulpits inside. The Medici Chapels, with Michelangelo's
famous tomb sculptures, are part of the church complex (see listing, later).

Cost and Hours: €3.50, buy ticket just inside cloister to the
left of the facade, €6 combo-ticket covers Laurentian Medici Library; Mon-Sat 10:00-17:30, Sun 13:30-17:30 March-Oct, closed

A Renaissance Walk Through Florence

During the Dark Ages, it was especially obvious to the people of Italy—sitting on the rubble of Rome—that there had to be a brighter age on the horizon. The long-awaited rebirth, or Renaissance, began in Florence for good reason. Wealthy because of its cloth industry, trade, and banking; powered by a fierce city-state pride (locals would pee into the Arno with gusto, knowing rival city-state Pisa was downstream); and fertile with more than its share of artistic genius (imagine guys like Michelangelo and Leonardo attending the same high school)—Florence was a natural home for this cultural explosion.

Take a two-hour walk through the core of Renaissance Florence from the Duomo (cathedral) to Ponte Vecchio on the Arno River. You can download a free Rick Steves audio tour of this walk (see page 9).

Begin at the Duomo to marvel at the dome that kicked off the architectural Renaissance. Step inside the Baptistery to view a ceiling covered with preachy, flat, 2-D, medieval mosaic art. Then, to learn what happened when art met math, check out the realistic 3-D reliefs on the doors; the man who painted them, Giotto, also designed the bell tower—an early example of a Renaissance genius who excelled in many areas.

Continue toward the river on Florence's great pedestrian mall, Via de' Calzaiuoli—part of the original grid plan given to the city by the ancient Romans. Stop by any gelato shop for some cool refreshment. Down a few blocks, compare medieval and Renaissance statues on the exterior of the Orsanmichele Church. Via de' Calzaiuoli connects the cathedral with the central square (Piazza della Signoria); the city palace (Palazzo Vecchio); and the Uffizi Gallery, which contains the greatest collection of Italian Renaissance paintings in captivity. Finally, walk through the Uffizi courtyard—a statuary think tank of Renaissance greats—to the Arno River and Ponte Vecchio.

Sun Nov-Feb; last entry 30 minutes before closing, on Piazza di San Lorenzo, tel. 055-214-042, www.operamedicealaurenziana.it.

Visiting the Church: The exterior is big, ugly, and unfinished because Pope Leo X (also a Medici) pulled the plug on the project due to dwindling funds—after Michelangelo had labored on a facade plan for four years (1516-1520). Inside, though, is the spirit of Florence in the 1420s, with gray-and-white columns and arches

in perfect Renaissance symmetry and simplicity. Brunelleschi designed the church interior to receive an even, diffused light. The Medici coat of arms (a gold shield with six round balls) decorates the ceiling, and everywhere are images of St. Lawrence, the Medici patron saint who was martyred on a grill.

Highlights of the church include two finely sculpted Donatello pulpits (in the nave). In the Martelli Chapel (left wall of the left transept), Filippo Lippi's *Annunciation* features a smiling angel greeting Mary in a sharply 3-D courtyard. Light shines through the vase in the foreground, like the Holy Spirit entering Mary's womb. The Old Sacristy (far-left corner), designed by Brunelleschi, was the burial chapel for the Medici. Bronze doors by Donatello flank the sacristy's small altar. Overhead, the dome above the altar shows the exact arrangement of the heavens on July 4, 1442, leaving scholars to hypothesize about why that particular date was used. Back in the nave, the round inlaid marble in the floor before the main altar marks where Cosimo the Elder—Lorenzo the Magnificent's grandfather—is buried. Assistants in the church provide information on request, and the information brochure is free and in English.

Other Church Sights: Outside the church, just to the left of the main door, is a **cloister** with peek-a-boo Duomo views and the **San Lorenzo Museum.** This collection of fancy reliquaries is included in your church admission, but is hardly worth the walk, except to see Donatello's grave. Also in the cloister is the **Laurentian Medici Library** (€3, €6 combo-ticket with church, generally open Mon-Sat 9:30-13:00, closed Sun, tel. 055-210-760, www.bmlonline.it). The library, largely designed by Michelangelo, stars his impressive staircase, which widens imperceptibly as it descends. Michelangelo also did the walls in the vestibule (entrance) that feature empty niches, scrolls, and oddly tapering pilasters. Climb the stairs and enter the Reading Room—a long, rectangular hall with a coffered-wood ceiling—designed by Michelangelo to host scholars enjoying the Medici's collection of manuscripts.

Nearby: A **street market** bustles outside the church (see listing, later). Around the back end of the church is the entrance to the Medici Chapels and the New Sacristy, designed by Michelangelo for a later generation of dead Medici.

▲▲Medici Chapels (Cappelle Medicee)

The burial site of the ruling Medici family in the Church of San Lorenzo includes the dusky Crypt; the big, domed Chapel of Princes; and the magnificent New Sacristy, featuring architecture, tombs, and statues almost entirely by Michelangelo. The Medici made their money in textiles and banking, and patronized a dream team of Renaissance artists that put Florence on the cultural map. Michelangelo, who spent his teen years living with the Medici, was commissioned to create the family's final tribute.

Cost and Hours: €6, €9 with mandatory exhibits, covered by Firenze Card; April-Oct Tue-Sat 8:15-16:50, Nov-March Tue-Sat 8:15-13:50; also open second and fourth Mon and first, third, and fifth Sun of each month; last entry 30 minutes before closing; reservations possible but unnecessary, audioguide-€6 (€10/2 people), modest dress required, no photos, tel. 055-238-8602, www.polomuseale.firenze.it.

▲San Lorenzo Market

Florence's vast open-air market sprawls around the Church of San Lorenzo. Most of the leather stalls are run by Iranians selling South American leather that was tailored in Italy. Prices are soft (daily 9:00-19:00, closed Mon in winter, between the Duomo and train station).

▲Mercato Centrale (Central Market)

Florence's giant iron-and-glass-covered central market, a wonderland of picturesque produce, is fun to explore. While the nearby San Lorenzo Market—with its garment stalls in the streets—feels like a step up from a haphazard flea market, the Mercato Centrale retains a Florentine elegance. Wander around. You'll see parts of the cow you'd never dream of eating (no, that's not a turkey neck), enjoy generous free samples, watch pasta being made, and have your pick of plenty of fun eateries sloshing out cheap and tasty pasta to locals (Mon-Fri 7:00-14:00, Sat 7:00-17:00, closed Sun). For eating ideas in and around the market, see "Eating in Florence," later.

▲Medici-Riccardi Palace (Palazzo Medici-Riccardi)

Lorenzo the Magnificent's home is worth a look for its art. The tiny Chapel of the Magi contains colorful Renaissance gems such as the *Procession of the Magi* frescoes by Benozzo Gozzoli. The former library has a Baroque ceiling fresco by Luca Giordano, a prolific artist from Naples known as "Fast Luke" *(Luca fa presto)* for his speedy workmanship. While the Medici

originally occupied this 1444 house, in the 1700s it became home to the Riccardi family, who added the Baroque flourishes. While the palace is rarely mobbed, you may encounter a slight bottleneck at the Chapel of the Magi (Cappella di Gozzoli). Only 10 people are allowed in at a time, but the line moves quickly.

Cost and Hours: €7, covered by Firenze Card, Thu-Tue 9:00-18:00, closed Wed, last entry 30 minutes before closing, ticket entrance is north of the main gated entrance, videoguide-€4, no photos in Chapel of the Magi, Via Cavour 3, tel. 055-276-0340, www.palazzo-medici.it.

Leonardo Museums

Two different-but-similar entrepreneurial establishments—Le Macchine di Leonardo da Vinci and Museo Leonardo da Vinci—are several blocks apart and show off reproductions of Leonardo's ingenious inventions. Either one is fun for anyone who wants to crank the shaft and spin the ball bearings of Leonardo's fertile imagination. While there are no actual historic artifacts, each museum shows several dozen of Leonardo's inventions and experiments made into working models. You might see a full-size armored tank, walk into a chamber of mirrors, operate a rotating crane, or watch experiments in flying. The exhibits are described in English, and you're encouraged to touch and play with many of the models—it's great for kids. The Museo has larger scale models; Le Macchine has better visitor information.

Cost and Hours: Le Macchine di Leonardo da Vinci—€7, €2 discount with this book, April-Oct daily 9:30-19:30; Nov-March Mon-Fri 11:00-17:00, Sat-Sun 9:30-19:30; for €1 extra they'll throw in a slice of pizza and a Coke, in Galleria Michelangelo at Via Cavour 21; tel. 055-295-264, www.macchinedileonardo.com. **Museo Leonardo da Vinci**—€7, €0.50 discount with this book, daily April-Oct 10:00-19:00, Nov-March 10:00-18:00, Via dei Servi 66 red, tel. 055-282-966, www.mostredileonardo.com.

Duomo and Nearby

The following Duomo-related sights are all covered by a single combo-ticket (€10, sold at all of the sights and also online, www.operaduomo.firenze.it). This ticket admits you to the Baptistery, Dome, Campanile, Duomo Museum, and church crypt (the Duomo itself is free). The rarely crowded Duomo Museum and the Centro Arte e Cultura (a few steps north of the Baptistery at Piazza di San Giovanni 7) can be good places to buy your ticket.

FLORENCE

The Firenze Card (see page 516) also covers all of these sights (except the uninteresting crypt).

▲▲Duomo (Cattedrale di Santa Maria del Fiore)

Florence's Gothic cathedral has the third-longest nave in Christendom. The church's noisy neo-Gothic facade from the 1870s is covered with pink, green, and white Tuscan marble. In the interior, you'll see a huge *Last Judgment* by Giorgio Vasari and Federico Zuccari (inside the dome). Much of the church's great art is stored behind the church in the Duomo Museum (which is partially closed for renovation until 2015).

The cathedral's claim to artistic fame is Brunelleschi's magnificent dome—the first Renaissance dome and the model for domes to follow. Think of the confidence of the age: The Duomo was built with a big hole in its roof, awaiting a dome...but it was built before the technology to span the hole with a dome even existed. No *problema.* They knew that someone soon could rise to the challenge...and local architect Filippo Brunelleschi did. First, he built the grand white skeletal ribs, which you can see, then filled them in with interlocking bricks in a herringbone pattern. The dome grew upward like an igloo, supporting itself as it proceeded from the base. When the ribs reached the top, Brunelleschi arched them in and fixed them in place with the cupola at the top. His dome, built in only 14 years, was the largest since Rome's Pantheon.

Massive crowds line up to see the huge church: Although it's a major sight (and free), it's not worth a long wait. To avoid the lines, go late, as crowds subside by late afternoon.

Cost and Hours: Cathedral interior—free; Mon-Fri 10:00-17:00, Thu until 16:00 May and Oct, until 16:30 Nov-April; Sat 10:00-

16:45, Sun 13:30-16:45, audioguide-€5, free English tours offered but fill up fast, modest dress code enforced, tel. 055-230-2885, www.operaduomo.firenze.it.

▲Climbing the Duomo's Dome

For a grand view into the cathedral from the base of the dome, a peek at some of the tools used in the dome's construction, a chance to see Brunelleschi's "dome-within-a-dome" construction, a glorious Florence view from the top, and the equivalent of 463 plunges on a Renaissance StairMaster, climb the dome. The wonder of the

FLORENCE

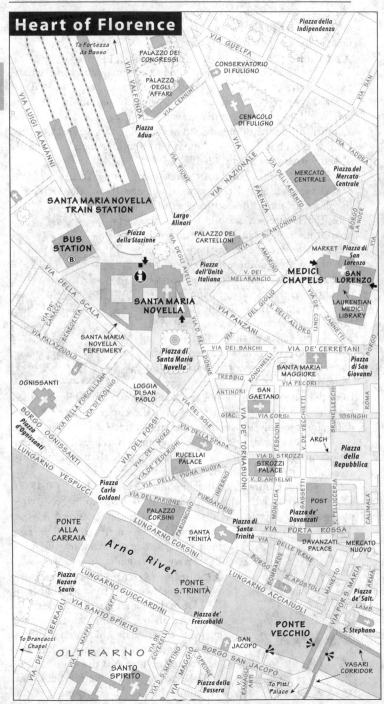

Heart of Florence

To Fortezza da Basso

VIA GUELFA

Piazza della Indipendenza

PALAZZO DEI CONGRESSI

CONSERVATORIO DI FULIGNO

VIA VALFONDA

PALAZZO DEGLI AFFARI

VIA CENNINI

CENACOLO DI FULIGNO

Piazza Adua

VIA FIUME

VIA NAZIONALE

VIA DELL'ARIENTO

MERCATO CENTRALE

Piazza del Mercato Centrale

VIA TADDEA

VIA SAN

BORGO LA NOCE

VIA LUIGI ALAMANNI

SANTA MARIA NOVELLA TRAIN STATION

Largo Alinari

PALAZZO DEI CARTELLONI

S. ANTONINO

P. AMORINO

MARKET

Piazza di San Lorenzo

VIA DELLA SCALA

BUS STATION
(B)

Piazza della Stazione

VIA DEGLI AVELLI

Piazza dell'Unità Italiana

V. DEI MELARANCIO

MEDICI CHAPELS

SAN LORENZO

VIA DE' ZANNETTI

LAURENTIAN MEDICI LIBRARY

VIA DE CANACCI

BENEDETTA

SANTA MARIA NOVELLA

VIA D. MELARANCIO

VIA PANZANI

VIA DEL GIGLIO

V. DE' CONTI

VIA DELL'ALLORO

VIA PALAZZUOLO

SANTA MARIA NOVELLA PERFUMERY

Piazza di Santa Maria Novella

VIA D. BELLE DONNE

VIA DEI BANCHI

VIA DE' CERRETANI

Piazza di San Giovanni

OGNISSANTI

VIA DELLA PORCELLANA

VIA DI PAOLINO

LOGGIA DI SAN PAOLO

TREBBIO

RONDINELLI

SANTA MARIA MAGGIORE

VIA PECORI

Piazza d'Ognissanti

BORGO OGNISSANTI

VIA DEL SOLE

ANTINORI

SAN GAETANO

BRUNELLESCHI

ROMA

LUNGARNO VESPUCCI

VIA DEL MORO

VIA DELLA SPADA

GIAC.

VIA DE' TORNABUONI

VIA CORSI

VIA D. VECCHIETTI

TOSINGHI

VIA DEL FOSSI

VIA DELLA VIGNA NUOVA

RUCELLAI PALACE

PESCIONI

ARCH

Piazza della Repubblica

Piazza Carlo Goldoni

VIA DE FEDERIGHI

INFERNO

VIA D. STROZZI

STROZZI PALACE

V. D. ANSELMI

BASSETTI

POST

VIA DELLA VIGNA NUOVA

PURGATORIO

PARDONCINO

MONALDA

Piazza de' Davanzati

V. PELLICCERIA

CALIMALA

PONTE ALLA CARRAIA

PALAZZO CORSINI

LUNGARNO CORSINI

SANTA TRINITÀ

Piazza di Santa Trinità

VIA PORTA ROSSA

DAVANZATI PALACE

MERCATO NUOVO

Arno River

LUNGARNO GUICCIARDINI

PONTE S. TRINITÀ

VIA DELLE TERME

BORGO S. APOSTOLI

LUNGARNO ACCIAIUOLI

BORGO BOMBARDE

MANETTO

Piazza de' Salt.

VIA POR S. MARIA

ARMA

LAMB.

Piazza Nazaro Sauro

VIA SANTO SPIRITO

Piazza de' Frescobaldi

VIA SANTO SPIRITO

SERRAGLI

VIA DE COVERELLI

BORGO SAN JACOPO

SAN JACOPO

PONTE VECCHIO

S. Stephano

To Brancacci Chapel

VIA MAFFIA

OLTRARNO

VIA D. R. S. MARTINO

VIA MAGGIO

SPRONE

VIA D. RAMAGLI-ANTI

To Pitti Palace

VASARI CORRIDOR

SANTO SPIRITO

Piazza della Passera

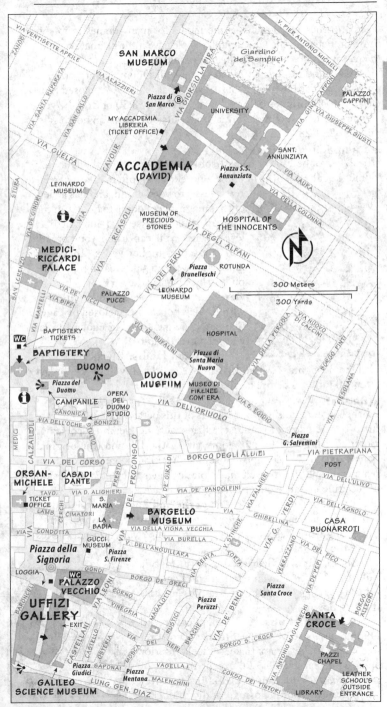

age, Brunelleschi's dome was the model for many domes to follow, from St. Peter's to the US Capitol. People gave it the ultimate compliment, saying, "Not even the ancients could have done it."

Cost and Hours: €10 ticket covers all Duomo sights, covered by Firenze Card, Mon-Fri 8:30-19:00, Sat 8:30-17:40, closed Sun, last entry 40 minutes before closing, arrive by 8:30 or drop by very late for the fewest crowds, enter from outside church on north side, tel. 055-230-2885.

▲Campanile (Giotto's Tower)

The 270-foot bell tower has 50-some fewer steps than the Duomo's dome (but that's still 414 steps—no elevator); offers a faster, rela-

tively less-crowded climb; and has a view of that magnificent dome to boot. On the way up, there are several intermediate levels where you can catch your breath and enjoy ever-higher views. The stairs narrow as you go up, creating a mosh-pit bottleneck near the very top—but the views are worth the hassle. While the various viewpoints are enclosed by cage-like bars, the gaps are big enough to let you snap great photos.

Cost and Hours: €10 ticket covers all Duomo sights, covered by Firenze Card, daily 8:30-19:30, last entry 40 minutes before closing.

▲Baptistery

Michelangelo said the bronze doors of this octagonal building were fit to be the gates of paradise. Check out the gleaming copies of Lorenzo Ghiberti's bronze doors facing the Duomo (the original panels are in the Duomo Museum). Making a breakthrough in perspective, Ghiberti used mathematical laws to create the illusion of receding distance on a basically flat surface.

The doors on the north side of the building were designed by Ghiberti when he was young; he'd won the honor and opportunity by beating Brunelleschi in a competition (the rivals' original entries are in the Bargello).

Inside, sit and savor the medieval mosaic ceiling, where it's always Judgment Day and Jesus is giving the ultimate thumbs-up and thumbs-down.

Cost and Hours: €10 ticket covers all Duomo sights, covered by Firenze Card (get free paper ticket from ticket office), interior open Mon-Sat 11:15-19:00 except first Sat of month 8:30-14:00, Sun 8:30-14:00, last entry 30 minutes before closing, audioguide-€2, photos allowed inside, tel. 055-230-2885. Buy your tickets at the office just across the piazza. The (facsimile) bronze doors are on the exterior, so they are always "open" and viewable.

▲▲▲**Duomo Museum (Museo dell'Opera del Duomo)**
The underrated cathedral museum, behind the church, is great if you like sculpture. It will be partially closed for renovation through 2015, so what's on display may change.

The museum is home to many of the original creations that defined the 1400s (the Quattrocento) in Florence, when the city blossomed and classical arts were reborn (parts of the museum may be closed for renovation during your visit). On the ground floor, look for a late Michelangelo *Pietà*, which was intended as his sculptural epitaph, and statues from the original Baptistery facade. The museum also features Ghiberti's original bronze "Gates of Paradise" panels (the ones on the Baptistery's doors today are replicas).

The original sculptured masterpieces that decorated the exterior of the Duomo and the Campanile are now restored and displayed safely indoors at the Duomo Museum (copies are installed on the cathedral and bell tower). Upstairs, you'll find Brunelleschi's models for his dome, as well as Donatello's anorexic *Mary Magdalene* and his playful choir loft. Though overlooked by most visitors to Florence, this museum is a delight.

Cost and Hours: €10 ticket covers all Duomo sights, covered by Firenze Card, Mon-Sat 9:00-19:30, Sun 9:00-13:45, last entry 45 minutes before closing, one of the few museums in Florence always open on Mon, audioguide-€5, guided tours-€3 summer only (schedule varies, stop by or call to ask), Via del Proconsolo 9, tel. 055-282-226 or 055-230-7885, www.operaduomo.firenze.it.

Nearby: If you find this church art intriguing, head to the left around the back of the Duomo to find Via dello Studio (near the south transept), then walk a block toward the river to #23a (freestanding yellow house on the right). You can look through the open doorway of the **Opera del Duomo art studio** and see workers sculpting new statues, restoring old ones, or making exact copies. They're carrying on an artistic tradition that dates back to the days of Brunelleschi. The "opera" continues.

Between the Duomo and Piazza della Signoria
▲▲▲**Bargello (Museo Nazionale del Bargello)**
This underappreciated sculpture museum is in a former police station-turned-prison that looks like a mini-Palazzo Vecchio. The

Renaissance began with sculpture—the great Florentine painters were "sculptors with brushes." You can see the birth of this revolution of 3-D in the Bargello (bar-JEL-oh), which boasts the best collection of Florentine sculpture. It's a small, uncrowded museum and a pleasant break from the intensity of the rest of Florence.

The Bargello has Donatello's very influential, painfully beautiful *David* (the first male nude to be sculpted in a thousand years), works by Michelangelo, and rooms of Medici treasures. Moody Donatello, who embraced realism with his lifelike statues, set the personal and artistic style for many Renaissance artists to follow. The best pieces are in the ground-floor room at the foot of the outdoor staircase (with fine works by Michelangelo, Cellini, and Giambologna) and in the "Donatello room" directly above (with plenty by Donatello, including two different *David*s, plus Ghiberti and Brunelleschi's revolutionary dueling door panels and yet another *David* by Verrocchio).

Cost and Hours: €4, €7 with mandatory exhibits, covered by Firenze Card, Tue-Sat 8:15-13:50, until 16:50 during special exhibits (generally April-Oct); also open first, third, and fifth Mon and the second and fourth Sun of each month; last entry 30 minutes before closing, reservations possible but unnecessary, audioguide-€6 (€10/2 people), photos in courtyard only, Via del Proconsolo 4, reservation tel. 055-238-8606, www.polomuseale.firenze.it.

Casa di Dante (Dante's House)

Dante Alighieri (1265-1321), the poet who gave us *The Divine Comedy*, is the Shakespeare of Italy, the father of the modern Italian language, and the face on the country's €2 coin. However, most Americans know little of him, and this museum is not the ideal place to start. Even though it has English information, this small museum (in a building near where he likely lived) assumes visitors have prior knowledge of the poet. It's not a medieval-flavored house with period furniture—it's just a small, low-tech museum about Dante. Still, Dante lovers can trace his interesting life and works through pictures, models, and artifacts. And because the ex-

hibits are as much about medieval Florence as they are about the man, novices can learn a little about the city Dante lived in.

Cost and Hours: €4, covered by Firenze Card, April-Sept daily 10:00-18:00; Oct-March Tue-Sun 10:00-17:00, closed Mon; last entry 30 minutes before closing, near the Bargello at Via Santa Margherita 1, tel. 055-219-416, www.museocasadidante.it.

▲Orsanmichele Church

In the ninth century, this loggia (covered courtyard) was a market used for selling grain (stored upstairs). Later, it was enclosed to make a church.

Outside are dynamic, statue-filled niches, some with accompanying symbols from the guilds that sponsored the art. Donatello's *St. Mark* and *St. George* (on the northeast and northwest corners) step out boldly in the new Renaissance style.

The interior has a glorious Gothic tabernacle (1359), which houses the painted wooden panel that depicts *Madonna delle Grazie* (1346). The iron bars spanning the vaults were the Italian Gothic answer to the French Gothic external buttresses. Look for the rectangular holes in the piers—these were once wheat chutes that connected to the upper floors. The museum upstairs (limited hours) displays most of the originals from the niches outside the building, by Ghiberti, Donatello, Brunelleschi, and others.

Cost and Hours: Free, daily 10:00-17:00 (except closed Mon in Aug), free upstairs museum open only Mon, niche sculptures always viewable from the outside. You can give the *Madonna della Grazie* a special thanks if you're in town when an evening concert is held inside the Orsanmichele (tickets sold on day of concert from door facing Via de' Calzaiuoli; also books Uffizi and Accademia tickets, ticket window open daily 10:00-17:00).

▲Mercato Nuovo (a.k.a. the Straw Market)

This market loggia is how Orsanmichele looked before it became a church. Originally a silk and straw market, Mercato Nuovo still functions as a rustic yet touristy market (at the intersection of Via Calimala and Via Porta Rossa). Prices are soft, but the San Lorenzo Market (listed earlier) is much better for haggling. Notice the circled *X* in the center, marking the spot where people hit the ground after being hoisted up to the top and dropped as punishment for bankruptcy. You'll also find *Il Porcellino* (a statue of a wild boar nicknamed "The Piglet"), which people rub and give coins to ensure their return to Florence. This new copy, while only a few years old, already has a polished snout. At the back corner, a wagon sells tripe (cow innards) sandwiches—a local favorite (daily 9:00-20:00).

▲Palazzo Davanzati

This five-story, late-medieval tower house offers a rare look at a noble dwelling built in the 14th century. Only the ground-floor loggia and

first floor are open to visitors, though the remaining floors (more living quarters and the kitchen) can be visited with an escort (usually at 10:00, 11:00, and 12:00; call ahead to be sure there's space or ask when you arrive). Like other buildings of the age, the exterior is festooned with 14th-century horse-tethering rings made from iron, torch holders, and poles upon which to hang laundry and fly flags. Inside, though the furnishings are pretty sparse, you'll see richly painted walls, a long chute that functioned as a well, plenty of fireplaces, a lace display, and even an indoor "outhouse." While there's little posted information, you can borrow English descriptions in each room.

Cost and Hours: €2, covered by Firenze Card, Tue-Sat 8:15-13:50; also open first, third, and fifth Sun and second and fourth Mon of each month; Via Porta Rossa 13, tel. 055-238-8610.

▲Piazza della Repubblica and Nearby

This large square sits on the site of the original Roman Forum. Florence was a riverside garrison town set below the older town

of Fiesole—essentially a rectangular fort with the square marking the intersection of the two main roads (Via Corso and Via Roma). The square's lone column—nicknamed the "belly button of Florence"—once marked the intersection (the Roman streets were about nine feet below the present street level). Above ground, all that survives of Roman Florence is this column and the city's street plan. But beneath the stones lie the remains of the ancient city. Look at any map of Florence today, and you'll see the ghost of Rome in its streets: a grid-plan city center surrounded by what was the Roman wall. The Braille model of the city (in front of the Paszkowski café) makes the design clear.

Venerable cafés and stores line the square. During the 19th century, intellectuals met in cafés here. Gilli, on the northeast corner, is a favorite for its grand atmosphere and tasty sweets (cheap if you stand at the bar, expensive to sit down) while the recommended Paszkowski has good lunch options (see page 572). The department store La Rinascente, facing Piazza della Repubblica, is one of the city's mainstays (WC on fourth floor, continue up the stairs from there to the bar with a rooftop terrace for great Duomo and city views).

Palazzo Strozzi

The former home of the wealthy Strozzi family, great rivals of the Medici, offers a textbook example of a Renaissance palace (built between 1489 and 1538). Peek into its grand courtyard and imagine how well-to-do families competed to commission grandiose structures (and artistic masterpieces) to promote their status and wealth. Today it hosts top-notch special exhibitions, usually un-crowded and well described in English.

Cost and Hours: Free entry to courtyard and café, both open daily 8:30-20:00; gallery—€12.50, price and hours can change with exhibits, but often daily 9:00-20:00, Thu until 23:00, last entry one hour before closing, discounts with train or bus tickets; just west of Piazza della Repubblica at Piazza Strozzi, tel. 055-264-5155, www.palazzostrozzi.org.

On and near Piazza della Signoria

The main civic center of Florence is dominated by the Palazzo Vec-chio, Uffizi Gallery, and marble greatness of old Florence littering the cobbles. Piazza della Signoria still vibrates with the echoes of the city's past—executions, riots, and great celebrations. Today, it's a tourist's world with pigeons, postcards, horse buggies, and tired hubbies. If it would make your weary companion happy, stop in at the recommended but expensive **Rivoire** café to enjoy its fine des-serts, pudding-thick hot chocolate, and the best view seats in town. It's expensive—but if you linger, it can be a great value.

▲▲▲Uffizi Gallery

This greatest collection of Italian paintings anywhere features works by Giotto, Leonardo, Raphael, Caravaggio, Titian, and

Michelangelo, and a roomful of Botticellis, including the *Birth of Venus*. Northern Renais-sance masters (Dürer, Rembrandt, and Ru-bens) are also well represented.

Cost and Hours: €6.50, €11 with manda-tory special exhibits, extra €4 for recommend-ed reservation, cash required to pick up tickets reserved by phone, covered by Firenze Card, Tue-Sun 8:15-18:35, closed Mon, last entry 30 minutes before closing, audioguide-€6, free Rick Steves audio tour available—see page 9, museum info tel. 055-238-8651, reservation tel. 055-294-883, www.uffizi.firenze.it. To avoid the long ticket lines, get a Firenze Card (see page 516) or make reservations (see page 518).

Getting In: There are several entrances. Which one you use de-pends on whether you have a Firenze Card, a reservation, or neither.

FLORENCE

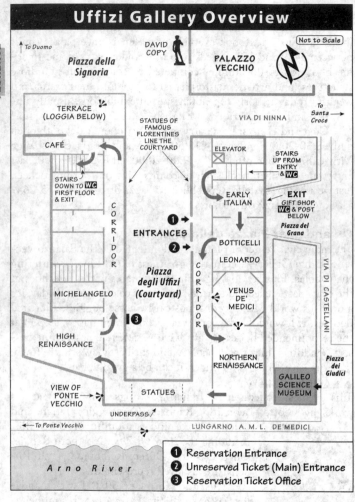

Uffizi Gallery Overview

↑ To Duomo

Piazza della Signoria

DAVID COPY

PALAZZO VECCHIO

Not to Scale

TERRACE (LOGGIA BELOW)

CAFÉ

STATUES OF FAMOUS FLORENTINES LINE THE COURTYARD

VIA DI NINNA

To Santa Croce →

ELEVATOR

STAIRS UP FROM ENTRY & WC

STAIRS DOWN TO WC FIRST FLOOR & EXIT

EARLY ITALIAN

EXIT
GIFT SHOP, WC & POST BELOW

Piazza del Grana

C O R R I D O R

❶ ENTRANCES

❷

BOTTICELLI

LEONARDO

MICHELANGELO

C O R R I D O R

VENUS DE' MEDICI

Piazza degli Uffizi (Courtyard)

❸

HIGH RENAISSANCE

NORTHERN RENAISSANCE

VIA DI CASTELLANI

Piazza dei Giudici

GALILEO SCIENCE MUSEUM

VIEW OF PONTE VECCHIO →

STATUES

UNDERPASS

← To Ponte Vecchio

LUNGARNO A. M. L. DE'MEDICI

Arno River

❶ Reservation Entrance
❷ Unreserved Ticket (Main) Entrance
❸ Reservation Ticket Office

Firenze Card holders enter at door #1 (labeled *Reservation Entrance*), close to the Palazzo Vecchio. Get in the line for individuals, not groups.

People **buying a ticket on the spot** line up with everyone else at door #2. (The wait can be hours long.)

To **buy a Firenze Card,** or to see if there are any **same-day reservations** available (€4 extra, but could save you time in the ticket line), enter door #2 to the left of the ticket-buying line (marked *Booking Service and Today*).

If you've **already made a reservation** and need to pick up your ticket, go to door #3 (labeled *Reservation Ticket Office,* across the courtyard from doors #1 and #2). Tickets are available for pickup 10 minutes before your appointed time. If you booked online and have already prepaid, you'll just exchange your voucher for a ticket. If you (or your hotelier) booked by phone, give them your confirmation number and pay for the ticket (cash only). Once you have your ticket, walk briskly past the 200-yard-long ticket-buying line —pondering the IQ of this gang—to door #1. Show your ticket and walk in.

Renovation: The Uffizi is undergoing a massive, years-long renovation that may affect your visit. Some of the artworks may be displayed in different rooms, on loan to other museums, or out for restoration—pick up a floor plan as you enter, and if you need help finding a particular piece of art, ask the guards in each room.

Visiting the Museum: The museum is not nearly as big as it is great. Few tourists spend more than two hours inside. Most of the paintings are displayed on one comfortable, U-shaped floor in chronological order from the 13th through 17th centuries. The left wing, starring the Florentine Middle Ages to the Renaissance, is the best. The connecting corridor contains sculpture, and the right wing focuses on the High Renaissance and Baroque.

Medieval (1200-1400): Paintings by **Duccio, Cimabue,** and **Giotto** show the baby steps being made from the flat Byzantine style toward realism. In his *Madonna and Child with Angels*, Giotto created a "stage" and peopled it with real beings. The triumph here is Mary herself—big and monumental, like a Roman statue. Beneath her robe, she has knees and breasts that stick out at us. This three-dimensionality was revolutionary, a taste of the Renaissance a century before it began.

Early Renaissance (mid-1400s): Paolo Uccello's *Battle of San Romano* is an early study in perspective with a few obvious flubs. Piero della Francesca's *Federico da Montefeltro and Battista Sforza* heralds the era of humanism and the new centrality of ordinary people in art, warts and all. Fra Filippo Lippi's radiantly beautiful Madonnas are light years away from the generic Marys of the medieval era.

Renaissance (1450-1500): The Botticelli room is filled with masterpieces and classical fleshiness (the famous *Birth of Venus* and *Allegory of Spring*), plus two minor works by Leonardo da Vinci. Here is the Renaissance in its first bloom, its "springtime" of innocence. Madonna is out, Venus is in. This is a return to the pre-Christian pagan world of classical Greece, where things of the flesh are not sinful.

Classical Sculpture: If the Renaissance was the foundation of the modern world, the foundation of the Renaissance was classical sculpture. Sculptors, painters, and poets alike turned for inspiration to ancient Greek and Roman works as the epitome of balance, 3-D perspective, human anatomy, and beauty.

In the octagonal classical sculpture room, the highlight is the *Venus de' Medici,* a Roman copy of the lost original of the great Greek sculptor Praxiteles' *Aphrodite.* Balanced, harmonious, and serene, this statue was considered the epitome of beauty and sexuality in Renaissance Florence.

The sculpture hall has the best view in Florence of the Arno River and Ponte Vecchio through the window, dreamy at sunset.

High Renaissance (1500-1550): Don't miss Michelangelo's *Holy Family,* the only surviving completed easel painting by the greatest sculptor in history; Raphael's *Madonna of the Goldfinch,* with Mary and the Baby Jesus brought down from heaven into the real world of trees, water, and sky; and Titian's voluptuous *Venus of Urbino.*

Wrap up your visit by enjoying Duomo views from the café terrace. The lower floor contains temporary exhibitions and works by Caravaggio and foreign painters.

In the Uffizi's Courtyard: Enjoy the courtyard (free), full of artists and souvenir stalls. (Swing by after dinner when it's completely empty.) The surrounding statues honor earthshaking Florentines: artists (Michelangelo); philosophers (Niccolò Machiavelli); scientists (Galileo); writers (Dante); cartographers (Amerigo Vespucci); and the great patron of so much Renaissance thinking, Lorenzo "the Magnificent" de' Medici.

Nearby: The Loggia dei Lanzi, across from the Palazzo Vecchio and facing the square, is where Renaissance Florentines once debated the issues of the day; a collection of Medici-approved sculptures, including Cellini's bronze *Perseus,* now stands (or writhes) under its canopy.

▲▲Palazzo Vecchio

This castle-like fortress with the 300-foot spire dominates Florence's main square. In Renaissance times, it was the Town Hall, where citizens pioneered the once-radical notion of self-rule. Its official name—the Palazzo della Signoria—refers to the elected members of the city council. In 1540, the tyrant Cosimo I de' Medici made the building his personal palace, redecorating the interior in lavish style. Today the building functions once again as the Town Hall.

Entry to the ground-floor courtyard is free, so even if you don't go upstairs to the museum, you can step inside and feel the essence of the Medici. Paying customers can see Cosimo's (fairly) lavish royal apartments, decorated with (fairly) top-notch paintings and statues by Michelangelo and Donatello. The highlight is the Grand Hall (Salone dei

Cinquecento), a 13,000-square-foot hall lined with huge frescoes and interesting statues.

Cost and Hours: Courtyard—free to enter, museum—€6.50, tower climb-€6.50 (418 steps), museum plus tower-€10, museum and tower covered by Firenze Card (first pick up ticket at ground-floor information desk before entering museum); Fri-Wed 9:00-19:00, until 24:00 April-Sept, Thu 9:00-14:00 year-round; tower keeps similar but shorter hours, ticket office closes one hour earlier, videoguide-€5, English tours available, Piazza della Signoria, tel. 055-276-8224, www.museicivicifiorentini.it.

Nighttime Terrace Visits: In summer you can join an escort for an unnarrated walk along the "patrol path"— the balcony that runs just below the crenellated top of the building (€2 plus regular admission ticket, every 30 minutes between 21:00 and 23:00, no tours Oct-March). Note that this tour doesn't go to the top of the tower, but just to the top of the main building.

▲Ponte Vecchio

Florence's most famous bridge has long been lined with shops. Originally these were butcher shops that used the river as a handy disposal system. Then, when the powerful and princely Medici built the Vasari Corridor (described next) over the bridge, the stinky meat market was replaced by the more elegant gold and silver shops that remain there to this day. A  statue of Benvenuto Cellini, the master goldsmith of the Renaissance, stands in the center, ignored by the flood of tacky tourism. This is a very romantic spot late at night (when lovers gather, and a top-notch street musician performs).

Vasari Corridor

This elevated and enclosed passageway, constructed in 1565, gave the Medici a safe, private commute over Ponte Vecchio from their Pitti Palace home to their Palazzo Vecchio offices. It's open only by special appointment, and though enticing to lovers of Florence, the actual tour experience isn't much. Entering from inside the Uffizi Gallery, you walk along a modern-feeling hall (wide enough to carry a Medici on a sedan chair) across Ponte Vecchio, and end in the Pitti Palace. Half the corridor is lined with Europe's best collection of self-portraits, along with other paintings (mostly 17th- and 18th-century) that seem like they didn't make the cut to be hung on the walls of the Uffizi. The best way to get inside the corridor is to go with a tour company such as Florencetown (€85, Tue-Sun at 15:30, tel. 055-012-3994, www.florencetown.com) or

ArtViva (€84, Tue and Sat at 13:30, tel. 055-264-5033, www.art-viva.com). The three-hour tours include a tour of the Uffizi.

▲▲Galileo Science Museum
(Museo Galilei e Istituto di Storia della Scienza)

When we think of the Florentine Renaissance, we think of visual arts: painting, mosaics, architecture, and sculpture. But when the

visual arts declined in the 1600s (abused and co-opted by political powers), music and science flourished in Florence. The first opera was written here. And Florence hosted many scientific breakthroughs, as you'll see in this fascinating collection of Renaissance and later clocks, telescopes, maps, and ingenious gadgets. Trace the technical innovations as modern science emerges from 1000 to 1900. Some of the most talked-about bottles in Florence are the ones here that contain Galileo's fingers. Exhibits include various tools for gauging the world, from a compass and thermometer to Galileo's telescopes. Other displays delve into clocks, pumps, medicine, and chemistry. It's friendly, comfortably cool, never crowded, and just a block east of the Uffizi on the Arno River.

Cost and Hours: €9, €22 family ticket, cash only, covered by Firenze Card, Wed-Mon 9:30-18:00, Tue 9:30-13:00, last entry 30 minutes before closing, Piazza dei Giudici 1, tel. 055-265-311, www.museogalileo.it.

Tours: The €5 **audioguide** is well-produced and offers both a highlights tour as well as dial-up info (with video) on each exhibit. The 1.5-hour English-language **guided tour** covers the collection plus behind-the-scenes areas, and includes hands-on demonstrations of some of the devices (€50 flat fee for 2-14 people, cash only, doesn't include museum entry, book at least a week in advance, great for kids, tel. 055-234-3723, groups@museogalileo.it).

East of Piazza della Signoria
▲▲Santa Croce Church

This 14th-century Franciscan church, decorated with centuries of precious art, holds the tombs of great Florentines. The loud 19th-century Victorian Gothic facade faces a huge square ringed with tempting shops and littered with tired tourists. Escape into the church and admire its sheer height and spaciousness.

FLORENCE

Cost and Hours: €6, €8.50 combo-ticket with Casa Buonarroti, covered by Firenze Card, Mon-Sat 9:30-17:30, Sun 14:00-17:30, last entry 30 minutes before closing, audioguide-€5 (€8/2 people), modest dress required, 10-minute walk east of Palazzo Vecchio along Borgo de' Greci, tel. 055-246-6105, www.santacroceopera.it. The **leather school** is free and sells church tickets—handy when the church has a long line (daily 10:00-18:00, closed Sun in fall/winter, has own entry behind church plus an entry within the church, www.scuoladelcuoio.com).

Visiting the Church: On the left wall (as you face the altar) is the tomb of **Galileo Galilei** (1564-1642), the Pisan who lived his last years under house arrest near Florence. His crime? Defying the Church by saying that the earth revolved around the sun. His heretical remains were only allowed in the church long after his death.

Directly opposite (on the right wall) is the tomb of **Michelangelo Buonarroti** (1475-1564). Santa Croce was Michelangelo's childhood church, as he grew up a block west of here. Farther up the nave is the tomb of **Niccolò Machiavelli** (1469-1527), a champion of democratic Florence and author of *The Prince,* a how-to manual on hardball politics.

The first chapel to the right of the main altar features the famous *Death of St. Francis* fresco by Giotto. With simple but eloquent gestures, Francis' brothers bid him a sad farewell. In the hallway near the bookstore, notice the photos of the devastating flood of 1966. Beyond that is the leather school (free entry).

Exit between the Rossini and Machiavelli tombs into the delightful cloister (open-air courtyard). On the left, enter Brunelleschi's Pazzi Chapel, which captures the Renaissance in miniature.

▲Casa Buonarroti (Michelangelo's House)

Fans enjoy a house standing on property once owned by Michelangelo. The house was built after Michelangelo's death by the artist's grand-nephew, who turned it into a little museum honoring his famous relative. You'll see some of Michelangelo's early, less-than-monumental statues and a few sketches. Be warned: Michelangelo's descendants sold off many of the drawings by their famous relative; only a few sketches and sculptures here are actually by Michelangelo.

Cost and Hours: €6.50, €8.50 combo-ticket with Santa Croce Church, covered by Firenze Card, Wed-Mon 10:00-17:00, closed Tue, English descriptions, Via Ghibellina 70, tel. 055-241-752, www.casabuonarroti.it.

FLORENCE

Santa Maria Novella Sights near the Train Station
▲▲Church of Santa Maria Novella

This 13th-century Dominican church is rich in art. Along with crucifixes by Giotto and Brunelleschi, it contains every textbook's

example of the early Renaissance mastery of perspective: *The Trinity* by Masaccio. The exquisite chapels trace art in Florence from medieval times to early Baroque. The outside of the church features a dash of Romanesque (horizontal stripes), Gothic (pointed arches), Renaissance (geometric shapes), and Baroque (scrolls). Step in and look down the 330-foot nave for a 14th-century optical illusion.

Next to the church are the cloisters and the **museum**, located in the old Dominican convent of Santa Maria Novella. The museum's highlight is the breathtaking Spanish Chapel, with walls covered by a series of frescos by Andrea di Bonaiuto.

Cost and Hours: Church and museum—€5, covered by Firenze Card, Mon-Thu 9:00-17:30, Fri 11:00-17:30, Sat 9:00-17:00, Sun 12:00-17:00 July-Sept (from 13:00 Oct-June), last entry 45 minutes before closing, audioguide-€5 (€8/2 people), modest dress required, no photos, main entrance on Piazza Santa Maria Novella, Firenze Card holders must enter behind the church at Piazza della Stazione 4, tel. 055-219-257, www.museicivicifiorentini.it or www.chiesasantamarianovella.it.

Farmacia di Santa Maria Novella

This palatial perfumery has long been run by the Dominicans of Santa Maria Novella. Thick with the lingering aroma of centuries of spritzes, it started as the herb garden of the Santa Maria Novella monks. Well-known even today for its top-quality products, it is extremely Florentine. Pick up the history sheet from the rack, and wander deep into the shop. The main sales room, where you can sample various cosmetics and perfumes, was originally a chapel; the middle (green) room offers items for the home; and the historic third room, which sells herbal products, is where the pharmacy was originally established in 1612. From here, you can peek at one of Santa Maria Novella's cloisters with its dreamy frescoes and imagine a time before Vespas and tourists.

Cost and Hours: Free but shopping encouraged, inconsistent hours but daily likely from 9:30 or 10:30 until 19:30, a block from Piazza Santa Maria Novella, 100 yards down Via della Scala at #16—see map on page 528, tel. 055-216-276, www.smnovella.com.

Sights South of the Arno River

To locate these sights, see the map on page 544.

▲▲Pitti Palace

The imposing Pitti Palace, several blocks southwest of Ponte Vecchio, is not only home to the second-best collection of paintings in town, the **Palatine Gallery**, but also happens to be the most sumptuous palace you can tour in Florence. The building itself is mammoth, holding several different museums and anchoring two gardens. Stick primarily to the gallery, forget about everything else, and the palace becomes a little less exhausting.

You'll walk through one palatial room after another, walls sagging with masterpieces by 16th- and 17th-century masters, including Rubens, Titian, and Rembrandt. Its Raphael collection is the second-biggest anywhere—the Vatican beats it by one. Each room has some descriptions in English, though the paintings themselves have limited English labels.

The collection is all on one floor. To see the highlights, walk straight down the spine through a dozen or so rooms. Before you exit, consider a visit to the Royal Apartments. These 14 rooms (of which only a few are open at any one time) are where the Pitti's rulers lived in the 18th and 19th centuries. Each room features a different color and time period. Here, you get a real feel for the splendor of the dukes' world.

The rest of the Pitti Palace is skippable, unless the various sights match your interests: the **Gallery of Modern Art** (second floor, features Romantic, Neoclassical, and Impressionist works by 19th- and 20th-century Tuscan painters), **Argenti/Silverworks Museum** (on the ground and mezzanine floors; displays Medici treasures from jeweled crucifixes to gilded ostrich eggs), **Costume Gallery, Porcelain Museum,** and **Boboli and Bardini gardens** (behind the palace; enter from Pitti Palace courtyard—be prepared to climb uphill).

The main reason to visit the Pitti Palace is to see the Palatine Gallery, but you can't buy a ticket for the gallery alone; to see it you'll need to buy ticket #1, which includes the Palatine Gallery, Royal Apartments, and Gallery of Modern Art. Ticket #2 covers the Boboli and Bardini Gardens, Costume Gallery, Argenti/Silverworks Museum, and Porcelain Museum. Behind door #3 is a combo-ticket covering the whole shebang.

Cost and Hours: Ticket #1—€8.50 (€13 with special exhibitions), Tue-Sun 8:15-18:50, closed Mon, last entry one hour before closing. Ticket #2—€7 (€10 with special exhibitions), daily

FLORENCE

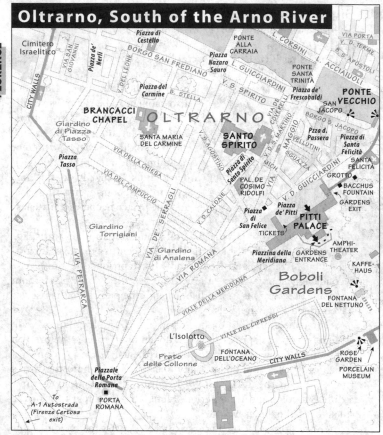

Oltrarno, South of the Arno River

June-Aug 8:15-19:30, April-May and Sept 8:15-18:30, March and Oct 8:15-17:30, Nov-Feb 8:15-16:30, closed first and last Mon of each month, last entry one hour before closing. Ticket #3—€11.50, valid 3 days, usually not available during special exhibitions. Reservations are possible but unnecessary, and everything is covered by the Firenze Card. The €6 audioguide (€10/2 people) explains the sprawling palace. No photos are allowed in the Palatine Gallery. Tel. 055-238-8614, www.polomuseale.firenze.it.

Getting In: If there's a long line, bypass it by making a €3 "reservation" on the spot for immediate entry (just march up to the head of the line and go to window 3 on the right, marked *reservation desk*). Once you have your ticket, enter through the main doorway in the center of the facade. Firenze Card holders should go directly to the main entrance (where you may be ushered to the head of the security checkpoint); then go to the bookstore on the left side of the courtyard to have your card swiped and get your tickets.

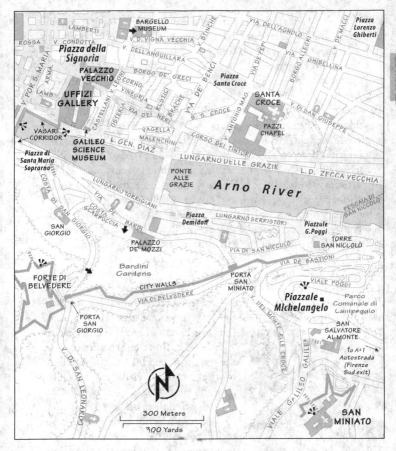

▲▲Brancacci Chapel

For the best look at works by Masaccio (one of the early Renaissance pioneers of perspective in painting), see his restored frescoes here. Instead of medieval religious symbols, Masaccio's paintings feature simple, strong human figures with facial expressions that

reflect their emotions. The accompanying works of Masolino and Filippino Lippi provide illuminating contrasts.

Your ticket includes a 20-minute film in English on the chapel, the frescoes, and Renaissance Florence. (If the film's not showing, consider the €1 videoguide.) Computer animation brings the paintings to 3-D life—they appear

FLORENCE

to move—while narration describes the events depicted in the panels. The film takes liberties with the art, but it's visually interesting and your best way to see the frescoes close up.

Cost and Hours: €6, cash only, covered by Firenze Card; free and easy reservations required if you don't have a Firenze Card (see next); Mon and Wed-Sat 10:00-17:00, Sun 13:00-17:00, closed Tue, last entry 30 minutes before closing; free 20-minute film, videoguide-€1, knees and shoulders must be covered; in Church of Santa Maria del Carmine, on Piazza del Carmine in the Oltrarno neighborhood; reservations tel. 055-276-8224 or 055-276-8558, ticket desk tel. 055-284-361, www.museicivicifiorentini.it.

Reservations: Although reservations are required, on weekdays and any day off-season, it's often possible to walk right up and get an entry time, especially if you come before 15:30. To reserve in advance, call the chapel a day ahead (tel. 055-276-8224 or 055-276-8558, English spoken, call center open Mon-Sat 9:30-13:00 & 14:00-17:00, Sun 9:30-12:30). You can also try via email—info.museoragazzi@comune.fi.it.

Santo Spirito Church

This church has a classic Brunelleschi interior—enjoy its pure Renaissance lines (and ignore the later Baroque altar that replaced

the original). Notice Brunelleschi's "dice"—the stone cubes added above the column capitals that contribute to the nave's playful lightness. The church's art treasure is a painted, carved wooden crucifix attributed to 17-year-old Michelangelo. The sculptor donated this early work to the monastery in appreciation for allowing him to dissect and learn about bodies. The Michelangelo *Crocifisso* is displayed in the sacristy, through a door midway down the left side of the nave (if it's closed, ask someone to let you in). Copies of Michelangelo's *Pietà* and *Risen Christ* flank the nave (near the main door). Beer-drinking, guitar-playing rowdies decorate the church steps.

Cost and Hours: Free, Mon-Tue and Thu-Sat 9:30-12:30 & 16:00-17:30, Sun 16:00-17:30 only, closed Wed, Piazza di Santo Spirito, tel. 055-210-030, www.basilicasantospirito.it.

▲Piazzale Michelangelo

Overlooking the city from across the river (look for the huge bronze statue of *David*), this square has a superb view of Florence and the stunning dome of the Duomo (see photo on page 498).

It's worth the 30-minute hike, drive (free parking), or bus ride (either #12 or #13 from the southeast corner of the train station, between the pine trees and the bikes—takes 20-30 minutes, longer in bad traffic). It makes sense to take a taxi or ride the bus up and then enjoy the easy downhill walk back into

town. An inviting café (open seasonally) with great views is just below the overlook. The best photos are taken from the street immediately below the overlook (go around to the right and down a few steps). Off the west side of the piazza is a somewhat hidden terrace, an excellent place to retreat from the mobs. After dark, the square is packed with school kids licking ice cream and each other. About 200 yards beyond all the tour groups and teenagers is the stark, beautiful, crowd-free, Romanesque San Miniato Church (next listing). A WC is located just off the road, halfway between the two sights.

The hike down is quick and enjoyable. Take the steps between the two bars on the San Miniato Church side of the parking lot (Via San Salvatore al Monte). At the first landing (marked #3), peek into the rose garden (Giardino delle Rose). After a few minutes, you'll walk through the old wall (Porta San Miniato) and emerge in the delightful little Oltrarno neighborhood of San Niccolò.

▲▲San Miniato Church

According to legend, the martyred St. Minias—this church's namesake—was beheaded on the banks of the Arno in A.D. 250.

He picked up his head and walked here (this was before the #12 bus), where he died and was buried in what became the first Christian cemetery in Florence. In the 11th century, this church was built to house Minias' remains. The church's green-and-white marble facade (12th century) is classic Floren-tine Romanesque, one of the oldest in town. Inside you'll find some wonderful 3-D paintings, a plush ceiling of glazed terra-cotta panels by Luca della Robbia, and an exquisite Renaissance chapel (on the left side of the nave). The highlight for me is the brilliantly preserved art in the sacristy (upstairs to right of altar, in the room on right) showing scenes from the life of St. Benedict (circa 1350, by a follower of Giotto).

Drop €2 into the electronic panel in the corner to light the room for five minutes. The evening vesper service with the monks chanting in Latin offers a meditative worship experience—a peaceful way to end your visit.

Cost and Hours: Free, daily Easter-mid-Oct 8:00-20:00, in winter 8:30-13:00 & 15:30-19:00, closed sporadically for special occasions, tel. 055-234-2731, www.sanminiatoalmonte.it.

Getting There: It's about 200 yards above Piazzale Michelangelo. From the station, bus #12 takes you right to the San Miniato al Monte stop (hop off and hike up the grand staircase); bus #13 from the station takes you to Piazzale Michelangelo, from which you'll hike up the rest of the way.

Gregorian Chants: To experience this mystical medieval space at its full potential, time your visit to coincide with a prayer service of Gregorian chants. In general, these are held each evening at 18:30 and last 30 minutes—but as the schedule is subject to change, double-check with any TI, the church's website, or call ahead.

Shopping in Florence

Florence is a great shopping town—known for its sense of style since the Medici days. Many people spend entire days shopping. Smaller stores are generally open 9:00-13:00 and 15:30-19:30, usually closed on Sunday, often closed on Monday, and sometimes closed for a couple of weeks around August 15. Many stores have promotional stalls in the market squares.

Busy street scenes and markets abound, especially near San Lorenzo, near Santa Croce, on Ponte Vecchio, and at Mercato Nuovo (the covered market square three blocks north of Ponte Vecchio, described on page 533). Prices are soft in the markets—go ahead and bargain. Leather, gold, silver, art prints, and tacky plaster mini-*David*s are most popular.

For shopping ideas, ads, and a list of markets, see *The Florentine* newspaper or *Florence Concierge Information* magazine (free from TI and many hotels). For a list of bookstores, see page 509. For ritzy Italian fashions, browse along Via della Vigna Nuova (runs west from Via de' Tornabuoni), Via del Parione, and Via Strozzi (runs east from Via de' Tornabuoni to Piazza della Repubblica).

The main **Ferragamo** store fills a classy 800-year-old building with a fine selection of shoes and bags (daily 10:00-19:30, Via de' Tornabuoni 2). Typical chain department stores are **Coin,** the Italian equivalent of Macy's (Mon-Sat 10:00-19:30, Sun 10:30-19:30, on Via de' Calzaiuoli, near Orsanmichele Church); the similar, upscale **La Rinascente** (Mon-Sat 9:00-22:00, Sun 10:00-21:00, on

Piazza della Repubblica); and **Oviesse,** a discount clothing chain, the local JCPenney (Mon-Sat 9:00-19:30, Sun 10:00-19:30, near train station at intersection of Via Panzani and Via del Giglio).

Sleeping in Florence

Competition among Florence's hotels is stiff. When things slow down, fancy hotels drop their prices and become a much better value for travelers than the cheap, low-end places. Nearly all of my recommended accommodations are located in the center of Florence, within minutes of the great sights. If arriving by train, you can either walk (usually around 10 minutes) or take a taxi (roughly €8-12) to reach most of my recommended accommodations, as buses don't cover the city center very well.

Florence is notorious for its mosquitoes. If your hotel lacks air-conditioning, request a fan and don't open your windows, especially at night. Many hotels furnish a small plug-in bulb *(zanzariere)*—usually set in the ashtray—that helps keep the blood-suckers at bay. If not, you can purchase one cheaply at any pharmacy *(farmacia)*.

Museumgoers take note: If you don't plan to get a Firenze Card (see page 516), you may want to ask if your hotelier will reserve entry times for you to visit the popular Uffizi Gallery and the Accademia (Michelangelo's *David*). Request this service when you book your room; it's fast, easy, and offered free or for a small fee by most hotels—the only requirement is advance notice. Ask them to reserve your visits for any time the day after your arrival. If you'd rather make the reservations yourself, see page 518 for details.

North of the Arno River
Near the Duomo

All of these places are within a block of Florence's biggest church and main landmark.

$$$ Palazzo Niccolini al Duomo, one of five elite Historic Residence Hotels in Florence, is run by Niccolini da Camugliano. The lounge (where free chamomile tea is served in the evenings) is palatial, but the 12 rooms, while splendid, vary wildly in size. If you have the money and want a Florentine palace to call home, this can be a good bet (Db-€150-€500 depending on type of room, ask for 10 percent Rick Steves discount when you book, check online to choose a room and consider last-minute deals, elevator, air-con, free guest computer, Wi-Fi, Via dei Servi 2, tel. 055-282-412, www.niccolinidomepalace.com, info@niccolinidomepalace.com).

$$$ Hotel Duomo, big and venerable, rents 24 slightly over-priced rooms four floors up. The Duomo looms like a monster outside the hotel's windows; most (but not all) rooms come with views.

The rooms are modern and comfortable enough, but you're paying for the location (Sb-€100, Db-€190, Tb-€230, 10 percent discount with this book if you pay cash, air-con, elevator, free Wi-Fi, Piazza del Duomo 1, tel. 055-219-922, www.hotelduomofirenze.it, info@ hotelduomofirenze.it; Paolo and Gilvaneide).

$$ Residenza dei Pucci rents 12 pleasant rooms (each one different) spread over three floors. The decor, a mix of soothing earth tones and aristocratic furniture, makes this place feel upscale for this price range (Sb-€135, Db-€150, Tb-€170, Qb suite-€238, 10 percent discount with this book if you pay cash, air-con, no elevator, free Wi-Fi, reception open 9:00-20:00, shorter hours off-season—let them know if you'll arrive late, Via dei Pucci 9, tel. 055-281-886, www.residenzadeipucci.com, residenzadeipucci@ residenzadeipucci.com, friendly Mirella and Marina).

$$ Soggiorno Battistero rents seven simple, airy rooms, most with great views, overlooking the Baptistery and the Duomo square. Choose a view or a quieter room in the back when you book by email, but keep in mind there's always some noise in the city center. It's a pristine and minimalist place run by Italian Luca and his American wife Kelly, who makes the hotel particularly welcoming (Sb-€83, Db-€110, Tb-€145, Qb-€155, 5 percent discount if you book direct and pay cash, breakfast served in room, air-con available June-Aug, elevator, free Wi-Fi, Piazza San Giovanni 1, third floor, tel. 055-295-143, www.soggiornobattistero.it, info@ soggiornobattistero.it).

$$ Residenza Giotto B&B offers the chance to stay on Florence's upscale shopping drag, Via Roma. Occupying the top floor of a 19th-century building, this place has six bright, smallish rooms and a terrace with knockout views of the Duomo's tower. Reception is generally open 9:00-17:00; let them know your arrival time in advance (Sb-€90, Db-€130, view rooms-€10 extra, extra bed-€25, 10 percent discount if you book direct and pay cash, air-con, elevator, free Wi-Fi, Via Roma 6, tel. 055-214-593, www.residenzagiotto.it, info@residenzagiotto.it, Giorgio).

$$ La Residenza del Proconsolo B&B, run by helpful Mariano, has five older-feeling rooms a minute from the Duomo (three rooms have Duomo views). The place lacks public spaces, but the rooms are quite large and nice—perfect for eating breakfast, which is served in your room (Sb-€90, Db-€120, Tb-€140, slightly larger "deluxe" with view-€20 more, air-con, no elevator, free Wi-Fi, Via del Proconsolo 18 black, tel. 055-264-5657, mobile 335-657-4840, www.proconsolo.com, info@proconsolo.com).

Sleep Code

(€1 = about $1.30, country code: 39)
S = Single, **D** = Double/Twin, **T** = Triple, **Q** = Quad, **b** = bathroom, **s** = shower only.

You can assume a hotel takes credit cards unless you see "cash only" in the listing. Unless otherwise noted, hotel staff speak basic English and breakfast is included.

Florence charges a hotel tax of €1 per star (according to the hotel's official star rating), per person, per night. So a couple staying at a three-star hotel would pay €3 each, or €6 total, per night. This tax is generally not included in the prices I've listed here.

To help you easily sort through these listings, I've divided the accommodations into three categories based on the price for a standard double room with bath during high season:

$$$ **Higher Priced**—Most rooms €160 or more.
  $$ **Moderately Priced**—Most rooms between €100-160.
    $ **Lower Priced**—Most rooms €100 or less.

Prices can change without notice; verify the hotel's current rates online or by email. For the best prices, always book direct.

North of the Duomo
North of the Mercato Centrale

After dark, this neighborhood can feel a little deserted, but I've never heard of anyone running into harm here. It's a short walk from the train station and an easy stroll to all the sightseeing action. While workaday, it's practical, with plenty of good budget restaurants and markets nearby.

$$ Grand Tour Firenze has six charming rooms on a nondescript street between the train station and the Accademia. This cozy B&B will make you feel right at home; it's thoughtfully appointed and the owners, Cristina and Giuseppe, live there. The delightful and spacious suites come with a garden ambience on the ground floor (Db-€115, suite-€130, 10 percent discount if you book direct and pay cash, includes breakfast voucher for the corner bar—or skip it to save €7/person, air-con, free Wi-Fi, Via Santa Reparata 21, tel. 055-283-955, www.florencegrandtour.com, info@florencegrandtour.com). They run another more romantic, pricier place a couple of blocks away.

$$ Galileo Hotel, a classy business hotel with 31 rooms on a chaotic and congested street, is run with familial warmth (Sb-€100, Db-€130, Tb-€160, Qb-€190, ask for 10 percent Rick Steves discount when you book direct and pay cash, quadruplepaned windows effectively shut out street noise, air-con, elevator, free guest computer, Wi-Fi, Via Nazionale 22a, tel. 055-496-645, www.galileohotel.it, info@galileohotel.it).

$ Hotel Il Bargellino, run by Bostonian Carmel and her Italian husband Pino, is in a residential neighborhood, still within walking distance of the center. They rent 10 summery rooms decorated with funky antiques and Pino's modern paintings. Guests enjoy Leopoldo, the parrot, and relaxing on the big, breezy, momentum-slowing terrace adorned with plants and lemon shrubs (S-€45, D-€80, Db-€90, €5-10 more for room facing terrace, book direct and ask for the Rick Steves rate, extra bed-€25, no breakfast, free Wi-Fi, north of the train station at Via Guelfa 87, tel. 055-238-2658, www.ilbargellino.com, carmel@ilbargellino.com).

$ Casa Rabatti is the ultimate if you always wanted to have a Florentine mama. Its four simple, clean rooms are run with warmth by Marcella. This is a great place to practice your Italian, as Marcella loves to chat and speaks minimal English. Seeing nearly two decades of my family Christmas cards on their walls, I'm reminded of how long she has been keeping budget travelers happy (D-€50, Db-€60, €25 extra per bed in shared quad or quint, prices good with this book, cash only but secure reservation with credit card, no breakfast, fans available, free Wi-Fi, 5 blocks from station at Via San Zanobi 48 black, tel. 055-212-393, casarabatti@inwind.it).

$ Hotel Enza rents 18 straightforward rooms, some recently renovated. The prices are reasonable for predictable hotel comfort (Sb-€55, Db-€80, Tb-€100, these prices promised through 2014 with this book, no breakfast, air-con, no elevator, free guest computer, Wi-Fi, Via San Zanobi 45 black, tel. 055-490-990, www.hotelenza.it, info@hotelenza.it, Diana).

Near the Accademia

$$$ Hotel Loggiato dei Serviti, at the most prestigious address in Florence on the most Renaissance square in town, gives you Old World romance with hair dryers. Stone stairways lead you under open-beam ceilings through this 16th-century monastery's monumental public rooms—it's so artful, you'll be snapping photos everywhere. The 38 cells—with air-conditioning, TVs, minibars, free Wi-Fi, and telephones—would be unrecognizable to their original inhabitants. The hotel staff is both professional and warm (Sb-€120, Db-€160, superior Db-€190, family suites from €280, ask for Rick Steves rate when you book, elevator, valet parking-€21/day, Piazza S.S. Annunziata 3, tel. 055-289-592, www.loggiatodeiservitihotel.it, info@loggiatodeiservitihotel.it; Simonetta, Gianni, and two Chiaras). When full, they rent five spacious and sophisticated rooms in a 17th-century annex a block away. While it lacks the monastic mystique, the annex rooms are bigger, gorgeous, and cost the same.

$$$ Hotel dei Macchiaioli offers 15 fresh and spacious rooms on one high-ceilinged, noble floor in a restored *palazzo* owned for generations by a well-to-do Florentine family. You'll eat breakfast under original frescoed ceilings while enjoying modern comforts (Sb-€100, Db-€180, Tb-€220, 10 percent Rick Steves discount if you book direct and pay cash, air-con, free Wi-Fi, Via Cavour 21, tel. 055-213-154, www.hoteldeimacchiaioli.com, info@hoteldei-macchiaioli.com, helpful Francesca and Paolo).

$$ Hotel Morandi alla Crocetta, a former convent, envelops you in a 16th-century cocoon. Located on a quiet street with 12 rooms, period furnishings, parquet floors, and wood-beamed or painted ceilings, it takes you back a few centuries and up a few social classes (Sb-€105, Db-€155, Tb-€185, Qb-€199, air-con, no elevator, free Wi-Fi, a block off Piazza S.S. Annunziata at Via Laura 50, tel. 055-234-4747, www.hotelmorandi.it, welcome@ho-telmorandi.it, well-run by Maurizio, Rolando, and Ertol).

$$ Hotel Europa, family run since 1970, has a welcoming atmosphere fostered by cheery Miriam, Roberto, and daughters Priscilla and Isabel. The breakfast room is spacious, and some of the 20 rooms have views of the Duomo (Sb-€89, Db-€150, Tb-€180, Qb-€250, slightly more for bigger "deluxe" room or a view, 10 percent discount if you pay cash, mention Rick Steves to get their best available room, air-con, old-timey elevator, free Wi-Fi, Via Cavour 14, tel. 055-239-6715, www.webhoteleuropa.com, firenze@webho-teleuropa.com).

East of the Duomo

$$ Residenza il Villino, popular and friendly, aspires to offer a Florentine home away from home. It has 10 charmingly rustic rooms and a picturesque, peaceful little courtyard. As it's in a "little villa" (as the name implies) set back from the street, this is a quiet refuge from the bustle of Florence (Sb-€100, small Db-€110, Db-€130, family suite that sleeps up to 6—price upon request, 5 percent discount with this book if you pay cash, air-con, free guest computer, Wi-Fi, just north of Via degli Alfani at Via della Pergola 53, tel. 055-200-1116, www.ilvillino.it, info@ilvillino.it; Sergio—who looks a bit like Henry Winkler, Elisabetta, and son Lorenzo).

$$ Panella's Residence, once a convent and today part of owner Graziella's extensive home, is a classy B&B, with six chic, romantic, and ample rooms, antique furnishings, and historic architectural touches (Db-€155, bigger "deluxe" Db-€180, extra bed-€40, book direct and mention Rick Steves for these prices, discounts for cash and stays of 3 or more nights, air-con, free Wi-

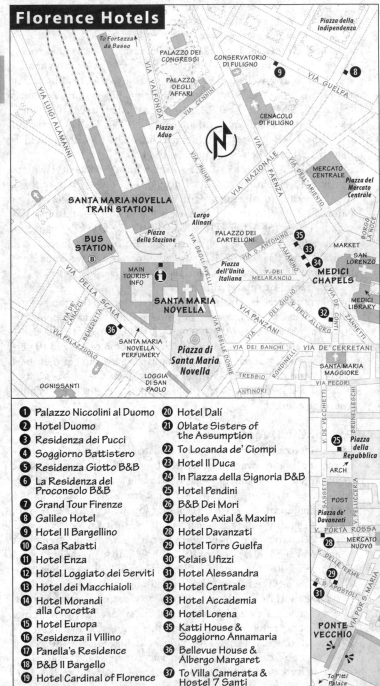

Florence Hotels

1 Palazzo Niccolini al Duomo
2 Hotel Duomo
3 Residenza dei Pucci
4 Soggiorno Battistero
5 Residenza Giotto B&B
6 La Residenza del Proconsolo B&B
7 Grand Tour Firenze
8 Galileo Hotel
9 Hotel Il Bargellino
10 Casa Rabatti
11 Hotel Enza
12 Hotel Loggiato dei Servizi
13 Hotel dei Macchiaioli
14 Hotel Morandi alla Crocetta
15 Hotel Europa
16 Residenza il Villino
17 Panella's Residence
18 B&B Il Bargello
19 Hotel Cardinal of Florence

20 Hotel Dalí
21 Oblate Sisters of the Assumption
22 To Locanda de' Ciompi
23 Hotel Il Duca
24 In Piazza della Signoria B&B
25 Hotel Pendini
26 B&B Dei Mori
27 Hotels Axial & Maxim
28 Hotel Davanzati
29 Hotel Torre Guelfa
30 Relais Uffizi
31 Hotel Alessandra
32 Hotel Centrale
33 Hotel Accademia
34 Hotel Lorena
35 Katti House & Soggiorno Annamaria
36 Bellevue House & Albergo Margaret
37 To Villa Camerata & Hostel 7 Santi

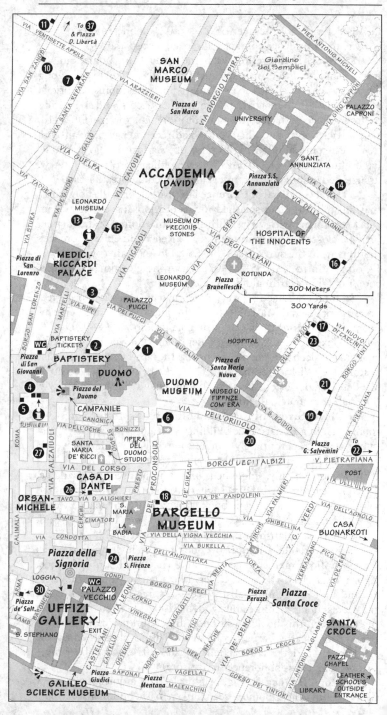

FLORENCE

Fi, Via della Pergola 42, tel. 055-234-7202, mobile 345-972-1541, www.panellaresidence.com, panella_residence@yahoo.it).

$$ B&B Il Bargello is a home away from home, run by friendly and helpful Canadian expat Gabriella. Hike up three long flights (no elevator) to reach six smart, relaxing rooms. Gabriella offers a cozy communal living room, kitchen access, and an inviting rooftop terrace with close-up views of Florence's towers (Db-€110, ask for Rick Steves rate when you book direct and pay cash, air-con, free guest computer, Wi-Fi, 20 yards off Via Proconsolo at Via de' Pandolfini 33 black, tel. 055-215-330, mobile 339-175-3110, www. firenze-bedandbreakfast.it, info@firenze-bedandbreakfast.it).

$ Hotel Cardinal of Florence is a third-floor walk-up with 17 spartan, tidy, and sun-splashed rooms overlooking either a silent courtyard (many with views of Brunelleschi's dome) or quiet street (may be closed for renovation in 2014). Relax and enjoy Florence's rooftops from the sun terrace (Sb-€60, Db-€95, air-con, free Wi-Fi, Borgo Pinti 5, tel. 055-234-0780, www.hotelcardinalofflorence. com, info@hotelcardinalofflorence.com).

$ Hotel Dalí has 10 cheery rooms in a nice location for a great price. Samanta and Marco, who run this guesthouse with a charming passion and idealism, are a delight to know (S-€40, D-€70, Db-€85, extra bed-€25, request quiet room when you book, nearby apartments sleep 2-6 people, no breakfast, fans but no air-con, elevator, free Wi-Fi, free parking, 2 blocks behind the Duomo at Via dell'Oriuolo 17 on the second floor, tel. 055-234-0706, www. hoteldali.com, hoteldali@tin.it).

$ Oblate Sisters of the Assumption run an institutional 30-room hotel in a Renaissance building with a dreamy garden, great public spaces, appropriately simple rooms, and a quiet, prayerful ambience (€45/person in single, double, triple, or quad rooms with bathrooms, cash only, single beds only, family discounts available, air-con, elevator, Wi-Fi with suggested donation, €10/day limited parking—request when you book, Borgo Pinti 15, tel. 055-248-0582, sroblateborgopinti@virgilio.it, sisters are likely to speak French but not English, Sister Theresa is very helpful).

$ Locanda de' Ciompi, overlooking the inviting Piazza dei Ciompi antique market in a young and lively neighborhood, is just right for travelers who want to feel like a part of the town. Alessio and Lisa run a minimalist place—just five quiet, clean, tasteful rooms along a thin hallway (Db-€100, Tb-€120, 10 percent discount with this book if you book direct and pay cash, includes breakfast at nearby bar, air-con, free Wi-Fi, 8 blocks behind the Duomo at Via Pietrapiana 28, tel. 055-263-8034, www.bbflorence-firenze.com, info@bbflorencefirenze.com).

$ Hotel Il Duca—a big, bright place on a quiet street a few blocks behind the Duomo—seems like a basic building wearing a fancy coat. Its 13 pleasant rooms are a great value, but don't expect a warm welcome or personal service (Sb-€85, Db-€90, third bed-€25, air-con, free Wi-Fi, Via della Pergola 34, tel. 055-906-2167, www.hotelilduca.it, info@hotelilduca.it, Angela).

South of the Duomo
Between the Duomo and Piazza della Signoria

These are the most central of my accommodations recommendations (and therefore a little overpriced). While worth the extra cost for many, given Florence's walkable, essentially traffic-free core, nearly every hotel I recommend can be considered central.

$$$ **In Piazza della Signoria B&B,** overlooking Piazza della Signoria, is peaceful, refined, and homey at the same time. Fit for a honeymoon, the 10 rooms come with all the special touches and little extras you'd expect in a top-end American B&B. However, the rates are high, and the "partial view" rooms, while slightly larger, require craning your neck to see anything—not worth the extra euros (viewless Db-€250, partial-view Db-€280, full-view "deluxe" Db-€300, Tb-€280, partial-view Tb-€300, ask for 10 percent discount when you book direct with this book, family apartments, lavish bathrooms, air-con, tiny elevator, free guest computer, Wi-Fi, Via dei Magazzini 2, tel. 055-239-9546, mobile 348-321-0565, www.inpiazzadellasignoria.com, info@inpiazzadellasignoria.com, Sonia and Alessandro).

$$$ **Hotel Pendini,** with three stars and 42 rooms (most of them recently renovated), fills the top floor of a grand building constructed to celebrate Italian unification in the late 19th century. It overlooks Piazza della Repubblica, and as you walk into the lobby, you feel as if you are walking back in time (Sb-€139, Db-€189, deluxe Db with square view and noise-€239, air-con, elevator, free guest computer, Wi-Fi, Via degli Strozzi 2, tel. 055-211-170, www.hotelpendini.it, info@hotelpendini.it).

$$ **B&B Dei Mori,** a peaceful haven with a convivial and welcoming living room, rents five tastefully appointed rooms ideally located on a quiet pedestrian street near Casa di Dante—within a five-minute walk of the Duomo, the Bargello, or Piazza della Signoria. Accommodating Daniele (Danny) and Peter pride themselves on offering personal service, including lots of tips on dining and sightseeing in Florence. But if they're full, I'd skip their offer of an apartment nearby (D-€110, Db-€130, minimum 2-night stay, 10 percent discount for Rick Steves' readers—ask when you book, air-con-€5, no elevator, free Wi-Fi, reception open 8:00-19:00, Via Dante Alighieri 12, tel. 055-211-438, www.deimori.com, deimori@bnb.it).

$$ **Hotel Axial,** on the main pedestrian drag, has 14 straightforward rooms, three-star amenities, and decent prices for the lo-

FLORENCE

cation (Sb-€84-104, Db-€139, book direct and use promo code "RICK" for 10 percent discount, air-con, elevator, free guest computer, Wi-Fi, Via de' Calzaiuoli 11, tel. 055-218-984, www.hotel-axial.it, info@hotelaxial.it, Nicola).

\$\$ Hotel Maxim, two floors above their sister Hotel Axial (and one star below), has 26 simpler rooms and even lower rates (Sb-€70, Db-€104, Tb-€124, Qb-€144, book direct and use promo code "RICK" for 10 percent discount, air-con, elevator, free guest computer, Wi-Fi, Via de' Calzaiuoli 11, tel. 055-217-474, www.hotelmaximfirenze.it, reservation@hotelmaximfirenze.it, Chiara).

Near Ponte Vecchio

\$\$\$ Hotel Davanzati, bright and shiny with artistic touches, has 25 cheerful rooms with all the comforts. The place is a family affair, thoughtfully run by friendly Tommaso and father Fabrizio, who offer drinks and snacks each evening at their candlelit happy hour, plus lots of other extras (Sb-€132, Db-€199, Tb-€259, family rooms available, these rates good with this book though prices soft off-season, 10 percent discount if you pay cash, free loaner laptop in every room, free on-demand videos—including Rick Steves' Italy shows—on your room TV, air-con, free Wi-Fi, next to Piazza Davanzati at Via Porta Rossa 5—easy to miss so watch for low-profile sign above the door, tel. 055-286-666, www.hoteldavanzati.it, info@hoteldavanzati.it).

\$\$\$ Hotel Torre Guelfa has grand (almost royal) public spaces and is topped by a fun medieval tower with a panoramic rooftop terrace. Its 31 pricey rooms vary wildly in size and layout. Room 315, with a private terrace (€260), is worth reserving several months in advance (Db-€170-200, Db junior suite-€250, ask for Rick Steves discount, family deals, check their website for promotions, air-con, elevator, free guest computer, Wi-Fi, a couple blocks northwest of Ponte Vecchio, Borgo S.S. Apostoli 8, tel. 055-239-6338, www.hoteltorreguelfa.com, info@hoteltorreguelfa.com, Niccolo and Barbara).

\$\$\$ Relais Uffizi is a peaceful little gem, with 15 classy rooms tucked away down a tiny alleyway off Piazza della Signoria. The lounge has a huge window overlooking the action in the square below (Sb-€120, Db-€180, Tb-€220, more for deluxe rooms, buffet breakfast, air-con, elevator, free Wi-Fi, off Chiasso de Baroncelli through arch to Chiasso del Buco 16, tel. 055-267-6239, www.relaisuffizi.it, info@relaisuffizi.it, charming Alessandro and Elizabetta).

\$\$ Hotel Alessandra is 16th-century, tranquil, and sprawling, with 27 big, tasteful rooms and an old-school, peeling-wallpaper vibe (S-€67-88, Sb-€110, D-€110, Db-€150, Tb-€195, Qb-€215, 5 percent cash discount, air-con, 30 steps to the elevator, free guest computer, Wi-Fi, Borgo S.S. Apostoli 17, tel. 055-283-438, www.hotelalessandra.com, info@hotelalessandra.com, Anna and son Andrea).

Between the Duomo and the Train Station

$$$ Hotel Centrale is indeed central, just a short walk from the Duomo. The 31 spacious but slightly overpriced rooms—with a tasteful mix of old and new decor—are over a businesslike conference center (Db-€190, bigger superior Db-€237, Tb-€236, suites available, 10 percent discount with this book, ask for Rick Steves rate when you reserve, 20 percent discount if booked 3 months in advance, air-con, elevator, free guest computer, Wi-Fi, Via dei Conti 3, check in at big front desk on ground floor, tel. 055-215-761, www .hotelcentralefirenze.it, info@hotelcentralefirenze.it, Margherita and Roberto).

$$ Hotel Accademia, which comes with marble stairs, parquet floors, and attractive public areas, has 21 pleasant rooms and a floor plan that defies logic (Db-€145, Tb-€170, 10 percent discount with this book if you book direct and pay cash, air-con, no elevator, free guest computer, Wi-Fi, Via Faenza 7, tel. 055-293-451, www.hotelaccademiafirenze.com, info@hotelaccademiafirenze.com, Tea).

$ Hotel Lorena, just across from the Medici Chapels, has 19 rooms (six of which have shared bathrooms), a tiny lobby, and is run with care by the Galli family. Though it's a bit like a youth hostel, it's cheap and conveniently located (S-€35, Sb-€50, D-€60, Db-€75, Tb-€95, very flexible rates, breakfast-€5, air-con, free Wi-Fi, Via Faenza 1, tel. 055-282-785, www.hotellorena.com, info@hotellorena.com).

$ Katti House and the nearby **Soggiorno Annamaria** are run by house-proud mama-and-daughter team Maria and Katti, who rent a total of 15 simple rooms on a bustling, sometimes-noisy pedestrian street. While both offer comparable comfort, Soggiorno Annamaria has a more historic setting, with frescoed ceilings, unique tiles, timbered beams, and quieter rooms. Katti House serves as reception for both places, but mostly you interact with Maria; while she's a fine hostess, she speaks virtually no English, so communication can be challenging (Sb-€85, D-€85, Db-€100, air-con, no elevator, free guest computer, Wi-Fi—only in Katti, Via Faenza 21, if no answer check in at Trattoria Katti next door, tel. 055-213-410, www.kattihouse.com, info@kattihouse.com). They also have several newer rooms located a five-minute walk north on busy Via Nazionale.

Near the Train Station

$$ Bellevue House is a third-floor (no elevator) oasis of tranquility, with six spacious, old fashioned rooms flanking a long, mellow-yellow lobby. It's a peaceful time warp thoughtfully run by the Michel family (Db-€110, Tb-€120, Qb-€140, 10 percent discount if you book direct and stay two nights, no breakfast, air-con, free Wi-Fi, Via della Scala 21, tel. 055-260-8932, www.bellevuehouse. it, info@bellevuehouse.it).

$ **Albergo Margaret,** homey yet minimalist, doesn't have a public lounge or offer breakfast. Run by the Cristantielli family, it has seven tidy, simple rooms (D-€40, Ds-€60, Db-€75, 10 percent discount if you book direct and pay cash, extra bed-€10, air-con, free Wi-Fi, near Santa Maria Novella at Via della Scala 25, tel. 055-210-138, www.hotel-margaret.it, info@hotel-margaret.it; Francesco, Anna, and Graziano).

Hostels away from the Center

These two hostels, northeast of downtown, are a bus ride from the action. A far more central hostel is in the Oltrarno (listed at the end of the next section).

$ **Villa Camerata,** classy for an IYHF hostel, is in a pretty villa three miles northeast of the train station, on the outskirts of Florence (€24/bed with breakfast, 4- to 6-bed rooms, members pay €3/night less, private rooms available, free Wi-Fi, self-serve laundry, Viale Augusto Righi 2—take bus #11 from the train station to Salviatino or bus #17 to Via Cento Stelle, tel. 055-601-451, www. aighostels.com, firenze@aighostels.com).

$ **Hostel 7 Santi** calls itself a "travelers' haven." It fills a former convent, but you'll feel like you're in an old school. Still, it offers some of the best cheap beds in town, is friendly to older travelers, and comes with the services you'd expect in a big, modern hostel, including free Wi-Fi and self-serve laundry. It's in a more residential neighborhood near the Campo di Marte stadium, about a 10-minute bus ride from the center (200 beds in 60 rooms, mostly 4- or 6-bed dorms with a floor of doubles and triples, €16-18/dorm bed, Sb-€45, Db-€60, Tb-€70, Qb-€80, includes sheets and towels, breakfast and dinner available but cost extra, no curfew, free guest computer, Wi-Fi; Viale dei Mille 11—from train station, take bus #10, #17, or #20, direction: Campo di Marte, to bus stop Chiesa dei Sette Santi; tel. 055-504-8452, www.7santi.com, info@7santi.com).

South of the Arno River, in the Oltrarno

Across the river in the Oltrarno area, between the Pitti Palace and Ponte Vecchio, you'll find small, traditional crafts shops, neighborly piazzas, and family eateries. The following places are an easy walk from Ponte Vecchio. Only the first two are real hotels—the rest are a ragtag gang of budget alternatives.

$$$ Hotel Silla is a classic three-star hotel with 36 cheery, spacious rooms. On the opposite side of the river from Santa Croce Church, it has a breezy terrace and faces the river, overlooking a small park. Still, it can get a bit noisy from the surrounding neighborhood (Db-€180, bigger "superior" Db-€210, Tb-€230, book direct and use promo code "RICK" for 10 percent discount, extra bed-€35, air con, elevator, free guest computer, Wi-Fi, parking-€19/day, Via dei Renai 5, tel. 055 234-2888, www.hotelsilla.it, hotelsilla@hotelsilla.it; Laura, Chiara, Massimo, and Stefano).

$$ Hotel la Scaletta has 28 functional but colorful rooms hiding in a tortured floor plan, plus a fabulous rooftop terrace overlooking the Boboli Gardens (Db-€125, slightly more for new "superior" rooms, third bed-€20, family suite that sleeps up to 6-€239, breakfast-€7, air-con, elevator, free guest computer, Wi-Fi, Via de' Guicciardini 13, tel. 055-283-028, www.hotellascaletta.it, info@hotellascaletta.it).

$ Soggiorno Alessandra has five bright, comfy, and smallish rooms. Because of its double-paned windows, you'll hardly notice the traffic noise (D-€70, Db-€75, Tb-€100, Qb-€130, includes basic breakfast in room, air-con-€5, free Wi-Fi, just past the Carraia Bridge at Via Borgo San Frediano 6, tel. 055-290-424, www.soggiornoalessandra.it, info@soggiornoalessandra.it, Alessandra).

$ Casa Santo Nome di Gesù is a grand, 29-room convent whose sisters—Franciscan Missionaries of Mary—are thankful to rent rooms to tourists. Staying in this 15th-century palace, you'll be immersed in the tranquil atmosphere created by a huge, peaceful garden, generous and prayerful public spaces, and smiling nuns. As with the Istituto Gould, below, it's a good value and understandably popular—it's best to reserve a couple of months in advance (D-€70, Db-€85, T-€100, Tb-€120, extra bed-€15, book direct to avoid fees, no air-con but rooms have fans, elevator, free Wi-Fi, memorable convent-like breakfast room, 1:00 in the morning curfew, parking-€10, Piazza del Carmine 21, tel. 055-213-856, www.fmmfirenze.it, info@fmmfirenze.it).

$ Istituto Gould is a Protestant Church-run place with 40 clean and spartan rooms that have twin beds and modern facilities. It's located in a 17th-century palace overlooking a beautiful garden courtyard. The complex also houses kids from troubled homes, and proceeds raised from renting rooms help fund that important work (Sb-€55, Db-€60, €20 more for garden rooms that are quieter and have air-con, Tb-€84, Qb-€100, breakfast-€6, non-air-con rooms have fans, free Wi-Fi in lobby, Via dei Serragli 49, tel. 055-212-576, www.istitutogould.it, foresteriafirenze@diaconiavaldese.org). You must arrive when the office is open (Mon-Fri 8:45-13:00 & 15:00-19:30, Sat 9:00-13:30 & 14:30-18:00, no live check-in on Sundays, but they'll email you a code).

Oltrarno Hotels & Restaurants

To
Porta
San
Frediano
& ⑩

BORGO SAN FREDIANO

③

To
Santa Maria
Novella

Arno

LUNGARNO GUICCIARDINI

Piazza
Nazaro
Sauro

⑧

VIA DI SANTO SPIRITO

VIA DELLE LEONE

Piazza del
Carmine

BORGO STELLA

VIA SANTA MONACA

④

⑥ O L T R A R N O

VIA DEI SERRAGLI

VIA MAFFIA

VIA DE' COVERELLI

BRANCACCI
CHAPEL

SANTA MARIA
DEL CARMINE

SANTO
SPIRITO

To ⑫

VIA S. AGOSTINO

⑤

Piazza di
Santo Spirito

VIA D. S. MARTINO

SDRUCCIOLO DE' PITTI

VIA DELLA CHIESA

VIA DELLA CALDAIE

Piazza di
Santo Spirito

⑭

TEGOLAIO

⑬

VIA MAGGIO

MICH.

VIA MARSILI

VIA DE'

VIA DEL CAMPUCCIO

PAL. DE
COSIMO
RIDOLFI

VIA MAZZETTA

BORGO

Giardino
Torrigiani

Piazza di
San Felice

TICKET
OFFICE

VIA ROMANA

Piazzina
della
Meridiana

To
Porta
Romana

VIALE DELLA MERIDIANA

L'Isolotto

VIALE DEL CIPRESSI

FONTANA
DELL'OCEANO

① To Hotel Silla & Il Gelato di Filo
② Hotel la Scaletta
③ Soggiorno Alessandra
④ Casa Santo Nome di Gesù
⑤ Istituto Gould
⑥ Ostello Santa Monaca
⑦ Golden View Open Bar
⑧ Il Santo Bevitore Ristorante &
   Enoteca Il Santino Gastronomia
⑨ Trattoria 4 Leoni
⑩ To Antico Ristoro Di' Cambi,
   Trattoria da Sergio & Trattoria
   Sabatino
⑪ Olio & Convivium Gastronomia
⑫ To Trattoria Al Tranvai
⑬ Trattoria Casalinga
⑭ Borgo Antico; Volume Bar;
   Rist. & Caffè Ricchi
⑮ Le Volpi e l'Uva Wine Bar
⑯ Sapori & Dintorni Conad
   (Supermarket)

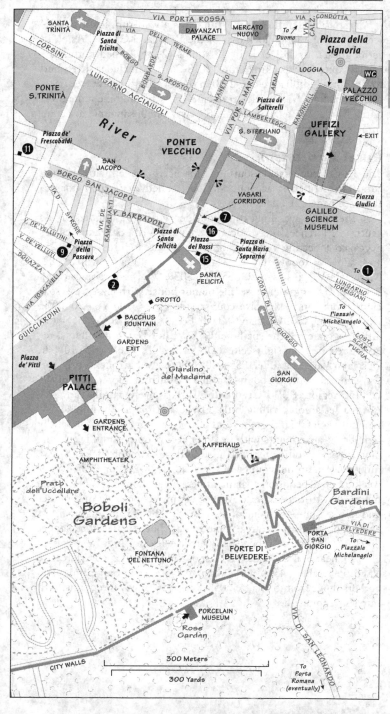

Hostel: **$ Ostello Santa Monaca** is a well-run, institutional-feeling hostel a long block east of the Brancacci Chapel. As clean as its guests, its 112 beds in 13 rooms (2- to 20-bed dorms) attract a young backpacking crowd (€18-26/bed, includes sheets and towel, 10:00-14:00 lock-out, 2:00 in the morning curfew, free guest computer, free Wi-Fi, self-serve laundry, kitchen, bike rental, Via Santa Monaca 6, tel. 055-268-338, www.ostellosantamonaca.com, info@ostellosantamonaca.com).

Rural *Agriturismi*

The Tuscan countryside south of Florence is loaded with enticing rural farms offering accommodations, called *agriturismi* (for details, see page 29).

There are several places to consider within 30 minutes or less south of Florence. The rustic and cozy **$$ Villa Salvadonica** has a gorgeous setting overlooking rolling Tuscan hills (Db-€125-150, superior rooms and suites also available, Via Grevigiana 82, Mercatale Val di Pesa, tel. 055-821-8039, www.salvadonica.com). **$$ Villa Il Poggiale** is a serene manor house with classy and spacious rooms and expansive countryside views (Db-€69-200, Via Empolese 69, San Casciano Val di Pesa, tel. 055-828-311, www.villailpoggiale.it). The spa hotel **$$$ Villa I Barronci** offers a relaxing respite from sightseeing (Db-€179-200, Via Sorripa 10, San Casciano Val di Pesa, tel. 055-820-598, www.ibarronci.com).

Another option about 45 minutes south of Florence is in the Chianti region: **$$$ I Greppi di Silli** is a lovely, family-run *agriturismo* set among rolling hills. Owners Anna and Giuliano Alfani cultivate Chianti grapes and olive trees, and offer six carefully remodeled apartments with beds for 2-6 people, some with panoramic views and/or terraces; a seventh apartment (sleeps 8) is a mile away in an old country house (Db-€115-280 or €735-1,900/week, price depends on apartment, less off-season; one-week minimum—Sat-to-Sat—in July-Aug, fewer nights possible in shoulder and low season—but generally still a 3-night minimum; breakfast extra, pool, kids' play area, table tennis, bocce ball court, loaner bikes, weekly farm dinners-€30/person—less for kids, Via Vallacchio 19, near San Casciano and just outside the village of Mercatale Val di Pesa, about 45 minutes' drive to Florence or San Gimignano and one hour from Siena, tel. 055-821-7956, www.igreppidisilli.it, info@igreppidisilli.it).

Eating in Florence

Remember, restaurants like to serve what's fresh. If you're into flavor, go for the seasonal best bets—featured in the *piatti del giorno*
("specials of the day") section on menus. For dessert, it's gelato (see
sidebar later in this section).

To save money and time for sights, keep lunches fast and simple, eating in one of the countless pizzerias and self-service cafeterias. Picnicking is easy—there's no shortage of corner *supermerca-
tos,* or you can picnic your way through the Mercato Centrale.

Foodies or those with more time (and a smartphone), consider
downloading Elizabeth Minchilli's excellent app, Eat Florence,
which has thorough descriptions of all things food-related in the
city (www.elizabethminchilliinrome.com).

North of the Arno River
Near the Church of Santa Maria Novella

Trattoria Marione serves sincerely home-cooked-style meals to
a mixed group of tourists and Florentines beneath hanging ham
hocks. The ambience is happy, crowded, food-loving, and a bit
frantic (€8-11 pastas, €10-12 *secondi,* daily 12:00-17:00 & 19:00-
23:00, Via della Spada 27 red, tel. 055-214-756, Fabio).

Trattoria al Trebbio serves traditional food, especially rabbit
and steak, in a throwback Florentine setting. Inside, enjoy the old
movie posters and garlands of garlic, or grab one of the few tables
outside in season (€7-10 pastas, €10-16 *secondi,* daily 12:00-15:00 &
19:15-23:00, half a block off of Piazza Santa Maria Novella at Via
delle Belle Donne 47, tel. 055-287-089, Antonio).

Trattoria "da Giorgio" is a family-style diner on a sketchy
street serving up piping-hot, simple home cooking to happy locals
and tourists alike. Their three-course, fixed-price meal, including
water and a drink, is a great value (€12 at lunch, €13 at dinner).
Choose from among the daily specials or the regular menu (Mon-
Sat 12:00-14:30 & 18:30-22:00, closed Sun, Via Palazzuolo 100
red, tel. 055-284-302, Silvano).

Trattoria Sostanza-Troia, characteristic and well-established, is famous for its beef. Hearty steaks and pastas are splittable. Whirling ceiling fans and walls strewn with old photos evoke
earlier times, while the artichoke pies remind locals of Grandma's
cooking. Crowded, shared tables with paper tablecloths give this
place a bistro feel. Reservations are always a good idea but essential
for dinner, during which they offer two seatings, at 19:30 and 21:00
(dinners for about €30 plus wine, cash only, lunch Mon-Sat 12:30-
14:00, closed Sun, closed Sat off-season, Via del Porcellana 25 red,
tel. 055-212-691).

Trattoria 13 Gobbi ("13 Hunchbacks") is a trendy and slightly self-important eatery, atmospherically cluttered and glowing with candles around a tiny garden. Romantic in front and more kid-friendly in back, it serves beautifully presented Tuscan food (they're enthusiastic about their steak) on big, fancy plates to a mostly tourist crowd (€10-12 pastas, €14-19 *secondi*, daily 12:30-15:00 & 19:30-23:00, Via del Porcellana 9 red, tel. 055-284-015, Enrico).

Near the Mercato Centrale

The following market-neighborhood eateries all have a distinct vibe. They're within a few blocks of each other; scout around and choose your favorite.

Trattoria Zà-Zà is a fun, high-energy place facing the Mercato Centrale. It offers a family-friendly festival of standard Tuscan dishes such as *ribollita* and *bistecca alla fiorentina*, plus a variety of big, splittable €8 salads. Though it's more touristy than ever, the food is still good, and everyone's happy. Arrive early or make a reservation. Choose between the colorful interior or the outdoor piazza. Understand your itemized bill, and don't mistake their outside seating with the neighboring restaurant's (€8-10 pastas, €10-16 *secondi*, daily 11:00-23:00, Piazza del Mercato Centrale 26 red, tel. 055-215-411). Their **bar/osteria,** nearby, has a similar menu (with a few differences, including more of an emphasis on seafood and *taglieri*—cheese-and-meat plates), a trendier-feeling interior, and a smaller, more open outdoor-dining zone.

Trattoria la Burrasca is Flintstone-chic. Friendly Elio and his staff offer a limited menu with good-value seasonal specials of Tuscan home cooking. It's small—14 tables—and often filled with my readers. If Archie Bunker were Italian, he'd eat at this trattoria for special nights out (€6 pastas, €7-15 *secondi*, no cover or service charge, Tue-Sun 12:00-15:00 & 19:00-22:30, closed Mon, Via Panicale 6, north corner of Mercato Centrale, tel. 055-215-827).

Trattoria Lo Stracotto is a truffle-colored eatery with sophisticated ambience just steps away from the Medici Chapels. It's run by cousins Francesco and Tommaso, who serve up tasty, traditional dishes such as *bistecca alla fiorentina* and *ribollita* (based on grandfather's recipe), and good chocolate soufflé. Enjoy the candlelit ambience and soft music as you sit either in the dining room or out on the terrace (€7-10 pastas, €10-17 *secondi*, daily 12:00-15:00 & 18:00-22:30, Piazza Madonna degli Aldobrandi 16/17, tel. 055-230-2062).

Osteria Vineria i'Brincello is a bright, happy, no-frills diner with tasty food, lots of spirit, friendly service, and no hint of snobbishness. It features a list of Tuscan daily specials hanging from the ceiling and great prices on good bottled wine (€7-8 pastas, €8-15 *secondi*, €5 takeout homemade pasta, daily 12:00-15:00 & 19:00-23:00, near corner of Via Nazionale and Via Chiara at Via Nazionale 110 red, tel. 055-282-645, Fredi cooks while Claudia serves). Their hole-in-the-wall across the street, **i'Brincellino,** serves several inexpensive hot dishes (from the same kitchen) and tasty sandwiches. You can eat in or get it to go (daily 11:00-23:00).

Trattoria Nerone Pizzeria, serving up cheap, hearty Tuscan dishes and decent pizzas, is a tourist-friendly, practical standby in the hotel district. The lively, flamboyantly outfitted space (once the garden courtyard of a convent—they still have a small, leafy seasonal terrace) feels like a good but kitschy Italian-American chain restaurant (€5-8 pizzas, €6-8 pastas, €8-12 *secondi*, daily 12:00-23:00, just north of Via Nazionale at Via Faenza 95-97 red, tel. 055-291-217, Tulio).

Eating Cheaply in or near the Mercato Centrale

Note that none of these eateries is open for dinner.

Mercato Centrale (Central Market) is great for an ad lib lunch. It offers colorful piles of picnic produce, people-watching, and rustic sandwiches (Mon-Sat 7:00-14:00, Sat in winter until 17:00, closed Sun, a block north of San Lorenzo street market). The thriving eateries within the market (such as Nerbone, described next) serve some of the cheapest hot meals in town. The fancy deli, Perini, is famous for its quality (pricey) products and enticing display. Buy a picnic of fresh mozzarella cheese, olives, fruit, and crunchy bread to munch on the steps of the nearby Church of San Lorenzo, overlooking the bustling street market.

Nerbone in the Market is a venerable café and the best place for a sit-down meal within the Mercato Centrale. Join the shoppers and workers who crowd up to the bar to grab their €4-7 plates, and then find a stool at the cramped shared tables nearby. Of the several cheap market diners, this feels the most authentic. As intestines are close to Florentines' hearts, it's a good place to try tripe. For the less adventurous, *porchetta* (roast pork with herbs) and *bollito* (stewed beef with broth) are tasty alternatives (lunch menu served Mon-Sat 12:00-14:00, sandwiches available from 8:00 until the bread runs out, closed Sun, cash only, inside Mercato Centrale on the side closest to the Church of San Lorenzo, mobile 339-648-0251).

Trattoria Mario's, around the corner from Trattoria Zà-Zà (listed earlier), has been serving hearty lunches to market-goers since 1953 (Fabio and Romeo are the latest generation). Their simple formula: no-frills, bustling service, old-fashioned good value, and shared tables. It's *cucina casalinga*—home cooking *con brio*. This place is high-energy and jam-packed. Their best dishes often sell out first, so go early. If there's a line, put your name on the list (€5-6 pastas, €8 *secondi*, cash only, Mon-Sat 12:00-15:30, closed Sun and Aug, no reservations, Via Rosina 2, tel. 055-218-550).

Casa del Vino, Florence's oldest operating wine shop, offers

FLORENCE

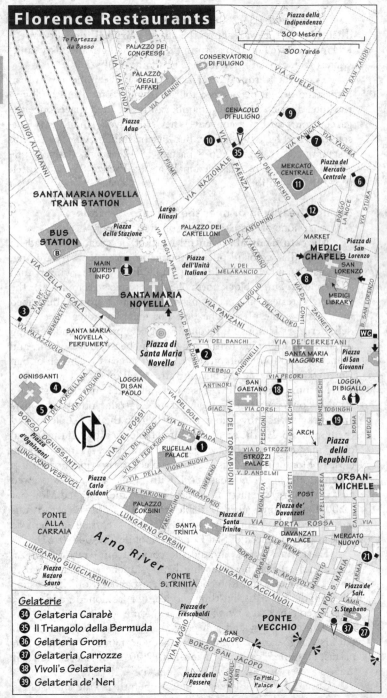

Florence Restaurants

Piazza della
Indipendenza

300 Meters

300 Yards

To Fortezza
da Basso

PALAZZO DEI
CONGRESSI

CONSERVATORIO
DI FULIGNO

VIA VALFONDA

VIA GUELFA

PALAZZO
DEGLI
AFFARI

VIA GENNINI

CENÁCOLO
DI FULIGNO

9

10

7

35

Piazza
Adua

VIA FIUME

VIA DELL'ARIENTO

MERCATO
CENTRALE

Piazza del
Mercato
Centrale

6

VIA NAZIONALE FAENZA

11

SANTA MARIA NOVELLA
TRAIN STATION

BORGO LA NOCE

12

Largo
Alinari

PALAZZO DEI
CARTELLONI

VIA S. ANTONINO

MARKET

BUS
STATION
B

Piazza
della Stazione

VIA DEGLI AVELLI

VIA S. AMARINO

MEDICI
CHAPELS

Piazza di
San
Lorenzo

Piazza
dell'Unità
Italiana

V. DEI
MELARANCIO

SAN
LORENZO

8

MAIN
TOURIST
INFO

i

VIA DEL GIGLIO

MEDICI
LIBRARY

3

SANTA MARIA
NOVELLA

V. DELL'ALLORO

VIA PANZANI

B. SAN LORENZO

VIA DE' CONTI

VIA PALAZZUOLO

VIA DELLA SCALA

SANTA MARIA
NOVELLA
PERFUMERY

Piazza di
Santa Maria
Novella

VIA D. BELLE DONNE

VIA DEI BANCHI

VIA DE' CERRETANI

WC

VIA DE' ZANNETTI

OGNISSANTI

4

2

TREBBIO

SANTA MARIA
MAGGIORE

Piazza
di San
Giovanni

LOGGIA
DI SAN
PAOLO

RONDINELLI

ANTINORI

VIA PECORI

5

VIA DEL PORCELLANA

VIA DI PAOLINO

SAN
GAETANO

18

LOGGIA
DI BIGALLO
&

VIA DEL SOLE

GIAC.

VIA CORSI

V. DE' VECCHIETTI

TOSINGHI

Piazza
d'Ognissanti

N

VIA DEL FOSSI

VIA DELLA SPADA

PESCIONI

BRUNELLESCHI

ROMA

19

MEDICI

BORGO OGNISSANTI

VIA DEL MORO

RUCELLAI
PALACE

1

ARCH

Piazza
della
Repubblica

LUNGARNO VESPUCCI

VIA DE' FEDERIGHI

VIA D. STROZZI

ORSAN-
MICHELE

Piazza
Carlo
Goldoni

VIA DELLA VIGNA NUOVA

STROZZI
PALACE

V. D. ANSELMI

CALIMALA

PALAZZO
CORSINI

VIA DEL PARIONE

PURGATORIO

PARIONCINO

INFERNO

MONALDA

SASSETTI

POST

Piazza de'
Davanzati

VIA

PONTE
ALLA
CARRAIA

LUNGARNO CORSINI

SANTA
TRINITA

Piazza di
Santa
Trinita

VIA PORTA ROSSA

PELLICCERIA

MERCATO
NUOVO

Arno River

DAVANZATI
PALACE

VIA DELLE TERME

21

LUNGARNO GUICCIARDINI

PONTE
S. TRINITA

VIA POR S. MARIA

BORGO S.S. APOSTOLI

ARMA

Piazza
Nazaro
Sauro

LUNGARNO ACCIAIUOLI

BORGO

S.S. APOSTOLI

LAMB

Piazza de'
Salt.

S. Stephano

Gelaterie

34 Gelateria Carabè

Piazza de'
Frescobaldi

PONTE
VECCHIO

37

27

35 Il Triangolo della Bermuda

SAN
JACOPO

36 Gelateria Grom

37 Gelateria Carrozze

BORGO SAN JACOPO

38 Vivoli's Gelateria

VIA MAGGIO

V.D.
RAMAGLI-
ANTI

To Pitti
Palace

39 Gelateria de' Neri

Piazza della
Passera

1. Trattoria Marione
2. Trattoria al Trebbio
3. Trattoria "da Giorgio"
4. Trattoria Sostanza-Troia
5. Trattoria 13 Gobbi
6. Trattoria Zà-Zà & Trattoria Mario's
7. Trattoria la Burrasca
8. Trattoria Lo Stracotto
9. Osteria Vineria i'Brincello & i'Brincellino
10. Trattoria Nerone Pizzeria
11. Mercato Centrale & Nerbone in the Market
12. Casa del Vino
13. Pugi Pizza
14. Pasticceria Robiglio
15. La Mescita Fiaschetteria
16. Il Centro Supermercati
17. To Antica Trattoria da Tito
18. Self-Service Rist. Leonardo
19. Paszkowski Café
20. Turkuaz Döner Kebab
21. Rivoire Café
22. Frescobaldi Ristorante & Wine Bar
23. Ristorante Paoli, Cantinetta dei Verrazzano & Perchè No! Gelateria
24. Osteria Vini e Vecchi Sapori
25. I Fratellini
26. L'Antico Trippaio, Pizzeria Totò & Supermarket
27. 'Ino Wine Bar
28. Ristorante del Fagioli
29. Boccadama Enoteca Ristorante
30. Trattoria Anita
31. Trattoria l'cche C'è C'è
32. Club del Gusto
33. All'Antico Vinaioi

Florentine and Tuscan Cuisine

While many restaurants in Florence and Tuscany serve your basic Italian fare—pasta and pizza, veal cutlets, and mixed salad—there are a few specialties you'll find without looking too hard. In general, the cuisine of this region is hearty, simple farmers' food: grilled meats, high-quality seasonal vegetables, fresh herbs, prized olive oil, and rustic bread. By the way, there's nothing wrong with your *pane alla toscana* (Tuscan bread)—it's supposed to taste that way. Tuscan bread is unsalted (from the days when salt was more valuable than gold) and nearly flavorless.

Many menus list dishes cooked *alla fiorentina*—"Florence-style," or *alla toscana*—"Tuscan style"; usually this means it's a rustic preparation highlighting local produce, but in practice these terms can mean almost anything.

A basic Tuscan **antipasto** (appetizer) is bread drenched in olive oil and sprinkled with salt. For something a bit more elaborate, bruschetta is toasted bread brushed with olive oil and rubbed with garlic, topped with chopped tomato, mushrooms, or whatever else sounds good. *Crostini* are small toasted bread rounds topped with meat or vegetable pastes (*alla toscana* generally means with chicken liver paste). *Panzanella* is a summer salad mixing day-old bread with chopped tomatoes, onion, basil, and a light vinaigrette. Tuscany is a land of great *salumi* (cold cuts, usually air- and/or salt-cured), such as prosciutto (air-cured ham hock), pancetta (cured pork belly), *lardo* (cured pork lard), and *finocchiona* (fennel salami); for a list of other *salumi*, see page 40. The cheese here is also excellent, specializing in pecorino, from ewe's milk (it comes either *fresco*—fresh, or *stagionato*—

glasses of wine from among 25 open bottles (see the list tacked to the bar). Owner Gianni, whose family has owned the Casa for more than 70 years, is a class act. Gianni's *carta dei panini* lists delightful €3.50 sandwiches and €1 crostini; the *I Nostri Panini* (classic sandwiches) richly reward adventurous eaters. During busy times, it's a mob scene. You'll eat standing outside alongside workers on a quick lunch break (Mon-Fri 9:30-20:00 year-round, Sat 9:30-17:00 Sept-June only, closed Sun year-round and Sat in summer, hidden behind stalls of San Lorenzo Market at Via dell'Ariento 16 red, tel. 055-215-609).

Near the Accademia
Budget Lunch Places Surrounding the Accademia
For pizza by the slice, try **Pugi**, at Piazza San Marco 9B.

Pasticceria Robiglio, a smart little café, opens up its stately dining area and sets out a few tables on the sidewalk for lunch. They have a small menu of daily pasta and *secondi* specials, and seem determined to do things like they did in the elegant, pre-tourism

aged). For variety, order a *tagliere*—a big wooden platter with a sampling of cold cuts and cheeses.

First courses *(primi)* include some tasty pastas, such as *pici al ragù* (fat, spaghetti-like hand-rolled pasta served with a meat-tomato sauce) and *pappardelle al sugo di lepre* (long, broad noodles with a rich sauce made from wild hare). *Ribollita* is a "re-boiled" soup traditionally made with leftovers, including white beans *(fagioli)*, seasonal vegetables, and olive oil, with layers of day-old Tuscan bread slices.

When it comes to **second courses** *(secondi)*, the local favorite is *bistecca alla fiorentina*: a thick T-bone steak, generally grilled very rare and lightly seasoned. (The best is from the white Chianina breed of cattle you'll see grazing throughout Tuscany.) This dish is often sold by weight (per *etto*, or 100 grams), not per portion; ask what the minimum amount costs. And don't confuse that dish with *trippa alla fiorentina*—tripe (intestines) and vegetables sautéed in a tomato sauce, sometimes baked with parmesan cheese. *Cinghiale* (boar) shows up all over menus, served grilled or in soups, stews, and pasta, as well as in sausages and salami. Also popular are various game birds: squab, pheasant, and guinea hen. *Arrosto misto* is an assortment of roasted meats, sometimes on a skewer *(spiedino)*.

For *dolci* (desserts), gelato is a local specialty; the Florentines claim they invented Italian-style ice cream (for some tips on enjoying it here, see page 576). Another popular and simple dessert is *cantucci* (crunchy almond cookies) dipped in Vin Santo (literally, "holy wine"), a sweet, golden dessert wine.

days (generous €9-10 plates, a great €8 *niçoise*-like "fantasy salad," pretty pastries, smiling service, daily 12.00-15.00, longer hours as a café, a block toward the Duomo off Piazza S.S. Annunziata at Via dei Servi 112 red, tel. 055-212-784). Before you leave, be tempted by their pastries, which are famous among Florentines.

La Mescita Fiaschetteria is a characteristic hole-in-the-wall just around the corner from *David*—but a world away from all the tourism. It's where locals and students enjoy daily pasta specials and hearty sandwiches with good €1.50 house wine. You can trust Mirco and Alessio (as far as you can throw them—check your bill)—just point to what looks good (such as their €5-6 pasta plate or €6-8 *secondi*), and you'll soon be eating well and inexpensively. The place can either be mobbed by students or in a peaceful time warp, depending on when you stop by (Mon-Sat 10:45-16:00, closed Sun, Via degli Alfani 70 red, mobile 347-795-1604 or 338-992-2640).

Picnic on the Ultimate Renaissance Square: **Il Centro Supermercati,** a handy supermarket a half-block north of the Accademia, has a curbside sandwich bar (Panineria) with an easy English menu that includes salads to go (Mon-Sat 9:00-19:30, Sun 10:00-19:00, Sat-Mon closed 15:00-16:30, sandwich bar may close earlier, Via Ricasoli 109). With your picnic in hand, hike around the block and join the bums on Piazza S.S. Annunziata, the first Renaissance square in Florence (don't confuse this with the less-interesting Piazza San Marco, closer to the supermarket). There's a fountain for washing fruit on the square. Grab a stony seat anywhere you like, and savor one of my favorite cheap Florence eating experiences. Or drop by any of the places listed earlier for an easy lunch (pizza, kebab, or sandwich plus juice) to go.

Dining with Bobo away from the Center

Antica Trattoria da Tito, a 10-minute hike from the Accademia along Via San Gallo, can be fun if you want a long, drawn-out event of a meal with a local crowd and smart-aleck service. The boss, Bobo, serves quality traditional food and lots of wine. While the food is good, there's no pretense—it's just a playground of Tuscan cuisine with "no romance allowed." The music is vintage 1980s and can be loud. To gorge on a feast of *antipasti* (cold cuts, cheeses, a few veggies, and bruschetta), consider ordering *fermami* (literally, "stop me")—for €14, Bobo brings you food until you say, *"Fermami!"* A couple can get *fermami,* desserts, and a nice bottle of wine for around €60 total (€10 pastas, €12 *secondi,* €14 *gran tagliere*—big plate of cheese and meat, travelers with this book get a free after-dinner drink, Mon-Sat 12:30-15:00 & 19:00-23:00, closed Sun, reservations generally necessary, Via San Gallo 112 red, tel. 055-472-475, www.trattoriadatito.it).

Fast and Cheap near the Duomo

Self-Service Ristorante Leonardo is an inexpensive, air-conditioned, quick, and handy cafeteria. Eating here, you'll get the sense that they're passionate about the quality of their food. Stefano and Luciano (like Pavarotti) run the place with enthusiasm and put out free pitchers of tap water. It's just a block from the Duomo, southwest of the Baptistery (€5 *primi,* €6 main courses, lots of veggies, Sun-Fri 11:45-14:45 & 18:45-21:45, closed Sat, upstairs at Via Pecori 11, tel. 055-284-446).

Paszkowski, a grand café on Piazza della Repubblica, serves up inexpensive, quick lunches. At the display case, order a salad or €7 plate of pasta or cooked veggies (or half and half), pay the cashier, and find a seat upstairs. Better yet, eat at one of the tables on the square. Note that table service prices are much more expensive (daily 7:00-24:00, lunch served 12:00-15:00, closed Mon off-season, Piazza della Repubblica 35 red—northwest corner, tel. 055-210-236).

Döner Kebab: A good place to try this cheap Middle Eastern specialty is **Turkuaz,** a couple blocks northeast of the Duomo (Via dei Servi 65).

Near Piazza della Signoria

Piazza della Signoria, the scenic square facing Palazzo Vecchio, is ringed by beautifully situated yet touristy eateries serving over-priced, bad-value, and probably microwaved food. If you're deter-mined to eat on the square, have pizza at Ristorante il Cavallino or bar food from the Irish pub next door. Piazza della Signoria's sav-ing grace is **Rivoire** café, famous for its fancy desserts and thick hot chocolate. While obscenely expensive, it has the best view tables on the square. Stand at the bar with the locals and pay way less (Tue-Sun 7:30-24:00, closed Mon, tel. 055-214-412).

Fine Dining near the Piazza

Frescobaldi Ristorante and Wine Bar, the showcase of Italy's aristocratic wine family, is a good choice for a formal dinner in Florence. Candlelight reflects off glasses of wine, and high-vaulted ceilings complement the sophisticated dishes. They offer the same seasonal menu in three different dining areas: cozy interior, woody wine bar, and breezy terrace. If coming for dinner, make a reserva-tion, dress up, and hit an ATM (€11-14 appetizers and pastas, €18-25 *secondi,* lighter wine-bar menu at lunch, daily 12:00-14:30 & 19:00-22:30, closed the middle of Aug, air-con, half a block north of Palazzo Vecchio at Via dei Magazzini 2-4 red, tel. 055-284-724, www.deifrescobaldi.it, Duccio).

Ristorante Paoli dishes up traditional cuisine to loads of cheerful eaters being served by jolly little old men under a richly frescoed Gothic vault. It feels old-school and Old World...it's all about the setting. Because of its fame and central location, it's filled mostly with tourists, but for a traditional Tuscan splurge meal, this is a fine choice. The walls are sweaty with memories that go back to 1824, and the service is flamboyant and fun-loving (but don't get taken—confirm prices). Woodrow Wilson slurped spaghetti here—his bust looks down on you as you eat (€10-15 pastas, €12-20 *secondi,* daily 12:00-15:00 & 19:00-23:00, reserve for dinner, between Piazza della Signoria and the Duomo at Via dei Tavolini 12 red, tel. 055-216-215, Antonio).

Cheap, Simple Eats near the Piazza

Cantinetta dei Verrazzano, a long-established bakery/café/wine bar, serves delightful sandwich plates in an old-time setting. Their *selezione Verrazzano* is a fine plate of four little crostini (like mini-bruschetta) proudly featuring different breads, cheeses, and meats from the Chianti region (€7.50). The *tagliere di focacce,* a sampler plate of mini-focaccia sandwiches, is also fun (€16 for big plate for two). Add a €5 glass of Chianti to either of these dishes to make a fine, light meal. Office workers pop in for a quick lunch, and it's traditional to share tables. Be warned: Prices can add up here in a hurry (Mon-Sat 8:00-21:00, Sun 10:00-16:30, no reservations taken, just off Via de' Calzaiuoli, across from Orsanmichele Church at Via dei Tavolini 18, tel. 055-268-590). They also have benches and tiny tables for eating at take-out prices. Simply step to the back and point to a hot *focacce* sandwich (€3), order a drink at the bar, and take away your food or sit with Florentines and watch the action while you munch.

Osteria Vini e Vecchi Sapori, half a block north of the Palazzo Vecchio, is a colorful eatery serving Tuscan food with a fun, accessible menu of delicious €8-10 pastas and €9-15 *secondi* (Mon-Sat 12:00-14:30 & 19:00-22:30, closed Sun, reserve for dinner; facing the bronze equestrian statue in Piazza della Signoria, go behind its tail into the corner and to your left; Via dei Magazzini 3 red, tel. 055-293-045, run by Mario while wife Rosanna cooks and son Thomas serves).

I Fratellini is a hole-in-the-wall where the "little brothers" have served peasants 29 different kinds of sandwiches and cheap glasses of Chianti wine (see list on wall) since 1875. Join the local crowd to order, then sit on a nearby curb to eat, placing your glass on the wall rack before you leave (€2.50-3 sandwiches, daily 9:00-19:30 or until the bread runs out, closed Sun in winter, 20 yards in front of Orsanmichele Church on Via dei Cimatori, tel. 055-239-6096). Be adventurous with the menu (easy-order by number). Consider *finocchiona e caprino* (#15, a Tuscan salami and soft goat cheese), *lardo di Colonnata* (#22, cured lard aged in Carrara marble), and *cinghiale* (#19, spicy wild boar salami) sandwiches. Order the most expensive wine they're selling by the glass (Brunello for €5; bottles are labeled).

Cheap Takeout on Via Dante Alighieri: Three handy places line up on this street, just a couple of blocks from the Duomo. **L'Antico Trippaio,** a tripe stand, is a fixture in the town center. Cheap and authentic as can be, this is where locals come daily for €4-7 sandwiches *(panino),* featuring specialties like *trippa alla fiorentina* (tripe), *lampredotto* (cow's stomach), and a list of more appetizing options. Lisa and Maurizio offer a free plastic glass of rotgut Chianti with each sandwich for travelers with this book (daily 9:00-21:00, on Via Dante Alighieri, mobile 339-742-5692). If tripe isn't your cup of offal, **Pizzeria Totò,** just next to the tripe stand, has good €2.50-3 slices (daily 10:30-23:00, Via Dante Alighieri 28 red, tel. 055-290-406). And a few steps in the opposite direction is a **Metà supermarket,** with cheap drinks and snacks and a fine *antipasti* case inside (daily 8:30-21:30, Sun from 9:00, Via

Dante Alighieri 20-24). If you pick up lunch at any of these, the best people-watching place to enjoy your sandwich is three blocks away, on Piazza della Signoria.

Wine Bar near Ponte Vecchio

'**Ino** is a mod little shop filled with gifty edibles. Alessandro and his staff serve sandwiches and wine—you'll get your €5-8 sandwich on a napkin with an included glass of their wine of the day as you perch on a tiny stool. They can also make a fine €12 *piatto misto* of cheeses and meats with bread (daily 11:30-16:30, immediately behind Uffizi Gallery on Ponte Vecchio side, between the olive tree and the river, Via dei Georgofili 7 red, tel. 055-219-208).

Between Palazzo Vecchio and Santa Croce Church

Ristorante del Fagioli is an enthusiastically run eatery where you feel the heritage. The dad, Gigi, commands the kitchen while family members Antonio, Maurizio, and Simone keep the throngs of loyal customers returning. The cuisine: home-style bread-soups, hearty steaks, and other Florentine classics. Don't worry—though *fagioli* means "beans," that's the family name, not the extent of the menu (€9 *primi*, €9-10 *secondi*, cash only, Mon-Fri 12:30-14:30 & 19:30-22:30, closed Sat-Sun, reserve for dinner, a block north of the Alle Grazie bridge at Corso dei Tintori 47, tel. 055-244-285).

Boccadama Enoteca Ristorante is a stylish, shabby-chic wine bistro serving an easy-to-navigate menu of capably executed traditional Tuscan fare based on seasonal produce. Eat in the intimate dining room with candles reflecting off bottle-lined walls or at one of the few tables on the dramatic Piazza Santa Croce. As this place is popular with groups, reservations are smart, especially for outside (€8-9 *primi*, €12-16 *secondi*, daily 11:00-23:00, on south side of Piazza Santa Croce at 25-26 red, tel. 055-243-640, Marco, www.boccadama.com).

Trattoria Anita, midway between the Uffizi and Santa Croce, feels old-school, with wood paneling and rows of wine bottles. Brothers Nicola, Gianni, and Maurizio offer a good-value lunch special: three hearty Tuscan courses for €10 on weekdays (€7-8 pastas, €7-13 *secondi*, Mon-Sat 12:00-14:30 & 19:00-22:15, closed Sun, on the corner of Via Vinegia and Via del Parlagio at #2 red, tel. 055-218-698).

Trattoria I'cche C'è C'è (EE-kay chay chay; dialect for "whatever there is, there is") is a small, family-style restaurant where fun-loving Gino and his wife Mara serve functional local food, including a €13 three-course, fixed-price meal. While filled with tourists, the place has a charming mom-and-pop warmth (€7-12 pastas, €12-18 *secondi*, Tue-Sun 12:30-14:30 & 19:30-22:30, closed

Gelato

Italy's best ice cream is in Florence. But beware of scams at touristy joints on busy streets that turn a simple request for a cone into a €10 "tourist special" rip-off. To avoid this, survey the size options and specify what you want—for example, *un cono da tre euro* (a €3 cone). For even more gelato tips, see page 42.

All of these places, which are a cut above, are open daily for long hours.

Near the Accademia: A Sicilian choice on a tourist thoroughfare, **Gelateria Carabè** is particularly famous for its luscious granite—Italian ices made with fresh fruit. A cremolata is a granita with a dollop of gelato—a delicious combination (from the Accademia, it's a block toward the Duomo at Via Ricasoli 60 red).

Near the Mercato Centrale: Il Triangolo della Bermuda is a hit both for its fresh ingredients and for the big-hearted energy of its owner, Vetulio (Via Nazionale 61 red, where it crosses Via Faenza, tel. 055-287-490).

Near the Duomo: Grom uses organic ingredients and seasonal fresh fruit, along with biodegradable spoons and tubs. This clever Italy-wide chain markets its traditional approach, although

Mon and two weeks in Aug, midway between Bargello and river at Via Magalotti 11 red, tel. 055-216-589).

Club del Gusto, a block behind the Palazzo Vecchio, is a low-key place with a friendly owner/chef. Grab a salad or sandwich to carry away, or enjoy a made-to-order pasta plate at a table in back (Via dei Neri 50 red, tel. 348-090-3142).

All'Antico Vinaio, a photogenic Florentine favorite, has two options: You can either stand in the street, grabbing a €5 sandwich and pouring your own wine (€2/glass), or head across the street to their *osteria* to sit down and order from a more extensive menu (Mon-Sat 12:00-23:00, Sun 12:00-16:00, Via dei Neri 65 red, tel. 055-238-2723).

South of the River, in the Oltrarno

In general, dining in the Oltrarno offers a more authentic experience; although it's quite close to the old center, tourists imagine that it's another world and tend to stay away. At many of these places, Florentines may even outnumber my readers. For locations, see the map on page 562.

purists grumble that a chain gelateria can't possibly compare with a local one-off. Still, it's good and has maintained a high quality—likely because the menu follows what's in season, changing every month (Via delle Oche 24 red).

Near Orsanmichele Church: **Perchè No!** is located just off the busy main pedestrian drag, Via de' Calzaiuoli, and serves a wide array of flavors (Via dei Tavolini 19).

Near Ponte Vecchio: **Gelateria Carrozze** is a longtime favorite (on riverfront 30 yards from Ponte Vecchio toward the Uffizi at Piazza del Pesce 3).

Near the Church of Santa Croce: The venerable favorite, **Vivoli's** still has great gelato—but it's more expensive, and stingy in its servings. Before ordering, try a free sample of their rice flavor—riso (closed Mon, Aug, and Jan; opposite the Church of Santa Croce, go down Via Torta a block and turn right on Via Stinche). Florentines flock to **Gelateria de' Neri** (Via dei Neri 22 red; if not there, it might have moved slightly east—ask a local).

Across the River: If you want an excuse to check out the little village-like neighborhood across the river from Santa Croce (or are walking to Piazzale Michelangelo), enjoy a gelato at the tiny **Il Gelato di Filo** (named for Filippo and Lorenzo) at Via San Miniato 5 red, a few steps toward the river from Porta San Miniato. Gelato chef Edmir is proud of his fruity sorbet as well.

Dining with a Ponte Vecchio View

Golden View Open Bar is a lively, trendy bistro, good for a romantic meal or just a salad, pizza, or pasta with fine wine and a fine view of Ponte Vecchio and the Arno River. Its white, minimalist interior is a stark contrast to atmospheric old Florence. Reservations for window tables are essential unless you drop in early for dinner (€10 pizzas, €11-15 pastas, big €11-14 salads, €20-30 *secondi*, daily 11:30-24:00, impressive wine bar, 50 yards east of Ponte Vecchio at Via dei Bardi 58, tel. 055-214-502, www.goldenviewopenbar.com, run by Antonio, Marco, and Tommaso). They have four seating areas (with the same menu and prices) for whatever mood you're in: a riverside pizza place, a classier restaurant, a jazzy lounge, and a wine bar (they also serve a buffet of appetizers free with your €10-12 drink from 19:00 to 21:00). Mixing their fine wine, river views, and live jazz makes for a wonderful evening (jazz Mon, Wed, Fri, and Sat nights at 21:00).

Dining Well in the Oltrarno

Of the many good and colorful restaurants in the Oltrarno, these are my favorites. Reservations are a good idea in the evening.

Il Santo Bevitore Ristorante, lit like a Rembrandt painting and filled with dressy tables, serves creative Tuscan cuisine. They're enthusiastic about matching quality produce from the area with the right wine. This is a good break from the big, sloppy plates of pasta you'll get at many Florence eateries (€9-12 pastas, €8-12 meat-and-cheese *taglieri*, €10-18 *secondi*, good wine list by the glass or bottle, daily 12:30-14:30 & 19:30-22:30, closed Sun for lunch, come early or make reservations, no outside seating, Via di Santo Spirito 64, tel. 055-211-264). Their smaller wine bar next door, **Enoteca Il Santino Gastronomia,** feels like the perfect after-work hangout for foodies who'd like a glass of wine and some light food. Tight, cozy, and atmospheric, one wall is occupied by the bar, where you can assemble an €8-12 *tagliere* of local cheeses and *salumi* (also available to take away). They also have a few €6-8 hot dishes. Both the food and the wine are locally sourced from small producers (daily 12:30-23:00, Via di Santo Spirito 60 red, tel. 055-230-2820).

Trattoria 4 Leoni creates the quintessential Oltrarno dinner scene, and it's understandably popular with tourists. The Tuscan-style food is made with an innovative twist and an appreciation for vegetables. You'll enjoy the fun energy and characteristic seating, both outside on the colorful square, Canto ai Quattro Pagoni, and inside, where you'll dine in exposed-stone sophistication. While the wines by the glass are pricey, the house wine is good (€8-10 *primi*, €10-15 *secondi*, daily 12:00-24:00, dinner reservations smart; from Ponte Vecchio walk four blocks up Via de' Guicciardini, turn right on Via dello Sprone, then slightly left to Via de' Vellutini 1; tel. 055-218-562, www.4leoni.com).

Antico Ristoro Di' Cambi is a meat lover's dream—thick with Tuscan traditions, rustic touches, and T-bone steaks. The bustling scene has a memorable, beer-hall energy. As you walk in, you'll pass a glass case filled with red chunks of Chianina beef that's priced by weight (for the famous *bistecca alla fiorentina*, €40/kilo, standard serving is half a kilo per person). Before you OK your investment, they'll show you the cut and tell you the weight. While the steak comes nearly uncooked, it's air-dried for 21 days so it's not really raw, just very tasty and tender—it'll make you happy you're at the top of the food chain. Sit inside the convivial woody interior or outside on a square (€8-10 pastas, €10-18 *secondi*, Mon-Sat 12:00-14:30 & 18:30-22:30, closed Sun, reserve on weekends and to sit outside, Via Sant'Onofrio 1 red, one block south of Ponte Amerigo Vespucci, tel. 055-217-134, run by Stefano and Fabio, the Cambi cousins).

Olio & Convivium Gastronomia is primarily a catering company for top-end events, and this is where they showcase their cooking. It started as an elegant deli whose refined olive-oil-tasting room morphed into a romantic, aristocratic restaurant. Their three intimate rooms are surrounded by fine *prosciutti*, cheeses, and wine shelves. It can seem intimidating and a little pretentious, but well-dressed foodies will appreciate this place for its quiet atmosphere. Their list of €14-25 *gastronomia* plates offers an array of taste treats and fine wines by the glass (€14-16 pastas, €20-22 *secondi*, stylish €18 lunches with wine, Tue-Sat 12:00-14:30 & 19:00-22:30, Mon 12:00-14:30 only, closed Sun, strong air-con, Via di Santo Spirito 4, tel. 055-265-8198, Monica).

Trattoria da Sergio is a tiny eatery about a block before Porta San Frediano, one of Florence's medieval gates. It has charm and a strong following, so reservations are a must. The food is on the gourmet side of home-cooking—mama's favorites with a modern twist—and therefore a bit more expensive (€9-10 *primi*, €12-18 *secondi*, Mon-Sat 12:00-14:00 & 19:30-22:45, Sun 12:00-14:00 only, Borgo San Frediano 145 red, tel. 055-223-449, Sergio and Marco, www.trattoriadasergio.it).

Trattoria Al Tranvai, with tight seating and small dark-wood tables, looks like an old-time tram filled with the neighborhood gang. A 10-minute walk from the river at the edge of the Oltrarno, it feels like a small town's favorite eatery (€8-10 pastas, €10-13 *secondi,* Mon 19:00-24:00, Tue-Sat 12:30-14:30 & 19:30-22:30, closed Sun; from the Brancacci Chapel, go south on Via del Leone 5 minutes to Piazza T. Tasso 14 red, tel. 055-225-197, www.altranvai.it).

Eating Cheaply in the Oltrarno

Trattoria Sabatino, farthest away and least touristy of my Oltrarno listings, is a spacious, brightly lit mess hall. You get the feeling it hasn't changed much since it opened—in 1956. It's disturbingly cheap, with family character and a simple menu—a super place to watch locals munch, especially since you'll likely be sharing a table. You'll find it just outside Porta San Frediano, a 15-minute walk from Ponte Vecchio (€4 pastas, €6 *secondi,* Mon-Fri 12:00-14:30 & 19:15-22:00, closed Sat-Sun, Via Pisana 2 red, tel. 055-225-955, little English spoken).

Trattoria Casalinga, an inexpensive standby, comes with aproned women bustling around the kitchen. Florentines and tourists alike pack the place and leave full and happy, with euros to spare for gelato (€7 pastas, €8-10 *secondi,* Mon-Sat 12:00-14:30 & 19:00-21:45, after 20:00 reserve or wait, closed Sun and Aug, just off Piazza di Santo Spirito, near the church at Via de' Michelozzi 9 red, tel. 055-218-624, Andrea and Paolo).

Borgo Antico is the hit of Piazza di Santo Spirito, with enticing pizzas, big deluxe plates of pasta, a delightful setting, and trendy and boisterous young crowd (€8-10 pizza, pasta, and salad, €14-18 *secondi,* daily 12:00-23:00, best to reserve for a seat on t square, Piazza di Santo Spirito 6 red, tel. 055-210-437, Andrea and Michele—feel his forearm). **Volume,** the bar next door, is run by the same gang.

Caffè Ricchi, next to Borgo Antico, has fine gelato, home-made desserts, shaded outdoor tables, and €4 pasta dishes at lunch. After noting the plain facade of the Brunelleschi church facing the square, step inside the café and pick your favorite picture of the many ways the church might be finished (daily 7:00-24:00, tel. 055-280-830). **Ristorante Ricchi,** its sister restaurant next door, is more formal, has a larger menu, and also has tables on the square.

Le Volpi e l'Uva, a wine bar just steps from Ponte Vecchio, has a limited menu of *affettati* (cold cuts), cheese, and *crostone* (hearty bruschetta)—a nice spot for a light lunch (Mon-Sat 11:00-21:00, closed Sun, Piazza dei Rossi 1).

Supermarket: **Sapori & Dintorni Conad,** just over Ponte Vecchio and to the left, has all you need for picnic (daily 9:30-20:00).

Florence Connections

Florence is Tuscany's transportation hub, with fine train, bus, and plane connections to virtually anywhere in Italy. The city has several train stations, a bus station (next to the main train station), and an airport (plus Pisa's airport is nearby). Livorno, on the coast west of Florence, is a major cruise-ship port for passengers visiting Florence, Pisa, and other nearby destinations.

By Train

From Florence by Train to: Pisa (2-3/hour, 45-75 minutes, €7.80), **Lucca** (2/hour, 1.5 hours, €6.40), **Siena** (direct trains hourly, 1.5-2 hours, €8.50; bus is better because Siena's train station is far from the center), **Camucia-Cortona** (hourly, 1.5 hours, €9.80), **Livorno** (hourly, 1.25 hours, some change in Pisa, €9), **La Spezia** (for the Cinque Terre, 5/day direct, 2.5 hours, otherwise nearly hourly with change in Pisa, €11.30), **Milan** (hourly, 1.75 hours, €53), **Milan's Malpensa Airport** (2/day direct, 2.75 hours, €58), **Venice** (hourly, 2-3 hours, may transfer in Bologna; often crowded—reserve ahead, €43), **Assisi** (8/day direct, 2-3 hours, €12), **Orvieto** (hourly, 2 hours, some with change in Campo di Marte or Rifredi station, €19), **Rome** (at least hourly, 1.5 hours, most connections require seat reservations, €45), **Naples** (hourly, 3 hours, €72), **Brindisi** (8/day, 8 hours with change in Bologna or Rome, €75), **Interlaken** (5/day, 5.5-6 hours, 2-3 changes), **Frankfurt** (1/day, 12 hours, 1-3 changes), **Paris** (3/day, 10-15 hours, 1-2 changes, important to reserve overnight train ahead), **Vienna** (1 direct overnight train, or 5/day with 1-3 changes, 10-16 hours).

Note that these departures are operated by Trenitalia; a competing private rail company called Italo offers additional high-speed connections to major Italian cities (including **Milan, Padua, Venice, Rome,** and **Naples**). While Italo is often cheaper (particularly if you book long in advance), it doesn't accept railpasses (for details on Italo, see page 1166 or visit www.italotreno.it).

By Bus

The BusItalia bus station (100 yards west of the Florence train station on Via Santa Caterina da Siena) is a big, old-school lot with numbered stalls and all the services you'd expect. Although the bus company's name recently changed, most buses and signs will probably still have the old *SITA* label. Schedules for regional trips are posted and TV monitors show imminent departures. Bus service drops dramatically on Sunday. Generally it's best to buy bus tickets in the station, as you'll pay 30 percent more if you buy tickets onboard. Bus info: tel. 800-373-760 (Mon-Fri 9:00-15:00, closed Sat-Sun), www.fsbusitalia.it.

From Florence by Bus to: San Gimignano (hourly, less on Sun, 1.5-2 hours, change in Poggibonsi, €6.80), **Siena** (about 2/hour, 1.25-hour *rapida/via superstrada* buses are faster than the train, avoid the slower *ordinaria* buses, €7.80, www.sienamobilita.it), **Volterra** (4/day Mon-Sat, 1/day Sun, 2 hours, change in Colle Val d'Elsa to CPT bus #770, €8.35, www.cpt.pisa.it), **Montepulciano** (2/day, 2 hours, LFI bus, €11.20, www.lfi.it), Florence's **Amerigo Vespucci Airport** (2/hour, 30 minutes, €6, pay driver and immediately validate ticket, usually departs from platform 1, first bus leaves for airport from Florence at 5:30).

By Taxi

For small groups with more money than time, zipping to nearby towns by taxi can be a good value (e.g., €120 from your Florence hotel to your Siena hotel).

A more comfortable alternative is to hire a private car service. Florence-based **Transfer Chauffeur Service** has a fleet of modern vehicles with drivers who can whisk you between cities, to and from the cruise-ship port at Livorno, and through the Tuscan countryside for around the same price as a cab (tel. 055-612-3659, mobile 338-862-3129, www.transfercs.com, marco.masala@transfercs.com, Marco). **Prestige Rent** also has friendly, English-speaking drivers and offers similar services (tel. 055-300-230, mobile 333-999-5929, US tel. 347/338-0972, www.prestigerent.com, usa@prestigerent.com, Saverio).

FLORENCE

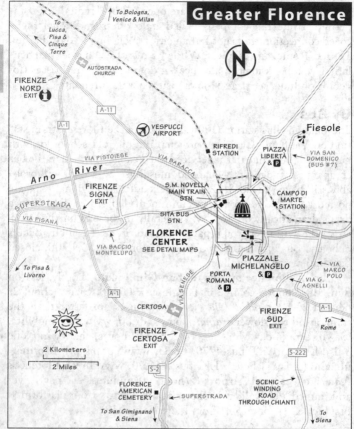

Greater Florence

To Bologna,
Venice & Milan

To Lucca, Pisa & Cinque Terre

AUTOSTRADA CHURCH

FIRENZE NORD EXIT

A-11

A-1

VIA PISTOIESE

VIA BARACCA

VESPUCCI AIRPORT

RIFREDI STATION

PIAZZA LIBERTÀ & P

Fiesole

VIA SAN DOMENICO (BUS #7)

Arno River

FIRENZE SIGNA EXIT

SUPERSTRADA

VIA PISANA

S.M. NOVELLA MAIN TRAIN STN.

SITA BUS STN.

FLORENCE CENTER
SEE DETAIL MAPS

CAMPO DI MARTE STATION

VIA BACCIO MONTELUPO

To Pisa & Livorno

PIAZZALE MICHELANGELO & P

VIA MARCO POLO

VIA G. AGNELLI

PORTA ROMANA & P

A-1

CERTOSA

VIA SENESE

FIRENZE SUD EXIT

A-1

To Rome

2 Kilometers

2 Miles

FIRENZE CERTOSA EXIT

S-222

S-2

FLORENCE AMERICAN CEMETERY

SUPERSTRADA

SCENIC WINDING ROAD THROUGH CHIANTI

To San Gimignano & Siena

To Siena

By Plane

For information on Florence's **Amerigo Vespucci Airport**, see page 505. For information on Pisa's **Galileo Galilei Airport**, see page 610.

By Cruise Ship

Florence's port is Livorno (sometimes called "Leghorn" in English), a coastal town located about 60 miles west of Florence. Of the excursion options, **Florence** is the most time-consuming to reach (roughly two hours each way by public transit); it will take you the whole day. **Pisa** is closer (about an hour each way), and—since Pisa is well-connected with **Lucca**—it's possible to combine those two cities into one long day. (If doing this, save Pisa until after lunch to avoid the cruise crowds in the morning, and be aware that most shops and restaurants in Lucca are closed Sun-Mon.) No matter where you go, if you're taking the train, keep in mind that it can take about 30 minutes just to get from Livorno's cruise port to the train station across town. Plan your day conservatively, as trains can be delayed.

Arrival in Livorno

Livorno's port (at the western edge of town) is vast and sprawling, but most cruise ships dock in one of two places: Molo 75, at the Porto Mediceo, or the adjacent Molo Capitaneria. Livorno's city center clusters around two nearby squares: Piazza del Municipio (TI, public WCs, shuttle-bus stop) and Piazza Grande (stop for buses #1 and #1R to train station). The squares are connected by a long, covered pedestrian mall (with the main TI inside).

Tours: The **TI** arranges local guides and has a free *Livorno* brochure with self-guided Livorno walks. They can also inform you about local tours, such as a boat trip around the canals of Livorno plus a visit to Pisa (€20). **Karin Kibby,** an Oregonian living in Livorno who leads Rick Steves tours, offers a morning "slice of Italian life" walk (including Livorno's fantastic food market) and day trips from the cruise port throughout Tuscany (2-10 people, mobile 333-108-6348, karinkintuscany@yahoo.it).

Connecting Livorno and Florence, Pisa, or Lucca

On Your Own: With a little patience, budget-minded travelers can use public transportation to go from Livorno to Florence, Pisa, or Lucca and back again before the ship departs.

First, ride the cruise line's **shuttle bus** from the port to downtown Livorno. It will drop you off at a bus stop near the TI on Piazza del Municipio (about €5-8 round-trip). Then ride public **bus** #1 and #1R to the Livorno Centrale Station (buses depart from the middle of Piazza Grande, in front of the cathedral).

From the station, **trains** zip to **Florence** (hourly, usually departs at :10 after the hour, arrive in Florence at :32 past the following hour—1 hour and 22 minutes total, €9 on a regional train; occasional departures are a few minutes shorter but require you to change trains at Pisa Centrale), **Pisa** (2-3/hour, 20 minutes, €2.50 on a regional train), **Lucca** (about hourly, 1-1.25 hours, transfer at Pisa Centrale, €5.10 on a regional train), and other points in Italy.

Note that Pisa is usually listed as an intermediate station (for example, on the way to Firenze, Milano, or Torino) rather than the final destination. All Florence-bound trains stop in Pisa. If you want to visit Lucca and Pisa in one day, take the train to Lucca first. A handy bus connects Lucca's Piazzale Giuseppe Verdi to Pisa's Field of Miracles (€3, hourly Mon-Sat, fewer on Sun, 30 minutes).

Taxi and Shared Minibus Excursions: Taxis meet arriving cruises and offer various day trips around the area (the cabbie drops you off for a designated amount of time in one or two cities). While a private taxi is costly, enterprising drivers with eight-seat mini-buses gather groups to split their €400 fee; €50/person is actually a great deal—you'll be driven one hour into Florence, dropped off near the center for four or five hours of free time, and then taken back to the port.

Here are some ballpark round-trip fares for a four-seat car: **Pisa**—€120, **Pisa and Lucca**—€220, **Florence**—€320. Ask if wait time is included—if not, it can cost about €30/hour. In general, drivers at the port prefer to take passengers who will pay them for the whole day, so it can be difficult to get someone to take you just one-way (especially the long haul into Florence).

Taxis both at the port and in the city offer the same rates. Clarify the fare beforehand, even though by law the driver must have the meter on (the quoted price will usually be less than the meter).

Cruise-Ship Excursions: Most cruise lines offer a "transportation-only" excursion from the ship to Florence. This includes a bus ride from the ship directly to a point in downtown Florence, free time to explore the city, then a bus ride back to your ship. This is extremely convenient but relatively expensive (around $100-125, which is about €75-95).

Near Florence: Fiesole

Perched on a hill overlooking the Arno valley, Fiesole (fee-AY-zoh-lay) gives weary travelers a break in the action and—during

the heat of summer—a breezy location from which to admire the city below. It's a small town with a main square, a few restaurants and shops, a few minor sights, and a great view. The ancient Etruscans knew a good spot when they saw one, and chose to settle here, establishing Fiesole about 400 years before the Romans founded Florence. Wealthy Renaissance families in pre-air-conditioning days also chose Fiesole as a preferred vacation spot, building villas in the surrounding hillsides. Later, 19th-century Romantics spent part of the Grand Tour admiring the vistas, much like the hordes of tourists do today. Most come here for the view—the actual sights pale in comparison to those in Florence. Shutterbugs visit in the morning for the best light, while some prefer the evening for sunset.

Getting to Fiesole: It's only a half-hour away by bus or taxi. From Florence's Piazza San Marco, take bus #7—enjoying a peek at gardens, vineyards, orchards, and villas—to the last stop, Piazza Mino (3-4/hour, fewer after 21:00 and on Sun, 30 minutes, €1.20, €2 if bought on bus, validate on board; departs Florence from Piazza San Marco to the right of the church; wear your money belt—thieves frequent this bus). Taxis from Florence cost about €25-35 (ride to highest point you want to visit—Ristorante La Reggia for nearby view terrace or Church of San Francesco—then explore downhill).

Tourist Information: The TI, immediately to the right of the Roman Archaeological Area, is a two-minute walk from the bus stop—head behind the church (flexible hours but generally April-Sept daily 10:00-19:00, March and Oct daily 10:00-18:00; Nov-Feb Wed-Mon 10:00-14:00, closed Tue; Via Portigiani 3, tel. 055-596-1311, www.fiesoleforyou.it).

Market Day: A modest selection of food and household items fills Via Portigiani, just off Piazza Mino, on Saturday mornings until 13:00.

Sights in Fiesole

Fiesole's main sights are either free or covered by one €10 combo-ticket, available at the Archaeological Area.

▲▲Terrace and Garden with a View
Catch the sunset (and your breath) from the sweeping view terrace just below Ristorante La Reggia, a steep seven-minute hike from the Fiesole bus stop. For overachievers in search of similar views—and a peek at residential Fiesole—climb up the opposite side of the square, along the equally steep road hugging the ridgeline.

Church of San Francesco
For even more hill-climbing, continue up from the view terrace to this charming little church. Its small scale and several colorful altar paintings make this church more enjoyable than Fiesole's Duomo.

Cost and Hours: Free, Mon-Sat 7:00-19:00, Sun 7:00-11:00 & 12:00-19:00, Via San Francesco 13, tel. 055-59-175.

Franciscan Ethnographic Missionary Museum (Museo Missionario Etnografico Francescano)
This eclectic little collection, hidden beneath the Church of San Francesco, includes an Egyptian mummy, ancient coins, Chinese Buddhas, and the in situ ruins of a third-century Etruscan wall.

Cost and Hours: Free but donation suggested, Tue-Sat 9:30-12:00 & 15:00-18:00, Sun 15:00-18:00, closed Mon, unmarked door inside church leads to cloisters and museum, tel. 055-59-175.

Duomo

While this church has a drab, 19th-century exterior, the interior is worth a look, if only for the blue-and-white glazed Giovanni della Robbia statue of St. Romulus over the entry door.

Cost and Hours: Free, daily 8:00-12:00, across Piazza Mino from the bus stop.

Archaeological Area and Museum

The chief attraction in the Archaeological Area is its Roman theater. Occasionally used today for plays and concerts, the well-preserved theater held up to 2,000 people in its heyday. The site's other ruins are, well, ruined, and lacking in explanation. But the valley view and peaceful setting are lovely.

The museum, located within the Archaeological Area, imparts insight into Fiesole's Etruscan and Roman roots with well-displayed artifacts and a few sheets of English description in the corners.

Cost and Hours: €8, except Fri-Sun when an obligatory combo-ticket (€10) adds the Bandini Museum (see next listing), buy tickets from the TI next door, covered by Firenze Card; April-Sept daily 10:00-19:00, March and Oct daily 10:00-18:00; Nov-Feb Wed-Mon 10:00-14:00, closed Tue; behind the Duomo at Via Portigiani 1, www.museidifiesole.it.

Bandini Museum

This petite museum displays the wooden panels of lesser-known Gothic and Renaissance painters as well as the glazed terra-cotta figures of Andrea della Robbia.

Cost and Hours: €5, covered by €10 combo-ticket with Archaeological Area and Museum, Fri-Sun 10:00-18:00, closed Mon-Thu, shorter hours off-season, behind Duomo at Via Dupre 1.

Eating in Fiesole

The first two restaurants are on Piazza Mino, where the bus from Florence stops; the other is near the view terrace above town.

Fiesolano (a.k.a. Ristorante Perseus), a local favorite, lacks views but serves authentic Tuscan dishes at a fair price in a rambling interior, at a few sidewalk tables, or on a shady garden terrace in fair weather (daily 12:30-14:30 & 19:30-23:30, Piazza Mino 9R, tel. 055-59-143, Leonardo).

Ristorante Aurora is an upscale alternative with a view terrace overlooking the city of Florence (daily 12:00-14:30 & 19:00-22:30, Piazza Mino 39, tel. 055-59-363).

Ristorante La Reggia has perhaps the best food (and highest prices) in town, as long as you're willing to make the steep walk up. Reserve a table at a window or on their terrace to enjoy the vista

FLORENCE

(*primi* €10-12, *secondi* €16-20, daily 11:00-15:00 & 18:00-23:00, Via San Francesco 18, tel. 055-59-385).

Picnics: Fiesole is made-to-order for a scenic and breezy picnic. Grab a simple sandwich and a pastry at Fiesole's best *pasticceria*, **Alcedo** (head up the main drag from the bus stop to Via Gramsci 27). Round out your goodies across the street at the **Coop** supermarket (Mon-Sat 8:00-13:00 & 16:00-20:00, closed Sun) before backtracking to the panoramic terrace. Or, for more convenience and less view, picnic at the shaded park on the way to the view terrace (walk up Via San Francesco about halfway to the terrace, and climb the stairs to the right).

Gelato: Your most convenient option is **Gelateria Il Tucano,** on the main drag, before the *pasticceria* (Via Gramsci 8, tel. 055-59-594).

PISA AND LUCCA

Florence is within easy striking distance of a number of great cities—as their fortifications attest. Along with Siena (see the Siena chapter), Pisa and Lucca show that Florence wasn't the only power and cultural star of the late Middle Ages and Renaissance.

Pisa's Leaning Tower is touristy but worth a visit. Many tourists are surprised to see that the iconic tower is only a small part of a gleaming white architectural complex—featuring a massive cathedral and baptistery—that dominates the grand green square, the Field of Miracles. The rest of the city is virtually tourist-free and merits a wander for its rich history, architecture, and student vibe.

Lucca, contained within its fine Renaissance wall, lacks any blockbuster sights, but has a charm that causes many connoisseurs of Italy to claim it as a favorite stop. The town's garden-topped city wall is perfect for a laid-back bike ride—the single must-do activity in this pleasant getaway.

The two towns are 30 minutes from each other by hourly bus. Each is about 1.5 hours (or less) by train from Florence and well-served by excellent highways.

Using public transportation, you could day-trip from Florence to both cities. But with more time, stay overnight in Lucca. Take the train to Pisa in the morning, do your sightseeing, catch the bus to Lucca late in the afternoon, enjoy the evening scene, and stay the night. Sightsee Lucca the next day, then move on to your next destination by train.

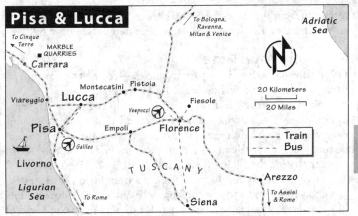

Pisa

In A.D. 1200, Pisa's power peaked. For nearly three centuries (1000-1300), Pisa rivaled Venice and Genoa as a sea-trading power, exchanging European goods for luxury items in Muslim lands. As a port near the mouth of the Arno River (six miles from the coast), the city enjoyed easy access to the Mediterranean, plus the protection of sitting a bit upstream. The Romans had made it a naval base, and by medieval times the city was a major player.

Pisa's 150-foot galleys cruised the Mediterranean, gaining control of the sea, establishing outposts on the islands of Corsica, Sardinia, and Sicily, and trading with other Europeans, Muslims, and Byzantine Christians as far south as North Africa and as far east as Syria. European Crusaders hired Pisan boats to carry them and their supplies as they headed off to conquer the Muslim-held Holy Land. The Pisan "Republic" prided itself on its independence from both popes and emperors. The city used its sea-trading wealth to build the grand monuments of the Field of Miracles, including the now-famous Leaning Tower. But the Pisan fleet was routed in battle by Genoa (1284, at Meloria, off Livorno), and their overseas outposts were taken away. Then the port silted up, and Pisa was left high and dry, with only its Field of Miracles and its university keeping it on the map.

Pisa's three important sights—the Duomo, Baptistery, and the Tower—float regally on the best lawn in Italy. The style throughout is Pisa's very own "Pisan Romanesque." Even as the church was being built, Piazza del Duomo was nicknamed the "Campo dei Miracoli," or Field of Miracles, for the grandness of the undertaking.

The Tower recently underwent a decade of restoration and

topple-prevention. To ascend, you have to get your ticket and book a time at least a few hours in advance (for details, see page 597).

Planning Your Time

For most visitors, Pisa is a touristy quickie—seeing the Tower, visiting the square, and wandering through the church are 90 percent of their Pisan thrills. But it's a shame to skip the rest of the city. Considering Pisa's historic importance and the wonderful ambience created by its rich architectural heritage and vibrant student population, the city deserves a half-day visit. For many, the lack of tourists outside the Field of Miracles is both a surprise and a relief.

·   If you want to climb the Tower, go straight to the ticket office upon your arrival to snag an appointment—usually for a couple of hours later, especially in summer (for directions to the Field of Miracles, see "Arrival in Pisa," later). You can also buy a ticket and book a time in advance online (no sooner than 20 days but at least 12 days beforehand) at www.opapisa.it. If you'll be seeing both the town and the Field of Miracles, plan on a six-hour stop. If just blitzing the Field of Miracles, three hours is the minimum. Spending the night lets you savor a great Italian city scene.

If you're day-tripping to Pisa from Lucca, or doing a Lucca/Pisa day trip from Florence, note that a handy bus runs hourly (less frequent on Sun) between the Field of Miracles and Lucca, saving time and hassle (see page 610).

Orientation to Pisa

The city of Pisa is framed on the north by the Field of Miracles (Leaning Tower) and on the south by the Pisa Centrale train station. The Arno River flows east to west, bisecting the city. Walking from Pisa Centrale directly to the Tower takes about 30 minutes (but allow up to an hour if you take my self-guided walk). The two main streets for  tourists and shoppers are Via Santa Maria (running south from the Tower) and Corso Italia/Borgo Stretto (running north from the station).

Tourist Information

The TI is about 200 yards from Pisa Centrale train station—exit and walk straight up the left side of the street to the big, circular Piazza Vittorio Emanuele II. The TI is on the left at #14 (daily April-Oct 9:00-18:00, Nov-March 9:00-17:00, tel. 050-42291, www.pisaunicaterra.it). There's also a TI at the airport, in the arrivals hall (daily April-Oct 9:00-23:00, Nov-March 9:00-20:00, tel. 050-502-518).

Arrival in Pisa

By Train

Most trains (and visitors) arrive at Pisa Centrale Station, about a mile south of the Tower and Field of Miracles. A few trains, particularly those from Lucca, also stop at the smaller Pisa San Rossore Station, which is just four blocks from the Tower (not all trains stop here, but if yours does, hop off).

Pisa Centrale: This station has a baggage-check desk—look for *deposito bagagli* (€3/bag for 12 hours, daily 6:00-21:00, they photocopy your passport to check ID). As you get off the train, it's to the right at the far end of platform 1, just after the police station.

To get from this station to the Field of Miracles, you can **walk** (get free map from TI, 30 minutes direct, 1 hour if you follow my self-guided walk), take a **taxi** (€7-10, tel. 050-541-600, taxi stand at station), or go by **bus.** At all bus stops in Pisa, be cautious of pickpockets, who take advantage of crowds to operate.

Bus **LAM Rossa** (4-6/hour, runs until 20:30, 15 minutes) stops across the street from the train station, in front of the NH Cavalieri Hotel. Buy a €1.10 bus ticket from the tobacco/magazine kiosk in the train station's main hall or at any tobacco shop (€1.50 if you buy it on board, smart to have exact change, good for 70 minutes, round-trip permitted). Before getting on the bus, confirm that it is indeed going to "Campo dei Miracoli" (ask driver, a local, or TI) or risk taking a long tour of Pisa's suburbs. The correct buses let you off at Piazza Manin, in front of the gate to the Field of Miracles; drivers make sure tourists don't miss the stop.

To return to the train station from the Tower, catch bus LAM Rossa in front of the BNL bank, across the street from where you got off (again, confirm the destination—"Stazione Centrale," staht-see-OH-nay chen-TRAH-lay). You'll also find a taxi stand 30 yards from the Tower (at Bar Duomo).

Pisa San Rossore: From this train station to the Field of Miracles, it's just a four-block walk. Take the underground walkway to Piazza Fancelli and turn left onto Via Andrea Pisano. Continue for about 150 yards, and you'll see the Tower ahead of you, a few minutes away.

By Car

It's best to leave your car at the big Pietrasantina parking lot, designed for tour buses (which pay €110 to park) and tourists with cars (who park for free). From there, a city bus shuttles you to the Field of Miracles (driving in the city center will likely net you a

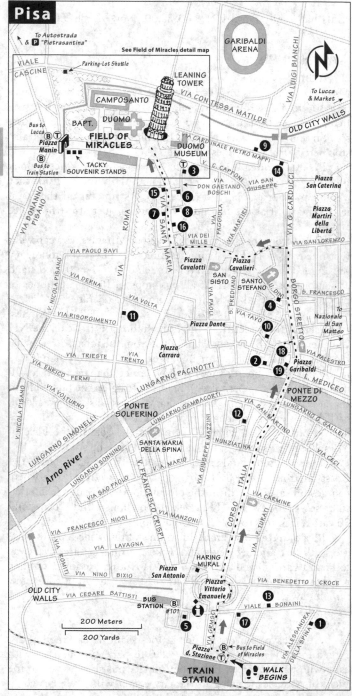

Pisa

To Autostrada & P "Pietrasantina"

See Field of Miracles detail map

Parking-Lot Shuttle

VIALE CASCINE

GARIBALDI ARENA

VIA LUIGI BIANCHI

LEANING TOWER

VIA CONTESSA MATILDE

CAMPOSANTO

DUOMO

BAPT.

FIELD OF MIRACLES

Bus to Lucca

Piazza Manin

Bus to Train Station

TACKY SOUVENIR STANDS

DUOMO MUSEUM

To Lucca & Market

OLD CITY WALLS

VIA CARDINALE PIETRO MAFFI

9

14

VIA G. CAPPONI

VIA SAN GIUSEPPE

Piazza San Caterina

VIA BONANNO PISANO

ROMA

VIA SANTA MARIA

15

7

6

8

16

VIA DON GAETANO BOSCHI

VIA FAGGIOLA

VIA MARTIRI

VIA G. CARDUCCI

VIA SAN LORENZO

Piazza Martiri della Libertà

VIA DEI MILLE

VIA PAOLO SAVI

VIA DERNA

V. VIA NICOLA PISANO

VIA RISORGIMENTO

11

VIA VOLTA

VIA

VIA TRIESTE

VIA TRENTO

Piazza Cavalotti

Piazza Cavaleri

SAN SISTO

S. FREDIANO

SANTO STEFANO

U. DINI

S. VIA TAVO

4

10

Piazza Dante

Piazza Carrara

2

18

19

Piazza Garibaldi

BORGO STRETTO

S. FRANCESCO

To Nazionale di San Matteo

VIA PALESTRO

L. MEDICEO

PONTE DI MEZZO

V. ENRICO FERMI

V. NICOLA PISANO

VIA VOLTURNO

LUNGARNO SIMONELLI

LUNGARNO PACINOTTI

PONTE SOLFERINO

LUNGARNO GAMBACORTI

LUNGARNO SONNINO

Arno River

SANTA MARIA DELLA SPINA

V. A. MARIO

12

VIA SAN MARTINO

LUNGARNO G. GALILEI

VIA CECI

LUNGARNO SAO PAOLO

VIA GIUSEPPE MAZZINI

NUNZIATINA

CORSO ITALIA

VIA CARMINE

VIA FRANCESCO CRISPI

VIA MANZONI

VIA FRANCESCO NIOSI

VIA LAVAGNA

VIA ROMITI

VIA NINO BIXIO

VIA E. FURATI

Piazza San Antonio

HARING MURAL

Piazza Vittorio Emanuele II

VIA BENEDETTO CROCE

13

VIALE

BONAINI

OLD CITY WALLS

VIA CESARE BATTISTI

BUS STATION #101

5

VIA ALESSANDRA DELLA SPINA

17

1

VIA ALESSANDRA DELLA SPINA

Piazza d. Stazione

Bus to Field of Miracles

WALK BEGINS

TRAIN STATION

200 Meters

200 Yards

N

3

Pisa Key

1. Hotel Alessandro della Spina
2. Hotel Royal Victoria & Caffè dell'Ussero
3. Hotel Villa Kinzica
4. Residenza Gorkij
5. Hotel Milano
6. Pensione Helvetia
7. Locanda La Lanterna
8. Antica Locanda San Ranieri
9. Two Steps from the Tower B&B
10. Antica Trattoria il Campano
11. Ristorante Masala
12. Ristorante Bagus
13. Da Michele
14. Pizzeria al Bagno di Nerone
15. Paninoteca il Canguro
16. Panetteria Antiche Tradizioni
17. La Lupa Ghiotta Tavola Calda
18. Via delle Colonne Produce Market & Restaurants
19. La Bottega del Gelato

steep fine—cameras catch you and the city sends you a ticket by mail).

To reach the parking lot, exit the autostrada at *Pisa Nord* and follow signs to *Pisa* (on the left). Pass the second traffic light and turn left toward the city center. Go straight, following the *Bus Parking* signs, until you see the gas station. The parking lot is on the left. Here you'll find a cafeteria, WC, lots of big buses, and a bus stop for the orange shuttle, labeled *navetta,* that goes back and forth between the lot and the Largo Cocco Griffi bus stop, just behind the walls of the Field of Miracles (6/hour, daily 8:30-19:20, €1, buy round-trip ticket on board with exact change). If you have more time and want to follow my self-guided walk through Pisa to the Field of Miracles, take bus LAM Rossa to Pisa Centrale train station (4-6/hour, runs until 20:00, €1.10 if you buy ticket at parking-lot cafeteria, €1.50 if purchased on board, also stops near the Tower at Piazza Manin en route).

By Plane
For details on Pisa's Galileo Galilei Airport, see page 610.

Helpful Hints
Markets: An open-air produce market attracts picnickers to Piazza della Vettovaglie, one block north of the Arno River near Ponte di Mezzo, and nearby Piazza Sant'Uomobuono (Mon-Sat 7:00-18:00, main section closes at 13:00, closed Sun). A street market—with more practical goods than food—bustles on Wednesday and Saturday mornings between Via del Brennero and Via Paparrelli (8:00-13:00, just outside of wall, about 6 blocks east of the Tower).

Festivals: The first half of June has many events, culminating in a celebration for Pisa's patron saint (June 16-17).

Local Guide: Dottore Vincenzo Riolo is a great guide for Pisa and the surrounding area (€130/3 hours, mobile 338-211-2939, www.pisatour.it, info@pisatour.it).

Tours: The TI coordinates with local guides to offer walking tours most days. The theme and schedule change every day; check with the TI for the latest information. Ask about touring the old city walls; if open, a walk up top offers great views.

Self-Guided Walk

From Pisa Centrale Train Station to the Tower

A leisurely one-hour stroll from the station to the Tower is a great way to get acquainted with the more subtle virtues of this Renaissance city. Because the hordes who descend daily on the Tower rarely bother with the rest of the town, you'll find most of Pisa to be delightfully untouristy—a student-filled, classy, Old World town with an Arno-scape much like its upstream rival, Florence. Pisa is pretty small, with just 100,000 people. But its 45,000 students keep it lively, especially at night.

• *From Pisa Centrale train station, walk north up Viale Antonio Gramsci to the circular square called...*

Piazza Vittorio Emanuele II

The Allies considered Pisa to be strategically important in World War II, and both the train station and its main bridge were tar-

geted for bombing. Forty percent of this district was destroyed. The piazza recently was rebuilt, and now this generous public space with grass and benches is actually a lid for an underground parking lot. The TI is on this piazza, in the arcade. The entire wall of a building just to the left of the piazza, by the Credito Artigiano bank, was painted by American artist Keith Haring in 1989 to create *Tuttomondo (Whole Wide World)*. Haring (who died of AIDS in 1990) brought New York City graffiti into the mainstream. This painting is a celebration of diversity, chaos, and the liveliness of our world, vibrating with energy.

• *Walk up Corso Italia to the river.*

Corso Italia

Cutting through the center of town, this is Pisa's main drag. As you leave Piazza Vittorio Emanuele II, look to the right to see the circa-1960 wall map of Pisa with a steam train (on the wall of the bar on the corner). You'll also see plenty of youthful fashions, as kids are out making the scene here. Be on guard for pickpockets—too young to arrest, they can only be kicked out of town. Pushed out of their former happy hunting grounds, the Field of Miracles, they now work the crowds here, often dressed as tourists.

• *Follow the pedestrianized Corso Italia straight north to the Arno River and Ponte di Mezzo. Stop in the center of the bridge.*

Ponte di Mezzo

This modern bridge, constructed on the same site where the Romans built one, marks the center of Pisa. In the Middle Ages, this bridge (like Florence's Ponte Vecchio) was lined with shops. It's been destroyed several times by floods and, in 1943, by British and American bombers. Enjoy the view from the center of the bridge of the elegant mansions that line the riverbank, recalling Pisa's days of trading glory—the cityscape feels a bit like Venice's Grand Canal. Pisa sits on shifting delta sand, making construction tricky. The entire town leans. With innovative arches above ground and below, architects didn't stop the leaning—but they have made buildings that wobble without being threatened.

• *Cross the bridge to...*

Piazza Garibaldi

This square is named for the charismatic leader of the Risorgimento, the unification movement that led to Italian independence in 1870. Knowing Pisa was strongly nationalist, Garibaldi came here when wounded to be nursed back to health; many Pisans died in the national struggle. **La Bottega del Gelato,** Pisa's favorite gelato place, is on Piazza Garibaldi (daily 11:00-24:00). You can side-trip about 100 yards downstream to **Caffè dell'Ussero** (famous for its fine 14th-century red terra-cotta original facade, at #28, Sun-Fri 7:00-21:00, closed Sat) and browse its time-warp interior, lined with portraits and documents from the struggle for Italian independence.

• *Continue north up the elegantly arcaded...*

Borgo Stretto

Welcome to Pisa's main shopping street. On the right, the Church of St. Michael, with its fine Pisan Romanesque facade, still sports some 16th-century graffiti. I'll bet you can see some modern graffiti across the street. Students have been pushing their causes here—or simply defacing things—for five centuries.

From here, look farther up the street and notice how it undulates like a flowing river. In the sixth century B.C., Pisa was born when two parallel rivers were connected by canals. This street echoes the flow of one of those canals. An 11th-century landslide rerouted the second river, destroying ancient Pisa, and the entire city had to regenerate.

• *After a few steps, detour left onto Via delle Colonne, and walk one block down to...*

Piazza delle Vettovaglie

Pisa's historic market square, Piazza delle Vettovaglie, is lively day and night. Its Renaissance loggia has hosted the fish and vegetable market for generations. The stalls are set up in this piazza during the morning (Mon-Sat 7:00-13:00, closed Sun) and stay open later in the neighboring piazza to the west (Piazza Sant'Uomobuono, Mon-Sat 7:00-18:00, closed Sun). You could cobble together a picnic from the sandwich shops and fruit-and-veggie stalls ringing these squares.

• *Continue north on Borgo Stretto another 100 yards, passing an ugly bomb site on the right, with its horrible 1960s reconstruction. Take the second left on nondescript Via Ulisse Dini (it's not obvious—turn left immediately at the arcade's end, just before the pharmacy). This leads to Pisa's historic core, Piazza dei Cavalieri.*

Piazza dei Cavalieri

With its old clock and colorfully decorated palace, this piazza was once the seat of the independent Republic of Pisa's government. In

around 1500, Florence conquered Pisa and made this square the training place for the knights of its navy. The statue of Cosimo I de' Medici shows the Florentine who ruled Pisa in the 16th century. With a foot on a dolphin, he reminded all who passed that the Florentine navy controlled the sea—at least a little of it. The frescoes on the exterior of the square's buildings, though damaged by salty sea air and years of neglect, reflect Pisa's fading glory under the Medici.

With Napoleon, this complex of grand buildings became part of the University of Pisa. The university is one of Europe's oldest, with roots in a law school that dates back as far as the 11th century. In the mid-16th century, the city was a hotbed of controversy, as spacey professors like Galileo Galilei studied the solar system—with results that challenged the church's powerful doctrine. More recently, the blind tenor Andrea Bocelli attended law school in Pisa before embarking on his well-known musical career.

From here, take Via Corsica (to the left of the clock). The

Field of Miracles Tickets

Pisa has a combo-ticket scheme designed to get you into its neglected secondary sights: the Baptistery, Camposanto Cemetery, Duomo Museum, and Museum of the Sinopias (fresco pattern museum). For €5, you get your choice of one of these sights; for two of these sights, the cost is €7; and for the works, you'll pay €9 (credit cards accepted except AmEx). No matter which ticket you get, you have to pay an additional €18 if you want to climb the Tower. Entry into the Duomo

is free, but you'll need a free voucher, or you can show your combo-ticket.

You can get the Duomo voucher (good for up to two people) and any of these tickets from either ticket office on the Field of Miracles: One is behind the Leaning Tower and the other is at the Museum of the Sinopias (near Baptistery, almost suffocated by souvenir stands). Both ticket offices have big, yellow, triangle-shaped signs. You can buy tickets in advance online at www.opapisa.it (no sooner than 20 days but at least 12 days ahead of your visit; the free voucher for the Duomo is not available online).

humble **Church of San Sisto,** ahead on the left (side entrance on Via Corsica), is worth a quick look. With simple bricks, assorted reused columns, heavy walls, and few windows, this was the typical Romanesque style that predated the more lavish Pisan Romanesque style of the Field of Miracles structures.

Follow Via Corsica as it turns into Via dei Mille, then turn right on Via Santa Maria, which leads north (and grab a quick bite at the recommended **Panetteria Antiche Tradizioni**). You'll pass through increasingly touristy claptrap, directly to the Field of Miracles and the Tower.

Sights in Pisa

▲▲▲Leaning Tower

A 15-foot lean from the vertical makes the Tower one of Europe's most recognizable images. You can see it for free; it's always viewable, or you can pay to climb its roughly 280 stairs to the seventh-floor viewing platform (one story below the top).

Cost and Hours: Free to look, €18 to go inside and climb to the seventh-floor viewing platform, one level below the top—the belfry is not currently accessible (see age restrictions in "Reservations to Climb the Tower," below), always viewable from the outside; open to climb daily April-Sept 8:00-20:00 (until 22:00 mid-June-Aug), Oct 9:00-19:00, Nov-Feb 10:00-17:00, March 9:00-18:00, ticket office opens 30 minutes early, last entry 30 minutes before closing. For details on how to get to the Tower from the train station, see page 591.

PISA & LUCCA

Reservations to Climb the Tower: Entry to the tower is by a timed ticket good for a 30-minute visit. Every 20 minutes, 45 people can clamber up the tilting steps (about 280 total—while belfry is closed). Children under age eight are not allowed to go up. Children ages 8-12 must be accompanied by—and hold hands at all times with—an adult. Teenagers (up to and including 18-year-olds) must also be accompanied by an adult.

Reserve your timed entry in person at either ticket office (see below), or choose your entry time and buy your ticket online at www.opapisa.it.

Online bookings are accepted no earlier than 20 days and no later than 12 days in advance. You must pick up your ticket(s) at least 30 minutes before your entry time. Show up 10 minutes before your appointment at the meeting point outside the ticket office.

To reserve in person, go to the **ticket office,** behind the Tower on the left (in the yellow building), or to the Museum of the Sinopias ticket office, hidden behind the souvenir stalls. In summer, for same-day entry, you'll likely need to wait a couple of hours before going up (see the rest of the monuments and grab lunch while waiting). The wait is usually much shorter at the beginning or end of the day.

At the Tower: In 2013, the room at the bottom of the tower, known as the *Sala del Pesce* for the Christian fish symbol on the wall, was opened to visitors after a long period of restoration. Here, guides offer a short explanation of the Tower's construction and history before you wind your way up the outside along a spiraling ramp, climbing 280 or so stairs. For your 30-minute time slot, figure about a 5-minute presentation by the guide, 10 minutes to climb, and 10 to descend. This leaves about 5 minutes for vertigo on the seventh-floor viewing platform. (The belfry at the top of the tower is currently not accessible.) Even though this is technically a "guided" visit, the "guide" is a museum guard who makes sure you don't stay past your scheduled time.

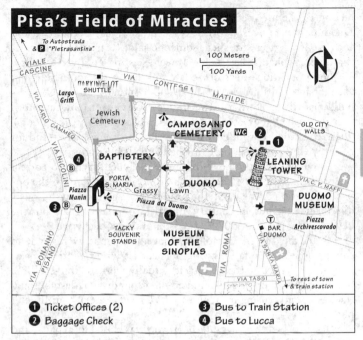

Pisa's Field of Miracles

To Autostrada & **P** "Pietrasantina"

100 Meters
100 Yards

VIALE CASCINE

VIA CARLO CAMMEO

VIA CONTESSA MATILDE

PARKING LOT SHUTTLE

Largo Griffi

Jewish Cemetery

CAMPOSANTO CEMETERY WC **②** **①**

OLD CITY WALLS

VIA NICOLINI

④ **B**

BAPTISTERY

PORTA S. MARIA

Piazza Manin

LEANING TOWER

DUOMO

VIA C. P. MAFFI

DUOMO MUSEUM

Piazza Archivescovado

③ **B** **T**

Grassy Lawn

Piazza del Duomo

TACKY SOUVENIR STANDS

①

MUSEUM OF THE SINOPIAS

VIA BONANNO PISANO

VIA ROMA

VIA SANTA MARIA

T BAR DUOMO

VIA TASSI

To rest of town & train station

① Ticket Offices (2)
② Baggage Check

③ Bus to Train Station
④ Bus to Lucca

PISA & LUCCA

Baggage Check: You can't take any bags up the Tower, but day-bag-size lockers are available at the ticket office—show your Tower ticket to check your bag. You may check your bag 10 minutes before your reservation time and must pick it up immediately after your Tower visit.

Caution: The railings are skinny, the steps are slanted, and rain makes the marble slippery. Anyone with balance issues of any sort should think twice before ascending.

❷ Self-Guided Tour: Rising up alongside the cathedral, the Tower is nearly 200 feet tall and 55 feet wide, weighing 14,000 tons and currently leaning at a five-degree angle (15 feet off the vertical axis). It started to lean almost immediately after construction began. Count the eight stories—a simple base, six stories of columns (forming arcades), and a belfry on top. The inner structural core is a hollow cylinder built of limestone bricks, faced with white marble barged here from San Giuliano, northeast of the city. The thin columns of the open-air arcades make the heavy Tower seem light and graceful.

The Tower was built over two centuries by at least three different architects. You can see how each successive architect tried to correct the leaning problem—once halfway up (after the fourth story), once at the belfry on the top.

The first stones were laid in 1173, probably under the direction of the architect Bonanno Pisano (who also designed the Duomo's bronze back door). Five years later, just as the base and the first arcade were finished, someone said, "Is it just me, or does that look crooked?" The heavy Tower—resting on a very shallow 13-foot foundation—was obviously sinking on the south side into the marshy, multilayered, unstable soil. (Actually, all the Campo's buildings tilt somewhat.) The builders carried on anyway, until they'd finished four stories (the base, plus three arcade floors). Then, construction suddenly halted—no one knows why—and for a century the Tower sat half-finished and visibly leaning.

Around 1272, the next architect continued, trying to correct the problem by angling the next three stories backward, in the opposite direction of the lean. The project then again sat mysteriously idle for nearly another century. Finally, Tommaso Pisano put the belfry on the top (c. 1350-1372), also kinking it backward.

After the Tower's completion, several attempts were made to stop its slow-motion fall. The architect/artist/writer Giorgio Vasari reinforced the base (1550), and it actually worked. But in 1838, well-intentioned engineers pumped out groundwater, destabilizing the Tower and causing it to increase its lean at a rate of a millimeter per year.

It got so bad that in 1990 the Tower was closed for repairs, and $30 million was spent trying to stabilize it. Engineers dried the soil with steam pipes, anchored the Tower to the ground with steel cables, and buried 600 tons of lead on the north side as a counterweight (not visible)—all with little success. The breakthrough came when they drilled 15-foot-long holes in the ground on the north side and sucked out 60 tons of soil, allowing the Tower to sink on the north side and straighten out its lean by about six inches.

In addition to gravity, erosion threatens the Tower. Since its construction, 135 of the Tower's 180 marble columns have had to be replaced. Stone decay, deposits of lime and calcium phosphate, accumulations of dirt and moss, cracking from the stress of the lean—all of these are factors in its decline.

Thanks to the Tower's lean, there are special trouble spots. The lower south side (which is protected from cleansing rain and wind) is a magnet for dirty airborne particles, while the stone on the upper areas has more decay (from eroding rain and wind).

The Tower, now stabilized, has been cleaned as well. Cracks were filled, and accumulations of dirt removed with carefully formulated atomized water sprays and poultices of various solvents.

All the work to shore up, straighten, and clean the Tower has probably turned the clock back a few centuries. In fact, art historians figure it leans today as much as it did when Galileo reputedly conducted his gravity experiments here some 400 years ago.

▲▲Duomo (Cathedral)

The huge Pisan Romanesque cathedral, with its carved pulpit by Giovanni Pisano, is artistically more important than its more famous bell tower.

Cost and Hours: Free; you can enter using any of the combo-tickets (see sidebar on page 597) or pick up a free voucher (valid for up to two people) at one of the ticket offices nearby; daily April-Sept 10:00-20:00, Oct 10:00-19:00, Nov-Feb 10:00-13:00 & 14:00-17:00, March 10:00-18:00, last entry 30 minutes before closing.

Information: Shorts are OK as long as they're not too short, and shoulders should be covered (although it's not really enforced). Big backpacks are not allowed, nor is storage provided. If you have a day bag, carry it. Don't let the sparkle of the new coin-operated "phone guides" tempt you. These €2 machines still use narration from a bygone era.

❍ Self-Guided Tour: Begun in 1063, the Duomo is the centerpiece of the Field of Miracles' complex of religious buildings. Start by admiring its facade.

Exterior: The architect Buschetto created the Pisan Romanesque style that set the tone for the Baptistery and Tower. Five decades later (1118), the architect Rainaldo added the impressive

main-entrance facade (which also leans out about a foot).

The **bronze back doors** (Porta San Ranieri, at the Tower end) were designed by Bonanno Pisano (c. 1186). The doors have 24 different panels that show Christ's story using the same simple, skinny figures found in Byzantine icons. (The doors are actually copies; the originals are housed—but not always on display—in the Duomo Museum.) Cast using the lost-wax technique, these doors were an inspiration for Lorenzo Ghiberti's bronze doors in Florence.

Nave: Inside, the 320-foot nave was the longest in Christendom when it was built. The striped marble and arches-on-columns give it an exotic, almost mosque-like feel. Dim light filters in from the small upper windows of the galleries, where the women worshipped.

PISA & LUCCA

At the center of the gilded coffered ceiling is the shield of Florence's Medici family. This powerful merchant and banking family took over Pisa after its glory days.

In the apse (behind the altar) is a **mosaic** (c. 1300, partly done by the great artist Cimabue) showing Christ as the Ruler of All (Pantocrator), between Mary and St. John the Evangelist. The Pantocrator image of Christ is standard fare among Eastern Orthodox Christians—that is, the "Byzantine" people who were Pisa's partners in trade.

Giovanni's Pulpit: The 15-foot-tall, octagonal pulpit is by Giovanni Pisano (c. 1250-1319), who left no stone uncarved in his pursuit of beauty. Four hundred intricately sculpted figures smother the pulpit, blurring the architectural outlines. In addition, the relief panels are actually curved, making it look less like an octagon than a circle. The creamy-white Carrara marble has the look and feel of carved French ivories, which the Pisanos loved. At the base, lions roar and crouch over their prey, symbolizing how Christ (the lion) triumphs over Satan (the horse, as in the Four Horsemen of the Apocalypse). Four of the pulpit's support "columns" are statues. The central "column" features three graceful ladies representing Faith, Hope, and Charity, the three pillars of Christianity. Around the top of the pulpit, Christ's life unfolds in a series of panels saturated with carvings.

Galileo's Lamp: The bronze incense burner that hangs from the ceiling of the north transept (to the left of the altar) is a replica of the one that supposedly caught teenage Galileo's attention when a gust of wind set the lamp swinging. He timed the swings and realized that the burner swung back and forth in the same amount of time regardless of how wide the arc. (This pendulum motion was a constant that allowed Galileo to measure our ever-changing universe.)

St. Ranieri's Body: In a glass-lined casket on the altar, Pisa's patron saint lies mummified, encased in silver at his head and feet, with his hair shirt covering his body. The silver, mask-like face dates from 2000 and is as realistic as possible—derived from an FBI-style computer scan of Ranieri's skull. The son of a rich sea-trader, Ranieri (1117-1161) was a hard-partying, touring musician who one night was inspired to set fire to his musical instrument, open his arms to the heavens (à la Jimi Hendrix), and return to his father's shipping business, where he amassed a fortune. He later gave away his money, joined a monastery, and delivered spirited sermons from the Duomo pulpit.

Tomb of Holy Roman Emperor Henry VII: Pause at the tomb of this German king (c. 1275-1313), who invaded Italy and was welcomed by the Pisans as a leader of unity and peace. Unfortunately, Henry took ill and died young, leaving Ghibelline Pisa at the mercy of its Guelph rivals, such as rising Florence. Pisa never recovered.

▲▲▲Field of Miracles (Campo dei Miracoli)

Scattered across a golf-course-green lawn are five grand buildings: the cathedral (or Duomo), its bell tower (the Leaning Tower), the

Baptistery, the hospital (today's Museum of the Sinopias), and the Camposanto Cemetery. The buildings are constructed from similar materials—bright white marble—and have comparable decoration. Each has a simple ground floor and rows of delicate columns and arches that form open-air arcades, giving the Campo a pleasant visual unity.

The style is called Pisan Romanesque. Unlike traditional Romanesque, with its heavy fortress-like feel—thick walls, barrel arches, few windows—Pisan Romanesque is light and elegant. At ground level, most of the structures have simple half-columns and arches. On the upper levels, you'll see a little of everything—tight rows of thin columns; pointed Gothic gables and prickly spires; Byzantine mosaics and horseshoe arches; and geometric designs (such as diamonds) and striped, colored marbles inspired by mosques in Muslim lands.

Architecturally, the Campo is unique and exotic. Theologically, the Campo's buildings mark the main events of every Pisan's life: christened in the Baptistery, married in the Duomo, honored in ceremonies at the Tower, healed in the hospital, and buried in the Camposanto Cemetery.

Lining this field of artistic pearls is a gauntlet of Europe's tackiest souvenir stands, as well as dozens of amateur mimes "propping up" the Leaning Tower while tourists take photos. Although the smooth green carpet looks like the ideal picnic spot, lounging on this lawn can result in a €25 fine.

Secondary Sights on the Field of Miracles

The next four sights—the Baptistery, Camposanto Cemetery, Museum of the Sinopias, and Duomo Museum—share the same pricing and schedule.

Cost and Hours: €9 combo-ticket includes all the sights, plus the Duomo (credit cards accepted; see sidebar on page 597 for run-down on various combo-tickets). Open daily April-Sept 8:00-20:00, Oct 9:00-19:00, Nov-Feb 10:00-17:00, March 9:00-18:00, last entry 30 minutes before closing.

Getting There: The Baptistery is located in front of the Duomo's facade. The Camposanto Cemetery is behind the church on the north side of the Field of Miracles. The Museum of the Sinopias is hidden behind souvenir stands, across the street from the Baptistery entrance. The Duomo Museum is housed behind the Tower.

▲**Baptistery**

The round Baptistery is the biggest in Italy. It's interesting for its superb acoustics and fine Pisano pulpit.

Visiting the Baptistery: The building is 180 feet tall—John the Baptist is almost eye-to-eye with the tourists looking out from the nearly 200-foot-tall Leaning Tower. Notice that the Baptistery leans nearly six feet to the north (the Tower leans 15 feet to the south). The building (begun in 1153) is modeled on the circular domed Church of the Holy Sepulchre in Jerusalem, seen by Pisan Crusaders who occupied Jerusalem in 1099.

Inside, it's simple, spacious, and baptized with light. Tall arches encircle just a few pieces of religious furniture. In the center sits the beautiful, marble **octagonal font** (1246). A statue of the first Baptist, John the Baptist, stretches out his hand and says, "Welcome to my Baptistery." The font contains plenty of space for baptizing adults by immersion (the medieval custom), plus four wells for dunking babies.

The **pulpit** by Nicola Pisano, Giovanni's father, is arguably the world's first Renaissance sculpture. It's the first authenticated (signed) work by the "Giotto of sculpture," working in what came to be called the Renaissance style. The free-standing sculpture has classical columns, realistic people and animals, and 3-D effects in the carved panels. The speaker's platform stands on columns that rest on the backs of animals, representing Christianity's triumph over paganism. The relief panels, with scenes from the life of Christ, are more readable than the Duomo pulpit. Read left to right, starting from the back: Nativity, Adoration of the Magi, Presentation in the Temple, Crucifixion, Last Judgment.

The **acoustics** are impressive. Make a sound in here and it echoes for a good 10 seconds. A priest standing at the baptismal font (or a security guard today) can sing three tones within the 10 seconds—"Ave Maria"—and make a chord, singing haunting harmonies with himself. This medieval form of digital delay is due to the 250-foot-wide dome. Recent computer analysis suggests that the 15th-century architects who built the dome intended this building to function not just as a Baptistery, but also as a musical instrument. A security guard sings every half-hour, starting when the doors open in the morning. Climb 75 steps to the interior gallery (midway up) for an impressive view back down on the baptismal font.

Camposanto Cemetery

This site has been a cemetery since at least the 12th century. The building's cloistered open-air courtyard, lined with traces of fresco on the bare-brick walls, is surrounded by an arcade with intricately carved tracery in the arches and dozens of ancient Roman sarcophagi. The courtyard's grass grows on special dirt (said to turn a body into bones in a single day), shipped here by returning Crusaders from Jerusalem's Mount Calvary, where Christ was crucified. The 1,000-square-foot fresco, *The Triumph of Death* (c. 1340), captures late-medieval Europe's concern with death—predating but still accurately depicting Pisa's mood in reaction to the bubonic plague (1348), which killed one in three Pisans. Grim stuff, but appropriate for the Camposanto's permanent residents.

In 1944, the Camposanto took a direct hit from an Allied incendiary grenade (the rest of the Field of Miracles was miraculously unscathed). It melted the lead-covered arcade roof and peeled historic frescoes from the walls—one of the many tragic artistic losses of World War II (look for photos of the bombed-out Camposanto at the back of the courtyard). The Americans liberated the city on September 2 and later rebuilt the Camposanto.

Museum of the Sinopias (Museo delle Sinopie)

Housed in a 13th-century hospital, this museum features the preparatory sketches (sinopias) for the Camposanto's WWII-damaged frescoes (including *The Triumph of Death,* described earlier). Sinopias are sketches made in red paint directly on the wall, designed to guide the making of the final colored fresco. The master always did the sinopia himself; if he liked the results, his assistants made a "cartoon" by tracing the sinopia onto large sheets of paper *(cartone)*. Then the sinopia was plastered over, and the assistants redrew the outlines, using the cartoon as a guide. While the plaster was still wet, the master and his team quickly filled in the color and details, producing the final frescoes (now on display at the Camposanto). These sinopias—never meant to be seen—were uncovered by the bombing and restoration of the Camposanto and brought here.

Whether or not you pay to go in, you can watch two free videos in the entry lobby that serve to orient you to the square: a 10-minute, 3-D computer tour of the complex, and a 15-minute story of the Tower, its tilt, and its fix.

Duomo Museum (Museo dell'Opera del Duomo)

This museum behind the Leaning Tower is big on Pisan art, displaying treasures of the cathedral, paintings, silverware, and sculptures (from the 12th to 14th centuries, particularly by the Pisano dynasty), as well as ancient Egyptian, Etruscan, and Roman artifacts. It houses many of the original statues and much of the artwork that once adorned the Campo's buildings (where copies stand today), notably the statues by Nicola and Giovanni Pisano. You can stand face-to-face with the Pisanos' very human busts, which once ringed the outside of the Baptistery.

Also on display are the Duomo's original 12th-century bronze doors of St. Ranieri, done by Bonanno Pisano, which feature scenes from the life of Jesus. You'll also see a mythical sculpted hippogriff (a medieval jackalope) and other oddities brought back from the Holy Land by Pisan Crusaders, along with several large-scale wooden models of the Duomo, Baptistery, and Tower. The museum's grassy interior courtyard has a two-story, tourist-free view of the Tower, Duomo, and Baptistery.

Beyond the Field of Miracles

Museo Nazionale di San Matteo

On the river and in a former convent, this art museum displays 12th- to 15th-century sculptures, illuminated manuscripts, and paintings on wood by pre- and early Renaissance masters Martini, Masaccio, and others. It's a fine collection—especially its painted wood crucifixes—and gives you a chance to see Pisan innovation in 11th- to 13th-century art, before Florence took the lead.

Cost and Hours: €5, Tue-Sat 8:30-19:00, Sun 8:30-13:00, closed Mon, near Piazza San Paolo at Lungarno Medicero, a 5-minute walk upriver (east) from the main bridge, tel. 050-541-865.

Sleeping in Pisa

To locate these hotels, see the map on page 592.

$$$ Hotel Alessandro della Spina, in a nondescript neighborhood near Pisa Centrale train station, has 16 elegant and colorful rooms, each named after a flower (Sb-€120, Db-€140, discounts off-season and online, air-con, guest computer, free Wi-Fi, parking-€10/day; head straight out of train station, turn right on Viale F. Bonaini, and take the third right on Via Alessandro della Spina to find the hotel on your left at #5; tel. 050-502-777, www.hoteldellaspina.it, info@hoteldellaspina.it).

$$ Hotel Royal Victoria, a classy place on the Arno River, has been run by the Piegaja family since 1837. With 48 creaky, historic rooms filled with antiques, it's ideal for romantics who missed out on the Grand Tour. The location, dead-center between the Tower and Pisa Centrale train station, is the most atmospheric of my listings (D-€80, standard Db-€110, better Db-€130, suite-€210, family room-€260, breakfast-€5, 10 percent discount with this book if you book direct, check website for special deals, air-con on request, Wi-Fi, parking garage-€20/day, lush communal terrace, Lungarno Pacinotti 12, tel. 050-940-111, www.royalvictoria.it, mail@royalvictoria.it).

$$ Hotel Villa Kinzica has 30 tired, worn rooms with high ceilings, and a prime location just steps from the Field of Miracles—ask for a room with a view of the Tower (Sb-€70, Db €95, Tb-€109, Qb-€119, better prices off-season, air-con, elevator, Piazza Arcivescovado 2, tel. 050-560-419, www.hotelvillakinzica.it, info@hotelvillakinzica.it).

$ Residenza Gorkij, recently opened by good-natured Lucca and his Russian wife, offers eight tasteful rooms—some with frescoed ceilings—in a converted historic building in the town center. Two minutes from Piazza dei Cavalieri and 10 minutes from the Leaning Tower, this is a comfortable, good-value option (Sb-€45, Db-€55, Tb-€65, show this book to get these reduced rates, air-con, Wi-Fi, elevator, 2 rooms have small kitchen, call or email ahead with your arrival time—there's no staff on-site, Piazza Donati 13, tel. 050-580-395, mobile 334-132-9859, www.gorkij.it, info@gorkij.it).

$ Hotel Milano, near Pisa Centrale train station, offers 10 simple, clean rooms (D-€55, Db-€78, 10 percent discount for Rick Steves readers if you book direct, breakfast extra, Wi-Fi, air-con, TV in rooms, Via Mascagni 14, tel. 050-23-162, www.hotelmilano.pisa.it, info@hotelmilano.pisa.it).

$ Pensione Helvetia is a no-frills, homey, clean, and quiet inn just 100 yards from the Tower. Its 29 economical rooms are spread over four floors (no elevator); the lower your room number, the lower your altitude (S-€45, Sb-€54, D-€54, Db-€60, Tb €75, no breakfast but small lounge with vending machines, ceiling fans, guest computer, free Wi-Fi, Via Don G. Boschi 31, reception around the corner at Hotel Francesco on Via Santa Maria, tel. 050-553-084, www.pensionehelvetiapisa.com, helvetiapisatravel@gmail.com, Maria Sandra and Micaele).

$ Locanda La Lanterna and **Antica Locanda San Ranieri** combine to offer 28 characteristic and comfortable rooms in their main location (on Via Santa Maria) and their less spacious Ranieri annex (in a narrow side street nearby). Both are run by down-to-earth Senora Angela (ask to see her old Italian lira-note collection).

Rooms are on three or four floors, with no elevator; the bathrooms are plain and cramped (Sb-€45, Db-€65, Tb-€75, annex-€10 less per room, air-con, Wi-Fi, street parking-€8, 5 minutes from the Tower on Via Santa Maria 113, tel. 050-830-305, www.locanda-lalanterna.com, info@anticalocandalalanterna.com).

$ Two Steps from the Tower B&B, in the historic center just a few blocks east of the Field of Miracles, offers three Ikea-style rooms in a modern apartment block (Sb-€30-40, Db-€55-70, extra bed-€15, weekly rates available, free Wi-Fi, kitchen use-€10/day, 2 rooms have access to small garden, Via Cardinale Pietro Maffi 6, tel. 347-394-6559, www.2stepsfromtower.com, info@2stepsfromtower.com).

Eating in Pisa

Antica Trattoria il Campano, just off the market square, has a typically Tuscan menu and a candlelit, stay-awhile atmosphere. Their €30-35 tasting menus include wine and generous portions of local specialties (Fri-Tue 12:30-15:00 & 19:30-22:45, Thu 19:30-22.45, closed Wed, reservations smart, Via Cavalca 19, tel. 050-580-585, Giovanna).

Ristorante Masala serves tasty, authentic Indian cuisine just a few blocks from the Tower. As there is a large Indian community in Pisa, this is a great place to take a break from pizza and pasta (€4-9 curries, vegetarian options, Tue-Sun 19:00-23:00, closed Mon, Via Roma 52, tel. 050-48513).

At **Ristorante Bagus** the specialties are an extra-rare burger made with the famous Chianina beef and trendy twists on typical Tuscan fare (€30 fixed-price meal, Mon-Fri 12:30-14:30 & 19:30-23:00, Sat 19:30-23:00 only, closed Sun; heading south on Corso Italia, turn right on Via Nunziata and take your first right after Piazza Griletti to Piazza dei Facchini 13; tel. 050-26196).

Da Michele is a handy choice if you are sleeping near the train station. A family-run, basic affair, the home-cooking is tasty and reasonably priced, and the place stays open late. The tiramisù is a classic (daily 12:00-15:00 & 18:00-23:00, except sometimes closed Wed; 3-minute walk from recommended Hotel Alessandro della Spina heading toward the station at Viale Bonaini 96/100, tel. 050-24128).

Pizzeria al Bagno di Nerone is a local favorite and particularly popular with students. Belly up to the bar and grab a slice to go, or sit in their small dining room for a whole pie. Try the *cecina*, a crepe-like garbanzo-bean cake (Wed-Mon 12:00-14:30 & 18:00-22:30, closed Tue, a 5-minute walk from the Tower at Largo Carlo Fedeli 26, tel. 050-551-085).

At **Paninoteca il Canguro,** Fabio makes warm, hearty sandwiches to order. Check the chalkboard for seasonal specials, such as *porchetta* (daily 9:00-24:00, may be closed Sun in winter, Via Santa Maria 151, tel. 050-561-942).

Panetteria Antiche Tradizioni—not to be confused with another panetteria across the street—is a sandwich/bread shop with complete fixings for a picnic. Build your own sandwich with homemade bread or focaccia, then choose fruit from the counter, fresh pastries from the window, and cold drinks or wine to round out your meal (daily 8:00-20:00, Via Santa Maria 66, mobile 327-570-5210).

Drop by cheery **La Lupa Ghiotta Tavola Calda** for a cheap, fast, and tasty meal a few steps from Pisa Centrale train station. It's got everything you'd want from a *ristorante* at half the price and with faster service (build your own salad—five ingredients for €4.50; Mon-Sat 12:15-15:00 & 19:15-23:30, closed Sun, Viale F. Bonaini 113, tel. 050-21018).

The street that houses the daily market, **Via delle Colonne** (a block north of the Arno, west of Borgo Stretto), has a few atmospheric, mid-priced restaurants and several fun, greasy take-out options.

Pisa Connections

Pisa is well-connected by trains, buses (particularly with Lucca), and highways, with a busy airport nearby.

From Pisa Centrale Station by Train to: Florence (2-3/hour, 45-75 minutes, €7.80), **Livorno** (2-3/hour, 20 minutes, €2.50), **Rome** (2/hour, many change in Florence, 3-4 hours), **La Spezia,** gateway to Cinque Terre (about hourly, 1-1.5 hours), **Siena** (2/hour, 1.75 hours, change at Empoli, €9.80), **Lucca** (1-2/hour, 30 minutes, bus is better except on Sun—see below, €3). Even the fastest trains stop in Pisa, so you might change trains here whether you plan to stop or not.

By Bus to Lucca: A handy bus connects the Field of Miracles with Lucca's Piazzale Giuseppe Verdi in 30 minutes (Mon-Sat hourly, fewer on Sun; in Pisa, wait at the Vai Bus signpost, immediately outside the wall behind the Baptistery on the right; also stops at Pisa's airport, buy €3 ticket on bus). This makes a half-day side-trip to Pisa from Lucca particularly easy.

By Car: The drive between Pisa and Florence is that rare case where the non-autostrada highway (free, more direct, and at least as fast) is a better deal than the autostrada.

By Plane: Pisa's **Galileo Galilei Airport** handles more and more international and domestic flights (daily April-Oct 9:00-23:00, Nov-March 9:00-20:00, tel. 050-502-518; cash machine, car-rental agencies, baggage storage from 9:00-19:00 only—€7/bag, self-service cafeteria; airport code: PSA, tel. 050-849-300, www.pisa-airport.com).

To get into **Pisa,** you can take bus LAM Rossa (4-6/hour, runs until 20:30, 15 minutes, pay €1.50 on board or €1.10 if you purchase ticket in advance at kiosk, departs from in front of arrivals hall); a train (departs from the far left of the arrivals hall as you face the exits); or a taxi (€10-12).

You can connect from Pisa's airport to **Florence** easily by train (2-3/hour, 1.25 hours, €7.80, most transfer at Pisa Centrale) or by Terravision bus (about hourly, 1.25 hours, €5 one-way, ticket kiosk is at the right end of the arrivals hall as you're facing the exits, catch bus outside and to the far right of the bus parking lot, leaves you at Santa Maria Novella station, www.terravision.eu).

Lucca

Surrounded by well-preserved ramparts, layered with history, alternately quaint and urbane, Lucca charms its visitors. The city is a paradox. Though it hasn't been involved in a war since 1430, it is Italy's most impressive fortress city, encircled by a perfectly intact wall. Most cities tear down their wall to make way for modern traffic, but Lucca's effectively keeps out both traffic and, it seems, the stress of the modern world. Locals are very protective of their wall, which they enjoy like a community roof garden. Lucca, known for being Europe's leading producer of toilet paper and tissue (with a monopoly on the special machinery that makes it), is nothing to sneeze at. However, the town has no single monumental sight to attract tourists—it's simply a uniquely human and undamaged, never-bombed city. Romanesque churches seem to be around every corner, as do fun-loving and shady piazzas filled with soccer-playing children.

Locals say Lucca is like a cake with a cherry filling in the middle...every slice is equally good. Despite Lucca's charm, few tourists seem to put it on their maps, and it remains a city for the Lucchesi (loo-KAY-zee).

Planning Your Time

Low-impact Lucca has no must-see sights, but its pleasant ambience, ample churches, and pristine piazzas reward any time you've got. With the better part of a day, stroll through the town center, dipping into the sights that interest you. Once you've had your fill, rent a bike and do a few spins around the ramparts (or do the loop in slow motion, by foot) before dinner.

Orientation to Lucca

Tourist Information

Lucca has two TIs. The main TI, on **Piazzale Giuseppe Verdi,** offers city information and a no-fee room-booking service (daily

April-Oct 9:00-19:00, Nov-March 9:00-17:00, futuristic WC-€0.60, tel. 0583-583-150, www.luccaitinera. it). It also has Internet access, baggage storage, and bike rentals (all described under "Helpful Hints," later) and guided city walks (see "Tours in Lucca," later).

The second TI, which may be useful for drivers, is west of town on Via

Luporini (between Via Parri and Via delle Città Gemelle), at the tourist-bus checkpoint and near parking (April-Sept 9:00-17:00, tel. 0583-583-462).

Arrival in Lucca

By Train: There is no baggage check at the train station, but you can leave luggage at Tourist Center Lucca (near the station) or at the main TI on Piazzale Guiseppe Verdi (see "Helpful Hints" for specifics on both).

To reach the city center from the train station, walk toward the walls and head left, to the entry at Porta San Pietro. Taxis are sparse, but try calling 025-353 (ignore any recorded message—just wait for a live operator); a ride from the station to Piazza dell'Anfiteatro costs about €10.

By Bus: Buses from Pisa, Viareggio, and from nearby villages arrive inside the walls at Piazzale Giuseppe Verdi, where the main TI is located.

By Car: The key for drivers—don't try to drive within the walls. The old town is ringed by parking lots (with two just inside the walls, both usually full).

An easy option is to park near the tour-bus lot and second TI, not far from the southwest wall. As you leave the autostrada, follow signs for *Bus Turistico Checkpoint*, which will lead you to parking lots on Via Luporini—one is for buses, but the other has free and paid parking for cars. White lines denote free parking, and blue lines are paid parking (daily 8:00-20:00, €1-1.50/hour, pay at automated kiosks). Avoid the yellow lines—these spots are for locals only. From here it's about a five-minute walk to Porta Sant'Anna.

Parking is always free in Piazzale Don Franco, a five-minute walk north of the city walls. If you must park inside the city walls, try just inside Porta Santa Maria (€1.50/hour). Or consider parking outside the gates near the train station or on the boulevard surrounding the city (meter rates vary; also about €1/hour). Overnight parking (20:00-8:00) on city streets and in city lots is usually free. Check with your hotelier to be sure.

Helpful Hints

Combo-Tickets: A €7 combo-ticket includes visits to the Ilaria del Carretto tomb in San Martino Cathedral (€3), Cathedral Museum (€4), and San Giovanni Church (€4). A €6 combo-ticket combines the Guinigi Tower (€4) and the Clock Tower (€4). Yet another combo-ticket covers Palazzo Mansi and Villa Guinigi for €6.50 and is valid for three days (€4 each if purchased separately).

Shops and Museums Alert: Shops close most of Sunday and Monday mornings. Many museums are closed on Monday as well.

Markets: Lucca's atmospheric markets are worth visiting. Every third weekend of the month (whenever the third Sun falls), one of the largest **antique markets** in Italy sprawls in the blocks between Piazza Antelminelli and Piazza San Giovanni (8:00-19:00). The last weekend of the month, local artisans sell **arts and crafts** around town, mainly near the cathedral (also 8:00-19:00). At the **general market,** held Wednesdays and Saturdays, you'll find produce and household goods (8:30-13:00, from Porta Elisa to Porta San Jacopo on Via dei Bacchettoni).

Concerts: San Giovanni Church hosts one-hour concerts featuring a pianist and singers performing highlights from hometown composer Giacomo Puccini (€20 at the door, €18 advance purchase at TI and some hotels, daily April-Oct at 19:00, Nov-March check schedule and location at www.puccinielasualucca.com).

Festival: On September 13 and 14, the city celebrates Volto Santo ("Holy Face"), with a procession of the treasured local crucifix and a fair in Piazza Antelminelli.

Internet Access: You can get online (you need your ID or a copy of your passport) at the main TI on Piazzale Giuseppe Verdi (€2/hour, two terminals, Wi-Fi same price) or at **Betty Blue,** a wine bar handy to the recommended launderette (€3.50/hour, two terminals and cables to plug in your laptop, Thu-Tue 13:00-24:00, closed Wed, Via del Gonfalone 18, tel. 0583-492-166).

Baggage Storage: For train travelers, the most convenient storage spot is **Tourist Center Lucca** (on the left side of the square as you exit the train station, daily April-Oct 9:00-20:00, Nov-March 9:00-18:00, €3-9). The main TI on **Piazzale Giuseppe Verdi** is more convenient to buses (2 bags for €4.50/5 hours, €7/day, daily 9:00-17:30, they need to photocopy your passport). In a pinch, you may be able to store bags at the recommended Hotel Rex (near the train station).

Laundry: Lavanderia Self-Service Niagara is just off Piazza Santa Maria at Via Rosi 26 (€9 wash and dry, daily 7:00-23:00).

Bike Rental: A one-hour rental (ID required) gives you time for two leisurely loops around the ramparts. Several places with identical prices cluster around Piazza Santa Maria (€3/hour, €15/day, tandem bikes available, helmets available on request, daily about 9:00-19:00 or sunset). Try these easygoing shops: **Antonio Poli** (Piazza Santa Maria 42, tel. 0583-493-787, enthusiastic Cristiana) and, right next to it, **Cicli Bizzarri** (Piazza Santa Maria 32, tel. 0583-496-682, Australian Dely). At the west end of town, the **TI** on Piazzale Giuseppe Verdi rents

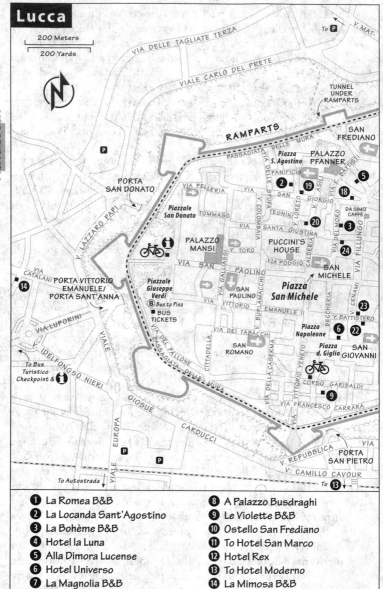

Lucca

200 Meters
200 Yards

V. MAT-

To P

VIA DELLE TAGLIATE TERZA

VIALE CARLO DEL PRETE

TUNNEL
UNDER
RAMPARTS

RAMPARTS

PASSAGGIATA DELLE MURA

SAN
FREDIANO

P

PORTA
SAN DONATO

VIA PELLERIA

VIA DELLA STUA

VIA C. BATTISTI

Piazza
S. Agostino

PALAZZO
PFANNER

Panificio

2

19

VIA SAN
GIORGIO

VIA FILLUNGO

5

18

VIA C. ASILI

VIA LORETO

Piazzale
San Donato

TOMMASO

VIA COLOMBAIA

VIA TEGNINI

SANTA GIUSTINA

DA SIMO
CAFFÈ

VIA DEL MORO

3

PALAZZO
MANSI

VIA S. GIROLAMO

VIA TORO

VIA POGGIO

CALDERIA

24

SAN
MICHELE

V. LAZZARO PAPI

VIA
CATALANI

PORTA VITTORIO
EMANUELE/
PORTA SANT'ANNA

Piazzale
Giuseppe
Verdi

B Bus to Pisa

BUS
TICKETS

VIA SAN
PAOLINO

VIA GALLI E ASSI

SAN
PAOLINO

VIA VITTORIO EMANUELE II

VIA BURLAMACCHI

Piazza
San Michele

VIA CENAMI

VIA BECCHERIA

23

V. BATTISTERO

14

VIA LUPORINI

V. IDELFONSO NIERI

To Bus
Turistico
Checkpoint &

VIA DEI TABACCHI

SAN
ROMANO

CITTADELLA

VIA DELLA CASERMA

VIA DEL FOSSO

Piazza
Napoleone

6

22

Piazza
d. Giglio

SAN
GIOVANNI

9

VIA EUROPA

VIALE GIOSUÈ

VIA VITTORIO VENETO

CORSO GARIBALDI

VIA FRANCESCO CARRARA

CARDUCCI

To Autostrada

P

P

To 13

PORTA
SAN PIETRO

V. REPUBBLICA

VIA

V. CAMILLO CAVOUR

PISA & LUCCA

PASSAGGIATA DELLE MURA

PUCCINI'S
HOUSE

❶ La Romea B&B	❽ A Palazzo Busdraghi
❷ La Locanda Sant'Agostino	❾ Le Violette B&B
❸ La Bohème B&B	❿ Ostello San Frediano
❹ Hotel la Luna	⓫ To Hotel San Marco
❺ Alla Dimora Lucense	⓬ Hotel Rex
❻ Hotel Universo	⓭ To Hotel Moderno
❼ La Magnolia B&B	⓮ La Mimosa B&B

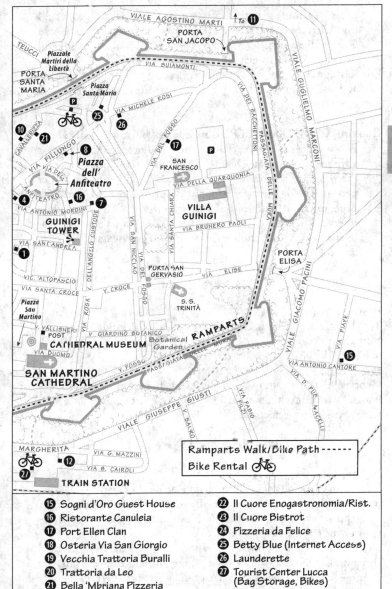

15 Sogni d'Oro Guest House	**22** Il Cuore Enogastronomia/Rist.
16 Ristorante Canuleia	**23** Il Cuore Bistrot
17 Port Ellen Clan	**24** Pizzeria da Felice
18 Osteria Via San Giorgio	**25** Betty Blue (Internet Access)
19 Vecchia Trattoria Buralli	**26** Launderette
20 Trattoria da Leo	**27** Tourist Center Lucca
21 Bella 'Mbriana Pizzeria	(Bag Storage, Bikes)

Within the map:

VIALE AGOSTINO MARTI

↑ To **11**

PORTA
SAN JACOPO

TEUCCI

Piazzale
Martiri della
Libertà

VIA BUIAMONTI

VIALE GUGLIELMO MARCONI

PORTA
SANTA
MARIA

Piazza
Santa Maria

VIA MICHELE ROSI

VIA DEI BACCHETTONI

PASSEGGIATA DELLE MURA

25

26

10

CAVALLERIZZA

VIA FILLUNGO

21

8

Piazza
dell'
Anfiteatro

VIA DELL' ANFITEATRO

VIA DEL FOSSO

17

SAN
FRANCESCO

P

VIA DELLA QUARQUONIA

VILLA
GUINIGI

VIA SANTA CHIARA

VIA BRUNERO PAOLI

4

16

7

VIA ANTONIO MORDINI

GUINIGI
TOWER

VIA SANT'ANDREA

1

DELL'ANGELO CUSTODE

VIA SAN NICCLAO

VIA DEL FOSSO

PORTA SAN
GERVASIO

VIA ELISE

PORTA
ELISA

VIC. ALTOPASCIO

VIA SANTA CROCE

V. CROCE

S. S.
TRINITÀ

Piazza
San
Martino

V. VALLISNERI

POST

V. GIARDINO BOTANICO

Botanical
Garden

RAMPARTS

VIA PIAVE

15

VIALE GIACOMO PACINI

CATHEDRAL MUSEUM

VIA DUOMO

PASSEGGIATA DELLE MURA

VIA ANTONIO CANTORE

VIA D. PUB. MACELLI

SAN MARTINO
CATHEDRAL

V. FOSSO

VIALE GIUSEPPE GIUSTI

V. SALSO

VIA FABIO
FILZI

MARGHERITA

VIA G. MAZZINI

12

VIA B. CAIROLI

27

TRAIN STATION

Ramparts Walk/Bike Path - - - - - -

Bike Rental

bikes (€3/hour). At the south end, at Porta San Pietro, you'll find **Chrono** (same rates and hours as the competition, Corso Garibaldi 93, tel. 0583-490-591, www.chronobikes.com) and **Tourist Center Lucca** (near the train station).

Local Magazine: For insights into American and British expat life and listings of concerts, markets, festivals, and other special events, pick up a copy of the *Grapevine* (€2), available at newsstands.

Cooking Class: Gianluca Pardini invites you to the hills above Lucca to learn to make Tuscan fare. You prepare and then eat a three-course meal. Depending on how many others attend, the price ranges from €50 (a steal) to a whopping €125 per person. This is great for groups of four or more (€14 cab ride from town, 3-hour lesson plus time to dine, includes wine, reserve at least 2 days in advance, Via di San Viticchio 414, tel. 0583-378-071, mobile 347-678-7447, www.italiancuisine. it, info@italiancuisine.it).

Tours in Lucca

Walking Tours
The TI offers two-hour city walks with a local guide, departing from the office on Piazzale Giuseppe Verdi (€10, daily at 14:00, tel. 0583-583-150).

Local Guide
Gabriele Calabrese knows and shares his hometown well (€120/3 hours, by foot or bike, mobile 347-788-0667, www.turislucca.com, turislucca@turislucca.com).

Sights in Lucca

▲▲Bike the Ramparts
Lucca's most remarkable feature, its Renaissance wall, is also its most enjoyable attraction—especially when circled on a rental bike. Stretching for 2.5 miles, this is an ideal place to come for an overview of the city by foot or bike.

Lucca has had a protective wall for 2,000 years. You can read three walls into today's map: the first rectangular Roman wall, the later medieval wall (nearly the size of today's), and the 16th-century Renaissance wall that still survives.

With the advent of cannons, thin medieval walls were suddenly vulnerable. A new design—the same one that stands today—was state-of-the-art when it was built (1550-1650). Much of the old medieval wall (look for the old stones) was incorporated into the Renaissance wall (with uniform bricks). The new wall was squat: a 100-foot-wide mound of dirt faced with bricks, engineered to absorb a cannonball pummeling. The townspeople cleared a wide no-man's-land around the town, exposing any attackers from a distance. Eleven heart-shaped bastions (now inviting picnic areas) were designed to minimize exposure to cannonballs and to maximize defense capabilities. The ramparts were armed with 130 cannons.

The town invested a third of its income for more than a century to construct the wall, and—since it kept away the Florentines and nasty Pisans—it was considered a fine investment. In fact, nobody ever bothered to try to attack the wall. Locals say that the only time it actually defended the city was during an 1812 flood of the Serchio River, when the gates were sandbagged and its ramparts kept out the high water.

Today, the ramparts seem made-to-order for a leisurely bike ride (20-minute pedal, wonderfully smooth). You can rent bikes cheaply and easily from one of several bike-rental places in town (listed earlier, under "Helpful Hints").

Piazza dell'Anfiteatro

Just off the main shopping street, the architectural ghost of a Roman amphitheater can be felt in the delightful Piazza dell'Anfiteatro.

With the fall of Rome, the theater (which seated 10,000) was gradually cannibalized for its stones and inhabited by people living in a mishmash of huts. The huts were cleared away at the end of the 19th century to better appreciate the town's illustrious past. Today the square is a circle of touristy shops and mediocre restaurants that becomes a lively bar-and-café scene after dark. The modern street level is nine feet above the original arena floor. The only bits of surviving Roman stonework are a few arches on the northern exterior (at Via Fillungo 42 and on Via dell'Anfiteatro).

Via Fillungo

This main pedestrian drag stretches southwest from Piazza dell'Anfiteatro. *The* street to stroll, Via Fillungo takes you from the amphitheater almost all the way to the cathedral. Along the way, you'll get a taste of Lucca's rich past, including several elegant, century-old storefronts. Many of the original storefront paintings, reliefs, and mosaics survive—even if today's shopkeeper sells something entirely different.

The History of Lucca

Lucca began as a Roman settlement. In fact, the grid layout of the streets (and the shadow of an amphitheater) survives from Roman times. Trace the rectangular Roman wall—indicated by today's streets—on the map. As in typical Roman towns, two main roads quartered the fortified town, crossing at what was the forum (main market and religious/political center)—today's Piazza San Michele.

Christianity came here early; it's said that the first bishop of Lucca was a disciple of St. Peter. While churches were built here as early as the fourth century, the majority of Lucca's elegant Romanesque churches date from about the 12th century.

Feisty Lucca, though never a real power, enjoyed a long period of independence (maintained by clever diplomacy). Aside from 30 years of being ruled from Pisa in the 14th century, Lucca was basically an independent city-state until Napoleon came to town.

In the Middle Ages, wealthy Lucca's economy was built on the silk industry, dominated by the Guinigi (gwee-NEE-gee) family. Without silk, Lucca would have been just another sleepy Italian town. In 1500, the town had 3,000 silk looms employing 25,000 workers. Banking was also big. Many pilgrims stopped here on their way to the Holy Land, deposited their money for safety...and never returned to pick it up.

In its heyday, Lucca packed 160 towers—one on nearly every corner—and 70 churches within its walls. Each tower was the home of a wealthy merchant family. Towers were many stories tall, with single rooms stacked atop each other: ground-floor shop, upstairs living room, and top-floor fire-safe kitchen, all connected by exterior wooden staircases. The rooftop was generally a vegetable garden, with trees providing shade. Later, the wealthy city folk moved into the countryside, trading away life in their city palazzos to establish farm estates complete with fancy villas. (You can visit some of these villas today—the TI has a brochure—but they're convenient only for drivers and are generally not worth the cost of admission.)

In 1799, Napoleon stormed into Italy and took a liking to Lucca. He liked it so much that he gave it to his sister as a gift (who ruled 1805-14). After Napoleon was toppled, Europe's ruling powers gave Lucca to Maria Luisa, the daughter of the king of Spain. Duchess Maria Luisa (who ruled 1817-24) was partially responsible for turning the city's imposing (but no longer particularly useful) fortified wall into a fine city park that is much enjoyed today. Her statue stands on Piazza Napoleone, near Palazzo Ducale.

At #97 is a classic old **jewelry store** with a rare storefront that has kept its T-shaped arrangement (when it's closed, you see a wooden T, and during open hours it unfolds with a fine old-time display). This design dates from a time when the merchant sold his goods in front, did his work in the back, and lived upstairs.

Di Simo Caffè, at #58 (but currently closed), has long been the hangout of Lucca's artistic and intellectual elite. Composer and hometown boy Giacomo Puccini tapped his foot while sipping coffee here.

A surviving five-story **tower house** is at #67. There was a time when nearly every corner sported its own tower (see the sidebar). The stubby stones that still stick out once supported wooden staircases (there were no interior connections between floors). So many towers cast shadows over this part of town that the street just before it is called Via Buia (Dark Street). Look away from this tower and down Via San Andrea for a peek at the town's tallest tower, Guinigi, in the distance—with its characteristic oak trees sprouting from the top.

At #45 and #43, you'll see two more good examples of tower houses. Across the street, the **Clock Tower** (Torre delle Ore) has

a hand-wound Swiss clock that has clanged four times an hour since 1754 (€4 to climb up and see the mechanism flip into action on the quarter-hour—if it's actually working, €6 combo-ticket includes Guinigi Tower, daily April-Oct 9:30-18:30, Nov-March 9:30-17:30, last entry 20 minutes before closing, corner of Via Fillungo and Via del'Arancio).

The intersection of Via Fillungo and Via Roma/Via Santa Croce marks the center of town (where the two original Roman roads crossed). As you go right down Via Roma, you'll pass the fine Edison Bookstore on your left before reaching Piazza San Michele.

Piazza San Michele

This square has been the center of town since Roman times, when it was the forum. It's dominated by the Church of San Michele. Towering above the church's fancy Pisan Romanesque facade, the archangel Michael stands ready to flap his wings—which he was known to do on special occasions.

The square is surrounded by an architectural hodgepodge. The loggia, which dates from 1495, is the first Renaissance building in town. There's a late-19th-century interior in Buccellato Taddeucci, a 130-year-old pastry shop (#34). The left section of the BNL bank (#5; in front of the church) sports an Art Nouveau facade that celebrates both Amerigo Vespucci and Cristoforo Colombo.

Perhaps you've noticed that the statues of big shots that decorate many an Italian piazza are mostly absent from Lucca's squares. That's because, unlike Venice, Florence, and Milan—which were dominated by a few powerful dynasties—Lucca was traditionally run by an oligarchy of a hundred leading families, with no one central figure to commemorate in stone. But after Italian unification, when leaders were fond of saying, "We have created Italy...now we need to create Italians," stirring statues of national heroes popped up everywhere—even in Lucca. The statue on Piazza San Michele is a two-bit local guy, dredged up centuries after his death because he favored strong central government.

Look back at the church facade, which also has an element of patriotism—designed to give roots and legitimacy to Italian statehood. Perched above many of the columns are the faces of heroes in the Italian independence and unification movement: Victor Emmanuel II (above the short red column on the right), the Count of Cavour (next to Victor, above the column with black zigzags), and Giuseppe Mazzini.

▲San Martino Cathedral

This cathedral, begun in the 11th century, is an entertaining mix of architectural and artistic styles. It's also home to the exquisite 15th-century tomb of Ilaria del Carretto, who married into the wealthy Guinigi family.

Cost and Hours: Cathedral—free, Ilaria tomb—€3, €7 combo-ticket includes Cathedral Museum and San Giovanni Church; Mon-Fri 9:30-17:45, Sat 9:30-18:45; Sun 11:00-17:00; Piazza San Martino.

Visiting the Cathedral: The cathedral's elaborate Pisan Romanesque **facade** features Christian teaching scenes, animals, and candy-cane-striped columns.

The central figure is St. Martin, a Roman military officer from Hungary who, by offering his cloak to a beggar, more fully understood the beauty of Christian compassion. (The impressive original, a fine example of Romanesque sculpture, hides from pollution just inside, to the right of the main entrance.) Each column on the facade is unique. Notice how the facade is asymmetrical: The 11th-century bell tower was already in place when the rest of the cathedral was built, so the builders cheated on the right side to make it fit the space. Over the right portal (as if leaning against the older tower), the architect Guideo from Como holds a document declaring that

he finished the facade in 1204. On the right (at eye level on the pilaster), a labyrinth is set into the wall. The maze relates the struggle and challenge our souls face in finding salvation. (French pilgrims on their way to Rome could relate to this, as it's the same pattern they knew from the floor of the church at Chartres.) The Latin plaque just left of the main door is where money changers and spice traders met to seal deals (on the doorstep of the church—to underscore the reliability of their promises). Notice the date: *An Dni MCXI* (A.D. 1111).

The interior features Gothic arches, Renaissance paintings, and stained glass from the 19th century. On the left side of the nave, a small, elaborate, birdcage-like temple contains the wooden crucifix—beloved by locals—called **Volto Santo.** It's said to have been sculpted by Nicodemus in Jerusalem and set afloat in an unmanned boat that landed on the coast of Tuscany, from where wild oxen miraculously carried it to Lucca in 782. The sculpture (which is actually 12th-century Byzantine-style) has quite a jewelry collection, which you can see in the Cathedral Museum (described next).

On the right side of the nave, the sacristy houses the enchantingly beautiful **memorial tomb of Ilaria del Carretto** by Jacopo della Quercia (1407). Pick up a handy English description to the right of the door as you enter the sacristy. This young bride of silk baron Paolo Guinigi is decked out in the latest, most expensive fashions, with the requisite little dog (symbolizing her loyalty) curled up at her feet in eternal sleep. She's so realistic that the statue was nicknamed "Sleeping Beauty." Her nose is partially worn off because of a long-standing tradition of lonely young ladies rubbing it for luck in finding a boyfriend.

Cathedral Museum (Museo della Cattedrale)

This beautifully presented museum houses original paintings, sculptures, and vestments from the cathedral and other Lucca churches. The first room displays jewelry made to dress up the Volto Santo crucifix (described above), including gigantic gilded silver shoes. Upstairs, notice the fine red brocaded silk—a reminder that this precious fabric is what brought riches and power to the city. The exhibits in this museum have very brief descriptions and are meaningful only with the slow-talking €1 audioguide—if you're not in the mood to listen, skip the place altogether.

Cost and Hours: €4, €7 combo-ticket includes Ilaria tomb and San Giovanni Church; April-Oct daily 10:00-18:00; Nov-March Mon-Fri 10:00-14:00, Sat-Sun 10:00-17:00; to the left of the cathedral as you're facing it, Piazza Antelminelli, tel. 0583-490-530, www.museocattedralelucca.it.

San Giovanni Church

This first cathedral of Lucca is interesting only for its archaeological finds. The entire floor of the 12th-century church has been excavated in recent decades, revealing layers of Roman houses, ancient hot tubs that date back to the time of Christ, early churches, and theological graffiti. Sporadic English translations help you understand what you're looking at. As you climb under the church's present-day floor and wander the lanes of Roman Lucca, remember that the entire city sits on similar ruins. If it's open, climb the *campanile* (bell tower) of the church for a panoramic view of the city.

Cost and Hours: €4, €7 combo-ticket includes Ilaria tomb and Cathedral Museum, audioguide-€1; mid-March-Oct daily 10:00-18:00; Nov-mid-March Sat-Sun 10:00-17:00, closed Mon-Fri; see concert info on page 613; kitty-corner from cathedral at Piazza San Giovanni.

Church of San Frediano

This impressive church was built in 1112 by the pope to counter Lucca's bishop and his spiffy cathedral. Lucca was the first Mediterranean stop on the pilgrim route from northern Europe, and the pope wanted to remind pilgrims that the action, the glory, and the papacy awaited them in Rome. Therefore, he had the church made "Roman-esque." The pure marble facade frames an early Christian Roman-style mosaic of Christ with his 12 apostles. Step inside and you're struck by the sight of 40 powerful (if recycled) ancient Roman columns. The message: Lucca may be impressive, but the finale of your pilgrimage—in Rome—is worth the hike.

Inside, there's a notable piece of art in each corner: At rear left is the 12th-century baptistery, with some interesting Church propaganda showing the story of Moses (the evil Egyptians are played by Holy Roman Empire troops). At rear right is St. Zita's actual body, put there in 1278. At front left is a particularly elegant Virgin Mary, depicted at the moment she gets the news that she'll bring the Messiah into the world (carved and painted by Lucchesi artist Matteo Civitali, c. 1460). And at front right is a painting on wood of the *Assumption of the Virgin* (c. 1510), with Doubting Thomas receiving Mary's red belt as she ascends so he'll doubt no more. The pinball-machine composition serves as a virtual catalog of the fine silk material produced in Lucca—a major industry in the 16th century.

Cost and Hours: Free, Mon-Sat 8:30-12:00 & 15:00-17:30, Sun 9:00-11:30 & 15:00-17:30, Piazza San Frediano, tel. 0583-493-627.

Palazzo Mansi

Minor paintings by Tintoretto, Pontormo, Veronese, and others vie for attention, but the palace itself—a sumptuously furnished and decorated 17th-century confection—steals the show. This is your chance to appreciate the wealth of Lucca's silk merchants. Since all visitors must be accompanied by a museum employee, during high season you may have to wait a bit for your chance to enter.

Cost and Hours: €4, €6.50 combo-ticket includes Villa Guinigi, hours prone to change but generally Tue-Sat 8:30-19:30, Sun 8:30-13:30, closed Mon, no photos, request English booklet at ticket desk, Via Galli Tassi 43, tel. 0583-55-570.

Guinigi Tower (Torre Guinigi)

Many Tuscan towns have towers, but none is quite like the Guinigi family's. Up 227 steps is a small garden with fragrant trees, surrounded by fantastic views.

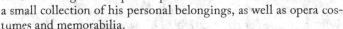

Cost and Hours: €4, €6 combo-ticket includes Clock Tower, daily April-May 9:30-18:30, June-Sept 9:30-19:30, March and Oct 9:30-17:30, Nov-Feb 9:30-16:30, Via Sant'Andrea 41.

Puccini's House

Opera enthusiasts (but nobody else) will want to visit the home where Giacomo Puccini (1858-1924) grew up. The museum has the great composer's piano and a small collection of his personal belongings, as well as opera costumes and memorabilia.

Cost and Hours: €7; April-Oct Wed-Mon 10:00-18:00, Nov-March Wed-Mon 11:00-17.00, closed Tue year-round; Corte San Lorenzo 9, ring to be let in, tel. 0583-584-028, www.puccinimuseum.it.

Palazzo Pfanner

Garden enthusiasts (and anyone needing a break from churches) will enjoy this 18th-century palace built for a rich Swiss expat who came to Lucca to open a brewery. His sudsy legacy includes Baroque furniture, elaborate frescoes, a centuries-old kitchen, and a lavish garden.

Cost and Hours: Garden or residence-€4.50 apiece, €6 for both, April-Oct daily 10:00-18:00, closed Nov-March, Via degli Asili 33, tel. 0583-954-029, www.palazzopfanner.it.

Villa Guinigi

Built by Paolo Guinigi in 1418, the family villa is now a stark, abandoned-feeling museum displaying a hodgepodge of Etruscan artifacts, religious sculptures, paintings, inlaid woodwork, and ceramics. Monumental paintings by the multitalented Giorgio Vasari are the best reason to visit.

Cost and Hours: €4, €6.50 combo-ticket includes Palazzo Mansi, Tue-Sat 8:30-19:30, Sun 8:30-13:30, closed Mon, may have to wait in high season for a museum employee to accompany you, Via della Quarquonia, tel. 0583-496-033.

Sleeping in Lucca

Fancy Little Boutique B&Bs Within the Walls

$$$ **La Romea B&B,** in an air-conditioned, restored, 14th-century palazzo near Guinigi Tower, feels like a royal splurge. Its four posh rooms and one suite are lavishly decorated in handsome colors and surround a big, plush lounge with stately Venetian-style floors (Db-€100-135 depending on season, big suite-€160, extra bed-€20-25; 10 percent discount when you book direct, show this book, and pay cash; Wi-Fi; from the train station, take Via Fillungo, turn right on Via Sant'Andrea, then take the second right to Vicolo delle Ventaglie 2; tel. 0583-464-175, www.laromea.com, info@laromea.com, Giulio and wife Gaia).

$$$ **La Locanda Sant'Agostino** has three romantic, bright, and palatial rooms. The vine-draped terrace, beautiful breakfast spread, and quaint views invite you to relax (Db-€160, extra bed-€25, air-con, guest computer, Wi-Fi, from Via Fillungo take Via San Giorgio to Piazza Sant'Agostino 3, best to reserve by email, tel. 0583-443-100, mobile 347-989-9069, www.locandasantagostino.it, info@locandasantagostino.it).

$$ **La Bohème B&B** has a cozy yet elegant ambience, offering six large, charming, chandeliered rooms, each painted with a different rich color scheme (Db-€125, less off-season, 10 percent discount with this book if you pay cash and book direct, air-con, free Wi-Fi, Via del Moro 2, tel. 0583-462-404, www.boheme.it, info@boheme.it, Sara).

Sleeping More Forgettably Within the Walls

$$ **Hotel la Luna,** run by the Barbieri family, has 29 rooms in a great location, right in the heart of the city. Updated rooms are split between two adjacent buildings just off of the main shopping street. The annex may have an elevator, but I prefer the rooms in the main building, which are larger and classier (Sb-€90, Db-€125, suite-€190, these prices for Rick Steves readers who book direct, air-con, pay guest computer and Wi-Fi, parking-€20/day, Via Fillungo at Corte Compagni 12, tel. 0583-493-634, www.hotellaluna.com, info@hotellaluna.com, Sara).

$$ **Alla Dimora Lucense**'s seven newer rooms are bright, modern, clean, and peaceful, with all the comforts. Enjoy their relaxing, sunny interior courtyard (Db-€125, suite for 2-4 people-€150-200; 5 percent discount if you pay cash, book direct, and show this book; air-con, Wi-Fi, half a block from Via Fillungo at Via Fontana 19, tel. 0583-495-722, www.dimoralucense.it, info@dimoralucense.it).

$$ **Hotel Universo,** renting 55 rooms right on Piazza Napo-

leone and facing the theater and Palazzo Ducale, is a 19th-century
town fixture. While it clearly was once elegant, now it's old and
tired, with a big Old World lounge and soft prices ("comfort" Db-
€100, "superior" Db with updated bath-€130, Wi-Fi, Piazza del
Giglio 1, tel. 0583-493-678, www.universolucca.com, info@uni-
versolucca.com)

$$ **La Magnolia B&B** offers five basic rooms with an inti-
mate atmosphere and relaxing garden. It's buried in a ramshackle
old palace in a central location (Sb-€70, Db-€90, a block behind
amphitheater at Via Mordini 63, tel. 0583-467-111, www.lamag-
nolia.com, info@lamagnolia.com).

$$ **A Palazzo Busdraghi** has seven comfortable, pastel-col-
ored rooms with modern baths (some with Jacuzzi–style tubs) in
a tastefully converted 13th-century palace inside a courtyard just
off Via Fillungo (Sb-€120, Db-€150-170, extra bed-€10, cheaper
prices off-season, air-con, Wi-Fi, parking-€15, Via Fillungo 170,
tel. 0583-950-856, www.apalazzobusdraghi.it, info@apalazzobus-
draghi.it, Marta).

$ At **Le Violette B&B,** friendly Anna (who's still learning
English) will settle you into one of her six homey rooms near the
train station inside Porta San Pietro (S-€40, D-€60, Db-€75, extra
bed-€15, Wi-Fi, communal kitchen, €5 to use washer and dryer,
Via della Polveriera 6, tel. 0583-493-594, mobile 349-823-4645,
www.leviolette.it, leviolette@virgilio.it).

$ **Ostello San Frediano,** in a central, sprawling ex-convent
with a peaceful garden, is a cut above the average hostel, though
it's still filled mainly with a young crowd. Its 29 rooms are bright
and modern, and some have fun lofts (€20 beds in 6- to 8-person
dorms, 140 beds, Db-€65, Tb-€80, Qb-€105, includes sheets, €2
extra/night for nonmembers, cash only, breakfast extra, no curfew,
lockers, guest computer, Wi-Fi, cheap restaurant, free parking,
Via della Cavallerizza 12, tel. 0583-469-957, www.ostellolucca.it,
info@ostellolucca.it).

Outside the Walls

$$$ **Hotel San Marco,** a seven-minute walk outside the Porta
Santa Maria, is a postmodern place decorated à la Stanley Kubrick.
Its 42 rooms are sleek, with all the comforts (Sb-€87, Db-€136,
extra bed-€10, includes nice breakfast spread, air-con, Wi-Fi, ele-
vator, pool, bikes-€6/half-day, free parking, taxi from station-€10,
Via San Marco 368, tel. 0583-495-010, www.hotelsanmarcolucca.
com, info@hotelsanmarcolucca.com).

$$ **Hotel Rex** rents 25 rooms in a practical, contemporary
building on the train station square. While in the modern world,
you're just 200 yards away from the old town and get more space

for a better price (Db-€80-100; 10 percent discount with this book if you pay cash and book direct, does not apply to prepaid/nonrefundable rooms booked online; air-con, Wi-Fi, free bike rental, a few steps from the train station at Piazza Ricasoli 19, tel. 0583-955-443, www.hotelrexlucca.com, info@hotelrexlucca.com).

$$ Hotel Moderno is indeed modern, with 12 good-value rooms tastefully decorated in shades of white. Although it backs up to the train tracks, the rooms are quiet (Sb-€70, Db-€90, air-con, Wi-Fi, Via Vincenzo Civitali 38—turn left out of train station and go over bridge across tracks, tel. 0583-55-840, www.albergomodernolucca.com, info@albergomodernolucca.com).

$ La Mimosa B&B has five cozy rooms a 10-minute walk west of Porta Sant'Anna. Most practical if you're arriving or leaving Lucca by bus, this trendy little house is run by the Zichi cousins, Giuseppe and Stefano, and decorated with modern paintings by Uncle Zichi. It's located on a main road, but double-paned windows reduce traffic noise (Sb-€50, Db-€80, Qb-€120, cheaper prices off-season, air-con, Wi-Fi, free street parking nearby, Via Pisana 66; leave Piazzale Giuseppe Verdi through Porta Sant'Anna, swing right, then cross road, walk straight down Via Catalani, and take second road on the left; tel. 0583-583-121, www.bblamimosa.it, info@bblamimosa.it).

$ Sogni d'Oro Guest House ("Dreams of Gold"), run by Davide, is a handy budget option for drivers, with five basic rooms and a cheery communal kitchen (grocery store next door). It's a 10-minute walk from the train station and a 5-minute walk from the city walls (D-€50, Db-€65, Q-€70, 10 percent discount with cash; free ride to and from station with advance notice—then call when your train arrives in Lucca; from the station, head straight out to Viale Regina Margherita and turn right, follow the main boulevard as it turns into Viale Giuseppe Giusti, at the curve turn right onto Via Antonio Cantore to #169; tel. 0583-467-768, mobile 329-582-5062, www.bbsognidoro.com, info@bbsognidoro.com).

Eating in Lucca

Ristorante Canuleia is run by enthusiastic Matteo and Eleonora, who make everything fresh in their small kitchen. You can eat tasty Tuscan cuisine in a dressy little dining room or outside on the garden courtyard (€10 pastas, €17 *secondi*, Tue-Sun 12:00-14:30 & 19:00-22:00, closed Mon, Via Canuleia 14, tel. 0583-467-470, call to reserve for dinner).

Port Ellen Clan is an unusual concept in traditional Lucca—a combination restaurant, wine bar, and whisky bar (featuring more than 150 types of whisky). Though the cuisine is typically Tuscan, the theme is creative and original, with a Scottish twist (€9 pastas, €15 *secondi*, Wed-Sun 12:30-15:00 & 19:30-24:00, closed Mon-Tue, Via del Fosso 120, tel. 0583-493-952 or 329-245-2762, www.portellenclan.com).

Osteria Via San Giorgio, owned by Daniela and her brother Piero, is a cheery family eatery that satisfies both fish-lovers and meat-lovers. Sample the splittable *antipasti*—small courses such as *ceviche* (seafood salad), scallops au gratin, squid sautéed with potatoes, or whatever else was caught that day in Viareggio; they also offer a meatier version. Dinner-size salads are bright and fresh, pasta is homemade, and Daniela's desserts tempt (daily 12:00-16:00 & 19:00-23:00, Via San Giorgio 26, tel. 0583-953-233).

Vecchia Trattoria Buralli, on quiet Piazza Sant'Agostino, is a good bet for traditional cooking and juicy steaks, with fine indoor and piazza seating (€7 pastas, €10 *secondi*, €12-30 fixed-price meals, Thu-Tue 12:00-14:45 & 19:00-22:30, closed Wed, Piazza Sant'Agostino 10, tel. 0583-950-611).

Trattoria da Leo packs in chatty locals for typical, cheap home-cooking in a hash-slingin' Mel's-diner atmosphere. This place is a high-energy winner...you know it's going to be good as soon as you step in. Arrive early or reserve in advance (€6 pastas, €10 *secondi*, daily 12:00-14:30, Mon-Sat also 19:30-22:30, cash only, leave Piazza San Salvatore on Via Asili and take the first left to Via Tegrimi 1, tel. 0583-492 236).

Bella 'Mbriana Pizzeria focuses on doing one thing very well: turning out piping-hot, wood-fired pizzas to happy locals in a welcoming wood-paneled dining room. Order and pay at the counter, take a number, and they'll call you when your pizza's ready. Consider take-out to munch on the nearby walls (Wed-Mon 12:30-14:30 & 18:30-23:00, closed Tue, to the right as you face the Church of San Frediano, Via della Cavallerizza 29, tel. 0583-495-565).

Il Cuore Enogastronomia/Ristorante includes a delicatessen and restaurant. For a fancy picnic, drop in the deli for ready-to-eat lasagna, saucy meatballs, grilled and roasted vegetables, vegetable soufflés, Tuscan bean soup, fruit salads, and more, sold by weight and dished up in disposable trays to go. Ask them to heat your order *(riscaldare),* then picnic on nearby Piazza Napoleone. For curious traveling foodies on a budget who want to eat right there, they can assemble a €10 "degustation plate"—just point to what you want from among the array of tasty treats under the glass (Tue-Sun 9:30-19:30, closed Mon, Via del Battistero 2, tel. 0583-493-196, Cristina).

Specialties in Lucca

Lucca has some tasty specialties worth seeking out. *Ceci* (CHEH-chee), also called *cecina* (cheh-CHEE-nah), makes an ideal cheap snack any time of day. This garbanzo-bean crepe is sold in pizza shops and is best accompanied by a nip of red wine.

Farro, a grain (spelt) dating back to ancient Roman cuisine, shows up in restaurants in soups or as a creamy rice-like dish *(risotto di farro)*.

Tordelli, the Lucchesi version of *tortelli*, is homemade ravioli. It's traditionally stuffed with meat and served with more meat sauce, but chefs creatively pair cheeses and vegetables, too.

Meat, not fish, is the star at most restaurants, especially steak, which is listed on menus as *filetto di manzo* (filet), *tagliata di manzo* (thin slices of grilled tenderloin), or the king of steaks, *bistecca alla fiorentina*. Order *al sangue* (rare), *medio* (medium rare), *cotto* (medium), or *ben cotto* (well). Anything more than *al sangue* is considered a travesty for steak connoisseurs.

Note that steaks (as well as fish) are often sold by weight, noted on menus as *s.q.* (according to quantity ordered) or *l'etto* (cost per 100 grams—250 grams is about an 8-ounce steak).

For something sweet, bakeries sell *buccellato,* bread dotted with raisins, lightly flavored with anise, and often shaped like a wreath. It's sold only in large sizes, but luckily it stays good for a few days (and it also pairs well with *vin santo*—fortified Tuscan dessert wine). An old proverb says, "Coming to Lucca without eating the *buccellato* is like not having come at all." *Buon appetito!*

Il Cuore Bistrot, located across the way, is a trendy find for wine-tasting or a meal on a piazza. Try the €8 *aperitivo* (available 18:00-20:00), which includes a glass of wine and a plate of cheese, *salumi,* and snacks, or feast on fresh pastas and other high-quality dishes from their lunch and dinner menus (Wed-Sun 12:00-22:00 with limited menu 15:00-19:30, Tue 12:00-15:00, closed Mon, Via del Battistero, tel. 0583-493-196).

Pizzeria da Felice is a little mom-and-pop hole-in-the-wall serving *cecina* (garbanzo-bean crepes) and slices of freshly baked pizza to throngs of snackers. Grab an *etto* of *cecina* and a short glass of wine for €2.50 (Mon-Sat 10:00-20:30, closed Sun and 3 weeks in Aug, Via Buia 12, tel. 0583-494-986).

Lucca Connections

From Lucca by Train to: Florence (2/hour, 1.5 hours), **Pisa** (roughly 1-2/hour, 30 minutes, bus is better except on Sun), **Livorno** (about hourly, 1-1.25 hours, transfer at Pisa Centrale, €5.10),

Milan (2/hour except Sun, 4-5 hours, transfer in Florence), **Rome** (1/hour except Sun, 3-4 hours, change in Florence).

From Lucca by Bus to Pisa: Direct buses from Lucca's Piazzale Giuseppe Verdi drop you right at the Leaning Tower, making Pisa an easy day trip (Mon-Sat hourly, fewer on Sun, 30 minutes, also stops at Pisa's airport, €3). Even with a car, I'd opt for this much faster and cheaper option.

SIENA

Siena was medieval Florence's archrival. And while Florence ultimately won the battle for political and economic superiority, Siena still competes for the tourists. Sure, Florence has the heavyweight sights. But Siena seems to be every Italy connoisseur's favorite town. In my office, whenever Siena is mentioned, someone exclaims, "Siena? I looove Siena!"

Once upon a time (about 1260-1348), Siena was a major banking and trade center, and a military power in a class with Florence, Venice, and Genoa. With a population of 60,000, it was even bigger than Paris. Situated on the north-south road to Rome (Via Francigena), Siena traded with all of Europe. Then, in 1348, the Black Death (bubonic plague) swept through Europe, hitting Siena and cutting the population by more than a third. Siena never recovered. In the 1550s, Florence, with the help of Philip II's Spanish army, conquered the flailing city-state, forever rendering Siena a non-threatening backwater. Siena's loss became our sightseeing gain, as its political and economic irrelevance pickled the city in a purely medieval brine. Today, Siena's population is still 60,000.

Siena, situated atop three hills, qualifies as Italy's ultimate "hill town" (though it's much larger than its cousins covered in the Hill Towns of Central Italy chapter). Its thriving historic center, with red-brick lanes cascading every which way, offers Italy's best medieval city experience. Most people do Siena, just 35 miles south of Florence, as a day trip, but it's best experienced at twilight. While Florence has the blockbuster museums, Siena has an easy-to-enjoy soul: Courtyards sport flower-decked wells, alleys dead-end at rooftop views, and the sky is a rich blue dome.

For those who dream of a Fiat-free Italy, Siena is a haven. Pedestrians rule in the old center of town, as the only drivers allowed are residents and cabbies. Sit at a café on the main square. Wander narrow streets lined with colorful flags and studded with iron rings to tether horses. Take time to savor the first European city to eliminate automobile traffic from its main square (1966), and then, just to be silly, wonder what would happen if they did it in your hometown.

Planning Your Time

On a quick trip, consider spending two nights in Siena (or three nights with a whole-day side-trip into Florence). Whatever you do, be sure to enjoy a sleepy medieval evening in Siena. The next morning, you can see the city's major sights in half a day.

Orientation to Siena

Siena lounges atop a hill, stretching its three legs out from Il Campo. This main square, the historic meeting point of Siena's neighborhoods, is pedestrian-only—and most of those pedestrians are students from the university.

Just about everything mentioned in this chapter is within a 15-minute walk of the square. Navigate by three major landmarks (Il Campo, Duomo, and Church of San Domenico), following the excellent system of street-corner signs. The typical visitor sticks to the Il Campo-San Domenico axis. Make a point to stray from this main artery. Sienese streets go in anything but a straight line, so it's easy to get lost—but equally easy to get found. Don't be afraid to explore.

Siena itself is one big sight. Its individual sights come in two little clusters: the square (Civic Museum and City Tower) and the cathedral (Baptistery and Duomo Museum, with its surprise viewpoint). Check these sights off, and then you're free to wander.

Tourist Information

The TI on Il Campo can be an exasperating place. Think about the importance of tourism to this town—and yet this office charges €0.50 for a map and lets tour commissions color its advice (Mon-Sat 9:30-18:30, Sun 9:30-17:00, on Il Campo at #56, tel. 0577-280-551, www.terresiena.it). They hand out a few pretty booklets (including *Siena* and the regional *Terre di Siena* guide), sell maps and books, and may be able to answer a few questions. The TI also organizes walking tours (described later, under "Tours in Siena").

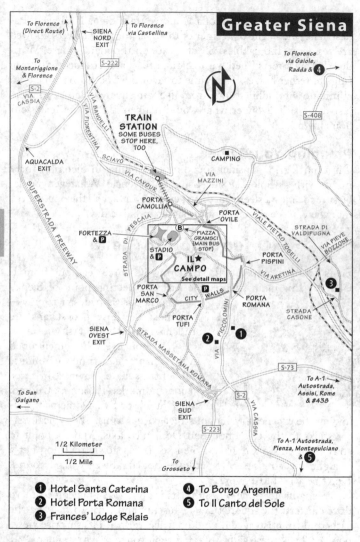

Greater Siena

To Florence (Direct Route)

To Florence via Castellina

SIENA NORD EXIT

To Monteriggione & Florence

S-222

VIA CASSIA

S-2

VIA BANDELLI

VIA FIORENTINA

To Florence via Gaiole, Radda & ④

S-408

TRAIN STATION SOME BUSES STOP HERE, TOO

AQUACALDA EXIT

SCIAVO

VIA CAVOUR

CAMPING

VIA MAZZINI

SUPERSTRADA FREEWAY

STRADA DI PESCAIA

PORTA CAMOLLIA

FORTEZZA & P

Ⓑ

STADIO & P

PIAZZA GRAMSCI (MAIN BUS STOP)

PORTA OVILE

VIALE PIETRO TOGELLI

STRADA DI VALDIFUGNA

VIA PIEVE BOZZONE

IL★ CAMPO See detail maps

PORTA PISPINI

VIA ARETINA

③

PORTA SAN MARCO

CITY WALLS

P

PORTA ROMANA

STRADA CASONE

SIENA OVEST EXIT

STRADA MASSETANA ROMANA

PORTA TUFI

VIA PICCOLOMINI

② ①

S-73

To A-1 Autostrada, Assisi, Rome & #438

To San Galgano

SIENA SUD EXIT

S-2

S-223

VIA CASSIA

To Grosseto

To A-1 Autostrada, Pienza, Montepulciano & ⑤

1/2 Kilometer

1/2 Mile

① Hotel Santa Caterina
② Hotel Porta Romana
③ Frances' Lodge Relais
④ To Borgo Argenina
⑤ To Il Canto del Sole

Ignore the second "TI" across from the Church of San Domenico, which is a useless private agency run by the local hotel association.

Arrival in Siena

By Train

The small train station, located at the base of the hill on the edge of town, has a bar, a bus office (Mon–Fri 7:15–19:30, Sat 7:15–17:45, Sun 8:30–12:30 & 14:30–18:30), and a newsstand (which sells local bus tickets—buy one now if you're taking the city bus into town), but no baggage check or lockers (stow bags at Piazza Gramsci—

see "By Intercity Bus," later). A shopping mall with a supermarket (handy for picnic supplies) is across the plaza right in front of the station.

Getting from the Train Station to the City Center: To reach central Siena, you can hop aboard the city bus, ride a long series of escalators (which involves a bit of walking along a picturesque street), or take a taxi.

By Bus or Escalator: To reach either the bus or the escalators, head for the shopping mall across the plaza. From the tracks, go down the stairs into the tunnel that connects the platforms; this leads (with escalators) right up into the mall. Alternatively, you can exit the station out the front door, cross over to the plaza, turn left and walk to the far end of the plaza, then turn right to enter the mall's glass doors.

To ride the **city bus,** go through the shopping mall's right-hand door and use the elevator to go down to the subterranean bus stop. If you didn't buy bus tickets in the train station, you can get them from the blue machine (press "F" to toggle to English, then select "A" for type of ticket). Buses leave frequently (6/hour, fewer on Sun and after 22:00, €1.10, about a 10-minute ride into town depending on route). Smaller shuttle buses go up to Piazza del Sale, while bigger city buses head to nearby Piazza Gramsci (both are at the north end of town, walkable to most of my recommended hotels). Before boarding, double-check the destination with the driver by asking *"Centro?"* Punch your ticket in the machine onboard to validate it.

Riding the **escalator** into town takes a few minutes longer and requires more walking than the bus. From the station, follow the instructions above and enter the mall at the far-left end. Once inside, go straight ahead and ride the escalators up two floors to the food court. Continue directly through the glass doors to another escalator (marked *Porta Camollia/Centro*) that takes you gradually up, up, up into town (free). Exiting the escalator, turn left down the big street, bear left at the fork, then continue straight through the town gate. From here, landmarks are well-signed (go up Via Camollia).

By Taxi: The taxi stand is to your right as you exit the train station, but as the city is chronically short on cabs, getting one here can take a while (about €11 to Il Campo, taxi tel. 0577-49222).

Getting to the Train Station from the City Center: If you're leaving Siena by train, you can ride a smaller shuttle bus from Piazza del Sale (which goes straight to the station), or catch an orange or red-and-silver city bus from Piazza Gramsci (which may take a more roundabout route). Multiple bus routes make this trip—look for *Ferrovia* or *Stazione* on schedules and marked on the bus. City buses drop off right in front of the station. Confirm with the driver that the bus is going to the *stazione* (staht-see-OH-nay); remember to purchase your ticket in advance from a tobacco shop or blue machine, then validate it on board.

By Intercity Bus

Most buses arrive in Siena at Piazza Gramsci, a few blocks north of the city center. (Some buses only go to the train station; others go first to the train station, then continue to Piazza Gramsci—to find out, ask your driver, "pee-aht-sah GRAHM-chee?") The main bus companies are Sena and Tiemme/Siena Mobilità (formerly called Tra-In). Day-trippers can store baggage in the Sottopassaggio la Lizza passageway underneath Piazza Gramsci at the Tiemme/Siena Mobilità office (€5.50/day, open daily 7:00-19:00, carry-on-sized luggage no more than 33 pounds, no overnight storage). From Piazza Gramsci, it's an easy walk into the town center—just head in the opposite direction of the tree-filled park. For more on buses, see page 670.

By Car

Siena is not a good place to drive. Plan on parking in a big lot or garage and walking into town.

Drivers coming from the autostrada take the *Siena Ovest* exit and follow signs for *Centro*, then *Stadio* (stadium). The soccer-ball signs take you to the stadium lot (Parcheggio Stadio, €1.70/hour, pay when you leave) near Piazza Gramsci and the huge, bare-brick Church of San Domenico. The nearby Fortezza lot charges the same amount. Another good option is the underground Santa Caterina garage (you'll see signs on the way to the stadium lot, same price). From the garage, hike 150 yards uphill through a gate to an escalator on the right, which carries you up into the city. If you're staying in the south end of town, try the Il Campo lot, near Porta Tufi.

On parking spots, blue stripes mean pay and display; white stripes mean free parking. You can park for free in the lot west of the Fortezza; in white-striped spots behind the Hotel Villa Liberty (south of the Fortezza); and overnight in most city lots from 20:00 to 8:00. Watch for signs showing a street cleaner and a day of the week—that's when the street is closed to cars for cleaning.

Driving within Siena's city center is restricted to local cars and policed by automatic cameras. If you drive or park anywhere marked *Zona Traffico Limitato (ZTL)*, you'll likely have a hefty ticket waiting for you in the mail back home.

Technically, hotel customers are allowed to drop off bags at their hotel before finding a place to park overnight, but getting permission to do so isn't worth the trouble.

Helpful Hints

Combo-Tickets: Siena always seems to be experimenting with different combo-tickets, but in general, only two are worth considering: the €12 Opa Si combo-ticket that includes the Duomo, Duomo Museum, Crypt, and Baptistery (a savings of at least €9 if you plan on seeing all of those sights; sold only at the ticket office just right of the Duomo, near the Duomo Museum entrance), and the €13 combo-ticket covering the Civic Museum and City Tower (a €3 savings; must purchase at City Tower on Il Campo).

Wednesday Morning Market: The weekly market (clothes, knick-knacks, and food) sprawls between the Fortezza and Piazza Gramsci along Viale Cesare Maccari and the adjacent Viale XXV Aprile. The fact that this is more local than touristy makes it, for some, even more interesting.

Internet Access: In this university town, there are lots of places to get plugged in. **Cheap Phone Center** is hidden in a small shopping mall near Il Campo (€2/hour to use terminals, €1/hour for Wi-Fi, Mon-Sat 10:00-22:00, Sun 12:00-22:00; coming from Il Campo, go uphill past recommended Albergo Tre Donzelle, turn left at Via Cecco Angiolieri, after 20 yards look for #16). **Internet Point** is located upstairs at Via di Città 80, with the entrance around the corner on Via delle Campane (€3/hour, daily 9:00-21:00). See the map on page 642 for locations.

Post Office: It's on Piazza Matteotti (Mon-Fri 8:15-19:00, Sat 8:15-13:30, closed Sun).

Books: Libreria Senese sells books (including my guidebooks), newspapers, and magazines in English, with an emphasis on Italian-related topics (Mon-Sat 9:00-20:00, Sun 10:00-20:00, Via di Città 62, tel. 0577-280-845). The **Feltrinelli** bookstore at Banchi di Sopra 52 also sells books and magazines in English (Mon-Sat 9:00-19:30, closed Sun, tel. 0577-271-104; the bigger Feltrinelli branch farther down the street at #64 has no English books). See the map on page 642 for locations.

Laundry: Onda Blu is a modern, self-service launderette just 50 yards from Il Campo (about €6 wash and dry, daily 8:00-21:15, last load at 20:15, Via del Casato di Sotto 17—see map on page 642).

Travel Agency: Palio Viaggi, on Piazza Gramsci, sells plane tickets upstairs. Their downstairs office (go down the ramp to the door below the arch) sells train tickets, railpass reservations, and some bus tickets (only for the longer-distance Sena buses, not the regional Tiemme/Siena Mobilità buses). They charge a €1 fee per bus or train ticket, but this saves you a trip to the train station (Mon-Fri 9:00-12:45 & 15:00-18:30, Sat 9:00-

12:30, closed Sun, opposite the columns of NH Excelsior Hotel at La Lizza 12—see map on page 642, tel. 0577-280-828).

Wine Classes: The **Tuscan Wine School** gives two-hour classes in English on Italian wine and food. Morning classes (11:00) cover rotating topics: wines from all over Italy, olive-oil tasting, or a "Savor Siena" food tour that visits several vendors around town (check website for specific schedule). Afternoon classes (16:00) focus on Tuscan wines, including samples of five vintages. They also offer a one-hour "crash course" at 14:00. Rebecca and her fellow sommeliers keep things entertaining and offer classes for as few as two people (€40/person, 20 percent student discount to anyone with this book, €25 for one-hour course, classes offered Mon-Sat, closed Sun, reservations recommended—especially in peak season, Via di Stalloreggi 26, 30 yards from recommended Hotel Duomo, see map on page 642 for location, tel. 0577-221-704, mobile 333-722-9716, www.tuscanwineschool.com, info@tuscanwineschool.com). Their outlet store sells wine from local producers at cost (Mon-Sat 11:00-18:00, closed Sun).

Tours in Siena

Roberto's Tuscany Tours
Roberto Bechi, a hardworking Sienese guide, specializes in off-the-beaten-path, ecologically friendly minibus tours of the surrounding countryside (up to eight passengers, convenient pickup at hotel). Married to an American (Patti) and having run restaurants in Siena and the US, Roberto communicates well with Americans. His passions are Sienese culture, Tuscan history, and local cuisine. It's ideal to book well in advance, but you might be able to schedule a tour if you call the day before (seven different tours—explained on his website, €90/person for full-day tours, €60/person for off-season four-hour tours, entry fees extra, assistant Carolina can schedule city tours as well as other guides if Roberto is booked, Carolina's mobile 320-147-6590, Roberto's mobile 328-425-5648, www.toursbyroberto.com, toursbyroberto@gmail.com). Roberto also offers multiday tours. If you book any tour with Roberto, he can advise you on other aspects of your trip.

Other Local Guides
Federica Olla, who leads walking tours of Siena, is a smart, youthful guide with a knack for creative teaching (€55/hour, mobile 338-133-9525, info@ollaeventi.com).

GSO Guides Co-op is a group of 10 young professional guides who offer good tours covering all of Tuscany and Umbria (€130/half-day, €260/full day, 10 percent discount for Rick Steves readers, www.guidesienaeoltre.com). Among them, charming Stefania Fabrizi specializes in Siena (mobile 338-640-7796, stefania-fabrizi@kata.com; if unavailable call Silvia, mobile 338-611-0127).

Walking Tours
The TI offers walking tours of the old town. Guides usually conduct their walks in both English and Italian (€20, daily April-Oct at 11:00, 2 hours, no interiors, depart from TI, Il Campo 56, tel. 0577-280-551).

Bus Tours
Somehow a company called My Tour has a lock on all hotel tour-promotion space. Every hotel has a rack of their brochures, which advertise a variety of five-hour big-bus tours into the countryside (€38, depart from Piazza Gramsci).

Sights in Siena

On Il Campo, the Main Square

▲▲▲Il Campo

This square is the heart, both geographically and metaphorically, of Siena. It fans out from City Hall (Palazzo Pubblico) to create an amphitheater. It's the only town square I've ever seen where people stretch out as if at the beach. Il Campo's shining moment is the famous Palio horse races, which take place in summer (see sidebar on page 646).

Originally, this area was just a field (campo) located outside the former city walls. Bits of those original walls, which circled the Duomo (and curved against today's square), can be seen above the pharmacy (the black-and-white stones, to the right as you face City Hall). In the 1200s, with the advent of the Sienese Republic, the city expanded—once a small medieval town circling its cathedral, it became a larger, humanistic city gathered around its towering City Hall. In this newer and relatively secular age, the focus of power shifted from the bishop to the city council.

As the city expanded, Il Campo eventually became the historic junction of Siena's various competing *contrade* (neighborhood districts) and the old marketplace. The brick surface is divided into nine sections, representing the council of nine merchants and city bigwigs who ruled medieval Siena. The square and its buildings are the color of the soil upon which they stand—a color known to artists and Crayola users as "Burnt Sienna."

City Hall: This secular building, with its 330-foot tower,

Siena at a Glance

▲▲▲**Il Campo** Best square in Italy. **Hours:** Always open. See page 637.

▲▲▲**Duomo** Art-packed cathedral with mosaic floors and statues by Michelangelo and Bernini. **Hours:** March-Oct Mon-Sat 10:30-19:00, Sun 13:30-18:00; Nov-Feb Mon-Sat 10:30-17:30, Sun 13:30-17:30. See page 644.

▲▲**Civic Museum** City museum in City Hall with Sienese frescoes, the *Effects of Good and Bad Government*. **Hours:** Daily mid-March-Oct 10:00-19:00, Nov-mid-March 10:00-18:00. See page 639.

▲▲**Duomo Museum** Siena's best museum, displaying cathedral art (including Duccio's *Maestà*) and offering sweeping Tuscan views. **Hours:** Daily March-Oct 10:30-19:00, Nov-Feb 10:30-17:30. See page 650.

▲**City Tower** 330-foot tower climb. **Hours:** Daily March-mid-Oct 10:00-19:00, mid-Oct-Feb 10:00-16:00. See page 640.

▲**Pinacoteca** Fine Sienese paintings. **Hours:** Tue-Sat 8:15-19:15, Sun-Mon 9:00-13:00. See page 641.

▲**Baptistery** Cave-like building with baptismal font decorated by Ghiberti and Donatello. **Hours:** Daily March-Oct 10:30-19:00, Nov-Feb 10:30-17:30. See page 652.

▲**Santa Maria della Scala** Museum with vibrant ceiling and wall frescoes depicting day-to-day life in a medieval hospital, much of the original *Fountain of Joy*, and an Etruscan artifact exhibit. **Hours:** May be closed for renovation—if open, likely daily March-Oct 10:30-18:00, Nov-Feb 10:30-16:00. See page 652.

Crypt Site of 12th-century church, housing some of Siena's oldest frescoes. **Hours:** Daily March-Oct 10:30-19:00, Nov-Feb 10:30-17:30. See page 652.

Church of San Domenico Huge brick church with St. Catherine's head and thumb. **Hours:** Daily 7:00-18:30. See page 653.

Sanctuary of St. Catherine Home of St. Catherine. **Hours:** Daily 9:00-18:00, church closed 12:30-15:00. See page 655.

dominates the square. In medieval Siena, this was the center of the city, and the whole focus of Il Campo still flows down to it.

The **City Tower** (Torre del Mangia) is Italy's tallest secular tower. It was named after a hedonistic watchman who consumed his earnings like a glutton consumes food. His chewed-up statue is in the courtyard, to the left as you enter. (For details on climbing the tower, see "City Tower" listing, later.)

The open **chapel** located at the base of the tower was built in 1348 as thanks to God for ending the Black Death (after it killed more than a third of the population). It should also be used to thank God that the top-heavy tower—just plunked onto the building with no extra foundation and no iron reinforcement—still stands. These days, the chapel is used solely to bless the Palio contestants, and the tower's bell rings only for the race.

Fountain of Joy (Fonte Gaia): This 15th-century work by Jacopo della Quercia marks the square's high point. The joy is all about how the Sienese Republic blessed its people with water. Notice Lady Justice with her scales (also holding a sword, right of center), overseeing the free distribution of water to all. Imagine residents gathering here in the 1400s to fill their jugs. The Fountain of Joy still reminds locals that life in Siena is good. Notice the pigeons politely waiting their turn to tightrope gingerly down slippery

spouts to slurp a drink from wolves' snouts. The relief panel on the left shows God creating Adam by helping him to his feet. It's said that this reclining Adam influenced Michelangelo when he painted his Sistine Chapel ceiling. This fountain is a copy—you can see most of the original fountain in an interesting exhibit at Siena's Santa Maria della Scala (described later).

▲▲Civic Museum (Museo Civico)

At the base of the tower is Siena's City Hall, the spot where secular government got its start in early Renaissance Europe. There you'll find city government still at work, along with a sampling of local art, including Siena's first fresco (with a groundbreaking down-to-earth depiction of the Madonna). While pricey, it's worth strolling through the dramatic halls to see fascinating frescoes and portraits extolling Siena's greats, saints, and the city-as-utopia.

Cost and Hours: €8, €13 combo-ticket with tower (must be purchased at the tower), daily mid-March-Oct 10:00-19:00, Nov-mid March 10:00-18:00, last entry 45 minutes before closing, tel. 0577-292-615, www.comune.siena.it.

Visiting the Museum: Start in the Sala del Risorgimento, with dramatic scenes of Victor Emmanuel II's unification of Italy (surrounded by statues that don't seem to care).

Passing through the chapel, where the city's governors and bureaucrats prayed, enter the Sala del Mappamondo. On opposite walls are two large frescoes. The beautiful *Maestà* (*Enthroned Virgin*, 1315), by Siena's great Simone Martini (c. 1280-1344), is groundbreaking as Siena's first fresco showing a Madonna not in a faraway, gold-leaf heaven, but under the blue sky of the real world that we inhabit. Facing the *Maestà* is the famous *Equestrian Portrait of Guidoriccio da Fogliano* (1330), which depicts a mercenary general surveying the imposing castle that his armies have just conquered.

Next is the Sala della Pace—where the city's fat cats met. Looking down on the oligarchy during their meetings was a fascinating fresco series showing the *Effects of Good and Bad Government,* by Sienese painter Ambrogio Lorenzetti. Compare the whistle-while-you-work happiness of the utopian community ruled by the utopian government (in the better-preserved fresco) against the crime, devastation, and societal mayhem of a community ruled by politicians with more typical values. The message: Without justice, there can be no prosperity.

On your way out, climb up to the loggia (using the stairs just before the Sala del Risorgimento) for a sweeping view of the city and its surroundings. (For a less impressive version of this view, you could skip the stairs and simply peek behind the curtains in the Sala della Pace.)

▲City Tower (Torre del Mangia)

Siena gathers around its City Hall more than its church. Medieval Siena was a proud republic, and this tall tower is the exclamation point of its "declaration of independence." Its 300 steps get pretty skinny at the top, but the reward is one of Italy's best views.

Cost and Hours: €8, €13 combo-ticket with

Civic Museum, daily March-mid-Oct 10:00-19:00, mid-Oct-Feb 10:00-16:00, last entry 45 minutes before closing, closed in rain, free and mandatory bag check.

Crowd Alert: Admission is limited to 50 people at a time, so be prepared for long lines or for tickets to be sold out. Wait at the bottom of the stairs for the green *Avanti* light. Try to avoid midday crowds (up to an hour wait at peak times).

Near Il Campo
▲Pinacoteca

If you're into medieval art, you'll likely find this quiet, uncrowded, colorful museum delightful. The museum walks you through Siena's art chronologically, from the 12th through the 16th centuries, when a revolution in realism was percolating in Tuscany.

Cost and Hours: €4, Tue-Sat 8:15-19:15, Sun-Mon 9:00-13:00, last entry 30 minutes before closing, free and mandatory bag check (must leave ID); from Il Campo, walk out Via di Città and go left on Via San Pietro to #29; tel. 0577-281-161 or 0577-286-143, www.pinacotecanazionale.siena.it.

Visiting the Museum: In general, the collection lets you follow the evolution of painting styles from Byzantine to Gothic, then to International Gothic, and finally to Renaissance.

As you walk through the museum, take time to trace the delicate features with your eyes. Long after Florentine art went realistic, the Sienese embraced a timeless, otherworldly style glittering with lots of gold. But Sienese art features more than just paintings. In this city of proud craftsmen, the gilding and carpentry of the frames almost compete with the actual paintings. The exquisite attention to detail gives a glimpse into the wealth of the 13th and 14th centuries, Siena's Golden Age. The woven silk and gold clothing you'll see was worn by the very people who once walked these halls, when this was a private mansion (appreciate the colonnaded courtyard).

The core of the collection is on the second floor, in Rooms 1-19. Works by Duccio (artist of the *Maestà* in the Duomo Museum) feature groundbreaking innovations that are subtle to the layman's eyes: less gold-leaf background, fewer gold creases in robes, transparent garments, inlaid-marble thrones, and a more human Mary and Jesus. Notice that the Madonna-and-Bambino pose is eerily identical in each version.

St. Augustine of Siena, by Duccio's assistant, Simone Martini (who did the *Maestà* and possibly the Guidoriccio frescoes the Civic Museum), sets the saint's life in pretty realistic Siena streets, buildings, and landscapes. In each panel, the saint pop at the oddest (difficult to draw) angles to save the day.

Also look for religious works by the hometown Lor

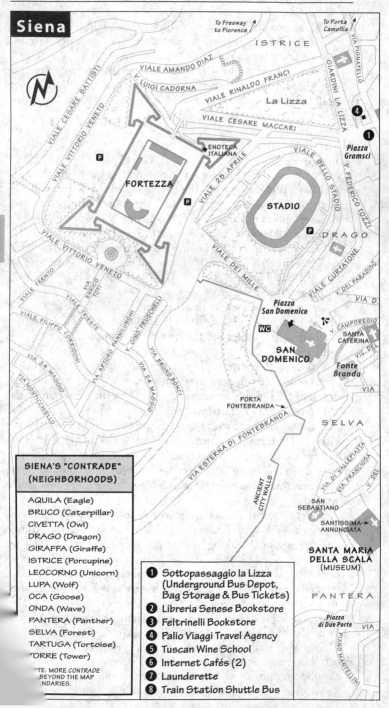

Siena

To Freeway
to Florence

To Porta
Camollia

ISTRICE

VIALE AMANDO DIAZ

V. LUIGI CADORNA

VIALE RINALDO FRANCI

La Lizza

VIALE CESARE MACCARI

GIARDINI LA LIZZA

VIA PIGNATTELLO

Piazza
Gramsci

❹

❶

VIALE VITTORIO VENETO

VIALE CESARE BATTISTI

ENOTECA
ITALIANA

FORTEZZA

VIALE 25 APRILE

VIALE DELLO STADIO

V. FEDERICO TOZZI

STADIO

DRAGO

P

VIALE DEI MILLE

VIALE CURTATONE

VIA DEL PARADISO

VIA D.

VIALE VITTORIO VENETO

VIALE TRENTO

VIALE TRIESTE

VIALE FILIPPO CORRIDONI

VIA ENRICO TOTI

VIA ARTURO PANNILUNGHI

VIA GINO FRUSCHELLI

VIA BRUNO BONCI

VIA 24 MAGGIO

VIA MONTICCHIELLO

VIA 24 MAGGIO

Piazza
San Domenico

WC

SAN
DOMENICO

V. CAMPOREGIO

SANTA
CATERINA

VIC. DEL

Fonte
Branda

VIA

PORTA
FONTEBRANDA

SELVA

VIA ESTERNA DI FONTEBRANDA

ANCIENT
CITY WALLS

VIA DI VALLEPIATTA

VIA FRANCIOSA

V. DEL

SAN
SEBASTIANO

SANTISSIMA
ANNUNCIATA

SANTA MARIA
DELLA SCALA
(MUSEUM)

PANTERA

Piazza
di Due Porte

VIA

PIANO MANTELLINI

SIENA'S "CONTRADE" (NEIGHBORHOODS)

AQUILA (Eagle)
BRUCO (Caterpillar)
CIVETTA (Owl)
DRAGO (Dragon)
GIRAFFA (Giraffe)
ISTRICE (Porcupine)
LEOCORNO (Unicorn)
LUPA (Wolf)
OCA (Goose)
ONDA (Wave)
PANTERA (Panther)
SELVA (Forest)
TARTUGA (Tortoise)
TORRE (Tower)

NOTE: MORE CONTRADE
BEYOND THE MAP
BOUNDARIES.

❶ Sottopassaggio la Lizza
   (Underground Bus Depot,
   Bag Storage & Bus Tickets)
❷ Libreria Senese Bookstore
❸ Feltrinelli Bookstore
❹ Palio Viaggi Travel Agency
❺ Tuscan Wine School
❻ Internet Cafés (2)
❼ Launderette
❽ Train Station Shuttle Bus

SIENA

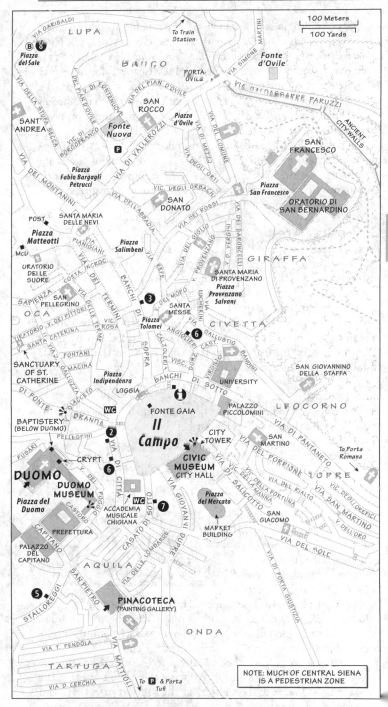

SIENA

brothers (Ambrogio is best known for the secular masterpiece, the *Effects of Good and Bad Government,* in the Civic Museum). *Città sul Mare (City by the Sea)* and *Castello in Riva al Lago (Castle on the Lakeshore)* feature the strange, medieval landscape Cubism seen in the work of the contemporaneous *Guidoriccio da Fogliano* (in the Civic Museum). Notice the weird, melancholy light that captures the sense of the Dark Ages. These images are replicated on postcards found throughout the city.

Several colorful rooms on the first floor are dedicated to Domenico Beccafumi (1486-1551), who designed many of the Duomo's inlaid pavement panels (including *Slaughter of the Innocents*). With strong bodies, twisting poses, and dramatic gestures, Beccafumi's works epitomize the Mannerist style.

Cathedral Area

Each of the first four sights (Duomo, Duomo Museum, Crypt, and Baptistery) is covered by a separate ticket, or by the €12 Opa Si combo-ticket. If you're planning to visit only the Duomo and Duomo Museum, this ticket doesn't add up; but if you're curious about the Crypt and Baptistery, the combo-ticket lets you peek into those sights for just €1 more. Separate tickets and the Opa Si combo-ticket are sold only at the ticket office near the entrance to the Duomo Museum—to the right as you face the cathedral facade (no tickets sold at sight entrances).

▲▲▲Duomo

If the Campo is the heart of Siena, the Duomo (or cathedral) is its soul. The white-and-dark-green striped church, sitting on an ar-

tificial platform atop Siena's highest point, is visible for miles around. This ornate but surprisingly secular shrine to the Virgin Mary is stacked with colorful art inside and out, from the inlaid-marble floors to the stained-glass windows. The interior is a Renaissance riot of striped columns, intricate marble inlays, Michelangelo statues, and Bernini sculptures. In the Piccolomini Library, a series of captivating frescoes by the Umbrian painter Pinturicchio tells the story of Aeneas Piccolomini, Siena's consummate Renaissance Man, who became Pope Pius II.

Cost: €4 includes cathedral and Piccolomini Library, buy ticket at Duomo Museum entrance (facing the cathedral entry, the museum is 100 yards to the right, near the south transept). To add

SIENA

the Duomo Museum, Crypt, and Baptistery, consider the €12 Opa Sì combo-ticket. Check the line to get into the Duomo before buying tickets   if there's a long wait, you can pay an extra €1 for a (misnamed) "reservation" that lets you skip the line (not possible to book in advance—just buy it on the spot).

Hours: March-Oct Mon-Sat 10:30-19:00, Sun 13:30-18:00; Nov-Feb Mon-Sat 10:30-17:30, Sun 13:30-17:30; last entry 30 minutes before closing.

Information: Tel. 0577-286-300, www.operaduomo.siena.it. Inside the Duomo are €2 video terminals that give a history of the cathedral floor.

Dress Code: Modest dress is required, but stylish paper ponchos are provided for the inappropriately clothed.

Tours: The Porta Del Cielo ("Heaven's Gate") **guided tour** includes a 45-minute visit to the dome's cupola and roof for spectacular interior and exterior views, along with a 45-minute guided tour of the rest of the cathedral. Tours must be reserved at least 48 hours in advance and might be in Italian only (ask about English tours). When you reserve, you will be given a reference number, which you must show on arrival at the ticket office; pay before meeting your guide (€25, April-Oct Fri-Sun only; call for tour times—tel. 0577-286-300 Mon-Fri between 9:00 and 17:00).

The **videoguide** (rent in the nave) is informative but extremely dry. I'd stick with the commentary in this chapter (for Duomo only: €6, €10/2 people; for Duomo plus Duomo Museum, Crypt, and Baptistery: €8, €14/2 people).

⊙ Self-Guided Tour: Grab a spot on a stone bench opposite the entry to take in this architectural festival of green, white, pink, and gold.

Exterior: Like a medieval altarpiece, the facade is divided into sections, each frame filled with patriarchs and prophets, studded with roaring gargoyles, and topped with prickly pinnacles. Imagine pilgrims arriving at this church, its facade trumpeting the coming of Christ and the correct path to salvation.

The current structure dates back to 1215, with the major decoration done during Siena's heyday (1250-1350). The lower story, by Giovanni Pisano (who worked from 1284 to 1297), features remnants of the fading Romanesque style (round arches over the doors), topped with the pointed arches of the new Gothic style that was seeping in from France. The upper half, in full-blown Gothic, was designed and built a century later.

• *Step inside, putting yourself in the mindset of a pilgrim as you take in this trove of religious art. (With a maximum capacity of 700 visitors, you may have to wait—the current number is indicated on a computer screen at the turnstile. Remember, if the line is dreadfully long, you can pay €1 for a "reservation" at the ticket office and go right in.)*

Siena's Palio

In the Palio, the feisty spirit of Siena's 17 neighborhoods lives on. Each neighborhood, or *contrada*, has a parish church, well or fountain, and sometimes even a historical museum. Each is represented by a mascot (porcupine, unicorn, wolf, etc.) and unique colors worn proudly by residents.

Contrada pride is evident year-round in Siena's parades and colorful banners, lamps, and wall plaques. (If you hear the thunder of distant drumming, run to it for some medieval action—there's a good chance it'll feature flag throwers.) You are welcome to participate in these lively neighborhood festivals. Buy a scarf in *contrada* colors, grab a glass of Chianti, munch on some *panforte*, and join in the merriment.

Contrada passion is most visible twice a year—on July 2 and August 16—when the city erupts during its world-famous horse race, the Palio di Siena. Ten of the 17 neighborhoods compete (chosen by rotation and lot), hurling themselves with medieval abandon into several days of trial races and traditional revelry. Jockeys—usually from out of town—are considered hired guns, no better than paid mercenaries. Bets are placed on which *contrada* will win...and lose. Despite the shady behind-the-scenes dealing, on the big day the horses are taken into their contrada's church to be blessed. ("Go and return victorious," says the priest.) It's considered a sign of luck if a horse leaves droppings in the church.

On the evening of the race, Il Campo is stuffed to the brim with locals and tourists. Dirt is brought in and packed down over the gray pavement of the perimeter to create the track's surface, while mattresses pad the walls of surrounding buildings. The most treacherous spots are the sharp corners, where many a rider

Nave: The heads of 172 popes—who reigned from Peter's time to the 12th century—peer down from above, looking over the fine inlaid art on the floor. With a forest of striped columns, a coffered dome, a large stained-glass window at the far end (described later), and an art gallery's worth of early Renaissance art, this is one busy interior. If you look closely at the popes, you'll see the same four faces repeated over and over.

For almost two centuries (1373-1547), 40 artists paved the marble floor with scenes from the Old Testament, allegories, and intricate patterns. The series starts near the entrance with historical allegories; the larger, more elaborate scenes surrounding the altar are mostly stories from the Old Testament. Many of the floor

has bitten the dust.

Picture the scene: Ten snorting horses and their nervous riders line up near the pharmacy (on the west side of the square) to await the starting signal. Then they race like crazy while

 spectators wave the scarves of their neighborhoods. Every possible vantage point and perch is packed with people straining to see the action. One lap around the course is about a third of a mile (350 meters); three laps make a full circuit. In this literally no-holds-barred race—which lasts just over a minute—a horse can win even without its rider (jockeys perch precariously without saddles on the sweaty horses' backs, and often fall off).

When the winner crosses the line, 1/17th of Siena—the prevailing neighborhood—goes berserk. Winners receive a *palio* (banner), typically painted by a local artist and always featuring the Virgin Mary. But the true prize is proving that your *contrada* is *numero uno* and mocking your losing rivals.

All over town, sketches and posters depict the Palio. This is not some folkloric event—it's a real medieval moment. If you're packed onto the square with 60,000 people, all hungry for victory, you won't see much, but you'll feel it. Bleacher and balcony seats are expensive, but it's free to join the masses in the square. Be sure to go with an empty bladder as there are no WCs, and be prepared to surrender any sense of personal space.

While the actual Palio packs the city, you could side trip in from Florence to see the horse-race trials—called *prove* (proh-vay)—on any of the three days before the main event (usually at 9:00 and after 19:00, free seats in bleachers). For more information, visit www.ilpalio.org.

---

panels are roped off— and occasionally even covered—to prevent further wear and tear.

• *Look for the marble altarpiece decorated with statues.*

Piccolomini Altar: This was designed for the tomb of the Sienese-born Pope Pius III (born Francesco Todeschini Piccolomini). It was commissioned when he was the cardinal of Siena, but because he later became a pope (see the fresco of his coronation with Pius wearing the golden robe—above and to the right of the Michelangelo statue), he was buried in the Vatican, and this fancy tomb was never used. It's most interesting for its statues: one by Michelangelo, and three by his students. Michelangelo was originally contracted to do 15 statues, but another sculptor had started the marble blocks, and Michelangelo's heart was never in the project. He personally finished only one—the figure of St. Paul (lower right, clearly more interesting than the bland, bored popes above him).

• *Now grab a seat under the...*

Dome: The dome sits on a 12-sided base, but its "coffered" ceiling is actually a painted illusion. Get oriented to the array of sights by thinking of the church floor as a big 12-hour clock. You're the middle, and the altar is high noon: You'll find the *Slaughter of the Innocents* roped off on the floor at 10 o'clock, Pisano's pulpit between two pillars at 11 o'clock, a copy of Duccio's round stained-glass window at 12 o'clock, Bernini's chapel at 3 o'clock, the Piccolomini Altar at 7 o'clock, the Piccolomini Library at 8 o'clock, and a Donatello statue at 9 o'clock.

Pisano's Pulpit: The octagonal Carrara marble pulpit (1268) rests on the backs of lions, symbols of Christianity triumphant. Like the lions, the Church eats its catch (devouring paganism) and nurses its cubs. The seven relief panels tell the life of Christ in rich detail. The pulpit is the work of Nicola Pisano (c. 1220-1278), the "Giotto of sculpture," whose revival of classical forms (columns, sarcophagus-like relief panels) signaled the coming Renaissance. His son Giovanni (c. 1240-1319) carved many of the panels, mixing his dad's classicism and realism with the decorative detail and curvy lines of French Gothic—a style that would influence Donatello and the other Florentines.

Duccio's Stained-Glass Rose Window: This is a copy of the original window, which was moved to the Duomo Museum a couple of years ago. The famous rose window was created in 1288 and dedicated to the Virgin Mary (for more details, see page 650).

Slaughter of the Innocents: This pavement panel shows Herod (left), sitting enthroned amid Renaissance arches, as he orders the massacre of all babies to prevent the coming of the promised Messiah. It's a chaotic scene of angry soldiers, grieving mothers, and dead babies, reminding locals that a republic ruled by a tyrant will experience misery.

• *Step into the chapel just beyond the pavement panel (next to the Piccolomini Library) to see the...*

St. John the Baptist Statue: The statue of the rugged saint in his famous rags was created by Donatello. The aging Florentine sculptor, whose style was now considered passé in Florence, came here to build bronze doors for the church (similar to Ghiberti's in

Florence). He didn't complete the door project, but he did finish this bronze statue (1457). Notice the cherubs high above it, playfully dangling their feet.

• *Cross beneath the dome to find the Chigi Chapel, also known as the...*

Chapel of the Madonna del Voto: To understand why Gian Lorenzo Bernini (1598-1680) is considered the greatest Baroque sculptor, step into this sumptuous chapel (designed in the early 1660s for Fabio Chigi, a.k.a. Pope Alexander VII). Move up to the altar and look back at the two Bernini statues: Mary Magdalene in a state of spiritual ecstasy, and St. Jerome playing the crucifix like a violinist lost in beautiful music. It's enough to make even a Lutheran light a candle.

The painting over the altar is the *Madonna del Voto*, a Madonna and Child adorned with a real crown of gold and jewels (painted by an unknown Italian master in the mid-13th century). In typical medieval fashion, the scene is set in the golden light of heaven. Mary has the almond eyes, long fingers, and golden folds in her robe that are found in orthodox icons of the time. Still, this Mary tilts her head and looks out sympathetically, ready to listen to the prayers of the faithful. This is the Mary to whom the Palio is dedicated, dear to the hearts of the Sienese. In thanks, they give **offerings** of silver hearts and medallions, many of which hang now on the wall just to the left as you exit the chapel.

• *Cross back to the other side of the church to find the...*

Piccolomini Library: Brilliantly frescoed, the library captures the exuberant, optimistic spirit of the 1400s, when humanism and the Renaissance were born. The never-restored frescoes look nearly as vivid now as the day they were finished 550 years ago. (With the bright window light, candles were unnecessary in this room— and didn't sully the art with soot.) The painter Pinturicchio (c. 1454-1513) was hired to celebrate the life of one of Siena's hometown boys—a man many call "the first humanist," Aeneas Piccolomini (1405-1464), who became Pope Pius II. Each of the 10 scenes is framed with an arch, as if Pinturicchio were opening a window onto the spacious 3-D world we inhabit.

The library also contains intricately decorated, illuminated music scores and a statue (a Roman copy of a Greek original) of the Three Graces, who almost seem to dance to the beat. The oddly huge sheep-skin sheets of music are from the days before individual hymnals—they had to be big so that many singers could read the music at the same time from a distance. Appreciate the fine painted decorations on the music—the gold-leaf highlights, the newly discovered (and quite expensive) cobalt for blue tones, and the miniature figures. All of this exquisite detail was lovingly crafted by Benedictine monks for the glory of God. Find your favorite—I like the blue, totally wild god of wind with the big hair (in the fourth case).

• *Exit the Duomo and make a U-turn to the left, walking alongside the church to Piazza Jacopo della Quercia.*

Unfinished Church: After rival republic Florence began its grand cathedral (1296), proud Siena planned to build one even bigger, the biggest church in all Christendom.

Construction began in the 1330s on an extension off the right side of the existing Duomo (today's cathedral would have been used as a transept). The nave of the Duomo

was supposed to be where the piazza is today. Worshippers would have entered the church from the far end of the piazza through the unfinished wall. (Look way up at the highest part of the wall. That's the viewpoint accessible from inside the Duomo Museum.) Some of the nave's green-and-white-striped columns were built, and are now filled in with a brick wall. White stones in the pavement mark where a row of pillars would have been.

The vision was grand, but it underestimated the complexity of constructing such a building without enough land for it to sit upon. That, coupled with the devastating effects of a plague, killed the city's ability and will to finish the project. Look through the unfinished entrance facade, note blue sky where the stained-glass windows would have been, and ponder the struggles, triumphs, and failures of the human spirit.

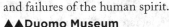

▲▲Duomo Museum (Museo dell'Opera e Panorama)

Located in a corner of the Duomo's grand but unfinished extension (to the right as you face the main facade), Siena's most enjoyable museum was built to house the cathedral's art. Here you can stand eye-to-eye with the saints and angels who once languished unknown in the church's upper reaches (where copies are found today).

Cost and Hours: €7, covered by

Opa Si combo-ticket, buy tickets near Duomo Museum entry, daily March-Oct 10:30-19:00, Nov-Feb 10:30-17:30, last entry 30 minutes before closing, videoguide-€4 (€6/2 people); next to the Duomo, in the skeleton of the unfinished part of the church on the Il Campo side—look for the white banner, tel. 0577-286-300, www.operaduomo.siena.it.

Audioguides: You can rent a videoguide on a tablet computer for €4 (€6/2 people). A pricier option also covers the Duomo and other sights, but you have to pick it up and drop it off inside the cathedral (for details, see page 644).

❍ Self-Guided Tour: Start your tour at the bottom and work your way up.

Ground Floor: This floor is filled with the cathedral's original Gothic sculptures by Giovanni Pisano, who spent 10 years in the late 1200s carving and orchestrating the decoration of the cathedral with saints, prophets, sibyls, animals, and the original she-wolf with Romulus and Remus.

On the ground floor you'll also find Donatello's fine, round *Madonna and Child* carved relief. A slender, tender Mary gazes down at her chubby-cheeked baby, as her sad eyes say that she knows the eventual fate of her son.

On the opposite side of the room is Duccio's original stained-glass window, which until recently was located above and behind the Duomo's altar. Now the church has a copy, and art lovers can enjoy a close-up look at this masterpiece. The rose window—20 feet across, made in 1288—is dedicated (like the church and the city itself) to the Virgin Mary. The work was designed by Siena's most famous artist, Duccio di Buoninsegna (c. 1255-1319), and combines elements from rigid Byzantine icons (Mary's almond-shaped bubble, called a *mandorla*, and the full frontal saints that flank her) with a budding sense of 3-D realism (the throne turned at a three-quarter angle to simulate depth, with angels behind).

Duccio's *Maestà*: Upstairs awaits a private audience with the *Maestà* (*Enthroned Virgin*, 1311), whose panels were once part of the Duomo's main altarpiece. Although the former altarpiece was disassembled (and the frame was lost), most of the pieces are displayed here, with the front side (*Maestà*, with Mary and saints) at one end of the room, and the back side (26 Passion panels) at the other.

The *Maestà* was revolutionary for the time in its sheer size and opulence, and in Duccio's budding realism, which broke standard conventions. Duccio, at the height of his powers, used every innovative arrow in his quiver. He replaced the standard gold-leaf background (symbolizing heaven) with a gold, intricately patterned curtain draped over the throne. Mary's blue robe opens to reveal her body, and the curve of her knee suggests real anatomy beneath the

SIENA

robe. Baby Jesus wears a delicately transparent garment. Their faces are modeled with light—a patchwork of bright flesh and shadowy valleys, as if lit from the left (a technique he likely learned from his contemporary Giotto during a visit to Florence).

The flip side of the *Maestà* featured 26 smaller panels—the medieval equivalent of pages—showing colorful scenes from the Passion of Christ.

Panorama dal Facciatone: About 60 claustrophobic spiral stairs take you to the first viewpoint. You can continue up another similar spiral staircase to reach the very top. Standing on the wall from this high point in the city, you're rewarded with a stunning view of Siena...and an interesting perspective. Look toward the Duomo and consider this: If Siena's grandiose plans to expand the cathedral had come to fruition, you'd be looking straight down the nave toward the altar.

▲Baptistery

Siena is so hilly that there wasn't enough flat ground on which to build a big church. What to do? Build a big church anyway and prop up the overhanging edge with the Baptistery. This dark and quietly tucked-away cave of art is worth a look for its cool, tranquil bronze panels and angels by Ghiberti, Donatello, and others that adorn the pedestal of the baptismal font.

Cost and Hours: €4, covered by Opa Si combo-ticket, buy tickets near Duomo Museum entry, daily March-Oct 10:30-19:00, Nov-Feb 10:30-17:30, last entry 30 minutes before closing.

Crypt

The cathedral "crypt" is archaeologically important. The site of a small 12th-century Romanesque church, it was filled in with dirt a century after its creation to provide a foundation for the huge church that sits atop it today. Recently excavated, the several redis-covered frescoed rooms show off what are likely the oldest frescoes in town. Religious art exhibitions are sometimes held here.

Cost and Hours: €6, €8 during special exhibitions, covered by Opa Si combo-ticket, buy tickets near Duomo Museum entry, daily March-Oct 10:30-19:00, Nov-Feb 10:30-17:30, last entry 30 minutes before closing, entrance is halfway up the stairs between the Baptistery and Duomo Museum.

▲Santa Maria della Scala

This museum, opposite the Duomo entrance, was used as a hospital until the 1980s (though it may be closed for renovation during your visit). Its labyrinthine 12th-century cellars—carved out of volcanic tuff and finished with brick—go down several floors and during medieval times were used to store supplies for the hospital upstairs. Today, the hospital and its cellars are filled with exhibits (well-described in English) and can be a welcome refuge from the hot streets. Stop in for a cool and quiet break in the air-conditioned lobby, which offers a fine bookshop and big, comfy couches, all under great 15th-century timbers.

Cost and Hours: If open, likely around €6, daily March-Oct 10:30-18:00, Nov-Feb 10:30-16:00, last entry 30 minutes before closing, bookstore, tel. 0577-534-511, www.santamariadellascala. com.

Visiting the Museum: It's easy to get lost in this gigantic complex, so stay focused on the main attractions—the fancily frescoed Pellegrinaio Hall (ground floor), most of the original *Fountain of Joy* (first basement), and the Etruscan collection in the Archaeological Museum (second basement). Just inside the complex (enter from the square) is the Church of the Santissima Annunziata.

From the entrance, walk down the lengthy hall to the long room with the colorful frescoes. The sumptuously frescoed walls of **Pellegrinaio Hall** show medieval Siena's innovative health care and social welfare system in action (c. 1442, wonderfully described in English). Starting in the 11th century, the hospital nursed the sick and cared for abandoned children, as is vividly portrayed in these frescoes. The good works paid off, as bequests and donations poured in, creating the wealth that's evident throughout this building.

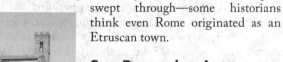

Head down the stairs, then continue straight into the darkened rooms with pieces of Siena's landmark fountain—follow signs to *Fonte Gaia*. An engaging exhibit explains Jacopo della Quercia's early 15th-century **Fountain of Joy** *(Fonte Gaia)*—and displays the disassembled pieces of the original fountain itself. In the 19th century, after serious deterioration, the ornate fountain was dismantled, and plaster casts were made. (From these casts, they formed the replica that graces Il Campo today.) Here you'll see the eroded original panels paired with their restored casts, along with the actual statues that once stood on the edges of the fountain.

Descend into the cavernous second basement. Under the groin vaults of the **Archaeological Museum,** you're alone with piles of ancient Etruscan stuff excavated from tombs dating centuries before Christ (displayed in a labyrinthine exhibit). Remember, the Etruscans dominated this part of Italy before the Roman Empire swept through—some historians think even Rome originated as an Etruscan town.

San Domenico Area
Church of San Domenico
This huge brick church is worth a quick look. The spacious, plain interior (except for the colorful flags of the city's 17 *contrade,* or neighborhoods) fits the austere philosophy of

SIENA

St. Catherine of Siena
(1347-1380)

The youngest of 25 children born to a Sienese cloth dyer, Catherine began experiencing heavenly visions as a child. At  16 she became a Dominican nun, locking herself away for three years in a room in her family's house. She lived the life of an ascetic, which culminated in a vision wherein she married Christ. Catherine emerged from solitude to join her Dominican sisters, sharing her experiences, caring for the sick, and gathering both disciples and enemies. At age 23, she lapsed into a spiritual coma, waking with the heavenly command to spread her message to the world. She wrote essays and letters to kings, dukes, bishops, and popes, imploring them to find peace for a war-ravaged Italy. While visiting Pisa during Lent of 1375, she had a vision in which she received the stigmata, the wounds of Christ.

Still in her twenties, Catherine was invited to Avignon, France, where the pope had taken up residence. With her charm, sincerity, and reputation for holiness, she helped convince Pope Gregory XI to return the papacy to the city of Rome. Catherine also went to Rome, where she died young. She was canonized in the next generation (by a Sienese pope), and her relics were distributed to churches around Italy.

Because of her intervention in the papal schism, today Catherine is revered (along with St. Benedict) as the patron saint of Europe and remembered as a rare outspoken medieval woman still appreciated for her universal message: that this world is not a gift from our fathers, but a loan from our children.

the Dominicans and invites meditation on the thoughts and deeds of St. Catherine. Walk up the steps in the rear to see paintings from her life. Halfway up the church on the right, find a metal bust of St. Catherine, a small case housing her thumb (on the left), and a glass box on the lowest shelf containing the chain she used to scourge herself. In the chapel (15 feet to the left) surrounded with candles, you'll see Catherine's actual head atop the altar. Through the door just beyond are the sacristy and the bookstore.

Cost and Hours: Free, daily 7:00-18:30, gift shop tel. 0577-286-848, www.basilicacateriniana.com. A WC (€0.50) is at the far end of the parking lot, to the right as you face the church entrance.

Sanctuary of St. Catherine (Santuario di Santa Caterina)

Step into the cool and peaceful site of Catherine's home. Siena remembers its favorite hometown gal, a simple, unschooled, but mystically devout soul who, in the mid-1300s, helped convince the pope to return from France to Rome. Pilgrims have visited this place since 1464, and architects and artists have greatly embellished what was probably once a humble home (her family worked as wool dyers). You'll see paintings throughout showing scenes from her life.

Enter through the courtyard, and walk down the stairs at the far end. The church on your right contains the wooden crucifix upon which Catherine was meditating when she received the stigmata. Take a pew, gaze at it, and try to imagine the scene. Back outside, the oratory across the courtyard stands where the kitchen once was. Go down the stairs (left of the gift shop) to reach the saint's room. Catherine's bare cell is behind wrought-iron doors.

Cost and Hours: Free, daily 9:00-18:00, church closed 12:30-15:00, a few downhill blocks toward the center from San Domenico—follow signs to *Santuario di Santa Caterina*—at Costa di Sant'Antonio 6, tel. 0577-288-175.

Shopping in Siena

The main drag, Via Banchi di Sopra, is a cancan of fancy shops. Here are some things to look for:

Flags: For easy-to-pack souvenirs, get some of the large, colorful scarves/flags that depict the symbols of Siena's 17 different neighborhoods (such as the wolf, the turtle, or the snail). They're good for gifts or to decorate your home (sold in varying sizes at souvenir stands).

Sweets: All over town, Prodotti Tipici shops sell Sienese specialties. Siena's claim to caloric fame is its *panforte*, a rich, chewy concoction of nuts, honey, and candied fruits that impresses even fruitcake haters. There are a few varieties: *Margherita*, dusted in powdered sugar, is more fruity, while *panpepato* has a spicy, peppery crust. Locals prefer a chewy, white macaroon-and-almond cookie called *ricciarelli*.

Sleep Code

(€1 = about $1.30, country code: 39)
S = Single, **D** = Double/Twin, **T** = Triple, **Q** = Quad, **b** = bathroom, **s** = shower only.

Unless otherwise noted, credit cards are accepted, English is spoken, and breakfast is included. If your hotel doesn't provide breakfast, eat at a bar on Il Campo or near your hotel. Many cities in Italy levy a hotel tax of €2 per person, per night, which must be paid in cash (not included in the rates I've quoted).

To help you easily sort through these listings, I've divided the accommodations into three categories based on the price for a standard double room with bath during high season:

$$$ **Higher Priced**—Most rooms €130 or more.
 $$ **Moderately Priced**—Most rooms between €90-130.
  $ **Lower Priced**—Most rooms €90 or less.

Prices can change without notice; verify the hotel's current rates online or by email. For the best prices, always book direct.

Sleeping in Siena

Finding a room in Siena is tough during Easter (April 20 in 2014) or the Palio (July 2 and Aug 16). Many hotels won't take reservations until the end of May for the Palio, and even then they might require a four-night stay. While day-tripping tour groups turn the town into a Gothic amusement park in midsummer, Siena is basically yours in the evenings and off-season.

Part of Siena's charm is its lively, festive character—this means that all hotels can be plagued with noise, even (and sometimes especially) the hotels in the pedestrian-only zone. If tranquility is important for your sanity, ask for a room that's off the street, or consider staying at one of the recommended places outside the center.

Fancy Sleeps, Southwest of Il Campo

These well-run places are a 10-minute walk from Il Campo.

$$$ Pensione Palazzo Ravizza is elegant and friendly, with 38 rooms and an aristocratic feel—fitting, as it was once the luxurious residence of a noble. Guests enjoy a peaceful garden set on a dramatic bluff, along with a Steinway in the upper lounge (Sb-€180, small loft Db-€140, standard Db-€180, superior Db-€220, Tb-€255, family suites-€300, rates can vary, see website for room differences, rooms in back overlook countryside, air-con, elevator, free Wi-Fi, Via Piano dei Mantellini 34, tel. 0577-280-462, www.palazzoravizza.it, bureau@palazzoravizza.it). As parking is free and the hotel is easily walkable from the center, this is a particularly good value for drivers.

$$$ Hotel Duomo has 20 spacious but slightly dated rooms, a picnic-friendly roof terrace, and a bizarre floor plan (Sb-€105, Db-€130, Db suite-€180, Tb-€180, Qb-€230, elevator with some stairs, air-con, free Wi-Fi, discounted parking-€20/day; follow Via di Città, which becomes Via di Stalloreggi, to #38; tel. 0577-289-088, www.hotelduomo.it, booking@hotelduomo.it, Alessandro). If you're arriving by train, take a taxi (€12) or ride bus #3 to the Porta Tufi stop, just a few minutes' walk from the hotel; you can also arrange to have Alessandro take you to/from the train station or airport (with this book: train station-€10, Florence's Vespucci Airport-€105, Pisa's Galilei Airport-€165; he'll also take you to nearby hill towns, e.g. Florence-€105 and Pisa-€165). If you're driving, go to Porta San Marco, turn right, and follow signs to the hotel—drop your bags, then park in the nearby Il Campo lot near Porta Tufi.

Simple Places near Il Campo

Most of these listings are forgettable but well-priced, and just a horse wreck away from one of Italy's most wonderful civic spaces.

$$ Piccolo Hotel Etruria, with 20 simple, recently redecorated rooms, is well-located and restful (S-€50, Sb-€60, Db-€90-110, Tb-€120-138, Qb-€145-166, higher rates are for peak-of-peak times, 10 percent discount with this book, optional breakfast-€5, air-con May-Oct only, elevator, Wi-Fi, next to recommended Albergo Tre Donzelle at Via delle Donzelle 1-3, tel 0577-288-088, www.hoteletruria.com, info@hoteletruria.com, friendly Conti family)

$ Albergo Tre Donzelle is a fine budget value with 20 plain, well-worn rooms. Although the showers have seen better days, these may be the cheapest rooms in the center. Don't hang out here...think of Il Campo, a block away, as your terrace (S-€38, D-€49, Db-€60, T-€70, Tb-€85, no rooms available for Palio, breakfast-€5, free Wi-Fi; with your back to the tower, head away from Il Campo toward 2 o'clock to Via delle Donzelle 5; tel. 0577-280-358, www.tredonzelle.com, info@tredonzelle.com).

$ Hotel Cannon d'Oro, a few blocks up Via Banchi di Sopra, is a labyrinthine slumbermill renting 30 institutional, overpriced rooms (Sb-€71, Db-€90, Tb-€115, Qb-€136, these discounted prices good with this book through 2014, fans, free Wi-Fi in lobby and some rooms, a couple of blocks from the bus hub at Via dei Montanini 28, tel. 0577-44-321, www.cannondoro.com, info@cannondoro.com; Maurizio, Tommaso, and Rodrigo).

B&Bs in the Old Center

$$ Antica Residenza Cicogna is a seven-room guesthouse with a homey elegance and an ideal location. It's warmly run by the young

Siena Hotels & Restaurants

SIENA

100 Meters
100 Yards

To Porta
Camollia

ISTRICE

VIALE AMANDO DIAZ
V. LUIGI CADORNA
VIALE RINALDO FRANCI
VIALE CESARE MACCARI

La Lizza

SOTTOPASSAGGIO
LA LIZZA

Piazza
Gramsci

FORTEZZA

STADIO

DRAGO

VIALE DEI MILLE

Piazza
San Domenico

WC

SAN
DOMENICO

Fonte
Branda

PORTA
FONTEBRANDA

VIA ESTERNA DI
FONTEBRANDA

ANCIENT
CITY WALLS

SELVA

NOTE: MUCH OF CENTRAL SIENA
IS A PEDESTRIAN ZONE

SAN
SEBASTIANO

SANTISSIMA
ANNUNCIATA

SANTA MARIA
DELLA SCALA
(MUSEUM)

PANTERA

Piazza
di Due Porte

Eateries & Nightlife

17 Antica Osteria Da Divo
18 Taverna San Giuseppe
19 Compagnia dei Vinattieri
20 Hostaria Il Carroccio
21 Trattoria La Torre, Ciao Cafeteria & Spizzico Pizza
22 Osteria del Gatto
23 Ristorante Guidoriccio
24 Trattoria Papei
25 Osteria Trombicche
26 La Taverna Di Cecco
27 Il Pomodorino
28 Rist. Alla Speranza & Bar Paninoteca San Paolo

29 Il Bandierino
30 Bar Il Palio
31 Osteria Liberamente
32 Costarella Gelateria
33 Key Largo Bar
34 Antica Pizzicheria al Palazzo della Chigiana
35 Pizzeria San Martino
36 Rosticceria Vitti
37 Consorzio Agrario Siena Grocery
38 Nannini Pastry Shop
39 Gelateria Grom
40 Un Tubo
41 Enoteca Italiana

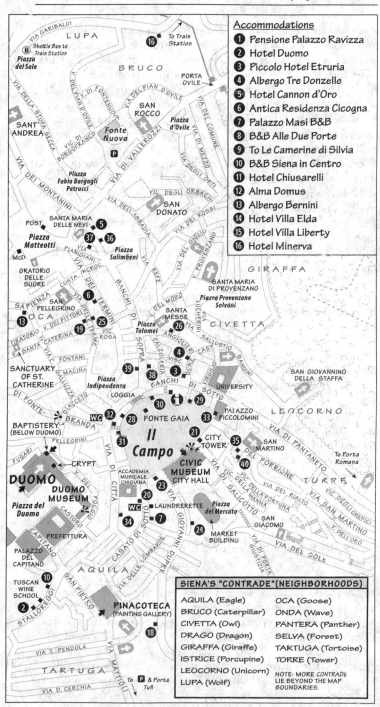

Accommodations

1. Pensione Palazzo Ravizza
2. Hotel Duomo
3. Piccolo Hotel Etruria
4. Albergo Tre Donzelle
5. Hotel Cannon d'Oro
6. Antica Residenza Cicogna
7. Palazzo Masi B&B
8. B&B Alle Due Porte
9. To Le Camerine di Silvia
10. B&B Siena in Centro
11. Hotel Chiusarelli
12. Alma Domus
13. Albergo Bernini
14. Hotel Villa Elda
15. Hotel Villa Liberty
16. Hotel Minerva

SIENA'S "CONTRADE" (NEIGHBORHOODS)

AQUILA (Eagle)	OCA (Goose)
BRUCO (Caterpillar)	ONDA (Wave)
CIVETTA (Owl)	PANTERA (Panther)
DRAGO (Dragon)	SELVA (Forest)
GIRAFFA (Giraffe)	TARTUGA (Tortoise)
ISTRICE (Porcupine)	TORRE (Tower)
LEOCORNO (Unicorn)	
LUPA (Wolf)	NOTE: MORE CONTRADE LIE BEYOND THE MAP BOUNDARIES.

SIENA

and charming Elisa and her dad, Fabio, who set out biscotti, *vin santo*, and tea all day for their guests. With artfully frescoed walls and ceilings, this is remarkably genteel for the price (Db-€95, suite Db-€120, third bed-€15, air-con, free guest computer, free Wi-Fi, Via delle Terme 76, tel. 0577-285-613, mobile 347-007-2888, www.anticaresidenzacicogna.it, info@anticaresidenzacicogna.it).

$$ Palazzo Masi B&B, run by Alizzardo and Daniela, is just below Il Campo. They rent six pleasant, spacious, antique-furnished rooms with shared common areas on the second and third floors of an old building. While a bit pricey, the fine location and warm welcome are appreciated (D-€80, Db-€120 if you book direct, discounts for 4 or more nights, cash only, breakfast-€8, free Wi-Fi, discounted parking at nearby Il Campo lot-€25/24 hours; from City Hall, walk 50 yards down Via del Casato di Sotto to #29; mobile 349-600-9155, www.palazzomasi.com, info@palazzomasi.it). The place is sometimes unstaffed, so it's important to phone upon arrival.

$ B&B Alle Due Porte is a charming little establishment renting four big rooms with sweet furniture under big medieval beams. The shared breakfast room is delightful. The manager, Egisto, is a phone call and five-minute scooter ride away (Db-€85, windowless Db with small bed-€65, Tb-€110, air-con in two rooms, free Wi-Fi, Via di Stalloreggi 51, tel. 0577-287-670, mobile 368-352-3530, www.sienatur.it, soldatini@interfree.it).

$ Le Camerine di Silvia, a romantic hideaway perched near a sweeping, grassy olive grove, rents five simple but cozy rooms in a converted 16th-century building. A small breakfast terrace with fruit trees and a private hedged garden lends itself to contemplation (Db-€50-€80, rate depends on season, cash only, ask for a view room, fans, Wi-Fi, shared microwave and small fridge, nearby parking-€12, free parking a 10-minute walk away, Via Ettore Bastianini 1-3, just below recommended Pensione Palazzo Ravizza—see listing earlier, mobile 338-761-5052 or 339-123-7687, www.lecamerinedisilvia.com, info@lecamerinedisilvia.com, Conti family).

$ B&B Siena in Centro is a clearinghouse managing five good and centrally located private apartments. Their handy office functions as a reception renting out a total of about 20 rooms; stop by here to pick up your key and be escorted to your apartment. The rooms are generally spacious, quiet, and comfortable, but with no air-conditioning or Wi-Fi. Their website lets you visualize your options (Sb-€45-60, Db-€70-90, Tb-€90-120, reception open 9:00-13:30 & 15:00-19:00, later in high season, other times by phone request, OK to leave bags at reception, Via di Stalloreggi 14, tel. 0577-43041, mobile 331-281-0136 or 347-465-9753, www.bbsienaincentro.com, info@bbsienaincentro.com, Gioia or Michela).

Near San Domenico Church

These hotels are within a 10-minute walk northwest of Il Campo. Both Albergo Bernini and Alma Domus offer fine panoramas of the old town for reasonable prices.

$$$ Hotel Chiusarelli, with 48 classy rooms in a beautiful Neoclassical villa, has a handy location but is on a very busy street. Expect traffic noise at night—ask for a quieter room in the back (can be guaranteed with reservation). The bells of San Domenico are your 7:00 wake-up call (Sb-€105, Db-€150, Tb-€190, ask for 10 percent Rick Steves discount when you book, air-con, free Wi-Fi with this book, across from San Domenico at Viale Curtatone 15, tel. 0577-280-562, www.chiusarelli.com, info@chiusarelli.com).

$ Alma Domus is a church-run hotel featuring 43 spartan rooms with quaint balconies, some fantastic views (ask for a room *con vista*), stately public rooms, and a pleasant atmosphere. However, the thin doors, echoey halls, and nearby church bells can be drawbacks; ask for a room with double-paned windows or bring earplugs. The 10:00 checkout time is strict, but they will store your luggage in their secure courtyard (Sb-€48, Db-€85, Tb-€110, air-con, elevator, pay guest computer, pay Wi-Fi; from San Domenico, walk downhill toward the view with the church on your right, turn left down Via Camporegio, make a U-turn down the brick steps to Via Camporegio 37; tel. 0577-44-177, www.hotelalmadomus.it, info@hotelalmadomus.it, Luigi).

$ Albergo Bernini makes you part of a Sienese family in a modest, clean home with 10 traditional rooms. Giovanni, charming wife Daniela, and their three daughters welcome you to their spectacular view terrace for breakfast and picnic lunches and dinners (S-€55, D-€65, Sb or small Db with view-€78, Db-€85, less in winter, optional breakfast-€3.50/small or €7.50/big, cash only, free Wi-Fi, on the main Il Campo-San Domenico drag at Via della Sapienza 15, tel. 0577-289-047, www.albergobernini.com, hbernin@tin.it).

Farther from the Center

These options, a 10- to 20-minute walk from the center, are great for drivers.

Near Porta Romana City Gate

These two fine spots are about 200 yards outside the Porta Romana (for locations, see the map on page 632). To get to downtown Siena from here, catch minibus line A uphill to Piazza al Mercato, just behind Il Campo (€1.10). To reach the bus and train stations, take bus #2 (which becomes #17 at Piazza del Sale; when arriving, catch #17 from the station). If driving, from the freeway, take the Siena Sud exit, continue in direction Romana, then at the first light turn left, following *Pta Romana/Centro* signs for about half a mile until you see the big city gate.

$$$ Hotel Santa Caterina is a three-star, 18th-century place renting 22 comfy rooms. It's professionally run with real attention to quality. While it's on a big city street, it has a delightful garden terrace with views over the countryside (Sb-€125, four small Db-€125, Db-€165, split-level Tb or Qb-€215, prices promised with this book through 2014, can be cheaper in low season, garden side is quieter, air-con, fridge in room, elevator, free Wi-Fi, parking-€15/day—request when you reserve, Via E.S. Piccolomini 7, tel. 0577-221-105, www.hscsiena.it, info@hscsiena.it, Lorenza and her crew).

$$ Hotel Porta Romana is at the edge of town, off a busy road. Some of its 15 rooms face the open countryside (request one of these), and breakfast is served in the garden (Sb-€90, Db-€110, extra person-€20, 10 percent Rick Steves discount if you book direct and pay cash, air-con in most rooms, free guest computer, free Wi-Fi, free parking, inviting sun terrace, outdoor hot tub-€10/person per stay, Via E.S. Piccolomini 35, tel. 0577-42299, www.hotelportaromana.com, info@hotelportaromana.com; Marco and Evelia).

In the Posh Neighborhood South of the Fortress

These two places are in a villa-studded residential neighborhood across a gully from San Domenico Church. They're about 5-10 minutes farther than the listings under "Near San Domenico Church," earlier, but the extra walking gets you to a swankier address.

$$$ Hotel Villa Elda rents 11 bright and light rooms in a recently renovated villa. It's classy, stately, pricey, and run with a feminine charm (Db-€140-170, about €20 more for view, extra person-€30, air-con, free Wi-Fi, garden and view terrace, Viale Ventiquattro Maggio 10, tel. 0577-247-927, www.villaeldasiena.it, info@villaeldasiena.it).

$$$ Hotel Villa Liberty, across a busy street from the fortress, is a former private mansion. It has 17 big, bright, comfortable rooms and some road noise (Sb-€80, Db-€150, Tb-€180, €10 more for superior room, air-con, elevator, free Wi-Fi, bar, courtyard, free and easy street parking, facing fortress at Viale Vittorio Veneto 11, tel. 0577-44-966, www.villaliberty.it, info@villaliberty.it).

Just Inside Porta Ovile, at the North End of Town

$$ Hotel Minerva is your big, professional, plain, efficient option. It's the most impersonal of my listings, with zero personality but predictable comfort. While its 56 rooms are boring, they don't hide any unpleasant surprises. It works best for those with cars—parking is reasonable (€12/day), and it's only a 10-minute walk from

SIENA

the action (Sb-€76, Db-€122, Tb-€168, bigger suites available for more, ask for a view room, air-con, elevator, free guest computer, pay Wi-Fi, Via Garibaldi 72, tel. 0577-284-474, www.albergominerva.it, info@albergominerva.it).

East of Siena

$$$ **Frances' Lodge Relais** is a tranquil and delightfully managed farmhouse B&B a mile out of Siena. Each of its six rooms is bursting with character (all well-described on their website). Franca and Franco run this rustic-yet-elegant old place, which features a 19th-century orangery that's been made into a "better homes and palaces" living room, as well as a peaceful garden, eight acres of olive trees and vineyards, and great views of Siena and its countryside—even from the swimming pool (small Db-€170, Db-€190, Db suite-€220, Tb-€210-220, Tb suite-€280, Qb suite-€340, these prices promised to Rick Steves readers through 2014 if you book direct, possibly cheaper for longer stays, air-con, free guest computer, free Wi-Fi, free parking, Strada di Valdipugna 2, tel. 0577-42379, mobile 337-671-608, www.franceslodge.it). To the center, it's a five-minute bus ride (€1.10, they'll call to arrange) plus a five-minute walk, or €10 by taxi. Consider having an al fresco dinner in the gazebo, complete with view (make your own picnic, or have your hosts assemble a very fancy one for €20/person).

Outside Siena

The following accommodations are set in the lush, peaceful countryside surrounding Siena, and are best for those traveling by car (see locations on the map on page 632).

$$$ **Borgo Argenina** has seven rooms in a well-maintained, pricey splurge of a B&B. Run by helpful Elena Nappa, it's 20 minutes north of Siena by car in the Chianti region (Db-€170, beautiful gardens, free Wi-Fi, mobile 345-353-7673, www.borgoargenina.it, info@borgoargenina.it).

$$ **Il Canto del Sole** is a restored 18th-century farmhouse turned family-friendly B&B located about six miles outside the Porta Romana city gate. Run by Laura, Luciano, and their son Marco, it features 10 bright and airy rooms and two apartments with original antique furnishings, a saltwater swimming pool, a game room, and bike rentals (Db-€120, Tb-€140, extra bed-€30, apartment-€180-220, air-con, free Wi-Fi, free parking, dinner cooked on request, Val di Villa Canina 1292, 53014 Loc. Cuna, tel. 0577-375-127, www.ilcantodelsole.com, info@ilcantodelsole.com).

Eating in Siena

Sienese restaurants are reasonable by Florentine and Venetian standards. You can enjoy ordering high on the menu here without going broke. For me, the best €5 you can spend in Siena is on a cocktail at Bar Il Palio, overlooking Il Campo. For pasta, a good option is *pici* (PEE-chee), a thick Sienese spaghetti that seems to be at the top of every menu.

Fine Dining in the Old Town

For only a few euros more, these four places deliver a more upscale ambience and generally better food than my later recommendations.

Antica Osteria Da Divo is *the* place for a dressy and atmospheric €45 meal. The kitchen is creative, the ambience is flowery and candlelit, some of the seating fills old Etruscan tombs, and the food is fresh, delicate, and top-notch. While the cuisine is flamboyant and almost over-the-top, Chef Pino and his wife Susanna serve up my favorite splurge dinner in town. Pino is a fanatic for fresh ingredients, enjoys giving traditional dishes his creative spin, and is understandably proud of his desserts. The wine is good, too—you can order it by the glass (€4-7) if you ask (€10-12 pastas, €20-26 *secondi*, €3 cover, Wed-Mon 12:00-14:30 & 19:00-22:30, closed Tue, reservations smart; facing Baptistery door, take the far right street and walk one long curving block to Via Franciosa 29; tel. 0577-284-381, www.osteriadadivo.it). Those dining here with this book can finish with a complimentary biscotti and *vin santo* or coffee (upon request).

Taverna San Giuseppe, a local favorite, offers modern Tuscan cuisine in a chic grotto atmosphere. While the vibe is high energy and casual, the food compares favorably with the slightly more upscale places listed here. The wine-and-cheese cellar in back is cut from an Etruscan tomb. Check the posters tacked around the entry for daily specials. Reserve or arrive early to get a table (€8-10 pastas, €15-20 *secondi*, Mon-Sat 12:00-14:30 & 19:00-22:00, closed Sun, air-con, 7-minute climb up street to the right of City Hall at Via Giovanni Dupre 132, tel. 0577-42-286, www.tavernasangiuseppe.it, Matteo).

Compagnia dei Vinattieri serves modern Tuscan dishes with a creative twist. In this elegantly unpretentious space, you can enjoy a quiet and romantic meal under graceful brick arches. The menu is small and accessible, and the young staff will help you match your meal with the right wine. Marco, the owner, is happy to take you down to the marvelous wine cellar (€9-12 pastas, €16-18 *secondi*, leave this book on the table for a complimentary *aperitivo* or dessert drink, daily 12:30-15:00 & 19:30-23:00, near Via dei Pittori at Via delle Terme 79, tel. 0577-236-568, www.vinattieri.net).

Hostaria Il Carroccio, artsy and convivial, seats guests in a tight, sea-foam-green dining room and serves elegantly presented, traditional "slow food" recipes with innovative flair at affordable prices (€8 pastas, €14-18 *secondi*, €30 tasting *menu*—minimum two people, cash only, reservations wise, Thu-Tue 12:30-15:00 & 19:30-22:00, closed Wed, Via del Casato di Sotto 32, tel. 0577-41-165, sweet Renata and Mauro).

Traditional and Rustic Places in the Old Town

Trattoria La Torre is a thriving, unfussy *casalinga* (home-cooking) eatery, popular for its homemade pasta, plates of which entice customers as they enter. The sound of its busy open kitchen adds to the conviviality. Ten tables are packed under one medieval brick arch. Service is brisk and casual, and despite its priceless position below the namesake tower, it feels more like a local hangout than a tourist trap. Study the menu in the window before entering; otherwise, the owner likes to just recite his long list of dishes (€7-8 pastas, €8-10 *secondi*, €2 cover, Fri-Wed 12:00-15:00 & 19:00-22:00, closed Thu, just steps below Il Campo at Via di Salicotto 7, tel. 0577-287-548, Alberto Buccini).

Osteria del Gatto is a classic little hole-in-the-wall, thriving with townspeople and powered by a passion for serving good Sienese cuisine. Marco Coradeschi and his engaged staff cook and serve daily specials with attitude. As it's so small and popular, it can get loud (€8-9 pastas, €8-10 *secondi*, Mon-Fri 12:30-15:00 & 19:30-22:00, Sat 19:30-22:00 only, closed Sun, 5-minute walk away from the center at Via San Marco 8, tel. 0577-287-133).

Ristorante Guidoriccio, just a few steps below Il Campo, feels warm and welcoming. You'll get smiling service from Ercole and Elisabetta. While mostly filled with tourists, the place has a charm—especially if you let gentle Ercole explore the menu with you, and follow his suggestions (€9 pastas, €13-15 *secondi*, Mon-Sat 12:30-14:30 & 19:00-22:30, closed Sun, air-con, Via Giovanni Dupre 2, tel. 0577-44-350).

Trattoria Papei is a Sienese favorite, featuring a casual, rollicking family atmosphere and friendly servers dishing out generous portions of rib-stickin' Tuscan specialties and grilled meats. This big, sprawling place under tents in a parking lot is in all the guidebooks and often jammed—so call to reserve (€7 pastas, €8-12 *secondi*, daily 12:00-15:00 & 19:00-22:30, on the market square directly behind City Hall at Piazza del Mercato 6, tel. 0577-280-894; for 50 years Signora Giuliana has ruled her kitchen, Amadeo and Eduardo speak English).

Osteria Trombicche takes you back to another age—cheap and small, with tight indoor seating and two tiny outdoor tables from which to watch the street scene. Alessandro serves fast, hearty food to a local crowd (€6.50 *ribollita*—bean-and-vegetable soup—in winter, €5 *panzanella*—bread salad with tomato and basil—in summer, €8-10 mixed-vegetable antipasto plates, hand-cut prosciutto, Mon-Sat 11:00-15:00 & 18:00-22:00, Sun 11:00-15:00, Via delle Terme 66, tel. 0577-288-089).

La Taverna Di Cecco is a simple, comfortable little eatery on an uncrowded back lane where earnest Luca and Gianni serve tasty salads and Sienese specialties made by their grandmother from fresh ingredients (€8-12 pastas, €10-20 *secondi*, daily 12:00-16:00 & 19:00-24:00, Via Cecco Angiolieri 19, tel. 0577-288-518).

Il Pomodorino is a lively restaurant with a great view of the Duomo from its outdoor terrace. Tasty €8 pizzas pair well with a beer from their wide selection. The more intimate interior has Italian proverbs on the walls (daily 12:30-24:00 or later, a few steps from the recommended Alma Domus hotel at Via Camporegio 13, tel. 0577-286-811, mobile 345-026-5865).

Places on Il Campo

If you choose to eat on perhaps the finest town square in Italy, you'll pay a premium, meet waiters who don't need to hustle, and get mediocre food. And yet I recommend it. The clamshell-shaped square is lined with venerable cafés, bars, restaurants, and pizzerias.

To experience Il Campo without paying for a full meal, consider having drinks or breakfast on the square. Some bars serve food. And if your hotel doesn't include breakfast or if you'd like something more memorable, Il Campo has plenty of options. A cappuccino and a *cornetto* (croissant) run about €5-6.

Dining and Drinks on the Square

Ristorante Alla Speranza has perhaps the best view in all of Italy. If you're looking to eat reasonably on Il Campo, this is your place (€8-10 pastas and pizzas, €13-15 *secondi*, €3 cover charge, daily 9:00-late, tel. 0577-280-190). It's smart to reserve the view table of your choice by phone—or simply stop by earlier in the day while you're sightseeing in the square.

Il Bandierino is another decent option with an angled view of City Hall (€8-12 salads, €11-12 pizzas, €13-15 pastas; no cover but a 20 percent service fee, daily 11:00-23:00, tel. 0577-282-217, Hugo).

Bar Il Palio is the best bar on Il Campo for a pre- or post-dinner drink: It has straightforward prices, no cover, decent waiters, and a fantastic perspective out over the square.

Dynamic little **Osteria Liberamente** (on the square, not above it) has a trendy vibe and is popular with young people (fine wine by the glass, €7 cocktails with good tapas, Wed-Mon 8:00 until late, closed Tue, Pino).

Nightlife in Siena

Evenings are a wonderful time to be out and about in Siena, after the tour groups have left for the day.

Join the evening *passeggiata* (peak strolling time is 19:00) along Via Banchi di Sopra with gelato in hand. I like **Gelateria Grom,** which serves "Gelato like it used to be." Its seasonal flavors and all-natural ingredients make it a popular stop for any Sienese in need of something cool and sweet to lick while strolling (a little pricier than the competition, daily 11:00-24:00, Banchi di Sopra 13).

A fun trend in Siena is the *aperitivo*. All over town, you'll find bars attracting an early-evening crowd by serving a free buffet of food with the purchase of a drink. For many, this can be a light dinner for the cost of a drink. Or consider starting or ending a meal with a drink or dessert on Il Campo. For suggestions, see "Places on Il Campo."

Un Tubo is a chic little bar tucked away in a mysterious alley just five minutes from Il Campo. It's perched on top of Etruscan caves, which are open to visitors and serve as a cellar for their many international wines. The scene—mainly local artsy types—is sometimes accompanied by live music or a DJ playing lounge music (daily 13:00 until late, light snacks available, Via del Luparello 2; from Il Campo, head down Via Porrione and turn right on Via del Luparello, just after San Martino church; tel. 0577-271-312). Giandomenico speaks English and will make you feel welcome.

Enoteca Italiana is a good wine bar in a cellar in the Fortezza, funded in part by the government to promote Italian wine production. They have about 15 different bottles open on any given day, and they offer tastings for €3-10. To get there, enter the Fortezza via the bridge, cross the running track, and—after passing a tree—go left down a ramp (Mon-Sat 12:00-24:00, closed Sun, snacks served when the bar's pricey restaurant is between mealtimes, outside terrace, tel. 0577-228-832).

Drinks or Snacks from Balconies Overlooking Il Campo

Three places have skinny balconies with benches overlooking the main square for their customers. Sipping a coffee or nibbling a pastry here while marveling at the Il Campo scene is one of my favorite things to do in Europe. And it's very cheap. Survey these three places from Il Campo (with your back to the tower, they are at 10 o'clock, high noon, and 3 o'clock, respectively).

The little **Costarella Gelateria,** on the corner of Via di Città and Costa dei Barbieri, has good drinks and light snacks, such as cute little €3.50 sandwiches, though the gelato tastes artificial (daily 8:00-late, Via di Città 33). While the restaurant is for regular service, you're welcome to take anything from the bar out to the simple benches (just walk through the "table service only" section upstairs) and eat with a grand view overlooking Il Campo.

Bar Paninoteca San Paolo has a youthful pub ambience and a row of stools lining a skinny balcony overlooking the square. It serves big €7 salads and 50 kinds of €4 sandwiches, hot and cold—not authentic Italian, but quick and filling (order and pay at the counter, food served daily 12:00-2:00 in the morning, on Vicolo di San Paolo, tel. 0577-226-622).

Key Largo Bar has two long, second-story benches in the corner offering a wonderful secret perch. Buy your drink or snack at the bar (no cover and no extra charge to sit on balcony), climb upstairs, and slide the ancient bar to open the door. Enjoy stretching out, and try to imagine how, during the Palio, three layers of spectators cram into this space—note the iron railing used to plaster the top row of sardines up against the wall. Suddenly you're picturing Palio ponies zipping wildly around the corner (€4 cocktails, daily 7:00-24:00, on the corner of Via Rinaldini). If you can't get a seat on the outdoor benches, skip the otherwise nondescript, youthful interior.

Eating Cheaply in the Center

Antica Pizzicheria al Palazzo della Chigiana (look for the sign reading *Pizzicheria de Miccoli*) may be the official name, but I bet locals just call it Antonio's. For most of his life, frenzied Antonio has carved salami and cheese for the neighborhood. Most of the day, a hungry line spills onto the street as people wait for their sandwiches—meat and cheese sold by weight—with a good €10 bottle of Chianti (Italian law dictates that he must sell you a bottle of wine—cheap and good—and lend you the glasses). Antonio and his boys offer a big cheese-and-meat plate (about €18 gets you 30 minutes of eating) and pull out a tiny tabletop in the corner so you can munch or sip while standing and watching the ham-hock-y scene. Or just grab a €4-5 sandwich. Even if you don't eat here, pop in to inhale the commotion or peruse Antonio's gifty traditional edibles (daily 8:00-20:00, Via di Città 95, tel. 0577-289-164).

Ciao Cafeteria, at the bottom of Il Campo, offers good-value, self-service lunches, but no ambience or views (hearty €5-7 meals, daily 12:00-15:00). The crowded **Spizzico,** a pizza counter in the front half of Ciao, serves huge €4-5 quarter-pizzas. For both places, the food and ambience recall a cut-rate truck stop—but on sunny days, people take the pizza out on Il Campo for a memorable picnic (daily 11:00-21:00, to left of City Tower as you face it).

Pizza: Spizzico (listed above) is worth considering only if you're standing on Il Campo, desperate for pizza, and unashamedly lazy. Budget eaters look for *pizza al taglio* shops, scattered throughout Siena, selling better pizza by the slice. One good bet, **San Martino,** a couple blocks behind Il Campo, is a local-feeling spot with €2-3 slices and sandwiches (Mon-Sat 8:00-14:30 & 16:30-21:00, closed Sun, Via del Porrione 64).

Rosticcerie: For cheap take-out food, look for a *rosticceria* (explained on page 39). One affordable, central option that feels at least partly untouristed is **Rosticceria Vitti,** near Piazza Gramsci's bus terminus (point to what you want in the glass case, figure €5 for a light meal, Sun-Fri 9:00-21:30, until 16:00 off-season, closed Sat, Via dei Montanini 14/16, tel. 0577-289-291).

Supermarket: You won't find many cheap grocery shops in the touristy center of Siena. But one handy (if fancy) option is **Consorzio Agrario Siena.** Ask them to make you up a *panino*. As this place specializes in artisanal Tuscan foods, both the quality and prices are high (Mon-Sat 8:00-19:00, sometimes open Sun from 9:30, a block off Piazza Matteotti, toward Il Campo at Via Pianigiani 5).

Desserts and Treats

For a special dessert or a sweet treat any time of day, stop by **Nannini**—considered the top-end pastry shop and *the* place to go for quality local specialties (Mon-Sat 7:30-21:00, Sun 8:00-21:00, *aperitivo* happy hour 18:00-21:00, Banchi di Sopra 24). Across the street is the wonderful **Gelateria Grom** (see "Nightlife in Siena" sidebar)—but you have my permission to sample every gelateria in town to pick your favorite.

Siena Connections

Siena has sparse train connections but is a great hub for buses to the hill towns, though frequency drops on Sundays and holidays. For most, Florence is the gateway to Siena. Even if you are a railpass-user, connect these two cities by bus—it's faster than the train, and Siena's bus station is more convenient and central than its train station. (Note: Many travelers mistake old signs for a former bus company, Tra-In, as signs for trains or the train station. Those buses have nothing to do with the railway.)

By Train

Siena's train station is at the edge of town. For details on getting between the town center and the station, see page 632.

From Siena by Train to: Florence (direct trains hourly, 1.5-2 hours, €8.50; bus is better), **Pisa** (2/hour, 1.75 hours, change at Empoli, €9.80), **Assisi** (8/day, 4-5 hours, most involve 2 changes, from €13, bus is faster), **Rome** (1-2/hour, 3-3.5 hours, change in Florence or Chiusi, €26-53), **Orvieto** (12/day, 2-2.5 hours, change in Chiusi, €15.80). For more information, visit www.trenitalia.com.

By Bus

The main bus companies are **Tiemme** (part of a larger company called Siena Mobilità and formerly called Tra-In; mostly handles buses to regional destinations, tel. 0577-204-246, www.sienamobilita.it) and **Sena** (for long-distance connections, tel. 0577-208-282, www.sena.it). On schedules, the fastest buses are marked *rapida*. I'd stick with these. Most buses depart Siena from Piazza Gramsci; others leave from the train station (confirm when you buy your ticket).

SIENA

Tiemme/Siena Mobilità Buses to: Florence (roughly 2/hour, 1.25-hour *rapida/via superstrada* buses are faster than the train, avoid the 2-hour *ordinaria* buses unless you have time to enjoy the beautiful scenery en route, €7.80; if there are lines at bus-ticket office, tickets also available at tobacco shops/*tabacchi*; generally leaves from Piazza Gramsci as well as train station), **San Gimignano** (8/day direct, no direct service on Sun, 1.25 hours, €6, leaves from Piazza Gramsci), **Volterra** (4/day Mon-Sat, no buses on Sun, 2 hours, change in Colle Val d'Elsa, €6.15, leaves from Piazza Gramsci), **Montepulciano** (8/day, none on Sun, 1.25 hours, €6.60, leaves from train station), **Pienza** (6/day, none on Sun, 1.5 hours, €4.40, leaves from train station), **Montalcino** (6/day Mon-Sat, 4/day Sun, 1.25 hours, €4.90, leaves from train station or Piazza del Sale), and **Pisa's Galileo Galilei Airport** (3/day, 1.75 hours, €14, one direct, two via Poggibonsi).

Sena Buses to: Rome (9-10/day, 3 hours, €23, from Piazza Gramsci, arrives at Rome's Tiburtina station on Metro line B with easy connections to the central Termini train station), **Naples** (2/day, 6.5 hours, one at 17:00 and an overnight bus that departs at 23:59, €33), and **Milan** (6/day, 4 hours, €36, departs from Piazza Gramsci, arrives at Milan's Cadorna Station with Metro access and direct trains to Malpensa Airport).

To reach the town center of **Pisa,** the train is better (described earlier).

Tickets and Information: You can buy tickets in the underground passageway (called Sottopassaggio la Lizza) beneath Piazza Gramsci—look for stairwells in front of NH Excelsior Hotel. The larger office (marked *Siena Mobilità*) handles Tiemme/Siena Mobilità buses (Mon-Fri 6:30-19:30, Sat-Sun 7:00-19:30). The smaller one is for Sena buses (Mon-Sat 8:30-19:45; on Sun, when the Sena bus ticket office is closed, buy tickets next door at Tiemme/Siena

HILL TOWNS OF CENTRAL ITALY

San Gimignano • Volterra • Montepulciano • Pienza •
Montalcino • Cortona • More Hill Towns and Sights

The sun-soaked hill towns of central Italy offer what to many is the quintessential Italian experience: sun-dried tomatoes, homemade pasta, wispy cypress-lined driveways following desolate ridges to fortified 16th-century farmhouses, atmospheric *enoteche* serving famously tasty wines, and dusty old-timers warming the same bench day after day while soccer balls buzz around them like innocuous flies.

Hill towns are best enjoyed by adapting to the pace of the countryside. So, slow...down...and savor the delights that this region offers. Spend the night if you can, as many hill towns are mobbed by day-trippers.

Planning Your Time

How in Dante's name does a traveler choose from Italy's hundreds of hill towns? I've listed some of my favorites in this chapter. The one(s) you visit will depend on your interests, time, and mode of transportation.

Multi-towered San Gimignano is a classic, but because it's such an easy hill town to visit (about 1.5 hours by bus from Florence), peak-season crowds can overwhelm its charms. For rustic vitality not completely trampled by tourist crowds, out-of-the-way Volterra is the clear winner. Wine aficionados head for Montalcino and Montepulciano—each a happy gauntlet of wine shops and art galleries (Montepulciano being my favorite). Fans of architecture and urban design appreciate Pienza's well-planned streets and squares. Those enamored by Frances Mayes' memoir *(Under the Tuscan Sun)* make the pilgrimage to Cortona. Urbino, well off the tourist track and quite remote, is known for its huge Ducal Palace.

Mobilità office; Sena office also has a desk selling *Eurolines* tickets for bus connections to other countries). Both offices accept credit cards. You can also get tickets for both Tiemme/Siena Mobilità buses and Sena buses at the train station (look for bus-ticket kiosk just inside main door—see page 634 for hours). If necessary, you can buy tickets from the driver, but it costs €3 extra.

Services: Sottopassaggio la Lizza also has luggage storage (see page 634 for details), posted bus schedules, TV monitors listing imminent departures for several bus companies, and WCs (€0.50).

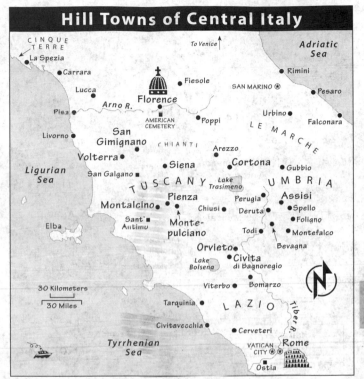

Hill Towns of Central Italy

CINQUE TERRE
La Spezia
Carrara
Lucca
Pisa
Arno R.
Florence
AMERICAN CEMETERY
Poppi
Fiesole
SAN MARINO ⊛
To Venice
Adriatic Sea
Rimini
Pesaro
Urbino
Falconara
LE MARCHE
Livorno
San Gimignano
Volterra
CHIANTI
Arezzo
Cortona
Gubbio
Ligurian Sea
San Galgano
Siena
Lake Trasimeno
UMBRIA
TUSCANY
Pienza
Perugia
Assisi
Montalcino
Chiusi
Deruta
Spello
Foligno
Elba
Sant' Antimo
Monte-pulciano
Todi
Montefalco
Orvieto
Civita di Bagnoregio
Bevagna
Lake Bolsena
30 Kilometers
30 Miles
Viterbo
Bomarzo
N
Tarquinia
LAZIO
Tiber R.
Civitavecchia
Cerveteri
Tyrrhenian Sea
VATICAN CITY ⊛⊛
Rome
Ostia

And Assisi, Siena, and Orvieto—while technically hill towns—are in a category by themselves: Bigger and with more major artistic and historic sights, they each get their own chapter. (The Orvieto chapter also includes my all-around favorite hill town, the stranded-on-a-hilltop Civita di Bagnoregio.)

For a relaxing break from big-city Italy, settle down in an *agriturismo*—a farmhouse that rents out rooms to travelers (usu-

ally for a minimum of a week in high season). These rural B&Bs—almost by definition in the middle of nowhere—provide a good home base from which to find the magic of Italy's hill towns. I've listed several good options throughout this chapter (for more information, see "Agritourism" on page 29).

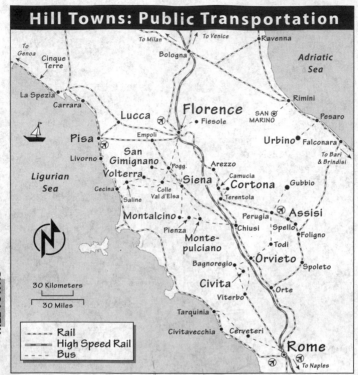

Hill Towns: Public Transportation

HILL TOWNS

Getting Around the Hill Towns

While you can reach just about any place with public buses, taxis, and loads of patience, most hill towns are easier and more efficient to visit by car.

By Bus or Train

Traveling by public transportation is cheap and connects you with the locals. While trains link some of the towns, hill towns—being on hills—don't quite fit the railroad plan. Stations are likely to be in the valley a couple of miles from the town center, usually connected efficiently by a local bus. Buses are often the only public-transportation choice to get between small hill towns. But, as with trains, they don't always drive up into the town itself. Fortunately, bus stations are sometimes connected to the town by escalator or elevator. (For more on traveling by train and bus in Italy, see the appendix.) If you're pinched for time, it makes sense to narrow your focus to one or two hill towns, or rent a car to see more.

By Car

Exploring the hill towns by car can be a great experience. But since

Driving in Tuscany: Distance & Time

EMILIA - ROMAGNA

To Milan

To Venice

To Cinque Terre
(La Spezia)

20 Kilometers

20 Miles

N

LE
MARCHE

50m · 1h
50m · 1h

Lucca
50m · 1h
Florence
190m · 3.5h
160m · 2.5h

Pisa
20m · .5h

70m · 1.25h
(via FIPILI)

70m · 1.5h

Livorno
15m · .5h
60m · 1.25h

55m · 1.5h

40m · 75h
(via S-2)

45m · 1h (via superstrada)

45m · 1.5h
(via S-222)

75m · 1.5h
(via A-1)

70m · 1.5h

San
Gimignano
20m
.5h

Cortona
40m · 1h

Volterra

30m · .75h

Siena
45m · 1h

50m · 1h
40m · 1.5h
(via S-438)
20m · 75h

30m · .75h
40m · 1h

To
Assisi

40m · 1h
30m · .75h
35m · 1h
San Galgano
Monastery
55m · 1.5h
30m · 1h
15m · .5h
Montalcino
10m · .25h
Pienza
75m · .5h
Chiusi

Monte-
pulciano

UMBRIA
To Assisi
35m · 1h
60m · 1.5h

Mediterranean
Sea

m = miles h = hours
Note: Your times may
vary based on traffic,
construction and
road conditions.

210m · 4h

60m · 1.5h

Bagnoregio
(Civita)

Orvieto
15m · .5h
75m · 1.5h

To
Rome

LAZIO
To
Rome

a car is an expensive, worthless headache in cities like Florence and Rome, wait to pick up your car until the last sizeable town you visit (or pick it up at the nearest airport to avoid big-city traffic). Then use the car for lacing together the hill towns and exploring the countryside. For more on car rentals and driving in Italy, see the appendix.

A big, detailed regional road map (buy one at a newsstand or gas station) and a semiskilled navigator are essential. Freeways (such as the toll autostrada and the non-toll *superstrada*) provide the fastest way to connect two points, but the smaller roads, including the super-scenic S-222, which runs through the heart of the Chianti region (connecting Florence and Siena), are more rewarding. For more joyrides—from Siena to

Montalcino, and from Montalcino to Montepulciano—see "The Crete Senese" on page 738.

Parking throughout this region can be challenging. Some towns don't allow visitors to park in the city center, so you'll need to leave your car outside the walls and walk into town. Signs reading *Zona Traffico Limitato (ZTL)*—often above a red circle—mark areas where no driving or parking is allowed. Parking lots, indicated by big blue *P* signs, are usually free and plentiful outside city walls (and in some cases are linked to the town center by elevators or escalators). In some towns, you can park on the street; nearby kiosks sell "pay and display" tickets. In general, white lines indicate free parking, blue lines mean you have to pay, and yellow lines are spaces reserved for local residents. To reduce the threat of theft (no guarantees, though), choose a parking lot instead of street parking when possible. Your hotelier can also recommend safe parking options.

Between Florence and Siena

Two fine hill towns—one famous, the other underrated—sit in the middle of the triangle formed by three major destinations: Florence, Siena, and Pisa. If driving between those cities, it makes sense to detour either to picturesque but touristy San Gimignano, or charming and authentic-feeling Volterra. (Or you could use one of them as a home base for reaching the bigger towns.) While they're only about a 30-minute drive apart, they're poorly connected to each other by public transit (requiring an infrequent two-hour connection); if you're relying on buses, San Gimignano is easier to reach, but Volterra rewards the additional effort.

San Gimignano

The epitome of a Tuscan hill town, with 14 medieval towers still standing (out of an original 72), San Gimignano (sahn jee-meen-YAH-noh) is a perfectly pre-

served tourist trap. There are no important interiors to sightsee, and the town is packed with crass commercialism. The locals seem spoiled by the easy money of tourism, and most of the rustic is faux. The fact that this small town supports two torture museums is a comment on the caliber of the masses who choose to visit. But San Gimignano is so easy to reach and visually so beautiful that it remains a good stop. It's enchanting at night, when it's yours alone. For this reason, San Gimignano is an ideal place to go against the touristic flow—arrive late in the day, enjoy it at twilight, then take off in the morning before the deluge begins.

In the 13th century—back in the days of Romeo and Juliet—feuding noble families ran the hill towns. They'd periodically battle things out from the protection of their respective family towers. Pointy skylines like San Gimignano's were the norm in medieval Tuscany.

San Gimignano's cuisine is mostly what you might find in Siena—typical Tuscan home cooking. *Cinghiale* (cheeng-GAH-lay, boar) is served in almost every way: stews, soups, cutlets, and, my favorite, salami. Most shops will give you a sample before you commit to buying. The area is well known for producing some of the best saffron in Italy (collected from the purple flowers of *Crocus sativus*); you'll find the spice for sale in shops (it's fairly expensive) and as a flavoring in meals at finer restaurants. Although Tuscany is normally a red-wine region, the most famous Tuscan white wine comes from here: the inexpensive, light, and fruity Vernaccia di San Gimignano. Look for the green "DOCG" label around the neck for the best quality (see "Wines Labels and Lingo" on page 45).

Orientation to San Gimignano

While the basic ▲▲▲ sight here is the town of San Gimignano itself, there are a few worthwhile stops. From the town gate, head straight up the traffic-free town's cobbled main drag to Piazza della Cisterna (with its 13th-century well). The town sights cluster around the adjoining Piazza del Duomo.

Tourist Information

The helpful TI is in the old center on Piazza del Duomo (daily March-Oct 10:00-13:00 & 15:00-19:00, Nov-Feb 10:00-13:00 & 14:00-18:00, free maps, sells bus tickets, books rooms, handles VAT refunds, tel. 0577-940-008, www.sangimignano.com).

If interested, ask if the TI is still offering a two-hour **guided walk** in English and Italian on weekends; if they are, book it the day before by 18:00 (April-Oct Sat-Sun at 11:00, €20; includes admission either to the Duomo or to the Civic Museum and Tower; pay and meet at TI). They also offer a two-hour minibus tour to a countryside winery (€20, April-Oct Tue and Thu at 17:00).

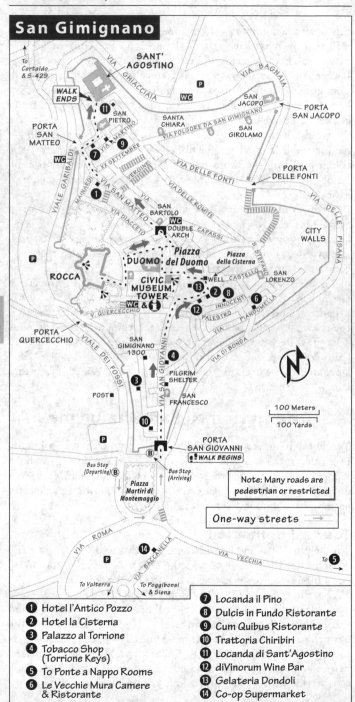

San Gimignano

1. Hotel l'Antico Pozzo
2. Hotel la Cisterna
3. Palazzo al Torrione
4. Tobacco Shop (Torrione Keys)
5. To Ponte a Nappo Rooms
6. Le Vecchie Mura Camere & Ristorante
7. Locanda il Pino
8. Dulcis in Fundo Ristorante
9. Cum Quibus Ristorante
10. Trattoria Chiribiri
11. Locanda di Sant'Agostino
12. diVinorum Wine Bar
13. Gelateria Dondoli
14. Co-op Supermarket

Arrival in San Gimignano

The **bus** stops at the main town gate, Porta San Giovanni. There's no baggage storage anywhere in town, so you're better off leaving your bags in Siena or Florence.

You can't **drive** within the walled town. There are three pay lots a short walk outside the walls: The handiest is Parcheggio Montemaggio, just outside Porta San Giovanni (€2/hour, €20/day). The one below the roundabout and Co-op supermarket, called Parcheggio Giubileo, is least expensive (€1.50/hour, €6/day). And at the north end of town, by Porta San Jacopo, is Parcheggio Bagnaia (€2/hour, €15/day). Note that some lots—including the one directly in front of the Co-op and the one just outside Porta San Matteo—are designated for locals and have a one-hour limit for tourists.

Helpful Hints

Market Day: Thursday is market day on Piazza del Duomo (8:00-13:00), but for local merchants, every day is a sales frenzy.

Services: A public **WC** is just off Piazza della Cisterna (€0.50); others are at the Rocca fortress, just outside Porta San Matteo, and at the Parcheggio Bagnaia parking lot.

Shuttle Bus: A little electric shuttle bus does its laps all day from Porta San Giovanni to Piazza della Cisterna to Porta San Matteo. Route #1 runs back and forth through town; route #2—which runs only in summer—conveniently connects the three parking lots to the town center. Each route runs about hourly (€0.75 one-way, €1.50 for all-day pass, buy ticket in advance from TI or tobacco shop, possible to buy all-day pass on bus).

Self-Guided Walk

Welcome to San Gimignano

This quick walking tour will take you across town, from the bus stop at Porta San Giovanni through the town's main squares to the Duomo, and on to the Sant'Agostino Church.

• *Start, as most tourists do, at the Porta San Giovanni gate at the bottom end of town.*

Porta San Giovanni: San Gimignano lies about 25 miles from both Siena and Florence, a good stop for pilgrims en route to those cities, and on a naturally fortified hilltop that encouraged settlement. The town's walls were built in the 13th century, and gates like this helped regulate who came and went. Today, modern posts keep out all but service and emergency vehicles. The small square just outside the gate features a memorial to the town's WWII dead.

Follow the pilgrims' route (and flood of modern tourists) through the gate and up the main drag.

About 100 yards up, on the right, is a pilgrims' shelter (12th-century, Pisan Romanesque). The eight-pointed Maltese cross indicates that this was built by the Knights of Malta, whose early mission (before they became a military unit) was to provide hospitality for pilgrims. It was one of 11 such shelters in town. Today, only the wall of this shelter remains.

• *Carry on past all manner of touristy rip-off shops, up to the town's central Piazza della Cisterna. Sit on the steps of the well.*

Piazza della Cisterna: The piazza is named for the cistern that is served by the old well standing in the center of this square. A clever system of pipes drained rainwater from the nearby rooftops into the underground cistern. This square has been the center of the town since the ninth century. Turn in a slow circle and observe the commotion of rustic-yet-proud facades crowding in a tight huddle around the well. Imagine this square in pilgrimage

times, lined by inns and taverns for the town's guests. Now finger the grooves in the lip of the well and imagine generations of maids and children fetching water. Each Thursday, the square fills with a market—as it has for more than a thousand years.

• *Notice San Gimignano's famous towers.*

The Towers: Of the original 72 towers, only 14 survive. Before effective city walls were developed, rich people fortified their

own homes with these towers: They provided a handy refuge when ruffians and rival city-states were sacking the town. If under attack, tower owners would set fire to the external wooden staircase, leaving the sole entrance unreachable a story up; inside, fleeing nobles pulled up behind them the ladders that connected each level, leaving invaders no way to reach the stronghold at the tower's top. These towers became a standard part of medieval skylines. Even after town walls were built, the towers continued to rise—now to fortify noble families feuding within a town (Montague and Capulet-style).

In the 14th century, San Gimignano's good times turned very bad. In the year 1300, about 13,000 people lived within the walls. Then, in 1348, a six-month plague decimated the population, leaving the once-mighty town with barely 4,000 survivors. Once fiercely independent, now crushed and demoralized, San Gimignano came under Florence's control and was forced to tear down its towers. (The Banca CR Firenze building occupies the remains of one such toppled tower.) And, to add insult to injury, Florence redirected the vital trade route away from San Gimignano. The town never recovered, and poverty left it in a 14th-century architectural time warp. That well-preserved cityscape, ironically, is responsible for the town's prosperity today.

• *From the well, walk 30 yards uphill to the adjoining square with the cathedral.*

Piazza del Duomo: The square faces the former cathedral. The twin towers to the right are 10th century, among the first in town.

The stubby tower opposite the church is typical of a merchant's tower: main door on ground floor, warehouse upstairs, holes to hold beams that once supported wooden balconies and exterior staircases, heavy stone on the first floor, cheaper and lighter brick for upper stories.

• *On the piazza are the Civic Museum and Tower, worth checking out (see "Sights in San Gimignano," later). You'll also see the...*

Duomo (or Collegiata): Inside San Gimignano's Romanesque cathedral, Sienese Gothic art (14th century) lines the nave with parallel themes—Old Testament on the left and New Testament on the right. (For example, from back to front: Creation facing the Annunciation, the birth of Adam facing the Nativity, and the suffering of Job opposite the suffering of Jesus.) This is a classic use of art to teach. Study the fine Creation series (top left). Many scenes are portrayed with a local 14th-century "slice of life" setting, to help lay townspeople relate to Jesus—in the same way that many white Christians are more comfortable thinking of Jesus as Caucasian (€3.50, €5.50 combo-ticket includes mediocre Religious Art Museum—skip it; April-Oct Mon-Fri 10:00-19:10, Sat 10:00-17:10, Sun 12:30-19:10; Nov-March Mon-Sat 10:00-16:40, Sun 12:30-16:40; last entry 20 minutes before closing, buy ticket and enter from the courtyard around the left side).

• *From the church, hike uphill (passing the church on your left), following signs to* Rocca e Parco di Montestaffoli. *Keep walking until you enter a peaceful hilltop park and olive grove within the shell of a 14th-century fortress.*

Hilltop Views at the Rocca: On the far side, 33 steps take you to the top of a little tower (free) for the best views of San Gimi-

HILL TOWNS

gnano's skyline; the far end of town and the Sant'Agostino Church (where this walk ends); and a commanding 360-degree view of the Tuscan countryside. San Gimignano is surrounded by olives, grapes, cypress trees, and—in the Middle Ages—lots of wild dangers. Back then, farmers lived inside the walls and were thankful for the protection.

• *Return to the bottom of Piazza del Duomo, turn left, and continue your walk across town, cutting under the double arch (from the town's first wall). In around 1200, this defined the end of town. The* **Church of San Bartolo** *stood just outside the wall (on the right). The Maltese cross over the door indicates that it likely served as a hostel for pilgrims. As you continue down Via San Matteo, notice that the crowds have dropped by at least half. Enjoy the breathing room as you pass a fascinating array of stone facades from the 13th and 14th centuries—now a happy cancan of wine shops and galleries. Reaching the gateway at the end of town, follow signs to the right to reach...*

Sant'Agostino Church: This tranquil church, at the far end of town (built by the Augustinians who arrived in 1260), has fewer crowds and more soul. Behind the altar, a lovely fresco cycle by Benozzo Gozzoli (who painted the exquisite Chapel of the Magi in the Medici-Riccardi Palace in Florence) tells of the life of St. Augustine, a North African monk who preached simplicity. The kind, English-speaking friars (from Britain and the US) are happy to tell you about their church and way of life, and also have Mass in English on Sundays at 11:00. Pace the peaceful cloister before heading back into the tourist mobs (free, €0.50 lights the frescoes; April-Oct daily 7:00-12:00 & 15:00-19:00; Nov-March Tue-Sun 7:00-12:00 & 15:00-18:00, Mon 16:00-18:00). Their fine little shop, with books on the church and its art, is worth a look.

Sights in San Gimignano

▲Civic Museum and Tower
(Museo Civico and Torre Grossa)

This small, fun museum, consisting of just three unfurnished rooms and a tower, is inside City Hall (Palazzo Comunale). The main room (across from the ticket desk), called the **Sala di Consiglio** (a.k.a. Dante Hall), is covered in festive frescoes, including the *Maestà* by Lippo Memmi. This virtual copy of Simone Martini's *Maestà* in Siena proves that Memmi didn't have quite the same talent as his famous brother-in-law.

Upstairs, the **Pinacoteca** displays a classy little painting collection of mostly altarpieces. The highlight is a 1422 altarpiece by Taddeo di Bartolo honoring St. Gimignano (far end of last room). You can see the saint, with the town—bristling with towers—in his hands, surrounded by events from his life.

Before going back downstairs, be sure to stop by the **Mayor's Room** (Camera del Podestà, across the stairwell from the Pinacoteca). Frescoed in 1310 by Memmo di Filippuccio, it offers an intimate and candid peek into the 14th century. The theme: profane love. As you enter, look to the left corner where a young man is ready to experience the world. He hits his parents up for a bag of money and is free. On the opposite wall (above the window), you'll see a series of bad decisions: Almost immediately he's entrapped by two prostitutes, who lead him into a tent where he loses his money, is turned out, and is beaten. Above the door, from left to right, you see a parade of better choices: marriage, the cradle of love, the bride led to the groom's house, and newlyweds bathing together and retiring happily to their bed.

The highlight for most visitors is a chance to climb the **Tower** (Torre Grossa, entrance halfway down the stairs from the Pina

coteca). The city's tallest tower, 200 feet and 218 steps up, rewards those who climb it with a commanding view. See if you can count the town's 14 towers (yes, that includes the stubby little one just below this tower). It's a sturdy, modern staircase most of the way, but the last stretch is a steep, ladder-like climb.

HILL TOWNS

Coming back down to earth, you leave the complex via a delightful stony loggia and courtyard out back.

Cost and Hours: €5 includes museum and tower, daily April-Sept 9:30-19:00, Oct-March 11:00-17:30, Piazza del Duomo, tel. 0577-990-312.

San Gimignano 1300

This small but interesting attraction, located inside the Palazzo Ficarelli on a quiet street a block over from the main street, is a trip back in time. When possible, attendants like to lead visitors on individual tours around the small exhibit. The highlight is a painstakingly rendered 1:100 scale clay model of San Gimignano at the turn of the 14th century. You can see the 72 original "tower houses" and marvel at how unchanged the street plan remains today. You'll peek into cross-sections of buildings, view scenes of medieval life both within and outside the city walls, and watch videos about town history and the making of the model. After walking through a gallery of modern Italian sculpture, your visit ends in the ceramics workshop next door, where models like this one are created from wet lumps of clay. (Conveniently, the "workshop" is one corner of a ceramics shop.) While cynics might view this as little more than a gimmick to sell more little ceramic buildings, the detail of the model is truly enchanting.

Cost and Hours: €5; April-Oct daily 10:00-19:00; Nov-March Mon-Fri 10:00-17:00, Sat-Sun until 18:00; Via Berignano 23, tel. 0577-941-078, www.sangimignano1300.com.

Sleeping in San Gimignano

Although the town is a zoo during the daytime, locals outnumber tourists when evening comes, and San Gimignano becomes mellow and enjoyable. Drivers can unload near their hotels, then park outside the walls in recommended lots. Hotel websites provide instructions.

$$$ Hotel l'Antico Pozzo is an elegantly restored, 15th-century townhouse with 18 tranquil, comfortable rooms, a peaceful interior courtyard terrace, and an elite air (Sb-€95, small Db-€120, standard Db-€140, big Db-€180, includes breakfast, air-con, elevator, free Wi-Fi, near Porta San Matteo at Via San Matteo 87, tel. 0577-942-014, www.anticopozzo.com, info@anticopozzo.com; Emanuele, Elisabetta, and Mariangela). If arriving by bus, save a crosstown walk by asking for the Porta San Matteo stop (rather than getting off at the main stop near Porta San Giovanni).

$$$ Hotel la Cisterna, right on Piazza della Cisterna, feels old and stately, with 49 predictable rooms, some with panoramic view terraces—a scene from the film *Tea with Mussolini* was filmed from one (Sb-€78, Db-€100, Db with view-€125, Db with view terrace—€140, 10 percent discount with this book when you book direct, includes buffet breakfast, air-con, elevator, free Wi-Fi, good restaurant with great view, closed Jan-Feb, Piazza della Cisterna 23, tel. 0577-940-328, www.hotelcisterna.it, info@hotelcisterna.it, Alessio).

$$$ Ponte a Nappo, run by enterprising Carla Rossi (who doesn't speak English) and her sons Francesco and Andrea (who do), has seven comfortable rooms and two apartments in a kid-friendly farmhouse. Located a long half-mile below town (best for drivers, but doable for hardy walkers), this place has killer views. A picnic dinner lounging on their comfy garden furniture as the sun sets is good Tuscan living (Db-€100-130, 2-6 person apartment-€130-250, price depends on season and length of stay, for best price book direct and mention Rick Steves, air-con mid-June-mid-Sept only, free Wi-Fi, free parking, pool, free loaner bikes, lunch and dinner sometimes available to guests, 15-minute walk or 5-minute drive from Porta San Giovanni, tel. 0577-907-282, mobile 349-882-1565, www.accommodation-sangimignano.com, info@rossicarla.it). About 100 yards below the monument square at Porta San Giovanni, find Via Vecchia (not left or right, but down

---

Sleep Code

(€1 = about $1.30, country code: 39)

S = Single, **D** = Double/Twin, **T** = Triple, **Q** = Quad, **b** = bathroom, **s** = shower only. Unless otherwise noted, credit cards are accepted, English is spoken, and breakfast is included (but usually optional). Many towns in Italy levy a hotel tax of about €2 per person, per night, which is generally not included in the rates I've quoted.

To help you sort easily through these listings, I've divided the accommodations into three categories based on the price for a standard double room with bath:

$$$ Higher Priced—Most rooms €100 or more.

$$ Moderately Priced—Most rooms between €70-100.

$ Lower Priced —Most rooms €70 or less.

Prices can change without notice; verify the hotel's current rates online or by email. For the best prices, always book direct.

---

a tiny road) and follow it down a dirt road for five minutes by car. They also rent a dozen or so rooms and apartments in town (including some in the Palazzo Tortoli, a stone tower right on the main square, Db-€75-110, pay Wi-Fi, each room is described on their website).

$$ Palazzo al Torrione, on an untrampled side street just inside Porta San Giovanni, is quiet and handy, and generally better than most hotels (even though they don't have a full-time reception). Their 10 modern rooms are spacious and tastefully appointed (Db-€90, terrace Db-€110, Tb-€100, terrace Tb-€120, Qb-€120-130, 10 percent discount with this book when you book direct, breakfast-€7, communal kitchen with Wi-Fi, parking-€6/day, inside and left of gate at Via Berignano 76; operated from tobacco shop 2 blocks away, on the main drag at Via San Giovanni 59; tel. 0577-940-480, mobile 338-938-1656, www.palazzoaltorrione. com, palazzoaltorrione@palazzoaltorrione.com, Vanna and Francesco).

$ Le Vecchie Mura Camere offers three good rooms above their restaurant in the old town (Db-€65, no breakfast, air-con, free Wi-Fi, Via Piandornella 15, tel. 0577-940-270, www.vecchiemura.it, info@vecchiemura.it, Bagnai family).

$ Locanda il Pino has just seven rooms and a big living room. It's dank but clean and quiet. Run by English-speaking Elena and her family, it sits above their elegant restaurant just inside Porta San Matteo (Db-€55, no breakfast, free Wi-Fi in lobby, easy parking just outside the gate, Via Cellolese 4, tel. 0577-940-415, locanda@ ristoranteilpino.it). If you're arriving by bus, ask for the Porta San Matteo stop, rather than the main stop near Porta San Giovanni.

Eating in San Gimignano

My first two listings cling to quiet, rustic lanes overlooking the Tuscan hills (yet just a few steps off the main street); the rest are buried deep in the old center.

Dulcis in Fundo Ristorante, small and family-run, proudly serves modest portions of "revisited" Tuscan cuisine (with a modern twist and gourmet presentation) in a jazzy ambience. This enlightened place, whose menu identifies the sources of their ingredients, offers lots of vegetarian options and gladly caters to gluten-free diets—rare in Tuscany (€12 pastas, €13-16 *secondi,* meals served 12:30-14:30 & 19:15-21:30, closed Wed, Vicolo degli Innocenti 21, tel. 0577-941-919, Roberto and Cristina).

Le Vecchie Mura Ristorante has good and fast service, great prices, tasty if unexceptional home cooking, and the ultimate view. It's romantic indoors or out. They have a dressy, modern interior where you can dine with a view of the busy stainless-steel kitchen under rustic vaults, but the main reason to come is for the incredible cliffside garden terrace. Cliffside tables are worth reserving in advance by calling or dropping by: Ask for "front view" (€8-11 pastas, €12-15 *secondi,* open only for dinner from 18:00, last order at 22:00, closed Tue, Via Piandornella 15, tel. 0577-940-270, Bagnai family).

Cum Quibus ("In Company"), tucked away near Porta San Matteo, has a smallish dining room with soft music, beamed ceilings, and modern touches; it also offers al fresco tables in its interior patio in summer. Lorenzo and Fabiana produce tasty Tuscan cuisine, fresh truffle specialties, and artistic desserts (€10 pastas, €15 *secondi,* truffle dishes more expensive, Wed-Mon 12:30-14:30 & 19:00-22:00, closed Tue, reservations advised, Via San Martino 17, tel. 0577-943-199, www.cumquibus.it).

Trattoria Chiribiri, just inside Porta San Giovanni on the left, serves homemade pastas and desserts at remarkably fair prices. While its petite size and tight seating make it hot in the summer, it's a good budget option—and, as such, it's in all the guidebooks (€8 pastas, €10 *secondi,* daily 11:00-23:00, Piazza della Madonna 1, tel. 0577-941-948, Maria and Maurizio).

Locanda di Sant'Agostino spills out onto the peaceful square, facing Sant'Agostino Church. It's cheap and cheery, serving lunch and dinner daily—big portions of basic food in a restful setting. Dripping with wheat stalks and atmosphere on the inside, there's shady on-the-square seating outside (€8 pizzas, pastas, and *brus-*

chette; €9-15 *secondi*, daily 11:00-22:00, closed Tue off-season and Jan-Feb, Piazza Sant'Agostino 15, tel. 0577-943-141, Genziana and sons).

Enoteca: **diVinorum,** a cool wine bar with a small entrance right on Piazza Cisterna, has a contemporary cellar atmosphere and—best of all—a row of tables out back overlooking rolling Tuscan hills (just downhill and toward the main drag from Dulcis in Fundo, recommended earlier; at mealtimes, you'll have to order food to sit at the outdoor tables). They have local wines by the glass (€3-5) as well as snacks that can easily make a light meal (€10-15 *antipasti* plates, €7-8 *bruschette* and warm plates, daily 11:00-21:30, Nov-April until 20:00, Piazza Cisterna 30 or Via degli Innocenti 5, tel. 0577-907-192, Matteo).

Picnics: The big, modern **Co-op supermarket** sells all you need for a nice spread (Mon-Sat 8:30-20:00, Sun 8:30-12:30 except closed Sun Nov-March, at parking lot below Porta San Giovanni). Or browse the little shops guarded by boar heads within the town walls; they sell pricey boar meat *(cinghiale)*. Pick up 100 grams (about a quarter pound) of boar, cheese, bread, and wine and enjoy a picnic in the garden at the Rocca or the park outside Porta San Giovanni.

Gelato: To cap the evening and sweeten your late-night city stroll, stop by **Gelateria Dondoli** on Piazza della Cisterna (at #4). Gelato-maker Sergio was a member of the Italian team that won the official Gelato World Cup—and his gelato really is a cut above (daily 8:00-24:00, closes at 19:00 off-season, tel. 0577-942-244, Dondoli family).

San Gimignano Connections

Bus tickets are sold at the bar just inside the town gate or at the TI. Many connections require a change at Poggibonsi (poh-jee-BOHN-see, with a soft "g"), which is also the nearest train station.

From San Gimignano by Bus to: Florence (hourly, less on Sun, 1.5-2 hours, change in Poggibonsi, €6.80), **Siena** (8/day direct, on Sun must change in Poggibonsi, 1.25 hours, €6), **Volterra** (4/day Mon-Sat; on Sun only 1/day—in the late afternoon and usually crowded—with no return to San Gimignano; 2 hours, change in Colle Val d'Elsa, €6.15). Note that the bus connection to Volterra is four times as long as the drive; if you're desperate to get there faster, you can pay about €70 for a taxi.

By Car: San Gimignano is an easy 45-minute drive from Florence (take the A-1 exit marked *Firenze Certosa,* then a right past tollbooth following *Siena per 4 corsie* sign; exit the freeway at Poggibonsi). From San Gimignano, it's a scenic and windy half-hour drive to Volterra.

Volterra

Encircled by impressive walls and topped with a grand fortress, Volterra sits high above the rich farmland surrounding it. More

than 2,000 years ago, Volterra was one of the most important Etruscan cities, and much larger than we see today. Greek-trained Etruscan artists worked here, leaving a significant stash of art, particularly funerary urns. Eventually Volterra was absorbed into the Roman Empire, and for centuries it was an independent city-state. Volterra fought bitterly against the Florentines, but like many Tuscan towns, it lost in the end and was given a fortress atop the city to "protect" its citizens.

Unlike other famous towns in Tuscany, Volterra feels neither cutesy nor touristy...but real, vibrant, and almost oblivious to the allure of the tourist dollar. This probably stems from the Volterrans' feisty resistance to change. (At a recent town meeting about whether to run high-speed Internet cable to the town, a local grumbled, "The Etruscans didn't need it—why do we?") This stubbornness helps make Volterra a refreshing change of pace from its more commercial neighbors. It also boasts some particularly fine sights for a small town, from a remarkably intact ancient Roman theater, to a finely decorated Pisan Romanesque cathedral, to an excellent museum of Etruscan artifacts. All in all, Volterra is my favorite small town in Tuscany.

Orientation to Volterra

Compact and walkable, the city stretches out from the pleasant Piazza dei Priori to the old city gates.

Tourist Information

The helpful TI is on the main square, at Piazza dei Priori 19 (daily 9:00-13:00 & 14:00-18:00, tel. 0588-87257, www.volterratur.it). The TI's excellent €5 audioguide narrates 20 stops (2-for-1 discount on audioguides with this book).

Arrival in Volterra

By Public Transport: Buses stop at Piazza Martiri della Libertà in the town center. Train travelers can reach the town with a short bus ride (see "Volterra Connections," later.)

By Car: Drivers will find the town ringed with easy numbered parking lots (#5, #6, and #8 are free; #3 is for locals only). The most central lots are the pay lots at Porta Fiorentina and underground at Piazza Martiri della Libertà (€1.50/hour, €11/24 hours).

Helpful Hints

Market Day: The market is on Saturday morning near the Roman Theater (8:00-13:00, at parking lot #5; in winter, it's right on Piazza dei Priori). The TI hands out a list of other market days in the area.

Festivals: Volterra's Medieval Festival takes place the third and fourth Sundays of August. Fall is a popular time for food festivals—check with the TI for dates and events planned.

Internet Access: Web & Wine has a few terminals, fine wine by the glass, and organic vegetarian food (€3/hour, no minimum, summer daily 9:30-1:00 in the morning, closed Thu in Sept-May, Via Porta all'Arco 11-15, tel. 0588-81531, Lallo speaks English). **Enjoy Café Internet Point** has a couple terminals in their basement (€3/hour, daily 6:30-1:00 in the morning, Piazza dei Martiri 3, tel. 0588-80530).

Laundry: The handy self-service **Lavanderia Azzurra** is just off the main square (€4 wash, €4 dry, daily 7:00-23:00, Via Roma 7, tel. 0588-80030).

Tours in Volterra

▲▲Guided Volterra Walk

Annie Adair (also listed individually, next) and her colleagues offer a great one-hour, English-only introductory walking tour of Volterra for €10. The walk touches on Volterra's Etruscan, Roman, and medieval history, as well as the contemporary cultural scene (April-July and Sept-Oct daily, rain or shine, at 18:00; meet in front of alabaster shop on Piazza Martiri della Libertà, no need to reserve—just show up, they need a minimum of 3 people, or €30—to make the tour go, www.volterrawalkingtour.com or www.tuscantour.com, info@volterrawalkingtour.com). There's no better way to spend €10 and one hour in this city.

Local Guide

American **Annie Adair** is an excellent city guide. She and her husband Francesco, a sommelier, organize private history and wine tours and even Tuscan weddings for Americans (€50/hour, minimum 2 hours, tel. 0588-086-201, mobile 347-143-5004, www.tus-

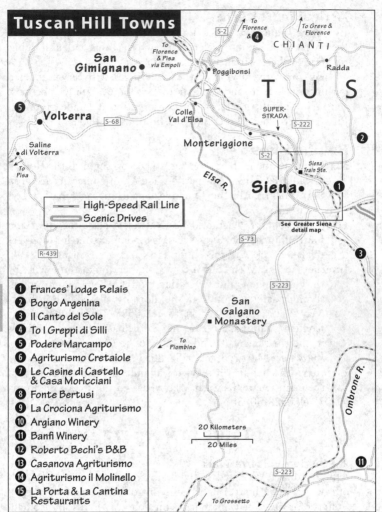

Tuscan Hill Towns

To Florence & ④
To Greve & Florence
S-2
CHIANTI

San Gimignano
To Florence & Pisa via Empoli
Poggibonsi
Radda

T U S

⑤ Volterra
S-68
Colle Val d'Elsa
SUPER-STRADA
S-222

Saline di Volterra
Monteriggione
②

To Pisa
Elsa R.
S-2
Siena Train Stn.
①

Siena •

High-Speed Rail Line
Scenic Drives

See Greater Siena detail map

R-439
S-73
③

S-223

① Frances' Lodge Relais
② Borgo Argenina
③ Il Canto del Sole
④ To I Greppi di Silli
⑤ Podere Marcampo
⑥ Agriturismo Cretaiole
⑦ Le Casine di Castello & Casa Moricciani
⑧ Fonte Bertusi
⑨ La Crociona Agriturismo
⑩ Argiano Winery
⑪ Banfi Winery
⑫ Roberto Bechi's B&B
⑬ Casanova Agriturismo
⑭ Agriturismo il Molinello
⑮ La Porta & La Cantina Restaurants

San Galgano ■ Monastery

To Piombino

Ombrone R.

20 Kilometers
20 Miles

S-223

⑪

To Grosseto

HILL TOWNS

cantour.com, info@tuscantour.com). Francesco leads a crash one-hour "Wine Tasting 101" class in sampling Tuscan wines, held at a local wine bar (€50 per group plus cost of wine).

Sights in Volterra

I've arranged these sights as a handy little town walk, connected by directions on foot. Not all the sights will interest everyone, so skim the listings to decide which detours appeal to you.

• *Begin your visit of town at the Etruscan Arch. To find it, go all the way down to the bottom of Via Porta all'Arco (you'll find the top of this street*

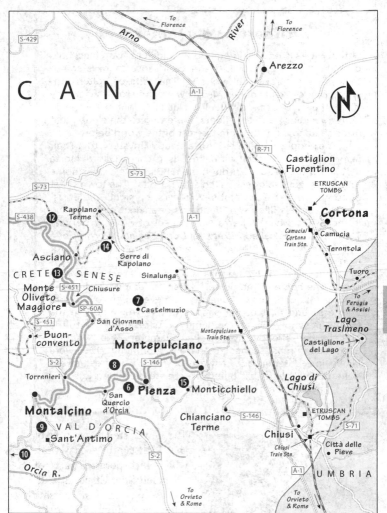

between Piazza Martiri della Libertà, with the town bus stop, and the main square, Piazza dei Priori).

▲Etruscan Arch (Porta all'Arco)

Volterra's most famous sight is its Etruscan arch, built of massive, volcanic tuff stones in the fourth century B.C. (for more information on tuff, see the sidebar on page 696). Volterra's original wall was four miles around—twice the size of the wall that encircles it today. With 25,000 people, Volterra was a key trading center and one of 12 leading towns in the confederation of *Etruria Propria*. The three seriously eroded heads, dating from the first century B.C., show what happens when you leave something outside for 2,000 years.

Otherworldly Volterra

Sitting on its stony main square at midnight, watching bats dart about as if they own the place, I sense there is something supernatural about Volterra. The cliffs of Volterra inspired Dante's "cliffs of hell." In the winter, the town's vibrancy is smothered under a deadening cloak of clouds. The name Volterra means "land that floats"—referring to the clouds that often seem to cut it off from the rest of the world below.

The people of Volterra live in a cloud of mystery, too. Their favorite cookie, crunchy with almonds, is called Ossi di Morta ("bones of the dead"). Through the 1980s, Volterra was home to Italy's second-biggest psychiatric hospital. The town's first disco was named Catacombs. Volterra's top sight—the Etruscan Museum—is filled with hundreds of ancient caskets. And in the 1970s, when Volterra was the set of a wildly popular TV horror series called *Ritratto di Donna Velata (Portrait of a Veiled Woman)*, all of Italy tuned in to Volterra every week for a good scare.

Fans of the *Twilight* books and films may recognize Volterra as the home of the powerful clan of vampires called the Volturi. Author Stephanie Meyer had never been to Volterra before setting part of her second novel, *New Moon*, in the town; she simply picked the name for its resemblance to the one she had already given to her characters, the "Volturi." Even though most scenes in the *New Moon* film (2009) were filmed in Montepulciano, a wave of *Twilight* interest swept Volterra. *Twilight* is just one more chapter in a long tale of a town that revels in being otherworldly.

The newer stones are part of the 13th-century city wall, which incorporated parts of the much older Etruscan wall.

A plaque just outside remembers June 30, 1944. That night, Nazi forces were planning to blow up the arch to slow the Allied advance. To save their treasured landmark, Volterrans ripped up the stones that pave Via Porta all'Arco and plugged the gate, managing to convince the Nazi commander that there was no need to blow up the arch. Today, all the stones are back in their places, and like silent heroes, they welcome you through the oldest standing Etruscan gate into Volterra. Locals claim this as the only surviving round arch of the Etruscan age; most experts believe this is where the Romans got the idea for using a keystone in their arches.

• *Go through the arch and head up Via Porta all'Arco, which I like to call...*

"Artisan Lane" (Via Porta all'Arco)

This steep and atmospheric strip is lined with interesting shops featuring the work of artisans and producers. Because of its alabaster heritage, Volterra attracted craftsmen and artists, who brought with them a rich variety of handiwork (shops generally open Mon-Sat 10:00-13:00 & 16:00-19:00, closed Sun; the TI produces a free booklet called *Handicraft in Volterra*).

From the Etruscan Arch, browse your way up the hill, checking out these shops and items (listed from bottom to top): La Mia Fattoria—a co-op of producers of cheese, salami, and olive oil lets you buy direct at farm prices (just up Via Laberinti near #52); alabaster shops (#57, #50, and #45); book bindery and papery (#26); jewelry (#25); etchings (#23); Web & Wine (Internet access; #11-15); and bronze work (#6).

• *Reaching the top of Via Porta all'Arco, turn left and walk a few steps into Volterra's main square, Piazza dei Priori. It's dominated by the...*

Palazzo dei Priori

Volterra's City Hall (c. 1209) claims to be the oldest of any Tuscan city state. It clearly inspired the more famous Palazzo Vecchio in Florence. Town halls like this are emblematic of an era when city-states were powerful. They were architectural exclamation points declaring that, around here, no pope or emperor called the shots. Towns such as Volterra were truly city-states—proudly independent and relatively democratic. They had their own armies, taxes, and even weights and measures. Notice the horizontal "cane" cut into the City Hall wall (right of the door). For a thousand years, this square hosted a market, and the "cane" was the local yardstick. When not in use for meetings or weddings, the city council chambers—lavishly painted and lit with fun dragon lamps, as they have been for centuries of town meetings—are open to visitors.

The tower was recently opened to the public. For the adventurous, 70 or so steps take you up a tight, winding, metal staircase to a small platform with great panoramic views of the city and surrounding countryside. Be aware that this is the bell tower; expect loud chimes if you visit on the hour or half-hour.

Cost and Hours: €1.50, €2.00 additional for tower, mid-March-Oct daily 10:30-17:30, Nov-mid-March Sat-Sun only 10:00-17:00.

• *Facing the City Hall, notice the black-and-white-striped wall to the right (set back from the square). The door in that wall leads into Volterra's...*

Duomo

This church is not as elaborate as its cousin in Pisa, but the simple 13th-century facade and the interior (rebuilt in the late 16th cen-

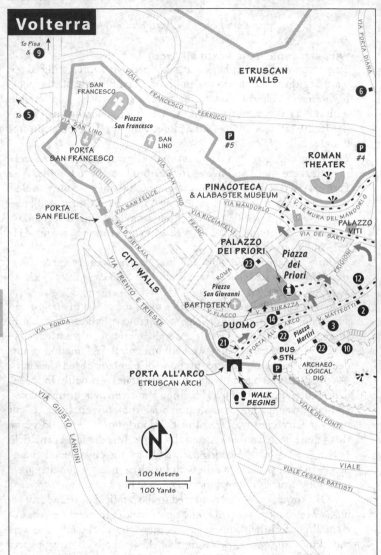

Volterra

To Pisa & 9

San Francesco

Piazza San Francesco

To 5

San Lino

ETRUSCAN WALLS

6

P #5

PORTA SAN FRANCESCO

VIALE FRANCESCO

FERRUCCI

VIA SAN LINO

VIA SAN LINO

VIA SAN FELICE

VIA RICCIARELLI

FRANC.

VIA MANDORLO

ROMAN THEATER

P #4

PINACOTECA & ALABASTER MUSEUM

V. LE MURA DEL MANDORLO

VIA PORTA DIANA

PALAZZO VITI

VIA DEI SARTI

PORTA SAN FELICE

PALAZZO DEI PRIORI

Piazza dei Priori

VIA D. PIETRAIA

VIA TRENTO E TRIESTE

CITY WALLS

VIA FONDA

VIA GIUSTO LANDINI

ROMA

23

Piazza San Giovanni

BAPTISTERY

DUOMO

V. FLACCO

14

V. TURAZZA

21

V. PORTA ALL'ARCO

PORTA ALL'ARCO ETRUSCAN ARCH

WALK BEGINS

22

PRIGIONI

12

2

V. MATTEOTTI

3

Piazza Martiri

22

10

BUS STN.

P #1

ARCHAEO-LOGICAL DIG

VIALE DEI PONTI

VIALE

VIALE CESARE BATTISTI

N

100 Meters

100 Yards

1 Hotel La Locanda

2 Albergo Etruria

3 Albergo Nazionale

4 To Park Hotel Le Fonti

5 To Albergo Villa Nencini & Old Etruscan Wall

6 La Primavera B&B

7 Seminario Vescovile Sant'Andrea

8 To Chiosco delle Monache Hostel, Hotel Foresteria & Trattoria da Bado

9 To Podere Marcampo

10 Ristorante Enoteca del Duca

11 Trattoria Don Beta

12 La Vecchia Lira

HILL TOWNS

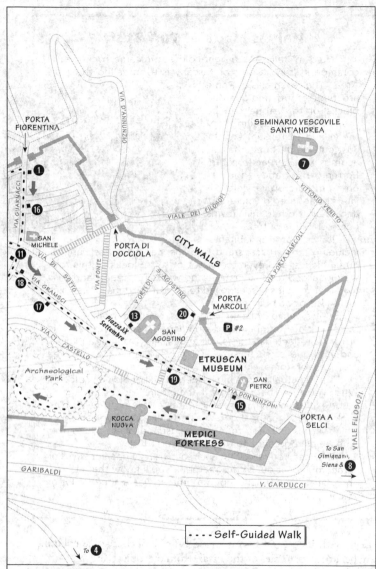

PORTA
FIORENTINA

❶

⓰

SAN
MICHELE

VIA GUARNACCI

VIA D'ANNUNZIO

SEMINARIO VESCOVILE
SANT'ANDREA

✚

❼

V. VITTORIO VENETO

VIALE DEI FILOSOFI

PORTA DI
DOCCIOLA

CITY WALLS

⓫

⓲

VIA DI SOTTO

VIA FONTE

V. ORTI DI S. AGOSTINO

PORTA
MARCOLI

VIA PORTA MARCOLI

⓱

VIA GRAMSCI

Piazza XX
Settembre

⓭

SAN
AGOSTINO

⓴

Ⓟ #2

VIA DI CASTELLO

Archaeological
Park

ETRUSCAN
MUSEUM

⓳

SAN
PIETRO

VIA DON MINZONI

⓯

PORTA A
SELCI

ROCCA
NUOVA

MEDICI
FORTRESS

VIALE FILOSOFI

To San
Gimignano,
Siena & ❽

GARIBALDI

V. CARDUCCI

- - - - Self-Guided Walk

To ❹

⓭ La Carabaccia

⓮ Ristorante il Sacco
Fiorentino

⓯ La Vena di Vino
Wine Bar

⓰ Ombra della Sera &
Pizzeria Tavernetta

⓱ Despar Market

⓲ L'Isola di Gusto Gelato

⓳ Alab'Arte Alabaster
Showroom

⓴ Alab'Arte Alabaster
Workshop

㉑ "Artisan Lane"

㉒ Internet Cafés (2)

㉓ Launderette

Italy Is Made of Tuff Stuff

Tuff (*tufo* in Italian) is a light-colored volcanic rock that is common in Italy. A part of Tuscany is even called the "Tuff Area." The seven hills of Rome are made of tuff, and quarried blocks of this stone can be seen in the Colosseum, Pantheon, and Castel Sant'Angelo. Just outside of Rome, the catacombs were carved from tuff. Sorrento rises above the sea on a tuff outcrop. Orvieto, Civita di Bagnoregio (pictured), and many other hill towns perch on bluffs of tuff.

Italy's early inhabitants, including the Etruscans and Romans, carved caves, tunnels, burial niches, and even roads out of tuff. Blocks of this rock were quarried to make houses and walls. Tuff is soft and easy to carve when it's first exposed to air, but hardens later, which makes it a good building stone.

Italy's tuff-producing volcanoes resulted from a lot of tectonic-plate bumping and grinding. This violent geologic history is reflected in Italy's volcanoes, like Vesuvius and Etna, and earthquakes such as the 2009 quake in the L'Aquila area northeast of Rome.

Tuff is actually just a big hardened pile of old volcanic ash. When volcanoes hold magma that contains a lot of water, they erupt explosively (think heat + water = steam = POW!). The exploded rock material gets blasted out as hot volcanic ash, which settles on the surrounding landscape, piles up, and over time welds together into the rock called tuff.

So when you're visiting an area in Italy of ancient caves or catacombs built out of this material, you'll know that at least once (and maybe more) upon a time, it was a site of a lot of volcanic activity.

tury), with its central nave flanked by monolithic stone columns, are beautiful examples of the Pisan Romanesque style.

Cost and Hours: Free, daily 8:00-12:30 & 15:00-18:00, Nov-March until 17:00, closed Fri 15:00-16:00 while the cleaners religiously perform their duties.

Visiting the Church: Enter through the door off Piazza dei Priori (technically the back door) and take a moment to let your eyes adjust to this dark, Romanesque space. (If you come through the main door around on Piazza San Giovanni, do this tour in reverse.) The interior was decorated mostly in the late 16th century, during Florentine rule under the Medici family. Their coat of arms, with its distinctive balls (called *palle*), is repeated multiple times throughout the building.

Head down into the nave to face the main altar. Up the stairs just to the right is a dreamy painted and gilded-wood *Deposition* (Jesus being taken down from the cross), restored to its original form. Carved in 1228, a generation before Giotto, it shows emotion and motion way ahead of its time (€1 buys some light).

The glowing **windows** in the transept and behind the altar are sheets of alabaster. These, along with the recorded Gregorian chants, add to the church's wonderful ambience.

The 12th-century marble **pulpit** is also beautifully carved. In the relief panel of the Last Supper, all the apostles are together except Judas, who's under the table with the evil dragon (his name is the only one not carved into the relief).

Just past the pulpit on the right (at the Rosary Chapel), check out the *Annunciation* by Fra Bartolomeo (who was a student of Fra Angelico and painted this in 1497). Bartolomeo delicately gives worshippers a way to see Mary "conceived by the Holy Spirit." Note the vibrant colors, exaggerated perspective, and Mary's *contrapposto* pose—all attributes of the Renaissance.

At the end of the nave, the **chapel** to the right of the doors has painted terra-cotta statue groups of the Nativity and the Adoration of the Magi, thought to be the work of master ceramists Luca and Andrea della Robbia. Luca is credited with inventing the glazing formula that makes his inventive sculptures shine even in poorly lit interiors.

To see a classically Pisan space, step outside the door into Piazza San Giovanni. A common arrangement in the Middle Ages was for the church to face the baptistery (you couldn't enter the church until you were baptized)...and for the hospital to face the cemetery (now the site of the local ambulance corps). These buildings all overlooked the same square. That's how it is in Pisa, and that's how it is here.

• *Exit the cathedral out the back door into the main square, Piazza dei Priori. Face the City Hall, and go down the street to the left; after one short block, you're standing at the head (on the left) of...*

▲Via Matteotti

The town's main drag, named after the popular Socialist leader Giacomo Matteotti (killed by the Fascists in 1924), provides a good cultural scavenger hunt.

At #1 is a typical Italian bank security door. (Step in and say, "Beam me up, Scotty.") Back outside, stand at the corner and look up and all around. Find the medieval griffin torch holder—symbol of Volterra—and imagine it holding a lit torch. The pharmacy sports the symbol of its medieval guild. Across the street from the bank, #2 is the base of what was a San Gimignano-style fortified

Tuscan tower. Look up and imagine heavy beams cantilevered out, supporting extra wooden rooms and balconies crowding out over the street. Throughout Tuscany, today's stark and stony old building fronts once supported a tangle of wooden extensions.

As you head down Via Matteotti, notice how the doors show centuries of refitting work. Doors that once led to these extra rooms are now partially bricked up to make windows. Contemplate urban density in the 14th century, before the plague thinned out the population. Be careful: There's a wild boar (a local delicacy) at #10.

At #12, notice the line of doorbells: This typical palace, once the home of a single rich family, is now occupied by many middle-class families. After the social revolution in the 18th century and the rise of the middle class, former palaces were condominiumized. Even so, like in *Dr. Zhivago*, the original family still lives here. Apartment #1 is the home of Count Guidi.

At #16, pop in to an alabaster showroom. Alabaster, mined nearby, has long been a big industry here. Volterra alabaster—softer and more porous than marble—was sliced thin to serve as windows for Italy's medieval churches.

At #19, the recommended La Vecchia Lira is a lively cafeteria. The Bar L'Incontro across the street is a favorite for pastries; in the summer, they sell homemade gelato, while in the winter they make chocolates.

Across the way, up Vicolo delle Prigioni, is a fun bakery *(panificio)*. They're happy to sell small quantities if you want to try the local *cantuccini* (almond biscotti) or another treat (closed 14:00-17:30, Sat after 14:00, and all day Sun).

Continue to the end of the block. At #51, a bit of Etruscan wall is artfully used to display more alabaster art. And #56A is the alabaster art gallery of Paolo Sabatini.

Locals gather early each evening at Osteria dei Poeti (at #57) for some of the best cocktails in town—served with free munchies. The cinema is across the street. Movies in Italy are rarely in *versione originale;* Italians are used to getting their movies dubbed into Italian. To bring some culture to this little town, they also show live transmissions of operas and concerts (advertised in the window).

At #66, another Tuscan tower marks the end of the street. This noble house has a ground floor with no interior access to the safe upper floors. Rope ladders were used to get upstairs. The tiny door was wide enough to let in your skinny friends...but definitely not anyone wearing armor and carrying big weapons.

Across the street stands the ancient Church of St. Michael. After long years of barbarian chaos, the Lombards moved in from the north and asserted law and order in places like Volterra. That generally included building a Christian church on the old Roman

HILL TOWNS

forum to symbolically claim and tame the center of town. (Locals still call this San Michele in Foro—"in the forum.") The church standing here today is Romanesque, dating from the 12th century. Around the right side, find the crude little guy and the smiling octopus under its eaves—they've been making faces at the passing crowds for 800 years.

• *Three more sights Palazzo Viti (fancy old palace), the Pinacoteca (gallery of gilded altarpieces), and the Alabaster Museum (within the Pinacoteca building)—are a short stroll down Via dei Sarti: From the end of Via Matteotti, turn left. If you want to skip straight down to the Roman Theater, just head straight from the end of Via Matteotti onto Via Guarnacci, then turn left when you get to the Porta Fiorentina gate. To head directly to Volterra's top sight, the Etruscan Museum, just turn around, walk a block back up Via Matteotti, turn left on Via Gramsci, and follow it all the way through Piazza XX Settembre up Via Don Minzoni to the museum.*

Palazzo Viti

Go behind the rustic, heavy stone walls of the city and see how the nobility lived (in this case, rich from 19th-century alabaster wealth). One of the finest private residential buildings in Italy, with 12 rooms open to the public, Palazzo Viti feels remarkably lived in—because it is. You'll also find Signora Viti herself selling admission tickets. It's no wonder this time warp is so popular with Italian movie directors. Remember, you're helping keep a noble family in leotards.

Cost and Hours: €5, pick up the loaner English description, April-Oct daily 10:00-13:00 & 14:30-18:30, closed Nov-March, Via dei Sarti 41, tel. 0588-84047, www.palazzoviti.it.

• *A block past Palazzo Viti, also on Via dei Sarti, is the...*

Pinacoteca and Alabaster Museum

The Pinacoteca fills a 15th-century palace with fine paintings that feel more Florentine than Sienese—a reminder of whose domain this town was in. You'll see roomfuls of gilded altarpieces and saintly statues. Head upstairs to the first floor. If you go left, you'll circle all the way around and save the best for last—but to cut to the chase, turn right at the landing and go directly into the best room, with Luca Signorelli's beautifully lit *Annunciation* (1491), an example of classic High Renaissance (from the town cathedral), and (to the right) *Deposition from the Cross* (1521), the groundbreaking Mannerist work by Rosso Fiorentino (note the elongated bodies and harsh emotional lighting and colors). In the adjacent room, see Ghirlandaio's *Christ in Glory* (1492). The two devout-looking kneeling women are actually pagan, pre-Christian Etruscan demi-goddesses, Attinca and Greciniana, but the church identified them as obscure saints to make the painting acceptable. Rather than attempt to get locals to stop venerating them (as their images were all over town), the church simply sainted them. Upstairs, the second floor has three more rooms of similar art.

A new staircase leads down to the recently opened **Alabaster Museum.** With alabaster sculptures spread over four floors, the museum contains examples from Etruscan times until the present (and lacked English descriptions when I visited). The top floor shows tools used to work the stone. Etruscan pieces are on the third floor, and modern sculptures—including an intriguing alabaster fried egg—are on the lower floors. As you leave, note the fine, tranquil, cloister-like courtyard with the remains of its original well.

Cost and Hours: €6 for Pinacoteca, €8 for Alabaster, €10 combo-ticket covers both museums plus Etruscan Museum, daily 9:00-18:45, Nov-mid-March until 13:45, Via dei Sarti 1, no photos permitted, tel. 0588-87580.

• *Exiting the Pinacoteca, turn right, then right again down the Passo del Gualduccio passage into the parking-lot square; at the end of this square, turn right and walk along the wall, with fine views of the...*

Roman Theater

Built in about 40 B.C., this well-preserved theater has good acoustics. Because a fine aerial view is available from the city wall promenade, you may find it unnecessary to pay admission to enter. Belly up to the 13th-century wall and look down. The wall that you're standing on divided the theater from the town center...so, naturally, the theater became the town dump. Over time, the theater was forgotten—covered in the garbage of Volterra. Luckily, it was rediscovered in the 1950s, by an administrator (and armchair historian) at the local mental hospital. Since they couldn't secure government funding for the dig, the theater was first excavated by mental patients who found the activity therapeutic.

The stage wall was standard Roman design—with three levels from which actors would appear: one level for mortals, one for heroes, and the top one for gods. Parts of two levels still stand. Gods leaped out onto the third level for the last time around the third century A.D., which is when the town began to use the theater stones to build fancy baths instead. You can see the remains of the baths behind the theater, including the round sauna with brick supports that raise the heated floor.

From the vantage point on the city wall promenade, you can trace Volterra's vast Etruscan wall. Find the church in the distance, on the left, and notice the stones just below. They are from the Etruscan wall that followed the ridge into the valley and defined Volterra in the fourth century B.C.

Cost and Hours: €3.50, but you can view the theater free from Via Lungo le Mure; the entrance is near the little parking lot just outside Porta Fiorentina—you can see the entry to the right as you survey the theater from above; mid-March-Oct daily 10:30-17:30,

Nov-mid-March Sat-Sun only 10:00-16:00, may be closed in bad weather.

• *From the Roman Theater, make your way back to Via Matteotti (follow Via Guarnacci straight up from Porta Fiorentina). A block down Via Matteotti, you can't miss the wide, pedestrianized shopping street called Via Gramsci. Follow this up to Piazza XX Settembre, walk through that leafy square, and continue uphill on Via Don Minzoni. Watch on your left for the...*

▲▲Etruscan Museum (Museo Etrusco Guarnacci)

Filled top to bottom with rare Etruscan artifacts, this museum—even with few English explanations and its dusty, almost neglectful, old-school style—makes it easy to appreciate how advanced this pre-Roman culture was.

Cost and Hours: €8, €10 combo-ticket includes the Pinacoteca and Alabaster Museum; daily mid-March-Oct 9:00-19:00, Nov-mid-March 10:00-16:00; ask at the ticket window for mildly interesting English pamphlet, audioguide-€3, Via Don Minzoni 15, tel. 0588-86347, www.comune.volterra.pi.it/english.

Visiting the Museum: The museum's three floors feel dusty and disorganized. As there are scarcely any English explanations, consider the serious but interesting €3 audioguide; the information below hits the highlights.

Ground Floor: The collection starts with a small gathering of pre-Etruscan Villanovian artifacts (c. 1500 B.C., to the left as you enter), but its highlight is straight ahead, sprawling through several rooms: a seemingly endless collection of Etruscan **funerary urns** (dating from the seventh to the first century B.C.). Designed to contain the ashes of cremated loved ones, each urn is tenderly carved with a unique scene, offering a peek into the still-mysterious Etruscan society. Etruscan urns have two parts: The casket on the bottom contained the remains (with elaborately carved panels), while the lid was decorated with a sculpture of the departed.

First pay attention to the people on top. While contemporaries of the Greeks, the Etruscans were more libertine. Their religion was less demanding, and their women were a respected part of both the social and public spheres. Women and men alike are depicted lounging on Etruscan urns. While they seem to be just hanging out, the lounging dead were actually offering the gods a banquet—in order to gain their favor in the transition to the next life. The banquet—where Etruscans really did lounge like this in front of a table—was the epitome of their social structure. But the outcome of this particular banquet had eternal consequences. The dearly departed are often depicted holding scrolls, blank wax tablets (symbolizing blank new lives in the next world), and containers that would generally be used at banquets, including libation cups for offering wine to the gods. The women in particular are finely dressed, sometimes holding a pomegranate (symbolizing fertility) or a mirror. Look at the faces, and imagine the lives they lived and the loved ones they left behind.

Now tune into the reliefs carved into the fronts of the caskets. The motifs vary widely, from floral patterns to mystical animals (such as a Starbucks-like mermaid) to parades of magistrates. Most show journeys on horseback—appropriate for someone leaving this world and entering the next. The most evocative scenes show the fabled horseback-and-carriage ride to the underworld, where the dead are greeted by Charon, an underworld demon, with his hammer and pointy ears.

While the finer urns are carved of alabaster, most are made of limestone. Originally they were colorfully painted. Many lids are mismatched—casualties of reckless 18th- and 19th-century archaeological digs.

First Floor: You'll enter a room with a circular mosaic in the floor (a Roman original, found in Volterra and transplanted here). Turn left into a series of green rooms—the best presented (and most important) of the museum.

The first room, Sala XIV, collects scenes of Ulysses carved into the fronts of caskets. Turn left and head into Sala XV, with the museum's prize piece. Fans of Alberto Giacometti will be amazed at how the tall, skinny figure called *The Evening Shadow* (*L'Ombra della Sera*, third century B.C.) looks just like the modern Swiss sculptor's work—but is 2,500 years older. This is an exceptional example of the *ex-voto* bronze statues that the Etruscans created in thanks to the gods. With his supremely lanky frame, distinctive wavy hairdo, and inscrutable Mona Lisa smirk, this Etruscan lad captures the illusion of a shadow stretching long late in the day. Admire the sheer artistry of the statue; with its right foot shifted slightly forward, it even hints at the *contrapposto* pose that would become common in this same region during the Renaissance, two millennia later.

Continue circling clockwise, through Sala XVI (alabaster urns with more Greek myths), Sala XVII (ex-voto water-bearer statues, kraters—vases with handles, and bronze hand mirrors), and Sala XVIII (golden jewelry). Sala XIX shows off the museum's other top piece, the *Urn of the Spouses* (*Urna degli Sposi*, first century B.C.). It's unique for various reasons, including its material (it's in terra-cotta—a relatively rare material for these funerary urns) and its depiction

of two people rather than one. Looking at this elderly couple, it's easy to imagine the long life they spent together and their desire to pass eternity lounging with each other at a banquet for the gods.

The rest of this floor has black glazed pottery; thousands of Etruscan, Greek, and Roman coins; and many more bronze ex-votos and jewelry.

Top Floor: From the top of the stairs, turn right, then immediately right again to find a re-created grave site, with several neatly aligned urns and artifacts that would have been buried with the deceased. Some of these were funeral dowries (called *corredo*) that the dead would pack along. You'll see artifacts such as mirrors, coins, hardware for vases, votive statues, pots, pans, and jewelry. On the landing are fragments from Volterra's acropolis—a site now occupied by the Medici Fortress.

• *After your visit, duck across the street to the alabaster showroom and the wine bar (both described next).*

▲Alabaster Workshop

Alab'Arte offers a fun peek into the art of alabaster. Their showroom is across from the Etruscan Museum, but to find their powdery workshop, go a block downhill, in front of Porta Marcoli, where you can watch Roberto Chiti and Giorgio Finazzo at work. They are delighted to share their art with visitors. (Everything—including Roberto and Giorgio—is covered in a fine white

dust.) Lighting shows off the translucent quality of the stone and the expertise of these artists. This is not a touristy guided visit, but something far more special: the chance to see busy artisans practicing their craft. For more such artisans in action, visit "Artisan Lane" (Via Porta all'Arco) described earlier, or ask the TI for their list of the town's many workshops open to the public.

Cost and Hours: Free, showroom—daily 10:30-13:00 & 15:30-19:00, Via Don Minzoni 18; workshop—March-Oct Mon-Sat 9:30-13:00 & 15:00-19:00, closed Sun, usually closed Nov-Feb—call ahead, Via Orti Sant'Agostino 28; tel. 0588-87968, www.alabarte.com.

▲La Vena di Vino (Wine-Tasting with Bruno and Lucio)

La Vena di Vino, also just across from the Etruscan Museum, is a fun *enoteca* where two guys who have devoted themselves to the wonders of wine share it with a fun-loving passion. Each day Bruno and Lucio open six or eight bottles, serve your choice by the glass, pair it with characteristic munchies, and offer fine music (guitars

Under the Etruscan Sun

Around 550 B.C.—just before the Golden Age of Greece—the Etruscan people of central Italy had their own Golden Age. Though their origins are mysterious, their mix of Greek-style art with Roman-style customs helped lay a civilized foundation for the rise of the Roman Empire. As you travel through Italy—particularly in Tuscany (from "Etruscan")—you'll find traces of this long-lost people.

Etruscan tombs and artifacts are still being discovered, often by farmers in the countryside. Museums in Volterra and Cortona house fine collections of urns, pottery, and devotional figures. You can visit several domed tombs outside Cortona.

The Etruscans first appeared in the ninth century B.C., when a number of cities sprouted up in sparsely populated Tuscany and Umbria, including today's hill towns of Cortona, Chiusi, and Volterra. Possibly immigrants from Turkey, but more likely local farmers who moved to the city, they became traders and craftsmen, and welcomed new ideas from Greece.

More technologically advanced than their neighbors, the Etruscans mined metal, exporting it around the Mediterranean, both as crude ingots and as some of the finest-crafted jewelry in the known world. They drained and irrigated large tracts of land, creating the fertile farmland of central Italy's breadbasket. With their disciplined army, warships, merchant vessels, and (from the Greek perspective) pirate galleys, they ruled central Italy and the major ports along the Tyrrhenian Sea. For nearly two centuries (c. 700-500 B.C.), much of Italy lived a Golden Age of peace and prosperity under the Etruscan sun.

Judging from the frescoes and many luxury items that have survived, the Etruscans enjoyed the good life: They look healthy and vibrant as they play flutes, dance with birds, or play party games. Etruscan artists celebrated individual people, showing their wrinkles, crooked noses, silly smiles, and funny haircuts.

Scholars today have deciphered the Etruscans' Greek-style alphabet and some individual words, but they have yet to fully crack the code. Much of what we know of the Etruscans comes from their tombs. The tomb was a home in the hereafter, complete with all of the deceased's belongings. The sarcophagus might have a statue on the lid of the deceased at a banquet—lying across a dining couch, spooning with his wife, smiles on their faces, living the good life for all eternity.

Seven decades of wars with the Greeks (545-474 B.C.) disrupted their trade routes and drained the Etruscan League, just as a new Mediterranean power was emerging: Rome. In 509 B.C., the Romans overthrew their Etruscan king, and Rome expanded, capturing Etruscan cities one by one (the last in 264 B.C.). Etruscan resisters were killed, the survivors intermarried with Romans, and their kids grew up speaking Latin. By Julius Caesar's time, the only remnants of Etruscan culture were its priests, who be-

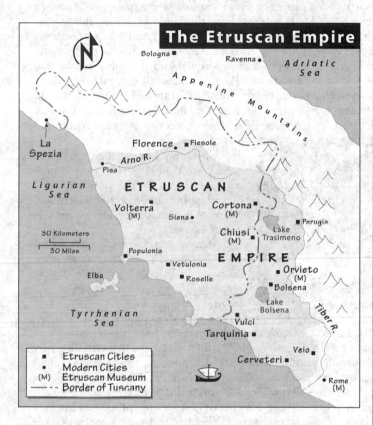

The Etruscan Empire

Bologna ■
Ravenna •
Adriatic Sea

Appenine Mountains

La Spezia
Florence ■ Fiesole
Arno R.
Pisa •

Ligurian Sea

ETRUSCAN

Volterra ■
(M)
Siena •
Cortona ■
(M)
■ Perugia

Chiusi ■
(M)
Lake Trasimeno

30 Kilometers
30 Miles
Populonia •

EMPIRE

Vetulonia ■
Orvieto •
(M)

Elba
Roselle •
■ Bolsena

Lake Bolsena

Tyrrhenian Sea
Tiber R.

Vulci ■
Tarquinia ■

Veio ■
Cerveteri ■
• Rome
(M)

■ Etruscan Cities
• Modern Cities
(M) Etruscan Museum
--- Border of Tuscany

came Rome's professional soothsayers. Interestingly, the Etruscan prophets had foreseen their own demise, having predicted that Etruscan civilization would last 10 centuries.

But Etruscan culture lived on in Roman religion (pantheon of gods, household gods, and divination rituals), art (realism), lifestyle (the banquet), and in a taste for Greek styles—the mix that became our "Western civilization."

Etruscan Sights in Italy

Rome: Traces of original Etruscan engineering projects (e.g., Circus Maximus), Vatican Museum artifacts, and Villa Giulia Museum, with the famous "husband and wife sarcophagus."

Orvieto: Archaeological Museum (coins, dinnerware, and a sarcophagus), necropolis, and underground tunnels and caves.

Volterra: Etruscan gate (Porta all'Arco, from fourth century B.C.) and Etruscan Museum (funerary urns).

Chiusi: Museum, tombs, and tunnels.

Cortona: Museum and dome-shaped tombs.

available for patrons) and an unusual decor (the place is strewn with bras). Hang out here with the local characters. This is your chance to try the Super Tuscan wine—a creative mix of international grapes grown in Tuscany. According to Bruno, the Brunello (€7/glass) is just right with wild boar, and the Super Tuscan (€6) is perfect for meditation. Food is served all day, including some microwaved hot dishes or a plate of meats and cheeses. Although Volterra is famously quiet late at night, this place is full of action. Downstairs is a rustic cellar that doubles on weekend nights as a sort of disco.

Cost and Hours: Pay per glass, open Wed-Mon 11:30-1:00 in the morning, closed Tue, 3- to 5-glass wine tastings, shipping options available, Via Don Minzoni 30, tel. 0588-81491, www.lavenadivino.com.

• *Volterra's final sight is perched atop the hill just above the wine bar. Climb up one of the lanes nearby, then walk (to the right) along the formidable wall to find the park.*

Medici Fortress and Archaeological Park

The Parco Archeologico marks what was the acropolis of Volterra from 1500 B.C. until A.D. 1472, when Florence conquered the pesky city and burned its political and historic center, turning it into a grassy commons and building the adjacent Medici Fortezza. The old fortress—a symbol of Florentine dominance—now keeps people in rather than out. It's a maximum-security prison housing only about 150 special prisoners. (When you're driving from San Gimignano to Volterra, you pass another big, modern prison—almost surreal in the midst of all the Tuscan wonder.) Authorities prefer to keep organized crime figures locked up far away from their family ties in Sicily.

The park sprawling next to the fortress (toward the town center) is a rare, grassy meadow at the top of a rustic hill town—a favorite place for locals to relax and picnic on a sunny day. Nearby are the remains of the acropolis (€3.50 to enter, ticket also includes the Roman Theater), but these can be viewed through a fence for free.

Cost and Hours: Park—free to enter, closes at 20:00 in summer, 17:00 in winter.

Countryside Strolls

All these sights are in a tight little zone of the old town, about a 10-minute walk from each other. But if you have time for a stroll, Volterra—perched on a ridge overlooking pristine Tuscan hills—has countryside galore to explore. Get some advice from the TI.

One popular walk is to head to the west end of town, out Porta San Francesco, into a workaday area (dubbed "Borghi," literally, "neighborhoods") that sees few tourists. Continuing downhill (past the Church of San Giusto), you'll come to a cliff with a stretch of the original fourth-century B.C. Etruscan wall. Peering over the cliff from here, you can see that Volterra sits upon orange sandy topsoil packed onto clay cliffs, called Le Balze. At various points in its history, the town has been threatened by landslides, and parts of its hilltop have simply disappeared. The big church you see in the distance was abandoned in the late 1800s for fear that it would be swallowed up by the land. The distinctive cliffs surrounding Volterra are called *calanchi* (similar to the French *calanques* that slash the Mediterranean coast).

Sleeping in Volterra

Predictably for a small town, Volterra's accommodations are limited, and all have their quirks—but there are plenty of places offering a good night's sleep at a fair price. While it's convenient to stay inside the old town, the lodgings that are a short walk away are generally a bit cheaper (and much easier for drivers).

Inside Volterra's Old Town

$$$ **Hotel La Locanda** feels stately and old-fashioned. This well-located place (just inside Porta Fiorentina) rents 18 decent rooms with flowery decor and modern comforts (Db-€104, less off-season, 10 percent Rick Steves discount, includes breakfast, air-con, free Wi-Fi, Via Guarnacci 24/28, tel. 0588-81547, www.hotel-lalocanda.com, staff@hotel-lalocanda.com, Giulia, Stefania, and Irina).

$$ **Albergo Etruria,** on Volterra's main drag, rents 21 fresh, modern, and spacious rooms within an ancient stone structure. They have a welcoming TV lounge and a peaceful rooftop garden (Sb-€75, Db-€95, Tb-€115, 10 percent discount with cash and this book when you book direct, includes breakfast, fans, free but spotty Wi-Fi, Via Matteotti 32, tel. 0588-87377, www.albergoetruria.it, info@albergoetruria.it, Lisa and Giuseppina are fine hosts).

$$ **Albergo Nazionale,** with 38 big rooms, is simple, a little musty, short on smiles, popular with school groups, and steps from the bus stop. While the place feels dated, it's an exceptionally handy location (Sb-€55-70, Db-€70-90, Tb-€90-105, 10 percent discount with cash and this book if you book direct, reception closes at midnight, includes breakfast, free Wi-Fi, Via dei Marchesi 11, tel. 0588-86284, fax 0588-84097, www.hotelnazionale-volterra.it, info@hotelnazionale-volterra.it).

Just Outside the Old Town

These accommodations are within a 5- to 15-minute walk of the city walls.

$$$ Park Hotel Le Fonti, a dull 10-minute walk downhill from Porta all'Arco, can't decide whether it's a business hotel or a resort. The spacious, imposing building feels old and stately, and has 64 rooms, many with views. While generally overpriced (the management knows it's the only hotel of its kind in Volterra), it can be a good value if you manage to snag a deal. In addition to the swimming pool, guests can use a small spa with sauna, hot tub, and an intriguing "emotional shower" (Db-€89-165, average is about Db-€129 but prices vary wildly depending on season, "superior" room is identical to others but has a view for €20 extra, "deluxe" room with terrace costs €30 extra, includes breakfast, elevator, pay Wi-Fi in lobby, on-site restaurant, wine bar, free parking, Via di Fontecorrenti 5, tel. 0588-85219, www.parkhotellefonti.com, info@hotellefonti.com).

$$ Albergo Villa Nencini, just outside of town, is big, professional, and older-feeling, with 36 cheaply furnished rooms. A few rooms have terraces, and many have views. Guests also enjoy the large pool and free parking (Sb-€67, Db-€88, Tb-€115, 10 percent discount with cash and this book, includes breakfast, pay Wi-Fi, Borgo Santo Stefano 55, a 15-minute uphill walk to main square, tel. 0588-86386, www.villanencini.it, info@villanencini.it, Nencini family).

$ La Primavera B&B is a great value just a few minutes' walk outside Porta Fiorentina (near the Roman Theater). Silvia rents five charming, tidy rooms that share a cutesy-country, heavily perfumed lounge. The house is along a fairly busy road, but set back along a pleasant courtyard (Db-€75, Tb-€100, includes breakfast, free Wi-Fi, free parking, Via Porta Diana 15, tel. 0588-87295, mobile 328-865-0390, www.affittacamere-laprimavera.com, info@affittacamere-laprimavera.com).

$ Seminario Vescovile Sant'Andrea has been training priests for more than 500 years. Today, the remaining eight priests still train students, but when classes are over, their 16 rooms—separated by vast and holy halls in an echoing old mansion—are rented very cheaply. Look for the 15th-century Ascension ceramic by Andrea della Robbia, tucked away in a corner upstairs (S-€17, Sb-€22, D-€32, Db-€40, T-€48, Tb-€60, no breakfast, closed Oct-March, elevator, closes at 24:00, groups welcome, free parking, 10-minute walk from Etruscan Museum, Viale Vittorio Veneto 2, tel. 0588-86028, semvescovile@diocesivolterra.it; Alberto, Angela, and Sergio).

$ Chiosco delle Monache, Volterra's youth hostel, fills a wing of the restored Convent of San Girolamo with 68 beds in 23 rooms.

It's modern, spacious, and very institutional, with lots of services and a tranquil cloister to wander. However, it's about a 20-minute hike out of town, in a boring area near deserted hospital buildings (bed in 6-bed dorm-€18, breakfast-€6 extra, lockers; Db-€69, includes breakfast; reception closed 13:00-15:00 and after 22:00, elevator, pay Wi-Fi, free parking, Via dell Teatro 4, look for hospital sign from main Volterra-San Gimignano road, tel. 0588-86613, www.ostellovolterra.it, info@ostellovolterra.it). Nearby and run by the same organization, **$ Hotel Foresteria** has 35 big, utilitarian, new-feeling rooms with great prices but the same location woes as the hostel; it's worth considering for budget travelers, families, and drivers (Sb-€58, Db-€82, Tb-€103, Qb-€122, includes breakfast, air-con, elevator, pay Wi-Fi, restaurant, free parking, Borgo San Lazzaro, tel. 0588-80050, www.foresteriavolterra.it, info@foresteriavolterra.it).

Near Volterra

$$ Podere Marcampo is a newer *agriturismo* about 2.5 miles outside Volterra on the road to Pisa. Run by Genuino (owner of the recommended Ristorante Enoteca del Duca), his wife Ivana, and their English-speaking daughter Claudia, this peaceful spot has three well-appointed rooms and three apartments, plus a swimming pool with panoramic views. Genuino produces his award-winning Merlot on site and offers €20 wine-tastings with cheese and home-made salami. Cooking classes at their restaurant in town are also available (Db-€94, apartment-€118-195, more expensive mid-July-Aug, includes breakfast with this book, air-con, free Wi-Fi, free parking, tel. 0588-85393, Claudia's mobile 328-174-4605, www.agriturismo-marcampo.com, info@agriturismo-marcampo.com).

Eating in Volterra

Menus feature a Volterran take on regional dishes. *Zuppa alla Volterrana* is a fresh vegetable-and-bread soup, similar to *ribollita* (except that it isn't made from leftovers). *Torta di ceci*, also known as *cecina*, is a savory pancake-like dish made with garbanzo beans. Those with more adventurous palates dive into *trippa* (tripe; comes in a bowl like stew), the traditional breakfast of the alabaster carvers. *Fegatelli* are meatballs made with liver.

Ristorante Enoteca del Duca, with a locally respected chef named Genuino, serves well-presented and creative Tuscan cuisine. You can dine under a medieval arch with walls lined with wine bottles, in a sedate, high-ceilinged dining room (with an Etruscan statuette at each table), on a nice little patio out back, or in their little *enoteca* (wine cellar). It's a good place for truffles, and has a friendly staff and a fine wine list (which includes Genuino's own merlot, plus several much pricier options—choose carefully). The spacious seating, dressy clientele, and calm atmosphere make this a good choice for a romantic splurge (€42 food-sampler fixed-price meal, €10-15 pastas, €15-22 *secondi*, Wed-Mon 12:30-15:00 & 19:30-22:00, closed Tue, near City Hall at Via di Castello 2, tel. 0588-81510, www.enoteca-delduca-ristorante.it).

Trattoria da Bado, a 10-minute hike out of town, is every local's favorite for its *tipica cucina Volterrana.* Giacomo and family offer a rustic atmosphere and serve food with no pretense—"the way you wish your mamma cooks" (meals from 12:30 and 19:30, closed Wed, Borgo San Lazzero 9, tel. 0577-80402, reserve before you go as it's often full).

Don Beta is a family-run trattoria on the main drag, popular with travelers for its stylish home cooking. Mirko supervises the lively young team as they whisk out steaming plates of pasta and homemade desserts (€6-10 pastas, €12-18 *secondi,* daily 12:00-14:30 & 19:00-23:00, reservations smart, Via Matteotti 39, tel. 0588-86730, www.donbeta.it).

La Vecchia Lira, bright and cheery, is a classy self-serve eatery that's a hit with locals as a quick and cheap lunch spot by day (with €5-10 meals) and a fancier restaurant at night (€9-10 pastas, €11-18 *secondi;* Fri-Wed 11:30-14:30 & 19:00-22:30, closed Thu, Via Matteotti 19, tel. 0588-86180, Lamberto and Massimo).

La Carabaccia feels like an old-school Italian eatery, with a 1950s turquoise color scheme, a deli up front, and a country-rustic dining room in back. They serve only two pastas and two *secondi* on any given night, so check the menu by the door to be sure you like the choices. Committed to tradition, on Fridays they serve only fish. They whip up €3-4 take-away sandwiches at the deli up front (€7-9 pastas and *secondi,* Tue-Sun 12:30-14:30 & 19:30-22:00, closed Mon, Piazza XX Settembre 4/5, tel. 0588-86239).

Ristorante il Sacco Fiorentino is a local favorite for traditional cuisine and seasonal seafood specials (€8-10 pastas, €10-15 *secondi,* Thu-Tue 12:00-15:00 & 19:00-22:00, closed Wed, Via Giusto Turazza 13, tel. 0588-88537).

La Vena di Vino is an *enoteca* serving up simple and traditional dishes and the best of Tuscan wine in a fun atmosphere. As their hot dishes are microwaved (there's no real kitchen), come here more for the wine and ambience than for the food (€8-12 meals, closed Tue, Via Don Minzoni 30, tel. 0588-81491). For more details, read the description on page 703.

Pizzerias: **Ombra della Sera** dishes out what local kids consider the best pizza in town. At €6-9 a pop, their pizzas make for a cheap date (Tue-Sun 12:00-15:00 & 19:00-22:00, closed Mon, Via

Guarnacci 16, don't confuse this with their second, pricier location on Via Gramsci; tel. 0588-85274). **Pizzeria Tavernetta,** next door, is more romantic, with delightful indoor and on-the-street seating. Its romantically frescoed dining room upstairs is the classiest I've seen in a pizzeria. Marco, who looks like a younger Billy Joel, serves €5-8 pizzas (Thu-Tue 12:00-16:00 & 18:30-22:00, closed Wed, Via Guarnacci 14, tel. 0588-87630).

Picnic: You can assemble a picnic at the few *alimentari* around town (try Despar Market at Via Gramsci 12, Mon-Sat 7:30-13:00 & 16:00-20:00, Sun 8:30-13:00) and eat in the breezy Archaeological Park.

Gelato: Of the many ice-cream stands in the center, I've found **L'Isola di Gusto** to be reliably high quality (daily 11:00-late, Via Gramsci 3).

Volterra Connections

In Volterra, buses come and go from Piazza Martiri della Libertà (buy tickets at the tobacco shop right on the piazza; if it's closed, purchase on board for small extra charge). Most connections—except to Pisa—are with the C.P.T. bus company (www.cpt.pisa.it) through Colle Val d'Elsa ("koh-leh" for short), a workaday town in the valley (4/day Mon-Sat, 1/day Sun, 50 minutes, €2.75). Once in Colle, you must buy another ticket (from another bus company) at the newsstand near the bus stop, or from the blue automated machine at the bus stop (press "F" to toggle to English, then punch in the number for your destination). I've listed total journey fares below. The nearest train station is in Saline di Volterra, a 15-minute bus ride away (7/day, 2/day Sun); however, trains from Saline run only to the coast, not to the major bus destinations listed next.

From Volterra by Bus to: Florence (4/day Mon-Sat, 1/day Sun, 2 hours, change in Colle Val d'Elsa, €8.35), **Siena** (4/day Mon-Sat, no buses on Sun, 2 hours, change in Colle Val d'Elsa, €6.15), **San Gimignano** (4/day Mon-Sat, 1/day Sun, 2 hours, change in Colle Val d'Elsa, €6.15), **Pisa** (9/day, 2 hours, change in Pontedera, €5.50).

South of Siena

Just an hour south of Siena (or two hours south of Florence), you'll find a trio of inviting hill towns, with an emphasis on good wine and scenic country drives: The biggest and most interesting, Montepulciano, has an engaging medieval cityscape draped in a Renaissance coat, wine cellars that plunge deep down into the cliffs it sits upon, and a classic town square. Pienza is a tidily planned Renaissance town that once gave the world a pope. And mellow Montalcino is (even more than most towns around here) all about its wine: Brunello di Montalcino. All three are within about a half-hour drive of each other, making any one of them a good home base for the entire region. Just to the north are the rippling hills of the Crete Senese. Dressed in vibrant green in spring and parched brown in fall, this area is blessed with quintessential Tuscan scenery and dotted with worthwhile countryside accommodations. While my favorite home base for the region is the most interesting town, Montepulciano, you can't go wrong staying in the countryside or in Montalcino.

Montepulciano

Curving its way along a ridge, Montepulciano (mohn-teh-pull-chee-AH-noh) delights visitors with *vino* and views. Alternately

under Sienese and Florentine rule, the city still retains its medieval *contrade* (districts), each with a mascot and flag. The neighborhoods compete the last Sunday of August in the Bravio delle Botti, where teams of men push large wine casks uphill from Piazza Marzocco to Piazza Grande, all hoping to win a banner and bragging rights. The entire last week of August is a festival: Each *contrada* arranges musical entertainment and serves food at outdoor eateries along with generous tastings of the local *vino*.

The city is a collage of architectural styles, but the elegant San Biagio Church, at the base of the hill, is its best Renaissance building. Most visitors ignore the architecture and focus more on the city's other creative accomplishment, the tasty Vino Nobile di Montepulciano red wine.

Orientation to Montepulciano

The commercial action in Montepulciano centers in the lower town, mostly along Via di Gracciano nel Corso (nicknamed "Corso"). This stretch begins at the town gate called Porta al Prato (near the TI, bus station, and some parking) and winds slowly up, up, up through town—narrated by my self-guided walk, later. Strolling here, you'll find eateries, gift shops, and tourist traps. The back streets are worth exploring. The main square, at the top of town (up a steep switchback lane from Corso), is Piazza Grande. Standing proudly above all the touristy sales energy, it has a noble, Florentine feel.

Tourist Information

The helpful TI is just outside the Porta al Prato city gate, directly underneath the small tree-lined parking lot. It offers a paltry town map for €0.50, books hotels and rooms for no fee, sells train tickets (€1 fee), has an Internet terminal (€3.50/hour), and can book one of the town's few taxis (Mon-Sat 9:30-12:30 & 15:00-18:00, Sun 9:30-12:30, daily until 20:00 in July-Aug, Piazza Don Minzoni, tel. 0578-757-341, www.prolocomontepulciano.it, info@proloco-montepulciano.it).

Note that on the main square there is an office that looks like a TI, but this is actually a privately run "Strada del Vino" (Wine Road) agency. They don't have city info, but they do provide wine-road maps, organize **wine tours** in the city, and lead minibus winery tours farther afield. They also offer other tours (olive oil, cheese, and slow food), cooking classes, and more, depending on season and demand (Mon-Fri 10:00-13:00 & 15:00-18:00, closed Sat-Sun but likely open both days in summer, Piazza Grande 7, tel. 0578-717-484, www.stradavinonobile.it).

Arrival in Montepulciano

Buses leave passengers at the station on Piazza Nenni, steeply downhill from the Porta al Prato gate. From the station, cross the street and head inside the modern orange-brick structure burrowed into the hillside, where there's an elevator. Ride to level 1, walk straight ahead down the corridor (following signs for *centro storico*), and ride another elevator to level 1. You'll pop out at the Poggiofanti Gardens; walk to the end of this park and hook left to find the gate. From here, it's a 15-minute walk uphill along the Corso, the bustling main drag, to the main square, Piazza Grande (following my self-guided walk, described later). Alternatively, you can wait for the orange shuttle bus that takes you all the way up to Piazza Grande (2/hour, €1.10, buy tickets at bars or tobacco shops); it's a good strategy to take the bus up and walk back down. There's a bus stop just before the TI, beside a gray metal canopy over a hotel-booking booth.

Drivers arriving by car should park outside the walls. The city center is a "ZTL" zone—marked with a red circle—where you'll be fined if you drive; even if you were allowed, you wouldn't want to tackle the tiny roads inside the city. In general, white lines indicate free parking and blue lines mean pay parking. (If you're sleeping in town, your hotelier will give you a permit to park within the walls; be sure to get very specific instructions.) Well-signed pay-and-display parking lots ring the city center, usually €1.30/hr. To get the full Montepulciano experience of walking the entire length of the town up the Corso, park just outside the Porta al Prato gate (#1 is handiest, but may be full; #2, #3, and #4 are nearby—#3 has a maximum of 1 hour; #5 is near the bus station—you can ride up to the gate on the elevator described earlier). For a quick surgical strike, make a beeline to the lots up at the top end of town. Follow signs for *centro storico, duomo,* and *Piazza Grande,* and use the *Fortezza* or *San Donato* lots (flanking the fortress at the top of town). Drivers, be aware that Montepulciano is a very vertical town, and it's easy to get turned around. Mercifully, it's also a small town, so backtracking isn't too time-consuming. Just avoid the ZTL areas, and don't park on yellow lines.

Helpful Hints

Market Day: It's on Thursday morning (8:00-13:00), near the bus station.

Services: There's no official **baggage storage** in town, but the TI might let you leave bags with them if they have space and you ask nicely. Public **WCs** are located at the TI, to the right of Palazzo Comunale, and at the Sant'Agostino Church.

Laundry: A self-service launderette is at Via del Paolino 2, just around the corner from the recommended **Camere Bellavista** (€4 wash, €4 dry, daily 8:00-22:00, tel. 0578-717-544).

Taxis: To reach the English-speaking **Eurospin** taxi hotline, call 330-732-723 (€10 for short trips up or down hill; they also provide rides to other towns). For a private taxi, try 348-702-4124. Montepulciano has only a few taxis, so be sure to book well in advance.

Self-Guided Walk

Welcome to Montepulciano

This two-part walk traces the spine of the town, from its main entrance up to its hilltop seat of power. Part 1 begins at Porta al Prato (where you'll enter if arriving at the bus station, parking at certain lots, or visiting the TI). Note that this part of the walk is uphill;

if you'd rather skip straight to the more level part of town, ride the twice-hourly shuttle bus up, or park at one of the lots near the Fortezza. In that case, you can still do Part 1, backwards, on the way down.

Part 1: Up the Corso

This guided stroll takes you up through Montepulciano's commercial (and touristic) gamut, which curls ever so gradually from the bottom of town to the top. While the street is lined mostly with gift shops, you'll pass a few relics of an earlier, less commercial age.

Begin in front of the imposing Porta al Prato, one of the many stout city gates that once fortified this highly strategic town. Facing the gate, find the sign for the Porta di Bacco *"passagio secreto"* on the left. While Montepulciano did have secret passages tunneled through the rock beneath it for coming and going in case of siege, this particular passage—right next to the city's front door—was probably no *secreto*...though it works great for selling salami.

Walk directly below the entrance to the **Porta al Prato,** and look up to see the slot where the portcullis (heavily fortified gate) could slide down to seal things off. Notice that there are two gates, enabling defenders to trap would-be invaders in a no-man's land where they could be doused with hot tar (sticky and painful). Besides having a drop-down portcullis, each gate also had a hinged door—effectively putting four barriers between the town and its enemies.

Pass through the gate and head a block uphill to reach the **Colona dell' Marzocco.** This column, topped with a lion holding the Medici shield, is a reminder that Montepulciano existed under the auspices of Florence—but only for part of its history. Originally the column was crowned by a she-wolf suckling human twins, the civic symbol of Siena. At a strategic crossroads of mighty regional powers (Florence, Siena, and the papal states), Montepulciano often switched allegiances—and this column became a flagpole where the overlords du jour could tout their influence.

The column is also the starting point for Montepulciano's masochistic tradition, **Bravio delle Botti,** held on the last Sunday of August, in which each local *contrada* (fiercely competitive neighborhood, like Siena's) selects its two stoutest young men to roll a 180-pound barrel up the hill through town. If the vertical climb through town wears you out, be glad you're only toting a camera.

A few steps up, on the right (at #91), is one of the many fine noble palaces that front Montepulciano's main strip. The town is fortunate to be graced with so many bold and noble palazzos—Florentine nobility favored Montepulciano as a breezy and relaxed place for a secondary residence. Grand as this palace is, with its stylized lion heads, it's small potatoes—the higher you go

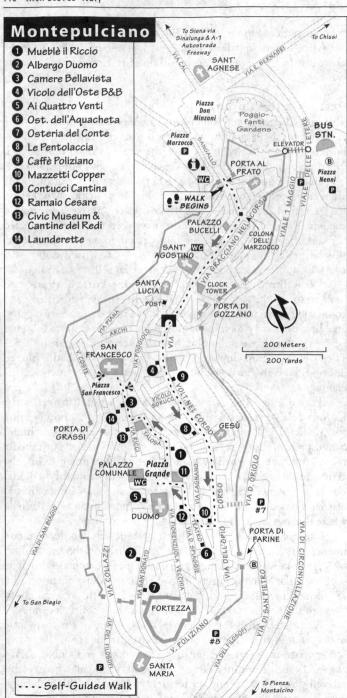

Montepulciano

1. Mueblè il Riccio
2. Albergo Duomo
3. Camere Bellavista
4. Vicolo dell'Oste B&B
5. Ai Quattro Venti
6. Ost. dell'Aquacheta
7. Osteria del Conte
8. Le Pentolaccia
9. Caffè Poliziano
10. Mazzetti Copper
11. Contucci Cantina
12. Ramaio Cesare
13. Civic Museum & Cantine del Redi
14. Launderette

To Siena via Sinalunga & A-1 Autostrada Freeway

To Chiusi

SANT' AGNESE

Piazza Don Minzoni

Poggio-fanti Gardens

BUS STN.

ELEVATOR

Piazza Nenni

Piazza Marzocco

PORTA AL PRATO

WALK BEGINS

PALAZZO BUCELLI

COLONA DELL' MARZOCCO

SANT' AGOSTINO

WC

SANTA LUCIA

POST

CLOCK TOWER

PORTA DI GOZZANO

200 Meters
200 Yards

SAN FRANCESCO

Piazza San Francesco

PORTA DI GRASSI

GESÙ

PALAZZO COMUNALE

Piazza Grande

WC

DUOMO

PORTA DI FARINE

FORTEZZA

To San Biagio

SANTA MARIA

To Pienza, Montalcino

- - - - Self-Guided Walk

VIALE DELLE LETERE

VIA E BERNABEI

VIA CAL

SANGALLO

VIA DI GRACCIANO NEL CORSO

VIALE 1 MAGGIO

VIA DI VOLTAIA NEL CORSO

VICOLO SDRUCO

VIA DELL'OPIO NEL CORSO

VIA TALOSA

VIA RICCI

V. COSTE

VIA PIANA

VIA D. ORIOLO

VIA DI CIRCONVALLAZIONE

VIA CAGNANO

VIA DI SAN PIETRO

VIA DEL FILOSOFI

VIA DI SAN BIAGIO

VIA COLLAZZI

VIA SAN DONATO

VIA FIORENZUOLA VECCHIA

VIA D. SPAGGIE

VIA D. TEATRO

V. POLIZIANO

VIA DEL FILOSOFI

ARCHI

VIA POGGIOLO

P #7

P #8

HILL TOWNS

in Montepulciano, the closer you are to the town center...and the fancier the mansions.

Farther up on the right, at #75 (Palazzo Bucelli), take a moment to examine the **Etruscan and Roman fragments** embedded in the wall (left here by a 19th-century antiques dealer). You can quickly distinguish which pieces came from the Romans and those belonging to the earlier Etruscans by the differences in their alphabets: The "backwards" Etruscan letters (they read from right to left) look closer to Greek than the more modern Roman letters. Many of the fragments show a circle flanked by a pair of inward-facing semicircular designs. The circle represents the libation cup used for drinking at an Etruscan banquet. Banquets were at the center of Etruscan social life, and burial urns depict lounging nobles presenting a feast for the gods.

At the top of the block on the right, pass by the Baroque-style Church of Sant'Agostino. Huff up a few more steps (imagine pushing a barrel now), then take a breather to look back and see the **clock tower** in the middle of the street. The bell ringer at the top takes the form of the character Pulcinella, one of the wild and carefree revelers familiar from Italy's comedy theater *(commedia dell'arte)*.

Keep on going, bearing right (uphill) at the fork. At the *alimentari* on the right (at #23), notice the classic old sign advertising milk, butter, margarine, and olive and canola oil. Soon after, you'll pass under another sturdy **gateway**—indicating that this city grew in concentric circles. Passing through the gate and facing the loggia (with the Florentine Medici seal—a shield with balls), turn left and keep on going.

As you huff and puff, notice (on your right, and later on both sides) the steep, narrow, often-covered lanes called *vicolo* ("little street"). You're getting a peek at the higgledy-piggledy medieval Montepulciano. Only when the rationality of Renaissance aesthetics took hold was the main street realigned, becoming symmetrical and pretty. Beneath its fancy suit, though, Montepulciano remains a rugged Gothic city.

On the left, watch for the hulking former palace (I told you they'd get bigger) that's now home to Banca Etruria. "Etruria"—a name you'll see everywhere around here—is a term for the Etruscan territory of today's Tuscany.

Just after is a fine spot for a coffee break (on the left, at #27): **Caffè Poliziano,** the town's most venerable watering hole (from 1868). Step inside to soak in the genteel atmosphere, with a busy espresso machine, newspapers on long sticks, and a little terrace with spectacular views (open long hours daily; it also has free Wi-Fi). It's named for a famous Montepulciano-born 15th-century poet who was a protégé of Lorenzo the Magnificent de Medici and tutored his two sons. So important is he to civic pride that towns-people are nicknamed *poliziani*.

A bit farther up and on the right, notice the precipitous Vicolo dello Sdrucciolo—literally, "slippery lane." Any *vicolo* on the right can be used as a steep shortcut to the upper part of town, while those on the left generally lead to fine views. Many of these side lanes are spanned by brick arches, allowing the centuries-old buildings to lean on each other for support rather than toppling over—a fitting metaphor for the tight-knit communities that vitalize Italian small towns.

Soon the street levels out. Near the end, on the right (at #64), look for the **Mazzetti** copper shop, crammed full of both decorative and practical items. Because of copper's unmatched heat conductivity, it's a favored material in premium kitchens. The production of hand-hammered copper vessels like these is a dying art; in this shop, you can meet gregarious Cesare, who makes them in his workshop just up the street.

To get there, go up the covered lane just after the copper shop (Vicolo Benci, on the right). You'll emerge partway up the steep street just below the main square. Cesare's workshop and museum are across the street and a bit to the left (look for *Ramaio;* for details on him, see page 721). Steeply uphill, on the right just before reaching the square, Cesare's buddy Adamo loves to introduce travelers to Montepulciano's fine wines at the Contucci Cantina (described on page 720). Visit Cesare and Adamo now, or head up to the square for Part 2 of this walk before coming back down.

Either way, Montepulciano's main square is just ahead. You made it!

Part 2: Piazza Grande and Nearby

This pleasant, lively piazza is surrounded by a grab bag of architectural sights. If the medieval **Palazzo Comunale,** or town hall, reminds you of Palazzo Vecchio in Florence, it's because Florence

dominated Montepulciano in the 15th and 16th centuries. The crenellations along the roof were never intended to hide soldiers—they're just meant to symbolize power. But the big, square central tower makes it clear that the city is keeping an eye out in all directions.

Take a moment to survey the square, where the town's four great powers stare each other down. Face the Palazzo Comunale, and keep turning to the right to see: the one-time building of the courts (Palazzo del Capitano); the noble Palazzo Tarugi, a Renaissance-arcaded confection; and the aristocratic Palazzo Contucci, with its 16th-century Renaissance facade. (The Contucci family still lives in their palace, producing and selling their own wine.) Continuing your spin, you see the unfinished Duomo looking glumly on, wishing the city hadn't run out of money for its facade. (Its interior, described later under "Sights and Experiences in Montepulciano," looks much better.)

A cistern system fed by rainwater draining from the roofs of surrounding palaces supplied the fine **well** in the corner. Check out its 19th-century pulleys, the grills to keep animals from contaminating the water supply, and the Medici coat of arms (with lions symbolizing the political power of Florence).

Climbing the town hall's **tower** rewards you with a windy but commanding view from the terrace below the clock. Go into the Palazzo Comunale, head up the stairs to your left, and pay on the second floor (€3, daily 10:00-18:00, closed in winter).

The street to the left as you face the tower leads to the **Fortez-za,** or fortress. While you might expect the town to be huddled protectively around its fortress, in Montepulciano's case, it's built on a distant ledge at the very edge of town. That's because this fort wasn't meant to protect the townspeople, but to safeguard its rulers by keeping an eye on those townspeople.

Detour to the Church of San Francesco and Views: From the main square, it's a short, mostly level walk to a fine viewpoint. You could head down the wide street to the right as you face the tower. But for a more interesting look at Montepulciano behind its pretty palaces, go instead up the narrow lane between the Palazzo... steps... but by a mishmash of brick and stone. Pause at the Mueblè il Riccio B&B (with a fine courtyard—peek inside) and look high up across the street to see how centuries of structures have been stitched together, sometimes gracelessly.

Follow along this lane as it bends left, and eventually you'll pop out just below the main square, facing the recommended Cantine del Redi wine cellar (described later). Turn right and head down toward the church. At #21 (on the left), look for a red-and-gold shield, over a door, with the name *Talosa*. This marks the home of one of Montepulciano's *contrade,* or neighborhoods; birth and death announcements for the *contrada* are posted on the board next to the door.

Soon you'll come to a viewpoint (on the right) that illustrates Montepulciano's highly strategic position. The ancient town sitting on this high ridge was surrounded by powerful forces—everything you see in this direction was part of the Papal States, ruled from

Rome. In the distance is Lake Trasimeno, once a notorious swamp-land that made it even harder to invade this town.

Continue a few steps farther to the big parking lot in front of the church. Head out to the terrace for a totally different view: the rolling hills that belonged to Siena. And keep in mind that Montepulciano itself belonged to Florence. For the first half of the 16th century, those three formidable powers—Florence, Siena, and Rome (the papacy)—vied to control this small area. Take in the view of Montepulciano's most impressive church, San Biagio—well worth a visit for drivers or hikers (described later).

From here, you can head back up to the main square, or drop into Cantine del Redi to spelunk its wine cellars.

Sights and Experiences in Montepulciano

These are listed in the order you'll reach them on the self-guided walk, above. For me, Montepulciano's best "experiences" are personal: dropping in on either Adamo, the winemaker at Contucci Cantina; or Cesare, the coppersmith at Ramaio Cesare. Either one will greet you with a torrent of cheerful Italian; just smile and nod, pick up what you can from gestures, and appreciate this rare opportunity to meet a true local character.

▲▲Contucci Cantina

Montepulciano's most popular attraction isn't made of stone...it's the famous wine, Vino Nobile. This robust red can be tasted in any of the cantinas lining Via Ricci and Via di Gracciano nel Corso, but the cantina in the basement of Palazzo Contucci is both historic and fun. Skip the palace, formal wine-tasting showroom facing the square, and instead head down the lane on the right to the actual cellars, where you'll meet lively Adamo (ah-DAH-moh), who has been making wine since 1953 and welcomes tourists into his cellar. While at the palace, you may meet Andrea Contucci, whose family has lived here since the 11th century. He loves to share his family's products with the public. Adamo and Signor Contucci usually have a dozen bottles open.

After sipping a little wine with Adamo, explore the palace basement, with its 13th-century vaults. Originally part of the town's wall, these chambers have been filled since the 1500s with huge barrels of wine. Dozens of barrels of Croatian, Italian, and French oak (1,000-2,500 liters each) cradle the wine through a two-year in-the-barrel aging process, while the wine picks up the personality of the wood. After about 35 years, an exhausted barrel has nothing left to offer its wine, so it's retired. Adamo explains that the French oak gives the wine "pure elegance," the Croatian is more masculine, and the Italian oak is a marriage of the two. Each barrel is labeled with the size in liters, the year the wine was barreled, and the percentage of alcohol (determined by how much sun shone in that year). "Nobile"-grade wine needs a minimum of 13 percent alcohol.

Cost and Hours: Free drop-in tasting, daily 8:30-12:30 & 14:30-18:30, Sat-Sun from 9:30, Piazza Grande 13, tel. 0578-757-006, www.contucci.it.

▲Ramaio Cesare

Cesare (CHEH-zah-ray) the coppersmith is an institution in Montepulciano, carrying on his father's and grandfather's trade by hammering into existence an immense selection of copper objects in his cavernous workshop. Though his English is limited, he's happy to show you photos of his work—including the copper top of the Duomo in Siena and the piece he designed and personally delivered to Pope Benedict. Next door, he has assembled a fine museum with items he and his relatives have made, as well as pieces from his personal collection. Cesare is evangelical about copper, and if he's not too busy, he'll create personalized mementoes for visitors—he loves meeting people from around the world who appreciate his handiwork (as his brimming photo album demonstrates). Cesare's justifiable pride in his vocation evokes the hardworking, highly skilled craft guilds that once dominated small-town Italy's commercial and civic life.

Cost and Hours: Demonstration and museum are free; Cesare is generally in his workshop Mon-Sat 8:00-12:30 & 14:30-18:30, Piazzetta del Teatro, tel. 0578-758-753, www.rameria.com. Cesare's shop *(negozio)* is on the main drag, just downhill at Corso #64—look for Rameria Mazzetti, open long hours daily.

Duomo

This church's unfinished facade—rough stonework left waiting for the final marble veneer—is not that unusual. Many Tuscan churches were built just to the point where they had a functional interior, and then, for various practical reasons, the facades were left unfinished. But step inside and you'll be rewarded with some fine art. A beautiful Andrea della Robbia blue-and-white, glazed-terra-cotta *Altar of the Lilies* is behind the baptismal font (on the left as you enter). The high altar, with a top like a pine forest, features a luminous, early-Renaissance Assumption triptych by the Sienese artist Taddeo di Bartolo. Showing Mary in her dreamy eternal sleep as she ascends to be crowned by Jesus, it illustrates how Siena clung to the Gothic aesthetic—elaborate gold leaf and lacy pointed arches—to show heavenly grandeur at the expense of realism.

Cost and Hours: Free, daily 9:00-13:00 & 15:00-18:30.

▲Cantine del Redi

The most impressive wine cellars in Montepulciano sit below the Palazzo Ricci, just a few steps off the main square (toward the Church of San Francesco). Enter through the unassuming door and find your way down a spiral staircase—with rounded steps designed to go easy on fragile noble feet, and lined with rings held in place by finely crafted tiny wrought-iron goat heads. You'll wind up in the dramatic cellars, with gigantic barrels under even more gigantic vaults—several stories high. As you go deeper and deeper into the cellars, high up, natural stone seems to take over the brick. At the deepest point, the atmospheric cave, surrounding a filled-in well, a warren of corridors holds fine wine aging in bottles. Finally you wind up in the shop, where you're welcome to taste two or three Redi wines for free—or, if you show them this book, they'll offer you the free wines along with some light food in their spacious tasting room.

Cost and Hours: Free tasting, €7-20 bottles, affordable shipping, daily 10:30-19:00, next to Palazzo Ricci, tel. 0578-757-166, www.dericci.it.

Civic Museum (Museo Civico)

Eclectic and surprisingly modern, but small and ultimately forgettable, this museum collects bits and pieces of local history with virtually no English explanation. The ground floor and cellar hold ancient artifacts and vases, including some Etruscan items. The next two floors are the pinacoteca (art gallery); the highlight is the first-floor room filled with colorful Andrea della Robbia ceramic altarpieces. You'll find a similar della Robbia altarpiece in situ, in the Duomo, for free.

Cost and Hours: €5, Tue-Sun 10:00-13:00 & 15:00-18:00, closed Mon, Via Ricci 10, tel. 0578-717-300.

Just Outside Montepulciano

San Biagio Church

At the base of Montepulciano's hill, down a picturesque driveway lined with cypresses, this church—designed by Antonio da Sangallo and built of locally quarried travertine—is Renaissance perfection. The proportions of the Greek cross floor plan give the building a pleasing rhythmic quality. Bramante, who designed St. Peter's at the Vatican in 1516, was inspired by this dome. The lone tower was supposed to have a twin, but it was never built. The soaring interior, with a high dome and lantern, creates a fine Renaissance space. Walk around the building to study the freestanding towers, and consider a picnic or snooze on the grass in back. The street called Via di San Biagio, leading from the church up into town, makes for an enjoyable, if challenging, walk.

Cost and Hours: Free, normally open daily 8:30-18:30.

Sleeping in Montepulciano

$$$ Mueblè il Riccio ("Hedgehog") is medieval-elegant, with 10 modern and spotless rooms, an awesome roof terrace, and friendly owners. Five are new "superior" rooms with grand views across the Tuscan valleys (Sb-€80, Db-€100, view Db-€110, superior Db-€150, superior Db with balcony-€160, Tb-€116, superior Tb-€180, superior Qb-€200, breakfast-€8, air-con, guest computer and Wi-Fi, limited free parking—request when you reserve, a block below the main square at Via Talosa 21, tel. 0578-757-713, www.ilriccio.net, info@ilriccio.net, Gió and Ivana speak English). Gió and his son Iacopo give tours of the countryside (€50/hour) in one of their classic Italian cars; for details, see their website. Ivana makes wonderful breakfast tarts.

$$ Albergo Duomo is big, modern, and nondescript, with 13 rooms (with small bathrooms) and a comfortable lounge downstairs (small Db-€75, standard Db-€95, Tb-€115, family deals, elevator, air-con in some rooms for €5 extra, free Wi-Fi, loaner laptops, free parking nearby, Via di San Donato 14, tel. 0578-757-473, www.albergoduomo.it, albergoduomo@libero.it, Elisa and Saverio).

$$ Camere Bellavista has 10 charming, tidy rooms. True to its name, each room has a fine view—though some are better than others. Room 6 has a view terrace worth reserving (Db-€80, terrace Db-€100, cash only, optional €3-10 breakfast at a bar in the piazza, lots of stairs with no elevator, free Wi-Fi, Via Ricci 25, no reception—call before arriving or ring bell, mobile 347-823-2314, www.camerebellavista.it, bellavista@bccmp.com, Gabriella speaks only a smidgen of English).

$$ Vicolo dell'Oste B&B, just off the main drag halfway up through town, has five modern rooms with fully outfitted kitchenettes (Db-€95-100, Tb-€130, Qb-€140, includes breakfast at nearby café, free Wi-Fi, on Via dell'Oste 1—an alley leading right off the main drag just after Caffè Poliziano and opposite the *farmacia* at #47, tel. 0578-758-393, www.vicolodelloste.it, info@vicolodelloste.it, Luisa and Giuseppe).

Countryside Options near Montepulciano: If you'd rather be in the country than in town, don't miss the nearby options listed under "Sleeping near Pienza," later—about a 15-minute drive from Montepulciano.

Eating in Montepulciano

Ai Quattro Venti is fresh, flavorful, fun, and right on Piazza Grande, with a simple dining room and outdoor tables right on the square. It distinguishes itself by offering reasonable portions of tasty, unfussy Tuscan food in an unpretentious setting. Try their very own organic olive oil and wine (€8-9 pastas, €9-10 *secondi*, Fri-Wed 12:30-14:30 & 19:30-22:30, closed Thu, next to City Hall on Piazza Grande, tel. 0578-717-231, Chiara).

Osteria dell'Aquacheta is a carnivore's dream come true, famous among locals for its excellent beef steaks. Its long, narrow room is jammed with shared tables and tight seating, with an open fire in back and a big hunk of red beef lying on the counter like a corpse on a gurney. Giulio, with a pen tucked into his ponytail, whacks off slabs with a cleaver, confirms the weight and price with the diner, and tosses the meat on the grill—seven minutes per side. Steaks are sold by weight (€3/100 grams, or *etto*, one kilo is about the smallest they serve, two can split it for €30). They also serve hearty €6 pastas and salads and a fine house wine. In the tradition of old trattorias, they serve one glass, which you use alternately for wine and water (Wed-Mon 12:30-15:00 & 19:30-22:30, closed Tue, Via del Teatro 22, tel. 0578-758-443 or 0578-717-086).

Osteria del Conte, an attractive but humble family-run bistro, offers a €30 *menù del Conte*—a four-course dinner of local specialties including wine—as well as à la carte options and cooking like mom's. While the interior is very simple, they also have outdoor tables on a stony street at the edge of the historic center (€7-8 pastas, €9-14 *secondi*, Thu-Tue 12:30-14:30 & 19:30-21:30, closed Wed, Via San Donato 19, tel. 0578-756-062).

Le Pentolaccia is a small, family-run restaurant at the upper, relatively untouristy end of the main drag. With both indoor and outdoor seating, they make tasty traditional Tuscan dishes as well as daily fish specials. Cristiana serves, and husband-and-wife team Jacobo and Alessia stir up a storm in the kitchen (€8-10 pastas, €8-15 *secondi*, Fri-Wed 12:00-15:00 & 19:30-22:30, closed Thu, Corso 86, tel. 0578-757-582).

Near Montepulciano, in Monticchiello

If you'd enjoy getting out of town for dinner—but not too far—consider the 15-minute drive to the smaller, picturesque hill town of Monticchiello. Just inside the town's gate is the highly regarded

La Porta restaurant, where Daria pleases diners either indoors or out with well-executed traditional Tuscan dishes (€9 pastas, €12-15 *secondi*, reservations smart; seatings at 12:30, 14:00, 19:30, and 21:30; closed Thu, Via del Piano 1, tel. 0578-755-163, www.osteri-alaporta.it). If La Porta is closed, or you want a bit more contemporary preparation in a modern atmosphere, continue 50 yards up into town and turn right to find **La Cantina,** run by daughter Deborah (similar prices, Tue-Thu 12:30-15:00 & 19:30-22:00, closed Wed, Via San Luigi 3, tel. 0578-755-280).

Getting There: It's a straight shot to Monticchiello, but finding the road is the hard part. At the base of Montepulciano, head toward Pienza. Shortly after passing the road to San Biagio Church (on the right), watch on the left for the Albergo San Biagio. Turn off and take the road that runs up past the left side of this big hotel, and follow it all the way to Monticchiello. This is a rough (gravel at times), middle-of-nowhere drive. As a bonus, right near Monticchiello is a twisty serpentine section lined with stoic cypress trees—one of those classic Tuscan images you'll see on calendars and postcards. It's also possible to reach Monticchiello more directly from Pienza (ask locals for directions).

Montepulciano Connections

Schedule information and bus tickets are available at the TI. All buses leave from Piazza Pietro Nenni. The bus station seems to double as the town hangout, with a lively bar and locals chatting inside. In fact, there's no real ticket window—you'll buy your tickets at the bar. Check www.sienamobilita.it for schedules.

From Montepulciano by Bus to: Florence (2/day, 2 hours, LFI bus, €11.20, www.lfi.it), **Siena** (8/day, none on Sun, 1.25 hours, €6.60), **Pienza** (8/day, 30 minutes, €2.50), **Montalcino** (4/day Mon-Fri, 3/day Sat, none Sun, change in Torrenieri, 1-1.25 hours total, €4.90). There are hourly bus connections to **Chiusi,** a town on the main Florence-Rome rail line (40 minutes, €3.40); Chiusi is a much better bet than the distant Montepulciano station (5 miles away), which is served only by milk-run trains, but it is handy on Sundays if you want to go to Siena. Buses connect Montepulciano's bus station and its train station (6/day, none on Sun).

To Montalcino: This connection is problematic by public transportation—consider asking at the TI for a **taxi,** or call **Eurospin** taxi company, listed under "Helpful Hints" earlier. Although expensive (about €70), a taxi could make sense for two or more people. Otherwise you can take a bus to Torrenieri, then change to get to Montalcino (2 hours). **Drivers** find route S-146 to Montalcino particularly scenic (see "The Crete Senese" on page 738). **Cortona** is another awkward connection, involving a bus to

Chiusi, then a 30-minute train ride to the Camuccia-Cortona train station, four miles below town with poorly timed bus connections to Cortona itself. Consider taking a taxi (about €40).

Pienza

Set on a crest and surrounded by green, rolling hills, the small town of Pienza packs a lot of Renaissance punch. In the 1400s,

locally born Pope Pius II of the Piccolomini family decided to remodel his birthplace in the style that was all the rage: Renaissance. Propelled by papal clout, the town of Corsignano was transformed—in only five years' time—into a jewel of Renaissance architecture. It

was renamed Pienza, after Pope Pius. The plan was to remodel the entire town, but work ended in 1464 when both the pope and his architect, Bernardo Rossellino, died. Their vision—what you see today—was completed a century later. The architectural focal point is the square, Piazza Pio II, surrounded by the Duomo and the pope's family residence, Palazzo Piccolomini. While Piazza Pio II is Pienza's pride and joy, the entire town—a mix of old stonework, potted plants, and grand views—is fun to explore, especially with a camera or sketchpad in hand. You can walk every lane in the tiny town in a few minutes.

Cute as the town is, it's far from undiscovered; tourists can flood Pienza in peak season, and boutiques selling gifty packages of pecorino cheese and local wine greatly outnumber local shops. While it offers fine views of the surrounding countryside, Pienza is situated on a relatively flat plateau rather than the steep pinnacle of more dramatic towns like Montepulciano and Montalcino. For these reasons, it's made to order as a stretch-your-legs break to enjoy the setting, and perhaps tour the palace, but it's not ideal for lingering overnight.

Nearly every shop sells the town's specialty: pecorino cheese. This pungent sheep's cheese is available fresh *(fresco)* or aged *(secco)*, and sometimes contains other ingredients, such as truffles or peppers. Look on menus for warm Pecorino *(al forno* or *alla griglia)*, often topped with honey or pears and served with bread. Along with a glass of local wine, this just might lead you to a new understanding of *la dolce vita.*

Orientation to Pienza

Tourist Information: The TI is 10 yards up the street from Piazza Pio II, inside the Diocesan Museum (Wed-Mon 10:00-13:00 & 14:30-18:00, closed Tue, Sat-Sun only in Nov-March, Corso il Rossellino 30, tel. 0578-749-905). Ignore the kiosk just outside the gate, labeled *Informaturista*, which is a private travel agency.

Arrival in Pienza: Buses drop you just a couple of blocks directly in front of the town's main entrance. If **driving**, read signs carefully—some parking spots are reserved for locals, others require the use of a cardboard clock, and others are pay-and-display. Parking is tight, so if you don't see anything quickly, head for the large lot at Piazza del Mercato near Largo Roma outside the old town: As you approach town and reach the "ZTL" cul-de-sac (marked with a red circle) surrounding the park right in front of the town gate, head up the left side of town and look for the turn-off on the left for parking (€1.50/hour, closed Fri morning during market).

Helpful Hints: Market day is Friday morning at Piazza del Mercato, just outside the town walls. A public **WC,** marked *gabinetti pubblici,* is on the right as you face the town gate from outside, on Piazza Dante Alighieri (down the lane next to the faux TI).

Sights in Pienza

▲Piazza Pio II

One of Italy's classic piazzas, this square is famous for its elegance and artistic unity. The square and the surrounding buildings were

all designed by Rossellino to form an "outdoor room." Spinning around clockwise, you'll see City Hall (13th-century bell tower with a Renaissance facade and a fine loggia), the Bishop's Palace (now the Diocesan Museum), the Duomo, and the Piccolomini family palace. Just to the left of the church, a lane leads to the best viewpoint in town (described later).

Duomo

Its classic, symmetrical Renaissance facade—dated 1462 with the Piccolomini family coat of arms immodestly front and center—dominates Piazza Pio II. The interior is charming, with several Gothic altarpieces and painted arches. Windows feature the crest of Pius II, with five half-moons advertising the number of crusades that his family funded. The interior art is Sienese Gothic, on the cusp of the Renaissance. As the local clay and *tufo* stone did not make an ideal building foundation, the church is slouching. The church's cliff-hanging position bathes the interior in light, but also makes it feel as if the building could break in half if you jumped up and down. See the cracks in the apse walls, and get seasick behind the main altar.

Cost and Hours: Free, generally open daily 7:00-13:00 & 14:30-19:00.

▲Palazzo Piccolomini

The home of Pius II (see page 649) and the Piccolomini family (until 1962) can only be visited on an escorted audioguide tour (about 30 minutes total). You'll see six rooms (dining room, armory, bedroom, library, and so on), three galleries (art-strewn hallways), and the panoramic loggia before being allowed to linger in the beautiful hanging gardens. The drab interiors, faded paintings, coffered ceilings, and scuffed furniture have a mothballed elegance that makes historians wish they'd seen it in its heyday. The audioguide very dryly identifies each item in each room but (sadly) does little to muster enthusiasm for this small-town palace that once hosted a big-name player in European politics. While it's not quite the fascinating slice of 15th-century aristocratic life that it could be (I'd like to know more about the pope's toilet), this is still the best small-town palace experience I've found in Tuscany (it famously starred as the Capulets' home in Franco Zeffirelli's 1968 Academy Award-winning *Romeo and Juliet*). You can peek inside the door for free to check out the well-preserved, painted courtyard. In Renaissance times, most buildings were covered with elaborate paintings like these.

Cost and Hours: €7, Tue-Sun 10:00-13:00 & 14:00-18:30, first tour departs at 10:30, last tour at 18:00, closed Mon, Piazza Pio II 2, tel. 0578-748-392, www.palazzopiccolominipienza.it.

Diocesan Museum (Museo Diocesano)

This measly collection of religious paintings, ecclesiastical gear, altarpieces, and old giant hymnals from local churches fills one room of the cardinal's Renaissance palace. The art is provincial Sienese, displayed in chronological order from the 12th through 17th centuries (but with no English information).

Cost and Hours: €4.50, same hours as TI—which is where you'll buy the ticket, Corso il Rossellino 30.

View Terrace

As you face the church, the upper lane leading left brings you to the panoramic promenade. Views from the terrace include the Tuscan countryside and, in the distance, Monte Amiata, the largest mountain in southern Tuscany. You can exit the viewpoint down the first alley, Via del'Amore—the original Lover's Lane—which leads back to the main drag.

Sleeping near Pienza

While I wouldn't hang my hat in sleepy Pienza itself, some fine countryside options sit just outside town—including one of my favorite Italian *agriturismo* experiences, Cretaiole. Location-wise, this is an ideal home base: midway between Montepulciano and Montalcino, and immersed in Tuscan splendor. Three or four of *the* iconic Tuscan landscape vistas are within 10 or 15 minutes' drive of Pienza; you'll make your sightseeing commute along extremely scenic roads with plenty of strategically located pullouts.

$$$ Agriturismo Cretaiole, in pristine farmland just outside Pienza, is a terrific value if you want to call Tuscany home for a long stay It's warmly run by reformed city-slicker Isabella, her country-boy husband Carlo, and their family. This family-friendly farm welcomes visitors for weeklong stays (generally Sat-Sat) in six comfortable apartments. Eager  to share their local traditions, they offer travelers a rich cultural education. Carlo is a professional olive-oil taster. Carlo's father, Luciano, is in charge of the grappa and tends the vegetable garden (take your pick of the free veggies). And Isabella is a tireless Jill-of-all-trades, who prides herself on personally assisting each of her guests to find exactly the Tuscan experience they're dreaming of. While there's no swimming pool—for philosophical reasons—many thoughtful touches and extras, such as Wi-Fi, mountain bikes, and loaner mobile phones, are provided. Isabella also organizes fairly priced optional activities such as pasta-making and olive-oil tasting classes, family-style Tuscan dinners, winery tours, truffle hunts and grape and olive harvesting (in season), visits to the studios of local artisans, side-trips to Siena, watercolor classes, dinner at a local monastery, and more (Db-€825/week, small Db apartment-€990/week, large Db apartment-€1,290/week, same apartment for four-€1,595/week, these prices promised with this book in 2014, fewer activities and lower prices mid-Nov-mid-March, tel. 0578-748-083, Isabella's mobile 338-740-9245, www.cretaiole.it, info@cretaiole.it). It's on the Montalcino-Pienza road (S-146), about 11 miles out of Montalcino, and about 2.5 miles from Pienza. While they prefer weeklong stays, when things are slow they may accept guests for as few as three nights (for this you must book less than a month in advance, Db-€120, 3-night minimum). The same family runs two other properties, with the same activities and personal attention as the main *agriturismo:* **Le Casine di Castello** is a townhouse with two units and the same prices as Cretaiole, but guests have more independence. The more upscale **Casa Moricciani** is a swanky villa featuring dreamy views, plush interiors, loads of extras, and pure Tuscan luxury (€2,900/week upstairs or €3,900/week downstairs, each with 2 bedrooms and 2 bathrooms). Both properties are in the untouristy medieval village of Castelmuzio, five miles north of Pienza; for details, see www.buongiornotoscana.com.

$$$ Fonte Bertusi, nearly across the road from Cretaiole, is well-run by young couple Manuela and Andrea, Andrea's father Eduardo, and their attention-starved cats. This imaginative family has scattered vivid, whimsical bits and pieces of artwork around the grounds and in the rooms. The eight apartments are simple—mixing rustic decor with avant-garde creations—and a bit pricey, but the setting is sublime (nightly rate: 1-bedroom apartment-€130, 2-bedroom apartment-€260, includes breakfast; weekly rate: €710-1,010, €40 extra per person for breakfast all week; free Wi-Fi, laundry service, swimming pool, communal BBQ and outdoor kitchen, just outside Pienza toward San Quirico d'Orcia on the right—don't confuse it with the turnoff for "Il Fonte" just before, tel. 0578-748-077, www.fontebertusi.it, info@fontebertusi.it).

Pienza Connections

Bus tickets are sold at the bar/café (marked *Il Caffè,* closed Tue) just outside Pienza's town gate (or pay a little extra and buy tickets from the driver). Buses leave from a few blocks up the street, directly in front of the town entrance. Montepulciano is the nearest transportation hub to other points.

From Pienza by Bus to: Siena (6/day, none on Sun, 1.5 hours, €4.40), **Montepulciano** (8/day, 30 minutes, €2.50), **Montalcino** (4/day Mon-Fri, 3/day Sat, none sun, change in Torrenieri, 45-60 minutes total, €3.40).

Montalcino

On a hill overlooking vineyards and valleys, Montalcino—famous for its delicious and pricey Brunello di Montalcino red wines—is a must for wine lovers. It's a pleasant, low-impact town with a fine ambience but little sightseeing. Everyone touring this area seems to be relaxed and in an easy groove...as if enjoying a little wine buzz.

In the Middle Ages, Montalcino (mohntahl-CHEE-noh) was considered Siena's biggest ally. Originally aligned with Florence, the town switched sides after the Sienese beat up Florence in the Battle of Montaperti in 1260. The Sienese persuaded the Montalcini to join their side by forcing them to sleep one night in the bloody Florentine-strewn battlefield.

Montalcino prospered under Siena, but like its ally, it waned after the Medici family took control of the region. The village became a humble place. Then, in the late 19th century, the Biondi Santi family created a fine, dark red wine, calling it "the brunette" (Brunello). Today's affluence is due to the town's much-sought-after wine.

If you're not a wine lover, you may find Montalcino a bit too focused on *vino*, but one sip of Brunello makes even wine skeptics believe that Bacchus was onto something. Note that Rosso di Montalcino (a younger version of Brunello) is also very good, at half the price. Those with a sweet tooth will enjoy crunching the Ossi di Morta ("bones of the dead") cookies popular in Tuscany.

Orientation to Montalcino

Sitting atop a hill amidst a sea of vineyards, Montalcino is surrounded by walls and dominated by the Fortezza (a.k.a. "La Rocca"). From here, roads lead down into the two main squares: Piazza Garibaldi and Piazza del Popolo.

Tourist Information: The helpful TI, just off Piazza Garibaldi in City Hall, can find you a room for no fee. They sell bus tickets; can call ahead to book a visit at a countryside winery (€1-per-person service fee); and have information on taxi service to nearby towns, abbeys, and monasteries (daily 10:00-13:00 & 14:00-17:30, tel. 0577-849-331, www.prolocomontalcino.com).

Arrival in Montalcino: The **bus** station is on Piazza Cavour, about 300 yards from the town center. From here, simply follow Via Mazzini straight into town.

Drivers coming in for a short visit should drive around the old gate under the fortress, take the first right (follow signs to *Fortezza;* it looks almost forbidden), and grab a spot in the pay lot at the fortress (€1.50/hour, free 20:00-8:00). If you miss this lot—or if it's full—follow the town's western wall toward the Madonna del Socorrso church and a long pay lot with the same prices. Otherwise, park for free a short walk away.

Helpful Hints: Market day is Friday (7:00-13:00) on Viale della Libertà (near the Fortezza). Day-trippers be warned: Montalcino has **no baggage storage.**

Montalcino

PORTA BURELLI

VIA LAPINI

Piazza Cavour

BUS STATION

VIALE ROMA

LAPINI

MADONNA DEL SOCCORSO

CITY WALLS

SAN FRANCESCO

VIA DEL PINO

VIA CIALDINI

VIA MAZZINI

VIA MOGLIO

VIA D. MISTERO

VIA CASTELLANA

VIA S. LUCIA

PORTA CASTELLANA

CITY WALLS

VIALE DELLA LIBERTA

VIA SPAGNI

Piazza Santa Catarina

COSTA SPAGNI

VIA FONTE BULA

DUOMO

VIA SPAGNI

Piazza del Popolo

CITY HALL, TOWER & ℹ

VIALE PIERO STROZZI

VIALE DELLA LIBERTA

FREE

SANT' AGOSTINO

CIVIC MUSEUM

VIA RICASOLI

Piazza Garibaldi

V. BOLDRINI

VIA DONNOLI

C. GATTOLI

PAN.

V. DELLE CASERME

V. SOCCORSO SALONI

V. LANDI

VIA LANDI

PORTA GATTOLI

PORTA AL CASSERO

Piazzale Fortezza

WC

FORTEZZA

VIA ALDO MORO

PORTA CERBAIA

100 Meters
100 Yards

VIA OSTIUCCIO

VIA CIRCONVALLAZIONE

To Via Cassia, Siena, Pienza & Montepulciano

To 13

To Sant'Antimo & 5

1 Hotel Dei Capitani
2 Palazzina Cesira
3 Albergo Giardino
4 Affittacamere Mariuccia
5 To La Crociona Agriturismo
6 Re di Macchia Ristorante
7 Taverna il Grappolo Blu

8 Ristorante-Pizzeria San Giorgio
9 Co-op Supermarket
10 Enoteca la Fortezza di Montalcino
11 Caffè Fiaschetteria Italiana
12 Enoteca di Piazza
13 To Banfi & Argiano Wineries

Sights in Montalcino

Fortezza

This 14th-century fort, built under the rule of Siena, is now little more than an empty shell. People visit for its wine bar (see page 736). You can climb the ramparts to enjoy a panoramic view of the Asso and Orcia valleys, or enjoy a picnic in the park surrounding the fort.

Cost and Hours: €4 for rampart walk—buy ticket and enter in the wine bar, €6 combo-ticket includes Civic Museum (sold only at museum), daily 9:00-20:00, until 18:00 Nov-March, last entry 30 minutes before closing.

Piazza del Popolo

All roads in tiny Montalcino seem to lead to the main square, Piazza del Popolo ("People's Square").

Since 1888, the recommended **Caffè Fiaschetteria Italiana** has been *the* elegant place to enjoy a drink. Its founder, inspired by Caffè Florian in Venice, brought fine coffee to this humble town of woodcutters.

City Hall was the fortified seat of government. It's decorated by the coats of arms of judges who, in the interest of fairness, were from outside of town. Like Siena, Montalcino was a republic in the Middle Ages. When Florentines took Siena in 1555, Siena's ruling class retreated here and held out for four more years. The Medici coat of arms (with the six pills), which supersedes all the others, is a reminder that in 1559 Florence finally took Montalcino.

The one-handed **clock** was the norm until 200 years ago. For five centuries the arcaded **loggia** hosted the town market. And, of course, it's fun to simply observe the *passeggiata*—these days mostly a parade of tourists here for the wine.

Montalcino Museums (Musei di Montalcino)

While it's technically three museums in one (archaeology, medieval art, and modern art), and it's surprisingly big and modern for this little town, Montalcino's lone museum ranks only as a decent bad-weather activity. The archaeology collection, filling the cellar, includes interesting artifacts from the area dating back as far as—gulp—200,000 B.C. With good English explanations, this section also displays a mannequin dressed as an Etruscan soldier and a model of the city walls in early Roman times. The ground, first, and second floors hold the medieval and modern art collections, with an emphasis on Gothic sacred art (with works from Montalcino's heyday, the 13th to 16th centuries). Most of the art was created by local artists. The ground floor is best, with a large collection of crucifixes and the museum's highlights, a glazed-terra-cotta altarpiece and statue of St. Sebastian, both by Andrea della Robbia.

Cost and Hours: €4.50, €6 combo-ticket includes rampart

walk at Fortezza, Tue-Sun 10:00-13:00 & 14:00-17:50, closed Mon, Via Ricasoli 31, to the right of Sant'Agostino Church, tel. 0577-846-014.

Sleeping in Montalcino

$$$ Hotel Dei Capitani, at the end of town near the bus station, has plush public spaces, an inviting pool, and a cliffside terrace offering plenty of reasons for lounging. About half of the 29 rooms come with vast Tuscan views for the same price (request a view room when you reserve), the nonview rooms are bigger, and everyone has access to the terrace (Db-€138 with this book in 2014, extra bed-€40, air-con, elevator, free guest computer and Wi-Fi, limited free parking—first come, first served, Via Lapini 6, tel. 0577-847-227, www.deicapitani.it, info@deicapitani.it).

$$ Palazzina Cesira, right in the heart of the old town, is a gem renting five spacious and tastefully decorated rooms in a fine 13th-century residence with a palatial lounge and a pleasant garden. You'll enjoy a refined and tranquil ambience, a nice breakfast (with eggs), and the chance to get to know Lucilla and her American husband Roberto, who are generous with local advice (Db-€105, suites-€125, cash only, 2-night minimum, 3-night minimum on holiday weekends, air-con, free guest computer and Wi-Fi, free off-street parking, Via Soccorso Saloni 2, tel. 0577-846-055, www.montalcinoitaly.com, p.cesira@tin.it).

$ Affittacamere Mariuccia has three small, colorful, good-value, Ikea-chic rooms on the main drag over a heaven-scented bakery (Sb-€40, Db-€50, air-con, breakfast-€10 extra, check in across the street at Enoteca Pierangioli before 20:00 or let them know arrival time, Piazza del Popolo 16, rooms at #28, tel. 0577-849-113, mobile 348-392-4780, www.affittacameremariuccia.it, enotecapierangioli@hotmail.com, Alessandro and Stefania speak English).

$ Albergo Giardino, old and basic, has nine big simple rooms, no public spaces, and a convenient location near the bus station (Db-€55-60, 10 percent discount with this book outside May and Sept, no breakfast, Piazza Cavour 4, tel. 0577-848-257, mobile 338-684-3163, albergoilgiardino@virgilio.it; Roberto speaks English; dad Mario doesn't).

Near Montalcino

$$ La Crociona, an *agriturismo* farm and working vineyard, rents seven fully equipped apartments. Fiorella Vannoni and Roberto and Barbara Nannetti offer cooking classes and tastes of the Brunello wine grown and bottled on the premises (Db-€95, or €65 in Oct-mid-May; Qb-€130, or €95 in Oct-mid-May; lower weekly rates, metered gas heating, laundry-€8/load, covered pool, hot tub, fitness room, La Croce 15, tel. 0577-847-133 or 0577-848-007, www.lacrociona.com, info@lacrociona.com). The farm is two miles south of Montalcino on the road to the Sant'Antimo Monastery; don't turn off at the first entrance to the village of La Croce—wait for the second one, following directions to Tenuta Crocedimezzo e Crociona). A good restaurant is next door.

Eating in Montalcino

Restaurants

Re di Macchia is an invitingly intimate restaurant where Antonio serves up the Tuscan fare Roberta cooks. Look for their seasonal menu and Montalcino-only wine list. Try the €25 fixed-price meal, and for €17 more, have it paired with local wines carefully selected to accompany each dish (€9-10 pastas, €16 *secondi*, Fri-Wed 12:00-14:00 & 19:00-21:00, closed Thu, reservations strongly recommended, Via Soccorso Saloni 21, tel. 0577-846-116).

Taverna il Grappolo Blu is unpretentious, friendly, and serious about its wine, serving local specialties and vegetarian options to an enthusiastic crowd (€8-9 pastas, €9-14 *secondi*, daily 12:00-15:00 & 19:00-22:00, reservations smart, near the main square, a few steps off Via Mazzini at Scale di Via Moglio 1, tel. 0577-847-150, Luciano, www.grappoloblu.it).

Ristorante-Pizzeria San Giorgio is a homey trattoria/pizzeria with kitschy decor and reasonable prices. It's a reliable choice for a simple meal (€4-7 pizzas, €8 pastas, €8-12 *secondi*, daily 12:00-15:00 & 19:00-22:30, Via Soccorso Saloni 10-14, tel. 0577-848-507, Mara).

Picnic: Gather ingredients at the **Co-op supermarket** on Via Sant'Agostino (Mon-Sat 8:30-13:00 & 16:00-20:00, closed Sun, just off Via Ricasoli in front of Sant'Agostino Church), then enjoy your feast up at the Madonna del Soccorso Church, with vast territorial views.

Wine Bars: Note that two of the places listed under "Wine Bars *(Enoteche)* in Town," later, also serve light food.

Wine Tasting and Wineries

There are two basic approaches for sampling Montalcino's wines: at an *enoteca* in town, or at a countryside winery. Serious wine connoisseurs will enjoy a day of winery-hopping, sipping the wines right where they were created. But if you don't have the time, or want to try more than one producer's wines, you might prefer to simply visit a wine bar in town, where you can comfortably taste a variety of vintages before safely stumbling back to your hotel.

Wine Bars *(Enoteche)* in Town

Enoteca la Fortezza di Montalcino offers a chance to taste top-end wines by the glass, each with an English explanation. While wine snobs turn up their noses, the medieval setting inside Montalcino's fort is a hit for most visitors. Spoil yourself with Brunello in the cozy *enoteca* or at an outdoor table (€13 for 3 tastings, or €22 for 3 "top-end" tastings; €10-18 two-person sampler plates of cheeses, *salumi,* honeys, and olive oil; daily 9:00-20:00, closes at 18:00 Nov-March, inside the Fortezza, tel. 0577-849-211, www.enotecalafortezza.com, info@enotecalafortezza.com).

Caffè Fiaschetteria Italiana, a classic, venerable café/wine bar, was founded by Ferruccio Biondi Santi, the creator of the famous Brunello wine. The wine library in the back of the café boasts many local choices. A meeting place since 1888, this grand café also serves light lunches and espresso to tourists and locals alike (€6-12 Brunellos by the glass, €3-5 light snacks, €8-12 plates; same prices inside, outside, or in back room; daily 7:30-23:00, closed Thu Nov-Easter, free Wi-Fi, Piazza del Popolo 6, tel. 0577-849-043). And if it's coffee you need, this place—with its classic 1961 espresso machine—is considered the best in town.

Enoteca di Piazza is one of a chain of wine shops with a system of mechanical dispensers. A "drink card" (like a debit card) keeps track of the samples you take, for which you'll pay from €1 to €9 for each 50-milliliter taste of the 100 different wines, including some whites—rare in this town. The only nibbles are saltine-type crackers. They hope you'll buy a bottle of the samples you like and are happy to educate you in English. (Rule of thumb: A bottle costs about 10 times the cost of the sample. If you buy a bottle, the sample of that wine is free.) While the place feels a little formulaic, it can be fun—the wine is great, and the staff is casual and helpful (daily 9:00-20:00, near Piazza del Popolo at Via Matteotti 43, tel. 0577-848-104, www.enotecadipiazza.com). Confusingly, there are three similarly named places in this same area—this tasting room is a block below the main square.

Wineries in the Countryside

The surrounding countryside is littered with wineries, some of which offer tastings. A few require an appointment, but many are happy to serve a glass to potential buyers and show them around. The Montalcino TI can give you a list of more than 150 regional wineries and will call ahead for you (€1 fee per person). Or check with the vintners' consortium (tel. 0577-848-246, www.consorzio-brunellodimontalcino.it, info@consorziobrunellodimontalcino.it). These two places listed below are big and capable of handling a steady flow of international visitors; they don't offer an "authentic" Tuscan or cozy experience, but they are convenient and user-friendly.

Argiano claims to be one of the oldest working wineries in the region, dating back to 1580. About a 10-minute drive south of Montalcino at Sant'Angelo in Colle, their one-hour tour in English includes the vineyards, the exterior of a historic villa, and ancient moldy cellars full of wine casks. They also rent on-site apartments—handy for those who have oversampled (€20 tour includes 6 wine samples, reserve in advance, tel. 0577-844-037, www.argiano.net, coming by car the last 2 miles are along a rough-but-drivable track through vineyards).

Banfi, run by the Italian-American Mariani brothers, is huge and touristy. While it's not an intimate family winery, the grounds are impressive and they're well set up to introduce the passing hordes to their wines (€15 for 3 tastings, €3.50-25 per glass, daily 10:00-19:00, free tours Mon-Fri at 16:00—reserve in advance, 10-minute drive south of Montalcino in Sant'Angelo Scalo, tel. 0577-877-500, www.castellobanfi.com, reservations@banfi.it).

Bus Tour: If you lack a car (or don't want to drive), you can take a tour on the **Brunello Wine Bus,** which laces together a variety of wineries (€25, mid-June-Oct Tue, Thu, and Sat, departs at 9:00, returns at 20:00, tel. 0577-846-021, www.lecameredibacco.com, info@lecameredibacco.com).

Montalcino Connections

Montalcino is poorly connected to just about everywhere except Siena— making it a good day trip if Siena is your base—but other connections are generally workable. Montalcino's bus station is on Piazza Cavour, within the town walls. Bus tickets are sold at the bar on Piazza Cavour, at the TI, and at some tobacco shops, but not on board (except for the bus to Sant'Antimo). Check schedules at the TI, at the bus station, or at www.sienamobilita.it. The nearest train station is a 20-minute bus ride away, in Buonconvento (bus runs nearly hourly, €2.05).

From Montalcino by Bus: The handiest direct bus is to **Siena** (6/day Mon-Sat, 4/day Sun, 1.5 hours, €4.90). To reach **Pienza** or **Montepulciano,** ride the bus to Torrenieri (5/day Mon-Sat, none on Sun, 20 minutes), where you'll switch to line #114 for the rest of the way (from Torrenieri: 25 minutes and €3.40 total to Pienza; 45 minutes and €4.90 total to Montepulciano). A local bus runs to **Sant'Antimo** (3/day Mon-Fri, 2/day Sat, none on Sun, 15 minutes, €1.50, buy tickets on board). Anyone going to **Florence** by bus changes in Siena; since the bus arrives at Siena's train station, it's handier to go the rest of the way to Florence by train. Alternatively, you could take the bus to Buonconvento (described earlier), and catch the train there to Florence.

The Crete Senese

Between Siena and the trio of towns I've described (Montepulciano, Pienza, Montalcino), the hilly area known as the "Sienese Clay Hills" is full of colorful fields and curvy, scenic roads. The Crete Senese (KRAY-teh seh-NAY-zeh) begins at Siena's doorstep and tumbles south through some of the most eye-pleasing scenery in Italy. You'll see an endless parade of classic Tuscan scenes, rolling hills topped with medieval towns, olive groves, rustic stone farmhouses, and a skyline punctuated with cypress trees. You won't find many wineries here, since the clay soil is better for wheat and sunflowers, but you will find the pristine, panoramic Tuscan countryside featured on countless calendars and postcards.

During the spring, the fields are painted in yellow and green with fava beans and broom, dotted by red poppies on the fringes. Sunflowers decorate the area during June and July, and expanses of windblown grass fill the landscape for much of the early spring and summer.

Most roads to the southeast of Siena will give you a taste of this area, but one of the most scenic stretches is the Lauretana road (Siena-Asciano-San Giovanni d'Asso, S-438, S-451, and SP-60a on road maps; the numbering changes as you drive, but it feels like the same road). To find the Lauretana road from Siena, follow signs for the A-1 expressway; you'll turn off onto S-438 (look for the sign for *Asciano*) well before you reach the expressway. You'll come across plenty of turnouts for panoramic photo opportunities on this road, as well as a few roadside picnic areas and several good accommodations (see "Sleeping in the Crete Senese," later).

For a break from the winding road, about 15 miles from Siena, you'll find the quaint and non-touristy village of **Asciano.** With a medieval town center and several interesting churches and museums, this town offers a rare look at everyday Tuscan living—and it's a great place for lunch (TI open Tue-Sun 10:30-13:00 & 15:00-18:00, Mon 10:00-13:00, at Corso Matteotti 18, tel. 0577-718-811). If you're in town on Saturday, gather a picnic at the outdoor market (Via Amendola, 8:00-13:00).

A bit farther along, in **Chiusure** (about 6 miles south of Asciano, on S-451), follow signs up a steep driveway to the *casa di reposo* (nursing home) for a fine viewpoint over the Crete Senese, including classic views of jagged *calanchi* cliffs. From that hilltop,

The Beauty of Tuscany's Geology (and Vice Versa)

While North Americans have romanticized notions of the "Tuscan" landscape, there's a surprisingly wide variety of land forms in the region. Never having been crushed by a glacier, Tuscany is anything but flat. The hills and mountains scattered around the area are made up of different substances, each of which is ideal for very different types of cultivation.

The Chianti region (between Florence and Siena) is rough and rocky, with an inhospitable soil that challenges grape vines to survive while coaxing them to produce excellent wine grapes.

Farther south, the soil switches from rock to clay, silt, and sand. The region called the Crete Senese is literally translated as the "Sienese Clay Hills"—a perfect description of the landscape. Seen from a breezy viewpoint, it's easy to imagine that these clay hills were once at the bottom of the sea floor. The soil here is the yin to Chianti's yang: not ideal for wine, but perfect for truffles and for vast fields of cereal crops such as wheat, fava beans, and sun-yellow rapeseed (for canola oil). In the spring and summer, the Crete Senese is blanketed with brightly colorful crops and flowers. But by the fall, after the harvest, it's a brown and dusty desolate wasteland punctuated with pointy cypress trees—still picturesque, but in a surface-of-the-moon way. Within the Crete Senese, you can distinguish two types of hills shaped by erosion: smooth, rounded *biancane* and pointy, jagged *calanchi*.

The area around Montepulciano and Montalcino is more varied, with rocky protuberances breaking up the undulating clay hills (and providing a suitable home for wine grapes). Even farther south is the Val d'Orcia, the valley of the Orcia River, with its own beauty that mixes clay hills and jutting rock.

You'll see many hot springs in this part of Tuscany, as well as town names with the word *Terme* (for "spa" or "hot spring"). These generally occur where clay meets rock: Water moving through the clay encounters a barrier and gets trapped. Aside from hot water, another byproduct of this change in landscapes is travertine, explaining the quarries you may see in or near spa towns.

you can also see the **Abbey of Monte Oliveto Maggiore.** Located 1.5 miles west of Chiursure, the abbey houses a famous fresco cycle of the life of St. Benedict, painted by Renaissance masters Il Sodoma and Luca Signorelli (free, daily 9:15-12:00 & 15:15-18:00, Nov-March until 17:00, Gregorian chanting Sat-Sun at 18:30, Sun also at 11:00, Mon-Fri at 18:15, call to confirm, tel. 0577-707-611, www.monteolivetomaggiore.it).

Once you reach the town of **San Giovanni d'Asso**—in the

heart of the truffle region—it's a short drive southwest to Montalcino, or southeast to Pienza (each about 12 miles away).

Another scenic drive is the lovely stretch between Montalcino and Montepulciano. This route (S-146 on road maps) alternates between the grassy hills of the Crete Senese and sunbathed vineyards of the Orcia River valley. Stop by Pienza en route.

Sleeping in the Crete Senese

If pastoral landscapes and easy access to varied towns are your goals, you can't do much better than sleeping in the Crete Senese. These countryside options sit between Siena, Montepulciano, Pienza, and Montalcino (a 15- to 45-minute drive from any of them). These options line up on (or just off) the scenic roads (S-438 and S-451) south of Siena; I've listed them from north to south.

$$$ Recommended local guide **Roberto Bechi** (see page 636) has designed and built a new house from scratch that's immersed in gorgeous Crete Sense scenery (about 15 minutes south of Siena). With five spacious rooms, the house is entirely "green," with a zero-carbon footprint (Db-€100, mobile 328-425-5648, www.toursby-roberto.com, toursbyroberto@gmail.com). It's just off road S-438; take the turnoff for Fontanelle.

$ **Casanova Agriturismo** is for people who *really* want to stay on an authentic, working farm. This rustic place comes with tractors, plenty of farm smells and noises, and a barn full of priceless Chianina cows. If the five simple rooms and one apartment take a back seat to the farm workings, the lodgings are accordingly inexpensive, and you'll appreciate the results of their hard work when you dig into one of their fine farm-fresh dinners (€20/person). German Wiebke (who speaks great English and runs the accommodations), her Tuscan husband Bartolo (who works the fields), his mama Paola (who cooks), and the rest of the Conte clan make this a true *agriturismo* experience (Db-€60, apartment-€80 for 2 and €10 per additional person up to 4, breakfast-€8, free Wi-Fi in some areas, swimming pool, just outside Asciano on road S-451 toward Chiusure, tel. 0577-718-324, mobile 346-792-0859, www.agriturismo-casanova.it, info@agriturismo-casanova.it).

$$ **Agriturismo il Molinello** ("Little Mill") rents six apartments, two built over a medieval mill, on the grounds of a working farm with organic produce, olives, and a truffle ground. Hardworking Alessandro and Elisa share their organic produce and offer weekly wine and olive-oil tastings for a minimum of four people; they also lead cooking classes on request. From May through October, they give free guided tours of Siena on Tuesday afternoons. More rustic than romantic, and lacking the dramatic views of some places, this is a nice mix of farm and style. With children, friendly

dogs, toys, and a swimming pool, it's ideal for families (Db-€50-80, Qb-€70-100, apartment for up to 8-€160-200 depending on season and number of people, optional organic breakfast-€9.50, one-week stay required in July-Aug, discounts and no minimum stay off-season, free Wi-Fi in public areas, mountain-bike rentals, biking maps and guided bike tours, between Asciano and the village of Serre di Rapolano—on the road toward Rapolano, 30 minutes southeast of Siena, tel. 0577-704-791, mobile 335-692-5720, www.molinello.com, info@molinello.com).

Cortona

Cortona blankets a 1,700-foot hill surrounded by dramatic Tuscan and Umbrian views. Frances Mayes' book *Under the Tuscan Sun*

placed this town in the touristic limelight, just as Peter Mayle's books popularized the Luberon region in France. But long before Mayes ever published a book, Cortona was popular with Romantics and considered one of the classic Tuscan hill towns. Although it's unquestionably touristy, unlike San Gimignano, Cortona maintains a rustic and gritty personality—even with its long history of foreigners who, enamored with its Tuscan charm, made this their adopted home.

The city began as one of the largest Etruscan settlements, the remains of which can be seen at the base of the city walls, as well as in the nearby tombs. It grew to its present size in the 13th to 16th centuries, when it was a colorful and crowded city, eventually allied with Florence. The farmland that fills almost every view from the city was marshy and uninhabitable until about 200 years ago, when it was drained and turned into some of Tuscany's most fertile land.

Art lovers know Cortona as the home of Renaissance painter Luca Signorelli, Baroque master Pietro da Cortona (Berretini), and the 20th-century Futurist artist Gino Severini. The city's museums and churches reveal many of the works of these native sons.

Orientation to Cortona

Most of the main sights, shops, and restaurants cluster around the level streets on the Piazza Garibaldi-Piazza del Duomo axis, but Cortona will have you huffing and puffing up some steep hills. From Piazza Garibaldi, it's a level five-minute walk down bustling shop-lined Via Nazionale to Piazza della Repubblica, the heart of the town, which is dominated by City Hall (Palazzo del Comune). From this square, a two-minute stroll leads you past the TI, the interesting Etruscan Museum, and the theater to Piazza del Duomo, where you'll find the recommended Diocesan Museum. These sights are along the more-or-less level spine that runs through the bottom of town; from here, Cortona sprawls upward. Steep streets, many of them stepped, go from Piazza della Repubblica up to the San Niccolò and Santa Margherita churches and the Medici Fortress (a 30-minute climb from Piazza della Repubblica). In this residential area, you'll see fewer tourists and get a better sense of the "real" Cortona.

In the flat valley below Cortona sprawls the modern, workaday town of Camucia (kah-moo-CHEE-ah), with the train station and other services (such as launderettes) that you won't find in the hill town itself.

Tourist Information

To reach the helpful TI, head to Piazza Signorelli, then walk through the courtyard of the Etruscan Museum and up a short flight of steps, at the back (mid-May-Oct Mon-Sat 9:00-13:00 & 15:00-18:00, Sun 9:00-13:00, Nov-mid-May Mon-Fri 9:00-13:00 & 15:00-18:00, Sat 9:00-13:00, closed Sun, tel. 0575-637-223 or 0575-637-276, www.turismo.provincia.arezzo.it).

Arrival in Cortona

Cortona is challenging but doable by public transportation. There are few intercity buses, so your best bet for reaching the town is by train or by car.

By Train: Trains arrive at the unstaffed Camucia station, in the valley four miles below Cortona. Sporadic local buses connect the train station and Piazza Garibaldi in Cortona in about 10 minutes. (If you choose to walk, it's a long, steep climb, and there are no sidewalks.) From the station, walk out the front door and look left to find the bus shelter (with schedules posted). Unfortunately, buses depart only about once per hour—and only twice daily on Sundays—and the schedule is not well-coordinated with train times (purchase €1.60 from driver; you want a bus marked for Cortona rather than the opposite direction, Terontola). On the schedule, departures marked with S do not run during school vacations; those marked with N run only during school vacations. Buses usually drop off at Piazza Garibaldi, but may stop instead at Piazza del Mercato (just outside the city walls near Porta Santa Maria), requiring a 10-minute uphill walk to Piazza Signorelli (for the TI and the Etruscan Museum).

If you'd rather not wait, consider taking a taxi into town (€10,

call for Dejan and his seven-seater cab, mobile 348-402-3501—
Dejan also arranges day trips, see "Local Guides," later; or you can
ask your hotel to arrange a taxi).

By Car: You'll find several lots ringing the walls; some are free
(white lines), others require payment (blue lines), and still others
are for local residents only (yellow lines), so check signs carefully.
Your best bet is the large, free lot on Viale Cesare Battisti, just after
the big Santo Spirito Church. From here, a series of stairs and escalators take you steeply up to Piazza Garibaldi. Piazza Garibaldi
itself may have a handful of pay spots available (marked by blue
lines, pay & display, free 20:00-8:00). The small town is actually
very long, and it can be smart to drive to the top for sightseeing up
there (free parking at Santa Margherita Basilica).

Helpful Hints

Market Day: The market is on Saturday on Piazza Signorelli (from
early morning until 14:00).

Services: The town has **no baggage storage,** so try asking nicely at
a hotel to leave your bag there. The best public **WC** is located
in Piazza del Duomo, under Santa Margherita's statue.

Tuscan Cooking School: Husband-and-wife team **Romano and
Agostina** hold morning hands-on cooking and cheesemak-
ing classes, as well as wine-, cheese-, and oil-tasting courses,
six mornings a week in the converted cellar of a 16th-century
monastery, just behind their recommended Ristorante La Bucaccia (closed Mon). In the five-hour class, you'll prepare two
antipasti, two types of pasta, an entrée, and a dessert, which
you then get to eat (roughly €90/person, price includes wine,
5 percent discount if you show this book, classes start at 9:30).
A three-hour version starts at 11:00 (€70/person; try to book
at least a month in advance, evening and personalized classes
available). They also offer Italian snack tastings with Romano's
homemade cheeses and cold meats (17:00-23:00, €15—includes a free glass of wine with this book; Via Ghibellina 17,
tel. 0575-606-039, www.labucaccia.it, info@labucaccia.it).

Local Guides: Giovanni Adreani exudes energy and a love of his
city and Tuscan high culture. He is great at bringing the fine
points of the city to life and can take visitors around in his car
for no extra charge. As this region is speckled with underappreciated charms, having Giovanni for a day as your driver/
guide promises to be a fascinating experience (€110/half-day,
€200/day, tel. 0575-630-665, mobile 347-176-2830, www.
adreanigiovanni.com, adreanigiovanni@libero.it). Reliable,
English-speaking taxi driver **Dejan** (DAY-zhan) **Prvulovic**
can also take you on full-day tours to Pienza, Montalcino,
Siena, Assisi, and Chianti—email him and devise your own

itinerary (€250/day depending on number of passengers, mobile 348-402-3501, dejanprvi70@yahoo.it).

Self-Guided Walk

Welcome to Cortona

This introductory walking tour will take you from Piazza Garibaldi and up the main strip to the town center, its piazzas, and the Duomo. (If your bus drops off at Piazza del Mercato, see the map on page 746 to locate Piazza Garibaldi.)

• *Start at the bus stop in...*

Piazza Garibaldi: Many visits start and finish in this square, thanks to its bus stop. While the piazza, bulging out from the town fortifications like a big turret, looks like part of an old rampart, it's really a souvenir of those early French and English Romantics— the ones who first created the notion of a dreamy, idyllic Tuscany. During the Napoleonic Age, the French built this balcony (and the scenic little park behind the adjacent San Domenico Church) simply to enjoy a commanding view of the Tuscan countryside.

With Umbria about a mile away, Cortona marks the end of Tuscany. This is a major cultural divide, as Cortona was the last town in Charlemagne's empire and the last under Medici rule. Umbria, just to the south, was papal territory for centuries. These deep-seated cultural disparities were a great challenge for the visionaries who unified the fractured region to create the modern nation of Italy during the 1860s. An obelisk in the center of this square honors one of the heroes of the struggle for Italian unification—the brilliant revolutionary general, Giuseppe Garibaldi.

Enjoy the commanding view from here. Assisi is just over the ridge on the left. Lake Trasimeno peeks from behind the hill, looking quite normal today. But, according to legend, it was blood-red after Hannibal defeated the Romans here in 217 B.C., when 15,000 died in the battle. The only sizable town you can see, on the right, is Montepulciano. Cortona is still defined by its Etruscan walls—remnants of these walls, with stones laid 2,500 years ago, stretch from here in both directions.

Frances Mayes put Cortona on the map for many Americans with her book (and later movie) *Under the Tuscan Sun.* The book describes her real-life experience buying, fixing up, and living in a run-down villa in Cortona with her husband, Ed. The movie romanticized the story, turning Frances into a single, recently divorced writer who restores the villa and her peace of mind. Mayes' villa isn't "under the Tuscan sun" very often; it's named "Bramasole"—literally, "craving sun." On the wrong side of the hill, it's in the shade after 15:00. She and her husband still live there part of each year and are respected members of their adopted community (outside the walls, behind the hill on the left—a 20-minute walk away; ask at the TI for directions if you'd like to see it up close).

• *From this square, head into town along...*

Via Nazionale: The only level road in town, locals have nicknamed Via Nazionale the *ruga piana* (flat wrinkle). This is the main commercial street in this town of 2,500, and it's been that way for a long time. Every shop seems to have a medieval cellar or an Etruscan well. Notice the crumbling sandstone door frames. The entire town is constructed from this grainy, eroding rock.

• *Via Nazionale leads to...*

Piazza della Repubblica: City Hall faces Cortona's main square. Note how City Hall is a clever hodgepodge of twin medieval towers, with a bell tower added to connect them, and a grand staircase to lend some gravitas. Notice also the fine wood balconies on the left. In the Middle Ages, wooden extensions like these were common features on the region's stone buildings. These balconies (not original, but rebuilt in the 19th century) would have fit right into the medieval cityscape. These days, you usually see only the holes that once supported the long-gone wooden beams.

This spot has been the town center since Etruscan times. Four centuries before Christ, an important street led from here up to the hill-capping temple. Later, the square became the Roman forum. Opposite City Hall is the handy, recommended Despar Market Molesini, good for cheap sandwiches. Above that is the loggia—once a fish market, now the recommended Ristorante La Loggetta.

• *The second half of the square, to the right of City Hall, is...*

Piazza Signorelli: Dominated by Casali Palace, this square was the headquarters of the Florentine captains who used to control the city. Peek into the palace entrance (under the MAEC sign) for a look at the coats of arms. Every six months, Florence would send a new captain to Cortona, who would help establish his rule by inserting his family coat of arms into the palace's wall. These date from the 15th to the 17th century, and were once painted with bright colors. Cortona's fine Etruscan Museum (described later, under "Sights in Cortona") is in the Casali Palace courtyard, which is lined with many more of these family coats of arms. The inviting Caffè del Teatro fills the loggia of the theater that is named for the town's most famous artist, Luca Signorelli.

• *Head down the street, just to the right of the museum, to...*

Piazza del Duomo: Here you'll find the Diocesan Museum (listed later, under "Sights in Cortona"), cathedral, and (closer to the top of the square) a statue of Santa Margherita. The cathedral's

Cortona

facade, though recently renovated, still seems a little underwhelming and tucked away. Cortona so loves its hometown saint, Margherita, that it put the energy it would otherwise have invested in its cathedral into the Santa Margherita Basilica, at the top of the hill (at the other end of town—not visible from here). Margherita was a 13th-century rich girl who took good care of the poor and was an early follower of St. Francis and St. Clare. Many locals believe that Margherita protected Cortona from WWII bombs.

The Piazza del Duomo terrace comes with a commanding view of the Tuscan countryside. Notice the town cemetery in the foreground. If you were standing here before the time of Napoleon, you'd be surrounded by tombstones. But Cortona's graveyards—like other urban graveyards throughout Napoleon's realm—were cleaned out in the early 1800s to reclaim land and improve hygiene.

• Next, enter the...

Duomo: The Cortona cathedral is not, strictly speaking, a cathedral, because it no longer has a bishop. The white-and-gray Florentine Renaissance-style interior is mucked up with lots of Ba-

TUSCAN SUN

PORTA MONTANINA

VIA PORTA MONTANINA

To Medici Fortress

SAN CRISTOFORO

BAR

VIA SANTA CROCE

SANTA MARGHERITA

SAN NICCOLÒ

VIA SANTA MARGHERITA

VIA ORIO DELLA CERA

VIA SAN NICCOLÒ

VIA CANTUCCE

VIA DELLA SANTISSIMI TRINITA

SAN MARCO

PORTA BERADA

VIA SANTA MARGHERITA

CITY WALLS

SAN DOMENICO

VIA DEL CROCIFISSO

Public Gardens

VIA L'ESARE BATTISTI

VIA SEVERINI

VIALE DEI GIARDINI PUBBLICA

100 Meters

100 Yards

1. Hotel San Luca
2. Dolce Maria B&B & Locanda al Pozzo Antico
3. San Marco Hostel
4. Hotel Villa Marsili
5. Casa Betania
6. Villa Santa Margherita
7. Casa Kita
8. Ristorante La Bucaccia
9. Trattoria la Grotta
10. Ristorante La Loggetta & Despar Market Molesini
11. Fufluns Tavern Pizzeria
12. Osteria del Teatro
13. Fiaschetteria Fett'unta
14. Enoteca la Saletta

roque chapels filling once-spacious side niches. In the rear (on the right) is an altar cluttered with relics. Technically, any Catholic altar, in order to be consecrated, needs a relic embedded in it. Gently lift up the tablecloth (go ahead—the priest here doesn't mind), and you'll see a little marble patch that holds a bit of a saint (daily in summer 7:30-13:00 & 15:00-18:30, daily in winter 8:00-12:30 & 15:00-17:30, closed during Mass).

• *From here, you can visit the nearby Diocesan Museum, or head back toward Piazza della Repubblica to visit the Etruscan Museum in Piazza Signorelli (both listed next) or to get a bite to eat (see "Eating in Cortona," later).*

Sights in Cortona

▲Etruscan Museum (Museo dell'Accademia Etrusca e della Città di Cortona)

Located in the 13th-century Casali Palace and called MAEC for short, this fine gallery (established in 1727) is one of the first dedicated to artifacts from the Etruscan civilization. (In the logo, notice the E is backwards—in homage to the Etruscan alphabet.) This sprawling collection is nicely installed on four big floors with plenty of English information. The bottom two floors (underground) are officially the "Museum of the Etruscan and Roman City of Cortona." You'll see an exhibit on the Roman settlement and take a virtual tour of the Etruscan "Il Sodo" tombs (in the nearby countryside). The Cortona Tablet (*Tabula Cortonensis*, second century B.C.), a 200-word contract inscribed in bronze, contains dozens of Etruscan words archaeologists had never seen before its discovery in 1992. Along with lots of gold and jewelry, you'll find a seventh-century B.C. grater (for some *very* aged Parmesan cheese). The top two floors, called the "Accademia," display an even more eclectic collection, including more Etruscania, Egyptian artifacts, fine Roman mosaics, and a room dedicated to 20th-century abstract works by Severini, all lovingly described in English. A highlight is the magnificent fourth-century B.C. bronze oil lamp chandelier with 16 spouts. On the top floor, peek into the classic old library of the Etruscan Academy, founded in 1727 to promote an understanding of the city through the study of archaeology.

Cost and Hours: €10, €13 combo-ticket includes Diocesan Museum; April-Oct daily 10:00-19:00; Nov-March Tue-Sun 10:00-17:00, closed Mon; Casali Palace on Piazza Signorelli, tel. 0575-637-235, www.cortonamaec.org.

▲Diocesan Museum (Museo Diocesano)

This small collection contains some very choice artworks from the town's many churches, including works by Fra Angelico and Pietro Lorenzetti, and masterpieces by hometown hero and Renaissance master Luca Signorelli.

Cost and Hours: €5, €13 combo-ticket includes Etruscan Museum, helpful audioguide-€3; April-Oct daily 10:00-19:00; Nov-March Tue-Sun 10:00-17:00, closed Mon; Piazza del Duomo 1, tel. 0575-62-830.

Visiting the Museum: From the entrance, head straight into the Signorelli Room (Sala 4). Signorelli was a generation ahead of Michelangelo and, with his passion for painting ideas, was an inspiration for the younger artist (for more on Signorelli, visit the San Niccolò Church, described later). Take a slow stroll past his very colorful canvases, mostly relocated here from local churches. Among the most striking is *Lamentation over the Dead Christ* (*Compianto sul Cristo Morto*, 1502). Everything in Signorelli's painting has a meaning: The skull of Adam sits under the sacrifice of Jesus; the hammer represents the Passion (the Crucifixion leading to the Resurrection); the lake is blood; and so on. I don't understand all the medieval symbolism, but it is intense.

Then cut across the top of the stairwell into Sala 3, which was once the nave of the Gesù Church (look up at the beautiful wood-carved ceiling). In Fra Angelico's sumptuous *Annunciation* (c. 1430), Mary says "Yes," consenting to bear God's son. The angel's words are top and bottom, while Mary's answer is upside down (logically, since it's directed to God, who would be reading while looking down from heaven). Notice how the house sits on a pillow of flowers...the new Eden. The old Eden, featuring the expulsion of Adam and Eve from Paradise, is in the upper left. The bottom edge of the painting comes with comic strip-like narration of scenes from Mary's life. On the wall to the right, the crucifix (by Pietro Lorenzetti, c. 1325) is striking in its severity. Notice the gripping realism—even the tendons in Jesus' arms are pulled tight.

Now head back to the stairwell, which is lined with colorful Stations of the Cross scenes by another local but much later artist, the 20th-century's Gino Severini. These are actually "cartoons," models used to create permanent pieces for the approach up to the Santa Margherita Basilica. Downstairs, the lower refectory (Sala 6) has a vault with beautiful frescoes (1545) designed by Giorgio Vasari. Back up near the entrance, another staircase leads down to an important but dull collection of vestments and ecclesiastical gear.

San Francesco Church

Established by St. Francis' best friend, Brother Elias, this church dates from the 13th century. The wooden beams of the ceiling are original. While the place was redecorated in the Baroque age, some of the original frescoes that once wallpapered the church peek through the whitewash in the second chapel on the left. Francis fans visit for its precious Franciscan relics. To the left of the altar, you'll find one of Francis' tunics, his pillow (inside a fancy cover), and his gospel book. Notice how the entire high altar seems designed to frame its precious relic— a piece of the cross Elias brought back from his visit to the patriarch in Constantinople. You're welcome to climb the altar for a close-up look. In the humble choir area behind the main altar is Elias' very simple tomb (just a stone slab in the middle of the floor—on a nearby slab, see the *Frate Elia da Cortona* plaque).

Cost and Hours: Free, daily 9:00-17:30, often open until 19:00 in summer, check with TI; Mass on Sun at 10:00, Mon-Sat at 17:30.

San Niccolò Church

Although this tiny church is rarely open, Signorelli enthusiasts may want to make the pilgrimage—a steep 10-minute walk above the San Francesco Church. While it's not worth going out of the way for (the picturesque neighborhood surrounding it is, for many, more interesting), it's an easy detour if you're hiking up to Santa Margherita. The highlight of this humble church is an altarpiece painted on both sides by Signorelli; it's usually pulled halfway open so you can see both sides.

Cost and Hours: €1 donation, check with TI before making the trip to make sure it's open.

Santa Margherita Basilica

From San Niccolò Church, another steep path leads uphill 10 minutes to this basilica, which houses the remains of Margherita, the town's favorite saint. The red-and-white-striped interior boasts some colorfully painted vaults. Santa Margherita, an unwed mother from Montepulciano, found her calling with the Franciscans in Cortona, tending to the sick and poor. The well-preserved and remarkably emotional 13th-century crucifix on the right is the cross that, according to legend, talked to Margherita.

Cost and Hours: Free, daily 9:00-12:00 & 15:00-19:00 except closed Mon morning, tel. 0575-603-116.

Nearby: Still need more altitude? Head uphill five more minutes to the **Medici Fortezza Girifalco** (though may be closed—check with TI; if open, likely to be €3, daily late April-Sept 9:00-13:00 & 15:00-18:00, often later in July-Aug, closed Oct-late April, sometimes closed for rehearsals by Italian rock legend Jovanotti, who lives in a villa beyond San Niccolò Church). The views are stunning, stretching all the way to distant Lago Trasimeno.

Etruscan Tombs near Cortona

Guided tours to the tombs (called *melone* for their melon-like shape), in the locality of Sodo, are complicated to arrange. But the excavation site and bits of the ruins are easy to visit and can be seen even from outside the fence. In the mornings, the guardian often opens the gates for a closer inspection (8:30-13:30). It's just a couple of miles northwest of Cortona on the Arezzo road (R-71), at the foot of the Cortona hill; ask anyone for "Il Sodo."

Sleeping in Cortona

Inside the Old Town

$$$ Hotel San Luca, perched on the side of a cliff, has 54 impersonal business-class rooms, half with stunning views of Lago Trasimeno. While the hotel feels tired and the rooms have seen better days, it's friendly and conveniently located, right on Piazza Garibaldi at the entrance to the Old Town (Sb-€70, Db-€100, Tb-€130, request a view room when you reserve for no extra charge, popular with Americans and groups, air-con, elevator, free Wi-Fi, Piazza Garibaldi 2, tel. 0575-630-460, www.sanlucacortona.com, info@sanlucacortona.com). If driving, you might find a spot at the small public parking lot at the hotel; otherwise you can park at the big lot down below and ride the escalator up.

$$ Dolce Maria B&B is located in a 16th-century building with high-beamed ceilings. The six rooms are good-value, luminous, and spacious, with tasteful period furnishings and modern bathrooms. The B&B is run by warm and efficient Paola, who also runs the Antico Pozzo restaurant next door—the two businesses share a patio (Db-€80-100, air-con, free Wi-Fi, Via Ghini 12, tel. 0575-601-577, www.cortonastorica.com, info@cortonastorica.com).

$ San Marco Hostel, at the top of town, is housed in a remodeled 13th-century palace (bunk in 4- to 6-bed dorm-€18, in 2-bed room-€25, includes breakfast, lunch or dinner-€11, lockout 10:00-13:00; from Piazza Garibaldi head up steep Via Santa Margherita, then turn left to find Via Maffei 57; tel. 0575-601-765, www.cortonahostel.com, ostellocortona@libero.it).

Outside the Old Town

These accommodations line up along the road that angles downhill from Piazza Garibaldi, within a 10-minute (uphill) walk to the entrance to the Old Town. Drivers may find these handier than the places in town.

$$$ Hotel Villa Marsili is a comfortable splurge just below town. It was originally a 15th-century church, then an elegant 18th-century home. Its 26 rooms and public areas have been recently redecorated and restored, and come with lots of thoughtful little touches. Guests can enjoy an evening aperitif with free snacks on the panoramic terrace. In general, the higher up the room, the fancier the decor and the higher the price. Diane Lane slept in one of the suites while filming *Under the Tuscan Sun* (Sb-€110, small standard Db-€150, superior Db-€180, deluxe Db-€230, Db suite-€350, extra bed-€25/child or €50/adult, Jacuzzi in deluxe room and suites, air-con, elevator, free guest computer and Wi-Fi, free street parking nearby—first come, first served, otherwise €12, Viale Cesare Battisti 13, tel. 0575-605-252, fax 0575-605-618, www.villamarsili.net, info@villamarsili.net, Marina).

$ Casa Betania, a big, wistful convent with an inviting view terrace, rents 30 fine rooms (mostly twin beds) for the best price in town. While it's primarily for "thoughtful travelers," anyone looking for a peaceful place to call home will feel welcome in this pilgrims' resort. Marco, a big-city lawyer escaping from the rat race, has taken over this place and turned it into an impressive retreat facility, with conference rooms, a chapel, wine cellar, cooking classes, and more (S-€32, D-€44, Db-€48, Tb-€66, extra bed-€20, breakfast-€4, free Wi-Fi, free parking, about a third of a mile out of town, a few minutes' walk below Piazza Garibaldi and through iron gates on the right at Via Gino Severini 50, tel. 0575-630-423, www.casaperferiebetania.com, info@casaperferiebetania.com).

$ Villa Santa Margherita, run by the Serve di Maria Riparatrici sisters, rents 22 nicely renovated rooms in a smaller and more traditional-feeling convent just up the street from Casa Betania (Sb-€50, Db-€66, Tb-€86, Qb-€98, elevator, pay Wi-Fi, free parking, Viale Cesare Battisti 17, tel. 0575-178-7203 or 0575-630-336, fax 0575-630-549, www.villasm.it, info@villasm.it).

$ Casa Kita, renting five slightly quirky rooms, is a homey place just below Piazza Garibaldi with fine views from its terrace. You'll really feel like you're staying in someone's home, but the prices are good (Db-€65, free Wi-Fi, 100 yards below Piazza Garibaldi at Vicolo degli Orti 7, tel. 389-557-9893, www.casakita.com, info@casakita.com, Lorenzini family).

Eating in Cortona

Ristorante La Bucaccia is a family-run eatery set in a rustic medieval wine cellar. It's dressy and romantic. Taking an evangelical pride in their Chianina beef dishes and homemade pastas, Romano hosts and his wife Agostina cooks. Reservations are required for dinner—and worth making (€8-9 pastas, €12-15 *secondi*, Tue-Sun 12:30-15:30 & 19:00-23:00, closed Mon, show this book for a 5 percent discount and a small free appetizer, Via Ghibellina 17, tel. 0575-606-039, www.labucaccia.it).

Trattoria la Grotta, just off Piazza della Repubblica, is a traditional place serving daily specials to an enthusiastic clientele under grotto-like vaults (€7-9 pastas, €7-20 *secondi*, good wine by the glass, Wed-Mon 12:00-14:30 & 19:00-22:00, closed Tue, Piazza Baldelli 3, tel. 0575-630-271).

Locanda al Pozzo Antico offers an affordable menu of Tuscan fare, with a focus on fresh, quality produce, and using their own homemade olive oil. Eat in a classy, minimalist dining room or tucked away in a tranquil secret courtyard. Paola is a charming hostess; ask about her cooking classes (€6-9 pastas, €10-16 *secondi*, Fri-Wed 12:30-14:30 & 19:30-22:00, closed Thu, Via Ghini 12, tel. 0575-62091 or 0575-601-577; Paola, husband Franco, and son Gianni).

Ristorante La Loggetta serves up big portions of well-presented Tuscan cuisine on the loggia overlooking Piazza della Repubblica. While they have fine indoor seating under stone vaults, I'd eat here for the chance to gaze at the square over a meal (€8-10 pastas, €8-15 *secondi*, Thu-Tue 12:30-15:00 & 19:30-23:00, closed Wed, Piazza Pescheria 3, tel. 0575-630-575).

Fufluns Tavern Pizzeria (that's the Etruscan name for Dionysus) is easy-going, friendly, and remarkably unpretentious for its location in the town center. It's popular with locals for its good, inexpensive Tuscan cooking, friendly staff, and stone-and-beam-cozy interior (€5-7 pizza and €6-10 pastas plus big salads, good house wine, Wed-Mon 12:15-14:30 & 19:15-22:30, closed Tue, a block below Piazza della Repubblica at Via Ghibellina 3, tel. 0575-604-140).

Osteria del Teatro tries very hard to create a romantic Old World atmosphere, and does it well. Chef and owner Emiliano serves nicely presented and tasty Italian and local cuisine (taking creative liberties with traditions). There's good outdoor seating, too. It feels upscale and a bit self-important (€8-9 pastas, €11-16 *secondi*, Thu-Tue 12:30-14:30 & 19:30-22:00, closed Wed, 2 blocks uphill from the main square at Via Maffei 2—look for the gnomes on the steps, tel. 0575-630-556, www.osteria-del-teatro.it). They also own the bright little restaurant just opposite, **Fiaschetteria Fett'unta,** which has traditional light snacks and sandwiches.

Enoteca la Saletta, dark and classy with a nice, mellow vibe, is good for fine wine and a light meal. You can sit inside surrounded by wine bottles or outside to people-watch on the town's main drag (€3-5 sandwiches and pizzas, €7-12 pastas and *secondi*, daily 7:30-24:00, meals served 12:00-24:00, closed Wed in winter, free Wi-Fi, Via Nazionale 26, tel. 0575-603-366).

Picnic: On the main square, the chic little **Despar Market Molesini** makes tasty sandwiches, served with a smile (see list on counter and order by number, or invent your own), and sells whatever else you might want for a picnic (Mon-Sat 7:00-13:30 & 16:00-20:00, Sun 9:30-13:30, Piazza della Repubblica 23). Munch your picnic across the square on the steps of City Hall, or just past Piazza Garibaldi in the public gardens behind San Domenico Church.

Cortona Connections

Cortona has good train connections with the rest of Italy through its Camucia-Cortona station. The station is usually unstaffed, but it has two ticket machines: One is in front as you enter the station, and one is outside on platform 1. They take credit cards and cash (change is given). When purchasing, choose the British flag for English, and then follow the clear instructions, delivered with a charming Italian accent. After buying your ticket, immediately validate it in one of the green boxes next to the ticket machine in the main station or on platforms 1 and 3.

To get to the train station at the foot of the hill, take a €10 taxi or hop the €1.20 bus (see "Arrival in Cortona," earlier; runs only about once hourly; buy tickets at a newsstand or tobacco shop, or buy from driver for €0.40 more). Be sure to confirm with the TI whether these buses leave from Piazza Garibaldi or Piazza del Mercato, outside Porta Santa Maria. Some buses take you only as far as the newsstand that's 200 yards in front of the station.

From Camucia-Cortona by Train to: Rome (9/day, 2.5 hours, 4 direct, others with change, €11.35), **Florence** (hourly, 1.5 hours, €9.80), **Assisi** (every 2 hours, 70 minutes, €5.55), **Montepulciano**

(9/day, 1.5-2 hours, change in Chiusi; because few buses serve Montepulciano's town center from its distant train station, it's better to go by train to Chiusi, then by hourly 40-minute bus to Montepulciano, or easier still to take a taxi for about €40), **Chiusi** (9/day, 40 minutes).

Most trains stop at the Camucia-Cortona train station, but each day, two or three high-speed trains to/from Rome, Florence, and Assisi stop at **Terontola,** 10 miles away (buses go about hourly to Terontola, leaves from Piazza Garibaldi, 25-30 minutes, €2, check the schedule at the bus stop or pick up printed bus schedule from the TI).

More Hill Towns and Sights

These are listed roughly from north to south.

▲Florence American Cemetery and Memorial

The compelling sight of endless rows of white marble crosses and Stars of David recalls the heroism of the young Americans who fought so valiantly in World War II to free Italy (and ultimately Europe) from the grip of fascism. This particular cemetery is the final resting place of more than 4,000 Americans who died in the liberation of Italy. Climb the hill past the perfectly manicured lawn lined with grave markers, to the memorial, where maps and a history of the Italian campaign detail the Allied advance.

Cost and Hours: Free, daily 9:00-17:00; 7.5 miles south of Florence, off Via Cassia, which parallels the *superstrada* between Florence and Siena, 2 miles south of Florence Certosa exit on A-1 autostrada; buses from Florence stop just outside the cemetery; tel. 055-202-0020, www.abmc.gov.

▲San Galgano Monastery

Of southern Tuscany's several evocative monasteries, San Galgano is the best. Set in a forested area called the Montagnolo ("Medium-Size Mountains"), the isolated abbey and chapel are postcard-perfect, though you'll need a car to get here. Other, more accessible Tuscan monasteries worth visiting include Sant'Antimo (6 miles south of Montalcino) and Monte Oliveto Maggiore (15 miles south of Siena, mentioned in "The Crete Senese," earlier).

Cost and Hours: €2, June-Aug daily 9:00-20:00, shoulder

season until 19:00, Nov-Feb daily 9:30-17:30, tel. 0577-756-738, www.prolocochiusdino.it; concerts sometimes held here in summer—info tel. 055-597-8309, www.festivalopera.it. For a quick snack, a small, touristy bar at the end of the driveway is your only option.

Getting There: Although a bus reportedly comes here from Siena, this sight is realistically accessible only for drivers. It's just outside Monticiano (not Montalcino), about an hour southwest of Siena. A warning to the queasy: These roads are curvy.

Visiting the Monastery: St. Galgano was a 12th-century saint who renounced his past as a knight to become a hermit. Lacking a cross to display, he created his own by miraculously burying his sword up to its hilt in a stone, à la King Arthur, but in reverse. After his death, a large Cistercian monastery complex grew. Today, all you'll see is the roofless, ruined abbey and, on a nearby hill, the Chapel of San Galgano with its fascinating dome and sword in the stone.

This picturesque Cistercian **abbey** was once a powerful institution in Tuscany. Known for their skill as builders, the Cistercians oversaw the construction of Siena's cathedral. But after losing most of its population in the plague of 1348, the abbey never really recovered and was eventually deconsecrated.

The Cistercian order was centered in France, and the architecture of the abbey shows a heavy French influence. Notice the large, high windows and the pointy, delicate arches. This is pure French Gothic, a style that never fully caught on in Italy (compare it with the chunky, elaborately decorated cathedral in Siena, built about the same time).

As you enter the church, look to the left to see a small section of the cloister wall. This used to surround the garden and was the only place where the monks were allowed to talk, for one hour each day. From inside the church, the empty windows frame the view of the chapel up on the hill.

The upper floor of the actual monks' quarters (to the side of the abbey) may now be open to the public.

A path from the abbey leads up the hill to the **Chapel of San Galgano.** The unique, beehive-like interior houses St. Galgano's sword and stone, recently confirmed to date back to the 12th century. Don't try and pull the sword from the stone—the small chapel to the left displays the severed arms of the last guy who tried. The chapel also contains some deteriorated frescoes and more interesting *sinopie* (fresco sketches). The adjacent gift shop sells a little bit of everything, from wine to postcards to herbs, some of it monk-made.

▲Urbino

If you're driving through central Italy, Urbino is worth a stop for its sprawling, fascinating Ducal Palace. Although Urbino is the hometown of the artist Raphael and the architect Donato Bramante, it's better known for the Duke of Montefeltro, a mercenary general who built the palace and turned Urbino into an important Renaissance center. For my expanded coverage of Urbino, see www.ricksteves.com/urbino.

A classic hill town, Urbino has a medieval wall with four gates and two main roads that crisscross at the town's main square, Piazza della Repubblica. The tiny **TI** is just across from the Ducal Palace (mid-March-Oct daily 9:00-13:00 & 15:00-18:30, but closed Mon afternoons; Nov-mid-March daily 9:00-13:00, Mon and Fri also 15:00-18:00; Piazza Duca Federico 35, tel. 0722-2613, www.turismo.pesarourbino.it, info@turismo.pesarourbino.it).

The **Ducal Palace** (Palazzo Ducale), which has more than 300 rooms, was built in the mid-1400s. While the rooms are fairly bare, the palace holds a few very special paintings, as well as exquisite inlaid-wood decorations. It's a monument to how one man—the Duke of Montefeltro—brought the Renaissance to his small town (€5, but sometimes €9 for special exhibits, Mon 8:30-13:00, Tue-Sun 8:30-19:00, last entry one hour before closing, tel. 072-232-2625). The highlights of the palace include great paintings such as Raphael's *Portrait of a Gentlewoman* (a.k.a. *La Muta*); the Renaissance courtyard patterned after the trendsetting Medici-Riccardi Palace in Florence; the richly paneled and inlaid-wood walls of the duke's study; and the vast cellars that include a giant stable with a clever horse-pie disposal system.

Stop by the **Oratory of St. John** to see its remarkable frescoed interior that tells the story of the life of St. John the Baptist (€2.50, Mon-Sat 10:00-13:00 & 15:00-18:00, Sun 10:00-13:00, 5-minute walk from main square—follow signs, Piazza Baricci 31; if no one's there, find attendant at the Oratory of San Giuseppe a few steps away; mobile 347-671-1181).

Finally, for the ultimate Urbino view, climb up to the grassy park surrounding the **fortress** (interior closed, but grounds open to the public). The Franciscan church spire, on the left, marks the main square.

Getting There: Urbino is easier for drivers, but public transportation is an option. Buses link Urbino with Pesaro, on the Ravenna-Pescara train line (buses run hourly, 1-hour trip). From Venice, Florence, or Rome, trains leave for Pesaro almost hourly (taking 3-5 hours). In Urbino, buses come and go from the Piazza Mercatale parking lot below the town, where an elevator lifts you up to the base of the Ducal Palace (or take a 5-minute steep walk up Via Mazzini to Piazza della Repubblica).

Sleeping in Urbino: The hotel scene is limited to a few comfortable, expensive places, including **Albergo San Domenico** (www.viphotels.it), **Hotel Raffaello** (www.albergoraffaello.com), and **Albergo Italia** (www.albergo-italia-urbino.it). The TI has a line on lots of families renting rooms.

Eating in Urbino: Try **Taverna degli Artisti** (Via Donato Bramante 52) and **Il Coppiere** (Via Santa Margherita 1), or **Ristorante/Pizzeria Le Tre Piante** (Via Voltaccia della Vecchia 1).

▲Chiusi

This small hill town (rated ▲▲ for Etruscan fans) was once one of the most important Etruscan cities. Today it's a key train junction and a pleasant, workaday Italian village with an enjoyable historic center and few tourists. The hill upon which Chiusi sits is honeycombed with Etruscan tunnels, which you can see in a variety of ways.

Tourist Information: The well-organized TI faces the main square (April-Aug daily 9:00-13:00 & 15:00-17:00, Sept daily 9:00-13:00 & 15:00-17:00, Oct-March Tue-Sun 9:30-12:30, closed Mon, Via Porsenna 79, tel. 0578-227-667, www.prolocochiusi.it).

Arrival in Chiusi: The region's **trains** (to Florence, Siena, and Rome—each of these is about an hour away) go through or change at this hub, making Chiusi an easy day trip. There's no luggage storage at the station, but the TI may be willing to take your bags for a short time. Buses link the train station with the town center two miles away (every 40 minutes, buy tickets at tobacco shop, bus doesn't run during a gap in the afternoon, taxi costs €10). All buses from the station drop off at a stop just below the center of town (follow well-marked pedestrian signs up to the TI and museums); about half continue on to a stop near the town theater, right downtown. **Drivers** follow signs for *centro storico*, then the TI. Easy and free parking lots are a five-minute walk from the center; pay spaces (marked with blue lines) are right downtown, next to the TI and museums. Hertz has a rental-car office near the train station (Via M. Buonarroti 21, tel. 057-822-3000).

Sights in Chiusi: All the town's sights are within a five-minute walk of each other and the TI.

The **Archaeological Museum** (Museo Archeologico Nazionale, a.k.a. the Etruscan Museum) thoughtfully presents a high-quality collection with plenty of explanations in English. The collection of funerary urns, some in painted terra-cotta and some in *pietra fetida* ("stinky stone"), are remarkably intact. You'll also see exhibits on two tombs in the nearby countryside: a model of the Tomba della Pellegrina, and small-scale reproductions of the frescoes from the Tomba della Scimmia—both mentioned below (€6, daily 9:00-20:00, in the stately Neoclassical-looking building just off the main square at Via Porsenna 93, tel. 0578-20177, www.archeotoscana.beniculturali.it).

The museum also arranges tours to visit the actual Pellegrina and Scimmia **tombs;** to take part, you'll need to have your own car and to join a guide (meet at the museum 15 minutes before the tour time). For the Tomba della Pellegrina (Tomb of the Pilgrim), from the Hellenistic period (4th century B.C.), tours depart daily at 11:00 and 16:00 (or 14:30 in winter). This is included in museum admission, and no reservations are necessary—just ask when you arrive. The other, the Tomba della Scimmia (Tomb of the Monkey), is a century earlier and has some well-preserved frescoes (€2; Tue, Thu, and Sat only; March-Oct at 11:00 and 16:00, Nov-Feb at 11:00 and 14:30; this tomb requires an advance reservation).

Troglodyte alert! The **Cathedral Museum** on the main square has a dark, underground labyrinth of Etruscan tunnels. The mandatory guided tour of the tunnels ends in a large Roman cistern, from which you can climb the church bell tower for an expansive view of the countryside (museum-€2, labyrinth-€3, combo-ticket-€4, daily June-mid-Oct 9:45-12:45 & 16:00-18:30, mid-Oct-May 9:45-12:45 only, 30-minute tunnel tours run every 40 minutes during museum hours, Piazza Duomo 1, tel. 0578-226-490).

Craving more underground fun? The **Museo Civico** provides hourly tours of the Etruscan water system, which includes an underground lake (€4; May-Oct Tue-Sun at 10:15, 11:30, 12:45, 15:15, 16:30, and 17:45; closed Mon, fewer tours and closed Mon-Wed off-season, call to confirm times, Via II Ciminia 1, tel. 0578-20530, mobile 334-626-6851).

▲Gubbio

This handsome town climbs Monte Ingino in northeast Umbria. Tuesday is market day, when Piazza 40 Martiri (named for 40 local martyrs shot by Nazis) bustles. Nearby are the ruins of the Roman amphitheater, and a park that's perfect for a picnic. Head up Via della Repubblica to the main square with the imposing Palazzo dei Consoli. Farther up, Via San Gerolamo leads to the funky lift that will carry you up the hill, in two-person "baskets," for a stunning view  from the top, where the Basilica of San Ubaldo is worth a look. The **TI** is at Via della Repubblica 15 (daily April-Sept 8:30-13:45 &

15:30-18:30, Oct-March closes at 18:00 daily; tel. 075-922-0693, www.gubbio-altochiascio.umbria2000.it). Buses from Gubbio run directly to Rome and Perugia (where you can transfer to Florence).

▲Bevagna

This sleeper of a town south of Assisi has Roman ruins, interesting churches, and more. Locals offer their guiding services for free (usually Italian-speaking only) and are excited to show visitors their town. Get a map at the **TI** at Piazza Silvestri 1 (daily 9:30-12:30 & 15:30-19:30, tel. 074-236-1667) and wander. Highlights are the Roman mosaics, remains of the arena, a paper-making workshop, the Romanesque Church of San Silvestro, and a gem of a 19th-century theater. Bevagna has all the elements of a hill town except one: a hill. You can see the main sights easily in a couple of hours.

▲Spello

Umbrian hill town aficionados always include Spello on their list. Just six miles south of Assisi, this town is much less touristy than its neighbor to the north. Spello will give your legs a workout. Via Consolare goes up, up, up to the top of town. Views from the terrace of the **Il Trombone** restaurant will have you singing a tune (Via Fontanello 1, tel. 074-265-1069). The **TI** is on Piazza Matteotti 3 (daily 9:30-12:30 & 16:00-18:00, afternoons 15:30-17:30 in winter, tel. 074-230-1009, www.prospello.it). Spello is on the Perugia-Assisi-Foligno train line.

HILL TOWNS

ASSISI

Assisi is famous for its hometown boy, St. Francis, who made very good. While Francis the saint is interesting, Francesco Bernardone the man is even more so, and mementos of his days in Assisi are everywhere—where he was baptized, a shirt he wore, a hill he prayed on, and a church where a vision changed his life.

About the year 1200, this simple friar from Assisi countered the decadence of Church government and society in general with a powerful message of non-materialism and a "slow down and smell God's roses" lifestyle. Like Jesus, Francis taught by example, living without worldly goods and aiming to love all creation. A huge monastic order grew out of his teachings, which were gradually embraced (some would say co-opted) by the Church. Christianity's most popular saint and its purest example of simplicity is now glorified in beautiful churches, along with his female counterpart, St. Clare. In 1939, Italy made Francis one of its patron saints; in 2013, the newly elected pope took his name.

Francis' message of love, simplicity, and sensitivity to the environment has a broad and timeless appeal. But every pilgrimage site inevitably gets commercialized, and Francis' legacy is now Assisi's basic industry. In summer, this Umbrian town bursts with flash-in-the-pan Francis fans and Franciscan knickknacks. Those able to see past the glow-in-the-dark rosaries and bobblehead friars can actually have a "travel on purpose" experience. Even a block or two off the congested main drag, you'll find pockets of serenity that, it's easy to imagine, must have made Francis feel at peace.

Planning Your Time

Assisi is worth a day and a night. Its old town has a half-day of sightseeing and another half-day of wonder. The essential sight is the Basilica of St. Francis. For a good visit, take my self-guided "Welcome to Assisi" walk, ending at the Basilica of St. Francis. With more time, be sure to wander the back streets and linger on the main square, Piazza del Comune.

Most visitors are day-trippers. While the town's a zoo by day, it's a delight at night. Assisi after dark is closer to a place Francis could call home.

Orientation to Assisi

Crowned by a ruined castle, Assisi spills downhill to its famous Basilica of St. Francis. The town is beautifully preserved and rich in history. A 5.5-magnitude earthquake in 1997 did more damage to the tourist industry than to the town's buildings. Fortunately, tourists—whether art lovers, pilgrims, or both—have returned, drawn by Assisi's special allure.

The city stretches across a ridge that rises from a flat plain. The Basilica of St. Francis sits at the low end of town; Piazza Matteotti (bus stop and parking lot) is at the high end; and the main square, Piazza del Comune, lies in between. The main drag (called Via San Francesco for most of its course) runs from Piazza del Comune to the basilica. Capping the hill above the town is the ruined castle, called the Rocca Maggiore, and rising above that is Mount Subasio. The town is smaller than its fame might lead you to think: Walking uphill from the basilica to Piazza Matteotti takes 30 minutes, while the downhill journey takes about 15 minutes. Some Francis sights lie outside the city walls, in the valley beneath the ridge (the modern part of town, called Santa Maria degli Angeli) and in the hills above.

Tourist Information

The TI, which hands out free maps, is in the center of town on Piazza del Comune (Mon-Fri 8:00-14:00 & 15:00-18:00—until 18:30 July-early Oct, Sat-Sun 9:30-17:00—until 18:00 in April-Oct, tel. 075-813-8680). There's also a branch down in the valley, across the street from the big piazza in front of the Basilica of St. Mary of the Angels.

Arrival in Assisi

By Train: The train station is about two miles below Assisi, in Santa Maria degli Angeli. You can check bags at the station's newsstand (€3/12 hours, daily 6:30-13:00 & 14:30-19:00), but not in the old town.

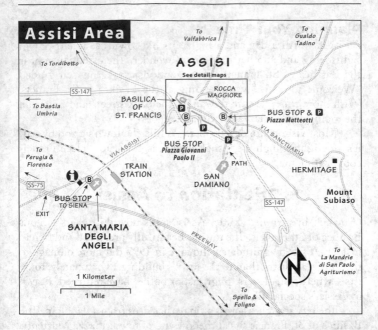

Assisi Area

To Valfabbrica

To Gualdo Tadino

ASSISI

See detail maps

To Tordibetto

SS-147

BASILICA OF ST. FRANCIS

ROCCA MAGGIORE

To Bastia Umbria

BUS STOP & Piazza Matteotti

VIA SANCTUARIO

To Perugia & Florence

VIA ASSISI

BUS STOP Piazza Giovanni Paolo II

PATH

HERMITAGE

SS-75

TRAIN STATION

SAN DAMIANO

Mount Subiaso

EXIT

BUS STOP TO SIENA

SANTA MARIA DEGLI ANGELI

SS-147

FREEWAY

N

To La Mandrie di San Paolo Agriturismo

1 Kilometer

1 Mile

To Spello & Foligno

Orange city **buses** connect the station with the old town on the hilltop. Buses (line #C) usually leave at :16 and :46 past the hour from the bus stop immediately to your left as you exit the station (daily 5:30-23:00, 15 minutes; buy tickets at the newsstand inside the train station for €1, or on board the bus for €1.50—exact change only, valid for 70 minutes after being stamped, good for any bus within the old town). On the way up into town, buses stop at Piazza Giovanni Paolo II (near Basilica of St. Francis), then Largo Properzio (just outside the Porta Nuova city gate), and finally Piazza Matteotti (top of old town).

Going from the old town to the train station, the orange buses usually run from Piazza Matteotti at :10 and :40 past the hour (stopping outside Porta Nuova at Largo Properzio a couple of minutes later, and in Piazza Giovanni Paolo II a few minutes after that).

Taxis from the train station to the old town cost about €15. You can be charged extra for luggage, night service, additional people (four is customary)...and sometimes just for being a tourist. When departing the old town, you'll find taxi stands at Piazza Giovanni Paolo II, the Basilica of St. Francis, the Basilica of St. Clare, and Piazza del Comune (or have your hotel call for you, tel. 075-813-100). Expect to pay a minimum of €10 for any ride.

By Bus: Buses from Siena arrive at the stop next to the Basilica of St. Mary of the Angels, near the train station (for directions from there to town, see page 761). Most other intercity buses arrive in the old town.

By Car: Drivers coming in for the day can follow the signs to several handy parking lots *(parcheggi)*. Piazza Matteotti's wonderful underground parking garage (#C) is at the top of the town and comes with bits of ancient Rome in the walls. Another big lot, Parcheggio Giovanni Paolo II (#A), is at the bottom end of town, 200 yards below the Basilica of St. Francis. Between them is the unlettered Parcheggio Mojano; although outside the town wall, this comes with an escalator that transports you near the Basilica of St. Clare. At Parcheggio Porta Nuova (#B), an elevator delivers you to Porta Nuova near St. Clare's. The lots vary in price (€1.30-1.60/hour, most €10-12/day but Matteotti costs €19/day). For day-trippers, the best plan is to park at Piazza Matteotti, follow my self-guided town walk, tour the basilica, and then either catch a bus back to Piazza Matteotti or simply wander back up through town to your car.

Helpful Hints

Best Shopping: Tacky knickknacks line the streets leading to the Basilica of St. Francis. For better shops (with local handicrafts), head to Via San Rufino and Corso Mazzini (both just off Piazza del Comune, shops described later in the "Welcome to Assisi" self-guided walk). A Saturday-morning market fills Via Borgo San Pietro (along the bottom edge of town).

Festivals: Assisi annually hosts several interesting festivals commemorating St. Francis and life in the Middle Ages. **Festa di Calendimaggio** is a springtime medieval festival featuring costume parades, concerts, and competitions among Assisi's rival neighborhoods (www.calendimaggiodiassisi.it). Rustic medieval "taverns" pop up around the center offering *porchetta* (roasted pig) and *vino* (starts the first Thu-Sat in May; if one of these days is already a public holiday, it's held the following week). The **Settimana Francescana** commemorates the beginning of the end of Francis' life, when he made his way for the last time to the Porziuncola Chapel (Sept 28). This week-long celebration culminates in the **Festa di San Francesco,** which marks his death with religious processions, special services, and an arts, crafts, and folklore fair. The TI has a monthly *Assisi Informa* leaflet with details on upcoming festivals and celebrations; see also the event listings at www.assisi.regioneumbria.eu.

Internet Access: Facing the Cathedral of San Rufino, **Caffè Duomo** has free Wi-Fi and Internet access for customers (daily 7:00-23:00, snacks, Piazza San Rufino 5, tel. 075-813-023).

Laundry: 3elleblu' Lavanderia can do a load of laundry for you at a reasonable price on the same day, if they're not too busy (€5/

ASSISI

St. Francis of Assisi (1181-1226)

In 1202, young Francesco Bernardone donned armor and rode out to battle the Perugians (residents of Umbria's capital city).

The battle went badly, and Francis was captured and imprisoned for a year. He returned a changed man. He avoided friends and his father's lucrative business and spent more and more time outside the city walls fasting, praying, and searching for something.

In 1206, a vision changed his life, culminating in a dramatic confrontation. He stripped naked before the town leaders, threw his clothes at his father—turning his back on the comfortable material life—and declared his loyalty to God alone.

Idealistic young men flocked to Francis, and they wandered Italy like troubadours, spreading the joy of the Gospel to rich and poor. Francis became a cult figure, attracting huge crowds. They'd never seen anything like it—sermons preached outdoors, in the local language (not Church Latin), making God accessible to all. Francis' new order of monks was also extremely unmaterialistic, extolling poverty and simplicity. Despite their radicalism, the order eventually gained the pope's approval and spread through the world. Francis, who died in Assisi at the age of 45, left a legacy of humanism, equality, and love of nature that would eventually flower in the Renaissance.

In Francis' Sandal-Steps

1. Baptized in Assisi's **Cathedral of San Rufino** (then called St. George's).
2. Raised in the family home just off Piazza del Comune (now the **Chiesa Nuova**).
3. Heard call to "rebuild church" in **San Damiano.** (The crucifix of the church is now in the **Basilica of St. Clare.**)
4. Settled and established his order of monks at the **Porziuncola Chapel** (inside today's St. Mary of the Angels Basilica).
5. Met Clare. (Her tomb and possessions are at the **Basilica of St. Clare.**)
6. Received the pope's blessing for his order (1223 document in the reliquary chapel at the **Basilica of St. Francis**).
7. Had many visions and was associated with miracles during his life (depicted in **Giotto's frescoes** in the Basilica of St. Francis' upper level).
8. Died at the **Porziuncola,** his body later interred beneath the **Basilica of St. Francis.**

wash, €4.50/dry, Mon-Fri 9:00-18:00, Sat 9:00-13:00, closed Sun, Via Borgo Aretino 6a, tel. 075-816-084).

Travel Agencies: You can purchase train and bus tickets at **Agenzia Viaggi Stoppini,** centrally located between Piazza del Comune and the Basilica of St. Clare. Manager Fabrizio is patient with tourists' needs (€1 surcharge for train tickets, Mon-Fri 9:00-12:30 & 15:30-19:00, Sat 9:00-12:30, closed Sun, Corso Mazzini 31, tel. 075-812-597). For more information, see "Assisi Connections," at the end of this chapter.

Local Guides: Giuseppe Karabotis is a good licensed guide (€130/2.5 hours, €260/6 hours, mobile 328-867-0567, iokarabot@libero.it). **Daniela Moretti** is a hardworking young guide from Perugia who knows both Assisi and all of Umbria (€120/half-day, €240/day, mobile 335-829-9984, www.danyguide.com, danyguide@hotmail.com). If they're busy, they can recommend other guides.

Getting Around Assisi

Most visitors need only their feet to get everywhere in Assisi, except to the train station and nearby Basilica of St. Mary of the Angels (via bus #C—see directions in "Arrival in Assisi").

Within the old town, pale-yellow minibuses #A and #B run every 20-40 minutes, linking the lower end (near the Basilica of St. Francis) with the middle (Piazza del Comune) and the top (Piazza Matteotti). While it's only a 15-minute stroll from the upper end to the lower, the climb back up can have you looking for a lift. Hop on a bus marked *Piazza Matteotti* if you're exhausted after your basilica visit and need a sweat-free five-minute return to the top of the old town (near many of my recommended hotels). Before boarding, confirm the destination (catch the bus below the Basilica of St. Francis at the Porta San Francisco).

You can buy a bus ticket (good on any city bus) at a newsstand or kiosk for €1, or get a ticket from the driver for €1.50 (exact change only). After you've stamped your ticket on board the bus, it's valid for 70 minutes.

Self-Guided Walk

▲▲Welcome to Assisi

There's much more to Assisi than just St. Francis and what the blitz tour groups see. This walk covers the town from top (Piazza Matteotti) to bottom (Basilica of St. Francis). To get to Piazza Matteotti, ride the bus from the train station (or from Piazza Giovanni Paolo II) to the last stop; drive up (and park in the underground lot); or hike five minutes uphill from Piazza del Comune.

ASSISI

You can download a free Rick Steves audio tour of this walk; see page 9.
• *Start 50 yards beyond Piazza Matteotti (away from city center—see map).*

❶ The Roman Amphitheater (Anfiteatro Romano)

A lane named Via Anfiteatro Romano skirts the cozy neighborhood built around a Roman amphitheater—a reminder that Assisi was once an important Roman town. Circle the amphitheater counterclockwise. Imagine how colorful the town laundry basin (on the right) must have been in previous generations, when the women of Assisi gathered here to do their wash. Just beyond the basin is a small rectangular pool; above it are the coats of arms of Assisi's leading families. A few steps farther, leave the amphitheater, hiking up the stairs on the right to the top of the hill, for an aerial view of the ancient oval. The Roman stones have long been absorbed into the medieval architecture. It was Roman tradition to locate the amphitheater outside of town, which this used to be. While the amphitheater dates from the first century A.D., the buildings filling it today were built in the 13th and 14th centuries.
• *Continue on, enjoying the grand view of the fortress in the distance. The lane leads down to a city gate and an...*

❷ Umbrian View

Step outside of Assisi at the Porta Perlici for a commanding view. Umbria, called the "green heart of Italy," is the country's geographical center and only landlocked region. Enjoy the various shades of green: silver green on the valley floor (olives), emerald green (grapevines), and deep green on the hillsides (evergreen oak trees). Also notice Rocca Maggiore ("big fortress"), which provided townsfolk a refuge in times of attack, and, behind you atop the nearer hill, Rocca Minore ("little fortress"), which gives the town's young lovers a little privacy. The quarry (under the Rocca Maggiore) was a handy source for Assisi's characteristic pink limestone.

• *Go back through the gate and follow Via Porta Perlici—it's immediately on your right—downhill into town (toward Hotel La Rocca). Enjoy the higgledy-piggledy architecture (this neighborhood has some of the most photogenic back lanes in town). Keep an eye out for a wall containing an aqueduct (on the left, at the arch before #52) that goes back to Roman times. It still brings water from a*

mountain spring into the city (push the brass tap for a taste). After another 50 yards, turn left through a medieval town gate (with Hotel La Rocca on your right). Just after the hotel, you'll pass a second gate dating from Roman times. Follow Via Porta Perlici downhill until you hit a fine square facing a big church.

❸ Cathedral of San Rufino (Cattedrale San Rufino)

Trick question: Who's Assisi's patron saint? While Francis is one of Italy's patron saints, Rufino (the town's first bishop, martyred and buried here in the third century) is Assisi's. The cathedral (seat of the local bishop) is 11th-century Romanesque with a Neoclassical interior. Although it has what is considered to be one of the best and purest Romanesque facades in all of Umbria, the big triangular top of it (just a decorative

wall) was added in Gothic times. Study the lions at the base of the facade, flanking each door. One is eating a Christian martyr, reminding worshippers of the courage of early Christians.

Enter the church. While the front of the church is an unremarkable mix of 17th- and 18th-century Baroque and Neoclassical, the rear (near where you enter) has several points of interest. Notice first the two fine statues: *St. Francis* and *St. Clare* (by Giovanni Dupré, 1888). To your right is an old baptismal font (in the corner with the semicircular black iron grate). In about 1181, a baby boy was baptized in this font. His parents were upwardly mobile Francophiles who called him Francesco ("Frenchy"). In 1194, a nobleman baptized his daughter Clare here. Eighteen years later, their paths crossed in this same church, when Clare attended a class and became mesmerized by the teacher—Francis. Traditionally, the children of Assisi are still baptized here.

The striking glass panels in the floor reveal foundations preserved from the ninth-century church that once stood here. You're walking on history. After the 1997 earthquake, structural inspectors checked the church from ceiling to floor. When they looked under the paving stones, they discovered graves (until Napoleon decreed otherwise, it was common practice to bury people in churches). Underneath that level, they found Roman foundations and some animal bones (suggesting the possibility of animal sacrifice). There might have been a Roman temple here; churches were often built upon temple ruins. Stand at the back of the church fac-

ASSISI

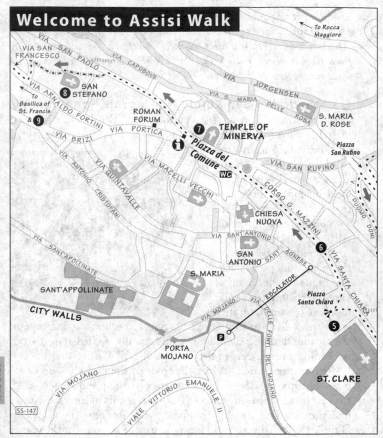

ing the altar, and look left to the Roman cistern (inside the great stone archway, next to where you entered). Take the three steps down (to trigger the light) and marvel at the fine stonework and Roman engineering. In the Middle Ages, this was the town's emergency water source when under attack.

Underneath the church, incorporated into the Roman ruins, are the foundations of an earlier Church of San Rufino, now the crypt and **Diocesan museum.** When it's open, you can go below to see the saint's sarcophagus and the small museum featuring the cathedral's art from centuries past.

Cost and Hours: Cathedral—free, daily 7:30-19:00, Nov-mid-March closed Mon-Fri 12:30-14:30, tel. 075-812-283; crypt/museum—€3.50, mid-March-mid-Oct Thu-Tue 10:00-13:00 & 15:00-18:00, longer hours in Aug, shorter hours mid-Oct-mid-March, closed Wed except in Aug, tel. 075-812-712, www.assisi-museodiocesano.com.

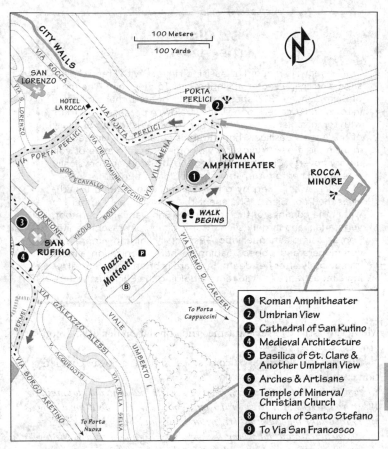

• *Leaving the church, take a sharp left (at the pizza-by-the-slice joint, on Via Dono Doni). After 20 yards, take a right and go all the way down the stairway to see some...*

❹ Medieval Architecture

At the bottom of the stairs, notice the pink limestone pavement, part of the surviving medieval town. The arches built over door-ways indicate that the buildings date from the 12th through the 14th centuries, when Assisi was booming. Italian cities such as Assisi—thriving on the north-south trade between northern Europe and Rome—were in the process of inventing free-market capitalism, dabbling in democratic self-rule, and creating the modern urban lifestyle. The vaults you see that turn lanes into tunnels are reminders of medieval urban expansion—creating more living space (mostly 15th century). While the population grew, people wanted to live within the town's protective walls.

St. Clare
(1194-1253)

The 18-year-old rich girl of Assisi fell in love with Francis' message, and made secret arrangements to meet him. The night of Palm Sunday, 1212, she slipped out of her father's mansion in town and escaped to the valley below. A procession of friars with torches met her and took her to (what is today) St. Mary of the Angels Basilica. There, Francis cut her hair, clothed her in a simple brown tunic, and welcomed her into a life of voluntary poverty. Clare's father begged, ordered, and physically threatened her to return, but she would not budge.

Clare was joined by other women who banded together as the Poor Clares. She spent the next 40 years of her life within the confines of the convent of San Damiano: barefoot, vegetarian, and largely silent. Her regimen of prayer, meditation, and simple manual labor—especially knitting—impressed commoners and popes, leading to her canonization almost immediately after her death. St. Clare is often depicted carrying a monstrance (a little temple holding the Eucharist wafer).

Medieval Assisi had several times the population density of modern Assisi.

Notice the blooming balconies; Assisi holds a flower competition each June.

• *From the bottom of the stairs, head to the left and continue downhill. When you arrive at a street, turn left, going slightly uphill for a long block, then take the low road (right) at the Y, and head down Via Sermei. Continue ahead, following the* S. Chiara *sign downhill to the big church. Cross the street and walk under the three massive buttresses to Piazza Santa Chiara and the front of the church.*

❺ Basilica of St. Clare (Basilica di Santa Chiara)

Dedicated to the founder of the Order of the Poor Clares, this Umbrian Gothic church is simple, in keeping with the nuns' dedication to a life of contemplation. In Clare's lifetime, the order was located in the humble Church of San Damiano, in the valley below, but after Clare's death, they needed a bigger and more glorious building. The church was built in 1265, and the huge buttresses were added in the next century.

The interior's fine frescoes were whitewashed in Baroque times. The battered remains of one on the left shows how the fresco surface was hacked up so whitewash would stick. Imagine all the pristine frescoes hiding behind the whitewash (here and all over Europe).

The Chapel of the Crucifix of San Damiano, on the right, has the wooden crucifix that changed Francis' life. In 1206, an emaciated, soul-searching, stark-raving Francis knelt before this crucifix (then located in the Church of San Damiano) and asked for guidance. The crucifix spoke: "Go and rebuild my Church, which you can see has fallen into ruin." Francis followed the call.

Stairs lead from the nave down to the tomb of St. Clare. Her tomb is at the far end (the image is wax; her bones lie underneath). As you circulate with the crowd of pilgrims, notice the paintings on the walls depicting spiritual lessons from Clare's life and death. At the opposite end of the crypt (back between the stairs, in a large glassed-in area) are important relics: the saint's robes, hair (in a silver box), and an enormous tunic she made—along with relics of St. Francis (including a blood-stained stocking he wore after receiving the stigmata). The attached cloistered community of the Poor Clares has flourished for 700 years.

Cost and Hours: Free, daily 6:30-12:00 & 14:00-19:00, until 18:00 in winter.

• *Leave the church and belly up to the viewpoint at the edge of the square for...*

Another Umbrian View: On the left is the convent of St. Clare (global headquarters of all the Poor Clares). Below you lies the olive grove of the Poor Clares, which has been there since the 13th century. In the distance is a grand Umbrian view. Assisi overlooks the richest and biggest valley in otherwise hilly and mountainous Umbria. The municipality of Assisi has a population of 25,000, but only 3,500 people live in the old town. The lower town, called Santa Maria degli Angeli, grew up with the coming of the railway in the 19th century. In the haze, the blue-domed church is St. Mary of the Angels (described later), the cradle of the Franciscan order. A popular pilgrimage site today, it marks the place where St. Francis lived and worked.

Spanish-speaking Franciscans settled in California. Three of their missions grew into major cities: Los Angeles (named after this church), San Francisco (named after St. Francis), and Santa Clara (named after St. Clare).

• *From the church square, step out into Via Santa Chiara.*

❻ Arches and Artisans

Notice the three medieval town gates (two behind the church, and one uphill toward the town center). The gate over the road behind the church dates from 1265. (Farther on, you can just see the crenellations of the 1316 Porta Nuova, which marks the final medieval expansion of Assisi.) Toward the city center (on Via Santa Chiara, the high road), an arch marks the site of the Roman wall. These three gates represent the town's three walls, illustrating how much the city has grown since ancient times.

Walk uphill along Via Santa Chiara (which becomes Corso Mazzini) to the city's main square. The street is lined with interesting shops selling traditional embroidery, religious souvenirs, and gifty local edibles. The shops on Corso Mazzini, on the stretch between the gate and the Piazza del Comune, show off many local crafts. As you browse, watch for the following shops: Galleria d'Arte Perna (on the left, #20) sells the medieval fantasy townscapes of Paolo Grimaldi, a local painter who runs this shop with his brother, Alessandro. A helpful travel agency is across the street and a few steps up (at #31, Agenzia Viaggi Stoppini; see "Helpful Hints," earlier).

Next, the shop L'Ulivo Sculture (on the left at #14D) sells olive-wood carvings, as does Poiesis, across the street at #23. It's said that St. Francis made the first nativity scene to help humanize and, therefore, teach the Christmas message. That's why you'll see so many crèches in Assisi. (Even today, nearby villages are enthusiastic about their "living" manger scenes, and Italians everywhere enjoy setting up elaborate crèches in churches for Christmas.) Adjacent to #14 is a bakery, Bar Sensi, selling the traditional raisin-and-apple strudel called *rocciata* (roh-CHAH-tah, €3.50 each). Farther along on the left (at #2) is Il Duomo, selling religious art, manger scenes, and crucifixion figurines. Across the street, on the right, is Centro Ricami, a respected embroidery shop. And on the square (at #34, opposite the flags), the recommended La Bottega dei Sapori is worth a visit for edible and drinkable souvenirs.

You've walked up what was, in ancient times, the main drag into town. Ahead of you, the six fluted Corinthian columns of the Temple of Minerva marked the forum (today's Piazza del Comune). Sit at the fountain on the piazza for a few minutes of people-watching—don't you just love Italy? Within a few hundred yards of this square, on either side, were the medieval walls. Imagine the commotion of 5,000 people confined within these walls. No wonder St. Francis needed an escape for some peace and quiet.

• *Now, head over to the temple on the square.*

❼ Temple of Minerva/Christian Church

Assisi has always been a spiritual center. The Romans went to great lengths to make this first-century B.C. Temple of Minerva a centerpiece of their city. Notice the columns that cut into the stairway. It was a tight fit here on the hilltop. In ancient times, the stairs went down—about twice as far as they do now—to the main drag, which has gradually been filled in over time. The Church of Santa Maria sopra ("over") Minerva was added in the ninth century. The bell tower is from the 13th century.

Pop inside the temple/church. Today's interior is 17th-century Baroque. Walk to the front. Flanking the altar are the original Roman temple floor stones. You can even see the drains for the bloody sacrifices that took place here. Behind the statues of Peter and Paul, the original Roman embankment peeks through.

Cost and Hours: Free, Mon-Sat 7:15-19:30, Sun 8:00-19:30, in winter closes at sunset and midday.

• *Across the square at #11, step into the 16th-century frescoed vaults of the...*

Old Market: Notice the Italian flair for design. Even this smelly market was once finely decorated. The art style is called "grotesque"—literally from a cave (grotto-esque), named for the fanciful Roman paintings found on the walls of Italian caves. This scene was indisputably painted after 1492. How do they know? Because it features turkeys—first seen in Europe after Columbus returned from the Americas with his bag of exotic souvenirs. The turkeys painted here may have been that bird's European debut.

• *From the main square, hike past the temple up the high road, Via San Paolo. After 200 yards (across from #24), a sign directs you down a stepped lane to the...*

❽ Church of Santo Stefano (Chiesa di Santo Stefano)

Surrounded by cypress, fig, and walnut trees, Santo Stefano—which used to be outside the town walls in the days of St. Francis—is a delightful bit of offbeat Assisi. Legend has it that Santo Stefano's bells miraculously rang on October 3, 1226, the day St. Francis died. Step inside. This is the typical rural Italian Romanesque church—no architect, just built by simple stonemasons who put together the most basic design. Hundreds of years later, it still stands.

Cost and Hours: Free, daily 8:30-21:30, Sept-May until 18:30.

• *The lane zigzags down to Via San Francesco. Turn right and walk under the arch toward the Basilica of St. Francis.*

❾ Via San Francesco

This main drag leads from the town to the basilica holding the body of St. Francis. Francis was a big deal even in his own day. He was made a saint in 1228—the same year that the basilica's foundations were laid—and his body was moved here by 1230. Assisi was a big-time pilgrimage center, and this street was its booming hub. The arch marks the end of what was Assisi in St. Francis' day.

Notice the fine medieval balcony immediately past the arch. About 30 yards farther down (on the left), cool yourself at the fountain, as medieval pilgrims might have. The hospice next door was built in 1237 to house pilgrims. Notice the three surviving faces of its fresco: Jesus, Francis, and Clare. Farther down, across from #12a (on the left), is the Oratorio dei Pellegrini, dating from the 1450s. A brotherhood ran a hostel here for travelers passing through to pay homage to St. Francis. The chapel offers a richly frescoed space in which to contemplate the saint's message.

• *Continuing on, you'll eventually reach Assisi's main sight, the Basilica of St. Francis. For the start of my self-guided tour, walk downhill to the basilica's lower courtyard.*

Self-Guided Tour

▲▲▲Basilica of St. Francis (Basilica di San Francesco)

The basilica is one of the artistic and religious highlights of Europe. It rises where, in 1226, St. Francis was buried (with the outcasts

he had stood by) outside of his town on the "Hill of the Damned"—now called the "Hill of Paradise." The basilica is frescoed from top to bottom with scenes by the leading artists of the day: Cimabue, Giotto, Simone Martini, and Pietro Lorenzetti. A 13th-century historian wrote, "No more exquisite monument to the Lord has been built."

From a distance, you see the huge arcades "supporting" the basilica. These were 15th-century quarters for the monks. The arcades that line the square and lead to the church housed medieval pilgrims.

Cost and Hours: Free entry; lower basilica daily 6:00-18:45, until 17:45 in Nov-March; reliquary chapel in lower basilica generally open Mon-Fri 9:00-18:00, often closed Sat-Sun and occasionally at other times for religious services; upper basilica daily 8:30-18:45, until 17:45 in Nov-March. Modest dress is required to enter the church—no sleeveless tops or shorts for men, women, or children.

Information: The church courtyard at the entrance of the lower basilica has an info office, often staffed by native English-speaking friars (Mon-Sat 9:15-12:00 & 14:15-17:30, closed Sun, tel. 075-819-0084, www.sanfrancescoassisi.org). Call or check the website to find out about upcoming concerts at the basilica.

Tours: Audioguides (boring and old-school) are available at the kiosk located outside the entrance of the upper basilica (€6 donation requested, €7/2 people, daily 9:00-17:00, 45 minutes). You can download a free Rick Steves audio version of this chapter's tour of the basilica (see page 9). You can also take an English tour, offered daily except Sunday (€10 donation requested, call or email the information office to reserve, tel. 075-819-0084, www.sanfrancescoassisi.org, assisisanfrancesco@libero.it).

Bookstore: The church bookshop is in the inner courtyard behind the upper and lower basilica. It sells an excellent guidebook, *The Basilica of Saint Francis: A Spiritual Pilgrimage* (€3, by Goulet, McInally, and Wood; I used this book, and a tour with Brother Michael, as sources for this self-guided tour).

Services: Go before you enter, as there aren't any WCs inside. There are two different pay WCs within a half-block of the lower entrance—up the road in a squat building, and halfway down the big piazza on the left.

Attending Mass: To worship in the basilica, consider joining the Franciscan brothers in the lower basilica in the morning at 7:15 or 11:00, or experience a Mass sung by the basilica choir many Sundays at 10:30. On Sundays in summer (Easter-Oct), there's an English Mass in the upper basilica at 9:00. Additional English and sung Masses don't follow a set schedule. Call the basilica to find out when English-speaking pilgrimage groups or choirs have reserved Masses, and attend with them—although groups change their plans fairly often (tel. 075-819-0084).

Overview

The Basilica of St. Francis, a theological work of genius, can be difficult for the 21st-century tourist/pilgrim to appreciate.

Since the basilica is the reason that most people visit Assisi, and the message of St. Francis has even the least devout sightseers blessing the town Vespas, I've designed this self-guided tour with an emphasis on the place's theology (rather than art history).

A disclaimer before we start: Just as Francis used many biblical legends to help teach the Christian message, legends from the life of Francis were told in later ages to teach the same message. Are they true? In general, probably not. Are they in keeping with Francis' message? Yes. Do I share legends here as if they are historic? Sure.

The church has three parts: the upper basilica, the lower basilica, and the saint's tomb (below the lower basilica). To get oriented, stand at the lower entrance in the courtyard. While empty today, centuries ago this main plaza was cluttered with pilgrim services

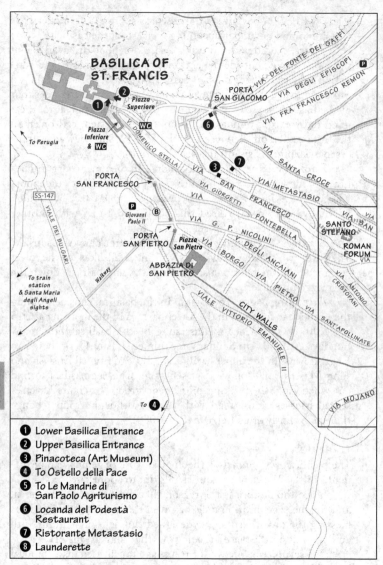

ASSISI

1 Lower Basilica Entrance
2 Upper Basilica Entrance
3 Pinacoteca (Art Museum)
4 To Ostello della Pace
5 To Le Mandrie di
  San Paolo Agriturismo
6 Locanda del Podestà
  Restaurant
7 Ristorante Metastasio
8 Launderette

and the medieval equivalent of souvenir shops. Opposite the entry to the lower basilica is the information center.

Enter through the grand doorway of the lower basilica. Just inside, decorating the top of the first arch, look up and see St. Francis, who greets you with a Latin inscription. Sounding a bit like John Wayne, he says the equivalent of, "Slow down and be joyful, pilgrim. You've reached the Hill of Paradise. And, if you're observant and thoughtful, this church will knock your spiritual socks off."

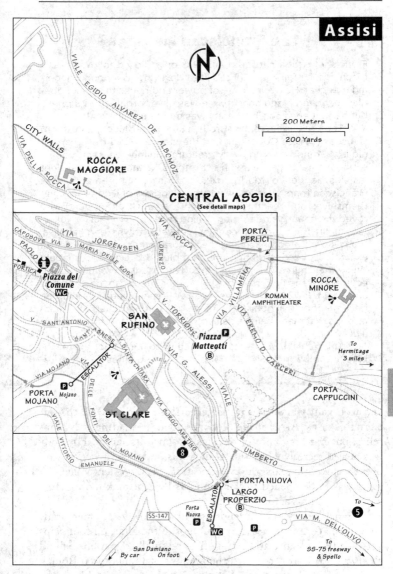

• *Start with the tomb. To get there, turn left into the nave. Midway down, follow the signs and go right, to the tomb downstairs.*

The Tomb

The saint's remains are above the altar in the stone box with the iron ties. In medieval times, pilgrims came to Assisi because St. Francis was buried here. Holy relics were the "ruby slippers" of medieval Europe. Relics gave you power—they answered your prayers

The Franciscan Message

Francis' message caused a stir. Not only did he follow Christ's teachings, he followed Christ's lifestyle, living as a poor, wandering preacher. He traded a life of power and riches for one of obedience, poverty, and chastity. He was never ordained as a priest, but his influence on Christianity was monumental.

The Franciscan realm (Brother Sun, Sister Moon, and so on) is a space where God, man, and the natural world frolic harmoniously. Francis treated every creature—animal, peasant, pope—with equal respect. He and his "brothers" (*fratelli,* or friars) slept in fields, begged for food, and exuded the joy of non-materialism. Franciscan friars were known as the "Jugglers of God," modeling themselves on French troubadours (*jongleurs,* or jugglers) who roved the countryside singing, telling stories, and cracking jokes.

In an Italy torn by conflict between towns and families, Francis promoted peace and the restoration of order. (He set an example by reconstructing the crumbled San Damiano chapel.) While the Church was waging bloody Crusades, Francis pushed ecumenism and understanding. And the Franciscan message had an impact. In 1288, just 62 years after Francis died, a Franciscan became pope (Nicholas IV). Francis' message also led to Church reforms that many believe delayed the Protestant Reformation by a century.

This richly decorated basilica seems to contradict the teachings of the poor monk it honors, but it was built as an act of re-

and won your wars—and ultimately helped you get back to your eternal Kansas. Assisi made no bones about promoting the saint's relics, but hid his tomb for obvious reasons of security. His body was buried secretly while the basilica was under construction, and over the next 600 years, the exact location was forgotten. When the tomb was to be opened to the public in 1818, it took more than a month to find his actual remains.

Francis' four closest friends and first followers are memorialized in the corners of the room. Opposite the altar, up four steps between the entrance and exit, notice the small copper box behind the metal grill. This contains the remains of Francis' rich Roman patron, Jacopa dei Settesoli. She traveled to see him on his deathbed but was turned away because she was female. Francis waived the rule and welcomed "Brother Jacopa" to his side. These five tombs—in the Franciscan spirit of being with your friends—were added in the 19th century.

The candles you see are the only real candles in the church (others are electric). Pilgrims pay a coin, pick up a candle, and place it in the small box on the side. Franciscans will light it later.

• *Climb back up to the lower nave.*

ligious and civic pride to remember the hometown saint. It was also designed—and still functions—as a pilgrimage center and a splendid classroom. Though monks in robes may not give off an "easy-to-approach" vibe, the Franciscans of today are still God's jugglers (and many of them speak English).

Here is Francis' message, in his own words:

The Canticle of the Sun

Good Lord, all your creations bring praise to you!

Praise for Brother Sun, who brings the day. His radiance reminds us of you!

Praise for Sister Moon and the stars, precious and beautiful.

Praise for Brother Wind, and for clouds and storms and rain that sustain us.

Praise for Sister Water. She is useful and humble, precious and pure.

Praise for Brother Fire who cheers us at night.

Praise for our sister, Mother Earth, who feeds us and rules us.

Praise for all those who forgive because you have forgiven them.

Praise for our sister, Bodily Death, from whose embrace none can escape.

Praise and bless the Lord, and give thanks, and, with humility, serve him.

ASSISI

Lower Basilica

Appropriately Franciscan—subdued and Romanesque—this nave is frescoed with parallel scenes from the lives of Christ (right) and Francis (left), connected by a ceiling of stars. The Passion of Christ and the Compassion of Francis lead to the altar built over Francis' tomb. After the church was built and decorated, side chapels were erected to provide mausoleums for the rich families that patronized the work of the order. Unfortunately, in the process, huge arches were cut out of some frescoed scenes, but others survive. In the fresco directly above the entry to the tomb, Christ is being taken down from the cross (just the bottom half of his body can be seen, on the left), and it looks like the story is over. Defeat. But in the opposite fresco (above the tomb's exit), we see Francis preaching to the birds, reminding the faithful that the message of the Gospel survives.

These stories directed the attention of the medieval pilgrim to the altar, where he could meet God through the sacraments. The church was thought of as a community of believers sailing toward God. The prayers coming out of the nave (*navis*, or ship) fill the triangular sections of the ceiling—called *vele*, or sails—with spiritual

Basilica of St. Francis—Lower Level

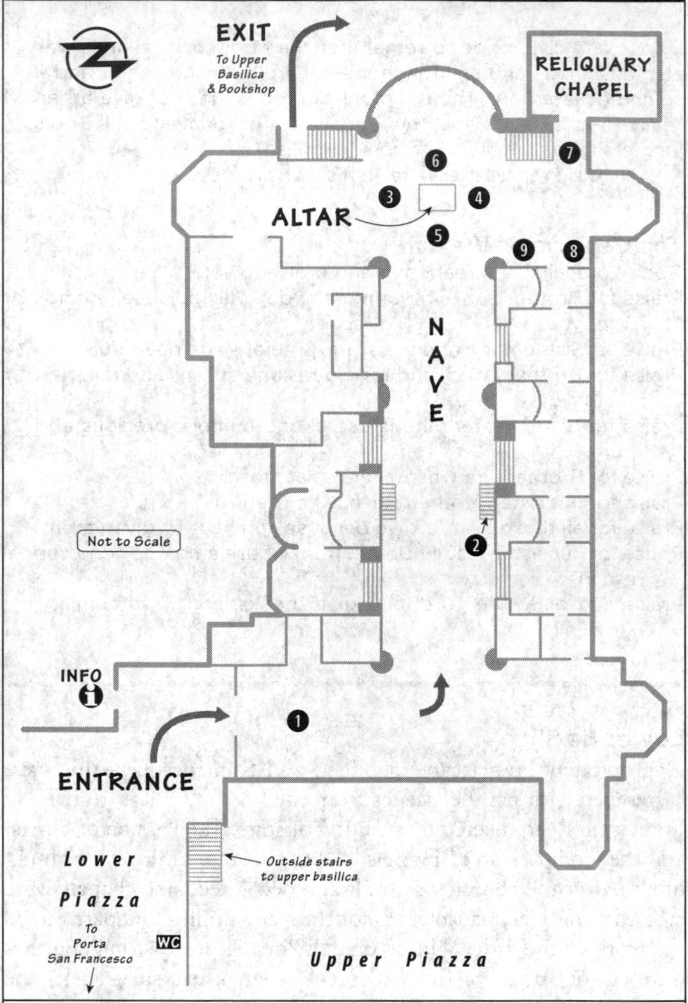

EXIT
To Upper
Basilica
& Bookshop

RELIQUARY
CHAPEL

6

3 **4**

ALTAR

5

9 **8**

N
A
V
E

Not to Scale

2

INFO

ENTRANCE

1

Lower

Piazza

To
Porta
San Francesco

WC

Outside stairs
to upper basilica

Upper   Piazza

ASSISI

1 St. Francis (on ceiling)   **6** Francis on a Heavenly Throne
2 Stairs to Tomb   **7** Reliquary Chapel
3 Obedience (on ceiling)   **8** GIOTTO – Crucifixion
4 Chastity (on ceiling)   **9** CIMABUE – St. Francis
5 Poverty (on ceiling)

wind. With a priest for a navigator and the altar for a helm, faith propels the ship.

Stand behind the altar (toes to the bottom step, facing the entrance) and look up. The three scenes above you represent the creed of the Franciscans: Directly above the tomb of St. Francis, to the right, **Obedience** (Francis appears twice, wearing a rope harness and kneeling in front of Lady Obedience); to the left, **Chastity** (in her tower of purity held up by two angels); and straight ahead, **Poverty.** Here Jesus blesses the marriage as Francis slips a ring on Lady Poverty. In the foreground, two "self-sufficient" yet pint-size merchants (the new rich of a thriving northern Italy) are throwing sticks and stones at the bride. But Poverty, in her patched wedding dress, is fertile and strong, and even bare brambles blossom into a rosebush crown.

The three knots in the rope that ties the Franciscan robe symbolize the monks' vows of obedience, chastity, and poverty. St. Francis called money the "devil's dung." The jeweled belt of a rich person was all about material wealth. A bag of coins hung from it, as did a weapon to protect that person's wealth. Franciscans instead bound their tunics with a simple rope, its three knots a constant reminder of their vows.

Now put your heels to the altar and—bending back like a drum major—look up for a peek at the reward for a life of obedience, chastity, and poverty: **Francis on a heavenly throne** in a rich, golden robe. He traded a life of earthly simplicity for glory in heaven.

• *Turn to the right and march to the corner, where steps lead down into the...*

Reliquary Chapel

This chapel is filled with fascinating relics (which a €0.50 flier explains in detailed English; often closed Sat-Sun). Step in and circle the room clockwise. You'll see the silver chalice and plate that Francis used for the bread and wine of the Eucharist (in a small, dark, windowed case set into wall, marked *Calice e Patena*). Francis believed that his personal possessions should be simple, but the items used for worship should be made of the finest materials. Next, the Veli di Lino is a cloth Jacopa wiped her friend's brow with on his deathbed. In the corner display case is a small section of the itchy haircloth *(cilizio)*—not sheep's wool, but cloth made from scratchy horse or goat hair—worn by Francis as penance (the cloth he chose was the opposite of the fine fabric his father sold). In the next corner are the tunic and slippers that Francis donned during his last days. Next, find a prayer (in a fancy silver stand) that St. Francis wrote for Brother Leo and signed with a T-shaped character—his tau cross. The last letter in the Hebrew alphabet, tav ("tau" in Greek) is symbolic of faithfulness to the end, and Francis adopted it for his signature. Next is a papal document (1223) legitimizing the Franciscan order and assuring his followers that they were not risking a (deadly) heresy charge. Finally, just past the altar, see the tunic that was lovingly patched and stitched by followers of the five-foot, four-inch-tall St. Francis.

Before leaving the chapel, notice the modern paintings done in the last year or so by local artists. Over the entrance, Francis is shown being born in a stable like Jesus (by Capitini). Scenes from the life of Clare and Padre Pio (a Capuchin priest, very popular in Italy, who was sainted in 2002) were painted by Stefanelli and Antonio.

• *Return up the stairs, stepping into the...*

Lower Basilica's Transept

The decoration of this church brought together the greatest Sienese (Lorenzetti and Simone Martini) and Florentine (Cimabue and Giotto) artists of the day. Look around at the painted scenes. In 1300, this was radical art—believable homespun scenes, landscapes, trees, real people. Directly opposite the reliquary chapel, study **Giotto's painting of the Crucifixion,** with the eight sparrow-like angels. For the first time, holy people are expressing emotion: One angel turns her head sadly at the sight of Jesus, and another scratches her hands down her cheeks, drawing blood. Mary (lower left), previously in control, has fainted in despair. The Franciscans, with their goal of bringing God to the people, found a natural partner in Europe's first naturalist (and therefore modern) painter, Giotto.

To grasp Giotto's artistic leap, compare his work with the painting to the right, by Cimabue. It's Gothic, without the 3-D architecture, natural backdrop, and slice-of-life reality of Giotto's work. **Cimabue's St. Francis** (far right) shows the saint with the stigmata—Christ's marks of the Crucifixion. Contemporaries described Francis as being short, with a graceful build, dark hair, and sparse beard. (This is considered the most accurate portrait of Francis—done according to the description of one who knew him.) The sunroof haircut (tonsure) was

standard for monks of the day. According to legend, the brown robe and rope belt were inventions of necessity. When Francis stripped naked and ran away from Assisi, he grabbed the first clothes he could, a rough wool peasant's tunic and a piece of rope, which became the uniform of the Franciscan order. To the left, at eye level under the sparrow-like angels, are paintings of saints and their exquisite halos (by Simone Martini or his school). To the right of the door at the same level, see five of Francis' closest followers—clearly just simple folk.

Francis' friend, "Sister Bodily Death," was really not all that terrible. In fact, Francis would like to introduce you to her now (above and to the right of the door leading into the reliquary chapel). Go ahead, block the light from the door with this book and meet her. Before his death, Francis added a line to *The Canticle of the Sun:* "Praise for our sister, Bodily Death, from whose embrace none can escape."

• *Now cross the transept to the other side of the altar (enjoying some of the oldest surviving bits of the inlaid local-limestone flooring—c. 13th century), and find the staircase going up. Immediately above the stairs is Pietro Lorenzetti's* Francis Receiving the Stigmata. *(Francis is considered the first person ever to earn the marks of the cross through his great faith and love of the Church.) Make your way to the...*

Courtyard

The courtyard overlooks the 15th-century cloister, the heart of this monastic complex. Pope Sixtus IV (of Sistine Chapel fame) had it built as a secure retreat for himself. Balanced and peaceful by design, the courtyard also functioned as a cistern to collect rainwater, supplying enough for 200 monks (today, there are about 40). The Franciscan order emphasizes teaching. This place functioned as a kind of theological center of higher learning, which rotated monks in for a six-month stint, then sent them back home more prepared and better inspired to preach effectively. That explains the complex narrative of the frescoes wallpapering the walls and halls here.

The **treasury** *(Museo del Tesoro)* to the left of the bookstore features ornately decorated chalices, reliquaries, vestments, and altarpieces (free but donation requested, April-Oct Mon-Sat 10:30-13:00 & 14:00-17:30, Sun 10:00-17:30, closed Nov-March).

• *From the courtyard, climb the stairs (next to the bookshop) to the...*

Upper Basilica

Built later than its counterpart below, the brighter upper basilica is considered the first Gothic church in Italy (started in 1228). You've followed the intended pilgrims' route, entering the lower church and finishing here. Notice how the pulpit (embedded in the corner pillar) can be seen and heard from every spot in the packed church. The spirit of the order was to fill the church and preach. See also the design in the round window in the west end

Basilica of St. Francis—Upper Level

ALTAR

Entrance from bookstore

21 Three "post mortem miracles" associated with St. Francis

20 Francis' death, funeral, and canonization

Not to Scale

19 Francis receives the stigmata

18 The apparition at Arles

17 Preaching for Pope Honorius III

16 The Knight of Celano invites Francis to his deathbed

15 Sermon to the birds →

Stairs down to lower basilica

To Piazza Comune & the rest of Assisi

S O U T H   W A L L

N A V E

N O R T H   W A L L

1 A common man spreads his cape before Francis

2 Francis offers his cape to a needy stranger

3 Francis is visited by the Lord in a dream

4 Francis prays to the crucifix

5 Francis relinquishes his possessions

6 The pope has a dream

7 The pope confirms the Franciscan order

8 A vision of the flaming chariot

9 A vision of thrones

10 Exorcism of demons in Arezzo

11 St. Francis before the sultan

12 Ecstasy of St. Francis

13 The crèche at Greccio

14 ← Miracle of the spring

22 Tan patches on ceiling

MAIN ENTRANCE

L a w n
WITH TAU CROSS
& "PAX"

ASSISI

(high above the entry). The tiny centerpiece reads "IHS" (the first three letters of Jesus' name in Greek). And, as you can see, this trippy kaleidoscope seems to declare that all light radiates from Jesus. The windows here are treasures from the 13th and 14th centuries. Those behind the apse are among the oldest and most precious in Italy. Imagine illiterate medieval peasants entranced by these windows, so full of meaning that they were nicknamed "Bibles of the Poor." But for art lovers, the basilica's draw is that Giotto and his assistants practically wallpapered it circa 1297-1300. Or perhaps the job was subcontracted to other artists—scholars debate it (for more on Giotto, see page 174). Whatever the case, the anatomy, architectural depth, and drama of these frescoes helped to kick off the Renaissance. The gallery of frescoes shows 28 scenes from the life of St. Francis. The events are a mix of documented history and folk legend.

• *Working clockwise, start on the north wall (to the left, if you just climbed the stairs from the bookstore) and follow along with the help of the numbered map key. The subtitles in the black strip below the frescoes describe each scene in clear Latin—and affirm my interpretation.*

ASSISI

❶ **A common man spreads his cape before Francis** in front of the Temple of Minerva on Piazza del Comune. Before his conversion, young Francis was the model of Assisian manhood—handsome, intelligent, and well dressed, befitting the son of a wealthy cloth dealer. Above all, he was liked by everyone, a natural charmer who led his fellow teens in nights of wine, women, and song. Medieval pilgrims understood the deeper meaning of this scene: The "eye" of God (symbolized by the rose window in the Temple of Minerva) looks over the young Francis, a dandy "imprisoned" in his own selfishness (the Temple—with barred windows—was once a prison).

❷ **Francis offers his cape to a needy stranger.** Francis was always generous of spirit. He became more so after being captured in battle and held for a year as a prisoner of war, then suffering from illness. Charity was a Franciscan forte.

❸ **Francis is visited by the Lord in a dream.** Still unsure of his calling, Francis rode off to the Crusades. One night, he dreams of a palace filled with armor marked with crosses. Christ tells him to leave the army—to become what you might consider the first "conscientious objector"—and go home to wait for a non-military assignment in a new kind of knighthood. He returned to Assisi and, though reviled as a coward, would end up fighting for spiritual wealth, not earthly power and riches.

❹ **Francis prays to the crucifix** in the Church of San Damiano. After months of living in a cave, fasting, and meditating, Francis kneels in the run-down church and prays. The crucifix speaks, telling him: "Go and rebuild my Church, which you can see has fallen into ruin." Francis hurried home and sold his father's cloth to pay for God's work. His furious father dragged him before the bishop.

❺ **Francis relinquishes his possessions.** In front of the bishop and the whole town, Francis strips naked and gives his dad his clothes, credit cards, and time-share on Capri. Francis raises his hand and says, "Until now, I called you father. From now on, my only father is my Father in Heaven." Notice God's hand blessing the action from above. Francis then ran off into the hills, naked and singing. In this version, Francis is covered by the bishop, symbolizing his transition from a man of the world to a man of the Church. Notice the disbelief and concern on the bishop's advisors' faces; subtle expressions like these wouldn't have made it into other medieval frescoes of the day.

❻ **The pope has a dream.** Francis headed to Rome, seeking the pope's blessing on his fledgling movement. Initially rebuffing Francis, the pope then dreams of a simple, barefooted man propping up his teetering Church, and then...

❼ **The pope confirms the Franciscan order,** handing Francis and his gang the document now displayed in the reliquary chapel.

Francis' life was peppered with visions and miracles, shown in three panels in a row: ❽ **vision of the flaming chariot,** ❾ **vision of thrones,** and ❿ **exorcism of demons in Arezzo.**
• *Next see...*

⓫ **St. Francis before the sultan.** Francis' wandering ministry took him to Egypt during the Crusades (1219). He walked unarmed into the Muslim army camp. They captured him, but the sultan was impressed with Francis' manner and let him go, reportedly whispering, "I'd convert to your faith, but they'd kill us both." Here the sultan gestures from his throne.

⓬ **Ecstasy of St. Francis.** This oft-painted scene shows the mystic communing with Christ.

⓭ **The crèche at Greccio.** A creative teacher, Francis invents the tradition of manger scenes.
• *Around the corner, see the...*

⓮ **Miracle of the spring.** Shown here getting water out of a rock to quench a stranger's thirst, Francis felt closest to God when in the hills around Assisi, seeing the Creator in the creation.
• *Cross over to the far side of the entrance door.*

⑮ Sermon to the birds. In his best-known miracle, Francis is surrounded by birds as they listen to him teach. Francis embraces all levels of creation. One interpretation of this scene is that the birds, which are of different species, represent the diverse flock of humanity and nature, all created and beloved by God and worthy of one another's love.

This image of well-fed birds is an appropriate one to take with you. It's designed to remind pilgrims that, like the birds, God gave us life, plenty of food, feathers, wings, and a world to fly around in. Francis, patron saint of the environment and animals, taught his followers to count their blessings. A monk here reminded me that even a student backpacker today eats as well as the wealthiest nobleman in the days of Francis.

• *Continue to the south wall for the rest of the panels.*

Despite the hierarchical society of his day, Francis was welcomed by all classes, shown in these three panels: **⑯ the knight of Celano invites Francis to his deathbed; ⑰ preaching for Pope Honorius III,** who listens intently; and **⑱ the apparition at Arles,** which illustrates how Francis could be in two places at once (something only Jesus and saints can pull off). The proponents of Francis, who believed he was destined for sainthood, show him performing the necessary miracles.

⑲ Francis receives the stigmata. It's September 17, 1224, and Francis is fasting and praying on nearby Mount Alverna when a six-winged angel (called a seraph) appears with holy laser-like powers to burn in the marks of the Crucifixion, the stigmata. For the strength of his faith, Francis is given the marks of his master, the "battle scars of love." These five wounds suffered by Christ (nails in palms and feet, lance in side) marked Francis' body for the rest of his life.

The next panels deal with **⑳ Francis' death, funeral, and canonization.** The last panels show **㉑ miracles** associated with the saint after his death, proving that he's in heaven and bolstering his eligibility for sainthood.

Francis died thanking God and singing his *Canticle of the Sun.* Just as he referred to the sun as his brother and the moon as his sister, Francis called his body "brother." On his deathbed he conceded, "Maybe I was a bit tough on brother ass." Ravaged by an asceticism extreme enough to earn him the stigmata and tuberculosis, Francis died in 1226.

Before leaving through the front entrance, look up at the ceiling and the walls near the rose window to see **㉒ large tan patches.** In 1997, when a 5.5-magnitude quake hit Assisi, it shattered the upper basilica's frescoes into 300,000 fragments. Shortly after the quake, an aftershock shook the ceiling frescoes down, killing two monks and two art scholars standing here. Later, the fragments were meticulously picked up and pieced back together.

Outside, on the lawn, the Latin word *pax* (peace) and the Franciscan tau cross are sculpted from shrubbery. For a drink or snack, the Bar San Francesco (facing the upper basilica) is handy. For *pax,* take the high lane back to town, up to the castle, or into the countryside.

More Sights in Assisi

▲Roman Forum (Foro Romano)
For a look at Assisi's Roman roots, tour the Roman Forum, which is underneath Piazza del Comune. The floor plan is clearly explained in English, as are the surviving odd bits and obscure pieces. During your visit, you'll walk on an ancient Roman road.

Cost and Hours: €4, included in €8 combo-ticket that also covers next two sights daily March-Oct 10:00-13:00 & 14:30-18:00—until 19:00 in June-Aug, Nov-Feb 10:30-13:00 & 14:00-17:00; from Piazza del Comune, go a half-block down Via Portica—it's on your right; tel. 075-815-5077.

Pinacoteca
This small, unexciting museum attractively displays its 13th- to 17th-century art (mainly frescoes), with general English information in nearly every room. There's a damaged Giotto Madonna and a rare secular fresco (to the right of the Giotto art), but it's mainly a peaceful walk through a pastel world—best for art lovers.

Cost and Hours: €3, included in €8 combo-ticket, same hours as Roman Forum, Via San Francesco, across from #13C—look for banner above entryway, on main drag between Piazza del Comune and Basilica of St. Francis, tel. 075-815-5077.

▲Rocca Maggiore
The "big castle" offers a good look at a 14th-century fortification and a fine view of Assisi and the Umbrian countryside. If you're pinching your euros, skip it—the view is just as good from outside the castle. There's talk of restoring some rooms in their original medieval style, possibly in time for your visit.

Cost and Hours: €5, included in €8 combo-ticket, daily from 10:00 until an hour before sunset—about 19:15 in summer, tel. 075-815-5077.

Church of San Damiano (Chiesa di San Damiano)
Located on the slope steeply below the Basilica of St. Clare, this church and convent was where Francis received his call and where Clare spent her days as mother superior of the Poor Clares. Today, there's not much to see, but it's a relatively peaceful escape from touristy Assisi. Drivers can zip right there (watch for the turnoff on

the road up to Piazza Matteotti), while walkers descend pleasantly from Assisi for 15 minutes through an olive grove.

In 1206, Francis was inside the church when he heard the wooden crucifix order him to rebuild the church. (The crucifix in San Damiano is a copy; the original is now displayed in the Basilica of St. Clare.) Francis initially interpreted these miraculous words as a call to rebuild crumbling San Damiano. He sold his father's cloth for money to fix the church. (The church we see today, however, was rebuilt later by others.) Eventually, Francis realized his charge was to revitalize the Christian Church at large.

As he approached the end of his life, Francis came to San Damiano to visit his old friend Clare. She set him up in a simple reed hut in the olive grove, where he was inspired to write his poem *The Canticle of the Sun* (see page 779).

Cost and Hours: Free, daily, convent open 10:00-12:00 & 14:00-18:00, closes at 16:30 in winter, church opens at 6:15, start walking from the Porta Nuova parking lot at the south end of Assisi and follow the signs, tel. 075-812-273, www.assisiofm.it.

Commune with Nature
For a picnic with the same birdsong and views that inspired St. Francis, leave the tourists behind and hike to the Rocca Minore (small private castle, not tourable) above Piazza Matteotti.

In Santa Maria degli Angeli
This modern part of Assisi sits in the flat valley below the hill town (see "Assisi Area" map, earlier). Whether you're arriving by car or by train, it's practical to visit these sights on the way into or out of Assisi (they're an easy walk from the train station—which has baggage storage—and there's ample, well-marked parking).

▲▲Basilica of St. Mary of the Angels
(Basilica di Santa Maria degli Angeli)
This huge basilica, towering above the buildings below Assisi, marks the spot where Francis lived, worked, and died. It's a grandi-

ose church built around a humble chapel—reflecting the monumental impact of this simple saint on his town and the world.

Cost and Hours: The basilica is free to enter and open Mon-Sat 6:15-12:50 & 14:30-19:30, Sun 6:45-12:50 & 14:30-19:30 (tel. 075-805-11). A little TI kiosk is across the street from the souvenir stands (generally daily 10:00-13:00 & 15:30-18:30 but hours a bit erratic, tel. 075-

ASSISI

804-4554). As you face the church, the best WC is on your right (€0.50).

Getting There: From Assisi's train station, it's a five-minute walk to the basilica (exit station left, after 50 yards take the underground pedestrian walkway—*sottopassaggio*—on your left, then walk straight ahead, passing several handy eateries).

From the old town, you can reach the basilica on the same orange bus (line #C) that runs down to the train station (stay on one more stop to reach the basilica). In the opposite direction, buses from the basilica up to the old town run twice hourly, usually at :14 and :44 after the hour. Leaving the church, the stop is on your right, by the side of the building. For information on tickets, see "Getting Around Assisi," earlier.

Visiting the Basilica: This grand church was built in the 16th century around the tiny but historic **Porziuncola Chapel** (now directly under the dome), after the chapel

became too small to accommodate the many pilgrims wanting to pay homage to St. Francis. Some local monks had given Francis this *porziuncola,* or "small portion," after his conversion—a little land with a fixer-upper chapel. Francis lived here after he founded the Franciscan Order, and this was where he consecrated St. Clare as a Bride of Christ. What would humble Francis think of the huge church—Christianity's 10th largest—built over his tiny chapel?

Behind the Porziuncola Chapel on the right, find the **Cappella del Transito,** which marks the site of Francis' death on October 3, 1226. Francis died as he'd lived—simply, in a small hut located here. On his last night on earth, he invited some friars to join him in a Last Supper-style breaking of bread. Then he undressed, lay down on the bare ground, and began to recite Psalm 141: "Lord, I cry unto thee." He spoke the last line, "Let the wicked fall into their own traps, while I escape"...and he passed on.

From the right transept, follow *Roseto* signs to the rose garden. You'll walk down a passage with gardens on either side (viewable through the windows)—on the left, a tranquil park with a statue of Francis petting a sheep, and on the right, the **rose garden.** Francis, fighting a temptation that he never named, once threw himself onto the roses. As the story goes, the thorns immediately dropped off. Thornless roses have grown here ever since.

Exiting the passage, turn right to find the **Rose Chapel** (Cappella delle Rose), built over the place where Francis lived.

In the autumn, a room in the next **hallway** displays a giant animated nativity scene (a reminder to pilgrims that Francis first established the tradition of manger scenes as a teaching aid). You'll pass a room with a free 10-minute video about the church (ask for English, daily 10:00-12:30 & 16:00-18:00). The bookshop has some works in English and an "old pharmacy" selling herbal cures.

Continuing on, you'll pass the **Porziuncola Museum,** featuring early depictions of St. Francis by 13th-century artists, a model of Assisi during Francis' lifetime, and religious art and objects from the basilica. On the museum's upper floor are some monks' cells, which provide intriguing insight into the spartan lifestyles of the pious and tonsured (€4 to see both floors, ask for English brochure, museum open April-Oct Tue-Sun 9:30-12:30 & 15:30-19:00, Nov-March until 18:00, closed Mon, tel. 075-805-1419, www.porziuncola.org).

Museo Pericle Fazzini

This small museum, housed in the arcaded building across the street from the basilica, features works by the contemporary Italian sculptor Pericle Fazzini. His works feature elongated, wildly distorted, and very expressive figures. The permanent collection, on the first floor, includes bronzes, wooden sculptures (including one of St. Francis), and the original bronze casting of *The Risen Christ*—a miniature of Fazzini's famous bronze of Jesus rising from a nuclear-bomb crater, commissioned by the pope for the Sala Nervi audience hall of the Vatican. Biographical information on the sculptor is provided in English. Upstairs on the second floor are temporary exhibits.

Cost and Hours: €5, Tue-Sun 10:00-13:00 & 16:00-19:00, closed Mon, tel. 075-804-4586, www.museo.periclefazzini.it.

Outside of Assisi

Hermitage (Eremo delle Carceri)

If you want to follow further in St. Francis' footsteps, take a trip up the rugged slopes of nearby Mount Subasio to the humble hermitage where Francis and his followers retreated for solitude. Today the spot is marked by a 14th-century convent. The highlight is a look at the tiny, dank cave where Francis would retire for private prayer.

Cost and Hours: Free, daily 6:30-19:00, until 18:00 in winter, last entry 30 minutes before closing, tel. 075-812-301, www.eremocarceri.it.

Getting There: There is no public transportation; either drive, take a taxi, or hike. Starting from Assisi's Porta Cappuccini gate, it's a stiff 3-mile, 1.5-hour hike with an elevation gain of about 1,000 feet. You'll walk along a narrow, switchbacked, paved road enjoying brisk air and sporadic views. A souvenir kiosk at the entrance sells drinks and sandwiches.

Sleep Code

(€1 = about $1.30, country code: 39)
S = Single, **D** = Double/Twin, **T** = Triple, **Q** = Quad, **b** = bathroom, **s** = shower only. Unless otherwise noted, credit cards are accepted, English is spoken, and breakfast is included. Many cities in Italy levy a hotel tax of €2 per person, per night, which must be paid in cash (not included in the rates I've quoted).

To help you sort easily through these listings, I've divided the accommodations into three categories based on the price for a standard double room with bath:

$$$ **Higher Priced**—Most rooms €100 or more.
$$ **Moderately Priced**—Most rooms between €55-100.
$ **Lower Priced**—Most rooms €55 or less.

Prices can change without notice; verify the hotel's current rates online or by email. For the best prices, always book direct.

Sleeping in Assisi

Assisi accommodates large numbers of pilgrims on religious holidays (see list on page 1189). Finding a room at any other time should be easy. I've listed prices for spring (April-mid-June) and fall (mid-Aug-Oct). At most places, expect slightly lower rates in midsummer and winter. Breakfast is often included in the room rate—I've noted where it costs extra.

Few hotels are air-conditioned. Locals suggest that you keep your windows closed through the middle of the day so that your room will be as cool as possible in the evening.

Hotels and Rooms

$$$ Hotel Umbra, a quiet villa in the middle of town, has 24 spacious but overpriced rooms with great views, thinning carpets, and older decor (Sb-€75, standard Db-€110, bigger "superior" Db with better views-€125, Tb-€155, 10 percent discount with this book if you pay cash and stay for 2 or more nights, air-con, elevator, free Wi-Fi, peaceful garden and view sun terrace, most rooms have views—request when you reserve, closed Dec-March, just off Piazza del Comune under the arch at Via degli Archi 6, tel. 075-812-240, www.hotelumbra.it, info@hotelumbra.it, family Laudenzi).

$$ Hotel Ideale, on a ridge overlooking the valley, offers 14 airy rooms with simple modern furnishings (most with views and balconies), a tranquil garden setting, and free parking (Sb without view-€50, nicer Sb-€65, Db-€85, Tb-€100, prices good with this book through 2014, 10 percent discount for stays of 3 or more nights, air-con, free Wi-Fi, confirm your arrival time—especially if it's after 17:00, Piazza Matteotti 1, tel. 075-813-570, www.hotelideale.it, info@hotelideale.it, friendly sisters Lara and Ilaria and their monolingual family). The hotel is across the street from the bus stop (and parking lot) at Piazza Matteotti, at the top end of town.

$$ Hotel Belvedere, a great value, is a modern building with 12 spacious, classic-feeling rooms; eight come with sweeping views (Sb-€50, Db-€70, Tb-€85, Qb-€100, breakfast-€5, elevator, free Wi-Fi, large communal view terrace, 2 blocks past Basilica of St. Clare at Via Borgo Aretino 13, tel. 075-812-460, www.assisihotel-belvedere.com, hotelbelvedereassisi@yahoo.it, thoughtful Enrico speaks fluent New Jerseyan). Coming by bus from the train station, get off at Porta Nuova; the hotel is steps away.

$$ La Pallotta offers seven fresh, bright, small rooms and a shared top-floor lounge with view. They provide guests with a loaner Assisi guidebook, map, and audioguide, as well as a bus ticket and English helpline number (Sb-€45, Db-€79, free guest computer and Wi-Fi, free use of washer and drying rack, free hot drinks and cake at teatime; a block off Piazza del Comune at Via San Rufino 6—go up a short flight of stairs outside building, above the arch, to reach entrance; tel. 075-812-307, www.pallottaassisi.it, pallotta@pallottaassisi.it; helpful Stefano, Serena, and family). If you're driving, head to Piazza San Rufino, where they'll meet you (call ahead). They also have a good restaurant (see "Eating in Assisi," later).

$$ Hotel San Rufino offers a great locale, solid stone quality, and 11 comfortable rooms (Sb-€46, Db-€58, Tb-€78, Qb-€92, breakfast-€5, elevator, free Wi-Fi; from Cathedral of San Rufino, follow sign to Via Porta Perlici 7; tel. 075-812-803, www.hotelsanrufino.it, info@hotelsanrufino.it). Their nine-room annex, Albergo Il Duomo (listed later), saves you about €5 a night for a double with no loss in comfort.

$$ Hotel La Rocca, on the peaceful top end of town, has 32 solid and modern rooms in a medieval shell (Sb-€46, Db-€59, Tb-€79, breakfast-€5, air-con, elevator, pay Wi-Fi, parking-€7, sunny rooftop terrace, decent restaurant upstairs, 3-minute walk from Piazza Matteotti at Via Porta Perlici 27, tel. 075-812-284, www.hotelarocca.it, info@hotelarocca.it, Carlo).

$$ Hotel Sole, renting 38 rooms in a 15th-century building, is well-worn and forgettable, but the location is central. Half of its rooms are in a newer annex across the street (Sb-€50, Db-€70, Tb-€90, ask for a discount, breakfast-€5, air-con-€5 extra, free Wi-Fi in common areas, public parking nearby, 100 yards before Basilica of St. Clare at Corso Mazzini 35, tel. 075-812-373, www.assisihotelsole.com, info@assisihotelsole.com).

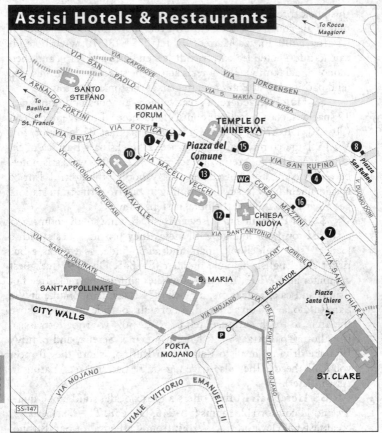

Assisi Hotels & Restaurants

$ Camere Carli has six shiny, spacious, new rooms in a solid, minimalist place above a shop (Sb-€35, Db-€48, Tb-€60, Qb-€70, no breakfast, show this book to get these prices, family lofts, lots of stairs and no elevator, free Wi-Fi, free parking 150 yards away, facing the Duomo at Via Porta Perlici 1, tel. 075-812-490, mobile 339-531-1366, www.camerecarli.it, carliarte@live.it, pleasant Carli speaks limited English).

$ Albergo Il Duomo's nine rooms are tidy and *tranquillo*. Located on a stair-stepped lane one block up from Hotel San Rufino, it's more atmospheric and has nicer bathrooms than its parent hotel (Sb-€43, Db-€55, Tb-€68, breakfast-€5, free Wi-Fi in Hotel San Rufino lobby, Vicolo San Lorenzo 2 but check in at Hotel San Rufino—see earlier, tel. 075-812-742, www.hotelsanrufino.it, info@hotelsanrufino.it).

$ Camere Annalisa Martini is a cheery home amid vines and roses in the town's medieval core. This is a good budget choice—

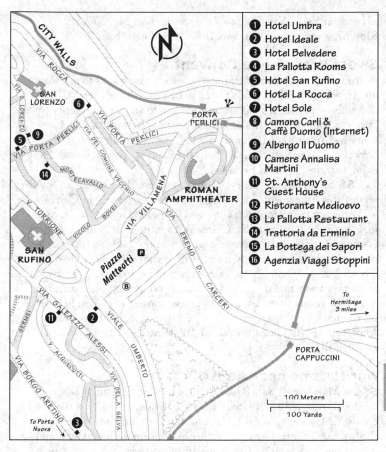

① Hotel Umbra
② Hotel Ideale
③ Hotel Belvedere
④ La Pallotta Rooms
⑤ Hotel San Rufino
⑥ Hotel La Rocca
⑦ Hotel Sole
⑧ Camoro Carli & Caffè Duomo (Internet)
⑨ Albergo Il Duomo
⑩ Camere Annalisa Martini
⑪ St. Anthony's Guest House
⑫ Ristorante Medioevo
⑬ La Pallotta Restaurant
⑭ Trattoria da Erminio
⑮ La Bottega dei Sapori
⑯ Agenzia Viaggi Stoppini

Annalisa enthusiastically accommodates her guests with a picnic garden, a washing machine (€7/small load, includes line drying), a communal refrigerator, and six homey rooms (S-€27, Sb-€30, D-€40, Db-€42, Tb-€58, Qb-€68, rates soft for last-minute bookings, cash only, 3 rooms share 2 bathrooms, no breakfast, free Wi-Fi; 1 block from Piazza del Comune—go downhill toward basilica, turn left on Via San Gregorio to #6; tel. 075-813-536, cameremartini@libero.it, Mamma Rosignoli—"roh-sin-YOH-lee"—doesn't speak English, but Annalisa does).

Hostel: Francis probably would have bunked with the peasants in Assisi's 65-bed **$ Ostello della Pace** (€17 beds in 4- to 8-bed rooms, €20-22/person in private 2- to 4-person rooms with bath, dinner-€10.50, laundry service-€4, pay guest computer, free Wi-Fi, free parking, lockout 10:00-16:00, midnight curfew, closed Nov-Feb; take orange shuttle bus from station to Piazza Giovanni Paolo II, then walk 15 minutes downhill on via Marconi, then left at bend on Via di Valecchie to #4—see map on page 777; tel. 075-816-767, www.assisihostel.com, info@assisihostel.com).

Sweet Dreams in a Convent

Assisi is filled with convents, most of which rent rooms to pilgrims and travelers. While you don't need to be a pilgrim or even a Christian to be welcome, it's just common sense to stay in a convent *only* if you're approaching Assisi with a contemplative mindset. Convents feel institutional, house many groups, and are not particularly cheap—but they come with all the facilities you might need to enjoy a spirit-filled visit to Assisi.

$$ **St. Anthony's Guest House** is where the Franciscan Sisters of the Atonement (including several Americans and Canadians) offer a very warm and tranquil welcome. Their oasis of peace is just above the Basilica of St. Clare. With only 35 beds in 19 rooms (some with great views—request when you reserve) at a reasonable price, they book up literally months in advance (Sb-€45, Db-€65, Tb-€85, 2-night minimum, cash only for short stays, no problem if couples want to share a bed, elevator, no air-con but fans, free Wi-Fi in common areas, 23:00 curfew, closed mid-Nov-Feb, library, views, picnic garden, parking-€3 donation, just below Piazza Matteotti at Via Galeazzo Alessi 10, tel. 075-812-542, atoneassisi@tiscali.it).

Agriturismo near Assisi

$$ **Le Mandrie di San Paolo** ("The Herd of St. Paul") is a meticulously restored 1,000-year-old stone house renting 13 rustic but comfortable rooms. Soulful Alex and the Damiani family are justifiably proud of their fine craftsmanship, passion for hospitality, and connection to the land. They have an olive grove (ask Alex if he'll give you a tour of their modern mill in the valley), lots of animals, a beautiful swimming pool, sauna/steam room, fine restaurant, and spectacular views over Assisi and the valleys of Umbria (Db-€90; 2-bedroom apartments: Db-€105, Qb-€130; family deals, 3-night minimum in June-mid-Sept, free Wi-Fi, mobile 349-821-7867, tel. 075-806-4070, www.agriturismomandriesanpaolo.it, mandrie10@gmail.com). Their restaurant is a great choice, and worth considering for non-guests who just want to get out of town—they produce their own olive oil and flour, and fire their bread ovens with their own wood (€25-30 for four-course meal, daily 19:30-22:00, in winter on request, reservations preferred). It's about a 10-minute drive from Assisi, on the hill high above the village of Viole (a.k.a. San Vitale). Just head southeast of Assisi following signs for *Viole*; when you enter town, before you reach the arch, turn left and follow signs up the hill.

Eating in Assisi

I've listed decent, central, good-value restaurants. Assisi's food is heavy and rustic. Locals brag about their sausage and love to grate truffles on pasta. Many restaurants in town offer a fixed-price *menù turistico* for €18—for the best value, find one that includes dessert and something to drink, such as at La Pallotta.

To bump up any meal, consider a glass or bottle of the favorite homegrown red wine, Sagrantino de Montefalco. Sagrantino is Umbria's answer to Brunello (although many wine lovers around here would say that it's vice versa). Before or after dinner, enjoy a drink on the main square facing the Roman temple...or hang out with the local teens with a take-away beer under the temple's columns.

Fine Dining

Ristorante Medioevo is my vote for your best splurge. With heavy but spacious cellar vaults, William Ventura's restaurant is an elegant, accessible playground of gastronomy. Maître d' Massimo will guide you to the best of Umbrian cuisine. He features traditional cuisine with a modern twist, dictated by what's in season. While his first passion is cooking, his second is music—mellow jazz and bossa nova give a twinkle to the medieval atmosphere. Dishes are well-presented; beef and game dishes are the specialties, and the wonderful Sagrantino wine is served by the glass. As a special treat for readers of this book, when you order a glass of Sagrantino, you'll receive a small slice of just the right strong pecorino cheese—to better understand the Italian fascination with "a good marriage" between food and wine (€9-13 pastas, €12-16 *secondi*, Tue-Sun 12:30-15:00 & 19:30-22:45, closed Mon, in winter open weekends only; from the fountain on Piazza del Comune, hike downhill two blocks to Via Arco dei Priori 4; tel. 075-813-068).

Casual Eateries

La Pallotta, a local favorite run by a friendly and hardworking family—with Margarita in charge of the kitchen—offers delicious, well-presented regional specialties, such as *piccione* (squab, a.k.a. pigeon) and *coniglio* (rabbit). And they like to serve split courses *(bis)* featuring the two local pastas. Reservations are smart (€5-9 pastas, €8-15 *secondi*, €18 fixed-price meal includes dessert and wine or water, better €27 fixed-price meal showcases local specialties, Wed-Mon 12:15-14:30 & 19:00-23:00, last orders at 21:30, closed Tue, vegetarian options, a few steps off Piazza del Comune across from temple/church at Vicolo della Volta Pinta 2, tel. 075-812-649).

At **Locanda del Podestà,** chef Stelvio cooks up tasty grilled Umbrian sausages, *gnocchi alla locanda,* and all manner of truffles, while Romina graciously serves happy diners who know a good value. Try the tasty *scottaditto* ("scorch your fingers") lamb chops (€5-9 pastas, €7-16 *secondi*, €18 fixed-price meal includes coffee, Thu-Tue 12:00-14:30 & 19:00-21:30, closed Wed and Feb, 5-minute walk uphill along Via Cardinale Merry del Val from basilica, Via San Giacomo 6c—see map on page 777, tel. 075-816-553).

Ristorante Metastasio, just up the street from Podestà, offers a pricey, traditional menu and Assisi's best view terrace for dining (€9-13 pastas, €10-18 *secondi*, Thu-Tue 12:00-14:30 & 19:00-21:30, closed Wed, terrace closed in bad weather, Via Metastasio 9, tel. 075-816-525).

Trattoria da Erminio has peaceful tables on a tiny square, and indoor seating under a big, medieval (but air-conditioned) brick vault. Run by Federico and his family for three generations, it specializes in local meat cooked on an open-fire grill. They have good Umbrian wines—before you order, ask Federico or Giuliana for a taste of the Petranera wine (€8-11 pastas, €9-14 grilled meats, €18 fixed-price meal changes weekly, Fri-Wed 12:00-14:30 & 19:00-21:00, closed Thu; from Piazza San Rufino, go a block up Via Porta Perlici and turn right to Via Montacavallo 19; tel. 075-812-506).

Picnic on the Main Square

There are many little grocery stores *(alimentari)* near Piazza del Comune (one is a block uphill from the main square, at Via San Rufino 19), plus bakeries selling pizza by the slice. But try **La Bottega dei Sapori** to assemble a picnic of Umbrian treats: good prosciutto sandwiches and specialty items, including truffle paste and olive oil. Friendly Fabrizio, who is a slow-food enthusiast, may give you a taste. He also stocks the best Umbrian wines at good-to-go prices—nice if you have an appointment with your terrace for sunset (€3-4 sandwiches, daily 9:30-20:00, until 21:00 in summer, closed Jan-Feb, Piazza del Comune 34, tel. 075-812-294).

Assisi Connections

From Assisi by Train to: Rome (nearly hourly, 2-3.5 hours, 5 direct, most others change in Foligno; train timetables change frequently—double-check details), **Florence** (8/day direct, 2-3 hours), **Orvieto** (roughly hourly, 3 hours, with transfer in Terantola or Orte), **Siena** (hourly, 3.25-4.25 hours, most involve 2 transfers; bus is faster), **Cortona** (every 2 hours, 70 minutes to Camucia-Cortona station). The train station's ticket office is often open only Mon-Fri 12:00-20:00, closed Sat-Sun; when the office is closed, use the ticket machine (may only accept credit cards; newsstands sell only regional tickets and accept cash). Up in Assisi's old town, you can get train information and tickets from Agenzia Viaggi Stoppini (see "Helpful Hints" on page 763). Also try online, at www.trenitalia.com.

By Bus: Service to **Rome** is operated by the Sulga bus company (2/day, 3 hours, pay driver, departs from Piazza San Pietro, arrives at Rome's Tiburtina station, where you can connect with the train to Fiumicino airport, tel. 800-099-661, www.sulga.it). A bus for **Siena** (1/day at 10:20, 2 hours, www.sena.it) departs from the stop next to the Basilica of St. Mary of the Angels, near the train station; you can't buy Siena tickets from the driver—buy them at Assisi's Agenzia Viaggi Stoppini (see "Helpful Hints" on page 763).

Don't take the bus to **Florence;** the train is better. To see either **Gubbio** (described on page 758) or **Todi** as a side-trip from Assisi, you'll need a car—bus schedules don't accommodate day-trippers. Day trips to **Spello** (described on page 759) and **Lake Trasimeno** work by train, but not by bus. A day trip to **Perugia** is possible with buses operated by Umbria Mobilità (www.umbriamobilita.it). For nearby day-trip options like these, you could also consider taking a tour; the recommended Agenzia Viaggi Stoppini offers several (see page 765, www.viaggistoppiniassisi.it).

By Plane: Perugia/Assisi Airport, about 10 miles from Assisi, has daily connections to London Stansted and Brussels (on Ryanair), and to a few Mediterranean destinations (airport code: PEG, tel. 075-592-141, www.airport.umbria.it). Bus service between Assisi and the airport is so sporadic (just a few times a day— see www.umbriamobilita.it) that you should plan on taking a taxi (about €30).

ASSISI

ORVIETO AND CIVITA

While Tuscany is justifiably famous for its many fine hill towns, Umbria, just to the south, has some stellar offerings of its own. Assisi (covered in its own chapter) is a must for nature lovers and Franciscan pilgrims. But if you're after views, wine, and charming villages, you'll find Umbria's best in Orvieto and in Civita di Bagnoregio (which is technically just across the border in Lazio, the same region as Rome). About a 30-minute drive apart, these hill towns—one big, one small—perch high above scenic plains. Pleasant Orvieto is best known for its colorful-inside-and-out cathedral and its fine Orvieto Classico wine. Tiny Civita di Bagnoregio, my favorite hill town, is an improbable pinnacle of traditional Italian village culture, just accessible enough that modern tourists are keeping it going. Taken together, Orvieto and Civita make a perfect duet for experiencing what all the hill-town fuss is about.

Planning Your Time

The town of Orvieto and the village of Civita deserve at least an overnight, although even a few hours in each is enough to sample what they have to offer. Both are also great places to slow down and relax. Stay in one, and side-trip to the other (Orvieto has more restaurants and other amenities and is easier to reach, while Civita really lets you get away from it all). The two towns are connected by a 30-minute drive or a 45-minute bus ride, and Orvieto is conveniently close to Rome (about an hour away by train or expressway).

Orvieto

Just off the freeway and the main train line, Umbria's grand hill town entices those heading to and from Rome. While no secret, it's well worth a visit. The town sits majestically on its *tufo* throne a thousand feet above the valley floor (for more on volcanic tuff, see the sidebar on page 696). Orvieto became a regional power in the Middle Ages, and even earlier, a few centuries before Christ, it was one of a dozen major Etruscan cities. Some historians believe Orvieto may have been a religious center—a kind of Etruscan Mecca (locals are looking for archaeological proof—the town and surrounding countryside are dotted with Etruscan ruins).

Orvieto has three popular claims to fame: cathedral, Classico wine, and ceramics. Drinking a shot of the local white wine in a ceramic cup as you gaze up at the cathedral lets you experience Orvieto's three C's all at once. (Is the cathedral best in the afternoon, when the facade basks in golden light, or early in the morning, when it rises above the hilltop mist? You decide.) Though loaded with tourists by day, Orvieto is quiet by night, and a visit here comes with a wonderful bonus: close proximity to the unforgettable Civita di Bagnoregio (covered later in this chapter).

Orientation to Orvieto

Orvieto has two distinct parts: the old-town hilltop and the dreary new town below (called Orvieto Scalo). Whether coming by train or car, you first arrive in the nondescript, modern lower part of town. From there you can drive or take the funicular, elevator, or escalator up to the medieval upper town, an atmospheric labyrinth of streets and squares where all the sightseeing action is.

Tourist Information

The TI is on the cathedral square at Piazza del Duomo 24 (Mon-Fri 8:15-13:50 & 16:00-19:00, Sat-Sun 10:00-13:00 & 15:00-18:00, tel. 0763-341-772). Pick up the free city map and their green city guide, and ask about train and bus schedules. The ticket office next to the main TI sells combo-tickets and books reservations for the underground tours (tel. 0763-340-688). Depending on funding, the town may also have a branch TI at Piazza Cahen (at the top of the funicular) during summer.

Combo-Ticket: The €18 **Carta Unica** combo-ticket covers Orvieto's top sights (virtually every sight recommended here, including Underground Orvieto Tours) and includes one round-trip on the bus and/or funicular (www.cartaunica.it). To cover your funicular ride, you can buy the combo-ticket on your arrival in the

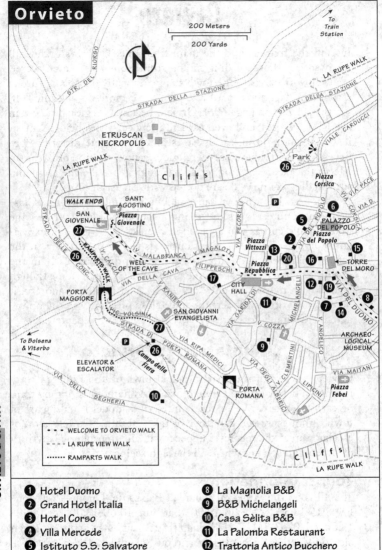

Orvieto

200 Meters
200 Yards

To Train Station

STR. DEL KIORSO

STRADA DELLA STAZIONE

STRADA DELLA STAZIONE

VIALE CARDUCCI

ETRUSCAN NECROPOLIS

LA RUPE WALK

Cliffs

Park

Piazza Corsica

VIA PACE

VIA CORSI

VIA D.

WALK ENDS

SANT' AGOSTINO

Piazza S. Giovenale

SAN GIOVENALE

STRADA DELLE CONC.

RAMPARTS WALK

V. CACCIA

V. MALABRANCA

V. MAGALOTTI

VIA PECORELLI

VIA DEL POPOLO

PALAZZO DEL POPOLO

Piazza del Popolo

Piazza Vittozzi

WELL OF THE CAVE

VIA DELLA CAVA

FILIPPESCHI

Piazza Repubblica

TORRE DEL MORO

PORTA MAGGIORE

V. VOLSINIA

V. RANIERI

SAN GIOVANNI EVANGELISTA

VIA GARIBALDI

MICHELANGELI

VIA DEL DUOMO

CITY HALL

To Bolsena & Viterbo

STRADA DI PORTA ROMANA

VIA RIPA MEDICI

V. COZZA

V. ANGELICO

ARCHAEO-LOGICAL MUSEUM

ELEVATOR & ESCALATOR

Campo della Fiera

VIA DEGLI ALBERICI

CLEMENTINI

LIPIGINI

VIA MAITANI

Piazza Febei

VIA DELLA SEGHERIA

PORTA ROMANA

Cliffs

LA RUPE WALK

ORVIETO & CIVITA

- - - WELCOME TO ORVIETO WALK
- - - LA RUPE VIEW WALK
····· RAMPARTS WALK

1 Hotel Duomo
2 Grand Hotel Italia
3 Hotel Corso
4 Villa Mercede
5 Istituto S.S. Salvatore
6 Affitacamere Valentina
7 Hotel Posta

8 La Magnolia B&B
9 B&B Michelangeli
10 Casa Sèlita B&B
11 La Palomba Restaurant
12 Trattoria Antico Bucchero
13 L'Antica Trattoria dell'Orso
14 Trattoria la Grotta & Despar Supermarket

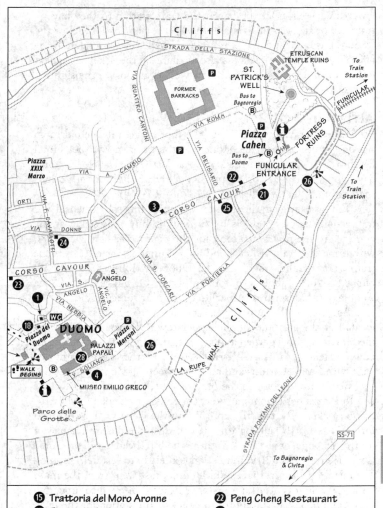

⑮ Trattoria del Moro Aronne	㉒ Peng Cheng Restaurant
⑯ Trattoria da Carlo	㉓ Metà Supermarket
⑰ Pizzeria & Rest. Charlie	㉔ Internet Café
⑱ Enoteca al Duomo &	㉕ Tobacco Shop (Bus Tickets)
Pasqualetti Gelateria	㉖ La Rupe View Walk Access (5)
⑲ L'Oste del Re	㉗ Romantic Rampart Stroll
⑳ Caffé Montanucci	㉘ MoDo Art Galleries &
㉑ Idea Pizza	National Arch. Museum

lower town—either at the bar at the train station (if they haven't run out), or at a seasonal ticket office in the parking lot (below the station, Easter-Sept daily 9:00-16:00, closed Oct-Easter, tel. 0763-302-378). The combo-ticket is also available at the ticket office next to the TI on Piazza del Duomo, as well as at most of the sights it covers.

Arrival in Orvieto

By Train: The train station is at the foot of the hill the old town sits on. There's no baggage storage at the train station, but Hotel Picchio, 300 yards from the station at Via G. Salvatori 17, stores day-trippers' luggage for €5 per bag (leaving the station, go left, then right up Via G. Salvatori, tel. 0763-301-144).

The easiest way to the top of town (including the cathedral and my recommended hotels) is by **funicular:** Buy your ticket at the entrance to the *funiculare;* look for the *biglietteria* sign (€1, €0.80 with same-day train ticket, good for 70 minutes, includes minibus from Piazza Cahen to Piazza del Duomo, Mon-Sat 7:20-20:30, Sun 8:00-20:30, about every 10 minutes). Or buy a Carta Unica combo-ticket (described earlier) to cover your funicular ride.

As you exit the funicular at the top, you're in Piazza Cahen, located at the east end of the upper town. To your left is a ruined fortress with a garden and a commanding view. To your right, down a steep path, is St. Patrick's Well. Farther to the right is a park with Etruscan ruins and another sweeping view.

Just in front of you is the orange **shuttle bus,** waiting to take you to Piazza del Duomo at no extra charge (included in your funicular ticket). The bus fills up fast, but the views from the ruined fortress are worth pausing for—if you miss the bus, you can wait for the next one, or just walk to the cathedral (head uphill on Corso Cavour; after about 10 minutes, take a left onto Via del Duomo). The bus drops you in Piazza del Duomo, just steps from the main TI and within easy walking distance of most of my recommended sights and hotels. If you forgot to check at the station for the train schedule to your next destination, no problem—the schedule is posted at the top of the funicular and is also available at the TI.

If you arrive outside the funicular's operating hours, you can reach the upper part of town by **taxi** (figure about €12—see later) or **bus** to Piazza della Repubblica (buses run roughly 2/hour until midnight, buy €1.50 ticket from driver).

By Car: For free parking, use the huge lot below the train station (5 minutes off the autostrada; follow the *P funiculare* signs). Walk through the station and ride the funicular up the hill (see "By Train," above).

It's also possible to park in the old town. Some free parking is available in the north half (white lines) of Piazza Cahen (at the top end of the funicular). There are also several pay options: the small lot in Piazza Marconi, near Orvieto's cathedral (€1.50 for first hour, €1/hour thereafter); the south half (blue lines) of Piazza Cahen (€1.20/hour); and the Campo della Fiera lot just below the west end of town (€1/hour; from top level of lot, walk up into town or take escalator—7:00-21:00—or elevator—7:00-24:00; both free). Generally, white lines indicate free parking, and blue lines require you to buy a "pay and display" slip from a nearby machine.

While you can drive up Via Postierla and Via Roma to get to central parking lots, Corso Cavour and other streets in the old center are closed to traffic and monitored by cameras (look for red lights, and avoid streets marked by a red circle).

By Taxi: Taxis line up in front of the train station and charge about €12 for a ride to the cathedral (a ridiculous price considering the ease and pleasure of the €1 funicular/shuttle-bus ride to the cathedral square; mobile 360-433-057).

Helpful Hints

Market Days and Festivals: On Thursday and Saturday mornings, Piazza del Popolo becomes a busy farmers' market. The same square hosts an arts-and-crafts market some Sundays. Orvieto is also busy during the Umbria Jazz festival that takes place for a few days before New Year's (www.umbriajazz.com).

Internet Access: Caffè Montanucci has four terminals (€2.50/30 minutes, free if you buy food, daily 7:00-24:00, Corso Cavour 21), and **Copisteria ESPA** has two (€3/30 minutes, Mon-Fri 9:00-13:00 & 16:00-19:40, Sat 9:00-13:00, closed Sun, Via Felice Cavallotti 9).

Laundry: There's a coin launderette in the lower town, a 10-minute walk from the train station, in the complex on top of the big Co-op supermarket. It's a bit of a haul from central hotels, and instructions are in Italian only, but it's workable if you're desperate (daily 7:00-22:00, Piazza del Comercio, off via Monte Nibbio, mobile 393-758-6120).

Car/Minibus Service: Giuliotaxi is run by charming, English-speaking Giulio and his sister, Maria Serena. They have a car (for up to 4) and a minibus (for up to 8). I've organized two special excursions with them that offer great efficiency and value for couples and small groups going from Orvieto to Civita: Rather than hassle with a bus and long walks, book Giulo for the drive to Civita, a two-hour wait, and the return to Orvieto (€80/car, €100/minibus). For a longer trip, book a drive to Civita, visit for two hours, explore around Lake Bolsena for a couple more hours, and then head back to Orvieto (5 hours total, €150/car, €180/minibus). If you assemble a small group at your hotel and split the cost, this service becomes an even better deal. They can take you to other destinations, as well (mobile 360-433-057, www.italy-driver.com, giuliotaxi@ libero.it).

Local Guide: Manuela del Turco is good (€120/2.5-hour tour, mobile 333-221-9879, manueladel@virgilio.it).

After Dark: In the evening, there's little going on other than strolling and eating. The big *passeggiata* scene is down Via del Duomo and Corso Cavour. See page 823 for good places to enjoy the show.

Self-Guided Walk

Welcome to Orvieto

This quickie L-shaped walk takes you from the Duomo through Orvieto's historic center. Each evening, this route is the scene of the local *passeggiata*.

Facing the cathedral, head left. Stroll past the clock tower (first put here in 1347 for the workers building the cathedral), which marks the start of Via del Duomo, lined with shops selling ceramics. **Via dei Magoni** (second left) has several artisan shops and the crazy little Il Mago di Oz ("Wizard of Oz") shop, a wondrous toyland created by eccentric Giuseppe Rosella (Via dei Magoni 3, tel. 0763-342-063). Have Giuseppe push a few buttons, and you're far from Kansas (no photos allowed).

Via del Duomo continues to Orvieto's main intersection, where it meets Corso Cavour and a tall, stark tower—the **Torre del Moro.** The tower marks the center of town, serves as a handy orientation tool, and is decorated by the coats of arms of past governors. The elevator leaves you with 173 steps still to go to earn a commanding view (€3, daily March-Oct 10:00-19:00, May-Aug until 20:00, Nov-Feb 10:30-17:00).

This crossroads divides the town into **four quarters** (notice the *Quartiere* signs on the corners). In the past, residents of these four districts competed in a lively equestrian competition on Piazza del Popolo during the annual Corpus Christi celebration. Historically, the four streets led from here to the market and the fine palazzo on Piazza del Popolo, the well, the Duomo, and City Hall.

Before heading left down Corso Cavour, side-trip a block farther ahead, behind the tower, for a look at the striking **Palazzo del Popolo.** Built of local *tufo,* this is a textbook example of a fortified medieval public palace: a fortress designed to house the city's leadership and military, with a market at its base, fancy meeting rooms upstairs, and aristocratic living quarters on the top level.

Return to the tower and head down Corso Cavour (turning right) past classic storefronts to **Piazza della Repubblica** and City Hall. The original vision—though it never came to fruition—was for City Hall to have five arches flanking the main central arch (marked by the flags today). The Church of Sant'Andrea (left of City Hall) sits atop an Etruscan temple that was likely the birthplace of Orvieto centuries before Christ. Inside is an interesting architectural progression: Romanesque (with few frescoes surviving), Gothic (the pointy vaults over the altar), and a Renaissance barrel vault in the apse (behind the altar)—all lit by fine alabaster windows.

From City Hall, you can continue to the far end of town to the **Church of Sant'Agostino,** where you can see the statues of the apostles that once stood in the Duomo (included in the MoDo ticket; see page 812). From here you can take a left and walk the cliffside ramparts (see "View Walks," later).

Sights in Orvieto

▲▲▲Duomo

Oriveto's cathedral has Italy's liveliest facade. This colorful, prickly Gothic facade, divided by four pillars, has been compared to a me-

dieval altarpiece. The optical-illusion interior features some fine art, including Luca Signorelli's lavishly frescoed Chapel of San Brizio.

Cost and Hours: €3; April-Sept Mon-Sat 9:30-19:00, Sun 13:00-17:30 or until 18:30 July-Sept; March and Oct Mon-Sat 9:30-18:00, Sun 13:00-17:30; Nov-Feb Mon-Sat 9:30-13:00 & 14:30-17:00, Sun 14:30-17:30; last entry 30 minutes before closing. A €5 combo-ticket includes the Duomo, the chapel, and the Museo dell'Opera del Duomo, called the "MoDo" (available at the chapel; MoDo alone costs €4). Admission is also covered by the €18 Carta Unica combo-ticket.

◐ Self-Guided Tour: Begin by viewing the **exterior facade.** Study this gleaming mass of mosaics, stained glass, and sculpture (c. 1300, by Lorenzo Maitani and others).

At the base of the cathedral, the four broad **marble pillars** carved with biblical scenes tell the history of the world in four acts, from left to right. The relief on the far left shows the Creation (see God creating Eve from Adam's rib, and the snake tempting Eve). Next is the Tree of Jesse (Jesus' family tree—with Mary, then Jesus on top) flanked by Old Testament stories, then the New Testament (look for the unique manger scene, and other events from the life of Christ). On the far right is the Last Judgment (Christ judging on top, with a commotion of sarcophagi popping open and all hell breaking loose at the bottom).

Each pillar is topped by a bronze symbol of one of the Evangelists: angel (Matthew), lion (Mark), eagle (John), and ox (Luke). The bronze doors are modern, by the Sicilian sculptor Emilio Greco. (A gallery devoted to Greco's work is to the immediate right of the church; see page 813.) In the mosaic below the rose window, Mary is transported to heaven. In the uppermost mosaic, Mary is crowned.

• *Now step inside.*

The **nave** feels spacious and less cluttered than most Italian churches. Until 1877, it was much busier, with statues of the apostles at each column and fancy chapels. Then the people decided they wanted to "un-Baroque" their church. (The original statues are now on display in the Church of Sant'Agostino, at the west end of town.)

The interior is warmly lit by **alabaster windows,** highlighting the black-and-white striped stonework. Why such a big and impressive church in such a little town? First of all, it's not as big as it looks. The architect created an illusion—with the nave wider at the back and narrower at the altar, the space seems longer than it is. Still, it's a big and rich cathedral—the seat of a bishop. Its historic importance and wealth is thanks to a miracle that happened nearby in 1263. According to the story, a skeptical priest named Peter of Prague passed through Bolsena (12 miles from Orvieto) while on a pilgrimage to Rome. He had doubts that the bread used in communion could really be transformed into the body of Christ. But during Mass, as he held the host aloft and blessed it, the bread began to bleed, running down his arms and dripping onto a linen cloth (a "corporal") on the altar. That miraculously blood-stained cloth is now kept here, in the Chapel of the Corporal.

• *We'll tour the church's interior. First, find the chapel in the north transept, left of the altar. (You'll see lots of pilgrims here celebrating the 750th anniversary of the Miracle of Bolsena. There's likely a black metal railing where pilgrims come in from outside without a ticket. Cross into this zone, then return to the rest of the church by showing your ticket.)*

Chapel of the Corporal: The bloody cloth from the miracle is displayed in the turquoise frame atop the chapel's altar. It was brought from Bolsena to Orvieto, where Pope Urban IV happened to be visiting. The amazed pope proclaimed a new holiday, Corpus Christi (Body of Christ), and the Orvieto cathedral was built (begun in 1290) to display the miraculous relic. Find the fine reliquary in a glass case on the left. Until the 1970s, this silver-and-blue enamel reliquary—made in the early 1300s, and considered one of the finest medieval jewels in Italy—held the linen relic as if in a frame. Notice how it evokes the facade of this cathedral. For centuries, the precious linen was paraded through the streets of Orvieto in this ornate reliquary.

Orvieto's Duomo

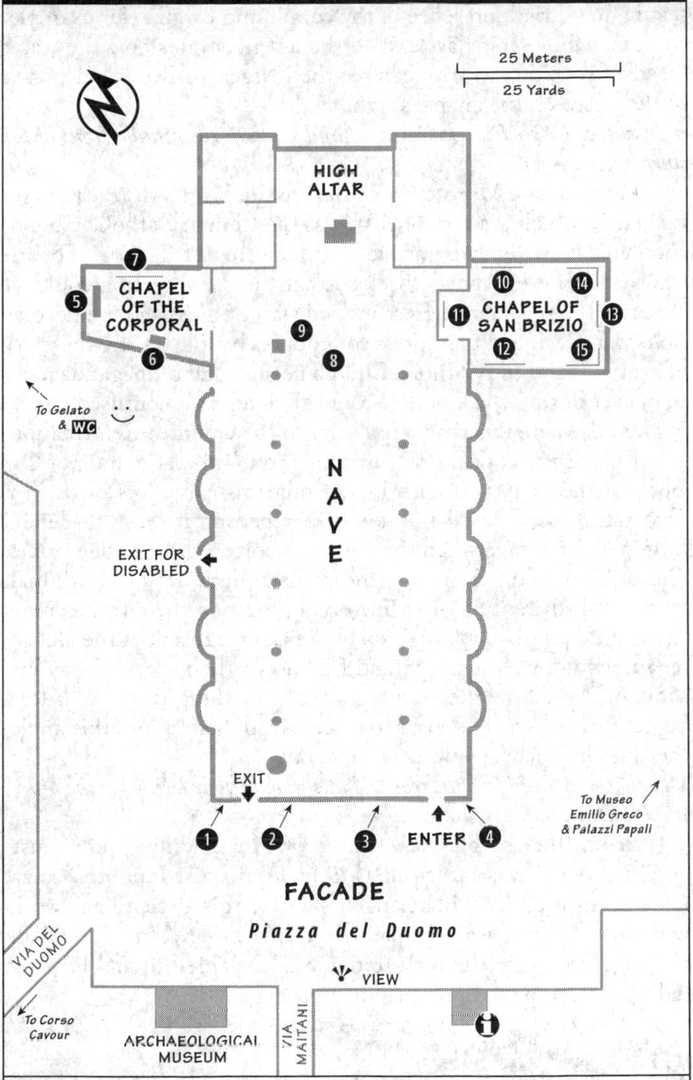

25 Meters
25 Yards

HIGH ALTAR

7 CHAPEL OF THE CORPORAL

5

6

To Gelato & WC

9

8

10 **14**
11 CHAPEL OF SAN BRIZIO **13**
12 **15**

N A V E

EXIT FOR DISABLED

EXIT

1 **2** **3** ENTER **4**

To Museo Emilio Greco & Palazzi Papali

FACADE

Piazza del Duomo

VIA DEL DUOMO

To Corso Cavour

ARCHAEOLOGICAL MUSEUM

VIA MAITANI

VIEW

ORVIETO & CIVITA

1 Creation
2 Tree of Jesse & Old Testament Stories
3 New Testament Stories
4 Last Judgment
5 "Corporal" (Linen Cloth)
6 Reliquary
7 Miracle of Bolsena Fresco
8 Marble Floor Patch
9 Pietà
10 Sermon of the Antichrist
11 End of the World (above doorway)
12 Resurrection of the Bodies
13 Last Judgment
14 Elect in Heaven
15 Damned in Hell

The room was frescoed in the 14th century with scenes attesting to Christ's presence in the communion wafer (for example, the panel above the glass case to the left illustrates how the wafer bleeds if you cook it). You can see the Miracle of Bolsena depicted in the fresco on the chapel's right wall.

• *Leave the Chapel of the Corporal and walk to the middle front of the church, where you'll see a...*

Patch in the Marble Floor Before the High Altar: Stand on the patch, which is a reminder that as the Roman Catholic Church countered the Reformation, it made reforms of its own. For instance, altars were moved back so that the congregation could sit closer to the spectacular frescoes and stained glass. (These decorations were designed to impress commoners by illustrating the glory of heaven—and the Catholic Church needed that propaganda more than ever during the Counter-Reformation.) This confused patching marks where the altar stood prior to the Counter-Reformation.

Enjoy the richness that surrounds you. This cathedral put Orvieto on the map, and with lots of pilgrims came lots of wealth. Two future popes used the town—perched on its easy-to-defend hilltop—as a refuge when their enemies forced them to flee Rome. The brilliant stained glass is the painstakingly restored original, from the 14th century. The fine organ, high on the left, has more than 5,000 pipes. Look high up in the right transept at the alabaster rose window. Then turn and face down the nave, the way you came in. Note how the architect's trick—making the church look bigger from the rear—works in reverse from here. From this angle, the church appears stubbier than it actually is.

• *Turn around and face the front. A few steps to your left, near the pillar, is a beautiful white-marble statue.*

Pietà: The marble *pietà* (statue of Mary holding Jesus' just-crucified body) was carved in 1579 by local artist Ippolito Scalza. Clearly inspired by Michelangelo's *Pietà*, this exceptional work, with four figures, was sculpted from one piece of marble. Walk around it to notice the texture that Scalza achieved, and how the light plays on the sculpture from every angle.

• *To the right of the main altar is Orvieto's one must-see artistic sight, the...*

Chapel of San Brizio: This chapel features Luca Signorelli's brilliantly lit frescoes of the Day of Judgment and Life after Death (painted 1499-1504). Step into the chapel and you're surrounded by vivid scenes crammed with figures. Although the frescoes refer to themes of resurrection and salvation, they also reflect the turbulent political and religious atmosphere of late 15th-century Italy.

The chapel is decorated in one big and cohesive story. Start with the wall to your left as you enter, and do a quick counter-clockwise spin to get oriented to the basic plot: Antichrist (a false prophet), end of the world (above the arch leading to the nave), Resurrection of the Bodies, hell, Judgment Day (Fra Angelico painted Jesus above the window), and finally heaven.

Now do a slower turn to take in the full story: In the **Sermon of the Antichrist** (left wall), a crowd gathers around a man preaching from a pedestal. It's the Antichrist, who comes posing as Jesus to mislead the faithful. This befuddled Antichrist forgets his lines mid-speech, but the Devil is on hand to whisper what to say next. His words sow wickedness through the world, including executions (upper right). The worried woman in red and white (foreground, left of pedestal) gets money from a man for something she's not proud of (perhaps receiving funds from a Jewish moneylender—notice the Stars of David on his purse).

Most likely, the Antichrist himself is a veiled reference to Savonarola (1452-1498), the charismatic Florentine monk who defied the pope, drove the Medici family from power, and riled the populace with apocalyptic sermons. Many Italians—including the painter Signorelli—viewed Savonarola as a tyrant and heretic, the Antichrist who was ushering in the Last Days.

In the upper left, notice the hardworking angel. He looks as if he's at batting practice, hitting followers of the Antichrist back to earth as they try to get through the pearly gates. In the bottom left is a self-portrait of the artist, **Luca Signorelli** (c. 1450-1523), well-dressed in black with long golden hair. Signorelli, from nearby Cortona, was at the peak of his powers, and this chapel was his masterpiece. He looks out proudly as if to say, "I did all this in just five years, on time and on budget," confirming his reputation as a speedy, businesslike painter. Next to him (also in black) is the artist Fra Angelico, who started the chapel decoration five decades earlier but completed only a small part of it.

Around the arch, opposite the windows, are signs of the **end of the world:** eclipse, tsunami, falling stars, earthquakes, violence in the streets, and a laser-wielding gray angel.

On the right wall (opposite the Antichrist) is the **Resurrection of the Bodies.** Trumpeting angels blow a wake-up call, and the dead climb dreamily out of the earth to be clothed with new bodies. On the same wall (below the action, at eye level) is a gripping *pietà*. Also by Signorelli, this *pietà* gives an insight into the artist's genius and personality. Look at the emotion in the faces of the two Marys and consider that Signorelli's son had just died. The Deposition scene (behind Jesus' leg) seems inspired by ancient

Greek scenes of a pre-Christian hero's death. In the confident spirit of the Renaissance, the artist incorporates a pagan scene to support a Christian story. This 3-D realism in a 2-D sketch shows the work of a talented master.

The altar wall (with the windows) features the **Last Judgment.** To the left of the altar (and continuing around the corner, filling half the left wall) are the **Elect in Heaven.** They spend eternity posing like bodybuilders while listening to celestial Muzak. To the right (and continuing around the corner on the right wall) are the **Damned in Hell,** in the scariest mosh pit ever. Devils torment sinners in graphic detail, while winged demons control the airspace overhead. In the center, one lusty demon turns to tell the frightened woman on his back exactly what he's got planned for their date. (According to legend, this was Signorelli's lover, who betrayed him...and ended up here.) Signorelli's ability to tell a story through human actions and gestures, rather than symbols, inspired his younger contemporary, Michelangelo, who meticulously studied the elder artist's nudes.

In this chapel, Christian theology sits physically and figuratively upon a foundation of classical logic. Below everything are Greek and Latin philosophers, plus Dante, struggling to reconcile Classic truth with Church doctrine. You can see the intellectual challenge on their faces as they ponder this puzzle. They're immersed in fanciful Grotesque (i.e., grotto-esque) decor. Dating from 1499, this is one of the first uses of the frilly, nubile, and even sexy "wallpaper pattern" so popular in the Renaissance. (It was inspired by the decorations found in Nero's Golden House in Rome, which had been discovered under street level just a few years earlier and was mistaken for an underground grotto.)

During the Renaissance, nakedness symbolized purity. When attitudes changed during the Counter-Reformation, the male figures in Signorelli's frescoes were given penis-covering sashes. During a 1982 restoration, most—but not all—of the sashes were removed. A little of that prudishness survives to this day, as those in heaven were left with their sashes modestly in place.

• *Our tour is finished. Leaving the church, turn left (passing a small parking lot and WC) to reach a park that affords a fine Umbrian view. Turn left twice, and you'll circle behind the church to reach the cathedral's art collections (part of MoDo, described next).*

Near the Duomo: MoDo and Other Museums

▲▲MoDo City Museum (Museo dell'Opera del Duomo)

This museum is a confusing ensemble of three different sights scattered around town: the cathedral art collection behind the cathedral; the Emilio Greco collection (next to the cathedral, in Palazzo Soliano); and, at the far end of town, the Church of Sant'Agostino,

ORVIETO & CIVITA

which has statues of the 12 apostles that were added to the Duomo in the Baroque Age (c. 1700) and removed in the late 1800s.

Cost and Hours: €4 MoDo ticket covers all MoDo sights (or get the €5 combo-ticket that includes the Duomo); April-Sept daily 9:30-19:00; March and Oct Wed-Mon 10:00-17:00, closed Tue; Nov-Feb Wed-Mon 10:00-13:00 & 14:00-17:00, closed Tue; last entry 30 minutes before closing, Piazza Duomo, tel. 0763-343-592, www.operadelduomo.it.

Cathedral Art Collections: Behind the Duomo, a complex of medieval palaces called Palazzi Papali shows off the city's best devotional art. It comes in two parts: the skippable collection of frescos on the ground floor, and a delightful collection up the metal staircase. Climb the stairs to buy your ticket. The highlight is just inside the upstairs entrance: a marble Mary and Child who sit beneath a bronze canopy, attended by exquisite angels. This proto-Renaissance ensemble, dating from around 1300, once filled the niche in the center of the cathedral's facade (where a replica sits today). In several art-filled rooms on this floor, you'll find Baroque paintings from the late 1500s that decorated the side chapels with a harsh Counter-Reformation message; a *Madonna and Child* from 1322 by the Sienese great Simone Martini, who worked in Orvieto; other saintly statues and fine inlaid woodwork from the original choir; a carved 14th-century Crucifixion that shows the dead Christ in gripping detail; and more church art surrounded by *sinopias* (preliminary drawings for the frescoes decorating the cathedral's Chapel of the Corporal, with a roughed-up surface so the wet plaster would stick).

Museo Emilio Greco: This fresh little collection shows off the work of Emilio Greco (1913-1995), a Sicilian artist who designed the modern doors of Orvieto's cathedral. His sketches and about 30 of his bronze statues are on display here, showing his absorption with gently twisting and turning nudes. Greco's sketchy outlines of women are simply beautiful. The artful installation of his work in this palazzo, with walkways and a spiral staircase up to the ceiling, is designed to let you view his sculptures from different angles.

National Archaeological Museum of Orvieto (Museo Archeologico Nazionale di Orvieto)

This small five-room collection, immediately behind the cathedral in the ground floor of Palazzi Papali (under MoDo), beautifully shows off a trove of well-preserved Etruscan bronzes, terra-cotta objects, and ceramics—many from the necropolis at the base of Orvieto, and some with painted colors surviving from 500 B.C. To see the treasure of this museum, ask an attendant for the Golini tombs (named after the man who discovered them in 1836). She'll escort you to the reconstructed, forth-century B.C. tombs, frescoed with scenes from an Etruscan banquet in the afterlife.

Cost and Hours: €3, daily 8:30-19:30, tel. 0763-341-039. For background on the Etruscans, see page 704.

Etruscan Museum (Museo Claudio Faina e Museo Civico)

This 19th-century, Neoclassical nobleman's palace stands on the main square facing the cathedral. Its elegantly frescoed rooms hold an impressive Etruscan collection. The ground floor features the "Museo Civico," with fragments of Etruscan sculpture. On the first floor is the "Collezione Conti Faina," with Etruscan jewelry and an extensive array of Roman coins (push the brass buttons and the coins rotate so you can see both sides). The top floor features the best of the Etruscan and proto-Etruscan (from the ninth century B.C.) vases and bronzes, lots of votives found buried in nearby tombs, and fine views of the Duomo.

Cost and Hours: €4.50; April-Sept daily 9:30-18:00; Oct-March Tue-Sun 10:00-17:00, closed Mon; English descriptions throughout, tel. 0763-341-511, www.museofaina.it.

Underground Orvieto

▲▲St. Patrick's Well (Pozzo di San Patrizio)

Modern engineers are impressed by this deep well—175 feet deep and 45 feet wide—designed in the 16th century with a double-helix pattern. The two spiral stairways allow an efficient one-way traffic flow: intriguing now, but critical then. Imagine if donkeys and people, balancing jugs of water, had to go up and down the same stairway. At the bottom is a bridge that people could walk on to scoop up water.

The well was built because a pope got nervous. After Rome was sacked in 1527 by renegade troops of the Holy Roman Empire, the pope fled to Orvieto. He feared that even this little town (with no water source on top) would be besieged. He commissioned a well, which was started in 1527 and finished 10 years later. It was a huge project. (As it turns out, the town was never besieged, but supporters believe that the well was worth the cost and labor because of its deterrence value—attackers would think twice about besieging a town with a reliable water source.) Even today, when a local is faced with a difficult task, people say, "It's like digging St. Patrick's Well." It's a total of 496 steps up and down—lots of exercise and not much to see other than some amazing 16th-century engineering.

Cost and Hours: €5, interesting €1 audioguide, daily May-Aug 9:00-19:45, March-April and Sept-Oct 9:00-18:45, Nov-Feb 10:00-16:45, the well is to your right as you exit the funicular, Viale

Sangallo, tel. 0763-343-768. Bring a sweater if you plan to descend to the chilly depths.

Well of the Cave (Pozzo della Cava)

While renovating its trattoria, an Orvieto family discovered a vast underground network of Etruscan-era caves, wells, and tunnels. The excavation started in 1984 and continues to this day. It's well-explained in English and makes for a fun subterranean wander.

Cost and Hours: €3, €2 if you have a St. Patrick's Well or funicular ticket, Tue-Sun 9:00-20:00, closed Mon, Via della Cava 28, tel. 0763-342-373, www.pozzodellacava.it.

Underground Orvieto Tours (Parco delle Grotte)

Guides weave archaeological history into a good look at about 100 yards of Etruscan and medieval caves. You'll see the remains of an old olive press, an impressive 130-foot-deep Etruscan well shaft, what's left of a primitive cement quarry, and an extensive dove-cote (pigeon coop) where the birds were reared for roasting (pigeon dishes are still featured on many Orvieto menus; look for—or avoid—*piccione*).

Cost and Hours: €6; 45-minute English tours depart at 11:15, 12:30, 16:15, and 17:30; more often with demand, book tour and depart from ticket office at Piazza Duomo 23 (next to main TI); confirm times at TI or by calling 0763-340-688, www.orvietounderground.it.

Etruscan Necropolis
(Necropoli Etrusca di Crocifisso del Tufo)

Below town, at the base of the cliff, is a remarkable "city of the dead" that dates back to the sixth to third century B.C. The tombs, which are laid out in a kind of street grid, are empty, and there's precious little to see here other than the basic stony construction. But it is both eerie and fascinating to wander the streets of an Etruscan cemetery.

Cost and Hours: €3, daily April-Sept 8:30-19:00, Oct-March 8:30-17:00.

View Walks

▲Hike Around the City on the Rupe

Orvieto's Rupe is a peaceful paved path that completely circles the town at the base of the cliff upon which it sits. With the help of the TI's *Anello delle Rupe* map, you'll see there are five access points from the town for the three-mile walk (allow about two hours round-trip). Once on the trail, it's fairly level and easy to

follow. On one side you have the
cliff, with the town high above.
On the other side you have Umbrian views stretching into the
distance. I'd leave Orvieto at
Piazza Marconi and walk left
(counterclockwise) three-quarters of the way around the town
(there's a fine view down onto
the Etruscan Necropolis mid-

way), and ride the escalator and elevator back up to the town from
the big Campo della Fiera parking lot. If you're ever confused about
the path, follow the *la Rupe* signs.

▲Shorter Romantic Rampart Stroll

Thanks to its dramatic hilltop setting, several fine little walks wind
around the edges of Orvieto. My favorite after dark, when it's
lamp-lit and romantic, is along the ramparts at the far west end of
town. Start at the Church of Sant'Agostino. With your back to the
church, go a block to the right to the end of town. Then head left
along the ramparts, with cypress-dotted Umbria to your right, and
follow Vicolo Volsinia to the Church of San Giovanni Evangelista,
where you can re-enter the old town center near several recommended restaurants.

Near Orvieto

Wine-Tasting

Orvieto Classico wine is justly famous. Two inviting wineries sit
just outside Orvieto on the scenic Canale route to Bagnoregio; if
you're side-tripping to Civita, it's easy to stop at either or both for a
tasting (but call ahead).

For a short tour of a winery with Etruscan cellars, visit **Tenuta
Le Velette,** where English-speaking Corrado and Cecilia (cheh-
CHEEL-yah) Bottai will welcome you if you've set up an appointment (€8-21 for tour and tasting, price varies depending on wines
and number of people, Mon-Fri 8:30-12:00 & 14:00-17:00, Sat
8:30-12:00, closed Sun, also has accommodations—see listing on
page 820, tel. 0763-29090, mobile 348-300-2002, www.levelette.
it). From their sign (5-minute drive past Orvieto at top of switchbacks just before Canale, on road to Bagnoregio), cruise down a
long tree-lined drive, then park at the striped gate (must call ahead;
no drop-ins).

Custodi is another respected family-run winery that produces
Orvieto Classico, grappa, and olive oil on their 140-acre estate.
Helpful Chiara and Laura Custodi speak English. Reserve ahead
for a tour of their cantina, an explanation of the winemaking process, and a tasting of four of their wines. An assortment of *salumi*

and local cheeses to go with your wine-tasting is possible on request (€7/person for wines only, €16/person with light lunch, daily
8:30-12:30 & 15:30-18:30 except closed Sun afternoons, Viale
Venere S.N.C. Loc. Canale; on the road from Orvieto to Civita,
a half-mile after Le Velette, it's the first building before Canale;
tel. 0763-29053, mobile 392-161-9334, www.cantinacustodi.com,
info@cantinacustodi.com).

Sleeping in Orvieto

The prices I've listed are for high season—roughly May to early July
and in September and October, as well as during the Umbria Jazz
festival in the days before New Year's.

In the Town Center

$$$ Hotel Duomo is centrally located and modern, with splashy
art and 17 rooms. Double-paned windows keep the sound of the
church bells well-muffled (Sb-€80, Db-€120, Db suite-€140, Tb-
€150, extra bed-€10, 10 percent discount with this book if you
pay cash and book direct, air-con, elevator, free guest computer
and Wi-Fi, private parking-€10, sunny terrace, a block from the
Duomo at Vicolo di Maurizio 7, tel. 0763-341-887, www.orvi-
etohotelduomo.com, info@orvietohotelduomo.com, Gianni and
Maura Massaccesi don't speak English, daughter Elisa does). The
Massaccesi family also owns a three-room B&B 50 yards from the
hotel (Sb-€70, Db-€90, Tb-€110, breakfast and Wi-Fi at the main
hotel).

$$$ Grand Hotel Italia feels businesslike, bringing predict-
able modern class to this small town. The 46 rooms are spacious
and well-located in the heart of Orvieto (Sb-€80, Db-€140, extra
bed-€30, air-con, elevator, stay-awhile lobby and terrace, free guest
computer and Wi-Fi, parking-€10—reserve ahead, Via di Piazza
del Popolo 13, tel. 0763-342-065, www.grandhotelitalia.it, hoteli-
ta@libero.it).

$$ Hotel Corso is friendly, with 18 frilly and flowery rooms—
a few with balconies and views. Their sunlit little terrace is enjoy-
able, but the location—halfway between the center of town and the
funicular—feels less convenient than others (Sb-€70, Db-€95, Tb-
€120, 10 percent discount for my readers if you book direct, buffet
breakfast-€6.50, ask for quieter room off street, air-con, elevator,
free Wi-Fi, free public parking nearby and on main street, reserved
parking-€7, up from funicular toward Duomo at Corso Cavour
343, tel. 0763-342-020, www.hotelcorso.net, info@hotelcorso.net,
Carla).

$ Villa Mercede, a good value, is owned by a religious institu-
tion and offers 23 cheap, simple, mostly twin-bedded rooms, each

Sleep Code

(€1 = about $1.30, country code: 39)
S = Single, **D** = Double/Twin, **T** = Triple, **Q** = Quad, **b** = bathroom, **s** = shower only. Unless otherwise noted, credit cards are accepted, English is spoken, and breakfast is included (but usually optional). Many towns in Italy levy a hotel tax of about €2 per person, per night, which is generally not included in the rates I've quoted.

To help you sort easily through these listings, I've divided the accommodations into three categories based on the price for a standard double room with bath:

$$$ Higher Priced—Most rooms €100 or more.
  $$ Moderately Priced—Most rooms between €70-100.
    $ Lower Priced—Most rooms €70 or less.

Prices can change without notice; verify the hotel's current rates online or by email. For the best prices, always book direct.

with a big modern bathroom and many with glorious Umbrian views (Sb-€50, Db-€70, Tb-€90, elevator, free Wi-Fi, free parking, a half-block from Duomo at Via Soliana 2, reception upstairs, tel. 0763-341-766, www.villamercede.it, info@villamercede.it).

$ Istituto S.S. Salvatore rents nine spotless twin rooms and five singles in their convent, which comes with a peaceful terrace and garden, great views, and a 22:30 curfew. Though the nuns don't speak English, tech-savvy Sister Maria Stella has mastered Google Translate, and will happily use it to answer your questions (Sb-€38, Db-€58, €5 less per person Oct-March, cash only, no breakfast, elevator, free parking, no Internet access, just off Piazza del Popolo at Via del Popolo 1, tel. 0763-342-910, istitutosansalvatore@tiscali.it).

$ Affittacamere Valentina rents six clean, airy, well-appointed rooms, all with big beds and antique furniture. Her place is located in the heart of Orvieto, behind the palace on Piazza del Popolo (Db-€58/€65, Tb-€75/€85, studio with kitchen-€80/€90, lower rates are cash only and good with this book for stays of 2 or more nights; breakfast at nearby cafe-€5, air-con-€5, free Wi-Fi, parking-€10/day, Via Vivaria 7, tel. 0763-341-607, mobile 393-970-5868, www.bandbvalentina.com, valentina.z@tiscalinet.it). Valentina also rents three rooms across the square (D-€58, shared bath and kitchen, no air-con) and three offsite apartments (€170/night with 3-night minimum).

$ Hotel Posta is a dumpy, long-ago-elegant palazzo renting

20 quirky rooms with vintage furniture. The rooms without private bath are among the cheapest in town. It's clean, relatively well-maintained, and centrally located (S-€31, Sb-€37, D-€44, Db-€57, T-€60, Tb-€75, breakfast-€6, cash only, elevator, free Wi-Fi in common areas, Via Luca Signorelli 18, tel. 0763-341-909, www. orvietohotels.it, hotelposta@orvietohotels.it, Alessia).

$ La Magnolia B&B has lots of fancy terra-cotta tiles, a couple of rooms with frescoed ceilings, terraces, and other welcoming touches. Its seven unique rooms, some like mini-apartments with kitchens, are cheerfully decorated and on the town's main drag. The three units facing the busy street are air-conditioned and have good double-paned windows (Db-€65, plush Db apartment-€75, extra person-€15, family deals; book direct, pay cash, and stay at least 2 nights to get a 10 percent Rick Steves discount; no elevator, free Wi-Fi, use of washer-€3.50, Via Duomo 29, tel. 0763-342-808, mobile 349-462-0733, www.bblamagnolia.it, info@bblamagnolia. it, Serena and Loredana).

$ B&B Michelangeli offers two comfortable and well-appointed apartments hiding along a residential lane a few blocks from the tourist scene. It's run by eager-to-please Francesca, who speaks limited English but provides homey touches and free tea, coffee, and breakfast supplies. This is a good choice for families (Db-€70, kids-€10 extra, fully equipped kitchen, free Wi-Fi, washing machine, private parking-€5, Via dei Saracinelli 20—ring bell labeled *M. Michelangeli*, tel. 0763-393-862, mobile 347-089-0349, www.bbmichelangeli.com, f_michelangeli@alice.it).

Just Outside the Town Center: **$$ Casa Sèlita B&B,** a peaceful country house, offers easy access to Orvieto (best for drivers, but workable for adventurous train travelers). It's nestled in an orchard just below the town cliffs; to get to town, you'll climb a steep path through their fields to reach the big Campo della Fiera parking lot, with its handy escalator taking you the rest of the way up into Orvieto. Its five rooms with terraces are airy and fresh, with dark hardwood floors, fluffy down comforters, and modern baths. Enjoy the views from the relaxing garden. Conscientious Sèlita, her husband Ennio, and daughter Elena are gracious hosts (Sb-€55, Db-€80, Tb-€90, €5 less with stays of two or more nights, €5 more off-season for heat, these prices promised to my readers through 2014 if you book direct, cash preferred, fans, free Wi-Fi, free parking, Strada di Porta Romana 8, don't use GPS—sends you to the wrong location, mobile 339-225-4000 or 328-611-2052, tel. 0763-344-218, www.casaselita.com, info@casaselita.com).

Near Orvieto

All of these (except the last one) are within a 20-minute drive of Orvieto, in different directions, and require a car.

$$$ La Rocca Orvieto, run by Emiliano and Sabrina, is a fancy spa-type "country resort," located 15 minutes north of Orvieto by car. They produce their own olive oil and wine and have nine rooms and 10 apartments—all with air-conditioning and Wi-Fi (Db-€90-150, 10 percent discount with this book—mention when you reserve, pool, panoramic view restaurant, wellness center with Jacuzzi and steam room, gym, mountain bikes, bocce court, hiking paths, tel. 0763-344-210 or 0763-393-437, mobile 348-640-0845, www.laroccaorvieto.com, info@laroccaorvieto.com).

At **$$$ Agriturismo Locanda Rosati,** you'll be greeted by friendly hosts Giampiero Rosati and niece Cristiana, who rent 10 tastefully decorated rooms in a pleasant, homey atmosphere (Db-€110-140, Tb-€140-160, full traditional dinners for €35 on request with this book, air-con, swimming pool, 5 miles from Orvieto on the road to Viterbo, tel. 0763-217-314, www.locandarosati.it, info@locandarosati.it).

$$$ Borgo Fontanile is a vacation home with a swimming pool, terrace, and kids' play area. Its five new apartments with rustic wood beams and terra-cotta tile floors sleep up to four people (€40-50/night per person, discounts for longer stays, €400-800/apartment per week, air-con, Vocabolo Fornace 159, Loc. Baschi, tel. 074-495-7342, www.borgofontanile.com, info@borgofontanile.com).

$$ Tenuta le Velette is a sprawling, family-run farmhouse. Cecilia and Corrado Bottai rent six fully furnished apartments and villas scattered over their expansive and scenic grounds. They range wildly in size—accommodating from 2 to 14 people—but they all nestle in perfect Umbrian rural peace and tranquility (Db apartment-€90-110, see website for details on various villas, 2-night minimum, 10 percent discount for weekly stay, free Wi-Fi, pool, bocce court, 5 minutes from Orvieto—drive toward Bagnoregio-Canale and follow *Tenuta le Velette* signs, tel. 0763-29090, mobile 348-300-2002, www.levelette.it, cecilialevelette@libero.it). They also offer wine-tastings (see listing on page 816).

$$ Agriturismo Cioccoleta ("Little Stone") has eight rooms with cozy country decor, each named after one of the grapes grown in the *agriturismo*'s vineyards. It's family-run and offers sweeping views of Orvieto and the pastoral countryside (Db-€75, Tb-€96, Qb-€110, 10 percent discount with this book—mention when you reserve, includes breakfast, free Wi-Fi, 3 miles north of Orvieto at Località Bardano 34 in Bardano, tel. 0763-316-011, mobile 349-860-9780, www.cioccoleta.it, info@cioccoleta.it, Angela Zucconi).

$$ Agriturismo Poggio della Volara, 12 miles southeast of Orvieto, has seven apartments (sleeping from two to five people) and seven rooms in two buildings overlooking a swimming pool (Db-€100, Tb-€120, smaller apartment-€100, larger apartment-€160, room rates include breakfast but costs €8 extra in apartments, air-con in all but four rooms, free Wi-Fi, tel. 0744-951-820, mobile 347-335-2523, www.poggiodellavolara.it, info@poggiodellavolara.it, Marco).

Farther Out, Northwest of Todi: **$$$ Agriturismo Fattoria di Vibio** produces olive oil and honey, sells organic products, and offers classes and spa services. In August, its 14 rooms rent at peak prices (and for one week during the month they require a minimum seven-night stay, with arrivals and departures on Saturdays). The rest of the year, no minimum stay is required, although rates drop dramatically for longer visits (Db-€200-300, includes breakfast and dinner). Its three cottages sleep from four to six people and rent only by the week (€1,260-2,100/week depending on amenities, see complicated rate table on website, farthest cottage is 20 miles northeast of Orvieto, tel. 075-874-9607, www.fattoriadivibio.com, info@fattoriadivibio.com).

Eating in Orvieto

Trattorias in the Center

La Palomba features game and truffle specialties in a wood-paneled dining room. Giampiero, Enrica, and the Cinti family enthusiastically take care of their regulars and visiting travelers, offering both a fine value and a classy conviviality. Truffles are shaved right at your table—try the *ombricelli al tartufo* (homemade pasta with truffles) or *spaghetti dall'Ascavo* (with truffles), then perhaps follow that with *piccione* (pigeon). As firm believers in the slow-food movement, they use ingredients that are mostly organic and locally sourced (€10 pastas, €9-15 *secondi*, 10 percent service charge, Thu-Tue 12:30-14:15 & 19:30-22:00, closed Wed and July, reservations smart, just off Piazza della Repubblica at Via Cipriano Manente 16, tel. 0763-343-395).

Trattoria Antico Bucchero, elegant under a big white vault, makes for a nice memory with its candlelit ambience and delicious food (€9 pastas, €12 *secondi,* no cover, daily 12:00-15:00 & 19:00-23:00—but closed Wed Nov-March, seating indoors and on a peaceful square in summer, air-con, a half-block south of Corso Cavour, between Torre del Moro and Piazza della Repubblica at Via de Cartari 4, tel. 0763-341-725; Piero and Silvana, plus sons Fabio and Pericle).

L'Antica Trattoria dell'Orso offers well-prepared Umbrian cuisine paired with fine wines in a homey, bohemian-chic, peaceful atmosphere. Ciro and chef Gabriele enjoy getting to know their diners, and will steer you toward the freshest seasonal plates of their famous pastas and passionately prepared vegetables. Gabriele—who loves to put together a "trust your chef" multicourse tasting *menu*—offers an amazing value for my readers: €30 for two people, including their fine house wine and water—my vote for the best dining value in town (€10-12 pastas, €12-16 *secondi*, Wed-Sat 12:00-14:00 & 19:30-22:00, Sun 12:00-14:00, closed Mon-Tue, just off Piazza della Repubblica at Via della Misericordia 18, tel. 0763-341-642).

Trattoria la Grotta prides itself on serving only the freshest food and finest wine. The decor is Signorelli-mod, and the ambience is quiet, with courteous service. Owner-chef Franco has been at it for 50 years, and promises diners a free coffee, grappa, *limoncello,* or Vin Santo with this book (€8 pastas, €14-18 *secondi*, Wed-Mon opens at 12:00 for lunch and at 19:00 for dinner, closed Tue, Via Luca Signorelli 5, tel. 0763-341-348).

Trattoria del Moro Aronne is a long-established family bistro run by Cristian and his mother Rolanda, who lovingly prepare homemade pasta and market-fresh meats and produce for their typical Umbrian specialties. Be sure to sample the *nidi*—folds of fresh pasta enveloping warm, gooey Pecorino cheese sweetened with honey. The crème brûlée is a winner for dessert. Three small and separate dining areas make the interior feel intimate. It's touristy and not particularly atmospheric, but this place is known locally as an excellent value (€7-10 pastas, €10-14 *secondi*, Wed-Mon 12:30-14:30 & 19:30-22:00, closed Tue, free Wi-Fi, Via San Leonardo 7, tel. 0763-342-763).

Trattoria da Carlo, hiding on its own little piazzetta between Via Corso Cavour and Piazza del Popolo, is a cozy spot with a charming interior and inviting tables outside. Animated and opinionated Carlo—a likeable loudmouth—holds court, chatting up his diners as much as he cooks, while his mama scuttles about taking orders, bussing dishes, and lovingly rolling her eyes at her son's big personality. The short, pricey menu changes constantly. Pasta with pork cheeks and fennel is a favorite here (€9 pastas, €12-16 *secondi*, daily 12:00-15:00 & 19:00-24:00, Vicolo del Popolo 1/9, tel. 0763-343-916).

Pizzeria & Restaurant Charlie is a local favorite. Its noisy dining hall and stony courtyard are popular with families and students for casual dinners of wood-fired €6-8 pizzas, big salads, homemade €7-9 pastas, or €12-15 grilled meat dishes. In a quiet courtyard guarded by a medieval tower, it's centrally located a block southwest of Piazza della Repubblica (Wed-Mon 12:30-14:30 & 19:00-23:00, closed Tue, dinner only Nov-Feb, Via Loggia dei Mercanti 14, tel. 0763-344-766).

Enoteca al Duomo, to the left of the Duomo with pleasant outdoor seating, is run by Roman transplants Emilano and Ilaria. They serve rustic *panini* (€6 to eat in, €4 to go), wines by the glass, and a full menu of local dishes in a wine-bar atmosphere (€10 pastas and meal-size salads, €10-19 *secondi*, daily 10:00-24:00, Piazza del Duomo 13, tel. 0763-344-607).

Fast and Cheap Eats

L'Oste del Re is a simple trattoria on Corso Cavour, with hearty sandwiches and pizza to go. They serve a two-course lunch-of-the-day (a pasta and a *secondo*) for about €15, and €7.50 pizza in the evenings (no cover, daily 11:00-15:30 & 19:00-22:30 but closed weekday evenings Oct-April, Corso Cavour 58, tel. 0763-343-846).

For lunch each day, **Caffè Montanucci,** along the main street, lays out an appetizing display of pastas (€7) and main courses (€10) behind the counter. Choose one (or mix—called a *bis*), find a seat in the modern interior, and they'll bring it out on a tray. You'll eat among newspaper-reading locals on lunch break (no cover, daily 7:00-24:00, Corso Cavour 21, tel. 0763-341-261).

Takeout Pizza: **Idea Pizza,** a few doors from Piazza Cahen, has the old town's biggest selection of pizza-by-weight (about €1.50/slice, also tables, Mon and Wed-Sat 10:00-14:00 & 17:00-21:00, Sun 17:00-21:00, closed Tue, Corso Cavour 326, tel. 0763-342-177).

Asian Food: **Peng Cheng** has an inexpensive menu of standard Chinese dishes (take out or indoor/outdoor seating, daily 11:00-15:00 & 18:00-21:30, close to Piazza Cahen at Corso Cavour 443, tel. 0763-343-355).

Groceries: Two smallish markets, both tucked away two minutes from the Duomo, have what you need to put together a functional picnic or stock your hotel room pantry: **Metà** (Mon-Sat 8:30-20:00, Sun 8:30-13:00, Corso Cavour 100, opposite Piazza Cesare Fracassini) and **Despar** (Mon-Sat 8:00-13:30 & 16:30-19:30, Sun 9:00-13:00, just past recommended Trattoria la Grotta at Via Luca Signorelli 23). A full-size supermarket is in the lower town, a few minutes' walk from the train station, near the laundry (see "Helpful Hints," earlier).

Gelato: For dessert, try the deservedly popular *gelateria* **Pasqualetti** (daily 11:30-21:00, open later June-Aug, closed Dec-Feb, next to left transept of church, Piazza del Duomo 14; another branch is at Corso Cavour 56, open daily 11:00-23:00, closes at 21:00 in winter).

Café Scene along Corso Cavour

Orvieto has a charming, traffic-free, pedestrian-friendly vibe. To enjoy it, be sure to spend a little time savoring *la dolce far niente* while sitting at a café. There are inviting places all over town. The first three listed below are along Corso Cavour, the main strolling drag, and offer the very best people-watching.

Café Clan Destino is the town hotspot, with a youthful

energy. It's well-located, with plenty of streetside seating and endless little bites served with your drink (Corso Cavour 42). **Café Barrique** is less crowded, less trendy, and quieter, with nice outdoor tables and good free snacks with your drink (Corso Cavour 111). **Caffé Montanucci,** where locals go to read their newspaper, is the town's venerable place for a coffee and pastry, but it has no on-street seating (Corso Cavour 21). **Bar Palace,** on Piazza del Popolo, is a sunny, relaxed perch facing a big square that's generally quiet (except on market day), with free Wi-Fi and quality coffee and pastries.

Cafés Facing the Cathedral: Several cafés on Piazza del Duomo invite you to linger over a drink with a view of Orvieto's amazing cathedral.

Orvieto Connections

From Orvieto by Train to: Rome (roughly hourly, 1-1.5 hours), **Florence** (hourly, 2 hours, use Firenze S.M.N. train station—see page 503), **Siena** (12/day, 2.5 hours, change in Chiusi, all Florence-bound trains stop in Chiusi), **Assisi** (roughly hourly, 3 hours, 1 or 2 transfers), **Milan** (3/day direct, 5.5 hours; otherwise about hourly with a transfer in Florence, Bologna, or Rome, 4.75-5 hours). The train station's Buffet della Stazione is surprisingly good if you need a quick *focaccia* sandwich or pizza picnic for the train ride.

Tip for Drivers: If you're thinking of driving to Rome, consider stashing your car in Orvieto instead. You can easily park the car, safe and free, in the big lot below the Orvieto train station (for up to a week or more), and zip effortlessly into Rome by train (1.25 hours).

Getting to Civita di Bagnoregio

To reach Civita, you'll first head for the adjacent town of Bagnoregio. From there, it's a 30-minute walk or five-minute drive to Civita.

By Bus to Bagnoregio: The trip from Orvieto to Bagnoregio takes about 45 minutes (€2.20 one-way if bought in advance from bar or tobacco shop, €7 one-way if purchased from driver—this includes a fine for not buying your ticket in advance).

Here are likely departure times (but confirm) from Orvieto's Piazza Cahen on the blue Cotral bus, daily except Sunday (when this bus does not run at all): 6:20, *7:25, *7:50, 12:45, 15:45, and 18:20; slower buses depart at *13:55 and 17:40. Departures marked with an asterisk (*) run only during the school year (roughly Sept-June). It's nice to get up early, take the *7:50 bus, and see Civita in the cool morning calm. If you take the 12:45 bus, you can make the last (17:25) bus back, but your time in Civita may feel a little rushed.

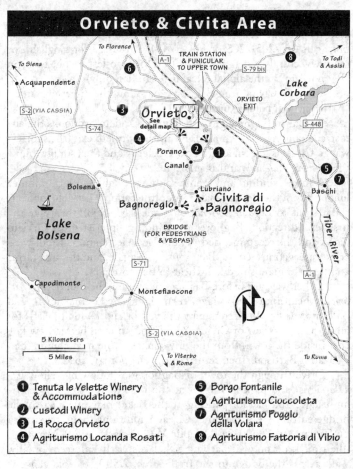

Orvieto & Civita Area

To Florence

TRAIN STATION
& FUNICULAR
TO UPPER TOWN

To Todi
& Assisi

A-1

S-79 bis

❽

To Siena

❻

Acquapendente

ORVIETO
EXIT

Lake
Corbara

S-2 (VIA CASSIA)

❸

Orvieto
See
detail map

ORVIETO
EXIT

S-448

S-74

❹

Porano

❷

❶

Canale

Bolsena

Lubriano

Civita di
Bagnoregio

❺

Baschi

❼

Bagnoregio

BRIDGE
(FOR PEDESTRIANS
& VESPAS)

Lake
Bolsena

Tiber River

S-71

Capodimonte

Montefiascone

N

A-1

5 Kilometers

5 Miles

S-2 (VIA CASSIA)

To Viterbo
& Rome

To Rome

❶ Tenuta le Velette Winery
   & Accommodations

❷ Custodi Winery

❸ La Rocca Orvieto

❹ Agriturismo Locanda Rosati

❺ Borgo Fontanile

❻ Agriturismo Cioccoleta

❼ Agriturismo Poggio
   della Volara

❽ Agriturismo Fattoria di Vibio

ORVIETO & CIVITA

Buy your ticket at the tobacco shop at Corso Cavour 306, a block up from the funicular (daily 8:00-13:00 & 16:00-20:00)—otherwise you'll pay the premium ticket price on board the bus. If you'll be returning to Orvieto by bus, it's simpler to get a return ticket now rather than in Bagnoregio.

Officially, the bus stop is at the far left end of Piazza Cahen (across the street from the bus section of the parking lot; see map on page 802). The schedule is posted at the stop—look for the *A.co. tra.l. Capolinea* sign. Buses actually stop in the bus spaces in the parking lot (yellow lines). The bus you want says *Bagnoregio* in the window. You'll see lots of buses marked *Umbria Mobilità* stopping in front of the funicular; because Civita is in Lazio, it's served by a different bus company (Cotral).

Buses departing Piazza Cahen stop five minutes later at Orvieto's train station—to catch the bus there, wait to the left of the funicular station (as you're facing it); schedule and tickets are available in the tobacco shop/bar in the train station. For more information, call 06-7205-7205 or 800-174-471 (press 7 for English), or see www.cotralspa.it (click on "Orari" in the left menu, then on "Bagnoregio" in the alphabetical list—Italian only).

To reach Civita from Bagnoregio, follow the directions under "Arrival in Bagnoregio, near Civita," later.

By Car to Bagnoregio and Civita: Orvieto overlooks the autostrada (and has its own exit). From the Orvieto exit, the shortest way to Civita is to turn left (below Orvieto), and then simply follow the signs to *Lubriano* and *Bagnoregio*.

A more winding and scenic route takes about 10-15 minutes longer: From the freeway, pass under hill-capping Orvieto (on your right, signs to *Lago di Bolsena*, on Viale I Maggio), then take the first left (direction: Bagnoregio), winding up past great Orvieto views and the recommended Tenuta Le Velette and Custodi wineries (reservations required) en route to Canale, and through farms and fields of giant shredded wheat to Bagnoregio.

Either way, just before Bagnoregio, follow the signs left to *Lubriano*, head into that village, turn right as you enter town, and pull into the first little square by the yellow church (on the left) for a breathtaking view of Civita. You'll find an even better view farther inside the town, from the tiny square at the next church (San Giovanni Battista). Then return to the Bagnoregio road.

Drive through the town of Bagnoregio (following yellow *Civita* signs) and park in the lot at the base of the steep pedestrian bridge. You pay for parking at the ticket machine next to the bridge entrance (€2/first hour, €1/each additional hour, maximum €6.50/day, free 20:00-8:00, public WC at parking lot). Warning: The time limit on your parking ticket is strictly enforced. Finally, walk across the bridge to the traffic-free, 2,500-year-old canyon-swamped pinnacle town of Civita di Bagnoregio.

If the parking lot by the bridge is full, you can park at the belvedere overlook (above the lot) and take the stairs down to the bridge.

By Taxi or Shared Taxi: If you can share the cost, a **taxi** from Orvieto to Civita is perhaps the best deal of all. Giulio taxi service can take a group of up to four in a car (€80) or eight in a mini-bus (€100) to the base of the pedestrian bridge at Civita, wait two hours, and then bring you back to Orvieto (see page 805 for more details).

Civita di Bagnoregio

Perched on a pinnacle in a grand canyon, the traffic-free village of Civita di Bagnoregio is Italy's ultimate hill town. In the last decade, the old, self-sufficient Civita (CHEE-vee-tah) has died—the last of its lifelong residents have passed on, and the only work here is in serving visitors. But relatives and newcomers are moving in and revitalizing the village, and it remains an amazing place to visit. (It's even become popular as a backdrop for movies, soap operas, and advertising campaigns.) Civita's only connection to the world and the town of Bagnoregio is a long pedestrian bridge.

Civita's history goes back to Etruscan and ancient Roman times. In the early Middle Ages, Bagnoregio was a suburb of Civita, which had a population of about 4,000. Later, Bagnoregio surpassed Civita in size—especially following a 1695 earthquake, after which many residents fled Civita to live in Bagnoregio, fearing their houses would be shaken off the edge into the valley below. You'll notice Bagnoregio is dominated by Renaissance-style buildings while, architecturally, Civita remains stuck in the Middle Ages.

While Bagnoregio lacks the pinnacle-town romance of Civita, it's actually a healthy, vibrant community (unlike Civita, the suburb now nicknamed "the dead city"). In Bagnoregio, get a haircut, sip a coffee on the square, and walk down to the old laundry (ask, *"Dov'è la lavanderia vecchia?"*).

Orientation to Civita

Arrival in Bagnoregio, near Civita

By Bus: If you're taking the bus from Orvieto, you'll get off at the bus stop in Bagnoregio. Look at the posted bus schedule and write down the return times to Orvieto, or check with the driver. If you have heavy bags, leave them with Mauro—see "Helpful Hints," later.

Once in Bagnoregio, you have to get to Civita, which sits at the opposite end of town, about a mile away from the bus stop. Whether you cover this mile by foot, bus, or car, you'll have another 10-minute walk from the base of Civita's bridge up to its main square.

Walking is the simplest way to get from the Bagnoregio bus stop to the base of Civita's bridge (20-30 minutes, slightly uphill at first, but downhill overall). The walk through Bagnoregio also offers a delightful look at a workaday Italian town. Take the road going uphill, Via Garibaldi (overlooking the big parking lot). Once on the road, take the first right, and then an immediate left, to cut

Civita di Bagnoregio

Note: Map not to scale; a walk across civita takes approx. 5 minutes—but don't rush it!

To Lubriano Town

Cliffs

Cliffs

OSTERIA AL FORNO DI AGNESE

ANTICO FORNO TRATTORIA & CIVITA B&B

LOCANDA DELLA BUONA VENTURA

CAMPANILE (BELL TOWER)

CHURCH

ANTICO FRANTOIO OLIVE PRESS & BRUSCHETTERIA

Piazza

WC

ETRUSCAN COLUMNS

ALMA CIVITA

OLD LAUNDRY

MAIN   STRADA

ARCH

ANTICA CIVITA MUSEUM

FOOTBRIDGE

SNACK BAR

CANTINA DE ARIANNA

To Bagnoregio

WINE BAR DA PEPPONE & GEOLOGICAL MUSEUM

PALACE (PRIVATE)

CAVES & CHAPEL CARVED IN ROCK

Cliffs

Trail to Etruscan tunnel under Civita

RUINS OF HOUSE OF ST. BONAVENTURE

over onto the main drag, Via Roma. Follow this straight out to the belvedere for a superb viewpoint. From there, backtrack a few steps (staircase at end of viewpoint is a dead end) and take the stairs down to the road leading to the bridge.

There is also a **shuttle bus** to the base of the bridge to Civita, with a stop just 20 yards from where the bus from Orvieto drops you (in Piazzale Battaglini). However, by this stop you'll see large signs in English saying that you can board the bus only at another stop, which is halfway along the walking route to Civita (Piazza Sant'Agostino). Locals say the reason for this is to make visitors more likely to patronize the stores along the main street in Bagnoregio. Unless it's pouring rain, skip the shuttle bus, but do take advantage of the shuttle back *uphill* from the Civita bridge. On the return, the shuttle brings you all the way back to the Orvieto-bound bus stop. Note the return times on the schedule posted by the base of the bridge—if you forget, ask at the recommended Trattoria Antico Forno (usually 1-2/hour, but no buses 13:15-15:30, 5-minute ride, €0.70 one-way, €1 round-trip, pay driver, first bus runs at about 7:30, last at 18:15, no buses on Sun Oct-March).

By Car: Drive through Bagnoregio and park under the bridge at the base of Civita (for more driving tips, see "Orvieto Connections," earlier).

Helpful Hints

Market Day: A lively market fills the Bagnoregio bus-station parking lot each Monday.

Baggage Storage: While there's no official baggage-check service in Bagnoregio, I've arranged with Mauro Laurenti, who runs the **Bar/Enoteca/Caffè Gianfu** and **Cinema Alberto Sordi,** to let you leave your bags there (€1/bag, Fri-Wed 6:00-13:00 & 13:30-24:00, closed Thu, mobile 339-697-9340). As you get off the bus, go back 50 yards or so in the direction that the Orvieto bus just came from, and go right around corner.

Food near Bagnoregio Bus Stop: Across the street from Mauro's bar/cinema and baggage storage is **L'Arte del Pane,** with fresh pizza by the slice (Via Matteotti 5). On the other side of the old-town gate (Porta Albana), in the roundabout, is a small grocery store.

Orvieto Bus Tickets: To save money on bus fare to Orvieto, buy a ticket before boarding from the newsstand (with the awning marked *art.regalo edicola cartoleria*) near the Bagnoregio bus stop, across from the gas station (€2.20 one way in advance; €7 from driver).

Self-Guided Walk

Welcome to Civita

Civita was once connected to Bagnoregio, before the saddle between the separate towns eroded away. Photographs around town show the old donkey path, the original bridge. It was bombed in World War II and replaced in 1966 with the new footbridge that you're climbing today.

• *Entering the town, you'll pass through Porta Santa Maria, a 12th-century Romanesque arch. This stone passageway was cut by the Etrus-*

cans 2,500 years ago, when this town was a stop on an ancient trading route. Inside the archway, you enter a garden of stones. Stand in the little square—the town's antechamber—facing the Bar La Piazzetta. To your right are the remains of a...

Renaissance Palace: The wooden door and windows (above the door) lead only to thin air. They were part of the facade of one of five palaces that once graced Civita. Much of the palace fell into the valley, riding a chunk of the ever-eroding rock pinnacle. Today, the door leads to a remaining section of the palace—complete with Civita's first hot tub, as it was once owned by the "Marchesa," a countess who married into Italy's biggest industrialist family.

• *A few steps uphill, farther into town (on your left, beyond the Bottega souvenir store), notice the two shed-like buildings.*

Old WC and Laundry: In the nearer building (covered with ivy), you'll see the town's old laundry, which dates from just after World War II, when water was finally piped into the town. Until a few years ago, this was a lively village gossip center. Now, locals park their mopeds here. Just behind that is another stone shed, which houses a poorly marked and less-than-pristine WC.

• *The main square is just a few steps farther along, but we'll take the scenic circular route to get there, detouring around to the right. Belly up to the...*

Canyon Viewpoint: Lean over the banister and listen to the sounds of the birds and the bees. Survey old family farms, noticing how evenly they're spaced. Historically, each one owned just enough land to stay in business. Turn left along the belvedere and walk a few steps to the site of the long-gone home of Civita's one famous son, St. Bonaventure, known as the "second founder of the Franciscans" (look for the small plaque on the wall).

• *From here, a lane leads past delightful old homes and gardens, and then to...*

Civita's Main Square: The town church faces Civita's main piazza. Grab a stone seat along the biggest building fronting the

square (or a drink at Peppone's bar) and observe the scene. They say that in a big city you can see a lot, but in a small town like this you can feel a lot. The generous bench is built into the long side of the square, reminding me of how, when I first discovered Civita back in the 1970s and 1980s, the town's old folks would gather here every night. The piazza has been integral to Italian culture since ancient Roman times. While Civita is humble today, imagine the town's former wealth, when mansions of the leading families faced this square, along with the former city hall (opposite the church, to your left). The town's history includes a devastating earthquake in 1695. Notice how stone walls were reinforced with thick bases, and how old stones and marble slabs were recycled and built into walls.

Here in the town square, you'll find Bar Da Peppone (open daily, local wines and microbrews, inviting fire in the winter) and two restaurants. There are wild donkey races on the first Sunday of June and the second Sunday of September. At Christmastime, a living nativity scene is enacted in this square, and if you're visiting at the end of July or beginning of August, you might catch a play here. The pillars that stand like giants' bar stools are ancient Etruscan. The church, with its *campanile* (bell tower), marks the spot where an Etruscan temple, and then a Roman temple, once stood. Across from Peppone's, on the side of the former city hall, is a small, square stone counter. Old-timers remember when this was a meat shop, and how one day a week the counter was stacked with fish for sale.

The humble **Geological Museum,** next to Peppone's, tells the story of how erosion is constantly shaping the surrounding "Bad Lands" valley, how landslides have shaped (and continue to threaten) Civita, and how the town plans to stabilize things (€3, June-Sept Tue-Sun 9:30-13:00 & 14:00-18:30, closed Mon, weekends only off-season, closed Jan-Feb, mobile 328-665-7205).

• *Now step inside...*

Civita's Church: A cathedral until 1699, the church houses records of about 60 bishops that date back to the seventh century (church open daily 10:00-13:00 & 15:00-17:00, often closed Jan-Feb). Inside you'll see Romanesque columns and arches with faint Renaissance frescoes peeking through Baroque-era whitewash. The central altar is built upon the relics of the Roman martyr St. Victoria, who once was the patron saint of the town. St. Marlonbrando served as a bishop here in the ninth century; an altar dedicated to him is on the right. The fine crucifix over this altar, carved out of pear wood in the 15th century, is from the school of Donatello. It's remarkably expressive and greatly venerated by locals. Jesus' gaze is almost haunting. Some say his appearance changes based on what angle you view him from: looking alive from the front, in agony from the left, and dead from the right. Regardless, his eyes follow you from side to side. On Good Friday, this crucifix goes out and is the focus of the midnight procession.

On the left side, midway up the nave above an altar, is an intimate fresco of the *Madonna of the Earthquake*, given this name because—in the great shake of 1695—the whitewash fell off and revealed this tender fresco of Mary and her child. (During the Baroque era, a white-and-bright interior was in vogue, and churches such as these—which were covered with precious and historic frescoes—were simply whitewashed over. Look around to see examples.) On the same wall—just toward the front from the *Madonna*—find the faded portrait of Santa Apollonia, the patron saint of your teeth; notice the scary-looking pincers.

• *From the square, you can follow...*

The Main Street: A short walk takes you from the church to the end of the town. Along the way, you'll pass a couple of little eateries (described later, under "Eating in Civita"), olive presses, gardens, a rustic town museum, and valley views. The rock below Civita is honeycombed with ancient tunnels, caverns (housing olive presses), cellars (for keeping wine at a constant temperature all year), and cisterns (for collecting rainwater, since there was no well in town). Many date from Etruscan times.

ORVIETO & CIVITA

Wherever you choose to eat (or just grab a *bruschetta* snack), be sure to take advantage of the opportunity to poke around—every place has a historic cellar. At the trendy **Alma Civita,** notice the damaged house facing the main street—broken since the 1695 earthquake and scarred to this day. Just beyond, the rustic **Antico Frantoio Bruschetteria** serves bruschetta in an amazing old space. Whether or not you buy food, venture into their back room to see an interesting collection of old olive presses (if you're not eating here, a €1 donation is requested). The huge olive press in the entry is about

1,500 years old. Until the 1960s, blindfolded donkeys trudged in the circle here, crushing olives and creating paste that filled the circular filters and was put into a second press. Notice the 2,500-year-old sarcophagus niche. The hole in the floor (with the glass top) was a garbage hole. In ancient times, residents would toss their jewels down when under attack; excavations uncovered a windfall of treasures.

In front is the well head of an ancient cistern—designed to collect rain water from neighboring rooftops—carved out of *tufo* and covered with clay to be waterproof.

• *Across the street and down a tiny lane, find...*

Antica Civita: This is the closest thing the town has to a history museum. The humble collection is the brainchild of Felice, the old farmer who's hung black-and-white photos, farm tools, olive presses, and local artifacts in a series of old caves. Climb down to the "warm blood machine" (another donkey-powered grinding wheel) and a viewpoint and to see rooms where a mill worker lived until the 1930s. Felice wants to give visitors a feeling for life in Civita when its traditional economy was strong (€1, daily 10:00-19:00, until 17:00 in winter, some English explanations).

• *Another few steps along the main street take you to...*

The End of Civita: Here the road is literally cut out of the stone, with a dramatic view of the Bad Lands opening up. Pop in to the cute "Garden of Poets" (immediately on the left just outside town, with the tiny local crafts shop) to savor the view. Then, look back up at the end of town and ponder the precarious future of Civita. There's a certain stillness here, far from the modern world and high above the valley.

Continue along the path a few steps toward the valley below the town, and you come to some shallow caves used as stables until a few years ago. The third cave, cut deeper into the rock, with a barred door, is the **Chapel of the Incarcerated** (Cappella del Carcere). In Etruscan times, the chapel—with a painted tile depicting the Madonna and child—may have been a tomb, and in medieval times, it was used as a jail (which collapsed in 1695).

Although it's closed to the public now, an Etruscan tunnel just beyond the Chapel of the Incarcerated cuts completely through the hill. Tall enough for a woman with a jug on her head to pass through, it may have served as a shortcut to the river below. It was widened in the 1930s so that farmers could get between their scattered fields more easily. Later, it served as a refuge for frightened villagers who huddled here during WWII bombing raids.

• *Hike back into town. Make a point to take some time to explore the peaceful back lanes before returning to the modern world.*

Sleeping in Civita or Bagnoregio

Civita has nine B&B rooms up for grabs. Bagnoregio has larger lodgings, and there are plenty of *agriturismi* nearby; otherwise, there's always Orvieto. Off-season, when Civita and Bagnoregio are deadly quiet—and cold—I'd side-trip in from Orvieto rather than spend the night here. Those staying overnight in Civita may be able to get a discount on parking at the base of the bridge—ask when you reserve.

In Civita

$$$ Locanda della Buona Ventura rents four overpriced rooms with tiny bathrooms, up narrow stairs, decorated in medieval rustic-chic, and overlooking Civita's piazza. Because you're not likely to see the owner, the shop across the square functions as the reception (Db-€120, or €100 in Oct-May, extra bed-€20, skimpy breakfast at nearby restaurant, no Internet access, tel. 0761-792-025, mobile 347-627-5628, www.locandabuonaventura.it, info@locandabuonaventura.it).

$$ Alma Civita is a classic old stone house that was recently renovated by a sister-and-brother team, Alessandra and Maurizio (hence the name: Al-Ma). These are Civita's two most comfortable, modern, and warmly run rooms (Db-€100, no Internet access, tel. 0761-792-415, mobile 347-449-8892, www.almacivita.com, prenotazione@almacivita.com). They also have a restaurant (see later).

$ Civita B&B, run by gregarious Franco Sala, has three little rooms above Trattoria Antico Forno, each overlooking Civita's main square. Two are doubles with private bath. The third is a triple (with one double and one kid-size bed), which has its own bathroom across the hall (S-€50, Sb-€55, D-€70, Db-€75, T-€95, continental breakfast, free Wi-Fi, Piazza del Duomo Vecchio, tel.

076-176-0016, mobile 347-611-5426, www.civitadibagnoregio.it, fsala@pelagus.it).

In Bagnoregio

$$ Romantica Pucci B&B is a haven for city-weary travelers. Its five spacious rooms are indeed romantic, with canopied beds and flowing veils (Db-€80, extra bed-€25, air-con, free guest computer and Wi-Fi, free parking, Piazza Cavour 1, tel. 0761-792-121, www.hotelromanticapucci.it, hotelromanticapucci@gmail.com). It's just above the public parking lot you see when you arrive in Bagnoregio. From the bus stop, take Via Garibaldi uphill above the parking lot, and then bear right at the tobacco shop onto Via Roma.

$ Hotel Divino Amore has 23 bright, modern rooms, four with perfect views of a miniature Civita. These view rooms, and the ones with air-conditioning, cost no extra—but are booked first (Sb-€50, Db-€70, Tb-€80, Qb-€90, air-con in seven rooms, no Internet access, closed Jan-Mar, Via Fidanza 25-27, tel. 076-178-0882, mobile 329-344-8950, www.hoteldivinoamore.com, info@hoteldivinoamore.com). From the bus stop, follow Via Garibaldi uphill above the parking lot for 200 yards.

Eating in Civita or Bagnoregio

In Civita

Osteria Al Forno di Agnese is a delightful spot where Manuela and her friends serve visitors simple yet delicious meals on a covered patio just off Civita's main square (nice €7 salads, €9 pastas—including gluten-free options, €7-12 *secondi*, good selection of local wines, opens daily at 12:00 for lunch, June-Sept also at 19:00 for dinner, closed Tue in winter and sometimes in bad weather, tel. 0761-792-571, mobile 340-1259-721).

Trattoria Antico Forno serves up rustic dishes, homemade pasta, and salads at affordable prices. Try their homemade pasta with truffles (€7 pastas, €7-12 *secondi*, €15 fixed-price meal, daily for lunch 12:30-15:30 and dinner 19:00-22:00, on main square, also rents rooms—see Civita B&B listing earlier, tel. 076-176-0016, Franco and his assistants Nina and Fiorella).

La Cantina de Arianna Trattoria Bruschetteria is a family affair, with a busy open fire specializing in grilled meat and wonderful bruschetta. It's run by Arianna, her sister Antonella, and their parents, Rossana and Antonio. After eating, wander down to their cellar, where you'll see traditional winemaking gear and provisions for rolling huge kegs up the stairs. Tap on the kegs in the bottom level to see which are full (daily 11:00-17:00, tel. 0761-793-270).

Alma Civita, a lunch-only place, feels like a fresh, new take on old Civita. It's owned by two of its longtime residents: Alessandra (an architect) and her brother Maurizio (who runs the restaurant). Choose from one of three different seating areas: outside on a stony lane, in the modern and trendy-feeling main-floor dining room, or in the equally modern but atmospheric cellar. Even deeper is an old Etruscan tomb that's now a wine cellar (€3-5 *bruschette* and *antipasti*, €7 pastas, €6-10 *secondi*, May-Oct Wed-Mon 10:30-18:00, closed Tue, Nov-April Fri-Sun only, tel. 0761-792-415).

Antico Frantoio Bruschetteria, the last place in town, is a rustic, super-atmospheric spot for a bite to eat. The specialty here: delicious bruschetta toasted over hot coals. Peruse the menu, choose your toppings (chopped tomato is super), and get a glass of wine for a fun, affordable snack or meal (roughly 10:00-18:00 in summer, off-season open weekends only 10:00-17:00, mobile 328-689-9375, Fabrizio).

At the Foot of the Bridge

Hostaria del Ponte is a more serious restaurant than anything in Civita itself. It offers creative and traditional cuisine with a great view terrace at the parking lot at the base of the bridge to Civita. Big space heaters make it comfortable to enjoy the wonderful view as you dine from their rooftop terrace, even in spring and fall (€9 pastas, €12-13 *secondi,* reservations often essential, Tue-Sun 12:30-14:30 & 19:30-21:30, closed Mon, Nov-April also closed Sun eve, tel. 076-179-3565, Lorena).

In Bagnoregio

The recommended **Romantica Pucci B&B** offers a small restaurant with tables in its private garden (€25-30 meals, closed Mon, see contact details earlier).

Bagnoregio Connections

From Bagnoregio to Orvieto: Public Cotral buses (45 minutes, €2.20 one-way if purchased in advance, €7 one-way from driver) connect Bagnoregio to Orvieto. Departures from Bagnoregio—Monday to Saturday only (no buses on Sunday or holidays)—are likely to be at the following times (but confirm): 5:30, *6:30, 6:50, 9:55, *10:10 or 10:25, 13:00, *13:35, 14:25, and 17:25. Departures marked with an asterisk (*) operate only during the school year (roughly Sept-June). For more information, call 06-7205-7205 or 800-174-471 (press 7 for English), or see www.cotralspa.it (click on "Orari" in the left-hand menu, then on "Bagnoregio" in the alphabetical list—Italian only). For info on coming from Orvieto, see "Orvieto Connections" (page 824).

Remember to save money by buying your ticket in Bagnoregio

before boarding the bus—purchase one from the newsstand near the bus stop, across from the gas station. Better yet, if you're side-tripping from Orvieto, buy two tickets in Orvieto so you already have one when you're ready to come back.

From Bagnoregio to Points South: Cotral buses also run to **Viterbo,** which has a good train connection to Rome (buses go weekdays at 5:10, 6:30, 7:15, 7:40, 8:10, 10:00, 12:55, 13:45, and 14:50; less frequent Sat-Sun, 35 minutes, see phone number and website earlier).

ROME

Roma

Rome is magnificent and brutal at the same time. It's a showcase of Western civilization, with astonishingly ancient sights and a modern vibrancy. But if you're careless, you'll be run down or pickpocketed. And with the wrong attitude, you'll be frustrated by the kind of chaos that only an Italian can understand. On my last visit, a cabbie struggling with the traffic said, *"Roma chaos."* I responded, *"Bella chaos."* He agreed.

While Paris is an urban garden, Rome is a magnificent tangled forest. If your hotel provides a comfortable refuge; if you pace yourself; if you accept—and even partake in—the siesta plan, if you're well-organized for sightseeing; and if you protect yourself and your valuables with extra caution and discretion, you'll love it. (And Rome is much easier to live with if you can avoid the mid-summer heat.)

For me, Rome is in a three-way tie with Paris and London as Europe's greatest city. Two thousand years ago the word "Rome" meant civilization itself. Everything was either civilized (part of the Roman Empire, Latin- or Greek-speaking) or barbarian. Today, Rome is Italy's political capital, the capital of Catholicism, and the center of its ancient empire, littered with evocative remains. As you peel through its fascinating and jumbled layers, you'll find Rome's buildings, cats, laundry, traffic, and 3.4 million people endlessly entertaining. And then, of course, there are its stupendous sights.

Visit St. Peter's, the greatest church on earth, and scale Michelangelo's 448-foot-tall dome, the world's tallest. Learn something about eternity by touring the huge Vatican Museum. You'll find the story of creation—bright as the day it was painted—in the restored Sistine Chapel. Do the "Caesar Shuffle" through ancient

Rome's Neighborhoods

Rome's Forum and Colosseum. Savor Europe's most sumptuous building, the Borghese Gallery, and take an early evening "Dolce Vita Stroll" down Via del Corso with Rome's beautiful people. Enjoy an after-dark walk from Campo de' Fiori to the Spanish Steps, lacing together Rome's Baroque and bubbly nightspots. Dine well at least once.

Planning Your Time

Rome is wonderful, but it's huge and exhausting. On a first-time visit, many travelers find that Rome is best done quickly—Italy is more charming elsewhere. But whether you're here for a day or a week, you won't be able to see all of these sights, so don't try—you'll keep coming back to Rome. After several dozen visits, I still have a healthy list of excuses to return.

Rome in a Day: Some people actually try to "do" Rome in a day. Crazy as that sounds, if all you have is a day, it's one of the most exciting days Europe has to offer. Start at 8:30 at the Colosseum. Then explore the Forum, hike over Capitoline Hill, and cap your "Caesar Shuffle" with a visit to the Pantheon. After a quick lunch, taxi to the Vatican Museum (the lines usually die down mid-afternoon, or you can reserve a visit online in advance). See the Vatican Museum, then St. Peter's Basilica (open until 19:00 April-Sept). Taxi back to Campo de' Fiori to find dinner. Finish your day lacing together all the famous floodlit spots (follow my self-guided "Heart of Rome Walk"). Note: This busy plan is possible only if you ace the line-avoidance tricks.

Rome in Two to Three Days: On the first day, do the "Caesar Shuffle" from the Colosseum to the Forum, then over Capitoline Hill to the Pantheon. After a siesta, join the locals strolling from Piazza del Popolo to the Spanish Steps (follow my self-guided "Dolce Vita Stroll"). On the second day, see Vatican City (St. Peter's, climb the dome, tour the Vatican Museum). Have dinner on the atmospheric Campo de' Fiori, and then walk to the Trevi Fountain and Spanish Steps (following my "Heart of Rome Walk"). With a third day, add the Borghese Gallery (reservations required) and the Capitoline Museums.

Orientation to Rome

Sprawling Rome actually feels manageable once you get to know it. The old core, with most of the tourist sights, sits in a diamond formed by Termini train station (in the east), the Vatican (west), Villa Borghese Gardens (north), and the Colosseum (south). The Tiber River runs through the diamond from north to south. In the center of the diamond sits Piazza Venezia, a busy square and traffic hub. It takes about an hour to walk from Termini Station to the Vatican.

Think of Rome as a series of neighborhoods, huddling around major landmarks.

Ancient Rome: In ancient times, this was home for the grandest buildings of a city of a million people. Today, the best of the classical sights stand in a line from the Colosseum to the Forum to the Pantheon.

Pantheon Neighborhood: The Pantheon anchors the neighborhood I like to call the heart of Rome. It stretches eastward from the Tiber River through Campo de' Fiori and Piazza Navona, past the Pantheon to the Trevi Fountain.

Vatican City: Located west of the Tiber, it's a compact world of its own, with two great, huge sights: St. Peter's Basilica and the Vatican Museum.

North Rome: With the Spanish Steps, Villa Borghese Gardens, and trendy shopping streets (Via Veneto and the "shopping triangle"—the area between the Spanish Steps, Piazza Venezia, and Piazza del Popolo), this is a more modern, classy area.

ROME

East Rome: This includes the area around Termini Station, with its many recommended hotels and public-transportation connections. Nearby is the neighborhood I call "Pilgrim's Rome," with several prominent churches dotting the area south of the station.

South Rome: South of Vatican City is Trastevere, the colorful, wrong-side-of-the-river neighborhood that provides a look at village Rome. It's the city at its crustiest—and perhaps most "Roman." Across the Tiber River, directly south of the city center, are the gritty/colorful Testaccio neighborhood, the 1930s suburb of E.U.R., and the Appian Way, home of the catacombs.

Within each of these neighborhoods, you'll find elements from the many layers of Rome's 2,000-year history: the marble ruins of ancient times; tangled streets of the medieval world; early Christian churches; grand Renaissance buildings and statues; Baroque fountains and church facades; 19th-century apartments; and 20th-century boulevards choked with traffic.

Since no one is allowed to build taller than St. Peter's dome, and virtually no buildings have been constructed in the city center since Mussolini got distracted in 1938, central Rome has no modern skyline. The Tiber River is basically ignored—after the last floods (1870), the banks were built up very high, and Rome turned its back on its naughty river.

Tourist Information

Rome has two TI offices and several TI kiosks. The TI offices are at the airport (Terminal 3, daily 8:00-19:30) and Termini train station (daily 8:00-19:30, 100 yards down track 24, look for signs). Little kiosks (generally open daily 9:30-19:00) are near the Forum (on Piazza del Tempio della Pace), on Via Nazionale (at Palazzo delle Esposizioni), near Castel Sant'Angelo (at Piazza Pia), near Piazza Navona (at Piazza delle Cinque Lune), and near the Trevi Fountain (at Via del Corso and Via Minghetti). The TI's website is www.turismoroma.it. The TIs don't offer room-booking services. If a commercial info-center offers to book you a room, just say no—you'll save money by booking direct.

At any TI, ask for a city map and a listing of sights and hours (in the free *Evento* booklet with English-language pages listing the month's cultural events—also includes a bus map; if they're out, ask for last month's issue as much of the info is still valid). Your hotel will have a freebie map and may also have the free *Evento* booklet. The best map I found is published by Rough Guide (€9 in bookstores).

Rome's single best source of up-to-date tourist information is its **call center**, with English-speakers on staff. Dial 06-0608 (answered daily 9:00-21:00, press 2 for English, www.060608.it).

Several English-oriented **websites** provide insight into events and daily life in the city: www.inromenow.com (light tourist info

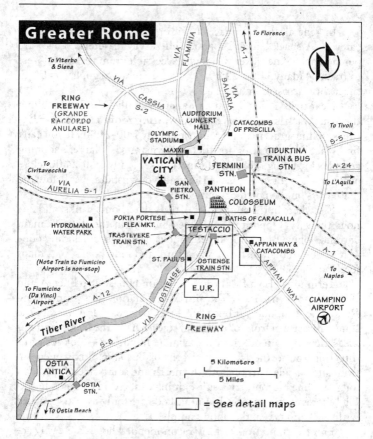

Greater Rome

on lots of topics), www.wantedinrome.com (events and accommodations), and www.rome.angloinfo.com (on living in and moving to Rome).

Arrival in Rome

By Train at Termini Station

Termini, Rome's main train station, is a buffet of tourist services. However, it's undergoing renovation, so services might have moved by the time you visit. The customer service and ticket windows can be jammed with travelers (take a number and wait). For simple questions, several handy red info kiosks are located near the head of the tracks. The ticket machines can also be helpful for checking schedules.

Along track 24, about 100 yards down, you'll find the **TI** (daily 8:00-19:30), a **hotel booking** office, and **car rental** desks. The **baggage storage** *(deposito bagagli)* is downstairs (€5/5 hours, then cheaper, daily 6:00-23:00). The **Leonardo Express train** to Fiumicino Airport runs from track 24 (see page 991).

ROME

In general, the best places to sit in the station are in one of its eateries. A snack bar and a good self-service **cafeteria** (Ciao) are perched above the ticket windows, accessible from the side closest to track 24 (daily 11:00-22:30). For **sandwiches** to go, try VyTA in the atrium across from track 1.

Near track 1, you'll find a **pharmacy** (daily 7:30-22:00); along the same track is an often cramped **waiting room** and **Despar Express,** selling groceries and toiletries (daily 7:00-21:30). If you can't find what you're looking for there, downstairs is a larger shopping complex including the **Conad** supermarket (daily 6:00-24:00; closest to track 1). Pricey **WCs** (€1) are also downstairs, just below the main exits on the north or south side.

Elsewhere in the station are **ATMs,** late-hours banks, and 24-hour thievery. Opposite the ticket windows in the station's main entrance lobby, **Borri Books** sells books in English, including popular fiction, Italian history and culture, and kids' books, plus maps (daily 7:00-23:00).

Termini is also a local transportation hub. Metro lines A and B intersect downstairs at Termini Metro station. Buses (including Rome's hop-on, hop-off bus tours—see page 859) leave across the square directly in front of the main station hall. The Metro and bus areas are a work in progress and change frequently—look for signs directing you to the Metro platform or bus stop. Taxis queue in front and outside exits on both the north and south sides; if there's a long taxi line in front, try a side exit instead. Avoid con men hawking "express taxi" services in unmarked cars (only use cars marked with the word *taxi* and a phone number).

From Termini, most of my recommended hotels are easily accessible by foot (for those near this train station) or by Metro (for those in the Colosseum and Vatican neighborhoods).

The station has some sleazy sharks with official-looking business cards; avoid anybody selling anything unless they're in a legitimate shop at the station. Other shady characters linger around the ticket machines—offers to help usually come with the expectation of a "tip."

By Train or Bus at Tiburtina Station

Tiburtina, Rome's second-largest train station, is located in the city's northeast corner. Recently rebuilt, it's a sleek and modern complex but still a work in progress. In general, slower trains (from Milan, Bolzano, Bologna, Udine, and Reggio di Calabria) and some night trains (from Munich, Milan, Venice, Innsbruck, and Udine) use Tiburtina, as does the night bus to Fiumicino Airport. Direct night trains from Paris and Vienna use Termini train station instead.

Tiburtina has been newly redeveloped for high-speed rail, including some Frecce trains and the Italo service. A separate "Casa Italo" area has dedicated service counters, red ticket machines, and a small waiting area (in the upper part of the station, across from track 23). For more on Italo, see page 1166.

Tiburtina is also known as a hub for bus service to destinations all across Italy. Buses depart from the piazza in front of the station. Ticket offices are located in the piazza and around the corner on Circonvallazione Nomentana (just beyond the elevated freeway).

Tiburtina is on Metro line B, with easy connections to Termini (a straight shot, four stops away) and the entire Metro system (note that when going to Tiburtina, Metro line B splits—you want a train signed *Rebibbia*). Or take bus #492 from Tiburtina to various city-center stops (such as Piazza Barberini, Piazza Venezia, and Piazza Cavour) and the Vatican neighborhood (as you emerge from the station, the bus stop is to the left).

By Car

The Grande Raccordo Anulare circles greater Rome. This ring road has spokes that lead you into the center. Entering from the north, leave the autostrada at the Settebagni exit. Following the ancient Via Salaria (and the black-and-white *Centro* signs), work your way doggedly into the Roman thick of things. This will take you along the Villa Borghese Gardens and dump you right on Via Veneto in downtown Rome. Avoid rush hour and drive defensively: Roman cars stay in their lanes like rocks in an avalanche.

Parking in Rome is dangerous. Park near a police station or get advice at your hotel. Garages charge about €24 per day. The Villa Borghese underground garage is handy (Metro: Spagna), or park at Tiburtina Station (€1/hour, www.atac.roma.it) and take a 10-minute ride on the Metro line B into the center. Consider this: Your car is a worthless headache in Rome. Avoid a pile of stress and save money by parking at the huge, easy, and relatively safe lot behind the train station in the hill town of Orvieto (follow *P* signs from autostrada) and catching the train to Rome (hourly, 1-1.5 hours).

By Plane or Cruise Ship

For information on Rome's airports and Civitavecchia's cruise-ship terminal, see the end of this chapter.

Helpful Hints

Sightseeing Tips: Avid sightseers can save money by buying the Roma Pass (see "Tips on Sightseeing in Rome" sidebar, later), available at TIs and participating sights—buy one before visiting the Colosseum or Forum, and you can skip the long lines there. Another way to bypass lines at the Colosseum and Forum is to buy a ticket online in advance (see page 886). If

Daily Reminder

Sunday: These sights are closed: the Vatican Museum (except for last Sun of the month, when it's free and even more crowded), Villa Farnesina (except for second Sun of the month), and the Catacombs of San Sebastiano. In the morning, the Porta Portese flea market hops, and the old center is delightfully quiet. The Via dei Fori Imperiali and much of the Appian Way are closed to traffic and fun to stroll.

Monday: Many sights are closed, including the National Museum of Rome, Borghese Gallery, Capitoline Museums, Catacombs of Priscilla, Museum of the Imperial Forums (includes Trajan's Market and Trajan's Forum), Castel Sant'Angelo, Ara Pacis, Montemartini Museum, E.U.R.'s Museum of Roman Civilization, Etruscan Museum, Museum of the Liberation of Rome, MAXXI, some Appian Way sights (Tomb of Cecilia Metella; Circus and Villa of Maxentius; and the San Sebastiano Gate and Museum of the Walls), and Ostia Antica.

Major sights that are open include the Colosseum, Forum, and Vatican Museum, among others. Churches are open as usual. The Baths of Caracalla close early in the afternoon.

Tuesday: All sights are open in Rome. This isn't a good day to side-trip to Naples because its Archaeological Museum is closed.

Wednesday: All sights are open, except the Catacombs of San Callisto. St. Peter's Basilica may be closed in the morning for a papal audience.

Thursday/Friday: All sights are open.

Saturday: Most sights are open in Rome, except the Synagogue and Jewish Museum.

you want to see the Borghese Gallery, remember to reserve ahead (see page 920). To sidestep the long Vatican Museum line, reserve an entry time online (see page 910 for details).

Internet Access: Most hotels have Wi-Fi, but if yours doesn't, your hotelier can point you to the nearest Internet café.

Bookstores: The following stores sell travel guidebooks, including mine (all open daily except Anglo American and Open Door closed Sun). The first two are chains, while the others have a more personal touch. **Borri Books** is at Termini Station, and **Feltrinelli** has two branches (at Largo Argentina 11, with a limited English section, and the larger Feltrinelli International, just off Piazza della Repubblica at Via Vittorio Emanuele Orlando 78-81, tel. 06-487-0171). **Anglo American Bookshop** has great art and history sections (closed all day

Sun and Mon morning, a few blocks south of Spanish Steps at Via della Vite 102, tel. 06-679-5222). **Libreria Fanucci** has a small selection, but is centrally located (a block toward the Pantheon from Piazza Navona at Piazza Madama 8, tel. 06-686-1141). In Trastevere, Irishman Dermot at the **Almost Corner Bookshop** stocks an Italian-interest section (Via del Moro 45, tel. 06-583-6942), and the **Open Door Bookshop** carries the only used books in English in town (closed Sun, Via della Lungaretta 23, tel. 06-589-6478).

Laundry: Your hotelier can direct you to the nearest launderette. The **Ondablu** chain usually comes with Internet access (€2/hour); one of their more central locations is near Termini Station (about €8 to wash and dry a 15-pound load, usually open daily 8:00-22:00, Via Principe Amedeo 70b, tel. 06-474-4647).

Travel Agencies: You can get train tickets and railpass-related reservations and supplements at travel agencies (at little or no additional cost), avoiding a trip to a train station. Your hotelier will know of a convenient agency nearby.

Updates to This Book: For updates to this book, check www.ricksteves.com/update.

Dealing with (and Avoiding) Problems

Theft Alert: While violent crime is rare in the city center, petty theft is rampant. With sweet-talking con artists meeting you at the station, well-dressed pickpockets on buses, and thieving gangs of children at the ancient sites, Rome is a gauntlet of rip-offs. Although it's not as bad as it was a few years ago, and pickpockets don't want to hurt you—they usually just want your money—green or sloppy tourists will be scammed. Thieves strike when you're distracted. Don't trust kind strangers. Keep nothing important in your pockets.

Be most on guard while boarding and leaving buses and subways. Thieves crowd the door, then stop and turn while others crowd and push from behind. You'll find less crowding and commotion—and less risk—waiting for the end cars of a subway rather than the middle cars. The sneakiest thieves pretend to be well-dressed businessmen (generally with something in their hands), or tourists wearing fanny packs and toting cameras and even Rick Steves guidebooks.

If you know what to look out for, fast-fingered moms with babies and gangs of children picking the pockets and handbags of naive tourists are not a threat, but an interesting, albeit sad, spectacle. Pickpockets troll through the tourist crowds around the Colosseum, Forum, Vatican, and train and Metro stations. Watch them target tourists who are overloaded with

Tips on Sightseeing in Rome

These tips will help you use your time and money efficiently, making the Eternal City seem less eternal and more entertaining. For general advice on sightseeing, see page 19.

Passes

Roma Pass: Rome offers several sightseeing passes to help you save money. For most visitors, the Roma Pass (www.romapass.it) is the clear winner. The Roma Pass costs €34 and is valid for three days, covering public transportation and free or discounted entry to Roman sights.

You get free admission to your first two sights (where you also get to skip the ticket line) and then a discount on the rest within the three-day window. Sights covered (or discounted) by the pass include the following: Colosseum/Palatine Hill/Roman Forum, Borghese Gallery (though you still must make a reservation), Capitoline Museums, Castel Sant'Angelo, Montemartini Museum, Ara Pacis, Museum of Roman Civilization, Etruscan Museum, Baths of Caracalla, Trajan's Market, and some of the Appian Way sights. The pass also covers four branches of the National Museum of Rome, considered as a single "sight": Palazzo Massimo (the most important of the lot), Crypta Balbi (medieval art), Palazzo Altemps (sculpture collection), and Museum of the Bath (ancient inscriptions). The pass does not cover the Vatican Museum (which contains the Sistine Chapel).

If you'll be using public transportation and visiting any two of the major sights in a three-day period, get the pass. It's sold at participating sights, TIs, and many tobacco shops and newsstands all over town (look for a *Roma Pass* sign; all should offer the same price). Try to buy it at a less crowded TI or sight (you can buy it at a sight even if you don't intend to use it there). Don't bother to order it online—you have to physically pick up the pass in Rome, which negates any time-saving advantage.

Validate your Roma Pass by writing your name and validation date on the card. Then insert it directly into the turnstile at your first two (free) sights. At other sights, show it at the ticket office to get your reduced (*ridotto*) price—about 30 percent off.

To get the most of your pass, visit the two most expensive sights first—for example, the Colosseum (€12) and the National Museum of Rome (€10). Definitely use it to bypass the long ticket-buying line at the Colosseum. For sights that normally sell a combined ticket (such as the Colosseum/Palatine Hill/Roman Forum or the National Museum branches), visiting the combined sight counts as a single entry.

The Roma Pass comes with a three-day transit pass. Write your name and birthdate on the transit pass, validate it on your

first bus or Metro ride by passing it over a sensor at a turnstile or validation machine (look for a yellow circle), and you can take unlimited rides within Rome's city limits until midnight of the third day.

Combo-Ticket for Colosseum, Forum, and Palatine Hill: A €12 combo-ticket covers these three adjacent sights (no individual tickets are sold). The combo-ticket allows one entry per sight and is valid for two days. Note that these sights are also covered by the Roma Pass. To avoid ticket-buying lines at the Colosseum and Forum, purchase your combo-ticket or Roma Pass at the lesser-visited Palatine Hill.

Top Tips

Museum Reservations: The marvelous Borghese Gallery requires reservations in advance (for specifics, see page 920). You can reserve online to avoid long lines at the Vatican Museum (see page 910).

Opening Hours: Rome's sights have notoriously variable hours from season to season. Get a current listing of opening times—ask for the free booklet *Evento* at a TI or your hotel. On holidays, expect shorter hours or closures.

Churches: Many churches, which have divine art and free entry, open early (around 7:00-7:30), close for lunch (roughly 12:00-15:00), and close late (about 19:00). Kamikaze tourists maximize their sightseeing hours by visiting churches before 9:00 or late in the day; during the siesta, they see major sights that stay open all day (St. Peter's, Colosseum, Forum, Capitoline Museums, Pantheon, and National Museum of Rome). Dress modestly for church visits.

Picnic Discreetly: Public drinking and eating is not allowed at major sights, though the ban has proven difficult to enforce. To avoid the risk of being fined, choose an empty piazza for your picnic, or keep a low profile.

Miscellaneous Tips: I carry a plastic water bottle and refill it at Rome's many public drinking spouts. Because public restrooms are scarce, use toilets at museums, restaurants, and bars.

ROME

bags or distracted with a video camera. The kids look like beggars and hold up newspapers or cardboard signs to confuse their victims. They scram like stray cats if you're on to them.

Scams abound: Always be clear about what paper money you're giving someone, demand clear and itemized bills, and count your change. Don't give your wallet to self-proclaimed "police" who stop you on the street, warn you about counterfeit (or drug) money, and ask to see your cash. If a bank machine eats your ATM card, see if there's a thin plastic insert with a tongue hanging out that thieves use to extract it.

Reporting Losses: To report lost or stolen items, file a police report (at Termini Station, with *polizia* at track 11 or with Carabinieri at track 20; offices are also at Piazza Venezia). You'll need the report to file an insurance claim for lost gear, and it can help with replacing your passport—first file the police report, then call your embassy to make an appointment (US embassy: Tel. 06-46741, Via Vittorio Veneto 121, www.usembassy.it). For information on how to report lost or stolen credit cards, see page 17.

Emergency Numbers: Police—tel. 113. Ambulance—tel. 118.

Pedestrian Safety: Your main safety concern in Rome is crossing streets safely. Use extreme caution. Scooters don't need to stop at red lights, and even cars exercise what drivers call the "logical option" of not stopping if they see no oncoming traffic. Each year, as noisy gasoline-powered scooters are replaced by electric ones, the streets get quieter (hooray) but more dangerous for pedestrians. Follow locals like a shadow when you cross a street (or spend a good part of your visit stranded on curbs). When you do cross alone, don't be a deer in the headlights. Find a gap in the traffic and walk with confidence while making eye contact with approaching drivers—they won't hit you if they can tell where you intend to go.

Staying/Getting Healthy: The siesta is a key to survival in summertime Rome. Lie down and contemplate the extraordinary power of gravity in the Eternal City. I drink lots of cold, refreshing water from Rome's many drinking fountains (the Forum has three).

There's a pharmacy (marked by a green cross) in every neighborhood. Pharmacies stay open late in Termini Station (daily 7:30-22:00) and at Piazza dei Cinquecento 51 (Mon-Fri 7:00-23:30, Sat-Sun 8:00-23:00, next to Termini Station on the corner of Via Cavour, tel. 06-488-0019). There's also a 24-hour pharmacy several blocks down from Piazza della Repubblica at Via Nazionale 228 (tel. 06-488-4437).

Embassies and hotels can recommend English-speaking

ROME

doctors. Consider MEDline, a 24-hour home-medical service; doctors speak English and make calls at hotels for €150 (tel. 06-808-0995). Anyone is entitled to free emergency treatment at public hospitals. The hospital closest to Termini Station is Policlinico Umberto 1 (entrance for emergency treatment on Via Lancisi, translators available, Metro: Policlinico). Readers report that the staff at Santa Susanna Church, home of the American Catholic Church in Rome, offers useful advice and medical referrals (see page 931).

Getting Around Rome

Sightsee on foot, by city bus, by Metro, or by taxi. I've grouped your sightseeing into walkable neighborhoods. Make it a point to visit sights in a logical order. Needless backtracking wastes precious time.

The public transportation system, which is cheap and efficient, consists primarily of buses, a few trams, and the two underground subway (Metro) lines. Consider it part of your Roman experience.

The walking-tour company, Rome Walks, has produced an orientation video to Rome's transportation system; find it on YouTube by searching for "Understanding Rome's Public Transport."

For information, visit www.atac.roma.it, which has a useful route planner in English, or call 06-57003. If you have a smartphone and an international data plan, consider downloading the free Roma Bus app by Movenda, which also has a route planner and real-time updates on the bus schedule. The ATAC mobile website has similar info (www.muovi.roma.it).

Buying Tickets

All public transportation uses the same ticket. It costs €1.50 and is valid for one Metro ride— including transfers underground—plus unlimited city buses and trams during a 100-minute period. Passes good on buses and the Metro are sold in increments of one day (€6, good until midnight), three days (€16.50), one week (€24, about the cost of three taxi rides), and one month (€35, valid for a calendar month).

You can purchase tickets and passes at some newsstands, tobacco shops (*tabacchi*, marked by a black-and-white *T* sign), and major Metro stations and bus stops, but not on board. It's smart to

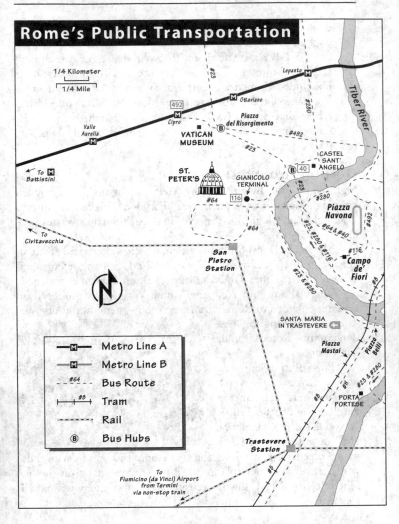

Rome's Public Transportation

1/4 Kilometer

1/4 Mile

Tiber River

Lepanto Ⓜ

#23

#280

Ⓜ Ottaviano

492

Ⓜ Cipro

Piazza
del Risorgimento
Ⓑ

#492

Valle
Aurelia Ⓜ

VATICAN
MUSEUM

#23

CASTEL
SANT'
ANGELO

← To Ⓜ
Battistini

ST.
PETER'S

GIANICOLO
TERMINAL

Ⓑ 40

#23

#280

#64

116

Piazza
Navona

#23 #280 & #116

#64 & #40

#280

To
Civitavecchia

#64

San
Pietro
Station

#23 & #280

#116

Campo
de'
Fiori

#8

#23 & #280

N

SANTA MARIA
IN TRASTEVERE ◁

Piazza
Mastai

Piazza
Belli

Metro Line A

Metro Line B

#64 **Bus Route**

#8 **Tram**

Rail

Ⓑ **Bus Hubs**

#H

#8

#23 & #280

PORTA
PORTESE

Trastevere
Station

#8

To
Fiumicino (da Vinci) Airport
from Termini
via non-stop train

ROME

stock up on tickets early, or to buy a pass or a Roma Pass (which includes a three-day transit pass—see page 846). That way, you don't have to run around searching for an open tobacco shop when you spot your bus approaching. Metro stations rarely have human ticket-sellers, and the machines are unreliable (it helps to insert your smallest coin first).

Validate your ticket by sticking it in the Metro turnstile (magnetic-strip-side up, arrow-side first) or in the machine when you board the bus (magnetic-strip-side down, arrow-side first)—watch others and imitate. It'll return your ticket with your expiration time printed. To get through a Metro turnstile with a transit pass or Roma Pass, use it just like a ticket; on buses and trams,

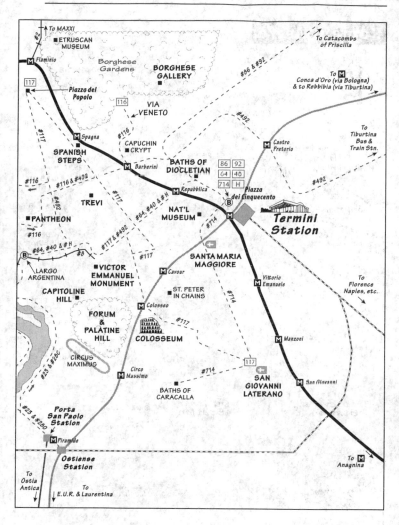

however, you need to validate your pass only if that's your first time using it.

By Metro

The Roman subway system (Metropolitana, or "Metro") is simple, with two clean, cheap, fast lines—A and B—that intersect at Termini Station. The Metro runs from 5:30 to 23:30 (Fri-Sat until 1:30 in the morning). Remember, the subway's first and last compartments

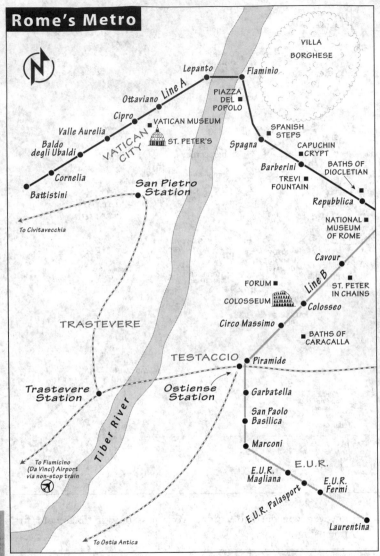

Rome's Metro

are generally the least crowded, and the least likely to harbor pickpockets.

You'll notice lots of big holes in the city while a new line is being built to run across town, including the historic heart. It likely will not be completed until 2020.

While much of Rome is not served by its skimpy subway, the following stops are helpful:

Termini (intersection of lines A and B): Termini Station,

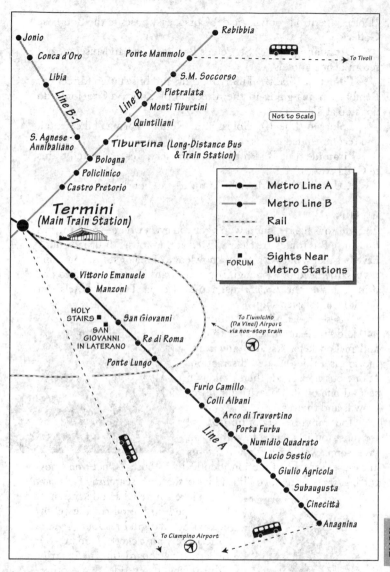

shuttle train to airport, National Museum of Rome, and recommended hotels

Repubblica (line A): Baths of Diocletian, Via Nazionale, and recommended hotels

Barberini (line A): Capuchin Crypt, Trevi Fountain, and Villa Borghese

Spagna (line A): Spanish Steps and classy shopping area

Flaminio (line A): Piazza del Popolo, start of recommended

"Dolce Vita Stroll" down Via del Corso, easy buses to the Borghese Gallery

Ottaviano (line A): St. Peter's Basilica, Vatican Museum, and recommended hotels

Tiburtina (line B): Tiburtina train and bus station (direction: Rebibbia; trains going in the direction of Conca d'Oro/Jonio do not stop at Tiburtina)

Colosseo (line B): Colosseum, Roman Forum, bike rental, and recommended hotels

Piramide (line B): Protestant Cemetery, Testaccio, and trains to Ostia Antica

E.U.R. (line B): Mussolini's futuristic suburb

By Bus

The Metro is handy, but it won't get you everywhere—take the bus (or tram). Bus routes are clearly listed at the stops. TIs usually don't have bus maps, but with some knowledge of major stops, you won't necessarily need one (though if you do want a route map, find one printed inside the *Evento* magazine—free at TIs and hotels—or buy it from tobacco shops).

Buses—especially the touristy #40 and #64—are havens for thieves and pickpockets. Assume any commotion is a thief-created distraction. If one bus is packed, there's likely a second one on its tail with far fewer crowds and thieves.

The tram lines are of limited use for most tourists, but a few lines can save some walking. For all intents and purposes, they function identically to buses. Once you know the bus/tram system, you'll find it's easier than searching for a cab.

Tickets have a barcode and must be stamped on the bus in the yellow box with the digital readout (be sure to retrieve your ticket). Validate your ticket as you board (magnetic-strip-side down, arrow-side first), otherwise you're cheating. While relatively safe, riding without a stamped ticket on the bus is stressful. Inspectors fine even innocent-looking tourists €50. There's no need to validate a transit pass or Roma Pass on the bus, unless your pass is new and hasn't yet been stamped elsewhere in the transit system. Bus etiquette (not always followed) is to board at the front or rear doors and exit at the middle.

Regular bus lines start running at about 5:30, and during the day they run every 5-10 minutes. After 23:30, and sometimes earlier (such as on Sundays), buses are less frequent but still dependable. Night buses are also reliable, and are marked with an *N* and an owl symbol on the bus-stop signs.

These are the major bus routes:

Bus #64: This bus cuts across the city, linking Termini Station with the Vatican, stopping at Piazza della Repubblica (sights), Via Nazionale (recommended hotels), Piazza Venezia (near Forum), Largo Argentina (near Pantheon and Campo de' Fiori), St. Peter's Basilica (get off just past the tunnel), and San Pietro Station. Ride it for a city overview and to watch pickpockets in action. The #64 can get horribly crowded.

Bus #40: This express bus, which mostly follows the #64 route (but ends near the Castel Sant'Angelo on the Vatican side of the river), is especially helpful—fewer stops and crowds.

The following routes conveniently connect Trastevere with other parts of Rome:

Bus #H: This express bus, linking Termini Station and Trastevere, makes a stop near Piazza Repubblica and at the bottom of Via Nazionale (for Trastevere, get off at Piazza Belli/Sonnino, just after crossing the Tiber River).

Tram #2: Leaving from near the Flaminio Metro stop, this route gives easy access to the Etruscan Museum and MAXXI, Rome's contemporary art museum.

Tram #8: This tram connects Piazza Venezia and Largo Argentina with Trastevere (get off at Piazza Belli).

Buses #23 and #280: These link the Vatican with Trastevere and Testaccio, stopping at the Vatican Museum (nearest stop is Via Leone IV), Castel Sant'Angelo, Trastevere (Piazza Belli), Porta Portese (Sunday flea market), and Piramide (Metro and gateway to Testaccio).

Other useful routes include:

Bus #62: Largo Argentina to St. Peter's Square.

Bus #81: San Giovanni in Laterano, Largo Argentina, and Piazza Risorgimento (Vatican).

Buses #85 and #87: Piazza Venezia, Colosseum, San Clemente, and San Giovanni in Laterano.

Bus #492: Travels east-west across the city, connecting Tiburtina (train and bus stations), Largo Santa Susanna (near Piazza della Repubblica), Piazza Barberini, Piazza Venezia, Largo Argentina, Piazza Cavour (Castel Sant'Angelo), and Piazza Risorgimento (St. Peter's Basilica and Vatican).

Bus #714: Termini Station, Santa Maria Maggiore, San

Giovanni in Laterano, Terme di Caracalla (Baths of Caracalla), and on to E.U.R.

Elettrico Minibuses: Two cute *elettrico* minibuses that wind through the narrow streets of old and interesting neighborhoods are great for transport or simple joyriding. *Elettrico* **#116** runs through the medieval core of Rome: Ponte Vittorio Emanuele II (near Castel Sant'Angelo) to Campo de' Fiori, Pantheon, Piazza Barberini, and the southern edge of the scenic Villa Borghese Gardens. *Elettrico* **#117** connects San Giovanni in Laterano, Colosseo, Via dei Serpenti, Trevi Fountain, Piazza di Spagna, and Piazza del Popolo—and vice versa. Where Via del Corso hits Piazza del Popolo, a #117 is usually parked and ready to go. Riding it from here to the end of the line, San Giovanni in Laterano, makes for a fine joyride that leaves you, conveniently, at a great sight.

By Taxi

I use taxis in Rome more often than in other cities. They're reasonable and useful for efficient sightseeing in this big, hot metropolis.

Taxis start at €3, then charge about €1.50 per kilometer (surcharges: €1.50 on Sun, €3.50 for nighttime hours of 22:00-7:00, one regular suitcase or bag rides free, tip by rounding up to the nearest euro). Sample fares: Termini area to Vatican-€11; Termini area to Colosseum-€7; Termini area to the Borghese Gallery-€8; Colosseum to

Trastevere-€8 (or look up your route at www.worldtaximeter.com). Three or four companions with more money than time should taxi almost everywhere.

It's tough to wave down a taxi in Rome, especially at night. Find the nearest taxi stand by asking a passerby or a clerk in a shop, *"Dov'è una fermata dei taxi?"* (doh-VEH OO-nah fehr-MAH-tah DEH-ee TAHK-see). Some taxi stands are listed on my maps. To save time and energy, have your hotel or restaurant call a taxi for you; the meter starts when the call is received (generally adding a euro or two to the bill). To call a cab on your own, dial 06-3570, 06-4994, or 06-6645. It's routine for Romans to ask the waiter in a restaurant to call a taxi when they ask for the bill. The waiter will tell you how many minutes you have to enjoy your coffee.

Beware of corrupt taxis. First, make sure the meter *(tassametro)* is turned on. If it isn't, get out and hail another cab. Check that the meter is reset to the basic drop charge (should be around €3, or around €5 if you or your hotelier phoned for the taxi). Many meters show both the fare and the time elapsed during the ride, and some tourists—mistaking the time for the fare—end up paying more than the fair meter rate. Keep an eye on the fare on the meter as you near your destination; some cabbies turn the meter off instantly when they stop and tell you a higher price.

When you arrive at the train station or airport, beware of hustlers conning naive visitors into unmarked, rip-off "express taxis." Only use official taxis, with a *taxi* sign and phone number marked on the door. By law, they must display a multilingual official price chart; point to the chart and ask the cabbie to explain it if the fare doesn't seem right. A common cabbie scam is to take your €20 note, drop it, and pick up a €5 note (similar color), claiming that's what you gave him. To avoid this scam, pay in small bills; if you only have a large bill, show it to the cabbie as you state its face value.

If you encounter any problems with a taxi, making a show of writing down the taxi number (to file a complaint) can motivate a driver to quickly settle the matter.

If you take a Rome city cab from Fiumicino Airport to anywhere in central Rome within the old city walls, the cost should be €48 (covering up to four people and their bags); however, every year some readers report being ripped off. The catch is that cabbies *not* based in Rome or Fiumicino can charge €70. At the airport, look specifically for a Rome city cab, with the words "Roma Capitale" and a "SPQR" shield on the door. By law, they can charge only €48 for the ride (still, be sure to establish the price before you get in).

Tired travelers arriving at the airport will likely find it less stressful to take an airport shuttle van to their hotel, or catch the train to Termini Station and take the Metro or a cheaper taxi from there (see page 991 for details on getting from the airport to downtown Rome via taxi, shuttle, or train).

By Bike

Biking in the big city of Rome can speed up sightseeing or simply be an enjoyable way to explore. Though Roman traffic can be stressful, Roman drivers are respectful of cyclists. Still, use caution and never assume the right of way. The best rides are on small streets in the city center. A bike path along the banks of the Tiber River makes a good 20-minute ride (easily accessed from the ramps at Porta Portese and Ponte Regina Margherita near Piazza del Popolo). Get a bike with a well-padded seat—the little stones that pave Roman streets are unforgiving.

Top Bike Rental and Tours is professionally run by Roman bike enthusiasts who want to show off their city. Your rental comes with a helmet, a lock, and a handy map that suggests a route and indicates less-trafficked streets. They also offer four-hour-long

English-only guided tours around the city and the Appian Way; check their website for itineraries and schedules (rental: €15/day, 10 percent discount with this book, best to reserve in advance via email; bike tours: start at €39, reservations required; daily 10:00-19:00, bring ID for deposit, from Santa Maria Maggiore go up Via dell'Olmata and turn left at the end of the block, Via dei Quattro Cantoni 40, tel. 06-488-2893, www.topbikerental.com, info@top-bikerental.com).

Cool Rent, near the Colosseo Metro stop, is cheaper but less helpful and has more basic bikes (€4/hour, €12/day, 3-person bike cart €10/hour, daily April-Oct 9:00-20:00, Nov-March 9:00-18:00, driver's license or other ID for deposit, 10 yards to the right as you exit the Metro). A second outlet is just off Via del Corso (on Largo di Lombardi, near corner of Via del Corso and Via della Croce, mobile 388-695-9303, Sasin).

Tours in Rome

Walking Tours

Finding the best guided tours in Rome is challenging. Local guides are good but pricey. Tour companies are cheaper, but quality and organization are unreliable. To sightsee on your own, download my series of free audio tours that illuminate some of Rome's top sights and neighborhoods (see sidebar on page 9 for details).

If you do hire a private Italian guide, consider organizing a group of four to six people from your hotel to split the cost (around €180 for a three-hour tour); this ends up costing about the same per person as going on a scheduled tour from one of the walking-tour companies listed below (about €25, generally expat guides).

Local Guides

I've worked with each of these licensed independent local guides. They're worth every euro. They speak excellent English and enjoy tailoring tours to your interests. Their prices (roughly €55-60/hour) flex with the day, season, and demand. Arrange your date and price by email.

Francesca Caruso loves to teach and share her appreciation of her city, and has contributed generously to this chapter (www.francescacaruso.com, francescainroma@gmail.com). Popular with my readers, Francesca understandably books up quickly; if she's busy, she'll recommend one of her colleagues. **Carla Zaia** is an engaging expert on all things Roman (carlaromeguide@gmail.com). **Cristina Giannicchi** has an archaeology background (mobile 338-111-4573, www.crisromanguide.com, crisgiannicchi@gmail.com). **Sara Magister,** a Roman with doctorates in art history and archaeology, leads tours throughout the city (a.magister@iol.it). **Giovanna Terzulli** is a personable, knowledgeable art historian

ROME

(gioterzulli@gmail.com). **Alessandra Mazzoccoli** is experienced, easygoing, and good with all ages (alemazzoccoli@gmail.com). Italian-American **Sean Finelli,** known as "The Roman Guy," offers several walking tours and a trip-planning service (www.theromanguy.com).

Walking-Tour Companies

Rome has many highly competitive tour companies, each offering a series of themed walks through various slices of Rome. Three-hour guided walks generally cost €25-30 per person. Guides are usually native English speakers, often American expats. Tours are limited to small groups, geared to American tourists, and given in English only. I've listed some here, but without a lot of details on their offerings. Before your trip, spend some time on these companies' websites to get to know your options, as each company has a particular teaching and guiding personality. Some are highbrow, and others are less scholarly. It's sometimes required, and always smart, to book a spot in advance (easy online). I must add that we get a lot of negative feedback on some tour companies. Readers report that advertising can be misleading, and scheduling mishaps are common. Make sure you know what you are booking and when.

Context Rome's walking tours are more intellectual than most, designed for travelers with longer-than-average attention spans. They are more expensive than others and are led by "docents" rather than guides (tel. 06-9672-7371, US tel. 800-691-6036, www.contextrome.com). **Enjoy Rome** offers a number of different walks and a website filled with helpful information (Via Marghera 8a, tel. 06-445-1843, www.enjoyrome.com, info@enjoyrome.com). **Rome Walks** has put together several particularly creative itineraries (mobile 347-795-5175, www.romewalks.com, info@romewalks.com, Annie). **Europe Odyssey,** formerly named Roman Odyssey, gives readers of this book a 10 percent discount on their walks (tel. 06-580-9902, mobile 328-912-3720, www.europeodyssey.com, Rahul). **Through Eternity** offers travelers with this book a 10 percent discount on most group tours and a 20 percent discount on its Underground Rome; book through their website ("Group Tours Rome" tab) and enter the promotional code "RICKSTEVES" for the best discount (tel. 06-700-9336, mobile 347-336-5298, www.througheternity.com, office@througheternity.com, Rob). **Walks of Italy** has fun guides who lead a variety of good walks for groups of no more than 12 people at a time (10 percent discount for readers of this book, US tel. 202/684-6916, Italian mobile 334-974-4274, tel. 06-9558-3331, www.walksofitaly.com, Jason Spiehler).

ROME

Hop-on, Hop-off Bus Tours

Several different agencies, including the ATAC public bus company, run hop-on, hop-off tours around Rome. These tours are constantly evolving and offer varying combinations of sights. You can grab one (and pay as you board) at any stop; Termini Station and Piazza Venezia are handy hubs. Although the city is perfectly walkable, and traffic jams can make the bus dreadfully slow, these open-top bus tours remain popular.

The **110open Bus** seems to be the best. Operated by the ATAC city-bus lines, it offers an orientation tour on big red double-decker buses with an open-air upper deck. In less than two hours, you'll have 80 sights pointed out to you, with a next-to-worthless recorded narration. While you can hop on and off, the service can be erratic (mobbed midday, not ideal in bad weather), and it can be very slow in heavy traffic. It's  best to think of this as a 90-minute quickie orientation with scant information and lots of images. Stops include the Colosseum, Circus Maximus, Bocca della Verità (the Mouth of Truth from *Roman Holiday* fame), Piazza Venezia, St. Peter's Square, Via del Tritone (Trevi Fountain), and Piazza Barberini. The 110open Bus departs roughly every 20 minutes (less frequent off-season). You can catch it at any stop, including Termini Station. Buy the ticket as you board (runs daily April-Oct 8:30-20:30, Nov-March 8:30-19:00, single tour-€12, 1-day ticket-€15, 48-hour ticket-€20, family tickets available, kids 9 and under ride free, tel. 800-281-281, www.trambusopen.com).

Archeobus is an open-top bus, also operated by ATAC, that runs twice hourly from Termini Station out to the Appian Way  (with stops at the Colosseum, Baths of Caracalla, San Callisto, San Sebastiano, and the Tomb of Cecilia Metella). This is a handy way to see the sights down this ancient Roman road, but it can be frustrating for various reasons—sparse narration, sporadic service, and not ideal for hopping on and off (single tour-€10, 48-hour ticket-€12, €25 combo-ticket with 110open Bus valid 72 hours, deals for families and children, 1.5-hour loop, daily April-mid-Oct 9:00-16:30, bus runs Fri-Sun only mid-Oct-March, from Termini Station and Piazza Venezia, tel. 800-281-281, www.trambusopen.com). A similar bus laces together all the Christian sights.

Car and Minibus Tours

Autoservizi Monti Concezio, run by gentle, capable, and English-speaking Ezio, offers private cars or minibuses with driver/guides (car–€40/hour, minibus–€45/hour, 3-hour minimum for city sightseeing, long rides outside Rome are more expensive, mobile 335-636-5907 or 349-674-5643, www.tourservicemonti.it, info@tourservicemonti.it).

Miles & Miles Private Tours, a family-run company, offers a number of tours (all explained on their website) in Mercedes vans and cars, all with good English-speaking driver/guides (€60/hour for up to 8 people, 5-hour minimum, mention Rick Steves when booking direct then show the book on the day of service to get a discount, mobile 331-466-4900, www.milesandmiles.net, info@milesandmiles.net, Francesco answers the mobile phone, while Kimberly—an American—runs the office). They can also provide unguided long-distance transportation; if traveling with a small group or a family from Rome to Florence, the Amalfi Coast, or elsewhere, consider paying extra to turn the trip into a memorable day tour with door-to-door service.

Weekend Tour Packages for Students

Andy Steves (my son) runs **Weekend Student Adventures,** offering active and experiential three-day weekend tours from €199, designed for American students studying abroad; see www.wsaeurope.com for details on tours of Rome and other great cities.

Self-Guided Walks in Rome

Here are three walks that give you a moving picture of Rome, an ancient yet modern city. You'll walk through history (Roman Forum Walk), take a refreshing early-evening walk (Dolce Vita Stroll), and enjoy the thriving local scene, best at night (Heart of Rome Walk).

Roman Forum Walk

The Forum was the political, religious, and commercial center of

the city. Rome's most important temples and halls of justice were here. This was the place for religious processions, political demonstrations, elections, important speeches, and parades by conquering generals. As Rome's empire expanded, these few acres of land became the center of the civilized world.

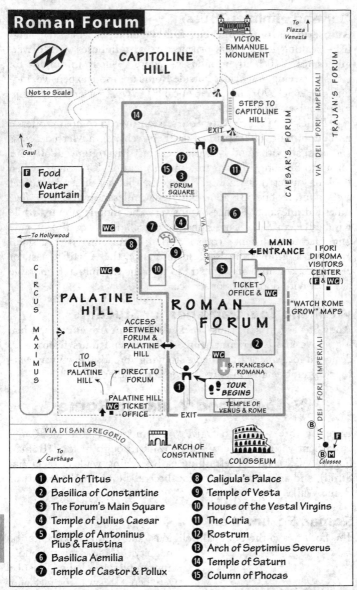

Roman Forum

Not to Scale

CAPITOLINE HILL

VICTOR EMMANUEL MONUMENT

To Piazza Venezia

TRAJAN'S FORUM

VIA DEI FORI IMPERIALI

CAESAR'S FORUM

STEPS TO CAPITOLINE HILL

EXIT

To Gaul

F Food
● Water Fountain

FORUM SQUARE

WC

To Hollywood

CIRCUS MAXIMUS

PALATINE HILL

ROMAN FORUM

MAIN ENTRANCE

I FORI DI ROMA VISITORS CENTER (**F** & **WC**)

"WATCH ROME GROW" MAPS

TICKET OFFICE & **WC**

WC

ACCESS BETWEEN FORUM & PALATINE HILL

TO CLIMB PALATINE HILL

DIRECT TO FORUM

PALATINE HILL **WC** TICKET OFFICE

S. FRANCESCA ROMANA

TOUR BEGINS

TEMPLE OF VENUS & ROME

EXIT

VIA DI SAN GREGORIO

To Carthage

ARCH OF CONSTANTINE

COLOSSEUM

VIA DEI FORI IMPERIALI

Ⓑ

F
Ⓑ **M**
Colosseo

❶ Arch of Titus
❷ Basilica of Constantine
❸ The Forum's Main Square
❹ Temple of Julius Caesar
❺ Temple of Antoninus Pius & Faustina
❻ Basilica Aemilia
❼ Temple of Castor & Pollux

❽ Caligula's Palace
❾ Temple of Vesta
❿ House of the Vestal Virgins
⓫ The Curia
⓬ Rostrum
⓭ Arch of Septimius Severus
⓮ Temple of Saturn
⓯ Column of Phocas

ROME

Cost: €12 combo-ticket covers both the Roman Forum/Palatine Hill (grouped as one sight for the purposes of the ticket) and the Colosseum; also covered by the Roma Pass. The combo-ticket is valid two consecutive days, but once your ticket is scanned for either the Forum/Palatine Hill or the Colosseum, you can't re-enter that sight (even the next day).

Hours: The Roman Forum, Palatine Hill, and Colosseum are all open daily 8:30 until one hour before sunset: April-Aug until 19:15, Sept until 19:00, Oct until 18:30, Nov-mid-Feb until 16:30, mid-Feb-mid-March until 17:00, mid-March-late March until 17:30; last entry one hour before closing.

Avoiding Lines: See tips on page 886.

Getting There: The closest Metro stop is Colosseo. The Forum has two entrances. The main entrance is on Via dei Fori Imperiali ("Road of the Imperial Forums"). From the Colosseo Metro stop, walk away from the Colosseum on Via dei Fori Imperiali to find the low-profile Forum ticket office (look closely), located where Via Cavour spills into Via dei Fori Imperiali. Buses #53, #85, #87, and #175 stop along Via dei Fori Imperiali near the entrance, the Colosseum, and Piazza Venezia.

While the Forum has four exits, there are only two ways in. The second entrance—which may be more convenient if you're coming from the Colosseum—is at the Palatine Hill ticket office on Via di San Gregorio. After buying your ticket, take the path to the right (not up the hill), which leads to the Forum at the Arch of Titus.

Information: A free visitors center (called I Fori di Roma), located across Via dei Fori Imperiali from the Forum's main entrance, has a TI (which sells the Roma Pass), bookshop, small café, WCs, and a film (daily 9:30-18:30). A bookstore is at the Forum entrance. Vendors outside sell *Rome: Past and Present* books with plastic overlays that restore the ruins (includes DVD; smaller book marked €15, prices soft, so offer €10). Info office tel. 06-3996-7700, http://archeoroma.beniculturali.it/en.

Tours: An unexciting yet informative **audioguide** helps decipher the rubble (€5/2 hours, €7 version includes Palatine Hill and lasts 3 hours, must leave ID), but you'll have to return it to one of the Forum entrances instead of being able to exit directly to Capitoline Hill or the Colosseum. Official **guided tours** in English might be available (inquire at ticket office). You can download this walk as a free Rick Steves **audio tour** (see page 9).

Length of This Walk: Allow 1.5 hours. If you have less time, end the walk at the Arch of Septimius Severus. Don't miss the Basilica of Constantine hiding behind the trees.

Services: WCs are at the main entrance, near the Arch of Titus (in the "Soprintendenza" office), and in the middle of the Forum, near #8 on the map.

Plan Ahead: The ancient paving at the Forum is uneven; wear sturdy shoes. I carry a water bottle and refill it at the Forum's public drinking fountains.

Improvise: Because of ongoing restoration, paths through the

Forum are often rerouted. Use this walk as a starting point, but be prepared for a few detours and backtracking.

The Walk Begins

• *Start at the Arch of Titus (Arco di Tito). It's the white triumphal arch that rises above the rubble on the east end of the Forum (closest to the Colosseum). Stand at the viewpoint alongside the arch and gaze over the valley known as the Forum.*

Viewing the Ruins: As you begin this Forum tour, here's a hint for seeing things with "period eyes." We imagine the structures in ancient Rome as mostly white, but ornate buildings and monuments like the Arch of Titus were originally more colorful. Through the ages, builders scavenged stone from the Forum, and the finest stone—the colored marble—was cannibalized first. If any was left, it was generally the white stone. Statues that filled the niches were vividly painted, but the organic paint rotted away as statues lay buried for centuries. Lettering was inset bronze and eyes were inset ivory. Even seemingly intact structures, like the Arch of Titus, have been reassembled. Notice the columns are half smooth and half fluted. The fluted halves are original; the smooth parts are reconstructions—intentionally not trying to fake the original.

❶ Arch of Titus (Arco di Tito): The Arch of Titus commemorated the Roman victory over the province of Judaea (Israel) in A.D. 70. The Romans had a reputation as benevolent conquerors who tolerated the local customs and rulers. All they required was allegiance to the empire, shown by worshipping the emperor as a god. No problem for most conquered people, who already had half a dozen gods on their prayer lists anyway. But Israelites believed in only one god, and it wasn't the emperor. Israel revolted. After a short but bitter war, the Romans defeated the rebels, took Jerusalem, destroyed their temple (leaving only the foundation wall—today's revered "Wailing Wall"), and brought home 50,000 Jewish slaves...who were forced to build this arch (and the Colosseum).

• *Walk down Via Sacra into the Forum. Imagine Roman sandals on these original basalt stones—the oldest street you'll ever walk. After about 50 yards, turn right and follow a path uphill to the three huge arches of the...*

❷ Basilica of Constantine (Basilica Maxentius): Yes, these are big arches. But they represent only one-third of the original Basilica of Constantine, a mammoth hall of justice. The arches were matched by a similar set along the Via Sacra side (only a few squat brick piers remain). Between them ran the central hall, which was spanned by a roof 130 feet high—about 55 feet higher than the side arches you see. (The stub of brick you see sticking up began an arch that once spanned the central hall.) The hall itself was as long as a football field, lavishly furnished with colorful inlaid marble, a gild-

Rome: Republic and Empire
(500 B.C.-A.D. 500)

Ancient Rome spanned a thousand years, from about 500 B.C. to A.D. 500. During that time, Rome expanded from a small tribe of barbarians to a vast empire, then dwindled slowly to city size again. For the first 500 years, when Rome's armies made her ruler of the Italian peninsula and beyond, Rome was a republic governed by elected senators. Over the next 500 years, a time of world conquest and eventual decline, Rome was an empire ruled by a military-backed dictator.

Julius Caesar bridged the gap between republic and empire. This ambitious general and politician, popular with the people because of his military victories and charisma, suspended the Roman constitution and assumed dictatorial powers in about 50 B.C. A few years later, he was assassinated by a conspiracy of senators. His adopted son, Augustus, succeeded him, and soon "Caesar" was not just a name but a title.

Emperor Augustus ushered in the Pax Romana, or Roman peace (A.D. 1-200), a time when Rome reached her peak and controlled an empire that stretched even beyond Eurail—from England to Egypt, Turkey to Morocco.

ed bronze ceiling, and statues, and filled with strolling Romans. At the far (west) end was an enormous marble statue of Emperor Constantine on a throne. (Pieces of this statue, including a hand the size of a man, are on display in Rome's Capitoline Museums.)

The basilica was begun by the emperor Maxentius, but after he was trounced in battle (see page 887), the victor Constantine completed the massive building. No doubt about it, the Romans built monuments on a more epic scale than any previous Europeans, wowing their "barbarian" neighbors.

• Now stroll deeper into the Forum, downhill along Via Sacra, through the trees. Many of the large basalt stones under your feet were walked on by Caesar Augustus 2,000 years ago. Pass by the only original bronze door still swinging on its ancient hinges (the green door at the Tempio di Romolo, on the right—if it happens to be open, peek in), and continue between ruined buildings until Via Sacra opens up to a flat, grassy area.

❸ The Forum's Main Square: The original Forum, or main square, was this flat patch about the size of a football field, stretching to the foot of Capitoline Hill. Surrounding it were temples, law courts, government buildings, and triumphal arches.

Rome was born right here. According to legend, twin brothers Romulus (Rome) and Remus were orphaned in infancy and raised by a she-wolf on top of Palatine Hill. Growing up, they found it hard to get dates. So they and their cohorts attacked the nearby Sabine tribe and kidnapped their women. After they made peace,

ROME

this marshy valley became the meeting place and then the trading center for the scattered tribes on the surrounding hillsides.

The square was the busiest and most crowded—and often the seediest—section of town. Besides the senators, politicians, and currency exchangers, there were even sleazier types—souvenir hawkers, pickpockets, fortune-tellers, gamblers, slave marketers, drunks, hookers, lawyers, and tour guides.

Ancient Rome's population exceeded one million, more than any city until London and Paris in the 19th century. All those Roman masses lived in tiny apartments as we would live in tents at a campsite, basically just to sleep. The public space—their Forum, today's piazza—is where they did their living. To this day, urban Italians have a passion for spending a major part of their time in the streets and squares.

The Forum is now rubble, but imagine it in its prime: blindingly brilliant marble buildings with 40-foot-high columns and shining metal roofs; rows of statues painted in realistic colors; processional chariots rattling down Via Sacra. Mentally replace tourists in T-shirts with tribunes in togas. Imagine the buildings towering and the people buzzing around you while an orator gives a rabble-rousing speech from the Rostrum. If things still look like just a pile of rocks, at least tell yourself, "But Julius Caesar once leaned against these rocks."

• At the near (east) end of the main square (the Colosseum is to the east) are the foundations of a temple now capped with a peaked wood-and-metal roof.

❹ Temple of Julius Caesar (Tempio del Divo Giulio, or Ara di Cesare): On March 15, in 44 B.C., Julius Caesar was stabbed 23 times by political conspirators. After his assassination, Caesar's body was cremated on this spot (under the metal roof). Afterward, this temple was built to honor him. Peek behind the wall into the small apse area, where a mound of dirt usually has fresh flowers—given to remember the man who, more than any other, personified the greatness of Rome.

Caesar (100-44 B.C.) changed Rome—and the Forum—dramatically. He cleared out many of the wooden market stalls and began to ring the square with even grander buildings. Caesar's house was located behind the temple, near that clump of trees. He walked right by here on the day he was assassinated ("Beware the Ides of March!" warned a street-corner Etruscan preacher).

Though he was popular with the masses, not everyone liked Caesar's urban design or his politics. When he assumed dictatorial powers, he was ambushed and stabbed to death by a conspiracy of senators, including his adopted son, Brutus ("Et tu, Brute?").

The funeral was held here, facing the main square. The citizens gathered, and speeches were made. Mark Antony stood up to say (in Shakespeare's words), "Friends, Romans, countrymen, lend me your ears. I come to bury Caesar, not to praise him." When Caesar's body was burned, his adoring fans threw anything at hand on the fire, requiring the fire department to come put it out. Later, Emperor Augustus dedicated this temple in his name, making Caesar the first Roman to become a god.

• *Behind and to the left of the Temple of Julius Caesar are 10 tall columns. These belong to the...*

❺ Temple of Antoninus Pius and Faustina: The Senate built this temple to honor Emperor Antoninus Pius (A.D. 138-161) and his deified wife, Faustina. The 50-foot-tall Corinthian (leafy) columns must have been awe-inspiring to out-of-towners who grew up in thatched huts. Although the temple has been inhabited by a church, you can still see the basic layout—a staircase led to a shaded porch (the columns), which admitted you to the main building (now a church), where the statue of the god sat. Originally, these columns supported a triangular pediment decorated with sculptures.

Picture these columns, with gilded capitals, supporting brightly painted statues in the pediment, and the whole building capped with a gleaming bronze roof. The stately gray rubble of today's Forum is a faded black-and-white photograph of a 3-D Technicolor era.

The building is a microcosm of many changes that occurred after Rome fell. In medieval times, the temple was pillaged. Note the diagonal cuts high on the marble columns—a failed attempt by scavengers to cut through the pillars to pull them down for their precious stone. (They used vinegar and rope to cut the marble... but because vinegar also eats through rope, they abandoned the attempt.) In 1550, a church was housed inside the ancient temple. The green door shows the street level at the time of Michelangelo. The long staircase was underground until excavated in the 1800s.

• *Next, explore the ruins of the Basilica Aemilia. You can view it from a ramp next to the Temple of Antoninus Pius and Faustina, or find the entrance near the Curia.*

❻ Basilica Aemilia: A basilica was a covered public forum, often serving as a Roman hall of justice. In a society that was as legal-minded as America is today, you needed a lot of lawyers—and a big place to put them. Citizens came here to work out matters such as inheritances and building permits, or to sue somebody.

Notice the layout. It was a long, rectangular building. The stubby columns all in a row form one long, central hall flanked by two side aisles. Medieval Christians required a larger meeting hall for their worship services than Roman temples provided, so they used the spacious Roman basilica as the model for their churches. Cathedrals from France to Spain to England, from Romanesque to Gothic to Renaissance, all have the same basic floor plan as a Roman basilica.

• *Return again to the Temple of Julius Caesar. To the right of the temple are the three tall columns of the...*

❼ Temple of Castor and Pollux: These three columns—all that remain of a once-prestigious temple—have become the most photographed sight in the Forum. The temple was one of the city's oldest, built in the fifth century B.C. It commemorated the Roman victory over the Tarquin, the notorious Etruscan king who oppressed them. As a symbol of Rome's self-governing Republic, the temple was often used as a meeting place of senators, and its front steps served as a podium for free speech. The three columns are Corinthian style, featuring leafy capitals and fluting. They date from a later incarnation of the temple (first century).

• *Beyond the three columns is Palatine Hill, the corner of which may have been...*

❽ Caligula's Palace (Palace of Tiberius): Emperor Caligula (ruled A.D. 37-41) had a huge palace on Palatine Hill overlooking the Forum. It actually sprawled down the hill into the Forum (some supporting arches remain in the hillside).

Caligula was not a nice person. He tortured enemies, stole senators' wives, and parked his chariot in handicap spaces. But Rome's luxury-loving emperors only added to the glory of the Forum, with each one trying to make his mark on history.

• *To the left of the Temple of Castor and Pollux, find the remains of a small, white circular temple.*

❾ Temple of Vesta: This is perhaps Rome's most sacred spot. Rome considered itself one big family, and this temple represented a circular hut, like the kind that Rome's first families lived in. Inside, a fire burned, just as in a Roman home. And back in the days before lighters and butane, you never wanted your fire to go out. As long as the sacred flame burned, Rome would stand. The flame was tended by priestesses known as Vestal Virgins.

• *Around the back of the Temple of Vesta, you'll find two rectangular brick pools. These stood in the courtyard of the...*

❿ House of the Vestal Virgins: The Vestal Virgins lived in a two-story building surrounding a long central courtyard with two pools at one end. Rows of statues depicting leading Vestal Virgins flanked the courtyard. This place was the model—both architecturally and sexually—for medieval convents and monasteries.

Chosen from noble families before they reached the age of 10, the six Vestal Virgins served a 30-year term. Honored and revered by the Romans, the Vestals even had their own box opposite the emperor in the Colosseum. The statues that line the courtyard honor dutiful Vestals.

As the name implies, a Vestal took a vow of chastity. If she served her term faithfully—abstaining for 30 years—she was given a huge dowry and allowed to marry. But if they found any Virgin who wasn't, she was strapped to a funeral car, paraded through the streets of the Forum, taken to a crypt, given a loaf of bread and a lamp...and buried alive. Many women suffered the latter fate.

• *Return to the Temple of Julius Caesar and head to the Forum's west end (opposite the Colosseum). As you pass alongside the big, open space of the Forum's main square, consider how the piazza is still a standard part of any Italian town. It has reflected and accommodated the gregarious and outgoing nature of the Italian people since Roman times.*

Stop at the big, well-preserved brick building (on right) with the triangular roof—the Curia. (Ongoing archaeological work may restrict access to the Curia, as well as the Arch of Septimius Severus—described later—and the exit to Capitoline Hill.)

⓫ The Curia (Senate House): The Curia was the most important political building in the Forum. While the present building dates from A.D. 283, this was the site of Rome's official center of government since the birth of the republic. Three hundred senators, elected by the citizens of Rome, met here to debate and create the laws of the land. Their wooden seats once circled the building in three tiers; the Senate president's podium sat at the far end. The marble floor is from ancient times. Listen to the echoes in this vast room—the acoustics are great.

Rome prided itself on being a republic. Early in the city's history, its people threw out the king and established rule by elected representatives. Each Roman citizen was free to speak his mind and have a say in public policy. Even when emperors became the supreme authority, the Senate was a power to be reckoned with. The Curia building is well-preserved, having been used as a church since early Christian times. In the 1930s, it was restored and opened to the public as a historic site. (Note: Although Julius Caesar was assassinated in "the Senate," it wasn't here—the Senate was temporarily meeting across town.)

A statue and two reliefs inside the Curia help build our mental image of the Forum. The statue, made of porphyry marble in about A.D. 100 (with its head, arms, and feet now missing), was a tribute to an emperor, probably Hadrian or Trajan. The two relief panels may have decorated the Rostrum. Those on the left show people (with big stone tablets) standing in line to burn their debt records following a government amnesty. The other shows the distribution of grain (Rome's welfare system), some buildings in the background, and the latest fashion in togas.

• *Go back down the Senate steps and find the 10-foot-high wall just to the left of the big arch, marked...*

⓬ Rostrum: Nowhere was Roman freedom more apparent than at this "Speaker's Corner." The Rostrum was a raised plat-

Rome Falls

Remember that Rome lasted 1,000 years—500 years of growth, 200 years of peak power, and 300 years of gradual decay. The fall had many causes, among them the barbarians who pecked away at Rome's borders. Christians blamed the fall on moral decay. Pagans blamed it on Christians. Socialists blamed it on a shallow economy based on the spoils of war. (Republicans blamed it on Democrats.)

Whatever the reasons, the far-flung empire could no longer keep its grip on conquered lands, and it pulled back. Barbarian tribes from Germany and Asia attacked the Italian peninsula and even looted Rome itself in A.D. 410, leveling many of the buildings in the Forum. In 476, when the last emperor checked out and switched off the lights, Europe plunged into centuries of ignorance, poverty, and weak government—the Dark Ages.

But Rome lived on in the Catholic Church. Christianity was the state religion of Rome's last generations. Emperors became popes (both called themselves "Pontifex Maximus"), senators became bishops, orators became priests, and basilicas became churches. The glory of Rome remains eternal.

form, 10 feet high and 80 feet long, decorated with statues, columns, and the prows of ships.

On a stage like this, Rome's orators, great and small, tried to draw a crowd and sway public opinion. Mark Antony rose to offer Caesar the laurel-leaf crown of kingship, which Caesar publicly (and hypocritically) refused while privately becoming a dictator. Men such as Cicero railed against the corruption and decadence that came with the city's newfound wealth. In later years, daring citizens even spoke out against the emperors, reminding them that Rome was once free. Picture the backdrop these speakers would have had—a mountain of marble buildings piling up on Capitoline Hill.

In front of the Rostrum are trees bearing fruits that were sacred to the ancient Romans: olives (provided food, light, and preservatives), figs (tasty), and wine grapes (made a popular export product).

• *The big arch to the right of the Rostrum is the...*

🅐 **Arch of Septimius Severus:** In imperial times, the Rostrum's voices of democracy would have been dwarfed by images of the empire, such as the huge six-story-high Arch of Septimius Severus (A.D. 203). The reliefs commemorate the African-born emperor's battles in Mesopotamia. Near ground level, see soldiers marching captured barbarians back to Rome for the victory parade. Despite Severus' efficient rule, Rome's empire was crumbling under the weight of its own corruption, disease, decaying infrastructure, and the constant attacks by foreign "barbarians."

• *Pass underneath the Arch of Septimius Severus and turn left. If the path is blocked, backtrack toward the Temple of Julius Caesar and around the square. On the slope of Capitoline Hill are the eight remaining columns of the...*

⓮ Temple of Saturn: These columns framed the entrance to the Forum's oldest temple (497 B.C.). Inside was a humble, very old wooden statue of the god Saturn. But the statue's pedestal held the gold bars, coins, and jewels of Rome's state treasury, the booty collected by conquering generals.

• *Standing here, at one of the Forum's first buildings, look east at the lone, tall...*

⓯ Column of Phocas: This is the Forum's last monument (A.D. 608), a gift from the powerful Byzantine Empire to a fallen empire—Rome. Given to commemorate the pagan Pantheon's becoming a Christian church, it's like a symbolic last nail in ancient Rome's coffin. After Rome's 1,000-year reign, the city was looted by Vandals, the population of a million-plus shrank to about 10,000, and the once-grand city center—the Forum—was abandoned, slowly covered up by centuries of silt and dirt. In the 1700s, an English historian named Edward Gibbon overlooked this spot from Capitoline

Hill. Hearing Christian monks singing at these pagan ruins, he looked out at the few columns poking up from the ground, pondered the decline and fall of the Roman Empire, and thought, "Hmm, that's a catchy title..."

• *From here, you have several options:*

    1. *Exiting past the Arch of Titus lands you at the Colosseum (page 882).*

    2. *Exiting past the Arch of Septimius Severus leads you to the stairs up to Capitoline Hill (page 895).*

    3. *The Forum's main entrance spills you back out onto Via dei Fori Imperiali, from where you can head to Trajan's Column, Trajan's Market, and Museum of the Imperial Forums (page 893).*

    4. *From the Arch of Titus, you can climb Palatine Hill to the top (page 891).*

The *Passeggiata*

Throughout Italy, early evening is time to stroll. While elsewhere in Italy this is called the *passeggiata*, in Rome it's a cruder, big-city version called the *struscio* (meaning "to rub").

Unemployment among Italy's youth is very high; many stay with their parents even into their thirties. They spend a lot of time being trendy and hanging out. Like American kids gathering at the mall, working-class suburban youth *(coatto)* converge on the old center, as there's little to keep them occupied in Rome's dreary outskirts (which lack public spaces). The hot *vroom-vroom* motor scooter is their symbol; haircuts and fashion are follow-the-leader.

In a more genteel small town, the *passeggiata* comes with sweet whispers of *"bella"* and *"bello"* ("pretty" and "handsome"). In Rome, the admiration is stronger, oriented toward consumption—they say *"buona"* and *"buono"*—meaning, roughly, "tasty." But despite how lusty this all sounds, you'll see just as many chunky, middle-aged Italians out and about as hormone-charged youth.

▲▲Dolce Vita Stroll

This is the city's chic stroll, from Piazza del Popolo (Metro: Flaminio) down a wonderfully traffic-free section of Via del Corso, and up Via Condotti to the Spanish Steps. It takes place from around 17:00 to 19:00 each evening (Fri and Sat are best), except on Sunday, when it occurs earlier in the afternoon. Leave before 18:00 if you plan to visit the Ara Pacis (Altar of Peace), which closes at 19:00 and is closed Monday.

As you stroll, you'll see shoppers, people-watchers, and flirts on the prowl filling this neighborhood of some of Rome's most fashionable stores (some open after siesta 16:30-19:30). While both the crowds and the shops along Via del Corso have gone downhill recently, elegance survives in the grid of streets between here and the Spanish Steps. If you get hungry during your stroll, see page 982 for descriptions of neighborhood wine bars and restaurants.

To reach **Piazza del Popolo,** where the stroll starts, take Metro line A to Flaminio and walk south to the square. Delightfully car-free, Piazza del Popolo is marked by an obelisk that was brought to Rome by Augustus after he conquered Egypt. (It used to stand in the Circus Maximus.) In medieval times, this area was just inside Rome's main entry (for more background on the square, see page 924).

If starting your stroll early enough, the Baroque church of **Santa Maria del Popolo** is worth popping into (Mon-Sat until 19:00, Sun until 19:30, next to gate in old wall on north side of

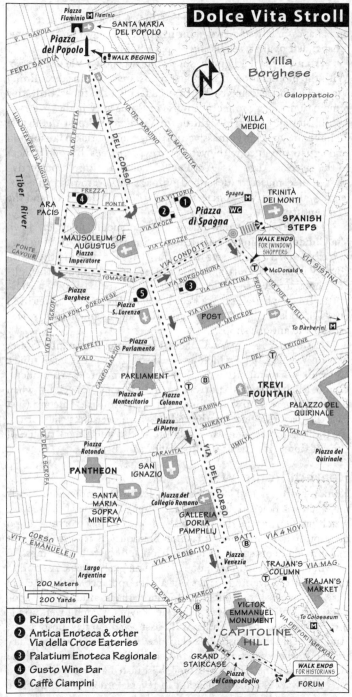

Dolce Vita Stroll

Piazza Flaminio — Flaminio

SANTA MARIA DEL POPOLO

Piazza del Popolo

WALK BEGINS

Villa Borghese

Galoppatoio

V. L. SAVOIA

FERD. SAVOIA

VIA DEL BABUINO

VIA DI RIPETTA

VIA DEL CORSO

VIA MARGUTTA

LUNGOTEVERE IN AUGUSTA

Tiber River

VILLA MEDICI

FREZZA

PONTE

❹

ARA PACIS

MAUSOLEUM OF AUGUSTUS

Piazza Imperatore

PONTE CAVOUR

VIA VITTORIA

❶

❷

VIA CROCE

Piazza di Spagna

Spagna — M

WC

TRINITÀ DEI MONTI

SPANISH STEPS

VIA CAROZZE

WALK ENDS FOR (WINDOW) SHOPPERS

VIA SISTINA

TOMACELLI

VIA CONDOTTI

VIA BORGOGNONA

❸

VIA FRATTINA

PROPA.

VIA DUE MACELLI

McDonald's

Piazza Borghese

Piazza S. Lorenzo

❺

VIA FONT. BORGHESE

VIA VITE

V. MERCEDE

POST

To Barberini — M

VIA DELLA SCROFA

PREFETTI

VALD

Piazza Parlamento

V. CON.

VIA DEL T

TRITONE

CAMPO MARZIO

PARLIAMENT

Piazza di Montecitorio

Piazza Colonna

T B

SABINA

TREVI FOUNTAIN

PALAZZO DEL QUIRINALE

Piazza di Pietra

MURATTE

UMILTA

DATARIA

Piazza del Quirinale

Piazza Rotonda

CARAVITA

VIA DEL CORSO

PANTHEON

SAN IGNAZIO

Piazza del Collegio Romano

SANTA MARIA SOPRA MINERVA

GALLERIA DORIA PAMPHILJ

VIA 4 NOV.

CORSO VITT. EMANUELE II

Largo Argentina

VIA PLEBISCITO

BATT.

Piazza Venezia

TRAJAN'S COLUMN

VIA MAG.

T

TRAJAN'S MARKET

200 Meters

200 Yards

VIA D'ARACOELI

SAN MARCO

B

VICTOR EMMANUEL MONUMENT

To Colosseum — M

VIA DEI FORI IMPERIALI

CAPITOLINE HILL

GRAND STAIRCASE

Piazza del Campodoglio

WALK ENDS FOR HISTORIANS

FORUM

❶ Ristorante il Gabriello
❷ Antica Enoteca & other Via della Croce Eateries
❸ Palatium Enoteca Regionale
❹ Gusto Wine Bar
❺ Caffè Ciampini

ROME

square). Inside, look for Raphael's Chigi Chapel (KEE-gee, second chapel on left) and two paintings by Caravaggio (in the Cerasi Chapel, left of altar; see listing on page 925).

From Piazza del Popolo, shop your way down **Via del Corso.** With the proliferation of shopping malls, many chain stores lining Via del Corso are losing customers and facing hard times. Still, this remains a fine place to feel the pulse of Rome at twilight.

Historians side-trip right down Via Pontefici past the fascist architecture to see the massive, rotting, round-brick **Mausoleum of Augustus,** topped with overgrown cypress trees. Beyond it, next to the river, is Augustus' **Ara Pacis,** enclosed within a protective glass-walled museum (described on page 927). From the mausoleum, walk down Via Tomacelli to return to Via del Corso and the 21st century.

From Via del Corso, window-shoppers should take a left down **Via Condotti** to join the parade to the **Spanish Steps,** passing big-name boutiques. The streets that parallel Via Condotti to the south (Borgognona and Frattina) are also elegant and filled with high-end shops. A few streets to the north hides the narrow Via Margutta. This is where Gregory Peck's *Roman Holiday* character lived (at #51); today it has a leafy tranquility and is filled with pricey artisan and antique shops.

Historians: Ignore Via Condotti and forget the Spanish Steps. Stay on Via del Corso, which has been straight since Roman times, and walk a half-mile down to the Victor Emmanuel Monument. Climb Michelangelo's stairway to his glorious (especially when floodlit) square atop Capitoline Hill. Stand on the balcony (just past the mayor's palace on the right), which overlooks the Forum. As the horizon reddens and cats prowl the unclaimed rubble of ancient Rome, it's one of the finest views in the city.

Heart of Rome Walk

Rome's most colorful neighborhood features narrow lanes, intimate piazzas, fanciful fountains, and some of Europe's best people-watching. During the day, this walk shows off the colorful Campo de' Fiori market and trendy fashion boutiques as it meanders past major monuments such as the Pantheon and the Spanish Steps.

But, when the sun sets, unexpected magic happens. A stroll in the cool of the evening brings out all the romance of the Eternal City. Sit so close to a bubbling fountain that traffic noise evaporates. Jostle with kids to see the gelato flavors. Watch lovers straddling more than the bench. Jaywalk past *polizia* in flak-proof vests. And marvel at the ramshackle elegance that softens this brutal city for those who were born here and can't imagine living anywhere else. These are the flavors of Rome, best tasted after dark.

This walk is equally pleasant in reverse order. You could ride the Metro to the Spanish Steps and finish at Campo de' Fiori, near many recommended restaurants. To lengthen this walk, you could start in Trastevere; see directions on page 934.

• *Start this walk at Campo de' Fiori, my favorite outdoor dining room (especially after dark—see "Eating in Rome," page 973). It's a few blocks west of Largo Argentina, a major transportation hub. Buses #40, #64, and #492 stop at both Largo Argentina and along Corso Vittorio Emanuele II, a long block north of Campo de' Fiori. A taxi from Termini Station costs about €8.*

Campo de' Fiori: One of Rome's most colorful spots, this bohemian piazza hosts a fruit and vegetable **market** in the morn-

ing, cafés in the evening, and pub-crawlers at night. In ancient times, the "Field of Flowers" was an open meadow. Later, Christian pilgrims passed through on their way to the Vatican, and a thriving market developed.

Lording over the center of the square is a statue of **Giordano Bruno,** an intellectual heretic who was burned on this spot in 1600. The pedestal shows scenes from Bruno's trial and execution, and reads, "And the flames rose up." When this statue honoring a heretic was erected in 1889, the Vatican protested, but they were overruled by angry Campo locals. The neighborhood is still known for its free spirit and anti-authoritarian demonstrations.

Campo de' Fiori is the product of centuries of unplanned urban development. At the east end of the square (behind Bruno), the ramshackle apartments are built right into the old outer wall of ancient Rome's mammoth Theater of Pompey. This entertainment complex covered several city blocks, stretching from here to Largo Argentina. Julius Caesar was assassinated in the Theater of Pompey, where the Senate was renting space.

The square is surrounded by fun eateries, great for people-watching. Bruno faces the bustling **Forno** (in the left corner of the square, closed Sun), where take-out *pizza bianco* is sold hot out of the oven. On weekend nights, when the Campo is packed with beer-drinking kids, the medieval square is transformed into one vast Roman street party.

• *If Bruno did a hop, step, and jump forward, then turned right on Via dei Baullari and marched 200 yards, he'd cross the busy Corso Vittorio Emanuele; then, continuing another 150 yards on Via Cuccagna, he'd find...*

Piazza Navona: This oblong square retains the shape of the original racetrack that was built around A.D. 80 by the emperor

ROME

Heart of Rome Walk

N

ARA PACIS

MAUSOLEUM OF AUGUSTUS

V. PONT.

Piazza Cavour

PONTE CAVOUR

VIA DI RIPETTA

Piazza Augusto Imperatore

PALACE OF JUSTICE

Tiber River

Piazza Borghese

LUNGOTEVERE MARZIO

CLEMENTINO

PONTE UMBERTO

MONTE BRIANZO

VIA DELLA SCROFA

PREFETTI

Piazza Ponte Umberto I

STELLETTA

VIA DI RIPETTA

CAMPO

To Ponte Sant'Angelo

VIA DEL CORONARI

UFFICI

GIOLITTI

VOLPE

ANCIENT STADIUM ENTRANCE

T
i

VIA DELLE COPPELLE

LA MADDE-LENA

Piazza Fico

Navona

SAN LUIGI

VIA IN AQUIRO

SAN CRISPINO

TRE SCALINI

SALVATORE ITALY'S SENATE

T

VIA GIUSTINIANI

Piazza Rotunda

CHIESA NUOVA

SANT' AGNESE

Piazza

FOUR RIVERS FOUNTAIN

SANT' EUSTACHIO

MONTE-FORTE

PANTHEON

Piazza della Chiesa Nuova

Piazza Pasquino

SANT' IVO

Piazza Sant'Eustachio

PASQUINO STATUE

CITY MUSEUM

CORSO DEL RINASCIMENTO

ARGENTINA

VIA DE CESTARI

CORSO   VITTORIO

B

EMANUELE II

SANT ANDREA DELLA VALLE

VICE

Largo Argentina

VIA D.BAULLARI

VIA CHIAVARI

B   T

LARGO ARGENTINA RUINS

WALK BEGINS

BRUNO STATUE

Campo de' Fiori

Largo Pallaro

VIA GIUBBONARI

PALAZZO FARNESE

Piazza Farnese

To Trastevere

ROME

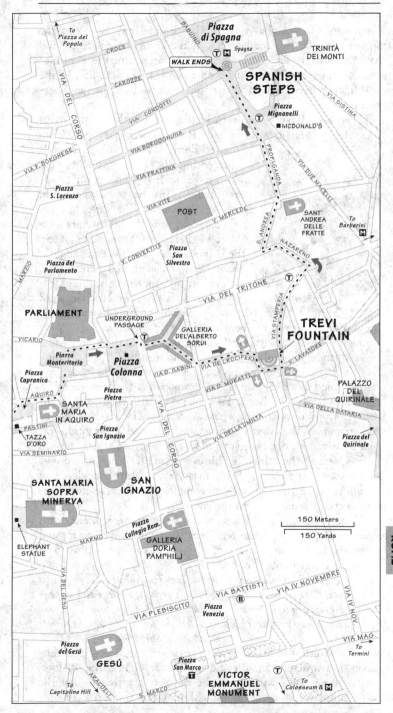

To Piazza del Popolo

CROCE

CAROZZE

VIA DEL CORSO

BABUINO

Piazza di Spagna

Spagna

WALK ENDS

TRINITÀ DEI MONTI

SPANISH STEPS

VIA SISTINA

VIA CONDOTTI

Piazza Mignanelli

■McDONALD'S

VIA BORGOGNONA

VIA FRATTINA

PROPAGANDA

VIA DUE MACELLI

VIA F. BORGHESE

Piazza S. Lorenzo

VIA VITE

POST

Y. MERCEDE

S. ANDREA

SANT' ANDREA DELLE FRATTE

To Barberini

M

V. CONVERTITE

Piazza San Silvestro

NAZARENO

MARZIO

Piazza del Parlamento

VIA DEL TRITONE

VIA STAMPERIA

TREVI FOUNTAIN

PARLIAMENT

UNDERGROUND PASSAGE

GALLERIA DEL'ALBERTO SORDI

VICARIO

Piazza Monteritorio

Piazza Colonna

VIA D. SABINI

VIA DE CROCIFERI

V. LAVATORE

Piazza Caprica

AQUIRO

Piazza Pietra

VIA D. MURATTE

PALAZZO DEL QUIRINALE

PASTINI

SANTA MARIA IN AQUIRO

VIA DELLA DATARIA

TAZZA D'ORO

Piazza San Ignazio

VIA DELL'UMILTÀ

VIA SEMINARIO

Piazza del Quirinale

VIA DEL CORSO

SANTA MARIA SOPRA MINERVA

SAN IGNAZIO

MARMO

ELEPHANT STATUE

Piazza Collegio Rom.

GALLERIA DORIA PAMPHILJ

150 Meters

150 Yards

VIA DEL GESÙ

VIA BATTISTI

VIA IV NOVEMBRE

VIA IV NOV.

VIA PLEBISCITO

Piazza Venezia

B

VIA MAG.

To Termini

Piazza del Gesù

GESÙ

Piazza San Marco

VICTOR EMMANUEL MONUMENT

To Capitoline Hill

ARACOELI

S. MARCO

To Colosseum & M

Domitian. (To see the ruins of the original entrance, exit the square at the far—or north—end, then take an immediate left and look down to the left 25 feet below the current street level.) Since ancient times, the square has been a center of Roman life. In the 1800s, the city would flood the square to cool off the neighborhood.

The **Four Rivers Fountain** in the center is the most famous fountain by the man who remade Rome in Baroque style, Gian

Lorenzo Bernini. Four burly river gods (representing the four continents that were known in 1650) support an Egyptian obelisk. The water of the world gushes everywhere. The Nile has his head covered, since the headwaters were unknown then. The Ganges holds an oar. The Danube turns to admire the obelisk, which Bernini had moved here from a stadium on the Appian Way. And Uruguay's Río de la Plata tumbles backward in shock, wondering how he ever made the top four. Bernini enlivens the fountain with horses plunging through the rocks and exotic flora and fauna from these newly discovered lands. Homesick Texans may want to find the armadillo. (It's the big, weird, armor-plated creature behind the Plata river statue.) The Plata river god is gazing upward at the **Church of St. Agnes,** worked on by Bernini's former student-turned-rival, Francesco Borromini. Borromini's concave facade helps reveal the dome and epitomizes the curved symmetry of Baroque. Tour guides say that Bernini designed his river god to look horrified at Borromini's work. Or maybe he's shielding his eyes from St. Agnes' nakedness, as she was stripped before being martyred. But either explanation is unlikely, since the fountain was completed two years before Borromini even started work on the church.

Piazza Navona is Rome's most interesting night scene, with street music, artists, fire-eaters, local Casanovas, ice cream, and outdoor cafés that are worthy of a splurge if you've got time to sit and enjoy Italy's human river.

• *Leave Piazza Navona directly across from Tre Scalini (famous for its rich chocolate ice cream), and go east down Corsia Agonale, past rose peddlers and palm readers. Jog left around the guarded building (the Palazzo Madama, where Italy's senate meets), and follow the brown sign to the Pantheon, which is straight down Via del Salvatore.*

The Pantheon: Sit for a while under the portico of the Pantheon (romantically floodlit and moonlit at night). The 40-foot, single-piece granite columns of the Pantheon's entrance show the scale the ancient Romans built on. The columns support a triangu-

lar Greek-style roof with an inscription that says "M. Agrippa" built it. In fact, it was built *(fecit)* by Emperor Hadrian (A.D. 120), who gave credit to the builder of an earlier structure. This impressive entranceway gives no clue that the greatest wonder of the building is inside—a domed room that inspired later domes, including Michelangelo's St. Peter's and Brunelleschi's Duomo (in Florence).

If it's open, pop into the Pantheon for a look around (interior described on page 900). If you have extra time, consider detouring to several interesting churches near the Pantheon (listed on page 902).

• *With your back to the Pantheon, veer to the right, uphill toward the yellow sign that reads* Casa del Caffè *at the Tazza d'Oro coffee shop on Via Orfani.*

From the Pantheon to the Trevi Fountain: Tazza d'Oro Casa del Caffè, one of Rome's top coffee shops, dates back to the days when this area was licensed to roast coffee beans. Locals come here for a shot of espresso or, when it's hot, a refreshing *granita di caffè con panna* (coffee slush with cream).

• *Continue up Via Orfani to...*

Piazza Capranica is home to the big, plain Florentine Renaissance-style Palazzo Capranica (directly opposite as you enter the square). Big shots, like the Capranica family, built towers on their palaces—not for any military use, but just to show off.

• *Leave the piazza to the right of the palace, heading down Via in Aquiro.*

The street Via in Aquiro leads to a sixth-century B.C. **Egyptian obelisk** taken as a trophy by Augustus after his victory in Egypt over Mark Antony and Cleopatra. The obelisk was set up as a sundial. Follow the zodiac markings to the well-guarded front door. This is Italy's **parliament building,** where the lower house meets; you may see politicians, political demonstrations, and TV cameras.

• *To your right is Piazza Colonna, where we're heading next—unless you like gelato...*

A one-block detour to the left (past Albergo Nazionale) brings you to Rome's most famous *gelateria*. **Giolitti's** is cheap for takeout or elegant and splurge-worthy for a sit among classy locals (open daily until past midnight, Via Uffici del Vicario 40); get your gelato in a cone *(cono)* or cup *(coppetta)*.

Piazza Colonna features a huge second-century column. Its reliefs depict the victories of Emperor Marcus Aurelius over the barbarians. When Marcus died in A.D. 180, the barbarians began to get the upper hand, beginning Rome's long three-century fall. The big, important-looking palace houses the headquarters for the prime minister's cabinet.

Noisy **Via del Corso** is Rome's main north-south boulevard. It's named for the Berber horse races—without riders—that took place here during Carnevale. This wild tradition continued until the late 1800s, when a series of fatal accidents (including, reportedly, one in front of Queen Margherita) led to its cancellation. Historically the street was filled with meat shops. When it became one of Rome's first gas-lit streets in 1854, these butcher shops were banned and replaced by classier boutiques, jewelers, and antique dealers. Nowadays the northern part of Via del Corso is closed to traffic, and for a few hours every evening it becomes a wonderful parade of Romans out for a stroll (see the "Dolce Vita Stroll," earlier).

• *Cross Via del Corso to enter a big palatial building with columns, which houses the Galleria Alberto Sordi shopping mall (with convenient WCs). Inside, take the fork to the right and exit at the back. (If you're here after 22:00, when the mall is closed, circle around the right side of the Galleria on Via dei Sabini.) Once out the back, head up Via de Crociferi, to the roar of the water, lights, and people at the...*

Trevi Fountain: The Trevi Fountain shows how Rome took full advantage of the abundance of water brought into the city by

its great aqueducts. This fountain celebrated the reopening of several of ancient Rome's aqueducts in the Renaissance and Baroque eras. After a thousand years of surviving on poor-quality well water, Romans could once again enjoy pure water brought from the distant hills east of the city. This watery Baroque avalanche

by Nicola Salvi was completed in 1762. Salvi used the palace behind the fountain as a theatrical backdrop for the figure of "Ocean," who represents water in every form. The statue surfs through his wet kingdom—with water gushing from 24 spouts and tumbling over 30 different kinds of plants—while Triton blows his conch shell.

The magic of the square is enhanced by the fact that no streets directly approach it. You can hear the excitement as you draw near, and then—*bam!*—you're there. The scene is always lively, with lucky Romeos clutching dates while unlucky ones clutch beers. Romantics toss a coin over their shoulder, thinking it will give them a wish and assure their return to Rome. That may sound silly, but every year I go through this tourist ritual...and it actually seems to work.

Take some time to people-watch (whisper a few breathy *bellos* or *bellas*) before leaving. There's a peaceful zone at water level on the far right.

• *From the Trevi Fountain, we're 10 minutes from our next stop, the Spanish Steps. Just use a map to get there, or follow these directions: Facing the Trevi Fountain, go forward, walking along the right side of the fountain on Via della Stamperia. Cross busy Via del Tritone. Continue 100 yards and veer right at Via delle Fratte, a street that changes its name to Via Propaganda before ending at the...*

Spanish Steps: Piazza di Spagna, with the very popular Spanish Steps, is named for the Spanish Embassy to the Vatican, which has been here for 300 years. It's been the hangout of many Romantics over the years (Keats, Wagner, Openshaw, Goethe, and others). In the 1700s, British aristocrats on the "Grand Tour" of Europe came here to ponder Rome's decay. The British poet John Keats pondered his mortality, then died of tuberculosis at age 25 in the pink building on the right side of the steps. Fellow Romantic Lord Byron lived across the square at #66.

The wide, curving staircase is one of Rome's iconic sights. Its 138 steps lead sharply up from Piazza di Spagna, forming a butterfly shape as they fan out around a central terrace. The design culminates at the top in an obelisk framed between two Baroque church towers.

The **Sinking Boat Fountain** at the foot of the steps, built by Bernini or his father, Pietro, is powered by an aqueduct. Actually, all of Rome's fountains are aqueduct-powered; their spurts are determined by the water pressure provided by the various aqueducts. This one, for instance, is much weaker than Trevi's gush.

The piazza is a thriving scene at night. Window-shop along Via Condotti, which stretches away from the steps. This is where Gucci and other big names cater to the trendsetting jet set. It's clear that the main sight around here is not the famous steps, but the people who sit on them.

• *Our walk is finished. If you'd like to reach the top of the steps sweat-free, take the free elevator just outside the Spagna Metro stop (to the left, as you face the steps; elevator closes at 21:00). A free WC is underground in the piazza near the Metro entrance, by the middle palm tree (10:00-19:30). The nearby McDonald's (as you face the Spanish Steps, go right one block) is big and lavish, with a salad bar and WC. When you're ready to leave, you can zip home on the Metro (usually open until 23:30, Fri-Sat until 1:30 in the morning), or grab a taxi at either the north or south side of the piazza.*

Sights in Rome

I've clustered Rome's sights into walkable neighborhoods, some quite close together (see "Rome's Neighborhoods" map on page 838). Save transit time by grouping your sightseeing according to location. For example, the Colosseum and the Forum are a few minutes' walk from Capitoline Hill; a 15-minute walk beyond that is the Pantheon. I like to tour these sights in one great day, starting at the Colosseum and ending at the Pantheon.

Ancient Rome

The core of ancient Rome, where the grandest monuments were built, is between the Colosseum and Capitoline Hill. Among the ancient forums, a few modern sights have popped up.

The Colosseum and Nearby
▲▲▲Colosseum (Colosseo)

This 2,000-year-old building is the classic example of Roman en-

gineering. Used as a venue for entertaining the masses, this colossal, functional stadium is one of Europe's most recognizable landmarks. Whether you're playing gladiator or simply marveling at the remarkable ancient design and construction, the Colosseum gets a unanimous thumbs-up.

Built when the Roman Empire was at its peak, in A.D. 80, the Colosseum represents Rome at its grandest. The Flavian Amphitheater (the Colosseum's real name) was an arena for gladiator contests and public spectacles. When killing became a spectator sport, the Romans wanted to share the fun with as many people as possible, so they stuck two semicircular theaters together to create a freestanding amphitheater. The outside (where slender cypress trees stand today) was decorated with a 100-foot-tall bronze statue of Nero that gleamed in the sunlight. In a later age, the colossal structure was nicknamed a "coloss-eum," the wonder of its age. Towering 150 feet high, it could accommodate 50,000 roaring fans (100,000 thumbs). This was where ancient Romans—whose taste for violence was the equal of modern America's—enjoyed their *Dirty Harry*s and *Terminator*s. Gladiators, criminals, and wild animals fought to the death in every conceivable scenario.

The Romans pioneered the use of concrete and the rounded arch, which enabled them to build on this tremendous scale. The exterior is a skeleton of 3.5 million cubic feet of travertine stone. (Each of the pillars flanking the ground-level arches weighs five

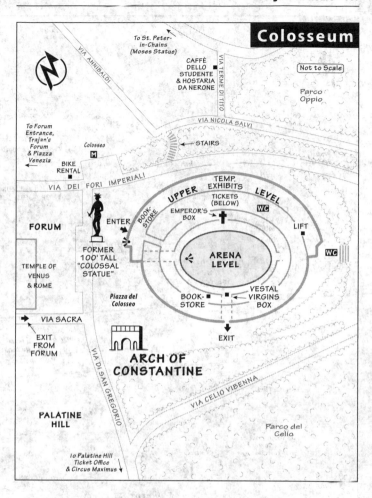

Colosseum

Not to Scale

To St. Peter-in-Chains (Moses Statue)

VIA ANNIBALDI

VIA TERME DI TITO

CAFFÈ DELLO STUDENTE & HOSTARIA DA NERONE

Parco Oppio

VIA NICOLA SALVI

To Forum Entrance, Trajan's Forum & Piazza Venezia

Colosseo M

BIKE RENTAL

← STAIRS

VIA DEI FORI IMPERIALI

UPPER LEVEL

TEMP. EXHIBITS

TICKETS (BELOW)

WC

ENTER

BOOK-STORE

EMPEROR'S BOX

LIFT

FORUM

FORMER 100' TALL "COLOSSAL STATUE"

ARENA LEVEL

WC

TEMPLE OF VENUS & ROME

Piazza del Colosseo

BOOK-STORE

VESTAL VIRGINS BOX

VIA SACRA

EXIT

EXIT FROM FORUM

VIA DI SAN GREGORIO

ARCH OF CONSTANTINE

VIA CELIO VIBENNA

PALATINE HILL

Parco del Celio

To Palatine Hill Ticket Office & Circus Maximus ↓

---

tons.) It took 200 ox-drawn wagons shuttling back and forth every day for four years just to bring the stone here from Tivoli. They stacked stone blocks (without mortar) into the shape of an arch, supported temporarily by wooden scaffolding. Finally, they wedged a keystone into the top of the arch—it not only kept the arch from falling, it could bear even more weight above. Iron pegs held the larger stones together; notice the small holes—the result of medieval peg poachers—that pockmark the sides.

The exterior says a lot about the Romans. They were great engineers, not artists, and the building is more functional than beautiful. (If ancient Romans visited the US today as tourists, they might send home postcards of our greatest works of "art"—freeways.) While the essential structure of the Colosseum is Roman, the four-story facade is decorated with mostly Greek columns—Doric-like

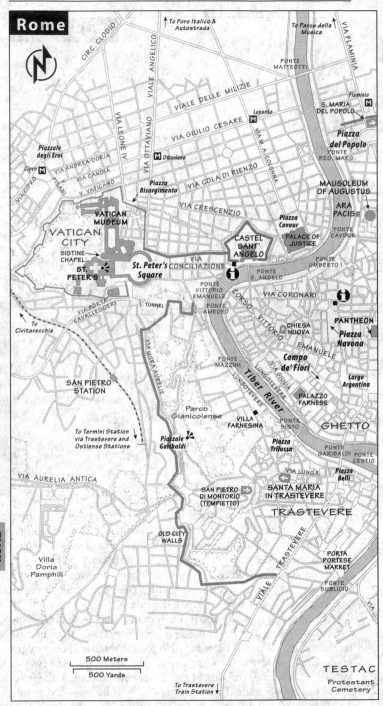

Rome

To Foro Italico &
Autostrada

To Parco della
Musica

VIA FLAMINIA

CIRC. CLODIO

PONTE
MATTEOTTI

VIA ANGELICO

VIALE DELLE MILIZIE

Flaminio

S. MARIA
DEL POPOLO

Piazza
del Popolo

VIA GIULIO CESARE   Lepanto

VIA LEONE IV

VIA OTTAVIANO

VIA M.A. COLONNA

PONTE
REG. MARG.

Piazzale
degli Eroi

VIA ANDREA DORIA

Ottaviano

VIA COLA DI RIENZO

MAUSOLEUM
OF AUGUSTUS

Cipro

VIA GANDIA

Piazza
Risorgimento

ARA
PACIS

V. VATICANO

VIA CIPRO

VIA TRIONFALE

VIA CRESCENZIO

PONTE
CAVOUR

VATICAN
MUSEUM

Piazza
Cavour

PALACE OF
JUSTICE

PONTE
UMBERTO I

VATICAN CITY

CASTEL
SANT'
ANGELO

VIA
CONCILIAZIONE

SISTINE
CHAPEL

ST.
PETER'S

St. Peter's
Square

PONTE
S. ANGELO

VIA CORONARI

VIA PORTA
CAVALLEGGERI

PONTE
VITTORIO
EMANUELE

CORSO VITTORIO

PANTHEON

To
Civitavecchia

TUNNEL

PONTE
AMEDEO

CHIESA
NUOVA

EMANUELE

Piazza
Navona

SAN PIETRO
STATION

VIA GIULIA

Campo
de' Fiori

Largo
Argentina

PONTE
MAZZINI

Tiber River

LUNGOTEVERE

LUNGOTEVERE

PALAZZO
FARNESE

To Termini Station
via Trastevere and
Ostiense Stations

Parco
Gianicolense

VILLA
FARNESINA

PONTE
SISTO

GHETTO

VIA MURA AURELIE

Piazzale
Garibaldi

Piazza
Trilussa

PONTE
GARIBALDI

PONTE
CESTIO

VIA AURELIA ANTICA

VIA LUNGA

Piazza
Belli

SAN PIETRO
DI MONTORIO
(TEMPIETTO)

SANTA MARIA
IN TRASTEVERE

Villa
Doria
Pamphili

OLD CITY
WALLS

TRASTEVERE

VIALE TRASTEVERE

PORTA
PORTESE
MARKET

PONTE
SUBLICIO

500 Meters

500 Yards

TESTAC

Protestant
Cemetery

To Trastevere
Train Station

ROME

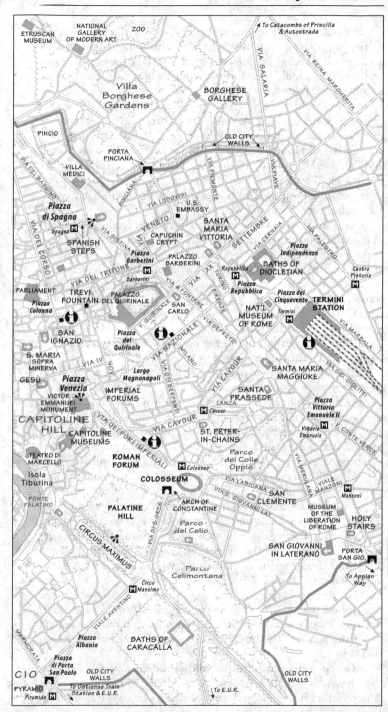

Tuscan columns on the ground level, Ionic on the second story, Corinthian on the next level, and, at the top, half-columns with a mix of all three. Originally, copies of Greek statues stood in the arches of the middle two stories, giving a veneer of sophistication to this arena of death.

Only a third of the original Colosseum remains. Earthquakes destroyed some of it, but most was carted off as easy pre-cut stones for other buildings during the Middle Ages and Renaissance.

Cost and Hours: €12 combo-ticket includes Roman Forum and Palatine Hill (see page 846), open daily 8:30 until one hour before sunset—for specifics, see "Hours" on page 863, last entry one hour before closing, Metro: Colosseo, tel. 06-3996-7700, www.archeoroma.beniculturali.it/en.

Avoiding Lines: Crowds tend to be thinner (and lines shorter) in the afternoon (especially after 15:00 in summer); this is also true at the Forum. You can save lots of time by buying your combo-ticket in advance (www.ticketclic.it) or by having the Roma Pass (see page 846). Buy either of these at the less-crowded Palatine Hill entrance, 150 yards away on Via di San Gregorio (facing the Forum, with Colosseum at your back, go left down the street). You can also buy a Roma Pass at the tobacco shop in the Colosseo Metro station, the I Fori di Roma visitors center on Via dei Fori Imperiali (see page 863), or other sights around town.

It's also possible to bypass the ticket lines by booking a guided tour or renting an audioguide or videoguide (get in the much shorter lines for *Tours* or *Visite Guidate*), or by hiring a private walking-tour guide. For more on these options, see "Tours," later.

Warning: Beware of the **greedy gladiators.** For a fee, the incredibly crude, modern-day gladiators snuff out their cigarettes and pose for photos. They're officially banned from panhandling in this area, but you may still see them, hoping to intimidate easy-to-swindle tourists into paying too much money for a photo op. (If you go for it, €4-5 for one photo usually keeps them appeased.) Also, look out for **pickpockets** and con artists in this prime tourist spot.

Getting There: The Colosseo Metro stop on line B is just across the street from the monument. Buses #53, #85, #87, and #175 stop along the Via dei Fori Imperiali near the entrance, the Colosseum, and Piazza Venezia.

Getting In: If you need to buy a ticket or sign up for a guided tour, follow the signs for the appropriate line. With a combo-ticket or Roma Pass in hand, look for signs for *ticket holders* or *Roma Pass*.

Information: Tel. 06-3996-7700, www.archeoroma.beniculturali.it/en.

Tours: A dry but fact-filled **audioguide** is available just past the turnstiles (€5.50/2 hours). A handheld **videoguide** senses where you are in the site and plays related video clips (€6). Official

guided tours in English depart nearly hourly between 10:00 and 17:00, and last 45-60 minutes (€5 plus Colosseum ticket, purchase inside the Colosseum near the ticket booth marked *Visite Guidate;* if you're lost, ask a guard to direct you to the desk).

A 1.5-hour **"Colosseum, Underground and Third Ring" tour** takes you through restricted areas, including the top floor and underground passageways, which are off-limits to regular Colosseum visitors. While interesting, this tour certainly isn't essential to appreciating the Colosseum. Although it's possible to sign up for the tour at the Colosseum's guided tours window, it's strongly advised you reserve at least a day in advance, either by phone or on-line. The tour is operated by CoopCulture, a private company (€8 plus Colosseum ticket, www.coopculture.it). Call 06-3996-7700 during business hours: Mon-Fri 9:00-18:00, Sat 9:00-14:00 (closed Sun, no same-day reservations). After dialing, wait for English instructions on how to reach a live operator, then reserve a time and pay with a credit card.

Private guides stand outside the Colosseum looking for business (€25-30/2-hour tour of the Colosseum, Forum, and Palatine Hill). If booking a private guide, make sure that your tour will start right away and that the ticket you receive covers all three sights: the Colosseum, Forum, and Palatine Hill.

You can also download a free Rick Steves **audio tour** of the Colosseum to your mobile device; see page 9.

Services: There's a WC (often crowded) inside the Colosseum.

▲Arch of Constantine

If you are a Christian, were raised a Christian, or simply belong to a so-called "Christian nation," ponder this arch. It marks one of the great turning points in history: the military coup that made Christianity mainstream. In A.D. 312, Emperor Constantine defeated his rival Maxentius in the crucial Battle of the Milvian Bridge. The night before, he had seen a vision of a cross in the sky. Constantine—whose mother and sister had already become Christians—became sole emperor and legalized Christianity. With this one battle, a once-obscure Jewish sect with a handful of followers became the state religion of the entire Western world. In A.D. 300, you could be killed for being a Christian; a century later, you could be killed for *not* being one. Church enrollment boomed.

The restored arch is like an ancient museum. It's decorated entirely with recycled carvings originally made for other buildings. By covering it with exquisite carvings of high Roman art—works

ROME

Rome at a Glance

▲▲▲**Colosseum** Huge stadium where gladiators fought. **Hours:** Daily 8:30 until one hour before sunset: April-Aug until 19:15, Sept until 19:00, Oct until 18:30, off-season closes as early as 16:30. See page 882.

▲▲▲**Roman Forum** Ancient Rome's main square, with ruins and grand arches. **Hours:** Same hours as Colosseum. See page 890.

▲▲▲**Pantheon** The defining domed temple. **Hours:** Mon-Sat 8:30-19:30, Sun 9:00-18:00, holidays 9:00-13:00, closed for Mass Sat at 17:00 and Sun at 10:30. See page 900.

▲▲▲**St. Peter's Basilica** Most impressive church on earth, with Michelangelo's *Pietà* and dome. **Hours:** Church—daily April-Sept 7:00-19:00, Oct-March 7:00-18:00, often closed Wed mornings; dome—daily April-Sept 8:00-18:00, Oct-March 8:00-16:45. See page 903.

▲▲▲**Vatican Museum** Four miles of the finest art of Western civilization, culminating in Michelangelo's glorious Sistine Chapel. **Hours:** Mon-Sat 9:00-18:00. Closed on religious holidays and Sun, except last Sun of the month (open 9:00-14:00). May be open some Fri nights by online reservation only. Hours are subject to change. See page 910.

▲▲▲**Borghese Gallery** Bernini sculptures and paintings by Caravaggio, Raphael, and Titian in a Baroque palazzo. Reservations mandatory. **Hours:** Tue-Sun 9:00-19:00, closed Mon. See page 920.

▲▲▲**National Museum of Rome** Greatest collection of Roman sculpture anywhere. **Hours:** Tue-Sun 9:00-19:45, closed Mon. See page 928.

▲▲▲**Capitoline Museums** Ancient statues, mosaics, and expansive view of Forum. **Hours:** Tue-Sun 9:00-20:00, closed Mon. See page 896.

▲▲**Palatine Hill** Ruins of emperors' palaces, Circus Maximus view, and museum. **Hours:** Same hours as Colosseum. See page 891.

▲▲**Museo dell'Ara Pacis** Shrine marking the beginning of Rome's Golden Age. **Hours:** Tue-Sun 9:00-19:00, closed Mon. See page 927.

▲▲**Dolce Vita Stroll** Evening passeggiata, where Romans strut their stuff. **Hours:** Roughly Mon-Sat 17:00-19:00 and Sun afternoons. See page 872.

▲▲**Catacombs** Underground tombs, mainly Christian, some outside the city. **Hours:** Generally open 10:00-12:00 & 14:00-17:00 See pages 925 and 950.

▲**Arch of Constantine** Honors the emperor who legalized Christianity. **Hours:** Always viewable. See page 887.

▲**St. Peter-in-Chains** Church with Michelangelo's Moses. **Hours:** Daily 8:00-12:30 & 15:00-19:00, until 18:00 in winter. See page 890.

▲▲**Trajan's Column, Market, and Forum** Tall column with narrative relief, forum ruins, and museum with entry to Trajan's Market. **Hours:** Forum and column always viewable; museum open Tue-Sun 9:00-19:00, closed Mon. See page 893.

▲**Piazza del Campidoglio** Square atop Capitoline Hill, designed by Michelangelo, with a museum, grand stairway, and Forum overlooks. **Hours:** Always open. See page 895.

▲**Victor Emmanuel Monument** Gigantic edifice celebrating Italian unity, with Rome from the Sky elevator ride up to 360-degree city view. **Hours:** Monument open daily 9:30-18:30; elevator open Mon-Thu 9:30-18:30, Fri-Sun 9:30-19:30. See page 899.

▲**Trevi Fountain** Baroque hot spot into which tourists throw coins to ensure a return trip to Rome. **Hours:** Always flowing. See page 903.

▲**Castel Sant'Angelo** Hadrian's Tomb turned castle, prison, papal refuge, now museum. **Hours:** Tue-Sun 9:00-19:30, closed Mon. See page 918.

▲**Baths of Diocletian** Once ancient Rome's immense public baths, now a Michelangelo church. **Hours:** Mon-Sat 7:00-18:30, Sun 7:00-19:30, closed to sightseers during Mass. See page 930.

▲**Santa Maria della Vittoria** Church with Bernini's swooning *St. Teresa in Ecstasy*. **Hours:** Mon-Sat 8:30-12:00 & 15:30-18:00, Sun 15:30-18:00. See page 931.

▲**Capuchin Crypt** Decorated with the bones of 4,000 Franciscan friars. **Hours:** Daily 9:00-19:00. See page 923.

ROME

that glorified previous emperors—Constantine put himself in their league. Hadrian is featured in the round reliefs, with Marcus Aurelius in the square reliefs higher up. The big statues on top are of Trajan and Augustus. Originally, Augustus drove a chariot similar to the one topping the modern Victor Emmanuel II Monument. Fourth-century Rome may have been in decline, but Constantine clung to its glorious past.

▲St. Peter-in-Chains Church (San Pietro in Vincoli)

Built in the fifth century to house the chains that held St. Peter, this church is most famous for its Michelangelo statue of Moses, intended for the tomb of Pope Julius II. Although the artist worked on the tomb in fits and starts for over 40 years, it was never completed. Check out the much-venerated chains under the high altar, then focus on mighty Moses. (Note that this isn't the famous St. Peter's Basilica, which is at Vatican City.)

Pope Julius II commissioned Michelangelo to build a massive tomb, with 48 huge statues, topped with a grand statue of this egomaniacal pope. The pope had planned to have his tomb placed in the center of St. Peter's Basilica. When Julius died, the work had barely been started, and no one had the money or necessary commitment to Julius to finish the project.

In 1542, some of the remnants of the tomb project were brought to St. Peter-in-Chains and pieced together by Michelangelo's assistants. Some of the best statues ended up elsewhere, such as the *Prisoners* in Florence and the *Slaves* in the Louvre. *Moses* and the Louvre's *Slaves* are the only statues Michelangelo personally completed for the project. Flanking *Moses* are the Old Testament sister-wives of Jacob, Leah (to our right) and Rachel, both begun by Michelangelo but probably finished by pupils.

The powerful statue of Moses—mature Michelangelo—is worth studying. Moses has received the Ten Commandments. As he holds the stone tablets, his eyes show a man determined to stop his tribe from worshipping the golden calf and idols...a man determined to win salvation for the people of Israel. Why the horns? Centuries ago, the Hebrew word for "rays" was mistranslated as "horns."

Cost and Hours: Free, daily April-Sept 8:00-12:30 & 15:00-19:00, Oct-March 8:00-12:30 & 15:00-18:00, modest dress required; the church is a 10-minute uphill walk from the Colosseum, or a shorter, simpler walk from the Cavour Metro stop.

The Roman Forum and Nearby

▲▲▲Roman Forum (Foro Romano)

This is ancient Rome's birthplace and civic center, and the common ground between Rome's famous seven hills. As just about anything important that happened in ancient Rome happened here, it's arguably the most important piece of real estate in Western civilization.

ROME

While only a few fragments of that glorious past remain, history seekers find plenty to ignite their imaginations amid the half-broken columns and arches.

Cost and Hours: €12 combo-ticket includes Colosseum and Palatine Hill (see page 846), open daily 8:30 until one hour before sunset—for specifics, see "Hours" on page 863, last entry one hour before closing, audioguide-€5, Metro: Colosseo, tel. 06-3996-7700, www.archeoroma.beniculturali.it/en.

Visiting the Forum: See my self-guided walk on page 861.

▲▲Palatine Hill (Monte Palatino)

The hill overlooking the Forum is jam-packed with history—"the huts of Romulus," the huge Imperial Palace, a view of the Circus Maximus—but there's only the barest skeleton of rubble left to tell the story.

We get our word "palace" from this hill, where the emperors chose to live. It was once so filled with palaces that later emperors had to build out. (Looking up at it from the Forum, you see the substructure that supported these long-gone palaces.) The Palatine museum contains statues and frescoes that help you imagine the luxury of the imperial Palatine. From the pleasant garden, you'll get an overview of the Forum. On the far side, look down into an emperor's private stadium and then beyond at the grassy Circus Maximus, once a chariot course. Imagine the cheers, jeers, and furious betting.

While many tourists consider Palatine Hill just extra credit after the Forum, it offers an insight into the greatness of Rome that's well worth the effort. (And, if you're visiting the Colosseum or Forum, you've got a ticket whether you like it or not.)

Cost and Hours: €12 combo-ticket includes Roman Forum and Colosseum—see page 846, open same hours as Forum and Colosseum, audioguide-€5, guided tours may be available—ask, Metro: Colosseo, tel. 06-3996-7700, www.archeoroma.beniculturali.it/en.

Getting In: The main entrance is on Via di San Gregorio (facing the Forum with the Colosseum at your back, it's down the street to your left). You can also enter Palatine from within the Roman Forum—just climb the hill from the Arch of Titus.

Services: WCs are at the ticket office when you enter, up the

ROME

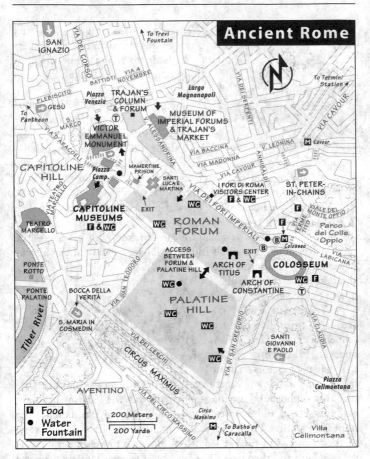

Ancient Rome

F Food
● Water Fountain

200 Meters
200 Yards

hill near the stadium, at the museum in the center of the site, and hiding among the orange trees in the Farnese Gardens.

Mamertine Prison

This 2,500-year-old cistern-like prison is where, according to Christian tradition, the Romans imprisoned Saints Peter and Paul. Though it was long a charming and historic sight, its artifacts have been removed, and today it's run by a commercial tour-bus company charging €5 for a cheesy "multimedia" walk-through. Don't go in. Instead, stand outside and imagine how this dank cistern once housed prisoners of the emperor. Amid fat rats and rotting corpses, unfortunate humans awaited slow deaths. It's said that a miraculous fountain sprang up inside so Peter could convert and baptize his jailers, who were also subsequently martyred.

Bocca della Verità

The legendary "Mouth of Truth" at the Church of Santa Maria in Cosmedin draws a playful crowd. Stick your hand in the mouth of

the gaping stone face in the porch wall. As the legend goes (and was popularized by the 1953 film *Roman Holiday*, starring Gregory Peck and Audrey Hepburn), if you're a liar, your hand will be gobbled up. The mouth is only accessible when the church gate is open, but it's always (partially) visible through the gate, even when closed. If the church itself is open, step inside to see one of the few unaltered medieval church interiors in Rome. Notice the mismatched ancient columns and beautiful cosmatesque floor—a centuries-old example of recycling.

Cost and Hours: €0.50 suggested donation, daily 9:30-17:50, closes earlier off-season, Piazza Bocca della Verità, near the north end of Circus Maximus, tel. 06-678-7759.

Imperial Forums

As Rome grew from a village to an empire, it outgrew the Roman Forum. Several energetic emperors built their own forums—which stood in a line from the Colosseum to Trajan's Column—complete with temples, shopping malls, government buildings, statues, monuments, and piazzas. While the Roman Forum (which gets all the touristic focus) was built with no grand plan over 1,200 years, these new imperial forums were distinct modules, with a cohesive plan stamped with the emperor's unique personality. Julius Caesar built the first one (46 B.C.), and over the next 150 years, it was added onto by Augustus (2 B.C.), Vespasian (A.D. 75), Nerva (A.D. 97), and Trajan (A.D. 112). What you see today are mostly the remains of Trajan's great building campaign.

Visiting the Ruins: The ruins are always visible and free to look at from viewpoints at Piazza Venezia, along Via dei Fori Imperiali, and at Via IV Novembre. Trajan's Forum, with its impressive column and market, is the main sight to see. To view other (heavily ruined) forums, stroll down Via dei Fori Imperiali. Visiting here is especially nice, because the once-busy street is now closed to private car traffic. If you want a close-up look at some excavated statues and more information about the forums, you can pay admission to the Museum of the Imperial Forums (see listing later). If not paying to go in, the best original ancient street is perfectly viewable from Via IV Novembre.

▲▲Trajan's Column, Market, and Forum

Rome peaked under Emperor Trajan (ruled A.D. 98-117), when the empire stretched from England to the Sahara, from Spain to the Fertile Crescent. A triumphant Trajan returned to Rome with his booty and shook it all over the city. He extended the Forum by

ROME

building his own commercial, political, and religious center near-by, complete with temples, law courts, and a semicircular shopping mall.

Trajan's Column, rising 140 feet, is the world's grandest column from antiquity. Decorated with a spiral relief of 2,500 figures trumpeting the emperor's exploits, it has stood for centuries as a symbol of a truly cosmopolitan civilization. At one point, the ashes of Trajan and his wife were held in the base, and the sun glinted off a polished bronze statue of Trajan at the top. (Today, St. Peter is on top.)

Nestled into the cutaway curve of Quirinal Hill, **Trajan's Market** was likely part shopping mall, part warehouse, and part administration building and/or government offices. For now the conventional wisdom holds that at ground level, the 13 tall (shallow) arches housed shops selling fresh fruit, vegetables, and flowers to people who passed by on the street. The 26 arched windows (above) lit a covered walkway lined with shops that sold wine and olive oil. On the roof (now lined with a metal railing) ran a street that likely held still more shops, making about 150 in all. Shoppers could browse through goods from every corner of Rome's vast empire—exotic

fruits from Africa, spices from Asia, and fish-and-chips from Londinium.

The extensive remains of **Trajan's Forum** (on the northeast side of Via dei Fori Imperiali) start at Trajan's Column and run about 120 yards southeast toward the Colosseum. It's mostly rubble today, except for Trajan's Market, rising up the flank of Quirinal Hill.

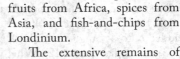

Museum of the Imperial Forums (Museo dei Fori Imperiali)
The museum, housed in buildings from Trajan's Market, features discoveries from the forums built by the different emperors. Though its collection of statues is not impressive compared to Rome's other museums, it's well displayed, and it's your only chance to get up close to Trajan's Market and Forum. Focus on the big picture to mentally resurrect the fabulous forums.

Cost and Hours: €9.50, Tue-Sun 9:00-19:00, closed Mon, last entry one hour before closing, tel. 06-0608, www.mercatiditraiano.it. Skip the museum's slow, dry €4 audioguide (you'll find some English descriptions within the museum); enter at Via IV Novembre 94 (up the staircase from Trajan's Column).

Capitoline Hill

Of Rome's famous seven hills, this is the smallest, tallest, and most famous—home of the ancient Temple of Jupiter and the center of city government for 2,500 years. There are several ways to get to the top of Capitoline Hill. If you're coming from the north (from Piazza Venezia), take Michelangelo's impressive stairway to the right of the big, white Victor Emmanuel Monument. Coming from the southeast (the Forum), take the steep staircase near the Arch of Septimius Severus. From near Trajan's Forum along Via dei Fori Imperiali, take the winding road. All three converge at the top, in the square called Campidoglio (kahm-pee-DOHL-yoh).

▲Piazza del Campidoglio

This square atop the hill, once the religious and political center of ancient Rome, is still the home of the city's government. In the 1530s, the pope called on Michelangelo to re-establish this square as a grand center. Michelangelo placed the ancient equestrian statue of Marcus Aurelius as its focal point. Effective. (The original statue is now in the adjacent museum.) The twin buildings on either side are the Capitoline Museums. Behind the replica of the statue is the mayoral palace (Palazzo Senatorio).

Michelangelo intended that people approach the square from his grand stairway off Piazza Venezia. From the top of the stairway, you see the new Renaissance face of Rome, with its back to the Forum. Michelangelo gave the buildings the "giant order"—huge pilasters make the existing two-story buildings feel one-storied and more harmonious with the new square. Notice how the statues atop these buildings welcome you and then draw you in.

The terraces just downhill (past either side of the mayor's palace) offer grand views of the Forum. To the left of the mayor's palace is a copy of the famous she-wolf statue on a column. Farther down is *il nasone* ("the big nose"), a refreshing water fountain (see photo). Block the spout with your fingers, and water spurts up for drinking. Romans joke that a cheap Roman boy takes his date out for a drink at *il*

Capitoline Hill & Piazza Venezia

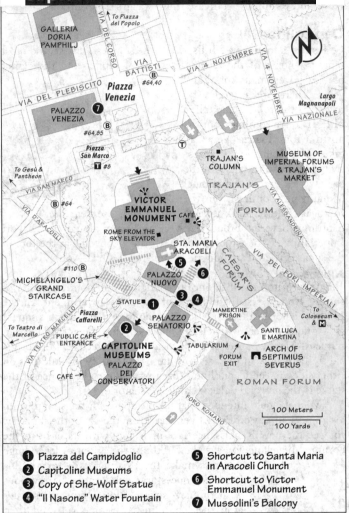

1. Piazza del Campidoglio
2. Capitoline Museums
3. Copy of She-Wolf Statue
4. "Il Nasone" Water Fountain
5. Shortcut to Santa Maria in Aracoeli Church
6. Shortcut to Victor Emmanuel Monument
7. Mussolini's Balcony

nasone. Near the she-wolf statue is the staircase leading to a short-cut to the Victor Emmanuel Monument (see sidebar).

▲▲▲Capitoline Museums (Musei Capitolini)

Some of ancient Rome's most famous statues and art are housed in the two palaces (Palazzo dei Conservatori and Palazzo Nuovo) that flank the equestrian statue in the Campidoglio. They're connected by an underground passage that leads to the Tabularium, an ancient building with panoramic views of the Roman Forum.

Cost and Hours: €12, Tue-Sun 9:00-20:00, closed Mon, last

Shortcut to the Victor Emmanuel Monument and Aracoeli Church

A clever shortcut lets you go directly from Piazza del Campidoglio, the square atop Capitoline Hill, to Santa Maria in Aracoeli Church and an upper level of the Victor Emmanuel Monument, avoiding long flights of stairs. Facing the square's equestrian statue, head to the left, climbing the wide set of stairs near the she-wolf statue. Midway up the stairs (at the column), turn left to reach the back entrance to the Aracoeli Church. To reach the Victor Emmanuel Monument, pass the column and continue to the top of the steps, pass through the iron gate, and enter the small unmarked door at #13 on the right. You'll soon emerge on a café terrace that leads to the monument and the Rome from the Sky elevator.

entry one hour before closing, audioguide-€5, tel. 06-8205-9127, www.muscicapitolini.org.

Visiting the Museums: Enter at the Palazzo dei Conservatori, which is on your right as you face the equestrian statue (you'll exit from the Palazzo Nuovo, on your left).

With lavish rooms and several great statues, the worthwhile **Palazzo dei Conservatori** claims to be one of the world's oldest museums, founded in 1471 when a pope gave ancient statues to the citizens of Rome. Many of the museum's statues have gone on to become instantly recognizable cultural icons, including the 13th-century *Capitoline She-Wolf* (the little statues of Romulus and Remus were added in the Renaissance). Don't miss the *Boy Extracting a Thorn* and the enchanting *Commodus as Hercules*. Behind Commodus is a statue of his dad, Marcus Aurelius, on a horse. The greatest surviving equestrian statue of antiquity, this was the original centerpiece of the square (where a copy stands today). Christians in the Dark Ages thought that the statue's hand was raised in blessing, which probably led to their misidentifying him as Constantine, the first Christian emperor. While most pagan statues were destroyed by Christians, "Constantine" was spared.

The museum's second-floor café, **Caffè Capitolino**, has a splendid patio offering city views. It's lovely at sunset (public entrance for non-museum-goers off Piazza Caffarelli and through door #4).

The **Tabularium,** built in the first century B.C., once held the archives of ancient Rome. (The word "Tabularium" comes from "tablet," on which Romans wrote their laws.) You won't see any tablets, but you will see a stunning head-on view of the Forum from the windows. The **Palazzo Nuovo** houses mostly portrait busts of forgotten emperors. But it also has two must-see statues: the *Dying Gaul* and the *Capitoline Venus* (both on the first floor up).

Santa Maria in Aracoeli Church

The church atop Capitoline Hill is old and dear to the hearts of Romans. It stands on the site where Emperor Augustus (supposedly) had a premonition of the coming of Mary and Christ standing on an "altar in the sky" *(ara coeli)*. The church is Rome in a nutshell, where you can time-travel across 2,000 years by standing in one spot.

Cost and Hours: Free, daily April-Oct 9:00-12:30 & 15:00-18:30, Nov-March 9:00-12:30 & 14:30-17:30, tel. 06-6976-3839.

Piazza Venezia

This vast square, dominated by the big, white Victor Emmanuel Monument, is a major transportation hub and the focal point of modern Rome.

With your back to the monument (you'll get the best views from the terrace by the guards and eternal flame), look down Via del Corso, the city's axis, surrounded by Rome's classiest shopping district. In the 1930s, Benito Mussolini whipped up Italy's nationalistic fervor from a balcony above the square (it's the less-grand balcony on the left). Fascist masses filled the square screaming, "Four more years!"—or something like that. Mussolini created the boulevard Via dei Fori Imperiali (to your right, capped by Trajan's Column) to open up views of the Colosseum in the distance. Mussolini lied to his people, mixing fear and patriotism to push his country to the right and embroil the Italians in expensive and regrettable wars. In 1945, they shot Mussolini and hung him from a meat hook in Milan.

With your back still to the monument, circle around the left side. At the back end of the monument, look down into the ditch on your left to see the ruins of an ancient apartment building from the first century A.D.; part of it was transformed into a tiny church (faded frescoes and bell tower). Rome was built in layers—almost everywhere you go, there's an earlier version beneath your feet. (The hop-on, hop-off 110open Bus stops just downhill from here.)

Continuing on, you reach two staircases leading up Capitoline Hill. One is Michelangelo's grand staircase up to the Campidoglio. The steeper of the two leads to Santa Maria in Aracoeli, a good example of the earliest style of Christian church (described earlier). The contrast between this climb-on-your-knees ramp to God's house and Michelangelo's elegant stairs illustrates the changes Renaissance humanism brought civilization.

ROME

From the bottom of Michelangelo's stairs, look right several blocks down the street to see a condominium actually built upon the surviving ancient pillars and arches of Teatro di Marcello.

▲Victor Emmanuel Monument

This oversize monument to Italy's first king, built to celebrate the 50th anniversary of the country's unification in 1861, was part of Italy's push to overcome the new country's strong regionalism and create a national identity.
The scale of the monument is over-the-top: 200 feet high, 500 feet wide. The 43-foot-long statue of the king on the horse is one of the biggest equestrian statues in the world. The king's

moustache forms an arc five feet long, and a person could sit within the horse's hoof. At the base of this statue, Italy's Tomb of the Unknown Soldier (flanked by Italian flags and armed guards) is watched over by the goddess Roma (with the gold mosaic background).

Cost and Hours: Monument—Free, daily 9:30-18:30, a few WCs scattered throughout, tel. 06-679-3598. Elevator—€7, Mon-Thu 9:30-18:30, Fri-Sun 9:30-19:30, ticket office closes 45 minutes earlier, WC at entrance, tel. 06-6920-2049; follow *ascensori panoramici* signs inside the Victor Emmanuel Monument or take the shortcut from Capitoline Hill (no elevator access from street level).

Background: With its gleaming white sheen (from a recent scrubbing) and enormous scale, the monument provides a vivid sense of what Ancient Rome looked like at its peak—imagine the Forum filled with shiny, grandiose buildings like this one. It's also lathered in symbolism meant to connect the modern city and nation with its grand past: The eternal flames are reminiscent of the Vestal Virgins and the ancient flame of Rome. And it's crowned by glorious chariots like those that topped the ancient Arch of Constantine.

Locals have a love/hate relationship with this "Altar of the Nation." Many Romans say it's a "punch in the eye" and regret its unfortunate, clumsy location atop precious antiquities. Others consider it a reminder of the challenge that followed the creation of the modern nation of Italy: actually creating "Italians."

Visiting the Monument: To see the "Vittoriano" (as locals call it) up close, simply climb the front stairs, or go inside from one of several entrances: midway up the monument through doorways flanking the central statue, on either side at street level, and at the base of the colonnade (two-thirds of the way up, near the shortcut from Capitoline Hill). The little-visited **Museum of the Risorgimento** fills several floors with displays (well-described in English) on the movement and war that led to the unification of Italy in 1870.

ROME

A section on the lower east side hosts temporary exhibits of minor works by major artists (free to enter museum, exhibits around €10, tel. 06-322-5380, www.comunicareorganizzando.it). A café is at the base of the top colonnade, on the monument's east side.

Best of all, the monument offers a grand view of the Eternal City. You can climb the stairs to the midway point for a decent view, keep climbing to the base of the colonnade for a better view,

or, for the best view, ride the **Rome from the Sky** (Roma dal Cielo) elevator, which zips you from the top of the stair climb (at the back of the monument) to the rooftop for the grandest, 360-degree view of the center of Rome—even better than from the top of St. Peter's dome. Once on top, you stand on a terrace between the monument's two chariots. You can look north up Via del Corso to Piazza del Popolo, west to the dome of St. Peter's Basilica, and south to the Roman Forum and Colosseum. Helpful panoramic diagrams describe the skyline, with powerful binoculars available for zooming in on particular sights. It's best in late afternoon, when it's beginning to cool off and Rome glows.

Pantheon Neighborhood

Besides being home to ancient sights and historic churches, this neighborhood gives Rome its urban-village feel. Wander narrow streets, sample the many shops and eateries, and gather with the locals in squares marked by bubbling fountains. Exploring is especially good in the evening, when the restaurants bustle and streets are jammed with foot traffic. For a self-guided walk of this neighborhood, from Campo de' Fiori to the Trevi Fountain, see my "Heart of Rome Walk" on page 874.

Getting There: The Pantheon neighborhood is a 15-minute walk from Capitoline Hill. Taxis and buses stop at a chaotic square called Largo Argentina, a few blocks south of the Pantheon—from here you can walk north on either Via dei Cestari or Via di Torre Argentina to the Pantheon. Buses #40 and #64 carry tourists and pickpockets frequently between the Termini train station and Vatican City (#492 serves the same areas via a different route). Bus #87 connects to the Colosseum. The elettrico minibus #116 runs between Campo de' Fiori and Piazza Barberini via the Pantheon.

▲▲▲Pantheon

For the greatest look at the splendor of Rome, antiquity's best-preserved interior is a must. Built two millennia ago, this influential

ROME

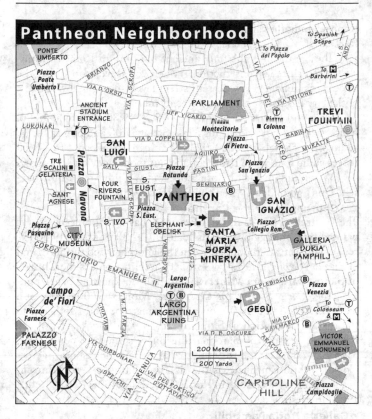

Pantheon Neighborhood

domed temple served as the model for Michelangelo's dome of St. Peter's and many others.

Because the Pantheon became a church dedicated to the martyrs just after the fall of Rome, the barbarians left it alone, and the locals didn't use it as a quarry. The portico is called "Rome's umbrella"—a fun local gathering in a rainstorm. Walk past its one-piece granite columns (biggest in Italy, shipped from Egypt) and through the original bronze doors. Sit inside under the glorious skylight and enjoy classical architecture at its best.

The dome, 142 feet high and wide, was Europe's biggest until the Renaissance. Michelangelo's dome at St. Peter's, while much higher, is about three feet narrower. The brilliance of this dome's construction astounded architects through the ages. During the Renaissance, Brunelleschi was given permission to cut into the dome (see the little square hole above and to the right of the entrance) to analyze the material. The concrete dome gets thinner and lighter with height—the highest part is volcanic pumice.

This wonderfully harmonious architecture greatly inspired

ROME

Raphael and other artists of the Renaissance. Raphael, along with Italy's first two kings, chose to be buried here.

The Pantheon is the only ancient building in Rome continuously used since its construction. When you leave, notice that the building is sunken below current street level, showing how the rest of the city has risen on 20 centuries of rubble.

Cost and Hours: Free, Mon-Sat 8:30-19:30, Sun 9:00-18:00, holidays 9:00-13:00, closed for Mass Sat at 17:00 and Sun at 10:30, audioguide-€5, tel. 06-6830-0230. You can download a free Rick Steves audio tour of the Pantheon to your mobile device; see page 9.

When to Go: Visit before 9:00, and you'll have it all to yourself. Don't go midday, when the Pantheon is packed.

▲▲Churches near the Pantheon

The **Church of San Luigi dei Francesi** has a magnificent chapel painted by Caravaggio (free, daily 10:00-12:30 & 15:00-19:00 except closed Thu afternoon, between the Pantheon and the north end of Piazza Navona). The only Gothic church in Rome is the **Church of Santa Maria sopra Minerva,** with a little-known Michelangelo statue, *Christ Bearing the Cross* (free, Mon-Sat 7:00-19:00, Sun 8:00-12:00 & 14:00-19:00, on a little square behind Pantheon, to the east). The **Church of San Ignazio,** several blocks east of the Pantheon, is a riot of Baroque illusions with a false dome (free, Mon-Sat 7:30-19:00, Sun 9:00-19:00). A few blocks away, across Corso Vittorio Emanuele, is the rich and Baroque **Gesù Church,** headquarters of the Jesuits in Rome (free, daily 7:00-12:30 & 16:00-19:45, interesting daily service at 17:30).

▲Galleria Doria Pamphilj

This underappreciated gallery, in the heart of the old city, offers a rare chance to wander through a noble family's lavish rooms with the prince who calls this downtown mansion home. Well, almost. Through an audioguide, the prince lovingly narrates his family's story as you tour the palace and its world-class art. Don't miss Velázquez's intense, majestic, ultra-realistic portrait of Pope Innocent X (1574-1655), patriarch of the Pamphilj (pahm-FEEL-yee) family. It stands alongside an equally impressive bust of the pope by Bernini. Stroll through a mini-Versailles-like hall of mirrors to more paintings, including works by Titian and Raphael. Finally, relax along with Mary, Joseph, and Jesus, and let the angel serenade you in Caravaggio's *Rest on the Flight to Egypt.*

Cost and Hours: €11, includes worthwhile 1.5-hour audioguide, daily 9:00-19:00, last entry one hour before closing, elegant café, from Piazza Venezia walk 2 blocks up Via del Corso to #305, tel. 06-679-7323, www.dopart.it/roma.

Piazza di Pietra (Piazza of Stone)

The square was actually a quarry set up to chew away at the abandoned Temple of Hadrian, dedicated to the emperor responsible for building the Pantheon (look for his bust and a model of the temple in a window on the square). You can still see the holes that hungry medieval scavengers chipped into the columns to steal the metal pins that held the slabs together. Look over the railing to see ground level 1,900 years ago. (The piazza is two blocks toward Via del Corso from the Pantheon.)

▲Trevi Fountain

The bubbly Baroque fountain, worth ▲▲ by night, is a minor sight to art scholars...but a major nighttime gathering spot for teens on the make and tourists tossing coins. Those coins are collected daily to feed Rome's poor (for more on the fountain, see page 880).

Vatican City

Vatican City, the world's smallest country, contains St. Peter's Basilica (with Michelangelo's exquisite *Pietà*) and the Vatican Museum

(with Michelangelo's Sistine Chapel). A helpful **TI** is just to the left of St. Peter's Basilica as you're facing it (Mon-Sat 8:30-18:15, closed Sun, tel. 06-6988-1662, Vatican switchboard tel. 06-6982, www.vatican.va). The entrances to St. Peter's and to the Vatican Museum are a 15-minute walk apart (follow the outside of the Vatican wall, which links the two sights). The nearest Metro stop—Ottaviano—still involves a 10-minute walk to either sight.

Modest dress is required of men, women, and children throughout Vatican City, even outdoors. Otherwise, the Swiss Guard can turn you away. Cover your shoulders; bring a light jacket or cover-up if you're wearing a tank top. Wear long pants instead of shorts. Skirts or dresses should extend below your knee.

▲▲▲St. Peter's Basilica (Basilica San Pietro)

There is no doubt: This is the richest and grandest church on earth. To call it vast is like calling Einstein smart. Plaques on the floor show you where other, smaller churches would end if they were placed inside. The ornamental cherubs would dwarf a large man. Birds roost inside, and thousands of people wander about, heads craned heavenward, hardly noticing each other. Don't miss Michelangelo's *Pietà* (behind bulletproof glass) to the right of the entrance. Bernini's altar work and twisting, towering canopy are brilliant.

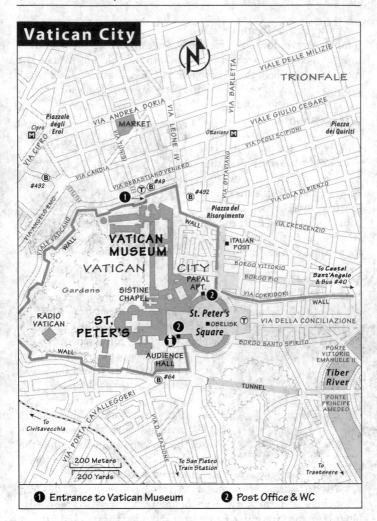

Vatican City

TRIONFALE

VIALE DELLE MILIZIE

VIA BARLETTA

VIALE GIULIO CESARE

Piazzale degli Eroi

Cipro M

VIA ANDREA DORIA

MARKET

VIA TUNISI

VIA LEONE IV

Ottaviano M

VIA DEGLI SCIPIONI

Piazza dei Quiriti

VIA CIPRO

VIA CANDIA

VIA OTTAVIANO

VIA COLA DI RIENZO

#492 B

VIA SEBASTIANO VENIERO

❶ T B #49

B #492

Piazza del Risorgimento

VIA CRESCENZIO

VIA ANGELO EMO

WALL

WALL

ITALIAN POST

VATICAN MUSEUM

VATICAN   CITY

BORGO VITTORIO

To Castel Sant'Angelo & Bus #40

VIALE VATICANO

PAPAL APT.

BORGO PIO

VIA CORRIDORI

WALL

Gardens

SISTINE CHAPEL

❷

RADIO VATICAN

ST. PETER'S

❷

St. Peter's Square

OBELISK T

VIA DELLA CONCILIAZIONE

BORGO SANTO SPIRITO

PONTE VITTORIO EMANUELE II

WALL

❶

AUDIENCE HALL

Tiber River

B #64

TUNNEL

PONTE PRINCIPE AMEDEO

VIA DI PORTA CAVALLEGGERI

To Civitavecchia

VIA D. STAZIONE

200 Meters

200 Yards

To San Pietro Train Station

To Trastevere

❶ Entrance to Vatican Museum   ❷ Post Office & WC

Cost: Free entry to basilica and crypt. Dome climb-€5 if you take the stairs all the way up, or €7 to ride an elevator partway (to the roof), then climb to the top of the dome (for details, see "Dome Climb," later). Treasury Museum-€7 (cash only).

Hours: Church—daily April-Sept 7:00-19:00, Oct-March 7:00-18:00, closed Wed mornings during papal audiences; dome *(cupola)*—daily April-Sept 8:00-18:00, Oct-March 8:00-16:45 (last entry 30 minutes before closing); treasury museum—daily April-Sept 9:00-18:15, Oct-March 9:00-17:15; crypt *(grotte)*—daily April-Sept 7:00-18:00, Oct-March 7:00-17:00.

Avoiding Lines: The security-checkpoint lines can get quite long and there's no sure-fire way to avoid them. Note that the checkpoint can switch locations; it's typically on the north side of the square, but can be closer to the church or tucked under the south colonnade. Occasionally, St. Peter's is accessible directly from the Sistine Chapel inside the Vatican Museum—a great time-saving trick, but unfortunately not a reliable one (for details, see page 910). Avoid the worst crowds by visiting before 10:00 or after 16:00. After around 16:00, the area around the altar is often roped off to prepare for Mass. (For a Mass schedule, see "Church Services," below.)

Dress Code: No shorts, above-the-knee skirts, or bare shoulders (this applies to men, women, and children). Attendants strictly enforce this dress code, even in hot weather.

Getting There: Take the Metro to Ottaviano, then walk 10 minutes south on Via Ottaviano. The #40 express bus drops off at Piazza Pio, next to Castel Sant'Angelo—a 10-minute walk from St. Peter's. The more crowded bus #64 is convenient for pickpockets and stops just outside St. Peter's Square to the south (get off the bus after it crosses the Tiber, at the first stop past the tunnel; backtrack toward the tunnel and turn left when you see the rows of columns). Bus #492 heads through the center of town, stopping at Largo Argentina, and gets you near Piazza Risorgimento (get off when you see the Vatican walls). A taxi from Termini train station to St. Peter's costs about €11.

Information: The TI on the left (south) side of the square is excellent (Mon-Sat 8:30-18:15, closed Sun, free Vatican and church map). Tel. 06-6988-1662, www.saintpetersbasilica.org (this unofficial site provides a detailed map and latest opening hours and Mass times).

Church Services: Mass is performed daily, generally in Italian and in just a small area of the vast church: usually either in the south (left) transept, the Blessed Sacrament Chapel (on right side of nave), or the apse (where the 17:00 service is held Mon-Sat). Sunday-morning Mass tends to take place at the main altar. Typical schedule: Mon-Sat at 8:30, 9:00, 10:00, 11:00, 12:00, and 17:00 (in Latin, in the apse); and on Sun and holidays at 9:00, 10:30 (in Latin), 11:30, 12:15, 13:00, 16:00, and 17:45.

Tours: The Vatican TI conducts free 1.5-hour **tours of St. Peter's** (depart from TI Mon-Fri at 14:15, plus Tue and Thu at 9:45, confirm schedule at TI, tel. 06-6988-1662). **Audioguides** can be rented near the checkroom (€5 plus ID, for church only, daily 9:00-17:00). Or you can download a free Rick Steves **audio tour** of St. Peter's to your mobile device; see page 9.

To see St. Peter's original grave, you can take a "Scavi" (excavations) tour into the **Necropolis** (€12, 1.5 hours, ages 15 and older only, no photos). Book at least two months in advance by phone (tel. 06-6988-5318), email (scavi@fsp.va), or fax (06-6987-3017), following the detailed instructions at www.vatican.va (click "site

ROME

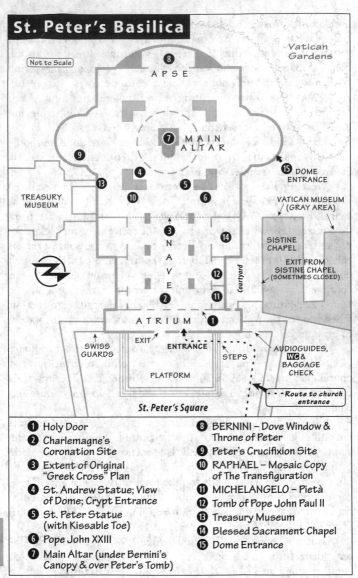

St. Peter's Basilica

Not to Scale

Vatican Gardens

APSE

MAIN ALTAR

TREASURY MUSEUM

NAVE

ATRIUM

Courtyard

DOME ENTRANCE

VATICAN MUSEUM (GRAY AREA)

SISTINE CHAPEL

EXIT FROM SISTINE CHAPEL (SOMETIMES CLOSED)

BLESSED SACRAMENT CHAPEL

SWISS GUARDS

EXIT   **ENTRANCE**   STEPS

AUDIOGUIDES, **WC** & BAGGAGE CHECK

PLATFORM

St. Peter's Square

- - - *Route to church entrance*

1 Holy Door
2 Charlemagne's Coronation Site
3 Extent of Original "Greek Cross" Plan
4 St. Andrew Statue; View of Dome; Crypt Entrance
5 St. Peter Statue (with Kissable Toe)
6 Pope John XXIII
7 Main Altar (under Bernini's Canopy & over Peter's Tomb)
8 BERNINI – Dove Window & Throne of Peter
9 Peter's Crucifixion Site
10 RAPHAEL – Mosaic Copy of The Transfiguration
11 MICHELANGELO – Pietà
12 Tomb of Pope John Paul II
13 Treasury Museum
14 Blessed Sacrament Chapel
15 Dome Entrance

ROME

map," then navigate to "Excavations Office"); no response means they're booked up.

To walk through the **Vatican Gardens,** you must book a guided tour at (the very) least a day in advance at http://biglietteriamusei.vatican.va. No response means they're booked up (€32, 2 hours, usually daily except Wed and Sun, includes entry to Vatican Museum; tours start at 9:30 or 10:00 at Vatican Museum tour desk).

Dome Climb: You can take the elevator or stairs to the roof (231 steps), then climb another 323 steps to the top of the dome. The entry to the elevator is just outside the basilica, on the north side of St. Peter's (near the secret exit from the Sistine Chapel). Look for signs to the *cupola*.

Length of This Tour: Allow one hour, plus another hour if you climb the dome (or a half-hour to the roof). If you have less time, skip the crypt and the dome climb, but at least stroll the nave, glance up at the dome and down at the marker of St. Peter's tomb. Don't miss the *Pietà*.

Baggage Check: The free bag check (mandatory for bags larger than a purse or daypack) is outside the basilica (to the right as you face the entrance), just inside the security checkpoint.

Services: WCs are to the right and left on St. Peter's Square (just outside the security checkpoint and exit), near baggage storage down the steps on the right side of the entrance, and on the roof.

❍ Self-Guided Tour: For a quick walk through the basilica, follow these points:

❶ The atrium itself is bigger than most churches. The huge white columns on the portico date from the first church (fourth century). Notice the historic doors (the Holy Door, on the right, won't be opened until the next Jubilee Year, in 2025).

❷ The purple, circular porphyry stone marks the site of Charlemagne's coronation in A.D. 800 (in the first St. Peter's church that stood on this site). From here, get a sense of the immensity of the church, which can accommodate 60,000 worshippers standing on its six acres.

❸ Michelangelo planned a Greek-cross floor plan, rather than the Latin-cross standard in medieval churches. A Greek cross, symbolizing the perfection of God, and by association the goodness of man, was important to the humanist Michelangelo. But accommodating—and impressing—large crowds was important to the Church in the fancy Baroque age, which followed Michelangelo, so the original nave length was doubled. Stand halfway up the nave and imagine the stubbier design that Michelangelo had in mind.

❹ View the magnificent dome from the statue of St. Andrew. See the vision of heaven above the windows: Jesus; Mary; a ring of saints; rings of angels; and, on the very top, God the Father.

Visitors can go down to the foundations of Old St. Peter's, containing tombs of popes and memorial chapels. The crypt entrance (labeled *Grotte* or *Tombe*) is usually beside the statue of St. Andrew, to the left of the main altar. Stairs lead you down to the floor level of the previous church, where you'll pass the sepulcher of Peter. This lighted niche with an icon is not Peter's actual tomb, but part of a shrine that stands atop Peter's tomb. The walk through

ROME

Pope Francis I

In 2013, Cardinal Jorge Bergoglio of Argentina became Francis I, the Catholic Church's 266th pope. His election represented three "firsts" that signaled a new direction for the Church: As the first pope from the Americas, Francis personifies the 80 percent of Catholics who now live outside Europe. As the first Jesuit pope—from the religious order known for education—he stands for spreading the faith through teaching, not aggression. And as the first Francis—named after St. Francis of Assisi—he calls to mind that medieval friar's efforts to return a corrupt church to simple Christian values of poverty and humility. In addition, Francis is in the unusual position of sharing the world stage with "pope emeritus" Benedict XVI (who, rather than dying in office, decided to retire).

Born in 1936, Francis grew up in Buenos Aires in a family of working-class Italian immigrants. He spent his twenties in various jobs (chemist, high-school teacher) before entering the priesthood. Ordained a Jesuit in 1969, he would rise to become Archbishop of Buenos Aires. He first came to the world's attention in 2005, when he was the runner-up in the election of Pope Benedict. While bishop in Argentina, he worked in the worst of slums, and denounced (though some say not loudly enough) Argentina's bloody dictatorship during the Dirty War of the 1970s.

Now a resident of Vatican City, Francis lives simply, staying in a Vatican guesthouse rather than the official papal apartments overlooking St. Peter's Square. He reportedly eats leftovers. When people talk about Francis, the word that comes up time and again is "dialogue." He's known for listening to every point of view, whether mediating between dictators and union lead-

the crypt is free and quick (15 minutes)—but you won't see St. Peter's original grave unless you take a Scavi "Excavations" tour (explained earlier).

5 The statue of St. Peter, with an irresistibly kissable toe, is one of the few pieces of art that predate this church. It adorned the first St. Peter's church.

6 Circle to the right around the statue of Peter to find the lighted glass niche with the red-robed body of Pope John XXIII (r. 1958-1963), who presided over the landmark Vatican II Council that instituted major reforms, bringing the Church into the modern age.

7 The main altar sits directly over St. Peter's tomb and under Bernini's seven-story bronze canopy.

8 St. Peter's throne and Bernini's starburst dove window is the site of a daily Mass (for Mass times, see "Church Services," earlier).

9 This marks the exact spot (according to tradition) where Peter was killed 1,900 years ago. When the authorities told Peter he was to be crucified just like his Lord, Peter said essentially, "I'm not worthy" and insisted they nail him on the cross upside-down.

ers, sitting down with the Orthodox Patriarch, celebrating Rosh Hashanah with Jews, visiting a mosque, or speaking well of atheists. In Argentina, he was often seen sharing *mate* (the national tea) with people of every stripe. At the Vatican, his management style stresses the collegiality of the cardinals. He speaks a number of languages, including fluent Italian—the language of his parents and of the Vatican. As Francis himself has pointed out, the original Latin word for pope—"*pontifex*"—literally means "bridge builder."

But Francis is not a liberal. He strongly defends traditional Catholic beliefs. No one expects major changes under Francis in the Church's positions on abortion, gay marriage, contraception, or the celibate, male-only priesthood. He inherited a Catholic Church with many problems: financial shenanigans, charges that they've protected pedophile priests, and alleged blackmailing of gay priests (as exposed in the "Vatileaks" scandal). And though the Catholic religion is growing worldwide, its home base—Europe—is becoming increasingly secular.

As pope, Francis has made it clear that he wants the Church to focus less on money and power, and more on the poor and the outcast. Francis is skeptical of globalization, worldliness, and unchecked capitalism, with the economic inequality they bring. One of his favorite Christian rituals is to literally kneel down before the poor, sick, or imprisoned, and wash their feet. Francis' personal credo, "*Miserando atque eligendo*," focuses on how God shows "mercy"—*miserando*—and compassion by forgiving sinners and helping the downtrodden.

❿ The church is filled with mosaics, some of which are copies of famous paintings. Notice the mosaic copy of Raphael's *Transfiguration*.

⓫ Michelangelo sculpted his *Pietà* when he was 24 years old. (A *pietà* is a work that represents Mary with the body of Christ taken down from the cross.) Michelangelo's mastery of the body is obvious in this powerfully beautiful masterpiece. Jesus is believably dead, and Mary, the eternally youthful "handmaiden" of the Lord, accepts God's will...even if it means giving up her son.

⓬ The tomb of Pope John Paul II was moved to the chapel of San Sebastian in 2011, after he was beatified by Pope Benedict XVI (a step on the road to sainthood). He lies beneath a painting of the steadfast St. Sebastian, his favorite saint.

⓭ For most, the museum-treasury (on the left side of the nave, near the altar) is not worth the admission.

⓮ You're welcome to step through the metalwork gates into the Blessed Sacrament Chapel, an oasis of peace reserved for prayer

ROME

and meditation (on the right-hand side of the church, about midway to the altar).

⓯ Outside on the north side of St. Peter's, an elevator leads to the roof and the stairway up the dome. The dome, Michelangelo's last work, is (you guessed it) the biggest anywhere. Taller than a football field is long, it's well worth the sweaty climb for a great view of Rome, the Vatican grounds, and the inside of the basilica—particularly heavenly while there is singing. Look around—Rome has no modern skyline. No building in Rome is allowed to exceed the height of St. Peter's. The elevator takes you to the rooftop of the nave. From there, a few steps take you to a balcony at the base of the dome looking down into the church interior. After that, the one-way, 323-step climb (for some people, it's claustrophobic) to the cupola begins. The rooftop level (below the dome) has a gift shop, WC, drinking fountain, and a commanding view.

▲▲▲Vatican Museum (Musei Vaticani)

The four miles of displays in this immense museum—from ancient statues to Christian frescoes to modern paintings—culminate in the Raphael Rooms and Michelangelo's glorious Sistine Chapel. This is one of Europe's top three or four houses of art. It can be exhausting, so plan your visit carefully, focusing on a few themes. Allow two hours for a quick visit, three or four hours for enough time to enjoy it.

Cost and Hours: €16, €4 online reservation fee, Mon-Sat 9:00-18:00, last entry at 16:00 (though the official closing time is 18:00, the staff starts ushering you out at 17:30), closed on religious holidays and Sun except last Sun of the month (when it's free, more crowded, and open 9:00-14:00, last entry at 12:30); open Fri nights May-July and Sept-Oct 19:00-23:00 (last entry at 21:30) by online reservation only. Hours are subject to constant change and frequent holidays; check http://mv.vatican.va for current times.

The museum is closed on many holidays (mainly religious ones), including, for 2014: Jan 1 (New Year's), Jan 6 (Epiphany), Feb 11 (Vatican City established), March 19 (St. Joseph's Day), April 21 (Easter Monday), May 1 (Labor Day), June 29 (Sts. Peter and Paul), Aug 15 plus either Aug 14 or 16—it varies year to year (Assumption of the Virgin), Nov 1 (All Saints' Day), Dec 8 (Immaculate Conception), and Dec 25 and 26 (Christmas).

Reservations: Bypass the long ticket lines by reserving an entry time online at http://mv.vatican.va. It costs €20 (€16 ticket plus €4 booking fee, pay with credit card). It's easy. You choose your day and time, they email

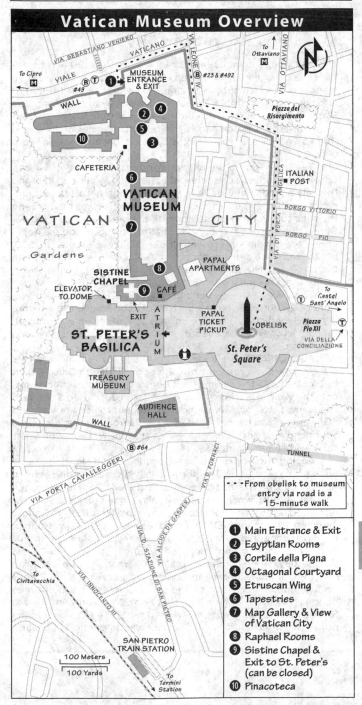

Vatican Museum Overview

1. Main Entrance & Exit
2. Egyptian Rooms
3. Cortile della Pigna
4. Octagonal Courtyard
5. Etruscan Wing
6. Tapestries
7. Map Gallery & View of Vatican City
8. Raphael Rooms
9. Sistine Chapel & Exit to St. Peter's (can be closed)
10. Pinacoteca

- - - From obelisk to museum entry via road is a 15-minute walk

ROME

Vatican City

This tiny independent country of little more than 100 acres, contained entirely within Rome, has its own postal system, armed guards, helipad, mini-train station, and radio station (KPOP). It also has two huge sights: St. Peter's Basilica (with Michelangelo's *Pietà*) and the Vatican Museum (with the Sistine Chapel). Politically powerful, the Vatican is the religious capital of 1.2 billion Roman Catholics. If you're not a Catholic, become one for your visit.

The pope is both the religious and secular leader of Vatican City. For centuries, locals referred to him as "King Pope." Italy and the Vatican didn't always have good relations. In fact, after unification (in 1870), when Rome's modern grid plan was built around the miniscule Vatican, it seemed as if the new buildings were designed to be just high enough so that no one could see the dome of St. Peter's from street level. Modern Italy was created in 1870, but the Holy See didn't recognize it as a country until 1929, when the pope and Mussolini signed the Lateran Pact, giving sovereignty and a few nearby churches to the Vatican.

Like every European country, Vatican City has its own versions of the euro coin (with a portrait of Pope Francis I and, before him, of Benedict XVI). You're unlikely to find one in your pocket, though, as they're snatched up by collectors before falling into circulation.

Post Offices: The Vatican postal service is famous for its stamps, which you can get from offices on St. Peter's Square (next to TI or between the columns just before the security checkpoint) or in the Vatican Museum (Mon-Sat 8:30-18:30, closed Sun). Vatican stamps are good throughout Rome, but to use the Vatican's mail service, you need to mail your cards from the Vatican; write your postcards ahead of time. (Note that the Vatican won't mail cards with Italian stamps.)

Seeing the Pope: Your best chances for a sighting are on Sunday or Wednesday. The pope usually gives a blessing at noon on Sunday from his apartment on St. Peter's Square (except in July and August, when he speaks at his summer residence at Castel Gandolfo, 25 miles from Rome, reachable by train from Rome's Termini train station). St. Peter's is easiest (just show up) and, for most, enough of a "visit." Those interested in a more formal appearance (though not more intimate) can get a ticket for the Wednesday general audience (at 10:30) when the pope, arriving in his Popemobile, greets and blesses the crowds at St. Peter's from a canopied platform on the square (except in winter, when he speaks at 10:30 in the 7,000-seat Paolo VI Auditorium, next to St. Peter's Basilica). If you only want to see St. Peter's—but not the pope—avoid these times (the basilica closes during papal audiences and crowds are substantial).

For the Wednesday audience, while anyone can observe from a distance, you need a (free) ticket to get close to the papal action (and get a seat). To find out the pope's schedule and request a ticket, see www.vatican.va (click on "Prefecture of the Papal Household") or call 06-6988-3114. Since the papal schedule is set only a month or two in advance, you may not be able to request tickets further out.

The American Catholic Church in Rome, Santa Susanna, lets you order tickets online (free, no booking fee, but donations appreciated) for the Wednesday general audience. Pick up your reserved tickets, or check for last-minute availability, at the church the Tuesday before the audience between 17:00 and 18:45—consider staying for the 18:00 English Mass (Via XX Settembre 15, near recommended Via Firenze hotels, Metro: Repubblica, tel. 06-4201-4554—charming Rosanna speaks English, details at www.santasusanna.org).

Probably less convenient—unless you're already at the basilica—is getting a ticket at St. Peter's Square from the Vatican guards at their station at the bronze doors (open Tue officially at 15:00—but can open as early as 12:00—and closes when church does; last-minute tickets may be available Wed morning—just join the line). It's under the "elbow" of Bernini's colonnade, on the right side of the square as you face the basilica—see map on page 911).

On Wednesday morning, you'll need to clear security (no big bags; lines tend to move more quickly on the side of the square farthest away from the Metro stop), be dressed appropriately (no short shorts or tank tops—long pants or knee-length skirts are safest), and then join the masses eagerly awaiting the pope's appearance. To get a seat, it's smart to be there a couple of hours early (bring reading material). If you just want to see the pope and get a good photo, you can show up later (though still at least 45 minutes early) and take your place in the standing-room section in the back half of the square. At around 10:00, after the names of attending pilgrim groups have been announced, the Popemobile appears, winding through the adoring crowd along the corridors blocked off by cloth-covered wooden fences (position yourself strategically). The multilingual message begins at 10:30 and lasts for about an hour; you're free to go at any time.

While many visitors come hoping for a more intimate audience, private audiences ended with the death of Pope John Paul II. Pope Benedict didn't do them, and as of this book's printing, Francis hasn't announced any plans to rekindle the tradition.

ROME

you a confirmation immediately, and you print out the voucher. At the Vatican Museum, bypass the ticket-buying line and queue up at the "Entrance with Reservations" line (to the right). Show your voucher to the guard and go in. Once inside the museum, present your voucher (and ID) at a ticket window *(cassa)*, either in the lobby or upstairs, and they'll issue your ticket.

When to Go: The museum is generally hot and crowded, with shoulder-to-shoulder sightseeing through much of it. There can be waits of up to two hours to buy tickets (figure about a 10-minute wait for every 100 yards in line). The best (or least-worst) time to visit is a weekday late-afternoon. The worst days are Saturdays, the last Sunday of the month (when it's free), Mondays, rainy days, and any day before or after a holiday closure. Mornings are most crowded.

More Line-Beating Tips: If you've booked a **guided tour** (see "Tours," next page), you can show the guard your voucher and go right in. You can often buy **same-day, skip-the-line tickets** (for the same €20 online price) through the TI in St. Peter's Square (to the left, as you face the basilica). Also, the "Roma Cristiana" tour company sells same-day tickets from their kiosk at St. Peter's Square (for a pricey €26.50, entrances almost hourly, tel. 06-6980-6380, www.operaromanapellegrinaggi.org). If their kiosk is closed, try the nearby storefront labeled *Opera Romana Pellegrini*, just in front of the square, which also sometimes sells these tickets.

If you don't have a reservation, **try arriving after 14:00,** when crowds subside somewhat. Another good time is during the papal audience, on Wednesday at 10:30, when many tourists are at St. Peter's Basilica.

Make sure you get in the right line. Generally, individuals without tickets line up against the Vatican City wall (to the left of the entrance as you face it), and reservation holders (both individuals and groups) enter on the right.

Dress Code: Modest dress is required (no shorts, above-knee skirts, or bare shoulders).

Getting There: The Ottaviano Metro stop is a 10-minute walk from the entrance. Bus #49 from Piazza Cavour/Castel Sant'Angelo stops at the Ottaviano Metro stop and continues right to the entrance. Bus #23 from Trastevere hugs the west bank of the Tiber and stops on Via Leone IV, just downhill from the entrance. Bus #492 heads from the city center past Piazza Risorgimento and the Vatican walls, and also stops on Via Leone IV. Bus #64 stops on the other side of St. Peter's Square, a 15- to 20-minute walk (facing the church from the obelisk, take a right through the colonnade and follow the Vatican Wall). Taxis are reasonable (hop in and say, "moo-ZAY-ee vah-tee-KAH-nee").

Tours: A €7 **audioguide** is available at the top of the spiral ramp/escalator (ID required). If you rent an audioguide, you lose the option of taking the shortcut from the Sistine Chapel to St. Peter's (described later, under "Museum Strategies"), since audioguides must be returned to the museum entrance/exit. You can download a free Rick Steves **audio tour** of the Sistine Chapel to your mobile device; see page 9.

The Vatican offers **English tours** that are easy to book online (€32, includes admission, http://mv.vatican.va). As with individual ticket reservations, present your confirmation voucher to a guard to the right of the entrance; then, once inside, go to the Guided Tours desk (in the lobby, up a few stairs). For a list of **private tour** companies and guides, see page 858.

Length of This Tour: Until you expire, the museum closes, or 2.5 hours, whichever comes first. If you're short on time, see the octagonal courtyard *(Laocoön),* then follow the crowd flow directly to the Sistine Chapel, sightseeing along the way; skip the Etruscan Wing and the Pinacoteca. From the Sistine Chapel, head straight to St. Peter's via the shortcut, if open (see "Museum Strategies," below).

Security and Baggage Check: To enter the museum, you pass through a metal detector (no pocket knives allowed). The baggage check (to the right after security) takes only bigger bags, not day bags.

Museum Strategies: The museum has two exits, and you'll want to decide which you'll take before you enter. The **main exit** is right near the entrance. Use this one if you want to rent an audioguide (which you must return at the entrance) or if you plan on following this self-guided tour exactly as laid out, visiting the Pinacoteca at the end (the Vatican's small but fine collection of paintings, with Raphael's *Transfiguration,* Leonardo's unfinished *St. Jerome,* and Caravaggio's *Deposition*).

The other exit is a handy (but sometimes closed) **shortcut** that leads from the Sistine Chapel directly to St. Peter's Basilica (spilling out alongside the church; see map on page 911). This route saves you a 30-minute walk (15 minutes back to the Vatican Museum entry/exit, then 15 minutes to St. Peter's) and lets you avoid the often-long security line at the basilica's main entrance. If you take this route, you'll have to forgo an audioguide and skip the Pinacoteca (or tour it earlier). Officially, this exit is for Vatican guides and their groups only. However, it's often open to anyone (depending on how crowded the chapel is and how the guards feel). It's worth a shot (try blending in with a group that's leaving), but be prepared for the possibility that you won't get through.

Photography: No photos allowed in the Sistine Chapel, but photos without flash are permitted elsewhere.

● **Self-Guided Tour:** Start, as civilization did, in **Egypt and Mesopotamia.** Decorating the museum's courtyard are some of the best **Greek and Roman statues** in captivity, including the *Laocoön* group (first century B.C., Hellenistic) and the *Apollo Belvedere* (a second-century Roman copy of a Greek original). The centerpiece of the next hall is the *Belvedere Torso* (just a 2,000-year-old torso, but one that had a great impact on the art of Michelangelo). Finishing off the classical statuary are two fine fourth-century porphyry sarcophagi. These royal purple tombs were made (though not used) for the Roman emperor Constantine's mother and daughter. They were Christians—and therefore outlaws—until Constantine made Christianity legal in A.D. 312, and they became saints. Both sarcophagi were quarried and worked in Egypt. The technique for working this extremely hard stone (a special tempering of metal was required) was lost after this, and porphyry marble was not chiseled again until Renaissance times in Florence.

After long halls of tapestries, old maps, broken penises, and fig leaves, you'll come to what most people are looking for: the Raphael Rooms and Michelangelo's Sistine Chapel.

The highlight of the **Raphael Rooms,** frescoed by Raphael and his assistants, is the restored *School of Athens.* It is remarkable for its blatant pre-Christian classical orientation, especially considering it originally wallpapered the apartments of Pope Julius II. Raphael honors the great pre-Christian thinkers—Aristotle, Plato, and company—who are portrayed as the leading artists of Raphael's day. There's Leonardo da Vinci, whom Raphael worshipped, in the role of Plato. Michelangelo broods in the foreground, added later. When Raphael snuck a peek at the Sistine Chapel, he decided that his arch-competitor was so good that he had to put their personal differences aside and include him in this tribute to the artists of his generation. Today's St. Peter's was under construction as Raphael was working. In the *School of Athens,* he gives us a sneak preview of the unfinished church.

Next is the brilliantly restored **Sistine Chapel.** This is the pope's personal chapel and also the place where, upon the death of the ruling pope, a new pope is elected (as in March of 2013).

The Sistine Chapel is famous for Michelangelo's pictorial culmination of the Renaissance, showing the story of creation, with a powerful God weaving in and out of each scene through that busy first week. This is an optimistic and positive expression of the High Renaissance and a stirring example of the artistic and theological maturity of the 33-year-old Michelangelo, who spent four years on this work.

The ceiling shows the history of the world before the birth of Jesus. We see God creating the world, creating man and woman, destroying the earth by flood, and so on. God himself, in his purple robe, actually appears in the first five scenes. Along the sides (where the ceiling starts to curve) are the Old Testament prophets and pagan Greek prophetesses who foretold the coming of Christ. Dividing these scenes and figures are fake niches (a painted 3-D illusion) decorated with nude statue-like figures with symbolic meaning.

When the ceiling was finished and revealed to the public, it simply blew 'em away. It both caps the Renaissance and turns it in a new direction. In perfect Renaissance spirit, it mixes Old Testament prophets with classical figures. But the style is more dramatic, shocking, and emotional than the balanced Renaissance works before it. This is a very personal work—the Gospel according to Michelangelo—but its themes and subject matter are universal. Many art scholars contend that the Sistine ceiling is the single greatest work of art by any one human being.

Later, after the Reformation wars had begun and after the Catholic army of Spain had sacked the Vatican, the reeling Church began to fight back. As part of its Counter-Reformation, a much older Michelangelo was commissioned to paint the *Last Judgment* (behind the altar).

It's Judgment Day, and Christ—the powerful figure in the center, raising his arm to spank the wicked— has come to find out who's naughty and who's nice. Beneath him, a band of angels blows its trumpets Dizzy Gillespie-style, giving a wake-up call to the sleeping dead. The dead at lower left leave their graves and prepare to be judged. The righteous, on Christ's right hand (the left side of the picture), are carried up to the glories of heaven. The wicked on the other side are hurled down to hell, where demons wait to torture them. Charon, from the underworld of Greek mythology, waits below to ferry the souls of the damned to hell.

When *The Last Judgment* was unveiled to the public in 1541, it caused a sensation. The pope is said to have dropped to his knees and cried, "Lord, charge me not with my sins when thou shalt come on the Day of Judgment."

And it changed the course of art. The complex composition, with more than 300 figures swirling around the figure of Christ, went far beyond traditional Renaissance balance. The twisted figures shown from every imaginable angle challenged other painters to try and top this master of 3-D illusion. And the sheer terror and drama of the scene was a striking contrast to the placid optimism of, say, Raphael's *School of Athens*. Michelangelo had Baroque-en all the rules of the Renaissance, signaling a new era of art.

For a **shortcut directly to St. Peter's Basilica** (see "Museum Strategies," earlier), exit at the far-right corner of the Sistine Chapel (with your back to the altar). If you exit here, you're done with the museum—you can't get back to the main entrance/exit (where audioguides are returned) or the Pinacoteca.

ROME

If you skip the shortcut and take the long march back, you'll find, along with the Pinacoteca, a cafeteria (long lines, uninspired food), the underrated early-Christian art section, and the exit via the souvenir shop.

Near Vatican City
▲Castel Sant'Angelo

Built as a tomb for the emperor, used through the Middle Ages as a castle, prison, and place of last refuge for popes under attack, and today a museum, this giant pile of ancient bricks is packed with history.

Cost and Hours: €10.50, Tue-Sun 9:00-19:30, closed Mon, last entry one hour before closing, near Vatican City, Metro: Lepanto or bus #40 or #64, tel. 06-681-9111, www.castelsantangelo.beniculturali.it.

Background: Ancient Rome allowed no tombs—not even the emperor's—within its walls. So Emperor Hadrian grabbed the most commanding position just outside the walls and across the river and built a towering tomb (c. A.D. 139) well within view of the city. His mausoleum was a huge cylinder (210 by 70 feet) topped by a cypress grove and crowned by a huge statue of Hadrian himself riding a chariot. For nearly a hundred years, Roman emperors (from Hadrian to Caracalla, in A.D. 217) were buried here.

In the year 590, the archangel Michael appeared above the mausoleum to Pope Gregory the Great. Sheathing his sword, the angel signaled the end of a plague. The fortress that was Hadrian's mausoleum eventually became a fortified palace, renamed for the "holy angel."

Castel Sant'Angelo spent centuries of the Dark Ages as a fortress and prison, but was eventually connected to the Vatican via an elevated corridor at the pope's request (1277). Since Rome was repeatedly plundered by invaders, Castel Sant'Angelo was a handy place of last refuge for threatened popes. In anticipation of long sieges, rooms were decorated with papal splendor (you'll see paintings by Carlo Crivelli, Luca Signorelli, and Andrea Mantegna). In 1527, during a sack of Rome by troops of Charles V of Spain, the pope lived inside the castle for months with his entourage of hundreds (an unimaginable ordeal, considering the food service at the top-floor bar).

Visiting the Castle: Touring the place is a stair-stepping workout. After you walk around the entire base of the castle, take the small staircase down to the original Roman floor (following the route of Hadrian's funeral procession). In the atrium, study the model of the mausoleum as it was in Roman times. Imagine being surrounded by a veneer of marble, and the niche in the wall filled with a towering "welcome to my tomb" statue of Hadrian. From here, a ramp leads to the right, spiraling 400 feet. While some of the fine original brickwork and bits of mosaic survive, the marble veneer is long gone (notice the holes in the wall from the pins that held it in place).

At the end of the ramp, a bridge crosses over the room where the ashes of the emperors were kept. From here, the stairs continue out of the ancient section and into the medieval structure (built atop the mausoleum) that housed the papal apartments. Don't miss the Sala del Tesoro (Treasury), where the wealth of the Vatican was locked up in a huge chest. (*Do* miss the 58 rooms of the military museum.) From the pope's piggy bank, a narrow flight of stairs leads to the rooftop and perhaps the finest view of Rome anywhere (pick out landmarks as you stroll around). From the safety of this dramatic vantage point, the pope surveyed the city in times of siege. Look down at the bend of the Tiber, which for 2,700 years has cradled the Eternal City.

Ponte Sant'Angelo

The bridge leading to Castel Sant'Angelo was built by Hadrian for quick and regal access from downtown to his tomb. The three middle arches are actually Roman originals and a fine example of the empire's engineering expertise. The statues of angels (each bearing a symbol of the passion of Christ—nail, sponge, shroud, and so on) are Bernini-designed and textbook Baroque. In the Middle Ages, this was the only bridge in the area that connected St. Peter's and the Vatican with downtown Rome. Nearly all pilgrims passed this bridge to and from the church. Its shoulder-high banisters recall a tragedy: During a Jubilee Year festival in 1450, the crowd got so huge that the mob pushed out the original banisters, causing nearly 200 to fall to their deaths.

ROME

North Rome

Borghese Gardens and Nearby

▲Villa Borghese Gardens

Rome's semi-scruffy three-square-mile "Central Park" is great for its shade and for people-watching plenty of modern-day Romeos and Juliets. The best entrance is at the head of Via Veneto (Metro:

Barberini, then 10-minute walk up Via
Veneto and through the old Roman wall
at Porta Pinciana, or catch a cab to Via
Veneto—Porta Pinciana). There you'll
find a cluster of buildings with a café, a
kiddie arcade, and bike rental (€4/hour).
Rent a bike or, for romantics, a pedaled
rickshaw *(riscio)*. Bikes come with locks
to allow you to make sightseeing stops.
Follow signs to discover the park's cafés,
fountains, statues, lake, great viewpoint

over Piazza del Popolo, and prime picnic spots. Some sights require paid admission, including Rome's zoo, the National Gallery
of Modern Art (which holds 19th-century art; not to be confused
with MAXXI, described later), and the Etruscan Museum described later.

▲▲▲Borghese Gallery
(Galleria Borghese)

More than just a great museum, the Borghese Gallery is a beautiful villa set in the greenery of surrounding gardens. You get to see
art commissioned by the luxury-loving Borghese family displayed
in the very rooms for which it was created. Frescoes, marble, stucco, and interior design enhance the masterpieces. This is a place
where—regardless of whether you learn a darn thing—you can sit
back and enjoy the sheer beauty of the palace and its world-class
Baroque sculpture as well as paintings by Caravaggio, Raphael,
Titian, and Rubens. The museum's mandatory reservation system
keeps crowds to a manageable size.

Cost and Hours: €13, drops to €9 when there's no temporary
exhibit, both prices include €2 reservation fee (see "Reservations,"
next), Tue-Sun 9:00-19:00, closed Mon, ticket office closes one
hour before museum.

Reservations: Reservations are mandatory and simple to get.
It's easiest to book online (www.galleriaborghese.it). You can also
reserve by telephone (tel. 06-32810, press 2 for English, pay for
tickets on arrival). Entry times are 9:00, 11:00, 13:00, 15:00, and
17:00. Reserve a *minimum* of several days in advance for a weekday visit, and at least a week ahead for weekends. For off-season
weekdays, your chances of getting a same-day reservation are fairly
high (but you must go in person—you can't call to reserve same-
day tickets). Be at the Borghese Gallery 30 minutes before your appointed time to pick up your ticket in the lobby on the lower level.
Arriving late can mean forfeiting your reservation.

You can use a Roma Pass for entry, but you're still required to
make a reservation (by phone only—not online; specify that you
have the Roma Pass). If you don't have a reservation, try arriving

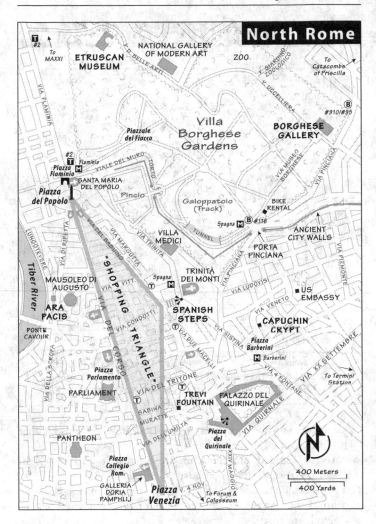

North Rome

near the top of the hour, when the museum sells unclaimed tickets to those standing by.

Getting There: The museum is set idyllically but inconveniently in the vast Villa Borghese Gardens. Bus #910 goes from

Termini train station (and Piazza Repubblica) to the Via Pinciana stop, 100 yards from the museum.

By Metro, from the Barberini Metro stop, walk 10 minutes up

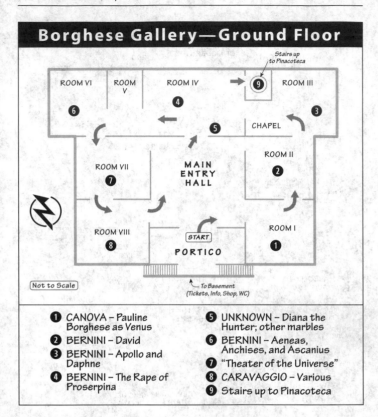

Borghese Gallery—Ground Floor

Stairs up to Pinacoteca

ROOM VI   ROOM V   ROOM IV   ❹   ⑨   ROOM III

❻   ❸

CHAPEL   ❺

ROOM VII   MAIN ENTRY HALL   ROOM II   ❷

❼

ROOM VIII   START   ROOM I   ❶

❽   PORTICO

Not to Scale

To Basement (Tickets, Info, Shop, WC)

❶ CANOVA – Pauline Borghese as Venus
❷ BERNINI – David
❸ BERNINI – Apollo and Daphne
❹ BERNINI – The Rape of Proserpina
❺ UNKNOWN – Diana the Hunter; other marbles
❻ BERNINI – Aeneas, Anchises, and Ascanius
❼ "Theater of the Universe"
❽ CARAVAGGIO – Various
⑨ Stairs up to Pinacoteca

Via Veneto, enter the park, and turn right, following signs another 10 minutes to the Borghese Gallery.

Tours: Guided English tours are offered at 9:10 and 11:10 (€6.50; may also be offered on busy weekends at 13:10 and 15:10). You can't book a tour when you make your museum reservation—sign up as soon as you arrive. Or consider the excellent 1.5-hour audioguide tour (€5).

Visiting the Museum: It's hard to believe that a family of cardinals and popes would display so many works with secular and sensual—even erotic—themes. But the Borgheses felt that all forms of human expression, including pagan myths and physical passion, glorified God.

The essence of the collection is the connection of the Renaissance with the classical world. As you enter, notice the second-century Roman reliefs with Michelangelo-designed panels above either end of the portico. The villa was built in the early 17th century by the great art collector Cardinal Scipione Borghese, who wanted to prove that the glories of ancient Rome were matched by the Renaissance.

In the main entry hall, high up on the wall, is a thrilling first-century Greek sculpture of a horse falling. The Renaissance-era rider was added by Pietro Bernini, father of the famous Gian Lorenzo Bernini.

Each room seems to feature a Baroque masterpiece. The best one of all is in Room III: Bernini's *Apollo and Daphne*. It's the perfect Baroque subject—capturing a thrilling, action-filled moment. In the mythological story, Apollo—made stupid by Cupid's arrow of love—chases after Daphne, who has been turned off by the "arrow of disgust." Just as he's about to catch her, she calls to her father to save her. Magically, her fingers begin to sprout leaves, her toes become roots, her skin turns to bark, and she transforms into a tree. Frustrated Apollo will end up with a handful of leaves. Walk slowly around the statue. It's more air than stone.

Etruscan Museum
(Museo Nazionale Etrusco di Villa Giulia)

The fascinating Etruscan civilization thrived in Italy around 600 B.C., when Rome was an Etruscan town. The Villa Giulia (a fine Renaissance palace in the Villa Borghese Gardens) hosts a museum that tells the story. The displays are clean and bright, with good English information.

The star of the museum is the famous "husband and wife sarcophagus"—a dead couple seeming to enjoy an everlasting banquet from atop their tomb (sixth century B.C. from Cerveteri). Historians also dig the gold sheets from Pyrgi, with inscriptions in two languages—the "Etruscan Rosetta Stone" that has helped scholars decipher their odd language, and the Apollo of Veio, which stood atop Apollo's temple. For more on the Etruscans, see the sidebar on page 704.

Cost and Hours: €8, Tue-Sun 8:30-19:30, closed Mon, last entry one hour before closing, good English information, 20-minute walk from Borghese Gallery or from most of the Villa Borghese Garden's entrances, Metro: Flaminio, then tram #2 to Viale delle Belli Arti and a 5-minute walk (east) to the museum, Piazzale di Villa Giulia 9, tel. 06-322-6571, www.villagiulia.beniculturali.it.

▲Capuchin Crypt

If you want to see artistically arranged bones, this is the place. The crypt is below the Church of Santa Maria della Immacolata Concezione on the tree-lined Via Veneto, just up from Piazza Barberini. Before getting to the crypt, you'll breeze through the new six-room museum that covers the history of the Capuchins, a branch of the Franciscans. The exhibits, featuring clothing, books, and other religious artifacts used by members of the order, are explained in English, but the only real artistic highlight is a painting of St. Francis in Meditation, once attributed to Caravaggio (but now thought to be a contemporary copy). For most travelers, however, the main attraction remains the morbid crypt. The bones of more than 4,000 friars who died between 1528 and 1870 are in the basement, all lined up in a series of six crypts for the delight—or disgust—of the always-wide-eyed visitor.

Cost and Hours: €6, daily 9:00-19:00, last entry 30 minutes before closing, modest dress required, no photos, Via Veneto 27, Metro: Barberini, tel. 06-4201-4995.

Piazza del Popolo

This vast oval square marks the traditional north entrance to Rome. From ancient times until the advent of trains and airplanes, this was just about any visitor's first look at Rome. Today the square, known for its symmetrical design and its art-filled churches, is the starting point for the city's evening *passeggiata* (see my "Dolce Vita Stroll" on page 872).

From the Flaminio Metro stop, pass through the third-century Aurelian Wall via the Porta del Popolo, and look south. The

10-story obelisk in the center of the square once graced the temple of Ramses II in Egypt and the Roman Circus Maximus racetrack. The obelisk was brought here in 1589 as one of the square's beautification projects. (The oval shape dates from the early 19th century.) At the south side of the square, twin domed churches mark the spot where three main boulevards exit the square and form a trident. The central boulevard (running between the churches) is Via del Corso, which since ancient times has been the main north-south drag through town, running to Capitoline Hill (the governing center) and the Forum. Along the north side of the square (flanking the Porta del Popolo) are two 19th-century buildings that give the square its pleasant symmetry: the Carabinieri station and the Church of Santa Maria del Popolo.

Two large fountains grace the sides of the square—Neptune to the west and Roma to the east (marking the base of Pincio Hill; steps lead up to the overlook with fine views to St. Peter's and the rest of the city). Though the name "Piazza del Popolo" means "Square of the People" (and it is a popular hangout), the word was probably derived from the Latin *populus,* after the poplar trees that once stood here.

ROME

Church of Santa Maria del Popolo

One of Rome's most overlooked churches, this features two cha-pels with top-notch art by Caravaggio and Bernini, and a facade

built of travertine scavenged from the Colosseum. The church is brought to you by the Rovere family, which pro-duced two popes, and you'll see their symbol—the oak tree and acorns—throughout.

Cost and Hours: Free but bring coins to illuminate the art, Mon-Sat 7:00-12:30 & 16:00-19:00, Sun 8:00-13:30 & 16:30-19:30, often partially closed to accommodate its busy schedule of Masses, on north side of Piazza del Popolo—as you face the gate in the old wall from the square, the church entrance is to your right.

Visiting the Church: Go inside. The Chigi Chapel (second on the left) was designed by Raphael and inspired (as Raphael was) by the Pantheon. Notice the Pantheon-like dome, pilasters, and capi-tals. Above, in the oculus, God looks in, aided by angels who power the eight known planets. Raphael built the chapel for his wealthy banker friend Agostino Chigi, buried in the pyramid-shaped tomb in the wall to the right of the altar. Later, Chigi's great-grandson hired Bernini to make two of the four statues, and Bernini deliv-ered a theatrical episode. In one corner, Daniel straddles a lion and raises his praying hands to God for help. Kitty-corner across the chapel, an angel grabs the prophet Habakkuk's hair and tells him to go take some food to poor Daniel in the lion's den.

In the Cerasi Chapel (left of altar), Caravaggio's *Conversion of St. Paul* shows the future saint sprawled on his back be-side his horse while his servant looks on. The startled Paul is blinded by the harsh light as Jesus' voice asks him, "Why do you persecute me?" In the style of the Counter-Reformation, Paul receives his new faith with open arms.

In the same chapel, Caravaggio's *Crucifixion of St. Peter* is shown as a banal chore; the workers toil like faceless animals. The light and dark are in high contrast. Caravaggio liked to say, "Where light falls, I will paint it."

▲▲Catacombs of Priscilla (Catacombe di Priscilla)

While most tourists and nearly all tour groups go out to the an-cient Appian Way to see the famous catacombs of San Sebastiano

ROME

and San Callisto, the Catacombs of Priscilla (on the other side of town) are less commercialized and less crowded—they just feel more intimate, as catacombs should.

You enter from a convent and explore the result of 250 years of tunneling that occurred from the second to the fifth century. Visits are by 30-minute guided tour only (English-language tours go whenever a small group gathers—generally every 20 minutes or so). You'll see a few thousand of the 40,000 niches carved here, along with some beautiful frescoes, including what is considered the first depiction of Mary nursing the baby Jesus.

Cost and Hours: €8, Tue-Sun 8:30-12:00 & 14:30-17:00, closed Mon, last entry 30 minutes before closing, closed one random month a year—check website or call first, tel. 06-8620-6272, www.catacombepriscilla.com.

Getting There: The catacombs are northeast of Termini train station (at Via Salaria 430), far from the center (a €15 taxi ride) but well-served by buses (20-30 minutes). From Termini, take bus #92 or #310 from Piazza Cinquecento. From Piazza Venezia, along Via del Corso or Via Barberini, take bus #63. Tell the driver "Piazza Crati" and "kah-tah-KOHM-bay" and he'll let you off near Piazza Crati (at the Nemorense/Crati stop). From there, walk through the little market in Piazza Crati, then down Via di Priscilla (about 5 minutes). The entrance is in the orange building on the left at the top of the hill.

For more information, see the "Catacombs" sidebar on page 950.

MAXXI

Rome's "National Museum of Art of the 21st Century" is the big news on the museum scene here—as you can imagine it would be, after the 10 years and €150 million it took to make it happen. Like many contemporary art museums, it's notable more for the building than the art inside. To me, it comes off as a second-rate Pompidou Center. While not to my taste, it's one of the few places in the city where fans of contemporary architecture can see the latest trends.

Cost and Hours: €11, Tue-Sun 11:00-19:00, Sat until 22:00, closed Mon, last entry one hour before closing; no permanent collection, several rotating exhibits throughout the year—preview on their website; tram #2 (direction: Mancini) from Piazza del Popolo to the Apollodoro stop, then walk west 5 minutes to Via Guido Reni 4a; to return (direction: Flaminio), the tram stop is 50 yards closer to MAXXI, tel. 06-322-5178, www.fondazionemaxxi.it.

From the Spanish Steps to the Ara Pacis

▲Spanish Steps

The wide, curving staircase, culminating with an obelisk between two Baroque church towers, makes for one of Rome's iconic sights. Beyond that, it's a people-gathering place. By day, the area hosts shoppers looking for high-end fashions; on warm evenings, it attracts young people in love with the city. For more, see my "Heart of Rome Walk" on page 874.

▲▲Museo dell'Ara Pacis (Museum of the Altar of Peace)

On January 30, 9 B.C., soon-to-be-emperor Augustus led a procession of priests up the steps and into this newly built "Altar of Peace." They sacrificed an animal on the altar and poured an offering of wine, thanking the gods for helping Augustus pacify barbarians abroad and rivals at home. This marked the dawn of the Pax Romana (c. A.D. 1-200), a Golden Age of good living, stability, dominance, and peace *(pax)*.

The Ara Pacis (AH-rah PAH-chees) hosted annual sacrifices by the emperor until the area was flooded by the Tiber River. Buried under silt, it was abandoned and forgotten until the 16th century, when various parts were discovered and excavated. Mussolini gathered the altar's scattered parts and reconstructed them in a building here in 1938. Today, the Altar of Peace stands in a pavilion designed by American architect Richard Meier (opened 2006). If this modern building seems striking, perhaps that's because it's about the only entirely new structure permitted in the old center of Rome since Mussolini's day.

Cost and Hours: €8.50 (more with special exhibits), tightwads can look in through huge windows for free; Tue-Sun 9:00-19:00, closed Mon, last entry one hour before closing; good €4 audioguide; good WC downstairs, tel. 06-0608, www.arapacis.it.

Getting There: The Ara Pacis is a long block west of Via del Corso on Via di Ara Pacis, on the east bank of the Tiber near Ponte Cavour, Metro: Spagna; a 10-minute walk down Via dei Condotti.

Visiting the Museum: Start with the model in the museum's lobby. The Altar of Peace was originally located east of here, along today's Via del Corso. The model shows where it stood in relation to the Mausoleum of Augustus (now next door) and the Pantheon. Approach the Ara Pacis and look through the doorway to see the raised altar. This simple structure has just the basics of a Roman temple: an altar for sacrifices surrounded by cubicle-like walls that enclose a consecrated space.

Climb the 10 steps and go inside. From here, the priest would ascend the eight altar steps to make sacrifices. The walls of the en-

ROME

closure are decorated with the kinds of things offered to the gods: animals (see the cow skulls), garlands of fruit, and ceremonial platters to present the offerings. The reliefs on the north and south sides probably depict the parade of dignitaries who consecrated the altar, while the reliefs on the west side (near the altar's back door) celebrate the two things Augustus brought to Rome: peace (goddess Roma as a conquering Amazon, right side) and prosperity (fertility goddess surrounded by children, plants, and animals).

East Rome

Near Termini Train Station

Most of these sights are within a 10-minute walk of the train station. By Metro, use the Termini stop for the National Museum and the Repubblica stop for the rest.

▲▲▲National Museum of Rome (Museo Nazionale Romano Palazzo Massimo alle Terme)

The National Museum's main branch, at Palazzo Massimo, houses the greatest collection of ancient Roman art anywhere. It's a historic yearbook of Roman marble statues with some rare Greek originals. On the ground floor alone, you can look eye-to-eye with Julius and Augustus Caesar, Alexander the Great, and Socrates.

Cost and Hours: €10 combo-ticket covers three other branches—all skippable, Tue-Sun 9:00-19:45, closed Mon, last entry one hour before closing, audioguide-€5, about 100 yards from train station, Metro: Repubblica or Termini, tel. 06-3996-7700, www.archeoroma.beniculturali.it/en.

Getting There: The museum is in Palazzo Massimo, situated between Piazza della Repubblica (Metro: Repubblica) and Termini Station (Metro: Termini). It's a few minutes' walk from either Metro stop. As you leave Termini, it's the sandstone-brick building on your left. Enter at the far end, at Largo di Villa Peretti.

Visiting the Museum: On the first floor, along with statues and busts showing such emperors as Trajan and Hadrian, you'll see the best-preserved Roman copy of the Greek *Discus Thrower*. Statues of athletes like this commonly stood in the baths, where Romans cultivated healthy bodies, minds, and social skills, hoping to lead well-rounded lives. Other statues on this floor originally stood in the pleasure gardens of the Roman rich—surrounded by greenery with the splashing sound of fountains, all painted in bright, lifelike colors. Though created by Romans, the themes are mostly Greek, with godlike humans and human-looking gods.

The second floor contains frescoes and mosaics that once decorated the walls and floors of Roman villas. They're remarkably realistic and unstuffy, featuring everyday people, animals, flowery patterns, and geometrical designs. The Villa Farnesina frescoes—in black, red, yellow, and blue—are mostly architectural designs, with

Near Termini Station

- - - Baroque Surprises
Self-Guided Walk

fake columns, friezes, and garlands. The Villa di Livia frescoes, owned by the wily wife of Augustus, immerse you in a leafy green garden full of birds and fruit trees, symbolizing the gods.

Finally, descend into the basement to see fine gold jewelry, dice, an abacus, and vault doors leading into the best coin collection in Europe, with fancy magnifying glasses maneuvering you through cases of coins from ancient Rome to modern times.

▲Baths of Diocletian (Terme di Diocleziano)

Of all the marvelous structures built by the Romans, their public baths were arguably the grandest, and the Baths of Diocletian were the granddaddy of them all.

Built by Emperor Diocletian around A.D. 300 and sprawling over 30 acres—roughly five times the size of the Colosseum—these baths could cleanse 3,000 Romans at once. They functioned until A.D. 537, when barbarians attacked and the

city's aqueducts fell into disuse, plunging Rome into a thousand years of poverty, darkness, and B.O. Today, tourists can visit one grand section of the baths, its former main hall. This impressive remnant of the ancient complex was later transformed (with help from Michelangelo) into the Church of Santa Maria degli Angeli.

Cost and Hours: Free, Mon-Sat 7:00-18:30, Sun 7:00-19:30. The entrance is on Piazza della Repubblica (Metro: Repubblica or buses #40 and #64).

Visiting the Baths: Start outside the church. The curved brick facade of today's church was once part of the *caldarium*, or steam room, of the ancient baths. Romans loved to sweat out last night's indulgences. After entering the main lobby (located where Piazza della Repubblica is today), they'd strip in the locker rooms, then enter the steam room. The *caldarium* had wood furnaces under the raised floors. Stoked by slaves, these furnaces were used to heat the floors and hot tubs. The low ceiling helped keep the room steamy.

Step into the vast and cool church. This round-domed room with an oculus (open skylight, now with modern stained glass) was once the *tepidarium*—the cooling-off room of the baths, where medium, "tepid" temperatures were maintained. This is where masseuses would rub you down and scrape you off with a stick (Romans didn't use soap).

Enter the biggest part of the church and stand under the towering vault on the inlaid marble cross. In ancient times, from the *tepidarium*, Romans would have continued on to this space, the **central hall** of the baths. While the decor around you dates from the 18th century, the structure dates from the fourth century. This hall retains the grandeur of the ancient baths. It's the size of a football field and seven stories high—once even higher, because the original ancient floor was about 15 feet below its present level. The ceiling's crisscross arches were an architectural feat unmatched for a thousand years. The eight red granite columns are original, from ancient Rome—stand next to one and feel its five-foot girth.

The church we see today was (at least partly) designed by Michelangelo (1561), who used the baths' main hall as the nave. Later, when Piazza della Repubblica became an important Roman intersection, another architect renovated the church. To allow people to enter from the grand new piazza, he spun it 90 degrees, turning Michelangelo's nave into a long transept.

▲**Church of Santa Maria della Vittoria**

This church houses Bernini's best-known statue, the swooning *St. Teresa in Ecstasy*. Inside the church, you'll find St. Teresa to the left of the altar. Teresa has just been stabbed with

God's arrow of fire. Now, the angel pulls it out and watches her reaction. Teresa swoons, her eyes roll up, her hand goes limp, she parts her lips...and moans. The smiling, cherubic angel understands just how she feels. Teresa, a 16th-century Spanish nun, later talked of the "sweetness" of "this intense pain," describing her oneness with God in ecstatic, even erotic, terms.

Bernini, the master of multimedia, pulls out all the stops to make this mystical vision real. Actual sunlight pours through the alabaster windows, and bronze sunbeams shine on a marble angel holding a golden arrow. Teresa leans back on a cloud, and her robe ripples from within, charged with her spiritual arousal. Bernini has created a little stage-setting of heaven. And watching from the "theater boxes" on either side are members of the family who commissioned the work.

The church, originally a poor Carmelite church, was slathered with Baroque richness in the 17th century. (It's grown popular lately for its part in Dan Brown's *Angels and Demons* book, something that serious historians scoff at.) At the altar, in the center of the starburst, is an icon of the Virgin Mary, considered miraculous for the military victories attributed to it during the Thirty Years' War (early 1600s). And, as the 17th century was a time when the Roman Catholic Church was threatened by Protestants, the ceiling shows Mary defeating (Protestant) snakes who grasp scriptures translated from the pope's Latin into the evil vernacular.

Cost and Hours: Free, pay €0.50 for light, Mon-Sat 8:30-12:00 & 15:30-18:00, Sun 15:30-18:00, about 5 blocks northwest of Termini train station at Via XX Settembre 17, Metro: Repubblica.

Santa Susanna Church

The facade of this church is considered the first in the Baroque style—see the date: MDCIII (1603). The architect (Carlo Maderno) added a new Baroque element—curves—seen in the scrollwork "shoulders." The home of the American Catholic Church in Rome, Santa Susanna holds Mass in English daily at 18:00 and on Sunday at 9:00 and 10:30. They arrange papal audience tickets (see page 913), and their excellent website contains tips for travelers and a list of convents that rent out rooms.

Cost and Hours: Free, Mon-Sat 9:00-12:00 & 16:00-18:00, open Sun only for Mass, Via XX Settembre 15, near recommended Via Firenze hotels, Metro: Repubblica, tel. 06-4201-4554, www.santasusanna.org.

Baroque Surprises Stroll on Via XX Settembre

When Pope Sixtus V developed an ambitious plan to reorganize Rome around key landmarks (c. 1580s), he transformed this formerly sleepy neighborhood near the Baths of Diocletian. Within three generations, it was a major traffic hub and the center of a new city water system. The streets were lined with grand fountains, obelisks, and churches, all decorated in the new style of the 1600s—Baroque.

For an enjoyable half-mile walk, start in Piazza di San Bernardo (near the Church of Santa Maria della Vittoria, with Bernini's famous St. Teresa statue and the Santa Susanna Church), stroll down Via XX Settembre (passing two Baroque churches—the **Church of San Carlo alla Quattro Fontane** and the **Church of Sant'Andrea al Quirinale**), and end at the Palazzo del Quirinale, which marks the summit of Quirinal Hill, the highest of Rome's fabled seven hills. The fountain in the middle of the square has colossal statues of horses and men (probably Castor and Pollux, third century); as part of his reordering of the city, Pope Sixtus V had the figures moved here from a spot near the Baths of Constantine. The obelisk, which formerly stood in front of the Mausoleum of Augustus, was erected here in the late 1700s. Take in the views—there's a fine vista of St. Peter's Basilica in the distance. From here, a set of stairs (in the direction of the dome) leads down to the Trevi Fountain. The big road continues on to Piazza Venezia.

Art Exhibitions

Two temporary exhibition spaces, near Palazzo del Quirinale and just a few blocks from each another, show top-notch art on a rotating basis. Scuderie del Quirinale typically focuses on the great masters (Titian, Vermeer, Caravaggio), while Palazzo delle Exposizioni favors contemporary artworks and photography.

Cost and Hours: €12 for each site, can be more with some exhibits, €20 combo-ticket for both is good for three days; both open Sun-Thu 10:00-20:00, Fri-Sat 10:00-20:30 except the Palazzo is closed Mon; last entry one hour before closing; Scuderie—Via XXIV Maggio 16, tel. 06-696-271, www.scuderiequirinale.it; Palazzo—Via Nazionale 194, tel. 06-399-6750, www.palazzoesposizioni.it.

Pilgrim's Rome

East of the Colosseum (and south of Termini train station) are several venerable churches that Catholic pilgrims make a point of visiting. Near one of the churches is a small WWII museum.

Church of San Giovanni in Laterano

Built by Constantine, the first Christian emperor, this was Rome's most important church through medieval times. A building alongside the church houses the Holy Stairs (Scala Santa) said to have been walked up by Jesus, which today are ascended by pilgrims on their knees.

Cost and Hours: Church—free, cloister-€5, audioguide available, daily 7:00-18:30; Holy Stairs—April-Sept Mon-Sat 6:00-12:00 & 15:30-18:45, Sun 7:00-12:30 & 15:30-19:00, Oct-

Pilgrim's Rome

Piazza Cinquecento

TERMINI STATION

Termini

Piazzale Sisto V

SANTA MARIA MAGGIORE

SANTA PRASSEDE

Piazza Vittorio Emanuele II

Vittorio Emanuele

ST. PETER-IN-CHAINS

MUSEUM OF ASIAN ART

Colosseo

Parco del Colle Oppio

←To Forum

COLOSSEUM

SAN CLEMENTE

Manzoni

MUSEUM OF THE LIBERATION OF ROME

ANCIENT ARCHES

Villa Wolkonski

SANTI GIOVANNI E PAOLO

HOLY STAIRS

Piazza San Giovanni in Laterano

Piazza di Porta San Giovanni

Piazza Celimontana

SAN GIOVANNI IN LATERANO

Piazzale di Appio

Villa Celimontana

San Giovanni

MARKET

250 Meters

250 Yards

March closes 30 minutes earlier, Piazza di San Giovanni in Laterano, Metro: San Giovanni, or bus #85 or #87; tel. 06-6988-6409, www.scalasanta.org.

Museum of the Liberation of Rome
(Museo Storico della Liberazione di Roma)

This small memorial museum, near the Church of San Giovanni in Laterano, is housed in the prison wing of the former Nazi police headquarters of occupied Rome. Other than a single pamphlet, there's little in English. Still, for those interested in resistance movements and the Nazi occupation, it's a stirring visit. You'll see a few artifacts, many photos of heroes, and a couple of cells preserved as they were found on June 4, 1944, when the city was liberated.

Cost and Hours: Free, Tue-Sun 9:30-12:30, Tue and Thu-Fri also 15:30-19:30, closed Mon and Aug, just behind the Holy Stairs, look for the flags at Via Tasso 145; tel. 06-700-3866.

Church of Santa Maria Maggiore

Some of Rome's best-surviving mosaics line the nave of this church built as Rome was falling. The nearby Church of Santa Prassede has still more early mosaics.

Cost and Hours: Free, daily 7:00-19:00, Piazza Santa Maria Maggiore, Metro: Termini or Vittorio Emanuele, tel. 06-6988-6802.

▲Church of San Clemente

Besides visiting the church itself, with frescoes by Masolino, you can also descend into the ruins of an earlier church. Descend yet one more level and enter the eerie remains of a pagan temple to Mithras.

Cost and Hours: Upper church—free, lower church-€5, both open Mon-Sat 9:00-12:30 & 15:00-18:00, Sun 12:00-18:00, last entry to lower church 20 minutes before closing; Via di San Giovanni in Laterano, Metro: Colosseo, or bus #85 or #87; tel. 06-774-0021, www.basilicasanclemente.com.

South Rome

The area south of the center contains some interesting but widely scattered areas, from Trastevere to the Jewish Quarter to Testaccio to E.U.R.

Trastevere and Nearby

Trastevere is the colorful neighborhood across *(tras)* the Tiber *(Tevere)* River. Trastevere (trahs-TAY-veh-ray) offers the best look at medieval-village Rome.

The action unwinds to the chime of the church bells. Go there and wander. Wonder. Be a poet. This is Rome's Left Bank. (You can download a free Rick Steves audio tour of this neighborhood to your mobile device; see page 9.)

This proud neighborhood was long a working-class area. Now that it's becoming trendy, high rents are driving out the source of so much color. Still, it's a great people scene, especially at night. Stroll the back streets (for restaurant recommendations, see page 970).

To reach Trastevere by foot from Capitoline Hill, cross the Tiber on Ponte Fabricio to Isola Tiberina; from there, Ponte Cestio takes you to Trastevere. You can also take tram #8 from Piazza Venezia or Largo Argentina, or bus #H from Termini or Piazza della Repubblica (get off at Sonnino/Piazza Belli). From the Vatican (Piazza Risorgimento), it's bus #23 or #271.

Linking Trastevere with the "Heart of Rome Walk": You can walk from Trastevere to Campo de' Fiori to link up with the beginning of my "Heart of Rome Walk" (see page 874). From Trastevere's church square (Piazza di Santa Maria), take Via del Moro to the river and cross at Ponte Sisto, a pedestrian bridge that has a good view of St. Peter's dome. Continue straight ahead for one block. Take the first left, which leads down Via di Capo di Ferro through the scary and narrow darkness to Piazza Farnese, with the imposing Palazzo Farnese. Michelangelo contributed to the facade of this palace, now the French Embassy. The fountains on the square feature huge one-piece granite hot tubs from the ancient Roman Baths of Caracalla. One block from there (opposite the palace) is the atmospheric square, Campo de' Fiori.

▲Church of Santa Maria in Trastevere

One of Rome's oldest church sites, a basilica was erected here in the fourth century, when Christianity was legalized. It is said to have

been the first church in Rome dedicated to the Virgin Mary. The structure you see today dates mainly from the 12th century. Its portico (covered area just outside the door) is decorated with fascinating fragments of stone—many of them lids from catacomb burial niches—and filled with early Christian symbolism. The incredibly expensive 13th-century floor is a fine example of Cosmati mosaic work—a style of mosaic featuring intricate geometric shapes (in this case, made with marble scavenged from Roman ruins).

Cost and Hours: Free, daily 7:30-21:00, on Piazza di Santa Maria.

▲Villa Farnesina

Here's a unique opportunity to see a sumptuous Renaissance villa in Rome decorated with Raphael paintings. It was built in the early 1500s for the richest man in Renaissance Europe, Sienese banker Agostino Chigi. Architect Baldassare Peruzzi's design—a U-shaped building with wings enfolding what used to be a vast garden— successfully blended architecture and nature in a way

ROME

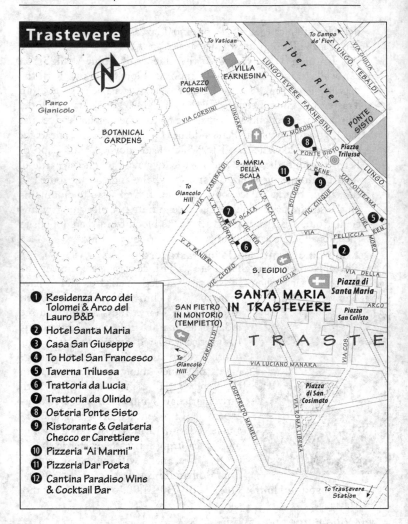

Trastevere

Legend:

1. Residenza Arco dei Tolomei & Arco del Lauro B&B
2. Hotel Santa Maria
3. Casa San Giuseppe
4. To Hotel San Francesco
5. Taverna Trilussa
6. Trattoria da Lucia
7. Trattoria da Olindo
8. Osteria Ponte Sisto
9. Ristorante & Gelateria Checco er Carettiere
10. Pizzeria "Ai Marmi"
11. Pizzeria Dar Poeta
12. Cantina Paradiso Wine & Cocktail Bar

that both ancient and Renaissance Romans loved. Orchards and flower beds flowed down in terraces from the palace to the riverbanks. Later construction of modern embankments and avenues robbed the garden of its grandeur, leaving it with a more melancholy charm. Inside, cavorting gods and goddesses cover the walls and ceilings, most famously Raphael's depiction of the sea nymph Galatea.

Cost and Hours: €6; Mon-Sat 9:00-14:00, closed Sun except open 9:00-17:00 on second Sun of month, last entry 30 minutes before closing; across the river from Campo de' Fiori, a short walk from Ponte Sisto and a block behind the river at 230 Via della Lungara; tel. 06-6802-7268, www.villafarnesina.it.

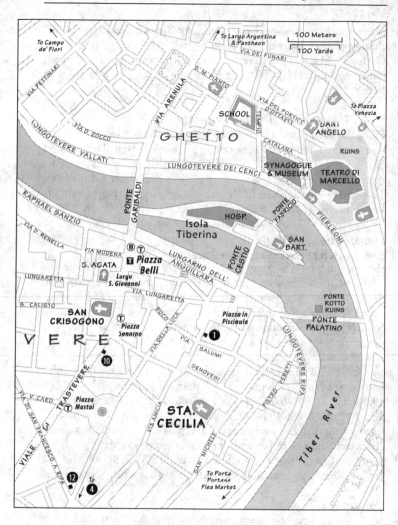

Gianicolo Hill Viewpoint

From this park atop a hill, the city views are superb, and the walk to the top holds a treat for architecture buffs. Start at Trastevere's Piazza di San Cosimato, and follow Via Luciano Manara to Via Garibaldi, at the base of the hill. Via Garibaldi winds its way up the side of the hill to the Church of San Pietro in Montorio. To the right of the church, in a small courtyard, is the Tempietto by Donato Bramante. This tiny church, built to commemorate the martyrdom of St. Peter, is considered a jewel of Italian Renaissance architecture.

Continuing up the hill, Via Garibaldi connects to Passeggiata del Gianicolo. From here, you'll find a pleasant park with panoramic city views. Ponder the many Victorian-era statues, including that of baby-carrying, gun-wielding, horse-riding Anita Garibaldi. She was the Brazilian wife of the revolutionary General Giuseppe Garibaldi, who helped forge a united Italy in the late 19th century.

Near Trastevere: Jewish Quarter

From the 16th through the 19th centuries, Rome's Jewish population was forced to live in a cramped ghetto at an often-flooded bend of the Tiber River. While the medieval Jewish ghetto is long gone, this area—just across the river and toward Capitoline Hill from Trastevere—is still home to Rome's synagogue and fragments of its Jewish heritage. You can download a free Rick Steves audio tour of this neighborhood to your mobile device; see page 9.

Synagogue (Sinagoga) and Jewish Museum (Museo Ebraico)

Rome's modern synagogue stands proudly on the spot where the medieval Jewish community was sequestered for more than 300 years. The site of a historic visit by Pope John Paul II, this synagogue features a fine interior and a museum filled with artifacts of Rome's Jewish community. Modest dress is required. The only way to visit the synagogue—unless you're here for daily prayer service—is with a tour.

Cost and Hours: €10 ticket includes museum and guided hourly tour of synagogue; mid-June-mid-Sept Sun-Thu 10:00-19:00, Fri 10:00-16:00, closed Sat; mid-Sept-mid-June Sun-Thu 10:00-17:00, Fri 9:00-14:00, closed Sat; last entry 45 minutes before closing, English tours usually at :15 past the hour, 30 minutes, check schedule at ticket counter; on Lungotevere dei Cenci, tel. 06-6840-0661, www.museoebraico.roma.it. Walking tours of the Jewish Ghetto are conducted at least once a day except Saturday.

Testaccio

In the gritty Testaccio neighborhood, several fascinating but lesser sights cluster at the Piramide Metro stop between the Colosseum and E.U.R. (This is a quick and easy stop as you return from E.U.R., or when changing trains en route to Ostia Antica.)

In ancient times (when Rome's population topped a million), wharves lined the banks of the Tiber River here. Back then, 90 percent of the city's food came through here, and the long tradition of Testaccio feeding Rome continues today. Long a working-class neighborhood, Testaccio has recently gone trendy-bohemian. Visitors wander through an awkward mix of yuppie and proletarian worlds, not noticing—but perhaps sensing—the "Keep Testaccio for the Testaccians" graffiti.

ROME

You can pick and choose among the Testaccio sights described here, or link them in the walk outlined next.

Testaccio Walk

To enjoy all the Testaccio sights, take this walk from the Piramide Metro stop to the Testaccio Market (just follow the map above): In the area around the Piramide Metro, view the pyramid and check out Porta San Paolo (and its free museum). Circle around to the Mussolini-era post office before walking down to the Protestant cemetery (enter to enjoy the park and views of the pyramid; handy WC). Continue down the same street (Via Caio Cestio) to loop around Monte Testaccio (the mound of broken ancient Roman pots now surrounded by a thriving nightclub scene). At the site of an old slaughterhouse (now a cultural complex with a contemporary art museum and music school), pick out the history of this spot—the ornamentation of the slaughterhouse, the *frigorifero* (ice house adjacent), and the fine view of the shard mountain. Finally, tour the modern Testaccio Market, finding the evocative spot where you can gaze down at the ancient Roman road littered with broken amphorae.

ROME

Pyramid of Gaius Cestius

An Egyptian-style pyramid from ancient Rome (first century B.C.) stands next to the Piramide Metro stop. The Roman occupation of Egypt brought exotic pharaonic styles into vogue. Stoking the fascination with Egypt even further was the love affair of Mark Antony and Cleopatra; this power couple was the ancient equivalent of Brangelina (Cleopantony?). A rich Roman magistrate, Gaius Cestius, had this pyramid built as his tomb, complete with a burial chamber inside. Made of brick covered in marble, the 90-foot structure was completed in just 330 days (as stated in its Latin inscription). While smaller than actual Egyptian pyramids, its proportions are correct. It was later incorporated into the Aurelian Wall, and it now stands as a marker to the entrance of Testaccio.

Porta San Paolo and Museo della Via Ostiense

This formidable gate (also next to the Piramide Metro stop) is from the Aurelian Wall, begun in the third century under Emperor Aurelian. The wall, which encircled the city, was 12 miles long and averaged about 26 feet high, with 14 main gates and 380 72-foot-tall towers. Most of what you'll see today is circa A.D. 400, but the barbarians reconstructed the gate later, in the sixth century.

Inside the gate is a tiny free museum (find entrance near pyramid; open Tue and Thu 9:00-13:30 & 14:30-16:30, Wed and Fri-Sat 9:00-13:30, open first and third Sun of month 9:00-13:30, closed Mon and second and fourth Sun of month, tel. 06-574-3193). The museum offers a chance to explore the gate and a few models of Rome's ancient port, Ostia Antica; its neighbor, Porto, with its famed hexagonal harbor; and the Ostian Way, the straight Roman road that paralleled the curvy Tiber for 15 miles from Rome to the sea.

For more on the Aurelian Wall, visit the San Sebastiano Gate and Museum of the Walls, described under "Appian Way" on page 948.

Protestant Cemetery

Lush and lovingly cared for, the Cemetery for the Burial of Non-Catholic Foreigners (Cimitero Acattolico per gli Stranieri al Testaccio) is a tomb-filled "park," running along the wall just beyond the pyramid. The cemetery is also the only English-style landscape (rolling hills, calculated vistas) in Rome, making it a favorite spot for a quiet stroll.

Cost and Hours: €3 suggested donation—leave in box by entrance, Mon-Sat 9:00-17:00, Sun 9:00-13:00, last entry 30 minutes before closing, nice WC inside, staff at info office can help you find specific graves, tel. 06-574-1900, www.cemeteryrome.it.

Visiting the Cemetery: From the Piramide Metro stop, walk between the pyramid and the Roman gate on Via Persichetti/Via Marmorata. Then go left on Caio Cestio to the gate of the cemetery.

Originally, none of the Protestant epitaphs were allowed to make any mention of heaven. Signs direct visitors to the graves of notable non-Catholics who have died in Rome since 1716. Many of the buried were diplomats. And many, such as the poets Percy Shelley (1792-1822) and John Keats (1795-1821), were from the Romantic Age. They came to Italy on the Grand Tour and—"captivated by the fatal charms of Rome," as Shelley wrote—never left.

Head 90 degrees left to find Keats' tomb, in the far corner. Keats died in his twenties, unrecognized. He wanted to be unnamed on a tomb that read, "Young English Poet, 1821. Here lies one whose name was writ in water." (To see Keats' tomb when the cemetery is closed, look through the tiny peephole on Via Caio Cestio, 10 yards off Via Marmarata.) Shelley's tomb is straight ahead from the entrance, up the hill, at the base of the stubby tower. Like so many Romantic age artists and writers, Shelley was enamored with Rome. In 1821 he wrote, "Go thou to Rome,—at once the Paradise, the grave, the city, and the wilderness" (from *Adonais*, his elegy on Keats' death).

Monte Testaccio

The area surrounding this small hill is a popular nightlife spot (as you leave the cemetery, turn left and continue two blocks down Caio Cestio). The hill, actually a 115-foot-tall ancient trash pile, is made of *testae*—broken shards of earthenware jars mostly used to haul oil 2,000 years ago, when this was a gritty port warehouse district. For 500 years, rancid oil vessels were discarded here. Slowly, Rome's lowly eighth hill was built. Because the caves dug into the hill stay cool (perfect for storing wine), trendy bars, clubs, and restaurants compete with gritty car-repair places for a spot. The neighborhood was once known for a huge slaughterhouse and a Roma (Gypsy) camp that squatted inside an old military base. Now it's home to the Testaccio Village (a site for summer concerts and techno raves—dead until late at night, when it thrives), a weekend farmers' market, and a branch of Rome's contemporary art museum (MACRO).

Testaccio Market (Mercato di Testaccio)

The covered and colorful market is a focal point of the neighborhood. It recently moved to this more modern and "hygienic" location—many say that it's lost some of its edgy charm. But while the structure may be new, the relationships are still old, as locals nurture close relationships with the merchants who sell them their favorite foods. A stroll through here affords a fine look at a traditional Roman market. Find the center (where the sky opens up) and look down at the ancient Roman road littered with the shards of broken amphorae.

Cost and Hours: Free, Mon-Sat until 14:00, closed Sun, WC on the north side (near the clothing stalls), across from Monte Testaccio on Via Galvani).

Eating in the Market: Testaccio has long been the neighborhood of slaughterhouses, and its restaurants are renowned for their ability to cook up the least palatable part of the animals...the "fifth quarter." Head toward the back of the market (the side closest to Via Beniamino Franklin) to search out a few favorites for a light lunch. At **Mordi & Vai** (stall 15), Sergio makes tasty €4 sandwiches; locals love the *trippa* (tripe), but I prefer the *panino con allesso* (boiled beef with the bread dipped in broth) and *picchiapò* (stewed beef in a mildly spicy tomato sauce). Nearby, **Dess'art** (stall 66) will satisfy your sweet tooth with their creative pastries. For olives, cheese, and cold cuts, try **Ferraro's** (stall 2-3, around the corner from Mordi & Vai). They're also a good bet for edible souvenirs—dried porcini mushrooms and sun-dried tomatoes, as well as other specialties, many from Calabria (think spicy).

South of Testaccio

You can ride the Metro to the Montemartini Museum and St. Paul's Outside the Walls, but if you prefer to stay above ground, buses #23, #271, and #769 run on Via Ostiense from the Piramide Metro stop to the museum (stop: Ostiense/Garbatella) and the church (stop: Viale S. Paolo).

▲Montemartini Museum
(Musei Capitolini Centrale Montemartini)

This museum houses a dreamy collection of 400 ancient statues, set evocatively in a classic 1932 electric power plant, among generators and *Metropolis*-type cast-iron machinery. While the art is not as famous as the collections you'll see downtown, the effect is fun and memorable—and you'll encounter absolutely no tourists. If you're tackling Rome with kids, this museum is ideal: It's uncrowded and cool, immersed in an old power plant, with art placed at kid level.

Cost and Hours: €7.50, Tue-Sun 9:00-19:00, closed Mon, last entry 30 minutes before closing, look for red banner marking

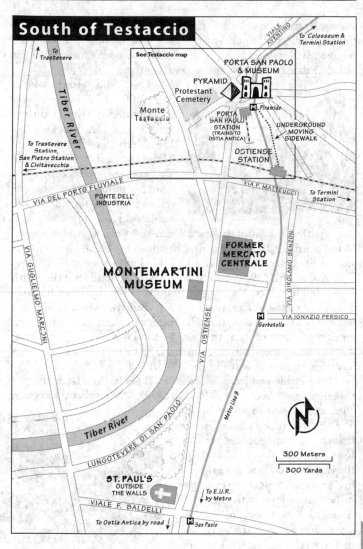

South of Testaccio

To Trastevere

Tiber River

To Colosseum &
Termini Station

VIALE
AVENTINO

See Testaccio map

PORTA SAN PAOLO
& MUSEUM

PYRAMID

Protestant
Cemetery

Monte
Testaccio

PORTA
SAN PAOLO
STATION
(TRAINS TO
OSTIA ANTICA)

M Piramide

UNDERGROUND
MOVING
SIDEWALK

OSTIENSE
STATION

To Trastevere
Station,
San Pietro Station
& Civitavecchia

VIA DEL PORTO FLUVIALE

VIA P. MATTEUCCI

To Termini
Station

PONTE DELL'
INDUSTRIA

VIA GUGLIELMO MARCONI

FORMER
MERCATO
CENTRALE

MONTEMARTINI
MUSEUM

VIA GIROLAMO BENZON

M VIA IGNAZIO PERSICO
Garbatella

VIA OSTIENSE

Tiber River

LUNGOTEVERE DI SAN PAOLO

Metro Line B

N

300 Meters

300 Yards

ST. PAUL'S
OUTSIDE
THE WALLS

To E.U.R.
by Metro

VIALE F. BALDELLI

To Ostia Antica by road

M *San Paolo*

Via Ostiense 106, a short walk from Metro: Garbatella, tel. 06-574-8030, www.centralemontemartini.org.

▲St. Paul's Outside the Walls
(Basilica San Paolo Fuori le Mura)

According to Christian tradition, the body of St. Paul was buried here, where a small shrine once stood. It was replaced by a much bigger church in around A.D. 380—in what was the last major construction project of Imperial Rome and the largest church in Christendom until St. Peter's. That church burned in 1823, and the stately, if stark, Neoclassical church you see today was built on its footprint. Pilgrims flock here to venerate the saint, especially since forensic experts concluded in 2009 that the bones interred under the altar date from the first or second century.

Cost and Hours: Free, daily 7:00-18:30, modest dress code enforced, dry audioguide-€5 plus ID, Via Ostiense 186, Metro: San Paolo, exit the Metro station following *via Ostiense* sign, and look for the church's round tower, the entrance is on the far side, www.basilicasanpaolo.org.

Visiting the Church: The column-lined courtyard leading up to the church is typical of early Christian churches—the first version of St. Peter's Basilica also had this kind of welcoming zone. The facade, while 19th century, is early Christian in its style—with Rome and Jerusalem flanking the Lamb of God. In the courtyard's center is a statue of Paul holding his trademark sword, the instrument of his martyrdom. The palm trees, while not native to Rome, remind pilgrims of what they saw in the Holy Land. The central door of bronze and silver, from the 1930s, is dedicated to Peter (crucified upside-down) and Paul (beheaded).

Step inside and feel as close as you'll get in the 21st century to experiencing a monumental Roman basilica. Marvel at the ceiling, with those massive wood beams.

The marble-inlaid floor is like that of the Pantheon and typically Roman. Alabaster windows light the vast interior. It feels sterile, but in a good way—as if you're already in heaven. Along with St. Peter's Basilica, San Giovanni in Laterano, and Santa Maria Maggiore, this church is, legally speaking, part of the Vatican rather than Italy. The triumphal arch leading to the altar has a fifth-century mosaic of Christ raising his hand in blessing.

The fine 13th-century mosaic filling the dome in the apse is Byzantine in style; it was likely created by the same craftsmen who decorated St. Mark's in Venice. Notice the tiny white bug-like creature washing Jesus' toe. It's Honorius III, the 13th-century pope who paid for the apse renovation—reminding people of his humbleness while getting some credit at the same time.

The church is built upon the supposed grave of St. Paul. Ac-

ROME

cording to tradition, Paul was decapitated two miles from this spot. His head was preserved at San Giovanni in Laterano, and his body was buried here under the altar. In 2009, archaeologists unearthed a sarcophagus with early inscriptions identifying it as Paul's, and carbon-dating on the bones inside confirmed their ancient origin. Ringing the upper part of the church are round mosaic portraits of 266 popes, from St. Peter (the first one in the right transept) to the present. Find the recent popes to the right of the altar—not in the nave, but farther to the right, under the arches of the dim right aisle. You'll see globetrotting John Paul II *(Jo Paulus II)* and progressive John XXIII, who oversaw the Vatican II changes of the 1960s. A portrait of Pope #266—Francis—was recently installed, alongside blank medallions for future popes.

The peaceful 13th-century cloister (€4) has elegant Romanesque columns and arches, and fragments of early Christian/Roman sarcophagi, a relic chapel, and a small painting gallery.

E.U.R.

In the late 1930s, Italy's dictator Benito Mussolini planned an international exhibition to show off the wonders of his fascist society.

But these wonders brought us World War II, and Il Duce's celebration never happened. The unfinished mega-project was completed in the 1950s, and today it houses government offices and big, obscure museums filled with important, rarely visited relics.

If Hitler and Mussolini had won the war, our world might look like E.U.R. (AY-oor). Hike down E.U.R.'s wide, pedestrian-mean boulevards. Patriotic murals, aren't-you-proud-to-be-an-extreme-right-winger pillars, and stern squares decorate the soulless planned grid and sterile office blocks. Patriotic quotes are chiseled into walls. Boulevards named for Astronomy, Electronics, Social Security, and Beethoven are more exhausting than inspirational. And, not to be outdone by the ancients, Mussolini had a towering fascist-style obelisk erected in the central Piazza Marconi.

Despite its grim past, E.U.R. is now an up-and-coming place with young people and trendy cafés. It's worth a trip for the Museum of Roman Civilization (described later). And because a few landmark buildings of Italian modernism are located here and there, E.U.R. has become an important destination for architecture buffs. The new futuristic convention center nicknamed "The Cloud" (it's meant to look like a cloud suspended in a glass box) promises to bring even more life to the district.

The Metro skirts E.U.R. with three stops (10 minutes from

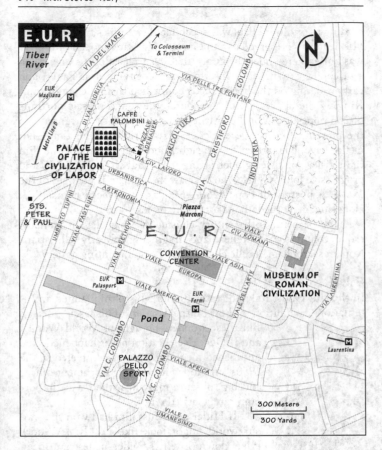

the Colosseum). Use E.U.R. Magliana for the Palace of the Civilization of Labor and E.U.R. Fermi for the Museum of Roman Civilization. Consider walking 20 minutes from the palace to the museum through the center of E.U.R.

Palace of the Civilization of Labor
(Palazzo della Civiltà del Lavoro)

From the Magliana Metro stop, stairs lead uphill to this epitome of fascist architecture. With its giant no-questions-asked patriotic statues and its stark simplicity, this is E.U.R.'s tallest building and key landmark. It's understandably nicknamed the "Square Colosseum." Closed to the public while they decide how to use it, it's still interesting to walk around. Downhill, in front of the palace, Caffè Palombini is a popular Roman institution; their buffet line is a hit with local workers for lunch (daily 7:00-22:00; good gelato, pastries, and snacks; Piazzale Adenauer 12, tel. 06-591-1700).

▲Museum of Roman Civilization (Museo della Civiltà Romana)

With dozens of rooms of plaster casts and models illustrating the greatness of classical Rome, this vast and dated museum gives a strangely lifeless, close-up look at Rome. It's calm and quiet, and lets you see virtually every ancient site intact. Each room has a theme, from military tricks to musical instruments, and is well described in English. One long hall is filled with casts of the reliefs of Trajan's Column. The highlight is the huge scale model of Constantine's Rome, circa A.D. 300. There are no ancient artifacts, but the various models can teach volumes about life and war in ancient Rome. The Planetarium and Astronomical Museum are mostly of interest to children—so don't bother with the €10.50 combo-ticket unless you have kids.

Cost and Hours: €8.50, Tue-Sun 9:00-14:00, closed Mon, last entry one hour before closing, Piazza G. Agnelli; leave the E.U.R. Fermi Metro station and head left on Viale America, toward McDonald's and the wide, narrow Eni skyscraper. At the T-intersection, turn left on Viale dell'Arte and go uphill three blocks—you'll see its colonnade on the right, beyond the trees; to return to the city center, access the Metro entrance across the street, on the side closest to the pond, tel. 06-5422-0919, www.museociviltaromana.it.

Ancient Appian Way

Southeast of the city center lie several ancient sights that make the trek here worthwhile.

Baths of Caracalla (Terme di Caracalla)

Inaugurated by Emperor Caracalla in A.D. 216, this massive bath complex could accommodate 1,600 visitors at a time. Today it's just a shell—a huge shell—with all of its sculptures and most of its mosaics moved to museums. You'll see a two-story roofless brick building surrounded by a garden, bordered by ruined walls. The two large rooms at either end of the building were used for exercise. In between the exercise rooms was a pool flanked by two small mosaic-floored dressing rooms. Niches in the walls once

ROME

held statues. The baths' statues are displayed elsewhere: For example, the immense *Toro Farnese* (a marble sculpture of a bull surrounded by people) snorts in Naples' Archaeological Museum.

In its day, this was a remarkable place to hang out. For ancient Romans, bathing was a social experience. The Baths of Caracalla functioned until Goths severed the aqueducts in the sixth century. In modern times, grand operas are performed here during the summer (www.operaroma.it).

Cost and Hours: €7, includes the Tomb of Cecilia Metella and the Villa dei Quintili on the Appian Way, Mon 9:00-14:00, Tue-Sun 9:00 until one hour before sunset (roughly April-Sept 19:00, Oct 18:30, Nov-mid-Feb 16:30, mid-Feb-March 17:00), last entry one hour before closing, audioguide-€5, good €8 guidebook; Metro: Circo Massimo, then a 5-minute walk south along Via delle Terme di Caracalla; bus #714 from Termini train station or bus #118 from the Appian Way—see "Getting There" on next page; tel. 06-3996-7700.

▲Appian Way

For a taste of the countryside around Rome and more wonders of Roman engineering, take the four-mile trip from the Colosseum out past the wall to a stretch of the ancient Appian Way, where the original pavement stones are lined by several interesting sights. Ancient Rome's first and greatest highway, the Appian Way once ran from Rome to the Adriatic port of Brindisi, the gateway to Greece. Today you can walk (or bike) some  stretches of the road, rattling over original paving stones, past crumbling monuments that once edged the sides.

The wonder of its day, Appian Way was the largest, widest, fastest road ever, called the "Queen of Roads." Begun in 312 B.C. and named after Appius Claudius Caecus (a Roman official), it connected Rome with Capua (near Naples), running in a straight line for much of the way, ignoring the natural contour of the land. Eventually, this most important of Roman roads stretched 430 miles to the port of Brindisi—the gateway to the East—where boats sailed for Greece and Egypt. Twenty-nine such roads fanned out from Rome. Just as Hitler built the Autobahn system in anticipation of empire maintenance, the expansion-minded Roman government realized the military and political value of a good road system.

Today the road and the landscape around it are preserved as a cultural park. For the tourist, the ancient Appian Way offers three attractions: the road itself, with its ruined monuments; the two

Ancient Appian Way

To
San Sebastiano Gate,
Museum of the Walls &
Central Rome

DOMINE
QUO VADIS
CHURCH

500 Meters

500 Yards

VIA DELLA CAFFARELLA

VIA ARDEANTINA

PEDESTRIAN WALKWAY (CLOSED WEDS.)

COLUMBARIUM

SECOND MILESTONE

CATACOMBS OF SAN CALLISTO

VIA APPIA

VIA APPIA PIGNATELLI

FOSSE ARDEANTINE

D. SETTE CHIESE

CATACOMBS OF SAN SEBASTIANO & WC

BASILICA DI SAN SEBASTIANO

VILLA OF MAXENTIUS

CIRCUS OF MAXENTIUS

VIA ARDEANTINA

VIA DI SAN SEBASTIANO

APPIA ANTICA

TOMB OF CECILIA METELLA

THIRD MILESTONE

VIA CECILIA METELLA

APPIA ANTICA CAFFÈ & BIKE RENTAL

Tu
Aqueduct
Park

ALIMENTARI

VIA APPIA ANTICA

TORRE DI CAPO DI BOVE

CAPO DI BOVE

SCENIC SECTION

To 4th through 11th
Milestones & Brindisi

A Bus #660 Stop
B Bus #118 Stops
C Bus #118 (Southbound Stop Only)
D Bus #218 Stop
E Archeobus Stops

ROME

major Christian catacombs open to visitors; and the peaceful atmosphere, which provides a respite from the city. Be aware, however, that the road today is busy with traffic—and actually quite treacherous in spots.

The road starts at the massive **San Sebastiano Gate and Museum of the Walls,** about two miles south of the Colosseum. The stretch that's of most interest to tourists starts another two miles south of the gate. I like to begin near the Tomb of Cecilia Metella, at the far (southern) end of the key sights, and work northward (mostly downhill) toward central Rome.

Catacombs

The catacombs are burial places for (mostly) Christians who died in ancient Roman times. By law, no one was allowed to be buried within the walls of Rome. While pagan Romans were into cremation, Christians preferred to be buried (so that they could be resurrected when the time came). But land was expensive, and most Christians were poor. A few wealthy, landowning Christians allowed their properties to be used as burial places.

The 40 or so known catacombs are scattered outside the ancient walls of Rome. From the first through the fifth centuries, Christians dug an estimated 375 miles of tomb-lined tunnels, with networks of galleries as many as five layers deep. The volcanic tuff that Rome sits atop—which is soft and easy to cut, but hardens when exposed to air—was perfect for the job. The Christians burrowed many layers deep for two reasons: to get more mileage out of the donated land, and to be near martyrs and saints already buried there. Bodies were wrapped in linen (like Christ's). Since they figured the Second Coming was imminent, there was no interest in embalming the body.

When Emperor Constantine legalized Christianity in A.D. 313, Christians had a new, interesting problem: There would be no more recently persecuted martyrs to bind them together and inspire them. Instead, the early martyrs and popes assumed more importance, and Christians began making pilgrimages to their burial places in the catacombs. In the 800s, when barbarian invaders started ransacking the tombs, Christians moved the relics of saints and martyrs to the safety of churches in the city center. For a thousand years, the catacombs were forgotten. In

Cost and Hours: San Sebastiano Gate and Museum of the Walls—€5, Tue-Sun 9:00-14:00, closed Mon, last entry 30 minutes before closing, tel. 06-7047-5284.

When to Go: Visit in the morning or late afternoon, since many of the sights—including the Catacombs of San Callisto—shut down from 12:00 to 14:00. All the recommended sights are open on Tuesday, Thursday, Friday, and Saturday. On Monday, several sights are closed, including Tomb of Cecilia Metella, Circus and Villa of Maxentius, and San Sebastiano Gate and Museum of the Walls. On Wednesday, Catacombs of San Callisto and the pedestrian path through the park are closed. On Sunday, the Catacombs of San Sebastiano are closed; however, Appian Way is closed to most car traffic, making it a great day for walking or biking (although the old stones can be bumpy).

Getting There: Bus #660 drops you off at the Tomb of Cecilia Metella. In Rome, take Metro line A to the Colli Albani stop, where you catch bus #660 (2/hour) and ride 15 minutes to the last

early modern times, they were excavated and became part of the Romantic Age's Grand Tour of Europe.

When abandoned plates and utensils from ritual meals were found, 18th- and 19th-century Romantics guessed that persecuted Christians hid out in these candlelit galleries. The popularity  of this legend grew, even though it was untrue: By the second century, more than a million people lived in Rome, and the 10,000 early Christians didn't need to camp out in the catacombs. They hid in plain view, melting into obscurity within the city itself.

The underground tunnels, while empty of bones, are rich in early Christian symbolism, which functioned as a secret language. The dove represented the soul. You'll see it quenching its thirst (worshipping), with an olive branch (at rest), or happily perched (in paradise). Peacocks, known for their purportedly "incorruptible flesh," embodied immortality. The shepherd with a lamb on his shoulders was the "good shepherd," the first portrayal of Christ as a kindly leader of his flock. The fish was used because the first letters of these words—"Jesus Christ, Son of God, Savior"—spelled "fish" in Greek. And the anchor is a cross in disguise. A second-century bishop had written on his tomb, "All who understand these things, pray for me." You'll see pictures of people praying with their hands raised—the custom at the time.

stop—Cecilia Metella/Via Appia Antica (at the intersection of Via Cecilia Metella and Via Appia Antica). The TI is about the only place to buy a bus ticket on the Appian Way—have one in hand for your return trip.

A **taxi** will get you from Rome to the Tomb of Cecilia Metella for about €20. However, to return by taxi, you'll have to phone for one; there are no taxi stands on Appian Way (or just take handy bus #118 back to Rome).

Bus #118 gets you to the sights on the northern part of Appian Way. In Rome, catch #118 from either the Piramide or Circo Massimo Metro stops; going away from the city center, it stops at the Baths of Caracalla, San Sebastiano Gate, Domine Quo Vadis Church, Catacombs of San Callisto, and Catacombs of San Sebastiano. Although bus #118 does not stop at Tomb of Cecilia Metella, the tomb is only 500 yards away from the San Sebastiano bus stop. Going back to Rome, bus #118 takes a somewhat different route (skipping Catacombs of San Sebastiano); catch this northbound bus just up the road at Catacombs of San Callisto or near Domine Quo Vadis.

Bus #218 goes from San Giovanni in Laterano to Domine Quo Vadis Church and the west entrance of Catacombs of San Callisto, but isn't that useful for other Appian Way sights.

The handy, but much more expensive, **Archeobus** runs from Termini train station to the major Appian Way sights (see "Tours in Rome," page 858). It stops at all the key attractions—you can hop off, tour the sights, and pick up a later bus (officially runs twice hourly during summer, but service can be spotty).

Getting Back: No matter how you arrive at Appian Way, **bus #118** is the easiest and cheapest way to return to Rome (get off at the end of the line, the Piramide Metro stop).

Information: The **Via Appia Antica TI** near Domine Quo Vadis Church gives out maps and information on the entire park, which stretches east and south of the visit outlined here (daily April-Oct 9:30-17:30, Nov-March 9:30-16:30, rents bikes, good €1 map, Via Appia Antica 58/60, tel. 06-513-5316, www.parcoappiaantica.it, general info at www.archeoroma.beniculturali.it/en). **Capo di Bove** has a small info center with a good €4 map/guide, active excavations, and a relaxing garden (Mon-Sat 10:00-16:00, Sun 10:00-18:00, closes earlier in winter, good place for discreet picnic, clean WCs, Via Appia Antica 222, tel. 06-3996-7700); it's 100 yards uphill from **Appia Antica Caffè,** which also sells maps.

Services: Free WCs are at the San Sebastiano and San Callisto catacombs and at Capo di Bove, and WCs for paying customers are at the Tomb of Cecilia Metella and the Appia Antica Caffè. There are several water fountains along the way to refill water bottles.

▲▲Catacombs of San Sebastiano

A guide leads you underground through the tunnels where early Christians were buried. You'll see faded frescoes and graffiti by early-Christian tag artists. Besides the catacombs themselves, there's a historic fourth-century basilica with holy relics. See the "Catacombs" sidebar for more information.

Cost and Hours: €8, includes 35-minute tour, 2/hour, Mon-Sat 10:00-17:00, closed Sun and late-Nov-late-Dec, last entry 30 minutes before closing, Via Appia Antica 136, tel. 06-785-0350, www.catacombe.org.

▲▲Catacombs of San Callisto

The larger of the two sets of catacombs, San Callisto also is the more prestigious, having been the burial site for several early popes.

Cost and Hours: €8, includes 30-minute tour, at least 2/hour, Thu-Tue 9:00-12:00 & 14:00-17:00, closed Wed and Feb, Via Appia Antica 110, tel. 06-5130-1580 or 06-513-0151, www.catacombe.roma.it.

Near Rome
▲▲Ostia Antica

For an exciting day trip, pop down to the Roman ___,
which is similar to Pompeii but a lot closer and, ... some ways,
more interesting. Because Ostia was a working port town, it shows
a more complete and gritty look at Roman life than wealthier Pompeii. Wandering around today, you'll see warehouses, apartment
flats, mansions, shopping arcades, and baths that served a once-thriving port of 60,000 people. Later, Ostia became a ghost town,
and it's now excavated. Buy a map, then explore the town, including the 2,000-year-old theater. Finish with its fine little museum.

Cost and Hours: €8 for the site and museum, €10 with special
exhibits, April-Sept Tue-Sun 8:30-19:00, Oct Tue-Sun 8:30-18:30,
Nov-mid-Feb Tue-Sun 8:30-16:30, mid-Feb-March Tue-Sun 8:30-17:00, closed Mon year-round, last entry one hour before closing.
The museum sometimes closes from 13:30 to 14:30 for lunch.

Information: Tel. 06-5635-0215. Helpful websites include
www.ostiaantica.beniculturali.it and www.ostia-antica.org. A map
of the site with suggested itineraries is available for €2 from the
ticket office.

Audio Tour: Although you'll see little audioguide markers
throughout the site, there may not be audioguides for rent. But you
can download a free Rick Steves audio tour of Ostia Antica to your
mobile device; see page 9.

Getting There: Getting to Ostia Antica from downtown
Rome is a snap—it's a 45-minute combination Metro/train ride.
(Since the train is part of the Metro system, it only costs one Metro
ticket each way—€3 total round-trip.)

From Rome, take Metro line B to the Piramide stop, which
is attached to the Roma Porta San Paolo train station. The train
tracks are just a few steps from the Metro tracks: Follow signs to
Lido—go up the escalator, turn left, and go down the steps into
the Roma-Lido station. All trains depart in the direction of Lido,
leave every 15 minutes, and stop at Ostia Antica along the way.
The lighted schedule reads something like, *"Prossima partenza alle
ore 13.25, bin 3,"* meaning, "Next departure at 13:25 from track 3."
Look for the next train, hop on, ride for about 30 minutes (no need
to stamp your Metro ticket again, but keep it handy in case they
decide to check), and get off at the Ostia Antica stop.

Leaving the train station in Ostia Antica, cross the road via
the blue skybridge and walk straight down Via della Stazione di
Ostia Antica, continuing straight until you reach the parking lot.
The entrance is to your left. (If you don't have a ticket to get back,
purchase one at the ticket window at the station, or from the nearby
snack bar.)

Tip: If you're using the Metro and want to maximize sightsee-

ROME

...g efficiency on your Ostia day trip, consider visiting the sights in south Rome on your return. The Piramide Metro stop—where you'll change trains—really *is* next to a pyramid, and is on the edge of the Testaccio neighborhood, which has several interesting sights. Other south Rome sights include St. Paul's Outside the Walls, E.U.R., and the Montemartini Museum (for more on all of these, see page 942).

Sleeping in Rome

Haggle if you arrive late in the day during off-season (roughly mid-July through August and November through mid-March). It's common for hotels in Rome to lower their prices 10-50 percent in the off-season, although prices at hostels and the cheaper hotels won't fluctuate much. Room rates are lowest in sweltering August.

Traffic in Rome roars. Thanks to double-paned windows and air-conditioning, night noise is not the problem it once was. Even so, light sleepers who ask for a *tranquillo* room will likely get a room in the back...and sleep better. Once you actually see your room, consider the potential problem of night noise. If necessary, don't hesitate to ask for a quieter room.

Almost no hotels have parking, but nearly all have a line on spots in a nearby garage (about €24/day).

For tips on making reservations, see page 26.

Convents: Although I list just a few, Rome has many convents that rent out rooms. See the Church of Santa Susanna's website for a list (www.santasusanna.org, select "Coming to Rome"). At convents, the beds are twins and English is often in short supply, but the price is right.

Consider these nun-run places, all listed in this chapter: the expensive but divine **Casa di Santa Brigida** (near Campo de' Fiori), **Suore di Santa Elisabetta** (near Santa Maria Maggiore), **Casa Santa Sofia** (near the Colosseum), **Casa Il Rosario** (near Piazza Venezia), and **Casa per Ferie Santa Maria alle Fornaci** (near the Vatican).

Hostels: If you're going the hostel route, consider the ones I list in this chapter (within a 10-minute walk of Termini train station), or check www.backpackers.it for more listings.

Near Termini Train Station

While not as atmospheric as other areas of Rome, the hotels near Termini train station are less expensive, and public-transportation options link these places easily with the entire city. The city's two Metro lines intersect at the station, and most buses leave from here. Piazza Venezia is a 20-minute walk down Via Nazionale.

Sleep Code

(€1 = about $1.30, country code: 39)

S = Single, **D** = Double/Twin, **T** = Triple, **Q** = Quad, **b** = bathroom, **s** = shower only. Unless otherwise noted, breakfast is included, hotel staff speak basic English, and credit cards are accepted. There's almost always Wi-Fi and/or a guest computer available, either free or for a fee. Rome charges a hotel tax of €2-3 per person, per night. This tax is typically not included in the prices I've listed here.

To help you easily sort through these listings, I've divided the accommodations into three categories based on the price for a double room with bath during high season:

$$$ **Higher Priced**—Most rooms €180 or more.
  $$ **Moderately Priced**—Most rooms between €125-180.
    $ **Lower Priced**—Most rooms €125 or less.

Prices can change without notice; verify the hotel's current rates online or by email. For the best prices, always book direct.

West of the Station

Most of these hotels are on or near Via Firenze, a safe, handy, central, and relatively quiet street that's a 10-minute walk from Termini train station and the airport train, and two blocks beyond Piazza della Repubblica. The Defense Ministry is nearby, so you've got heavily armed guards watching over you all night.

The neighborhood is well-connected by public transportation (with the Repubblica Metro stop nearby). Virtually all the city buses that rumble down Via Nazionale (#60, #64, #70, and the #40 express) take you to Piazza Venezia (Forum). From Piazza Venezia, bus #64 (jammed with people and thieves) and the #40 express bus continue to Largo Argentina (Pantheon, Campo de' Fiori) and the Vatican area. Or, at Piazza Venezia, you can transfer to tram #8 to Trastevere (get off at first stop after crossing the river). Bus #H also makes the journey to Trastevere, leaving from Piazza della Repubblica (on the northeast side of the square, near the entrance to Baths of Diocletian). If you are staying near the Santa Susanna and Santa Maria della Vittoria churches, buses from nearby Largo Santa Susanna (#62, #85, #116, #175, and #492) wind through the city center (leaving from the Bissolati stop; returning, the stop name is Largo S. Susanna).

To stock your closet pantry, pop over to **Despar Supermarket** (daily 8:00-21:00, Via Nazionale 213, at the corner of Via Venezia). A 24-hour **pharmacy** near the recommended hotels is Farmacia Piram (Via Nazionale 228, tel. 06-488-4437).

ROME

Hotels near Termini Station

1. Residenza Cellini, Target Inn, Bellesuite Rome & Hotel Adler
2. Hotel Modigliani
3. IQ Hotel & Hotel Opera Roma
4. Hotels Oceania & Nardizzi Americana
5. Hotel Aberdeen
6. Hotel Sonya
7. Hotel Selene Roma
8. Hotel Italia Roma
9. Hotel Margaret
10. Hotel Montreal
11. Suore di Sta. Elisabetta
12. Gulliver's Lodge
13. The Beehive
14. Hotel Select Garden
15. Hotel Sileo
16. Hotel Robinson
17. Funny Palace Hostel & Launderette/Internet Café
18. Yellow Hostel
19. Despar Supermarket

$$$ **Residenza Cellini** feels like the guest wing of a gorgeous Neoclassical palace. It offers 11 rooms, "ortho/anti-allergy beds," four-star comforts and service, and a breezy breakfast terrace (Db-€190, larger Db-€210, extra bed-€25, prices good through 2014 with this book and cash, air-con, elevator, guest computer, Wi-Fi, Via Modena 5, reception on third floor, use intercom after hours, tel. 06-4782-5204, www.residenzacellini.it, residenzacellini@tin.it, Barbara, Gaetano, and Donato).

$$$ Hotel Modigliani, a delightful 23-room place, is energetically run in a clean, bright, minimalist yet in-love-with-life style that its artist namesake would appreciate. It has a vast and plush lounge, a garden, and a newsletter introducing you to each of the staff (Db-€202, check website for deals and ask for a 10 percent Rick Steves discount when you book direct through 2014, air-con, elevator, Wi-Fi; northwest of Via Firenze—from Tritone Fountain on Piazza Barberini, go 2 blocks up Via della Purificazione to #42; tel. 06-4281-5226, www.hotelmodigliani.com, info@hotelmodigliani.com, Giulia and Marco).

$$$ IQ Hotel, facing the Opera House, opened in 2010 and feels almost Scandinavian in its efficiency, without a hint of the Old World. Its 88 rooms are fresh and spacious, the roof garden comes with a swing set, and vending machines dispense bottles of wine (Db-€100-230 depending on room size and season—likely €200 in peak season, €40 extra for 3rd and 4th person, 10 percent discount off best Web price for Rick Steves readers through 2014—must book direct and request at time of booking, breakfast-€10, air-con, elevator, guest computer, Wi-Fi, cheap self-service laundry, gym, Via Firenze 8, tel. 06-488-0465, www.iqhotelroma.it, info@iqhotelroma.it, manager Diego).

$$ Hotel Oceania is a peaceful slice of air-conditioned heaven. This 24-room manor house-type hotel is spacious and quiet, with tastefully decorated rooms. Stefano runs a fine staff, serves wonderful coffee, provides lots of thoughtful extra touches, and works hard to maintain a caring family atmosphere (Sb-€135, Db-€168, Tb-€198, Qb-€220, these prices good through 2014 with this book, 5 percent discount if you pay cash, deep discounts summer and winter, family suite, elevator, guest computer, Wi-Fi, videos in the TV lounge, Via Firenze 38, third floor, tel. 06-482-4696, www.hoteloceania.it, info@hoteloceania.it; Anna and Radu round out the staff).

$$ Hotel Aberdeen, which perfectly combines quality and friendliness, is warmly run by Annamaria, with support from sister Laura and cousin Cinzia, and staff members Mariano and Costel. The 37 comfy, modern rooms are a fine value (Sb-€102, Db-€170, Tb-€180, Qb-€200, for these rates—or better—book direct via email or use the "Rick Steves reader reservations" link on their website, air-con, guest computer, Wi-Fi, Via Firenze 48, tel. 06-482-3920, www.hotelaberdeen.it, info@hotelaberdeen.it).

$$ Hotel Opera Roma, with contemporary furnishings and marble accents, boasts 15 spacious, modern, and thoughtfully appointed rooms. It's quiet and just a stone's throw from the Opera House (Db-€150, Tb-€165, for these rates book direct and mention Rick Steves, 5 percent discount if you pay cash, air-con, elevator, guest computer, Wi-Fi, Via Firenze 11, tel. 06-487-1787, www.hoteloperaroma.com, info@hoteloperaroma.com, Rezza, Litu, and Federica).

$$ Hotel Sonya offers 34 well-equipped if small rooms, a hearty breakfast, and decent prices (Sb-€90, Db-€150, Tb-€165, Qb-€185, Quint/b-€200, 5 percent discount with this book and if you pay cash through 2014, air-con, elevator, guest computer, Wi-Fi, faces the Opera House at Via Viminale 58, Metro: Repubblica or Termini, tel. 06-481-9911, www.hotelsonya.it, info@hotelsonya.it, Francesca and Ivan).

$$ Hotel Selene Roma spreads its 40 rooms out on a few floors of a big palazzo. With elegant furnishings and room to breathe, it's a fine value (Db-€150, Tb-€165, email direct for 10 percent discount, 5 percent discount if you pay cash, air-con, elevator, free Wi-Fi, Via del Viminale 8, tel. 06-474-4781, www.hotelseleneroma.it, reception@hotelseleneroma.it).

$$ Bellesuite Rome offers six bright, modern rooms with all the comforts in a quiet building (Db-€150, Tb-€190, Qb-€215, 5 percent discount through 2014 if you show this book and pay cash, air-con, elevator, free Wi-Fi, Via Modena 5, tel. 06-9521-3049, www.bellesuiterome.com, mail@bellesuiterome.com).

$$ Target Inn is a sleek, practical six-room place next to Residenza Cellini (listed earlier). It's owned by the same people who run the recommended Target Restaurant nearby (Db-€150, air-con, elevator, free Wi-Fi, Via Modena 5, tel. 06-474-5399, www.targetinn.com, info@targetinn.com).

$ Hotel Adler features a small garden patio and eight basic rooms on a wide and elegant hall (Db-€125, Tb-€165, Qb-€190, Quint/b-€210, 5 percent off these prices with this book through 2014, additional 5 percent discount if you pay cash, air-con, elevator, guest computer, Wi-Fi, Via Modena 5, second floor, tel. 06-484-466, www.hoteladler-roma.com, info@hoteladler-roma.com).

$ Hotel Nardizzi Americana, with a small rooftop terrace and 40 standard rooms spread throughout the building, is another decent value (Sb-€95, Db-€125, Tb-€155, Qb-€175; to get the best rates, check their "Rick Steves readers reservations" link along with the rest of their website; additional 10 percent off any price if you pay cash, air-con, elevator, guest computer, Wi-Fi, Via Firenze 38, reception on fourth floor, tel. 06-488-0035, www.hotelnardizzi.it, info@hotelnardizzi.it; friendly Stefano, Fabrizio, Mario, and Giancarlo).

$ Hotel Italia Roma, in a busy and handy locale, is located safely on a quiet street next to the Ministry of the Interior. Thoughtfully run by Andrea, Sabrina, Abdul, and Gabriel, it has 35 modest but comfortable rooms (Sb-€80, Db-€120, Tb-€150, Qb-€180, book direct via email for these rates, air-con-€10 extra/day, elevator, guest computer, Wi-Fi, Via Venezia 18, just off Via

Nazionale, tel. 06-482-8355, www.hotelitaliaroma.it, info@hoteli-
taliaroma.it). The four "residenza" rooms upstairs on the third floor
are newer and a bit more expensive. They also have eight similar
annex rooms across the street.

$ Hotel Margaret offers few frills and 12 simple rooms at a
fair price (Db-€110, Tb-€140, Qb-€155, mention this book and
pay cash for best rates, air-con, elevator, free Wi-Fi, north of Piazza
Repubblica at Via Antonio Salandra 6, fourth floor, tel. 06-482-
4285, www.hotelmargaret.net, info@hotelmargaret.net, Emanuela).

Southwest of the Station
These good-value places cluster around the basilica of Santa Maria
Maggiore, on the edge of Rome's international district.

$ Hotel Montreal is a basic three-star place with 27 small
rooms on a big street a block southeast of Santa Maria Maggiore
(Sb-€90, Db-€110, Tb-€135, email direct and ask for a Rick Steves
discount, air-con, elevator, guest computer, Wi-Fi, small garden
terrace, good security, Via Carlo Alberto 4, 1 block from Metro:
Vittorio Emanuele, 3 blocks from Termini train station, tel. 06-
445-7797, www.hotelmontrealroma.it, info@hotelmontrealroma.
it, Pasquale).

$ Suore di Santa Elisabetta is a heavenly Polish-run con-
vent with a serene garden and 70 beds in tidy twin-bedded (only)
rooms. Often booked long in advance, with such tranquility it's a
super value (S-€40, Sb-€48, D-€66, Db-€85, Tb-€106, Qb-€128,
Quint/b-€142, fans but no air-con, elevator serves top floors only,
fine view roof terrace and breakfast hall, 23:00 curfew, a block
southwest of Santa Maria Maggiore at Via dell'Olmata 9, Metro:
Termini or Vittorio Emanuele, tel. 06-488-8271, www.csse-roma.
eu, ist.it.s.elisabetta@libero.it).

$ Gulliver's Lodge has four colorful rooms on the ground
floor of a large, secure building. While on a busy street, the rooms
are quiet. Although the public spaces are few, in-room extras like
DVD players (and DVDs, including my Italy shows) make it a fine
home base (Db-€120, Tb-€145, includes small breakfast at nearby
bar, mention this book for these prices through 2014, cash only,
air-con, guest computer, Wi-Fi, a 15-minute walk southwest of Termini train station at Via Cavour 101, Metro: Cavour, tel. 06-9727-
3787, www.gulliverslodge.com, info@gulliverslodge.com, Sara and
Mary).

Sleeping Cheaply, Northeast of
Termini Train Station
The cheapest beds in town are northeast of Termini train station
(Metro: Termini). Some travelers feel this area is weird and spooky

after dark, but these hotels feel plenty safe. With your back to the train tracks, turn right and walk two blocks out of the station. **Splashnet** launderette/Internet café is handy (€8 full-serve wash and dry, guest computer-€1.50/hour, €2 luggage storage per day—or free if you wash and go online, daily 8:30-23:00, just off Via Milazzo at Via Varese 33, tel. 06-4470-3523).

$ The Beehive gives vagabonds—old and young—a cheap, clean, and comfy home in Rome, thoughtfully and creatively run by Steve and Linda, a friendly American couple, and their hard-working staff. They offer six great-value artsy-mod double rooms (D-€80, T-€105) and an eight-bed dorm (€30 bunks). Their nearby annex, The Sweets, has similar style and several rooms with private baths (Sb-€60, Db-€100, air-con-€10, breakfast extra, guest computer, Wi-Fi, private garden terrace, 2 blocks from Termini train station at Via Marghera 8, tel. 06-4470-4553, www.the-bee-hive.com, info@the-beehive.com). They're also a good resource for apartments across the city (www.cross-pollinate.com).

$ Hotel Select Garden, a modern and comfortable 21-room hotel run by the cheery Picca family, boasts lively modern art adorning the walls and a beautiful lemon-tree garden. It's a safe, tranquil, and welcoming refuge just a couple blocks from the train station (Sb-€80, Db-€110, Tb-€130, book direct and mention Rick Steves for these prices through 2014, air-con, free Wi-Fi, Via V. Bachelet 6, tel. 06-445-6383, www.hotelselectgarden.com, info@hotelselectgarden.com, Cristina and Maurizia).

$ Hotel Sileo, with shiny chandeliers in dim rooms, is a homely little place renting 10 basic rooms (Db-€75, Tb-€90, air-con, elevator, free Wi-Fi, Via Magenta 39, fourth floor, tel. 06-445-0246, www.hotelsileo.com, info@hotelsileo.com). Friendly Alessandro and Maria Savioli don't speak English, but daughter Anna does.

$ Hotel Robinson is just a few steps from the station, but tucked away from the commotion. Set on an interior courtyard, it has 20 small and simple rooms that are a decent value (Sb-€65, Db-€85, Tb-€120, mention this book for these rates and a small breakfast, air-con-€10, Wi-Fi, Via Milazzo 3, tel. 06-491-423, www.hotelrobinsonrome.com, info@hotelrobinsonrome.com).

$ Yellow Hostel rents 240 beds in 4-, 6-, and 10-bed dorms to 18- through 39-year-olds only (they also have 11 private rooms that are open to all ages). Hip yet sane, it's well-run with fine facilities, including lockers and a café/late-night bar (€18-35/bed depending on plumbing, size, and season, Db-€140; reserve online—no telephone reservations accepted, free Wi-Fi, iPad rental available, no curfew, 6 blocks from station, just past Via Vicenza at Via Palestro 40/44, tel. 06-493-82682, www.yellowhostel.com).

$ Funny Palace Hostel, adjacent to Splashnet and run by

the same entrepreneurial owner, Mabri, rents dorm beds in quiet four-person rooms and 18 stark-but-clean private rooms (dorm beds-€30, Db-€100, cash only, free Wi-Fi, reception in the launderette—described earlier, Via Varese 33/31, tel. 06-4470-3523, www.hostelfunny.com).

Near Ancient Rome

Stretching from the Colosseum to Piazza Venezia, this area is central. Sightseers are a short walk from the Colosseum, Roman Forum, and Trajan's Column. While buses are your best bet here, I list a Metro stop if it's convenient.

$$$ Hotel Lancelot is a comfortable yet elegant refuge—a 60-room hotel with the ambience of a B&B. It's quiet and safe, with a shady courtyard, restaurant, bar, and tiny communal sixth-floor terrace. It's well-run by Faris and Lubna Khan, who serve a good €25 dinner—a chance to connect with your hotel neighbors and the friendly staff. No wonder it's popular with returning guests (Sb-€128, Db-€196, Tb-€226, Qb-€266, €20 extra for sixth-floor terrace room with a Colosseum view, 5 percent off these rates in 2014 if you book direct and mention Rick Steves, air-con, elevator, wheelchair-accessible, free Wi-Fi, parking-€10/day, 10-minute walk behind Colosseum near San Clemente Church at Via Capo d'Africa 47, tel. 06-7045-0615, www.lancelothotel.com, info@lancelothotel.com). Faris and Lubna speak the Queen's English.

$$$ Hotel Nerva is a recently renovated, modern slice of tranquility with 19 small, overpriced (but often discounted) rooms on a surprisingly quiet back street just steps away from the Roman Forum (Sb-€160, Db-€230, extra bed-€40, book direct and use promo code "RICKSTEVES" for an additional discount through 2014, air-con, elevator, free Wi-Fi, Via Tor de' Conti 3, tel. 06-678-1835, www.hotelnerva.com, info@hotelnerva.com, Antonio and Paolo).

$$ Hotel Paba has seven fresh rooms, chocolate-box-tidy and lovingly cared for by Alberta Castelli. It's just two blocks from the Forum. Although it overlooks busy Via Cavour, it's quiet enough (Db-€135, extra bed-€40, 5 percent discount if you pay cash, big beds, breakfast served in room, air-con, elevator, free Wi-Fi, Via Cavour 266, Metro: Cavour, tel. 06-4782-4902, www.hotelpaba.com, info@hotelpaba.com).

$$ Nicolas Inn Bed & Breakfast, a delightful little four-room place with thoughtful touches, is spacious and bright. It's run by François and American expat Melissa, who make you feel like you have caring friends in Rome (Db-€150-170, 10 percent Rick Steves discount with this book through 2014, cash only, included breakfast served at neighboring bar, air-con, free Wi-Fi, Via Cavour 295, tel. 06-9761-8483, www.nicolasinn.com, info@nicolasinn.com).

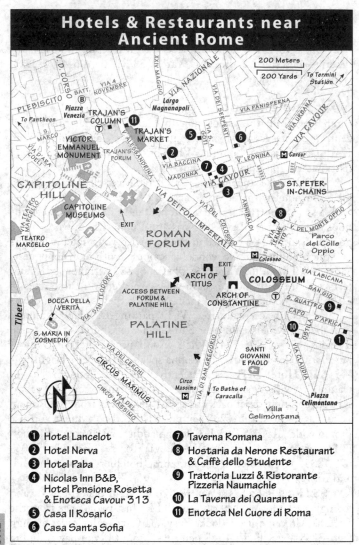

Hotels & Restaurants near Ancient Rome

1. Hotel Lancelot
2. Hotel Nerva
3. Hotel Paba
4. Nicolas Inn B&B, Hotel Pensione Rosetta & Enoteca Cavour 313
5. Casa Il Rosario
6. Casa Santa Sofia
7. Taverna Romana
8. Hostaria da Nerone Restaurant & Caffè dello Studente
9. Trattoria Luzzi & Ristorante Pizzeria Naumachie
10. La Taverna dei Quaranta
11. Enoteca Nel Cuore di Roma

$ Hotel Pensione Rosetta, homey and family-run, rents 15 simple rooms. It's pretty minimal, with no lounge and no breakfast, but has a good location and prices (Sb-€70, Db-€95, Tb-€110, air-con, free Wi-Fi, Via Cavour 295, tel. 06-4782-3069, www.rosettahotel.com, info@rosettahotel.com, Antonietta and Francesca).

$ Casa Il Rosario is a peaceful, well-run Dominican convent renting 40 rooms with monastic simplicity to both pilgrims and tourists in a good neighborhood (reserve several months in advance, S-€42, Sb-€56, Db-€94, Tb-€120, single beds only, fans, elevator, picnics welcome in small garden or on rooftop terrace, 23:00 curfew, midway between Quirinale and Colosseum near bottom of Via Nazionale at Via Sant'Agata dei Goti 10, bus #40 or #170 from Termini, tel. 06-679-2346, irodopre@tin.it).

$ Casa Santa Sofia, while stern and sterile, is still a welcoming and cozy convent that rents 54 rooms to travelers. Built for Ukrainian and Brazilian pilgrims, it's well-run and situated on a characteristic square near a Metro stop and the Roman Forum (Sb-€69, Db-€99, fans but no air-con, elevator, free Wi-Fi, Piazza della Madonna dei Monti 3, Metro: Cavour, tel. 06-485-778, www.casasantasofia.it).

In the Pantheon Neighborhood

Winding, narrow lanes filled with foot traffic and lined with boutique shops and tiny trattorias...this is village Rome at its best. And like a real village, buses are the only practical way to connect with other destinations. The atmosphere isn't cheap, but this is where you want to be—especially at night, when Romans and tourists gather in the floodlit piazzas for the evening stroll, the *passeggiata*.

Near Campo de' Fiori

You'll pay a premium (and endure a little extra night noise) to stay in the old center. But each of these places is romantically set deep in the tangled back streets near the idyllic Campo de' Fiori and, for many, worth the extra money.

$$$ Casa di Santa Brigida overlooks the elegant Piazza Farnese. With soft-spoken sisters gliding down polished hallways and pearly gates instead of doors, this lavish 20-room convent makes exhaust-stained Roman tourists feel like they've died and gone to heaven. If you don't need a double bed or a TV in your room, it's worth the splurge—especially if you luxuriate in its ample public spaces or on its lovely roof terrace (Sb-€120, twin Db-€200, book well in advance, air-con, elevator, guest computer, Wi-Fi, tasty €25 dinners, roof garden, plush library, Monserrato 54, tel. 06-6889-2596, www.brigidine.org, piazzafarnese@brigidine.org, many of the sisters are from India and speak English—pray you get to work with wonderful sister Gertrude).

$$$ Relais Teatro Argentina, a six-room gem, is steeped in tasteful old-Rome elegance, but has all the modern comforts. It's cozy and quiet like a B&B and couldn't be more centrally located (Db-€210, Tb-€255, discounts if you pay cash and stay 3 nights or more, air-con, no elevator, 3 flights of stairs, guest computer, Wi-Fi, Via del Sudario 35, tel. 06-9893-1617, www.relaisteatroargentina.com, info@relaisteatroargentina.com, Carlotta).

ROME

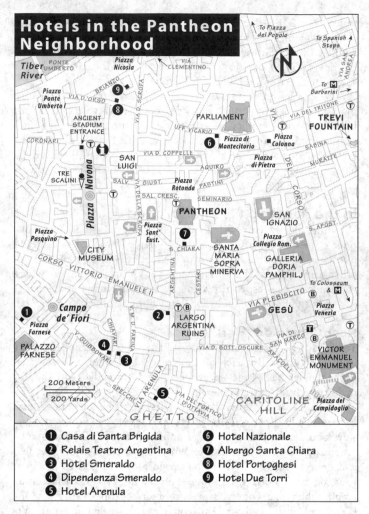

Hotels in the Pantheon Neighborhood

1. Casa di Santa Brigida
2. Relais Teatro Argentina
3. Hotel Smeraldo
4. Dipendenza Smeraldo
5. Hotel Arenula
6. Hotel Nazionale
7. Albergo Santa Chiara
8. Hotel Portoghesi
9. Hotel Due Torri

$$ Hotel Smeraldo, with 50 rooms, is strictly run by an impersonal staff, but it's clean and a reasonable deal (Sb-€110, Db-€150, Tb-€180, buffet breakfast free in 2014 if you show this book, air-con, elevator, guest computer, Wi-Fi, flowery roof terrace, midway between Campo de' Fiori and Largo Argentina at Vicolo dei Chiodaroli 9, tel. 06-687-5929, www.smeraldoroma.com, info@smeraldoroma.com, Massimo and Walter). Their **Dipendenza Smeraldo,** 10 yards around the corner at Via dei Chiavari 32, has 16 similar rooms (same price and free breakfast, same reception and contact info).

In the Jewish Ghetto

$$ Hotel Arenula, with 50 decent rooms, is the only hotel in Rome's old Jewish ghetto. Though it has the ambience of a gym and attracts lots of students, it is in the thick of old Rome (Sb-€100, Db-€140, 5 percent off with this book in 2014, extra bed-€21, aircon, no elevator, Wi-Fi, opposite the fountain in the park on Via Arenula at Via Santa Maria de' Calderari 47, tel. 06-687-9454, www.hotelarenula.com, info@hotelarenula.com).

Close to the Pantheon

These places are buried in the pedestrian-friendly heart of ancient Rome, each within about a five-minute walk of the Pantheon. You'll pay more here—but you'll save time and money by being exactly where you want to be for your early and late wandering.

$$$ Hotel Nazionale, a four-star landmark, is a 16th-century palace that shares a well-policed square with the Parliament building. Its 100 rooms are accentuated by lush public spaces, fancy bars, a uniformed staff, and a marble-floored restaurant. It's a big, stuffy hotel, but it's a worthy splurge if you want security, comfort, and the heart of Rome at your doorstep (Sb-€220, Db-€350, giant deluxe Db-€480, extra person-€70, check online for summer and weekend discounts—you'll typically save 30 percent off their sky-high rack rates, air-con, elevator, free Wi-Fi, Piazza Montecitorio 131, tel. 06-695-001, www.hotelnazionale.it, info@hotelnazionale.it).

$$$ Albergo Santa Chiara, in the old center, is big, solid, and hotelesque. Flavia, Silvio, and their fine staff offer marbled elegance (but basic furniture) and all the hotel services. Its ample public lounges are dressy and professional, and its 99 rooms are quiet and spacious (Sb-€138, Db-€215, Tb-€260, check website for discounts, book online direct and request special Rick Steves rates, elevator, air-con, free Wi-Fi, behind Pantheon at Via di Santa Chiara 21, tel. 06-687-2979, www.albergosantachiara.com, info@albergosantachiara.com).

$$$ Hotel Portoghesi is a classic hotel with 27 rooms in the medieval heart of Rome. It's peaceful, quiet, and calmly run, and comes with a delightful roof terrace—though you pay for the location (Sb-€160, Db-€200, Tb-€260, Qb suite-€300, breakfast on roof, air-con, elevator, free Wi-Fi, Via dei Portoghesi 1, tel. 06-686-4231, www.hotelportoghesiroma.it, info@hotelportoghesiroma.it).

$$$ Hotel Due Torri, hiding out on a tiny quiet street, is beautifully located. It feels professional yet homey, with an accommodating staff, generous public spaces, and 26 small rooms. While the location and lounge are great, the rooms are overpriced (Sb-€125, Db-€200, family apartment-€240 for 3 and €265 for 4,

ROME

check website for frequent discounts, air-con, elevator, free Wi-Fi, a block off Via della Scrofa at Vicolo del Leonetto 23, tel. 06-6880-6956, www.hotelduetorriroma.com, info@hotelduetorriroma.com, Cinzia).

In Trastevere

Colorful and genuine in a gritty sort of way, Trastevere is a treat for travelers looking for a less touristy and more bohemian atmosphere. Choices are few here, and public transit is limited to a few buses and trams. But by trekking across the Tiber, you can have the experience of being comfortably immersed in old Rome. To locate the following places, see the map on page 936.

$$$ **Residenza Arco dei Tolomei** is your most poetic Trastevere experience imaginable, with six small, unique, antique-filled rooms boasting fragrant balconies. With its quiet and elegant setting, you can pretend you're visiting aristocratic relatives (Db-€205, discounts if you pay cash and stay 3 nights or more, reserve well in advance, guest computer, Wi-Fi, from Piazza Piscinula a block up Via dell'Arco de' Tolomei at #27, tel. 06-5832-0819, www.bbarcodeitolomei.com, info@bbarcodeitolomei.com; Marco and Gianna Paola).

$$ **Hotel Santa Maria** sits like a lazy hacienda in the midst of Trastevere. Surrounded by a medieval skyline, you'll feel as if you're on some romantic stage set. Its 20 small but well-equipped, air-conditioned rooms—former cells in a cloister—are all on the ground floor, as are a few suites for up to six people. The rooms circle a gravelly courtyard of orange trees and stay-awhile patio furniture (Db-€170, Tb-€210; prices good through 2014 with this book, cash, and minimum stay of three nights; family rooms, free loaner bikes, guest computer, Wi-Fi, face church on Piazza Maria Trastevere and go right down Via della Fonte d'Olio 50 yards to Vicolo del Piede 2, tel. 06-589-4626, www.hotelsantamaria.info, info@hotelsantamaria.info). Some rooms come with family-friendly fold-down bunks for €30 extra per person. Their freshly renovated six-room **Residenza Santa Maria** is a couple of blocks away (same prices, www.residenzasantamaria.com).

$$ **Casa San Giuseppe** is down a characteristic laundry-strewn lane with a sunny roof terrace and views of Aurelian Walls. While convent-owned, it's a secular place renting 29 plain but peaceful, spacious, and spotless rooms (Sb-€115, Db-€155, Tb-€190, Qb-€220, garden-facing rooms are quiet, air-con, elevator, guest computer, Wi-Fi, parking-€15/day, just north of Piazza Trilussa at Vicolo Moroni 22, tel. 06-5833-3490, www.casasangiuseppe.it, info@casasangiuseppe.it, Matteo).

$$ **Arco del Lauro B&B** rents six white, minimalist rooms in a good location. Facing a courtyard (no views but little noise),

the friendly welcome and good value make up for the lack of public spaces (Db-€135, Qb-€185, prices good if booked direct, cash only, 3-4 night minimum stay over weekends in high season, includes breakfast served in a café, air-con, guest computer, Wi-Fi, from Piazza Piscinula a block up Via dell'Arco de' Tolomei at #29, tel. 06-9784-0350, mobile 346-244-3212, www.arcodellauro.it, info@arcodellauro.it, Lorenza and Daniela).

$$ Hotel San Francesco, big and blocky yet welcoming, stands like a practical and efficient oasis at the edge of all the Trastevere action. Renting 24 trim rooms in this authentic district, it comes with an inviting roof terrace and a helpful staff. Handy trams to Piazza Venezia are just a couple of blocks away (Db-€90-180, prices vary wildly, email direct and mention this book for best rates, air-con, elevator, free Wi-Fi, Via Jacopa de' Settesoli 7, tel. 06-5830-0051, www.hotelsanfrancesco.net, info@hotelsanfrancesco.net).

Near Vatican City

Sleeping near the Vatican is expensive, but some enjoy calling this more relaxed, residential neighborhood home. Even though it's handy to the Vatican (when the rapture hits, you're right there), everything else is a long way away. Fortunately, it's well-served by public transit—use the Metro (line A) and bus (ask your hotel for the most convenient routes) to easily connect with the center.

$$$ Hotel Alimandi Vaticano, facing the Vatican Museum, is beautifully designed. Run by the Alimandi family (Enrico, Irene, and Germano), it features four stars, 24 spacious rooms, and all the modern comforts you can imagine (Sb-€170, standard Db-€200, big Db with 2 double beds-€260, Tb-€260, 5 percent discount if you pay cash, air-con, elevator, guest computer, Wi-Fi, Viale Vaticano 99, Metro: Ottaviano, tel. 06-3974-5562, www.alimandi.com, alimandivaticano@alimandi.com).

$$$ Hotel Gerber, set in a quiet residential area, is family-run with 27 well-polished, businesslike rooms (Sb-€140, Db-€180, Tb-€200, Qb-€220, 10 percent high-season discount and 15 percent low-season discount off these prices with this book in 2014 when you book direct, air-con, elevator, free Wi-Fi, small leafy terrace; from Lepanto Metro station, go one block down Via M. Colonna and turn right to Via degli Scipioni 241; tel. 06-321-6485, www.hotelgerber.it, info@hotelgerber.it; Peter, Simonetta, and friendly dog Kira).

$$ Hotel Alimandi Tunisi is a good value, run by other members of the friendly and entrepreneurial Alimandi family—Paolo, Luigi, Marta, and Barbara. They have 27 modest but comfortable rooms and vast public spaces, including a piano lounge, pool table, and rooftop terrace where the grand buffet breakfast is served (Sb-

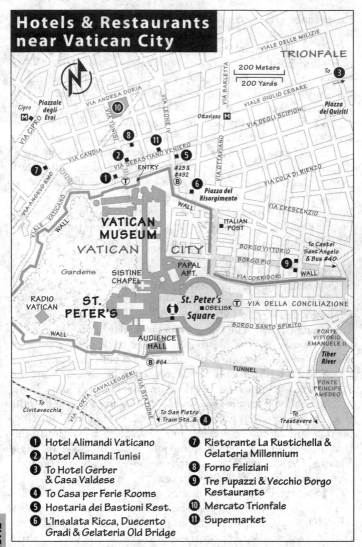

Hotels & Restaurants near Vatican City

1. Hotel Alimandi Vaticano
2. Hotel Alimandi Tunisi
3. To Hotel Gerber & Casa Valdese
4. To Casa per Ferie Rooms
5. Hostaria dei Bastioni Rest.
6. L'Insalata Ricca, Duecento Gradi & Gelateria Old Bridge
7. Ristorante La Rustichella & Gelateria Millennium
8. Forno Feliziani
9. Tre Pupazzi & Vecchio Borgo Restaurants
10. Mercato Trionfale
11. Supermarket

€90, Db-€175, 5 percent discount if you pay cash, elevator, air-con, guest computer, Wi-Fi, down the stairs directly in front of Vatican Museum, Via Tunisi 8, Metro: Ottaviano, tel. 06-3972-3941, www.alimandi.com, alimandi@tin.it).

$$ **Casa Valdese** is an efficient, well-managed, church-run hotel that's popular with Germans. Its 33 big, quiet rooms are located just over the Tiber River and near the Vatican. It feels safe if a bit institutional, with the bonus of two breezy, communal roof terraces with incredible views (two external Sb-€61, Db-€131, Tb-

€181, Qb-€211, discounts for 3-night stays, air-con, elevator, guest computer, Wi-Fi; from Lepanto Metro station, go one block down Via M. Colonna, turn left on Via degli Scipioni, then continue for a block to the intersection with Via Alessandro Farnese 18; tel. 06-321-5362, www.casavaldeseroma.it, reception@casavaldeseroma.it, Matteo).

$ Casa per Ferie Santa Maria alle Fornaci is simple and efficient, housing pilgrims and secular tourists just a short walk south of the Vatican in 54 identical, stark, utilitarian, mostly twin-bedded rooms. Reserve at least three months in advance (Sb-€70, Db-€100, Tb-€135, air-con, elevator, free Wi-Fi; take bus #64 from Termini train station to San Pietro train station, then walk 100 yards north along Via della Stazione di San Pietro to Piazza Santa Maria alle Fornaci 27; tel. 06-3936-7632, www.trinitaridematha.it, cffornaci@tin.it, Carmine).

More Hotels in Rome

If my listings are full, here are some others to consider. Rates vary with the season and demand.

Near Termini, family-friendly **$$ Hotel Rex** is between the Church of Santa Maria Maggiore and the Opera (Db-€120-230, at Via Torino 149, tel. 06-482-4828, www.hotelrex.net, rex@hotelrex.net).

In the Trastevere neighborhood, **$ Hotel Cisterna** has 19 spotless but tired rooms (Db-€80-105, Viale della Cisterna 7, tel. 06-581-7212, www.hotelcisternarome.com).

Near the Vatican, consider the the family-run **$$$ Hotel dei Consoli** with 26 rooms (Db-€200-250, Via Varrone 2D, tel. 06-6889-2972, www.hoteldeiconsoli.com, info@hoteldeiconsoli.com), the modern-style **$$$ Hearth Hotel** with 20 rooms (Db-€140-235, Via Santamaura 2, tel. 06-3903-8383, www.hearthhotel.com, info@hearthhotel.com), or the clean and handy **$$ Excel Rome St. Peter** with 24 rooms (Db-€78-310, Via Catone 34, tel. 06-3973-5082, www.excelstpeter.it, booking@excelstpeter.it).

Near the Spanish Steps, **$$$ Hotel Homs**' 53 pricey rooms are perfectly comfortable (Db-€150-250, Via della Vite 71, tel. 06-679-2976, www.hotelhoms.it, info@hotelhoms.it), while **$$ Hotel San Carlo**'s 50 rooms are a tranquil haven (Db-€117-216, Via delle Carrozze 92, tel. 06-678-4548, www.hotelsancarloroma.com, info@hotelsancarloroma.com).

ROME

Eating in Rome

I've listed a number of restaurants I enjoy. While most are in quaint and therefore pricey and touristy areas (Piazza Navona, the Pantheon neighborhood, Campo de' Fiori, and Trastevere), many are tucked away just off the tourist crush.

I'm impressed by how small the price difference can be between a mediocre Roman restaurant and a fine one. You can pay about 20 percent more for double the quality. If I had $100 for three meals in Rome, I'd spend $50 for one and $25 each for the other two, rather than $33 on all three. For splurge meals, I'd consider Gabriello, Fortunato, and Taverna Trilussa (in that order).

Rome's fabled nightspots (most notably Piazza Navona, near the Pantheon, and Campo de' Fiori) are lined with the outdoor tables of touristy restaurants with enticing menus and formal-vested waiters. The atmosphere is super-romantic: I, too, like the idea of dining under floodlit monuments, amid a constantly flowing parade of people. But you'll likely be surrounded by tourists, and noisy English-speakers can kill the ambience of the spot...leaving you with just a forgettable and overpriced meal. Restaurants in these areas are notorious for surprise charges, forgettable food, microwaved ravioli, and bad service.

I enjoy the view by savoring just a drink or dessert on a famous square, but I dine with locals on nearby low-rent streets, where the proprietor needs to serve a good-value meal and nurture a local following to stay in business. If you're set on eating—or just drinking and snacking—on a famous piazza, you don't need a guidebook listing to choose a spot; enjoy the ritual of slowly circling the square, observing both the food and the people eating it, and sit where the view and menu appeal to you. (And pizza is probably your best value and least risky bet.)

In Trastevere

Colorful Trastevere is now pretty touristy. Still, Romans join the tourists to eat on the rustic side of the Tiber River. Start at the central square, Piazza di Santa Maria. This is where the tourists dine, while others wander the back streets in search of mom-and-pop places with barely a menu. My recommendations are within a few minutes' walk of each other (between Piazza di Santa Maria in Trastevere and Ponte Sisto; see map on page 936).

Taverna Trilussa is your best bet for dining well in Trastevere. Brothers Massimo and Maurizio offer quality and value without pretense. With a proud 100-year-old tradition, this place has the right mix of style and informality. The service is fun-loving

The *Aperitivo* Tradition

Milan and northern Italian cities have long enjoyed the *aperitivo* tradition: Bars serve up an enticing buffet of small dishes, and anyone buying a drink (at an inflated price) gets to eat "for free." Now competition for customers in the early evening hours has driven bars in Rome to embrace the same practice. All over town, bars—from humble to chic and trendy—are offering a light meal with a cocktail during happy hour. Drinks generally cost €8-10, and the food's out from 18:00 to 21:00. Some places limit you to one plate; others allow refills. Either way, if you want a quick, light dinner with a drink, it's a great deal. You'll notice happy crowds all over town.

(they're happy to let you split plates into smaller portions to enjoy a family-style meal), yet professional. The menu celebrates local classics and seasonal specials, and comes with a big wine selection. The spacious dining hall is strewn with eclectic Roman souvenirs. For those who'd rather eat outdoors, Trilussa has an actual terrace rather than just tables jumbled together on the sidewalk (€15 pastas, €20 *secondi*, Mon-Sat from 19:30 for dinner, closed Sun, reservations very smart, Via del Politeama 23, tel. 06-581-8918, www.tavernatrilussa.it).

Trattoria da Lucia lets you enjoy simple, traditional food at a good price. It's your basic old-school, Trastevere dining experience, and has been family-run since World War II. You'll meet four generations of the family, including Giuliano and Renato, their uncle Ennio, and Ennio's mom—pictured on the menu in the 1950s. The family specialty is *spaghetti alla Gricia*, with *pancetta* (€9 pastas, €11 *secondi*, Tue-Sun 12:30-15:00 & 19:30-23:00, closed Mon and several weeks in Aug, cash only, evocative outdoor or comfy indoor seating—but avoid back room, just off Via del Mattonato at Vicolo del Mattonato 2, tel. 06-580-3601).

Trattoria da Olindo takes homey to extremes. You really feel like you dropped in on a family that cooks for the neighborhood to supplement their income—just don't expect any smiles (€8 pastas, €10 *secondi*, Mon-Sat dinner served 20:00-22:30, closed Sun, cash only, indoor and funky outdoor seating, on the corner of Vicolo della Scala and Via del Mattonato at #8, tel. 06-581-8835).

Osteria Ponte Sisto, small and Mediterranean, specializes in traditional Roman cuisine, but has frequent Neapolitan specials as well. Just outside the tourist zone, it caters mostly to Romans and offers beautiful desserts and a fine value (€9 pastas, €12-16 *secondi*, March-Oct Thu-Tue 12:30-23:30, closes between lunch and dinner off-season, closed Wed, Via Ponte Sisto 80, tel. 06-588-3411,

ROME

reservations smart for dinner, Oliviero). If you're coming from the city center, cross Ponte Sisto (pedestrian bridge) and continue across the little square (Piazza Trilussa). It's on the right.

Ristorante Checco er Carettiere is a big, family-run place that's been a Trastevere fixture for four generations—as the photos on the wall attest. With white tablecloths, well-presented food, and dressy local diners, this is a popular place for a special meal in Trastevere. While it's overpriced, you'll eat well amid lots of fun commotion (€18 pastas, €22 *secondi*, daily 12:30-15:00 & 19:30-23:15, Via Benedetta 10, tel. 06-580-0985, www.checcoercarettiere.it). Their *osteria* next door (at #13) shares the same kitchen and offers less ambience, lower prices, and a more basic menu (€11 pastas, €15 *secondi*). Many Romans consider their *gelateria* (next door at #7) to be among the best on this side of the river.

Pizzeria "Ai Marmi" is a bright and noisy festival of pizza, where the oven and pizza-assembly line are surrounded by marble-slab tables (hence the nickname "the Morgue"). It's a classic Roman scene, whether you enjoy the chaos inside or sit at a sidewalk table, with famously good €8 Roman-style pizza (thin and crispy) and very tight seating. Expect a long line between 20:00 and 22:00 (Thu-Tue 18:30-24:00, closed Wed, cash only, tram #8 from Piazza Venezia to first stop over bridge, just beyond Piazza Sonnino at Viale di Trastevere 53, tel. 06-580-0919).

Pizzeria Dar Poeta, tucked in a back alley and a hit with local students, cranks out less traditional, thick-crust, wood-fired pizza—some of the best I've had in Rome. It's run by three friends—Marco, Paolo, and another Marco—who welcome you into the informal restaurant beneath exposed brick arches. If you're in a spicy mood, order *lingua di fuoco* (tongue of fire). If you're extra hungry, pay an extra euro for *pizza alto* (even thicker crust). Choose between their classic, cramped interior and lively tables outside on the cobblestones. Their chocolate dessert calzone is a favorite (€6-9 pizza and salads, daily 12:00-24:00, Vicolo del Bologna 45, tel. 06-588-0516).

Cantina Paradiso Wine and Cocktail Bar, a block over Viale di Trastevere from the touristy action, has a funky romantic charm. During happy hour (18:00-21:00), the €8 drinks come with a well-made little buffet that can turn into a cheap, light dinner (€8 pastas, daily 18:00-24:00, Via San Francesco a Ripa 73, tel. 06-589-9799, Weronika).

And for Dessert: **Gelateria alla Checco er Carettiere,** run by and next door to the famous, recommended restaurant of the same name, is many locals' favorite spot for gelato in Trastevere (daily 12:00-24:00, Via Benedetta 7).

In the Jewish Ghetto
The Jewish Ghetto sits just across the river from Trastevere (see map on page 936).

Sora Margherita, hiding on a cluttered square, has been a rustic neighborhood favorite since 1927. Amid a picturesque commotion, families chow down on old-time Roman and Jewish dishes. It's technically not a real restaurant (it avoids red tape by officially registering itself an *associazione culturale*)—you can even sign a card to join the "cultural association" (don't worry; membership has no obligations except that you enjoy your meal). The menu's crude term for the fettuccini gives you some idea of the mood of this place: *nazzica culo* ("shaky ass"—what happens while it's made). Reservations are almost always necessary (€10-12 pastas, €12-14 *secondi*; Sept-May Mon-Sat 12:30-15:00, dinner seatings on Mon, Wed, Fri, and Sat at 20:00 and 21:30, closed Sun; June-July same hours except also closed Sat, closed in Aug, just south of Via del Portico d'Ottavia at Piazza delle Cinque Scole 30—look for the red curtain, tel. 06-687-4216).

In the Pantheon Neighborhood
For the restaurants in this central area, I've listed them based on which landmark they're closest to: Campo de' Fiori, Piazza Navona, the Trevi Fountain, or the Pantheon itself.

On and near Campo de' Fiori
By day, Campo de' Fiori hosts one of the few markets in downtown Rome, selling fruit and veggies (and an increasing number of tourist knickknacks; Mon-Sat closes around 13:30, closed Sun). Combined with a sandwich and sweet from the **Forno** (bakery) in the west corner of the square (behind the fountain), you can assemble a nice picnic.

By night, while it is touristy, Campo de' Fiori offers a sublimely romantic setting. And, since it's so close to the heart of the Roman people, it remains popular with locals, even though its restaurants offer greater atmosphere than food value. The square is lined with popular and interesting bars, pizzerias, and small restaurants—all great for people-watching over a glass of wine. Later at night it's taken over by a younger clubbing crowd.

Ristorante ar Galletto is nearby, on the more elegant and peaceful Piazza Farnese. Angelo entertains an upscale Roman clientele and has magical outdoor seating. Regrettably, service can be brusque, you need to double-check the bill, and single diners aren't treated very well. Still, if you're in no hurry and ready to savor my favorite al fresco setting in Rome (while humoring the waiters), this can be a good bet (€10-12 pastas, €16-22 *secondi*, daily 12:15-15:00 & 19:30-23:00, reservations smart for outdoor seating, Piaz-

Roman Cuisine

Here are a few food items to look for in the Eternal City:

For **antipasti,** Romans kick things off with *fritti* (little bread-ed-and-fried snacks—often olives stuffed with meat, potato croquettes, and mozzarella cheese). These include *supplì* (oval-shaped rice balls with tomato sauce and mozzarella) and *fiori di zucca* (squash blossoms filled with mozzarella and anchovies, then lightly fried).

Popular **first courses** *(primi)* include some delicious pastas: *spaghetti alla carbonara* (with a sauce of eggs, pancetta or cured pork cheek, cheese, and black pepper), *bucatini all'amatriciana* (thin pasta tubes with a sauce of tomatoes, onion, pancetta, and pecorino cheese on top), *penne all'arrabbiata* (tube pasta topped with a spicy tomato sauce of chili peppers and garlic), *spaghetti alle vongole veraci* (small clams in the shell sautéed with white wine and herbs, served over pasta), and *gnocchi alla romana* (small flattened dumpling made from semolina and baked with butter and cheese). For soup, try *stracciatella alla romana*, a meat broth with whipped eggs topped with parmesan cheese.

Roman **second courses** *(secondi)* include *saltimbocca alla romana* (literally "jump-in-the-mouth"—thinly sliced veal layered with prosciutto and sage, then lightly fried), *abbacchio alla scot-tadito* (baby lamb chops grilled and eaten as finger food), *trippa alla romana* (tripe braised with onions, carrots, and mint), *coda alla vaccinara* (oxtail braised with garlic, wine, tomato, and cel-

za Farnese 104, tel. 06-686-1714, www.ristoranteargallettoroma. com).

Vineria Salumeria Roscioli is an elegant *enoteca* that's a hit with local foodies, so reservations are a must. While it's just a sala-mi toss away from touristy Campo de' Fiori, you'll dine with classy locals and feel like you're sitting in a romantic (and expensive) deli after hours. They have a good selection of fine cheeses, meats, local dishes, and top-end wines by the glass (€15-25 plates, Mon-Sat 12:30-16:00 & 19:00-24:00, closed Sun, 3 blocks east of Campo de' Fiori at Via dei Giubbonari 21, tel. 06-687-5287, www.salu-meriaroscioli.com). Their nearby **Forno Roscioli** is a favorite for a quick slice of pizza or pastry to go (Mon-Sat 6:00-20:00, closed Sun, Via dei Chiavari 34, tel. 06-686-4045).

Trattoria der Pallaro, an eccentric and well-worn eatery that has no menu, has a slogan: "Here, you'll eat what we want to feed you." Paola Fazi—with a towel wrapped around her head turban-style—and her gang dish up a five-course meal of homey Roman food. You have three menu choices: €25 for the works; €20 for appe-tizers, *secondi*, and dessert; or €15 for appetizers and pasta. Any opery), *involtini di vitello al sugo* (veal cutlets rolled with prosciutto, celery, and cheese in a tomato sauce), *anguillette in umido* (stewed baby eels from nearby Lake Bracciano), and *filetti di baccalà* (salt cod fried in a batter—like "fish and chips" minus the chips). Popular *contorini* (side dishes) include *fave al guanciale* (fava beans simmered with cured pork cheek and onion), *misticanza* (mixed green salad of arugula and curly endive with anchovies), and *carciofi* (artichokes)—either *alla romana* (stuffed with garlic, mint, and parsley) or *alla giudia* (flattened and fried).

Dolci (desserts) can be a seasonal fruit, such as *fragole* (strawberries) or *pesche* (peaches), or even cheese, such as *pecorino romano* (made from ewe's milk) or *caciotta romana* (made from a combination of ewe's and cow's milk). *Crostata di ricotta* is a cheesecake-like dessert with ricotta, sweet Marsala wine, cinnamon, and bits of chocolate. *Bignè* are cream puff-like pastries filled with *zabaglione* (egg yolks, sugar, and Marsala wine). And *tartufo* is a rich dark-chocolate gelato ball with a cherry inside (*con panna* gets you whipped cream on top).

When it's hot outside, a shaved-ice-with-fruit-syrup concoction called a *grattachecca* (grah-tah-KEH-kah) cools you down fast. The vendors at the little booths scrape shavings off ice blocks and then flavor them with syrups. Try the combo-flavors such as *limoncocco*—lemon and coconut syrups with fresh chunks of coconut.

tion is filling, includes wine and coffee, and is capped with a thimble of mandarin juice. While the service can be odd and the food is rustic, the experience is fun (daily 12:00-16:00 & 19:00-24:00, reserve if dining after 20:00, cash only, indoor/outdoor seating on quiet square, a block south of Corso Vittorio Emanuele, down Largo del Chiavari to Largo del Pallaro 15, tel. 06-6880-1488).

Filetti di Baccalà is a cheap and basic Roman classic, where nostalgic regulars cram into wooden tables and savor their old-school favorites—fried cod finger-food fillets (€5 each) and raw, slightly bitter *puntarelle* greens (slathered with anchovy sauce, available in spring and winter). Study what others are eating, and order from your grease-stained server by pointing at what you want. Sit in the fluorescent-lit interior or try to grab a seat out on the little square, a quiet haven a block east of Campo de' Fiori (Mon-Sat 17:30-23:00, closed Sun, cash only, Largo dei Librari 88, tel. 06-686-4018). If you're not into greasy spoons, avoid this place.

Pizzeria da Baffetto 2 makes pizza Roman-style: thin crust, crispy, and wood-fired. Eat in the cramped informal interior, or outside on the busy square (€7-10 pizzas, daily 18:30-24:00, Sat-

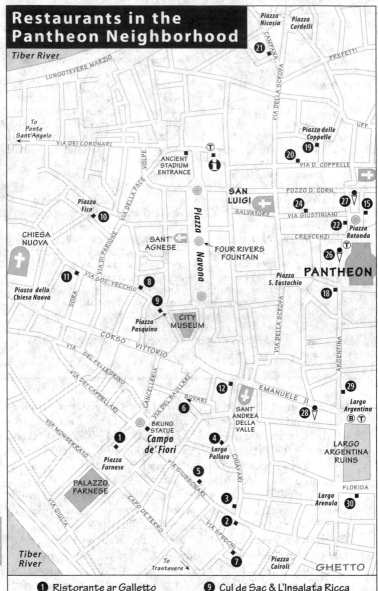

Restaurants in the Pantheon Neighborhood

1. Ristorante ar Galletto
2. Vineria Salumeria Roscioli
3. Forno Roscioli
4. Trattoria der Pallaro
5. Filetti di Baccalà
6. Pizzeria da Baffetto 2
7. Open Baladin Pub
8. Ciccia Bomba
9. Cul de Sac & L'Insalata Ricca
10. Rist. Pizzeria "da Francesco"
11. Pizzeria da Baffetto
12. L'Insalata Ricca
13. L'Antica Birreria Peroni
14. Rist. Pizzeria Sacro e Profano
15. Ristorante da Fortunato
16. Enoteca Corsi

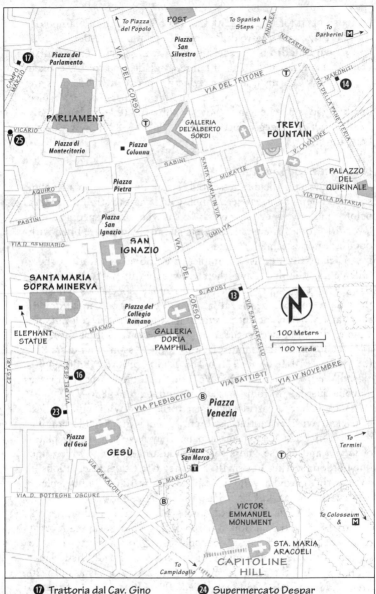

⑰ Trattoria dal Cav. Gino	㉔ Supermercato Despar
⑱ Miscellanea	㉕ Gelateria Giolitti
⑲ Osteria da Mario	㉖ Crèmeria Monteforte
⑳ Taverna le Coppelle	㉗ Gelateria San Crispino
㉑ Ristorante la Campana	㉘ Gelateria Vice
㉒ Antica Salumeria	㉙ Frullati Pascucci
㉓ Super Market Carrefour Express	㉚ Pizzeria Florida & Pane Più

ROME

Sun also open for lunch 12:30-15:30, a block north of Campo de' Fiori at Piazza del Teatro di Pompeo 18, tel. 06-6821-0807).

Open Baladin is a modern pub featuring a few dozen Italian craft beers on tap and menu of burgers, salads, and freshly cooked potato chips. As this is a relatively new concept in Italy, prices are somewhat high—and the food can be hit or miss—but it's a nice break if you're parched and ready for pub grub (€9-15 plates, daily 12:00-24:00, Via degli Specchi 5, tel. 06-683-8989, www.open-baladinroma.it).

Near Piazza Navona

Piazza Navona is the quintessential setting for dining on a Roman square. Whether you eat here or not, you'll want to stroll the piazza before or after your evening meal. This is where many people fall in love with Rome. The tangled streets just to the west are lined with popular eateries of many stripes.

Ciccia Bomba is a simple, traditional trattoria where Gianpaolo, Gianluca, and their crew serve up tasty homemade pasta, wood-fired pizza, and other Roman specialties (consider their daily-special sheet)—all at a good price. You can sit down-stairs at a table on ancient pavement next to your own column, but I prefer the ambience on the main level. Reserve at least a week in advance for their 45-minute pizza-making "lesson" that costs €25 (€8 pastas, €10-16 *secondi*, Thu-Tue 12:30-15:00 & 19:00-24:00, closed Wed, Via del Governo Vecchio 76, a block west of Piazza Navona, just north from Piazza Pasquino, tel. 06-6880-2108).

Cul de Sac, a corridor-wide trattoria lined with wine bottles, is packed with an enthusiastic crowd enjoying a wide-ranging menu, from pasta to homemade pâté. They have fun tasting-plates of *salumi* and cheese, more than a thousand different wines, and fine outdoor seating. It's small, and they don't take reservations—come early to avoid a wait (€7-15 plates, daily 12:00-24:00, a block off Piazza Navona on Piazza Pasquino, tel. 06-6880-1094).

Ristorante Pizzeria "da Francesco," bustling and authentic, has a 50-year-old tradition, a hardworking young waitstaff, great indoor seating, and classic outdoor seating on a cluttered little square that makes you want to break out a sketchpad. Their black-board explains the daily specials (€9 pizzas and pastas, €15-20 *secondi*, daily 12:00-15:30 & 19:00-24:00, 3 blocks west of Piazza Navona at Piazza del Fico 29, tel. 06-686-4009).

Pizzeria da Baffetto, buried deep in the old quarter behind Piazza Navona, is a Roman favorite, offering tasty pizza and surly service. Its tables are tightly arranged amid the mishmash of photos and sketches littering the walls. The pizza-assembly kitchen keeps things energetic, and the pizza oven keeps the main room warm (you can opt for a table on the cobbled street). Come early or late, or be prepared to wait (€7 pizzas, daily from 18:30, cash only; order "P," "M," or "D"—small, medium, or large; west of Piazza Navona on the corner of Via Sora at Via del Governo Vecchio 114, tel. 06-686-1617).

L'Insalata Ricca is a popular local chain that specializes in healthy, filling €8 salads and less-healthy pastas and main courses (daily March-Oct 12:00-24:00, closes between lunch and dinner in off-season). They have a handy branch on Piazza Pasquino (next to the recommended Cul de Sac, tel. 06-6830-7881) and a more spacious and enjoyable location a few blocks away, on a bigger square next to busy Corso Vittorio Emanuele (near Campo de' Fiori at Largo dei Chiavari 85, tel. 06-6880-3656).

Near the Trevi Fountain

The streets surrounding the Trevi Fountain are littered with mediocre restaurants catering exclusively to tourists—try one of these instead.

L'Antica Birreria Peroni is Rome's answer to a German beer hall. Serving hearty mugs of the local Peroni beer and lots of just plain fun beer-hall food and Italian classics, the place is a hit with Romans for a cheap night out (€7 pastas, €4-12 *secondi,* Mon-Sat 12:00-24:00, closed Sun, midway between Trevi Fountain and Capitoline Hill, a block off Via del Corso at Via di San Marcello 19, tel. 06-679-5310).

Ristorante Pizzeria Sacro e Profano fills an old church with spicy southern Italian (Calabrian) cuisine and satisfied tourists. Run with enthusiasm by Emiliano and friends, this is just far enough away from the Trevi mobs. Their pizza oven is wood-fired, and their hearty €15 *antipasti* plate is a filling montage of Calabrian taste treats (€10-12 pastas, €16-20 *secondi,* Tue-Sun 12:00-15:00 & 18:00-23:00, closed Mon, a block off Via del Tritone and Via della Panetteria at Via dei Maroniti 29, tel. 06-679-1836).

Close to the Pantheon

Eating on the square facing the Pantheon is a temptation, and I'd consider it just to relax and enjoy the Roman scene. But if you walk a block or two away, you'll get less view and better value. Here are some suggestions.

Ristorante da Fortunato is an Italian classic, with fresh flowers on the tables and white-coated, black-tie career waiters politely serving good meat and fish to politicians, foreign dignitaries, and tourists with good taste. Don't leave without perusing the photos of their famous visitors—everyone from former Iraqi Foreign Minister Tariq Aziz to Bill Clinton seems to have eaten here. All are pictured with the boss, Fortunato, who, since 1975, has been a master of simple edible elegance. (His son Jason is now on the team.) The

ROME

outdoor seating is fine for watching the river of Roman street life flow by, but the real atmosphere is inside. For a dressy night out, this is a reliable and surprisingly reasonable choice—but be sure to reserve ahead (plan to spend €45 per person, daily 12:30-15:30 & 19:30-23:30, a block in front of the Pantheon at Via del Pantheon 55, tel. 06-679-2788, www.ristorantefortunato.it).

Enoteca Corsi is a wine shop that grew into a thriving lunch-only restaurant. The Paiella family serves straightforward, traditional cuisine to an appreciative crowd of office workers. Check the board for daily specials (gnocchi on Thursday, fish on Friday, and so on). Friendly Giuliana, Claudia, Sara, and Manuela welcome eaters to step into their wine shop and pick out a bottle. For the cheap take-away price, plus €4-8 (depending on the wine), they'll uncork it at your table. With €9 pastas, €13 main dishes, and fine wine at a third of the price you'd pay in normal restaurants, this can be a good value. And guests with this book can finish their meal with a free glass of homemade *limoncello* (Mon-Sat 12:00-15:30, closed Sun, no reservations possible, a block toward the Pantheon from the Gesù Church at Via del Gesù 87, tel. 06-679-0821).

Trattoria dal Cavalier Gino, tucked away on a tiny street behind the Parliament, has been a favorite since 1963. Photos on the wall recall the days when it was the haunt of big-time politicians. Grandpa Gino shuffles around grating the parmesan cheese while his English-speaking children Carla and Fabrizio serve up traditional Roman favorites and make sure things run smoothly. Reserve ahead, even for lunch, as you'll be packed in with savvy locals (€8 pastas, €11 *secondi*, cash only, Mon-Sat 13:00-14:45 & 20:00-22:30, closed Sun, behind Piazza del Parlamento and just off Via di Campo Marzio at Vicolo Rosini 4, tel. 06-687-3434).

Miscellanea is run by much-loved Mikki, who's on a mission to keep foreign students well-fed. Welcoming travelers as well as locals, he offers hearty €4 sandwiches and a long list of €7 salads, along with pasta and other staples. This is a great value for a cheap and hearty dinner featuring typical rustic Roman cuisine. Mikki (and his son Romeo) often tosses in a fun little extra, including—if you have this book on the table—a free glass of Mikki's "sexy wine" (from *fragoline*—strawberry-flavored grapes). While basic, it's convenient (€7 pastas, €10 *secondi*, daily 11:00-24:00, indoor/outdoor seating, facing the rear of the Pantheon at Via della Palombella 34, tel. 06-6813-5318).

Osteria da Mario, a homey little mom-and-pop joint with a no-stress menu, serves traditional favorites in a fun dining room or on tables spilling out onto a picturesque old Roman square (€9 pastas, €12-15 *secondi*, Mon-Sat 12:30-15:30 & 19:00-23:00, closed Sun; from the Pantheon walk 2 blocks up Via del Pantheon, go left on Via delle Coppelle, and take first right to Piazza delle Coppelle 51; tel. 06-6880-6349, Marco).

Taverna le Coppelle is simple, basic, family-friendly, and inexpensive—especially for pizza—with a checkered-tablecloth ambience (€9 pizzas, daily 12:30-15:00 & 19:30-23:30, Via delle Coppelle 39, tel. 06-6880-6557, Alfonso).

Ristorante la Campana is a plain and honest little place—an authentic slice of Rome with a local following and no pretense. It serves classic dishes and daily specials, plus it has a good self-service *antipasti* buffet (€10 pastas, €15 *secondi*, Tue-Sun 12:30-15:00 & 19:30-23:00, closed Mon, inside seating only, reserve for dinner, just off Via della Scrofa and Piazza Nicosia at Vicolo della Campana 18, tel. 06-687-5273, www.ristorantelacampana.com).

Picnicking Close to the Pantheon

It's fun to munch a picnic with a view of the Pantheon. (Remember to be discreet.) Here are some options.

Antica Salumeria is an old-time *alimentari* (grocery store) on the Pantheon square. While they hustle most tourists into premade €5 sandwiches, you can make your own picnic. Find your way to the back to buy artichokes, mixed olives, bread, cheese, and meat (daily 8:00-21:00, mobile 334-340-9014).

Supermarkets near the Pantheon: Food is relatively cheap at Italian supermarkets. **Super Market Carrefour Express** is a convenient place for groceries a block from the Gesù Church (Mon-Sat 8:00-20:30, Sun 9:00-19:30, 50 yards off Via del Plebiscito at Via del Gesù 59). Another place, **Supermercato Despar,** is half a block from the Pantheon toward Piazza Navona (daily 8:30-22:00, Via Giustiniani 18).

Gelato Close to the Pantheon

Several fine *gelaterie* are within a five-minute walk of the Pantheon.

Giolitti is Rome's most famous and venerable ice-cream joint (although few would say it has the best gelato). Take-away prices are reasonable, and it has elegant Old World seating (daily 7:00-24:00, just off Piazza Colonna and Piazza Monte Citorio at Via Uffici del Vicario 40, tel. 06-699-1243).

Crèmeria Monteforte is known for its traditional gelato and super-creamy sorbets *(cremolati).* The fruit flavors are especially refreshing—think gourmet slushies (Tue-Sun 10:00-24:00, off-season closes earlier, closed Mon and Dec-Jan, faces the west side of the Pantheon at Via della Rotonda 22, tel. 06-686-7720).

Gelateria San Crispino serves small portions of particularly tasty gourmet gelato. Because of their commitment to natural ingredients, the colors are muted; gelato purists consider bright colors a sign of unnatural chemicals used to attract children (daily 12:00-

ROME

24:00, a block in front of the Pantheon on Piazza della Maddalena, tel. 06-6889-1310).

Gelateria Vice is a relative newcomer but might be the best of all. Using top-quality ingredients in innovative ways, the flavors change with the seasons (daily 11:00-24:00, around the northwest corner of Largo Argentina at Corso Vittorio Emanuele II 96, tel. 06-8117-3023).

Cheap Eats near Largo Argentina

The following are convenient choices for take-away; each offers just a few places to sit.

Frullati Pascucci is a hole-in-the-wall that's been making refreshing fruit *frullati* and frappés (like smoothies and shakes) for more than 75 years. Add a sandwich or fruit salad to make a healthy light meal (Mon-Sat 6:00-23:00, closed Sun, north of Largo Argentina at Via di Torre Argentina 20, tel. 06-686-4816).

Pizzeria Florida, on the south side of Largo Argentina, offers tasty, cheap pizza slices (Mon-Sat 10:00-22:00, closed Sun, Via Florida 25, tel. 06-6880-3236).

Pane Più, next door to Pizzeria Florida, is a good bet for gourmet *panini* and salads (€5 sandwiches, daily 11:30-16:00, Tue-Sat also 19:00-22:00, Via Florida 21, tel. 06-4542-7800).

In North Rome

Near the Ara Pacis and Spanish Steps

To locate these restaurants, see the "Dolce Vita Stroll" map on page 873.

Ristorante il Gabriello is inviting and small—modern under medieval arches—and provides a peaceful and local-feeling respite from all the top-end fashion shops in the area. Claudio serves with charisma, while his brother Gabriello cooks creative Roman cuisine using fresh, organic products from his wife's farm. Italians normally just trust their waiter and say, "Bring it on." Tourists are understandably more cautious, but you can be trusting here. Simply close your eyes and point to anything on the menu. Or invest €45 in "Claudio's Extravaganza" (not including wine). Specify whether you'd prefer fish, meat, or both. (Romans think raw shellfish is the ultimate in fine dining. If you differ, make that clear.) When finished, I stand up, hold my belly, and say, *"Ahhh, la vita è bella."* While you're likely to dine surrounded by my readers here (especially if eating before 21:00), the atmosphere is fun and convivial (€11-14 pastas, €14-20 *secondi*, dinner only, Mon-Sat 19:00-23:00, closed Sun, reservations smart, air-con, dress respectfully—no shorts, 3 blocks from Spanish Steps at Via Vittoria 51, tel. 06-6994-0810, www.ilgabriello.it).

Antica Enoteca, an upbeat, atmospheric 200-plus-year-old *enoteca,* has around 60 Italian-only wines by the glass (€4-10, listed on a big blackboard) and a full menu of eating options, from €8 salads to a €14 *antipasti* plate of veggies, *salumi,* and cheese. Very crowded on summer evenings, it comes with wonderful ambience both inside and out; its outside tables are set on a quiet cobbled street (daily 11:00-24:00, best to reserve for outdoor seating, Via della Croce 76b, tel. 06-679-0896, www.anticaenotecaroma.com).

Palatium Enoteca Regionale is a crisp, modern restaurant funded by the region of Lazio (home to Rome) to show off its finest agricultural fare. Surrounded by locals, you'll enjoy generous, shareable plates of cheeses and *salumi,* a limited menu of pasta and meat, and a huge selection of local wine (€12-16 plates, Mon-Sat 12:30-15:30 & 19:30-22:30, closed Sun and Aug, 5 blocks in front of the Spanish Steps at Via Frattina 94, tel. 06-6920-2132).

Gusto Wine Bar is a convenient choice for a glass of wine or a light meal. Popular with trendy locals, it gives a glimpse of today's Roman scene, though some of the decor has a 1930s ambience. While much of the food at their other nearby venues is pricey (and mediocre), the weekday €11 lunch buffet (12:30-15:30) is a good value. During happy hour (18:00-21:00) you get a light, self-service meal with your drink for €10-12 (daily 11:00-2:00 in the morning, kitchen closes at 24:00; just behind the Ara Pacis at Via della Frezza 23, tel. 06-322-6273).

Caffè Ciampini is delightfully set on one of my favorite traffic-free squares in the center of town. The food will win no awards—and you pay for the location—so I'd only stop here to sit outside and people-watch. This is a good place to make the scene with trendy and professional Romans. The cocktails come with a little tray of finger sandwiches and nuts; for some it's a light and inexpensive meal (€7-15 pizzas, salads, pastas, sandwiches; Piazza San Lorenzo in Lucina 29, tel. 06-687-6606, www.ciampini.com).

Eating Light on the Via della Croce: Two blocks north of the Spanish Steps, the Via della Croce offers a few simple options for a light meal or snack. **Pastificio** (#8) is a pasta shop that serves up two types of fresh pasta each day at 13:00. There are only a few stools, so you might be eating in the street (off a plastic plate), but for €4 you also get water and a "drop of wine for the most deserving"—be nice and say *per favore* (daily 13:00-16:00 or when the pasta is gone). **Pompi** (#82), the self-proclaimed "kingdom of tiramisu," features several flavors (classic, strawberry, pistachio) in €4 portions. Farther along, **Venchi** (#25-26) has chocolate in every form—good for their rich gelato and edible souvenirs. For more formal, sit-down options, **Antica Enoteca** (earlier) is also on this street. Tucked away in a quiet, vine-covered courtyard, **Trattoria Otello alla Concordia** (#81) is a decent choice for traditional food served in a slightly faded old-time atmosphere (€10-12 pastas, €12-

15 *secondi*, Mon-Sat 12:30-15:00 & 19:30-23:00, closed Sun, tel. 06-679-1178).

Near the Colosseum and Forum

Within a block of the Colosseum and Forum, you'll find convenient eateries catering to weary sightseers, offering neither memorable food nor good value. To get your money's worth, stick with one of these good choices or head farther away. The characteristic Monti neighborhood, with a number of casual options, is several blocks north of the Forum (head up Via Cavour and then left on Via dei Serpenti; the action centers on Piazza della Madonna dei Monti and unfolds along Via dei Serpenti, Via del Boschetto, and Via Leonina/Urbana). For locations, see the map on page 962.

Enoteca Cavour 313 is a wine bar with a mission: to offer good wine and food with an old-fashioned commitment to value and friendly service. Its slightly unconventional menu, ranging from couscous and salads to high-quality *affettati* (cold cuts) and cheese, makes a nice alternative to the usual pasta/pizza choices. With a mellow ambience under lofts of wine bottles, it's a favorite at any time, but especially for a convenient lunch (€7-14 basic plates, daily 12:30-14:45 & 19:00-24:00, 100 yards off Via dei Fori Imperiali at Via Cavour 313, tel. 06-678-5496, Angelo, Massimo, and Pulika).

Taverna Romana, run by the same folks as Cavour 313, is small and simple, serving traditional classics made with quality ingredients. Reserve for the earliest seating, or join the locals and add your name to the waitlist for the later seating (€8 pastas, €12 *secondi*, Mon-Sat 12:30-14:45 & 19:00-23:00, closed Sun, cash only, Via Madonna dei Monti 79, tel. 06-474-5325).

Hostaria da Nerone is a traditional place serving hearty classics, including tasty homemade pasta dishes. Their *antipasti* plate—with a variety of veggies, fish, and meat—is a good value for a quick lunch. While the *antipasti* menu indicates specifics, you can have a plate of whatever's out—just direct the waiter to assemble the €10 *antipasti* plate of your lunchtime dreams (€11 pastas, €13-15 *secondi*, Mon-Sat 12:00-15:00 & 19:00-23:00, closed Sun, indoor/outdoor seating, Via delle Terme di Tito 96, tel. 06-481-7952, Teo and Eugenio).

Caffè dello Studente, next door to Hostaria da Nerone, is popular with engineering students attending the nearby University of Rome. The owners—Pina, Mauro, their perky daughter Simona, and their son-in-law Emiliano (the last two speak English)—give my readers a friendly welcome. They serve average, microwaved *bar gastronomia* fare—toasted sandwiches, salads, and mixed bruschetta. If it's not busy, show this book when you order at the bar and sit at a table without paying extra (Mon-Sat 7:30-21:00, April-Oct

ROME

Sun 9:00-20:00, Nov-March closed Sun, Via delle Terme di Tito, tel. 06-488-3240).

Trattoria Luzzi is a well-worn, no-frills eatery serving simple food in a high-energy environment (as they've done since 1945). With good prices, big portions, and proximity to the Colosseum, it draws a crowd—reserve or expect a short wait at lunch and after 19:30 (€5-7 pastas, €7 pizzas, €7-12 *secondi*, Thu-Tue 12:00-24:00, closed Wed, Via San Giovanni in Laterano 88, tel. 06-709-6332). If Luzzi is jam-packed, as it often is, **Ristorante Pizzeria Naumachia** (next door at Via Celimontana 7, tel. 06-700-2764) is a bit more upscale and serves good-quality pizza and pastas at good prices.

La Taverna dei Quaranta, a casual neighborhood favorite, has a humble, red-checkered tablecloth ambience. In the evening, they fire up the wood oven for pizza, to go along with a basic menu of Roman classics and seasonal specialties. As the place caters mostly to locals, service can be a bit slow and straightforward—but it's a good bet in this touristy area (€8 pastas, €8-13 *secondi,* daily 12:00-15:30 & 19:00-23:30, Via Claudia 24, tel. 06-700-0550).

Enoteca Nel Cuore di Roma sits overlooking Trajan's Column. It's a modern little place with a cool, peaceful, and well-lit dining room and a few outside tables. It celebrates Roman cuisine with fresh local produce and daily €13 specials, including wine (daily 11:00-23:30, Foro Traiano 82, tel. 06-6994-0273).

Near Termini Station

These restaurants are near my recommended hotels on Via Firenze. Several are clustered on Via Flavia, others are nearby (Target, etc.), and a few, such as Bar Tavola Calda, are good options for quick meals.

On (or near) Via Flavia

To easily check out a fun and varied selection of eateries within a block of each other, walk to Via Flavia (a block behind the Church of Santa Maria della Vittoria of *St. Teresa in Ecstasy* fame) and survey these choices—an old-time restaurant, a good pizzeria, a small romantic place, and a friendly wine bar.

Ristorante da Giovanni, well-worn and old-fashioned, makes no concessions to tourism or the modern world—just hardworking cooks and waiters serving standard dishes at great prices to a committed clientele. It's simply fun to eat in the middle of this high-energy, Roman time warp (€6-12 pastas and *secondi,* daily specials, Mon-Sat 12:00-15:00 & 19:00-22:00, closed Sun and Aug, corner of Via XX Settembre at Via Antonio Salandra 1, tel. 06-485-950).

Ristorante la Pentolaccia, pricier and more romantic than the nearby Da Giovanni, is a dressy, tourist-friendly place with

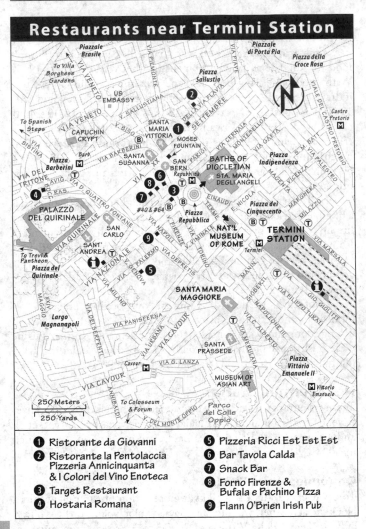

Restaurants near Termini Station

1 Ristorante da Giovanni

2 Ristorante la Pentolaccia
Pizzeria Annicinquanta
& I Colori del Vino Enoteca

3 Target Restaurant

4 Hostaria Romana

5 Pizzeria Ricci Est Est Est

6 Bar Tavola Calda

7 Snack Bar

8 Forno Firenze &
Bufala e Pachino Pizza

9 Flann O'Brien Irish Pub

tight seating and traditional Roman cooking—consider their daily specials. This is a local hangout, and reservations are smart (€8-12 pastas, €10-18 *secondi*, daily 12:00-15:00 & 17:30-23:00, a block off Via XX Settembre at Via Flavia 38, tel. 06-483-477, www.lapentolaccia.eu). To start things off with a free bruschetta, keep this book on the table.

Pizzeria Annicinquanta, big and classic, serves the neighborhood's favorite pizzas in a calm ambience with outdoor seating (€8 Neapolitan-style pizzas, €10-18 pastas and *secondi,* daily 12:15-15:30 & 19:30-24:00 except no lunch on Sat, Via Flavia 3, tel. 06-4201-0460).

I Colori del Vino Enoteca is a modern wine bar that feels like a laboratory of wine appreciation. It has woody walls of bottles, a creative menu of *affettati* (cold cuts) and cheeses with different regional themes, and a great list of fine wines by the glass. Helpful, English-speaking Marco carries on a long family tradition of celebrating the fundamentals of good nutrition: fine wine, cheese, meat, and bread (Mon-Fri 12.00-15.00 & 17:30-23:00, closed Sat-Sun because Marco doesn't cater to noisy weekend drinkers, corner of Via Flavia and Via Aureliana, tel. 06-474-1745). Remember Shakespeare's sage warning about drinking: "It provokes the desire, but it takes away the performance."

More Eateries near the Station

Target Restaurant seems to be the favorite recommendation of every hotel receptionist and tour guide for this neighborhood. It has a sleek look, capable service, and reliably good food (€8-12 salads, pastas, and pizzas; €17-20 *secondi*, daily 12:00-15:00 & 19:00-24:00 except no lunch on Sun, reserve to specify seating outside or inside—avoid getting seated in basement, Via Torino 33, tel. 06-474-0066, www.targetrestaurant.it).

Hostaria Romana is a busy bistro with a hustling and fun-loving gang of waiters, and noisy walls graffitied by happy eaters. As its menu specializes in traditional Roman dishes, it's a good place to try *saltimbocca alla romana* or *bucatini all'amatriciana*. Their €10 *antipasti* plate, with a variety of vegetables and cheeses, makes a hearty start to your meal (€9 pastas, €14 *secondi*, Mon-Sat 12:30-15:00 & 19:15-23:00, closed Sun and Aug, reservations smart, a block up the lane just past the entrance to the big tunnel near the Trevi Fountain, corner of Via Rasella and Via del Boccaccio, tel. 06-474-5284, www.hostariaromana.it).

Pizzeria Ricci Est Est Est, a venerable family-run pizzeria, has plenty of historical ambience, good €8 pizzas, and dangerously tasty *fritti*, such as fried *baccalà* (cod) and zucchini flowers (Tue-Sun 19:00-24:00, closed Mon and Aug, Via Genova 32, tel. 06-488-1107).

Fast, Simple Meals near the Station

Bar Tavola Calda is a workers' favorite for a quick, cheap lunch. They have good, fresh, hot dishes ready to go for a fine price. Head back past the bar to peruse their enticing display, point at what you want, then grab a seat and the young waitstaff will serve you (Mon-Fri 6:00-18:00, closed Sat-Sun, Via Torino 40, tel. 06-474-2767).

Snack Bar puts out a lunchtime display of inexpensive pastas, colorful sandwiches, fresh fruit, and salad. Their loyal customers appreciate the fruit salad with yogurt (daily 6:00-24:00, Via Firenze 33, tel. 06-9784-3866, Enrica).

ROME

Forno Firenze makes simple sandwiches, has a selection of well-priced wine, and stocks a few other goodies for a picnic to go (sandwiches priced by weight, Mon-Fri 7:00-19:00, Sat 8:00-14:00, closed Sun, Via Firenze 51-52, tel. 06-488-5035, Giovanni).

Bufala e Pachino Pizza is a convenient place for pizza by the slice *(al taglio)* and priced by weight—just point and tell them how much you'd like. Their *supplí* (fried rice balls filled with mozzarella), at just €1 each, make for cheap, filling snacks (daily 8:00-23:00, Via Firenze 54).

Flann O'Brien Irish Pub is an entertaining place for a light meal of pasta...or something *other* than pasta, such as grilled meats and giant salads, served early and late, when other places are closed. They have Irish beer, live sporting events on TV, and perhaps the most Italian crowd of all. Walk way back before choosing a table. Live bands often play on Thursday or Friday evenings (daily 7:00-24:00, Via Nazionale 17, at intersection with Via Napoli, tel. 06-488-0418).

Near Vatican City

As in the Colosseum area, eateries near the Vatican cater to exhausted tourists. Avoid the restaurant-pushers handing out fliers: They're usually hawking places with bad food and expensive menu tricks. Instead, tide yourself over with a slice of pizza or at any of these eateries (see map on page 968), and save your splurges for elsewhere.

Handy Lunch Places near Piazza Risorgimento

These are a stone's throw from the Vatican wall, located halfway between St. Peter's Basilica and the Vatican Museum. They're all fast and cheap, with a good *gelateria* next door.

Hostaria dei Bastioni, run by Antonio while Emilio cooks, has noisy street-side seating and a quiet interior (€8 pastas, €8-12 *secondi*, Mon-Sat 12:00-15:30 & 18:30-23:00, closed Sun, at corner of Vatican wall at Via Leone IV 29, tel. 06-3972-3034).

L'Insalata Ricca is another branch of the popular chain that serves hearty salads and pastas (daily April-Oct 12:30-23:30, closes between lunch and dinner in off-season, across from Vatican walls at Piazza Risorgimento 5, tel. 06-3973-0387).

Duecento Gradi is a good bet for fresh and creative €5 sandwiches. Munch your lunch on a stool or take it away (daily 11:00-24:00, Piazza Risorgimento 3, tel. 06-3975-4239).

Gelato: **Gelateria Old Bridge** scoops up hearty portions of fresh gelato for tourists and nuns alike—join the line (daily 10:00-23:00, just off Piazza Risorgimento across from Vatican walls at Via Bastioni 3).

Other Options in the Vatican Area

The first three listings—the restaurant, the streets with pizza shops, and the covered market—are near the Vatican Museum. The Borgo Pio eateries are near St. Peter's Basilica.

Ristorante La Rustichella serves tasty wood-fired pizza and the usual pasta in addition to their *antipasti* buffet (€8 for a single plate) in a no-frills, neighborhood setting. Do like the Romans do—take a moderate amount of *antipasti* and make one trip only (Tue-Sun 12:30-15:00 & 19:00-24:00, closed Mon, near Metro: Cipro, opposite church at end of Via Candia, Via Angelo Emo 1, tel. 06-3972-0649). Consider the fun and fruity **Gelateria Millennium** next door.

Viale Giulio Cesare and *Via Candia:* These streets are lined with cheap *pizza rustica* shops, self-serve places, and basic eateries. **Forno Feliziani** (Via Candia 61, tel. 06-3973-7362) is a good bet for pizza by the slice and simple cafeteria-style dishes.

Covered Market: As you collect picnic supplies, turn your nose loose in the wonderful **Mercato Trionfale** covered market. It's one of the best in the city, located three blocks north of the Vatican Museum (Mon-Sat roughly 7:00-14:00, Tue and Fri some stalls stay open until 19:00, closed Sun, corner of Via Tunisi and Via Andrea Doria). If the market is closed, try several nearby supermarkets; the most convenient is **Carrefour Express** (Mon-Sat 8:00-20:00, Sun 9:00-20:00, Via Sebastiano Veniero 16).

Along Borgo Pio: The pedestrians-only Borgo Pio—a block from Piazza San Pietro—has restaurants worth a look, such as **Tre Pupazzi** (Mon-Sat 12:00-15:00 & 19:00-23:00, closed Sun, at corner of Via Tre Pupazzi and Borgo Pio, tel. 06-686-8371). At **Vecchio Borgo,** across the street, you can get pasta, pizza slices, and veggies to go (Mon-Sat 9:00-21:00, closed Sun, Borgo Pio 27a, tel. 06-8117-3585).

Testaccio

Once a slaughterhouse district, working-class Testaccio is now going upscale. If your visit to the modern Testaccio Market makes you hungry, here are two options. For locations, see the map on page 939.

Flavio al Velavevodetto, partially set inside Monte Testaccio (windows reveal the ancient stacked pottery shards), is a good place to try traditional Roman classics like *coda alla vaccinara* (ox tail) or less adventurous options (€8-10 pastas, €12-18 *secondi*, daily 12:30-15:00 & 19:30-23:00, reservations smart for dinner, Via di Monte Testaccio 97, tel. 06-574-4194, www.flavioalvelavevodetto.it).

Volpetti Più is a fixture in this neighborhood of foodies for its great pizza and *tavola calda*. If you need a cheap, quick, and tasty lunch, drop by, pick up a tray, and point to what looks (and is) good (Mon-Sat 10:30-15:30 & 17:30-21:30, closed Sun, just off Via Marmorata at Via Alessandro Volta 8, tel. 06-574-2352). Their deli (similar hours) at Via Marmorata 47 is a sensory extravaganza for anyone enthusiastic about gourmet Italian cheeses, meats, and olive oils.

Rome Connections

Rome is well-connected with the rest of the planet: by train, bus, plane, car, and cruise ship. This section addresses your arrival and departure from the city. It explains the various options and gives a rundown on their points of departure.

By Train

Rome's main train station is the centrally located **Termini** train station, which has connections to the airport. Rome's other major station is the **Tiburtina** bus/train station, which is starting to get some high-speed rail connections, including privately run Italo trains (see page 1166). For in-depth descriptions of Termini and Tiburtina stations, see page 841.

Smaller stations include **Ostiense** (some high-speed rail service, mostly Italo) and its neighbor, **Porta San Paolo** (connections to Ostia Antica). If you're staying near the Vatican and taking a regional train, it saves time to get off at the **San Pietro** train station rather than at Termini. Cruise-ship passengers coming from Civitavecchia on a day trip usually use Ostiense or San Pietro.

The most convenient connections for travelers nearly always depart from Termini, but as a precaution, it's always smart to confirm whether your train departs from Termini or Tiburtina.

From Rome's Termini Station by Train to: Venice (roughly hourly, 3.5 hours, overnight possible), **Florence** (at least hourly, 1.5 hours, some stop at Orvieto en route), **Siena** (1-2/hour, 1 change, 3-3.5 hours), **Orvieto** (hourly, 1.25 hours), **Assisi** (hourly, 2-3.5 hours, 5 direct, most others change in Foligno), **Pisa** (2/hour, 3-4 hours, many change in Florence), **La Spezia** (7/day direct, more with transfers in Pisa, 3-4.5 hours), **Milan** (hourly, 3-8 hours, overnight possible), **Milan's Malpensa Airport** (1 direct express/day, 4.5 hours), **Naples** (at least hourly, 1.25 hours on Frecciarossa or Italo trains, otherwise 2 hours), **Civitavecchia** cruise-ship port (2-3/hour, 40-80 minutes), **Brindisi** (6/day, 3 direct, 6-9 hours, overnight possible), **Amsterdam** (6/day, 20 hours), **Interlaken** (5/day, 6.5-8 hours), **Frankfurt** (6/day, 11-12 hours), **Munich** (5/day, 10-11.5 hours, 1 direct night train, 11.5 hours), **Nice** (7/day, 8.75-10.5 hours), **Paris** (3/day, 11-12 hours, 1-2 changes; 1 night train, 14 hours, important to reserve ahead at www.thello.com), **Vienna** (2/day, 11.75 hours, 1 direct night train, 12 hours).

From Rome's **Tiburtina Station by Train to: Florence** (almost hourly, 1.5 hours), **Milan** (almost hourly, 3-3.5 hours), **Naples** (11/day, 1.25 hours), **Venice** (5/day, 3.5 hours).

By Bus

Long-distance buses (such as from Siena and Assisi) arrive at Rome's Tiburtina Station (described on page 812).

From Rome by Bus to: **Assisi** (2/day, 3 hours—the train makes much more sense), **Siena** (9-10/day, 3 hours), **Sorrento** (1-2/day, 4 hours; this is a cheap and easy way to go straight to Sorrento, buy tickets at Ticket Bus at Tiburtina, other travel agencies, or on board for a €3 surcharge; tel. 080-579-0111, www.marozzivt.it—in Italian only).

By Plane

Rome's two airports—**Fiumicino** (a.k.a. Leonardo da Vinci, airport code: FCO) and the small **Ciampino** (airport code: CIA)—share the same website (www.adr.it).

Fiumicino Airport

Rome's major airport has a TI (in Terminal 3, daily 8:00-19:30), ATMs, banks, luggage storage, shops, and bars. The Rome Walks website (www.romewalks.com) has a useful video on options for getting into the city from the airport. For airport information, call 06-65951. To inquire about flights, call 06-6595-3640.

The slick, direct **Leonardo Express train** connects the airport and Rome's central Termini train station in 30 minutes for €14. Trains run twice hourly in both directions from roughly 6:00 to 23:00 (leaving the airport usually at :08 and :38). From the airport's arrival gate, follow signs to the train car icon or *Stazione/Railway Station*. Buy your ticket from a machine, the Biglietteria office, or a newsstand near the platform; then validate it in a yellow machine near the track. Make sure the train you board is going to the central "Roma Termini" station, not "Roma Orte" or others.

Going from Termini train station to the airport, trains depart at about :22 and :52 past the hour, usually from track 24. Check the departure boards for "Fiumicino Aeroporto"—the local name for the airport—and confirm with an official or a local on the platform that the train is indeed going to the airport (€14, buy ticket from any tobacco shop or a newsstand in the station, or at the self-service machines, Termini-Fiumicino trains run 5:52-22:52). Read your ticket: If it requires validation, stamp it in the green or yellow machines near the platform before boarding. From the train station at the airport, you can access most of the terminals. American airlines flying direct to the US depart from Terminal 5, which is a separate building not connected to the rest of the terminals. If you arrive by train, catch the T5 shuttle bus *(navetta)* on the sidewalk in front of Terminal 3—it's too far to walk with luggage.

Allow lots of time going in either direction; there's a fair amount of transportation involved (e.g., getting from your hotel to Termini, the ride to the airport, the walk from the airport train station to check-in, etc.). Flying to the US involves an extra level of security—plan on getting to the airport even earlier than normal (flying transatlantic, I like to arrive 2.5 hours ahead of my flight; within Europe, 2 hours is usually sufficient).

The **Terravision Express bus** connects Fiumicino and Termini train station, departing roughly every 40 minutes (€6 one-way, €11 round-trip; leaves the airport from Terminal 3, leaves Termini Station from Via Marsala—just outside the exit closest to track 1; one hour, www.terravision.eu). The **SIT Bus Shuttle** also connects Fiumicino and Termini (€6 one-way, €11 round-trip, similar schedule and info to Terravision, tel. 06-592-3507, www.sitbusshuttle.com). While cheaper than the train, the buses take twice as long and can potentially fill up (allow plenty of extra time).

Shuttle van services run to and from the airport and can be economical for one or two people. It's cheaper from the airport to downtown, as several companies compete for this route; by surveying the latest deals, you should be able to snare a ride into town for around €10. To get from your hotel to the airport, consider Rome Airport Shuttle (€25/1 person, extra people-€6 each, by reservation only, tel. 06-4201-4507 or 06-4201-3469, www.airportshuttle.it).

A **taxi** between Fiumicino and downtown Rome takes 45 minutes in normal traffic (for tips on taxis, see page 856). If you're catching a taxi at the airport, be sure to wait at the taxi stand. Avoid unmarked, unmetered taxis; these guys will try to tempt you away from the taxi-stand lineup by offering an immediate (rip-off) ride. Rome's and Fiumicino's official taxis have a fixed rate to and from the airport (€48 for up to four people with normal-size bags).

Cabbies not based in Rome or Fiumicino are allowed to charge €70 for the ride. That sign is posted next to the €48-fare sign—confusing many tourists and allowing dishonest cabbies to overcharge. It's best to use a Rome city cab, with the words *"Rome Capitale"* and the "SPQR" shield on the door. They can only charge €48 for the ride to anywhere in the historic center (within the old city walls, where most of my recommended hotels are located).

If your cab driver tries to charge you more than €48 from the airport into town, say, *"Quarant'otto euro—è la legge"* (kwah-RAHN-OH-toh eh-OO-roh—eh lah LEH-jeh; which means, "Forty-eight euros—it's the law"), and they should back off.

To get from the airport into town cheaply by taxi, try teaming up with any tourist also just arriving (most are heading for hotels near yours in the center). When you're departing Rome, your hotel can arrange a taxi to the airport at any hour.

Ciampino Airport

Rome's smaller airport (tel. 06-6595-9515) handles charter flights and some budget airlines (including all Ryanair flights).

To get to downtown Rome from the airport, you can take the Cotral bus, which leaves every 40 minutes (€5, 20-minute ride, toll-free tel. 800-174-471, www.cotralspa.it), to the Anagnina Metro stop, where you can connect by Metro to the stop nearest your hotel. Rome Airport Shuttle also offers service to and from Ciampino (€25/1 person, listed earlier). The Terravision Express Shuttle connects Ciampino and Termini train station (€6 one-way, €8 round-trip, about 2/hour, 45 minutes, Termini to Ciampino pickup on Via Marsala outside the station next to the Terracafé, tel. 06-9761-0632, www.terravision.eu). The SIT Bus Shuttle also connects Termini to Ciampino (€6 one-way, €8 round-trip, about 2/hour, 45 minutes, pickup on Via Marsala just outside the train exit closest to track 1, tel. 06-592-3507, www.sitbusshuttle.com). A taxi should cost €30 to downtown (within the old city walls, including most of my recommended hotels).

By Cruise Ship

Hundreds of cruise ships—including Carnival, Royal Caribbean, Princess, and Celebrity lines—dock each year at the port of **Civitavecchia,** about 45 miles northwest of Rome. If your trip includes cruising beyond Rome, consider my guidebook, *Rick Steves' Mediterranean Cruise Ports.* Port facilities include a TI (tel. 0766-679-619), ATMs, Internet access, bag storage, and cafés.

To get from your ship to Civitavecchia's train station, take the free **shuttle bus** to the port entrance (some shuttles may take you all the way to the station—ask). From the shuttle-bus stop, walk through the security checkpoint at the port gate, and then walk about 10 minutes straight ahead up the main road with the sea on your right-hand side. After about three blocks, at Hotel de La Ville, bear left and uphill through a long parking lot to the pale-orange train station (marked *Civitavecchia*); if you get turned around, look for signs to *Stazione FF. SS.*

Taxis also wait at the port gate, attempting to extort €15 for the very short ride to the train station (tel. 076-626-121). A local bus to the train station only saves you a few minutes of walking; take one only if you're carrying heavy bags or have limited mobility. **Buses** #B, #C, and #D go from just above the port gate on Largo Plebiscito (Viale Garibaldi stop) one stop to the train station (Stazione FF. SS. stop; €1, 3-4/hour, 5 minutes, buy ticket at a tobacco shop before you board).

ROME

Getting Between Civitavecchia and Downtown Rome

The traffic between Civitavecchia and Rome is terrible, making trains faster and more economical than a taxi. Keep in mind that it takes approximately 1.5 hours each way to get between your ship and downtown Rome—so you'll need to mentally subtract at least three hours from the time you have in port.

By Train: The Civitavecchia train station has five main platforms (*binario*, or *bin*; numbered 1 through 5), connected by an underground tunnel. There are also two "short" *(tronco)* platforms, 1T and 2T, at the far-right end of the station as you face the tracks; these are *not* the same as tracks 1 and 2. Be sure you're waiting at the correct platform. For a useful video on taking the train from the port into the city, check out the Rome Walks website (www.romewalks.com).

Frequent trains (2-3/hour) connect Civitavecchia with several stations in Rome. Depending on your sightseeing plans, you'll likely be best off heading either to **Ostiense Station** (with a handy Metro station, just two stops from the Colosseum) or **San Pietro Station** (10-minute walk or a couple stops on bus #64 to get to St. Peter's Basilica). Termini Station, the main hub for the city's transit and for shuttle trains to the airport, overshoots the key city-center sights a bit.

Regional trains (marked *REG*) head into Rome roughly twice an hour, stopping at San Pietro and Ostiense stations on their way to Termini (40-55 minutes to San Pietro, 55-70 minutes to Ostiense, 65-80 minutes to Termini). The **Intercity train** (marked *IC*) is somewhat faster (40-50 minutes to Ostiense, 50 minutes to Termini), but doesn't stop at San Pietro, and isn't covered by the good-value BIRG ticket (described next). When there are enough ships in port to justify it, there's also a special **express "Vatican train non-stop"** to San Pietro, offering one daily round-trip designed for cruise travelers.

If you're taking a regional train, save money by getting the wonderful BIRG ticket: a €12 day pass covering second-class, round-trip train travel between Civitavecchia and Rome as well as unlimited travel on Rome's buses, Metro, and trams—a great convenience (not valid on fast Intercity trains or the express train to San Pietro). Otherwise, expect to pay about €5 each way for regional trains or €10 on the Intercity. All train tickets must be validated in the green or yellow box before you get on the train.

By Taxi: A taxi can run €110-150 one-way. Recommended driver Ezio of Autoservizi Monti Concezio takes cruise travelers to Rome in a private car (€130/2 people, €20 for each additional person) and offers full-day tours of the city (€380/2 people, €30 for each additional person; see "Car and Minibus Tours" on page 861).

ROME

Beware of unlicensed taxis offering a huge price break; local police sometimes follow these "gypsy" cabs in a scam that imposes hefty fines on both the driver and the passengers (the driver later gets a kickback from the cop).

Getting Between Civitavecchia and Fiumicino Airport

You'll need to take two **trains** to link Civitavecchia and Fiumicino Airport: one between Civitavecchia and Rome's Termini train station, and another between Termini and the airport. See "By Plane," earlier.

Shuttle van services run between the port and Rome's Fiumicino Airport. Try **Rome Airport Shuttle** (€90/1-2 people, €15 each additional person up to 8, share with others and save, much more for pickup between 21:00 and 7:00, tel. 06-4201-4507 or 06-4201-3469, www.airportshuttle.it). A **taxi** costs about €120 one-way between Civitavecchia and Fiumicino Airport.

NAPLES

Napoli

If you like Italy as far south as Rome, go farther south—it gets better. If Italy is getting on your nerves, don't go farther. Italy intensifies as you plunge deeper. Naples is Italy in the extreme—its best (birthplace of pizza and Sophia Loren) and its worst (home of the Camorra, Naples' "family" of organized crime).

Neapolis ("new city") was a thriving Greek commercial center 2,500 years ago. Today, it remains southern Italy's leading city. Naples impresses visitors with one of Europe's top archaeological museums (with the artistic treasures of Pompeii), fascinating churches that convey the city's unique personality and powerful devotion, an underground warren of Greek and Roman ruins, fine works of art (including pieces by Caravaggio, who lived here for a time), and evocative nativity scenes (called *presepi*). Naples, of course, makes the best pizza you'll find anywhere, and tasty pastries as well (try the crispy, ricotta-stuffed *sfogliatella*). But more than anything, Naples has a brash and vibrant street life—"Italy in your face" in ways both good and bad. Walking through its colorful old town is one of my favorite experiences anywhere in Europe. For a grand overlook, head to the hilltop viewpoint (San Martino) for sweeping views of the city and its bay.

Naples—Italy's third-largest city, with more than one million people—has almost no open spaces or parks, which makes its position as Europe's most densely populated city plenty evident. Watching the police try to enforce traffic sanity is almost comical in Italy's grittiest, most polluted, and most crime-ridden city. But Naples surprises the observant traveler with its impressive knack for living, eating, and raising children in the streets with good humor and decency. Overcome your fear of being run down or ripped off long enough to talk with people. Enjoy a few smiles and jokes with the man running the neighborhood tripe shop, or the woman taking her day-care class on a walk through the traffic.

The pulse of Italy throbs in Naples. Like Cairo or Mumbai, it's appalling and captivating at the same time, the closest thing to "reality travel" that you'll find in Western Europe. But this tangled mess still somehow manages to breathe, laugh, and sing—with a joyful Italian accent. Thanks to its reputation as a crime-ridden and dangerous place, Naples doesn't get nearly as many tourists as it deserves. While Naples has its problems, it has improved a lot in recent years. And even though it's a bit edgy, I feel comfortable here. Naples richly rewards those who venture in.

Naples is also the springboard for a full region of sightseeing treats (covered in the next three chapters): Just beyond Naples are the remarkable ruins of Pompeii and Herculaneum, and the brooding volcano that did them both in, Mount Vesuvius. A few more miles down the road is the pleasant resort town of Sorrento and the offshore escape isle of Capri. And plunging even farther south, you'll reach the dramatic scenery of the Amalfi Coast.

Planning Your Time

Naples makes an ideal day trip either from Rome or from the comfortable home base of Sorrento, located an hour south. Or stow your bag at the station and see Naples in a few hours while you change trains here on the way between Rome and Sorrento. A little Naples goes a long way; if you're not comfortable in chaotic and congested cities, think twice before spending the night here. But those who are intrigued by the city's sights and street life enjoy overnighting in Naples.

On a quick visit, start with the Archaeological Museum (closed Tue), follow my "A Slice of Neapolitan Life" self-guided walk, and celebrate your survival with pizza. With more time, dip into more churches, go underground to see Greek and Roman ruins, and consider ascending San Martino for the view. Of course, Naples is huge. But even with limited time, if you stick to the prescribed route and grab a cab when you're lost or tired, it's fun. Treat yourself well in Naples; the city is cheap by Italian standards. This is a place where splurging on a sane and comfortable hotel is a particularly worthwhile investment.

For a blitz tour from Rome, you could have breakfast on an early Rome-Naples express train (for example, Mon-Fri 7:35-8:45), do Naples and Pompeii in a day, and be back in Rome in time for bed. That's exhausting, but more memorable than a fourth day in Rome.

Remember that on summer afternoons, Naples' street life slows and many churches and museums close as the temperature soars. The city comes back to life in the early evening.

Orientation to Naples

Naples is set deep inside the large and curving Bay of Naples, with Mount Vesuvius looming just five miles away. Although Naples is a sprawling city, its fairly compact core contains the most interesting sights. The tourist's Naples is a triangle, with its points at the Centrale train station in the east, the Archaeological Museum to the west, and the Piazza del Plebiscito (with the Royal Palace) and the port to the south. Steep hills rise above this historic core, including San Martino, capped with a mighty fortress.

Tourist Information

Central Naples has six TIs (run variously by the city, the region, and a local business association), all of which are equally incapable of dispensing reliable advice. All are understaffed and have little to offer besides free maps. The most convenient—but perhaps least helpful—is in the **Centrale train station** (daily 9:00-18:00, near track 23, operated by a private agency, tel. 081-268-779). This is a convenient place to buy Campania ArteCard passes (see sidebar).

Other TIs are scattered around town: There are two near **Piazza del Plebiscito,** near the port: one right on the piazza at #14, under the arches to the right of church entrance (Mon-Fri 9:00-19:00, closed Sat-Sun, tel. 081-795-6162); and another by the entrance to the Galleria Umberto I shopping mall, across from Teatro di San Carlo (Mon-Sat 9:00-19:00, Sun 9:00-14:00, tel. 081-402-394). Along Spaccanapoli, there's an office across from the **Church of Gesù Nuovo** (Mon-Sat 9:00-19:00, Sun 9:00-14:00, tel. 081-551-2701). By the Museo Metro stop, in the park next to the **Archaeological Museum,** is a tiny information kiosk (Mon-Fri 10:00-17:00, Sat 10:00-14:00, closed Sun). And cruise-ship passengers exiting the **cruise terminal** complex pass through a little checkpoint (marked *Molo Angioino*) that has a small TI.

For information online, the best overall website is www.inaples.it. At www.inaples.it/eng/quinapoli.htm, you can download their big (100-plus-page, 50 MB) PDF version of the *Qui Napoli* booklet, which lists museum hours, events, and transportation info. (Due to funding cuts, the booklet is no longer distributed in paper form.)

NAPLES

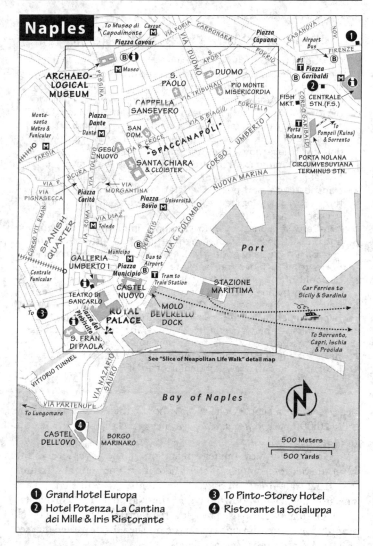

Naples

Legend:
1 Grand Hotel Europa
2 Hotel Potenza, La Cantina dei Mille & Iris Ristorante
3 To Pinto-Storey Hotel
4 Ristorante la Scialuppa

Arrival in Naples

By Train

There are several Naples train stations, but all trains coming into town stop at either Napoli Centrale or Garibaldi—which are essentially the same place, with Centrale on top of Garibaldi. Stretching in front of this station complex is the vast and gritty Piazza Garibaldi.

Centrale is the main station, serving trains on the main line. It's been spruced up in the last few years and has lots of facilities, including a small TI (near track 23), an ATM (at Banco di Napoli

Planning Your Time in the Region

On a quick trip, give the entire area—including Sorrento and Naples—a minimum of three days. If you use Sorrento as your sunny springboard (see Sorrento chapter), spend a day in Naples, a day exploring the Amalfi Coast, and a day split between Pompeii and the town of Sorrento. While Paestum (Greek temples), Mount Vesuvius, Herculaneum (an ancient Roman site like Pompeii), and the island of Capri are decent destinations, they are worthwhile only if you have more time. For a map, see page 999.

The **Campania ArteCard** regional pass may save you a few euros if you're here for two or three days, using public transportation, and plan to visit at least two of the region's three big sights: Pompeii (€11), Herculaneum (€11), and Naples' Archaeological Museum (€8). There are several Campania ArteCard versions, covering varying combinations of sights and public transportation. The three-day, €27 Tutta la Regione version is especially good if you'll be visiting both Naples and Sorrento; it includes free entry to two sights (plus a decent discount off others) and transportation within Naples, on the Circumvesuviana train, and on Amalfi Coast buses. The three-day, €30 Archeologia del Golfo version makes sense if you base yourself in Naples; it covers all three of the main archaeological sites plus several minor ones and transportation as far out as Pompeii. Cards are sold at some Naples TIs and at participating sights (cards activate on first use, expire 3 days later at midnight, www.campaniartecard.it).

near track 24), a baggage check (€5/5 hours, then €0.70/hour, daily 8:00-20:00, marked *deposito bagagli*, near track 5), and a ticket office (daily 5:50-21:10).

Garibaldi is a commuter rail station on the lower level of the Centrale Station complex. Get off here if arriving on the Circumvesuviana train line from Sorrento or Pompeii (the line terminates one stop deeper into downtown, at the Napoli Porta Nolana station). Garibaldi is also used by a few regular trains to make a quick stop as they barrel through. For more on the Circumvesuviana, see "Getting Around the Region," later.

By Ferry or Cruise Ship

Naples is a ferry hub with great boat connections to Sorrento, Capri, and other nearby destinations. Ferries use the Molo Beverello dock, while cruise ships use the nearby Stazione Marittima cruise terminal. The two docks are side-by-side at the port on the southeast edge of downtown Naples, near Castel Nuovo and the grand square called Piazza del Plebiscito. In the covered area between the cruise-terminal buildings, you'll find cafés and various shops, including a tobacco shop (where you can buy bus tickets).

NAPLES

Out by the street is the recommended Ontano Tours travel agency (see "Helpful Hints," later).

Whether arriving by ferry or cruise ship, you can get to the city center by taxi, bus, or on foot; the Alibus shuttle bus runs to the airport (see "By Plane," next; the stop is a couple of blocks inland from the port, between Castel Nuovo and Teatro di San Carlo).

The **taxi** stand is in front of the port area; figure €12-15 to get to the train station or to the Archaeological Museum (see "Getting Around Naples—By Taxi" on page 1005).

Tram #1 stops at the busy road directly in front of the cruise terminal and heads to Piazza Garibaldi and the train station, where you can connect to trains to sights outside of town (6/hour, 15 minutes, buy €1.20 ticket at tobacco shop, validate ticket in yellow box on the bus as you board); to reach the Circumvesuviana commuter line to Pompeii or Sorrento, you can hop off this tram a bit earlier, at Porta Nolana, to catch the train at its starting point.

Straight ahead across the road from the cruise terminal (on the right side of the big fortress) is a drab square called Piazza Municipio; from here, a **bus** stop to Naples' Archaeological Museum is a half-block down on Via Agostino Depretis (#R4, departs every 10-15 minutes, ride six stops to Piazza Museo). The new Municipio **Metro** stop, which may open here in 2014, will zip you to the museum faster (take line 1 three stops, to Museo).

On foot, it's a seven-minute **walk**—past the gigantic Castel Nuovo—to Piazza del Plebiscito and the old city center: After crossing the busy street in front of the port, head up the ramp just to the right of the castle. At the top, angle left, past Teatro di San Carlo, to Piazza del Plebiscito. From this square, you could do a truncated version of my self-guided walk (begin near the end of "Part 2," do that stretch backwards up the hill, then launch right into "Part 3").

By Plane

Naples International Airport (a.k.a. Capodichino, code: NAP) is located a few miles outside of town (tel. 081-789-6111 for operator, tel. 848-888-777 for info, www.gesac.it). Alibus shuttle buses zip you from the airport to Naples' Centrale train station/Piazza Garibaldi in 15 minutes, and then head to the port/Piazza Municipio for boats to Capri and Sorrento (buses run daily 6:30-24:00, 3/hour, less frequent early and late, 30 minutes to the port, €3, turn right as you exit and find platform #2 at the bus stop, pay driver, stops at train station and port only). It's tough to get a cabbie to use the meter from the airport, but a taxi ride should cost about €20 (see "Getting Around Naples—By Taxi" on page 1005).

To reach **Sorrento** from Naples Airport, take the direct Curreri bus (daily at 9:00, 11:00, 13:00, 14:30, 16:30, and 19:30; 1.25 hours, €10, pay driver, tel. 081-801-5420, www.curreriviaggi.it).

Helpful Hints

Theft Alert: While most travelers visit Naples completely safely, err on the side of caution. Don't venture into neighborhoods that make you uncomfortable. The areas close to the train station are especially seedy. Walk with confidence, as if you know where you're going and what you're doing. Touristy Spaccanapoli and the posh Via Toledo shopping boulevard are more upscale, but you'll still see rowdy kids and panhandlers. Assume able-bodied beggars are thieves.

Stick to busy streets and beware of gangs of hoodlums. A third of the city is unemployed, and past local governments have set an example that the Mafia would be proud of. Assume con artists are more clever than you. Any jostle or commotion is probably a thief-team smokescreen. To keep bags safe, it's probably best to leave them at your hotel or at the left-luggage office in Centrale Station.

Always walk on the sidewalk (even if the locals don't) and carry your bag on the side away from the street—thieves on scooters have been known to snatch bags as they swoop by. The less you have dangling from you (including cameras and necklaces), the better.

Perhaps your biggest risk of theft is while catching or riding the Circumvesuviana commuter train. If you're connecting from a long-distance express, you'll be stepping from a relatively secure compartment into an often crowded and dingy train, where disoriented tourists with luggage delicately mix with the residents of Naples' most down-at-heel districts. It's prime hunting ground for thieves. While I ride the Circumvesuviana comfortably and safely, each year I hear of many travelers who get ripped off on this ride. You won't be mugged—but you may be conned or pickpocketed. Especially late at night, the Circumvesuviana train is plagued by intimidating ruffians. For maximum safety and peace of mind, sit in the front car, where the driver will double as your protector, and avoid riding it after dark.

Con artists may say you need to "transfer" by taxi to catch the Circumvesuviana; you don't. Carry your own bags and keep valuables buttoned up.

Traffic Safety: In Naples, red lights are discretionary, and pedestrians need to be wary, particularly of motor scooters. Even on "pedestrian" streets, stay alert to avoid being sideswiped by scooters that nudge their way through the crowds. Keep children close. Smart tourists jaywalk in the shadow of bold and confident locals, who generally ignore crosswalks. Wait for a break in traffic, cross with confidence, and make eye contact with approaching drivers. The traffic will stop.

Supermarket: Superò is a block off Piazza Dante, close to my recommended hotels along Via Toledo and Spaccanapoli (Mon-
Sat 8:30-20:30, Sun 8:30-14:00, Via San Domenico Soriano
20e).

Laundry: Laundry DIY, between Piazza Dante and the Archaeological Museum, will—despite their name—do your laundry
for you (€8/load, Mon-Fri 8:00-19:30, Sat 8:00-13:15, closed
Sun, Via Vincenzo Bellini 50, mobile 339-318-0876).

Getting Around Naples

Naples' entire public transportation system—Metro, buses, funicular railways, and the single tram line—uses the same tickets,
which must be stamped as you enter (in the yellow machines). A
€1.30 single transit ticket gives you the run of the system for 1.5
hours, with unlimited changes. Tickets are sold at *tabacchi* stores
and (sometimes) at station windows; the few ticket machines you'll
see are usually out of order. A *giornaliero* day pass costs €3.70 (€3.10
on weekends) and pays for itself with three rides, but can be hard
to find; most *tabacchi* stores don't sell them. Many versions of the
Campania ArteCard (see sidebar on page 1000) include free public
transport in Naples, but the card doesn't work in the subway and
funicular turnstiles; you'll have to show it to the staff, who will
open the gate for you. For general information, maps, and fares in
English, visit www.unicocampania.it. For schedules, your only option is the Italian-only site www.anm.it.

By Subway: Naples' subway, the Metropolitana, has three
main lines. Line 1 is currently being extended, adding several new
stations that will make it very useful for tourists. Unless otherwise noted, the following stops are open (completion dates for the
rest are subject to change): From the Museo stop (Archaeological
Museum), line 1 heads to Dante (at Piazza Dante, between the
museum and Spaccanapoli), Toledo (south end of Via Toledo, near
Piazza del Plebiscito), Municipio (likely to open by 2014; at Piazza
Municipio, just above the harbor and cruise terminal), Università
(the university), Duomo (likely to open in 2015; near the cathedral
and the end of my self-guided walk), and Garibaldi (likely open by
late 2013; on Piazza Garibaldi in front of Centrale Station).

Line 2 (technically part of the Italian rail system) is most useful for getting from the train station to the Archaeological Museum
quickly: It runs from Centrale Station (catch it downstairs—the
stop is called Garibaldi) to Piazza Cavour (by the Archaeological
Museum). Other stops on line 2 include Montesanto (top of Spanish Quarter and Spaccanapoli street, and base of funicular up to
San Martino), and Amedeo (recommended hotel in the Chiaia district). The new line 6 is not yet complete; it will begin at Municipio
and head west—unlikely to be of much use to tourists.

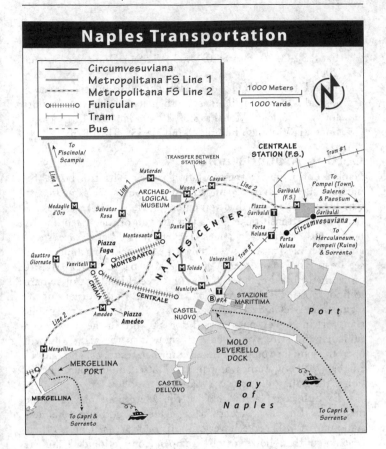

Naples Transportation

Circumvesuviana
Metropolitana FS Line 1
Metropolitana FS Line 2
Funicular
Tram
Bus

1000 Meters
1000 Yards

By Funicular: Central Naples' three funiculars *(funicolare)* carry commuters and sightseers into the hilly San Martino neighborhood just west of downtown. All three converge near Piazza Fuga, a short walk from the hilltop fortress and monastery/museum. The Centrale line runs from the Spanish Quarter, just near Piazza del Plebiscito and the Toledo Metro stop; the Montesanto line from the Montesanto Metro stop and Via Pignasecca market zone; and the Chiaia line from near the Piazza Amadeo Metro stop.

By Bus: Buses can be handy for certain trips, such as getting from the port to the Archaeological Museum (bus #R4), or if you need to curtail my self-guided walk from Via Toledo back to the station. But buses are crowded and poorly signed, and aren't a user-friendly option for uninitiated newcomers.

By Tram: The single tram line #1 runs along Corso Garibaldi (at the other end of the big square from Centrale Station) and down to the waterfront, terminating by the ferry and cruise terminals. It's useful if you're connecting from boat to train, or returning to the port after finishing my self-guided walk.

By Taxi: Taxi drivers in Naples are notorious for overcharging. A short ride in town should cost €10-12. Ask for the *tariffa predeterminata* (a fixed rate). Your hotel can tell you what a given ride should cost. There are some legitimate extra charges (baggage fees, €2.50 supplement after 22:00 or all day Sun and holidays).

Tours in Naples

Local Guides

Pina Esposito knows her ancient archaeology and art and does fine private walking and driving tours of Naples and the region (Pompeii, Capri, etc.), including Naples' Archaeological Museum (€60/ hour, 2-hour minimum, 10 percent off with this book, lower rates for full-day tours, mobile 366-622-8217, giuseppina.esposito20@ istruzione.it). The team at **Mondo Guide** also offers private tours of the museum (€120/2 hours), city (€240/4 hours), and region, along with a special deal for my readers—see next page (tel. 081-751-3290, www.mondoguide.it, info@mondoguide.it).

Hop-on, Hop-off Bus Tours

CitySightseeing Napoli tour buses make three different loops through the city, allowing riders to get on and off to explore. While the city's most engaging charms are buried in the tight tangle of lanes near Spaccanapoli, a bus tour does give you a better sense of the greater Naples that this chapter largely ignores (€22, tickets good for 24 hours, sparse frequency— 4-11/day depending on route, buy from driver or from kiosk at Piazza Municipio in front of Castel Nuovo near the port, scant recorded narration; for details, see the brochure at hotels and TI, tel. 081-551-7279, www.napoli. city-sightseeing.it).

Cruise-Ship Excursions

Convenient for cruise-ship passengers, consider the **Can't Be Missed** tour company, which gives you a quick look at Naples, Sorrento, and Pompeii with a small group and local guide for €65 (meet at 8:30 in front of port, bus leaves at 9:00, returns at 17:00, Pompeii ticket extra, mobile 329-129-8182, www.cantbemissedtours.com).

Self-Guided Tour

▲▲▲Archaeological Museum (Museo Archeologico)

This museum offers the best possible peek at the art and decorations of Pompeii and Herculaneum, the two ancient burgs that were buried in ash by the eruption of Mount Vesuvius in A.D. 79. For lovers of antiquity, this museum alone makes Naples a worth-

Mondo's Tours of Pompeii, Naples, and the Amalfi Coast for My Readers

Mondo Tours, a big Naples-based company (listed on previous page), offers co-op tours for Rick Steves readers. The idea—new for 2014—is to allow you the luxury of having a private, professional guide at a fraction of the usual cost (because you'll be sharing the expense with other travelers using this book). If you're willing to be a guinea pig for this experiment, sign up on their website, www.mondoguide.it (look for the Rick Steves tab). As they continually update departures on their online schedule, check the website to see the latest. Add your name as a promise to be there, then pay the guide (cash only) at the start of the tour. Pre-registration is required, and each tour will depart only if at least eight people have signed up (16-person maximum). Check the website the day before to be sure your tour received enough sign-ups to actually run (you can contact Mondo Tours at: tel. 081-751-3290, mobile 340-460-5254, info@mondoguide.it).

As this is a new system, please send your feedback—good or bad—to books@ricksteves.com. If you can't find the Rick Steves tab on Mondo's site, it means that the tours are no longer offered.

This program, which runs only from April through October of 2014, covers the tours in this region where travelers will get the most value out of this service.

Pompeii Tour: This two-hour guided walk brings to life the ruins of the excavated city (€12, doesn't include €11 Pompeii entry but guide will collect money and buy tickets, likely Mon-Fri at 10:30 but confirm schedule online; meet at Ristorante Suisse on Piazza Esedra (a 5-minute walk from the train station—exiting the

while stop. When Pompeii was excavated in the late 1700s, Naples' Bourbon king bellowed, "Bring me the best of what you find!" The finest art and artifacts ended up here, and today, the ancient sites themselves are impressive but barren. (If you'd like to visit those sites—both an easy train ride from Naples—see the next chapter.)

Cost and Hours: €8, sometimes more for temporary exhibits, Wed-Mon 9:00-19:30, closed Tue, last entry 30 minutes before closing. Early and temporary closures are noted on a board near the ticket office.

Getting There: To take the 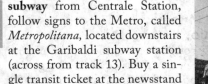 subway from Centrale Station, follow signs to the Metro, called *Metropolitana*, located downstairs at the Garibaldi subway station (across from track 13). Buy a single transit ticket at the newsstand or a tobacco shop (unless you're

NAPLES

station, turn right, pass the Porta Marina entrance, and continue down the hill to the restaurant, on the right).

Historic Naples Walk: Naples is a challenge to enjoy and understand; on this three-hour walk, a local Neapolitan guide helps you uncover the true character of the city (€20; likely Mon, Wed, and Fri at 15:00 but confirm schedule online). Tours meet at the steps of the National Museum of Archaeology (which is not included in the walk) in hopes that you can do the museum on your own before joining your guide.

Pompeii and Naples Combo: Combine the two tours listed above for €30 (only possible Mon, Wed, and Fri; you'll need to connect the two tours on your own; ideally, head straight from Pompeii to Naples in time to briefly tour the highlights of the National Museum of Archaeology before the Historic Naples Walk starts).

Full-Day Amalfi Coast Minibus Tour from Sorrento: The Amalfi Coast can be complicated and time-consuming to visit on your own, making a shared minibus the simplest and most affordable way to enjoy the sights. This nine-hour trip will save time and money and maximize your experience. It begins in Sorrento and heads south for the breathtaking drive (lightly narrated by your driver), photo stops, and an hour or two on your own in each of the three main towns—Positano, Amalfi, and Ravello—before returning to Sorrento (€45, likely Mon-Fri at 9:00 but confirm schedule online, meet overlooking the gorge in front of Hotel Antiche Mura, at Via Fuorimura 7, a block inland from Piazza Tasso).

getting a pass), and validate it in the small yellow boxes near the escalator going down to the tracks. You're looking for trains heading in the direction of Pozzuoli (generally depart from track 4). Hop on any train that comes through (confirm by its sign or with a local that it's going to Pozzuoli), and ride the subway one stop to Cavour. As you leave the Metro, exit and hike five minutes uphill through the park along the busy street. Look for a grand old red building located up a flight of stairs at the top of the block.

If taking the Metro back to Centrale Station, make sure to catch your train in the Cavour subway station, rather than at the connected Museo stop (which is on a different line).

Figure on €12 for a **taxi** from the train station to the museum.

Information: The shop sells a worthwhile *National Archaeological Museum of Naples* guidebook for €12. Tel. 081-442-2149.

Tours: My self-guided tour (below) covers all the basics. For more detail, the decent **audioguide** costs €5 (at ticket desk). If you want a **guided tour,** book Pina Esposito (see "Tours in Naples," earlier).

NAPLES

Baggage Check: Bag check is obligatory and free.

Photography: Photos are allowed without a flash.

Eating: The museum has no café, but vending machines sell drinks and snacks at reasonable prices. There are several good places to grab a meal within a few blocks; see page 1035.

Self-Guided Tour: Overview

Entering the museum, stand at the base of the grand staircase. To your right, on the ground floor, are the larger-than-life statues of

the Farnese Collection, starring the *Toro Farnese* and the *Farnese Hercules*. Up the stairs on the mezzanine level (turn left at the lion) are mosaics and frescoes from Pompeii, including the *Battle of Alexander* and the Secret Room of erotic art. On the top floor are more frescoes, a scale model of Pompeii, and bronze statues from Herculaneum. WCs are behind the staircase.

• *From the base of the grand staircase, turn right through the door marked* Collezione Farnese *and head to the far end—walking through a rich collection of idealistic and realistic ancient portrait busts—to reach the farthest room (Sala XIII).*

Ground Floor: The Farnese Collection

The museum's ground floor alone has enough Greek and Roman art to put any museum on the map. This floor has nothing from Pompeii; its highlight is the Farnese Collection, a grand hall of huge, bright, and wonderfully restored statues excavated from Rome's Baths of Caracalla. Peruse the larger-than-life statues filling the hall. They were dug up in the 1540s at the behest of Alessandro Farnese (by then Pope Paul III) while he was building the family palace on the Campo dei Fiori in Rome. His main purpose in excavating the baths was to scavenge quality building stone. The sculptures were a nice extra and helped the palace come in under budget on decorations. In the 1700s, the collection ended up in the hands of Charles, the Bourbon king of Naples (whose mother was a Farnese). His son, the next king, had it brought to Naples.

• *Quick—look down to the left end of the hall. There's a woman being tied to a snorting bull.*

The tangled *Toro Farnese* tells a thrilling Greek myth. At 13 feet, it's the tallest ancient marble group ever found, and the largest intact statue from antiquity. A third-century A.D. copy of a lost

bronze Hellenistic original, it was carved out of one piece of marble. Michelangelo and others "restored" it at the pope's request—meaning that they integrated surviving bits into a new work. Panels on the wall show which pieces were actually carved by Michelangelo (in blue on the chart): the head of the woman in back, the torso of the aunt under the bull, and the dog. (Imagine how the statue would stand out if it were thoughtfully lit and not surrounded by white walls.)

Here's the tragic story behind the statue: Once upon an ancient Greek time, King Lycus was bewitched by Dirce. He abandoned his pregnant wife, Antiope (standing regally in the background). The single mom gave birth to twin boys (shown here). When they grew up, they killed their deadbeat dad and tied Dirce to the horns of a bull to be bashed against a mountain. Captured in marble, the action is thrilling: cape flailing, dog snarling, hooves in the air. You can almost hear the bull snorting. And in the back, Antiope oversees this harsh ancient justice with satisfaction.

At the opposite end of the hall stands the **Farnese Hercules**. The great Greek hero is exhausted. He leans wearily on his club (draped with his lion skin) and bows his head. He's just finished the daunting Eleventh Labor, having traveled the world, fought men and gods, freed Prometheus from his rock, and carried Atlas' weight of the world on his shoulders. Now he's returned with the prize: the golden apples of the gods, which he cups behind his back. But, after all that, he's just been told he has to return the apples and do one final labor: descend into Hell itself. Oh, man.

The 10-foot colossus is a third-century A.D. Roman marble copy (signed by "Glykon") of a fourth-century B.C. Greek bronze original (probably by Lysippos). The statue was enormously famous in its day. Dozens of copies—some marble, some bronze—have been found in Roman villas and baths. This version was unearthed in Rome's Baths of Caracalla in 1546, along with the *Toro Farnese*.

The *Farnese Hercules* was equally famous in the 16th-18th centuries. Tourists flocked to Rome to admire it, art students studied

NAPLES

it from afar in prints, Louis XIV made a copy for Versailles, and petty nobles everywhere put small-scale knock-offs in their gardens. This curly-haired version of Hercules became the modern world's image of the Greek hero.

• *Backtrack to the main entry hall, then head up to the mezzanine level (turning left at the lion).*

Mezzanine: Pompeian Mosaics and the Secret Room

Most of these mosaics—of animals, musicians, and geometric designs—were taken from Pompeii's House of the Faun (see page 1052). Walk into the third room and look for the 20-inch-high statue in a freestanding glass case: the house's delightful centerpiece, the *Dancing Faun*. This rare surviving Greek bronze statue (from the fourth century B.C.) is surrounded by some of the best mosaics of that age.

A museum highlight, just beyond the statue, is the grand *Battle of Alexander*, a second-century B.C. copy of the original Greek fresco, done a century earlier. It decorated a floor in the House of the Faun and was found intact; the damage you see occurred as this treasure was moved from Pompeii to the king's collection here. Alexander (left side of the scene, with curly hair and sideburns) is about to defeat the Persians under Darius (central figure, in chariot with turban and beard). This pivotal victory allowed Alexander to quickly overrun much of Asia (331 B.C.). Alexander is the only one without a helmet...a confident master of the battlefield while everyone else is fighting for their lives, eyes bulging with fear. Notice how the horses, already in retreat, add to the scene's propaganda value. Notice also the shading and perspective, which Renaissance artists would later work so hard to accomplish. (A modern reproduction of the mosaic is now back in Pompeii, at the House of the Faun.)

Farther on, the **Secret Room** *(Gabinetto Segreto)* contains a sizable assortment of erotic frescoes, well-hung pottery, and perky statues that once decorated bedrooms, meeting rooms, brothels, and even shops at Pompeii and Herculaneum. These bawdy statues

NAPLES

and frescoes—many of them once displayed in Pompeii's grandest houses—were entertainment for guests. (By the time they made it to this museum, in 1819, the frescoes could be viewed only with permission from the king—see the letters in the glass case just outside the door.) The Roman nobles commissioned the wildest scenes imaginable. Think of them as ancient dirty jokes.

At the entrance, you're enthusiastically greeted by big stone penises that once projected over Pompeii's doorways. A massive phallus was not necessarily a sexual symbol, but a magical amulet used against the "evil eye." It symbolized fertility, happiness, good luck, riches, straight A's, and general well-being.

Circulating counterclockwise through this section, look for the following: a faun playfully pulling the sheet off a beautiful woman, only to be grossed out by a hermaphrodite's plumbing (perhaps the original *"Mamma mia!"*; #12); horny pygmies from Africa in action (#27); a toga with an embarrassing bulge (#34); a particularly high-quality statue of a goat and a satyr illustrating an act of sodomy (#36); and, watching over it all with remarkable aplomb, Venus, the patron goddess of Pompeii (#39).

The back room is furnished and decorated the way an ancient brothel might have been. The 10 frescoes on the wall functioned as both a menu of services offered and as a kind of *Kama Sutra* of sex positions. The glass cases contain more phallic art.

• So, *now that your travel buddy is finally showing a little interest in art...finish up your visit by climbing the stairs to the top floor.*

Top Floor: Frescoes, Statues, Artifacts, and a Model of Pompeii

At the top of the stairs, go through the center door to enter a grand, empty hall. This was the **great hall** of the university (17th and 18th centuries) until the building became the royal museum in 1777. Walk to the center. The sundial (from 1791) still works. Look up to the far-right corner of the hall and find the tiny pinhole. At noon (13:00 in summer), a ray of sun enters the hall and strikes the sundial, showing the time of the year...if you know your zodiac.

To your left, you'll see a door marked *affreschi*. This leads to eight rooms showing off the museum's impressive and well-described collection of (non-erotic) **frescoes** taken from the walls of Pompeii villas. Pompeiians loved to decorate their homes with scenes from mythology (Hercules' labors, Venus and Mars in love), landscapes, everyday market scenes, and faux architecture. Continue around this wing counterclockwise (with the courtyard on your left) through rooms of artifacts found at Pompeii. At the far end is a scale model of Pompeii as excavated in 1879 *(plastic di Pompeii)*. Another model (on the wall) shows the site in 2004, after more excavations.

• *Eventually you'll end up back in the great hall.*

Step out to the top landing of the staircase you climbed earlier. Turn left and go down, then up, 16 steps and into the wing labeled *La Villa dei Papiri.* This ex-

hibition shows off artifacts (particularly bronze statues) from the Herculaneum holiday home of Julius Caesar's father-in-law. In the second room (numbered CXVI), look into the lifelike blue eyes of the intense *Corridore* (athletes), bent on doing their best. The *Five Dancers,* with their inlaid-ivory eyes and graceful poses, decorated a portico. The next room (CXVII) has more fine works: *Resting Hermes* (with his tired little heel wings) is taking a break. Nearby, the *Drunken Faun* (singing and snapping his fingers to the beat, a wineskin at his side) is clearly living for today—true to the *carpe diem* preaching of the Epicurean philosophy. Caesar's father-in-law was a fan of Epicurean philosophy, and his library—containing 2,000 papyrus scrolls—supported his outlook. Back by the entrance, check out the plans of the villa, and in the side room, see how the half-burned scrolls were unrolled and (with luck) read after excavation in the 1750s.

• *Return to the ground floor. The exit hall (right) leads around the museum courtyard and to the gift shop.*

Doriforo

For extra credit on your way out, find **Doriforo.** He was last spotted on the right as you walk down the exit hall. (If he's been moved, ask a guard, *"Dov'è il Doriforo?"*) This seven-foot-tall "spear-carrier" (the literal translation of *doriforo*) just stands there, as if holding a spear. What's the big deal about this statue, which looks like so many others? It's a marble replica made by the Romans of one of the most-copied statues of antiquity, a fifth-century B.C. bronze Greek original by Polyclitus. This copy once stood in a Pompeii gym, where it inspired ancient athletes by showing the ideal proportions of Greek beauty. So full of motion, and so realistic in its *contrapposto* pose (weight on one foot), the *Doriforo* would later inspire Donatello and Michelangelo, helping

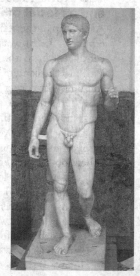

to trigger the Renaissance. And so the glories of ancient Pompeii, once buried and forgotten, live on today.

Self-Guided Walk

▲▲▲A Slice of Neapolitan Life

This walk takes you from the Archaeological Museum through the heart of town and back to Centrale Station. Allow at least three hours, plus time for pizza and sightseeing stops. If you're in a rush, do it in half the time by walking briskly and skipping Part 2.

Naples, a living medieval city, is its own best sight. Couples artfully make love on Vespas surrounded by more fights and smiles per cobblestone than anywhere else in Italy. Rather than seeing Naples as a list of sights, visit its one great museum and then capture its essence by taking this walk through the core of the city.

Part 1: From the Archaeological Museum to Piazza Bellini and Piazza Dante

The first two parts of this walk are a mostly straight one-mile ramble down a fine boulevard (with a few colorful detours) to the waterfront at Piazza del Plebiscito. Your starting point is the Archaeological Museum (at the top of Piazza Cavour, Metro: Cavour or Museo; for a self-guided tour of the museum, see earlier). As you stroll, remember that here in Naples, red traffic lights are considered "decorations." When crossing a street, try to tag along with a native.

• *From the door of the Archaeological Museum, cross the street, veer right, and pass through the fancy mall*

Galleria Principe di Napoli: This was named for the first male child of the royal Savoy family, the Prince of Naples. Walk directly through it, enjoying this fine shopping gallery from the late 19th century, similar to those popular in Paris and London. This is "Liberty Style," a variation of Art Nouveau (named for a British department store) that was in vogue at a time when Naples was nicknamed the "Paris of the South." Parisian artist Edgar Degas left Paris to adopt Naples—which he actually considered more cosmopolitan and sophisticated—as his hometown.

• *Leaving the gallery through the opposite end, walk one block downhill. At the fine Bellini Theater (in the Liberty Style), jog left one block, then turn right on Via Constantinopoli, continuing directly downhill to Piazza Bellini. As you walk, look up to enjoy architecture built in the late 19th century, when Naples was the last stop on Romantic Age travelers' Grand Tour of Europe. (From a tourism perspective, Sorrento only rose with the cultural and economic fall of Naples in the decades following Italian independence, around the early 20th century.)*

Soon you'll run into the ragtag urban park called...

A Slice of Neapolitan Life Walk

To Museo di Capodimonte

VIA STA. TERESA

Cavour

Piazza Cavour

VIA FORIA

VIA DUOMO

UNDERGROUND PASSAGE

One stop on Metro to Piazza Garibaldi & Centrale Station

ARCHAEOLOGICAL MUSEUM

Museo

V. DONNA

DUOMO

WALK BEGINS

GALLERIA PRINCIPE

V. PESSINA

V. BELLINI

BELLINI THEATER

VIA SAPIENZA

NAPOLI SOTTERRANEA

S. PAOLO

VIA DEI TRIBUNALI

G. G. MAGGIORE

S. LORENZO MAGGIORE

PIO MONTE MISERICORDIA

VIA VICARIA VECCHIA

FORCELLA

COLLETTA

CAFFÈ MEXICO

Piazza Bellini

V. PORT' ALBA

PORTA D'ALBA

VIA S.M. ARI

CAPPELLA SANSEVERO

VIA S. BIAGIO

POLO NORD GELATERIA

PIZZA

PIZZA

SUPER-MARKET

Piazza Dante

Dante

GESÙ NUOVO

VIA S. SEB.

SAN DOM.

CHAPEL OF MARADONA

DOLL HOSPITAL

WALK ENDS

To Montesanto (& funicular)

VIA TARSIA

Piazza Gesù Nuovo

VIA B. CROCE

"SPACCANAPOLI"

To Piazza Garibaldi & Centrale Station (10 min. walk)

VIA DUOMO

Piazza Sette Settembre

V. PIGNASECCA

VIA MADDALONI

SANTA CHIARA

CLOISTER

SCATURCHIO PASTICCERIA

VIA MEZZOCANNONE

CORSO UMBERTO I

VIA NUOVA MARINA

MONTEOLIVETO

CALATA TRINITÀ MAGGIORE

VIA TOLEDO

Piazza Carità

FASCIST BLDG.

VIA BATT.

VIA DONNALBINA

POST

Piazza Matteotti

VIA S. FELICE

Piazza Bovio

Università

SPANISH QUARTER

BNL BANK

VIA A. DIAZ

Toledo

VIA AGOSTINO DEPRETIS

VIA ALCIDE D. GASPERI

VIA CRISTOFORO COLOMBO

Port

VIA PORTA DI TAPPIA

BANCO DI NAPOLI

(B)

Municipio

Municipio

STAZIONE MARITTIMA (CRUISE TERMINAL)

BANCA INTESA SANPAOLO

GALLERIA UMBERTO I

Alibus Bus To Airport

(B)

Piazza Municipio

Tram #1 to Train Station

Centrale Funicular

TEATRO DI SAN CARLO

CASTEL NUOVO

MOLO BEVERELLO DOCK

GRAN CAFFÈ GAMBRINUS

ROYAL PALACE

V. AM. FERDINANDO

CONSOLE

To Sorrento & Capri

Piazza del Plebiscito

SAN FRANCESCO DI PAOLA

TUNNEL

VIA NAZARIO SAURO

Bay of Naples

300 Meters

300 Yards

To Castel dell'Ovo

NAPLES

Piazza Bellini: Walking between columns of two grand churches, suddenly you're in neighborhood Napoli. A statue of Vincenzo Bellini marks the center of Piazza Bellini. It's dedicated to the Sicilian opera composer who worked here in the early 1800s. Survey the many balconies—and the people who use them as a "backyard" in this densely packed city. The apartment flats were originally palaces of noble families, as indicated by the stately family crests above grand doorways. Look down below the square to see the ruined Greek walls: tuff blocks without mortar. This was the wall, and you're standing on land that was outside of the town. You can see the street level from the fifth century B.C., when Neapolis—literally, "the new city"—was founded. For 2,500 years, laundry has blown in the breeze right here.

• *Walk 30 yards downhill. Stop at the horseshoe-shaped Port'Alba gate (on the right). Spin slowly 360 degrees and take in the scene. The proud tile across the street shows Piazza Bellini circa 1890. Learn to ignore graffiti (as the locals do). Pass through the gate, and stroll past the book stalls down Via Port'Alba to the next big square...*

Piazza Dante: This square is marked by a statue of Dante, the medieval poet. Fittingly, half the square is devoted to bookstores. Old Dante looks out over an urban area that was once grand, then chaotic, and is now slowly becoming grand again.

While this square feels perfectly Italian to me, for many Neapolitans it represents the repression of the central Italian state. When Napoleon was defeated, Naples briefly became its own independent kingdom. But within a few decades of Italian unification, in 1861, Naples went from being a thriving cultural and political capital to a provincial town, its money used to help establish the industrial strength of the north, its dialect considered backward, and its bureaucrats transferred to Rome.

Originally, a statue of a Spanish Bourbon king stood in the square. (The grand red-and-gray building is typical of Bourbon structures from that period.) But with the unification of Italy, the king, symbolic of Naples' colonial subjugation, was replaced by Dante, the father of the unified Italian language—a strong symbol of nationalism (and yet another form of subjugation).

The Neapolitan people are survivors. A long history of corrupt and greedy colonial overlords (German, Norman, French, Austrian, and Spanish) has taught Neapolitans to deal creatively with authority. Many credit this aspect of Naples' past for the strength of organized crime here.

Across the street, **Caffè Mexico** (at #86) is an institution known for its espresso, which is served already sweetened—ask for *senza zucchero* if you don't want sugar (pay first, then take receipt to the counter and hand it over). Most Italians agree that Neapolitan coffee is the best anywhere.

NAPLES

• *Walk downhill on...*

Via Toledo: The long, straight street heading downhill from Piazza Dante is Naples' principal shopping drag. It originated as a military road built under Spanish rule (hence the name) in the 16th century. Via Toledo skirted the old town wall to connect the Spanish military headquarters (now the museum where you started this walk) with the Royal Palace (down by the bay, where you're heading). As you stroll, peek into lovely atriums, an ancient urban design feature providing a break from the big street.

After a couple of hundred yards, you'll reach Piazza Sette Settembre. In 1860, from the white marble balcony of the Neo-classical building overlooking the square, the famous revolutionary Giuseppe Garibaldi declared Italy united and Victor Emmanuel II its first king. Only in 1870, a decade later, was the dream of Italian unity fully realized when Rome fell to unification forces.

• *Continue straight on Via Toledo. About three blocks below Piazza Dante and a block past Piazza Sette Settembre, you'll come to Via Maddaloni, which marks the start of the long, straight, narrow street nicknamed...*

Spaccanapoli: Before crossing the street—whose name translates as "split Naples"—look left (toward the train station).

Then look right (to see San Martino hill rising steeply above the center). Since ancient times, this thin street has bisected the city. It changes names several times: Via Maddaloni (as it's called here), Via B. Croce, Via S. Biagio dei Librai, and Via Vicaria Vecchia. We'll return to this intersection later.

• *If you want to abbreviate this walk, turn left here and skip ahead to Part 3. Part 2, described next, is a bit of a detour, and requires backtracking uphill (or a short taxi ride) later. But if you have time, it's worth the effort.*

Part 2: Monumental Naples (Via Toledo, the Spanish Quarter, and Piazza del Plebiscito)

• *We'll detour off of Via Toledo for just a couple of blocks (rejoining it later). At the Spaccanapoli intersection, go right (toward the church facade on the hill, up Via Pasquale Scura). After about 100 yards, you hit a busy intersection. Stop. You're on one of Naples' most colorful open-air market streets...*

Via Pignasecca Market: Snoop around from here if you are so inclined. Then, turn left down Via Pignasecca and stroll this colorful strip. You'll pass meat and fish stalls, produce stands, street-food vendors, and much more. This is a taste of Naples' famous Spanish Quarter, which we'll experience more of later in this walk.

• *Via Pignasecca meets back up with Via Toledo at the square called...*

Piazza Carità: This square, built for an official visit by Hitler to Mussolini in 1938, is full of stern, straight, obedient lines. The big building belonged to an insurance company. (For the best fascist architecture in town, take a slight detour from here: With your back to Via Toledo, leave Piazza Carità downhill on the right-hand corner and walk a block to the Poste e Telegrafi building. There you'll see several government buildings with stirring reliefs singing the praises of lobotomized workers and a totalitarian society.)

In Naples—long a poor and rough city—rather than being heroic, people learn from the cradle the art of survival. The modern memorial statue in the center of the square celebrates Salvo d'Acquisto, a rare hometown hero. In 1943, he was executed after falsely confessing to sabotage...in order to save 22 fellow Italian soldiers from a Nazi revenge massacre.

• *From Piazza Carità, continue south down Via Toledo for a few blocks, looking to your left for more...*

Fascist Architecture (Banks): You can't miss the two big, blocky bank buildings. First comes the chalky-white BNL Bank. A bit farther down, past the Metro, imagine trying to rob the even more imposing Banco di Napoli (Via Toledo 178). Step across the street and check out its architecture: typical fascist arches and reliefs, built to celebrate the bank's 400th anniversary (est. 1539—how old is *your* bank?).

The street here was pedestrianized after the Toledo Metro stop opened in 2012. Now the street is even more popular for strolling, property values have risen, and international brands such as H&M and the Disney Store have moved in.

• *On the next block (at #184) is the...*

Banca Intesa Sanpaolo: This fills an older palace—take a free peek at the opulent atrium. In the entry hall, you can buy a ticket for the **Galleria d'Italia Palazzo Zevallos Stigliano,** a small collection located in the upper two floors. The gallery's only piece worth seeing—on the second floor—is a great late Caravaggio painting. *The Martyrdom of Saint Ursula* shows a terrible scene: His marriage proposal rejected, the king of the Huns shoots an arrow into Ursula's chest. Blood spurts, Ursula is stunned but accepts her destiny sweetly, and Caravaggio himself—far right, his last self-portrait—screams to symbolize the rejection of evil. The rest of the second floor holds opulent chandeliered apartments, a few Neapolitan landscapes, and little else. The first floor has temporary exhibits (€4, Tue-Sun 10:00-18:00, closed Mon; entry includes 40-minute audioguide, a look at old Naples paintings, and a fine WC; Via Toledo 185, tel. 800-454-229, www.palazzozevallos. com).

• *Feeling bold? From here, side-trip uphill a couple of blocks into the...*

Spanish Quarter: This is a classic world of *basso* (low) living. The streets—which were laid out in the 16th century for the Span-

ish military barracks outside the city walls—are unbelievably narrow (and cool in summer), and the buildings rise five stories high. In such tight quarters, life—flirting, fighting, playing, and loving—happens in the road. This is *the* cliché of life in Naples, as shown in so many movies. The Span-

ish Quarter is Naples at its most characteristic. The shopkeepers are friendly, and the mopeds are bold (watch out). Concerned locals will tug on their lower eyelids, warning you to be wary. Hungry? Pop into a grocery shop and ask the clerk to make you his best prosciutto-and-mozzarella sandwich (the price should be about €4).

• *Return to Via Toledo and work your way down. Near the bottom of the street, on the right, notice the station for the* **Centrale funicular.** *If you have extra time and enjoy city views, this can take you sweat-free up to the top of San Martino, the hill with a fortress and a monastery/ museum looming over town (covered by €1.30 single transit ticket; see page 1029 for details on fortress and museum). Across the street is the impressive Galleria Umberto I—but don't go in now, as you'll see it in a minute from the other side.*

For now, just keep heading down the main drag and through the smaller Piazza Trieste e Trento to the immense...

Piazza del Plebiscito: This square celebrates the 1861 vote (*plebiscito,* plebiscite) in which Naples chose to join Italy. Dominating the top of the square is the **Church of San Francesco di Paola,** with its Pantheon-inspired dome and broad, arcing colonnades. If it's open, step inside to ogle the vast interior—a Neoclassical recreation of one of ancient Rome's finest buildings (free, daily 8:30-12:00 & 16:00-19:00).

• *Opposite is the...*

Royal Palace (Palazzo Reale): Having housed Spanish, French, and even Italian royalty, this building displays statues of all those who stayed here. Look for eight kings in the niches, each from a different dynasty (left to right): Norman, German, French, Spanish, Spanish, Spanish, French (Napoleon's brother-in-law), and, finally, Italian—Victor Emmanuel II, King of Savoy. The statues were done at the request of V. E. II's son, so his dad is the most dashing of the group. While you could consider touring the interior, it's relatively unimpressive (described under "Sights in Naples," later).

• *Continue 50 yards past the Royal Palace (toward the trees) to enjoy a...*

Fine Harbor View: While boats busily serve Capri and Sorrento, Mount Vesuvius smolders ominously in the distance. Look back to see the vast "Bourbon red" palace—its color inspired by Pompeii. The hilltop above Piazza del Plebiscito is San Martino, with its Carthusian monastery-turned-museum and Castle of St. Elmo (remember, the Centrale funicular to the top is just across the square and up Via Toledo). This street continues to Naples' romantic harborfront—the fishermen's quarter (Borgo Marinaro)—a fortified island connected to the mainland by a stout causeway, with its fanciful, ancient Castel dell'Ovo (Egg Castle) and trendy harborside restaurants. Farther along the harborfront stretches the Lungomare promenade and Santa Lucia district. (The long harborfront promenade, Via Francesco Caracciolo, is a delightful people-watching scene on balmy nights.)

• *Head back through the piazza and pop into...*

Gran Caffè Gambrinus: This coffee house, facing the piazza, takes you back to the elegance of 1860. It's a classic place to sample a unique Neapolitan treat called *sfogliatella* (crispy scallop shell-shaped pastry filled with sweet ricotta cheese). Or you might prefer the mushroom-shaped, rum-soaked bread-like cakes called *babà*, which come in a huge variety. Stand at the bar *(banco)*, pay double to sit *(tavola)*, or just wander around as you imagine the café buzzing with the ritzy intellectuals, journalists, and artsy bohemian types who munched on *babà* here during Naples' 19th-century heyday (daily 7:00-24:00, Piazza del Plebiscito 1, tel. 081-417-582).

• *A block away, tucked behind the palace, you can peek inside the Neoclassical...*

Teatro di San Carlo: Built in 1737, 41 years before Milan's La Scala, this is Europe's oldest opera house and Italy's second-most-respected (after La Scala). The theater burned down in 1816, and was rebuilt within the year. Guided 35-minute visits in English basically just show you the fine auditorium with its 184 boxes—each with a big mirror to reflect the candlelight (€6; tours Mon-Sat at 10:30, 11:30, 12:30, 14:30, 15:30, and 16:30; Sun at 10:30, 11:30, and 12:30; tel. 081-797-468, www.teatrosancarlo.it).

Beyond Teatro di San Carlo and the Royal Palace is the huge, harborfront **Castel Nuovo,** which houses government bureaucrats and the **Civic Museum.** It feels like a mostly empty shell, with a couple of dusty halls of Neapolitan art, but the views over the bay from the upper terraces are impressive (€5, Mon-Sat 9:00-19:00, closed Sun, tel. 081-795-7722, www.comune.napoli.it).

Cross the street from Teatro di San Carlo and go through the tall yellow arch into the Victorian iron and glass of the 100-year-old shopping mall, **Galleria Umberto I.** It was built in 1892 to reinvigorate the district after a devastating cholera epidemic occurred here. Gawk up, then walk left to bring you back out on Via Toledo.

• *For Part 3 of this walk, double back up Via Toledo to Piazza Carità, veering right (just above the first big fascist-style building we saw earlier) on Via Morgantini through Piazza Monteoliveto. Cross the busy street, then angle up Calata Trinità Maggiore to the fancy column at the top of the hill. (To avoid the backtracking and uphill walk, catch a €10 taxi to the Church of Gesù Nuovo—JAY-zoo noo-OH-voh.)*

Part 3: Spaccanapoli Back to the Station

You're back at the straight-as-a-Greek-arrow Spaccanapoli, formerly the main thoroughfare of the Greek city of Neapolis.

• *Stop at...*

Piazza Gesù Nuovo: This square is marked by a towering 18th-century Baroque monument to the Counter-Reformation. Although the Jesuit order was powerful in Naples because of its Spanish heritage, locals never attacked Protestants here with the full fury of the Spanish Inquisition.

If you'd like, you can visit two bulky old churches, starting with the dark, fortress-like, 17th-century **Church of Gesù Nuovo,** followed by the simpler **Church of Santa Chiara** (in the courtyard across the street). Both are described in more detail later, under "Sights in Naples."

• *After touring the churches, continue along the main drag. Since this is a university district, you'll see lots of students and bookstores. This neighborhood is also famously superstitious. Look for incense-burning women with carts full of good-luck charms for sale.*

Farther down Spaccanapoli—passing Palazzo Venezia, the embassy of Venice to Naples when both were independent powers—you'll see the next square...

Piazza San Domenico Maggiore: This square is marked by an ornate 17th-century monument built to thank God for ending the plague. From this square, detour left along the right side of the castle-like church, then follow yellow signs, taking the first right and walking one block to the remarkable **Cappella Sansevero.** This Baroque chapel is well worth visiting (described later, under "Sights in Naples").

• *After touring the chapel, return to Via B. Croce (a.k.a. Spaccanapoli), turn left, and continue your cultural scavenger hunt. At the intersection of Via Nilo, find the...*

Statue of the Nile (on the left): A reminder of the multi-ethnic make-up of Greek Neapolis, this statue is in what was the Egyptian quarter. Locals like to call this statue *The Body of Naples*, with the overflowing cornucopia symbolizing the abundance of their fine city. (I once asked a Neapolitan man to describe the local women, who are famous for their beauty, in one word. He replied simply, "Abundant.") This intersection is considered the center of old Naples.

• *Directly opposite the statue, between the two doors of Bar Nilo, is the...*

"Chapel of Maradona": The small "chapel" on the wall is dedicated to Diego Maradona, a soccer star who played for Naples in the 1980s. Locals consider soccer almost a religion, and this guy was practically a deity. You can even see a "hair of Diego" and a teardrop from the city when he went to another team for more money. Unfortunately, his reputation has since been sullied by problems he's had with organized crime, drugs, and police. Perhaps inspired by Maradona's example, the coffee bar has posted a quadrilingual sign (though, strangely, not in English) threatening that those who take a picture without buying a cup of coffee may find their camera damaged...*Capisce?* (Note that this "chapel" is removable—if it's raining or they're just feeling grumpy, it may be gone.)

• *As you continue, you'll begin to see shops selling...*

Presepi (Nativity Scenes): Just as many Americans keep an eye out year-round for Christmas-tree ornaments, Italians regularly add pieces to the family *presepe*, the centerpiece of their holiday decorations. Stop after a few blocks at the tiny square, where Via San Gregorio Armeno leads left into a colorful district with the highest concentration of shops selling fantastic *presepi* and their tiny components, including figurines caricaturing local politicians and celebrities. Also in this neighborhood is the underground Napoli Sotteranea archaeological site (described later, under "Sights in Naples").

• *Back on Spaccanapoli, as Via B. Croce becomes Via S. Biagio dei Librai, notice the...*

Gold and Silver Shops: Some say stolen jewelry ends up here, is melted down immediately, and gets resold in some other form as soon as it cools. At #95, find the Compro Oro ("I Buy Gold") shop. This is one of many pawn shops that have appeared recently, in concert with Italy's economic tough times. At #81, the Ospedale delle Bambole (Doll Hospital) heals dolls that have been loved to pieces, and also sells restored classics.

• *Cross busy Via Duomo. If you have time and aren't already churched out, consider detouring five minutes north (left) up Via Duomo to visit*

Naples' **Duomo;** *just around the corner is the* **Pio Monte della Miseri-**
cordia Church, *with a fine Caravaggio painting (both described later,*
under "Sights in Naples"). Afterwards, continue straight along Via Vi-
caria Vecchia. As you stroll, ponder Naples' vibrant...

Street Life, Past and Present: Here along Via Vicaria Vecchia, the street and side-street scenes intensify. The area is said to
be a center of the Camorra (organized crime), but as a tourist, you
won't notice. Paint a picture with these thoughts: Naples has the
most intact street plan of any ancient Greek or Roman city. Imagine this city during those times (and retain these images as you visit
Pompeii), with streetside shop fronts that close up after dark, and
private homes on upper floors. What you see today is just one more
page in a 2,000-year-old story of a city: all kinds of meetings, beat-
ings, and cheatings; kisses, near misses, and little-boy pisses.

You name it, it occurs right on the streets today, as it has
since ancient times. People ooze from crusty corners. Black-and-

white death announcements
add to the clutter on the walls.
Widows sell cigarettes from
buckets. For a peek behind
the scenes in the shade of wet
laundry, venture down a few
side streets. Buy two carrots
as a gift for the woman on the
fifth floor, if she'll lower her
bucket to pick them up. The neighborhood action seems best at
about 18:00.

A few blocks on, at the tiny fenced-in triangle of greenery,
hang out for a few minutes to just observe the crazy motorbike action and teen scene.

• *From here, veer right onto Via Forcella (which leads to the busy boule-*
vard that takes you to Centrale Station). A block down, a tiny, fenced-in
traffic island protects a chunk of the ancient Greek wall of Neapolis. Turn
right here on Via Pietro Colletta, walk 40 yards, and step into the North
Pole, at the...

Polo Nord Gelateria: The oldest *gelateria* in Naples has had
four generations of family working here since 1931. Before you
order, sample a few flavors, including their *bacio* or "kiss" flavor
(chocolate and hazelnut)—all are made fresh daily. Low-sugar and
soy ice cream are also available (Via Pietro Colletta 41). Via Pietro
Colletta leads past two of Napoli's most competitive **pizzerias** (see
"Eating in Naples," later) to Corso Umberto I.

• *Turn left on the grand boulevard-like Corso Umberto I. From here to*
Centrale Station, it's at least a 10-minute walk (if you're tired, hop on
a bus; they all go to the station). To finish the walk, continue on Corso
Umberto I—past a gauntlet of purse/CD/sunglasses salesmen and shady

characters hawking stolen mobile phones—to the vast, ugly Piazza Garibaldi. On the far side is the station. You made it.

Sights in Naples

Churches on or near Spaccanapoli

These churches are linked—in this order—on Part 3 of my self-guided walk, earlier.

▲Church of Gesù Nuovo

This church's unique pyramid-grill facade survives from a fortified 15th-century noble palace. Step inside for a brilliant Neapolitan Baroque interior. The second chapel on the right features a much-adored **statue of St. Giuseppe Moscati** (1880-1927), a Christian doctor famous for helping the poor. In 1987, Moscati became the first modern doctor to be canonized. Sit and watch a steady stream of Neapolitans taking turns to kiss and touch the altar, then hold the good doctor's highly polished hand.

Continue on to the third chapel and enter the **Sale Moscati.** Look high on the walls of this long room to see hundreds of "Ex Votos"—tiny red-and-silver plaques of thanksgiving for prayers answered with the help of St. Moscati (each has a symbol of the ailment cured). Naples' practice of using Ex Votos, while incorporated into its Catholic rituals, goes back to its pagan Greek roots. Rooms from Moscati's nearby apartment are on display, and a glass case shows possessions and photos of the great doctor. As you leave the Sale Moscati, notice the big bomb casing that hangs in the left corner. It fell through the church's dome in 1943, but caused almost no damage...yet another miracle.

Cost and Hours: Free, daily 7:00-13:00 & 16:00-19:30, Piazza del Gesù Nuovo, www.gesunuovo.it.

Church of Santa Chiara

Dating from the 14th century, this church is from a period of French royal rule under the Angevin dynasty. Consider the stark contrast between this church (Gothic) and the Gesù Nuovo (Baroque), across the street. Inside, notice the huge inlaid-marble Angevin coat of arms on the floor. The faded Trinity on the back wall (on the right as you face the door), shows a dove representing the Holy Spirit between the heads of God the Father and Christ (c. 1414). This is an example of the fine frescoes that once covered the walls. Most were stuccoed over during Baroque times or destroyed in 1943 by Allied bombs. The altar is adorned with four finely carved Gothic tombs of Angevin kings. A chapel stacked with Bourbon royalty is just to the right.

Cost and Hours: Free, daily 7:00-13:00 & 16:30-20:00, Piazza del Gesù Nuovo. Its tranquil cloistered courtyard, around back, is not worth its €6 entry fee.

▲▲Cappella Sansevero

This small chapel is a Baroque explosion mourning the body of Christ, who lies on a soft pillow under an incredibly realistic veil. It's also the personal chapel of Raimondo de Sangro, an eccentric Freemason, containing his tomb and the tombs of his family. Like other 18th-century Enlightenment figures, Raimondo was a wealthy man of letters, scientist and inventor, and patron of the arts—and he was also a grand master of the Freemasons of the Kingdom of Naples. His chapel—filled with Freemason symbolism—is a complex ensemble, with statues representing virtues such as self-control, religious zeal, and the Freemason philosophy of freedom through enlightenment. Though it's a pricey private enterprise, the chapel is worth a visit.

Cost and Hours: €7, buy tickets at office at the corner, Mon and Wed-Sat 10:00-18:00, Sun 10:00-13:30, closed Tue, last entry 20 minutes before closing, no photos, Via de Sanctis 19, tel. 081-551-8470, www.museosansevero.it. Good English explanations are posted throughout; when you buy your ticket, pick up the free floor plan, which identifies each of the statues lining the nave.

Visiting the Chapel: Study the incredible *Veiled Christ* in the center. Carved out of marble, it's like no other statue I've seen (by Giuseppe "Howdeedoodat" Sammartino, 1753). The Christian message (Jesus died for our salvation) is accompanied by a Freemason message (the veil represents how the body and ego are obstacles to real spiritual freedom). As you walk from Christ's feet to his head, notice how the expression on Jesus' face goes from suffering to peace.

Raimondo's mom and dad are buried on either side of the **main altar.** To the right of the altar, marking his father's tomb, a statue representing *Despair* or *Disillusion* struggles with a marble rope net (carved out of a single piece of stone), symbolic of a troubled mind. The flames on the head of the winged boy represent human intellect—more Freemason symbolism, showing how knowledge frees the human mind. To the left of the main altar is a statue of *Modesty*, marking the tomb of Raimondo's mother (who died after his birth, and was only 20). The veiled woman fingers a broken tablet, symbolizing an interrupted life.

Raimondo de Sangro himself lies buried in a side altar (on the right). Among his inventions was the deep-green pigment used on the ceiling fresco. The inlaid M. C. Escher-esque maze on the floor around de Sangro's tomb is another Freemason reminder of how the quest for knowledge gets you out of the maze of life. This tilework once covered the floor of the entire chapel.

Your Sansevero finale is downstairs: two mysterious...**skeletons.** Perhaps another of the mad inventor's fancies: Inject a corpse with a fluid to fossilize the veins so that they'll survive the body's decomposition. While that's the legend, recent investigations have shown that the veins were artificial, and the models were created to illustrate how the circulatory system works.

▲Duomo

Naples' historic cathedral, built by imported French Anjou kings in the 14th century, boasts a breathtaking Neo-Gothic facade. Step into the vast interior to see the mix of styles along the side chapels—from pointy Gothic arches to rounded Renaissance ones to gilded Baroque decor.

Cost and Hours: Free, daily 8:30-13:30 & 14:30-20:00, Via Duomo.

Visiting the Church: Explore the two largest side-chapels—each practically a church in its own right. On the left, the Chapel of St. Restituta stands on the site of the original, early-Christian church that predated the cathedral (at the far end, you can pay €1.50 to see its sixth-century baptismal font under mosaics, and go downstairs to see its even earlier foundations; chapel open Mon-Sat 8:30-12:30 & 16:30-18:30, Sun 8:30-13:00). On the right is the Chapel of San Gennaro—dedicated to the beloved patron saint of Naples—decorated with silver busts of centuries of bishops, and seven paintings done on bronze.

Back out in the main nave, the altar at the front is ringed by carved wooden seats, filled three times a year by clergy to witness the Miracle of the Blood. Thousands of Neapolitans cram into this church for a peek at two tiny vials with the dried blood of St. Gennaro. As the clergy roots—or even jeers—for the miracle to occur, the blood temporarily liquefies. Neapolitans take this ritual with deadly seriousness, and believe that if the blood remains solid, it's terrible luck for the city. Sure enough, on the rare occasion that the miracle fails, locals can point to a terrible event soon after—such as an earthquake or an eruption of Mount Vesuvius.

The stairs beneath the altar take you to a crypt with the relics of St. Gennaro and (across the room) a statue of the bishop who rescued the relics from a rival town and returned them to Naples.

Pio Monte della Misericordia

Art lovers come to this small church (near the Duomo, and run by a charitable foundation) to appreciate one of the best works by Caravaggio, *The Seven Works of Mercy*, which hangs over the main altar. In one crowded canvas, the great early-Baroque artist illustrates seven virtues: burying the dead (the man carrying a corpse by the ankles), visiting the imprisoned, feeding the hungry (Pero breastfeeding her starving father—a scene from a famous Roman story), sheltering the homeless (a pilgrim on the Camino de Santiago, with his floppy hat, negotiates with an innkeeper), caring for the sick, clothing the naked (St. Martin offers part of his cloak to the injured man in the foreground), and giving drink to the thirsty

(Samson chugs from a jawbone in the background)—all of them set in a dark Neapolitan alley and watched over by Mary, Jesus, and a pair of angels. Caravaggio painted this work in Naples in 1607, while in exile from Rome, where he had been sentenced to death for killing a man in a duel. Your ticket also lets you in to the foundation's pleasant upper-floor museum, with some minor Neapolitan paintings.

Cost and Hours: €6, includes audioguide, Thu-Tue 9:00-14:30, closed Wed, Via dei Tribunali 253, tel. 081-446-944, www.piomontedellamisericordia.it.

In the City Center
Royal Palace (Palazzo Reale)
Facing Piazza del Plebiscito, this huge, lavish palace welcomes the public. The palace's grand Neoclassical staircase leads up to a floor with 30 plush rooms. You'll follow a one-way route (with some English descriptions) featuring the palace theater, paintings by "the Caravaggio Imitators," Neapolitan tapestries, fine inlaid-stone tabletops, chandeliers, gilded woodwork, and more. The rooms do feel quite grand, but they lack the personality and sense of importance of Europe's better palaces. Don't miss the huge, tapestry-laden Hercules Hall. On the way out, stop into the chapel, with a fantastic nativity scene—a commotion of 18th-century ceramic figurines.

Cost and Hours: €4, includes painfully dry audioguide, Thu-Tue 9:00-20:00, closed Wed, last entry one hour before closing, tel. 848-800-288.

▲Napoli Sotterranea
This archaeological site, a manmade underground maze of passageways and ruins from Greek and Roman times, can only be toured with a guide. You'll descend 121 steps under the modern city to explore two different underground areas. One is the old Greek tuff quarry used to build the city of Neapolis, which was later converted into an immense cistern by the Romans. The other is an excavated portion of the Greco-Roman theater that once seated 6,000 people. It's clear that this space has been encroached upon by modern development—some current residents' windows literally look down into the theater ruins. The tour involves a lot of stairs, as well as a long, narrow 20-inch-wide walkway—lit only by candlelight—that uses an ancient water channel (a heavyset person could not comfortably fit through this, and claustrophobes will be miserable). Although there's not much to actually see, the experience is fascinating and includes a little history from World War II—when the quarry/cistern was turned into a shelter to protect locals from American bombs.

Cost and Hours: €9.30; includes 1.5-hour tour. Visits in

English are offered daily at 10:00, 12:00, 14:00, 16:00, and 18:00. Bring a light sweater. Tel. 081-296-944, www.napolisotterranea. org.

Getting There: The site is at Piazza San Gaetano 68, along Via dei Tribunali. It's a 10-minute walk from the Archaeological Museum, and just a couple of blocks uphill from Spaccanapoli's statue of the Nile. The entrance is immediately to the left of the Church of San Paolo Maggiore (look for the *Sotterranea* signs).

Porta Nolana Open-Air Fish Market

Naples' fish market squirts and stinks as it has for centuries under the Porta Nolana (gate in the city wall), immediately in front of the

Napoli Porta Nolana Circum-vesuviana station and four long blocks from Centrale Station. Of the town's many boisterous outdoor markets, this will net you the most photos and memories. From Piazza Nolana, wander under the medieval gate and take your first left down Vico Sopramuro, enjoying this wild and entirely edible cultural scavenger hunt (Tue-Sun 8:00-14:00, closed Mon).

Two other markets with more clothing and fewer fish are at Piazza Capuana (several blocks northwest of Centrale Station and tumbling down Via Sant'Antonio Abate, Mon-Sat 8:00-18:00, Sun 9:00-13:00) and a similar cobbled shopping zone along Via Pignasecca (just off Via Toledo, west of Piazza Carità, described on page 1016).

Lungomare *Passeggiata*

Each evening, relaxed and romantic Neapolitans in the mood for a scenic harborside stroll do their *vasche* (laps) along the inviting Lungomare promenade. To join in this elegant people-watching scene (best after 19:00), stroll about 15 minutes from Piazza del Plebiscito along Via Nazario Sauro.

Detour out along the fortified causeway to poke around Borgo Marinaro ("fishermen's quarter"), with its striking Castel dell'Ovo and a trendy restaurant scene (see "Eating in Naples," later), where you can dine amidst yachts with a view of Vesuvius. This is known as the Santa Lucia district because this is where the song "Santa Lucia" was first performed. (The song is probably so famous in America because immigrants from Naples sang it to remember the old country.) Beyond that stretches the Lungomare, along Via Francesco Caracciolo. Taxi home or retrace your steps back to the old center.

On San Martino

The ultimate view overlooking Naples, its bay, and the volcano is from the hill called San Martino, just above (and west of) the city center. Up top you'll find a mighty fortress (which charges for entry but offers the best views from its ramparts) and the adjacent monastery-turned-museum. While neither of these sights is exciting in its own right, the views are. And the surrounding neighborhood (especially Piazza Fuga) has a classy "uptown" vibe compared to the gritty city-center streets below. Cheapskates can enjoy the views for free from the benches on the square in front of the monastery.

Getting There: From Via Toledo, the Spanish Quarter gradually climbs up San Martino's lower slopes, before steep paths take you up the rest of the way. But the easiest way to ascend San Martino is by funicular. Three different funicular lines lead from lower Naples to the hilltop: the Centrale line from near the bottom of Via Toledo, the Montesanto line from the Metro stop of the same name (near the top end of Via Toledo), and the Chiaia line from farther out, near Piazza Amadeo (all three are covered by any regular local transit ticket). Ride any of these three up to the end of the line. All three lines converge within a few blocks at the top of the hill—Centrale and Chiaia wind up at opposite ends of the charming Piazza Fuga, while Montesanto terminates a bit closer to the fortress and museum. Leaving any of the funiculars, head uphill, carefully tracking signs for *Castel S. Elmo* and *Museo di San Martino* (strategically placed escalators make the climb easier). You'll reach the castle first, and then the monastery/museum (both about 10 minutes' walk from Piazza Fuga).

Castel Sant'Elmo

While it's little more than an empty husk with a decent modern art museum, this 16th-century, Spanish-built, star-shaped fortress boasts commanding views over the city and the entire Bay of Naples. Buy your ticket at the booth, then ride the elevator up to the upper courtyard and climb up to the ramparts for a slow circle to enjoy the 360-degree views. In the middle of the yard is the likeable little Museo del Novecento, a gallery of works by 20th-century Neapolitan artists (last entry at 18:00, covered by same ticket); the castle also hosts temporary exhibits.

Cost and Hours: €5, open Wed-Mon 8:30-19:30, closed Tue, last entry one hour before closing, hours can be unreliable, Via Tito Angelini 22, tel. 081-229-4401.

▲San Martino Carthusian Monastery and Museum (Certosa e Museo di San Martino)

The monastery, founded in 1325 and dissolved in the early 1800s, is now a sprawling museum with several parts. The square out front has city views nearly as good as the ones you'll pay to see from inside, and a few cafés angling for your business.

Cost and Hours: €6, audioguide-€5, Thu-Tue 8:30-19:30, closed Wed, last entry one hour before closing, Largo San Martino 8, tel. 081-229-4502, http://museosanmartino.campaniabeniculturali.it.

Visiting the Monastery and Museum: If you want to tour the place, buy your ticket and head into the complex (which has some English information). Step into the church, a Baroque explosion with beautifully decorated chapels. Around the humble cloister are a variety of museum exhibits. The Naval Museum has nautical paintings, model boats, and giant ceremonial gondolas. In an adjacent hall is an excellent collection of *presepi* (nativity scenes), both life-size and miniature, including a spectacular one by Michele Cucinello—the best I've seen in this *presepi*-crazy city. Beyond that is the larger garden cloister, ringed with a painting gallery (with lots of antique maps and artifacts of old Naples), and an entrance to a pretty view terrace.

On Capodimonte

Another hilltop, about a mile due north from the Archaeological Museum, is home to Naples' top art museum—the **Museo di Capodimonte.** Its three floors of art include works by Raphael, Titian, Caravaggio, and Bellini. While most visitors to Naples prefer to focus on the city's uniquely vibrant street life, characteristic churches, and remarkable ancient artifacts—and there are far better art museums elsewhere in Italy—art lovers with some time to spare may find a visit to Capodimonte worth the trip. While bus #C63 does run to Capodimonte from Piazza Dante and the Archaeological Museum, it's easier to take a taxi (about €8-10 from downtown).

Cost and Hours: €7.50, Thu-Tue 8:30-19:30, closed Wed, last entry one hour before closing, Via Miano 2, tel. 081-749-9111.

Sleeping in Naples

As an alternative to intense Naples, most travelers prefer to sleep in mellow Sorrento, just over an hour away (see Sorrento chapter). But, if needed, here are a few good options. The prices listed are typical for high season (spring and late fall). In this business-oriented (rather than tourist-oriented) city, prices are particularly soft during the slow summer months (July-Sept).

Near Via Toledo and Spaccanapoli

$$$ **Decumani Hotel de Charme** is a classy oasis tucked away on a residential lane in the very heart of the city, just off Spaccanapoli. While the neighborhood is Naples-dingy, the 22 rooms—filling an elegant 18th-century palace with a gorgeous breakfast room—

Sleep Code

(€1 = about $1.30, country code: 39)

S = Single, **D** = Double/Twin, **T** = Triple, **Q** = Quad, **b** = bathroom, **s** = shower only. Unless otherwise noted, credit cards are accepted, English is spoken, and breakfast is included. Many cities in Italy levy a hotel tax of about €2 per person, per night, which must be paid in cash (not included in the rates I've quoted).

To help you sort easily through these listings, I've divided the accommodations into three categories based on the price for a standard double room with bath:

$$$ Higher Priced—Most rooms €130 or more.
  $$ Moderately Priced—Most rooms between €90-130.
   $ Lower Priced—Most rooms €90 or less.

Prices can change without notice; verify the hotel's current rates online or by email.

---

are an inviting retreat (standard Db-€134, bigger deluxe Db-€15 more, rates soft—check website for deals, air-con, elevator, free Wi-Fi, Via San Giovanni Maggiore Pignatelli 15—this lane is one street towards the station from Via Santa Chiara, second floor, tel. 081-551-8188, www.decumani.com, info@decumani.com).

$$$ Hotel Piazza Bellini is a newish hotel with 48 stripped-down-minimalist but comfy rooms surrounding a quiet courtyard. Two blocks below the Archaeological Museum and just off the lively Piazza Bellini, it offers modern sanity in the city center (generally Sb-€120, Db-€170, less if slow, bi-level "superior" Db-€20 more, extra bed-€20, air-con, elevator, free Internet access and Wi-Fi, Via Santa Maria di Constantinopoli 101, close to Metro: Dante, tel. 081-451-732, www.hotelpiazzabellini.com, info@hotelpiazzabellini.com).

$$ Chiaja Hotel de Charme, with the same owner as the Decumani (listed earlier), rents 33 less expensive rooms on the upscale Via Chiaia pedestrian shopping drag near Piazza del Plebiscito (smaller standard Db with interior view-€119, bigger Db with view of pedestrian street-€139, air-con, elevator, free Wi-Fi, Via Chiaia 216, first floor, tel. 081-415-555, www.hotelchiaia.it, info@hotelchiaia.it, Pietro Fusella).

$$ Art Resort Galleria Umberto has 15 rooms in two different buildings inside the Umberto I shopping gallery at the bottom of Via Toledo, just off Piazza del Plebiscito. This genteel-feeling place gilds the lily, with an aristocratic setting and decor but older

NAPLES

bathrooms. Consider paying €20 extra for a room overlooking the gallery (cheapest non-view Db-€109-120, elevator, air-con, free Wi-Fi, Galleria Umberto 83, fourth floor—ask at booth for coin to operate elevator if needed, tel. 081-497-6224, www.artresortgalleriaumberto.it, info@artresortgalleriaumberto.it).

$$ Hotel Il Convento, with 14 small but comfortable rooms with balconies, is a good choice for those who want to sleep in the gnarly, tight tangle of lanes called the Spanish Quarter—quintessential Naples. While the neighborhood can feel off-putting after dark, it's not especially unsafe. You're only a couple of short blocks off the main Via Toledo drag, and heavy-duty windows help block out some—but not all—of the scooter noise and church bells. A rare haven in this characteristic corner of town, it's in all the guidebooks (Sb-€80, Db-€120, Tb-€130, Qb-€160, €10-20 less if you prepay, elevator, air-con, free Wi-Fi, Via Speranzella 137A, tel. 081-403 977, www.hotelilconvento.com, info@hotelilconvento.com).

Near the Train Station

Although rates here are cheaper and it's very handy to the station, this area is relatively inconvenient for sightseeing and dining, less characteristic than the areas described earlier, and can feel unnerving—especially after dark.

$ Grand Hotel Europa, a gem on a seedy street right next to the station, has 89 decent rooms whimsically decorated with not-quite-right reproductions of famous paintings (Sb-€65, Db-€85, Tb-€109, book direct and ask for 15 percent Rick Steves discount off these prices or check website for special deals, air-con, elevator, free guest computer, free Wi-Fi near reception, restaurant, Corso Meridionale 14, tel. 081-267-511, www.grandhoteleuropa.com, info@grandhoteleuropa.com, well-run by Claudio). To find the hotel, exit the station on the north side, past track 5. You'll turn left and a right around a green *Polfer* sign, then exit through a gate. The hotel is across the street and a few doors down to the right.

$ Hotel Suite Esedra, with 17 small but tasteful rooms, is an affordable four-star charmer on a tiny square off busy Corso Umberto I, located just outside of the station-neighborhood sleaze (Sb-€60, Db-€80, these prices if you book direct and mention this book, air-con, elevator, free Wi-Fi, 10-minute walk from the station at Via Arnaldo Cantani 12—across the Corso from the Church of Santa Maria Egiziaca, tel. 081-287-451, www.hotelsuiteesedranapoli.it, info@hotelsuiteesedranapoli.it, Alessandro).

$ Hotel Potenza offers a rare bit of security and peace right on Piazza Garibaldi, 100 yards in front of the station. Its 26 pleasant rooms have good windows that help block out the bustle (Sb-€50, Db-€70, Tb-€75, Qb-€92, air-con, no elevator, free Wi-Fi, 100

Naples Hotels & Restaurants

To Museo di Capodimonte

VIA STA. TERESA

VIA FORIA

To Museo di Capodimonte

Piazza Cavour

Cavour Ⓜ

UNDERGROUND PASSAGE

One stop on Metro to Piazza Garibaldi & Centrale Station

ARCHAEOLOGICAL MUSEUM

VIA PESSINA

Ⓜ Museo Ⓑ 🛈

⑯

GALLERIA PRINCIPE

V. DONNA

DUOMO

PIO MONTE MISERICORDIA

VIA SAPIENZA

S. PAOLO

⑨

⑧ ⑩

VIA DEI TRIBUNALI

S. LORENZO MAGGIORE

VIA DUOMO

VIA VICARIA VECCHIA

FORCELLA

COLLETTA

PACE

CAFFÈ MEXICO

⑮ ②

Piazza Bellini

⑲

CAPPELLA SANSEVERO

VIA PORT' ALBA

VIA GREG ARMENO

S. GREG ARMENO

VIA S. BIAGIO

⑰

⑦

⑥

Piazza Dante

⑱

SAN SEBASTIANO

SAN DOM.

CHAPEL OF MARADONA

⑯ "SPACCANAPOLI"

To Piazza Garibaldi & Centrale Station (10 min. walk)

Dante Ⓜ

VIA TARSIA

GESÙ NUOVO

VIA B. CROCE

To Ⓜ Montesanto (& funicular)

Piazza Sette Settembre

VIA MADDALONI

Piazza Gesù Nuovo

SCATURCHIO PASTICCERIA

①

VIA MEZZOCANNONE

CORSO UMBERTO I

VIA NUOVA MARINA

V. PIGNASECCA

SANTA CHIARA

VIA MORG.

⑪

CALATA TRINITÀ MAGGIORE

Piazza Carità

⑫

MONTEOLIVETO

V. DONNALBINA

Piazza Bovio

Ⓜ Università

VIA BATT.

FASCIST BLDG.

POST

SPANISH QUARTER

BNL BANK

VIA A. DIAZ

Piazza Matteotti

VIA S. FELICE

Ⓜ Toledo

VIA AGOSTINO DEPRETIS

VIA ALCIDE D. GASPERI

VIA CRISTOFORO COLOMBO

Port

To Ⓜ

⑭

VIA TOLEDO

VIA PORTA DI TAPPIA

⑤ ⑬

BANCO DI NAPOLI

BANCA INTESA SANPAOLO

Centrale Funicular

GALLERIA UMBERTO I

Ⓑ Municipio

Municipio Ⓜ

Piazza Municipio

Ⓣ Tram #1 to Train Station

MOLO BEVERELLO DOCK

🛈

STAZIONE MARITTIMA (CRUISE TERMINAL)

③

GRAN CAFFÈ GAMBRINUS

④

Allibus Bus To Airport

🛈 Ⓑ

TEATRO DI SAN CARLO

CASTEL NUOVO

V. AM. FERDINANDO ACTON

To Sorrento & Capri

🛈

ROYAL PALACE

Piazza del Plebiscito

SAN FRANCESCO DI PAOLA

TUNNEL

CONSOLE

VIA NAZARIO SAURO

Bay of Naples

To Castel dell'Ovo

300 Meters

300 Yards

NAPLES

Naples Hotels & Restaurants Key

1. Decumani Hotel de Charme
2. Hotel Piazza Bellini & La Stanza del Gusto
3. Chiaja Hotel de Charme
4. Art Resort Galleria Umberto
5. Hotel Il Convento
6. Hotel Suite Esedra
7. Antica Pizzeria da Michele & Pizzeria Trianon
8. Gino Sorbillo Pizzeria
9. Pizzeria di Matteo
10. Pizzeria I Decumani & Trattoria Campagnola
11. Ecomesarà
12. Osteria il Garum
13. Valù
14. To Trattoria da Nonnolla
15. Caffetteria Angela
16. Salumeria Pasquale Carrino
17. Polo Nord Gelateria
18. Supermarket
19. Laundry

yards in front of the station at Piazza Garibaldi 120, tel. 081-286-330, www.hotelpotenza.com, info@hotelpotenza.com, Valenzano family).

In Chiaia, Farther Out

$$ Pinto-Storey Hotel seems a world away from the bustle of the city center. With 16 straightforward rooms in a relatively upscale neighborhood (three Metro stops from the train station), the hotel has an old-time charm (Sb-€78, Db-€98, Tb-€139, these prices if you book direct and mention this book, air-con-€8, elevator, expensive Wi-Fi, across the square from Metro line 2's Amedeo stop at Via Martucci 72, tel. 081-681-260, www.pintostorey.it, info@pintostorey.it).

Eating in Naples

Cheap and Famous Pizza

Naples is the birthplace of pizza. Its pizzerias bake just the right combination of fresh dough, mozzarella, and tomatoes in traditional wood-burning ovens. You can head for the famous, venerable places (I've listed five below), but these can have a long line stretching out the door, and a half-hour wait for a table. If you want to skip the hassle, just ask your hotel for directions to the neighborhood pizzeria. An average one-person pie costs €4-6; most places offer both take-out and eat-in.

Near the Station

These two pizzerias—the most famous—are both a few long blocks from the train station, and at the end of my "Slice of Neapolitan Life" self-guided walk.

Antica Pizzeria da Michele is for pizza purists. Filled with locals (and tourists), it serves just two varieties: *margherita* (tomato sauce and mozzarella) and *marinara* (tomato sauce, oregano, and garlic, no cheese). Come early to sit and watch the pizza artists in action. A pizza with beer costs €6-7. As this place is often jammed with a long line, arrive early or late to get a seat. If there's a mob, head inside to get a number. If it's just too crowded to wait, the less-exceptional Pizzeria Trianon (described next) generally has room (Mon-Sat 10:30-24:00, closed Sun; look for the vertical red *Antica Pizzeria* sign at the intersection of Via Pietro Colletta and Via Cesare Sersale at #1; tel. 081-553-9204).

Pizzeria Trianon, across the street and left a few doors, has been da Michele's archrival since 1923. It offers more choices, slightly higher prices (€5-7), air-conditioning, and a cozier atmosphere. For less chaos, head upstairs. While waiting for your meal, you can survey the transformation of a humble wad of dough into a smoldering bubbly feast in their entryway pizza kitchen (daily 11:00-15:30 & 19:00-23:00, Via Pietro Colletta 42, tel. 081-553-9426, Giuseppe).

On Via dei Tribunali

This street, which runs a couple of blocks north of Spaccanapoli, is home to several pizzerias that are more convenient to sightseeing. Three in particular are on all the "best pizza in Naples" lists...as you'll learn the hard way if you show up at peak mealtimes, when huge mobs crowd outside the front door waiting for a table. **Gino Sorbillo** is a local favorite (closed Sun, Via dei Tribunali 32—don't confuse this with his relatives' similarly named places on the same street, tel. 081-446-643). At **Pizzeria di Matteo,** people waiting out front snack on €0.50 croquettes *(crocché),* sold at the little window (closed Sun, Via dei Tribunali 94, tel. 081-455-262). **Pizzeria I Decumani** has a bit nicer seating and is open seven days a week (facing Piazza San Gaetano at Via dei Tribunali 58, tel. 081-557-1309).

Restaurants

If you want a full meal rather than a pizza, consider these options, which I've organized by neighborhood.

Near Spaccanapoli and Via Toledo

Ecomesarà serves up Neapolitan and *meridionale* (southern Italian) dishes in a modern setting just below the Santa Chiara cloister, a long block south of Spaccanapoli. The atmosphere is mellow, modern, and international. Cristiano and his staff are happy to explain the menu, which refreshingly dispenses with the traditional Italian *primi/secondi* distinction. Cristiano—who abides by the Slow Food ethic—explains that separate *contorni* (vegetable sides) aren't necessary because *all* of their dishes have vegetables (€9-16 main courses, Tue-Sun 13:00-15:00 & 19:30-23:00, closed Mon, Via Santa Chiara 49, tel. 081-1925-9353).

NAPLES

Trattoria Campagnola is a classic family place with a daily home-cooking-style chalkboard menu on the back wall, mama busy cooking in the back, and wine on tap. Here you can venture away from pastas, be experimental with a series of local dishes, and not go wrong (€7 main courses, Wed-Mon 12:00-16:00 & 19:00-23:00, closed Tue, between the famous pizzerias at Via Tribunali 47, tel. 081 459 034 but no reservations).

Osteria il Garum is great if you'd like to eat on a classic Neapolitan square. It's named for the ancient fish sauce that was widely used in Roman cooking. These days, mild-mannered Luigi and his staff inject their pricey local cuisine with centuries of tradition, served in a cozy split-level cellar or outside on a covered terrace facing a neighborhood church. It's just between Via Toledo and Spaccanapoli, a short walk from the Church of Gesù Nuovo (€9-13 pastas, €14-17 *secondi*, daily 12:00-15:30 & 19:00-23:30, Piazza Monteoliveto 2A, tel. 081-542-3228).

Valù, with a modern red-and-black color scheme and a wine-bar vibe, sits sane and romantic in the colorful and rowdy Spanish Quarter just a block off Via Toledo. This *risotteria* specializes in risotto (which is not a local dish), serving 20 different variations. Choose between the interior or a few outdoor tables along a tight alley (€10-12 risottos, €8-16 meat dishes, Mon-Sat 12:30-15:00 & 19:00-24:00, closed Sun, Vico Lungo del Gelso 80, up alley directly opposite Banco di Napoli entrance, tel. 081-038-1139).

Trattoria da Nennella is fun-loving chaos, with red-shirted waiters barking orders, a small festival anytime someone puts a tip in the bucket, and the fruit course served in plastic bidets. There's one price—€12 per person—and you choose three courses plus a fruit. House wine is served in tiny plastic cups, the crowd is ready for fun, and the food's good. It's buried in the Spanish Quarter. You can sit indoors, or on a cobbled terrace under a trellis (closed Sun, leave Via Toledo a block down from the BNL bank and walk up Vico Teatro Nuovo three blocks to the corner of Vico Lungo Teatro Nuovo, Vico Lungo Teatro Nuovo 103, tel. 081-414-338 but no reservations).

Near the Archaeological Museum

La Stanza del Gusto, two blocks downhill from the museum, tackles food creatively and injects crusty Naples with a little modern color and irreverence. The downstairs is casual, trendy, and playful, while the upstairs is more refined yet still polka-dotted (€5-8 *panini*, €10-15 *secondi*; fixed-price meals: €35 five-course vegetarian, €65 seven-course meat; Tue-Sat 12:00-15:30 & 19:30-23:30, closed Sun-Mon, Via Santa Maria di Constantinopoli 100, tel. 081-401-578).

Caffetteria Angela is a fun little eating complex: coffee bar;

Getting Around the Region

To connect Naples, Sorrento, and the Amalfi Coast, you can travel on land by train, bus, and taxi. Whenever possible, consider taking a boat—it's faster, cooler, and more scenic, and you can take coastline photos that you can't get from land. For specifics, check the "Connections" sections of the Naples, Sorrento, and Amalfi Coast chapters. Confirm times and prices locally.

By Circumvesuviana Train: This useful commuter train—popular with locals, tourists, and pickpockets—links Naples, Herculaneum, Pompeii, and Sorrento. At Naples' Centrale Station, follow *Circumvesuviana* signs downstairs and down the corridor to the Circumvesuviana ticket windows and turnstiles. When you buy your ticket, ask which track your train will depart from ("*Quale binario*?"; KWAH-lay bee-NAH-ree-oh). Insert your ticket at the turnstiles and find your platform (down another level).

Circumvesuviana tickets are covered by the Campania ArteCard (see page 1000), but not railpasses. All-day Circumvesuviana tickets are available, but—unless you're making several stops on a long round-trip—aren't worth considering, except on weekends, when they're nearly half-price (€12 Mon-Fri, €6.50 "weekend pass" available Sat-Sun). For schedules, see www.vesuviana.it.

If you're heading to **Pompeii** or **Herculaneum,** take any Circumvesuviana train marked *Sorrento*—they all stop at both places. Sorrento-bound trains depart twice hourly, and take about 20 minutes to reach Ercolano Scavi (for the Herculaneum ruins, €2.20 one-way), 40 minutes to reach Pompei Scavi-Villa Misteri (for the Pompeii ruins, €2.90 one-way), and 70 minutes to reach **Sorrento**, the end of the line (€4.20 one-way). Express trains to Sorrento marked *DD* (6/day) reach Sorrento 15 minutes sooner (and also stop at Herculaneum and Pompeii).

As you board, double-check with a local that the train goes to Sorrento, as the Circumvesuviana has several lines that branch out to other destinations. When returning to Naples on the Circumvesuviana, remember that the name of the Circumvesuviana stop at Centrale Station is "Garibaldi." Back in Naples, you can use your Circumvesuviana ticket to cover all public transit within three hours of validation (no need to validate again).

Be on guard: Many readers report being ripped off on the Circumvesuviana (see "Theft Alert," page 1002).

If you're **coming from Rome,** note that a different (non-Circumvesuviana) train—run by the national rail company—goes from Rome to Naples, then continues to the ugly modern city of Pompei. But there is almost no reason to go to Pompei city, where you'll face a long walk to the actual site. It's better to simply get off at Naples' Centrale Station and transfer to the Circumvesuviana (described above). The Pompei city train station is useful only if you need to travel directly between the ruins and Salerno (roughly hourly, 20 minutes) or Paestum (4 trains/day, 1 hour).

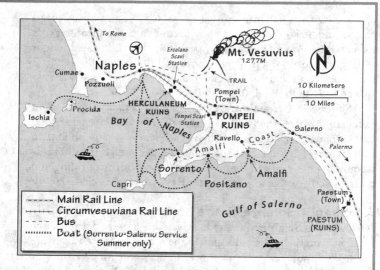

By Bus: Crowded SITA buses (often blue or green-and-white) are most useful for traversing the popular Amalfi Coast; see "Getting Around the Amalfi Coast—By Bus" on page 1101.

By Taxi: For €100, you can take a 30-mile taxi ride from Naples directly to your Sorrento hotel; agree on a set price without the meter and pay upon arrival. You can hire a cab on Capri for about €70/hour. Taxis in the Amalfi Coast are generally expensive, and more than willing to overcharge you, but they can be convenient, especially with a larger group. See "Getting Around the Amalfi Coast—By Taxi" on page 1102.

By Boat: Several ferry companies service the Naples, Sorrento, and Amalfi Coast areas. While these can change from year to year, major companies include Caremar (www.caremar.it), SNAV (www.snav.it), Gescab (a.k.a. NLG Jet, www.gescab.it), Metrò del Mare (www.metrodelmare.net), Navigazione Libera del Golfo (www.navlib.it), and Alilauro (www.alilauro.it). Each company has different destinations and prices; some compete for the same trips. The quicker the trip, the higher the price. A hydrofoil, called a "jet boat," skims between Naples and Sorrento—it's faster, safer from pickpockets, more scenic, and more expensive than the train (6/day, more in summer, departs roughly every 2 hours starting at 9:00, 35 minutes, €12-13). A taxi from Naples' Centrale train station to its port costs about €12-15.

For schedules to Capri, you can check online (www.capri-tourism.com; click "Shipping Timetable"), at any TI, or at Naples' Molo Beverello boat dock. Ticket windows clearly display the next available departure. The number of boats that run per day depends on the season. Trips are canceled in bad weather. Most boats charge €2 or so for luggage.

If you plan to arrive at and leave a destination by boat, note the return times—the last boat usually leaves before 19:00.

tavola calda with hot ready-to-eat dishes (€3-4); and a tiny meat, cheese, and bread shop with all you need for a cheap meal to go. It offers honest pricing and simple, peaceful, air-conditioned indoor seating (no cover, open Mon-Sat 7:00-21:00, Sun 9:00-14:00, 3 blocks below museum at Via Conte di Ruvo 21, between Via Pessina and Via Bellini, tel. 081-549-9660).

Salumeria Pasquale Carrino is a tiny *salumi* shop with an exuberant owner—the fun-loving and flamboyant Pasquale—who turns sandwich-making into a show (€3-7 sandwiches good for two people, Mon-Sat 8:00-15:00 & 17:00-20:00, closed Sun, 100 yards from museum—walk to the northwest corner of the building and cross two crosswalks to Via Salvator Rosa 10, tel. 081-564-0889).

A Romantic Splurge on the Harbor

Ristorante la Scialuppa ("The Rowboat") is a great bet for a fine local meal on the harbor. Located in the romantic Santa Lucia district, you'll walk across the causeway to the Castel dell'Ovo in the fisherman's quarter (the castle on the island) just off Via Partenope. They boast fine indoor and outdoor seating, attentive waitstaff, a wonderful assortment of *antipasti*, great seafood, and predictably high prices (€10 pizza, €14 pastas, €18 *secondi*, reservations smart, Borgo Marinari 4, tel. 081-764-5333, www.lascialuppa.it).

Near the Station

While far from high cuisine, these functional options are worth considering if you're on the way back to catch your train, or if you're sleeping in this neighborhood and don't want to venture far: **La Cantina dei Mille,** a block in front of the train station, is a traditional family-style place serving good, basic Neapolitan food to good, basic Neapolitans (€5-7 pizza, pasta, and *secondi*, hefty service charge, daily 12:00-16:00 & 17:00-24:00; with your back to the station, it's about halfway up the left side of Piazza Garibaldi at #126; tel. 081-283-448). Next door, **Iris** is another decent choice. The recommended **Grand Hotel Europa** has a restaurant peacefully buried in its basement, offering friendly service and a fine value (€18 fixed-price dinners include water and coffee, dinner served 19:00-22:30).

Naples Connections

From Naples by Boat to: Sorrento (6/day, more in summer, departs roughly every 2 hours starting at 9:00, 35 minutes, €12-13), **Capri** (roughly 2/hour, 45 minutes, €19-21); for more information, see www.snav.it and www.navlib.it. Seasonal boats to **Positano** (summer only, 4/day, 1.25-1.5 hours, €17) continue on to **Amalfi**

(1.5-2 hours, €18). For a map showing boat connections, see page 1100.

By Train to: Rome (at least hourly, 1.25 hours on Frecciarossa express trains, €45; otherwise 2 hours, €11-22), **Florence** (3/day direct, 3 hours, €72; otherwise about hourly with change in Rome, 4.25 hours, €56-59), **Salerno** (2/hour, 35-60 minutes, €7.50-17, change in Salerno for boats to Amalfi and Positano; avoid slower trains that leave from Garibaldi Station), **Paestum** (10/day, 1.5 hours, €7.50, tickets sold at ticket counter and tobacco shops but not from machines, direction: Sapri), **Brindisi** (8/day, 4.75-7 hours, overnight possible, €20-48 depending on speed; from Brindisi, ferries sail to Greece), **Milan** (direct trains hourly, 5 hours, €100, more frequent with change in Rome, overnight possible), **Venice** (almost hourly, 5.5-7 hours with changes in Bologna or Rome, €121, overnight possible), **Palermo** (2/day direct, 9-9.5 hours, €53, overnight possible), **Nice** (2/day, 12 hours with change in Genoa), **Paris** (3/day, 13-15 hours with change in Rome or Milan). Any train listed on the schedule as leaving Napoli PG or Napoli-Garibaldi departs not from Napoli Centrale, but from the adjacent Garibaldi Station.

Note that the departures listed above are Trenitalia connections; a private rail company called Italo offers additional options to **Rome, Salerno, Florence, Milan,** and **Venice.** While Italo may be cheaper (if you book long in advance), it doesn't accept railpasses (for details on Italo, see page 1166 or visit www.italotreno.it).

By Circumvesuviana Train: See the "Getting Around the Region" sidebar for information on getting to Herculaneum, Pompeii, and Sorrento.

To Pompeii: To visit the ancient site of Pompeii, don't use national train connections to the city of Pompei (which is far from the site). You're better off on the Circumvesuviana train, which takes you to the Pompei Scavi-Villa dei Misteri stop near the actual site.

POMPEII AND NEARBY

Pompeii • Herculaneum • Vesuvius

Stopped in their tracks by the eruption of Mount Vesuvius in A.D. 79, Pompeii and Herculaneum offer the best look anywhere at what life in Rome must have been like around 2,000 years ago. These two cities of well-preserved ruins are yours to explore. Of the two sites, Pompeii is grander, while Herculaneum is smaller and more intimate; both are easily reached from Naples on the Circumvesuviana commuter train (for details, see "Getting Around the Region" on page 1036). Vesuvius, still smoldering ominously, rises up on the horizon. It last erupted in 1944, and is still an active volcano. Buses from the train stations at Herculaneum or Pompeii drop you a steep half-hour hike from the summit.

Pompeii

A once-thriving commercial port of 20,000, Pompeii (worth ▲▲▲) grew from Greek and Etruscan roots to become an impor-

tant Roman city. Then, on August 24, A.D. 79, everything changed. Vesuvius erupted and began to bury the city under 30 feet of hot volcanic ash. For the archaeologists who excavated it centuries later, this was a shake-and-bake windfall, teaching them volumes about daily Roman life. Pompeii was accidentally rediscovered in 1599; excavations began in 1748.

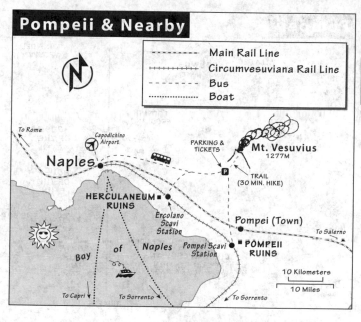

Pompeii & Nearby

- — · — · — Main Rail Line
- +++++++ Circumvesuviana Rail Line
- - - - - - Bus
- ·········· Boat

To Rome

Capodichino Airport

PARKING & TICKETS

Mt. Vesuvius 1277M

Naples

TRAIL (30 MIN. HIKE)

HERCULANEUM RUINS

Ercolano Scavi Station

Pompei (Town)

To Salerno

Bay   of   Naples

Pompei Scavi Station

POMPEII RUINS

10 Kilometers

10 Miles

To Capri   To Sorrento   To Sorrento

Orientation to Pompeii

Cost: €11, cash only; €20 combo-ticket includes Pompeii and three lesser sites (valid 3 consecutive days). Also consider the Campania ArteCard (see page 1000) if visiting other sites in the region.

Hours: Daily April-Oct 8:30-19:30, Nov-March 8:30-17:00 (last entry 1.5 hours before closing).

Closures: Be warned that some buildings and streets are bound to be closed for restoration when you visit.

Crowd-Beating Tips: On busy days, there can be a line of up to 30 minutes to buy a ticket. If you anticipate lines, buy your ticket at the "info point" kiosk at the train station (same price as at the site, credit cards accepted).

Getting There: Pompeii is roughly midway between Naples and Sorrento on the Circumvesuviana train line (2/hour, €2.90 and 40 minutes from Naples, one-way, not covered by railpasses). Get off at the Pompei Scavi-Villa dei Misteri stop; from Naples, it's the stop after Torre Annunziata. The DD express trains (6/day) bypass several stations but do stop at Pompei Scavi, shaving 10 minutes off the trip from Naples. From the Pompei Scavi train station, it's just a two-minute walk to the Porta Marina entrance: Turn right and walk down the road about a block to the entrance (on your left).

Pompei vs. Pompei Scavi: Pompei is the name of a separate train

POMPEII & NEARBY

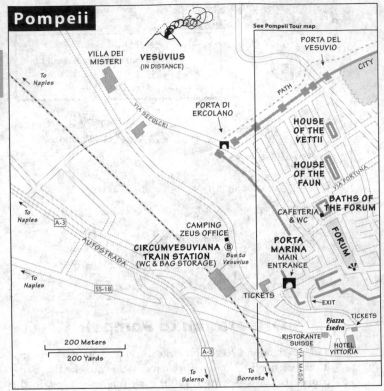

Pompeii

VILLA DEI MISTERI

VESUVIUS (IN DISTANCE)

See Pompeii Tour map

PORTA DEL VESUVIO

CITY

To Naples

VIA SEPOLCRI

PATH

PORTA DI ERCOLANO

HOUSE OF THE VETTII

HOUSE OF THE FAUN

VIA FORTUNA

BATHS OF THE FORUM

To Naples

A-3

AUTOSTRADA

CAFETERIA & WC

FORUM

CAMPING ZEUS OFFICE

CIRCUMVESUVIANA TRAIN STATION (WC & BAG STORAGE)

Bus to Vesuvius

PORTA MARINA MAIN ENTRANCE

To Naples

SS-18

TICKETS

EXIT

Piazza Esedra

TICKETS

200 Meters

200 Yards

A-3

RISTORANTE SUISSE

VIA MASS.

HOTEL VITTORIA

To Salerno

To Sorrento

station on the national rail network that's a long, dull walk from the ruins. Make sure you're taking the Circumvesuviana commuter train to Pompei Scavi (*scavi* means "excavations").

Parking: Parking is available at Camping Zeus, next to the Pompei Scavi train station (€2.50/hour, €10/12 hours, 10 percent discount with this book); several other campgrounds/parking lots are nearby.

Information: The "info point" kiosk at the station is a private agency selling tours (not a real TI; see "Tours," later), but they can provide some information and also sell tickets for the site.

Be sure to pick up the free, helpful map at the entrance (ask for it when you buy your ticket, or check at the info window to the left of the WCs—the maps aren't available within the walls of Pompeii). Tel. 081-857-5347, www.pompeiisites.org.

The bookshop sells the small Pompeii and Herculaneum *Past and Present* book. Its plastic overlays allow you to re-create the ruins (€12; if you buy from a street vendor, pay no more than that).

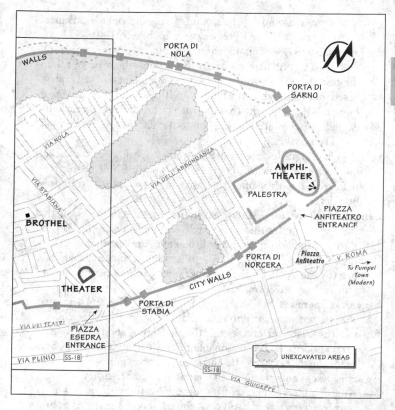

Tours: My **self-guided tour** in this chapter covers the basics and provides a good framework for exploring the site on your own. You can download this chapter as a free Rick Steves **audio tour**; see page 9.

    Guided tours leave every hour from the "info point" kiosk near the train station (€12). You can also sign up for a guided tour of Pompeii offered to Rick Steves readers through Naples-based Mondo Tours (€12, Mon-Fri at 10:00, meet at Ristorante Suisse, on Piazza Esedra, down the hill from the Porta Marina entrance, see page 1006).

    Private guides (around €110/2 hours) of varying quality— there really is no guarantee of what you're getting—cluster near the ticket booth at the site and may try to herd you into a group with other travelers, which makes the price more reasonable for you. For a private two-hour tour, consider **Gaetano Manfredi,** who is pricey but brings energy and theatricality to his tours (€120 for up to 4 people, book in advance by email, www.pompeii tourguide.com, gaetanoguide@hotmail.it). **Antonio Somma**

specializes in Pompeii (€120 for up to 8 people, book in advance, evening tel. 081-850-1992, daytime mobile 393-406-3824 or 339-891-9489, www.pompeitour.com, info@pompeitour.com). Antonio can organize transport for visitors who want to fill up the rest of the day with a trip to the Amalfi Coast. The Naples-based guides recommended on page 1005 can also guide you at Pompeii. Parents, note that the ancient brothel and its sexually explicit frescoes are included on tours; let your guide know if you'd rather skip that stop.

Audioguides are available from a kiosk near the ticket booth at the Porta Marina entrance (€6.50, €10/2 people, ID required), but they offer basically the same info as your free booklet.

Length of This Tour: Allow two hours, or three if you visit the theater and amphitheater. With less time, focus on the Forum, Baths of the Forum, House of the Faun, and brothel.

Baggage Check: The train station offers luggage storage for €3/bag (by the WC). Or use the free baggage check near the turn-stiles at the site entrance.

Services: There's a WC at the train station. The site has two WCs—one near the entrance and another in the cafeteria.

Eating: The Ciao cafeteria within the site serves good sandwiches, pizza, and pasta at a reasonable price. A few mediocre restaurants cluster between the entrance and the train station. Your cheapest bet may be to bring your own food for a discreet picnic.

Starring: Roofless (collapsed) but otherwise intact Roman buildings, plaster casts of hapless victims, a few erotic frescoes, and the dawning realization that these ancient people were not that different from us.

Background

Pompeii, founded in 600 B.C., eventually became a booming Roman trading city. Not rich, not poor, it was middle class—a perfect example of typical Roman life. Most streets would have been lined

with stalls and jammed with customers from sunup to sundown. Chariots vied with shoppers for street space. Two thousand years ago, Rome controlled the entire Mediterranean—making it a kind of free-trade zone—and Pompeii was a central and bustling port.

There were no posh neighborhoods in Pompeii. Rich and poor mixed it up as elegant houses existed side by side with simple homes. While nearby Herculaneum would have been a classier place to live (traffic-free streets, fancier houses, far better drainage), Pompeii was the place for action and shopping. It served an estimated 20,000 residents with more than 40 bakeries, 30 brothels, and 130 bars, restaurants, and hotels. With most of its buildings covered by brilliant white ground-marble stucco, Pompeii in A.D. 79 was an impressive town.

As you tour Pompeii, remember that its best art is in the Archaeological Museum in Naples (described in the previous chapter).

Self-Guided Tour

• *Just past the ticket-taker, start your approach up to the...*

❶ Porta Marina

The city of Pompeii was born on the hill ahead of you. This was the original town gate. Before Vesuvius blew and filled in the harbor, the sea came nearly to here. Notice the two openings in the gate (ahead, up the ramp). Both were left open by day to admit major traffic. At night, the larger one was closed for better security.

• *Pass through the Porta Marina and continue up to the top of the street, pausing at the three large stepping-stones in the middle.*

❷ Pompeii's Streets

Every day, Pompeiians flooded the streets with gushing water to clean them. These stepping-stones let pedestrians cross without

getting their sandals wet. Chariots traveling in either direction could straddle the stones (all had standard-size axles). A single stepping-stone in a road means it was a one-way street, a pair indicates an ordinary two-way, and three (like this) signifies a major thoroughfare. The basalt stones are the original Roman pavement. The sidewalks (elevated to hide the plumbing) were paved with bits of broken pots (an ancient form of recycling) and studded with reflective bits of white marble. These "cats' eyes" helped people get around after dark, either by moonlight or with the help of lamps.

• *Continue straight ahead, don your mental toga, and enter the city as the Romans once did. The road opens up into the spacious main square: the Forum. Stand at the near end of this rectangular space and look toward Mount Vesuvius.*

❸ The Forum (Foro)

Pompeii's commercial, religious, and political center stands at the intersection of the city's two main streets. While it's the most ruined part of Pompeii, it's grand nonetheless. Picture the piazza surrounded by two-story buildings on all sides. The pedestals that line the square once held statues (now safely displayed in the museum in Naples). In its heyday, Pompeii's citizens gathered here in the main square to shop, talk politics, and socialize. Business took place in the important buildings that lined the piazza.

The Forum was dominated by the **Temple of Jupiter,** at the far end (marked by a half-dozen ruined columns atop a stair-step base). Jupiter was the supreme god of the Roman pantheon—you might be able to make out his little white marble head at the center-rear of the temple.

At the near end of the Forum (behind where you're standing) is the **curia,** or city hall. Like many Roman buildings, it was built with brick and mortar, then covered with marble walls and floors. To your left (as you face Vesuvius and the Temple of Jupiter) is the **basilica,** or courthouse.

Since Pompeii was a pretty typical Roman town, it has the same layout and components that you'll find in any Roman city—main square, curia, basilica, temples, axis of roads, and so on. All power converged at the Forum: religious (the temple), political (the curia), judicial (the basilica), and commercial (this piazza was the main marketplace). Even the power of the people was expressed here, since this is where they gathered to vote. Imagine the hubbub of this town square in its heyday.

Look beyond the Temple of Jupiter. Five miles to the north looms the ominous backstory to this site: **Mount Vesuvius.** Mentally draw a triangle up from the two remaining peaks to reconstruct the mountain before the eruption. When it blew, Pompeians had no idea that they were living under a volcano, as Vesuvius hadn't erupted for 1,200 years. Imagine the wonder—then the horror—as a column of pulverized rock roared upward, and then ash began to fall. The weight of the ash and small rocks collapsed Pompeii's roofs later that day, crushing people who had taken refuge inside buildings instead of fleeing the city.

Pompeii Tour

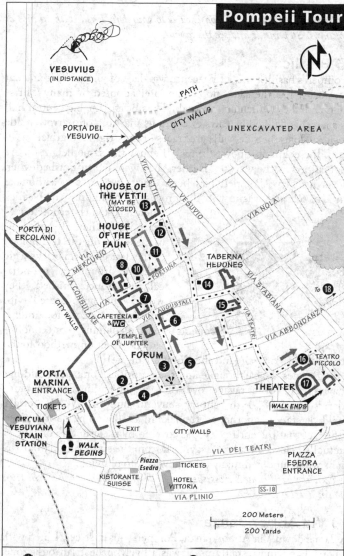

VESUVIUS
(IN DISTANCE)

N

PATH

CITY WALLS

UNEXCAVATED AREA

PORTA DEL
VESUVIO →

PORTA DI
ERCOLANO

HOUSE OF
THE VETTII
(MAY BE
CLOSED)

HOUSE
OF THE
FAUN

VIA MERCURIO

VIA CONSULARE

VIA VETTII

VIA VESUVIO

VIA NOLA

TABERNA
HEDONES

VIA STABIANA

To 18

VIA ABBONDANZA

CITY WALLS

VIA FORTUNA

CAFETERIA
& WC

TEMPLE
OF JUPITER

FORUM

PORTA
MARINA
ENTRANCE

TICKETS

CIRCUM
VESUVIANA
TRAIN
STATION

WALK
BEGINS

VIA AUGUSTALI

VIA TEATRI

THEATER

TEATRO
PICCOLO

WALK ENDS

EXIT

CITY WALLS

Piazza
Esedra

TICKETS

VIA DEI TEATRI

PIAZZA
ESEDRA
ENTRANCE

RISTORANTE
SUISSE

HOTEL
VITTORIA

SS-18

VIA PLINIO

200 Meters

200 Yards

1 Porta Marina
2 Pompeii's Streets
3 Forum
4 Basilica
5 Via Abbondanza
6 Fish & Produce Market;
Plaster Casts of Victims
7 Baths of the Forum
8 Fast-Food Joint
9 House of the Tragic Poet

10 Aqueduct Arch
11 House of the Faun
12 Original Lead Pipes
13 House of the Vettii
14 Bakery & Mill
15 Brothel
16 Temple of Isis
17 Theater &
Piccolo Theater
18 To Amphitheater

• *As you face Vesuvius, the basilica is to your left, lined with stumps of columns. Step inside and see the layout.*

❹ Basilica

Pompeii's basilica was a first-century palace of justice. This ancient law court has the same floor plan later adopted by many Christian churches (which are also called basilicas). The big central hall (or nave) is flanked by rows of columns marking off narrower side aisles. Along the side walls are traces of the original marble.

The columns—now stumps all about the same height—were not ruined by the volcano. Rather, they were left unfinished when Vesuvius blew. Pompeii had been devastated by an earthquake in A.D. 62, and was just in the process of rebuilding the basilica

when Vesuvius erupted, 17 years later. The half-built columns show off the technology of the day. Uniform bricks were stacked around a cylindrical core. Once finished, they would have been coated with marble dust stucco to simulate marble columns—an economical construction method found throughout Pompeii (and the Roman Empire).

Besides the earthquake and the eruption, Pompeii's buildings have suffered other ravages over the years, including Spanish plunderers (c. 1800), 19th-century souvenir hunters, WWII bombs, wild vegetation, another earthquake in 1980, and modern neglect. The fact that the entire city was covered by the eruption of A.D. 79 actually helped preserve it, saving it from the sixth-century barbarians who plundered many other towns into oblivion.

• *Exit the basilica and cross the short side of the square, where the city's main street hits the Forum.*

❺ Via Abbondanza

Glance down Via Abbondanza, Pompeii's main street. Lined with shops, bars, and restaurants, it was a lively, pedestrian-only zone. The three "beaver-teeth" stones are traffic barriers that kept chariots out. On the corner (just to the left), take a close look at the dark travertine column standing next to the white one. Notice that the marble drums of the white column are not chiseled entirely round—another construction project left unfinished when Vesuvius erupted.

• *Head toward Vesuvius, walking along the right side of the Forum. Immediately to the right of the Temple of Jupiter (just before the four round arches), a door leads into the market hall, where you'll find two glass cases.*

❻ Fish and Produce Market— Plaster Casts of Victims

As the frescoes on the wall (just inside on the left) indicate, this is where Pompeiians came to buy their food—fish, bread, chickens, and so on. These fine examples of Roman art—with their glimpses of everyday life and their mastery of depth and illusion—would not be matched until the Renaissance, a thousand years after the fall of Rome.

The glass cases hold casts of Pompeiians, eerily captured in their last moments. They were quickly suffocated by a superheated avalanche of gas and ash, and their bodies were encased in volcanic debris. While excavating, modern archaeologists detected hollow spaces underfoot, created when the victims' bodies decomposed. By gently filling the holes with plaster, the archaeologists were able to create molds of the Pompeiians who were caught in the disaster.

• *Continue on, leaving the Forum through an arch behind the Temple of Jupiter. Here you'll find a pedestrian-only road sign (ahead on the right corner, above the* REG VII INS IV *sign) and more "beaver-teeth" traffic blocks. The modern cafeteria is the only eatery inside the archaeological site (with a coffee bar and WC upstairs). Twenty yards past the cafeteria, on the left-hand side at #24, is the entrance to the...*

❼ Baths of the Forum (Terme del Foro)

Pompeii had six public baths, each with a men's and a women's section. You're in the men's zone. The leafy courtyard at the entrance was the gymnasium. After working out, clients could relax with a hot bath *(caldarium)*, warm bath *(tepidarium)*, or cold plunge *(frigidarium)*.

The first big, plain room you enter served as the **dressing room.** Holes on the walls were for pegs to hang clothing. High up, the window (with a faded Neptune underneath) was originally covered with a less-translucent Roman glass. Walk over the non-slip mosaics into the next room.

The *tepidarium* is ringed by mini-statues or *telamones* (male caryatids, figures used as supporting pillars), which divided the lockers. Clients would undress and warm up here, perhaps stretching out on one of the bronze benches near the bronze heater for a

The Eruption of Vesuvius

At about 1:00 in the afternoon on August 24, A.D. 79, Mount Vesuvius erupted, sending a mushroom cloud of ash, dust, and rocks 12 miles into the air. It spewed for 18 hours straight, as winds blew the cloud southward. The white-gray ash settled like a heavy snow on Pompeii, its weight eventually collapsing roofs and floors, but leaving the walls intact. And though most of Pompeii's 20,000 residents fled that day, about 2,000 stayed behind.

Although the city of Herculaneum was closer to the volcano—about four miles away—at first it largely escaped the rain of ash, due to the direction of the wind. However, 12 hours after Vesuvius awoke, the type of eruption suddenly changed. The mountain let loose a superheated avalanche of ash, pumice, and gas. This red-hot "pyroclastic flow" sped down the side of the mountain at nearly 100 miles per hour, engulfing Herculaneum and cooking its residents alive. Several more flows over the next few hours further entombed Herculaneum, burying it in nearly 60 feet of hot material that later cooled into rock, freezing the city in time. Then, at around 7:30 in the morning, another pyroclastic flow headed south and struck Pompeii, dealing a fatal blow to those who'd remained behind.

massage. Look at the ceiling—half crushed by the eruption and half intact, with its fine blue-and-white stucco work.

Next, admire the engineering in the steam-bath room, or *caldarium.* The double floor was heated from below—so nice with bare feet (look into the grate to see the brick support towers). The double walls with brown terra-cotta tiles held the heat. Romans soaked in the big tub, which was filled with hot water. Opposite the big tub is a fountain, which spouted water onto the hot floor, creating steam. The lettering on the fountain reminded those enjoying the room which two politicians paid for it...and how much it cost them (5,250 *sestertii*). To keep condensation from dripping annoyingly from the ceiling, fluting (ribbing) was added to carry water down the walls.

• *Today's visitors exit the baths through the original entry. If you're a bit hungry, immediately across the street is an ancient...*

❽ Fast-Food Joint

After a bath, it was only natural to want a little snack. So, just across the street is a fast-food joint, marked by a series of rectangular marble counters. Most ancient Romans didn't cook for themselves in their tiny apartments, so to-go places like this were commonplace. The holes in the counters held the pots for food. Each container was like a thermos, with a wooden lid to keep the soup hot, the wine cool, and so on. Notice the groove in the front doorstep and the holes out on the curb. The holes likely accommodated cords for stretching awnings over the sidewalk to shield the clientele from the hot sun, while the grooves were for the shop's folding accordion doors. Look at the wheel grooves in the pavement, worn down through centuries of use. Nearby are more stepping-stones for pedestrians to cross the flooded streets.

• *Just a few steps uphill from the fast-food joint, at #5 (with a locked gate), is the...*

❾ House of the Tragic Poet (Casa del Poeta Tragico)

This house is typical Roman style. The entry is flanked by two family-owned shops (each with a track for a collapsing accordion door). The home is like a train running straight away from the street: atrium (with skylight and pool to catch the rain), den (where deals were made by the shopkeeper), and garden (with rooms facing it and a shrine to remember both the gods and family ancestors). In the entryway is the famous "Beware of Dog" *(Cave Canem)* mosaic.

Today's visitors enter the home by the back door (circle around to the left). On your way there, look for the modern exposed pipe on the left side of the lane; this is the same as ones used in the ancient plumbing system, hidden beneath the raised sidewalk. Inside the house, the grooves on the marble well-head in the entry hall (possibly closed) were formed by generations of inhabitants dragging the bucket up by rope. The richly frescoed dining room is off the garden. Diners lounged on their couches (the Roman custom) and enjoyed frescoes with fake "windows," giving the illusion of a bigger and airier room. Next to the dining room is a humble BBQ-style kitchen with a little closet for the toilet (the kitchen and bathroom shared the same plumbing).

• *Return to the fast-food place and continue about 10 yards downhill to the big intersection. From the center of the intersection, look left to see a giant arch, framing a nice view of Mount Vesuvius.*

❿ Aqueduct Arch—Running Water

Water was critical for this city of 20,000 people, and this arch was part of Pompeii's water-delivery system. A 100-mile-long aqueduct carried fresh water down from the hillsides to a big reservoir perched at the highest point of the city wall. Since overall water pressure was disappointing, Pompeiians built arches like the brick one you see here (originally covered in marble) with hidden water tanks at the top. Located just below the altitude of the main tank, these smaller tanks were filled by gravity and provided each neighborhood with reliable pressure.

• *If you're thirsty, fill your water bottle from the modern fountain. Then continue straight downhill one block (50 yards) to #2 on the left.*

⓫ House of the Faun (Casa del Fauno)

Stand across the street and marvel at the grand entry with *"HAVE"* (hail to you) as a welcome mat. Go in. Notice the two shrines above the entryway—one dedicated to the gods, the other to this wealthy family's ancestors.

You are standing in Pompeii's largest home, where you're greeted by the delightful small bronze statue of the *Dancing Faun,* famed for its realistic movement and fine proportion. (The original, described on page 1010, is in Naples' Archaeological Museum.) With 40 rooms and 27,000 square feet, the House of the Faun covers an entire city block. The next floor mosaic, with an intricate diamond-like design, decorates the homeowner's office. Beyond that is the famous floor mosaic of the *Battle of Alexander.* (The original is also at the museum in Naples.) In 333 B.C., Alexander the Great beat Darius and the Persians. Romans had great respect for Alexander, the first great emperor before Rome's. While most of Pompeii's nouveau riche had notoriously bad taste and stuffed their palaces with over-the-top, mismatched decor, this guy had class. Both the faun (an ancient copy of a famous Greek statue) and the Alexander mosaic show an appreciation for history.

The house's back courtyard leads to the exit in the far-right corner. It's lined with pillars rebuilt after the A.D. 62 earthquake. Take a close look at the brick, mortar, and fake marble stucco veneer.

• *Sneak out of the House of the Faun through its back door and turn right. (If this exit is closed, return to the entrance and make a U-turn left, around to the back of the house.) Thirty yards down, along the right-hand side of the street are metal cages protecting...*

⓬ Original Lead Pipes

These 2,000-year-old pipes (made of lead imported from Britannia) were part of the city's elaborate water system. From the aqueduct-fed water tank at the high end of town, three independent pipe systems supplied water to the city: one for baths, one for private homes, and one for public water fountains. If there was a water shortage, democratic priorities prevailed: First the baths were cut off, then the private homes. The last water supply to go was the public fountains, where all citizens could get drinking and cooking water.

• *If the street's not closed off, take your first left (on Vicolo dei Vettii), walk about 20 yards, and find the entrance (on the left) to the next stop. (If the street is closed, turn right down the street marked REG VI INS XIV and skip down to the next set of directions.)*

⓭ House of the Vettii (Casa dei Vettii)

Pompeii's best-preserved home has been completely blocked off for years; unfortunately, it's unlikely to reopen in time for your visit.

The House of the Vettii was the bachelor pad of two wealthy merchant brothers. If you can see the entryway, you may spot the huge erection. This is not pornography. There's a meaning here: The penis and the sack of money balance each other on the goldsmith scale above a fine bowl of fruit. Translation: Only with a balance of fertility and money can you have abundance.

If it's open, step into the atrium with its ceiling open to the sky to collect light and rainwater. The pool, while decorative, was a functional water-supply tank. It's flanked by large money boxes anchored to the floor. The brothers were certainly successful merchants, and possibly moneylenders, too.

Exit on the right, passing the tight servant quarters, and go into the kitchen, with its bronze cooking pots (and an exposed lead pipe on the back wall). The passage dead-ends in the little Venus Room, which features erotic frescoes behind glass.

Return to the atrium and pass into the big colonnaded garden. It was replanted according to the plan indicated by the traces of roots that were excavated from the volcanic ash. Richly frescoed entertainment rooms ring this courtyard. Circle counterclockwise. The dining room is finely decorated in black and "Pompeiian red" (from iron rust). Study the detail. Notice the lead humidity seal between the wall and the floor, designed to keep the moisture-sensitive frescoes dry. (Had Leonardo da Vinci taken this clever step, his *Last Supper* in Milan might be in better shape today.) Continuing around, you'll see more of the square white stones inlaid in the floor. Imagine them reflecting like cats' eyes as the brothers and their friends wandered around by oil lamp late at night. Frescoes in the Yellow Room (near the exit) show off the ancient mastery of perspective, which would not be matched elsewhere in Europe for nearly 1,500 years.

• *Facing the entrance to the House of the Vettii, turn left and walk downhill one long block (along Vicolo dei Vettii) to a T-inter-section (Via della Fortuna), marked by a stone fountain with a bull's head for a spout. Intersections like this were busy neighbor-hood centers, where the rent was highest and people gathered. With the fountain at your back, turn left, then immediately right, walking along a gently curving road (Vicolo Storto). On the left side of the street, at #22, find four big stone cylinders.*

⓮ Bakery and Mill (Forno e Mulini)

The brick oven looks like a modern-day pizza oven. The stubby stone towers are flour grinders. Grain was poured into the top, and

donkeys or slaves pushed wood-en bars that turned the stones. The powdered grain dropped out of the bottom as flour—flavored with tiny bits of rock. Each neighborhood had a bakery like this.

Continue to the next in-tersection (Via degli Augustali, where there's another fast-food joint, at #32) and turn left. As you walk, look at the destructive power of all the vines, and notice how deeply the chariot grooves have worn into the pavement. Deep grooves could break wagon wheels. The suddenly ungroovy stretch indicates that this road was in the process of being repaved when the eruption shut everything down.

• *Head about 50 yards down this (obviously one-way) street to #44 (on the left). Here you'll find the Taberna Hedones (with a small atrium, den, and garden). This bar still has its original floor and, deeper in, the mosaic arch of a grotto fountain. Just past the tavern, turn right and walk downhill to #18, on the right.*

Possible detour: If the road past the tavern is blocked off, here's an-other way to reach the next stop: First, backtrack to the Forum—go back the way you came, turn left at the bull's-head fountain, then turn left again at the aqueduct arch. Back in the Forum, head down to the far end and turn left onto the main street, Via dell'Abbondanza (which we looked down earlier—remember the beaver teeth?). Follow this, turning left up the second street (after the fountain, marked REG VII INS I, with a small Vicolo del Lupanare *sign). This leads to the entrance of the...*

⓯ Brothel (Lupanare)

You'll find the biggest crowds in Pompeii at a place that was likely popular 2,000 ago, too—the brothel. Prostitutes were nicknamed *lupe* (she-wolves), alluding to the call they made when trying to attract business. The brothel was a simple place, with beds and pillows made of stone. The ancient graffiti includes tallies and exotic names of the women, indicating the prostitutes came from all corners of the Mediterranean (it also served as feedback from satisfied customers). The faded frescoes above the cells may have been a kind of menu for services offered. Note the idealized women (white, which was considered beautiful; one wears an early bra) and the rougher men (dark, considered horny). The bed legs came with little disk-like barriers to keep critters from crawling up.

• *Leaving the brothel, go right, then take the first left, and continue going downhill two blocks to the intersection with Pompeii's main drag, Via dell'Abbondanza. The Forum—and exit—are to the right, for those who may wish to opt out from here.*

The huge amphitheater—which is certainly skippable—is 10 minutes to your left. But for now, go left for 60 yards, then turn right just beyond the fountain, and walk down Via dei Teatri. Turn left before the columns, and head downhill another 60 yards to #28, which marks the...

⓰ Temple of Isis

This Egyptian temple served Pompeii's Egyptian community The little white stucco shrine with the modern plastic roof housed holy water from the Nile. Isis, from Egyptian myth, was one of many foreign gods adopted by the eclectic Romans. Pompeii must have had a synagogue, too, but it has yet to be excavated.

• *Exit the temple where you entered, and go right. At the next intersection, turn right again, and head downhill to the adjacent theaters. Your goal is the large theater down the corridor at #20, but if it's closed, look at the smaller but similar theater (Teatro Piccolo) just beyond at #19.*

⓱ Theater

Originally a Greek theater (Greeks built theirs with the help of a hillside), this was the birthplace of the Greek port here in 470 B.C. During Roman times, the theater sat 5,000 people in three sets of seats, all with different prices: the

five marble terraces up close (filled with romantic wooden seats for two), the main section, and the cheap nosebleed section (surviving only on the high end, near the trees). The square stones above the cheap seats once supported a canvas rooftop. Take note of the high-profile boxes, flanking the stage, for guests of honor. From this perch, you can see the gladiator barracks—the colonnaded court-yard beyond the theater. They lived in tiny rooms, trained in the courtyard, and fought in the nearby amphitheater.

• *You've seen Pompeii's highlights. When you're ready to leave, backtrack to the main road and turn left, going uphill to the Forum, where you'll find the main entrance/exit.*

However, there's much more to see—three-quarters of Pompeii's 164 acres have been excavated, but this tour has covered only a third of the site. After the theater—if you still have energy to see more—go back to the main road and take a right toward the eastern part of the site, where the crowds thin out. Go straight for about 10 minutes, likely jogging right after a bit (just follow the posted maps). You'll wind up passing through a pretty, forested area. At the far end is the...

⑱ Amphitheater

If you can, climb to the upper level of the amphitheater (though the stairs are often blocked). With Vesuvius looming in the back-ground, mentally replace the tourists below with gladiators and wild animals locked in combat. Walk along the top of the amphithe-ater and look down into the grassy rectangular area surrounded by columns. This is the **Pa-laestra,** an area once used for athletic training. (If you can't get to the top of the amphitheater, you can see the Palaestra from outside—in fact, you can't miss it, as it's right next door.) Facing the other way, look for the bell tower that tops the roofline of the modern city of Pompei, where locals go about their daily lives in the shadow of the volcano, just as their an-cestors did 2,000 years ago.

• *If it's too crowded to bear hiking back along uneven lanes to the en-trance, you can slip out the site's "back door," which is next to the amphi-theater. Exiting, turn right and follow the site's wall all the way back to the entrance.*

Herculaneum

Smaller, less crowded, and not as ruined as its famous big sister, Herculaneum (worth ▲▲, Ercolano in Italian) offers a closer, more intimate peek into ancient Roman life but lacks the grandeur of Pompeii (there's barely a colonnade).

Orientation to Herculaneum

Cost and Hours: €11, €20 combo-ticket includes Pompeii and three lesser sites (valid 3 consecutive days); also covered by the Campania ArteCard (see page 1000). Open daily April-Oct 8:30-19:30, Nov-March 8:30-17:00, ticket office closes 1.5 hours earlier.

Getting There: Ercolano Scavi, the nearest train station to Herculaneum, is about 20 minutes from Naples and 50 minutes from Sorrento on the same Circumvesuviana train that goes to Pompeii (for details on the Circumvesuviana, see page 1036). Walking from the Ercolano Scavi train station to the ruins takes 10 minutes: Leave the station and turn right, then left down the main drag; go eight blocks straight downhill to the end of the road, where you'll see the entrance to the ruins marked by a grand arch. (Skip Museo MAV.) Pass through the arch and continue 200 yards down the path to the ticket office in the modern building, taking in the bird's-eye first impression of the site to your right.

Information: Pick up a free, detailed map and excellent booklet at the info desk next to the ticket window. The booklet gives you a quick explanation of each building, keyed to the same numbers as the audioguides. (I've included some of these numbers in my self-guided tour, below.) There's a bookstore inside the site, next to the audioguide stand. Tel. 081-777-7008, www.pompeiisites.org.

Audioguide: The informative and interesting audioguide sheds light on the ruins and life in Herculaneum in the first century A.D. (€6.50, €10/2 people, ID required, cheaper version available for kids ages 4-10, pick up 100 yards after the ticket turnstiles, uses same numbers as info booklet).

Length of This Tour: Allow one hour.

Baggage Storage: Herculaneum is harder than Pompeii for those with luggage, but not impossible. Herculaneum's train station has lots of stairs and no baggage storage, but you can roll wheeled luggage down to the ruins and store it for free in a locked area in the ticket office building (pick up bags at least 30 minutes prior to site closing). To get back to the station, consider splurging on a €5 taxi (ask the staff to call one for you).

Services: There's a free WC in the ticket office building.

Eating: The site doesn't have a café of its own, but there are several eateries on the way from the train station.

Self-Guided Tour

Caked and baked by the same A.D. 79 eruption that pummeled Pompeii (see sidebar on page 1050), Herculaneum is a small community of intact buildings with plenty of surviving detail. While Pompeii was initially smothered in ash, Herculaneum was spared at first—due to the direction of the wind—but got slammed about 12 hours after the eruption started by a superheated avalanche of ash and hot gases roaring off the volcano. The city was eventually buried under nearly 60 feet of ash, which hardened into tuff, perfectly preserving the city until excavations began in 1748.

After leaving the ticket building, go through the turnstiles and walk the path below the site to the entrance. Look seawards and note where the shoreline is today; before the eruption, it was just where you are standing, a quarter-mile inland. This gives you a sense of just how much volcanic material piled up. The present-day city of Ercolano looms just above the ruins. The modern buildings don't look much different from their ancient counterparts.

As you cross the modern bridge into the excavation site, look down into the moat-like ditch. On one side, you see Herculaneum's seafront wall. On the other, the wall that you've just been walking on is the solidifed ash layer from the volcano and shows how deeply the town was buried.

After crossing the bridge, stroll straight to the end of the street and find the **Seat of the Augustali** (Sede degli Augustali, #24). Decorated with frescoes of Hercules (for whom this city was named), it belonged to an association of freed slaves working together to climb their way up the ladder of Roman society. Here and farther on, look around doorways and ceilings to spot ancient wood charred by the pyroclastic flows. Most buildings were made of stone, with wooden floors and beams (which were preserved here by the ash but rarely survive at ancient sites).

Leave the building through the back and go to the right, down the lane. The adjacent *thermopolium* (#22) was the Roman equivalent of a lunch counter or fast-food joint, with giant jars for wine, oil, and snacks. Most of the buildings along here were shops, with apartments above.

A few steps on, the **Bottega ad Cucumas** wine shop (#19) still has charred remains of beams, and its drink list remains frescoed on the outside wall (under glass).

Take the next right, go halfway down the street, and on the left find the **House of Neptune and Amphitrite** (Casa di Nettuno e Anfitrite, #29). Outside, notice the intact upper floor and imagine it going even higher. Inside, you'll see colorful mosaics and a unique "frame" made of shells.

Back outside, continue downhill to the intersection, then head left for a block and go straight across the street into the don't-miss-it **sports complex** (*palestra*; #12). First you'll see a row of "marble" columns, which (look closer) are actually made of rounded bricks covered with a thick layer of plaster, shaped to look like carved marble. While important buildings in Rome had solid marble columns, these fakes are typical of ordinary buildings.

Look for the hole in the hillside and walk through one of the triangular-shaped entrances to find the highlight: the Hydra of Lerna, a sculpted bronze fountain that features the seven-headed monster defeated by Hercules as one of his 12 labors. If this cavernous space is unlit, go to the second doorway on the left wall and press the light switch.

Go back out to the street and downhill to the **House of the Deer** (Casa dei Cervi, #8). It's named for the statues of deer being attacked by dogs in the garden courtyard (these are copies; the originals are in the Archaeological Museum in Naples). As you wander through the rooms, notice the colorfully frescoed walls. Ancient Herculaneum, like all Roman cities of that age, was filled with color, rather than the stark white we often imagine (even the statues were painted).

Continue downhill through the archway. The **baths** (Terme Suburbane, #3; enter near the side of the statue, sometimes closed) illustrate the city's devastation. After you descend into the baths, look back at the steps. You'll see the original wood charred in the disaster, protected by the wooden planks you just walked on. At the bottom of the stairs, in the waiting room to the right, notice where the floor collapsed under the sheer weight of the volcanic debris. (The sunken pavement reveals the baths' heating system: hot air generated by wood-burning furnaces and circulated between the different levels of the floor.) A doorway in front of the stairs is still filled with solidified ash. Despite the damage, elements of refinement remain intact, such as the delicate stuccoes in the *caldarium* (hot bath).

Back outside, make your way down the steps to the sunken area just below. As you descend, you're walking across what was formerly Herculaneum's beach. Looking back, you'll see **arches** that were part of boat storage areas. Archaeologists used to wonder why so few victims were found in Herculaneum. But during excavations in 1981, hundreds of skeletons were discovered here, between the wall of volcanic stone behind you and the city in front of you. Some of Herculaneum's 4,000 citizens tried to escape by sea, but were overtaken by the pyroclastic flows.

Thankfully, your escape is easier. Either follow the sounds of the water and continue through the tunnel; or, more scenically, backtrack and exit the same way you entered.

Vesuvius

The 4,000-foot-high Vesuvius, mainland Europe's only active volcano, has been sleeping restlessly since 1944. While Europe has

other dangerous volcanoes, only Vesuvius sits in the middle of a three-million-person metropolitan area that would be impossible to evacuate quickly. Many tourists don't know that you can easily visit the summit. Up top, it's desolate and lunar-like, and the rocks are newly created. Walk the entire accessible part of the crater lip for the most interesting views; the far end overlooks Pompeii. Be still. Listen to the wind and the occasional cascades of rocks tumbling into the crater. Any steam? Vesuvius is closed to visitors when erupting.

You can reach the volcano by bus, taxi, or private car (described below). No matter how you travel up, you'll land at the parking lot. From here it's a steep 30-minute hike (with a 950-foot elevation gain) to the top for a sweeping view of the Bay of Naples. Bring a coat; it's often cold and windy (especially Oct-April).

Cost and Hours: €10 covers entry to the national park (and a mandatory but brief introduction from a park guide, who then sets you free), daily April-Oct 9:30-17:00, until 18:00 in summer, Nov-March 9:30-15:00, last entry 1.5 hours before closing, no WC, tel. 081-865-3911 or 081-239-5653, www.parconazionaledelvesuvio.it.

Getting to Vesuvius

By Car or Taxi: Just drive to the end of the road and pay €2.50 to park. A taxi costs €90 round-trip from Naples, including a 2-hour wait; it's cheaper from Pompeii.

By Bus from Pompeii: From the Pompei Scavi train station on the Circumvesuviana line (just outside the main entrance to the Pompeii ruins), you have two bus services to choose from, each taking about three hours (40 minutes up, 40 minutes down, and about 1.5 hours at the summit).

Busvia del Vesuvio winds you up a bumpy private road through the back of the national park in a cross between a shuttle bus and a monster truck. It's a fun, more scenic way to go, but not for the easily queasy (€22 includes summit admission, runs hourly April-Oct daily 9:00-15:00, also at 16:00 and 17:00 June-Aug, rarely runs Nov-March—call for schedule, buy tickets at "info point" at Pompei Scavi train station, mobile 340-935-2616, www. busviadelvesuvio.com).

The old-fashioned **Vesuvius Trolley Tram** (Tramvia del Vesuvio) uses the main road up (€12 round-trip plus €10 summit admission, 10 percent discount with this book, 6/day, tickets sold at and departs from Camping Zeus next to Pompei Scavi train station, tel. 081-861-5320, www.campingzeus.it).

By Bus from Herculaneum: The quickest trip up is on the **Vesuvio Express**. These small buses leave from the Ercolano Scavi train station (on the Circumvesuviana line, where you get off for the Herculaneum ruins; €10 round-trip plus €10 summit admission, daily from 9:00, runs every 45 minutes based on demand, 20 minutes each way—about 2.5 hours total, office on square in front of train station, tel. 081-739-3666, www.vesuvioexpress.it).

SORRENTO AND CAPRI

Just an hour south of Naples and without a hint of big-city chaos, serene Sorrento makes an ideal home base for exploring this fascinating region, from Naples to the Amalfi Coast to Paestum. And the jet-setting island of Capri is just a short cruise from Sorrento, offering more charm and fun (outside of the crowded months of July and August) than its glitzy reputation would lead you to believe.

Sorrento

Wedged on a ledge under the mountains and over the Mediterranean, spritzed by lemon and olive groves, Sorrento is an attractive resort of 20,000 residents and, in summer, just as many tourists. It's as well-located for regional sightseeing as it is a fine place to stay and stroll. The Sorrentines have gone out of their way to create a completely safe and relaxed place for tourists to come and spend money. As 90 percent of the town's economy is tourism, everyone seems to speak fluent English and work for the Chamber of Commerce. This gateway to the Amalfi Coast has an unspoiled old quarter, a lively main shopping street, and a spectacular cliffside setting. Residents are proud of the many world-class romantics who've vacationed here, such as the famed tenor Enrico Caruso, who chose Sorrento as the place to spend his last weeks in 1921.

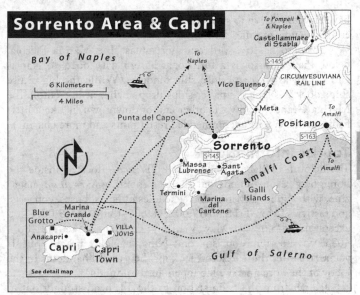

Sorrento Area & Capri

Bay of Naples

6 Kilometers

4 Miles

To Pompeii & Naples

Castellammare di Stabla

To Naples

S-145

CIRCUMVESUVIANA RAIL LINE

Vico Equense

Meta

To Amalfi

Positano

Punta del Capo

Sorrento

S-145

S-163

Massa Lubrense

Sant' Agata

Amalfi Coast

To Amalfi

Termini

Marina del Cantone

Galli Islands

Blue Grotto

Marina Grande

VILLA JOVIS

Anacapri

Capri

Capri Town

See detail map

Gulf of Salerno

Planning Your Time

Sorrento itself has no world-class sights, but can easily give you a few pleasant hours. More importantly, Sorrento is a fine base for visiting Naples (by boat or train); Pompeii, Herculaneum, and Mount Vesuvius (by train, plus a bus for Vesuvius); the Amalfi Coast (by bus); and the island of Capri (by boat). All of these destinations are within an hour or so of Sorrento. Of the region's attractions, only Paestum's Greek temples are a little hard to reach from Sorrento, and even they can be seen in a long day.

Sorrento hibernates in winter, and many places close down from November through February or March.

Orientation to Sorrento

Downtown Sorrento is long and narrow. Piazza Tasso marks the town's center. The main drag, Corso Italia, runs parallel to the

sea, passing 50 yards below the train station, through Piazza Tasso, and then out toward the cape, where the road's name becomes Via Capo. Nearly everything mentioned here (except Meta beach and the hotels on Via Capo) is within a 10-minute walk of the station. The town is perched on a cliff (some hotels have elevators down to sundecks on the water); the best real beaches are a couple of miles away.

Sorrento has two different port areas: The Marina Piccola, below Piazza Tasso, is a functional harbor with boats to Naples and Capri, as well as cruise-ship tenders. (While the big cruise ships dock in Naples, smaller ships drop anchor at Sorrento.) The Marina Grande, below the other end of downtown, is like a little fishing village, with recommended restaurants and more charm.

Tourist Information

The helpful TI (labeled *Soggiorno e Turismo*)—located inside the Foreigners' Club—hands out the free monthly *Surrentum* magazine, with a great city map and schedules of boats, buses, concerts, and festivals (Mon-Fri 8:30-19:00, Sat 9:00-13:00, Sun 9:00-13:00 except closed Sun Oct-May; Via Luigi de Maio 35, tel. 081-807-4033, www.sorrentotourism.com; Nino, Fabiola, and Peppe). If you arrive after the TI closes, look for their useful handouts in the lobby of the Foreigners' Club (open until midnight).

To get from the train station to the TI, head straight out to Corso Italia and turn left. Walk five minutes to Piazza Tasso, turn right at the end of the square, and go down Via Luigi de Maio through Piazza Sant'Antonino, bearing right downhill about 30 yards to the Foreigners' Club mansion at #35.

If you just need quick advice, the fake tourist office—located in a green caboose just outside the train station—can be of help. While they're a private business with hopes that you'll purchase one of their overpriced excursions, they're willing to give basic information on directions, buses, and ferries.

Arrival in Sorrento

By Train or Bus: Sorrento is the last stop on the Circumvesuviana train line. In front of the train station is the town's main bus stop, as well as taxis waiting to overcharge you (€15 minimum). All recommended hotels—except those on Via Capo—are within a 10-minute walk. For details on taking the bus to hotels on Via Capo, see page 1079.

By Boat: Passenger boats dock at Marina Piccola. To walk from the harbor to Piazza Tasso by the easiest route, follow the *Lift* signs a couple of hundred yards to the elevator. Pay €1 to ride it up into the Villa Comunale city park. From there, exit through the park gate and bear left; Piazza Tasso is about four blocks away. Or, if you don't mind a steep uphill hike, you can hike along the road for 15 minutes (free). Other options are the red-and-white city bus #B or #C (buy €1 tickets at the tobacco shop near the dock, 3/hour); or the small, blue private bus (€1, buy ticket from driver, passes not valid, 4/hour).

By Car: The Achille Lauro underground parking garage is centrally located, just a couple of blocks in front of the train station (€2/hour, €24/24 hours, on Via Correale).

Helpful Hints

Church Services: The **cathedral** hosts an English-language Anglican service at 17:00 most Sundays from June to August. At **Santa Maria delle Grazie** (perhaps the most beautiful Baroque church in town), cloistered nuns sing from above and out of sight during a Mass each morning at 7:30 (on Via delle Grazie).

Bookstore: Libreria Tasso has a decent selection of books in English, including this one (June-Sept daily 10:00-22:00; Oct-May Mon-Sat 9:45-13:00 & 16:00-20:30, Sun 11:00-13:00 & 17:00-20:00; Via San Cesareo 96, one block north of cathedral, near Sorrento Men's Club; tel. 081-807-1639).

Laundry: Sorrento has two handy self-service launderettes (both charge about €8/load wash and dry, includes soap). One launderette is just down the alley next to Corso Italia 30 (daily May-Sept 7:00-24:00, Oct-April 8:00-23:00, Vico I Fuoro 3, mobile 338-506-0942). The other is near the station, at the corner of Corso Italia and Via degli Aranci (daily 7:00-22:00).

Guided Tours of Pompeii, Naples, and Amalfi Coast: Naples-based **Mondo Tours** offers affordable tours of these destinations, including a nine-hour Amalfi Coast drive that starts from Sorrento. You'll sign up in advance and team up with fellow Rick Steves readers to split the cost (making it €45/person). For details, see page 1006.

Local Guides: Giovanna Donadio is a good tour guide for Sorrento, Amalfi, and Capri (€100/half-day, €160/day, same price for any size group, mobile 338-466-0114, giovanna_dona@hotmail.com). **Giovanni Visetti** is a nature lover, mapmaker, and orienteer who organizes hikes and has a fine website describing local trails (mobile 339-694-2911, www.giovis.com, giovis@giovis.com).

Getting Around Sorrento

By Bus: City buses (either orange or red-and-white) all stop near the main square, Piazza Tasso. Bus #A runs east to Meta beach or west to the hotels on Via Capo and beyond; buses #B and #C go to the port (Marina Piccola); and bus #D heads to the fishing village (Marina Grande). Buses #A and #D stop at the beginning of Corso Italia (west side of Piazza Tasso for Via Capo or Marina Grande, east side for Meta); #B and #C stop at the corner of Piazza Sant'Antonino, just down the hill toward the water. The trip between Piazza Tasso and Marina Piccola costs just €1; for other

Sorrento

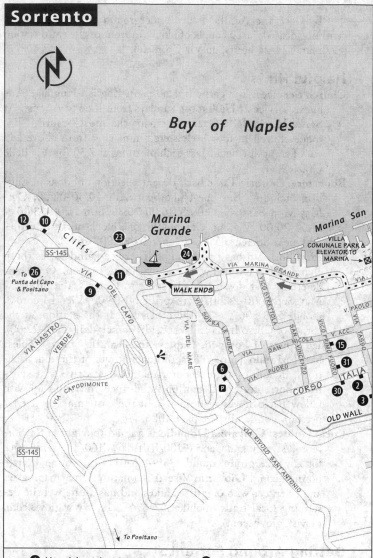

SORRENTO & CAPRI

Bay of Naples

Marina Grande

Marina San

VILLA COMUNALE PARK & ELEVATOR TO MARINA

Cliffs

SS-145

VIA DEL CAPO

VIA MARINA GRANDE

VIA

To Punta del Capo & Positano

VIA NASTRO VERDE

VIA CAPODIMONTE

B

WALK ENDS

VIA SOPRA LE MURA

VIA DEL MARE

VICO STRETTOLA

SAN VINCENZO

VIA SAN NICOLA

VIA FUORO

VICO PRIMO FUORO

V. ACC.

V. PAOLO

VIA TASSO

V. SAN

CORSO ITALIA

OLD WALL

SS-145

VIA RIVOLO SANT'ANTONIO

To Positano

1 Hotel Antiche Mura & Plaza Sorrento
2 Casa Astarita B&B
3 Hotel Mignon
4 Hotel Palazzo Tasso & Kebab Joint
5 Il Palazzo Starace B&B
6 Ulisse Deluxe Hostel
7 Hotel Nice & Penisola Rent
8 Grand Hotel Ambasciatori

9 Hotel Minerva
10 Hotel La Tonnarella & Hotel Désirée
11 Albergo Settimo Cielo
12 Hotel Elios
13 Ristorante il Buco & Teatro Tasso
14 L'Antica Trattoria
15 Inn Bufalito
16 Camera & Cucina Ristorante

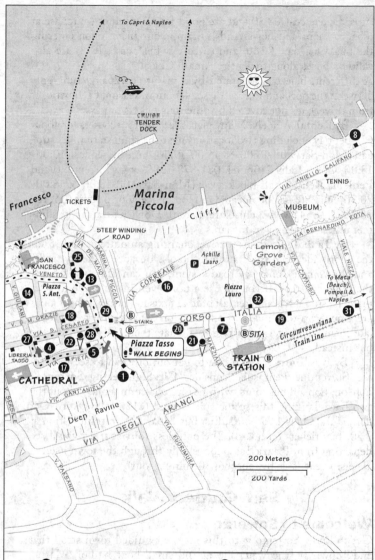

To Capri & Naples

CRUISE TENDER DOCK

Marina Piccola

Cliffs

TENNIS

MUSEUM

Lemon Grove Garden

STEEP WINDING ROAD

Francesco

TICKETS

SAN FRANCESCO

Piazza S. Ant.

Achille Lauro

Piazza Lauro

Piazza Tasso
WALK BEGINS

To Meta (Beach), Pompeii & Naples

CORSO ITALIA

Circumvesuviana Train Line

STAIRS

SITA

TRAIN STATION

CATHEDRAL

LIBRERIA TASSO

Deep Ravine

VIA DEGLI ARANCI

200 Meters
200 Yards

17 Chantecler's Trattoria & Meating
18 Rist. Pizzeria da Gigino
19 Pizzeria da Franco
20 Decò Supermarket
21 Gelateria David
22 Gelateria Primavera
23 Ristorante Delfino
24 Trattoria da Emilia
25 Foreigners' Club Rest.
26 Verde Mare
27 Sorrento Men's Club
28 The Fauno Bar
29 The Bagattelle American Bar
30 The English Inn
31 Launderettes (2)
32 Europcar

trips, tickets cost €2.50 and are good for 45 minutes (purchase at tobacco shops and newsstands). Stamp your ticket upon entering the bus. One-day (€7.60) and three-day bus passes (€18) are also valid on buses along the entire Amalfi Coast.

A different, blue bus (operated by a private company) runs only between the port and Piazza Tasso (4/hour in season, €1, buy ticket from driver); it's not covered by other bus tickets or passes.

By Rental Wheels: Many places rent motor scooters for about €35 per day, including two locations near the train station: **Europcar** (Mon-Sat 9:00-13:00 & 16:00-19:30, Sun by request 10:00-13:00, Corso Italia 210p, tel. 081-878-1386, www.sorrento.it) and **Penisola Rent,** a half-block away (Mon-Sat 9:00-13:00 & 16:00-20:30, Sun 9:00-13:00, located in Hotel Nice, Corso Italia 259, tel. 081-877-4664, www.penisolarent.com). Don't rent a car in summer unless you enjoy traffic jams.

By Taxi: Taxis are expensive, charging an outrageous €15 for the short ride from the station to hotels. Because of heavy traffic and the complex one-way road system, you can often walk faster than you can ride. If you do use a taxi, even if you agree to a set price, be sure it has a meter (all official taxis have one). I think taxis are a huge rip-off, since city officials don't have the nerve to regulate them, and hotels are afraid to alienate them. Walk or take the bus instead.

By Bus Tour: If you'd like to get out of town to see more of the Sorrentine Peninsula, consider **CitySightseeing Sorrento**'s hop-on, hop-off bus tours, with headphone commentary about the two bays flanking this scenic spit of land (€12, 4/day, April-Oct daily, full loop is 1.75 hours, first bus departs from train station at 9:30, buy tickets on board). The pointless **tourist train** you'll see departing from Piazza Tasso loops only through the town itself—all easily reachable by foot (€6, 30-minute tour).

Self-Guided Walk

Welcome to Sorrento

Get to know Sorrento with this lazy self-guided town stroll that ends down by the waterside at the small-boat harbor, Marina Grande.

• *Begin on the main square. Stand under the flags with your back to the sea, and face...*

Piazza Tasso: As in any southern Italian town, this "piazza" is Sorrento's living room. It may be noisy and congested, but locals want to be where the action is...and be part of the scene. The most expensive apartments and top cafés are on or near this square. City buses stop at or close to the square on their way to Marina Piccola and Via Capo. The train station is a five-minute walk to the left. A statue of St. Anthony, patron of Sorrento, faces north as if greeting those coming from Naples (he's often equipped with an armload of fresh lemons and oranges).

This square spans a gorge that divides downtown Sorrento. The newer section (to your left) was farm country just two centuries ago. The older part is to your right, with an ancient Greek gridded street plan (like much of southern Italy, Sorrento was Greek-speaking for centuries before it was Romanized). If you walk a block inland, go right up to the green railing, and look down, you'll see steps that were carved in the fifth century B.C. The combination of the gorge and the seaside cliffs made Sorrento easy to defend. A small section of wall (which you can find near Hotel Mignon) closed the landward gap in the city's defenses.

Sorrento's name may come from the Greek word for "siren," the legendary half-bird, half-woman who sang an intoxicating lullaby. According to Homer, the sirens lived on an island near here. No one had ever sailed by the sirens without succumbing to their incredible musical charms...and to death. But Homer's hero Ulysses was determined to hear the song. He put wax in his oarsmen's ears and had himself lashed to the mast of his ship. Oh, it was nice. The sirens, thinking they had lost their powers, threw themselves into the sea, and the place became safe to inhabit. Ulysses' odyssey was all about the westward expansion of Greek culture, and to the ancient Greeks, places like Sorrento were the wild, wild west.

• *With your back still to the sea, head to the far-right corner of the square, behind the statue of Torquato Tasso, the square's namesake. (A Sorrento native, he was a lively Renaissance poet—but today he seems only to wonder which restaurant to choose for dinner.) Peek into the big courtyard of Palazzo Correale (#18, behind the statue in the right corner) to get a feel for an 18th-century aristocratic palace's courtyard, its walls lined with characteristic tiles. In the same building, you'll see one of the zillions of fun, touristy shops in Sorrento that sells regional goodies and offers free biscuits and tastes of liqueurs. As you're leaving the courtyard, on your immediate left you'll see the narrow...*

Via Santa Maria della Pietà: Here, just a few yards off the noisy main drag, is a street that goes back centuries before Christ. About 100 yards down the lane, at #24 (on the left), find a 13th-century palace (no balconies back then...for security reasons), now an elementary school. A few steps farther on, you'll see a tiny shrine across the street. Typical of southern Italy, it's where the faithful pray to their saint, who contacts Mary, who contacts Jesus, who contacts God. This shrine is a bit more direct—it starts right with Mary.

• *Continue down the lane, which ends at the delightful...*

Cathedral: This is the seat of the local bishop. Pop in for a cool stroll around the ambulatory, checking out the impressive *in-*

tarsio (inlaid-wood) doors. There are two sets of doors—the main entry and the side entry, facing the big street. They're inlaid on both sides and show many scenes of the town and its industry. The doors facing the main street include an old-town map. These were made to celebrate the pope's visit in 1992. Also notice the intricate inlaid Stations of the Cross and the fine *presepe* (manger scene) in the back. This one takes Bethlehem on that first Christmas and sets it in Naples—with pasta, mozzarella, salami, and even Mount Vesuvius in the background (free, daily 8:00-12:30 & 16:30-20:30, no visits during Mass daily at 8:30 and 18:00, plus Sun at 11:00 and 12:15).

• *Backtrack 10 yards down Via Santa Maria della Pietà, turn left, and cross busy Corso Italia. In the summer, this stretch of road is closed to traffic each evening, when it hosts the best of the* passeggiata. *Look back at the bell tower, with the scavenged ancient Roman columns at its base. Then go straight on Via P. Reginaldo Giuliani (pausing to see who's died lately on the poster board on your right) and follow the...*

Old Greek Street Plan: Locals claim the ancient Greeks laid out the streets east-west for the most sunlight and north-south for the prevailing and cooling breeze.

• *One block ahead, on your right, the 14th-century loggia is home to the...*

Sorrento Men's Club: Once the meeting place of the town's nobles, this club has been a retreat for retired working-class men for generations. Strictly no women—and no phones.

Italian men venerate their mothers. (Italians joke that Jesus must have been a southern Italian because his mother believed her son was God, he believed his mom was a virgin, and he lived at home with her until he was 30.) But Italian men have also built into their culture ways to be on their own. Here, men play cards and gossip under a historic emblem of the city and a finely frescoed 16th-century dome, with its marvelous 3-D scenes.

• *Turn right for a better view of the Men's Club and a historical marker describing the building. Then continue along...*

Via San Cesareo: This touristy pedestrian-only shopping street leads back to Piazza Tasso. It's lined with competitive little shops where you can peruse (and sample) lemon products. Notice the huge ancient doorways with their tiny doors—to let the right people in, carefully, during a more dangerous age.

• *After a block, take a left onto Via degli Archi, go under the arch, and then hang a right (under another arch) to the square with the...*

Statue of St. Anthony (Antonino): Sorrento's town saint humbly looms among the palms, facing the basilica where the reliquary containing a few of his bones lies (free, downstairs in the crypt beneath the altar, surrounded by lots of votives).

• *Exit the square at the bottom-left (following the* lift to the port *signs; don't go down the street with the line of trees and the* porto *signs). After a block or so, on the right you'll see the trees in front of the Imperial Hotel Tramontano, and to their right a path leading to a...*

Cliffside Square: This fine public square, the Villa Comunale, overlooks the harbor. Belly up to the banister to enjoy the view of Marina Piccola and the Bay of Naples. From here, steps zigzag down to the harbor, where lounge chairs, filled by vacationers working on tans, line the sundecks (there's also a €1 elevator to the harbor). The Franciscan church fronting this square faces a fine modern statue of Francis across the street. Next to the church is a dreamy little cloister. Pop inside to see Sicilian Gothic—a 13th-century mix of Norman, Gothic, and Arabic styles, all around the old pepper tree. This is an understandably popular spot for weddings and concerts.

From here, you can quit the walk and stay in the town center, or continue another few minutes downhill to the waterfront at Marina Grande (if it's before 20:00, you'll be able to catch a bus back; otherwise, you'll have to walk back uphill).

• *Return to the road and continue downhill. At the next square (Piazza della Vittoria), which offers another grand view, cut over to the road closest to the water. After winding downhill for a few minutes, it turns into a wide stairway, and just before reaching the waterfront, you pass under an...*

Ancient Greek Gate: This gate marks the boundary between Sorrento and Marina Grande, technically a separate town with its own proud residents—it's said that even their cats look different. Because Marina Grande dwellers lived outside the wall and were more susceptible to rape, pillage, and plunder, Sorrentines believe that they come from Saracen (Turkish pirate) stock. Sorrentines still scare their children by saying, "Behave—or the Turks will take you away."

• *Now go all the way down the steps into Marina Grande, Sorrento's "big" small-boat harbor. (Confusingly, Capri also has a harbor called Marina Grande.)*

Marina Grande: Until recently, this little community was famously traditional, with its economy based on its fishing fleet. Locals recall when women wore black when a relative died (1 year for an uncle, aunt, or sibling; 2-3 years for a husband or parent). Men got off easy, just wearing a black memorial button.

There are two recommended restaurants on the harbor. **Trattoria da Emilia** has an old newspaper clipping, tacked near the door, about Sophia Loren filming here. On the far side of the harbor, **Ristorante Delfino** boasts a sundeck for a lazy drink before or after lunch.

• *From here, buses return to the center at Piazza Tasso every hour (€2.50, buy ticket at tobacco shop). Or you can walk back up.*

Sights in Sorrento

▲▲Strolling
Take time to explore the surprisingly pleasant old city between Corso Italia and the sea. Views from Villa Comunale, the public
park next to Imperial Hotel Tramontano, are worth the detour.
Each night in summer (May-Oct at 19:30; Nov-April weekends only), the police close off Corso Italia to traffic, and Sorrento's main drag becomes a thriving people scene. The *passeggiata* peaks at about 22:00. (When Piazza Tasso

and the main thoroughfare are closed to traffic, buses for Via Capo leave from up on Via degli Aranci, a short walk from Piazza Tasso along Via Fuorimura.)

Lemon Products Galore
Via San Cesareo is lined with hardworking rival shops selling a mind-boggling array of lemon products and offering samples of lots of sour goodies. Poke around for a pungent experience.

▲Lemon Grove Garden (Giardini di Cataldo)
This small park consists of an inviting organic lemon and orange grove lined with shady, welcoming paths. The owners of the grove are seasoned green thumbs, having worked the orchard through many generations. You'll see that they've even grafted orange-tree branches onto a lemon tree so that both fruits now grow on the same tree. The garden is dotted with benches, tables, and an inviting little tasting (and buying) stand. You'll get a chance to sniff and taste the varieties of lemons, and enjoy free samples of chilled *limoncello* along with various other homemade liqueurs made from basil, mandarins, or fennel (enthusiastically free, daily April-Sept 9:30-sunset, Oct-March 10:00-sunset, closed in rainy weather, tel. 081-807-4040, www.igiardinidicataldo.it). The main shop selling their organic homemade products, tasty gelato, and lemonade is across from the Corso Italia entrance at #267; a smaller stand is inside. Enter the garden either on Corso Italia (100 yards north of the train station—where painted tiles show lemon fantasies), or at the intersection of Via Capasso and Via Rota (next to the Hotel La Meridiana Sorrento).

Lemons

Around here, *limoni* are ubiquitous: screaming yellow painted on ceramics, dainty bottles of *limoncello,* and lemons the size of softballs at the fruit stand.

The Amalfi Coast and Sorrento area produces several different kinds of lemons. The gigantic, bumpy "lemons" are actually citrons, called *cedri*, and are more for show—they're pulpier than they are juicy, and make a good marmalade. The juicy *sfusato sorrentino,* grown only in Sorrento, is shaped like an American football, while the *sfusato amalfitano*, with knobby points on both ends, is less juicy but equally aromatic. These two kinds of luscious lemons are used in sweets such as *granita* (shaved ice doused in lemonade), *limoncello* (a candy-like liqueur with a big kick, called *limoncino* on the Cinque Terre), *delizia* (a dome of fluffy cake filled and slathered with a thick whipped lemon cream), *spremuta di limone* (fresh-squeezed lemon juice), and, of course, gelato or *sorbetto alla limone*.

▲**Swimming near Sorrento**

If you require immediate tanning, you can rent a chair on a pier by the port. There are no great beaches in Sorrento—the gravelly, jam-packed private beaches of **Marina Piccola** are more for partying than pampering, and there's just a tiny spot for public use. The elevator in Villa Comunale city park (next to the Church of San Francesco) gets you down for €1. At **Marina Grande,** Restaurant Delfino has a pier lined with lounge chairs for sunbathing (free for those with this book who buy lunch there).

There's a classic, sandy Italian beach two miles away at **Meta,** but it's generally overrun by teenagers from Naples. While the Meta Circumvesuviana stop is a very long walk from the beach (or a €25 cab ride), the red-and-white bus #A goes directly from Piazza Tasso to the Meta beach (last stop, schedule posted for hourly returns). At Meta, you'll find pizzerias, snack bars, and a little free section of beach, but the place is mostly dominated by several sprawling private-beach complexes—if you go, pay for a spot in one of these. Lido Metamare seems best (open May-Sept, €2.50 entry; lockable changing cabins, lounge chairs, and more available for an extra fee; tel. 081-532-2505). It's a very Italian scene—locals complain that it's "too local" (i.e., inundated with Naples' riffraff)—with light lunches, a playground, a manicured beach, loud pop music...and no international tourists.

Tarzan might take Jane to the wild and stony beach at **Punta del Capo,** a 15-minute bus ride from Piazza Tasso (the same bus #A explained above, but in the opposite direction from Meta; 2/ hour, get off at stop in front of the American Bar, then walk 10 minutes past ruined Roman Villa di Pollio).

Another good choice is **Marina di Puolo,** a tiny fishing town popular in the summer for its sandy beach, surfside restaurants, and beachfront disco (to get here, stay on bus #A a bit farther—ask driver to let you off at Marina di Puolo—then follow signs and hike down about 15 minutes).

Tennis
The Sorrento Sport Snack Bar has two fine courts open to the public (daily 9:30-23:00, until 20:00 in winter, €14/hour including rackets and balls for two people, call for reservation, across from recommended Grand Hotel Ambasciatori at Via Califano 5, tel. 081-807-1616).

Scuba Diving
To escape the shops, dive deep into the Mediterranean. PADI-certified Futuro Mare offers a one-hour boat ride out to the protected marine zone that lies between Sorrento and Capri, where you can try the beginners' dive (€90, includes instruction and complete supervision, April-Oct usually daily at 9:30). The boat also takes experienced certified divers (1 dive-€65, 2 dives-€95, April-Oct daily at 9:30 and 14:00). The whole experience takes about three hours. Prices include all equipment, transportation, and the dive itself, which lasts about 40 minutes for both novices and experts (call a day or two in advance to reserve, tel. 349-653-6323, www. sorrentodiving.it, info@futuromare.it).

Boat Rental
You can rent motor boats big enough for four people (€150/day, plus gas—figure about €30 for a trip to Capri, more with a skipper; with your back to the ferry-ticket offices, it's to the left around the corner at Via Marina Piccola 43; tel. 081-807-2283, www.nauticasicsic. com).

Nightlife in Sorrento

Pubs and Clubs
Sorrento is a fun place to enjoy a drink or some dancing after dinner. The crowd is older, and the many local English expats seem to have paved the way for you.

The Fauno Bar, which dominates Piazza Tasso with tables spilling onto the square, is a fine place to make the scene over a drink any time of day.

The Bagattelle American Bar, run by DJ Daniele, who tailors music to the audience, is the oldest club in town. The scene, while sloppy, is generally comfortable with the 30- to 60-year-old crowd. And if you're alone, there's a pole you can dance with (no cover charge, €4-7 drinks, no food, nightly from 21:30, down the steps from the flags at Piazza Tasso).

The English Inn offers both a streetside pub and a more re-fined-feeling garden out back—at least until the evening, when the music starts blaring. English vacationers come to Sorrento in droves (many have holidayed here annually for decades). Order up baked beans on toast, €10 fish-and-chips, or just a draft beer (near-ly all drinks-€5, daily, Corso Italia 55, tel. 081-878-2570).

Camera & Cucina, a sleek and modern photography-themed place, offers a snapshot of contemporary Italy with a creative food and drink menu, DJ music late at night, a secluded garden, and people-watching among stylish Italians on vacation (May-Nov daily 18:00-late, Dec-April open Fri-Sat only, reservations smart, Via Correale 19, 4-minute walk from Piazza Tasso, tel. 081-877-3686).

The Foreigners' Club offers live Neapolitan songs, Sinatra-style classics, and jazzy elevator music nightly at 20:00 throughout the summer. It's just right for old-timers feeling frisky (in the cen-ter; described earlier under "Helpful Hints").

Theater Show

At **Teatro Tasso,** a hardworking troupe puts on *The Sorrento Musi-cal,* a folk-music show that treats visitors to a schmaltzy dose of Neapolitan Tarantella music and dance—complete with "Funiculì Funiculà" and "Santa Loo-chee-yee-yah." The 75-minute Italian-language extravaganza features a cast of 14 playing guitar, violin, mandolin, and tambourines, and singing operatically from Nea-politan balconies...complete with Vesuvius erupting in the back-ground. Your €25 ticket (or €50 with four-course dinner) includes a drink before and after the show. Maurizio promises my readers a €5 discount if you buy direct from the box office and show this book (maximum 2 tickets per book; mid-April-June and Sept-Oct nightly at 21:30, July-Aug 3-4 nights per week at 21:30, bar opens 30 minutes before show, dinner starts at 20:00 and must be re-served in advance—in person or by email, box office open virtu-ally all day long, theater seats 500, facing Piazza Sant'Antonino in the old town, tel. 081-807-5525, www.teatrotasso.com, info@ teatrotasso.com).

Sleeping in Sorrento

Hotels here often charge the same for a room whether it has a view, balcony, or neither. At hotels that offer sea views, ask for a room *"con balcone, con vista sul mare"* (with a balcony, with a sea view). *"Tranquillo"* is taken as a request for a quieter room off the street.

Hotels listed are either near the train station and city center (where balconies overlook city streets) or on cliffside Via Capo (with sea-view balconies). Via Capo is a 20-minute walk—or short bus ride—from the station (for locations, see the map on page 1066).

You should have no trouble finding a room any time except in August, when the town is jammed with Italians and prices often rise above the regular high-season rates quoted here. Rates are soft in April and October, and tend to drop by about a third from November to March at the hotels that don't close for the winter. Always contact hotels directly, mention this book, and ask for their best rate. The two holdouts without air-conditioning (Désirée and Elios) are especially good values in April, May, September, and October, when hot temperatures are less likely.

Note: The spindly, more exotic, and more tranquil Amalfi Coast town of Positano (see next chapter) is also a good place to spend the night.

In the Town Center

$$$ **Hotel Antiche Mura,** with 50 rooms and four stars, is sophisticated, elegant, and plush. It offers all the amenities you could need, including an impressive breakfast buffet. Surrounded by lemon trees, the pool and sundeck are a peaceful oasis. Just a block off the main square, it's quieter than some central hotels because it's perched on the ledge of a dramatic ravine (small-windowed Db-€150, regular Db-€189, balcony Db-€250, Tb-€290, Qb-€340; Michele promises 15 percent off prevailing rates in 2014 if you reserve direct, mention this book, and pay cash; air-con, elevator, Wi-Fi, parking-€10/day, a block inland from Piazza Tasso at Via Fuorimura 7, tel. 081-807-3523, www.hotelantichemura.com, info@hotelantichemura.com).

$$$ **Plaza Sorrento** is a contemporary-feeling, upscale refuge in the very center of town (next door to Antiche Mura). Its 65 well-soundproofed rooms, arranged on color-coded floors, are mod and minimalist, and the rooftop swimming pool is inviting. Their "comfort" and "superior" rooms offer balconies for €20-40 more (standard Db-€180, elevator, air-con, free Wi-Fi, Via Fuorimura 3, tel. 081-877-1056, www.plazasorrento.com, info@plazasorrento.com).

$$ **Casa Astarita B&B** is a shining gem in the middle of

Sleep Code

(€1 = about $1.30, country code: 39)

S = Single, **D** = Double/Twin, **T** = Triple, **Q** = Quad, **b** = bathroom, **s** = shower only. Unless otherwise noted, credit cards are accepted, English is spoken, and breakfast is included. A local tax of €1 per person, per night (more for fancier hotels) is not included in these rates.

To help you sort easily through these listings, I've divided the accommodations into three categories based on the price for a standard double room with bath:

$$$ **Higher Priced**—Most rooms €140 or more.
$$ **Moderately Priced**—Most rooms between €85-140.
$ **Lower Priced**—Most rooms €85 or less.

Prices can change without notice; verify the hotel's current rates online or by email. For the best prices, always book direct.

town, with a crazy-quilt-tiled entryway. You'll find six bright, tranquil, air-conditioned rooms (three with little balconies) and a fully stocked communal fridge and sideboard for help-yourself breakfasts in the rustic-yet-elegant common room. Despite double-paned windows, pub noise can seep into the three front-facing, balcony rooms (Db-€115, Tb-€130, air-con, guest computer, free Wi-Fi, 50 yards past the cathedral on Corso Italia at #67, tel. 081-877-4906, www.casastarita.com, info@casastarita.com, Annamaria and Alfonso). If there's no one at reception, ask at Hotel Mignon (described next)—the same family runs both hotels.

$$ Hotel Mignon rents 24 soothing blue rooms with pretty, tiled public spaces in a quiet, central location near the cathedral (Sb-€80, Db-€105, big Db-€120, Tb-€130, these prices good with this book when you reserve direct, air-con, guest computer, free Wi-Fi, rooftop sundeck, some balconies but no views; from the cathedral, walk a block farther up Corso Italia and look for the hotel up a small gated lane to your left; Via Sersale 9, tel. 081-807-3824, www.sorrentohotelmignon.com, info@sorrentohotelmignon.com, Paolo).

$$ Hotel Palazzo Tasso is a simple, new place with a good location and 11 sleek, modern, reasonably priced rooms, though there's very little public space (Db-€90, up to €140 in peak season, air-con, small breakfast room on top floor, open all year, Via Santa Maria della Pietà 33, tel. 081-878-3579, www.palazzotasso.com, info@palazzotasso.com).

$$ Il Palazzo Starace B&B offers seven tidy rooms in a little alley off Corso Italia (opposite Hotel del Corso, listed earlier), one block from Piazza Tasso (Db-€90, nicer balcony Db-€110, five-bed family room-€150, 10 percent off with cash and this book in 2014, air-con, no elevator but a luggage dumbwaiter, free Wi-Fi; ring bell around corner from Via Santa Maria della Pietà 9, then climb 3 floors; tel. 081-807-2633, mobile 366-950-5377, www.palazzostarace.com, info@palazzostarace.com, Massimo).

$ Ulisse Deluxe Hostel is the best budget deal in town. This "hostel" is actually a hotel, with 56 marble-tiled rooms and elegant public areas, but also has two eight-bed dorm rooms (hotel: Db-€80, Tb-€120, Qb-€150; hostel: €25/bunk in single-sex dorm; both types of rooms include morning coffee, breakfast buffet-€7, these rates valid when you mention this book and reserve direct, air-con, elevator, free Wi-Fi, spa and pool use extra, parking-€10/day, Via del Mare 22, tel. 081-877-4753, www.ulissedeluxe.com, info@ulissedeluxe.com, Chiara). The hostel is a 5-minute walk from the old-town action, hiding beneath a big parking lot—go downhill along the right side of the lot to find the entrance.

$ Hotel Nice rents 29 simple, cramped, cheap rooms with high ceilings 100 yards in front of the train station on the noisy main drag. This last resort is worth considering only for its very handy-to-the-train-station location. Alfonso promises that you can have a quiet room—which is critical given the thin windows and busy location—if you request it with your booking email (Sb-€50, €60 in Aug; Db-€75, €85 in Aug; extra bed-€20; 10 percent discount when you book direct, mention this book, and pay cash; air-con, elevator, rooftop terrace, free Wi-Fi, closed Nov-March, Corso Italia 257, tel. 081-878-1650, www.hotelnice.it, info@hotel-nice.it).

At the East End of Town

This hotel is only a few minutes' walk beyond the town center. To reach it, head a block in front of the train station, turn right onto Corso Italia, then left down Via Capasso (which eventually winds right and becomes Via Califano).

$$$ Grand Hotel Ambasciatori is a sumptuous four-star hotel with 100 rooms, a cliffside setting, a sprawling garden, and a pool. This is Humphrey Bogart land, with plush public spaces, a relaxing stay-awhile ambience, and a free elevator to its "private beach"—actually a sundeck built out over the water (prices vary wildly, but in high season generally: viewless Db-€200, sea-view Db-€350, 10 percent discount with this book if you book direct, also check website for specials, elevator, air-con in summer, balconies in most rooms, pay guest computer, free Wi-Fi, parking-€20/day, closed Nov-March, Via Califano 18, tel. 081-878-2025, www.ambasciatorisorrento.com, ambasciatori@manniellohotels.com).

With a View on Via Capo

These cliffside hotels are outside of town, toward the cape of the peninsula (from the train station, go straight out Corso Italia, which turns into Via Capo). Once you're set up, commuting into town by bus or on foot is easy. Hotel Minerva is my favorite Sorrento splurge, while Hotel Désirée and Hotel Elios are super budget bets and have comparable views. If you're in Sorrento to stay put and luxuriate, especially with a car, these accommodations are perfect (although I'd rather luxuriate in Positano—see next chapter).

Getting to Via Capo: From the city center, it's a gradually uphill 15-minute walk (20 minutes from train station, last part is a bit steeper), a €20 taxi ride, or a cheap bus ride. If you're arriving with luggage, you can wait at the train station for one of the long-distance SITA buses (usually blue or green-and-white) that stop on Via Capo on their way to Massa Lubrense (about every 40 minutes; don't take the ones heading for Positano/Amalfi). Frequent Sorrento city buses leave from Piazza Tasso in the city center, a five-minute walk from the station (go down a block and turn left on Corso Italia; from far side of the piazza, look for red-and-white bus #A, about 3/hour). Tickets for either bus are sold at the station newsstand and tobacco shops (€2.50). Get off at the Hotel Belair stop for the hotels listed here. If you're headed to Via Capo after 19:30, when the center (and Piazza Tasso bus stop) is closed to traffic, catch the bus instead on Via degli Aranci (with your back to the station, wind left, up and around it; the bus stop is near Bar Paradise).

Getting from Via Capo into Town: Buses work great once you get the hang of them (and it's particularly gratifying to avoid the taxi racket). To reach downtown Sorrento from Via Capo, catch any bus heading downhill from Hotel Belair (3/hour, buses run all day and evening).

$$$ Hotel Minerva is like a sun-worshipper's temple. The road-level entrance (on a busy street) leads to an elevator that takes you to the fifth-floor reception. Getting off, you'll step onto a spectacular terrace with outrageous Mediterranean views. Bright common areas, a small rooftop swimming pool, and a cold-water Jacuzzi complement 60 large, tiled, colorful rooms with views, some with balconies (Db-€160, Tb-€200, these discounted prices promised through 2014 if you reserve direct and mention this book, can be cheaper in shoulder season, air-con, guest computer, free Wi-Fi, parking-€15/day, closed Nov-March, Via Capo 30, tel. 081-878-1011, www.minervasorrento.com, minerva@acampora.it).

$$$ Hotel La Tonnarella is an old-time Sorrentine villa turned boutique hotel, with several terraces, stylish tiles, and indifferent service. Eighteen of its 24 rooms have views of the sea (non-view Db-€140, "superior" sea-view or balcony Db-€180, "deluxe"

Db with view terrace-€205, exotic view suite with terrace-€320, email or check website for best rates, extra bed-€30, €30/person half-pension available, air-con, guest computer, free Wi-Fi, no elevator in building, parking-€5/day, small beach with private elevator access, closed Nov-March, Via Capo 31, tel. 081-878-1153, www.latonnarella.it, info@latonnarella.it).

$$ Albergo Settimo Cielo ("Seventh Heaven") is an old-fashioned, family-run cliff-hanger sitting 300 steps above Marina Grande. The reception is just off the waterfront side of the road, and the elevator passes down through four floors with 50 clean but spartan rooms—all with grand views, and many with balconies. The rooms feel dated for the price—you're paying for the views (Sb-€120, Db-€140, Tb-€180, Qb-€215, check website for specials, mention this book for 5 percent discount on these rates when reserving direct, air-con in summer, guest computer, free Wi-Fi, free parking with this book, inviting pool in the summer, sun terrace, closed Nov-March, Via Capo 27, tel. 081-878-1012, www.hotelsettimocielo.com, info@hotelsettimocielo.com; Giuseppe, sons Stefano and Massimo, and daughter Serena).

$$ Hotel Désirée is a modest affair, with reasonable rates, humbler vistas, and no traffic noise. The 22 basic rooms have high, ravine-facing or partial-sea views, and half come with balconies (all the same price). Most rooms have fans, and there's a fine rooftop sunning terrace and lovable cats. Owner Corinna (a committed environmentalist), daughter Cassandra, and receptionist Antonio serve an all-organic breakfast and are hugely helpful with tips on exploring the peninsula (Sb-€62, small Db-€77, Db-€87, Tb-€107, Qb-€117, lots of stairs with no elevator, guest computer, free Wi-Fi, laundry-€8, free parking, shares driveway and beach elevator with La Tonnarella, closed early Nov-mid-Dec and early Jan-Feb yet open for Christmas—rare for this area, Via Capo 31, tel. 081-878-1563, www.desireehotelsorrento.com, info@desireehotelsorrento.com).

$ Hotel Elios, warmly run by Gianna, is humble...much like a Sorrentine *nonna*'s house. It offers 14 simple but spacious rooms—12 with balconies and views—a panoramic sun terrace, and a quiet atmosphere. She serves a small continental breakfast, and you're welcome to use the kitchen and dining room (Sb-€55, Db-€85, Tb-€105, extra bed-€25, family rooms, cash only, free Wi-Fi in common areas, free parking, closed mid-Nov-mid-March, Via Capo 33, tel. 081-878-1812, www.hotelelios.it, info@hotelelios.it).

Eating in Sorrento

Gourmet Splurges Downtown

In a town proud to have no McDonald's, consider eating well for a few extra bucks. Both of these places are worthwhile splurges run by a hands-on boss with a passion for good food and exacting service. The first is gourmet and playful. The second is classic. Both are romantic. Be prepared to relax and stay a while.

Ristorante il Buco, once the cellar of an old monastery, is now a small, dressy restaurant that serves delightfully presented, playful, and creative modern Mediterranean dishes under a grand, rustic arch. Peppe and his staff love to explain exactly what's on the plate. The dashing team of cooks builds sophisticated dishes with an emphasis on seafood in a state-of-the-art kitchen. Peppe, who holds the only Michelin star in town, designs his menu around whatever's fresh. Reservations are often necessary to sit inside under their elegant vault (€18-24 pastas, €25-28 *secondi*, dinners run from about €50 plus wine, extravagant tasting *menus* for €60-100, 10 percent discount when you show this book, always a good vegetarian selection, Thu-Tue 12:30-14:30 & 19:30-22:30, closed Wed and Jan; just off Piazza Sant'Antonino—facing the basilica, go under the grand arch on the left and immediately enter the restaurant at II Rampa Marina Piccola 5; tel. 081-878-2354, www.ilbucoristorante.it).

L'Antica Trattoria serves more traditional cuisine from an inviting but pricey menu in a *romantico* candlelit ambience. The atmosphere is sedate and a bit old-school pretentious, with formally attired waiters. Run by the same family since 1930, the restaurant has a trellised garden outside and intimate nooks inside (perhaps too isolated for some, but ideal for small groups). Walk around the labyrinthine interior before you select a place to sit. Aldo and sons will take care of you while Vincenzo, the Joe Cocker-esque resident mandolin player, entertains. They offer several fixed-price meals (including a €20 two-course lunch and a €35 four-course dinner, 10 percent discount on these meals when you show this book), or you can order à la carte (€15-20 pastas, €26-29 *secondi*). Show this book for a free *limoncello* to cap the experience (always good vegetarian options, daily 12:00-23:30, closed Mon Nov-Feb, air-con, reservations smart, Via Padre R. Giuliani 33, tel. 081-807-1082).

Mid-Priced Restaurants Downtown

Inn Bufalito specializes in *mozzarella di bufala,* of course, but also features all things buffalo—steak, sausage, salami, carpaccio, buffalo-meat pasta sauce, and several different types of buffalo milk cheese. They serve more standard Italian food, too, but the buffalo theme is the reason to come. The smartly designed space has a modern, borderline-trendy, casual atmosphere and a fun indoor-outdoor vibe (€6-9 salads, €8-10 pastas, €9-14 *secondi*, no cover, don't miss the seasonal specialties on the blackboard, daily 12:00-24:00, closed Oct-April, Vico I Fuoro 21, tel. 081-365-6975).

Camera & Cucina is less traditional and more expensive, with mod atmosphere, a fine garden, and a creative menu that caters to trendy young locals (€9-13 pastas, €15-18 *secondi*, May-Nov daily 18:00-late, Dec-April open Fri-Sat only, reservations smart, Via Correale 19, 4-minute walk from Piazza Tasso, tel. 081-877-3686).

Chantecler's Trattoria, a hole-in-the-wall, family-run place on the narrow lane that leads to the cathedral, is particularly great for meat and vegetarian fare. They offer a €9 meal deal at lunch: your choice of one *primo* and one *secondo* (prices slightly higher at dinner—€7 pastas, €10 *secondi*, no cover charge, good vegetarian dishes, take out or eat in, Tue-Sun 12:00-15:00 & 19:00-24:00, closed Mon, Via Santa Maria della Pietà 38, tel. 081-807-5868, Luigi and family).

Ristorante Pizzeria da Gigino, lively and congested with a sprawling interior and tables spilling onto the street, makes huge, tasty Neapolitan-style pizzas in their wood-burning oven (€8-10 pizzas and pastas, €8-13 *secondi*, no cover charge, daily 12:00-24:00, closed Jan-Feb; just off Piazza Sant'Antonino—take first road to the left of Sant'Antonino as you face him, pass under the archway, and take the first left to Via degli Archi 15; tel. 081-878-1927, Antonino).

Meating, as its name implies, focuses on top-quality meats, from homemade sausages to giant steaks on a wood-fired grill. You'll find no seafood or pasta here, but there are a variety of vegetable dishes and delicious local cheeses, along with a reasonably priced selection of wine (€10-18 steaks, daily 18:00-24:00, Via Santa Maria della Pietà 20, tel. 081-878-2891).

With a Sea View: The **Foreigners' Club Restaurant** has some of the best sea views in town (with a sprawling terrace under breezy palms), live music nightly at 20:00 (May-mid-Oct), and passable meals. It's a good spot for dessert or an after-dinner *limoncello* (€9-14 pastas and pizzas, €12-23 *secondi*, daily, bar opens at 9:30, meals served 11:00-23:00, Via Luigi de Maio 35, tel. 081-877-3263). If you'd enjoy eating along the water (rather than just with a water view), see "Harborside in Marina Grande," later.

Cheap Eats Downtown

Pizza: **Pizzeria da Franco** seems to be Sorrento's favorite place for basic, casual pizza in a fun, untouristy atmosphere. There's nothing fancy about this place—just locals on benches eating hot sandwiches and great pizzas served on waxed paper in a square tin. It's packed to the rafters with a youthful crowd that doesn't mind the plastic cups (€6-8 pizzas and calzones, €5-7 salads, takeout possible, daily 8:00-2:00 in the morning, just across from Lemon Grove Garden on busy Corso Italia at #265, tel. 081-877-2066).

Kebabs: **Kebab Joint,** a little hole-in-the-wall, has a passionate following among eaters who appreciate Andrea's fresh bread, homemade sauces, and ethic of buying meat fresh each day (and closing when the supply is gone). This is your best non-Italian €5 meal in town. Choose beef or chicken—locals don't go for pork—and garnish as you like with fries and/or salad (nightly from 17:00, before the cathedral off Via Santa Maria della Pietà, at Vico il Traversa Pietà 23, tel. 081-807-4595).

Picnics: Get groceries at the **Decò supermarket** (Mon-Sat 8:30-20:30, Sun 9:30-13:00 & 16:30-20:00, Corso Italia 223).

Gelato: Near the train station, **Gelateria David** has many repeat customers (so many flavors, so little time). In 1957, Augusto Davide opened a *gelateria* in Sorrento, and his grandson, Mario, proudly carries on the tradition today (the gelato is still made on-site). Before choosing, sample *Profumi di Sorrento* (an explosive sorbet of mixed fruits), "Sorrento moon" (white almond with lemon zest), and lemon crème. They also serve sandwiches at fair prices (€2 cones, daily 9:00-24:00, shorter hours in spring and fall, closed Dec-Feb, a block below the train station at Via Marziale 19, tel. 081-807-3649). Mario also offers gelato-making classes for a behind-the-scenes look at Italy's favorite dessert (€10/person, 5-person minimum, 1 hour, call or email ahead to reserve, gelateria-david@yahoo.it). Don't mistake this place for the similarly named Gelateria Davide, in the town center—owned by a distant relative, but not as good.

At **Gelateria Primavera,** another local favorite, Antonio and Alberta whip up 70 exotic flavors—and still have time to make pastries for the pope (and everybody else—check out the photos). Try the *noci* (pronounced NO-chee) *di Sorrento,* made from local walnuts (€2.50 cones, daily 9:00-24:00, just west of Piazza Tasso at Corso Italia 142, tel. 081-807-3252).

Harborside in Marina Grande

For a decent dinner *con vista,* head down to either of these restaurants by Sorrento's small-boat harbor, Marina Grande. To get to Marina Grande, follow the directions from the cliffside square on the "Welcome to Sorrento" walk (described earlier). For a less scenic route, walk down Via del Mare, past the recommended Ulisse Deluxe Hostel, to the harbor. Either way, it's about a 15-minute stroll from downtown. You can also take bus #D from Piazza Tasso (€2.50).

Ristorante Delfino serves fish in big portions to hungry locals in a quiet and bright, Seattle-style pier restaurant. The cooking, service, and setting are all top-notch. The restaurant is lovingly run by Luisa, her brothers Andrea and Roberto, and her husband Antonio. Show this book for a free glass of *limoncello* to cap the meal. If you're here for lunch, take advantage of the sundeck—show this book to get an hour of relaxation and digestion on the lounge chairs (€11-16 pastas, €17-30 *secondi*, daily 11:30-15:30 & 18:30-23:00, closed Nov-March; at Marina Grande, facing the water, go all the way to the left and follow signs; tel. 081-878-2038).

Trattoria da Emilia, at the opposite end of the tranquil Marina Grande waterfront, is considerably more rustic, less expensive, and good for straightforward, typical Sorrentine home-cooking, including fresh fish, lots of fried seafood, and *gnocchi di mamma*—potato dumplings with meat sauce, basil, and mozzarella (€7-12 pastas, €11-15 *secondi*, daily 12:15-15:00 & 19:00-22:30, Sept-Oct closed Tue, closed Nov-Feb, no reservations taken, indoor and outdoor seating, tel. 081-807-2720).

On Via Capo

Verde Mare is the locals' pick for a reasonably priced meal (Thu-Tue 12:30-14:45 & 19:00-23:30, closed Wed, 300 yards uphill from La Tonnarella and other recommended hotels—see map on page 1066, tel. 081-878-2589).

Sorrento Connections

It's impressively fast to zip by boat from Sorrento to most coastal towns and islands during the summer, when there are many more departures. In fact, it's quicker and easier for residents to get around by fast boat than by car or train (see "By Boat," later, and the map on page 1063).

By Train and Bus

From Sorrento to Naples, Pompeii, and Herculaneum by Circumvesuviana Train: This commuter train runs twice hourly between Naples and Sorrento (www.vesuviana.it). From Sorrento, it's about 30 minutes to Pompeii, 50 minutes to Herculaneum (€2.20 one-way for either trip), and 70 minutes to Naples (€4.20 one-way). There's no round-trip discount, and the €12 all-day pass is generally not worthwhile (except on weekends, when it's called a "weekend pass" and is roughly half-price—€6.50). If there's a line at the train station, you can also buy tickets at the appropriately named Snack Bar (across from the main ticket office) or downstairs at the newsstand.

When returning to Naples' Centrale Station on the Circumvesuviana, get off at the next-to-the-last station, Garibaldi (Centrale Station is just up the escalator). Bonus: When returning from Sorrento, your Circumvesuviana ticket includes travel on the Naples Metro or bus system within three hours of validation (no need to validate again). The trip is also covered by the Campania ArteCard—see page 1000. The schedule is printed in the free *Surrentum* magazine (available at TI). For more information on the Circumvesuviana and theft precautions, see "Getting Around the Region" on page 1036 of the Naples chapter. Note that the risk of theft is mostly limited to suburban Naples, but can be a problem anywhere. Going between Sorrento and Pompeii or Herculaneum is generally safer.

From Sorrento to Naples Airport: Six Curreri buses run daily to and from the airport; confirm the schedule at the TI (€10, pay driver, daily at 6:30, 8:30, 10:30, 12:00, 14:00, and 16:30, likely 2 additional departures May-Oct, 1.5 hours, departs from in front of train station, tel. 081-801-5420, www.curreriviaggi.it). Although it's possible to connect through Naples (either take a jet boat/hydrofoil to Naples, then cross the street to catch the airport bus on Piazza Municipio; or ride the Circumvesuviana to Naples' Centrale Station to catch the airport bus from Piazza Garibaldi), the direct bus is more convenient and reliable.

From Sorrento to the Amalfi Coast: See page 1100.

From Sorrento to Rome: Most people ride the Circumvesuviana 70 minutes to Naples, then catch the Frecciarossa express train to Rome. However, the Sorrento-Rome bus is direct, cheaper, and all on one ticket—although the departure times can be inconvenient. Buses leave Sorrento's train station and arrive at Rome's Tiburtina station (€18, Mon-Sat at 6:00 and 17:00, Sun at 17:00, offseason at 6:00 only, 4 hours; buy tickets at www.marozzivt.it—in Italian only, at some travel agencies, or on board for a €3 surcharge; tel. 080-579-0111). A Curreri bus makes the trip as well, but only in the summer (departs Mon-Sat at 6:30, 4 hours, tel. 081-801-5420, www.curreriviaggi.it).

By Boat

The number of boats that run per day varies according to the season. The frequency indicated here is for roughly mid-May through mid-October, with more boats per day in the peak of summer and fewer off-season. Check all schedules with the TI, your hotel, or online (use the individual boat company websites—see below—or visit www.capritourism.com, select English, and click on "Shipping timetable"). The Caremar line, a subsidized state-run ferry company, takes cars, offers fewer departures, and is just a bit slower—but cheaper—than the hydrofoil. All of the boats take several hundred people each—and frequently fill up. Boat tickets are sold only at the port.

From Sorrento to Capri: Boats run at least hourly. Your options include a fast **ferry** (*traghetto* or *nave veloce*, 4/day, 25 minutes, €15, run by Caremar, tel. 081-807-3077, www.caremar.it) or a slightly faster, pricier **hydrofoil** (*aliscafi*, up to 20/day, 20 minutes, €17-18, run by Gescab, tel. 081-807-1812, www.gescab.it). To minimize the crowds on Capri, it's best to buy your ticket at 8:00 and take the 8:25 hydrofoil (if you miss it, try to depart by 9:30 at the very latest). These early boats can be jammed, but it's worth it once you reach the island.

From Sorrento to Other Points: Naples (6/day, departs roughly every 2 hours, 35 minutes, €12-13, starting at 7:20), **Positano** (mid-April-mid-Oct only, 2-4/day, 35 minutes, €16), **Amalfi** (mid-April-mid-Oct only, 2-4/day, 1.25 hours, €21).

Getting to Sorrento's Port: To walk from Sorrento's Piazza Tasso to Marina Piccola (the port), you have three options: Go down the stairs near the statue's left side (about 10 minutes); take the slightly longer road (with fewer stairs) that passes by the TI and Foreigners' Club; or find the Villa Comunale public park (see the self-guided tour, earlier) and take the stairs or elevator (€1) down from there. You also can take a bus: From Piazza Sant'Antonino, catch a red-and-white bus #B or #C (3/hour, €1, buy ticket at tobacco shop and specify that you're going to the *porto*) or the little blue bus (4/hour, €1, buy ticket from driver).

Capri

Capri was made famous as the vacation hideaway of Roman emperors Augustus and Tiberius. In the 19th century, it was the

haunt of Romantic Age aristocrats on their Grand Tour of Europe. Later it was briefly a refuge for Europe's artsy gay community: Oscar Wilde, D. H. Lawrence, and company hung out here back when being gay could land you in jail...or worse. And these days, the island is a world-class tourist trap, packed with gawky, nametag-wearing visitors searching for the rich and famous—and finding only their prices.

The "Island of Dreams" is a zoo in July and August—overrun with tacky, low-grade group tourism at its worst. At other times of year, though still crowded, it can provide a relaxing and scenic break from the cultural gauntlet of Italy.

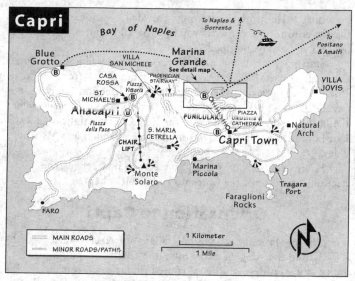

Planning Your Time

This is the best see-everything-in-a-day plan from Naples or Sorrento: Take an early hydrofoil to Capri (from Sorrento, buy ticket at 8:00, boat leaves at 8:25 and arrives at 8:45—smart). Go directly by boat to the Blue Grotto. Instead of taking the boat back, catch a bus from the grotto to Anacapri, which has two or three hours' worth of sightseeing. In Anacapri, see the town, ride the chairlift to Monte Solaro and back (or hike down), stroll out from the base of the chairlift to Villa San Michele for the view, and eat lunch. Afterward, catch a bus to Capri town, which is worth at least a half-hour. Finally, ride the funicular from Capri town down to the harbor and laze on the free beach or wander the yacht harbor while waiting for your boat.

If you're heading to Capri specifically to see the Blue Grotto, be sure to check the weather and sea conditions. If the tide is too high or the water too rough, the grotto can be closed. Ask the TI or your hotelier before going.

Efficient travelers can see Capri on the way between destinations: Sail from Sorrento, check your bag at the harbor, see Capri, and take a boat directly from there to Naples (or vice versa).

If you buy a one-way ticket to Capri (there's no round-trip discount anyway), you'll have maximum schedule flexibility and can take any convenient hydrofoil or ferry back. (Check times for the last return crossing upon arrival with any TI on Capri, or at www.capritourism.com; the last return trips usually leave between 18:30 and 19:30.) During July and August, however, it's wise to get a round-trip boat ticket with a late return time (ensuring you a spot on a boat at the time they're most crowded)—you can always use the ticket to return earlier if you like. Be 20 minutes early for the boat, or you can be bumped.

Starting your day as early as reasonably possible is key to an enjoyable trip to Capri. Day-trippers come down from as far as Rome, creating a daily rush hour in each direction (arriving between 10:00-11:00, leaving around 17:00). If you arrive before them, the entire trip to and into the Blue Grotto might take just a half-hour; arrive later and you might face as much as a two-hour delay.

For instructions on getting to Capri by boat, check the "Connections" sections of the Sorrento and Naples chapters.

Orientation to Capri

First thing—pronounce it right: Italians say KAH-pree, not kah-PREE like the song or the pants. The island is small—just four miles by two miles—and is separated from the Sorrentine Peninsula by a narrow strait. Home to 13,000 people, there are only two towns to speak of: Capri and Anacapri. The island also has some scant Roman ruins and a few interesting churches and villas. But its chief attraction is its famous Blue Grotto, and its best activity is the chairlift from Anacapri up the island's Monte Solaro.

Tourist Information

Capri's efficient English-speaking tourist information office has branches in Marina Grande, Capri town, and Anacapri. Their well-organized website has schedules and practical information in English (www.capritourism.com).

The **Marina Grande TI** is by the Motoscafisti Capri tour boat dock (May-Sept Mon-Sat 9:30-13:30 & 15:30-18:45, Sun 9:00-15:00; Oct-April generally daily 9:00-15:00; pick up free map—or the better €1 map if you'll be venturing to the outskirts of Capri town or Anacapri, tel. 081-837-0634).

The **Capri town TI** fills a closet under the bell tower on Piazza Umberto and is less crowded than its sister at the port (Mon-Sat 9:30-13:30 & 15:30-18:45, Sun 9:00-15:00, shorter hours off-season, WC and baggage storage downstairs behind TI, tel. 081-837-0686).

The tiny **Anacapri TI** is at Via Orlandi 59 (Mon-Sat 9:00-15:00, closed Sun, may be closed Nov-Easter, tel. 081-837-1524).

Arrival in Capri

Approaching Capri: Get oriented on the boat before you dock, as you near the harbor with the island spread out before you. The port is a small community of its own, called **Marina Grande,** con-

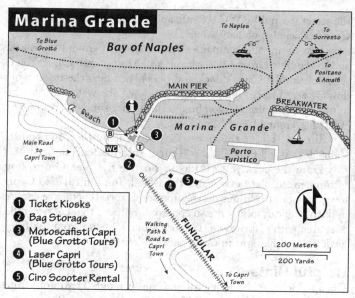

Marina Grande

Bay of Naples

To Blue Grotto

To Naples

To Sorrento

To Positano & Amalfi

MAIN PIER

BREAKWATER

Marina Grande

Beach

Main Road to Capri Town

Porto Turistico

1 **Ticket Kiosks**
2 **Bag Storage**
3 **Motoscafisti Capri (Blue Grotto Tours)**
4 **Laser Capri (Blue Grotto Tours)**
5 **Ciro Scooter Rental**

Walking Path & Road to Capri Town

FUNICULAR

To Capri Town

200 Meters
200 Yards

nected by a funicular and buses to the rest of the island. **Capri town** fills the ridge high above the harbor. The ruins of Emperor Tiberius' palace, **Villa Jovis,** cap the peak on the left. To the right, the dramatic *"Mamma mia!"* road arcs around the highest mountain on the island **(Monte Solaro),** leading up to **Anacapri** (the island's second town, just out of sight). Notice the old zigzag steps below that road. Until 1874, this was the only connection between Capri and Anacapri. (Though it's quite old, it's nowhere near as old as its nickname, "The Phoenician Stairway," implies.) The white house on the ridge above the zigzags is **Villa San Michele** (where you can go later for a grand view of boats like the one you're on now).

Arrival at Marina Grande: Upon arrival, get your bearings. Find the base of the **funicular railway** (signed *funicolare*) that runs up to Capri town, and stand facing it, with your back to the water.

The fourth little clothing-and-souvenir shop to the right of the funicular provides **baggage storage** (look inside for *left luggage* sign on far back wall, €3/bag, daily 9:00-18:00, tel. 081-837-4575). If it's closed, your best option is at the upper funicular station in Capri town (bag storage near public WCs, €3/bag, daily 7:00-20:00; be aware that you may have to pay extra to take big bags up the funicular).

To your right is a stand of ticket windows with counters for **funicular and bus tickets** (you can't buy tickets at the funicular itself) and for return **boat tickets** to Naples and Sorrento. Just beyond these is the **stop for buses** to the rest of the island. Across the street is a **public WC** (€0.50), and a little farther on is Marina Grande's pebbly public beach.

Two competing companies offer **boat trips** around the island and to the Blue Grotto: Laser Capri and Motoscafisti Capri. You'll see Motoscafisti Capri's dock and ticket shed near the ticket windows; Laser Capri's office is halfway down the waterfront to the left at Via Cristoforo Colombo 69. Both offer similar services (see "Getting Around Capri," later).

The **TI** is near the ticket kiosks, right by the Motoscafisti Capri dock (for TI details, see "Tourist Information," earlier).

From the port, you can take a boat to the Blue Grotto (my recommended plan) or around the island, the funicular to Capri town, or a bus to various destinations on Capri. If you have energy to burn, you can follow the steep paved footpath that connects the port area with Capri town. It starts a block inland from the ferry dock (follow the signs to *Capri centro*; allow 30 minutes).

Helpful Hints

Cheap Tricks: A cheap day trip to Capri is tough. Hydrofoils from Sorrento or Naples cost €15 to €20 each way, and Blue Grotto tickets (plus boat transportation) come to €26—that's €56-66 per person. Taking the slightly slower Caremar ferry to Capri instead of the hydrofoil saves about €3-5 per person each way, and using the bus to the Blue Grotto saves about €6 (see "Blue Grotto," later). After the boats stop running, anyone willing to swim the few yards in from the little dock can see the Blue Grotto for free (albeit illegally).

Best Real Hike: Serious hikers love the peaceful and scenic three-hour Fortress Hike, which takes you entirely away from the tourists. You'll walk under ruined forts along the rugged coast, from the Blue Grotto to the *faro* (lighthouse). From there, you can take a bus back to Anacapri (3/hour). The tourist office has a fine map/brochure.

Free Beach: Marina Grande has a free pebbly beach. You can get a shower at the bar for €1.

Local Guides: Anna Bilardi Leva lives on Capri and is licensed to guide both on the island, and elsewhere around Sorrento (€140/half-day, €220/day, mobile 339-712-7416, www.capritourinformation.com, annaleva@hotmail.it). **Giovanna Donadio** is a good tour guide for Sorrento, Amalfi, and Capri (€100/half-day, €160/day, same price for any size group, mobile 338-466-0114, giovanna_dona@hotmail.com). Naples-based **Pina Esposito** also does tours of the entire region (see listing on page 1005).

Getting Around Capri

By Bus and Funicular: Tickets for the island's buses and funicular cost €1.80 per ride or €8.60 for an all-day pass (includes deposit—turn it in at the end of the day to get €1 back). Single-ride tickets are available at newsstands, tobacco shops, official ticket offices, or from the driver. All-day passes and funicular tickets are usually sold only at official ticket offices. The all-day pass pays for itself if you take at least five rides on the buses and funicular (possible if you go by bus to the Blue Grotto and spend some time in both towns).

Schedules are clearly posted at all bus stations. Buses from the port to Capri town, and from Capri town to Anacapri, are frequent (4/hour, 10 minutes). The direct bus between the port to Anacapri runs less often (every 30-40 minutes, 25 minutes). From Anacapri, branch bus lines run to the parking lot above the Blue Grotto and to the Faro lighthouse. Buses are teeny (because of the island's narrow roads) and often packed. At most stops, you'll see ranks for passengers to line up in. Drivers can push a button to change the bus's display to *completo* (full), in which case you just have to wait for the next one.

By Taxi: Taxis have fixed rates (Marina Grande to Capri town-€15; Marina Grande to Anacapri-€20 for 3 people, €2/additional person). You can hire a taxi for about €70 per hour—negotiate.

Scooter Rental: If you are experienced at riding a scooter, this is the perfect way to have the run of the island. (For novice riders, Capri's steep and narrow roads aren't a good place to start.) **Ciro** proudly rents bright-yellow scooters with 50cc engines—strong enough to haul couples. Rental includes a map and instructions with parking tips and other helpful information (€15/hour, €55/day, €5 discount with this book for 2 hours or more in 2014; includes helmet, gas, and insurance; daily April-Oct 9:30-19:00, may open in good weather off-season, look for the Ferrari logo at Via Don Giobbe Ruocco 55, Marina Grande, tel. 081-837-8018, mobile 338-360-6918, www.capriscooter.com).

Boat Trips Around the Island: Both **Laser Capri** and **Motoscafisti Capri** run quick one-hour trips that circle the island, passing stunning cliffs, caves, and views that most miss when they go only to the Blue Grotto (€16-17; see contact details under "Blue Grotto," later). With both companies, you can combine the boat trip with a visit to the Blue Grotto at no extra charge (figure another hour). As the trip just to the grotto already costs €13.50, the island circle is well worth the extra €3 if you have an hour to spare (boats leave daily from 9:00 until 13:00 or possibly later—whenever Blue Grotto rowboats stop running).

Sights in Capri

Capri Town

This is a cute but extremely clogged and touristy shopping town. It's worth a brief visit, including the Giardini Augusto, before moving on to more interesting parts of the island.

The funicular drops you just around the corner from Piazza Umberto, the town's main square. With your back to the funicular, the bus stop is 50 yards straight ahead down Via Roma. You'll find the **TI** under the bell tower on Piazza Umberto (for TI details, see "Tourist Information," earlier). The footpath to the port starts just behind the TI, near the baggage storage (follow signs to *Il Porto*, 15-minute walk).

Capri town's multi-domed Baroque **cathedral,** which faces the square, is worth a quick look. (Its multicolored marble floor at the altar was scavenged from the Emperor Tiberius's villa in the 19th century.)

To the left of City Hall (Municipio, lowest corner), a lane leads into the medieval part of town, which has plenty of eateries and is the starting point for the walk to Villa Jovis.

The lane to the left of the cathedral (past Bar Tiberio, under the wide arch) is a fashionable shopping strip that's justifiably been dubbed "Rodeo Drive" by residents. Walk a few minutes down Rodeo Drive (past Gelateria Buonocore at #35, with its tempting fresh waffle cones) to Quisisana Hotel, the island's top old-time hotel. From there, head left for fancy shops and villas, and right for gardens and views. Downhill and to the right, a five-minute walk leads to a lovely public garden, Giardini Augusto, with superb views of the back side of the island (€1, April-Oct daily 9:00-19:30, May and early Nov daily 9:00-17:30, mid-Nov-March shorter hours and free admission, no picnicking).

Villa Jovis and the Emperor's Capri

Even before becoming emperor, Augustus loved Capri so much that he traded the family-owned Isle of Ischia to the (then-independent) Neapolitans in exchange for making Capri his personal property. Emperor Tiberius spent a decade here, A.D. 26-37. (Some figure he did so in order to escape being assassinated in Rome.)

Emperor Tiberius' ruined villa, Villa Jovis, is a scenic 45-minute hike from Capri town. You won't find any statues or mosaics here—just an evocative, ruined complex of terraces fitting a rocky perch over a sheer drop to the sea...and a lovely view. You can make out a large water reservoir for baths, the foundations of servants' quarters, and Tiberius' private apartments (fragments of marble flooring still survive). The ruined lighthouse dates from the Middle Ages.

Cost and Hours: €2, nearly daily 11:00-15:00, closed Tue from 1st to 15th of each month and closed Sun from the 16th to the end of each month, tel. 081-837-4549.

▲▲Blue Grotto

Three thousand tourists a day spend a couple of hours visiting Capri's Blue Grotto (Grotta Azzurra). I did—early (when the light is

best), without the frustration of crowds, and with choppy waves nearly making entrance impossible...and it was great.

The actual cave experience isn't much: a five-minute dinghy ride through a three-foot-high entry hole to reach a 60-yard-long cave, where the sun reflects brilliantly blue on its limestone bottom. But the experience—getting there, getting in, and getting back—is a scenic hoot. You get a fast ride on a 30-foot boat partway around the gorgeous island; along the way you see bird life and dramatic limestone cliffs with scant narration. You'll understand why Roman emperors appreciated the invulnerability of the island—it's surrounded by cliffs, with only one good access point, and therefore easy to defend.

Just outside the grotto, your boat idles as you pile into eight-foot dinghies that hold up to four passengers each. Next, you'll be taken to a floating ticket counter and asked to pass the €12.50 grotto entry fee over the side. From there, your ruffian rower will elbow his way to the tiny hole, then pull fast and hard on the cable at the low point of the swells to squeeze you into the grotto (keep your head down and hands in the boat). Then your man rows you around, spouting off a few descriptive lines and singing "O Sole Mio." Depending upon the strength of the sunshine that day, the blue light inside can be brilliant.

The grotto was actually an ancient Roman *nymphaeum*—a retreat for romantic hanky-panky. Many believe that, in its day, a tunnel led here directly from the palace, and that the grotto experience was enlivened by statues of Poseidon and company, placed half-underwater as if emerging from the sea. It was ancient Romans who smoothed out the entry hole that's still used to this day.

Sometimes, your boatman will try to extort an extra tip out of you before taking you back outside to your big boat (€1 is enough, but you don't need to pay a penny...you've already paid plenty). If you don't want to return by boat, ask your boatman to let you off at the little dock, where stairs lead up to a café and the Blue Grotto bus stop.

Cost: The €12.50 entry fee (separate from the €13.50 ride from Marina Grande) includes €8.50 for the rowboat service plus €4 to cover the admission to the grotto itself. Though signs forbid it, some people dive in for free from the little dock next to the grotto entrance after the boats stop running—a magical experience and a favorite among locals.

Timing: When the waves or high tide make entering dangerous, the boats don't go in—the grotto can close without notice, sending tourists (flush with anticipation) home without a chance to squeeze through the little hole. (If this happens to you, consider the one-hour boat ride around the island offered by both companies.)

If you're coming from Capri's port (Marina Grande), allow 1-3 hours for the entire visit, depending on the chaos at the caves. Going with the first trip will get you there at the same time as the boatmen in their dinghies—who hitch a ride behind your boat—resulting in less chaos and a shorter wait at the entry point.

Getting There: You can either take the boat directly from Marina Grande, as most people do, or save money by taking the bus via Anacapri.

By Boat from Marina Grande: Two companies make the boat trip from different parts of Marina Grande—Laser Capri and Motoscafisti Capri (€13.50 round-trip with either company, no discount for one-way; Motoscafista Capri—tel. 081-837-7714, www.motoscafisticapri.com; Laser Capri—tel. 081-837-5208, www.lasercapri.com). The first boats depart Marina Grande at 9:00, and they continue at least until 13:00—or often later, depending on when the rowboats stop running (likely 17:00 in summer, but earlier off-season).

By Bus via Anacapri: If you're on a budget, you can take the bus from Anacapri to the grotto (rather than a boat from Marina Grande). You'll save about €6 (assuming you take the direct Marina Grande-Anacapri bus and then change to the Anacapri-Blue Grotto bus), lose time, and see a beautiful, calmer side of the island.

Anacapri-Blue Grotto buses (roughly 3/hour, Nov-March 1-2/hour, 10 minutes) depart only from the Anacapri bus station at Piazza della Pace (not from the bus stop at Piazza Vittoria 200 yards away, which is more popular with tourists). If you're coming from Marina Grande or Capri town and want to transfer to the Blue Grotto buses, don't get off when the driver announces "Anacapri." Instead, ride one more stop to Piazza della Pace. If in doubt, ask the driver or a local.

Getting Back from the Blue Grotto: You can either take the boat back, or ask your boatman to drop you off on the small dock next to the grotto entrance, from where you climb up the stairs to the stop for the bus to Anacapri (if you came by boat, you'll still have to pay the full €13.50 round-trip boat fare).

Anacapri

Capri's second town has two or three hours' worth of interesting sights. Though higher up on the island ("ana" means "upper" in Greek), there are no sea views at street level in the town center.

When visiting Anacapri by bus, note that there are two stops: the bus stop by the cemetery (called Piazza della Pace—pronounced "PAH-chay"—though locals may call it by its former name, Piazza del Cimitero), and the more central Piazza Vittoria stop, 200 yards away, by the base of the chairlift to Monte Solaro. It doesn't matter which stop you get off at. But when leaving Anacapri for Capri town or Marina Grande, buses can be packed. Your best chance of getting a seat is to catch the bus from Piazza della Pace, one stop before where most people get on (stand at the street corner under the concrete awning).

Regardless of where you get off, make your way to Via Orlandi, Anacapri's pedestrianized main street. From Piazza della Pace, reach it via the crosswalk and then the small lane called Via Filietto; from Piazza Vittoria, head to the right of the statue of "Anacapri." Anacapri's tiny **TI** is at Via Orlandi 59 (Mon-Sat 9:00-15:00, closed Sun, may be closed Nov-Easter, tel. 081-837 1524, www.capritourism.com).

To see the town, walk on this street for 10 minutes or so. Signs suggest a quick circuit that links the Casa Rossa, St. Michael's Church, and peaceful side streets. You'll also find a number of shops and eateries, including a couple of good choices for quick, inexpensive pizza, *panini*, and other goodies: **Sciué Sciué** (same price for informal seating or take-away, no cover charge, daily April-Oct, closed Nov-March, near the TI at #73, tel. 081-837-2068) and **Pizza e Pasta** (take-away only, daily March-Nov, closed Dec-Feb, just before the church at #157, tel. 328-623-8460).

▲Villa San Michele

This is the 19th-century mansion of Axel Munthe, Capri's grand personality, an idealistic Swedish doctor who lived here until 1943 and whose services to the Swedish royal family brought him into contact with high society. At the very least, walk the path from Piazza Victoria past the villa to a superb, free viewpoint over Capri town and Marina Grande. Paying to enter the villa lets you see a few rooms with a well-done but ho-hum exhibit on Munthe, plus a delightful and extensive garden with a chapel, Olivetum (a tiny museum of native birds and bugs), and a view that's slightly better than the free one outside. A café (also with a view) serves €6 sandwiches. Walking to the villa from Piazza Victoria, you pass the deluxe Capri Palace Hotel—venture in if you can get past the treacherously eye-catching swimming pool windows.

Cost and Hours: €7, May-Sept daily 9:00-18:00, closes earlier Oct-April, last entry 20 minutes before closing, tel. 081-837-1401, www.villasanmichele.eu.

Casa Rossa (Red House)

This "Pompeiian-red," eccentric home, a hodgepodge of architectural styles, is the former residence of John Clay MacKowen, a Louisiana doctor and ex-Confederate officer who moved to Capri in the 1870s and married a local girl. (MacKowen and Axel Munthe loathed each other, and even tried to challenge each other to a duel.) Its small collection of 19th-century paintings of scenes from around the island recalls a time before mass tourism. Don't miss the second floor, with its four ancient, sea-worn statues, which were recovered from the depths of the Blue Grotto in the 1960s and '70s.

Cost and Hours: €3; free with ticket stub from Blue Grotto, Villa San Michele, or Monte Solaro chairlift; June-Sept Tue-Sun 10:00-13:30 & 17:30-20:00, closed Mon; April-May Tue-Sun 10:00-17:00, closed Mon; Oct Tue-Sun 10:00-16:00, closed Mon; closed Nov-March, Via Orlandi 78, tel. 081-838-2193.

▲Church of San Michele

This Baroque church in the village center has a remarkable majolica floor showing paradise on earth in a classic 18th-century Neapolitan style. The entire floor is ornately tiled, featuring an angel (with flaming sword) driving Adam and Eve from paradise. The devil is wrapped around the trunk of a beautiful tree. The animals—happily ignoring this momentous event—all have human expressions. For the best view, climb the spiral stairs from the postcard desk. Services are held only during the first two weeks of Advent, when the church is closed to visitors.

Cost and Hours: €2, daily April-Oct 9:00-19:00, Nov and mid-Dec-March 10:00-14:00, closed late Nov-mid Dec, in town center just off Via Orlandi—look for signs for *San Michele*, tel. 081-837-2396, www.chiesa-san-michele.com.

Faro

The lighthouse is a favorite place to enjoy the sunset, with a private beach, pool, small restaurants, and a few fishermen. Reach it by bus from Anacapri (3/hour, departs from Piazza della Pace stop).

▲▲Chairlift up to Monte Solaro

From Anacapri, ride the chairlift *(seggiovia)* to the 1,900-foot summit of Monte Solaro for a commanding view of the Bay of Naples.

Work on your tan as you float over hazelnut, walnut, chestnut, apricot, peach, kiwi, and fig trees, past a montage of tourists (mostly from cruise ships; when the grotto is closed—as it often is—they bring passengers here instead). Prospective smoochers should know that the lift seats are all single. As you ascend, consider how Capri's real estate has been priced out of the locals' reach. The ride takes 13 minutes each way, and you'll want at least 30 minutes on top, where there are picnic benches and a cafe with WCs.

Cost and Hours: €7.50 one-way, €10 round-trip, daily June-Oct 9:30-17:00, last run down at 17:30, closes earlier Nov-May, confirm schedule with TI, departs from top of the steps in Piazza Vittoria—the first Anacapri bus stop, tel. 081-837-1428, www.seggioviamontesolaro.it.

At the Summit: You'll enjoy the best panorama possible: lush cliffs busy with seagulls enjoying the ideal nesting spot. Find the Faraglioni Rocks—with tour boats squeezing through every few minutes—which are an icon of the island. The pink building nearest the rocks was an American R&R base during World War II. Eisenhower and Churchill met here. On the peak closest to Cape Sorrento, you can see the distant ruins of the Emperor Tiberius' palace, Villa Jovis. Pipes from the Sorrento Peninsula bring water to Capri (demand for fresh water here long ago exceeded the supply provided by the island's three natural springs). The Galli Islands mark the Amalfi Coast in the distance. Cross the bar terrace for views of Mount Vesuvius and Naples.

Hiking Down: A highlight for hardy walkers (provided you have strong knees and good shoes) is the 40-minute downhill hike from the top of Monte Solaro, through lush vegetation and ever-changing views, past the 14th-century Chapel of Santa Maria Cetrella (at the trail's only intersection, it's a 10-minute detour to the right), and back into Anacapri. The trail starts downstairs, past the WCs (last chance). Down two more flights of stairs, look for the sign to *Anacapri e Cetrella*—you're on your way. While the trail is well-established, you'll encounter plenty of uneven steps, loose rocks, and few signs.

Capri Connections

From Capri's Marina Grande by Boat to: Sorrento (fast ferry: 4/day, 25 minutes, €13; hydrofoil: up to 20/day, 20 minutes, €16-17), **Naples** (1-2/hour, hydrofoil: 50 minutes, €18-19; ferries: 60-80 minutes, €11-16); **Positano** (mid-April-mid-Oct, 2-4/day, 30-60 minutes, €17-19; less off-season), **Amalfi** (mid-April-mid-Oct, 1/day, 1.5 hours, €19). Confirm the schedule carefully at TIs or www.capritourism.org—last boats usually leave between 18:00 and 20:10.

AMALFI COAST AND PAESTUM

With its stunning scenery, hill- and harbor-hugging towns, and historic ruins, Amalfi is Italy's coast with the most. The bus trip from Sorrento to Salerno along the breathtaking Amalfi Coast is one of the world's great bus rides. It will leave your mouth open and your camera's memory card full. You'll gain respect for the 19th-century Italian engineers who built the roads—and even more respect for the 21st-century bus drivers who drive it. Cantilevered garages, hotels, and villas cling to the vertical terrain, and beautiful sandy coves tease from far below and out of reach. As you hyperventilate, notice how the Mediterranean, a sheer 500-foot drop below, really twinkles. All this beautiful scenery apparently inspires local Romeos and Juliets, with the latex evidence of late-night romantic encounters littering the roadside turnouts. Over the centuries, the spectacular scenery and climate have been a siren call for the rich and famous, luring Roman emperor Tiberius, Richard Wagner, Sophia Loren, Gore Vidal, and others to the Amalfi Coast's special brand of *la dolce vita*.

Amalfi Coast towns are pretty, but they're generally touristy, congested, overpriced, and a long hike above tiny, pebbly beaches. (For that reason, many visitors prefer side-tripping in from Sorrento.) Most beaches here are private, and access is expensive. Check and understand your bills in this greedy region.

Planning Your Time

On a quick visit, use Sorrento (described in the previous chapter) as your home base and do the Amalfi Coast as a day trip. But for a small-town vacation from your vacation, spend a few more days on the coast, perhaps sleeping in Positano or Amalfi town.

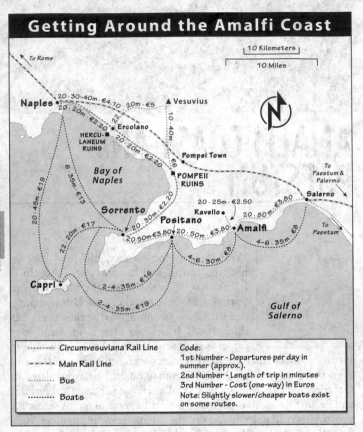

Getting Around the Amalfi Coast

To Rome

10 Kilometers

10 Miles

Naples
20·30-40m·€4.10   20·20m·€5
20·20m·€2.20   ▲ Vesuvius
Ercolano
HERCU-
LANEUM
RUINS
20·20m·€2.20
Pompei Town
■ POMPEII
RUINS

*Bay of
Naples*

6·35m·€13

20·45m·€19

22·20m·€17

Sorrento
20·30m·€2.20
20·50m·€3.80   20·50m·€3.80
Positano

20·25m·€2.50
Ravello
20·80m·€3.80
Amalfi
4-6·35m·€6

4-6·30m·€6

To
Paestum &
Palermo

Salerno

To
Paestum

Capri
2-4·35m·€16
2-4·35m·€19

*Gulf of
Salerno*

········· Circumvesuviana Rail Line
─·─·─ Main Rail Line
········· Bus
········· Boats

Code:
1st Number - Departures per day in
summer (approx.).
2nd Number - Length of trip in minutes
3rd Number - Cost (one-way) in Euros
Note: Slightly slower/cheaper boats exist
on some routes.

Trying to decide between staying in Sorrento, Positano, or Amalfi? Sorrento is the largest of the three, with useful services and the best transportation connections and accommodations. Positano is the most chic and picturesque, with a decent beach, but tiny and expensive. The town of Amalfi has the most actual sights and the best hiking opportunities, but lacks good-value places to stay.

Getting Around the Amalfi Coast

The real thrill here is the scenic Amalfi drive. This is treacherous stuff—even if you have a car, you may want to take the bus or hire a taxi. Brave souls enjoy seeing the coast by scooter or motorbike (rent in Sorrento). The most logical springboard for this trip is Sorrento, but Positano and Amalfi work, too.

Below, I've outlined your options by bus, boat, and taxi. Many travelers do the Amalfi Coast as a round-trip by bus, but a good strategy is to go one way by bus and return by boat. For example,

instead of busing from Sorrento to Salerno (end of the line) and back, consider taking the bus to Salerno, then catching the ferry back to Amalfi or Positano, and then, from either town, hopping another ferry to Sorrento. Perhaps the simplest option is to take the bus to Positano and boat from there back to Sorrento (or vice versa). Note that ferries run less often in spring and fall, and some don't run at all off-season (mid-Oct–mid-April). Boats don't run in stormy weather at any time of year.

Looking for exercise? Consider an Amalfi Coast hike (see "Hikes" on page 1122). Numerous trails connect the main towns along the coast with villages on the hills. Get a good map and/or book before you venture out.

By Bus

From Sorrento: SITA buses depart from Sorrento's train station nearly hourly (in peak season, 20/day, marked *Amalfi via Positano*) and stop at all Amalfi Coast towns (Positano in 50 minutes; Amalfi in another 50 minutes). To reach Salerno (3 hours), at the far end of the coast, you have to transfer in Amalfi. Ticket prices vary with trip length (45-minute ride, good for short hops–€2.50; 1.5-hour ride, good from Sorrento to Positano–€3.80; 24-hour day pass, good to Amalfi and beyond–€7.60; 3-day ticket–€18). For most trips, you'll want the 24-hour day pass.

In summer, buses start running as early as 6:30 and run as late as 22:00 (they stop running earlier off-season; check the schedule). Buy tickets at the tobacco shop nearest any bus stop before boarding.

An info booth is across from the bus stop at the Sorrento train station (mid-April–Oct daily 8:30-13:30), but the tobacco shop/newsstand at street level inside the station is more reliable (daily 7:00-13:30 & 14:30-20:00, also sells Circumvesuviana train tickets). If both are closed, try the appropriately named Snack Bar, upstairs in the station, or Bar Frisby, just down the hill.

Line up under the *Bus Stop SITA* sign (where a schedule is posted on the wall) across from the Sorrento train station (10 steps down). Carefully note the lettered codes that differentiate daily buses from weekend-only buses. *Giornaliero* means daily; *Feriale* denotes Monday-Saturday departures; and *Festivo* is for Sundays and holidays. After 19:30 (and occasionally on Sundays—check the sign at the main bus stop), buses may leave from Via degli Aranci (with your back to the station, go left and wind around it; the bus stop is near Bar Paradise).

Leaving Sorrento, grab a seat on the right for the best views. If you return by bus, it's fun to sit directly behind the driver for a box seat with a view over the twisting hairpin action. Sitting toward the front will also help minimize carsickness.

Avoiding Crowds on the Bus: Amalfi Coast buses are routinely unable to handle the demand during summer months and holidays. Occasionally, an extra bus is added to deal with the overflow. Generally, if you don't get on one bus, you're well-positioned to catch the next one (bring a book). Try to arrive early in the morning. Remember that buses start taking off as early as 6:30; beginning at 8:30, they leave about every 30 minutes. Departures between 9:00 and 11:00 are crowded and frustrating. Count the number of people in line: Buses pull into Sorrento empty and seat 48 (plus 25 standing). Remember that an eight-seater minibus and driver costs about €300 for the day—if you can organize a small group, €40 per person is a very good deal.

Returning to Sorrento: The congestion can be so bad in the summer—particularly July and August—that return buses don't even stop in Positano (because they've been filled in Amalfi). Those trying to get back to Sorrento are stuck with taking an extortionist taxi or, if in Positano, hopping a boat...if one's running. If touring the coast by bus, do Positano first and come home from Amalfi to avoid the problem of full buses.

By Boat

Several companies compete for passengers, and usually claim to know nothing about their rivals' services. It's wise to check posted schedules, pick up ferry schedules from the TI, and confirm times to figure out the best plan. Boats stop at Sorrento, Positano, Amalfi, and Salerno, generally from mid-April through mid-October (pick up schedule at TI, buy ticket on dock). Few boats run off-season.

By Taxi

Given the hairy driving, impossible parking, congested buses, and potential fun, you might consider splurging to hire your own car and driver for the Amalfi day. (Don't bother for Pompeii, as the Circumvesuviana train serves it conveniently and only licensed guides can take you into the site.)

The **Monetti family** car-and-driver service—Raffaele, brother-in-law Tony, and cousin Lorenzo—have long taken excellent care of my readers' transit needs from Sorrento. Sample trips and rates: all-day Amalfi Coast (Positano,

Amalfi, Ravello), eight hours, €280; Amalfi Coast and Paestum, 10 hours, €400; transfer to Naples airport or train station to Sorrento, €110 (these prices are for up to three people, more for a larger eight-seater van). Though Sorrento-based, they also do trips from Naples (more expensive). Payment is by cash only. Their reservation system is simple and reliable (Raffaele's mobile 335-602-9158 or 338-946-2860, "office" run by his English-speaking Finnish wife, Susanna, www.monettitaxi17.it, monettitaxi17@libero.it). Don't just hop into any taxi claiming to be a Monetti—call first. If you get into any kind of a serious jam in the area, you can call Raffaele for help.

Francesco del Pizzo is another smooth and honest driver. A classy young man who speaks English well, Francesco enjoys explaining things as he drives (nine hours or so in a car with up to four passengers, €280; up to eight passengers in a minibus, €320; mobile 333-238-4144, francescodelpizzo@yahoo.it).

Umberto and Giovanni Benvenuto offer transport, narrated tours, and shore excursions throughout the Amalfi Coast, as well as to Rome, Naples, Pompeii, and more. They are based in Praiano (near Positano). While as friendly as the Monettis, they're more upmarket and formal, with steeper rates explained on their website (tel. 081-007-2114, mobile 346-684-0226, US tel. 310-424-5640, www.benvenutolimos.com, info@benvenutolimos.com).

Sorrento Silver Star, with professional drivers and comfortable Mercedes cars and vans, offers custom trips throughout the area at prices between the Monettis' and Benvenutos' (tel. 081-877-1224, mobile 339-388-8143, www.sorrentosilverstar.com, luisa@sorrentosilverstar.com, Luisa).

Anthony Buonocore is based in Amalfi but does excursions and transfers anywhere in the region in his eight-person Mercedes van (rates vary depending on trip, tel. 349-441-0336, www.amalfitransfer.com, buonocoreanthony@yahoo.it).

Rides Only: If you're hiring a cabbie off the street for a ride and not a tour, here are sample fares from Sorrento to Positano: up to four people one-way for about €80 in a car, or up to six people for €90 in a minibus. Figure on paying 50 percent more to Amalfi. While taxis must use a meter within a city, a fixed rate is OK otherwise. Negotiate—ask about a round-trip.

By Tour

While hiring your own driver is convenient, it's also expensive. To bring the cost down, split the trip—and the bill—with other travelers using this book. Naples-based **Mondo Tour** offers an all-day, nine-hour, lightly guided minibus trip that departs from Sorrento and heads down the Amalfi Coast, with stops in Positano, Amalfi, and Ravello, before returning to Sorrento (€45/person). They also

AMALFI COAST

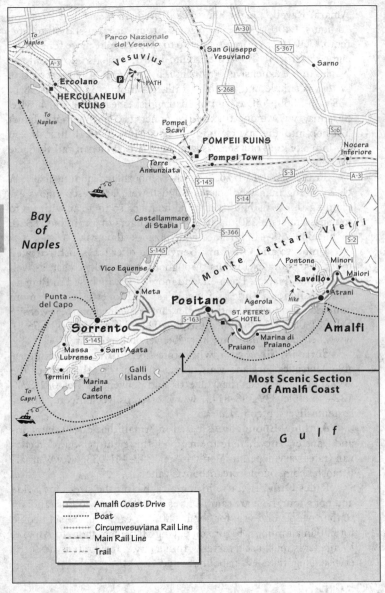

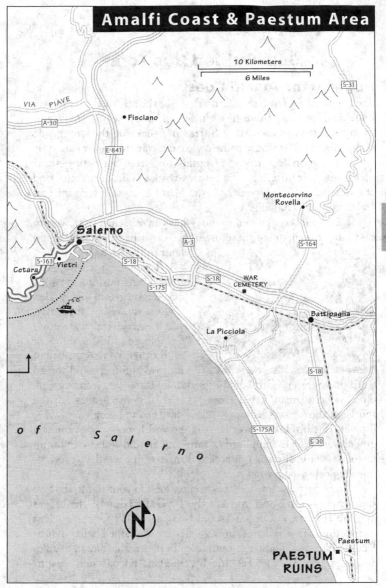

Amalfi Coast & Paestum Area

10 Kilometers

6 Miles

S-31

VIA PIAVE

A-30

• Fisciano

E-841

Montecorvino
Rovella

AMALFI COAST

Salerno

A-3

S-164

S-163

Vietri

S-18

Cetara

S-175

S-18

WAR
CEMETERY

Battipaglia

La Picciola

S-18

o f   S a l e r n o

S-175A

E 30

Paestum

**PAESTUM
RUINS**

offer Rick Steves readers shared tours in Pompeii and in Naples. For details, see page 1006.

Self-Guided Bus Tour

Hugging the Amalfi Coast

The trip from Sorrento to Salerno is one of the all-time great white-knuckle rides. Gasp from the right side of the bus as you go out and from the left as you return to Sorrento. (Those on the wrong side really miss out.) Traffic is so heavy that private tour buses are only allowed to go in one direction (southbound from Sorrento)—summer traffic is infuriating. Fluorescent-vested policemen are posted at tough bends during peak hours to help fold in side-view mirrors and keep things moving.

Here's a loosely guided tour of what you're seeing, from west to east (note that many of these towns are described in greater detail later in this chapter):

Leaving Sorrento, the road winds up into the hills past lemon groves and hidden houses. Traveling the coast, you'll see several watchtowers placed within sight of each other, so that a relay of rooftop bonfires could spread word of a Saracen (Turkish pirate) attack. The gray-green trees are olives. Dark, green-leafed trees planted in dense groves are the source of the region's lemons—many destined to become *limoncello* liqueur. The black nets over the orange and lemon groves create a greenhouse effect, trapping warmth and humidity for maximum tastiness, while offering protection from extreme weather (preserving the peels used for *limoncello*).

Atop the ridge outside of Sorrento, look to your right: The two small islands after Sorrento are the **Li Galli Islands;** the bigger one, on the left, is Ulysses Island (see page 1069 for the ancient connection). These islands, once owned by the famed ballet dancer Rudolf Nureyev, mark the boundary between the Bay of Naples and the Bay of Salerno. Technically, the Amalfi Coast drive begins here.

The limestone cliffs that plunge into the sea were traversed by an ancient trail that became a modern road in the mid-19th century. Fruit stands sell produce from farms and orchards just over the hill. Limestone absorbs the heat and rainwater, making this south-facing coastline a fertile suntrap, with temperatures as much as 10 degrees higher than in nearby Sorrento. Bougainvillea and geraniums grow like weeds here in the summer. Notice the nets—they're designed to catch rocks that often tumble loose after absorbing heavy rains.

As you approach the exotic-looking town of **Positano,** you know you've reached the scenic heart of the Amalfi Coast. Views of Positano, the main stop along the coast, are dramatic on either side of town. Just south of Positano, **St. Peter's Hotel** (Il San Pietro di Positano, camouflaged below the tiny St. Peter's church) is just about the most posh stop on the coast. Notice the elevator to the beach and dock. **Praiano** is notable for its cathedral, with the characteristic majolica-tiled roof and dome—a reminder of this region's respected ceramics industry. It's a spindly town, with most of its homes accessible only by tiny footpaths and staircases. Just past the tunnel stands another Saracen watchtower.

Marina di Praiano is a tiny and unique fishing hamlet wedged into a tight ravine with a couple of restaurants and some small ho-

tels.

The next Saracen tower guarded the harbor of the Amalfi navy until the fleet was destroyed in 1343 by a tsunami caused by an earthquake.

The most striking stretch of coastline ends at **Amalfi** and **Atrani.** As you leave Amalfi, look up to the left. The white house that clings to a cliff (Villa Rondinaia) was home for many years to the writer Gore Vidal. Atop the cliff is the town of **Ravello.** From here, the western half of the Amalfi Coast is mostly wild and unpopulated until you hit **Salerno,** and, farther south, the striking Greek temples at **Paestum.**

Positano

According to legend, the Greek god Poseidon created Positano for Pasitea, a nymph he lusted after. History says the town was found-

ed when ancient Greeks at Paestum decided to move out of the swamp (to escape the malaria carried by its mosquitoes). Specializing in scenery and sand, Positano hangs halfway between Sorrento and Amalfi town on the most spectacular stretch of the coast.

In antiquity, Positano was famed for its bold sailors and hearty fleet. But after a big 1343 tsunami and the pirate raids of the Middle Ages, its wealth and power declined. It flourished again as a favorite under the Bourbon royal family in the 1700s, when many of its fine mansions were built. Until the late 1800s, the only access was by donkey path or by sea. In the 20th century, Positano became a haven for artists and writers escaping Communist Russia or Nazi Germany. In 1953, American writer John Steinbeck's essay on the town popularized Positano among tourists, and soon after it became a trendy Riviera stop. That was when the town gave the world "Moda Positano"—a leisurely *dolce vita* lifestyle of walking barefoot; wearing bright, happy, colorful clothes; and sporting skimpy bikinis.

Today, the village, a breathtaking sight from a distance, is a pleasant gathering of cafés and expensive stores, with a good but pebbly beach. Positano is famous for its fashions—90 percent of its shops are women's clothing boutiques.

The "skyline" looks like it did a century ago. Notice the town's characteristic Saracen-inspired rooftop domes. Filled with sand, these provide low-tech insulation—to help buildings in the days before air-conditioning stay cool in summer and warm in winter. Traditionally, they were painted white in summer and black in winter.

It's been practically impossible to get a building permit in Positano for over 25 years now, and landowners who want to renovate can't make external changes. The steep stairs are a way of life for the 4,000 hardy locals. Only one street in Positano allows motorized traffic; the rest are steep pedestrian lanes. Because hotels don't take large groups (bus access is too difficult), this town—unlike Sorrento—has been spared the ravages of big-bus tourism.

Consider seeing Positano as a day trip from Sorrento: Take the bus out and the afternoon ferry home, but be sure to check the boat schedules when you arrive—the last ferry often leaves before 18:00, and doesn't always run in spring and fall. Or spend the night to enjoy the magic of Positano. The town has a local flavor at night, when the grown-ups stroll and the kids play soccer on the church porch.

Orientation to Positano

Squished into a ravine, with narrow alleys that cascade down to the harbor, Positano requires you to stroll, whether you're going up or heading down. The center of town has no main square (unless you count the beach). There's little to do here but eat, window-shop, and enjoy the beach and views...hence the town's popularity.

Tourist Information

The TI—which feels pulled out of a classic old Italian movie—is a half-block from the beach, in a small building at the bottom of the church steps (April-Sept Mon-Sat 8:30-19:00, Sun 9:00-14:00; Oct-March Mon-Sat 9:00-16:30, closed Sun; Via del Saracino 4, tel. 089-875-067, www.aziendaturismopositano.it).

Arrival in Positano

The main coast highway winds above the town. Regional SITA buses (blue or green-and-white) stop at two scheduled bus stops located at either end of town: Chiesa Nuova (at Bar Internazionale, near the Sorrento end of town; use this one only if you're staying at Brikette Hostel) and Sponda (nearer Amalfi town). Although both stops are near roads leading downhill through the town to the beach, Sponda is closer and less steep; from this stop, it's a 20-minute downhill stroll/shop/munch to the beach (and TI).

Neither bus stop has **baggage storage**, which makes it hard to visit Positano on the way (for example, between overnights in Sorrento and Amalfi). Your best bet is to get off at Chiesa Nuova and head for the Brikette Hostel, which offers day privileges for €10, including luggage storage, Wi-Fi, and showers. A last resort would be to get off at the Sponda stop and roll your bags all the way down to Piazza dei Mulini, where Positano's porters tend to hang out. They're usually willing to mind your luggage for €5/bag.

If you're catching the SITA bus back to Sorrento, be aware that it may leave from the Sponda stop up to five minutes before the printed departure. There's simply no room for the bus to wait, so in case the driver is early, you should be, too (€3.80, departures about hourly, daily 7:00-22:00, until 20:00 off-season). Buy tickets from the tobacco shop next to Bar Mulino Verde in the town center, or just below the Sponda bus stop at the Li Galli Bar or Total gas station (across from Hotel Marincanto).

If the walk up to the stop is too tough, take the dizzy little local red-and-white shuttle bus (marked *Interno Positano*), which constantly loops through Positano, connecting the lower town with the highway's two bus stops (2/hour, €1.20 at tobacco shop or €1.50 on board, catch it at convenient stop at the corner of Via Colombo and Via dei Mulini, heads up to Sponda). Bar Mulino Verde, located off Piazza dei Mulini (as close as cars, taxis, and the shuttle bus can get to the beach), is just across from the shuttle bus stop, with a fine, breezy terrace you can enjoy if you're waiting.

Drivers must go with the one-way flow, entering the town only at the Chiesa Nuova bus stop (closest to Sorrento) and exiting at Sponda. Driving is a headache here. Parking is even worse.

Tours in Positano

Local Guide

Christine Ornelas, an Australian lawyer who fell for a local and married into the Positano scene, has become the town historian. She weaves her interests into a fascinating three-hour walk through town. Christine's tour gives the town context and brings meaning to fun hidden history, while offering an overview of the local scene, tastings of local products, and tips on shopping, beaches, restaurants, and excursions (€25, 2 people-€45 with this book, April-mid-Nov daily at 10:30, email or call to confirm—she'll do the tour for even just a couple of people, mobile 334-232-2096, www. discoverpositano.it, christineornelas@gmail.com). Christine's walk starts at Piazza dei Mulini (outside the church, Chiesa del Rosario).

Self-Guided Walk

Welcome to Positano

While there's no real sightseeing in Positano, this short, guided stroll downhill will help you get your bearings from top to bottom.
• Start at...

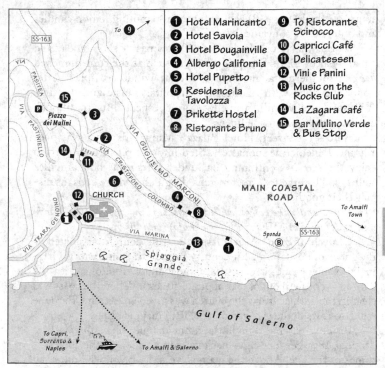

1 Hotel Marincanto
2 Hotel Savoia
3 Hotel Bougainville
4 Albergo California
5 Hotel Pupetto
6 Residence la Tavolozza
7 Brikette Hostel
8 Ristorante Bruno
9 To Ristorante Scirocco
10 Capricci Café
11 Delicatessen
12 Vini e Panini
13 Music on the Rocks Club
14 La Zagara Café
15 Bar Mulino Verde & Bus Stop

AMALFI COAST

Piazza dei Mulini: This is the upper-town meeting point—as close to the beach as vehicles can get—and is also the lower stop for the little red-and-white shuttle bus (2/hour, departs on the hour and half hour). Bar Mulino Verde is *the* local hangout—older people gather inside, while the younger crowd congregates on the wisteria-draped terrace across the street. In this small town, gossiping is a big pastime.

Positano's ceramic and linen industries boomed when tourists discovered the place in the 1970s. The beach-inspired Moda Positano fashion label was first created as a break from the rigid dress code of the '50s. On this piazza, and throughout town, you'll find lots of ceramic and linen shops (and an abundance of ATMs), along with galleries featuring the work of local artists.

• *Wander downhill to the "fork" in the road (stairs to the left, road to the right). You've reached...*

Midtown: At Enoteca Cuomo (#3), butcher Vincenzo stocks fine local red wines and is happy to explain their virtues. He also makes homemade sausages, salami, and *panini*—good for a quick lunch. The smaller set of stairs leads to the recommended Delicatessen grocery store, where Emilia can fix you a good picnic (see "Eating in Positano," later). Their downstairs café (enter past the stairs, on the left at #13) sells an array of tempting lemon candies and other edible souvenirs.

La Zagara (across the lane at #10) is a pastry shop by day and a piano bar by night. Tempting pastries such as the rum-drenched *babà* (a southern Italian favorite) fill the window display. After hours, it's filled with traditional Neapolitan music and dancing. A bit farther downhill, Brunella (#24) is respected for traditional, quality, and locally made linens.

Across the street, Hotel Palazzo Murat fills what was once a grand Benedictine monastery. Step into the plush courtyard to enjoy the scene. Continuing on, under a fragrant bougainvillea trellis, you'll come to "street merchants' gulch," where artisans display their goodies.

• *Continue under the bougainvillea trellis, turning right at the church, and go downstairs to Piazza Flavio Gioia, with the big...*

Church of Santa Maria Assunta: This church originated as the abbey of Positano's 12th-century Benedictine monastery. Originally Romanesque, it was eventually abandoned (along with the entire lower town) out of fear of pirate attacks. When the coast was clear in the 18th century, the church was given an extreme Baroque makeover. Its dome is covered in colorful majolica tiles.

Inside (first chapel on left) is a fine manger scene *(presepe)*. Its original 18th-century figurines give you an idea of the folk costumes of the age. Above the main altar is the Black Madonna, an icon-like Byzantine painting, which was likely brought here in the 12th century by Benedictine monks. But locals prefer the romantic legend: Saracen pirates had it on their ship as plunder. A violent storm hit—sure to sink the evil ship. The painting of Mary spoke, saying, *"Posa, posa"* (lay me down), and the ship glided safely to this harbor. The pirates were so stricken they became Christians. Locals kept the painting, and the town became known as *Posa-tano* (recalling Mary's command). To the right of the altar, a small chapel holds a silver and copper bust of St. Vitus—the town patron who brought Christianity here in about A.D. 300 (this may be displayed nearby in a freestanding wooden altar). In the adjacent niche (on the right) is a rare 1599 painting by Fabrizio Santafede of Baby Jesus being circumcised, considered the finest historic painting in town.

Back outside, you'll see the bell tower, dating from 1707. Above the door, it sports a Romanesque relief scavenged from the original church. The scene—a wolf mermaid with seven little fish—was a reminder to worshippers of how integral the sea was to their livelihood. Notice the characteristic shallow, white "insulation domes" on rooftops in front of the church.

• *Backtrack up the steps, circling around the church until you see an information board labeled* Villa Romana.

The information board describes, in English, how this spot once held a Roman villa, buried when Mount Vesuvius erupted in A.D. 79. Only a few minor rooms have been excavated (a photograph shows one of the preserved frescoes). The rest await discovery—digging has ceased until there are enough funds to do it properly. The stairs lead down to two glass doors that would (if this very rich town could afford to keep them open) offer a peek into the church's crypt—originally the early church's altar. According to local legend, the Benedictines sat their dead brothers on the stone choir chairs here to decompose and remind all of their mortality.

• *Continue climbing down the steps arcing to the right. You'll eventually come to the little square, with concrete benches, facing the beach.*

Piazzetta: This is the local gathering point in the evening, as local boys hustle tourist girls into the nearby nightclub. Residents traded their historic baptistery font with Amalfi town for the two iron lions you see facing the beach. From here, you can look up and admire the colorful majolica tiles so typical of church domes in this region. Positano was once a notable naval power, with many shipyards along this beach. These eventually became fishermen's quarters and storehouses, and later, today's tourist restaurants. The Positano **beach,** called Spiaggia Grande, is half public (with WC and €1 shower) and half private.

• *On the far left side of the beach is...*

Music on the Rocks: This chic, recommended club (below the Ristorante e Terrazze) is all that's left of the 1970s scene, when Positano really rocked. While it's dead until about 23:00, if you just want to stop for a drink, the cool troglo-disco interior opens at 21:00.

• *Wander across the beach. Beyond the kiosks that sell boat tickets, a path climbs up and over, past a 13th-century lookout fort from Saracen pirate days, to the next beach. It's a worthwhile little five-minute walk to...*

Fornillo Beach: This is where locals go for better swimming and to escape some of the tourist crowds. The walk over offers a welcome change of scene, as the path winds through a shady ravine.

• *Our walk is over. Time to relax.*

Sights in Positano

Beaches

Positano's pebbly and sandy primary beach, **Spiaggia Grande,** is colorful with umbrellas as it stretches wide around the cove. It's mostly private (€10-15/person, April-Oct, cost includes drink service and use of lounge chair and umbrella), with a free section near the middle, close to where the boats take off. The nearest WC is beneath the steps to the right (as you face the water).

Fornillo Beach, a less-crowded option just around the bend (to the west) of Spiaggia Grande, is favored by residents, with more affordable chair and umbrella rentals. This beach has a few humble snack bars and lunch eateries.

Boat Trips

At the west end of Spiaggia Grande (to the right as you face the sea), booths sell tickets to a number of destinations. Consider renting a rowboat or taking a boat tour to a nearby cave (La Grotta dello Smeraldo—Emerald Cave), fishing village (Nerano), or small islands.

Ferries run to Amalfi, Capri, and Sorrento; see "Positano Connections," page 1117.

Shopping

Locally produced linens and ceramics can be found at shops and galleries throughout town. **Ceramica Assunta,** one of the oldest ceramics stores in Positano, carries colorful Solimene dinnerware and more at two locations (Via Colombo 97 and Via Colombo 137, tel. 089-875-008). The young owner-artisan couple at **Sunflower Bottega d'Arte** make and paint their own ceramic designs. Two popular (and pricey) fashion boutiques are **Brunella** (Via Pasitea 72, tel. 089-875-228) and **Pepito's** (Via Pasitea 39, tel. 089-875-446).

Nightlife

The big-time action in the old town center is the impressive club **Music on the Rocks,** literally carved into the rocks on the beach (opens at 21:00 mid-April-Oct but party starts about 23:30, on summer weekends often a €10-20 cover charge that includes a drink, go to dance or just check out the scene, Via Grotte Dell'Incanto 51, tel. 089-875-874, www.musicontherocks.it). For a more low-key atmosphere, café/pastry shop **La Zagara** hosts music nightly in summer (June-Sept, starts around 21:00, Via dei Mulini 10, tel. 089-875-964).

Sleeping in Positano

These hotels (but not the hostel) are all on or near Via Colombo, which leads from the SITA Sponda bus stop down into the village. Prices given are for the highest season (May-Sept)—at other times, they become soft. Most places close in the winter (Dec-Feb or longer). Expect to pay more than €20 a day to park, except at Albergo California.

$$$ Hotel Marincanto is a recently restored, somewhat impersonal four-star hotel with 32 beautiful rooms and a bright breakfast terrace practically teetering on a cliff. Suites seem to be designed for a *luna di miele*—honeymoon (Db-€220, more expensive superior rooms and suites, extra bed-€70, air-con, elevator,

Sleep Code

(€1 = about $1.30, country code: 39)

S = Single, **D** = Double/Twin, **T** = Triple, **Q** = Quad, **b** = bathroom, **s** = shower only. Unless otherwise noted, credit cards are accepted, English is spoken, and breakfast is included. Many towns in Italy levy a hotel tax of €2 per person, per night, which must be paid in cash (not included in the rates I've quoted).

To help you sort easily through these listings, I've divided the accommodations into three categories based on the price for a standard double room with bath:

$$$ **Higher Priced**—Most rooms €180 or more.

$$ **Moderately Priced**—Most rooms between €130-180.

$ **Lower Priced**—Most rooms €130 or less.

Prices can change without notice; verify the hotel's current rates online or by email. For the best prices, always book direct.

guest computer, free Wi-Fi, pool, private stairs to beach, parking-€26/day, closed Nov-March, 50 yards below Sponda bus stop at Via Colombo 50, reception on bottom floor, tel. 089-875-130, www.marincanto.it, info@marincanto.it).

$$ Hotel Savoia is family-run, with 39 sizeable, breezy, bright, simple rooms with tiles and older furnishings (viewless Db-€120, view Db-€170, deluxe Db with balcony or terrace-€200, at least €10/day less with this book in 2014, extra bed-€50, air-con, elevator, free Wi-Fi in common areas, closed Nov-Feb, Via Colombo 73, tel. 089-875-003, www.savoiapositano.it, info@savoia-positano.it, Regina and daughters Mechy, Piera, and Cristina).

$$ Hotel Bougainville rents 16 comfortable rooms, half with balconies. Everything's bright, modern, and tasteful (small-windowed viewless economy Db-€119, regular viewless Db-€140, view Db-€185, 5 percent off these rates if you book direct with this book in 2014, check website for specials, air-con, guest computer, free Wi-Fi, closed Nov-March, Via Colombo 25, tel. 089-875-047, www.bougainville.it, info@bougainville.it, friendly Marella).

$$ Albergo California has 15 spacious rooms (all with lofty views), a grand terrace draped with vines, and full breakfasts. The Cinque family—including Maria, Bronx-born son John, and grandson Giuseppe—will welcome you (view Db-€160 June-Sept, €10 less April-May and Oct, these prices promised with this book through 2014, air-con, Wi-Fi, free parking, closed Nov-March,

Via Colombo 141, tel. 089-875-382, www.hotelcaliforniapositano.
it, info@hotelcaliforniapositano.it).

$ Hotel Pupetto is a family-run hotel for beach lovers. This
secluded waterfront spot is a 10-minute walk from Positano's
bustling harbor (Db-€95-120, Via Fornillo 37, tel. 089-875-087,
www.hotelpupetto.it, info@hotelpupetto.it).

$ Residence la Tavolozza is an attractive six-room hotel,
warmly run by Celeste (cheh-LEHS-tay) and daughters Francesca
(who speaks English) and Paola. Each cheerily tiled room comes
with a view, a terrace, and silence. This is a good value (Db-€95-120
depending on size, doesn't include breakfast, these prices promised
through 2014 with this book, families can ask for sprawling "Royal
Apartment"—price varies depending on occupancy, call to confirm
if arriving late, extra for lavish à la carte breakfast, air-con, free
Wi-Fi, closed Dec-Feb, Via Colombo 10, tel. 089-875-040, www.
latavolozzapositano.it).

$ Brikette Hostel offers your best cheap dorm-bed option in
this otherwise ritzy town. Renting 35 beds and offering a great sun
and breakfast terrace, it has a loose, youthful, rough-around-the-
edges ambience (bunk in humble 10-bed dorm-€25, bunk in 8-bed
dorm-€28, bunk in 5-bed dorm-€33, Db-€90, nicer Db-€120,
bigger family rooms; hearty breakfast-€5, €5-7 dinners; air-con in
a few rooms, free Wi-Fi; day privileges for day-trippers, including
luggage storage-€10; 11:00-14:30 lockout for cleaning, closed mid-
Nov-March, leave bus at Chiesa Nuova/Bar Internazionale stop
and backtrack uphill 500 feet to Via G. Marconi 358, tel. 089-875-
857, www.hostel-positano.com, hostelpositano@gmail.com).

Eating in Positano

Positano is an expensive place to dine. At the waterfront, several
interchangeable restaurants with view terraces leave people fat and
happy, albeit with skinnier wallets
(figure €15-20 pastas and *secondi*,
plus pricey drinks and sides, and a
cover charge). Little distinguishes
one place from the next; all are
pleasant, convenient, and overpriced.

"Uptown": The unassuming,
family-run **Ristorante Bruno** is
handy to my listed hotels. Consid-
er it if you want an expensive meal without hiking down into the
town center for dinner (€12-16 pastas, €16-22 *secondi*, daily 12:00-
23:00, closed Nov-Easter, near the top of Via Colombo at #157, tel.
089-875-179).

"Way Uptown": **Ristorante Scirocco** is a splurge, perched high above Positano with fantastic views and meals ranging from seafood to steak. Get there with enough daylight left to enjoy the scenery. New owners may mean changes to the menu or pricing in 2014 (€12 pastas, €18 *secondi*, €35 fixed-price meal, daily 12:00-15:00 & 19:00-24:00, closed Nov-Easter, Via Montepertuso 126, tel. 089-875-184).

Inexpensive Pizza & Pasta: **Capricci,** three doors from the TI, is budget-priced (for Positano). An informal café and *tavola calda* serves up €7.50 pizza and €8.50 main courses that you can eat on the spot or take away. If you sit down at their white-tablecloth restaurant across the street, you get the same food—but the pizza price jumps to €10, with a €2 cover (daily 9:00-23:00, Via Regina Giovanna 12, tel. 089-812-145). They deliver anywhere in Positano during slow hours for €3 (Tue-Sun 9:00-11:30 & 16:00-19:00, no delivery at other times or on Mon, menu at www.capriccipositano.it).

Picnics: If a picnic dinner on your balcony or the beach sounds good, sunny Emilia at the **Delicatessen** grocery store can supply the ingredients (*antipasto misto* to go at €1.40/100 grams, pasta for €1/100 grams, sandwiches made and sold by weight—about €3.50-4.50, she microwaves food and includes all the picnic ware, come early for best selection; daily March-Oct 7:00-22:00, Nov-Feb 8:00-20:00, just below car park at Via del Mulini 5, tel. 089-875-489).

Vini e Panini, another small grocery, is a block from the beach a few steps above the TI. Daniela, the fifth-generation owner, speaks English and happily makes sandwiches to order. Choose from the "Caprese" (mozzarella and tomato), the "Positano" (mozzarella, tomato, and ham), or create your own (priced by weight, around €3.50-4 each). They also have a nice selection of well-priced regional wines (daily 8:00-20:00, until 22:00 in summer, closed mid-Nov-mid-March, just off church steps, tel. 089-875-175).

Positano Connections

Always check boat schedules, since the last boats often leave Positano before 18:00. The schedule varies drastically according to time of year; it's more reliable in summer than off-season, but be sure to check it with the TI. There's no real dock, so stormy weather can disrupt schedules. If you're thinking of taking a Capri trip from Positano, consider a boat that goes directly to the Blue Grotto (rather than dropping you in the port to catch another boat from there).

From Positano by Boat to: Amalfi (4-6/day, 30 minutes, €8, on TravelMar), **Capri** (mid-April-mid-Oct, 2-4/day, 30-60 minutes, €17-19; less off-season), **Sorrento** (mid-April-mid-Oct only,

AMALFI COAST

2-4/day, 35 minutes, €16), **Salerno** (mid-April-Sept only, 4-6/day, 70 minutes, €12). Check schedules carefully as most boats run only mid-April to mid-October; few run off-season. Direct boats to **Naples** run several times a day in the summer (check with the TI); you can also change boats in Sorrento or Capri.

By Bus: See "Getting Around the Amalfi Coast—By Bus," on page 1101.

Amalfi Town

After Rome fell, the Amalfi Coast's namesake town was one of the first to trade goods—coffee, carpets, and paper—between Europe and points east. Its heyday was the 10th and 11th centuries,

when it was a powerful maritime republic—a trading power with a fleet that controlled this region and rivaled Pisa, Genoa, and Venice. The Republic of Amalfi founded a hospital in Jerusalem and claims to have founded the Knights of Malta order—even giving them the Amalfi cross, which became the famous Maltese cross. Amalfi minted its own coins and established "rules of the sea"—the basics of which survive today.

In 1343, this little powerhouse was suddenly destroyed by a tsunami caused by an undersea earthquake. That disaster, compounded by devastating plagues, left Amalfi a humble backwater. Today its 5,000 residents live off tourism. Amalfi is not as picturesque as Positano or as well-connected as Sorrento, but take some time to explore the town.

Amalfi's one main street runs up from the waterfront through a deep valley, with stairways to courtyards and houses on either side. It's worth walking uphill to the workaday upper end of town. If you hear water under a grate in the main street, it's the creek that runs through the ravine—a reminder that, originally, the town straddled the stream, and later paved over it to create a main drag. As you return downhill, be sure to explore up the winding and narrow lanes and arcaded passages on either side of the main street.

Though less touristy than Positano, Amalfi is packed during the day with big-bus tours (whose drivers pay €50 an hour to park while their groups shop for *limoncello* and ceramics). Amalfi's charms reveal themselves early and late in the day, when the tourist crowds dissipate.

Flavio Gioia

You'll see a statue of Flavio Gioia towering above the chaos of cars and buses on the seaside piazza. Amalfi residents credit this hometown boy with the invention of the magnetic compass back in 1302, but historians can't verify that he actually existed. While an improvement to the compass did occur in Amalfi during that time period, Chinese and Arab navigators had been using rudimentary compasses for years. In Gioia's time, seamen placed a magnetized needle on the surface of a container of water as a kind of medieval GPS. If Gioia existed at all, he probably just figured out how to secure that needle inside a little box. Locals, however, have no doubt that Flavio Gioia was an inventor extraordinaire.

Orientation to Amalfi Town

Amalfi's waterfront is the coast's biggest transport hub. The bus station, ferry docks, and a parking lot (€5/hour) are next to each other. A statue of local boy Flavio Gioia—the purported inventor of the compass (see sidebar)—overlooks them, and Amalfi's TI is just beyond, across the street.

Before you enter the town, notice the colorful tile above the Porta della Marina gateway, showing off the trading domain of the maritime Republic of Amalfi. Just to the left, along the busy road, is a series of arches that indicate the long, narrow, vaulted halls of its arsenal—where ships were built in the 11th century. One of these is now the fine little Arsenal Museum (described later).

Venture into the town, and you'll quickly come to Piazza Duomo, the main square, sporting a spring water-spewing statue of St. Andrew, and the cathedral—the town's most important sight.

The farther you get away from the water, the more traditional Amalfi becomes. The Paper Museum is a 10-minute walk up Via Lorenzo d'Amalfi, the main drag. From here, the road narrows and you can turn off onto a path leading to the shaded Valle dei Mulini; it's full of paper-mill ruins that recall this once proud and prosperous industry. The ruined castle clinging to the rocky ridge above Amalfi is Torre dello Ziro, a good lookout point for intrepid hikers (see "Hikes" on page 1122).

Tourist Information

The TI is about 100 yards from the bus station and ferry dock, next to the post office; facing the sea, it's to the left (April-Oct Mon-Fri 9:00-13:00 & 14:00-18:00, Sat 9:00-13:00; Nov-March Mon-

Sat 9:00-13:00; closed Sun year-round; Corso della Repubbliche Marinare 27, tel. 089-871-107, www.amalfitouristoffice.it).

Helpful Hints

Don't Get Stranded: Be warned—most of the year, the last bus back to Sorrento leaves at 20:00 (at 22:00 in June-July, at 23:00 in Aug, at 21:00 in April-May and Sept—but confirm times locally) and can be full. Without a public bus, your only option is a €100 taxi ride.

Internet Access: The travel agency **L'Altra Costiera,** on the main drag a block up from the church, has Wi-Fi and computers for use (€5/hour, daily 9:00-21:00, Via Lorenzo d'Amalfi 34, tel. 089-873-6082).

Baggage Storage: You can store your bag safely for €4 at the **Divina Costiera Travel Office** facing the waterfront square, across from the bus parking area (daily 8:00-13:00 & 14:00-19:30, tel. 089-872-467).

Speedboat Charters: To hire your own boat for a tour of the coastline from Amalfi (or to Capri), consider **Charter La Dolce Vita** (mobile 335-549-9365, www.amalficoastyacht.it).

Sights in Amalfi Town

Cathedral

This church is "Amalfi Romanesque" (a mix of Moorish and Byzantine flavors, built c. 1000-1300), with a fanciful Neo-Byzantine facade from the 19th century. Climb the imposing stairway, which functions as a handy outdoor theater for town events. The 1,000-year-old bronze door at the top was given to Amalfi by a wealthy local merchant who had it made in Constantinople.

Cost and Hours: €3, daily 10:00-17:00, open only for prayer 7:30-10:00 & 17:00-19:30, tel. 089-871-324. There's a fine, free WC at the top of the steps (through unmarked green door, just a few steps before ticket booth, ask for key at desk).

Visiting the Cathedral: Pick up the English flier as you enter. Visitors are directed on a one-way circuit through the cathedral complex with four stops.

This courtyard of 120 graceful columns—the **"Cloister of Paradise"**—was the cemetery for local nobles in the 13th century (note their stone sarcophagi). Don't miss the fine view of the bell tower and its majolica tiles.

The original ninth-century church, known as the **Basilica of the Crucifix,** is now a museum filled with the art treasures of the cathedral. The Angevin Mitre (Mitra Angioina), with a "pavement of tiny pearls" setting off its gold and gems, has been worn by bishops since the 14th century. Also on display is a carved wooden decoration from a Saracen pirate ship that wrecked just outside of town in 1544 during a freak storm. Believers credit St. Andrew with causing the storm that saved the town from certain Turkish pillage and plunder.

Just as Venice needed Mark to get on the pilgrimage map, Amalfi needed St. Andrew—one of the apostles who, along with his brother (St. Peter), left their fishing nets to become the original "fishers of men." What are believed to be his remains (in the **Crypt of St. Andrew,** under the huge bronze statue) were brought here from Constantinople in 1206 during the Crusades—an indication of the wealth and importance of Amalfi back then.

The **cathedral** interior is notable for its fine 13th-century wooden crucifix. The painting behind it shows St. Andrew martyred on an X-shaped cross flanked by two Egyptian granite columns supporting a triumphal arch. Before leaving, check out the delicate mother-of-pearl crucifix (right of door in back).

▲Paper Museum

Paper has been a vital industry here since Amalfi's glory days in the Middle Ages. They'd pound rags into pulp in a big vat, pull it up using a screen, and air-dry it to create paper (the same technique used to make paper sold today in Amalfi shops). At this cavernous, cool 13th-century paper mill-turned-museum, a multilingual guide collects groups at the entrance (no particular times) for a 25-minute tour. The guide recounts the history and process of papermaking, a longtime industry for the town of Amalfi, and turns on the museum's vintage water-powered machinery. Kids can dip a screen into the rag pool and make a sheet for themselves.

Cost and Hours: €4; March-Oct daily 10:00-18:30; Nov-Feb usually Tue-Sun 10:00-15:30, closed Mon; a 10-minute walk up the main street from the cathedral, look for signs to *Museo della Carta;* tel. 089-830-4561, www.museodellacarta.it. On the way up to the museum, don't miss the huge, outdoor *presepi* (nativity scenes) on your left.

Arsenal Museum

This small, underground museum just across the road from the bus station tells the history of Amalfi's maritime glory years. Stepping into the single long room under the dramatic vaulted stone ceiling, it sinks in: A thousand years ago, they made ships here. The collection (which is well-described in English) is small, but there are plenty of historic artifacts from Amalfi's city-state days of independence (839-1135). You'll learn about the early compass "invented" here in 1302, which ultimately opened up exploration of the New World. In 1080, it was written, "This city appears opulent and popular; no other city is as rich in silver, garments, and gold. Here dwells navigators very expert at pointing out the ways of the sea and the sphere of the heavens."

Cost and Hours: €2, Tue-Sun 10:00-13:30 & 15:30-19:00, closed Mon, shorter hours off-season, Piazza Flavio Gioia, tel. 089-871-170, www.museoarsenaleamalfi.it.

Hikes

Amalfi is the starting point for several fine hikes, two of which I've described here. The TI hands out photocopies of Giovanni Visetti's trail maps (or you can download them yourself at www.giovis.com). If you can find it, the best book on hiking is Julian Tippett's *Sorrento Amalfi Capri Car Tours and Walks*. It has useful color-coded maps and info on public transportation to the trailheads.

Hike #1: Pontone

This loop trail leads up the valley past paper-mill ruins, ending in the tiny town of Pontone; you can get lunch there, and head back down to the town of Amalfi (allow 3 hours total). Bring a good map, since it's easy to veer off the main route. Start your hike by following the main road (Via Lorenzo d'Amalfi) away from the sea.

After the Paper Museum, jog right, then left to join the trail, which runs through the shaded woods along a babbling stream. Heed the signs that warn people to stay away from the ruins of paper mills (no matter how tempting), since many are ready to collapse on unwary hikers. Continue up to Pontone, where Trattoria l'Antico Borgo offers wonderful cuisine and a great view (Via Noce 4, tel. 089-871-469). After lunch, return to Amalfi via a steep stairway.

If you're feeling ambitious, before you head back to Amalfi, add a one-hour detour (30 minutes each way) to visit the ridge-hugging **Torre dello Ziro** (ask a local how to find the trail to this tower). You'll be rewarded with a spectacular view.

Hike #2: Atrani

For an easier stroll, head to the nearby town of Atrani. This village, just a 15-minute stroll beyond Amalfi town, is a world apart; its 1,500 residents consider themselves definitely *not* from Amalfi. Leave Amalfi via the main road, and stay on the water side until the sidewalk ends. Cross the street and head up the stairs; the paved route takes you over the hill, and drops you into Atrani in about 15 minutes. Piazza Umberto is the core of town, with cafés and a little grocery store that makes sandwiches. Atrani has none of the trendy resort feel of Amalfi, with relatively few tourists, a delightful town square, and a free, sandy beach (if you drive here, pay for parking at harbor). This town also has some recommended accommodations.

From Atrani, you can theoretically continue up to **Ravello** (see page 1124). But be warned: Unless you're part mountain goat, you'll probably prefer catching the bus to Ravello from Amalfi town instead.

Sleeping in Amalfi Town

Sleeps are much better in Positano (nicer views) or Sorrento (lower prices), but if you're marooned in Amalfi, here are some options. Prices listed are for high season (roughly April-Oct), but can spike higher in August and drop in spring and fall.

$$ Hotel Aurora is a tranquil, bright, and cheery respite from Amalfi crowds just a 10-minute walk from the Duomo (Db-€149-189, Piazzale dei Protonini, tel. 089-871-209, www.aurora-hotel.it, info@aurora-hotel.it).

$$ Hotel Floridiana, just off the main drag and five minutes by foot from the harbor, is only three short flights of steps up from the street. Though lacking views, the 13 rooms are attractive and newly furnished and come with free garage parking—very unusual here (Db-€130-140, air-con, free Wi-Fi, Via Brancia 1; pass the Duomo, then take the next right through tiny arch—Salita Brancia—and up 30 steps; tel. 089-873-6373, www.hotelfloridiana.it, info@hotelfloridiana.it, Agnese).

$$ Hotel Lidomare's 18 rooms are decorated in traditional majolica tiles and rich antique furnishings just a few steps from the Duomo (Db-€90-145, Largo Piccolomini 9, tel. 089-871-332, www.lidomare.it, info@lidomare.it).

$ Hotel Centrale has incredible views of the cathedral in a handy, central, but noisy location (Db-€75-140, Largo Piccolomini 1, tel. 089-872-608, www.amalfihotelcentrale.it, info@amalfihotelcentrale.it).

$ Residenza del Duca is a little seven-room B&B with no views, up many flights of stairs in the heart of this touristy enclave (one minuscule Sb-€60, Db-€90—or €130 in Aug-Sept, €10 discount with this book and cash if you reserve direct, air-con, free Wi-Fi, no views but glimpses of ocean through the rooftops; 25 yards uphill from Piazza Duomo, take the first left, go up the stairs and follow the signs, then go up more stairs—over 70 total—to Via Mastalo II Duca 3; call for free luggage service—available April-Oct 8:00-20:00, tel. 089-873-6365, www.residencedelduca.it, info@residencedelduca.it, Andrea and Daniela).

Nearby, in Atrani

Atrani is a small-town hideaway without the glitz of Positano or the bustle of Amalfi. Atrani is a 15-minute hike from Amalfi (described under "Hike #2," earlier); Amalfi-Salerno buses also stop here.

$ A'Scalinatella is a dingy, informal backpackers' hostel, with a honeycomb of cramped 3- to 10-bed dorms, way-overpriced private rooms, and a communal kitchen (dorm bed-€25, D-€60, Db-€90, prices very soft—ask for Rick Steves discount on direct bookings, free Wi-Fi in common areas, 100 yards up from main square at #5 on Scalinatella Piazza Umberto I, tel. 089-871-492, www.hostelscalinatella.com, info@hostelscalinatella.com). It's run by English-speaking owners Filippo and Gabriele, who also rent rooms scattered all over town.

$ L'Argine Fiorito, which stands like a little castle overlooking a ravine at the top of town, rents five tidy and tiled rooms (Db-€105, extra bed-€35, tel. 089-873-6309, mobile 347-531-1158, www.larginefiorito.it, info@larginefiorito.it).

Eating in Amalfi Town

Amalfi, like Positano, has expensive, interchangeable restaurants along the waterfront. For a cheaper sit-down meal without a sea view, **Bar La Piazzetta** has €8-9 pasta, pizza, and salads at a dozen tables in a small, quiet square, reached through an archway directly across the main street from the cathedral steps (long hours daily, no cover, Piazza dei Dogi 5, tel. 089-871-585). Five minutes' walk up the main drag on the right (past the first archway) is **Pizza Express,** with honest €4-6 pies to go (Mon-Sat 9:00-21:00, closed Sun, Via Capuano 46, mobile 339-581-2336). The **Decò** supermarket, up an alley to the right off the main drag (by #34), is small but has a good selection (Mon-Sat 8:00-13:30 & 16:30-20:00, closed Sun, Via Dei Curiali 6).

Ravello

Ravello sits atop a lofty perch 1,000 feet above the sea. It offers an interesting church, two villas, and breathtaking views that have attracted celebrities for generations. Gore Vidal, Richard Wagner, D. H. Lawrence, M. C. Escher, Henry Wadsworth Longfellow, and Greta Garbo all have succumbed to Ravello's charms and called it home.

The town is like a lush and peaceful garden floating above it all. Wandering around, it seems there's nothing but tourists, cafés, stones, old villas-turned-luxury hotels, and grand views. It's one big place to convalesce. To me, it's more famous than enjoyable.

Ravello can make for a half-day outing

from Amalfi, or a full day from Positano with a stop in Amalfi. The views from the bus ride up and back are every bit as stunning as those along the coastal route.

To see the sights listed here, start at the bus stop and walk through the tunnel to the main square, where you'll find the Villa Rufolo on the left, the church on the right, and the **TI** down the street past the church (TI open daily May-Oct 10:00-18:00, shorter hours in winter, 100 yards from the square—follow signs to Via Roma 18, tel. 089-857-096, www.ravellotime.com). Villa Cimbrone is a 10-minute walk from the square (follow the signs).

Picnicking isn't allowed at the two villas, but there are benches with a view by the bus stop and on the main square.

Sights in Ravello

Piazza Duomo

The town's entry tunnel deposits you on the main square. Though perfectly peaceful today, the watchtower of Villa Rufolo—which used to keep an eye out for fires and invasions—is a reminder that it wasn't always postcards and *limoncello*. The facade of the cathedral is plain because the earlier, fancy west portal was destroyed in a 1364 earthquake. The front door is locked; to enter, you need to go through the museum on Viale Wagner, around the left side (described next). The fine pines on the square are pruned to look like umbrellas and provide a shady meeting place for strollers ending up here on the piazza. Opposite the church is a fine view of the terraced hillside and the community of Scala (which means "steps"—historically a way of life there). The terraces, supporting grapevines and lemon trees, mostly date from the 16th century. Viale Wagner climbs to the top of town for sea views and ruined villas that are now luxury hotels. The town is essentially traffic-free.

Duomo

Ravello's cathedral, overlooking the main square, is most memorable because its floor slopes upward. The key features of this church are its 12th-century bronze doors, with 54 Biblical scenes (from Constantinople); the carved marble pulpit supported by six lions; and the chance to climb behind the altar (left of the main altar) for a close-up look at the relic of holy blood. The geometric designs show Arabic influence. The humble cathedral museum, through which you'll enter, is two rooms of well-described carved marble that evoke the historical importance of the town.

Cost and Hours: €3 for the museum—which also gets you into the church, daily May-Oct 8:15-19:00, Nov-April 9:00-17:00, enter through the museum around the left side of the cathedral.

Villa Rufolo

The villa, built in the 13th-century ruins of a noble family's palace, presents wistful gardens among stony walls, with oh-my-God views. The Arabic/Norman gardens seem designed to frame commanding coastline vistas (you can enjoy the same view, without the entry fee, from the bus parking lot just below the villa). It's also one of the venues for Ravello's annual arts festival (July-Aug, www.ravellofestival.com) and music society performances (April-June and Sept-Oct, www.ravelloarts.org). Concertgoers perch on a bandstand on the edge of the cliff for a combination of wonderful music and dizzying views. Wagner visited here and was impressed enough to set the second act of his opera *Parsifal* in the villa's magical gardens. By all accounts, the concert on the cliff is a sublime experience.

Cost and Hours: €5, daily May-Sept 9:00-20:00, Oct-April 9:00 until sunset, may close earlier if hosting a concert, tel. 089-857-621, www.villarufolo.it.

Villa Cimbrone

This villa provides another romantic garden, this one built upon the ruins of an old convent. Located at the opposite end of Ravello, it was created in the 20th century by Englishman William Beckett. His mansion is now a five-star hotel. It's a longish walk to the end of town, where you explore a bluff dreamily landscaped around the villa. At the far end, above a sublime café on the lawn, "the Terrace of Infinity" dangles high above the sea.

Cost and Hours: €6, daily 9:00-sunset, tel. 089-858-072, www.villacimbrone.com.

▲Hike to Amalfi Town from Villa Cimbrone

To walk downhill from Ravello's Villa Cimbrone to the town of Amalfi (a path for hardy hikers only—follow the TI's map), retrace your steps back toward town. Take the first left, which turns into a stepped path winding its way below the cliff. Pause here to look back up at the rock with a big white mansion—Villa La Rondinaia, where Gore Vidal lived for many years. Continue down the fairly steep path about 40 minutes to the town of Atrani, where several bars on the main square offer well-deserved refreshment. From here, it's about a 15-minute walk back to Amalfi (see "Hike #2" on page 1122).

Eating in Ravello

Ristorante Da Salvatore serves a serious sit-down lunch that takes full advantage of the views that make a trip to Ravello worthwhile. Pino, the English-speaking owner of this formal restaurant, serves nicely presented, traditional Amalfi cuisine from a fun-if-pricey menu. Be adventurous when ordering and share dishes. Pato, the parakeet, is learning English (€17 pastas, €20 *secondi*, closed Mon, located at the spot where buses and taxis drop those visiting town, Via della Repubblica 2, tel. 089-857-227, reservations smart).

Ravello Connections

Ravello and the town of Amalfi are connected by a winding road and a bus. Coming from Amalfi town, buy your ticket at the bar on the waterfront, and ask where the bus stop is (normally by the statue on the waterfront, just to the statue's left as you face the water). In Ravello, line up early, since the buses are often crowded (2/hour, 25 minutes, €2.50, buy ticket in tobacco shop; catch bus 100 yards off main square, at other end of tunnel).

Paestum

The ruins at Paestum (PASTE-oom) include one of the best collections of Greek temples anywhere—and certainly the most accessible to Western Europe. Serenely situated, Paestum is surrounded by fields and wildflowers. It also has a functional zone that includes a bus stop, train station, church, and a straggle of houses and cafés that you could barely call a village.

This town was founded as Poseidonia by Greeks in the sixth century B.C., and became a key stop on an important trade route. In the fifth century B.C., the Lucanians, a barbarous inland tribe, conquered Poseidonia and tried to adopt the cultured ways of the Greeks. By the time of the Romans, who took over in the third century B.C., the name Poseidonia had been simplified to Paestum. The final conquerors of Paestum, malaria-carrying mosqui-

toes, kept the site wonderfully deserted for nearly a thousand years. The temples were never buried—just ignored. Rediscovered in the 18th century, Paestum today offers the only well-preserved Greek ruins north of Sicily.

While most visitors do Paestum as a day trip, it's not a bad place to stay overnight. Accommodations offer great value, and though it's a bit far, you could use Paestum as a base for day-tripping to Naples or the Amalfi Coast. There's a beach nearby, and hotels can help arrange visits to local buffalo-milk dairies.

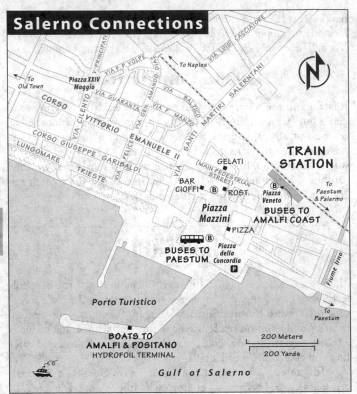

AMALFI COAST

Getting to Paestum

While Naples has direct connections to Paestum, from elsewhere you'll likely have to transfer in **Salerno** (see map).

The simplest way to reach Paestum is by **direct train from Naples' Centrale Station** (10/day, 1.5 hours, €7.50; no round-trip discount, but the €11.60 weekend-only day pass saves money, no day pass savings on weekdays). You'll need a U8 UnicoCampania regional ticket, available from *tabacchi* stores or the ticket windows at Naples' Centrale Station, which you must stamp before boarding. (Since trains to Paestum are "regional," you can't buy tickets from the automated machines at stations.) For a morning visit from Naples, you'll need to get an early start (always smart in warm weather): the first train leaves Naples at 6:30, and after the 8:30 departure, the next is at 12:52. The last three trains back from Paestum depart at 19:29, 20:45, and 21:48, arriving in Naples at 21:10, 22:26, and 23:06 (before setting off, check current times at stations or www.trenitalia.it).

From **Amalfi** or **Positano,** you can take either a bus or boat to Salerno, where you pick up the same train to Paestum on its way from Naples (35-40 minutes, €3.40). Buy your train ticket at the ticket office or the Il Globo Celeste travel agency in the Salerno train station (stamp before boarding). Buses from Amalfi terminate at the Salerno train station, but if you arrive in Salerno from the Amalfi Coast by boat, you will have to walk from the boat dock several blocks up to the train station (see the Salerno map). Alternatively, local CSTP bus #34 leaves from Piazza della Concordia in Salerno, by the base of the boat dock, for Paestum roughly every hour (1-hour trip, same €3.40 ticket). This Salerno-Paestum bus is slower than the train, and the stop is unmarked, with no posted schedule and no nearby ticket office. But it can be an option, especially during midday hours when trains are sparse. The bus brings you only slightly closer to the ruins at Paestum.

While it's technically possible to day-trip from **Sorrento** to Paestum by public transport, it makes for a very long day marred by worry about making connections back. Consider renting a car or hiring a taxi for the day. While the Amalfi Coast is a thrill to drive off-season, summer traffic is miserable. From Sorrento, Paestum is 60 miles and 3 hours via the coast, but a much smoother 2 hours by autostrada. To reach Paestum from Sorrento via the autostrada, drive toward Naples, catch the autostrada (direction: Salerno), skirt Salerno (direction: Reggio), exit at Battipaglia, and drive straight through the roundabout. During your ride, you'll see many signs for *mozzarella di bufala,* cheese made from the milk of water buffalo. Try it here—it can't be any fresher.

Planning Your Time

Allow two hours to see the ruins and the museum. Which one you see first depends on your interest and the heat. You'll enjoy the best light and smallest crowds late in the day.

Orientation to Paestum

Tourist Information: At the TI, next to the Paestum Archaeological Museum, pick up a free info booklet of the site (TI open daily 9:00-13:00 & 15:00-17:00, tel. 0828-811-016, www.infopaestum.it).

Arrival at Paestum: If you're arriving by train, exit the tiny station and walk through the old city gate; the ruins are an eight-minute walk straight ahead. (The station has no luggage storage, and its WC is usually locked.) Buses from Salerno (see "Getting to Paestum," earlier) stop near a corner of the ruins (at a little bar/café).

Cost: €10, includes site and museum.

Hours: Both museum and site are open daily at 8:30 (except the first and third Mon of each month, when the museum is closed). Year-round, the museum closes at 19:15 (last ticket sold at 18:45). The site closes one hour before sunset (as late as 19:30 June-July, as early as 15:00 in mid-Dec, last site ticket sold one hour before closing, tel. 0828-811-023).

Information: While there are scant descriptions at the site itself, this book provides all the information you need for both the site and the museum. The museum bookshop sells several mediocre guidebooks, including a €15 past-and-present guide. Dull €5 audioguides are available to rent at the museum or at site entrances (ID required). The €1.50 booklet, sold at the ticket desk, gives only general information and is more souvenir than guide.

Local Guide: Silvia Braggio is a good guide who gives a fine two-hour walk of the site and museum (special rate with this book—€100, must arrange in advance, mobile 347-643-2307, www.silviaguide.it, silvia@silviaguide.it).

Eating: La Basilica Café, between the parking lot and TI, is the most straightforward and reasonable option, with good €5-8 pizzas and other lunch fare, and free Wi-Fi (June-Sept daily 8:00-24:00, until 20:00 off-season, closed Jan, Via Magna Grecia 881, tel. 0828-811-301). **Ristorante Nettuno,** with quality food and good temple views, is more expensive and upscale (by the south entrance to the ruins).

Entry: The site and museum have separate entrances. The museum, just outside the ruins, is in a cluster with the TI and a small paleo-Christian basilica. Most visitors buy tickets at the museum and use the entrance across the street, but another ticket office and entrance is near the recommended Ristorante Nettuno (at the south end of the site). On days when the museum is closed (first and third Monday of each month), you have to buy tickets at the site entrances.

Self-Guided Tours

Paestum Archaeological Site

This tour starts at the entrance by the museum, visits the Temple of Ceres, goes through the center of the Roman town past the Greek Memorial Tomb, circles around the other two Greek temples, and then leaves the site to walk down the modern road to the Ekklesiasterion (which faces the museum).

Background: While Paestum is famous for its marvelous Greek temples, most of the structures you see are Roman. Five elements of Greek Paestum survive: three misnamed temples, a memorial tomb, and a circular meeting place (or Ekklesiasterion). The rest, including the wall that defines the site, is Roman.

Paestum was once a seaport (the ocean is now about a mile

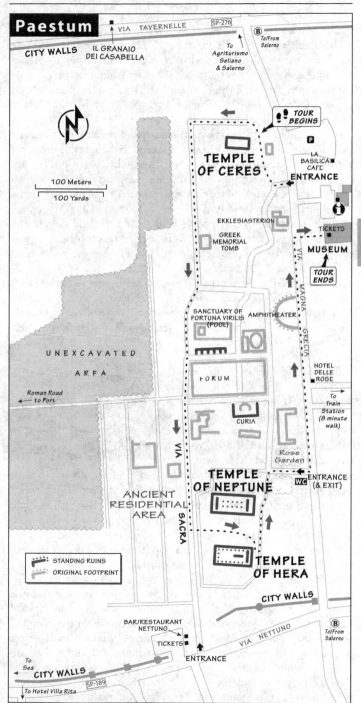

Paestum

VIA TAVERNELLE — SP-276

CITY WALLS

IL GRANAIO
DEI CASABELLA

To/From Salerno — (B)

To Agriturismo
Seliano
& Salerno

N

100 Meters

100 Yards

TOUR BEGINS

P

LA BASILICA CAFE

TEMPLE OF CERES

ENTRANCE

EKKLESIASTERION

TICKETS

GREEK MEMORIAL TOMB

MUSEUM

TOUR ENDS

VIA MAGNA GRECIA

SANCTUARY OF
FORTUNA VIRILIS
(POOL)

AMPHITHEATER

UNEXCAVATED
AREA

FORUM

HOTEL DELLE ROSE

Roman Road
to Port

To Train Station (8 minute walk)

CURIA

Rose Garden

ANCIENT
RESIDENTIAL
AREA

VIA SACRA

TEMPLE OF NEPTUNE

WC

ENTRANCE (& EXIT)

.... STANDING RUINS

—— ORIGINAL FOOTPRINT

TEMPLE OF HERA

CITY WALLS

BAR/RESTAURANT
NETTUNO

TICKETS

VIA NETTUNO

To/From Salerno — (B)

To Sea

CITY WALLS

SP-189

ENTRANCE

To Hotel Villa Rita

AMALFI COAST

away—the wall in the distance, which stretches about three miles, is about halfway to today's coastline). Only about a fifth of the site has been excavated. The Greek city, which archaeologists figure had a population of about 13,000, was first conquered by Lucanians (distant relatives of the Romans, who spoke a language related to Latin), and then by the Romans (who completely made it over and built the wall you see today).

The remaining Greek structures survive because the Romans were superstitious—they respected sacred areas, and didn't mess with temples and tombs. While most old Christian churches are built upon Roman temples (it's just what people do when they conquer another culture), no Roman temple is built upon a Greek temple. Romans appreciated how religion could function as the opiate of the masses. As long as people paid their taxes and obeyed the emperor's dictates, the practical Romans had no problem with any religion. The three Greek temples that you'll see here today have stood for about 2,500 years.

• *Buy your ticket at the museum, then head to the right to find the site's north entrance. Once inside, stand in front of the...*

Temple of Ceres: All three Paestum temples have inaccurate names, coined by 19th-century archaeologists who based their "discoveries" on wishful think-ing. (While the Romans made things easy by leaving lots of inscriptions, the Greeks did not.) Those 1800s archaeologists wanted this temple to be devoted to Ceres, the goddess of agriculture. However, all the little votive statues found later, when  modern archaeologists dug here, instead depicted a woman with a big helmet: Athena, goddess of wisdom and war. (The Greeks' female war goddess was also the goddess of wisdom—thinking...strategy...female. The Romans' masculine war god was Mars—just fighting.) Each temple is part of a sanctuary—an open, sacred space around the temple. Because regular people couldn't go into the temple, the altar logically stood outside.

The Temple of Ceres dates from 500 B.C. It's made of locally quarried limestone blocks. Good roads and shipping didn't come along until the Romans, so the Greeks' buildings were limited to local materials. The wooden roof is long gone. Like the other two temples, this one was once painted white, black, and red, and has an east-west orientation—facing the rising sun. This temple's *cella* (interior room) is gone, cleared out when it was used as a Christian church in the sixth century. In medieval times, Normans scavenged stones from here; chunks of these temples can be found in Amalfi's cathedral.

Walk around to the back side of the Temple of Ceres. The capitals broke in a modern earthquake, so a steel bar provides necessary support. Each of the Paestum temples is Doric style—with three stairs, columns without a base, and shafts that narrow at the top to a simple capital of a round then a square block. While there were no carved reliefs, colorful frescoes once decorated the pediments.

As you walk away, look back at the temple. Traditionally, Greeks would build a sanctuary of Athena on a city's highest spot (like the Parthenon in Athens, on the Acropolis). Paestum had no hill, so the Greeks created a mound. The hill was more impressive in its time because the Greek city level was substantially lower than the Roman pavement stones you'll walk on today.

• *From here, walk about 100 yards down the paving stones of Via Sacra toward the other Greek temples. To the left of the road, you'll see a little half-buried house with a tiled roof.*

Greek Memorial Tomb (Heroon): This tomb (from 500 B.C.) also survived because the Romans respected religious buildings. But the tomb was most inconveniently located, right in the middle of their growing city. So the practical Romans built a perimeter wall around it (visible today), added a fine tiled roof, and then buried the tomb.

There's a mystery here. Greeks generally buried their dead outside the city (as did Romans)—there are over a thousand ancient tombs outside Paestum's walls—yet this tomb was parked smack-dab in the center of town. When it was uncovered in 1952, no bodies were found inside. The tomb instead held nine perfectly preserved vases (now in the museum). Archaeologists aren't sure of the tomb's purpose. Perhaps it was a memorial dedicated to some great hero (like a city founder). Or perhaps it was a memorial to those lost when a neighboring community had to evacuate and settle as refugees here.

• *Continue walking down Via Sacra, the main drag of...*

Roman Paestum: Roman towns were garrison towns: rectangular with a grid street plan and two main streets cutting north-south and east-west, dividing the town into four equal sections. They were built by military engineers with a no-nonsense standard design. New excavations (on the left) have uncovered Roman-era lead piping. City administration buildings were on the left, and residential buildings were on the right.

Shortly after the road turns into a dirt path, you'll come to a big Roman pool that archaeologists believe was a sanctuary dedicated to Fortuna Virilis, goddess of luck and fertility. The strange stones likely supported a wooden platform for priests and statues of gods. Imagine young women walking down the ramp at the far end and through the pool, hoping to conceive a child.

The next big square was the Roman forum and ancient Paestum's main intersection. The road on the right led directly (and very practically) to the port. It made sense to have a direct connection to move freight between the sea and the center of town.

Until 2007, the vast field of ruins between the forum and the next temple (on the right) was covered in vegetation. It's since been cleared and cleaned of harmful lichen, which produce acids that dissolve limestone. Study the rocks: Yellow lichen is alive, black is dead. Even the great temples of Paestum were covered in this destructive lichen until 2000, when a two-year-long project cleaned them for the first time.

• *Ahead on the left are the so-called...*

Temples of Neptune and Hera: The **Temple of Neptune** dates from 450 B.C. and employs the Greek architectural trick where the

base line is curved up just a tad, to overcome the illusion of sagging caused by a straight base. The Athenians built their Parthenon (with a similar bowed-up base line) just 30 years after this. Many think this temple could have been their inspiration.

The adjacent **Temple of Hera,** dating from 550 B.C., is the oldest of Paestum's three temples and one of the oldest Greek temples still standing anywhere.

Notice the change 100 years makes in the architectural styles: Archaic Doric in 550 B.C. versus Classic Doric in 450 B.C.

Archaeologists now believe the "Temple of Neptune" was actually devoted to a different god. Votive statues uncovered here suggest that

Hera was the focus (perhaps this was a new and improved version of the adjacent, simpler, and older Temple of Hera). Or perhaps it was a temple to Zeus, Hera's husband, to honor the couple together.

Together, the two temples formed a single huge sanctuary with altars on the far (east) side. Walk around to the front. Notice how overbuilt the Temple of Hera appears. Its columns and capitals are closer together than necessary, as if the builders lacked confidence in their ability to span the distance between supports. Square pillars mark the corners of the *cella* inside. Temples with an odd number of columns (here, nine) had a single colonnade crossing in the center inside to support the wooden roof. More modern temples (such as the Temple of Neptune) had six columns, with two colonnades passing through the *cella*. This left a line of vision open through the middle so that worshippers could see the big statue of the god.

By the way, in 1943, Allied paratroopers dropped in near here during the famous "Landing of Salerno," when the Allies (who had already taken Sicily) invaded mainland Italy. Paestum was part of their first beachhead. The Temple of Hera served as an Allied military tent hospital. From here, the Allies pushed back the Nazis, marching to Naples, Cassino, and finally to Rome.

• *Leave the site and turn left on the modern road, Via Magna Grecia. The king of Naples had this Naples-to-Paestum road built in 1829 to inspire his people with ancient temples. While he was modern in his appreciation of antiquity, his road project destroyed a swath of the ancient city, as you'll see as you pass by half of the small amphitheater. Just past the amphitheater, you'll find the...*

Ekklesiasterion: Immediately across the street from the museum is what looks like a sunken circular theater. This rare bit of ancient Greek ruins was the Ekklesiasterion, a meeting place where the Greeks would get together to discuss things and vote. Archaeologists believe that the agora (market) would also have been located here.

• *Across the street is the...*

Paestum Archaeological Museum

Paestum's museum offers the rare opportunity to see artifacts—dating from prehistoric to Greek to Roman times—at the site where they were discovered. These beautifully crafted works (with good English descriptions throughout) help bring Paestum to life. Not everything you see here is from Paestum, though, as the museum also collects artifacts from other nearby sites.

Before stepping into the museum, notice the proud fascist architecture. Though the building dates from 1954, it was designed in 1938. It seems to command that you *will* enjoy this history lesson.

The exhibit is on several levels. You'll find mostly Greek pieces on the ground floor (artifacts from the Temple of Hera in front, frescoes from tombs in the back), Paleolithic to Iron Age artifacts on the mezzanine level, and Roman art on the top floor (statues, busts, and inscriptions dating from the time of the Roman occupation). While Roman art is not unique to Paestum, the Greek collection is—so that's what you should focus on. Here are the highlights:

Temple Reliefs: The museum's first room is designed like a Greek temple, with an inner *cella* that is used for temporary exhibitions. The large carvings overhead that wrap around this inner sanctum once adorned a sanctuary of the goddess Hera (wife of Zeus) five miles away. This sanctuary, called Heraion del Sele, was discovered and excavated in 1934. Some of the carvings show scenes from the life of Hercules. To the left side, displays tell the story of the excavation of both Heraion del Sele and Paestum.

• *Along the back wall of this room, find the glass case holding nine perfectly preserved...*

Vases: One ceramic and eight bronze, with artistic handles, these vases were found in Paestum's Greek Memorial Tomb (described earlier). Greek bronzes are rare because Romans often melted them down to make armor. These were discovered in 1952, filled with still-liquid honey and sealed with beeswax. The honey (as you can see in the display cases below) has since crystallized. Honey was a standard part of a funeral because, to ancient Greeks, honey symbolized immortality...it lasts forever.

• *The next room is filled with ancient Greek...*

Votive Offerings: These were dug up at Heraion del Sele (not at Paestum). Such offerings are a huge help to modern archaeologists, since the figures worshippers brought to a temple are clues as to which god the temple honored. These votives depict a woman with a crown on a throne—clearly Hera. The clay votives were simple, affordable, and accessible to regular people.

• *Now enter the large room (broken up by pillars and interior walls) that holds...*

Relics from the Temples at Paestum: This room displays smaller pieces that have been dug up at the site. Paestum's three temples were once adorned with decorations, such as ornamental spouts that spurted rainwater out of lions' mouths. Notice the bits of the surviving black, red, and white paint, and the reconstructions showing archaeologists' best guesses as to how the original decorations might have looked.

Displays (mostly in Italian) tell in which temple each relic was found. The Temple of Ceres is often referred to as the Temple of Athena or as the northern (*settentrionale*) sanctuary. The Temples of Neptune and Hera are spoken of as the southern (*meridionale*) sanctuaries. A fine drawing by Piranesi is on display, showing his visit to Paestum in 1777.

• *In a glass case nearby, find the statue of...*

Zeus: This painted clay statue of Zeus dates from 520 B.C. The king of the gods was so lusty with his antics, he's still smirking.

• *Look out the museum's back window for a good...*

View of Paestum's Walls: The walls of ancient Paestum reach halfway to the mountain—a reminder that most of the site is still private property and yet to be excavated. The town up on the mountainside is Capaccio, established in the eighth century when inhabitants of the original city of Paestum were driven out by malaria and the city was abandoned.

• *Walk along the corridor at the back of the museum, which shows...*

Objects from Tombs: Over 1,000 tombs have been identified outside of the ancient city's wall. About 100 were found decorated with frescoes or containing objects such as these.

• *At the far end of the corridor, turn left to see...*

The Tomb of the Diver: This is the museum's treasure and the most precious Paestum find. Dating from 480 B.C., it's not only the

sole ancient Greek tomb fresco in the museum—it's the only one ever found in southern Italy. Discovered in 1968, it has five frescoed slabs (four sides and a lid; the bottom wasn't decorated). The Greeks saw death as a passage: diving from mortality into immortality...into an un-

known world. Archaeologists believe that the pillars shown on the fresco represent the Pillars of Hercules at Gibraltar, which in ancient times defined the known world. The ocean beyond the Mediterranean was the great unknown...like the afterlife. The Greek banquet makes it clear that this was an aristocratic man.

• *After the Tomb of the Diver, the next room displays...*

Lucanian Tomb Frescoes: The many other painted slabs in the museum date from a later time, around 350 B.C., when Paestum fell under Lucanian rule. These frescoes are cruder than their earlier Greek counterpart. The people who conquered the Greeks tried to appropriate their art and style, but they lacked the Greeks' distinctive light touch. Still, these offer fascinating glimpses into ancient life here at Paestum.

• *Beyond this room, you'll find yourself back at the entrance. Before you leave, go up the stairs by the bookshop for a glimpse at the mezzanine level, which focuses on prehistoric archaeology. The exhibit here has much better English translations than the ground floor. At the very least, check out the...*

Film Footage from WWII: A 10-minute continuous film loop, subtitled in English, tells the story of Allied soldiers' encounters with the ruins in 1943. You'll see footage of soldiers hanging up their laundry and shaving in the temples, which they actually safeguarded well. Part of the film focuses on excavations directed by a British archaeologist who was attached to the invading forces.

Sleeping in Paestum

Paestum at night, with views of the floodlit ruins, is magic. Accommodations here offer great value. You can sleep in a mansion for the same price you'd pay for a closet in Positano. The prices

AMALFI COAST

listed are for high season (which rise further in August). All have free parking.

$ Il Granaio dei Casabella, a converted old granary with 14 attractive, reasonably priced rooms, is a 10-minute walk from the ruins. It has a beautiful garden and pretty common areas, and four rooms have views of one of the ancient temples (Sb-€70, Db-€90, Tb-€110, Qb-€130, about €20 more per room mid-July-Aug, 10 percent discount for Rick Steves readers, air-con, free Wi-Fi, just west of the bus stop closest to Salerno at Via Tavernelle 84, tel. 0828-781-014, www.ilgranaiodeicasabella.com, info@ilgranaio-deicasabella.com, hospitable Celardo family).

$ Hotel Villa Rita is a tidy, quiet country hotel set on two acres within walking distance of the beach and the temples. It has 22 rooms, a kid-friendly swimming pool, and attractive grounds with grassy lawns and a little soccer field (Sb-€70, Db-€90-100, €130 in Aug, third bed-€15, lunch or dinner-€16, Luigi promises a 10 percent discount with this book and cash in 2014, air-con, free Wi-Fi, closed Nov-Feb, Via Nettuno 9, tel. 0828-811-081, www.hotelvillarita.it, info@hotelvillarita.it). The hotel is a 10-minute walk west of the Hera entrance and public bus stop, and a 20-minute walk from the train station (they can usually pick you up, if you're arriving with luggage).

$ Hotel delle Rose, with 10 small, basic rooms with minuscule bathrooms, is near the Neptune entrance on the street bordering the ruins. It's an acceptable choice for those on a budget and is also the option closest to the ruins and the train station (Sb-€35, Db-€60, Tb-€70, Qb-€85, Luigi promises these prices in 2014 if you mention this book and reserve direct, Via Magna Grecia 943, tel. 0828-199-0692, www.hotelristorantedellerose.com, info@ho-telristorantedellerose.com).

Nearby

$ Agriturismo Seliano is a great option for drivers only. It offers plush public spaces, a pool, and 14 grand, spacious rooms on a peaceful, once-elegant farm estate that's been in the same family for 300 years (Db-€80-90, €110 in Aug, air-con, guest computer, free Wi-Fi, closed Nov-March; one mile north of ruins on main road—Via Magna Grecia—a small *Azienda Agrituristica Seliano* sign directs you down long dirt driveway; Via Seliano, tel. 0828-723-634, www.agriturismoseliano.it, seliano@agriturismoseliano.it). They serve a fine lunch or dinner with produce fresh from the garden (€20 for guests or €25 for non-guests, price includes all your drinks). The place is run by Cecilia, an English-speaking baroness, and her family—including about a dozen dogs.

Paestum Connections

By Train: Ten slow, milk-run trains a day head to Salerno (40 minutes, €3.40) and Naples (1.5 hours, €7.50). In Salerno, you can change for the bus to Amalfi, or walk down to the harbor to catch an Amalfi- or Positano-bound boat. Buy your train ticket at the bar-café near the Paestum TI or various souvenir shops—the station is not staffed. The last train out is at 21:48 (recheck times at station).

By Bus to Salerno: Buses from Paestum to Salerno run roughly every hour (1 hour, last departure about 20:00, €3.40). Buy a ticket from one of the bars in Paestum, then go to either of the intersections that flank the ruins (see map on page 1131), flag down any northbound bus, and ask, "Salerno?" From Salerno, you can continue on to Amalfi or Positano by boat, or walk up to the train station to catch an Amalfi-bound SITA bus or a train. Salerno's TI has bus, ferry, and train schedules (Mon-Sat 9:00-13:00 & 15:15-19:15, closed Sun, shorter hours off-season, on Piazza Veneto, just outside train station, tel. 089-231-432, toll-free 800-213-289, www.turismoinsalerno.it).

AMALFI COAST

ITALIAN HISTORY

Italy has a lot of history, so let's get started.

Origins of Rome (C. 753 B.C.-450 B.C.)

A she-wolf breastfed two human babies, Romulus and Remus, who grew to build the city of Rome in 753 B.C.—you buy that? Closer to fact, farmers and shepherds of the Latin tribe settled near the mouth of the Tiber River, a convenient trading location. The crude settlement was sandwiched between two sophisticated civilizations—Greek colonists to the south (Magna Grecia, or greater Greece), and the Etruscans of Tuscany, whose origins and language are largely still a mystery to historians (for more on the Etruscans, see page 704). Baby Rome was both dominated and nourished by these societies.

When an Etruscan king raped a Roman woman (509 B.C.), her husband led a revolt, driving out the Etruscan kings and replacing them with elected Roman senators and (eventually) a code of law ("Laws of the Twelve Tables," 450 B.C.). The Roman Republic was born.

The Roman Republic Expands (C. 509 B.C.- A.D. 1)

Located in the center of the peninsula, Rome was perfectly situated for trading salt and wine. Roman businessmen, backed by a disciplined army, expanded through the Italian peninsula, establishing a Roman infrastructure as they went. Rome soon swallowed up its northern Etruscan neighbors, conquering them by force and absorbing their culture.

Next came Magna Grecia, with Rome's legions defeating the Greek general Pyrrhus after several costly "Pyrrhic" victories (c. 275 B.C.). Rome now ruled a united federation stretching from Tuscany to the Italian peninsula, with a standard currency, a system of roads (including the Via Appia), and a standing army of a half-million soldiers ready for the next challenge: Carthage.

Carthage (modern-day Tunisia) and Rome fought the three bitter Punic Wars for control of the Mediterranean (264-201 B.C. and 146 B.C.). The balance of power hung precariously in the Second Punic War (218-201 B.C.), when Hannibal of Carthage crossed the sea to Spain with a huge army of men and elephants. He marched 1,200 miles overland, crossed the Alps, and forcefully penetrated Italy from the rear. Almost at the gates of the city of Rome, he was finally turned back. The Romans prevailed and, in the mismatched Third Punic War, they burned the city of Carthage to the ground (146 B.C.).

The well-tuned Roman legions easily subdued sophisticated Greece in three Macedonian Wars (215-146 B.C.). Though Rome conquered Greece, Greek culture dominated the Romans. From hairstyles to statues to temples to the evening's entertainment, Rome was forever "Hellenized," becoming the curators of Greek culture, passing it down to future generations.

By the first century B.C., Rome was master of the Mediterranean. Booty, cheap grain, and thousands of captured slaves poured in, transforming the economic model from small farmers to unemployed city dwellers living off tribute from conquered lands. The Republic had changed.

Civil Wars and the Transition to Empire (First Century B.C.)

With easy money streaming in and traditional roles obsolete, Romans bickered among themselves over their slice of the pie. Wealthy landowners (patricians, the ruling Senate) wrangled with the middle and working classes (plebeians) and with the growing population of slaves, who demanded greater say-so in government. In 73 B.C., Spartacus—a Greek-born soldier-turned-Roman slave who'd been forced to fight as a gladiator—escaped to the slopes of Mount Vesuvius, where he amassed an army of 70,000 angry slaves. After two years of fierce fighting across Italy, the Roman legions crushed the revolt and crucified 6,000 rebels along the Via Appia as a warning.

Amid the chaos of class war and civil war, charismatic generals who could provide wealth and security became dictators—men such as Sulla, Crassus, Pompey...and Caesar. Julius Caesar (100-44 B.C.) was a cunning politician, riveting speaker, conqueror of Gaul, author of *The Gallic Wars*, and lover of Cleopatra, Queen of Egypt. In his four-year reign, he reformed and centralized the government around himself. Disgruntled Republicans feared that he would make himself king. At his peak of power, they surrounded

The Roman Empire at Its Peak: Pax Romana A.D. 120

CALEDONIA

HIBERNIA

HADRIAN'S WALL

SCANDIA

BRITANNIA

BARBARIANS

RHINE RIVER

DANUBE RIVER

GAUL

GERMANIA

DACIA

ITALIA

ILLYRICUM

THRACE

HISPANIA

Roma

ASIA

CAPPADOCIA

ARMENIA

MEDIA

MESOPOTAMIA

MAURITANIA

Mediterranean Sea

SYRIA

AFRICA

EGYPT

Roman Empire

Caesar in the Senate on the "Ides of March" (March 15, 44 B.C.) and stabbed him to death.

Julius Caesar died, but the concept of one-man rule lived on in his adopted son. Named Octavian at birth, he defeated rival Mark Antony (another lover of Cleopatra, 31 B.C.) and was proclaimed Emperor Augustus (27 B.C.). Augustus outwardly followed the traditions of the Republic, while in practice he acted as a dictator with the backing of Rome's legions and the rubber-stamp approval of the Senate. He established his family to succeed him (making the family name "Caesar" a title), and set the pattern of rule by emperors for the next 500 years.

The Roman Empire (c. A.D. 1-500)

In his 40-year reign, Augustus ended Rome's civil wars and ushered in the Pax Romana: 200 years of prosperity and relative peace. Rome ruled an empire of 54 million people, stretching from Scotland to Africa, from Spain to the "Cradle of Civilization" (modern-day Iraq). Conquered peoples were welcomed into the fold of prosperity, linked by roads, common laws, common gods, education, and the Latin language. The city of Rome, with more than a million inhabitants, was decorated with Greek-style statues and monumental structures faced with marble. It was the marvel of the known world.

The empire prospered on a (false) economy of booty, slaves, and cheap imports. On the Italian peninsula, traditional small farms were swallowed up by large farming and herding estates. In this "global economy," the Italian peninsula became just one province of many in a worldwide Latin-speaking empire, ruled by an emperor who was likely born elsewhere. The empire even survived the often turbulent and naughty behavior of emperors such as Caligula (r. 37-41) and Nero (r. 54-68).

Decline and Fall (A.D. 200-500)

Rome peaked in the second century A.D. under the capable emperors Trajan (r. 98-117), Hadrian (r. 117-138), and Marcus Aurelius (r. 161-180). For the next three centuries, the Roman Empire declined, shrinking in size and wealth, a victim of corruption, disease, an overextended army, a false economy, and the constant pressure of "barbarian" tribes pecking away at its borders. By the third century, the army had become the real power, handpicking figurehead emperors to do its bidding—in a 40-year span, 15 emperors were first saluted and then assassinated by fickle generals.

Trying to stall the disintegration, Emperor Diocletian (r. 284-305) split the empire into two administrative halves under two equal emperors. Constantine (r. 306-337) solidified the divide by moving the capital of the empire from decaying Rome to the new city of Constantinople (330, present-day Istanbul). Almost instantly, the once-great city of Rome became a minor player in imperial affairs. (The eastern "Byzantine" half of the empire would thrive and live on for another thousand years.) Constantine also legalized Christianity (313), and the once-persecuted cult soon became virtually the state religion, the backbone of Rome's fading hierarchy.

By 410, "Rome" had shrunk to just the city itself, surrounded by a protective wall. Barbarian tribes from the north and east poured in to loot and plunder. The city was sacked by Visigoths (410), vandalized by Vandals (455), and the pope had to plead with Attila the Hun for mercy (451). The peninsula's population fell to six million, trade and agriculture were disrupted, schools closed, and the infrastructure collapsed. Peasants huddled near powerful lords for protection from bandits, planting the seeds of medieval feudalism.

In 476, the last emperor sold his title for a comfy pension, and Rome fell like a huge column, kicking up dust that would plunge Europe into a thousand years of darkness. For the next 13 centuries, there would be no "Italy," just a patchwork of rural dukedoms and towns, victimized by foreign powers. Italy lay in shambles, helpless.

Invasions (A.D. 500-1000)

In 500 years, Italy suffered through a full paragraph of invasions: Lombards (568) and Byzantines (under Justinian, 536) occupied the north. In the south, Muslim Saracens (827) and Christian Normans (1061) established thriving kingdoms. Charlemagne, King of the Franks (a Germanic tribe), defeated the Lombards, and on Christmas Day A.D. 800, he knelt before the pope in St. Peter's in Rome to be crowned "Holy Roman Emperor." For the next thousand years, Italians would pledge nominal allegiance to weak, distant German kings as their "Holy Roman Emperor," an empty title meant to resurrect the glory of ancient Rome united with medieval Christianity.

Through all of the invasions and chaos, the glory of ancient Rome was preserved in the pomp, knowledge, hierarchy, and wealth of the Christian Church. Strong popes (Leo I, 440-461, and Gregory the Great, 590-604) ruled like small-time emperors, governing territories in central Italy called the Papal States.

Prosperity and Politics (A.D. 1000-1300)

Italy survived Y1K, and the economy picked up. Sea-trading cities like Venice, Genoa, Pisa, Naples, and Amalfi grew wealthy as middlemen between Europe and the Orient. During the Crusades (e.g., First Crusade 1097-1130), Italian ships ferried Europe's Christian soldiers eastward, then returned laden with spices and highly marked-up luxury goods from the Orient. Trade spawned banking, and Italians became capitalists, loaning money at interest to Europe's royalty. Italy pioneered a new phenomenon in Europe—cities *(comuni)* that were self-governing commercial centers. The medieval prosperity of the cities laid the foundation of the future Renaissance.

Politically, the Italian peninsula was dominated by two rulers—the pope in Rome and the German "Holy Roman Emperor" (with holdings in the north). It split Italy into two warring political parties: supporters of the popes (called Guelphs, centered in urban areas) and supporters of the emperors (Ghibellines, popular with the rural nobility).

The Unlucky 1300s

In 1309, the pope—enticed by Europe's fast-rising power, France—moved from Rome to Avignon, France. At one point, two rival popes reigned, one in Avignon and the other in Rome, and they excommunicated each other. The papacy eventually returned to Rome (1377), but the schism had created a breakdown in central authority that was exacerbated by an outbreak of bubonic plague (Black Death, 1347-1348), which killed a third of the Italian population.

In the power vacuum, new powers emerged in the independent cities. Venice, Florence, Milan, and Naples were under the protection and leadership of local noble families *(signoria)* such as the Medici in Florence. Florence thrived in the wool and dyeing

Church Architecture

History comes to life when you visit a centuries-old church. Even if you wouldn't know your apse from a hole in the ground, learning a few simple terms will enrich your experience. Note that not every church has every feature, and that a "cathedral" isn't a type of church architecture, but rather a designation for a church that's a governing center for a local bishop.

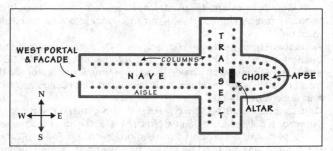

Aisles: The long, generally low-ceilinged arcades that flank the nave.

Altar: The raised area with a ceremonial table (often adorned with candles or a crucifix), where the priest prepares and serves the bread and wine for Communion.

Apse: The space beyond the altar, generally bordered with small chapels.

Barrel Vault: A continuous round-arched ceiling that resembles an extended upside-down U.

Choir: A cozy area, often screened off, located within the church nave and near the high altar, where services are sung in a more intimate setting.

Cloister: Covered hallways bordering a (usually square-shaped) open-air courtyard, traditionally where monks and nuns got fresh air.

Facade: The outer wall of the church's main (west) entrance, viewable from outside and generally highly decorated.

Groin Vault: An arched ceiling formed where two equal barrel vaults meet at right angles. Less common usage: term for a medieval jock strap.

Narthex: The area (portico or foyer) between the main entry and the nave.

Nave: The long, central section of the church (running west to east, from the entrance to the altar) where, in medieval times, the congregation stood through the service.

Transept: The north-south part of the church, which crosses (perpendicularly) the east-west nave. In a traditional Latin cross-shaped floor plan, the transept forms the "arms" of the cross.

West Portal: The main entry to the church (on the west end, opposite the main altar).

Top 10 Italians

Romulus: Breastfed on wolf milk, this legendary orphan grew to found the city of Rome (traditionally in 753 B.C.). Over the next seven centuries, his descendants dominated the Italian peninsula, ruling from Rome as a Republic.

Julius Caesar (100-44 B.C.): After conquering Gaul (France), subduing Egypt, and winning Cleopatra's heart, Caesar ruled Rome with king-like powers. In an attempt to preserve the Republic, senators stabbed him to death, but the concept of one-man rule lived on.

Augustus (born Octavian, 63 B.C.-A.D. 14): Julius' adopted son became the first of the Caesars that ruled Rome during its 500 years as a Europe-wide power. He set the tone for emperors both good (Trajan, Hadrian, Marcus Aurelius) and bad (Caligula, Nero, and dozens of others).

Constantine (c. 280-337 A.D.): Raised in a Christian home, this emperor legalized Christianity, almost instantly turning a persecuted sect into a Europe-wide religion. With the Fall of Rome, the Church was directed by strong popes and so guided Italians through the next thousand years of invasions, plagues, political decentralization, and darkness.

Lorenzo the Magnificent (1449-1492): Soldier, poet, lover, and ruler of Florence in the 1400s, this Renaissance Man embodied the "rebirth" of ancient enlightenment. Lorenzo's wealthy Medici family funded Florentine artists who pioneered a realistic 3-D style.

Michelangelo Buonarroti (1475-1564): His statue of David—slaying an ignorant brute—stands as a monumental symbol of Italian enlightenment. Along with fellow geniuses Leonardo da Vinci and Raphael, Michelangelo spread the Italian Renaissance (painting, sculpture, architecture, literature, and ideas) to a worldwide audience.

trade, which led to international banking, with branches in all of Europe's capitals. A positive side effect of the terrible Black Death was that the now-smaller population got a bigger share of the land, jobs, and infrastructure. By century's end, Italy was poised to enter its most glorious era since antiquity.

The Renaissance (1400s)

The Renaissance *(Rinascimento)*—the "rebirth" of ancient Greek and Roman art styles, knowledge, and humanism—began in Italy (c. 1400), and spread through Europe over the next two centuries. Many of Europe's most famous painters, sculptors, and thinkers—Michelangelo, Leonardo, Raphael, etc.—were Italian.

It was a cultural boom that changed people's thinking about

Giovanni Lorenzo Bernini (1598-1680): The "Michelangelo of Baroque" kept Italy a major exporter of sophisticated trends. Bernini's ornate statues and architecture decorated palaces of the rising power in France, even as Italy was reverting to an economically stagnant patchwork of foreign-ruled states.

Victor Emmanuel II (1820-1878): As the only Italian-born ruler on the peninsula, this King of Sardinia became the rallying point for Italian unification. Aided by the general Garibaldi, writer Mazzini, and politician Cavour (with a soundtrack by Verdi), he became the first ruler of a united, democratic Italy in September of 1870. (The preceding proper nouns have since come to adorn streets and piazzas throughout Italy.)

Benito Mussolini (1883-1945): A kinder, gentler Hitler, he derailed Italy's fledgling democracy, becoming dictator of a fascist state, leading the country into defeat in World War II. No public places honor Mussolini, but many streets and piazzas throughout Italy bear the name of Giacomo Matteotti (1885-1924), a politician whose outspoken opposition to Mussolini got him killed by Fascists.

Federico Fellini (1920-1993): Fellini's films (*La Strada*, *La Dolce Vita*, *8½*) chronicle Italy's postwar years in gritty black and white—the poverty, destruction, and disillusionment of the war followed by the optimism, decadence, and materialism of the economic boom. He captured the surreal chaos of Italy's abrupt social change from traditional Catholic to a secular, urban world presided over by Mafia bosses and weak government.

Top Italian Number 11 (?): Has Italy produced another recent citizen who's dominant enough to make his or her mark on the world? Could it be former Prime Minister Silvio Berlusconi, Italy's richest man? The late opera singer Luciano Pavarotti? Or big-pec'd model "Fabio" Lanzoni, named "Sexiest Man on Earth" by *Cosmopolitan* magazine? The world awaits.

every aspect of life. In politics, it meant democracy. In religion, it meant a move away from Church dominance and toward the assertion of man (humanism) and a more personal faith. Science and secular learning were revived after centuries of superstition and ignorance. In architecture, it was a return to the balanced columns and domes of Greece and Rome. In painting, the Renaissance meant 3-D realism.

Italians dotted their cities with publicly financed art—Greek gods, Roman-style domed buildings. They preached Greek-style democracy and explored the natural world. The cultural boom was financed by booming trade and lucrative banking. During the Renaissance, the peninsula once again became the trendsetting cultural center of Europe.

End of the Renaissance, France and Spain Invade (1500s)

In May of 1498, Vasco da Gama of Portugal landed in India, having found a sea route around Africa. Italy's monopoly on trade with the East was broken. Portugal, France, Spain, England, and Holland—nation-states under strong central rule—began to overtake decentralized Italy. Italy's once-great maritime cities now traded in an economic backwater, just as Italy's bankers (such as the Medici in Florence) were going bankrupt. While the Italian Renaissance was all the rage throughout Europe, it declined in its birthplace. Italy—culturally sophisticated but weak and decentralized—was ripe for the picking by Europe's rising powers.

France and Spain invaded (1494 and 1495)—initially invited by Italian lords to attack their rivals—and began divvying up territory for their noble families. Italy also became a battleground in religious conflicts between Catholics and the new Protestant movement. In the chaos, the city of Rome was brutally sacked by foreign mercenary warriors (1527).

Foreign Rule (1600-1800)

For the next two centuries, most of Italy's states were ruled by foreign nobles, serving as prizes for the winners of Europe's dynastic wars. Italy ceased to be a major player in Europe, politically or economically. Italian intellectual life was often cropped short by a conservative Catholic Church trying to fight Protestantism. Galileo, for example, was forced by the Inquisition to renounce his belief that the earth orbited the sun (1633). But Italy did export Baroque art (Giovanni Lorenzo Bernini) and the budding new medium of opera.

The War of the Spanish Succession (1713)—a war in which Italy did not participate—gave much of northern Italy to Austria's ruling family, the Habsburgs (who now wore the crown of "Holy Roman Emperor"). In the south, Spain's Bourbon family ruled the Kingdom of Naples (known after 1816 as the Kingdom of the Two Sicilies), making it a culturally sophisticated but economically backward area, preserving a medieval, feudal caste system.

In 1720, a minor war (the War of Austrian Succession) created a new state at the foot of the Alps, called the Kingdom of Sardinia (a.k.a. the Kingdom of Piedmont, or Savoy). Ruled by the Savoy family, this was the only major state on the peninsula that was actually ruled by Italians. It proved to be a toehold to the future.

Italy Unites—The Risorgimento (1800s)

In 1796, Napoleon Bonaparte swept through Italy and changed everything. He ousted Austrian and Spanish dukes, confiscated Church lands, united scattered states, and crowned himself "King

Italian Unification

NOTE: Dates indicate the year of annexation to the Kingdom of Sardinia. After 1861, this became the Kingdom of Italy

SWITZERLAND

VENETIA (1866)

AUSTRIA

LOMBARDY (1859)

PIEDMONT

Venice

FRANCE

PARMA

MODENA

Florence

TUSCANY (1860)

STATES OF THE CHURCH (1870)

Adriatic Sea

KINGDOM OF SARDINIA

Rome

Naples

SARDINIA

KINGDOM OF THE TWO SICILIES (1860)

Mediterranean Sea

SICILY

100 Kilometers
100 Miles

of Italy" (1805). After his defeat (1815), Italy's old ruling order (namely, Austria and Spain) was restored. But Napoleon had planted a seed: What if Italians could unite and rule themselves like Europe's other modern nations?

For the next 50 years, a movement to unite Italy slowly grew. Called the Risorgimento—a word that means "rising again"—the movement promised a revival of Italy's glory. It started as a revolutionary, liberal movement—taking part in it was punishable by death. Members of a secret society called the Carbonari (led by a professional revolutionary named Giuseppe Mazzini) exchanged secret handshakes, printed fliers, planted bombs, and assassinated conservative rulers. Their small revolutions (1820-1821, 1831, 1848) were easily and brutally slapped down, but the cause wouldn't die.

Gradually, Italians of all stripes warmed to the idea of unification. Whether it was a united dictatorship, a united papal state, a united kingdom, or a united democracy, most Italians could agree that it was time for Spain, Austria, and France to leave.

The movement coalesced around the Italian-ruled Kingdom of Sardinia and its king, Victor Emmanuel II. In 1859, Sardinia's prime minister, Camillo Cavour, cleverly persuaded France to drive Austria out of northern Italy, leaving the region in Italian hands. A plebiscite (vote) was held, and several central Italian states (including some of the pope's) rejected their feudal lords and chose to join the growing Kingdom of Sardinia.

After victory in the north, Italy's most renowned Carbonari general, Giuseppe Garibaldi (1807-1882), steamed south with a thousand of his best soldiers *(I Mille)* and marched on the Spanish-ruled city of Naples (1860). The old order simply collapsed. In two short months, Garibaldi had achieved a seemingly impossible victory against a far superior army. Garibaldi sent a one-word telegram to the king of Sardinia: *"Obbedisco"* (I obey). The following year, an assembly of deputies from throughout Italy met in Turin and crowned Victor Emmanuel II "King of Italy." Only the pope in Rome held out, protected by French troops. When the city finally fell—easily—to the unification forces on September 20, 1870, the Risorgimento was complete. Italy went ape.

The Risorgimento was largely the work of four men: Garibaldi (the sword), Mazzini (the spark), Cavour (the diplomat), and Victor Emmanuel II (the rallying point). Today, street signs throughout Italy honor them and the dates of their great victories.

Mussolini and War (1900-1950)

Italy—now an actual nation-state, not just a linguistic region—entered the 20th century with a progressive government (a constitutional monarchy), a collection of colonies, and a flourishing northern half of the country. In the economically backward south (the Mezzogiorno), millions of poor peasants emigrated to the Americas. World War I (1915-1918) left 650,000 Italians dead, but being on the winning Allied side, survivors were granted possession of the alpine regions. In the postwar cynicism and anarchy, many radical political parties rose up—Communist, Socialist, Popular, and Fascist.

Benito Mussolini (1883-1945), a popular writer for socialist and labor-union newspapers, led the Fascists. ("Fascism" comes from Latin *fasci*, the bundles of rods that symbolized unity in ancient Rome.) Though only a minority (6 percent of the parliament in 1921), they intimidated the disorganized majority with organized violence by black-shirted Fascist gangs. In 1922, Mussolini seized the government (see "The March on

The March on Rome

In October of 1922, Benito Mussolini, head of the newly formed Fascist Party, boldly proposed a coup d'état, saying: "Either the government will be given to us, or we will take it by marching on Rome." Throughout Italy, black-shirted Fascists occupied government buildings in their hometowns. Others grabbed guns, farming hoes, and kitchen knives and set off to converge on the outskirts of Rome. (Estimates of the size of the Fascist band range from 300 to the 300,000 of Fascist legend.) Mussolini sent the government an ultimatum to surrender. Though the Fascists were easily outmanned and outgunned by government forces, the show of force intimidated the king, Victor Emmanuel III, into avoiding a nasty confrontation. He invited Mussolini to Rome. Mussolini arrived the next day (by first-class train), was made prime minister, then marched his black-shirted troops triumphantly through the streets of Rome.

HISTORY

Rome" sidebar) and began his rule as dictator for the next two decades.

Mussolini solidified his reign among Catholics by striking an agreement with the pope (Concordato, 1929), giving Vatican City to the papacy, while Mussolini ruled Italy with the implied blessing of the Catholic Church. Italy responded to the great worldwide Depression (1930s) with big public works projects (including Rome's subway), government investment in industry, and an expanded army.

Mussolini allied his country with Hitler's Nazi regime, drawing an unprepared Italy into World War II (1940). Italy's lame army was never a factor in the war, and when Allied forces landed in Sicily (1943), Italians welcomed them as liberators. The Italians toppled Mussolini's government and surrendered to the Allies, but Nazi Germany sent troops to rescue Mussolini. The war raged on as Allied troops inched their way north against German resistance. Italians were reduced to dire poverty. In the last days of the war (April of 1945), Mussolini was captured by the Italian resistance. They shot him and his girlfriend and hung their bodies upside-down in a public square in Milan.

Postwar Italy

At war's end, Italy was physically ruined and extremely poor. The nation rebuilt in the 1950s and 1960s (the "economic miracle") with Marshall Plan aid from the United States. Many Italian men moved to northern Europe to find work; many others left farms and flocked to the cities. Italy regained its standing among nations, joining the United Nations, NATO, and what would later become the European Union.

However, the government remained weak, changing on average once a year, shifting from right to left to centrist coalitions (it's had 62 governments since World War II). All Italians acknowledged that the real power lay in the hands of backroom politicians and organized crime—a phenomenon called *Tangentopoli*, or "Bribe City." The country remained strongly divided between the rich, industrial north and the poor, rural south.

Italian society changed greatly in the 1960s and 1970s, spurred by the liberal reforms of the Catholic Church at the Vatican II conference (1962-1965). The once-conservative Catholic country legalized divorce and contraception, and the birth rate plummeted. In the 1970s, the economy slowed thanks to inflation, strikes, and the worldwide energy crisis. Italy suffered a wave of violence from left- and right-wing domestic terrorists and organized crime, punctuated by the assassination of Prime Minister Aldo Moro (1978). A series of coalition governments in the 1980s brought some stability to the economy.

Italy Today

In the early 1990s, the judiciary launched a campaign to rid politics of corruption and Mafia ties. Though still ongoing, the investigation sent a message that Italy would no longer tolerate evils that were considered necessary just a generation earlier. As home to the Vatican, Italy keeps a close watch on the Catholic Church's ongoing scandal of pedophile priests.

In 2001, controversial billionaire Silvio Berlusconi—the owner of many of Italy's media outlets and Italy's richest person—became prime minister, heading a center-right coalition. In 2003, he lost a close election, but in 2008, the 74-year-old Berlusconi was re-elected prime minister. Berlusconi's personal life made him a polarizing figure—he was accused of corruption and of consorting with women one-fourth his age—but his downfall came when Italy's economy started hitting the skids. By the end of 2011, Italy's debt load was the second worst in the euro zone, behind only Greece. To calm the markets, Berlusconi resigned. The government was taken over by former European Commissioner Mario Monti, who appointed a cabinet composed entirely of unelected professionals rather than politicians.

Like other European nations, Italy has run up big deficits by providing comfy social benefits without sufficient tax revenue, forcing the Italian government to tighten its belt. The Yale-trained

Monti has his hands full enforcing austerity while trying to promote growth.

As you travel through Italy today, you'll encounter a fascinating country with a rich history and a per-capita income that comes close to its neighbors to the north. Despite its ups and downs, Italy remains committed to Europe...yet it's as wonderfully Italian as ever.

HISTORY

APPENDIX

Contents

Tourist Information

The Italian national tourist offices **in the US** are a wealth of information. Before your trip, scan their website (www.italia.it) or contact the nearest branch to briefly describe your trip and request information. You can download many brochures free of charge or call to order a free, general Italy guide. If you have a specific problem, they're a good source of sympathy.

In New York: Tel. 212/245-5618, newyork@enit.it

In Chicago: Tel. 312/644-0996, chicago@enit.it

In Los Angeles: Tel. 310/820-1898, losangeles@enit.it

In **Italy,** your best first stop is generally the tourist information office (abbreviated **TI** in this book, and marked *i, turismo,* and *APT* in Italy). TIs are good places to get a city map and information on public transit (including bus and train schedules), walking tours, special events, and nightlife. While Italian TIs are about half as helpful as those in other countries, their information is twice as important. Prepare a list of questions and a proposed plan to double-check. Many TIs have information on the entire country or at least the region, so try to pick up maps for destinations you'll be visiting later in your trip. If you're arriving in town after the TI closes, call ahead or pick up a map in a neighboring town. Since Italy is ever-changing, ask the local TI for a current list of the city's sights, hours, and prices.

Be wary of the travel agencies or special information services that masquerade as TIs but serve fancy hotels and tour companies. They're in the business of selling things you don't need.

Communicating

Hurdling the Language Barrier

Many Italians—especially those in the tourist trade and in big cities—speak some English. Still, you'll get more smiles and results by using at least a few Italian pleasantries. In smaller, non-touristy towns, Italian is the norm. Italians have an endearing habit of talking to you even if they know you don't speak their language—and yet, thanks to gestures and thoughtfully simplified words, it somehow works. Don't stop them to say you don't understand every word—just go along for the ride. For a list of survival phrases, see page 1197.

Note that Italian is pronounced much like English, with a few exceptions, such as: c followed by e or i is pronounced ch (to ask, *"Per centro?"*—To the center?—you say, pehr CHEHN-troh). In Italian, ch is pronounced like the hard c in Chianti (*chiesa*—church—is pronounced kee-AY-zah).

Give it your best shot. Italians appreciate your efforts.

Telephones

Smart travelers use the telephone to reserve or reconfirm rooms, get tourist information, reserve restaurants, confirm tour times, or phone home. This section covers dialing instructions, phone cards, and types of phones (for more in-depth information, see www.ricksteves.com/phoning).

How to Dial

Calling from the US to Italy, or vice versa, is simple—once you break the code. The European calling chart later in this chapter will walk you through it.

Dialing Domestically Within Italy

The following instructions apply whether you're dialing from a landline (such as a pay phone or your hotel-room phone) or an Italian mobile phone.

Italy has a direct-dial phone system (no area codes). To call anywhere within Italy, just dial the number. For example, the number of one of my recommended Florence hotels is 055-289-592. That's the number you dial whether you're calling it from Florence's train station or from Rome.

Italy's landlines start with 0, and mobile lines start with 3. The country's toll-free lines begin with 80. These 80 numbers—called *freephone* or *numero verde* (green number)—can be dialed free from any phone without using a phone card. Note that you can't call Italy's toll-free numbers from the US, nor can you count on reaching American toll-free numbers from Italy. Any Italian phone number that starts with 8 but isn't followed by a 0 is a toll call, generally costing €0.10-0.50 per minute.

Italian phone numbers vary in length; a hotel can have, say, an eight-digit phone number and a nine-digit fax number.

If you're dialing within Italy using your US mobile phone, you may need to dial as if it's a domestic call, or you may need to dial as if you're calling from the US (described next). Try it one way, and if it doesn't work, try it the other way.

Dialing Internationally to or from Italy

If you want to make an international call, follow these steps:

• Dial the international access code (00 if you're calling from Europe, 011 from the US or Canada). If you're dialing from a mobile phone, you can replace the international access code with +, which works regardless of where you're calling from. (On many mobile phones, you can insert a + by pressing and holding the 0 key.)

• Dial the country code of the country you're calling (39 for Italy, or 1 for the US or Canada).

• Dial the local number. Note that in most European countries, you have to drop the zero at the beginning of the local number—but in Italy, you dial it. (For specifics per country, see the European calling chart in this chapter.)

Calling from the US to Italy: To call my recommended Florence hotel from the US, dial 011 (US access code), 39 (Italy's country code), then 055-289-592.

Calling from any European Country to the US: To call my office in Edmonds, Washington, from anywhere in Europe, I dial 00 (Europe's access code), 1 (US country code), 425 (Edmonds' area code), and 771-8303.

Mobile Phones

Traveling with a mobile phone is handy and practical. There are two basic options: roaming with your own phone (expensive but easy) or buying and using SIM cards with an unlocked phone (a bit more hassle, but potentially much cheaper).

European Calling Chart

Just smile and dial, using this key:
AC = Area Code, LN = Local Number.

European Country	Calling long distance within ...	Calling from the US or Canada to ...	Calling from a European country to ...
Austria	AC + LN	011 + 43 + AC (without initial zero) + LN	00 + 43 + AC (without initial zero) + LN
Belgium	LN	011 + 32 + LN (without initial zero)	00 + 32 + LN (without initial zero)
Bosnia-Herzegovina	AC + LN	011 + 387 + AC (without initial zero) + LN	00 + 387 + AC (without initial zero) + LN
Britain	AC + LN	011 + 44 + AC (without initial zero) + LN	00 + 44 + AC (without initial zero) + LN
Croatia	AC + LN	011 + 385 + AC (without initial zero) + LN	00 + 385 + AC (without initial zero) + LN
Czech Republic	LN	011 + 420 + LN	00 + 420 + LN
Denmark	LN	011 + 45 + LN	00 + 45 + LN
Estonia	LN	011 + 372 + LN	00 + 372 + LN
Finland	AC + LN	011 + 358 + AC (without initial zero) + LN	999 (or other 900 number) + 358 + AC (without initial zero) + LN
France	LN	011 + 33 + LN (without initial zero)	00 + 33 + LN (without initial zero)
Germany	AC + LN	011 + 49 + AC (without initial zero) + LN	00 + 49 + AC (without initial zero) + LN
Gibraltar	LN	011 + 350 + LN	00 + 350 + LN
Greece	LN	011 + 30 + LN	00 + 30 + LN
Hungary	06 + AC + LN	011 + 36 + AC + LN	00 + 36 + AC + LN
Ireland	AC + LN	011 + 353 + AC (without initial zero) + LN	00 + 353 + AC (without initial zero) + LN
Italy	LN	011 + 39 + LN	00 + 39 + LN

European Country	Calling long distance within ...	Calling from the US or Canada to ...	Calling from a European country to ...
Latvia	LN	011 + 371 + LN	00 + 371 + LN
Montenegro	AC + LN	011 + 382 + AC (without initial zero) + LN	00 + 382 + AC (without initial zero) + LN
Morocco	LN	011 + 212 + LN (without initial zero)	00 + 212 + LN (without initial zero)
Netherlands	AC + LN	011 + 31 + AC (without initial zero) + LN	00 + 31 + AC (without initial zero) + LN
Norway	LN	011 + 47 + LN	00 + 47 + LN
Poland	LN	011 + 48 + LN	00 + 48 + LN
Portugal	LN	011 + 351 + LN	00 + 351 + LN
Russia	8 + AC + LN	011 + 7 + AC + LN	00 + 7 + AC + LN
Slovakia	AC + LN	011 + 421 + AC (without initial zero) + LN	00 + 421 + AC (without initial zero) + LN
Slovenia	AC + LN	011 + 386 + AC (without initial zero) + LN	00 + 386 + AC (without initial zero) + LN
Spain	LN	011 + 34 + LN	00 + 34 + LN
Sweden	AC + LN	011 + 46 + AC (without initial zero) + LN	00 + 46 + AC (without initial zero) + LN
Switzerland	LN	011 + 41 + LN (without initial zero)	00 + 41 + LN (without initial zero)
Turkey	AC (if there's no initial zero, add one) + LN	011 + 90 + AC (without initial zero) + LN	00 + 90 + AC (without initial zero) + LN

- The instructions above apply whether you're calling to or from a European landline or mobile phone.

- If calling from any mobile phone, you can replace the international access code with "+" (press and hold 0 to insert it).

- The international access code is 011 if you're calling from the US or Canada.

- To call the US or Canada from Europe, dial 00, then 1 (country code for US and Canada), then the area code and number. In short, 00 + 1 + AC + LN = Hi, Mom!

Roaming with Your US Mobile Phone: This pricier option can be worthwhile if you won't be making or receiving many calls, don't want to bother with SIM cards, or want to stay reachable at your US number. Start by calling your mobile-phone service provider to ask whether your phone works in Europe and what the rates are (likely $1.29-1.99 per minute to make or receive calls, and 20-50 cents to send or receive text messages). Tell them to enable international calling on your account, and if you know you'll be making multiple calls, ask your carrier about any global calling deals to lower the per-minute costs. When you land in Europe, turn on your phone and—bingo!—you have service. Because you'll pay for receiving calls and texts, be sure your family knows to call only in an emergency. Note that Verizon and Sprint use a different technology than European providers, so their phones are less likely to work abroad; if yours doesn't, your provider may be able to send you a loaner phone (arrange in advance).

Buying and Using SIM Cards in Europe: If you're comfortable with mobile-phone technology, will be making lots of calls, and want to save some serious money, consider this very affordable alternative: Carry an unlocked mobile phone, and use it with a European SIM card to get much cheaper rates.

Getting an **unlocked phone** may be easier than you think. You may already have an old, unused mobile phone in a drawer somewhere. When you got the phone, it was probably "locked" to work only with one company—but if your contract is now up, your provider may be willing to send you a code to unlock it. Just call and ask. Otherwise, you can simply buy an unlocked phone: Search your favorite online shopping site for an "unlocked quad-band phone" before you go, or wait until you get to Europe and buy one at a mobile-phone shop there. Either way, a basic model costs less than $50.

Once in Europe, buy a **SIM card**—the little chip that inserts into your phone (either under the battery, or in a slot on the side)—to equip the phone with a European number. (Note that smaller "micro-SIM" or "nano-SIM" cards—used in some iPhones—are less widely available.) SIM cards are sold at mobile-phone shops, department-store electronics counters, and some newsstand kiosks for $5-10, and usually include about that much prepaid calling credit. Because SIM cards are prepaid, there's no contract and no commitment (in fact, they expire after just a few months of disuse); I buy one even if I'm in a country for only a few days.

In Italy, the major providers are Wind, TIM, Vodafone, and 3 ("Tre"). The vendor will make a copy of your passport to register the SIM card with the service provider. You'll receive a *Benvenuti!* text message once your service is activated (it can take a few hours).

When using a SIM card in its home country, it's free to receive calls and texts. In Italy, domestic and international calls average 20-30 cents per minute. Rates are higher if you're roaming in another country, but as long as you stay within the European Union, these fees are capped (about 30 cents per minute for making calls or 10 cents per minute for receiving calls). Texting is cheap even if roaming in another country.

When purchasing a SIM card, besides confirming the fees for domestic and international calls, ask about roaming charges, and how to check your credit balance, and how to buy more time. If text or voice prompts are in another language, ask the clerk whether they can be switched to English.

It's also possible to buy an **inexpensive mobile phone in Europe** that already comes with a SIM card. While these phones are generally locked to work with just one provider (and therefore can't be reused on future trips), they may be less hassle than buying an unlocked phone and a SIM card separately.

Mobile-Phone Calling Apps: If you have a smartphone, you can use it to make free or cheap calls in Europe by using a calling app such as Skype or FaceTime when you're on Wi-Fi; for details, see the next section.

Calling over the Internet

Some things that seem too good to be true...actually are true. If you're traveling with a smartphone, tablet, or laptop, you can make free calls over the Internet to another wireless device, anywhere in the world, for free. (Or you can pay a few cents to call from your computer or smartphone to a telephone.) The major providers are Skype, Google Talk, and (on Apple devices) FaceTime. You can get online at a Wi-Fi hotspot and use these apps to make calls without ringing up expensive roaming charges (though call quality can be spotty on slow connections). You can make Internet calls even if you're traveling without your own mobile device: Many European Internet cafés have Skype, as well as microphones and webcams, on their terminals—just log on and chat away.

Landline Telephones

Just like Americans, most Europeans these days make the majority of their calls on mobile phones. But you'll still encounter landlines in hotel rooms and at pay phones.

Hotel-Room Phones: Calling from your hotel room can be great for local calls and for international calls if you have an international phone card (described later). Otherwise, hotel-room phones can be an almost criminal rip-off for long-distance or international calls. Many hotels charge a fee for local and sometimes even "toll-free" numbers—always ask for the rates before you dial.

Public Pay Phones: Coin-op phones are becoming extinct in

Smartphones and Data Roaming

I take my smartphone to Europe, using it to make phone calls (sparingly) and send texts, but also to check email, listen to audio tours, and browse the Internet. You may have heard horror stories about people running up outrageous data roaming bills on their smartphones. But if you understand the options, it's easy to avoid these fees and still stay connected. Here's how.

For voice calls and text messaging, smartphones work like any mobile phone (as described under "Roaming with Your US Mobile Phone," earlier). To avoid roaming charges, connect to free Wi-Fi and use Skype, FaceTime, or other apps to make cheap or free calls (see "Calling over the Internet," earlier).

To get online with your phone, you have two options: Wi-Fi and mobile data. Because free Wi-Fi hotspots are generally easy to find in Europe (at most hotels, many cafés, and even some public spaces), the cheap solution is to use Wi-Fi wherever possible.

But what if you just can't get to a hotspot? Fortunately, most providers offer an affordable, basic data-roaming package for Europe: $25 or $30 buys you about 100 megabytes—enough to view 100 websites or send/receive 1,000 text emails. If you don't buy a data-roaming plan in advance, but use data in Europe anyway, you'll pay staggeringly high rates—about $20 per megabyte, or about 80 times what you'd pay with a plan.

While a data-roaming package is handy, your allotted megabytes can go quickly—especially if you stream videos or music.

Europe. To make calls from public phones, you'll need a prepaid phone card, described below.

Metered Phones: In Italy, some call shops have phones with meters. You can talk all you want, then pay the bill when you leave—but be sure you know the rates before you have a lengthy conversation. Note that charges can be "per unit" rather than per minute; find out the length of a unit.

Telephone Cards

There are two different kinds of phone cards: insertable (for pay phones) and international (cheap for overseas calls and usable from any type of phone). A phone card works only in the country where you bought it, so if you have a live card at the end of your trip, give it to another traveler to use. Most cards expire three to six months after the first use.

Insertable Phone Cards: This type of card, usable only at pay phones, is sold by Italy's largest phone company, Telecom Italia. They give you the best deal for calls within Italy and are reasonable for international calls. You can buy Telecom cards (in denominations of €5 or €10) at tobacco shops, post offices, and machines near

To keep a cap on usage and avoid incurring overage charges, I manually turn off data roaming on my phone whenever I'm not actively using it. (To turn off data and voice roaming, look in your phone's menu—try checking under "Cellular" or "Network," or ask your mobile-phone provider how to do it.) As I travel through Europe, I jump from hotspot to hotspot. But if I need to get online at a time when I can't easily access Wi-Fi—for example, to download driving directions when I'm on the road to my next hotel—I turn on data roaming just long enough for that task, then turn it off again. You can also limit how much data your phone uses by switching your email settings from "push" to "fetch" (you choose when to download messages rather than having them automatically "pushed" to your device). By carefully budgeting my data this way, my 100 megabytes last a long time.

If you want to use your smartphone exclusively on Wi-Fi—and not worry about either voice or data charges—simply turn off both voice and data roaming (or put your phone in "Airplane Mode," and then turn your Wi-Fi back on). If you're on a long trip, are positive you won't be using your phone for voice or data roaming, and want to save some money, ask your provider about suspending those services altogether while you're gone.

By sticking with Wi-Fi wherever possible and budgeting your use of data, you can easily and affordably stay connected while you travel.

phone booths (many phone booths have signs indicating where the nearest phone-card sales outlet is located).

Rip off the perforated corner to "activate" the card, and then physically insert it into a slot in the pay phone. It displays how much money you have remaining on the card. Then just dial away. The price of the call is automatically deducted while you talk.

International Phone Cards: With these cards, phone calls from Italy to the US can cost less than a nickel a minute. The cards can also be used to make local calls, and they work from any type of phone, including your hotel-room phone or a mobile phone with a European SIM card. To use the card, dial a local or toll-free access number, then enter your scratch-to-reveal PIN code. If you're calling from a hotel, be sure to dial the *freephone* number (starts with "80") provided on your card rather than the "local access" number (which will incur a charge). Some hotels block their phones from accepting these access numbers. (Ask your hotelier about access and rates before you call.)

You can buy the cards at small newsstand kiosks, tobacco shops, Internet cafés, hostels, and hole-in-the-wall long-distance phone shops. Because there are so many brand names, simply ask for an international phone card (*carta telefonica prepagata internazionale*, KAR-tah teh-leh-FOHN-ee-kah pray-pah-GAH-tah inter-naht-zee-oh-NAH-lay). Tell the vendor where you'll be calling the most (*"per Stati Uniti"*—to America), and he'll select the brand with the best deal.

Buy a lower denomination in case the card is a dud. I've had good luck with the Europa card, which offers up to 350 minutes from Italy to the US for €5. Some shops also sell cardless codes, printed right on the receipt. Since you don't need the actual card to use the account, you can write down the access number and code and share it with friends.

US Calling Cards: These cards, such as the ones offered by AT&T, Verizon, and Sprint, are a rotten value, and are being phased out. Try any of the options outlined earlier.

Useful Phone Numbers
Emergency Needs
English-Speaking Police Help: 113
Ambulance: 118
Road Service: 116

Embassies and Consulates
US Embassy in Rome: 24-hour emergency line—tel. 06-46741, non-emergency—tel. 06-4674-2420 answered Mon-Fri 15:00-17:00 (passport services Mon-Fri 8:30-12:00, Via Vittorio Veneto 121, http://italy.usembassy.gov)
US Consulates: Milan—tel. 02-290-351 (Via Principe Amedeo 2/10, http://milan.usconsulate.gov), **Florence**—tel. 055-266-951 (Lungarno Vespucci 38, http://florence.usconsulate.gov), **Naples**—tel. 081-583-8111 (Piazza della Repubblica, http://naples.usconsulate.gov)
Canadian Embassy in Rome: Tel. 06-854-441 (Via Zara 30, www.italy.gc.ca)

Travel Advisories
US Department of State: Tel. 888-407-4747, from outside US tel. 1-202-501-4444, www.travel.state.gov
Canadian Department of Foreign Affairs: Canadian tel. 800-387-3124, from outside Canada tel. 1-613-996-8885, www.travel.gc.ca
US Centers for Disease Control and Prevention: Tel. 800-CDC-INFO (800-232-4636), www.cdc.gov/travel

Directory Assistance
Telephone Help (in English; free directory assistance): 170

Directory Assistance (for €0.50, an Italian-speaking robot gives the number twice, very clearly): 12

Airports
Assisi: Perugia/Assisi Airport (airport code: PEG)—tel. 075-592-141, www.airport.umbria.it

Florence: Amerigo Vespucci Airport (airport code: FLR)—tel. 055-315-874 (for flight info, tel. 055-306-1700), www.aeroporto.firenze.it

Milan: Malpensa (airport code: MXP) and Linate (airport code: LIN) airports share the same phone number and website: tel. 02-74851, www.sea-aeroportimilano.it; Bergamo Airport (airport code: BGY)—tel. 035-326-323, www.sacbo.it

Naples: Naples International Airport (airport code: NAP)—tel. 081-789-6111, www.gesac.it

Pisa: Galileo Galilei Airport (airport code: PSA)—tel. 050-849-300, www.pisa-airport.com

Rome: Fiumicino Airport (airport code: FCO)—tel. 06-6595-3640; Ciampino Airport (airport code: CIA)—tel. 06-6595-9515. Both airports share the same website: www.adr.it

Venice: Marco Polo Airport (airport code: VCE)—tel. 041-260-9260, www.veniceairport.com; Treviso Airport (airport code: TSF)—tel. 042-231-5111, www.trevisoairport.it

Verona: Catullo Airport (also known as Verona-Villafranca, airport code: VRN)—tel. 045-809-5666, www.aeroportoverona.it

Internet Access
It's useful to get online periodically as you travel—to confirm trip plans, check train or bus schedules, get weather forecasts, catch up on email, blog or post photos from your trip, or call folks back home (explained earlier, under "Calling over the Internet").

Your Mobile Device: The majority of accommodations in Italy offer Wi-Fi, as do many cafés, making it easy for you to get online with your laptop, tablet, or smartphone. Access is often free, but sometimes there's a fee. At hotels that charge for a certain number of hours, you can save money by logging in and out of your account on an as-needed basis. You should be able to stretch a two-hour Wi-Fi pass over a stay of a day or two.

Some hotel rooms and Internet cafés have high-speed Internet jacks that you can plug into with an Ethernet cable.

Public Internet Terminals: Many accommodations offer a guest computer in the lobby with Internet access. If you ask politely, smaller places may sometimes let you sit at their desk for a few minutes just to check your email. If your hotelier doesn't have access, ask to be directed to the nearest place to get online. Italian keyboards are a little different from ours; to type an @ symbol, press the "Alt Gr" key and the key that shows the @ symbol.

Security: Whether you're accessing the Internet with your own device or at a public terminal, using a shared network or computer comes with the potential for increased security risks. If you're not convinced a connection is secure, avoid accessing any sites (such as online banking) that could be vulnerable to fraud.

Mail

You can mail one package per day to yourself worth up to $200 duty-free from Europe to the US (mark it "personal purchases"). If you're sending a gift to someone, mark it "unsolicited gift." For details, visit www.cbp.gov and search for "Know Before You Go."

Mail service in Italy has improved over the last few years, but even so, mail nothing precious from an Italian post office. For quick transatlantic delivery (in either direction), consider services such as DHL (www.dhl.com).

Transportation

By Car or Public Transportation?

Each has pros and cons. Public transportation is one of the few bargains in Italy. Cars are best for three or more traveling together (especially families with small kids), those packing heavy, and those scouring the countryside. Trains and buses are best for solo travelers, blitz tourists, city-to-city travelers, and those who don't want to drive in Europe. While a car gives you more freedom, trains and buses zip you effortlessly and scenically from city to city, usually dropping you in the center, often near a TI.

Considering how handy and affordable Italy's trains and buses are (and that you're likely to go both broke and crazy driving in Italian cities), I'd do most of Italy by public transportation. If you want to drive, consider doing the big, intense stuff (Rome, Naples area, Milan, Florence, and Venice) by train or bus and renting a car for the hill towns of central Italy and for the Dolomites. A car is a worthless headache on the Riviera and in the Lake Como area.

In this section, I'll cover specifics on traveling by train, bus, and car in Italy.

Public Transportation
Trains

To travel by train cheaply in Italy, you can simply buy tickets as you go. Ticket machines in stations are easy to use (see "Buying Tickets," later), so you can usually avoid long lines at ticket windows. Pay all ticket costs in the station before you board, or you'll pay a penalty on the train.

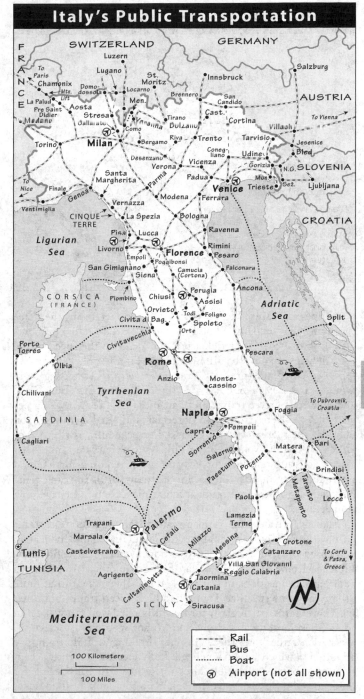

Italy's Public Transportation

FRANCE · SWITZERLAND · GERMANY · AUSTRIA · SLOVENIA · CROATIA

To Paris, Chamonix, Mtn. Lift, La Palud, Pre Saint Didier, Medano, Aosta, Stresa, Gallarate, Torino, To Nice, Finale, Genoa, Ventimiglia

Luzern, Lugano, St. Moritz, Locarno, Men., Domodossola, Varenna, Como, Bergamo, Milan, Desenzano, Santa Margherita, Parma, Vernazza, La Spezia

Innsbruck, Brennero, San Candido, Cast., Tirano, Bolzano, Riva, Trento, Cortina, Verona, Vicenza, Padua, Modena, Ferrara, Bologna

Salzburg, Villach, Tarvisio, Jesenice, Bled, Conegliano, Udine, Gorizia, N.G. SLOVENIA, Mon., Sez., Trieste, Ljubljana, To Vienna

Venice, Ravenna

Ligurian Sea

CINQUE TERRE, Pisa, Lucca, Livorno, Empoli, Florence, Poggibonsi, San Gimignano, Siena, Camucia (Cortona), Falconara, Rimini, Pesaro

CORSICA (FRANCE), Piombino, Chiusi, Orvieto, Civita di Bag., Todi, Foligno, Spoleto, Orte, Perugia, Assisi, Ancona, CROATIA

Adriatic Sea, Split

Civitavecchia, Pescara

Rome, Anzio, Montecassino

Porto Torres, Olbia, Chilivani, **Tyrrhenian Sea**, SARDINIA, Cagliari

To Dubrovnik, Croatia

Naples, Capri, Pompoii, Sorrento, Salerno, Paestum, Matera, Foggia, Bari, Potenza, Brindisi, Metaponto, Taranto, Lecce, Paola

Trapani, Marsala, Castelvetrano, Tunis, TUNISIA, Agrigento, Palermo, Cefalù, Milazzo, Messina, Caltanissetta, Taormina, Catania, Siracusa, Lamezia Terme, Crotone, Catanzaro, Villa San Giovanni, Reggio Calabria, SICILY

To Corfu & Patra, Greece

Mediterranean Sea

Rail
Bus
Boat
⊗ Airport (not all shown)

100 Kilometers
100 Miles

APPENDIX

Train Costs in Italy

Map key: Approximate point-to-point one-way second-class rail fares in US dollars. First class costs 50 percent more.

Before deciding to get a railpass, add up the approximate ticket costs for your itinerary. If you'll be making short, inexpensive trips each day, you'll probably find it's cheaper to buy tickets as you go in Italy.

Types of Trains: Most trains in Italy are operated by the state-run Trenitalia company (a.k.a. Ferrovie dello Stato Italiane, abbreviated FS or FSI). Since ticket prices depend on the speed of the train, it helps to know the different types of trains: pokey R or REG *(regionali)*; medium-speed RV *(regionale veloce)*, IR (InterRegio), D *(diretto)*, and E *(espresso)*; fast IC (InterCity) and EC (EuroCity); and super-fast Frecce trains: Frecciabianca ("White Arrow"), Frecciargento ("Silver Arrow"), and Frecciarossa ("Red Arrow"). (You may also see the Frecce trains marked on schedules as ES, AV, or EAV.) If you're traveling with a railpass (covered later), note that reservations are optional for IC trains, but required for EC and international trains (€5) and for Frecce trains (€10). You can't make reservations for regional trains, such as most Rome-Civitavecchia connections.

A new, private train company called **Italo** now runs fast trains on major routes in Italy (challenging Trenitalia's monopoly). Italo is focused on two high-speed corridors: Venice-Padua-Bologna-Florence-Rome and Turin-Milan-Bologna-Florence-Rome, with additional connections onward to Naples. The trains run at more or less the same speed as Trenitalia's high-speed trains, but often with lower fares, particularly for tickets booked well in advance. In some cities (most notably Rome and Milan), its trains use a secondary station rather than the main one: If taking an Italo train, pay attention to which station you need. Italo does not currently accept railpasses, but its affordable fares make it worth considering for point-to-point tickets. You can book in person (look for Italo ticket

APPENDIX

offices or machines—tickets not sold through Trenitalia), by phone (tel. 06-0708), or on their user-friendly website (www.italotreno.it).

Schedules: At the train station, the easiest way to check schedules is at a handy automated ticket machine (described later, under "Buying Tickets"). Enter the desired date, time, and destination to see all of your options. Printed schedules are also posted at the station (departure—*partenzi*—posters are always yellow).

Newsstands sell up-to-date regional and all-Italy timetables (€5, ask for the *orario ferroviaro*). On the Web, check www.trenitalia.com and www.italotreno.it (domestic journeys only); for international trips, use www.bahn.com (Germany's excellent all-Europe website). Trenitalia offers a single all-Italy telephone number for train information (24 hours daily, toll tel. 892-021, in Italian only, consider having your hotelier call for you). For Italo trains, call 06-0708.

Be aware that Trenitalia and Italo don't cooperate at all. If you buy a ticket for one train line, it's not valid on the other. Even if you just ask for information from one company, they will most likely ignore the other's options.

Point-to-Point Tickets

Train tickets are a good value in Italy. Sample fares are shown on the map on page 1168, though fares can vary for the same journey, mainly depending on the time of day, the speed of the train, and other factors. **First-class** tickets cost 30-50 percent more than **second-class.** While second-class cars go just as fast as their first-class neighbors, Italy is one country where I would consider the splurge of first class. The easiest way to "upgrade" a second-class ticket once on board a crowded train is to nurse a drink in the snack car. A *flessibile* (flexible) ticket costs more than a *base* (basic) fare—but special *promo* deals can drive the cost even lower. Fares labeled *servizi abbonati* are available only for locals with monthly passes—not tourists.

Speed vs. Savings: For point-to-point tickets on major routes, fast trains save time, but charge a premium. For example, super-fast Rome-Venice trains run hourly, cost €76 in second class, and make the trip in 3.75 hours, while infrequent InterCity trains (1-2/day) cost €46 and take 6 hours. Speedy Rome-Florence trains take 1.5 hours and cost €45 in second class, compared to InterCity trains that take 3 hours and cost €30. On routes like Verona-Padua-Venice in the north, regional trains cost considerably less than IC and ES express trains, and are only a little slower.

Discounts: Families with young children can get price breaks—kids ages 4 and under travel free; ages 4-11 travel at half-price. Ask for the "Offerta Familia" deal when buying tickets at a counter (or, at a ticket machine, choose "Yes" at the "Do you want

Deciphering Italian Train Schedules

At the station, look for the big yellow posters labeled *Partenze*—Departures. The white posters show arrivals.

Schedules are listed chronologically, hour by hour, showing the trains leaving the station throughout the day. Each schedule has columns:

- The first column *(Ora)* lists the time of departure.
- The next column *(Treno)* shows the type of train.
- The third column *(Classi Servizi)* lists the services available (first- and second-class cars, dining car, *cuccetta* berths, etc.) and, more important, whether you need reservations (usually denoted by an *R* in a box). All Frecce trains, many EuroCity (EC) trains, and most international trains require reservations.
- The next column lists the destination of the train *(Principali Fermate Destinazioni)*, often showing intermediate stops, followed by the final destination, with arrival times listed throughout in parentheses. Note that *your* final destination may be listed in fine print as an intermediate destination. For example, if you're going from Milan to Florence, scan the schedule and you'll notice that virtually all trains that terminate in Rome stop in Florence en route. Travelers who read the fine print end up with a far greater choice of trains.
- The next column *(Servizi Diretti e Annotazioni)* has pertinent notes about the train, such as "also stops in..." *(ferma anche a...)*, "doesn't stop in..." *(non ferma a...)*, "stops in every station" *(ferma in tutte le stazioni)*, "delayed..." *(ritardo...)*, and so on.
- The last column lists the track *(Binario)* the train departs from. Confirm the *binario* with an additional source: a ticket seller, the electronic board that lists immediate departures, TV monitors on the platform, or the railway officials who are usually standing by the train unless you really need them.

For any odd symbols on the poster, look at the key at the end. Some of the phrasing can be deciphered easily, such as *servizio periodico* (periodic service—doesn't always run). For the trickier ones, ask a local or railway official, try your *Rick Steves' Italian Phrase Book & Dictionary*, or simply take a different train.

You can also check schedules—for trains anywhere in Italy, not just from the station you're currently in—at the handy ticket machines. Enter the date and time of your departure (to or from any Italian station), and you can view all your options.

ticket issue?" prompt, then choose "Familia"). With the discount, families of three to five people with at least one kid (age 12 or under) get 50 percent off the child fare, and 20 percent off the adult fare. The deal doesn't apply to all trains at all times, but it's worth checking out.

Discounts for youths and seniors require purchase of a separate card (Carta Verde for ages 12-26 costs €40; Carta Argento for ages 60 and over is €30), but the discount on tickets is so minor (10-15 percent, respectively, for domestic travel), it's not worth it for most.

Buying Tickets: Avoid train-station ticket lines whenever possible by using the automated ticket machines found in station halls. You'll be able to easily purchase tickets for travel within Italy (not international trains), make seat reservations, and even book a *cuccetta* (koo-CHEH-tah; overnight berth). If you do use the ticket windows, be sure you're in the correct line. Key terms: *biglietti* (general tickets), *prenotazioni* (reservations), *nazionali* (domestic), and *internazionali*.

Trenitalia's automated ticket machines (usually green-and-white, marked *Biglietto Veloce/Fast Ticket*) are user-friendly and found in all but the tiniest stations in Italy. You can pay by cash (they give change) or by debit or credit card (even for small amounts). Select English, then your destination. If you don't immediately see the city you're traveling to, keep keying in the spelling until it's listed. You can choose from first- and second-class seats, request tickets for more than one traveler, and (on the high-speed Frecce trains) choose an aisle or window seat. Don't select a discount rate without being sure that you meet the criteria (for example, Americans are not eligible for any EU or resident discounts). If you need to validate your ticket, you can do it in the same machine if you're boarding your train right away.

For nearby destinations only, you can also buy tickets from the older, gray-and-blue machines marked *Rete regionale* (cash only, push button for English).

It's possible, but generally unnecessary, to buy Trenitalia tickets in advance online at www.trenitalia.com. Because most Italian trains run frequently and there's no deadline to buy tickets, you can keep your travel plans flexible by purchasing tickets as you go. (Any time you're ready to commit, you can buy several tickets at one station.) For busy weekend or holiday travel, however, it can be a good idea to buy tickets in advance, whether online or at a station. Also, some discounts may not be available at ticket machines.

To buy tickets for high-speed **Italo** trains, look for a dedicated service counter (in most major rail stations), or a red automated ticket machine labeled *Italo*. You can also book Italo tickets by phone (tel. 06-0708) or online (www.italotreno.it).

Open or Non-Reserved Ticket—Need to Validate

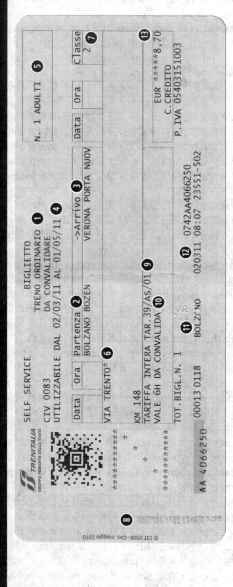

1 Open ticket for non-express trains, must be validated
2 Point of departure
3 Destination
4 Validity of ticket (use once within 2 months of purchase)
5 Number of passengers
6 Route
7 Class of travel (1 = 1st; 2 = 2nd)
8 Validation stamp
9 Full fare for non-express train
10 Once stamped, ticket is good for 1 trip within 6 hours
11 Location of ticket sale
12 Date ticket was purchased
13 Ticket cost

Reserved Ticket (Fast Train)—Need Not Validate

1 Departure date & time
2 Point of departure
3 Destination
4 "Ticket with reservation"
5 Number of passengers
6 Arrival date & time
7 Class of travel (1 = 1st; 2 = 2nd)
8 "Present to official if changing trains"
9 Train #, train car # & seat # (finestrino = window seat)
10 Fast-train fare (other types of trains can be cheaper and don't require reservations)
11 Location of ticket sale
12 Date ticket was purchased
13 Booking ID
14 Ticket cost
15 Amount of CO_2 usage reduced by this train trip

© GIT 2006 - Ord. maggio 2010

If you buy a ticket for one train line, you must travel with only that company—your ticket is not valid on the competitor's train line. Survey your options carefully before you choose.

Note that you can't buy international tickets from machines; for this and anything else that requires a real person, try a local travel agency, a good alternative to station ticket windows plagued by long lines. Agencies also sell domestic tickets and make reservations. The cost is only a little more (they charge a small fee, often €1-4 per ticket); it can be more convenient (if you find yourself near a travel agency while you're sightseeing); there are no crowds; and the language barrier can be smaller than at the station's ticket windows.

Validating Tickets: If your ticket includes a seat reservation on a specific train *(biglietto con prenotazione)*, you're all set and can just get on board. An open ticket with no seat reservation (it may say *da convalidare* or *convalida*) must always be validated—stamp it before you board in the machine near the platform (usually marked *convalida biglietti* or *vidimazione*). Once you validate a ticket, you must complete your trip within the timeframe shown on the ticket (within 6 hours for medium-distance trips; within 1.25 hours for short rides under 6 miles). If you forget to validate your ticket, go right away to the train conductor—before he comes to you—or you'll pay a fine.

Railpasses

The **Italy Pass** for Italian State Railways is generally no cheaper or easier than just buying point-to-point tickets. The pass may save you money if you're taking three long train rides or prefer first-class travel, but don't count on it for hop-on convenience on every train. Use the price map on page 1168 to add up your ticket costs (ticket prices on the map are for the fastest trains on a given route, many of which have reservation costs built in). Note that railpasses are not valid on Italo trains.

Railpass travelers must make separate seat reservations for the fastest trains between major Italian cities (Frecce trains, €10 each; EC trains, €5 each). Railpass travelers can just hop on InterCity trains (optional €5 reservation) and regional trains (no reservations possible). Making a reservation at a train station or travel agency is the same as the process to buy a ticket, so you may need to stand in line either way. Reservations for berths on overnight trains cost extra, aren't covered by railpasses, and aren't reflected on the ticket cost map.

A **Global Pass** can work well throughout most of Europe, but it's a bad value for travel exclusively in Italy. A cheaper version, the **Select Pass,** allows you to tailor a pass to your trip, provided you're traveling in three, four, or five adjacent countries directly

Railpasses

Prices listed are for 2013 and are subject to change. For the latest prices, details, and train schedules (and easy online ordering), see my comprehensive *Guide to Eurail Passes* at www.ricksteves.com/rail.

"Saver" prices are per person for two or more people traveling together. "Youth" means under age 26. The fare for children 4–11 is half the adult individual fare or Saver fare. Kids under age 4 travel free.

ITALY PASS

	Individual 1st Class	Individual 2nd Class	Saver 1st Class	Saver 2nd Class	Youth 2nd Class
3 days in 2 months	$295	$241	$252	$206	$196
Extra rail days (max 7)	41-47	37-41	37-41	32-37	29-33

ITALY RAIL & DRIVE PASS
Any 3 rail days and 2 car days in 2 months.

Car Category	1st Class	2nd Class	Extra Car Day
Economy 2-Door	$367	$311	$64
Economy 4-Door	375	320	72
Compact	394	339	92
Intermediate	420	365	118
Economy Automatic	403	347	100
Premium	520	464	217
Extra rail days (max 2)	32	26	

Prices are per person, two traveling together. Solo travelers pay about 20 percent more. To order a Rail & Drive pass, call your travel agent or Rail Europe at 800-438-7245. *This pass is not sold by Rick Steves' Europe.*

FRANCE–ITALY PASS

	Individual 1st Class	Individual 2nd Class	Saver 1st Class	Saver 2nd Class	Youth 2nd Class
4 days in 2 months	$411	$350	$350	$299	$269
Extra rail days (max 6)	44-51	30-41	30-41	32-37	29-33

Be aware of your route. Direct Paris–Italy trains (day and overnight) and trains via Switzerland aren't covered by this pass. Connections through Nice are ok.

GREECE–ITALY PASS

	Individual 1st Class	Individual 2nd Class	Saver 1st Class	Saver 2nd Class	Youth 2nd Class
4 days in 2 months	$381	$306	$325	$261	$249
Extra rail days (max 6)	37-40	30-32	32-34	26-27	25-27

Covers deck passage on overnight Superfast Ferries between Patras, Greece and Bari or Ancona, Italy (starts use of one travel day). Does not cover travel to or on Greek islands. Very few trains run in Greece.

SELECTPASS
This pass covers travel in three adjacent countries, not including France. Please visit **www.ricksteves.com/rail** for four- and five-country options.

	Individual 1st Class	Saver 1st Class	Youth 2nd Class
5 days in 2 months	$486	$414	$317
6 days in 2 months	536	457	350
8 days in 2 months	634	540	413
10 days in 2 months	735	625	479

connected by rail or ferry (but excluding France). For instance, with a three-country pass allowing ten days of train travel within a two-month period ($730 for a single adult in 2013), you could choose Switzerland-Italy-Greece or Germany-Austria-Italy. A **France and Italy Pass** combines just those two countries. Note that none of these passes cover direct day or night trains between Italy and Paris, which require a separate ticket. Before you buy a Select Pass or France and Italy Pass, consider how many travel days you'll really need. Use the pass only for travel days that involve long hauls or several trips. Pay out of pocket for tickets on days you're taking only short, cheap rides.

For a summary of railpass deals and the latest prices, check my Guide to Eurail Passes at www.ricksteves.com/rail. This guide will help you know you're getting the right railpass for your trip.

Train Tips

This section contains information on making seat reservations, storing baggage, avoiding theft, and dealing with strikes.

Seat Reservations: Trains can fill up, even in first class. If you're on a tight schedule, you'll want to reserve a few days ahead for fast trains (see "Types of Trains," earlier). Purchasing tickets or passholder reservations onboard a train comes with a nasty penalty. Buying them at the station can be a time-waster unless you use the ticket machines.

If you don't need a reservation, and if your train originates at your departure point (e.g., you're catching the Milan-Venice train in Milan), arriving at least 15 minutes before the departure time will help you snare a seat. Since most trains allow you to make reservations up to the time of departure, conductors post a list of the reservable and non-reservable seat rows (sometimes in English) in each train car's vestibule. This means that if you board a crowded train and get one of the last seats, you may be ousted when the reservation-holder comes along. Ask conductors for help selecting a seat that's not already spoken for.

On the platforms of some major stations, posters showing the train composition *(composizione principali treni)* indicate where first- and second-class cars will line up when the trains arrive (letters on the poster are supposed to correspond to letters posted over the platform—but they don't always).

Baggage Storage: Many stations have *deposito bagagli* where you can safely leave your bag for €8 per 12-hour period (payable when you pick up the bag, double-check closing hours). Because of security concerns, no Italian stations have lockers.

Theft Concerns: Italian trains are famous for their thieves. Never leave a bag unattended. Police do ride the trains, cutting down on theft. Still, for an overnight trip, I'd feel safe only in a *cuc-*

cetta (a bunk in a special sleeping car with an attendant who keeps track of who comes and goes while you sleep—approximately €21 in a 6-bed compartment, €26 in a less-cramped four-bed compartment, €50 in a more private, double compartment).

Strikes: Strikes, which are common, generally last a day (often a Friday). Train employees will simply explain, *"Sciopero"* (strike). But in actuality, sporadic trains, following no particular schedule, lumber down the tracks during most strikes. When a strike is pending, travel agencies (and hoteliers) can check online for you to see when the strike goes into effect and which trains will continue to run. Revised schedules may be posted in Italian at stations, and station personnel still working can often tell you what trains are expected to run. If I need to get somewhere and know a strike

is imminent, I leave early (heading off the strike, which often begins at 9:00), or I just go to the station with extra patience in tow and hop on anything rolling in the direction I want to go.

Buses

You can usually get anywhere you want to in Italy by bus...as long as you're not in a hurry and you plan ahead, using bus schedules (pick up at local TIs). For reaching small towns, buses are sometimes the only option if you don't have a car. In many hill towns, trains leave you at a station in the valley far below, while buses bring you right into the thick of things.

Larger towns have a long-distance bus station *(stazione degli autobus)*, with ticket windows and several stalls (usually labeled *corsia*, *stallo*, or *binario*). Smaller towns—where buses are more useful—just have a central bus stop *(fermata)*, likely along the main road or on the main square, and maybe several more scattered around town. In small towns, buy bus tickets at newsstands or tobacco shops (with the big *T* signs). When buying your ticket, confirm the departure point *("Dov'è la fermata?")*, and once there, double-check that the posted schedule lists your destination and departure time. In general, orange buses are local city buses, and blue buses are for long distances.

Once the bus arrives, confirm the destination with the driver.

You are expected to stow big backpacks underneath the bus (open the luggage compartment yourself if it's closed).

Sundays and holidays are problematic; even from large cities schedules are sparse, departing buses are jam-packed, and ticket offices are often closed. Plan ahead and buy your ticket in advance. Most travel agencies book bus (and train) tickets for just a small fee.

Renting a Car

If you're renting a car in Italy, bring your driver's license. You're also required to have an International Driving Permit—an official translation of your driver's license (sold at your local AAA office for $15 plus the cost of two passport-type photos; see www.aaa.com). While that's the letter of the law, I've often rented cars in Italy without having this permit. If all goes well, you'll likely never be asked to show the permit—but it's a must if you end up dealing with the police.

Rental companies require you to be at least 21 years old and to have held your license for one year. Drivers under the age of 25 may incur a young-driver surcharge, and some rental companies do not rent to anyone 75 or older. If you're considered too young or old, look into leasing (covered later), which has less-stringent age restrictions.

Research car rentals before you go. It's cheaper to arrange most car rentals from the US. Call several companies and look online to compare rates, or arrange a rental through your hometown travel agent.

Most of the major US rental agencies (including Avis, Budget, Enterprise, Hertz, and Thrifty) have offices throughout Europe. Also consider the two major Europe-based agencies, Europcar and Sixt. It can be cheaper to use a consolidator, such as Auto Europe (www.autoeurope.com) or Europe by Car (www.ebctravel.com), which compares rates at several companies to get you the best deal. However, my readers have reported problems with consolidators, ranging from misinformation to unexpected fees; because you're going through a middleman, it can be more challenging to resolve disputes that arise with the rental agency.

Regardless of the car-rental company you choose, always read the fine print carefully for add-on charges—such as one-way drop-off fees, airport surcharges, or mandatory insurance policies—that aren't included in the "total price." You may need to query rental agents pointedly to find out your actual cost.

For the best deal, rent by the week with unlimited mileage. To save money on fuel, ask for a diesel car. I normally rent the smallest, least-expensive model with a stick shift (generally much cheaper than an automatic). Almost all rentals are manual by default, so if you need an automatic, request one in advance; be aware that these cars are often larger models (not as maneuverable on narrow, winding roads).

Roads and parking spaces are narrow in Italy, so you'll do yourself a favor by renting the smallest car that meets your needs. For a one-week rental, allow roughly $400-500. Allow extra for insurance, fuel, tolls, and parking. For trips of three weeks or more, look into leasing (see page 1180); you'll save money on insurance and taxes.

You can sometimes get a GPS unit with your rental car or leased vehicle for an additional fee (around $15/day; be sure it's set to English and has all the maps you need before you drive off). Or, if you have a portable GPS device at home, consider taking it with you to Europe (buy and upload European maps before your trip). GPS apps are also available for smartphones, but downloading maps in Europe could lead to an exorbitant data-roaming bill (for more details, see the sidebar on page 1162).

Big companies have offices in most cities; ask whether they can pick you up at your hotel. Small local rental companies can be cheaper but aren't as flexible.

Compare pick-up costs (downtown can be less expensive than the airport) and explore drop-off options (south of Rome can be a problem). Always check the hours of the location you choose: Many rental offices close from midday Saturday until Monday morning and, in smaller towns, at lunchtime.

When selecting a location, don't trust the agency's description of "downtown" or "city center." In some cases, a "downtown" branch can be on the outskirts of the city—a long, costly taxi ride from the center. Before choosing, plug the addresses into a mapping website. You may find that the "train station" location is handier. But returning a car at a big-city train station or downtown agency can be tricky; get precise details on the car drop-off location and hours, and allow ample time to find it.

When you pick up the rental car, check it thoroughly and make sure any damage is noted on your rental agreement. Find out how your car's lights, turn signals, wipers, and fuel cap function, and know what kind of fuel the car takes. When you return the car, make sure the agent verifies its condition with you.

If you want a car for only a couple of days, a **rail-and-drive pass** (such as a EurailDrive, Select Pass Drive, or Italy Rail and Drive) can be put to thoughtful use. The basic Italy Rail and Drive Pass, which includes theft insurance and CDW (CDW described below), comes with two days of car rental and three days of rail in two months. While rail-and-drive passes are convenient, they're also pricey, particularly for solo travelers.

Car Insurance Options

Accidents can happen anywhere, but when you're on vacation, the last thing you need is stress over car insurance. When you rent a car, you're liable for a very high deductible, sometimes equal to the entire value of the car. Limit your financial risk in case of an accident by choosing one of these two options: Buy Collision Damage Waiver (CDW) coverage from the car-rental company (figure roughly 30 percent extra), or get coverage through your credit card (free, but more complicated).

In Italy, most car-rental companies' rates automatically include CDW coverage. Even if you try to decline CDW when you reserve your Italian car, you may find when you show up at the counter that you must buy it after all.

While each rental company has its own variation, basic CDW costs $15-35 a day and reduces your liability, but does not eliminate it. When you pick up the car, you'll be offered the chance to "buy down" the deductible to zero (for an additional $10-30/day; this is sometimes called "super CDW").

If you opt for credit-card coverage, there's a catch. You'll technically have to decline all coverage offered by the car-rental company, which means they can place a hold on your card for up to the full value of the car. In case of damage, it can be time-consuming to resolve the charges with your credit-card company. Before you decide on this option, quiz your credit-card company about how it works.

For more on car-rental insurance, see www.ricksteves.com/cdw.

Theft Insurance: Note that theft insurance (separate from CDW insurance) is mandatory in Italy. The insurance usually costs about $15-20 a day, payable when you pick up the car.

Leasing

For trips of three weeks or more, consider leasing (which automatically includes zero-deductible collision and theft insurance). By technically buying and then selling back the car, you save lots of money on tax and insurance. Leasing provides you a brand-new car with unlimited mileage and a 24-hour emergency assistance program. You can lease for as little as 21 days to as long as six months. Car leases must be arranged from the US. One of many companies offering affordable lease packages is Europe by Car (US tel. 800-223-1516, www.ebctravel.com).

Driving

Driving in Italy can be scary—a video game for keeps, and you only get one quarter. Italian drivers can be aggressive. They drive fast and tailgate as if it were required. They pass where Americans are taught not to—on blind corners and just before tunnels. Roads have narrow shoulders or none at all. Driving in the countryside is less stressful than driving through urban areas, but stay alert. On one-lane roads, larger vehicles have the right-of-way. If you're on a truckers' route, stifle your Good Samaritan impulse when you see provocatively dressed women standing by camper-vans at the side of the road; they're not having car trouble.

Road Rules: Stay out of restricted traffic zones or you'll risk huge fines. Car traffic is restricted in many city centers. Don't drive or park in any area that has a sign reading *Zona Traffico Limitato* (*ZTL*, often shown above a red circle—see image). If you do, your license plate can be photographed and a hefty (€100-plus) ticket mailed to your home without your ever having met a cop. Bumbling in and out of these zones can net you multiple fines. If your hotel is within a restricted area, it's best to ask your hotelier to direct you to parking outside the zone. (Although your hotelier can register your car as an authorized vehicle permitted to enter the zone, this usually isn't worth the hassle.) If you get a ticket, it could take months to show up (see www.bella-toscana.com/traffic_violations_italy.htm for all the gory details).

Be aware of typical European road rules. For example, many countries require headlights to be turned on at all times, and it's generally illegal to drive while using your mobile phone without a hands-free headset. Seatbelts are mandatory, and children under age 12 must ride in child-safety or booster seats. In Europe, you're not allowed to turn right on a red light, unless there is a sign or signal specifically authorizing it. Ask your car-rental company about these rules, or check the US State Department website (www.travel.state.gov, click on "International Travel," then specify "Italy" and click "Traffic Safety and Road Conditions").

Tolls: Italy's freeway system, the autostrada, is as good as our interstate system, but you'll pay about a dollar for every 10 minutes of use. (I paid €20 for the four-hour drive from Bolzano to Pisa.) While I favor the freeways because I feel they're safer, cheaper (saving time and gas), and less nerve-wracking than smaller roads, savvy local drivers know which toll-free *superstradas* are actually faster and more direct than the autostrada (e.g., Florence to Pisa). For more information, visit www.autostrade.it.

Fuel: Fuel is expensive—often about €2 per liter ($8.50/gallon). Diesel cars are more common in Europe than back home, so be sure you know what type of fuel your car takes before you fill up. Gas pumps are color-coded for unleaded *(senza piombo)* or diesel

APPENDIX

Driving in Italy

Note: Your times may vary based on traffic, construction and road conditions.

m = miles
h = hours

(gasolio). Autostrada rest stops are self-service stations open daily without a siesta break. Many 24-hour-a-day stations are entirely automated. Small-town stations are usually cheaper and offer full service but shorter hours.

Maps and Signage: A good map is essential. Learn the universal road signs (explained in charts in most road atlases and at service stations). Although roads are numbered on maps, actual road signs don't list route numbers. Instead, roads are indicated by blue signs with a city name on them (for example, if you were heading west out of Venice, the map would be marked "route S-11" on your map—but you'd follow signs to *Padua,* the next town along this road). The signs are inconsistent: They may direct you to the nearest big city or simply the next town along the route.

Theft: Cars are routinely vandalized and stolen. Thieves easily recognize rental cars and assume they are filled with a tourist's gear. Try to make your car look locally owned by hiding the "tourist-owned" rental-company decals and putting an Italian newspaper in your back window. Be sure all of your valuables are out of sight and locked in the trunk, or even better, with you or in your room.

Parking: White lines generally mean parking is free. Yellow lines mean that parking is reserved for residents only (who have permits). Blue lines mean you'll have to pay—usually €1.50 per hour (use machine, leave time-stamped receipt on dashboard). If there's no meter, there's probably a roving attendant who will take your money. Study the signs. Often the free zones have a 30- or 60-minute time limit. Signs showing a street cleaner and a day of the week indicate which day the street is cleaned; there's a €100 tow-fee incentive to learn the days of the week in Italian.

AND LEARN THESE ROAD SIGNS

Speed Limit (km/hr)	Yield	No Passing	End of No Passing Zone
One Way	Intersection	Main Road	Expressway
Danger	No Entry	Cars Prohibited	All Vehicles Prohibited
No Through Road	Restrictions No Longer Apply	Yield to Oncoming Traffic	No Stopping
Parking	No Parking	Customs	Peace

Zona disco has nothing to do with dancing. Italian cars come equipped with a time disk (a cardboard clock), which you set at your arrival time and lay on the dashboard so the attendant knows how long you've been parked. This is a fine system that all drivers should take advantage of. (If your rental car doesn't come with a *zona disco,* pick one up at a tobacco shop. In a pinch, just write your arrival time on a piece of paper and place it on the dashboard.)

Garages are safe, save time, and help you avoid the stress of parking tickets. Take the parking voucher with you to pay the cashier before you leave.

Cheap Flights

If you're visiting one or more cities on a longer European trip, or linking up far-flung Italian cities (such as Rome and Venice), consider the affordable intra-European airlines. While trains are still the best way to connect places that are close together, a flight can save both time and money on long journeys. When comparing your options, factor in the time it takes to get to the airport and how early you'll need to arrive to check in. Most flights make sense only as an alternative to a train ride five or more hours in length.

The best comparison search engine for both international and intra-European flights is www.kayak.com. For inexpensive flights within Europe, try www.skyscanner.com or www.hipmunk.com. If you're not sure who flies to your destination, check its airport's website for a list of carriers.

Well-known cheapo airlines include easyJet (www.easyjet.com) and Ryanair (www.ryanair.com).

Be aware of the potential drawbacks of flying on the cheap: nonrefundable and nonchangeable tickets, minimal or nonexistent customer service, treks to airports far outside town, and stingy baggage allowances with steep overage fees. If you're traveling with lots of luggage, a cheap flight can quickly become a bad deal. To avoid unpleasant surprises, read the small print before you book.

Resources

Resources from Rick Steves

Rick Steves' Italy 2014 is one of many books in my series on European travel, which includes country guidebooks, city guidebooks (Rome, Florence, Paris, London, etc.), Snapshot guides (excerpted chapters from my country guides), Pocket Guides (full-color little books on Rome and other big cities), and my budget-travel skills handbook, *Rick Steves' Europe Through the Back Door.* Most of my titles are available as ebooks. My phrase books—for Italian, French, German, Spanish, and Portuguese—are practical and budget-oriented. My other books include *Europe 101* (a crash course on art and history designed for travelers); *Mediterranean Cruise Ports* and *Northern European Cruise Ports* (how to make the most of your time in port); and *Travel as a Political Act* (a travelogue sprinkled with tips for bringing home a global perspective). A more complete list of my titles appears near the end of this book.

Video: My public television series, *Rick Steves' Europe,* covers European destinations in 100 shows, with 17 episodes on Italy. To watch episodes online, visit www.hulu.com; for scripts and local airtimes, see www.ricksteves.com/tv.

Audio: My weekly public radio show, *Travel with Rick Steves,* features interviews with travel experts from around the world. I've also produced free, self-guided **audio tours** of the top sights and

APPENDIX

Begin Your Trip at www.ricksteves.com

At our travel website, you'll discover a wealth of free information on European destinations, including fresh monthly news and helpful tips from thousands of fellow travelers. You'll find my latest guidebook updates (www.ricksteves.com/update), a monthly travel e-newsletter, my personal travel blog, and my free Rick Steves Audio Europe smartphone app (if you don't have a smartphone, you can access the same content via podcasts). You can also follow me on Facebook and Twitter.

Our **online Travel Store** offers travel bags and accessories that I've designed specifically to help you travel smarter and lighter. These include my popular bags (rolling carry-on and backpack versions), money belts, totes, toiletries kits, adapters, other accessories, and a wide selection of guidebooks, planning maps, and DVDs.

Choosing the right **railpass** for your trip—amid hundreds of options—can drive you nutty. We'll help you choose the best pass for your needs and ship it to you for free.

Want to travel with greater efficiency and less stress? We organize **tours** with more than three dozen itineraries and more than 600 departures reaching the best destinations in this book...and beyond. Our Italy tours include "the best of" in 17 days, Village Italy in 14 days, South Italy in 13 days, Sicily in 10 days, Venice-Florence-Rome in 10 days, the Heart of Italy in 9 days, a My Way: Italy "unguided" tour in 13 days, and a week-long Rome tour. You'll enjoy great guides, a fun bunch of travel partners (with small groups of 24 to 28 travelers), and plenty of room to spread out in a big, comfy bus. You'll find European adventures to fit every vacation length. For all the details, and to get our Tour Catalog and a free Rick Steves Tour Experience DVD (filmed on location during an actual tour), visit www.ricksteves.com or call us at 425/608-4217.

neighborhoods in Florence, Rome, Venice, Assisi, and more. All of this audio content is available for free at Rick Steves Audio Europe, an extensive online library organized by destination. Choose whatever interests you, and download it for free via the Rick Steves Audio Europe smartphone app, www.ricksteves.com/audioeurope, iTunes, or Google Play.

Maps

The black-and-white maps in this book are concise, simple, and tailored to my coverage. They're designed to help you locate recommended places and get to local TIs, where you can pick up more in-depth maps of cities and regions (usually free). Better maps are sold at newsstands and bookstores. Before you buy a map, look at it to be sure it has the level of detail you want. Drivers will want to pick up a good, detailed map in Europe (I'd recommend a 1:200,000- or 1:300,000-scale map).

Other Guidebooks

If you're like most travelers, this book is all you need. But if you're heading beyond my recommended destinations, $40 for extra maps and books can be money well spent. If you'll be spending a lot of time in Italian cities, consider *Rick Steves' Florence & Tuscany, Rick Steves' Venice,* or *Rick Steves' Rome.*

The following books are worthwhile, though most are not updated annually; check the publication date before you buy. Lonely Planet's *Italy* is thorough, well-researched, and packed with travel information, maps, and hotel recommendations for various budgets. The similar *Rough Guide to Italy* is also good and more insightful, updated by British researchers. The highly opinionated *Let's Go: Italy*, researched by Harvard students, is great for students and vagabonds. If you're a low-budget train traveler interested in hosteling and the youth and nightlife scene (which I have largely ignored), get *Let's Go: Italy*. The Italy section in the bigger *Let's Go: Europe* is sparse.

Cultural and Sightseeing Guides: The colorful Eyewitness series, which focuses mainly on sights, has editions on Italy, its various regions, and the major cities. They're fun for their great graphics and photos, but they're relatively skimpy on content and weigh a ton. You can buy them in Italy (no more expensive than in the US) or simply borrow a book for a minute from other travelers at certain sights to make sure that you're aware of that place's highlights. The tall, green Michelin guides to Italy and Rome have minimal information on room and board, but include great maps for drivers and lots of solid, encyclopedic coverage of sights, customs, and culture (sold in English in Italy). The Cadogan guides to various parts of Italy offer a thoughtful look at the rich and confusing local culture, as does *Culture Shock: Italy.*

Recommended Books and Movies

To learn more about Italy past and present, check out a few of these books or films.

Nonfiction

For the classics of Italian history, look to Machiavelli's *The Prince* and *Florentine Histories*. Written in the 18th century, Edward Gibbon's *Decline and Fall of the Roman Empire* is the landmark history of ancient Rome.

Travelers' Tales Italy (Calcagno) is an excellent compilation of travel writing. Susan Cahill collected travelogues by female authors in *Desiring Italy*. In *Italian Days,* Barbara Grizzuti Harrison crafts travel essays on destinations ranging from Milan to Naples.

Italian Neighbors (Parks) describes life as an Englishman in a small Italian town, while *The Italians* (Barzini), written by an Italian, sheds light on the national character of this fascinating country.

Florence history buffs would enjoy reading the story of the Renaissance city's first family, *The House of Medici* (Hibbert). *Brunelleschi's Dome* (King) describes the trials involved with building Florence's magnificent Duomo. *Under the Tuscan Sun* was a bestseller for Frances Mayes (and is better than the movie of the same name).

Out of Paul Hofmann's multiple books about Italy, *The Seasons of Rome* is the favorite among readers. Elizabeth Gilbert's eloquent *Eat, Pray, Love* describes her time in Rome (in the "Eat" section). David Macaulay's illustrated books about the Eternal City—*Rome Antics* and *City: A Story of Roman Planning and Construction*—please both kids and adults.

For a solid overview of Venice, try *A History of Venice* (Norwich). Mary McCarthy's *Venice Observed* is a well-written memoir. In *The City of Falling Angels,* John Berendt tells the real-life mystery of the La Fenice Opera House fire.

For a true story about the Sicilian Mafia, consider *Excellent Cadavers* (Stille). *Midnight in Sicily* (Robb) offers a good general history of the Mob. In the memoir *Christ Stopped at Eboli: The Story of a Year,* Carlo Levi describes his banishment to southern Italy.

Pomp and Sustenance: Twenty-Five Centuries of Sicilian Food (Simeti) is both a cookbook and an historical overview. Foodies also like *Italy for the Gourmet Traveler* (Plotkin) and *The Marling Menu-Master for Italy.*

Fiction

Fans of classical literature will want to read Dante's *Divine Comedy* and Boccaccio's *Decameron.* Among the Shakespeare plays set in Italy are *Romeo and Juliet* (Verona), *The Merchant of Venice, Much Ado About Nothing* (Sicily), *The Two Gentlemen of Verona,* and *The Taming of the Shrew* (Padua).

In his 18th-century collection of writings titled *Italian Journey,* Goethe describes his travels to Rome, Sicily, and Naples. Henry James often wrote stories with an Italian theme, and three recommended books—*The Wings of the Dove, Italian Hours,* and *The*

Aspern Papers and Other Stories—use Venice as their backdrop. Another classic tale is Thomas Mann's *Death in Venice*.

For historical fiction that brings ancient Rome to life, try *The First Man in Rome* (McCullough) and *I, Claudius* (Graves). *Pompeii* (Harris), set in the ancient doomed city, tells of a young man's rescue attempt. *The Agony and the Ecstasy* (Stone) recounts Michelangelo's struggle to paint the Sistine Chapel (and later became a Charlton Heston movie).

In the 19th and early 20th centuries, great European writers fell in love with Florence. Two great books from this time are George Eliot's *Romola* and E. M. Forster's *A Room with a View*. Modern novels with Florence as the setting include *The Passion of Artemisia* (Vreeland), *The Sixteen Pleasures* (Hellenga), *Birth of Venus* (Dunant), and *Galileo's Daughter* (Sobel).

If Venice is on your itinerary, consider reading *Invisible Cities* (Calvino), in which "Marco Polo" tells of fantastical cities that may simply be facets of Venice; *The Passion* (Winterson), a magical realist tale of love; and *In the Company of the Courtesan* (Dunant), a chronicle of romantic intrigue in Renaissance Venice.

Regarded as one of the most important works of Italian literature, *The Leopard* (di Lampedusa) describes Sicilian life during the Risorgimento. *A Bell for Adano,* set in Sicily, won John Hersey the Pulitzer Prize in 1945. *A Soldier of the Great War* (Helprin)—which takes place partially in the Italian Alps and partially in Sicily—is a brutal tale set in World War I. *A Thread of Grace* (Russell) follows a group of Jews trying to find a safe haven in WWII Italy.

One of the best (and bestselling) murder mysteries is Umberto Eco's *The Name of the Rose,* set in a 14th-century Italian monastery. Mystery fans should also consider the books by Michael Dibdin, including *Ratking* (set in Umbria) and *Cabal* (Rome), *A Full Rich Death* (Florence), and *Dead Lagoon* (Venice). Dan Brown, the author of *The Da Vinci Code,* used Rome as the backdrop for his earlier murder mystery, *Angels and Demons.* Two Florentine-based mysteries are *The Dante Game* (Langton) and *Bella Donna* (Cherne). Donna Leon's detective stories often take place in Venice; *Death at La Fenice* is one of her most popular.

Films

Roberto Rossellini's *Open City* (1945) and Vittorio de Sica's *Bicycle Thieves* (1949), both classics of Italian Neorealism, continue to inspire audiences today.

In *Roman Holiday* (1953), Audrey Hepburn and Gregory Peck sightsee the city on his scooter. Two campy, big-budget Hollywood flicks bring ancient Rome to life: *Ben-Hur* (1959) and *Spartacus* (1960). In *La Dolce Vita* (1961), Fellini captures the Roman character, while *Gladiator* (2000) was a crowd-pleaser and an Academy Award winner.

1900 (1977) is Bernardo Bertolucci's epic tale of life under fascism; it stars Robert De Niro and Gérard Depardieu.

A Room with a View (1986), a close adaptation of the classic novel, captures Florence's appeal to turn-of-the-century English travelers. The Oscar-winning *Life Is Beautiful* (1997) has sections set in a Tuscan town.

Cinema Paradiso (1990), about a film projectionist and a little boy in post-WWII Sicily, won the Oscar for Best Foreign Picture. In *Enchanted April* (1991), filmed in Portofino, an all-star British cast falls in love, discusses relationships, eats well, and takes naps in the sun. *Ciao, Professore!* (1994) shows the influence of a grade-school teacher in Southern Italy. In *Il Postino* (1995), poet Pablo Neruda befriends his Italian postman.

In *Bread and Tulips* (2000), a harassed Italian housewife discovers beauty, love, and her true self in Venice. For an adrenaline-laced chase scene through Venice's canals, see *The Italian Job* (2003). The 2006 James Bond film *Casino Royale* has several scenes set in Venice and on Lake Como.

The warmhearted epic *Best of Youth* (2003), a story of two brothers, takes place across many scenic Italian locations and gives you a good feel for the last several decades of Italian history. *Nuovomondo* (2006, also called *The Golden Door*) tells the story of Sicilian immigrants leaving home for Ellis Island.

Gorgeous Italian backdrops star in two 2010 movies: *Letters to Juliet,* shot in Verona and Siena; and the film adaptation of *Eat, Pray, Love,* with scenes in Naples and Rome.

Holidays and Festivals

In Italy, holidays seem to strike without warning. For instance, every town has a festival honoring its patron saint. The Vatican City in Rome closes for many lesser-known Catholic holidays—confirm their schedule at http://mv.vatican.va.

This list includes selected festivals in major cities in 2014, plus national holidays observed throughout Italy. Many sights and banks close down on national holidays—keep this in mind when planning your itinerary. Before planning a trip around a festival, verify its dates by checking the festival's website or TI sites (www.italia.it).

In Italy, hotels get booked up on Easter weekend (from Good Friday through Easter Monday), April 25 (Liberation Day), May 1 (Labor Day), November 1 (All Saint's Day), and on Fridays and Saturdays year-round. Some hotels require you to book the full three-day weekend around a holiday.

Jan 1	New Year's Day
Jan 6	Epiphany
Jan	Fashion convention, Florence
Feb 15-March 4	Carnevale (Mardi Gras, www.carnevale.venezia.it), Venice
Early Feb-early March	Carnevale Celebrations/Mardi Gras in Florence (costumed parades, street water fights, jousting competitions)
Early April	Vinitaly (wine festival), Verona
April	Italy's Cultural Heritage Week (www.beniculturali.it)
April 20	Easter Sunday (and Scoppio del Carro fireworks in Florence)
April 21	Easter Monday
April 21	City Birthday, Rome
April 25	Italian Liberation Day, St. Mark's Day, Venice
May 1	Labor Day
May 29	Feast of the Ascension Day
Mid-May	Cricket Festival, Florence (music, entertainment, food, crickets sold in cages)
Late May-early June	Fashion convention, Florence
Late May-early June	Vogalonga Regatta, Venice
June 1-30	Annual Flower Display, Florence (carpet of flowers on the main square, Piazza della Signoria)
June 2	Anniversary of the Republic
June 16-17	Festival of St. Ranieri, Pisa
June-Aug	Verona Opera season
June 24	St. John the Baptist Day, Rome; Festival of St. John the Baptist, Florence (parades, dances, boat races); and Calcio Fiorentino (costumed soccer game on Florence's Piazza Santa Croce)
June 29	Sts. Peter and Paul's Day, most fervently celebrated in Rome
Late June-early Sept	Florence's annual outdoor cinema season (contemporary films)
July 2	Palio horse race, Siena
Mid-July	Feast and Regatta of the Redeemer (held third weekend of month), Venice
July-Aug	Musical Weeks, Lake Maggiore
Aug 10	St. Lawrence Day, Rome
Aug 15	Feast of the Assumption (Ferragosto)

2014

JANUARY
S	M	T	W	T	F	S
			1	2	3	4
5	6	7	8	9	10	11
12	13	14	15	16	17	18
19	20	21	22	23	24	25
26	27	28	29	30	31	

FEBRUARY
S	M	T	W	T	F	S
						1
2	3	4	5	6	7	8
9	10	11	12	13	14	15
16	17	18	19	20	21	22
23	24	25	26	27	28	

MARCH
S	M	T	W	T	F	S
						1
2	3	4	5	6	7	8
9	10	11	12	13	14	15
16	17	18	19	20	21	22
23/30	24/31	25	26	27	28	29

APRIL
S	M	T	W	T	F	S
		1	2	3	4	5
6	7	8	9	10	11	12
13	14	15	16	17	18	19
20	21	22	23	24	25	26
27	28	29	30			

MAY
S	M	T	W	T	F	S
				1	2	3
4	5	6	7	8	9	10
11	12	13	14	15	16	17
18	19	20	21	22	23	24
25	26	27	28	29	30	31

JUNE
S	M	T	W	T	F	S
1	2	3	4	5	6	7
8	9	10	11	12	13	14
15	16	17	18	19	20	21
22	23	24	25	26	27	28
29	30					

JULY
S	M	T	W	T	F	S
		1	2	3	4	5
6	7	8	9	10	11	12
13	14	15	16	17	18	19
20	21	22	23	24	25	26
27	28	29	30	31		

AUGUST
S	M	T	W	T	F	S
					1	2
3	4	5	6	7	8	9
10	11	12	13	14	15	16
17	18	19	20	21	22	23
24/31	25	26	27	28	29	30

SEPTEMBER
S	M	T	W	T	F	S
	1	2	3	4	5	6
7	8	9	10	11	12	13
14	15	16	17	18	19	20
21	22	23	24	25	26	27
28	29	30				

OCTOBER
S	M	T	W	T	F	S
			1	2	3	4
5	6	7	8	9	10	11
12	13	14	15	16	17	18
19	20	21	22	23	24	25
26	27	28	29	30	31	

NOVEMBER
S	M	T	W	T	F	S
						1
2	3	4	5	6	7	8
9	10	11	12	13	14	15
16	17	18	19	20	21	22
23/30	24	25	26	27	28	29

DECEMBER
S	M	T	W	T	F	S
	1	2	3	4	5	6
7	8	9	10	11	12	13
14	15	16	17	18	19	20
21	22	23	24	25	26	27
28	29	30	31			

Aug 16	Palio horse race, Siena
Sept-Oct	Chestnut Festivals (festivals, chestnut roasts), most towns, mainly north of Rome
Early Sept	Historical Regatta (held first weekend of Sept), Venice; and Festa della Rificolona, Florence (children's procession with lanterns, street performances, parade)
Sept 13-14	Volto Santo (procession and fair), Lucca
Oct	Musica dei Popoli Festival, Florence (ethnic and folk music and dances)
Mid-Oct	Castelrotto Festival (held second weekend of Oct), Dolomites
Nov 1	All Saints' Day
Nov 21	Feast of Our Lady of Good Health, Venice

APPENDIX

Dec	Christmas Market, Rome, Piazza Navona; and crèches in churches throughout Italy
Dec 8	Feast of the Immaculate Conception
Dec 25	Christmas
Dec 26	St. Stephen's Day

Conversions and Climate

Numbers and Stumblers

- Europeans write a few of their numbers differently than we do. 1 = 1, 4 = 4, 7 = 7.
- In Europe, dates appear as day/month/year, so Christmas is 25/12/14.
- Commas are decimal points and decimals commas. A dollar and a half is $1,50, one thousand is 1.000, and there are 5.280 feet in a mile.
- When counting with fingers, start with your thumb. If you hold up your first finger to request one item, you'll probably get two.
- What Americans call the second floor of a building is the first floor in Europe.
- On escalators and moving sidewalks, Europeans keep the left "lane" open for passing. Keep to the right.

Metric Conversions

A kilogram is 2.2 pounds, and 1 liter is about a quart, or almost four to a gallon. A kilometer is six-tenths of a mile. I figure kilometers to miles by cutting them in half and adding back 10 percent of the original (120 km: 60 + 12 = 72 miles, 300 km: 150 + 30 = 180 miles).

1 foot = 0.3 meter	1 square yard = 0.8 square meter
1 yard = 0.9 meter	1 square mile = 2.6 square kilometers
1 mile = 1.6 kilometers	1 ounce = 28 grams
1 centimeter = 0.4 inch	1 quart = 0.95 liter
1 meter = 39.4 inches	1 kilogram = 2.2 pounds
1 kilometer = 0.62 mile	32°F = 0°C

Roman Numerals

In the US, you'll see Roman numerals—which originated in ancient Rome—used for copyright dates, clocks, and the Super Bowl. In Italy, you're likely to observe these numbers chiseled on statues and buildings. If you want to do some numeric detective work, here's how: In Roman numerals, as in ours, the highest numbers (thousands, hundreds) come first, followed by smaller numbers. Many numbers are made by combining numerals into sets: V = 5, so

VIII = 8 (5 plus 3). Roman numerals follow a subtraction principle for multiples of fours (4, 40, 400, etc.) and nines (9, 90, 900, etc.); the number four, for example, is written as IV (1 subtracted from 5), rather than IIII. The number nine is IX (1 subtracted from 10).

Rick Steves' Italy 2014—written in Italian with Roman numerals—would translate as *Rick Steves' Italia MMXIV*. Big numbers such as dates can look daunting at first. The easiest way to handle them is to read the numbers in discrete chunks. For example, Michelangelo was born in MCDLXXV. Break it down: M (1,000) + CD (100 subtracted from 500, or 400) + LXX (50 + 10 + 10, or 70) + V (5) = 1475. It was a very good year.

M = 1000	XL = 40
CM = 900	X = 10
D = 500	IX = 9
CD = 400	V = 5
C = 100	IV = 4
XC = 90	I = duh
L = 50	

Clothing Sizes

When shopping for clothing, use these US-to-European comparisons as general guidelines (but note that no conversion is perfect).

- Women's dresses and blouses: Add 30
  (US size 10 = European size 40)
- Men's suits and jackets: Add 10
  (US size 40 regular = European size 50)
- Men's shirts: Multiply by 2 and add about 8
  (US size 15 collar = European size 38)
- Women's shoes: Add about 30
  (US size 8 = European size 38-39)
- Men's shoes: Add 32-34
  (US size 9 = European size 41; US size 11 = European size 45)

Italy's Climate

First line, average daily high; second line, average daily low; third line, average days without rain. For more detailed weather statistics for destinations in this book (as well as the rest of the world), check www.wunderground.com.

APPENDIX

	J	F	M	A	M	J	J	A	S	O	N	D
Rome												
	52°	55°	59°	66°	74°	82°	87°	86°	79°	71°	61°	55°
	40°	42°	45°	50°	56°	63°	67°	67°	62°	55°	49°	44°
	13	19	23	24	26	26	30	29	25	23	19	21
Milan and Florence												
	40°	46°	56°	65°	74°	80°	84°	82°	75°	63°	51°	43°
	32°	35°	43°	49°	57°	63°	67°	66°	61°	52°	43°	35°
	25	21	24	22	23	21	25	24	25	23	20	24
Venice												
	42°	46°	53°	62°	70°	76°	81°	80°	75°	65°	53°	46°
	33°	35°	41°	49°	56°	63°	66°	65°	61°	53°	44°	37°
	25	21	24	21	23	22	24	24	25	24	21	23

Temperature Conversion:
Fahrenheit and Celsius

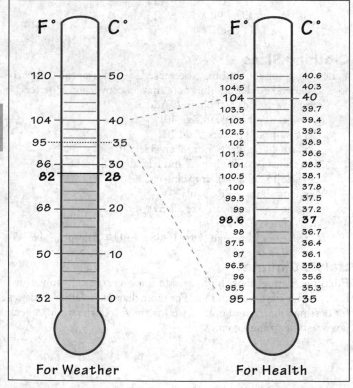

Europe takes its temperature using the Celsius scale, while we opt for Fahrenheit. For a rough conversion from Celsius to Fahrenheit, double the number and add 30. For weather, remember that 28°C is 82°F—perfect. For health, 37°C is just right.

Packing Checklist

Whether you're traveling for five days or five weeks, here's what you'll need to bring. Pack light to enjoy the sweet freedom of true mobility. Happy travels!

- ❑ 5 shirts: long- & short-sleeve
- ❑ 1 sweater or lightweight fleece
- ❑ 2 pairs of pants
- ❑ 1 pair of shorts
- ❑ 5 pairs of underwear & socks
- ❑ 1 pair of shoes
- ❑ 1 rainproof jacket with hood
- ❑ Tie or scarf
- ❑ Swimsuit
- ❑ Sleepwear
- ❑ Money belt
- ❑ Money—your mix of:
  - ❑ Debit card
  - ❑ Credit card(s)
  - ❑ Hard cash ($20 bills)
- ❑ Documents plus photo-copies.
  - ❑ Passport
  - ❑ Printout of airline eticket
  - ❑ Driver's license
  - ❑ Student ID, hostel card, etc.
  - ❑ Railpass/train reservations/car-rental voucher
  - ❑ Insurance details
- ❑ Guidebooks & maps
- ❑ Address list (for sending emails & postcards)
- ❑ Notepad & pen
- ❑ Journal
- ❑ Daypack
- ❑ Toiletries kit:
  - ❑ Toiletries
  - ❑ Medicines & vitamins
  - ❑ First-aid kit
  - ❑ Glasses/contacts/sunglasses (with prescriptions)
- ❑ Small towel/washcloth
- ❑ Laundry supplies:
  - ❑ Laundry soap
  - ❑ Clothesline
- ❑ Sewing kit

- ❑ Electronics—your choice of:
  - ❑ Camera (& related gear)
  - ❑ Mobile phone
  - ❑ Portable media player (iPod or other)
  - ❑ Laptop/netbook/tablet
  - ❑ Ebook reader
  - ❑ Headphones or earbuds
  - ❑ Chargers for each of the above
  - ❑ Plug adapter(s)
- ❑ Alarm clock
- ❑ Earplugs
- ❑ Sealable plastic baggies
- ❑ Empty water bottle
- ❑ Postcards & photos from home

If you plan to carry on your luggage, note that all liquids must be in 3.4-ounce or smaller containers and fit within a single quart-size sealable baggie. For details, see www.tsa.gov/travelers.

APPENDIX

Italian Survival Phrases

English	Italian	Pronunciation
Good day.	*Buon giorno.*	bwohn **jor**-noh
Do you speak English?	*Parla inglese?*	**par**-lah een-**glay**-zay
Yes. / No.	*Sì. / No.*	see / noh
I (don't) understand.	*(Non) capisco.*	(nohn) kah-**pees**-koh
Please.	*Per favore.*	pehr fah-**voh**-ray
Thank you.	*Grazie.*	**graht**-seeay
You're welcome.	*Prego.*	**pray**-go
I'm sorry.	*Mi dispiace.*	mee dee-spee**ah**-chay
Excuse me.	*Mi scusi.*	mee **skoo**-zee
(No) problem.	*(Non) c'è un problema.*	(nohn) cheh oon proh-**blay**-mah
Good.	*Va bene.*	vah **behn**-ay
Goodbye.	*Arrivederci.*	ah-ree-vay-**dehr**-chee
one / two	*uno / due*	**oo**-noh / **doo**-ay
three / four	*tre / quattro*	tray / **kwah**-troh
five / six	*cinque / sei*	**cheeng**-kway / **seh**ee
seven / eight	*sette / otto*	**seht**-tay / **ot**-toh
nine / ten	*nove / dieci*	**nov**-ay / dee**eay**-chee
How much is it?	*Quanto costa?*	**kwahn**-toh **kos**-tah
Write it?	*Me lo scrive?*	may loh **skree**-vay
Is it free?	*È gratis?*	eh **grah**-tees
Is it included?	*È incluso?*	eh een-**kloo**-zoh
Where can I buy / find...?	*Dove posso comprare / trovare...?*	**doh**-vay **pos**-soh kohm-**prah**-ray / troh-**vah**-ray
I'd like / We'd like...	*Vorrei / Vorremmo...*	vor-**reh**ee / vor-**ray**-moh
...a room.	*...una camera.*	**oo**-nah **kah**-meh-rah
...a ticket to ___.	*...un biglietto per ___.*	oon beel-**yeht**-toh pehr
Is it possible?	*È possibile?*	eh poh-**see**-bee-lay
Where is...?	*Dov'è...?*	**doh**-veh
...the train station	*...la stazione*	lah staht-see**oh**-nay
...the bus station	*...la stazione degli autobus*	lah staht-see**oh**-nay **dayl**-yee **ow**-toh-hoos
...tourist information	*...informazioni per turisti*	een-for-maht-see**oh**-nee pehr too-**ree**-stee
...the toilet	*...la toilette*	lah twah-**leht**-tay
men	*uomini, signori*	**woh**-mee-nee, seen-**yoh**-ree
women	*donne, signore*	**don**-nay, seen-**yoh**-ray
left / right	*sinistra / destra*	see-**nee**-strah / **dehs**-trah
straight	*sempre diritto*	**sehm**-pray dee-**ree**-toh
When do you open / close?	*A che ora aprite / chiudete?*	ah kay **oh**-rah ah-**pree**-tay / keeoo-**day**-tay
At what time?	*A che ora?*	ah kay **oh**-rah
Just a moment.	*Un momento.*	oon moh-**mayn**-toh
now / soon / later	*adesso / presto / tardi*	ah-**dehs**-soh / **prehs**-toh / **tar**-dee
today / tomorrow	*oggi / domani*	**oh**-jee / doh-**mah**-nee

In an Italian-speaking Restaurant

English	Italian	Pronunciation
I'd like...	*Vorrei...*	vor-**reh**ee
We'd like...	*Vorremmo...*	vor-**ray**-moh
...to reserve...	*...prenotare...*	pray-noh-**tah**-ray
...a table for one / two.	*...un tavolo per uno / due.*	oon **tah**-voh-loh pehr **oo**-noh / **doo**-ay
Non-smoking.	*Non fumare.*	nohn foo-**mah**-ray
Is this seat free?	*È libero questo posto?*	eh **lee**-bay-roh **kwehs**-toh **poh**-stoh
The menu (in English), please.	*Il menù (in inglese), per favore.*	eel may-**noo** (een een-**glay**-zay) pehr fah-**voh**-ray
service (not) included	*servizio (non) incluso*	sehr-**veet**-seeoh (nohn) een-**kloo**-zoh
cover charge	*pane e coperto*	**pah**-nay ay koh-**pehr**-toh
to go	*da portar via*	dah **por**-tar **vee**-ah
with / without	*con / senza*	kohn / **sehn**-sah
and / or	*e / o*	ay / oh
menu (of the day)	*menù (del giorno)*	may-**noo** (dayl **jor**-noh)
specialty of the house	*specialità della casa*	spay-chah-lee-**tah dehl**-lah **kah**-zah
first course (pasta, soup)	*primo piatto*	**pree**-moh pee**ah**-toh
main course (meat, fish)	*secondo piatto*	say-**kohn**-doh pee**ah**-toh
side dishes	*contorni*	kohn-**tor**-nee
bread	*pane*	**pah**-nay
cheese	*formaggio*	for-**mah**-joh
sandwich	*panino*	pah-**nee**-noh
soup	*minestra, zuppa*	mee-**nehs**-trah, **tsoo**-pah
salad	*insalata*	een-sah-**lah**-tah
meat	*carne*	**kar**-nay
chicken	*pollo*	**poh**-loh
fish	*pesce*	**peh**-shay
seafood	*frutti di mare*	**froo**-tee dee **mah**-ray
fruit / vegetables	*frutta / legumi*	**froo**-tah / lay-**goo**-mee
dessert	*dolci*	**dohl**-chee
tap water	*acqua del rubinetto*	**ah**-kwah dayl roo-bee-**nay**-toh
mineral water	*acqua minerale*	**ah**-kwah mee-nay-**rah**-lay
milk	*latte*	**lah**-tay
(orange) juice	*succo (d'arancia)*	**soo**-koh (dah-**rahn**-chah)
coffee / tea	*caffè / tè*	kah-**feh** / teh
wine	*vino*	**vee**-noh
red / white	*rosso / bianco*	**roh**-soh / bee**ahn**-koh
glass / bottle	*bicchiere / bottiglia*	bee-kee**ay**-ray / boh-**teel**-yah
beer	*birra*	**bee**-rah
Cheers!	*Cin cin!*	cheen cheen
More. / Another.	*Ancora un po.' / Un altro.*	ahn-**koh**-rah oon poh / oon **ahl**-troh
The same.	*Lo stesso.*	loh **stehs**-soh
The bill, please.	*Il conto, per favore.*	eel **kohn**-toh pehr fah-**voh**-ray
tip	*mancia*	**mahn**-chah
Delicious!	*Delizioso!*	day-leet-see**oh**-zoh

For more user-friendly Italian phrases, check out *Rick Steves' Italian Phrase Book & Dictionary* or *Rick Steves' French, Italian, and German Phrase Book*.

INDEX

INDEX

INDEX

MAP INDEX

MAP INDEX

Audio Europe™

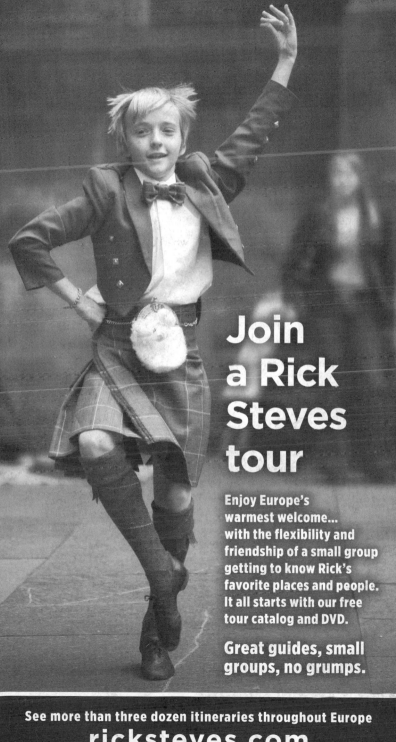

Join a Rick Steves tour

Enjoy Europe's warmest welcome... with the flexibility and friendship of a small group getting to know Rick's favorite places and people. It all starts with our free tour catalog and DVD.

Great guides, small groups, no grumps.

Start your trip at

Free information and great gear to

▶ Explore Europe

Browse thousands of articles, video clips, photos and radio interviews, plus find a wealth of money-saving tips for planning your dream trip. You'll find up-to-date information on Europe's best destinations, packing smart, getting around, finding rooms, staying healthy, avoiding scams and more.

▶ Travel News

Subscribe to our free Travel News e-newsletter, and get monthly updates from Rick on what's happening in Europe!

▶ Travel Forums

Learn, ask, share—our online community of savvy travelers is a great resource for first-time travelers to Europe, as well as seasoned pros.

Rick Steves' Europe Through the Back Door, Inc.

rickssteves.com

turn your travel dreams into affordable reality

▶ Rick's Free Audio Europe™ App

The Rick Steves Audio Europe™ app brings history and art to life. Enjoy Rick's audio tours of Europe's top museums, sights and neighborhood walks—plus hundreds of tracks including travel tips and cultural insights from Rick's radio show—all organized into geographic playlists. Learn more at rickssteves.com.

▶ Great Gear from Rick's Travel Store

Pack light and right—on a budget—with Rick's custom-designed carry-on bags, wheeled bags, day packs, travel accessories, guidebooks, journals, maps and Blu-ray/DVDs of his TV shows.

NOW AVAILABLE:
eBOOKS, DVD & BLU-RAY

TRAVEL CULTURE

Europe 101
European Christmas
Postcards from Europe
Travel as a Political Act

eBOOKS

*Nearly all Rick Steves guides
are available as eBooks. Check
with your favorite bookseller.*

RICK STEVES' EUROPE DVDs

11 New Shows 2013–2014
Austria & the Alps
Eastern Europe
England & Wales
European Christmas
European Travel Skills & Specials
France
Germany, BeNeLux & More
Greece, Turkey & Portugal
Iran
Ireland & Scotland
Italy's Cities
Italy's Countryside
Scandinavia
Spain
Travel Extras

BLU-RAY

Celtic Charms
Eastern Europe Favorites
European Christmas
Italy Through the Back Door
Mediterranean Mosaic
Surprising Cities of Europe

PHRASE BOOKS & DICTIONARIES

French
French, Italian & German
German
Italian
Portuguese
Spanish

JOURNALS

Rick Steves' Pocket Travel Journal
Rick Steves' Travel Journal

PLANNING MAPS

Britain, Ireland & London
Europe
France & Paris
Germany, Austria & Switzerland
Ireland
Italy
Spain & Portugal

Rick Steves books and DVDs are available at bookstores
and through online booksellers.

Rick Steves

www.ricksteves.com

EUROPE GUIDES

Best of Europe
Eastern Europe
Europe Through the Back Door
Mediterranean Cruise Ports
Northern European Cruise Ports

COUNTRY GUIDES

Croatia & Slovenia
England
France
Germany
Great Britain
Ireland
Italy
Portugal
Scandinavia
Spain
Switzerland

CITY & REGIONAL GUIDES

Amsterdam, Bruges & Brussels
Barcelona
Budapest
Florence & Tuscany
Greece: Athens & the Peloponnese
Istanbul
London
Paris
Prague & the Czech Republic
Provence & the French Riviera
Rome
Venice
Vienna, Salzburg & Tirol

SNAPSHOT GUIDES

Berlin
Bruges & Brussels
Copenhagen & the Best of
   Denmark
Dublin
Dubrovnik
Hill Towns of Central Italy
Italy's Cinque Terre
Krakow, Warsaw & Gdansk
Lisbon
Madrid & Toledo
Milan & the Italian Lakes District
Munich, Bavaria & Salzburg
Naples & the Amalfi Coast
Northern Ireland
Norway
Scotland
Sevilla, Granada & Southern Spain
Stockholm

POCKET GUIDES

Athens
Barcelona
Florence
London
Paris
Rome
Venice

Rick Steves guidebooks are published by Avalon Travel,
a member of the Perseus Books Group.

Credits

Researchers

To update his four books on Italy, Rick relied on the help of...

Ben Cameron

Ben experienced his first taste of European travel when he was three, exploring medieval castles with his parents. Returning after graduation, he was hooked and has spent much of his time since exploring Europe independently and leading tours for Rick Steves. When not living out of his backpack, Ben splits his time between Rome and Seattle.

Cameron Hewitt

Cameron writes and edits guidebooks for Rick Steves, specializing in Eastern Europe. For this book, he hiked the length of the Cinque Terre, rode *vaporetti* all over Venice, and rubbed elbows with students and pilgrims in Padua. When he's not traveling, Cameron lives in Seattle with his wife, Shawna.

Ian Watson

Ian has worked with Rick's guidebooks since 1993, after starting out with Let's Go and Frommer's guides. Originally from upstate New York, Ian speaks several European languages, including German, and makes his home in Reykjavík, Iceland.

Helen Inman

After graduating with a law degree, Helen left England for the Mediterranean, finding sunshine, vibrant energy, and Latin culture and languages. Currently working as a guide for Rick Steves tours and as a guidebook researcher, she enjoyed five years in *bella* Roma before moving to Spain, where she thrives on a diet of dancing, laughter, *cava,* and seafood.

Cary Walker

Cary discovered the power of international travel during her college years and has been feeding her wanderlust ever since. A former teacher, she believes that Europe is the best classroom for those willing to travel with an open mind. When not researching guidebooks or leading Rick Steves tours, she spends her time in Dallas planning her next European adventure.

Suzanne Kotz

Suzanne, an editor with Europe Through the Back Door, began her travel career riding in a station wagon with her six siblings from Michigan to Florida. Since then, she's broadened her destinations to include much of Europe and parts of Asia. A librarian by training and a longtime editor of art publications, she's happiest when she has a red pen in one hand and a book in the other. She lives in Seattle with her husband and son.

Marijan Kriskovic

As a child on the Adriatic island of Rab (Croatia), Marijan grew up in the shadows of Venetian campaniles. Enchanted by Italian culture and *dolce vita,* he's spent a good part of his adult life in search of the ultimate gelato. When he's not leading tours for Rick Steves, Marijan calls Ljubljana (Slovenia) home and indulges in his gelato passion with his wife, Barbara, and 26-year-old cat, John Travolta III.

Trish Feaster

As a high-school Spanish teacher, Trish enjoyed taking her students on summer trips to Europe, sharing her passion for language, history, culture, and cuisine. Trish later earned a degree in French, and now uses her language and teaching skills as a travel blogger, tour guide, and guidebook researcher. She and her partner enjoying traveling together, stand-up paddleboarding, and playing *pétanque* in their hometown of Edmonds.

Contributor
Gene Openshaw

Gene is the co-author of 10 Rick Steves' books. For this book, he wrote material on Italy's art, history, and contemporary culture. When not traveling, Gene enjoys composing music, recovering from his 1973 trip to Europe with Rick, and living everyday life with his daughter.

Images

Location	Photographer
Front color matter, title page: Varenna	David C. Hoerlein
Front color matter: Venice	Michael Potter
Front color matter: Venice	Laura VanDeventer
Venice: Church of San Giorgio Maggiore	David C. Hoerlein
Towns Near Venice: Verona's Roman Arena	David C. Hoerlein
The Dolomites: Alpe di Siusi	Julie Coen
The Lakes: Bellagio	Rick Steves
Milan: Cathedral (Duomo)	David C. Hoerlein
Cinque Terre: Corniglia	Rick Steves
Riviera Towns near the Cinque Terre: Portofino	David C. Hoerlein
Florence: View from Piazzale Michelangelo	Rick Steves
Pisa and Lucca: Pisa's Field of Miracles	Rick Steves
Siena: Il Campo	David C. Hoerlein
Hill Towns of Central Italy: San Gimignano	Rick Steves
Assisi: Basilica of St. Francis	Rick Steves
Orvieto & Civita: Civita di Bagnoregio	David C. Hoerlein
Rome: Piazza Navona	Rick Steves
Naples: Views from Certosa San Martino	Cameron Hewitt
Pompeii and Nearby: Mt. Vesuvius	David C. Hoerlein
Sorrento and Capri: Capri	David C. Hoerlein
Amalfi Coast and Paestum: Positano	David C. Hoerlein

Avalon Travel
a member of the Perseus Books Group
1700 Fourth Street
Berkeley, CA 94710

Printed in Canada by Friesens
First printing October 2013

ISBN 978-1-61238-659-1
ISSN 1084-4422

For the latest on Rick's lectures, guidebooks, tours, public radio show, and public television series, contact Europe Through the Back Door, Box 2009, Edmonds, WA 98020, tel. 425/771-8303, fax 425/771-0833, www.ricksteves.com, rick@ricksteves.com.

Europe Through the Back Door

Managing Editor: Risa Laib
Editorial & Production Manager: Jennifer Madison Davis
Editors: Glenn Eriksen, Tom Griffin, Cameron Hewitt, Suzanne Kotz, Cathy Lu, Carrie Shepherd, Gretchen Strauch
Editorial Assistant: Jessica Shaw
Editorial Intern: Alex Jacobs
Researchers: Ben Cameron, Cameron Hewitt, Helen Inman, Suzanne Kotz, Marijan Kriskovic, Cary Walker, Ian Watson
Maps & Graphics: David C. Hoerlein, Lauren Mills, Dawn Tessman Visser, Laura VanDeventer

Avalon Travel

Senior Editor and Series Manager: Madhu Prasher
Editor: Jamie Andrade
Associate Editors: Nikki Ioakimedes and Annette Kohl
Assistant Editor: Maggie Ryan
Copy Editor: Jennifer Malnick
Proofreader: Suzie Nasol
Indexer: Stephen Callahan
Cover Design: Kimberly Glyder Design
Maps & Graphics: Kat Bennett, Mike Morgenfeld

Front Matter Color Photos: p. I Varenna © David C. Hoerlein; p. XIV Venice © Michael Potter; p. XXIV, Venice © Laura VanDeventer
Front Cover Photo: Amalfi coast © Woldt/Getty Images
Additional Photography: Dominic Bonuccelli, Ben Cameron, Jennifer Hauseman, Cameron Hewitt, David C. Hoerlein, Anne Jenkins, Gene Openshaw, Michael Potter, Robyn Stencil, Rick Steves, Bruce VanDeventer, Laura VanDeventer, Les Wahlstrom, Ian Watson, Wikimedia Commons

ABOUT THE AUTHOR

RICK STEVES

Since 1973, Rick Steves has spent 100 days every year exploring Europe. Along with writing and researching a bestselling series of guidebooks, Rick produces a public television series (*Rick Steves' Europe*), a public radio show (*Travel with Rick Steves*), and an app and podcast (*Rick Steves Audio Europe*); writes a nationally syndicated newspaper column; organizes guided tours that take over ten thousand travelers to Europe annually; and offers an information-packed website (www.ricksteves.com). With the help of his hardworking staff of 80 at Europe Through the Back Door—in Edmonds, Washington, just north of Seattle—Rick's mission is to make European travel fun, affordable, and culturally enlightening for Americans.

Connect with Rick:

 facebook.com/RickSteves   twitter: @RickSteves

Foldout Color Map

The foldout map on the opposite page includes:
- **A map of Italy on one side**
- **City maps, including Rome, Florence, Venice, and Siena on the other side**